2002

The Dictionary of Art · volume one

The Dictionary of Art

CONSULTING EDITOR Hugh Brigstocke

EDITOR Jane Turner

1

A

TO

Anckerman

GROVE

The Dictionary of Art

edited by JANE TURNER, in thirty-four volumes, 1996

Reprinted with minor corrections, 1998

This edition is distributed within the United Kingdom and Europe
by Macmillan Publishers Limited, London, and within the United States and Canada by
Grove's Dictionaries Inc., New York.

Text keyboarded by Wearset Limited, Sunderland, England
Database management by Pindar plc, York, England
Imagesetting by William Clowes Limited, Suffolk, England
Printed and bound by China Translation and Printing Services Ltd, Hong Kong

British Library Cataloguing in Publication Data

The dictionary of art
1. Art - Dictionaries 2. Art - History -
Dictionaries
I. Turner, Jane
703

ISBN 1-884446-00-0

Library of Congress Cataloging in Publication Data

The dictionary of art / editor, Jane Turner.
p. cm.
Includes bibliographical references and index.
Contents: 1. A to Anckerman
ISBN 1-884446-00-0 (alk. paper)
1. Art—Encyclopedias.
I. Turner, Jane, 1956–
N31.D5 1996 96–13628
703—dc20 CIP

Contents

Preface

1. THE DICTIONARY OF ART. The title is deceptively simple. Yet when work began on the *Dictionary of Art* in the early 1980s, it was evident that it would not be a simple undertaking. Only after some time had elapsed, however, did we fully realize the enormity of the task on which we had embarked. The objective was clear enough: to produce, in 25 million words, an illustrated reference work that provided comprehensive coverage of the history of all the visual arts worldwide, from prehistory to the present. Like our renowned sister publication, the *New Grove Dictionary of Music and Musicians*, 20 vols (London, 1980), we aimed to present this comprehensive account using the highest possible standards of scholarship, while at the same time ensuring that entries were accessible to non-specialists. We have benefited enormously from the accumulated wisdom and experience of our Grove colleagues, but the preparation of these two publications has posed some quite different challenges. As Stanley Sadie, the editor of the *New Grove*, explained in his preface to the sixth edition of the music dictionary first prepared by Sir George Grove in the 1870s and 1880s, less than three percent of the entries in the *New Grove* were retained from earlier editions; the Grove editors did, however, have one distinct advantage over us—namely an existing product to revise and refine. We had to start more or less from scratch.

2. CONTENTS AND SCOPE. From the outset, we intended that the *Dictionary of Art* would take an entirely different approach from that of existing art reference works. Architecture and photography were certainly to be included, and the decorative arts would be treated as seriously as the traditional 'fine arts' of painting, sculpture and architecture, as would such contemporary art forms as performance art and multimedia installations, which do not fit easily into conventional categories. The only visual art form deliberately excluded was the history of film making, a subject that in itself would require a major reference work. (There is, however, an entry on Experimental film, and the film making activities of other kinds of artists are treated in their biographies.)

More importantly, if the *Dictionary* were to be truly comprehensive, its coverage could not be limited to biographies. Most ancient cultures and most civilizations outside the Western world simply do not lend themselves to a biographical approach. It was decided therefore that the *Dictionary* should offer as many types of article as possible in order to accommodate the wide range of topics of interest to modern students and historians of art. These articles vary in length from a few lines to hundreds of pages. (Indeed, some entries could be considered substantial books in their own right.) Combined with extensive cross-references and alternative headwords and an index of some 750,000 items, this diversity of approach is designed to enable readers to find information quickly and easily, from numerous points of access. Entries are further supplemented by detailed bibliographies, which have been carefully selected by the *Dictionary*'s authors and editors to reflect the most important past and recent scholarship.

A reference work is bound to reflect the attitudes and methodologies of the era in which it is created, and the *Dictionary of Art* is no exception. But there can have been few other times as exciting as the 1980s and the early 1990s in which to produce a work intended to be used well into the 21st century. When we began, we had little idea how momentous the political changes of the 1990s would prove to be, and just as the political map of the globe has been redrawn, so, too, have the boundaries of art history. Exactly when the latter process began cannot be pinpointed as accurately as the fall of the Berlin Wall in 1989, but it is certainly true that in the last quarter of the 20th century the ways in which art is studied have changed more dramatically than at any other time since the origins of the discipline in the late 19th century. Old assumptions have been questioned, opinions revised, new facts brought to light and whole new areas explored for the first time.

At no other period in this century has there been so much new evidence to consider, a phenomenon often referred to by the media as the 'information explosion' of recent decades. In 1974, for instance, the astonishing army of 10,000 Chinese terracotta warriors and horses, now seen as the quintessential embodiment of Qin-period sculpture, was excavated after having been buried for over 2000 years. Four years later workmen in Mexico City unearthed sculptures that led to the rediscovery of the Templo Mayor (or Great Temple) of the Aztecs. Moreover, it is not only in archaeological contexts that new 'finds' are made. Information continues to come to light about even the best-known artists and their work. New evidence concerning the possible identity of the sitter in one of the world's most famous paintings, Leonardo da Vinci's *'Mona Lisa'*, was published as recently as 1991. Since 1968 the entire corpus of paintings traditionally ascribed to Rembrandt has been systematically re-evaluated by a team of Dutch scholars, and the findings of this project (published from 1982 onwards) have led, controversially, to the reattribution of many works to Rembrandt's lesser-known pupils.

Along with the discovery of new facts have come fundamental changes in attitudes and understanding. Questions of authorship, formal analysis and stylistic development are no longer sufficient to satisfy the curiosity of today's art historians. They want to know more—for whom and how a work of art was produced, for instance. It has become clear that art objects can be fully understood only within the complete social, cultural, historical and economic context in which they were created. Subject-matter, iconography and patronage, as well as issues of gender, sexuality, politics and race, have thus taken their place among the many methodological approaches that have broadened our understanding of the history of artistic endeavour. In addition, forms of art, cultures and artists once completely neglected now attract the same professional interest as those areas making up the traditional Eurocentric canon. The history of architecture, photography and the decorative arts appear increasingly alongside the history of painting and sculpture in university syllabuses. Women artists of the past now receive the recognition they deserve, and, increasingly, the other roles women have played in the creation of art, as patrons for example, have begun to be better documented.

Perhaps the most significant advance in art-historical studies of the past several decades has been in our increased understanding of artistic practices in traditions outside the West. As long ago as 1749, the enlightened Dr Samuel Johnson, in the *Vanity of Human Wishes*, said: 'Let observation with extensive view survey mankind, from China to Peru.' Yet when it comes to standard art history reference books, little serious scholarly attention has been paid, in the intervening two and a half centuries, to the arts of China and Pre-Columbian Peru, let alone to those of Africa, the Pacific Islands and Native Americans, to name but a few of the areas only now finding their rightful place in a more universal history of art.

3. TYPES OF ARTICLE. The headings under which readers of the *Dictionary of Art* can look for information, though they appear in alphabetical order, can be grouped into some 12 broad categories. The largest group (numerically but not in extent) is that of biographies, which total about 20,800 of the 45,000 entries. About 17,300 biographies have been allocated to artists of all kinds: painters, sculptors, architects, illuminators, draughtsmen, silversmiths,

cabinetmakers, potters, industrial designers and so on. As far as possible, every aspect of an artist's career is touched on, including, where relevant, the person's character and personality, as well as related activities, such as designs for prints and the decorative arts, and art theory, collecting and dealing. There are also some 3500 biographies devoted to patrons, collectors, dealers, theorists, writers, art historians, museum officials, critics and teachers.

The selection of biographies to be included was among the most contentious tasks undertaken by our advisers and editors. The *Dictionary of Art* was never intended as a directory: it is a critically organized repository of historically significant information. Therefore the decision to include (or to exclude) an artist was inevitably a matter of scholarly and editorial judgement. Naturally the criteria for inclusion vary from century to century. Compared with modern periods, a greater percentage of those medieval or Renaissance artists whose names are known appear in the *Dictionary*'s pages because far fewer artists from these early periods are documented. In more recent times, the criteria have necessarily to be more closely linked with critical judgement. We have tried to compensate for this by increasing the number of artists included for each subsequent century, while reducing the length of the individual entries. There are thus more biographies of 20th-century artists (for whom there was no official cut-off date) than for any previous period. We were greatly helped in this difficult exercise by two factors—the large number of biographies that we were able to accommodate in this multivolume work and the expert advice and guidance we were given by our numerous regional advisers. Although we realize that no one person will agree with all the judgements we have made, we can only hope that most readers will find the selection reasonably consistent and intelligent.

The allocation of space to biographies had to be balanced against the pages given over to the achievements of groups whose individual identities might not be known, but whose activities or works still occupy an important place in the history of art. We have thus included many entries on non-Western peoples, such as the Nazca of Peru, the Yoruba of Africa and the Liao of China. The contribution of specific peoples can also be studied within the context of the substantial articles on the art of ancient cultures and civilizations outside the West, such as Aboriginal Australia, China, ancient Egypt and the Indian subcontinent. This aspect of our coverage extends to many millions of words and constitutes, we believe, the most comprehensive coverage of the arts of Asia, Africa, Australasia and the Americas ever published in one source.

Supplementing our coverage of the world's civilizations and peoples are articles on every modern country recognized by the United Nations (though in some cases, e.g. China and Japan, this will be combined with the history of the ancient civilization). Following a summary of geography and history, the modern country articles provide detailed historical surveys of architecture, painting and graphic arts, sculpture and the decorative arts. Sections on patronage, collecting and dealing, art education, museums, art libraries and photographic collections and historiography are also generally included.

There are many entries on cities and towns with significant artistic traditions, from every continent of the world. Each article discusses the history and urban development of the city or town, its art life and institutions and, where appropriate, the local production of decorative arts. Many city articles also include individual discussions of important buildings when these are the creations of anonymous artists (e.g. medieval cathedrals) or the result of collaborative efforts extending over many decades or centuries.

Entries on sites form another important category of our coverage. Site articles discuss the significance of archaeological excavations, and the monuments and artefacts found at locations as wide-ranging as Ayutthaya, Babylon or Great Zimbabwe. Another kind of site entry documents monuments and buildings that are not located in a modern city and therefore cannot be discussed under such a heading—for example the French château of Chenonceaux; the Spanish royal monastery and palace of the Escorial; and Monticello, the house designed by Thomas Jefferson near Charlottesville, Virginia. This category of entry also affords the opportunity to include factories and centres of production, for example tapestries at Cadillac, porcelain at Capodimonte, glass at Waterford and jet at Whitby.

In line with the tradition of many art dictionaries, we have individual entries on artistic styles, schools, groups and movements. Over 500 articles of this type—from Abstract Expressionism, the Ashcan school, Baroque and Brutalism to Donkey's Tail, Egyptian Revival, Estridentismo and the Utrecht Caravaggisti—offer a general definition and history of the style, school, group or movement in question, frequently situating its development within the wider social and political sphere. The origins and historical use of the term itself are often explained, especially for headings considered conceptually outmoded by some modern scholars. In a few cases, however, it seemed more appropriate to consider a particular style in the broader historical context of the relevant country article; thus, for example, Japanese painting and printmaking styles such as *Nihonga*, *ukiyoe* and *Zenga* are discussed in the relevant sections of the article on Japan (and can also be found by consulting the index).

The general trend away from basing art history primarily on stylistic analysis has coincided with greater attention being paid to the forms, themes and subject-matter of art. These topics are addressed in some 800 articles in the *Dictionary*, including Bed, Book, Carpet, Garden, Marine painting, Photography, Portraiture and Stele. Where appropriate, such articles attempt to provide a global account of their development (Altar, Garden, Mirror and Tomb being good examples). These articles illuminate key issues: design, taste, intention and function, patronage and cultural context. In other cases, the history and development of certain art forms and themes play such an integral role in the development of the arts of a particular culture or civilization that they are best studied under the latter heading. In the survey of Islamic art, for instance, no account of the development of textiles would be complete without a detailed study of Islamic carpets, and it is there that the principal discussion will be found. In the Carpet entry, by contrast, the reader is given technical information that applies to carpets in all regions and cultures (e.g. knotting and weaving techniques); this is followed by a short historical overview of carpets worldwide and a detailed history of Western carpets. Cross-references and the index will guide the reader to equally detailed discussions under other headings.

A similar category of art form entry discusses the history of building types (e.g. Airport, Church, Mosque and Palace), as well as parts of buildings, decorative features and construction techniques (e.g. Arch, Cantilever, Dome, Frieze, Machicolation, Moulding, Orders, Pinnacle and Vault). There is also a variety of related entries essential to the understanding of architecture (e.g. Building regulations, Lighting and Property development).

Another area of our coverage that we believe to be unprecedented is the series of some 600 entries devoted to the materials and techniques of art. Rather than being directed at the practising specialist, these articles are included to enable curators, scholars, students and collectors to understand technical issues related to how, and from what, works of art are made. Until now, standard art reference books have tended to neglect the interrelation between design, medium and technique. Articles such as Acrylic painting, Aluminium, Aquatint, Brass, Brush, Fresco, Glass, Glaze, Jade, Lithography, Panel, Stone and Wood typically discuss the properties, sources and manufacture of the material or technique concerned, the history of its use and its conservation. We have made every effort to ensure that difficult and complex scientific information is explained in clear and accessible language. Conservation issues are also covered in general entries such as Conservation and restoration, Heritage, and Technical examination, the last of which includes, among many others, detailed discussions of scientific dating methods and techniques for analysing the macrostructure of a work (e.g. by infra-red photography).

The history of art patronage is another area in which our treatment of the subject is intended to extend the boundaries of what is currently available in other reference sources, especially when the thousands of additional names of patrons found in the index are taken into account. Besides the individual biographies of patrons and ruling dynasties who commissioned works of art and the surveys of patronage found under each country heading, there are entries for all the major religions of the world. Articles on specific religious orders treat the history, iconography and patronage of each order, exploring in detail how each has influenced the production of art. Finally, there are substantial articles on many theoretical and general issues, such as Abstraction, Aesthetics, Anthropology and art, Art legislation, Authenticity, Colour, Connoisseurship, Decadence and decline, Display of art, Dissemination, Feminism and art, Forgery, Iconoclasm, Mass production, Ornament and pattern, Perspective, Semiotics and Sociology and art.

4. AUTHORS. Never before has the work of so many art historians—often with widely differing perspectives—been brought together in a single endeavour. Modern communications and the sweeping political changes that occurred during the course of our work resulted in unparalleled international scholarly cooperation. It enabled us to cast our net for advisers and authors far wider than we would have dreamt possible only a few years ago. The 6700 scholars whose names appear in vol. 33 came from over 120 countries. Not only did we have contributions from authors from all the former republics of the USSR (which still existed as a political bureaucracy when we began), but we were also lucky to have the enthusiastic participation of local scholars throughout Central and Eastern Europe, South America, Korea and the Caribbean—to isolate just a few of the places often overlooked by publishers. In many cases, the material they contributed has never before been available in English. The result of this extraordinary collaborative effort is, we hope, a reference work of which the whole is greater than the sum of the parts and in which 'new things are made familiar, and familiar things are made new' (Alexander Pope: *The Lives of the Poets*, 1779-81). Most of all, it is an achievement that is a tribute to the scholarship of today's international community of art historians.

With more than 45,000 entries, written by 6700 people over a period of 12 years, the *Dictionary of Art*, like the *New Grove*, 'no doubt embodies many contradictions'. But as Stanley Sadie went on to explain in his preface to the *New Grove*, 'contradictions on matters of interpretation are not of course unwelcome; it is part of a dictionary's role to represent a variety of standpoints'. Like our Grove colleagues, we have made every effort to compare related articles and to resolve apparent discrepancies, although the results are not always conclusive. Where differences of opinion do occur, we have endeavoured to respect the views of the author whose signature appears at the end of each article or subsection, while calling the reader's attention to other interpretations by means of parenthetical editorial comments and/or cross-references. Errors of fact are another matter, and users of the *Dictionary of Art* are asked to write to the editorial office, c/o Macmillan Publishers, 25 Eccleston Place, London, SW1, to notify us of any such sins of commission (or omission) so that they may be corrected in the future.

Jane Turner
London, 1996

Introduction

I. Alphabetization and identical headings. II. Article headings and structures. III. Standard usages. IV. Cross-references. V. Locations of works of art. VI. Illustrations. VII. Bibliographies and other sources. VIII. Authors. IX. Appendices. X. Index.

I. Alphabetization and identical headings.

All main headings in this dictionary are distinguished by bold typeface. Headings of more than one word are alphabetized letter by letter as if continuous, up to the first true mark of punctuation, and again thereafter: the comma in **Stam, Mart** therefore breaks the alphabetization, and his biography precedes the article on **Stamford**, whereas the full point of an abbreviation such as in **Cornelisz. van Haarlem** is ignored. Parenthesized letters or words and square-bracketed matter are also ignored in alphabetization: for example, the article **Barlow, (James) Alan (Noel)** precedes that on **Barlow, Francis**, which would come before **Barlow, F(aye) W(inifred)**. The reader who searches in the wrong place for a prefixed or double surname will be led to the correct location by a cross-reference. Abbreviations of 'Saint' and its foreign equivalents (S, SS, St, Ste etc) are alphabetized as if spelt out in full. The prefixes Mc and Mac where occurring as the first two or three letters of a name are alphabetized under Mac. The modified vowels ä, ö and ü are read as a, o and u, not as ae, oe and ue, and Dutch names with ij are alphabetized according to English usage rather than under y. Acronyms are alphabetized by initial, as if words, rather than by the full name (**CIAM** follows **Ciaccono** rather than **Congregation of the Oratory**). Artists active largely before *c.* 1500 for whom the second part of the name indicates a place of origin, domicile or profession etc are entered under the first name, so that, for example, **Leonardo da Vinci** is under 'L' not 'V'. If two headings are identical except for spacing, the spaced version appears first. Accented letters are treated like unaccented ones, although for headings identical except for the accents the unaccented form appears first. Numerals, except roman numeral epithets of generation, are alphabetized as if spelt out (**291** precedes **Tworkov, Jack**). Rulers and popes with roman numeral epithets are arranged numerically after any unnumbered rulers with that name and before any individuals with that name as a surname, as is illustrated by the following (incomplete) sequence of headings and cross-references:

Charles, Duc de Berry
Charles, Duke of Orléans
Charles, Prince of Wales
Charles I, Duke of Savoy
Charles I, King of England and Scotland
Charles I, King of Spain
Charles II, King of Naples and Jerusalem
Charles II, King of Spain
Charles III, King of Spain
Charles III, Margrave of Baden-Durlach
Charles V, Holy Roman Emperor
Charles VIII, King of France
Charles X, King of France
Charles, Richard
Charles Albert, King of Sardinia
Charles Augustus, Duke of Saxe-Weimar
Charles II Augustus, Duke of Zweibrucken
Charles Borromeo
Charles Eusebius, Prince of Liechtenstein
Charles of France
Charles the Bald
Charles Theodore, Elector Palatine of the Rhine
Charles the Wise, King of France
Charleston

Article headings that are truly identical are distinguished by the use of parenthesized small roman numerals; such articles are entered according to the following hierarchy: place, material, technique, art form, object, family entry, individual biography, peoples. If there are two articles on places with identical names, they are entered in chronological order by date of foundation. Where two or more unrelated people have identical names, also distinguished by small roman numerals, they are arranged chronologically by date of birth.

The entry **Masters, anonymous, and monogrammists** contains articles on all anonymous masters except ancient Greek and Roman vase painters, who appear under the entry **Vase painters**. The former is subdivided into: ***I. Anonymous masters***; ***II. Dated masters***; and ***III. Monogrammists***. Anonymous masters are alphabetized ignoring the title 'Master' and such intervening words as 'of' or 'the'; dated masters are organized chronologically; and the monogrammists alphabetically by initials. Vase painters appear in alphabetical order, ignoring the words 'Painter of'.

II. Article headings and structures.

1. BIOGRAPHICAL. All biographies in this dictionary start with the subject's name and, where known, the places and dates of birth and death and a statement of nationality and occupation. In the citation of a name in a heading, the use of parentheses indicates parts of the name that are not commonly used, while square brackets enclose variant names or spellings:

Jones, Charles (Thomas): full name Charles Thomas Jones, referred to as Charles Jones

Jones, C(harles) T(homas): full name Charles Thomas Jones, referred to as C. T. Jones

Smith [Smythe]**, Betty** [Elizabeth]: usually referred to as Betty Smith but sometimes in the form of Betty Smythe, Elizabeth Smith or Elizabeth Smythe

Smith, Betty [Smythe, Elizabeth]: Betty Smith's name has the alternative version of Elizabeth Smythe only

Smith [née Johnson], **Betty**: Smith is Betty Johnson's married name, by which she is generally known

Jones, Charles [Brown, William]: William Brown is known chiefly by his pseudonym of Charles Jones

Brown, William [pseud. Jones, Charles]: William Brown is referred to as such and is also known by the pseudonym of Charles Jones

Places of birth and death are cited according to the name current during the subject's lifetime, followed by the modern name, where that is different:

(*b* Constantinople [now Istanbul], . . .)

Statements of places and dates of birth and death are given with as much precision as the evidence allows and may be replaced or supplemented by dates of baptism (*bapt*), burial (*bur*), canonization (*can*), feast day (*fd*) or regnal years (*reg*). Where information is conjectural, a question mark is placed directly before the statement that it qualifies. Where dates of birth and death are unrecorded but there is documentary evidence for the subject's activity between certain fixed dates, *floruit* (*fl*) dates are given; when such evidence is circumstantial, as for instance in the case of an anonymous master, this is cited as '*fl c.*'.

A subject's nationality is stated as current at the time:

(*b* Antwerp, 2 May 1560; *d* Antwerp, 12 Aug 1625). Flemish architect.
(*b* Antwerp, 16 Sept 1835; *d* Brussels, 24 Feb 1910). Belgian painter.

If the subject changed nationality or country of activity, this is stated where significant, as may also be the subject's ancestry; otherwise this information is evident from the parenthesized matter after the heading or is conveyed in the text. The subject's nationality is followed by a definition of occupation, that is to say the activity (or activities) of art-historical significance that justified inclusion in the dictionary; for non-artists, the subject's profession is also stated (e.g. 'American banker and collector').

Biographies are generally structured to present information in chronological order. Longer biographies usually begin with a brief statement of the subject's significance and are then divided into sections, under such headings as 1. Life and work. 2. Working methods and techniques. 3. Character and personality. 4. Critical reception and posthumous reputation.; within sections there may be further divisions to aid the reader in finding specific information. The biographies of two or more related artists or patrons and collectors are gathered in 'family' entries, alphabetized under the main form of the surname; monarchs, popes, rulers and aristocrats who were members of a family of patrons and collectors appear under their dynastic or family name, rather than under their given name or title. (The reader looking under the given name or title will be directed to the correct location of the entry by a cross-reference.) Within a family article, individual members of significance have their own entries, beginning with an indented, numbered bold heading; for the second and subsequent members of the family, a statement of relationship to a previous member of the family is included wherever possible:

> **Smith.** English family of sculptors.
> **(1) John Smith** (*b* . . .; *d* . . .).
> **(2) Richard Smith** (*b* . . .; *d* . . .). Son of (1) John Smith.
> **(3) Edward Smith** (*b* . . .; *d* . . .). Brother of (2) Richard Smith.

The numbers allocated to family members are used in cross-references from other articles:

> 'He commissioned the sculptor Richard Smith (*see* SMITH, (2)) . . .'

Members of the same family with identical names are usually distinguished by the use of parenthesized small roman numerals after their names. Synonymous family members commonly differentiated in art-historical literature by large roman numerals appear as such in this dictionary in two cases: where a family entry does not contain the full sequence (e.g. **Karel van Mander I** and **Karel van Mander III**); and where there are two or more identical families whose surnames are distinguished by parenthesized small roman numerals (e.g. **Giovanni Battista I Carlone (ii)** and **Giovanni Battista II Carlone (ii)**).

2. NON-BIOGRAPHICAL. As with biographies, the headings of all non-biographical articles provide variant spellings, transliterations etc in square brackets, where relevant, followed by a definition. Longer articles are divided as appropriate for the topic and are provided with contents lists after the heading, introductory paragraph or each new major subheading. In all articles the hierarchy of subdivisions, from largest to smallest, is indicated by large roman numerals (I), arabic numerals (1), small roman numerals (i) and letters (a). A cross-reference within a long survey to another of its sections takes the form '*see* §I, 2(iii)(b) above'. The most extensive surveys, such as those of **China** or of **Islamic art**, include a detailed table of contents of all sections and subsections.

III. Standard usages.

For the sake of consistent presentation in this dictionary, certain standard usages, particularly in spelling and terminology, have been imposed throughout. In general, the rules of British orthography and punctuation have been applied, except that wherever possible original sources are followed for quoted matter and for specific names and titles. Many of the conventions adopted in the dictionary will become evident through use, for example the general abbreviations (which are listed at the front of each volume); some of the other editorial practices are explained below.

1. PLACE NAMES. While the dictionary was in production, there were rapid and momentous global political changes, many of which have affected the names of countries and cities. Every attempt has been made to cite these correctly as at the time of going to press, the standard for which has been the United Nations policy for officially recognized names (except that the use of Burma has been retained over the use of Myanmar). Variant versions of place names—alternative spellings, transliterations, foreign-language equivalents—appear in square brackets in the headings of country, civilization, city and site articles; all such variants have been indexed (*see* §X below). Cities are cited by their commonly used English-language names (e.g. Antwerp has been used instead of the Flemish Antwerpen or the French Anvers), but where there is no English name the usage of *The Times Atlas of the World* (London, 1992) has been followed for most Western place names. For references within the text of any entry to places that have changed name in the course of history (often more than once), the name historically correct for the context has been used, followed, after its first mention, by its modern name, as in 'Constantinople (now Istanbul)'.

2. RULERS' NAMES AND TITLES. As with some place names, certain biographical names have been standardized to their anglicized versions. This applies in particular to European regal and papal names of earlier periods, whereas names tend to be given in the vernacular form for modern rulers. Almost without exception, the forms chosen are based on those in R. F. Tapsell's *Monarchs, Rulers, Dynasties and Kingdoms of the World* (London, 1983). Rulers' titles are always cited in English. By contrast, members of the lesser nobility in France, German-speaking areas, Italy and Spain have both their name and title in the vernacular (for other countries, English-language equivalents are generally used).

3. FOREIGN TERMS AND TRANSLITERATION SYSTEMS. For citations of foreign-language material, a basic reading knowledge of art-historical terms in French, German, Italian and Spanish has been assumed (although wherever there is an exact English equivalent of a foreign term this has been used). Foreign words that have gained currency in English are cited in roman type, whereas those that have not are italicized and are qualified with a brief definition, unless this is clear from the context. The conventions of capitalization in foreign languages are generally adhered to within italicized matter (e.g. book titles) but not in running, roman text for job titles (e.g. Peintre du Roi), for names of institutions, professional bodies and associations and for recurring exhibitions. Abbreviations for foreign periodical titles cited in bibliographies (*see* §VII below) are capitalized, despite the relevant foreign-language conventions.

In languages with non-roman characters, every attempt has been made to employ consistently a system of romanization generally accepted by scholars in the relevant field of art history. The particular transliteration system adopted for each area is sometimes indicated in the introduction to the appropriate survey (e.g. under **China**, where the circumstances under which the *pinyin* and the Wade–Giles systems are used are explained).

4. WORKS OF ART. Titles of works of art are generally cited in italics and by their English names, unless universally known by a foreign title. Some subjects, religious and mythological in particular, have been given standard titles throughout. The use of 'left' and 'right' in describing a work of art corresponds to the spectator's left and right. For locations of works of art *see* §V below.

5. CALENDARS AND DATES. Dates after 1582 are given according to new style, following the Gregorian calendar, for all countries, including Russia (which changed to new style only

in 1917); the only exception is for Britain, for which dates are given according to the Julian calendar up to the change in 1752. Absolute consistency cannot be guaranteed, since usage varied and it is often impossible to tell which calendar is applicable.

Where non-Christian calendars are cited, their Christian era dates are generally given first, except for BP (before present, i.e. before 1950). Citations of other calendars are qualified by the appropriate abbreviation (e.g. AH for *Anno Hegirae*; BE for Buddhist era); AD is generally omitted for Christian era dates after *c.* 1000.

Generally accepted dates for chronological periods have been inserted where appropriate to provide a context for the use of conventional period and dynastic labels. In many cases, especially with reference to those ancient cultures and civilizations understood primarily on the basis of archaeological evidence, such as ancient Egypt, the Aegean Bronze Age, Pre-Columbian America and prehistoric Europe, these dates are provisional and subject to greater or lesser scholarly agreement. The same is true of dates for dynastic labels, which may not always accurately reflect the historical situation, since different areas may have been conquered at different times. For the benefit of the non-specialist reader and to avoid confusion, every effort has been made to cite dates consistently, but it should not be assumed that the author whose name follows a particular article (or sequence of articles) accepts in detail the chronologies chosen by the editors for use in the dictionary.

We have also attempted, wherever possible, to provide biographical dates in parentheses in running text at the first mention of all art-historically significant individuals who do not have their own entries in the dictionary. (For the citation of conjectural dates of birth and death *see* §II, 1 above.) The presence of parenthesized regnal dates for rulers and popes, however, does not necessarily indicate the lack of a biography of that person. Where no dates are provided, the reader may assume that there is a biography of that individual in the dictionary (or that the person is so obscure that dates are not readily available). The use of a question mark, for example in the date of a work of art, queries an indistinct digit(s), as in 148(?7), or an illegible one, as in 148(?).

6. MEASUREMENTS AND DIMENSIONS. All measurements are cited in metric, unless within quoted matter or if the archaic form is of particular historical interest. Where two dimensions are cited, height precedes width; for three dimensions, the order is height by width by depth. If only one dimension is given, it is qualified by the appropriate abbreviation for height, width, length, diameter etc.

IV. Cross-references.

This dictionary has been compiled in the spirit of creating an integrated and interactive whole, so that readers may gain the widest perspective on the issues in which they are interested. The cross-referencing system has been designed and implemented to guide the reader easily to the information required, as well as to complementary discussions of related material, and in some cases even to alternative views. External cross-references (i.e. those to a different heading) take several forms, all of which are distinguished by the use of small capital letters, with a large capital to indicate the initial letter of the entry to which the reader is directed. Such cross-references appear exactly as the bold headings (excluding parenthesized matter) of the entries to which they refer, though in running text they are not inverted (e.g. 'He collaborated on the project with ANTHONY VAN DYCK . . .'). The phrases 'see', 'see under' and 'see also' are always italicized when referring to another entry or another section of a multipartite article in the dictionary; where the word 'see' appears in roman type, the reference is to an illustration within the article or to another publication.

Given the comprehensiveness of the dictionary, cross-references are used sparingly between articles to guide readers to further discussions or to articles they may not have considered consulting; thus within a phrase such as 'He was influenced by Michelangelo' there is not a cross-reference to MICHELANGELO (though the reader can assume that there is a biography of Michelangelo, since there are no dates after his name), whereas 'Rosso Fiorentino and Francesco Primaticcio, through their work at FONTAINEBLEAU, introduced the Mannerist style into France (*see also* FRANCE, fig. 45)' alerts the reader to a useful description in the site entry and an illustration in the country survey. Cross-references have also been used to direct the reader to additional bibliography.

Another type of cross-reference appears as a main bold heading, to direct the reader to the place in the dictionary where the subject is treated:

> **Santi, Raffaello.** *See* RAPHAEL.
> **Holman Hunt, William.** *See* HUNT, WILLIAM HOLMAN.
> **Louis XIV.** *See* BOURBON, §I(9).
> **White, Stanford.** *See under* McKIM, MEAD & WHITE.
> **Watches.** *See under* CLOCKS AND WATCHES.

Some cross-references of this type include a short definition and guide the reader to a fuller discussion or illustration:

> **Bimah** [bema]. Raised pulpit in a synagogue, from which the Torah is read (*see* JEWISH ART, §II, 1(iii) and fig. 8).

V. Locations of works of art.

For each work of art mentioned specifically, every attempt has been made to cite its correct present location. In general this information appears in an abbreviated form, in parentheses, directly after the first mention of the work. The standard abbreviations used for locations are readily understandable in their short forms and appear in full in Appendix A in vol. 33. Pieces that are on loan or on deposit are duly noted as such, as are works that are *in situ.* Works in private collections are usually followed by the citation of a published illustration or a catalogue raisonné number to assist in identification. Similarly, objects produced in multiples, such as prints and medals, are identified with a standard catalogue number. Works for which the locations are unknown are cited as untraced or are supplied with the last known location or, in the case of pieces that appeared on the art market, are given the city, auction house or gallery name and, when known, the date of sale and lot number or a reference to a published illustration; works that have been destroyed are so noted.

VI. Illustrations.

As often as permissible, pictures have been integrated into the text of the article that they illustrate, and the wording of captions has been designed to emphasize the subject to which the picture is related. For an article with a single illustration, the textual reference appears as '(see fig.)'; multiple illustrations are numbered. Colour plates appear in many of the volumes; references to these are in the form '(see colour pl. XII, fig. 2)' or '(*see* GLASS, colour pl. V, fig. 1)'. There are frequent cross-references to relevant illustrations appearing in other articles, and all captions have been indexed.

VII. Bibliographies and other sources.

All but the shortest of entries in the dictionary are followed by bibliographies and may also have sections on unpublished sources, writings, photographic publications or prints and video recordings or films. These function both as guides to selected further reading and viewing and as acknowledgments of the sources consulted by authors. In some family entries and in longer surveys, bibliographies may be located directly after the introduction and/or at the end of each section. All bibliographies are chronologically arranged by the date of first edition (thus providing an abstract of the topic's historiography); longer bibliographies are divided into categories, in which the items are also in chronological order. Items published in the same year are listed alphabetically by authors' names and, where by the same author, alphabetically by title; items with named authors or editors take precedence over exhibition catalogues, which are cited by title first. Abbreviated references to certain alphabetically arranged dictionaries and encyclopedias (listed in full in vol. 33, Appendix C, List A) appear at the head of the bibliography (or section) in alphabetical order. The title of the article in such reference books is cited only if the spelling or form of the name differs from that used in this dictionary or if the reader is being referred to a different subject. Some other frequently cited works (*see* Appendix C, List B) are given in an abbreviated form, but in their correct chronological position within the bibliography and usually with their volume and page numbers. Appendix C also includes a list of the abbreviations used for works from publishers' series.

For books that have appeared in several editions, generally the first and most recent have been cited (unless there was a particular reason to include an intermediate edition), and where page numbers are provided these refer to the most recent edition. Revisions are indicated by the abbreviation 'rev.', reprints with '*R*' and translations with 'trans.' prefaced by an abbreviation to indicate the language of the translation. Where the place or date of publication does not appear in a book this is rendered as 'n.p.' or 'n.d.' as appropriate; where this information can be surmised it appears in square brackets. Volume numbers usually appear in small roman numerals, both for citations from multi-volume publications and for periodicals; issue numbers of periodicals are in arabic numerals. The titles of periodicals are cited in abbreviated forms, a full list of which appears in Appendix B in vol. 33. Exhibition catalogues are provided with the name of the host location (not the place of publication) according to the list of location abbreviations (*see* Appendix A). Collected papers from conferences and congresses are arranged chronologically by date of their oral presentation rather than by the date of their publication in hard copy. Dissertations are included in the bibliography sections (rather than as unpublished sources), with an abbreviated form of the degree (diss., MA, MPhil) and awarding institution; if available on microfilm, this is noted.

Lists of unpublished sources, apart from dissertations, include such material as manuscripts, inventories and diaries. They are organized alphabetically by the location of the holdings, with an indication of the contents given in square brackets. Lists of selected writings are included in biographies of subjects who wrote on art; these are ordered according to the same principles as the bibliographies. Sections of photographic publications and prints list published books or collections of work by the subject of the article. If there is a significant collection of material on video or film, this is listed in its own section, in chronological order.

Throughout the production time of this dictionary authors were asked to submit important new bibliography for addition to their articles. Some contributors did so, while others left updating to be done by the editors. For the additions that were made by the editorial staff in the final days before going to press, this may have resulted in the text of an article apparently failing to take into consideration the discoveries or opinions of the new publications; it was nevertheless felt useful to draw readers' attention to significant recent literature.

VIII. Authors.

Signatures of authors, in the form of their choice, appear at the end of the article or sequence of articles that they contributed. In multipartite articles, a section (or sections) that is unsigned is by the author of the next signed section. Where two authors have jointly written an article, their names appear in alphabetical order:

CHARLES JONES, BETTY SMITH

If, however, Smith was the main author and was assisted or had her text amended by Jones, their signatures appear as:

BETTY SMITH, with CHARLES JONES

In the event that Jones assisted with only the bibliography to Smith's text, this would be acknowledged as:

BETTY SMITH (bibliography with CHARLES JONES)

Where an article or introduction was compiled by the editors or in the few cases where an author has wished to remain anonymous, this is indicated by a square box (□) instead of a signature.

IX. Appendices.

Readers' attention is directed to the appendices in vol. 33. These comprise full lists of: abbreviated locations of works of art (A); abbreviated periodical titles (B); standard reference books and series (C); and authors' names (D).

X. Index.

All articles and illustrations in this dictionary have been indexed not only to provide volume and page numbers of the main headings but also to pinpoint variant names and spellings and specific information within articles and captions. Full guidelines for using the Index, located in the final volume, can be found as its preface.

Acknowledgements

Projects of this magnitude inevitably incur a multitude of debts. As is clear from the preface, the preparation of the *Dictionary of Art* represents an enormous collective effort, one that took over 14 years and involved literally a cast of thousands, from every corner of the globe. Here I can name only a selection of those who participated in the project in some capacity and apologize to those who cannot be mentioned individually. No single group deserves greater thanks than the countless unnamed contributors (our unsung heroes and heroines) who submitted their entries and proofs on schedule and followed the house-style notes for contributors. There were also many authors whose advice and support went far beyond the writing of their articles, for example in helping us to plan and commission large, complex multi-author articles. Other contributors (including a small army of in-house writers) agreed at short notice to provide entries when the original commissions failed to arrive. I should also like to thank many others who assisted us in innumerable ways: recommending authors, providing information, alerting us to discoveries, checking bibliographical details, securing photographs etc. We are most grateful to them all. The formal acknowledgements are divided into three sections: outside advisers, in-house staff and other outside sources. Unfortunately, for reasons of space, none of the lists can be fully comprehensive, and the extent and duration of each person's involvement has had to be weighed against those of hundreds of other individuals. However, we should like to express our thanks to everyone who participated in the creation of the *Dictionary*, whether mentioned below or not, for all the efforts they have put into making it a success.

1. OUTSIDE ADVISERS AND CONSULTANTS.

(i) Editorial Advisory Board. Our first debt of gratitude must go to the members of our distinguished Editorial Advisory Board for the guidance they provided on matters of general concept and approach.

Prof. Emeritus Terukazu Akiyama (formerly of the University of Tokyo)
Prof. Carlo Bertelli (Université de Lausanne)
Prof. Whitney Chadwick (San Francisco State University)
Prof. André Chastel (formerly of the Collège de France, Paris)†
Prof. Oleg Grabar (Institute for Advanced Study, Princeton)
Prof. Francis Haskell (University of Oxford)
Prof. Alfonso E. Pérez Sánchez (formerly of the Museo del Prado, Madrid)
Prof. Robert Rosenblum (New York University)
Dr Jessica Rawson (University of Oxford and formerly of the British Museum, London)
Prof. Willibald Sauerländer (formerly of the Zentralinstitut für Kunstgeschichte, Munich)
Mr Peter Thornton (formerly of the Sir John Soane's Museum, London)
Prof. Irene Winter (Harvard University, Cambridge, Massachusetts)

† deceased

In addition to informal advice over the years, a number of formal working seminars were arranged with advisory board members and other experts to examine particular areas of our coverage. I should like to thank, especially, Professor Akiyama for his continued advice on our coverage of Japanese art and art history; Whitney Chadwick for her help on contemporary and women artists; Francis Haskell for his assistance with patrons; Oleg Grabar for his advice on Islamic art, as well as on the balance of coverage between non-Western areas; and Peter Thornton for his constant support on matters pertaining to interior design and the decorative arts.

(ii) Area advisers. Once our general conceptual scheme had begun to take shape, outside experts were formally invited to develop plans for the coverage of the arts in their areas of specialization. Governed only by a general word allocation and suggestions for certain basic patterns of coverage, each was asked to prepare an outline (or report) with proposed headings, relative word lengths and names of potential authors. These area reports were then assigned to in-house area editors (see §2 below) to coordinate and supplement where necessary.

I. Ancient and non-Western cultures and civilizations.

Aboriginal art
Howard Morphy

Aegean Bronze Age art
Reynold Higgins†

Afghan art
David Macdowell

African art
John Picton

Ancient Cyprus
Nicolas Coldstream

Ancient Egyptian art
T. G. H. James

Ancient Greek and Roman jewellery
Reynold Higgins†

Ancient Greek and Roman sculpture
Geoffrey Waywell

Ancient Greek architecture
J. J. Coulton

Ancient Greek painting
Martin Robertson

Ancient Near Eastern art
Julian Reade

Ancient Roman architecture, painting and decorative arts
Margaret Lyttelton†

Armenian art
Lucy der Manuelian

Caribbean art
Dolores Yonker

Chinese and Korean art
Roderick Whitfield

† deceased

Chinese architecture
Nancy Shatzman Steinhardt

Chinese decorative arts
Jessica Rawson

Chinese general issues
Jonathan Hay

Chinese painting, sculpture and decorative arts
James Cahill

Early Christian and Byzantine art
Robin Cormack

Etruscan art
Tom Rasmussen

Indian art
Pramod Chandra
Vidya Dehejia
Robert Skelton

Islamic art
Robert Hillenbrand

Islamic carpets
Jon Thompson

Japanese art
David Waterhouse

Korean art and architecture
Youngsook Pak

Migration period art in Europe
John Mitchell

Mongolian art
Krystyna Chabros

Native North American art
Christian Feest
William Sturtevant
Richard Townsend

Nepalese art
Ian Alsop

Pacific Islands art
Peter Gathercole

Pre-Columbian Central and South American Art
Warwick Bray

Pre-Columbian Mesoamerican art
G. B. Nicholson

Prehistoric European art
Sara Champion
A. C. Renfrew

Pre-Islamic Arabian art
D. T. Potts

Sino-Central Asian art
Herbert Härtel

South-east Asian art
Robert Brown

Tibetan art
Jane Casey Singer
Frances Wood

Viking art
James Graham-Campbell

Western Central Asian art
Anatoly I. Ivanov

II. Medieval.

Architecture, sculpture and painting in Italy, 1200-1400
Julian Gardner

European medieval architecture
Paul Crossley

European medieval decorative arts and liturgical objects
Neil Stratford

European medieval stained glass
Jill Kerr

European medieval wall and panel painting
Paul Binski

Manuscript illumination in Italy, c. *800-1400*
Valentino Pace
Kay Sutton

Medieval architecture in Italy, 800-1200
Mario D'Onofrio

Medieval art in Scandinavia
Christopher Hohler

Painting and manuscript illumination in 15th-century France
Nicole Reynaud

Painting and mosaics in Italy, 300-1200
Caecilia Davis-Weyer

Sculpture in France, Spain, England and the Low Countries, 800-1500
Walter Cahn

Sculpture in Germany and Central Europe, 800-1200
Willibald Sauerländer

Sculpture in Italy, 800-1200
Dorothy Glass

Sculpture of the Holy Roman Empire, c. *1300-c. 1500*
Anton Legner

Western illuminated manuscripts
Christopher de Hamel

III. Regional surveys.

Albanian art
Gjergi Frashëri

American architecture, c. *1600-* c. *1914*
William Jordy

American decorative arts
Gerald Ward

American painting and sculpture, c. *1600-c. 1914*
Jules Prown

Art of the Holy Roman Empire in the 18th century
Alastair Laing

Arts of the (former) USSR
Mikhail N. Sokolov

Australian architecture
Conrad Hamann

Australian painting, sculpture and decorative arts
Patrick McCaughey
Terence Smith

Austrian and Hungarian sculpture in the 19th century
Walter Krause

Austrian art, 1500-1800
Kurt Woisetschläger

Austrian decorative arts
Elisabeth Scheicher

Belgian metalwork
Leo de Ren

Bohemian and Moravian painting and sculpture
Amanda Simpson

Bohemian Baroque architecture
Jirí Tomás Kotalík

British architecture, 1840-1914
J. Mordaunt Crook

British and early Netherlandish painting in the 16th century
Susan Foister

British and Irish painting in the 19th century
Marcia Pointon

British and Irish sculpture in the 18th and 19th centuries
Nicholas Penny

British painting in the 17th century
Sir Oliver Millar

British painting in the 18th century
John Hayes

British sculpture, 1500-1700
John Physick

Canadian archtitecture
Alan Gowans

Canadian painting, sculpture and decorative arts
Laurier Lacroix

Czech decorative arts
Dagmar Tucná

Dutch and Belgian architecture in the 19th century
Helen Searing

Dutch and Belgian painting, sculpture and the graphic arts in the 19th century
Ronald de Leeuw

Dutch and Flemish architecture and sculpture, 1550-1800
Kerry Downes

Dutch and Flemish ceramics
Mireille Jottrand

Dutch painting, drawing and graphic arts, 1550-1800
Christopher White

English and Welsh architecture, to c. *1840*
Howard Colvin

Flemish painting, drawing and graphic arts, 1550-1800
Kristin Belkin
Elizabeth McGrath

French and Italian architecture in the 18th and 19th centuries
Robin Middleton

French architecture in the 17th century
Neil MacGregor

French decorative arts
Pierre Ennès
Amaury Lefébure
Patricia Lemonnier

French furniture and interiors
Jean Nérée Ronfort

French painting, architecture and graphic arts in the 16th century
Jean Guillaume

French painting in the 17th century
Michael Kitson

French painting in the 18th century
Philip Conisbee

French painting, 1800-1870
Jon Whiteley

French painting and graphic arts, 1860-1900
Christopher Lloyd

French sculpture and decorative arts in the 16th century
Bertrand Jestaz

French sculpture in the 17th and 18th centuries
Geneviève Bresc

French sculpture in the 19th century
Anne Pingeot

German architecture, 1500-1700
Jürgen Zimmer

German architecture in the 19th century
Barry Bergdoll

German ceramics and glass
Walter Spiegl

German ivories and miniature sculpture, 1500-1800
Christian Theuerkauff

German painting and graphic arts in the 15th century
Kurt Löcher
Peter Strieder

German painting in the 16th and 17th centuries
Keith Andrews†

German painting in the 19th century
Will Vaughan

German sculpture in the 19th century
Peter Bloch
Sibylle Einholz

Greek art
Chrysanthos Christou

Icelandic art
Bera Nordal

Irish and Scottish architecture
Alistair Rowan

Italian architecture in the 15th and 16th centuries
Howard Burns

Italian architecture in the 17th century
Joseph Connors

Italian decorative arts
Renato Ruotolo

Italian painting in the 15th century
Jane Martineau

Italian painting in the 16th century
Martin J. Kemp

Italian painting in the 17th and 18th centuries
Hugh Brigstocke
Erich Schleier
Richard Spear

Italian painting and sculpture in the 19th century
Sandra Berresford

Italian sculpture in the 15th to 18th centuries
Charles Avery
Bruce Boucher
Anthony Radcliffe

Latin American art and architecture, to c. *1820*
John Bury

Netherlandish painting, 1400-1550
Lorne Campbell

† deceased

Polish art
Aleksander Gieysztor
Jerzy Pietrusinski
Andrezej Rottermund

Portuguese art, 1500-1800
Angela Delaforce
Hellmut Wohl

Portuguese art in the 19th century
José-Augusto França

Romanian art
Codruta Cruceanu

Russian and Soviet architecture from 1700
Catherine Cooke

Russian painting and sculpture from 1700
Larissa Haskell

Scandinavian architecture
Hakon Lund

Scandinavian painting and sculpture, 1400-1700
Torbjörn Fulton
Anna Nilsén

Scandinavian painting and sculpture, 1700-1900
Pontus Grate

Spanish architecture
Fernando Marías

Spanish architecture and decorative arts, 1490-1820
John Bury

Spanish architecture, c. *1820-*c. *1914*
Vicente Lleo Canal

Spanish painting in the 15th century
Santiago Alcolea

Spanish painting of the 16th to 18th centuries
Johnathan Brown

Spanish painting in the 19th century
Enrique Arias
Wifredo Rincón

Spanish sculpture
Juan José Martín González

Swedish decorative arts
Helena Dahlbäck-Lutteman

Swiss painting and sculpture, c. *1600-1900*
Hans A. Lüthy

Yugoslav art
Boris Vizintin

IV. 20th century.

Architecture after 1900
Gavin Stamp

Chinese art after 1900
Michael Sullivan

German and Austrian painting and sculpture since 1935
Richard Calvocoressi

Indian art after 1900
Geeta Kapur

Japanese art after 1900
Toru Asano
Shigeo Chiba
Yoshikazu Iwasaki
Kazu Kaido

Spanish art in the 20th century
Francisco Calvo Serraller

European, American and Japanese prints in the 20th century
Alexander Duckers

European, American and Russian painting and sculpture in the 20th century
Ronald Alley

European art, 1890-1920
Peter Vergo

V. Art forms and general issues.

Design and designers
Simon Jervis

Fans
Helene Alexander

Frames
Paul Mitchell

Gardens and garden design
John Dixon Hunt

Gems
Gertrud Seidmann

General Issues
David Freedberg
Henri Zerner

Jewellery
Diana Scarisbrick

Medals and plaquettes
Graham Pollard

Metalwork
Clare Le Corbeiller
Hannelore Müller
Anthony North

Painting materials and techniques
Joyce Plesters
Ashok Roy

Photography
Weston Naef

Printmaking
David Landau

Puppets
Henryk Jurkowski

Religion and art
Diane Apostolos-Cappadona

Sculpture and applied art materials and techniques
Jonathan Ashley-Smith

Tapestry
Candace Adelson

Wallpaper
Joanna Banham

2. EDITORIAL AND ADMINISTRATIVE STAFF. Among my colleagues, I must first acknowledge and express my gratitude to my predecessor as editor of the *Dictionary of Art*, Hugh Brigstocke, who was responsible for its overall plan. It was he who conceived the general intellectual framework, and, having argued the case in favour of an inclusive and broadly based theoretical approach (one that paid serious scholarly attention to architecture and the arts outside the West, among other things), he went on to establish the relative balance between the different areas of coverage. This basic plan, the result of four years of intensive work and consultation with many outside experts, was more or less finalized by the time of his departure in 1987, when the editing of the first texts got underway. It is a tribute to the coherence and intelligence of the plan that it has remained substantially unaltered since then. The task of planning the coverage and commissioning area reports was shared, in the early stages, with Jane Martineau, who joined the staff as Text Editor and was responsible for compiling the initial house-style rules based on those of the *New Grove*. In subsequent revisions to the house-style manual, I was greatly assisted by Ruth Thackeray, who, with Jane Martineau, was involved in the early training of desk editors.

In 1988 we reorganized the staff into editorial teams, as reflected in the list below. The success of this team approach to editing, in which copy editors and art historians worked together to prepare manuscripts for the typesetter, is due in large part to the support I received from our deputy editors. I should particularly like to thank Nicola Coldstream for her able supervision of the Classical and medieval teams; Marco Livingstone and, later, Samantha Roberts for ensuring that the coverage of 19th- and 20th- century art was thoughtful and well-balanced and that the articles themselves were free of unnecessary jargon; and, finally, Pat Barylski and, later, Diane Fortenberry for their sensitive guidance of the non-Western teams, who were grouped together (without an acceptable collective name) for reasons of the similar intellectual approach generally taken to their material rather than for any direct links between their areas. Besides contacting potential authors and preparing their articles for publication once they arrived, many members of the editorial staff, art historians in their own right, also contributed entries. Among our in-house writers, I should particularly mention the valuable contribution of Philip Cooper, who wrote more short biographies than any other author. After each article was edited for content and house-style, it was submitted to one of a small team of vetters before being sent to the typesetter; the *Dictionary* is undoubtedly a much more accurate and consistent work of reference due to their careful checking and high editorial standards.

The administration of a project this size is a formidable task. We are grateful to all those who played a part in the organization of commissions, contracts, payments, translations, illustrations, copyright permissions, proofs, author corrections, filing etc. The rules governing the compilation of the index were established by Ruth Levitt, who was succeeded by Gillian Northcott, under whose supervision a large team of indexers and checkers created some three quarters of a million index references. The final supervision of the illustrations database, which numbered some 15,000 items, was handled by Stephanie Farrow; she was ably assisted on matters of sizing and electronic digitization by Martyn Evans. Around 12,000 articles—over a quarter of the *Dictionary*—arrived in a language other than English, and among those involved in coordinating our team of outside translators, who had to cope with 30 different languages, were Paul Ratcliffe and Teresa Brown. For the proof stages of the project I am grateful to

Lucy Temperley, Jayne Bartholomew, Samantha Roberts and, most of all, Diane Fortenberry, who shared with me the task of checking the corrections to 30,000 page proofs in a period of just over ten weeks. On the production side, we greatly benefited from the expert experience of Macmillan's Production Director, John Peacock, who was assisted in our offices by Stephen Benaim. Among those involved in the typesetting at Pindar plc, special mention must be made of Vincent Loach, whose unstinting attention to technical details saved us much time and trouble; moreover, he and his colleagues managed to read enough of the *Dictionary of Art* in their spare time to compile the *Dictionary of Death: The Pindar Book of Bitter Ends*, an entertaining account of the often poignant but sometimes gruesome ways in which artists met their death.

(i) Editorial teams.

African and Australasian art
Jeremy Coote
Dunja Hersak

Ancient Egyptian art
Dominic Montserrat
Delia Pemberton
C. N. Reeves
Ian Shaw

Ancient Near Eastern art
Dominique Collon

Architecture
Val Clack (dep. ed.; vetter)
Paul Davies
David Hemsoll
Gordon Higgott
Charles Hind
Julian Honer (vetter)
Harold Meek
John Musgrove
Christine Stevenson
Alexandra Wedgwood
Robert Williams

British and French painting and northern European sculpture
Marc Jordan (dep. ed.)

Chinese, Korean and Mongolian art
Diane Fortenberry (dep. ed.; vetter)
Graham Hutt
Susan Pares
Susannah Perry
Sarah Waldram

Classical Greek and Roman art
Michael Bird (vetter)
David Hibler
Margaret Lyttelton†
Kim Richardson (vetter)

Decorative arts and materials and techniques
Michael Hall
Frankie Liebe (vetter)
Judith Neiswander

† deceased

Alexandra Pel (dep. ed.; vetter)
Liz Stubbs (vetter)
Lucy Trench
Sarah Yates (vetter)

Early Christian and Byzantine art
Kara Hattersley Smith
Valerie Nunn

Eastern European art
Anne Charvet
Kevin Halliwell (vetter)
Jeremy Howard

General issues and theory
Kevin Halliwell (vetter)
Richard Wollheim

Holy Roman Empire and Central European art
Alistair Laing
Dorothy Limouze

Islamic art
Sheila Blair
Jonathan Bloom
Roderick Brown
Godfrey Goodwin (dep. ed.)
Tim Stanley
Stephen Vernoit

Italian painting
Lucinda Collinge
Helen Langdon
Jane Martineau (dep. ed.; vetter)
Margaret Walker

Italian sculpture and Scandinavian art
Antonia Böstrom

Japanese art
Elizabeth Bennett
Kendall Brown
Eric Chaline
Ingrid Cranfield
Christine Guth
Amy Newland

Medieval art
Tanya Alfillé (dep. ed.; vetter)
Nicola Coldstream (dep. ed.; vetter)
Jill Franklin
Delia Gaze (vetter)
David Rose (vetter)
Kay Sutton

Netherlandish, Dutch and Flemish painting
Jane Turner (ed.; vetter)

19th- and 20th-century art
Francesca Calvocoressi
Elizabeth Clegg
Oliver Garnett
Marco Livingstone (dep. ed.; vetter)
Samantha Roberts (dep. ed.; vetter)
Matthew Taylor (vetter)

Patronage
Tanya Harrod
Janet Southorn†

Pre-Columbian art
Orianna Baddeley
Elizabeth Baquedano
David Jones

Prints
Katharina Mayer Haunton

South Asian art
Pat Barylski (dep. ed.; vetter)
Dan Ehnbom
Elizabeth Errington
Jenny Marsh (vetter)
Rekha Morris (dep. ed.)
Michael Willis

South-east Asian art
Angela Hobart
John Villiers

Spanish and Portuguese art
Angela Delaforce

† deceased

(ii) Non-editorial departments.

Administration
Christianne Bakker
Jayne Bartholomew
Victoria Boyd
Ian Critchley
Sara Cunningham
Sophie Durlacher
Caroline Jackson
Lucy Temperley

Index
Teresa Brown
Ruth Levitt
Gillian Northcott

Picture Department
Martyn Evans
Stephanie Farrow
Caroline Hensman
Lorraine Mallon
Philippa Thomson

Translations
Teresa Brown
Paul Ratcliffe

3. OTHER OUTSIDE SOURCES. Many people and organizations outside the *Dictionary* have provided generous help to us and to our contributors. We are particularly grateful to librarians in London, especially at the British Library, the Courtauld Institute, the Royal Institute of British Architects (RIBA), the School of Oriental and African Studies (SOAS), the Tate Gallery, the National Art Library at the Victoria and Albert Museum and the Warburg Institute, who facilitated the work of our staff and local authors. I should like to thank Noël Annesley, Deputy Chairman of Christie's, for his official support of staff members carrying out research for us on decorative art topics. For the commissioning of a number of short biographies of Dutch artists, we benefited from the services of the Stichting Postuniversitair Kunsthistorisch Onderzoek (SPKO), based in the Netherlands. We have enjoyed cordial and helpful relations with the editorial offices of a number of London art publications, such as *Apollo Magazine*, the *Art Newspaper* and the *Burlington Magazine*, who have patiently endured and resolved many a bibliographical query. The generosity of Her Majesty Queen Elizabeth II in waiving the reproduction fees for all works illustrated from the British Royal Collection is hereby gratefully acknowledged. Special thanks are also owed to several other photographic sources and copyright-holders, who processed especially large orders from us, including: the Archivi Alinari, Florence; the Bildarchiv Foto Marburg; the British Museum, London; Giraudon, Paris; the Kunsthistorisches Museum, Vienna; the Metropolitan Museum of Art, New York; and the Service Photographique de la Réunion des Museés Nationaux, Paris. The colour plates were designed by Robert Updegraff. The specific sources for all images in the *Dictionary*, both black-and-white and colour, are acknowledged in the list of picture credits appended to each volume.

A number of publishers and individuals kindly granted us permission to reuse and adapt material from previously published sources:

Annenberg School for Communication, University of Pennsylvania, and Oxford University Press: *The International Encyclopedia of Communications*, ed. Erik Barnouw (New York and London, 1989): **Printing**

Boston Museum of Fine Arts and the Pierpont Morgan Library, New York: *Rembrandt: Experimental Etcher* (exh. cat., 1969-70): **Rembrandt van Rijn, §II, 3**

British Museum Press: *The British Museum Book of Chinese Art* by Jessica Rawson (London, 1992), pp. 14-19: **China, §I, 1 and 3**

Editions d'Art Albert Skira S.A.: *Félix Bracquemond, le réalisme absolu: Oeuvre gravé, 1849-1859, catalogue raisonné* by Jean-Paul Bouillon (Geneva, 1987): **Félix Bracquemond**

George Weidenfeld & Nicolson Ltd.: *Who's Who in Architecture*, ed. J. M. Richards (London, 1977): **Mies van der Rohe**

Flammarion, Paris: *Les Manuscripts à peinture en France, 1440-1520* (exh. cat. by François Avril and Nicole Reynaud, Paris, Bib. N., 1993), pp. 109-20; 293-305: **Jean Bourdichon; Master of Jouvenel des Ursins**

Jane Voorhees Zimmerli Art Museum, Rutgers University, New Brunswick, NJ: *Haarlem: The Seventeenth Century* (exh. cat. by Frima Fox Hofrichter and others, 1983): **Haarlem, §2(i)**

Larousse plc: *Chambers Biographical Dictionary*, ed. Magnus Magnusson (5th edn, Edinburgh, 1990): **Max Uhle**

Los Angeles County Museum of Art: *Shippo: The Art of Enameling in Japan* (exh. cat., 1987): **Japan, §XV, 8**

National Gallery, London: *Art in the Making: Rembrandt* (exh. cat. by David Bomford, Christopher Brown and Ashok Roy, 1988): **Rembrandt van Rijn, §II, 2**

National Gallery, London, the Rijksmuseum, Amsterdam, and the Staatliche Museen Preussischer Kulturbesitz, Berlin: *The Master and his Workshop: Paintings* (exh. cat. by Christopher Brown, Jan Kelch and Pieter van Thiel, 1991-2) and *The Master and his Workshop: Drawings and Etchings* (exh. cat. by Holm Bevers, Peter Schatborn and B. Welzel, 1991-2): **Rembrandt van Rijn, §II, 1-2 and 4**

National Gallery of Art, Washington, DC: *Guercino: Drawings from Windsor Castle* (exh. cat. by Nicholas Turner, 1991-2): **Guercino, §1**

Oxford University Press: *The Oxford Companion to Gardens*, ed. Sir Geoffrey Jellicoe, Susan Jellicoe, Patrick Goode and Michael Lancaster (Oxford, 1986): **Powerscourt; Pratolino**

Palumbo, Peter: *Proof of Evidence* (London, 1990): **Mies van der Rohe**

Penn State Press: *The Painting of Baciccio* by Robert Enggass (University Park, 1964): **Giovanni Battista Gaulli**

Phaidon Press Ltd: *Mies van der Rohe at Work* by Peter Carter (New York and London, 1974): **Mies van der Rohe**

Princeton University Art Museum: *Images of the Mind: Selections from the Edward L. Elliot Family and John B. Elliot Collections of Chinese Calligraphy and Painting at the Art Museum, Princeton University* (exh. cat. by Wen Fong, 1984): **Daoji; Ni zan**

Sharp, Dennis: *The Rationalists* (London, 1987): **Mies van der Rohe**

The Free Press, a division of Macmillan Publishing Co.: *Macmillan Encyclopedia of Architects*, ed. Adolf K. Placzek, 4 vols (New York, 1982): **Francesco del Borgo; Ernest Cormier; Cornelius Gurlitt; Edwin Lutyens; Albert Speer**

* * *

On a personal note, I should like to thank all of my former secretaries, many of whose names appear in §2 above since their able skills enabled them to be moved into other roles; these include my first, Jayne Bartholomew (proof collation), and later Gillian Northcott (index), Rosalind Thiro (copy editor) and Kate Jaeger (marketing) and, lastly, my present assistant, Sally Meen. I am grateful also to Denise Smith, for ensuring that my first two and a half years of motherhood were entirely uncomplicated and pleasurable, and to my husband, Nicholas Turner, for his advice on countless art-historical matters and for his continued support, especially during the final editorial stages of this project. Finally, I am pleased to acknowledge the support that we have received from Macmillan Publishers Ltd. Their unwavering commitment to this ambitious academic undertaking is due in no small measure to the courage and vision of their chairman, Nicholas Byam Shaw, whose enthusiasm for progress was matched only by his commitment to quality. Among the other company directors, I should also like to thank Adrian Soar and Brian Stonier, as well as Richard Garnett, whose guidance was much appreciated in the early days of the project. In the day-to-day management since 1985, I have enjoyed the full cooperation and support of the Dictionary's Publisher, Ian Jacobs. The journey was made easier—and certainly more pleasant— in the company of such a sympathetic and tireless professional.

J. T.

General Abbreviations

The abbreviations employed throughout this dictionary, most of which are listed below, do not vary, except for capitalization, regardless of the context in which they are used, including bibliographical citations and for locations of works of art. The principle used to arrive at these abbreviations is that their full form should be easily deducible, and for this reason acronyms have generally been avoided (e.g. Los Angeles Co. Mus. A. instead of LACMA). The same abbreviation is adopted for cognate forms in foreign languages and in most cases for plural and adjectival forms (e.g. A.= Art, Arts, Arte, Arti etc). Not all related forms are listed below. Occasionally, if a name, for instance of an artists' group or exhibiting society, is repeated within the text of one article, it is cited in an abbreviated form after its first mention in full (e.g. The Pre-Raphaelite Brotherhood (PRB) was founded...); the same is true of archaeological periods and eras, which are abbreviated to initial letters in small capitals (e.g. In the Early Minoan (EM) period...). Such abbreviations do not appear in this list. For the reader's convenience, separate full lists of abbreviations for locations, periodical titles and standard reference books and series are included as Appendices A–C in vol. 33.

A.	Art, Arts
A.C.	Arts Council
Acad.	Academy
AD	Anno Domini
Add.	Additional, Addendum
addn	addition
Admin.	Administration
Adv.	Advances, Advanced
Aesth.	Aesthetic(s)
Afr.	African
Afrik.	Afrikaans, Afrikaner
A.G.	Art Gallery
Agrar.	Agrarian
Agric.	Agriculture
Agron.	Agronomy
Agy	Agency
AH	Anno Hegirae
A. Inst.	Art Institute
AK	Alaska (USA)
AL	Alabama (USA)
Alb.	Albanian
Alg.	Algerian
Alta	Alberta (Canada)
Altern.	Alternative
a.m.	ante meridiem [before noon]
Amat.	Amateur
Amer.	American
An.	Annals
Anatol.	Anatolian
Anc.	Ancient
Annu.	Annual
Anon.	Anonymous(ly)
Ant.	Antique
Anthol.	Anthology
Anthropol.	Anthropology
Antiqua.	Antiquarian, Antiquaries
app.	appendix
approx.	approximately
AR	Arkansas (USA)
ARA	Associate of the Royal Academy
Arab.	Arabic
Archaeol.	Archaeology
Archit.	Architecture, Architectural
Archv, Archvs	Archive(s)
Arg.	Argentine
ARHA	Associate of the Royal Hibernian Academy
ARIBA	Associate of the Royal Institute of British Architects
Armen.	Armenian
ARSA	Associate of the Royal Scottish Academy
Asiat.	Asiatic
Assist.	Assistance
Assoc.	Association
Astron.	Astronomy
AT&T	American Telephone & Telegraph Company
attrib.	attribution, attributed to
Aug	August
Aust.	Austrian
Austral.	Australian
Auth.	Author(s)
Auton.	Autonomous
Aux.	Auxiliary
Ave.	Avenue
AZ	Arizona (USA)
Azerbaij.	Azerbaijani
B.	Bartsch [catalogue of Old Master prints]
b	born
BA	Bachelor of Arts
Balt.	Baltic
bapt	baptized
BArch	Bachelor of Architecture
Bart	Baronet
Bask.	Basketry
BBC	British Broadcasting Corporation
BC	Before Christ
BC	British Columbia (Canada)
BE	Buddhist era
Beds	Bedfordshire (GB)
Behav.	Behavioural
Belarus.	Belarusian
Belg.	Belgian
Berks	Berkshire (GB)
Berwicks	Berwickshire (GB; old)
BFA	Bachelor of Fine Arts
Bibl.	Bible, Biblical
Bibliog.	Bibliography, Bibliographical
Biblioph.	Bibliophile
Biog.	Biography, Biographical
Biol.	Biology, Biological
bk, bks	book(s)
Bkbinder	Bookbinder
Bklore	Booklore
Bkshop	Bookshop
BL	British Library
Bld	Build
Bldg	Building

Bldr	Builder
BLitt	Bachelor of Letters/Literature
BM	British Museum
Boh.	Bohemian
Boliv.	Bolivian
Botan.	Botany, Botanical
BP	Before present (1950)
Braz.	Brazilian
BRD	Bundesrepublik Deutschland [Federal Republic of Germany (West Germany)]
Brecons	Breconshire (GB; old)
Brez.	Brezonek [lang. of Brittany]
Brit.	British
Bros	Brothers
BSc	Bachelor of Science
Bucks	Buckinghamshire (GB)
Bulg.	Bulgarian
Bull.	Bulletin
bur	buried
Burm.	Burmese
Byz.	Byzantine
C	Celsius
C.	Century
c.	*circa* [about]
CA	California
Cab.	Cabinet
Caerns	Caernarvonshire (GB; old)
C.A.G.	City Art Gallery
Cal.	Calendar
Callig.	Calligraphy
Cam.	Camera
Cambs	Cambridgeshire (GB)
can	canonized
Can.	Canadian
Cant.	Canton(s), Cantonal
Capt.	Captain
Cards	Cardiganshire (GB; old)
Carib.	Caribbean
Carms	Carmarthenshire (GB; old)
Cartog.	Cartography
Cat.	Catalan
cat.	catalogue
Cath.	Catholic
CBE	Commander of the Order of the British Empire
Celeb.	Celebration
Celt.	Celtic
Cent.	Centre, Central
Centen.	Centennial
Cer.	Ceramic
cf.	confer [compare]
Chap., Chaps	Chapter(s)
Chem.	Chemistry
Ches	Cheshire (GB)
Chil.	Chilean
Chin.	Chinese
Christ.	Christian, Christianity
Chron.	Chronicle
Cie	Compagnie [French]
Cinema.	Cinematography
Circ.	Circle
Civ.	Civil, Civic
Civiliz.	Civilization(s)
Class.	Classic, Classical
Clin.	Clinical
CO	Colorado (USA)
Co.	Company; County
Cod.	Codex, Codices
Col., Cols	Collection(s); Column(s)
Coll.	College
collab.	in collaboration with, collaborated, collaborative
Collct.	Collecting
Colloq.	Colloquies
Colomb.	Colombian
Colon.	Colonies, Colonial
Colr	Collector
Comm.	Commission; Community
Commerc.	Commercial
Communic.	Communications
Comp.	Comparative; compiled by, compiler
Concent.	Concentration
Concr.	Concrete
Confed.	Confederation
Confer.	Conference
Congol.	Congolese
Congr.	Congress
Conserv.	Conservation; Conservatory
Constr.	Construction(al)
cont.	continued
Contemp.	Contemporary
Contrib.	Contributions, Contributor(s)
Convalesc.	Convalescence
Convent.	Convention
Coop.	Cooperation
Coord.	Coordination
Copt.	Coptic
Corp.	Corporation, Corpus
Corr.	Correspondence
Cors.	Corsican
Cost.	Costume
Cret.	Cretan
Crim.	Criminal
Crit.	Critical, Criticism
Croat.	Croatian
CT	Connecticut (USA)
Cttee	Committee
Cub.	Cuban
Cult.	Cultural, Culture
Cumb.	Cumberland (GB; old)
Cur.	Curator, Curatorial, Curatorship
Curr.	Current(s)
CVO	Commander of the [Royal] Victorian Order
Cyclad.	Cycladic
Cyp.	Cypriot
Czech.	Czechoslovak
$	dollars
d	died
d.	denarius, denarii [penny, pence]
Dalmat.	Dalmatian
Dan.	Danish
DBE	Dame Commander of the Order of the British Empire
DC	District of Columbia (USA)
DDR	Deutsche Demokratische Republik [German Democratic Republic (East Germany)]
DE	Delaware (USA)
Dec	December
Dec.	Decorative
ded.	dedication, dedicated to
Democ.	Democracy, Democratic
Demog.	Demography, Demographic
Denbs	Denbighshire (GB; old)
dep.	deposited at
Dept	Department
Dept.	Departmental, Departments
Derbys	Derbyshire (GB)
Des.	Design
destr.	destroyed
Dev.	Development
Devon	Devonshire (GB)
Dial.	Dialogue
diam.	diameter
Diff.	Diffusion
Dig.	Digest
Dip. Eng.	Diploma in Engineering
Dir.	Direction, Directed
Directrt	Directorate
Disc.	Discussion
diss.	dissertation
Distr.	District
Div.	Division
DLitt	Doctor of Letters/Literature
DM	Deutsche Mark
Doc.	Document(s)
Doss.	Dossier
DPhil	Doctor of Philosophy
Dr	Doctor
Drg, Drgs	Drawing(s)
DSc	Doctor of Science/Historical Sciences
Dut.	Dutch
Dwell.	Dwelling
E.	East(ern)

EC	European (Economic) Community
Eccles.	Ecclesiastical
Econ.	Economic, Economies
Ecuad.	Ecuadorean
ed.	editor, edited (by)
edn	edition
eds	editors
Educ.	Education
e.g.	*exempli gratia* [for example]
Egyp.	Egyptian
Elem.	Element(s), Elementary
Emp.	Empirical
Emul.	Emulation
Enc.	Encyclopedia
Encour.	Encouragement
Eng.	English
Engin.	Engineer, Engineering
Engr., Engrs	Engraving(s)
Envmt	Environment
Epig.	Epigraphy
Episc.	Episcopal
Esp.	Especially
Ess.	Essays
est.	established
etc	*etcetera* [and so on]
Ethnog.	Ethnography
Ethnol.	Ethnology
Etrus.	Etruscan
Eur.	European
Evangel.	Evangelical
Exam.	Examination
Excav.	Excavation, Excavated
Exch.	Exchange
Excurs.	Excursion
exh.	exhibition
Exp.	Exposition
Expermntl	Experimental
Explor.	Exploration
Expn	Expansion
Ext.	External
Extn	Extension
f, ff	following page, following pages
F.A.	Fine Art(s)
Fac.	Faculty
facs.	facsimile
Fam.	Family
fasc.	fascicle
fd	feastday (of a saint)
Feb	February
Fed.	Federation, Federal
Fem.	Feminist
Fest.	Festival
fig.	figure (illustration)
Fig.	Figurative
figs	figures
Filip.	Filipina(s), Filipino(s)
Fin.	Finnish
FL	Florida (USA)
fl	*floruit* [he/she flourished]
Flem.	Flemish
Flints	Flintshire (GB; old)
Flk	Folk
Flklore	Folklore
fol., fols	folio(s)
Found.	Foundation
Fr.	French
frag.	fragment
Fri.	Friday
FRIBA	Fellow of the Royal Institute of British Architects
FRS	Fellow of the Royal Society, London
ft	foot, feet
Furn.	Furniture
Futur.	Futurist, Futurism
g	gram(s)
GA	Georgia (USA)
Gael.	Gaelic
Gal., Gals	Gallery, Galleries
Gaz.	Gazette
GB	Great Britain
Gdn, Gdns	Garden(s)
Gdnr(s)	Gardener(s)
Gen.	General
Geneal.	Genealogy, Genealogist
Gent.	Gentleman, Gentlemen
Geog.	Geography
Geol.	Geology
Geom.	Geometry
Georg.	Georgian
Geosci.	Geoscience
Ger.	German, Germanic
G.I.	Government/General Issue (USA)
Glams	Glamorganshire (GB; old)
Glos	Gloucestershire (GB)
Govt	Government
Gr.	Greek
Grad.	Graduate
Graph.	Graphic
Green.	Greenlandic
Gr.-Roman	Greco-Roman
Gt	Great
Gtr	Greater
Guat.	Guatemalan
Gym.	Gymnasium
h.	height
ha	hectare
Hait.	Haitian
Hants	Hampshire (GB)
Hb.	Handbook
Heb.	Hebrew
Hell.	Hellenic
Her.	Heritage
Herald.	Heraldry, Heraldic
Hereford & Worcs	Hereford & Worcester (GB)
Herts	Hertfordshire (GB)
HI	Hawaii (USA)
Hib.	Hibernia
Hisp.	Hispanic
Hist.	History, Historical
HMS	His/Her Majesty's Ship
Hon.	Honorary, Honourable
Horiz.	Horizon
Hort.	Horticulture
Hosp.	Hospital(s)
HRH	His/Her Royal Highness
Human.	Humanities, Humanism
Hung.	Hungarian
Hunts	Huntingdonshire (GB; old)
IA	Iowa
ibid.	*ibidem* [in the same place]
ICA	Institute of Contemporary Arts
Ice.	Icelandic
Iconog.	Iconography
Iconol.	Iconology
ID	Idaho (USA)
i.e.	*id est* [that is]
IL	Illinois (USA)
Illum.	Illumination
illus.	illustrated, illustration
Imp.	Imperial
IN	Indiana (USA)
in., ins	inch(es)
Inc.	Incorporated
inc.	incomplete
incl.	includes, including, inclusive
Incorp.	Incorporation
Ind.	Indian
Indep.	Independent
Indig.	Indigenous
Indol.	Indology
Indon.	Indonesian
Indust.	Industrial
Inf.	Information
Inq.	Inquiry
Inscr.	Inscribed, Inscription
Inst.	Institute(s)
Inst. A.	Institute of Art
Instr.	Instrument, Instrumental
Int.	International
Intell.	Intelligence
Inter.	Interior(s), Internal
Interdiscip.	Interdisciplinary
intro.	introduced by, introduction
inv.	inventory

Inven.	Invention
Invest.	Investigation(s)
Iran.	Iranian
irreg.	irregular(ly)
Islam.	Islamic
Isr.	Israeli
It.	Italian
J.	Journal
Jam.	Jamaican
Jan	January
Jap.	Japanese
Jav.	Javanese
Jew.	Jewish
Jewel.	Jewellery
Jord.	Jordanian
jr	junior
Juris.	Jurisdiction
KBE	Knight Commander of the Order of the British Empire
KCVO	Knight Commander of the Royal Victorian Order
kg	kilogram(s)
kHz	kilohertz
km	kilometre(s)
Knowl.	Knowledge
Kor.	Korean
KS	Kansas (USA)
KY	Kentucky (USA)
Kyrgyz.	Kyrgyzstani
£	libra, librae [pound, pounds sterling]
l.	length
LA	Louisiana (USA)
Lab.	Laboratory
Lancs	Lancashire (GB)
Lang.	Language(s)
Lat.	Latin
Latv.	Latvian
lb, lbs	pound(s) weight
Leb.	Lebanese
Lect.	Lecture
Legis.	Legislative
Leics	Leicestershire (GB)
Lex.	Lexicon
Lg.	Large
Lib., Libs	Library, Libraries
Liber.	Liberian
Libsp	Librarianship
Lincs	Lincolnshire (GB)
Lit.	Literature
Lith.	Lithuanian
Liturg.	Liturgical
LLB	Bachelor of Laws
LLD	Doctor of Laws
Lt	Lieutenant
Lt-Col.	Lieutenant-Colonel
Ltd	Limited
m	metre(s)
m.	married
M.	Monsieur
MA	Master of Arts; Massachusetts (USA)
Mag.	Magazine
Maint.	Maintenance
Malay.	Malaysian
Man.	Manitoba (Canada); Manual
Manuf.	Manufactures
Mar.	Marine, Maritime
Mason.	Masonic
Mat.	Material(s)
Math.	Mathematic
MBE	Member of the Order of the British Empire
MD	Doctor of Medicine; Maryland (USA)
ME	Maine (USA)
Mech.	Mechanical
Med.	Medieval; Medium, Media
Medic.	Medical, Medicine
Medit.	Mediterranean
Mem.	Memorial(s); Memoir(s)
Merions	Merionethshire (GB; old)
Meso-Amer.	Meso-American
Mesop.	Mesopotamian
Met.	Metropolitan
Metal.	Metallurgy
Mex.	Mexican
MFA	Master of Fine Arts
mg	milligram(s)
Mgmt	Management
Mgr	Monsignor
MI	Michigan
Micrones.	Micronesian
Mid. Amer.	Middle American
Middx	Middlesex (GB; old)
Mid. E.	Middle Eastern
Mid. Eng.	Middle English
Mid Glam.	Mid Glamorgan (GB)
Mil.	Military
Mill.	Millennium
Min.	Ministry; Minutes
Misc.	Miscellaneous
Miss.	Mission(s)
Mlle	Mademoiselle
mm	millimetre(s)
Mme	Madame
MN	Minnesota
Mnmt, Mnmts	Monument(s)
Mnmtl	Monumental
MO	Missouri (USA)
Mod.	Modern, Modernist
Moldav.	Moldavian
Moldov.	Moldovan
MOMA	Museum of Modern Art
Mon.	Monday
Mongol.	Mongolian
Mons	Monmouthshire (GB; old)
Montgoms	Montgomeryshire (GB; old)
Mor.	Moral
Morav.	Moravian
Moroc.	Moroccan
Movt	Movement
MP	Member of Parliament
MPhil	Master of Philosophy
MS	Mississippi (USA)
MS., MSS	manuscript(s)
MSc	Master of Science
MT	Montana (USA)
Mt	Mount
Mthly	Monthly
Mun.	Municipal
Mus.	Museum(s)
Mus. A.	Museum of Art
Mus. F.A.	Museum of Fine Art(s)
Music.	Musicology
N.	North(ern); National
n	refractive index of a medium
n.	note
N.A.G.	National Art Gallery
Nat.	Natural, Nature
Naut.	Nautical
NB	New Brunswick (Canada)
NC	North Carolina (USA)
ND	North Dakota (USA)
n.d.	no date
NE	Nebraska; Northeast(ern)
Neth.	Netherlandish
Newslett.	Newsletter
Nfld	Newfoundland (Canada)
N.G.	National Gallery
N.G.A.	National Gallery of Art
NH	New Hampshire (USA)
Niger.	Nigerian
NJ	New Jersey (USA)
NM	New Mexico (USA)
nm	nanometre (10^{-9} metre)
nn.	notes
no., nos	number(s)
Nord.	Nordic
Norm.	Normal
Northants	Northamptonshire (GB)
Northumb.	Northumberland (GB)
Norw.	Norwegian
Notts	Nottinghamshire (GB)
Nov	November
n.p.	no place (of publication)
N.P.G.	National Portrait Gallery
nr	near

Nr E.	Near Eastern
NS	New Style; Nova Scotia (Canada)
n. s.	new series
NSW	New South Wales (Australia)
NT	National Trust
Ntbk	Notebook
Numi.	Numismatic(s)
NV	Nevada (USA)
NW	Northwest(ern)
NWT	Northwest Territories (Canada)
NY	New York (USA)
NZ	New Zealand
OBE	Officer of the Order of the British Empire
Obj.	Object(s), Objective
Occas.	Occasional
Occident.	Occidental
Ocean.	Oceania
Oct	October
8vo	octavo
OFM	Order of Friars Minor
OH	Ohio (USA)
OK	Oklahoma (USA)
Olymp.	Olympic
OM	Order of Merit
Ont.	Ontario (Canada)
op.	opus
opp.	opposite; opera [pl. of opus]
OR	Oregon (USA)
Org.	Organization
Orient.	Oriental
Orthdx	Orthodox
OSB	Order of St Benedict
Ott.	Ottoman
Oxon	Oxfordshire (GB)
oz.	ounce(s)
p	pence
p., pp.	page(s)
PA	Pennsylvania (USA)
p.a.	per annum
Pak.	Pakistani
Palaeontol.	Palaeontology, Palaeontological
Palest.	Palestinian
Pap.	Paper(s)
para.	paragraph
Parag.	Paraguayan
Parl.	Parliament
Paroch.	Parochial
Patriarch.	Patriarchate
Patriot.	Patriotic
Patrm.	Patrimony
Pav.	Pavilion
PEI	Prince Edward Island (Canada)
Pembs	Pembrokeshire (GB; old)
Per.	Period
Percep.	Perceptions
Perf.	Performance, Performing, Performed
Period.	Periodical(s)
Pers.	Persian
Persp.	Perspectives
Peru.	Peruvian
PhD	Doctor of Philosophy
Philol.	Philology
Philos.	Philosophy
Phoen.	Phoenician
Phot.	Photograph, Photography, Photographic
Phys.	Physician(s), Physics, Physique, Physical
Physiog.	Physiognomy
Physiol.	Physiology
Pict.	Picture(s), Pictorial
pl.	plate; plural
Plan.	Planning
Planet.	Planetarium
Plast.	Plastic
pls	plates
p.m.	post meridiem [after noon]
Polit.	Political
Poly.	Polytechnic
Polynes.	Polynesian
Pop.	Popular
Port.	Portuguese
Port.	Portfolio
Posth.	Posthumous(ly)
Pott.	Pottery
POW	prisoner of war
PRA	President of the Royal Academy
Pract.	Practical
Prefect.	Prefecture, Prefectural
Preserv.	Preservation
prev.	previous(ly)
priv.	private
PRO	Public Record Office
Prob.	Problem(s)
Proc.	Proceedings
Prod.	Production
Prog.	Progress
Proj.	Project(s)
Promot.	Promotion
Prop.	Property, Properties
Prov.	Province(s), Provincial
Proven.	Provenance
Prt, Prts	Print(s)
Prtg	Printing
pseud.	pseudonym
Psych.	Psychiatry, Psychiatric
Psychol.	Psychology, Psychological
pt	part
Ptg(s)	Painting(s)
Pub.	Public
pubd	published
Publ.	Publicity
pubn(s)	publication(s)
PVA	polyvinyl acetate
PVC	polyvinyl chloride
Q.	quarterly
4to	quarto
Qué.	Québec (Canada)
R	reprint
r	*recto*
RA	Royal Academician
Radnors	Radnorshire (GB; old)
RAF	Royal Air Force
Rec.	Record(s)
red.	reduction, reduced for
Ref.	Reference
Refurb.	Refurbishment
reg	*regit* [ruled]
Reg.	Regional
Relig.	Religion, Religious
remod.	remodelled
Ren.	Renaissance
Rep.	Report(s)
repr.	reprint(ed); reproduced, reproduction
Represent.	Representation, Representative
Res.	Research
rest.	restored, restoration
Retro.	Retrospective
rev.	revision, revised (by/for)
Rev.	Reverend; Review
RHA	Royal Hibernian Academician
RI	Rhode Island (USA)
RIBA	Royal Institute of British Architects
RJ	Rio de Janeiro State
Rlwy	Railway
RSA	Royal Scottish Academy
RSFSR	Russian Soviet Federated Socialist Republic
Rt Hon.	Right Honourable
Rur.	Rural
Rus.	Russian
S	San, Santa, Santo, Sant', São [Saint]
S.	South(ern)
s.	solidus, solidi [shilling(s)]
Sask.	Saskatchewan (Canada)
Sat.	Saturday
SC	South Carolina (USA)
Scand.	Scandinavian
Sch.	School
Sci.	Science(s), Scientific
Scot.	Scottish
Sculp.	Sculpture

SD	South Dakota (USA)
SE	Southeast(ern)
Sect.	Section
Sel.	Selected
Semin.	Seminar(s), Seminary
Semiot.	Semiotic
Semit.	Semitic
Sept	September
Ser.	Series
Serb.	Serbian
Serv.	Service(s)
Sess.	Session, Sessional
Settmt(s)	Settlement(s)
S. Glam.	South Glamorgan (GB)
Siber.	Siberian
Sig.	Signature
Sil.	Silesian
Sin.	Singhala
sing.	singular
SJ	Societas Jesu [Society of Jesus]
Skt	Sanskrit
Slav.	Slavic, Slavonic
Slov.	Slovene, Slovenian
Soc.	Society
Social.	Socialism, Socialist
Sociol.	Sociology
Sov.	Soviet
SP	São Paulo State
Sp.	Spanish
sq.	square
sr	senior
Sri L.	Sri Lankan
SS	Saints, Santi, Santissima, Santissimo, Santissimi; Steam ship
SSR	Soviet Socialist Republic
St	Saint, Sankt, Sint, Szent
Staffs	Staffordshire (GB)
Ste	Sainte
Stud.	Study, Studies
Subalp.	Subalpine
Sum.	Sumerian
Sun.	Sunday
Sup.	Superior
suppl., suppls	supplement(s), supplementary
Surv.	Survey
SW	Southwest(ern)
Swed.	Swedish
Swi.	Swiss
Symp.	Symposium
Syr.	Syrian
Tap.	Tapestry
Tas.	Tasmanian
Tech.	Technical, Technique
Technol.	Technology
Territ.	Territory
Theat.	Theatre
Theol.	Theology, Theological
Theor.	Theory, Theoretical
Thurs.	Thursday
Tib.	Tibetan
TN	Tennessee (USA)
Top.	Topography
Trad.	Tradition(s), Traditional
trans.	translation, translated by; transactions
Transafr.	Transafrican
Transatlant.	Transatlantic
Transcarpath.	Transcarpathian
transcr.	transcribed by/for
Triq.	Triquarterly
Tropic.	Tropical
Tues.	Tuesday
Turk.	Turkish
Turkmen.	Turkmenistani
TV	Television
TX	Texas (USA)
U.	University
UK	United Kingdom of Great Britain and Northern Ireland
Ukrain.	Ukrainian
Un.	Union
Underwtr	Underwater
UNESCO	United Nations Educational, Scientific and Cultural Organization
Univl	Universal
unpubd	unpublished
Urb.	Urban
Urug.	Uruguayan
US	United States
USA	United States of America
USSR	Union of Soviet Socialist Republics
UT	Utah
v	*verso*
VA	Virginia (USA)
V&A	Victoria and Albert Museum
Var.	Various
Venez.	Venezuelan
Vern.	Vernacular
Vict.	Victorian
Vid.	Video
Viet.	Vietnamese
viz.	*videlicet* [namely]
vol., vols	volume(s)
vs.	versus
VT	Vermont (USA)
Vulg.	Vulgarisation
W.	West(ern)
w.	width
WA	Washington (USA)
Warwicks	Warwickshire (GB)
Wed.	Wednesday
W. Glam.	West Glamorgan (GB)
WI	Wisconsin (USA)
Wilts	Wiltshire (GB)
Wkly	Weekly
W. Midlands	West Midlands (GB)
Worcs	Worcestershire (GB; old)
Wtrcol.	Watercolour
WV	West Virginia (USA)
WY	Wyoming (USA)
Yb., Y.-b.	Yearbook, Year-book
Yem.	Yemeni
Yorks	Yorkshire (GB; old)
Yug.	Yugoslavian
Zamb.	Zambian
Zimb.	Zimbabwean

A Note on the Use of the Dictionary

This note is intended as a short guide to the basic editorial conventions adopted in this dictionary. For a fuller explanation, please refer to the Introduction, pp. xiii–xx.

Abbreviations in general use in the dictionary are listed on pp. xxix–xxxiv; those used in bibliographies and for locations of works of art or exhibition venues are listed in the Appendices in vol. 33.

Alphabetization of headings, which are distinguished in bold typeface, is letter by letter up to the first comma (ignoring spaces, hyphens, accents and any parenthesized or bracketed matter); the same principle applies thereafter. Abbreviations of 'Saint' and its foreign equivalents are alphabetized as if spelt out, and headings with the prefix 'Mc' appear under 'Mac'.

Authors' signatures appear at the end of the article or sequence of articles that the authors have contributed; in multipartite articles, any section that is unsigned is by the author of the next signed section. Where the article was compiled by the editors or in the few cases where an author has wished to remain anonymous, this is indicated by a square box (□) instead of a signature.

Bibliographies are arranged chronologically (within section, where divided) by order of year of first publication and, within years, alphabetically by authors' names. Abbreviations have been used for some standard reference books; these are cited in full in Appendix C in vol. 33, as are abbreviations of periodical titles (Appendix B). Abbreviated references to alphabetically arranged dictionaries and encyclopedias appear at the beginning of the bibliography (or section).

Biographical dates when cited in parentheses in running text at the first mention of a personal name indicate that the individual does not have an entry in the dictionary. The presence of parenthesized regnal dates for rulers and popes, however, does not necessarily indicate the lack of a biography of that person. Where no dates are provided for an artist or patron, the reader may assume that there is a biography of that individual in the dictionary (or, more rarely, that the person is so obscure that dates are not readily available).

Cross-references are distinguished by the use of small capital letters, with a large capital to indicate the initial letter of the entry to which the reader is directed; for example, 'He commissioned LEONARDO DA VINCI . . .' means that the entry is alphabetized under 'L'.

A

A.A.A. *See* ALLIED ARTISTS' ASSOCIATION and AMERICAN ABSTRACT ARTISTS.

Aachen [Fr. Aix-la-Chapelle]. City in Nordrhein-Westfalia, Germany. It was the birthplace and residence of Charlemagne, ruler of the Frankish Kingdom, and remained associated with German rulers throughout the Middle Ages; most Holy Roman emperors were crowned there until 1531. It was founded by the Romans in the 1st century AD as a modest military settlement. Its Roman name, Aquae Granni ('Waters of Granus'), was derived from a local Celtic deity and the area's abundant hot springs: the remains of three bath complexes have been uncovered in the centre of the city. Despite the collapse of the Roman Empire, the therapeutic waters encouraged continued habitation, and during the early 790s Charlemagne chose Aquisgranum, as it was then called, as his capital. Until his death in AD 814, he spent part of almost every year there and built an elaborate palace, of which the chapel survives (*see* §2 (ii) below). He gathered scholars and artists from all over Europe in order to promote the cultural revival known as the Carolingian *renovatio.* Between 1172 and 1176, by order of Emperor Frederick Barbarossa, fortification walls were built around the palace and burgeoning town, and between 1334 and 1349 Charlemagne's audience hall was replaced by an elegant town hall.

After a disastrous fire in 1656, much of the city was rebuilt in the Baroque style. Ceasing to be a Free Imperial city in 1794, Aachen was taken into Prussia in 1815. Now an industrial and mining city, it was badly damaged in World War II.

BIBLIOGRAPHY

K. Faymonville: *Die Kunstdenkmäler der Stadt Aachen*, 2 vols (Düsseldorf, 1916–22)

W. Kaemmerer: *Geschichtliches Aachen: Von Werden und Wesen einer Reichsstadt* (Aachen, 1955, rev. 2/1957)

H. Cüppers, ed.: *Aquae Granni: Beiträge zur Archäologie von Aachen*, Rheinische Ausgrabungen, xxii (Cologne, 1982)

L. Falkenstein: 'Charlemagne et Aix-la-Chapelle', *Byzantion*, lxi (1991), pp. 231–87

CHARLES B. McCLENDON

1. Centre of manuscript production. 2. Buildings.

1. CENTRE OF MANUSCRIPT PRODUCTION. Manuscripts produced at Aachen are those of a group of scribes of different origins and training rather than of a self-contained monastic scriptorium. The two groups of manuscripts associated with the royal court under Charlemagne, the 'Ada' and 'Coronation Gospels' groups, may well have been produced at Aachen itself, as could many of the liturgical, Classical and rare patristic texts produced for the court library. Under Louis the Pious (*reg* 814–40), on the other hand, evidence for the production at Aachen of legal manuscripts (the *leges* scriptorium group), of Classical and patristic texts (the Bamberg Pliny group) and of contemporary theology is substantial. As six extant manuscripts demonstrate, the court at Aachen continued to be a focus of fine book production in the reign of Emperor Lothair I (*reg* 840–55), but Aachen itself ceased for some decades thereafter to be a significant political or cultural focus.

See also CAROLINGIAN ART, §IV, 3.

BIBLIOGRAPHY

W. Koehler: *Die Karolingischen Miniaturen*, ii–iv (Berlin, 1958–82)

B. Bischoff: 'Die Hofbibliothek Karls des Grossen' and 'Die Hofbibliothek unter Ludwig dem Frommen', *Mittelalterliche Studien*, iii (Stuttgart, 1981), pp. 149–86

R. McKitterick: *The Carolingians and the Written Word* (Cambridge, 1989), pp. 57–9

——: 'Carolingian Uncial: A Context for the Lothar Psalter', *BL J.*, xvi (1990), pp. 1–15

ROSAMOND D. McKITTERICK

2. BUILDINGS.

(i) Palace. (ii) Palatine chapel.

(i) Palace. Charlemagne maintained many residences throughout his realm, all of which could be termed palaces because of their royal status, but none rivalled that at Aachen in size and splendour. Attracted by the site's natural hot springs and its strategic location between the Rhineland and northern France, his father, Pepin the Short (*reg* 754–68), spent winters at Aachen in 765, and Charlemagne followed suit in 769 and 787. Construction of a new palace was sufficiently advanced by 794 to allow it to be used regularly. Periodic excavation since the mid-19th century has uncovered the core of the complex (see fig. 1). To the south, a polygonal chapel (a) was flanked at the east end by two small basilican structures (b) and approached from the west by a monumental atrium (c). An audience hall (*aula regia*) stood *c.* 125 m to the north (d); its axis ran parallel to that of the chapel, but its main apse was at the west instead of the east. The audience hall and atrium of the chapel were in turn connected by a narrow, two-storey walkway (e), which was intersected midway by a massive rectangular gate-house (f). The layout of the palace followed a grid that seems to have been based on a module of 12 Carolingian feet (1 ft=330 mm) and diverged

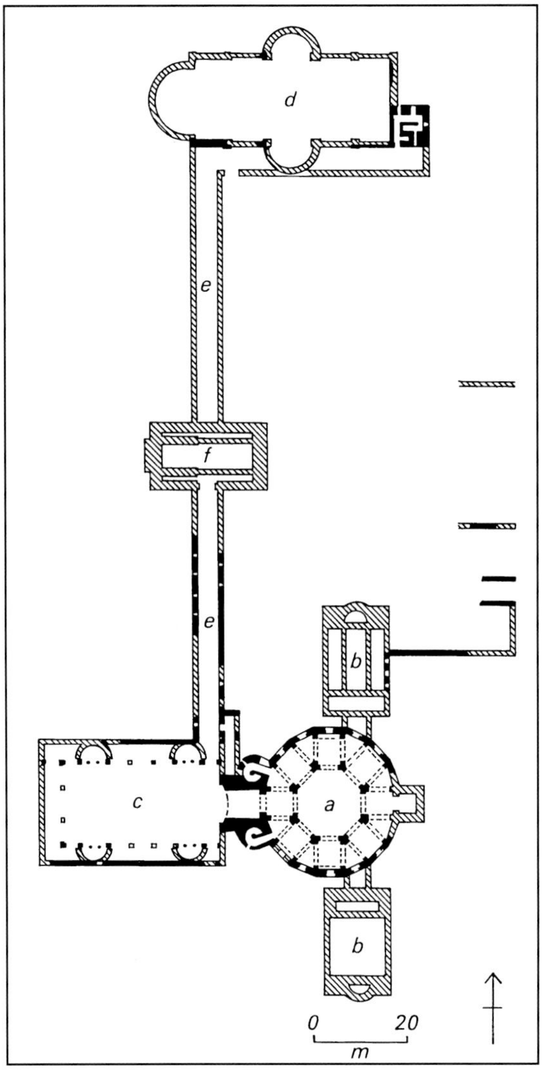

1. Aachen, plan of palace complex: (a) Palatine chapel; (b) basilican structures; (c) atrium; (d) audience hall; (e) walkway; (f) gate-house

from the Roman town's rectilinear street-plan by some 40°, in order to place the chapel on a strict east–west alignment. Around these ceremonial buildings of stone and mortar presumably stood subsidiary structures of wood—living quarters, workrooms and stables—but they have left no trace.

The audience hall was an aisleless building (47.42×20.76 m) with three apses, the largest to the west, and smaller ones in the middle of the north and south sides. At the east end, a massive stair-tower provided access to catwalks for maintenance. The exterior elevation was articulated at wide intervals by a series of thick pilasters and arches that framed one or more superimposed rows of round-arched windows. The long passageway between the audience hall and chapel was barrel-vaulted on the ground-floor, with mere slits for windows, and timber-roofed above, with broadly spaced tripartite windows looking out on to the west range of the complex. The thick foundations of the gate-house (29.57×15.10 m) indicate that it, too, was vaulted at ground-level and possessed a second storey, reached by stairs in its western corners.

The main buildings of the palace reflected Charlemagne's acclamation of Aachen as a new or second Rome. The audience hall with its three apses took the form of a triclinium, a structure traditionally used in Roman villas for reception or dining. This building type seems to have gone out of fashion in the Latin West in the 6th century AD, but it was revived in Rome in the mid-8th century for the papal palace adjoining the Lateran basilica. The blind arcading of the elevation was inspired by the audience hall of Constantine the Great at Trier. The reasons for this reference seem obvious. Charlemagne was described by contemporaries as a 'new Constantine', and Trier had served as Constantine's capital before he marched on Rome in AD 312. The arrangement of the monumental gateway and narrow corridor ultimately derived from Constantinople, where the Chalke Gate, built by Emperor Justinian, led to a covered passage that linked the imperial palace to Hagia Sophia (*see* ISTANBUL, §III, 12). Pope Zacharias (*reg* 741–52) erected a similar entrance tower in Rome, with a bronze gate leading to an elevated corridor that joined various parts of the Lateran palace. Thus, the design of the palace at Aachen was not only utilitarian in nature but also symbolized Charlemagne's political ties with both northern Europe and the Mediterranean.

(ii) Palatine chapel.

(a) Architecture. The best-preserved portion of the palace is the chapel, which, although partially obscured by later additions, still dominates the city. Dedicated to the Virgin, the chapel was nearing completion in 798, according to a letter of Alcuin (*c.* 735–804; Mnmt Ger. Hist., Epistolae, iv/2, p. 244). A 12th-century reference in the *Annales Tielenses* (Mnmt Ger. Hist., Scriptores, xxiv, p. 22) states that it was consecrated by Pope Leo III in 805, and a lost inscription inside the building ascribed its construction to Odo of Metz, an individual otherwise unknown (see Schlosser, 1896). The chapel (see fig. 2) is a complex double-shell design, composed of a domed octagonal core (diam. 14.46 m), with an enveloping aisle and upper gallery, and enclosed within a 16-sided outer wall. The east end was marked by a projecting square apse, replaced by the Late Gothic choir, while at the opposite end stands a multi-storey entranceway or westwork. The broad planes of the exterior are pierced by three tiers of individual round-arched windows. A cornice with brackets caps the outermost wall, while the octagonal drum of the dome is articulated at the corners by paired pilasters with Corinthian capitals, now badly eroded. The central octagon dominates the interior space, defined by eight massive piers that rise to form superimposed arches, squat at ground-level and attenuated above. The predominant impression is one of compression and lift, created by the lateral splaying of the piers and the tall proportions of the upper storey, which together lead the eye to the eight-sided cloister vault. The gallery, covered by a series of transverse barrel vaults, is divided into rectangular and triangular bays by heavy diaphragm arches. The ambula-

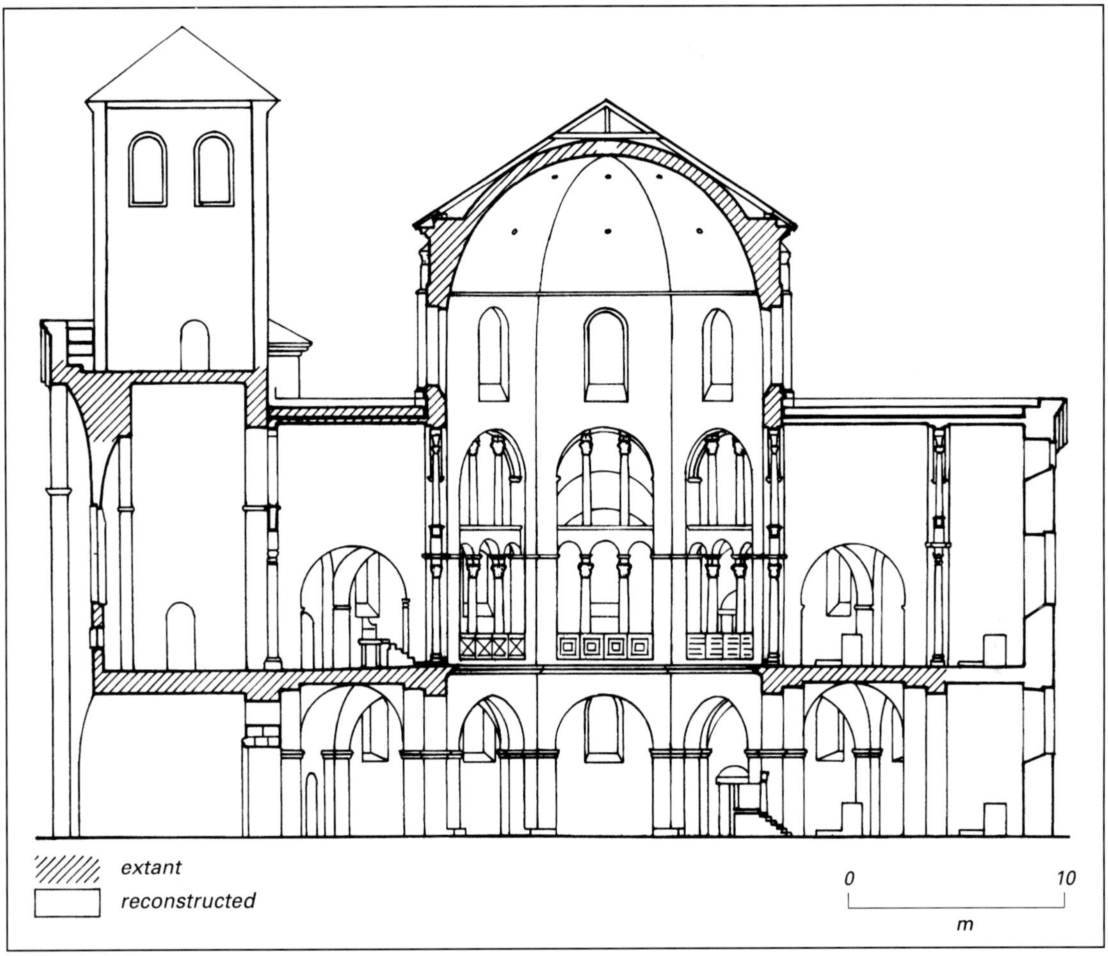

2. Aachen, section drawing of Palatine chapel

tory in contrast is low and dark, covered by an intricate sequence of groin vaults.

The current, resplendent interior decoration is not Carolingian but the result of a radical restoration carried out *c.* 1900 after late Baroque stucco had been stripped from the walls. It seems clear, nonetheless, that the walls were originally covered with rich marble revetment and the dome with mosaic (*see* CAROLINGIAN ART, §IV, 1), reviving the aesthetics of late antiquity. According to EINHARD, these luxurious materials, including marble columns, were imported from Rome and Ravenna. The current configuration of the throne in the gallery opposite the apse dates to the Ottonian period, but fragments of the original *opus sectile* floor show that this was a place of special prominence. From this vantage point, Charlemagne could look down to the main altar and up to the image of Christ in the dome, while the congregation below saw their king enthroned between heaven and earth.

The centralized design of the chapel, always rare in the West, also recalled Early Christian building traditions. Numerous models have been proposed, but the closest comparison, and the one most often cited, is S Vitale in Ravenna, dating from the reign of Justinian (*see* RAVENNA, §2(vii)). Their plans and elevations are strikingly similar, and Charlemagne's links with Ravenna are well known. Even so, the Early Christian model was not copied literally but transformed into a distinctly new and medieval form. The subtle interplay between curvilinear and angular patterns at S Vitale was replaced by a more ponderous and rectilinear approach. Billowing exedrae, framed by thin angular piers, became at Aachen flat screens sustained by massive, broad supports. In place of the undulating, free-flowing interior of S Vitale, that at Aachen is contained and defined through the compartmentalization of space, in keeping with the grid-like attitude toward planning that is characteristic of the layout of the whole palace. The construction techniques are also very different. S Vitale's brick-and-mortar masonry was translated at Aachen into the local idiom of rough-hewn stones and quoining. The WESTWORK, an element introduced to church architecture in Carolingian times, not only provided access to the gallery, as did the two stunted, cylindrical stair-towers flanking the entrance at S Vitale, but it also added a monumental vertical accent to the façade of the church (in place of a low narthex), marking the position of the king's throne by a great arch.

Like S Vitale and many other Early Christian churches, the chapel was preceded by an atrium, but one with its own distinctive characteristics. Long and low, the atrium was defined to the north and south by a solid outer wall, from which projected two large niches, screened off on the inside by rectangular piers and paired columns, forming a raised, covered platform that surrounded an open courtyard on three sides. Rather than a traditional quadriporticus, the atrium seems to have been designed as a place of assembly for the staging of such events as the annual gathering of nobles and the reception of foreign ambassadors. The remains of a water channel running diagonally across the courtyard indicate that a fountain stood at the centre, perhaps mounted by the bronze pine-cone that now stands in the vestibule of the chapel (*see* §(b) below). Two rectangular buildings set on a north–south axis either side of the chapel's east end were of similar dimensions (15×23 m), and each was connected to the gallery by a two-storey narthex, yet their exact functions remain unknown.

Charlemagne was buried in his chapel in 814. In 1165, through the instigation of Frederick Barbarossa, he was canonized, and his remains drew many pilgrims. From the start the palatine chapel was a focal-point of German kingship, and it inspired many copies until well into the 14th century. The gables were added to the roof in the 13th century and the dome rebuilt after the fire of 1656. Between 1355 and 1414 the eastern square apse was replaced by a double-bay apsed choir with extremely tall traceried windows and a quadripartite rib vault, the wall shafts of which are supported on angel-corbels. The chapel was designated the cathedral of a newly constituted diocese in 1802.

BIBLIOGRAPHY

Einhard: *Life of Charlemagne* (MS.; *c*. late 820s); ed. G. Pertz, Mnmt Ger. Hist., Scriptores, xxvi (Hannover, 1829), p. 457

J. von Schlosser: *Schriftquellen zur Geschichte der karolingischen Kunst* (Vienna, 1896), p. 28, n. 107 [Odo of Metz]

A. Haupt: *Die Pfalzkapelle Kaiser Karls des Grossen zu Aachen*, Monumenta Germaniae Architectonica, ii (Leipzig, 1913)

W. Braunfels and H. Schnitzler, eds: *Karl der Grosse: Lebenswerk und Nachleben*, 3 vols (Düsseldorf, 1965–7)

W. E. Kleinbauer: 'Charlemagne's Palace Chapel at Aachen and its Copies', *Gesta*, iv (1965), pp. 2–11

Karl der Grosse: Werk und Wirkung (exh. cat., Aachen, Rathaus, 1965)

F. Oswald, L. Schaeffer and H. R. Sennhauser: *Vorromanische Kirchenbauten: Katalog der Denkmäler bis zum Ausgang der Ottonen*, i (Munich, 1966), pp. 14–18

H. E. Kubach and A. Verbeek: *Romanische Baukunst an Rhein und Maas: Katalog der vorromanischen und romanischen Denkmäler*, i (Berlin, 1976), pp. 1–13

H. Belting: 'Das Aachener Münster im 19. Jahrhundert: Zur ersten Krise des Denkmal-Konzepts', *Wallraf-Richartz-Jb.*, xlv (1984), pp. 257–90

CHARLES B. MCCLENDON

(b) Sculpture. Among the columns and marbles brought by Charlemagne from Rome and Ravenna to Aachen was probably the late Antonine Proserpina Sarcophagus in which, according to tradition, Emperor Charlemagne was entombed. Antique columns and capitals survive in the chapel alongside Carolingian imitations. Antique bronzes were set up to vie with the authority of monuments at the Lateran palace: a *She-bear* from southern Gaul, now in the vestibule of the chapel, was to emulate the Roman *She-wolf*, and an equestrian statue (untraced) from Ravenna, thought to represent Theodoric (*reg* 489–526), was to parallel that of *Marcus Aurelius* on the Capitoline in Rome, then believed to depict Constantine the Great. A foundry brought to Aachen before 796 cast bronze doors and railings for the chapel, completing the work sometime after 800. Four surviving pairs of doors follow antique models, and the railings, originally gilt, still enclose the galleries. Changes in their design demonstrate a progressive mastery of the classicizing styles also developed in manuscript illumination at Charlemagne's court. It remains uncertain, however, whether the large bronze pine-cone in the chapel vestibule was made by this foundry or is a Roman casting set on a Carolingian base, which bears the four Rivers of Paradise and a fragmentary inscription naming an otherwise unknown Abbot Udalrich as donor. Whatever the case, it served as a fountain like the pine-cone (Rome, Vatican, Cortile Pigna) then in the atrium of Old St Peter's, Rome.

BIBLIOGRAPHY

W. Braunfels: 'Karls des Grossen Bronzewerkstatt', *Karolingische Kunst* (1965), iii of *Karl der Grosse: Lebenswerk und Nachleben*, ed. W. Braunfels and H. Schnitzler (Düsseldorf, 1965), pp. 168–202

Karl der Grosse: Werk und Wirkung (exh. cat., Aachen, Rathaus, 1965), nos 3–4, 6–7

P. Lasko: *Ars Sacra, 800–1200*, Pelican Hist. A. (Harmondsworth, 1972), pp. 14–16

(c) Treasury. Einhard's *Life of Charlemagne* relates that Charlemagne endowed his chapel with a rich treasure of liturgical objects and willed it to be kept from dispersal after his death. Other sources record that many relics were brought from Jerusalem, Constantinople, Rome and elsewhere and placed as objects of veneration into and above altars, encased in costly reliquaries and exhibited on special occasions. The location of a space reserved for the early medieval church treasure remains uncertain. From the early 15th century to the mid-19th it was kept in a large cabinet in the St Matthew Chapel (1379), which was used as a sacristy at the south junction of the choir and palatine chapel. In 1873 it was moved to the Charles Chapel (on the north-east side, 1455–74), in 1881 to the Hungarian Chapel (at the south-west, 1367) and in 1931 to the present site in a vaulted passage north of the Poor Souls' Chapel.

Of six objects surviving from Carolingian times, only three remain at Aachen: the Aachen Gospels, an ivory diptych depicting epiphanies of Christ and an early Byzantine silk (*see* EARLY CHRISTIAN AND BYZANTINE ART, §VII, 8). The Coronation Gospels and the burse reliquary of St Stephen (*c*. 830) were transferred to the imperial treasury in Vienna in 1798 (Vienna, Schatzkammer) and the 'Talisman (or Amulet) of Charlemagne' containing hair of the Virgin was given to Empress Josephine Bonaparte in 1804 and subsequently to Reims Cathedral.

Grimme lists 210 later additions to the treasury, of which the most significant were offerings from rulers seeking to legitimize their aspirations by claiming the heritage of Charlemagne. The Lothar Cross (*c*. 985–91), the Gospels of Otto III (Munich, Bayer. Staatsbib., Clm. 4453) and several Byzantine silks were donated by Otto III. An ivory situla may also have been given by him or by Henry II. The latter certainly donated the magnificent pulpit and the altar antependium known as the Pala d'Oro (both still in the chapel) and a golden book cover for the Aachen Gospels. Frederick Barbarossa, King of Germany, was responsible for the large Romanesque candelabrum (*c.* 1166) still hanging from the apex of the dome and the sumptuous shrine into which his grandson Frederick II placed Charlemagne's remains in 1215. In 1238 the shrine of the Virgin received Aachen's most sacred relics, the Virgin's robe, the swaddling clothes and loincloth of Christ, and the shroud of the head of John the Baptist. The Luxembourg emperor Charles IV presented the bust reliquary of Charlemagne and another reliquary formed like a small chapel the windowed base of which was seen part of Charlemagne's arm. In the late Middle Ages there were three more gifts to justify entitlement from the Carolingian past: in 1475 the crown of Margaret of York (1446–1503), wife of Charles the Bold, Duke of Burgundy; in 1481 an arm reliquary of Charlemagne given by King Louis XI of France; and, during the first quarter of the 16th century, several works by the Aachen goldsmith Hans von Reutlingen (*fl* 1497–1522) were presented by Maximilian I and one by Charles V.

From the 17th century numerous objects came to the treasury, each fashioned in the style of its period, from the Baroque to the Gothic Revival, the Romanesque Revival and the contemporary, the latest to be recorded being a chalice made in 1960 by Ewald Mataré.

BIBLIOGRAPHY

E. G. Grimme: *Der Aachener Domschatz*, Aachener Kunstblätter, xlii (Düsseldorf, 1972, rev. 2/1973)

JOACHIM E. GAEHDE

Aachen [Aach; Ach; Acha], **Hans** [Johann; Joan] **von** (*b* Cologne, 1552; *d* Prague, 4 March 1615). German painter and draughtsman, active also in Italy and Bohemia. One of the foremost painters of the circle gathered at the Prague court of Emperor Rudolf II (*see* HABSBURG, §I, (10)), he synthesized Italian and Netherlandish influences in his portraits and erudite allegories.

1. CAREER. Hans's surname is derived from his father's native town. According to Karel van Mander, he probably studied *c.* 1567–73 with the portrait painter Georg Jerrigh, who had trained in Antwerp. Von Aachen subsequently became a member of the Cologne guild of painters. He travelled to Italy *c.* 1574, first working in Venice as a copyist and for the painter Gaspar Rem (1542–1615/17), before going in 1575 to Rome, where he copied antique sculptures and the works of Italian masters; he also painted an *Adoration of the Shepherds* for the church of Il Gesù in Rome (1580s; untraced, but known from an engraving (1588) by Aegidius Sadeler; Hollstein, no. 32). In Rome, von Aachen joined the circle of northern artists that included Otto van Veen, Joris Hoefnagel, Jan Speeckaert, Paul and Matthijs Bril and Joseph Heintz (i). From 1582–3 he worked in Florence, obtaining numerous portrait commissions, including some from the Medici family, and met the sculptor Giambologna. In 1585 he again settled in Venice.

In 1587 von Aachen went to Augsburg, painting portraits for the Fugger family, and to Munich, where he produced two altarpieces for the church of St Michael (*in situ*). In 1588 he revisited Cologne and may have visited Prague for the first time in the train of Duke William V of Bavaria; he also went back to Venice and gave up his home there. From 1589 he was working in Munich, where he produced portraits of the ducal family, altarpieces and allegories. Further portraits were painted for the Fuggers in Augsburg *c.* 1591–2. While based in Munich, Hans von Aachen was in contact with figures such as Friedrich Sustris, Peter Candid and Christoph Schwartz, as well as the engravers Jan and Raphael Sadeler.

1. Hans von Aachen: *Bacchus, Ceres and Cupid*, oil on canvas, 1.63×1.13 m, *c.* 1600 (Vienna, Kunsthistorisches Museum)

On 1 January 1592 in Prague, Emperor Rudolf II appointed von Aachen 'Kammermaler von Haus aus'—a court painter who need not be present at court. In 1594 he made another journey to Prague, and after his marriage on 1 July 1596 to the daughter of Orlando di Lasso (*c.* 1530/32–1595), conductor of the Munich court orchestra, he finally settled there permanently. In Prague, von Aachen worked not only as a painter for Rudolf II, but also as an art agent, making frequent journeys abroad, for instance once to Besançon in 1597 to purchase pictures from the estate of Cardinal Antoine Perronet de Granvelle and again in 1600 to transport the collection, returning via Freiburg im Breisgau; in 1602 he travelled to Brunswick, Wolfenbüttel, Wittenberg and Dresden, and between 1603 and 1605 to Innsbruck, Venice, Turin, Mantua and Modena, partly in order to arrange the painting of portraits of possible future consorts for the Emperor. In 1604 he returned to Brunswick, and in 1605 he was in Vienna. Throughout these travels he worked not only as an art agent but also as a diplomat and envoy of the Emperor. He meanwhile continued to execute commissions for the

2. Hans von Aachen: *Triumph of Truth and Dominion* (*Allegory of the Truth of the Imperial Cause*), oil on copper, 560×470 mm, 1598 (Munich, Alte Pinakothek)

court in Munich, as well as for Augsburg clients. On 14 May 1605 Emperor Rudolf II conferred a knighthood on him. In 1610 von Aachen bought a house on the Hradčany.

After Rudolf's death in 1612, von Aachen was reappointed by his successor, Matthias, and given an estate in Raussnitz. The Emperor sent him to Dresden and Vienna in 1612, while 1613 saw him back in Augsburg, and 1614 again in Dresden. Von Aachen had several pupils, of whom Pieter Isaacsz. is the most famous—he was apprenticed to von Aachen while he was still in Italy. In Prague, Andreas Vogel (*b c.* 1588; *fl* 1638), Christian Buchner (*fl* 1600–20) and Hans Christoph Schürer (*fl* 1609–22) studied under him.

2. Work. Along with Bartholomäus Spranger and Joseph Heintz (i), Hans von Aachen was the main representative of the late Mannerist, internationally influenced style of art at the court of Rudolf II in Prague *c.* 1600. His works—portraits, paintings of historical and religious subjects, genre pictures and allegories—veer between an idealized style of painting indebted to Roman and Florentine Mannerism as well as to Venetian models (Titian, Veronese, Tintoretto) and the newly emerging tradition of Dutch realism.

(i) Portraits and related work. Von Aachen's portraits are remarkable for their psychological sensitivity. One of the earliest, of his teacher in Venice *Gaspar Rem* (*c.* 1574–5; Vienna, Ksthist. Mus.), clearly shows the influence of Venetian portrait painting (e.g. Jacopo Bassano). In Munich and Augsburg he painted numerous formal court portraits in which Flemish and Italian influences were intermingled, as for example in *Octavian Secundus Fugger* and *Hans Fugger* (both 1592; Babenhausen, Fugger-Mus.). In 1586–8 he created a memorial altar with the *Discovery and Examination of the Holy Cross by Empress Helena* (priv. col.; preparatory drawing, Leiden, Rijksuniv. Prentenkab.) for the burial chapel of the Grafen von Schwarzenburg in the Franziskanerkirche in Munich. This early work was also clearly influenced by Venetian painting: areas in deep shadow are effectively contrasted with bright areas emphasized by applied highlights, thoroughly demonstrating his familiarity with the work of Tintoretto and Veronese. Otto Heinrich, Graf zu Schwarzenberg (1535–90), who commissioned the painting, and his wife are depicted in the Empress's retinue, and on the right-hand edge of the picture by way of signature there is a self-portrait of the painter.

At the court of Rudolf II a great many portraits of officers were painted in connection with the Turkish wars, such as von Aachen's full-length portrait of *Adolf von Schwarzenberg* (after 1599; Győr, János Xantus Mus.). He also painted several portraits of the Emperor, for example one in an allegorical framework, symbolizing both current political events and the apotheosis of the Emperor (known only through an engraving made by Aegidius Sadeler II in 1603; Hollstein, no. 68). On the back of another portrait of *Rudolf II* (*c.* 1603–4; Nuremberg, Ger. Nmus.), painted on alabaster, there is an *Allegory on the Wars against the Turks*, inspired by the Gemma Augustea, a famous antique gemstone in the Emperor's collection. Hans von Aachen also painted many portraits at the court in Prague, such as those of *Johannes Kepler* (1603–4; Rychnov nad Kněžnou, Château A.G.), one of the most important scientists of Rudolf II's reign, and his fellow painter *Bartholomäus Spranger* (*c.* 1608–9; Florence, Uffizi). Von Aachen also executed several portraits of *Emperor Matthias* (Vienna, Ksthist. Mus.).

(ii) History and genre paintings. Along with some genre scenes with Dutch colouring, Hans von Aachen's finest achievements in painting are undoubtedly his mythological and historical compositions, which represent Rudolfine court art at its most sublime. Pictures of the gods as lovers are subtly linked in meaning to the subject-matter and radiate sensuality. The figures of Minerva as protectress of the arts and sciences and Venus are often central. Frequently too Rudolf II's qualities as a ruler are emphasized: the arts, sciences and love prosper in the land of the sovereign who has prevailed against the Turks.

In *Bacchus, Ceres and Cupid* (*c.* 1600; Vienna, Ksthist. Mus.; see fig. 1) deities important for the existence of love are portrayed. The nude figure of a woman viewed from behind, a favourite motif in Rudolfine art, is represented here in a sensually suggestive way. The elongation of the female body is characteristic of the excessively refined Mannerist art and culture prevalent at the court in Prague *c.* 1600 and can also be found in the work of von Aachen's contemporaries at court, Bartholomäus Spranger and Joseph Heintz (i). From a series of what must originally have been twelve compositions of *Allegories on the Wars against the Turks* (1593–1606), painted on parchment and assembled in book form, seven oil sketches have been preserved (Vienna, Ksthist. Mus.; Budapest, Mus. F.A.), one composition is known from an engraving (Hollstein, nos 7–9) and four others from drawn copies of which there are eleven in all, likewise bound together as a book (Dresden, Kupferstichkab.).

Two allegories created in 1598 are tributes to Rudolf II: the *Triumph of Dominion over Time* (Stuttgart, Staatsgal.) and the *Triumph of Truth and Dominion* (or *Allegory of the Truth of the Imperial Cause*; Munich, Alte Pin.; see fig. 2). The first picture should be understood as an allegory on the rule of Rudolf II: if time conquers his enemies (the Turks), love, prosperity and the arts will flourish in his realm. In the second painting, personifications of fertility, peace and harmony symbolize the fruits of the just rule of Rudolf II. Again von Aachen features a strongly sensual nude female figure viewed from behind (Truth).

Hans von Aachen's allegorical paintings, with their often complicated encoding, carried an intellectual stamp, powerfully influenced by the personality of the Emperor and by his high level of culture. After Rudolf II's death, von Aachen continued to paint in a similar fashion, though the colouring became darker in his late works, as if he were trying to convey the slow decline of Rudolfine art. During the reign of Emperor Matthias he painted *Bathsheba Bathing* (1612–15; Vienna, Ksthist. Mus.), a tribute to the ideal of female beauty of Prague Mannerism; here again the naked female body is at the centre of the narrative. The boundary between mythological and religious painting is blurred in favour of extremely sensual eroticism. The objects surrounding Bathsheba, arranged in a still-life manner, are reminiscent of Netherlandish models, to which Hans von Aachen was also indebted in his few genre paintings, such as the *Brothel Scene with Two Ill-matched Lovers* (two versions, both *c.* 1600; Karlsruhe, Staatl. Ksthalle; Linz, Oberösterreich. Landesmus.) and a *Young Couple* (Vienna, Ksthist. Mus.).

BIBLIOGRAPHY

Hollstein: *Ger.*; Thieme–Becker
R. A. Peltzer: 'Der Hofmaler Hans von Aachen; Seine Schule und seine Zeit', *Jb. Ksthist. Samml. Allhöch. Ksrhaus.*, xxx (1911–12), pp. 59–182
——: 'Hans von Aachen: Eine Nachlese', *Wallraf-Richartz-Jb.*, v (1928), pp. 75–84
R. Chadabra: 'Die Gemma Augustea und die Rudolfinische Allegorie', *Umění*, xviii (1970), pp. 289–97
E. Fučíková: 'Über die Tätigkeit Hans von Aachens in Bayern', *Münchn. Jb. Bild. Kst*, xxi (1970), pp. 129–42
R. an der Heiden: 'Die Porträtmalerei des Hans von Aachen', *Jb. Ksthist. Samml. Wien*, lxvi (1970), pp. 135–226
E. Fučíková: 'Quae praestat invenis vix potuere viri: Hans von Aachens Selbstbildnis in Köln', *Wallraf-Richartz-Jb.*, xxxiii (1971), pp. 115–21
R. an der Heiden: 'Zu neu aufgefundenen Gemälden Hans von Aachens', *Pantheon*, xxii (1974), pp. 249–54
H. J. Ludwig: *Die Türkenskizzen des Hans von Aachen für Rudolf II* (diss., U. Frankfurt am Main, 1977)
Zeichnung in Deutschland: Deutsche Zeichner, 1540–1640, i (exh. cat., Stuttgart, Staatsgal., 1979–80), nos B14–19
T. daCosta Kaufmann: *L'Ecole de Prague: La Peinture à la cour de Rodolphe II* (Paris, 1985; trans. and rev. Chicago and London, 1988)
Prag um 1600: Kunst und Kultur am Hofe Kaiser Rudolfs II (exh. cat., Vienna, Ksthist. Mus., 1988), i, nos 89–110, 176–87; ii, nos 543–53, 608–15
J. Müller: *Concordia Pragensis: Die Stellung der rudolfinischen Hofkünstler im Schilder-Boeck Carel van Manders. Ein Beitrag zur Rhetorisierung von Kunst und Leben um 1600* (diss., U. Bochum, 1991)

C. HÖPER

Aagaard Andersen, Gunnar (*b* Ordrup, 14 July 1919; *d* Munkerup, nr Dronningmølle, Hillerød, 29 June 1982). Danish painter, sculptor, designer and writer. He studied at the Kunsthåndvaerkerskole (1936–9) and the Kongelige Danske Kunstakademi (1939–46), both in Copenhagen. He experimented with non-figurative forms of expression in numerous media. He was a co-founder of Groupe Espace in 1951, and his work was important for the development of Concrete art internationally.

From 1947 to 1950 Aagaard Andersen developed a new, pure pictorial dynamic, moving from fine-lined drawings and faceted landscapes towards an abstract formal language that explored form in terms of light, shadow and reflection. His 'picture boxes', in which various elements manifested rhythmic and dynamic growth, explored the concept of painting as object. He began to use the techniques of folding and pleating (e.g. *Black Picture Surface with Three Folded Sections*, 1964; Esbjerg, Kstpav.), and his work was dominated by his interest in light and shadow.

Besides paintings, Aagaard Andersen produced a number of sculptures, for example the abstract steel work *Interferences* (1972) for the platform of the railway station at Fredericia. He also executed decorative projects for buildings, for example the Koncerthus in Odense (1982), for which he produced a colossal copper sculpture in the foyer, 20 black-and-white marble reliefs and an acoustic ceiling. He also illustrated books and designed textiles, furniture and glass, and wrote many articles on art.

BIBLIOGRAPHY

Aagaard Andersen (exh. cat., Lyngby, Sophienholm; Århus, Kstmus.; 1977)
Thorsen and Mollerup: *Aagaard Andersen* (Copenhagen, 1985) [contains several articles by Aagaard Andersen]
J. J. Thorsen: 'Aagaard Andersen dans l'Art International: Aagaard le novateur', *ICSAC Cah.*, 5 (1986), pp. 49–52
——: *Modernisme i Dansk Malerkunst*, ii (Copenhagen, 1987), pp. 185–97

RIGMOR LOVRING

Aalto, (Hugo) Alvar (Henrik) (*b* Kuortane, 3 Feb 1898; *d* Helsinki, 11 May 1976). Finnish architect and designer. His success as an architect lay in the individual nature of his buildings, which were always designed with their surrounding environment in mind and with great attention to their practical demands. He never used forms that were merely aesthetic or conditioned by technical factors but looked to the more permanent models of nature and natural forms. He was not anti-technology but believed that technology could be humanized to become the servant of human beings and the promoter of cultural values. One of his important maxims was that architects have an absolutely clear mission: to humanize mechanical forms.

1. Training and early years, to 1927. 2. Influence of Rationalism, 1927–32. 3. International recognition, 1933–49. 4. Later years: the 1950s and after. 5. Influence.

1. TRAINING AND EARLY YEARS, TO 1927. His father was a government surveyor working in the lake district of central Finland and became a counterforce to his son's

strong artistic calling. Instead of becoming a painter, which tempted him for a long time, Alvar chose the career of architect as a possible compromise. He never became a planner dominated by technological thinking, however, but always gave his creations an artistic, humanistic character. He studied at the Technical College in Helsinki (1916–21), with one of the foremost proponents of National Romantic architecture, Armas Lindgren, as his principal teacher. This instilled in him not only the national fervour of Lindgren and his colleague Eliel Saarinen but also the tendency of the Art Nouveau school towards live, dynamic forms, and a striving to adapt architecture to the natural environment. During his period of study, however, another style became dominant, formally, in Scandinavia, namely a sophisticated neo-classicism associated with Scandinavia in the 18th century. The chief proponent of this school was the Swedish architect Gunnar Asplund, who soon became an admired model for Aalto and a close personal friend to him. In 1923 Aalto established a modest architects' office in the town where he grew up, Jyväskylä in central Finland. The buildings that he planned there bear the stamp not only of Asplund but also a powerful Italian influence, which he brought back with him from his first trip there in 1924. The early Renaissance of central and northern Italy, with masters such as Brunelleschi and urban environments such as Florence, Siena and Venice, remained a frequently visited source of inspiration for Aalto all his life. The most important works from Aalto's neo-classical period, which lasted until the summer of 1927, include the Workers' Club in Jyväskylä with the town's theatre of that time (planned in 1924), the Defence Corps building (1926) in the same town, the church in Muurame (1926), reminiscent of an Italian provincial church, and the Defence Corps building (1924) in Seinäjoki. He also took part in several of the architectural competitions that are common in Scandinavia and enable young, untried architects to receive important commissions. Though unsuccessful in the competition in 1923–4 for the Finnish Parliament building, in 1927 he won first prize in the competition for Viipuri City Library; this library was not, however, built until 1934–5, to entirely new plans bearing the stamp of Aalto's change-over to Rationalism. Another competition that Aalto won in 1927 was for a multi-purpose building, the Agricultural Co-operative building in Turku, which housed shops, offices, restaurants, hotels, private dwellings and, in particular, the town theatre. This great volume of building work caused Aalto to move his office to Turku in 1927.

2. Influence of Rationalism, 1927–32. The new architecture launched from the beginning of the 1920s by Le Corbusier in France, the De Stijl group in the Netherlands and the Bauhaus in Germany reached Scandinavia in the late 1920s. However, in 1927 Aalto and his Swedish colleague Sven Markelius were drawn along with the new tendency, soon to be followed by Gunnar Asplund. Aalto's Agricultural Co-operative building shows the earliest signs of this innovation. In 1928 he was ready to design Finland's first completely Functionalist building, the newspaper group Turun Sanomat's building in Turku. It was completed in 1930 and fulfilled all of the criteria for a rationalist building that had been formulated by Le Corbusier, even though at that time Aalto knew Functionalism only through books and journals. With Erik Bryggman, he also planned the large open-air exhibition with pavilions, inspired by Soviet Constructivism and by modern typography, which was organized in the summer of 1929 in Turku to celebrate the 700th anniversary of the town. However, it was not so much the formal goals of the new architecture as its social goals to which Aalto and his Scandinavian colleagues were attracted. The Bauhaus and its programme of social reform, therefore, became a more important model for them to follow than the work of the French and Dutch Modernists.

In 1929 Aalto was invited to join CIAM. He went to Frankfurt to attend the second congress and established friendly relations, not only with older colleagues such as Le Corbusier and Walter Gropius but also with László Moholy-Nagy (who was the same age and who gave him important artistic inspiration) and with the group secretary Siegfried Giedion and the English architectural critic Philip Morton Shand who became a warm and influential supporter in the international arena. The same year Aalto made an international breakthrough when he won an architectural competition for the large tuberculosis sanatorium in Paimio outside Turku, a building commission that he completed in 1932 (*see* International style, fig. 1). In it he broke away from the strict principles of early Rationalism, grouping the various building lengths in a non-geometrical, organic way and giving consideration more to the psychological needs of the users than to the functional aspects and technical and constructional factors. For the Paimio Sanatorium he designed buildings and all of the interior equipment, ranging from furniture and lamps to door handles, glassware and porcelain. His transformation of the newly invented tubular steel furniture into modern wooden furniture, manufactured by compression-moulding laminated wood, was particularly significant. In collaboration with master joiner Otto Korhonen (1884–1935) and his furniture factory in Turku, he had already created a chair in 1929, on which the press-moulded back and seat of plywood are supported by tubular-steel legs. For the sanatorium he invented a chair without any tubular steel at all, the so-called Paimio Chair, the back and seat of which are supported by a laminated wood frame that provides both arm supports and legs. This creation, perfect in form, competed successfully against Marcel Breuer's famous tubular steel construction, the so-called Wassili Chair, in realizing the dream of a modern lifestyle. The cantilevered tubular steel chair that the Bauhaus launched was also matched in 1932 by a corresponding Aalto-style product, the elegant armchair of curved wood, which was soon imitated by many other furniture designers but which remained most sought after in its original models with both hard or soft seat and high or low back. The basic design element for Aalto's standard furniture is the chair- or table-leg, which he jokingly called the 'column's little sister' and which was designed in three variants, the L-leg, the Y-leg and the X-leg.

3. International recognition, 1933–49. Aalto's international reputation was initially founded very much on the furniture that, in contrast to the buildings erected in Finland, could be exhibited to an international

public, for example at a show in London in 1933 that attracted attention, and at the Triennale exhibitions in Milan. In 1933 he moved to Helsinki, where two years later he erected his own residential and office building in the district of Munkkiniemi.

An important event for Aalto's career was meeting the factory-owning couple Maire and Harry Gullichsen in 1935. His friendship with them made possible the foundation of the Artek furniture design company, which began to sell Aalto's furniture in Finland and abroad and in general promoted a modern lifestyle, introducing modern international art into the country at the same time. Through Harry Gullichsen, Aalto soon received important large-scale planning and building commissions for Finnish industry. In 1937 he planned extensive residential areas and an industrial complex for the sulphate cellulose mill in Sunila near Kotka. Shortly afterwards he planned the paper mill and different types of dwellings for the industrial town of Inkeroinen. After World War II he was commissioned to build a complete industrial community on virgin land in Summa near Hamina on the south coast of Finland.

The commission of 1938 to design a private residence in Noormarkku near Pori for Maire and Harry Gullichsen was even more significant. The result, Villa Mairea, is one of the young Aalto's major works and shows his revolt against rigid Rationalism. On the one hand, he mixed folk traditions in Finnish building with the classical heritage of architectural history and with the formal concerns of Rationalism, producing a unique collage; on the other, he defined a new spatial concept that is related to both the forest as a felt environment and to the type of spatial openness that Cézanne introduced and that the Cubist painters developed further. Taking into account the experience of the materials' textures, the ceiling and floor of wood, walls of lime-washed tiles, slabs of natural stone and folkloric textiles, a better understanding is gained of the warm, harmonious atmosphere that characterizes this home, where everything is of exquisite quality without being ostentatious.

The first opportunity for an international public to become aware of Aalto's architecture was in 1937 at the Exposition Internationale des Arts et Techniques dans la Vie Moderne in Paris, where he was responsible for the Finnish Pavilion. Its ground-plan of structures freely grouped around an inner garden gave it a more open character than the Villa Mairea. The success of the pavilion led MOMA, New York, to invite Aalto to mount a one-man show there. In the following year (1939) he was given the responsibility for the Finnish Pavilion at the World's Fair in New York, although this involved fitting up a sector of the unit-hall shared by the small countries, in which Finland with her limited resources rented a stand. In the enclosed interior (see fig. 1) he created one of his most original works, raising a freely curving, forward-leaning 'auroral frontage' within the limited space, where the exhibits of Finland, a timber-exporting country, formed an assemblage. At both expositions Aalto also displayed the glassware he created during the 1930s, in particular the Savoy Vase with serpentine curved sides, all of which was influential on the international successes of Finnish arts and crafts during the post-war decades.

1. Alvar Aalto: interior of Finnish Pavilion, World's Fair, New York, 1939

In 1940 Aalto was appointed research professor in architecture at the Massachusetts Institute of Technology (MIT), Cambridge, but he managed to teach for only a short time in the USA before he was summoned back to his homeland. He was employed on the reconstruction of Finland's towns and cities after war damage. He had been occupied with urban and regional planning before World War II. Faced with the risk that reconstruction would be based, frighteningly, on a stereotyped technological standardization, he advocated the development of what he called 'flexible standardization'. It accepted large-scale industrialized building, since only this could remedy the housing shortage, but required the building elements to be made sufficiently flexible to be combined in innumerable different ways in accordance with the possibilities afforded by the environment and the individual users' needs.

In 1945 Aalto was commissioned to draw up a general plan for the province of Lappland and a new city plan for the totally destroyed provincial capital, Rovaniemi. His principles for urban and regional planning amounted to maintaining contact with nature and the countryside, favouring small-scale grouping of dwellings and, if possible, breaking down large industrial plants, office complexes, government departments and shopping centres into smaller interrelated units. For the new town of Imatra (also known as Vuoksenniska), which was founded after the cession of areas of land to the USSR, he drew up a general plan (1947–53; published in book form in 1957) with very sparse grouping of buildings. (For the same town he later, in 1955, designed one of his most notable works, the church of the Three Crosses, assymetrical and with variable dimensions.)

2. Alvar Aalto: town hall, Säynätsalo, 1949–52; view across the elevated courtyard

In 1946 Aalto resumed his teaching at MIT but confined his stays there to three or four months in a year. His most important contribution there was the building of Baker House Dormitory (1947–9). This building of red tiles, with its huge serpentine façade facing the river and steps rising in cascade form on the inner frontage, is the realization of Aalto's dream of flexible standardization, based on nature's principle of individualization: all 260 of the students' rooms with a view over the river have different shapes and therefore varied interior fixtures and furniture. However, the death of his wife and collaborator of many years, Aino Aalto (1894–1949), who devoted herself especially to tasks of interior equipment in conjunction with the couple's buildings, caused him deep depression, leading him to abandon all his work in the USA.

4. Later years: the 1950s and after. The 1950s became a great, vital creative period in Aalto's life after he met the young architect Elissa Mäkiniemi (*b* 1922), his wife from 1952. The important monumental buildings that he was commissioned to design include the Kansaneläkelatos (National Pensions Insurance Institute) in Helsinki and the new buildings of the Technical College in Otaniemi outside Helsinki. These were two major tasks, which occupied him for a long time, and they were executed during 1952–6 and 1962–8 respectively. In both of them he used richly textured red tiles for the façades. In order to be able to build even more curved tile surfaces than in Baker House and in the main building of the Technical College in Otaniemi, he invented a triangular tile, which in 1955–8 enabled him to build the auditorium for Helsinki's House of Culture in the form of a gently rounded shell. In addition, the university in Jyväskylä (1951–6), with several buildings grouped around a campus, uses red tile-surfaces and offers various free-form interiors with the unlimited space characteristic of Aalto's work.

A key work of Aalto's architecture of the 1950s is the small civic centre for the industrial town of Säynätsalo outside Jyväskylä, where the moderate scale and grouping of the cubic structures around a small inner courtyard are reminiscent of Italian small towns such as San Gimignano. The synthesis between old building traditions of the Mediterranean countries and an uncompromising Modernism also characterizes the two buildings that Aalto built for himself in the 1950s, namely his summer holiday residence and studio in the wilderness of the island of Muuratsalo in the lake district of central Finland, rising like a Byzantine monastery on the rock-strewn shore, and his new office building in Munkkiniemi outside Helsinki, which combines the form of an ancient theatre auditorium with modern office premises.

It was during the 1950s that Aalto really began to receive commissions outside Finland. In 1953 he won the competition for the Vogelweidplatz sports hall in Vienna, with what was technically a very daring (and therefore unexecuted) project. In 1955 he and a dozen of the world's best-known architects were each invited to design a block of flats in the Hansaviertel in Berlin. When the project was formally opened in 1957 as the *Interbauausstellung*, Aalto's building was one of those that received most attention and praise. In 1959 he won the competition for an opera house in Essen, in which he combined his shell-like, asymmetrical auditorium, known from Helsinki's House of Culture, with a series of three-tiered, serpentine balconies that are mirrored in the tall foyer situated behind them. The opera house was eventually built between 1981 and 1988, but Aalto had already used its basic shape in his project for Helsinki's Finlandiatalo, which was completed in 1971. Between 1958 and 1962 he built a marble-clad, fan-shaped house of culture in Wolfsburg in Germany, where he also erected a church between 1960 and 1963. His Neue Vahr tower block in Bremen, fan-shaped in plan, was completed in 1962. Several of Aalto's best projects remained unrealized unfortunately, including the competition design of 1958 for a town hall in Kiruna in Sweden, which won first prize; his winning proposal from the same year for a museum of art in Ålborg, Denmark, was built ten years later, as was his church in Detmerode (1963–9), Germany.

In 1956 Aalto planned a very lavishly endowed residence in the village of Bazoches-sur-Guyonne outside Paris for the art dealer Louis Carré. The building's sloping roof covered with Normandy slate repeats the rhythm of the surrounding landscape, while every detail of the interior, which offers rooms of varying height, is specially designed. Nordens hus (1964–9) in Reykjavik, Iceland, can also be counted among Aalto's important works abroad. Its outline repeats the rhythm of the surrounding mountain ridges, while the interior, with a library and various assembly rooms, has a cosy, intimate character. For the Mount Angels Monastery in Oregon, USA, he designed in 1964 a small library in the form of a sloping theatre auditorium (completed 1968), and in the mountain village of Riola, south of Bologna in Italy, a church based on his designs, with stepped dormer windows and asymmetrical in plan, was built between 1975 and 1980.

One of Aalto's lasting ambitions was to build whole city centres with several public buildings grouped around squares. He planned such centres both for the place where he grew up, Jyväskylä, for Helsinki and for many other towns in Finland and abroad. In many instances he was commissioned to execute only a part of these projects: the town hall in Säynätsalo (1949–52; see fig. 2); a theatre

(1964–86) and a police station (1967–70) in Jyväskylä; the magnificent Finlandiatalo and its conference wing (1962–76) in Helsinki. In only two cases was Aalto's centre project fully implemented. Possibly Aalto's most beautiful library was erected around the central square of Rovaniemi between 1961 and 1966, with a crystal-like exterior and a bookpit inside. From 1969 to 1971 the theatre and radio building Lapponia was added, and from 1986 to 1988 the town hall, designed in 1963. However, the most richly endowed centre by Aalto was built in the town of Seinäjoki in central Finland, where the church (1951–60) was accompanied by a town hall (1958–62), a library (1960–65) and a theatre (1961–87), all of them grouped around a series of open spaces, testifying to the fact that Aalto welcomed the principle in the urban environment of unlimited space, more like the countryside than the city or town.

5. INFLUENCE. Aalto was an outgoing and spontaneous person with humour, charm and a great gift for relating to people, which contributed greatly towards his successes. Despite his bohemian living habits, lack of interest in financial gain and not very efficiently organized architect's bureau, during his career he managed to execute *c.* 1000 projects, always working with uninhibited pleasure and a wealth of ideas. Over the years he accepted more than 300 young architects from both Finland and abroad (particularly Switzerland, Italy, Scandinavia and the USA) as assistants for short or long periods of time. With his pronounced scepticism of theorizing, he refrained from writing books on architecture and from academic lecturing; however, he loved to converse about architectural matters that were at the same time social and cultural. He thought that the practical work in his office—which he called his 'academy'—was the best way to pass on professional knowledge: that is to say, a teaching method corresponding to what Renaissance painters and architects applied in their workshops where they were surrounded by apprentices and assistants.

BIBLIOGRAPHY

S. Giedion: *Space, Time and Architecture* (Cambridge, MA, 1944, rev. 3/1954), pp. 565–604
B. Zevi: *Storia dell'architettura moderna* (Turin, 1950), pp. 283–307
Archit. Aujourd'hui, xxix (1950) [special issue on Aalto]
E. Neuenschwander and C. Neuenschwander: *Finische Bauten: Atelier Alvar Aalto, 1950–51* (Zurich, 1954)
F. Gutheim: *Alvar Aalto*, Masters of World Architecture (New York and London, 1960)
Arquitectura [Madrid], ii (1960) [special issue on Aalto]
Quad. Arquit., xxxix (1960) [special issue on Aalto]
K. Fleig, ed.: *Alvar Aalto*, 3 vols (Zurich, 1963–78)
L. Mosso: *L'opera di Alvar Aalto* (Milan, 1965)
R. Venturi: *Complexity and Contradiction in Architecture* (New York, 1966)
Arkitekten [Stockholm], iv (1969) [special issue on Aalto]
B. Hoesli, ed.: *Alvar Aalto Synopsis: Painting Architecture Sculpture* (Zurich, 1970) [incl. writings, chronological list of works and bibliog., richly illus.; in Fr., Ger. and Eng.]
G. Baird: *Alvar Aalto* (New York, 1971) [photographs by Y. Futugawa]
G. Schildt, ed.: *Alvar Aalto luonnoksia* [Alvar Aalto sketches] (Helsinki, 1972; Eng. trans., 1978) [contains a selection of Aalto's articles and lectures]
C. Jencks: *Modern Movements in Architecture* (New York, 1973), pp. 167–83
C. Cresti: *Alvar Aalto*, Maestri del novecento, 25 (Florence, 1975; Eng. and Sp. trans., 1976)
Arkkitehti/Arkitekten, vii–viii (1976) [memorial issue on Aalto]
Archit. Aujourd'hui, cxci (1977) [special issue on Aalto]
Parametro, lxii (1977)
Prog. Archit., iv (1977) [special issue on Aalto]
Space Des., i–ii (1977) [special issue on Aalto]
A. Gozak: *Arhitektura i gumanizm* [Architecture and humanism] (Moscow, 1978)
P. D. Pearson: *Alvar Aalto and the International Style* (New York, 1978)
B. Zevi: *The Modern Language of Architecture* (Seattle, 1978)
Alvar Aalto, Architectural Monographs and Academy Editions, 4 (London, 1978) [texts by D. Porphyrios and R. L. Heinonen]
Alvar Aalto, 1898–1976 (exh. cat., ed. A. Ruusuvuori; Helsinki, Mus. Fin. Archit., 1978) [incl. writings]
Archit. Des., xii (1979) [special issue on Aalto]
K. Frampton: *Modern Architecture: A Critical History* (New York, 1980), pp. 192–202
L. Rubino: *Aino e Alvar Aalto: Tutto il disegno* (Rome, 1980)
W. Blaser: *Il design di Alvar Aalto* (Milan, 1981)
D. Porphyrios: *Sources of Modern Eclecticism: Studies on Alvar Aalto* (London, 1982)
G. Schildt: *Det vita bordet: Alvar Aaltos ungdom och grundlaggande konstnarliga ideer* (Helsinki, 1982); Eng. trans. as *Alvar Aalto: The Early Years* (New York, 1984) [biog. up to 1927]
M. Quantrill: *Alvar Aalto: A Critical Study* (London, 1983)
A & U, v (1983) [special issue on Aalto]
W. C. Miller: *Alvar Aalto: An Annotated Bibliography* (New York, 1984)
J. Pallasmaa, ed.: *Alvar Aalto Furniture*, Helsinki, Mus. Fin. Archit. cat. (Helsinki, 1984)
G. Schildt: *Moderna tider* (Helsinki, 1985); Eng. trans. as *Alvar Aalto: The Decisive Years* (New York, 1986) [biog. 1927–39]
——: *Den mänshliga fahtorn* (Helsinki, 1990); Eng. trans. as *Alvar Aalto: The Mature Years* (New York, 1991) [biog. 1940–76]
——: *Alvar Aalto: The Complete Catalogue of Architecture, Design and Art* (London and New York, 1994)

GÖRAN SCHILDT

Aaltonen, Wäinö (Waldemar) (*b* Marttila [Swed. St Mårtens], 8 March 1894; *d* Helsinki, 30 May 1966). Finnish sculptor and painter. He was the most significant sculptor of the early decades of Finnish independence (after 1917). His style combined classical tranquillity with a modern sensitivity and disclosed the beauty of granite as a sculptural material. He studied painting at the School of Drawing of the Turku Art Association between 1910 and 1915 but on graduation began to practise moulding techniques and to teach himself stone sculpting. In 1916 his firm instincts and talent for monumental sculpture were remarked on at a general exhibition. His *Granite Boy* (1917–20; Helsinki, Athenaeum A. Mus.) is one of the masterpieces of his youth, the timid austerity of the child's figure conveying an Egyptian quality. The marble sculptures *Little Wader* (1917–22; priv. col., see Okkonen, 1926) and *Wader* (1924; Helsinki, Athenaeum A. Mus.) are both good examples of Aaltonen's tonal carving. His main concerns were light and shadow and the atmosphere they create around the sculpture. In 1923 he made his first trip abroad, to Rome, followed by trips to France and England in 1925. In 1924 he was commissioned by the State to produce the statue of *Paavo Nurmi Running* (1925), although it was not erected outdoors until the 1950s (versions in Turku, outside the Olympic Stadium in Helsinki, Lausanne (1994)). As early as 1926 the influential critic Onni Okkonen published a book about Aaltonen's art that proposed his status as one of Finland's most important living artists.

The 1920s were Aaltonen's most effective period of creativity. Influenced by both Classical and modernist ideas, he captured incorporeality in gilded wooden sculptures such as *Girl's Head* (1925; Helsinki, Athenaeum A. Mus.) and experimented with Cubism, as in *The Dancer*

(1928; Turku, Aaltonen Mus.) and *Cubist Aleksis Kivi, Writer* (1927; Turku, Aaltonen Mus.). The memorial to Aleksis Kivi, the *Poet and his Genius* (1926–8; Tampere, Library Park), which symbolically depicts the poet's inspiration, also signified a breakthrough in Aaltonen's career. At this time he began to design Cubist book covers, as well as the sets for the avant-garde plays of Hagar Olsson. In exhibitions at that time he was noted for his sensuous interpretations in stone.

In the 1930s Aaltonen produced the figures for the Assembly Hall of the Parliament in Helsinki, the statue of *Aleksis Kivi* (1930–9; Helsinki, Railway Station Square) and the marble relief in Helsinki University, the *Goddess of Liberty Crowning Youth* (1938–40; damaged 1944). These, together with his many sculpted heads, such as that of *Jean Sibelius* (1935; Helsinki, Athenaeum A. Mus), strengthened Aaltonen's position as the creator of a national style of classicism. After the war, Aaltonen produced a number of memorials. The granite memorial to the war heroes in Lahti, entitled *Peace* (1950–52), conveys a tranquil nobility, and among the best works of his later period is the bronze statue of two horsemen *Establishing Friendship* (1951; Turku, Aninkainen Square). Before his death he produced a few abstract pieces, of which *Genius montanus I* (1961) was placed over his grave in the Maaria Cemetery, near Turku. Before World War II Aaltonen also painted a great deal, especially figure studies (e.g. *In the Concert*, 1926; priv. col., see 1988 exh. cat., p. 31). Apart from a few Cubist collages, he rarely attained the same standard as in his sculpture. His work covered a broad range, from medals to official portraits of presidents, book covers and theatre sets, which bears witness to his faith in his wide creative ability, apparently reinforced by the deafness he suffered from his youth. He was appointed a member of the Finnish Academy in 1948, and in 1967 the Wäinö Aaltonen Museum opened in Turku (*see* TURKU, §2).

BIBLIOGRAPHY

O. Okkonen: *Wäinö Aaltonen, 1915–1925: Tutkielma* [Wäinö Aaltonen, 1915–1925: a study] (Porvoo, 1926)

——: *Wäinö Aaltonen* (Porvoo, 1945)

Börje Sandberg, ed.: *Wäinö Aaltonen* (Helsinki, 1948)

G. Schildt: *Modern Finnish Sculpture* (New York, 1970)

L. Ahtola-Moorhouse: 'Review of Finnish Sculpture, 1910–80', *Suomalaista veistotaidetta—Finnish Sculpture*, The Association of Finnish Sculptors (Helsinki, 1980)

Wäinö Aaltonen vareissä: Maalauksia ja piirustuksia / Wäinö Aaltonen i färg: Målningar och teckningar [Wäinö Aaltonen in colour: paintings and drawings] (exh. cat., Helsinki, Acad. F.A., 1988)

Wäinö Aaltonen, 1894–1966 (exh. cat., ed. H. Pfäffli; Turku, Wäinö Aaltonen Mus., 1994)

LEENA AHTOLA-MOORHOUSE

Aarschot, Dukes of. *See* CRÖY, DE.

Aarts, Johannes Josephus (*b* The Hague, 18 Aug 1871; *d* Amsterdam, 19 Oct 1934). Dutch printmaker and painter. He trained at the Academie voor Beeldende Kunsten in The Hague, where he subsequently taught graphic art (1893–1911). In 1911 he succeeded Pieter Dupont as professor in graphics at the Rijksakademie in Amsterdam under the directorship of Antoon Derkinderen. In the early years of his career Aarts produced some paintings using the pointillist technique, mostly landscapes (The Hague, Gemeentemus.); he also carved some sculptures in wood. He is, however, best known for his graphic work. In technique and subject-matter, his prints have a great deal in common with those of Dupont. As the latter's successor he devoted himself to the revival of engraving, which his predecessor had reintroduced; his own experiments in this medium (in particular his scenes with diggers and beggars, all *c.* 1900) are considered milestones in early 20th-century Dutch printmaking. He also applied his skills to etching, lithography, woodcutting and wood-engraving; of the latter his *Dance of Death* series (*c.* 1915–20) is particularly well known. His subject-matter varies, from scenes from the lives of ordinary people to themes from literature and the Bible. An almost complete collection of his prints is housed in the Rijksmuseum in Amsterdam, and the Gemeentemuseum in The Hague holds some of his paintings.

BIBLIOGRAPHY

H. de Boer: 'J. J. Aarts', *Elsevier's Geillus. Mdschr.*, xvii (1907), pp. 34, 217–30 [with illus.]

Johannes Joseph Aarts (exh. cat., intro. G. Knuttel Willemszoon; The Hague, Gemeentemus., 1936)

A. J. Vernoorn: *Nederlandse prentkunst, 1840–1940* (Lochem, 1983), pp. 41, 70, 93 [with illus.]

M. Kersten: *De Nederlandse kopergravure, 1900–1975* (The Hague, 1989), pp. 26–33, 91–5 [with illus.]

JAN JAAP HEIJ

Aas, Nils (Sigurd) (*b* Inderøy, Nord-Trøndelag, 21 April 1933). Norwegian sculptor, designer and medallist. He became familiar with handicraft in his father's furniture workshop. In 1954 he began five years' study as a commercial artist at the Håndverks- og Kunstindustriskole in Oslo and from 1957 to 1963 he worked as an illustrator for a newspaper. He studied at the Kunstakademi in Oslo from 1959 to 1962 under the sculptor Per Palle Storm (1910–94) who advocated naturalism in sculpture. As an assistant to Arnold Haukeland from 1961 to 1964, Aas lost his apprehension of the untried and cultivated his sense of daring, as he gained experience with welding techniques. Highly imaginative and versatile, Aas worked in both abstract and figurative modes and is reckoned one of the foremost sculptors in Norway; in 1990 he was honoured with St Olav.

Aas's first sculpture was an equestrian monument in snow, made in Inderøy while he was a schoolboy. His first public project was the abstract steel figure *Bird* (1966–7), which is outside the Symra Cinema in Lambertseter, Oslo. The cinema and film suggested to Aas the subjects of the bird and flight. The sculpture, made of steel plates, stands on a concrete base 4 m high, the cinema's large brick wall forming a background. In 1967 he won the competition for a monument in Oslo to *King Haakon VII* (7 June Square). His unorthodox monumental bronze (h. *c.* 4.5 m including base, unveiled 1972) marked an artistic breakthrough for Aas. The King is shown standing, in a long coat, with his head raised and his right arm by his side: he holds his military cap in his left arm, bent in front of his breast. Although the sculpture was criticized for its non-militaristic posture, Aas wanted to convey the King's humility in the face of the people he was to serve. The tall, slender figure is simplified to grand lines of pivoting form, which convey the King's strong and steadfast character. At the same time, the sculpture reveals Aas's interest in the work of Alberto Giacometti. Aas was also influenced by the work of Constantin Brancusi, Giacomo Manzù, Marino Marini and Henry Moore.

Aas worked with a variety of materials and forms. In 1971 his sculpture *Beacon* was erected on Mølleråsen, north of Sandefjord. A stylized steel bird 3.5 m high on top of a 10 m base, it stands like a landmark on an elegantly formed column in light concrete. Aas got the idea for the wall sculpture *Northern light* (5×16.5 m, 1976–8) while sitting and twisting matchsticks between his fingers. It hangs in the Hall of the Council of Ministers in the Palais du Conseil de L'Europe in Strasbourg and consists of 100 pieces of Norwegian laminated spruce, each 150×200 mm in thickness. In 1981 a large granite monument to *Henrik Ibsen* (h. 3.6 m) was erected in Teaterparken (the theatre park) in Bergen. A life-size plaster model was made before the stone was cut; Aas worked on the granite and undertook the final polishing of this unorthodox sculpture, which was installed in three sections. Aas made Ibsen as he understood him to have been: a reserved, sensitive and timid person, short and stocky. It was particularly important for him to convey Ibsen's roles as a prophet and castigator of society. The character of the stone is thus brought forth in this highly stylized figure. A pen held in one lowered arm indicates the activity of the author. Aas has also made highly original sculptures in cut paper, steel thread or wood.

Aas began modelling busts in 1963. Bronze portraits of the author *Johan Borgen* (1965; Oslo, N.G.) and the government minister *Trygve Bratteli* (1982; Oslo, Norske Arbeiderparti) show his firm grasp of characterization. The surface planes have clear structures and show the traces of his work with tools and clay. A sculpture of Marilyn Monroe (1994) is situated in Haugesund. He is also internationally known for his engraved and cast commemorative medallions and in 1994 designed two Norwegian coins, the 10 and 20 kroner.

BIBLIOGRAPHY

Meissner; *NKL*

Fédération internationale de la médaille (exh. cats, Helsinki, 1973; Kraków, 1975; Budapest, 1977; Lisbon, 1979; Florence, 1983)

E. Dæhlin: 'Nils Aas', *Kst & Kult.*, iii/4 (1980), pp. 582–6

K. Berg and others, eds: *Inn i en ny tid* [Into a new era], vii of *Norges kunsthistorie* (Oslo, 1981–3), pp. 317, 323–7

B. Rostad: *Nils Aas: Et billedhuggerportrett* [Nils Aas: portrait of a sculptor] (Oslo, 1987)

INGEBORG WIKBORG

A(rt and) A(rchitecture) T(hesaurus). Ongoing American project, belonging to the Getty Art History Information Program (AHIP), intended as the first comprehensive thesaurus for the fields of art and architecture. Its aims are to promote consistency and compatibility among art-historical databases by providing a standardized, controlled vocabulary for use in bibliographic and visual databases and in the documentation of object collections. The AAT's terminology, arranged both alphabetically and hierarchically by concept, reflects the 'common usage' of scholars and cataloguers. Advisory boards composed of experts in the fields of architecture, decorative and fine arts, along with archivists and information managers in these fields, have reviewed and approved terminology for inclusion in the thesaurus.

The AAT was founded by Dora Crouch, Pat Molholt (*b* 19 Oct 1943) and Toni Petersen (*b* 13 May 1933) and was housed first at Rensselaer Polytechnic Institute in Troy, NY, and then at Bennington College in Bennington, VT. Initial work (1980–83) was funded by the Council on Library Resources, the National Endowment for the Humanities, the Andrew W. Mellon Foundation and the J. Paul Getty Trust. In 1983 the AAT became an AHIP project. In 1986 it moved to Williamstown, MA, under the directorship of Toni Petersen. The first edition of the AAT, published in 1990 by Oxford University Press in three volumes, received an award from the Association of American Publishers. The AAT was mounted as an online authority reference tool in the Research Libraries Information Network (RLIN) of the Research Libraries Group in 1990. An electronic edition on diskette, with accompanying browsing tool for use with personal computers, was developed in 1992; the complete second edition, in print and electronic form, was published in 1994 by Oxford University Press.

TONI PETERSEN

Abacco, Antonio. *See* LABACCO, ANTONIO.

Abacus. Uppermost element of a capital on a column or pilaster (*see* GREECE, ANCIENT, fig. 9n; ORDERS, ARCHITECTURAL, fig. 1xii). On the Doric, Ionic and Tuscan orders of architecture it is square in plan, but on the Corinthian each face is convex.

Abada, Tell. *See under* HAMRIN REGION.

Abadie, Paul (*b* Paris, 9 Nov 1812; *d* Chatou, 2 Aug 1884). French architect and restorer. He was the son of a Neo-classical architect of the same name (1783–1868), who was a pupil of Charles Percier and architect to the département of Charente. The younger Paul Abadie began studying architecture in 1832 by joining the atelier of Achille Leclère and then entered the Ecole des Beaux-Arts in 1835. While he was following this classical training, he participated in the rediscovery of the Middle Ages by going on archaeological trips and then, from 1844, in his capacity as attaché to the *Commission des Monuments Historiques*. He undertook his first restoration work at Notre-Dame de Paris, under the direction of Jean-Baptiste-Antoine Lassus and Viollet-le-Duc. Abadie was appointed deputy inspector at Notre-Dame in 1845, and in 1848, when the department responsible for diocesan buildings was created, he was appointed architect to the dioceses of Périgueux, Angoulême and Cahors. He subsequently completed about 40 restoration projects, mainly on Romanesque churches in Charente, in the Dordogne and the Gironde, and as a diocesan architect he was put in charge of two large cathedrals in his district: St Pierre d'Angoulême and St Front de Périgueux. In the former he undertook a huge programme of 'completion', returning to a stylistic unity that was in line with current episcopal policy (*see* ARCHITECTURAL CONSERVATION AND RESTORATION, fig. 2). He worked there from 1849 to 1880, rebuilding the upper levels of the north tower, restoring the central portal on the façade and building superstructures to replace those of the 16th century. He also undertook considerable restoration work on the rest of the building, suppressing post-Romanesque additions and constructing a new dome at the transept crossing. Abadie worked on St-Front de Périgueux from 1851 until his death. The project involved a difficult underpinning of the building (south wing, 1852–4), but work progressed rapidly towards an almost complete reconstruction that rationalized the architectural outline. In Bordeaux, where Abadie was appointed diocesan architect for the cathedral in 1862, he again took part in a sizeable programme of restoration work that was designed to symbolize the revival of Catholicism in the diocese. This included the restoration of the bell-tower of St Michel (1857–69) and the much-debated restoration of the façade of Sainte Croix (1859–65).

While he was carrying out this restoration work, Abadie planned or built around 40 new buildings, most of which were religious, including in Angoulême, the churches of St Martial (1849–56) and St Ausone (1856–68); in the Dordogne, the churches of Notre-Dame de Bergerac (1851–66), St Georges de Périgueux (1852–70) and Villefranche-de-Périgord (1855–70); and in Bordeaux, Ste Marie à La Bastide (1860–86) and St Ferdinand (1862–7). The church of St Martial in Angoulême is one of the first examples of 'archaeological' neo-Romanesque, while Notre-Dame de Bergerac is based on 13th-century Gothic examples and was inspired by a preceding project by Viollet-le-Duc. He also built a few residential properties (notably in the Rue Paul-Abadie in Angoulême) and several civic edifices. The most significant of the latter is Angoulême Town Hall (1854–69), where he used the remains of a former château and made stylistic reference to the town halls in medieval communes.

In 1874 Abadie won the competition to build the Eglise du Vœu National au Sacré-Coeur, the celebrated basilica in Montmartre, Paris. This was to be erected to fulfil a vow that had been made at the time of France's defeat in the Franco-Prussian war of 1870–71. Abadie's project, which has been rather hurriedly described as Romanesque Byzantine, represents, in the reworking of the Romanesque style of south-west France, the outcome of formal research by the restorer and the builder. Work began in 1875, the year in which Abadie was elected to the Institut de France. The basilica was not completed until around 1919, long after the architect's death, with modifications to the original plan that varied in significance according to the personalities of his successors, who included Honoré Daumet, Jean Charles Laisné, H.-P.-M. Rauline (*b* 1848), L. Magne (1849–1916) and L.-J. Hulot (1871–1959). With this monument, Abadie gave the Romanesque Revival its most notable expression and gave a decisive victory to the 'diocésains', a group composed mostly of rationalists that grew up under the influence of Viollet-le-Duc. Abadie was less militant and less of a theoretician than Viollet-le-Duc, however, and he produced at Montmartre and elsewhere a more equivocal achitecture that reflected his training, in which the rediscovery of the Middle Ages and the academic tradition existed side by side.

BIBLIOGRAPHY

C. Laroche: 'L'Oeuvre d'architecture de Paul Abadie (1812–1884): Situation culturelle et inventaire raisonné', *Bull. Soc. Hist. A. Fr.* (1981), pp. 219–38

Entre archéologie et modernité: Paul Abadie architecte, 1812–1884 (exh. cat., ed. C. Laroche; Angoulême, Mus. Mun., 1984)

Paul Abadie, architecte, 1812–1884 (exh. cat., ed. C. Laroche; Paris, Mus. Mnmts Fr., 1988)

J. Benoist: *Le Sacré-Coeur de Montmartre de 1870 à nos jours*, 2 vols (Paris, 1992)

CLAUDE LAROCHE

Abaj Takalik. Pre-Columbian MAYA site in Retalhuleu, in the Highland Maya region, near the Pacific coast of Guatemala. It is best known for its monumental stone sculptures, some of which were recorded in the 19th century. The site lies partly on the Finca San Isidro Piedra Parada, and it was known by this name when Eric Thompson published a description of some of the sculpture in 1943. 'Abaj Takalik' ('standing stone') is a translation of 'Piedra Parada' into Quiché Maya. It was occupied during the Pre-Classic (*c.* 2000 BC–*c.* AD 250) and Classic (*c.* AD 250–*c.* 900) periods. The site lies on a fertile slope between the mountains and the sea; there are remains of steep, manmade earthen terraces on which its structures were built. The earth removed to create the terraces may have been used to construct the various mounds at Abaj Takalik, a number of which were faced with stone cobbles. Adobe bricks were also used, and local volcanic material provided flooring. The site was covered in 1902 by volcanic ash, and much of the area is now used for growing coffee.

Abaj Takalik produced truly monumental stone sculptures, weighing between one and nearly twenty tons. Several hundred monuments, both plain and worked, and mostly of the abundant local andesite, are known. They include petroglyphs, a large number of boulder sculptures, 'potbelly' figures, sculptures in the round, silhouettes, and altars and stelae carved in low relief, the last two types often found in association. They vary greatly in their quality and degree of preservation. Style and iconography are also varied. Some monuments are finely carved with elaborate reliefs of human figures with symbolic paraphernalia, while others are simply incised boulders. Some of the sculptural styles and motifs are closely related to the late Olmec sculpture of the Mexican Gulf Coast (*see* MESOAMERICA, PRE-COLUMBIAN, §IV, 2(i)) and of CHALCATZINGO in central Mexico. During the Late Pre-Classic period (*c.* 300 BC–*c.* AD 250), Abaj Takalik was one of the most important centres in the Pacific region, together with KAMINALJUYÚ and IZAPA, sites with which its sculpture shows affinity. During the Early Classic period (*c.* AD 250–*c.* 600) the Abaj Takalik style closely resembled that of nearby SANTA LUCÍA COTZUMALHUAPA. Abaj Takalik Stele 2 has one of the earliest known dates of the Maya Long Count calendar (*see* MESOAMERICA, PRE-COLUMBIAN, §II), corresponding to the last half of the 1st century BC. The sculpture depicts two standing figures with feather headdresses facing a column of hieroglyphs. A similar composition appears on Stele 5, which has an inscription corresponding to AD 126. Hieroglyphs also appear on Stele 1 and on Altar 12.

There has been a degree of controversy over the dating of some Abaj Takalik sculptures. The resetting of some of the monuments during the Late Classic period (*c.* AD 600–*c.* 900) complicates the issue. John A. Graham of the University of California, Berkeley, who worked at the site from 1976, believed that the boulder and 'potbelly' sculptures of Abaj Takalik precede those of the Early Pre-Classic period (*c.* 2000–*c.* 1000 BC) OLMEC sites of the Gulf Coast; others consider that they belong to the Middle Pre-Classic period (*c.* 1000–*c.* 300 BC) or later.

BIBLIOGRAPHY

J. E. S. Thompson: *Some Sculptures from Southeastern Cevetzaltenango, Guatemala*, Notes on Middle American Archaeology and Ethnology, xvii, Carnegie Institution of Washington, DC, Division of Historical Research (Cambridge, MA, 1943), pp. 100–12

S. W. Miles: 'Sculpture of the Guatemala–Chiapas Highlands and Pacific Slopes, and Associated Hieroglyphs', *Hb. Mid. Amer. Ind.*, ii (1965), pp. 237–75

J. A. Graham, R. F. Heizer and E. M. Shook: 'Abaj Takalik 1976', *Studies in Ancient Mesoamerica*, iii, ed. J. A. Graham (Berkeley, 1978), pp. 85–110

J. A. Graham: 'Antecedents of Olmec Sculpture at Abaj Takalik', *Pre-Columbian Art History*, ed. A. Cordy-Collins (Palo Alto, 1982), pp. 7–22

L. A. Parsons: *The Origins of Maya Art*, Studies in Pre-Columbian Art and Archaeology, xxviii (Washington, DC, 1986)

J. A. Graham and L. Benson: 'Escultura olmeca y maya sobre canto in Abaj Takalik', *Arqueólogia*, iii (1990), pp. 77–84

ELIZABETH P. BENSON

Abakanowicz, Magdalena (*b* Felenty, nr Warsaw, 1930). Polish textile artist. She studied at the College of Fine Arts, Sopot, and graduated in 1955 from the Academy of Fine Arts, Warsaw. At the beginning of her career she was interested in drawing, painting and sculpture, but after 1960 she concentrated on textile arts in the broad sense of the term. Breaking with tradition, she initiated bold experiments with fibre and fabric. Her work contributed to the revolutionary textile movement known as FIBRE ART and finally entered the domain of modern sculpture.

Abakanowicz's début, with a composition of forms made of white fabrics, was in 1962 at the first Biennale Internationale de la Tapisserie in Lausanne. At that time she also experimented with tapestry, giving it three-dimensional relief by introducing non-woven shapes. In the late 1960s her development of three-dimensional textiles was fully realized in her 'abakans' (*see* TAPESTRY, fig. 15). These took various forms—winged, open or round—and were red, orange or white. She also created fifteen heavy, monolithic 'black forms' and three large 'black garments'. In 1971 she entwined Edinburgh Cathedral with rope, and the following year she repeated this happening with a fountain in Bordeaux. Ropes became a favourite material in various exhibition compositions. In the 1970s she experimented further with textile sculpture, using burlap, string and cotton gauze. She started with the *Deviations* series, followed by the *Alterations* series, featuring 'faces' and 'schizophrenic heads'. After this period her work concentrated on fragmented human figures (heads without trunks, bodies without heads, torsos without legs) placed singly or in large groups. The human body as a structure became her chief interest, and for her research she visited scientific laboratories and dissecting rooms, consulted the most advanced scientists and studied slides of the brain. She also travelled to Arizona for discussions with Paolo Soleri and to New Guinea to see the initiation ceremonies. Between 1976 and 1980 she created the *Human Backs* series of 80 figures, followed by the *Embryology* series (1980; oval forms made of linen, rags and cord) and the *Syndromes* series (16 brains made of clay). She made multiple casts of real human beings and individualized each form with a particular texture and pattern. The creases, ridges and veins of the resin-hardened fibre surface imitate organic characteristics, recalling the earth's rough surface or the cellular composition of human skin. The *Androgyn* series (1985) features torsos perched on low stretchers of wooden logs, which fill in for the missing legs; through such provocative images she expressed her view of the physical and spiritual condition of mankind. The *Catharsis* series (1986; 33 figures, each *c.* 3 m tall), made for the Fondazione Giuliano Gori, Florence, progressed a stage further and was cast in bronze.

Abakanowicz had more than 40 one-woman exhibitions all over the world, and her work is in many international museums, as well as in Poland (Warsaw, N. Mus.; Łódź, Cent. Mus. Textiles; Łódź, Mus. A.). In 1965 she was made a professor at the Stage College of Fine Arts, Poznań.

BIBLIOGRAPHY

Contemp. Artists

Polska tkanina awangardowa [Modern Polish art textiles] (exh. cat. by K. Kondratiuk, Poznań, 1969)

M. Constantine and J. L. Larsen: *Beyond Craft: The Art Fabric* (New York, 1973)

Magdalena Abakanowicz (exh. cat., Warsaw, Zachęta Gal., 1975)

Annu. Skira, i (1975)

Annu. Skira, ii (1976)

I. Huml: *Polska sztuka stosowana XX wieku* [20th-century Polish applied art] (Warsaw, 1978)

Annu. Skira, v (1979)

'Magdalena Abakanowicz: About the 1970s', *Annu. Skira*, vi (1980), pp. 130–31

Magdalena Abakanowicz, Polonia (exh. cat., Venice, Biennale, 1980)

Z. Żygulski jr: *An Outline History of Polish Applied Art* (Warsaw, 1987), p. 100

VIDEO RECORDINGS

Wytwórnia Filmów Oświatowych [Educational film workshop]: *Abakany* (Łódź, 1969)

Film Australia: *Abakanowicz in Australia* (Sydney, 1976)

——: *Division of Space* (Sydney, 1976)

Sydney Film and Television School: *Abakanowicz* (Sydney, 1976)

ZDZISŁAW ŻYGULSKI JR

Abaneri [anc. Abhānagari]. Temple site in north-eastern Rajasthan, India. It contains the fragmentary remains of two major monuments of the 8th century AD. The Chand Baori, a stepped ritual bathing tank *c.* 19 m deep, was probably built by Raja Chandra, from whom its name derives; an enclosing verandah dates to the 17th century. Although the Harshatmata Temple also dates to the 8th century, or early 9th, according to some scholars, a modern temple has been built over the original foundations, which include a broad platform and the lower walls of the original monument. A remarkable sequence of sculptures, showing primarily secular scenes, survives. These include kings with courtiers, musicians and couples (*see* INDIAN SUB-CONTINENT, fig. 186). The figural scenes are framed by pilasters carved with floral motifs and capped by elaborate interlaced pediments employing the *gavākṣa* (Skt: 'cow's-eye') motif.

The sculpture of Abaneri extensively illustrates a phase of sculptural development midway between the Gupta style of the Mathura region and the abstracted linearized style adopted in northern India from the 10th century. Its style, often referred to as naturalistic, renders the figure with an energetic elasticity conveying both potential and actual movement. The profuse details, including facial expressions and gestures, are carved with great delicacy, and the high relief utilizes deep undercutting. Several of the ancient sculptures have been embedded into the walls of the modern temple, and numerous fragments—possibly from other temples no longer extant—lie about the site. Other pieces, including images of deities such as Ganesha, Durga and Gaja-Lakshmi and scenes from the life of Krishna, have been removed to the Archaeological Museum in Amer.

BIBLIOGRAPHY
R. C. Agrawala: 'Sculptures from Abaneri, Rajasthan', *Lalit Kala*, i–ii (1955–6), pp. 130–35
P. Jayakar: 'Notes on Some Sculptures *in situ* at Abaneri, Rajasthan', *Lalit Kala*, i–ii (1955–6), pp. 139–44
K. C. Jain: *Ancient Cities and Towns of Rajasthan* (Delhi, 1972)
S. Gupta: *Jaipur*, Rajasthan District Gazetteer (Jaipur, 1987)

WALTER SMITH

Aba-Novák, Vilmos (*b* Budapest, 15 March 1894; *d* Budapest, 29 Sept 1941). Hungarian painter, draughtsman and etcher. He trained as a drawing teacher at the College of Fine Arts, Budapest (1912–14). In 1913 he worked at the Szolnok colony and he served in World War I. He taught drawing for a while at the Technical University, Budapest. In 1922 he learnt etching from Viktor Olgyay at the College of Fine Arts. His early works show an affinity with the Group of Eight; later he moved closer to the work of the Activists, especially József Nemes Lampérth and Béla Uitz. He instinctively sought a dynamic and powerful form of expression. His pen-drawings and etchings are frequently based on biblical subjects and are characterized by a heroic conception, an illusory atmosphere and romantic associations. The etching *Savonarola* (1925; Budapest, N.G.) reveals his extraordinary compositional abilities, especially in the rendering of crowds, and his use of strong chiaroscuro. His landscapes are dominated by carefully composed, naturalist details and the exploitation of the dramatic effect of reflections. In his drawings, Cubist arrangements gradually gave way to a more diffuse composition. His nudes in the landscape (e.g. *Bathers*, pen-and-ink, 1922; Budapest, N.G.) evoke an air of serenity. He soon sought more emotional and dramatic themes, however, becoming preoccupied with the search for a psychologically authentic depiction of apocalyptic events and mass ecstasy, and looking to his more immediate environment for models and themes.

In 1929–30 he spent two years in Italy on a scholarship, which greatly contributed to the development of his mature style. He studied medieval and early Renaissance painters and decided to paint in tempera. Most of his major works were created between 1930 and 1936. He favoured bright colours, depicting Italian town squares, travelling circuses, village fairs, peasant festivals and church ceremonies. Typical characters reappear again and again. With this work he continued the tradition of Hungarian genre-painting. After receiving an award in 1932 at an exhibition of ecclesiastical art in Padua, he was offered large-scale commissions by the state and the church. His wall painting for the church of Jászszentandrás summarizes in its depiction of the blessed and the damned all his previous achievements in the drawing of space and the representation of character types. The composition is at once archaic and modern and there is drama and forcefulness in the exaggerated gestures and lively mimicry, and an emphasis on theatrical effects. The wall paintings of the *Heroes' Gate* (1934) in Szeged represent realistically the horrors of World War I. In the last part of his life he continued to work, although worsening health, growing demands, changes in his ambitions and new experiments in technique all affected his output. His wall paintings became increasingly like large-scale coloured drawings, for example the *Creation* cycle (1938) for the ceiling of the church in the Buda City Park, Budapest. He continued to depict in bright colours jovial characters bursting with vitality. From 1938 until his death he taught at the College of Fine Arts, Budapest.

WRITINGS

'Vallomás' [Confession], *Magyar Művészet* (1931), pp. 189–212

BIBLIOGRAPHY
E. Ybl: 'Aba-Novák Vilmos', *Magyar Művészet* (1931), pp. 137–46
T. Gerevich: 'Aba-Novák Vilmos', *Szépművészet* (1940–41), pp. 261–6
M. B. Supka: 'Aba-Novák Vilmos festészetének nemzeti sajátosságairól' [On the national characteristics of Vilmos Aba-Novák's painting], *Magyar nemzeti Gal. Közleményei* [Publications of the Hungarian National Gallery], ii (1961), pp. 175–7
——: *Aba-Novák Vilmos* (Budapest, 1971)
S. Kontha, ed.: *Magyar Művészet, 1919–1945* [Hungarian art, 1919–45] (Budapest, 1985), pp. 418–26

S. KONTHA

Abarca de Bolea, Pedro Pablo. *See* ARANDA.

Abarquh [Abarqūh]. Iranian town in northern Fars province. A prosperous centre in medieval times, by the 10th century it was fortified with a citadel and had a congregational mosque. The octagonal tower of mortared stone known as the Gunbad-i 'Ali was erected, according to its inscription, by a Daylamite prince in 1056–7 to contain the remains of his parents. The Masjid-i Birun, a mosque to the south of the town, may be slightly earlier, although it has many later additions. The congregational mosque (rest.), with four iwans around a rectangular court, dates mostly to the 14th century, although the base of the dome chamber probably belongs to the 12th-century mosque. The many mihrabs within the mosque include a particularly fine stucco example (1338). There are also several mud-brick tombs in the town. These square structures have plain exteriors and plastered and painted interiors. One of the earliest is the tomb of Pir Hamza Sabzpush (12th century); the finest was that of Hasan ibn Kay Khusraw (1318; destr.). In the 18th century, the town suffered first in the Afghan invasion and then in the fighting between the Zands and Qajars.

BIBLIOGRAPHY
Enc. Iran.
A. Godard: 'Abarḳūh (Province de Yazd)', *Āthār-ē Īrān*, i (1936), pp. 47–72
D. N. Wilber: *The Architecture of Islamic Iran: The Il Khānid Period* (Princeton, 1955)
I. Afshar: *Yādgārhā-yi Yazd* [Monuments of Yazd], 3 vols (Tehran, Iran. Solar 1348–54/1970–76)
S. S. Blair: *The Monumental Inscriptions of Early Islamic Iran and Transoxiana* (Leiden, 1992)

□

Abarshahr. *See* NISHAPUR.

Abate, Giulio Camillo dell'. *See under* MASTERS, ANONYMOUS, AND MONOGRAMMISTS, §I: MASTER OF FLORA.

1. Nicolò dell'Abate: *Card-players* (*c.* 1550; detail), frescoed frieze, Palazzo Poggi, Bologna

Abate [Abbate]**, Nicolò** [Niccolò] **dell'** (*b* Modena, 1509–12; *d* ?Fontainebleau, 1571). Italian painter and draughtsman. He was one of the most important artists of the first FONTAINEBLEAU SCHOOL, which was developed at the French court by Rosso Fiorentino and Francesco Primaticcio, and he introduced the Italian Mannerist landscape into France.

1. ITALY, BEFORE 1552. He was almost certainly trained by his father, Giovanni dell'Abate (*d* 1559), a stuccoist, and by the sculptor Antonio Begarelli. Apparently after a period as a soldier, by 1537 he was working in Modena as a painter under Alberto Fontana (*fl* 1518–58). There the two artists decorated the façade of the Beccherie (Slaughterhouse) from which certain paintings survive (e.g. *St Geminian* and an allegory of the *Wine Harvest*; both Modena, Gal. & Mus. Estense). His early paintings clearly show the influence of Correggio and of such Ferrarese artists as Dosso Dossi. They also display a love of the picturesque and the pastoral, with frequent variations on the theme of the concert, as in the fragment of a concert scene (Reggio Emilia, Mus. Civ. & Gal. A.) from the façade decorations of the Palazzo Pratonieri in Reggio Emilia. Around 1540 he painted a series of frescoes based on Virgil's *Aeneid* in a study of a castle owned by the Boiardo family at Scandiano, near Modena. Some of these paintings survive (Modena, Gal. & Mus. Estense) but greatly altered by damage and restoration. Engravings after the paintings (published by G. B. Venturi, Modena, 1821) give some indication of their original state. The scheme of the room probably included 12 paintings, each representing a book of the *Aeneid*, many depicting several events. Below these were battle scenes; above them were lunettes containing landscapes. In the spandrels were eight female figures reaching up to the octagon of the ceiling, where dell'Abate painted portraits of members of the Boiardo family playing instruments and singing, a scene recalling the oculus of Andrea Mantegna's *Camera picta* (Mantua, Pal. Ducale). Although Dosso's *Aeneas* cycle (dispersed, U. Birmingham, Barber Inst.; Ottawa, N.G.; Washington, DC, N.G.A.), painted *c.* 1520 for Alfonso I d'Este, probably influenced dell'Abate, the Scandiano frescoes were the most extensive treatment of the Virgilian narrative in the period. They show dell'Abate's love of landscape, both for its own sake and to enhance narrative compositions. The figure style in these works suggests the influence of Parmigianino and Correggio.

The Scandiano project was undoubtedly instrumental in gaining other large commissions for dell'Abate. In 1546 he and Fontana were employed to decorate the Sala dei Conservatori of the Palazzo Pubblico in Modena. This decoration includes scenes from Roman history, once again set in idyllic landscapes. The treatment of landscape reflects Venetian and Emilian traditions, which in turn were shaped by those of northern European art. The decorations are restricted to a frieze under the cornice, a form often found in Emilian Renaissance palazzi. While this format is in the local tradition, the border of flowers and fruit underlining it shows an awareness of decorative schemes derived from those of Giulio Romano at the Palazzo del Te in Mantua or of Raphael at the Villa Farnesina in Rome.

Although dell'Abate was most influential for his contribution to large-scale decorative schemes, he executed a variety of other works, including altarpieces, for example that with a martyrdom of saints for SS Pietro e Paolo, Modena, in 1547 (ex-Gemäldegal., Dresden, destr.). In the same year he went to Bologna, where he encountered works by Lorenzo Costa, Francesco Salviati, Giorgio Vasari and, most importantly, Parmigianino. In Bologna he developed the decorative skills he later used in France. One of the most important schemes he worked on in Bologna was the Palazzo Torfanini (now Zucchini-Solomei), where his decorations included stories from Ludovico Ariosto's *Orlando furioso*. A series of arches frame the narrative scenes, which again have fantastical and elaborate settings, both natural and architectural. Garlands suspended between the arches are held by draped and nude figures sitting in the spandrels. Their poses recall figures by Michelangelo on the ceiling of the Sistine Chapel, Vatican, Rome, but they are treated with a more mannered

2. Nicolò dell'Abate: *Story of Aristaeus* (or *Death of Eurydice*), oil on canvas, 1.9×2.3 m, *c.* 1565 (London, National Gallery)

elegance. It is difficult to assess the effect of the scheme, as only two of the eight scenes are well preserved. Around 1550 dell'Abate was commissioned to decorate four rooms in the Palazzo Poggi, Bologna. These decorations, again limited to friezes (see fig. 1), include episodes from the *Life of Camilla*, from the *Aeneid*, as well as simple decorative landscapes and such ornamental devices as groups of putti playing with huge garlands. The landscapes are set in a fictive architectural structure, with garlands draped along the bottom cornice. The scheme is reminiscent of Baldassare Peruzzi's illusionistic decorations in the Sala delle Prospettive in the Villa Farnesina, Rome. Although the decorations are all painted, they appear to be composed of sculpted, painted and real elements. The scenes are separated by putti or larger figures, in rather disdainful poses, which are Mannerist in their elongation and refinement. The decorative works dell'Abate executed in Bologna were influential for future generations of artists there, including the Carracci family. They probably also helped him procure the appointment as assistant to the Bolognese artist Francesco Primaticcio in France, at the court of Henry II.

2. France, from 1552. Dell'Abate was in France from 1552 until his death in 1571, mainly working at the royal château of Fontainebleau. He was involved in major decorative projects there, following the precedent set by Rosso Fiorentino in the Galerie François I. Initially dell'Abate seems to have been subordinate to Primaticcio, whose influence on him is often noted. Writers, including Béguin (see 1969 exh. cat.), however, also stress dell'Abate's impact on Primaticcio, who increasingly concentrated on design, producing drawings for projects that dell'Abate executed. Dell'Abate's contributions to the schemes designed by Primaticcio have been identified mainly on stylistic grounds, as few are documented. Many of the large-scale projects do not survive or are in poor condition. Dell'Abate was largely responsible for the execution of the decoration of the Galerie d'Ulysse, for example, which was destroyed in 1738. The decorations, a complex programme of stories from the *Life of Ulysses*, are recorded in a series of preparatory drawings, mostly by Primaticcio (e.g. Florence, Uffizi; Paris, Louvre), and prints, notably Théodore van Thulden's *Les Travaux d'Ulysse* (Paris, 1633). It may have been dell'Abate's handling of paint and fine touch that provoked Vasari's comment that the Galerie seemed to have been painted in just one day. Another large-scale project on which dell'Abate worked was the decoration of the Galerie Henri II or Salle de Bal (1552–6). The theme of music appears

throughout the scheme, which has been heavily damaged and repainted. In the Chambre de la Duchesse d'Etampes (Escalier du Roi), the fresco of *Alexander Preserving the Works of Homer* is attributed to dell'Abate alone; no drawing for it by Primaticcio survives.

Dell'Abate's commissions apart from those at Fontainebleau included frescoes (before 1558) for the château of Fleury-en-Bière, for which drawings survive (e.g. Paris, Louvre). The constable, Anne, Duc de Montmorency, was a valuable patron, and dell'Abate's drawings (e.g. Paris, Louvre) for his Paris residence (destr.) show the artist's adoption of the rich decorative style developed at Fontainebleau by Rosso and Primaticcio. He also painted portraits in France, for example the enamelled double portrait of *Henry II and Catherine de' Medici* (1553; Paris, Louvre) for the Sainte-Chapelle in Paris. As a court artist, he designed tapestries and ephemeral decorations for court celebrations and for triumphal entries, such as that of Charles IX into Paris in 1571.

In addition, dell'Abate produced small-scale paintings, often of mythological subjects. In some examples the narrative is almost completely subordinated to the landscape, as in the *Story of Aristaeus* (or *Death of Eurydice*; *c.* 1565; London, N.G.; see fig. 2), in which the sky and the fantastical background, littered with figures derived from the Antique, appear agitated. In the *Continence of Scipio* (*c.* 1555; Paris, Louvre) the figures dominate the composition, their poses and attitudes interlocking across the picture plane. The elegant forms and the softness of the treatment are reminiscent of Salviati, who was in France in this period. The idyllic classical style, derived from Italian Mannerism, that dell'Abate brought to France greatly influenced the treatment of landscape in French art. After his death, painting at Fontainebleau was supervised by his son, Giulio Camillo dell'Abate (1552–82), who is one of those identified with the MASTER OF FLORA (*see* MASTERS, ANONYMOUS, AND MONOGRAMMISTS, §I).

BIBLIOGRAPHY

G. Vasari: *Vite* (1550, rev. 2/1568); ed. G. Milanesi (1878–85), vi, pp. 481–2; vii, pp. 410–11

L. Dimier: 'Niccolò dell'Abate et les tapisseries de Fontainebleau', *An. Soc. Hist. & Archéol. Gâtinais*, xiii (1895)

A. Venturi: 'Il Mauriziano. Casa Fioribelli: Affreschi di Nicolò dell'Abate', *L'Arte*, iv/9–10 (1901), p. 356

C. Gamba: 'Un ritratto e un paesaggio di Nicolò dell'Abate', *Cron. A.*, i (1924), pp. 77–89

G. Zucchini: 'La scoperta di affreschi di Nicolò dell'Abate in Bologna', *Com. Bologna* (June 1929)

G. Fabrizi: 'L'*Eneide* nei dodici quadri di Nicolò dell'Abate', *Capitolium*, vi/9 (1930), pp. 504–16

W. Bombe: 'Gli affreschi dell'*Eneide* di Nicolò dell'Abate nel Palazzo di Scandiano', *Boll. A.*, x (1931), pp. 529–53

E. Bodmer: 'L'attività artistica di Niccolò dell'Abate a Bologna', *Com. Bologna*, i–ii (1934), pp. 3–39

H. Tietze and E. Tietze Conrat: 'Some Drawings by Niccolò dell'Abate', *Gaz. B.-A.*, n. s. 5, xxviii (1945), pp. 378–9

S. Béguin: *L'Ecole de Fontainebleau: Le Maniérisme à la cour de France* (Paris, 1960)

——: 'Niccolò dell'Abbate en France', *A. France*, ii (1962), pp. 112–45

E. H. Langmuir: 'Nicolò dell'Abate at Bologna', *Burl. Mag.*, cxi (1969), pp. 635–9

A. Paolucci: 'Nicolò dell'Abate', *A. Illus.*, ii/23–4 (1969), pp. 90–93

Mostra di Nicolò dell'Abate (exh. cat., ed. S. Béguin; Bologna, Pal. Archiginnasio, 1969)

A. Mezzetti: *Per Nicolò dell'Abate, affreschi restaurati* (Modena, 1970)

A. Ottani Cavina: 'Il paesaggio di Nicolò dell'Abate', *Paragone*, 245 (1970), pp. 8–19

L'Ecole de Fontainebleau (exh. cat., ed. S. Béguin; Paris, Grand Pal., 1972)

Fontainebleau: L'Art en France, 1528–1610 (exh. cat., ed. S. Béguin; Ottawa, N.G., 1973)

G. Godi: *Nicolò dell'Abate e la presunta attività del Parmigianino a Soragna* (Parma, 1976)

I. Wardropper: 'Le Voyage italien de Primatice en 1550', *Bull. Soc. Hist. A. Fr.* (1981), pp. 27–31

S. Béguin, J. Guillaume and A. Roy: *La Galerie d'Ulysse à Fontainebleau* (Paris, 1985)

DORIGEN CALDWELL

ʿAbbās. *See* SAFAVID, (2).

ʿAbbasi, Shaykh. *See* SHAYKH ʿABBASI.

Abbasid [ʿAbbasid]. Islamic dynasty that ruled from several capitals in Iraq between AD 749 and 1258. The Abbasids traced their descent from al-ʿAbbas, the uncle of the Prophet Muhammad, and were thus able to claim a legitimacy that their predecessors had lacked (*see* UMAYYAD, §1). The Abbasids rose to power in north-east Iran by channelling disaffection with Umayyad rule, but they soon established their capitals in a more central location, founding BAGHDAD in 762. Although they initially encouraged the support of Shiʿites, the Abbasids quickly distanced themselves from their erstwhile allies to become champions of orthodoxy. Upon accession, each caliph adopted an honorific title, somewhat like a regnal name, by which he was later known. For the first two centuries, the Abbasids' power was pre-eminent, and their names were invoked from the Atlantic to western Central Asia. From the middle of the 10th century, however, real power was transferred to a succession of Persian and Turkish dynasts (*see* SAMANID, BUYID, GHAZNAVID and SALJUQ, §1), who paid lip-service to a series of puppet caliphs. After the fall of Baghdad to the Mongols in 1256, a nominal Abbasid caliphate was maintained in Cairo until 1517.

The shift in the centre of gravity from the Umayyad capital at Damascus to Baghdad involved not merely a geographical adjustment of 500 miles but had potent repercussions in politics, culture and art. Baghdad became, in a way that Damascus had not, an Islamic Rome. It absorbed ideas, artefacts and influences from the Islamic world, India, China and the Eurasian steppe and then exported them, transformed, throughout the Islamic world, stamped with its own unique cachet and glamour. Nine-bay mosques in Afghanistan and Spain, iridescent lustreware in Tunisia and Sind, Baghdadi textiles laboriously copied in Andalusia—even down to the inscription identifying the piece as made in Baghdad—and Iraqi stucco forms in Egypt and Central Asia all attest the unchallenged cultural dominance of Baghdad. The cumulative gravitational pull exerted by the eastern territories broke the grip of Mediterranean culture, and specifically of Greco-Roman Classicism and its Byzantine descendant, on Islamic art. Classical forms can still be dimly discerned on occasion—the triumphal arch underlies the portals of Abbasid palaces, and all three styles of Abbasid stucco-carving (*see* BEVELLED STYLE) are foreshadowed in early Byzantine art—but they have undergone a sea-change. New contexts and new functions transform them. In architecture (*see* ISLAMIC ART, §II, 4(i)(b)), the secluded, relatively small-scale splendours of the classically inspired Umayyad desert residences gave way to vast sprawling palaces or rather palace-cities at Baghdad, UKHAYDIR and Samarra' (*see* SAMARRA', §2), mostly urban and conceived on the Perso-Sasanian model, where massive scale is the dominant factor. Proportional ratios (often 3:2) and strict axiality hold these structures together. Inferior building materials—principally mud-brick—are disguised by lavish revetments, and acres of less important wall surface were cheaply and expeditiously covered with moulded and painted stucco featuring increasingly abstract vegetal and geometric patterns.

The figural iconography of these palaces (e.g. the Dar al-Khilafa or Jawsaq al-Khaqani at Samarra') attests the gradual consolidation and refinement of a cycle of princely pleasures (music, banqueting, hunting, wrestling, dancing and the like) to be interpreted not literally but as a sequence of coded references to a luxurious royal lifestyle (summarized by the 11th-century Persian poet Manuchihri in the rhyming jingle *sharāb u rabāb u kabāb* ('wine, music and meat'). This cycle was assiduously copied by Abbasid successor states or rival polities from Spain (Córdoba and Játiva: *see* UMAYYAD, §2) and Sicily (Palermo, Cappella Palatina) to Armenia (*see* AGHT'AMAR) and Afghanistan (*see* LASHKARI BAZAR). It occurs on marble troughs and ivory boxes (*see* ISLAMIC ART, §VIII, 7(ii)), on bronze buckets and ceremonial silks, on the exteriors and interiors of Christian churches, and of course in numerous palaces.

The immense financial resources of the early Abbasid empire generated luxury arts galore. Rock crystal workshops flourished in Basra (*see* ISLAMIC ART, §VIII, 13(i)). Gold and silver vessels with figural decoration including hunting scenes and dancing girls are described in the Bacchic poetry of the court laureate Abu Nuwas (*d c.* 813). Byzantine ambassadors marvelled at the 38,000 precious curtains displayed in a caliphal palace. Textiles bearing laudatory or benedictory inscriptions with the name of the ruling caliph (*see* TIRAZ) made the courtiers who wore them walking advertisements for their monarch. Moulded two-tone glass with relief inscriptions and lustre painting typified the technical advances achieved by Islamic craftsmen (*see* ISLAMIC ART, §VIII, 5(i)). Nearly all the objects in such precious materials as ebony, ivory or alabaster described in medieval texts have vanished, but they must be borne in mind when reconstructing the ambience of Abbasid art. It is all the more regrettable that the fullest sequence of any imperial Abbasid art form should survive in the humblest material of all—pottery (*see* ISLAMIC ART, §V, 2(ii)). Yet this material provides a paradigm of the radical innovation that characterizes this period. Pottery was suddenly promoted from largely domestic use to an art form. The impact of Chinese ceramics—porcelain, stoneware and glazed earthenware—was probably the galvanizing factor. Abbasid wares valiantly imitated Tang splashwares and celadons but with a diagnostic change: the Chinese emphasis on form, body, touch—even the sound a piece made when struck—was replaced, at least in part, by applied decoration not encountered in the prototype. This change of emphasis lays bare the profoundly different principles of Abbasid taste. The Islamic invention of the technically difficult craft of lustre painting transformed pottery and allowed for the vulgarization of more expensive art forms and materials that became characteristic of Islamic art.

The other art form that has survived in substantial quantity is calligraphy (*see* ISLAMIC ART, §III, 2(ii)). Under Abbasid patronage the somewhat haphazard penmanship of the earliest manuscripts of the Koran, expressed in irregular letter forms, skewed lines of taut spasmodic illumination and a general indifference to visual effect, was replaced by a solemn discipline appropriate to holy writ and redolent of epigraphy on paper. Horizontal parchment sheets often accommodated no more than four lines of text, so spaced and with letter forms subject to such extremes of stylization as to slow down recognition of the words themselves: an objective correlative to the awesome enigmas found in the text itself. A supple system of extension allowed calligraphers to balance words on a page with the utmost finesse and thus create striking visual harmonies. This style spread throughout the Abbasid dominions with only minor local variations. It thus typifies the prestige and paramount authority enjoyed by the art of Baghdad: a fact of life epitomized by the courtier Ziryab, the Baghdad *arbiter elegantiarum* who imported the lifestyle of the Iraqi capital in food, language, clothing and art to far-off Córdoba in the 10th century.

BIBLIOGRAPHY

A. Mez: *Die Renaissance des Islams* (Heidelberg, 1922); Eng. trans. by S. Khuda Bukhsh and D. S. Margoliouth as *The Renaissance of Islam* (Patna, 1938)
K. A. C. Creswell: *Early Muslim Architecture*, ii (Oxford, 1940/*R* New York, 1979)
R. Ettinghausen: 'The "Beveled Style" in the Post-Samarra Period', *Archaeologica Orientalia in Memoriam Ernst Herzfeld* (Locust Valley, NY, 1952), pp. 72–83
D. Sourdel: *Le Vizirat 'abbâside de 749 à 936*, 2 vols (Damascus, 1959–60)
D. Sourdel and J. Sourdel: *La Civilisation de l'Islam classique* (Paris, 1968)
L. Golombek: 'Abbasid Mosque at Balkh', *Orient. A.*, n. s., xv (1969), pp. 173–89
J. Lassner: *The Topography of Baghdad in the Early Middle Ages* (Detroit, 1970)
M. A. Shaban: *The 'Abbāsid Revolution* (Cambridge, 1970)
M. M. Ahsan: *Social Life under the Abbasids* (London, 1979)
J. Lassner: *The Shaping of 'Abbasid Rule* (Princeton, 1980)
H. Philon: *Early Islamic Ceramics: Ninth to Late Twelfth Centuries* (London, 1980)
H. Kennedy: *The Early Abbasid Caliphate* (London and Sydney, 1981)
R. Hillenbrand: "Abbasid Mosques in Iran', *Riv. Stud. Orient.*, lix (1985), pp. 175–212
T. Allen: *Five Essays on Islamic Art* (Sebastopol, CA, 1988)
J. Bloom: *Minaret: Symbol of Islam* (Oxford, 1989)
F. Déroche: *The Abbasid Tradition: Qur'ans of the 8th to the 10th Centuries AD* (1992), i of *The Nasser D. Khalili Collection of Islamic Art*, ed. J. Raby (London and Oxford, 1992–)

ROBERT HILLENBRAND

Abbate, Nicolò dell'. *See* ABATE, NICOLÒ DELL'.

Abbatini, Guido Ubaldo (*b* Città di Castello, *c.* 1600–05; *d* Rome, 1656). Italian painter and mosaicist. He trained in the Roman studio of Cavaliere d'Arpino. He is principally known for executing fresco decorations in several chapels in Rome to designs by Bernini. Independent commissions, such as the frescoes depicting the *Life of Charlemagne* (1635–7; Rome, Vatican, Sala di Carlo Magno), reveal, however, that despite his collaboration with Bernini and later with Cortona, his preference was for a restrained classical style, close to that of more conservative contemporaries such as Andrea Camassei and Giovanni Francesco Romanelli. He assisted Bernini with the vault of the Raimondi Chapel in S Pietro in Montorio (1642–4) and that of the Pio Chapel in S Agostino (*c.* 1644–5). He also painted the vision of clouds and angels in the vault above Bernini's marble group of *St Teresa in Ecstasy* (*c.* 1647; Rome, S Maria della Vittoria, Cornaro Chapel). In 1650 he executed independently the decorative frescoes on the ceiling and side walls of the sacristy of S Spirito in Sassia, Rome. He also executed mosaics in St Peter's, after his own designs and those of Cortona (e.g. 1654–6; chapel of S Sebastiano), as well as carrying out many modest artistic chores in St Peter's and the Vatican during Urban VIII's papacy, from gilding and marbling to painting topographical views (*see also* ITALY, fig. 104).

BIBLIOGRAPHY

G. B. Passeri: *Vite* (1679); ed. J. Hess (1934), pp. 234–40
O. Pollak: *Die Kunsttätigkeit unter Urban VIII*, 2 vols (Vienna, 1928–31)
E. K. Waterhouse: *Baroque Painting in Rome* (London, 1937, 2/1976), p. 49
B. Toscano: 'Il pittore del Cardinal Poli: Guidobaldo Abbatini', *Paragone*, 177 (1964), pp. 36–42
I. Lavin: *Bernini and the Unity of the Visual Arts* (New York, 1980), pp. 54, 56, 188, 189, 193, 200

ANN SUTHERLAND HARRIS

Abbaye de Créteil. Community of French writers, artists and composers in operation from November 1906 to February 1908, located in a villa on the banks of the Marne at Créteil, south-east of Paris. Their choice of name paid homage to François Rabelais, whose Gargantua had established the Abbey of Thelema as a model monastery, a self-supporting commune whose members devoted part of each day to group labour and the rest to perfecting the self intellectually. The Abbaye de Créteil numbered among its members the painters Albert Gleizes, Charles Berthold-Mahn and Jacques d'Otemar, the poets Charles Vildrac (*b* 1882), Georges Duhamel (1884–1966), René Arcos, Alexandre Mercereau, JULES ROMAINS, Henri-Martin Barzun (*b* 1881), the composer Albert Doyen, and the printer Lucien Linard, whom Gleizes had met while doing his military service. It was through Linard's trade of printing and publishing that the Abbaye hoped to secure its material future.

Only a few of the Abbaye's members lived there full-time, with cells available for associates who were only occasionally in residence. Until March 1907 Mercereau was in Russia, where as Eshmer Valdor he served as secretary to the review *Zolotoye Runo* (*see* GOLDEN FLEECE); Romains, still a medical student, may have particularly identified with the poet-physician Rabelais. Romains's collection of poems *La Vie unanime*, the first publication printed at the Abbaye, gave rise to the impression that all the members of the community subscribed to Unanimism, a belief that the reality of modern group life had permanently altered individual experience. In general the themes explored by the group's members did relate to the interconnected, epic qualities of modern life, to cities, crowds, machines, commerce, agriculture and shared emotions, especially in work done after the dissolution of the Abbaye, such as Gleizes's *Football Players* (1912–13; Washington, DC, N.G.A.). The multiplicity and simultaneity of experience, however, suggested not only new themes but also new methods in writing and painting, entailing a simplicity of imagery and a search for basic volumes. Filippo Tommaso Marinetti, who visited the Abbaye in the summer of 1907, drew much of his programme for Futurism from the thinking of Romains and the Abbaye circle.

Its radical nature notwithstanding, the Abbaye's programme nevertheless owed much to an older generation of late Symbolist poets, especially to Emile Verhaeren, Paul Adam and René Ghil (1862–1925), all of whom were active supporters of the Abbaye. Verharen's modern literary themes were borrowed by Romains, while Adam's idea of multiple perspectives, formulated as early as 1905, and Ghil's emphasis on elemental sounds, divorced from their customary linguistic meaning, were sources for abstract art and an influence on the subsequent work of Gleizes.

During its brief existence, the Abbaye published important works by Roger Allard, who later made his name as a supporter of Cubism, and Pierre-Jean Jouve. Its spirit survived in a circle around the review *Les Bandeaux d'or* in Paris, through which Gleizes met Henri Le Fauconnier in 1908. Gleizes and other former members later attained prominence as artists or men of letters. The group's influence was recognized in England in the lead article of the first issue of *Rhythm*, a review inaugurated by John Middleton Murray and Katherine Mansfield. The Abbaye idea, an optimistic mix of modernism and late medievalism, of Symbolism and ideas leading to Cubism, of individual creativity blended into group activity, continued to exert appeal until World War I.

BIBLIOGRAPHY

F. Goodyear: 'The New Thelema', *Rhythm*, i/1 (1911)
A. Gleizes: 'The Abbaye of Créteil: A Communistic Experiment', *The Modern School*, ed. C. Zigrosser (Stelton, NJ, 1918)
A. Mercereau: *L'Abbaye et le bolchevisme* (Paris, ?1922)
H. Clouard: *Histoire de la littérature française, du Symbolisme à nos jours, 1885–1914* (Paris, 1947), pp. 542ff
G. Duhamel: *Le Temps de la recherche* (1947), iii of *Lumières sur ma vie* (Paris, 1947)
D. Robbins: 'From Symbolism to Cubism: The Abbaye of Créteil', *A. J.* [New York], xxiii (Winter 1963–4), pp. 111–16
For further bibliography *see* GLEIZES, ALBERT, and ROMAINS, JULES.

DANIEL ROBBINS

Abbe, James (Edward) (*b* Alfred, ME, 17 July 1883; *d* San Francisco, 11 Nov 1973). American photographer. Self-taught, he started to produce photographs at the age of 12. From 1898 to 1910 he worked in his father's bookshop and then worked as a reporter for the *Washington Post*, travelling to Europe in 1910. Having earlier produced photographs of ships and sailors for tourist cards, from 1913 to 1917 he worked as a freelance photojournalist in Virginia. In 1917 he set up a studio in New York, where he produced the first photographic cover for the *Saturday Evening Post* as well as photographs for *Ladies Home Journal*, the *New York Times* and other publications. From 1922 to 1923 he worked as a stills photographer, actor and writer for film studios. Though this was mainly for Mack Sennett in Hollywood, he also worked for D. W. Griffiths as a stills photographer on *Way Down East* (1920) and accompanied Lilian Gish to Italy to provide stills for Griffiths's *The White Sister* (1923). After establishing a studio in Paris in 1924 he had his photographs published in such journals as *Harper's Bazaar*, *L'Illustration*, *New York Herald Tribune*, *The Tatler*, *Vanity Fair*, *Vogue* and *Vu*. He photographed film stars and the Moulin Rouge in Paris and also produced fashion pictures, such as *Natasha Rambova in Fortuny Gown* (*c.* 1924; see Hall-Duncan, p. 41).

From 1929 until 1932 Abbe travelled extensively in Europe, Mexico, the USA and the USSR as one of the first photojournalists, working for the *Berliner illustrierte Zeitung*. During this period he covered the Mexican Revolution of 1932 as well as crime and prohibition in Chicago. He photographed Hitler and Mussolini during their rise to power, and in 1932 he was the first foreign correspondent to photograph Stalin (among other images published in his book *I Photograph Russia*, 1934). In 1934 he returned to the USA, working in Larkspur, CO, as a freelance photojournalist until 1936. In the latter year he went to Spain as a war correspondent for the *Alliance* newspaper, covering the Civil War from General Franco's side. After this he ceased work as a photographer and became, in turn, a rancher, radio broadcaster and television critic.

PHOTOGRAPHIC PUBLICATIONS

I Photograph Russia (New York, 1934)
Stars of the '20s (London, 1975) [text by M. D. Early]

BIBLIOGRAPHY

C. Beaton and G. Buckland: *The Magic Image: The Genius of Photography from 1939 to the Present Day* (London, 1975), p. 185
N. Hall-Duncan: *The History of Fashion Photography* (New York, 1979), pp. 41, 43, 224
G. Walsh, C. Naylor and M. Held, eds: *Contemporary Photographers* (New York, 1982)

□

Abbey, Edwin Austin (*b* Philadelphia, PA, 1 April 1852; *d* London, 1 Aug 1911). American painter and illustrator, active in England. He began his artistic training in 1866, studying drawing with the Philadelphia portrait and landscape painter Isaac L. Williams (1817–95). In 1868 he attended evening classes in drawing at the Pennsylvania Academy of the Fine Arts under Christian Schussele (?1824–79). In the same year Abbey began to work as an illustrator for the Philadelphia publishers Van Ingen & Snyder. In 1870 *Harper's Weekly* published the *Puritans' First Thanksgiving*, and in 1871 Abbey moved to New York to join the staff of Harper & Brothers, thus inaugurating his most important professional relationship. Throughout the 1870s Abbey's reputation grew, both for his detailed exhibition watercolours and for his elegant line drawings, which, translated to wood-engravings in numerous periodicals, illustrated both factual and fictional events of the past and present. The influences on him were mainly English, in particular the works of the Pre-Raphaelite Brotherhood and illustrations in the English press, which he studied avidly. The success of his illustrations to some of Robert Herrick's poems, such as *Corinna's Going A-Maying* in *Harper's New Monthly Magazine* (May 1874), prompted Harper & Brothers in 1878 to send Abbey to England to do a complete series of drawings for an illustrated gift-book, *Selections from the Poetry of Robert Herrick* (New York, 1882). On his arrival in England, Abbey found his spiritual home, and except for a few trips, he never left.

Abbey, a small, handsome, athletic man, had a genius for forging long-lasting and often profitable friendships. In 1877 he helped to found the Tile Club, which included among its members the architect Stanford White, Augustus Saint-Gaudens and Winslow Homer, whose activities resulted in gift-books and lengthy magazine articles. Abbey's most intense friendship was with the English landscape painter and illustrator Alfred Parsons (1847–1920). The two artists shared studios and gallery exhibitions, travelled together widely and collaborated on several projects, most notably the gift-books *Old Songs* (New York, 1889) and *The Quiet Life* (New York, 1890). Abbey derived much of the inspiration for these from his long sojourns in the English countryside, especially, from 1885 to 1889, as one of the central figures in the artists' colony at Broadway (Hereford & Worcs), along with Parsons, Frank Millet (1846–1912) and John Singer Sargent.

Abbey undertook illustrative commissions throughout his life (his illustrations to Shakespeare's plays being

Edwin Austin Abbey: mural from the cycle of the *Quest for the Holy Grail* (1890–1901), h. 2.44 m, delivery room of the Boston Public Library, Boston, Massachusetts

especially noteworthy), but from 1889 on he devoted more time to mural projects and oil paintings. In 1890 he sent his first major oil, *May Day Morning* (New Haven, CT, Yale U. A.G.), based on one of the Herrick illustrations, to the Royal Academy Summer Exhibition, where it was favourably received. Until 1910 Abbey exhibited there frequently, and he was elected ARA in 1896 and RA in 1898. His exhibited works were usually based on Shakespearean, troubadour or Renaissance themes. Large and richly coloured, the paintings reflect Abbey's fascination with the stage, particularly in the arrangement of the figures, their poses and sumptuously coloured costumes (Abbey designed the costumes for John Hare's *Tosca* (1889) and Sir Henry Irving's *Richard II* (1898), among other productions). Although he received many honours and awards, the signal event of Abbey's career was the commission in 1902 to paint Edward VII's coronation (London, Buckingham Pal., Royal Col.).

The major projects of Abbey's later life were commissions for murals. He decorated the delivery room of McKim, Mead & White's Boston Public Library with a 15-panel series (1890–1901) based on the *Quest for the Holy Grail* (see fig.). Works for the Royal Exchange, London, and other commissions followed. In 1902 Abbey began the decorations for the Pennsylvania State Capitol at Harrisburg. An allegory of the state's history and its resources, Abbey's work here departed from the schematic narrative of his other murals and adopted a full-blown rhetorical style related to the work of Kenyon Cox and Edwin Blashfield.

BIBLIOGRAPHY

E. V. Lucas: *Edwin Austin Abbey, Royal Academician: The Record of his Life and Work*, 2 vols (London, 1921)

Edwin Austin Abbey (1852–1911) (exh. cat., ed. K. A. Foster and M. Quick; New Haven, CT, Yale U. A.G., 1973)

Unfaded Pageant: Edwin Austin Abbey's Shakespearean Subjects (exh. cat. by L. Oakley, New York, Columbia U., Miriam & Ira D. Wallach Gal., 1994)

MARC SIMPSON

Abbey, John Roland (*b* Brighton, 23 Nov 1894; *d* London, 24 Dec 1969). English collector. Educated privately, he was commissioned to the Rifle Brigade in 1914. He was invalided home in November 1916 and made a director in his family's brewing firm. He began his book collection in 1929, at first with an interest in modern bindings. In 1931 he commissioned Sybil Pye and R. de Coverley and Sons to produce a binding to his own design for Siegfried Sassoon's *Memoirs of an Infantry Officer*. Consistently stressing the importance of appearance and condition, Abbey began buying antiquarian books in 1933 and manuscripts (of which he ultimately owned 143) in 1946, with advice from Sydney Cockerell. After World War II he had the largest private collection of his time, including 1914 18th- and 19th-century books of watercolour prints.

Auctions of his collection were held between 1965 and 1967 (buyers included Paul Mellon and the Landesbibliothek, Stuttgart) and, after his death, between 1970 and 1975. He bequeathed books and manuscripts to the British Museum and Eton College.

WRITINGS

Travels in Aquatint and Lithography, 1770–1860 (London, 1953)

A Bibliographical Catalogue, 2 vols (London, 1956–7)

BIBLIOGRAPHY

DNB

J. J. G. Alexander and A. C. De la Mare: *The Italian Manuscripts in the Library of Major John Roland Abbey* (London, 1969)

JACQUELINE COLLISS HARVEY

Abbondi, Antonio. *See* SCARPAGNINO, ANTONIO.

Abbott, Berenice (*b* Springfield, OH, 17 July 1898; *d* 9 Dec 1991). American photographer. She spent a term at the Ohio State University in Columbus (1917–18) and then studied sculpture independently in New York (1918–21) where she met Marcel Duchamp and Man Ray. She left the USA for Paris in 1921 where she studied at the Académie de la Grande Chaumière before attending the Kunstschule in Berlin for less than a year in 1923. From 1924 to 1926 she worked as Man Ray's assistant and first saw photographs by Eugène Atget in Man Ray's studio in 1925. Her first one-woman show, at the gallery Le Sacre du Printemps in Paris in 1926, was devoted to portraits of avant-garde personalities such as Jean Cocteau, James Joyce and André Gide. She continued to take portraits until leaving Paris in 1929, such as that of *James Joyce* (1927; see *Berenice Abbott: Photographs*, p. 26). After Atget's death (1927) she bought most of his negatives and prints in 1928, and in 1929 she returned to New York. There she began a series of documentary photographs of the city and from 1935 to 1939 directed the 'Changing New York' project for the Works Progress Administration Federal Art Project, which resulted in the book of photographs *Changing New York* (1939). Like Atget's views of Paris these covered both the people and architecture of New York in a methodical and detached way. The images in *Greenwich Village Today and Yesterday* (1949) were motivated by a similar spirit. She also took various portrait photographs in the 1930s and 1940s, such as that of *Max Ernst* (1941; see O'Neal, p. 182).

From 1947 to 1958 Abbott ran the House of Photography, a firm established to develop and sell her photographic inventions, although it proved a financial failure. At a conference at the Aspen Institute for Humanistic Studies in Colorado (1951) she caused a storm by criticizing the Pictorialism of such photographers as Alfred Stieglitz, Edward J. Steichen and Paul Strand. Instead she advocated a documentary style, exemplified by her images of urban America, such as *American Shops* (1954; see O'Neal, p. 197). In 1956 she printed and published 100 sets of Atget's photographs in New York as *Eugène Atget Portfolio: Twenty Photographic Prints from his Glass Negatives*. Having experimented with scientific photography since 1939, from 1958 to 1961 she worked for the Physical Science Study Committee of Educational Services, taking photographs to illustrate the laws of physics. These were used in three books, published in Cleveland, OH, with texts by E. G. Valens: *Magnet* (1964), *Motion* (1965) and *The Attractive Universe* (1969). Continuing her championship of Atget, in 1964 she published *The World of Atget*, writing the text herself. In 1966 she moved to Abbot Village, ME, where she continued producing documentary photographs, such as those for *A Portrait of Maine* (1968). In later life she occupied herself increasingly with organizing and printing her earlier work, and from the late 1970s and into the 1980s several portfolios of earlier photographs were published by the Parasol Press in New York.

WRITINGS

A Guide to Better Photography (New York, 1941)

A New Guide to Better Photography (New York, 1953)

PHOTOGRAPHIC PUBLICATIONS

Changing New York, text by E. McCausland (New York, 1939)

Greenwich Village Today and Yesterday, text by H. W. Lanier (New York, 1949)

The World of Atget (New York, 1964)

Berenice Abbott: Photographs, text by D. Vestal and M. Rukeyser (New York, 1970, rev. Washington, DC, and London, 1990)

Berenice Abbott: The Red River Photographs, text by H. O'Neal (Provincetown, MA, 1979)

BIBLIOGRAPHY

Berenice Abbott: The 20's and 30's (exh. cat. by B. Shissler Nosanow, New York, Int. Cent. Phot.; Washington, DC, N. Mus. Amer. A.; 1981–2)

H. O'Neal: *Berenice Abbott: Sixty Years of Photography*, intro. by J. Canaday (New York and London, 1982)

□

Abbott, John White (*b* Exeter, 13 May 1764; *d* Exeter, 1851). English watercolourist, painter and apothecary. He was nephew of the prominent lawyer John White (1744–1825). An important patron of Francis Towne, he spent his entire career in Exeter as an apothecary and surgeon. Abbot was a keen amateur artist, taking lessons from Towne, but although he was an Honorary Exhibitor of landscape oils at the Royal Academy, London, from 1793 to 1805 and again in 1810 and 1812, he never sold a picture. His oil *Fordland* (1791; priv. col., see Oppé, pl. xxxii) is a *plein-air* study of woodland that owes much to Gainsborough's early work in its naturalism and broken, delicate handling.

In 1791 Abbott toured Scotland, the Lake District, Lancashire, Derbyshire and Warwickshire. He toured Monmouthshire in 1797, and again in 1827, as well as Gloucestershire and Wiltshire. He also made studies of Richmond, Surrey, in 1842, but the bulk of his work was done in the vicinity of Exeter. The *Mouth of the Exe* (priv. col., see Oppé, pl. xxxv, b) shows him adopting Towne's method of bold pen outline and monochrome wash to create a drawing that is topographically accurate and yet sensitive to the effects of light on foliage. The brightly coloured forest watercolour *Kerswell, Devon* (1813; London, V&A) has the classical grandeur of woodlands by Claude Lorrain. He made many imaginary Claudean-style landscapes, as well as watercolour copies of Towne's Italian drawings and a number of landscape etchings (London, BM). Watercolours such as *Exeter Cathedral* (Eton, Berks, Coll. Lib.) show an acute observation of figures that has more in common with Paul Sandby than with Towne. Abbott's watercolours are less bold in composition than Towne's but display a sensitivity to nature, particularly to tree formations, that is part of the intense exploration of landscape by English artists in the late 18th century and the early 19th. In 1825 Abbott inherited his uncle's property and retired to Fordland, near Exeter; in 1831 he was made Deputy Lieutenant of Devonshire.

BIBLIOGRAPHY

A. P. Oppé: 'John White Abbott of Exeter', *Walpole Soc.*, xiii (1924–5), pp. 67–84

I. A. Williams: 'John White Abbott: A Devonshire Artist', *Apollo*, xvii (1933), pp. 84–6

M. Hardie: *The Eighteenth Century* (1966), i of *Water-colour Painting in Britain* (London, 1965–9)

Paintings and Drawings by Francis Towne and John White Abbott (exh. cat., Exeter, Royal Albert Mem. Mus., 1971)

SUSAN MORRIS

Abbott, Lemuel Francis (*b* Leics, *c.* 1760; *d* London, 5 Dec 1802). English painter. He was the son of a clergyman and went to London to study with Francis Hayman shortly before the latter's death in 1776; he may have completed his studies in Derby with Joseph Wright of Derby. By the early 1780s Abbott had established a busy portrait practice in London. The formula he adopted for most of his head-and-shoulder portraits can be seen in *Sir William Herschel* (1785; London, N. Mar. Mus.): the body is parallel to the picture plane, and the sitter's head is moved into three-quarter profile, as if his attention has been suddenly distracted. In later portraits, such as those of fellow artists *Francesco Bartolozzi* (*c.* 1792; London, Tate) or *Joseph Nollekens* (*c.* 1797; London, N.P.G.), the sitter's hand or some attribute balances the movement of the head. Only male portraits by Abbott are known, and his patrons were mostly drawn from the professional classes, particularly the Navy; there are several versions of *Lord Nelson* (e.g. 1798; London, N. Mar. Mus.). His style is crisp but scratchy in technique, and often the anatomy of his figures is inaccurate. Paint is handled in a manner comparable with that of Gainsborough Dupont, but Abbott's sense of composition is superior. In 1798 he was certified insane, but he continued to exhibit at the Royal Academy in London for two further years. Several of his works were probably finished by another hand.

BIBLIOGRAPHY

Waterhouse: *18th C.*

A. C. Sewter: 'Some New Facts about Lemuel Francis Abbott', *Connoisseur*, cxxxv (1955), pp. 178–83

R. Walker: *Regency Portraits* (London, 1985)

HUGH BELSEY

Abd, Tell al-. *See* UBAID, TELL AL-.

ʿAbd al-Hayy [Khwāja ʿAbd al-Ḥayy] (*fl c.* 1374; *d* Samarkand, 1405). Illustrator and painter. According to the Safavid chronicler Dust Muhammad, ʿAbd al-Hayy trained under Shams al-Din at Baghdad during the reign of the Jalayirid sultan Uways I (*reg* 1356–74) and became the leading painter under his son Ahmad, who was also ʿAbd al-Hayy's pupil. When Timur took Baghdad, ʿAbd al-Hayy was sent to Samarkand, either in 1393 or in 1401, where he spent the rest of his life. He seems to have specialized in monochrome ink drawings: Dust Muhammad recorded that ʿAbd al-Hayy's pupil, Ahmad Jalayir, contributed a black-and-white drawing to a manuscript of the *Abūsaʿīdnāma* ('Book of Abu Saʿid'), and a number of examples attributed to the late 14th century and preserved in various albums (e.g. Berlin, Staatsbib. Preuss. Kultbes., Orientabt. Diez A. 70–73) bear the notation that they were copied from ʿAbd al-Hayy's drawings by Muhammad ibn Mahmud Shah Khayyam. In his album (Istanbul, Topkapı Pal. Lib., H. 2154), Dust Muhammad attributed one painting (fol. 20*v*) to ʿAbd al-Hayy. It was detached from a copy (London, BL, Add. MS. 18113) of the *Dīvān* ('Collected poems') of Khwaju Kirmani copied at Baghdad in 1396. The scene of a sleeping youth visited by angels is in the same style as the other paintings in the manuscript, one of which (fol. 45*v*) is signed by JUNAYD. Dust Muhammad may have attributed the painting to ʿAbd al-Hayy because it includes a drawing on the wall of a woman holding an infant and standing in a rocky landscape. According to the Timurid chronicler Ibn ʿArabshah (1392–1450), ʿAbd al-Hayy was a skilled painter who worked for Timur on wall paintings at Timurid palaces. The wall painting of the woman and child is similar to marginal drawings in a copy (Washington, DC, Freer, 32.30–37) of Ahmad Jalayir's *Dīvān*, which have also been attributed to ʿAbd al-Hayy. According to Dust Mohammad, one of ʿAbd al-Hayy's outstanding students was Pir Ahmad Baghshimali. After ʿAbd al-Hayy's death his work remained a source of inspiration, and his purity, delicacy and firmness of brush were considered unrivalled.

See also ISLAMIC ART, §III, 4(v)(c).

BIBLIOGRAPHY

Enc. Iran.
Dūst Muḥammad: 'Preface to the Bahram Mirza Album' (1544); Eng. trans., ed. W. M. Thackston, in *A Century of Princes: Sources on Timurid History and Art* (Cambridge, MA, 1989), p. 345
D. E. Klimburg-Salter: 'A Sufi Theme in Persian Painting: The Diwan of Sultan Ahmad Gala'ir in the Freer Gallery of Art, Washington, DC', *Kst Orients*, xi (1977), pp. 43–84
V. A. Prentice: 'A Detached Miniature from the *Masnavis* of Khwaju Kermani', *Orient. A.*, xxvii (1981), pp. 60–66
B. W. Robinson: 'Persian Painting under the Zand and Qājār Dynasties', *From Nadir Shah to the Islamic Republic* (1991), vii of *The Cambridge History of Iran* (Cambridge, 1968–91), pp. 870–90

S. J. VERNOIT

ʿAbd al-Jalil Čelebi. *See* LEVNI.

ʿAbdallah Khan [ʿAbdallāh Khān] (*fl c.* 1810–50). Persian painter. His major work was a large mural with 118 life-size figures covering three walls in the interior of the Nigaristan Palace at Tehran (destr.; *see* ISLAMIC ART, §VIII, 11(i)). On the end wall the Qajar monarch Fath ʿAli Shah (*reg* 1797–1834) was depicted enthroned in state surrounded by his sons; on the side walls he was attended by a double row of courtiers and foreign ambassadors, including the British ambassador Sir Gore Ouseley (1770–1844) and Napoleon's envoy C. M. Gardane (1766–1818). Most 19th-century European travellers attributed this mural to the painter MUHAMMAD HASAN KHAN, but in the late 1880s the scholar E. G. Browne read the inscription below the painting stating that it was done by ʿAbdallah Khan in 1812–13. The mural is known through several small-scale copies (e.g. London, India Office Lib., Add. Or. 1239–1242). A full-length portrait of Fath ʿAli Shah in a red robe and bejewelled astrakhan cap (London, V&A, 707–1876) has been ascribed to the artist. In 1813–14 he executed murals depicting the courts of the Qajar rulers Agha Muhammad (*reg* 1779–97) and Fath ʿAli Shah on the walls of the Sulaymaniyya Palace (destr.) at Karaj near Tehran, of which a few fragments were preserved in the library of the National School of Agriculture there.

BIBLIOGRAPHY

B. W. Robinson: 'The Court Painters of Fatḥ ʿAlī Shāh', *Eretz-Israel*, vii (1964), pp. 94–105
——: *Persian Paintings in the India Office Library* (London, 1976), pp. 250–53
——: 'Persian Painting in the Qajar Period', *Highlights of Persian Art*, ed. R. Ettinghausen and E. Yarshater (Boulder, 1979), pp. 331–62
M. A. Karimzada Tabrizi: *Aḥvāl u āthār-i naqqāshān-i qadīm-i īrān* [The lives and art of old painters of Iran] (London, 1985), no. 540

ʿAbdallah Sayrafi [ʿAbdallāh al-Ṣayrafī] (*b* ?Tabriz; *fl* 1310–44). Calligrapher. The son of Khwaja Mahmud Sarraf al-Tabrizi, he was a pupil of HAYDAR, one of the six followers of YAQUT AL-MUSTAʿSIMI. ʿAbdallah Sayrafi spent his life in the Ilkhanid capital of Tabriz where he designed inscriptions in glazed tile for two buildings, the Dimishqiyya Madrasa and the building called 'The Master and the Pupil' (both destr.). He wrote a short treatise on calligraphy (Berlin, Staatsbib. Preuss. Kultbes., Orientabt., MS. or. oct. 48); a page of calligraphy in *thuluth*, *naskh*, and *riqāʿ* (Baghdad, Iraq Mus., 1324) shows that he had mastered the six classical scripts (*see* ISLAMIC ART, §III, 2(iii)(c)). He penned several manuscripts of the Koran, including one in *naskh* (Mashhad, 1320; Imam Riza Shrine Mus.) and another in *muḥaqqaq* (1327; Dublin, Chester Beatty Lib., MS. 1468). His work was still renowned in the 15th century, and his style was followed by JAʿFAR (*see also* ISLAMIC ART, §III, 2(iv)(b)). When the Timurid prince Ibrahim Sultan restored the Friday Mosque at Shiraz in 1417–18, he had a stone with a Koranic inscription carved by ʿAbdallah Sayrafi transported there from Tabriz.

BIBLIOGRAPHY

Enc. Iran.
Qāżī Aḥmad ibn Mīr Munshī: *Gulistān-i hunar* [Rose-garden of art] (*c.* 1606); Eng. trans. by V. Minorsky as *Calligraphers and Painters* (Washington, DC, 1959), pp. 61–3
S. S. Blair: *The Ilkhanid Shrine Complex at Natanz, Iran* (Cambridge, MA, 1986), p. 13

NABIL SAIDI

ʿAbd al-Samad [(Khwāja) ʿAbd al-Ṣamad; ʿAbd as-Ṣamad; Abdus Ṣamad] (*fl c.* 1540–95). Iranian miniature painter and calligrapher, active also in India. Trained in Safavid Iran, ʿAbd al-Samad migrated to India, where he became director of the Mughal painting workshops under the emperor Akbar (*reg* 1556–1605). In this key position, he influenced the development of Mughal painting in the second half of the 16th century more than any other artist (*see* INDIAN SUBCONTINENT, §VI, 4(i)(b)).

1. IRAN AND WESTERN CENTRAL ASIA, BEFORE 1555. No inscribed works by ʿAbd al-Samad are known from the period when he worked in Safavid Iran, though attributions have been proposed. Already a mature painter, he paid homage in 1544 to Akbar's father, the Mughal emperor Humayun (*reg* 1530–40; 1555–6), when the exiled ruler was given refuge at the court of the Safavid shah Tahmasp I at Tabriz. In 1550 ʿAbd al-Samad joined Humayun in Kabul, where an interim capital had been established. During the immediately succeeding years, together with other painters, he regularly presented works to the Emperor on various occasions including Nawruz, the Persian New Year. *Two Young Men in a Garden*, dated 1551, is one such illustration by the artist later mounted in the *Muraqqaʿ-i gulshan* (Tehran, Gulistan Pal. Lib., MSS 1663–4), an album of pictures and calligraphic pieces of various dates formed by Humayun's grandson Jahangir (*reg* 1605–27). Several literary references to New Year's presentations can be matched with paintings included in

the *Muraqqaʿ-i gulshan*, all of which are in a conservative Persian style. In fact, it is primarily through the patron and subjects that the Mughal designation can be given; in style they remain strongly Safavid.

2. INDIA, 1555 AND AFTER. ʿAbd al-Samad travelled to India with the imperial party in 1555 and under Akbar became a leading member of the imperial workshops. The young Akbar himself studied painting with ʿAbd al-Samad, one of whose greatest works of this time is *Akbar Presenting a Painting to Humayun in a Tree House* (Tehran, Gulistan Pal. Lib., MSS 1663–4). In about 1569 ʿAbd al-Samad succeeded MIR SAYYID ʿALI as director of a 14-year project to copy and illustrate for the young Akbar the great *Dastan-i Amir Hamza* ('Legend of Amir Hamza') or *Ḥamzanāma* ('Tales of Hamza'; dispersed). In contrast to his predecessor, ʿAbd al-Samad oversaw the completion of ten volumes and one thousand illustrations in a seven-year period; Mir Sayyid ʿAli had directed the completion of only four volumes in the same length of time. Perhaps in part because of this organizational ability, ʿAbd al-Samad took on increasingly prominent administrative roles: director of the imperial mint (1577), overseer of commerce (1582), manager of the royal household (1583) and finance minister for the province of Multan (1586). His son, Muhammad Sharif, became a friend of the young Prince Salim, later Jahangir. Like his father, he too was an artist given important administrative responsibilities within the governmental hierarchy. No other painter's family is known to have held comparable power.

ʿAbd al-Samad was an extraordinary craftsman and his pictures are full of minute detail describing the patterns of architectural tilework, for example, or costumes and foliage. A contemporary account also praises his ability to paint elaborate scenes on grains of rice. All of this evidently appealed to Humayun, although Akbar, in his early years as Emperor, demanded lively narrative scenes rather than virtuoso displays of technique.

The earliest work made by ʿAbd al-Samad for Akbar may be *Prince Akbar Hunting* (Los Angeles, Benkaim priv. col.), datable to about 1556. The attribution is suggested by a comparison with the last work known by the artist, *Khusrau Hunting*, from a *Khamsa* ('Five poems') of Nizami manuscript (1595; London, BL, Or. MS. 12208, fol. 82a). That the paintings are so close in sensibility and style is evidence of the painter's tremendous conservatism. Yet, while his own style is not innovative, he clearly encouraged experimentalism and novelty among those painters whose work he directed. The *Ḥamzanāma* is the single most vital and inventive Mughal manuscript, and it is in the last ten volumes—the portion of the project that he oversaw—that this character is firmly established. Over 100 artists and craftsmen were involved in this effort, and in many cases they had been brought to the imperial studios from elsewhere. That a new and original style evolved during this process is testament as much to ʿAbd al-Samad's organizational skills as to his artistic abilities.

There are relatively few works attributable to ʿAbd al-Samad during the early years of Akbar's reign, perhaps because he was so involved with the completion of the *Ḥamzanāma*. Among works of his middle period in India is *Two Camels Fighting* (USA, priv. col.), an important copy and adaptation of a famous work by the great 15th-century Persian painter Bihzad. A popular motif in Mughal art, the work also bears an important inscription noting the painter's advanced age and paying homage to his son Muhammad Sharif.

ʿAbd al-Samad was clearly a strong personality who influenced both his son and other artists. When Akbar discovered the painter Daswanth, he sent him to ʿAbd al-Samad for training, and the younger artist's early works show that he initially adopted a style recognizably close to that of ʿAbd al-Samad, whose use of dark tonalities, especially for landscape, and lack of interest in adopting techniques drawn from European prints (widely available and highly influential with other painters) were personal characteristics. Also typical was ʿAbd al-Samad's insistence on the prime importance of the picture surface. This is shown in *Jamshid Writing on a Rock* (1588; Washington, DC, Freer; see fig.), in which the solid gold sky negates spatial depth. The gold also creates a sense of opulence and wealth, another important element of ʿAbd al-Samad's style. His figures, however, do not have the individualized personality so effortlessly created by such artists as Basawan or Bishan Das. Faces represent types.

This and ʿAbd al-Samad's other late works, such as the scene of *Khusrau Hunting*, were again in the mainstream

ʿAbd al-Samad (attrib.): *Jamshid Writing on a Rock*, opaque colour on paper, 420×265 mm; *verso* of single leaf from a Jahangir-period album, 1588 (Washington, DC, Freer Gallery of Art, MS. 63.4)

of Mughal art. This is not because he had changed, but because by the 1590s Mughal painting had come to have many of those values that he had so long championed. Just as the technical skills of Mughal artists developed and matured, so too imperial taste became more epicurean. Densely detailed, technically immaculate compositions in which no individual detail predominates became the rule and replaced the earlier taste for compositional excitement and strong colour.

On the other hand, painting at the end of the Akbar period (*c.* 1600) moved away from the style of ʿAbd al-Samad, presenting instead compositionally simple scenes that stress the definition and interaction of human personalities—a skill in which ʿAbd al-Samad showed little interest. That this could not happen until after his death is further evidence of the power he held over the imperial workshops.

See also INDIAN SUBCONTINENT, §VI, 4(i)(b).

BIBLIOGRAPHY

EWA: 'Abdu 's-Samad'
W. Staude: "Abd us-Samad, der Akbar Maler, und das Millionenzimmer in Schönbrunn', *Belvedere*, x (1931), pp. 155–60
M. B. Dickson and S. C. Welch: 'Abdus Samad', *The Houghton Shahnameh* (Cambridge, MA, 1981), pp. 192–200
M. C. Beach: *Early Mughal Painting* (Cambridge, MA, 1987)

MILO CLEVELAND BEACH

Abdülaziz. *See* OTTOMAN, §II(7).

ʿAbdülcelil Çelebi. *See* LEVNI.

Abedin, Zainul (*b* Kishorganj, East Pakistan [now Bangladesh], 18 Nov 1914; *d* Dhaka, 28 May 1976). Bangladeshi painter and printmaker. He studied painting at the Government School of Art in Calcutta from 1933 to 1938, and then taught there until 1947. His work first attracted public attention in 1943 when he produced a powerful series of drawings of the Bengal famine. After the partition of India and Pakistan in 1947 he worked as chief designer in the Pakistan government's Information and Publications Division, and also became principal of the Institute of Fine Arts in Dhaka (later known as the Bangladesh College of Arts and Crafts), which he helped to found in 1948 and where he remained until 1967. From 1951 to 1952 he visited Europe and, in addition to exhibiting his work at several locations, worked at the Slade School of Art in London, and represented Pakistan at the UNESCO art conference in Venice in 1952. An exhibition of his work in Lahore in 1953 became the starting-point for a series of exhibitions aimed at promoting contemporary Pakistani art. In 1956–7 he travelled to Japan, the United States, Canada, Mexico and Europe on a Rockefeller Foundation fellowship and in 1960 visited the Soviet Union. Since Bangladesh became independent in 1971, he has been regarded as the founding-figure of modern Bangladeshi art. His works embraced a variety of styles (*see* BANGLADESH, fig. 3), from the realistic sketches of the Bengal famine to semi-abstract and abstract paintings. Examples are preserved in a number of collections including the Zainul Abedin Sangrahashala at Mymensingh, the Academy of Fine Arts in Calcutta and the Lahore Museum.

BIBLIOGRAPHY

Zainul Abedin [Pakistan art folios] (Karachi, 1968)
B. K. Jahangir: *Contemporary Painters: Bangladesh* (Dhaka, 1974), pp. 5–9, 57
M. S. Islam: *Zainul Abedin* (Dhaka, 1977)

□

Abeele, Pieter van (*b* Amsterdam, 1608; *d* Amsterdam, after 1677). Dutch medallist. One of the foremost Dutch medallists of the 17th century, he was influential in developing a style that was more sculptural than before. Most of his medals consist of two silver plates of repoussé work, chased and joined together at the rim to create a hollow medal. This novel technique allowed the artist to create portraits in very high relief. His medals date from the late 1640s to the 1670s. One of the earliest, probably of 1647, portrays on one side *Prince Frederick Henry of Orange* and on the other *Prince Maurice of Orange*. More usually, the reverses of his medals bear a coat of arms, as for example the medal commemorating the settlement of the disputes between William II of Orange and the States of Holland (1650). Here the reverse bears William's armorial shield, a crown, and the English garter. The ground of the obverse is covered with orange branches in the manner typical of van Abeele and demonstrates his mastery of chasing. On his medal of *Admiral Maarten Tromp* (1653) the armorial reverse incorporates a scene from a naval battle. On others, such as the well-known medals commemorating the departure of Charles II for Britain from Scheveningen (1660), with their grim portrait of the King on the obverse, the scene occupies the whole of the reverse. On these medals the reverse is usually of a small-scale figurative type popular in Dutch medals, but executed with a vigour that is van Abeele's own. He also devised allegorical reverses, such as the charming marriage medal in which a couple on the obverse and a figure of Motherhood on the reverse are surrounded by garlands of flowers.

BIBLIOGRAPHY

Forrer; Thieme–Becker
E. Hawkins, A. W. Franks and H. A. Grueber: *Medallic Illustrations of the History of Great Britain and Ireland* (London, 1885)

PHILIP ATTWOOD

Abel, Josef (*b* Aschach, 22 Aug 1764; *d* Vienna, 4 Oct 1818). Austrian painter. He studied at the Akademie der Bildenden Künste in Vienna under Jakob Matthias Schmutzer (1733–1811) from 1783. On the advice of his mentor, Heinrich Füger, Abel turned from landscape to history painting, winning a gold medal in 1794 for *Daedalus and Icarus* (Vienna, Akad. Bild. Kst.). He was invited to Poland in 1795 by Prince Adam Casimir Czartoryski, and he produced numerous family portraits for the prince in a variety of media. In 1797 he returned to Vienna, where he taught, as well as undertaking commissions for paintings and for prints (e.g. *Portrait of the Artist's Father*, see Aurenhammer, fig. 7).

Abel had a preference for Classical subject-matter during his early training, and this was reinforced by his stay in Rome from 1801 to 1807. During this period he painted his most important work, *F. G. Klopstock in Elysium* (1803–7; Vienna, Belvedere), in collaboration with his friend Johann Christian Reinhart, who painted the landscape background. In 1815 Abel was elected a member of the academy in Vienna on the strength of *Cato of Utica* (completed 1817; Vienna, Akad. Bild. Kst.). In addition to his portraits and history paintings, he also produced theatre curtains, for example the main curtain for the theatre in Pest (1810; drawing, Vienna, Albertina, 14611), as well as a curtain (1794; destr. 1945) for the Burgtheater in Vienna, based on Füger's designs.

BIBLIOGRAPHY

Meissner

H. Aurenhammer: 'Josef Abel, 1764–1818', *Mitt. Österreich. Gal.*, x (1966), pp. 3–26 [18 pict.]

ANDRZEJ RYSZKIEWICZ

Abela, Eduardo (*b* San Antonio de los Baños, nr Güines, 1889; *d* Havana, 1965). Cuban painter and caricaturist. He graduated from the Academia de S Alejandro in Havana in 1920 and lived in Paris from 1927 to 1929. There he studied at the Académie de la Grande Chaumière and abandoned academicism, developing a modernist 'Cuban' style, in which folkloric scenes of peasant life were depicted in a colourful, energetic, pseudo-naive manner reminiscent of Jules Pascin and Amedeo Modigliani. An outstanding work of this period is *Triumph of the Rumba* (*c.* 1928; Havana, Mus. N. B.A.). After a trip to Italy in the early 1930s, Abela began to paint canvases such as *Guajiros* ('peasants'; 1938; Havana, Mus. N. B.A.), in which the Classical sobriety and order is the result of his contact with Italian medieval and Renaissance art. His style underwent a radical change in the early 1950s, and from this time until his death he painted small works that recall the drawings of children as well as the works of Marc Chagall in their use of fantasy.

Abela was a noted caricaturist early in his career, which contributed to the informal, whimsical quality of his painting. His most famous cartoon series, *The Fool*, helped bring about the overthrow of the Machado regime in Cuba in 1933.

BIBLIOGRAPHY

L. de la Torriente: 'El mundo ensoñado de Abela', *Rev. Inst. N. Cult.*, i/1 (1956), pp. 41–56

O. Hurtado and others: *Pintores cubanos* (Havana, 1962)

Abela: Magic and Fable (exh. cat., ed. C. Luis; Miami, FL, Cub. Mus. A. & Cult., 1983)

J. A. Martínez: *Cuban Art and National Identity: The Vanguardia Painters, 1927–1950* (Gainsville, 1994)

GIULIO V. BLANC

Abel de Pujol, Alexandre [Abel, Alexandre-Denis] (*b* Douai, 30 Jan 1785; *d* Paris, 28 Sept 1861). French painter. He was the natural son of Alexandre de Pujol de Mortry, a nobleman and provost of Valenciennes, but did not use his father's name until after 1814. He trained first at the Académie de Valenciennes (1799–1803), then at the Ecole des Beaux-Arts, Paris, and in the studio of Jacques-Louis David. At the end of 1805 it seemed he would have to end his apprenticeship for lack of money but David let him continue free of charge, so impressed had he been by *Philopoemen... Splitting Wood* (1806; ex-Delobel priv. col., Valenciennes). The astonishing *Self-portrait* (Valenciennes, Mus. B.-A.), showing the artist as the very image of a romantic hero, dates from this period.

From 1808 Abel exhibited history paintings at the Salon, making his living, however, by painting shop signs. In 1811 he won the prestigious Prix de Rome and his father subsequently permitted him to adopt his name. Thus from 1814 he signed his pictures *Abel de Pujol.* His stay in Italy was brief; he returned to Paris in 1812 and painted portraits in a finely executed Neo-classical style (e.g. *Nicolas Legrand and his Grandson*, exh. Salon, 1817; ex-Heim Gal., London, see 1978 exh. cat., no. 14). He won the prize for history painting at the Salon of 1817, with *St Stephen Preaching* (Paris, St Thomas d'Aquin), a representative work, characterized by impeccable drawing, clear composition, broad light effects and an evident predilection for painting beautiful drapery. At the Salon of 1819 he won acclaim for the *Death of the Virgin* (untraced), commissioned for the cathedral of Notre-Dame, and the *Renaissance of the Arts*, a ceiling painting over the grand staircase at the Louvre (destr. 1855; fragments, Valenciennes, Acad.). These anticipate the two main aspects of his future work: religious paintings and ceiling paintings with allegorical (e.g. *Egypt Saved by Joseph*, 1827; Paris, Louvre) or mythological subjects (e.g. decoration for the Galerie de Diane, 1822–4; Fontainebleau, Château). The grisaille decoration he executed in collaboration with Charles Meynier in 1826 on the coving in the great hall of the Bourse, Paris, was much acclaimed and won him a reputation as a painter in grisaille.

The revival of the use of frescoes in churches was another aspect of his work, first realized in the chapel of St Roch in the church of St Sulpice (1819–22) in which he modified his palette and simplified his forms to obtain monumental effects. His technical inventiveness was demonstrated again in 1828 when he painted the antependium made from lava in the church of St Elisabeth, Paris, where he also designed three stained-glass windows. Further experimental work was his participation in research into encaustic techniques of decoration (King's staircase, 1835; Fontainebleau, Château). Meanwhile he continued to execute numerous large-scale decorations in public buildings, two examples being the *Apocalypse* (2.5×13 m, 1837; Paris, Notre-Dame de Bonne-Nouvelle) and *St Denis Preaching in Gaul* (3.5×14 m, 1838–40; Paris, St Denys du St Sacrement). These are linked to the Nazarenes in the austerity of their frieze composition and the choice of archaic subject-matter. More striking is his unusual use of grisaille in more intimate works, such as the portrait of *Mademoiselle de L* (exh. Salon, 1831; Valenciennes, Mus. B.-A.).

In 1835 Abel de Pujol was elected to a chair in the Académie. His studio, which was particularly popular between 1817 and 1830, was attended, among others, by Camille Roqueplan, Alexandre-Gabriel Decamps, Adrienne Grandpierre-Deverzy (*b* 1798)—his second wife—and Théophile Vauchelet (1802–73). His son, Alexandre (1816–84), was also a pupil and exhibited at the Salons of 1847 and 1850. Alexandre's works, particularly his portraits, have been attributed to his father, but his signature, 'Adre de Pujol', identifies them securely as his own.

BIBLIOGRAPHY

De David à Delacroix (exh. cat., Paris, Grand Pal., 1974)

Trésors des musées du Nord de la France, II: Peinture française, 1770–1830 (exh. cat., Calais, Mus. B.-A.; Arras, Mus. B.-A.; Douai, Mus. Mun.; Lille, Mus. B.-A.; 1975–6) [notes on Abel de Pujol by D. Vieville]

Forgotten French Art from the First to the Second Empire (exh. cat., London, Heim Gal., 1978)

P. Grunchec: *Le Concours des Prix de Rome, 1797–1863* (Paris, 1986)

B. Foucart: *Le Renouveau de la peinture religieuse en France, 1800–1860* (Paris, 1987)

ISABELLE DENIS

Abercrombie, Sir **(Leslie) Patrick** (*b* Ashton-upon-Mersey, 6 June 1879; *d* Aston Tirrold, Oxon, 23 March 1957). English urban planner, architect and writer. He was educated at Uppingham, Leics, and was an apprentice in architectural offices, first in Manchester and then in Liverpool. In 1907 Charles H. Reilly appointed him to the School of Architecture at the University of Liverpool, and in 1909, following the foundation of the School of Civic Design, the first urban planning school in Britain, he became deputy to its professor, S. D. Adshead. He helped found its publication, the *Town Planning Review*, and became a major contributor; he wrote a series of articles on American and European cities, giving a detailed account of his conception of history, architectural styles and the analysis of urban planning. In 1915 he became Professor of Civic Design and was nominated Librarian for the Town Planning Institute. He was active as an editor and conference organizer as well as a teacher and practising architect, involved in work stimulated by the Housing and Town Planning Act of 1909; for example he produced various schemes for low-cost housing in established and new towns in Yorkshire.

In 1916, with Arthur and Sidney Kelley, he won the international competition for a new city plan for Dublin; the jury included Patrick Geddes and John Nolen. Abercrombie's plan addressed the problems relating to such a large-scale project, utilizing working models previously employed by eminent urban planners such as Georges-Eugène Haussmann, Eugène Alfred Hénard and Camillo Sitte. Abercrombie's subsequent plan for Doncaster (1922), the first English regional plan to be published, also embodied the first complete application of Geddes's regional planning concepts (*see* GEDDES, PATRICK). This plan, and those for Deeside (1923; with Sidney Kelley and Theodore Fyfe) and Tees-side (1925; with Adshead) in the north of England reveal a marked increase in the scale of planning through the application of Geddes's principles of conurbation, and, in so doing, they forged a link between urban and economic planning.

Abercrombie refined and articulated his planning methodology in later schemes: for example, in his plan for Sheffield (1924; with R. H. Mattocks) he introduced an elaborate preliminary analysis that allowed him to test the effectiveness of civic surveys. He also became a defender of the environment, a pioneering activity that began with the plan for Stratford-on-Avon (1923; with Lascelles Abercrombie) and culminated with the foundation of the Council for the Preservation of Rural England (1926), of which he was chairman and president for life. His planning methodology revolved around analysis, preservation and development, retaining old structures where possible and making them workable under modern conditions, as seen in the plans for East Kent (1925–8; with John Archibald), Thames Valley (1929; with Walter Mayo), Bristol and Bath (1930; with Bertrand Brueton) and Cumberland (1932).

Abercrombie was regarded as one of the most important urban planners in the country. He was committed to comprehensive planning, seeing in the urban planner a new type of intellectual whose interdisciplinary skills enabled him to carry out painless social transformation. His *Town and Country Planning* (1933) reveals just such a vision, the roots of which can be traced back to the Utopias of William Morris and the industrial philanthropy of the 19th century. This manual formed a central point of reference in the English and international literature of urban planning, which had never before been taken seriously by architectural historians.

In 1935 Abercrombie replaced Adshead in the Chair of Town Planning at the University of London, and in 1937 he participated in the Barlow Commission, which thoroughly criticized the existing planning legislation. This gave him the opportunity to carry out the London County Plan (1943; with J. H. Forshaw), for which competing proposals were produced by the MARS Group and the Royal Academy, and the Greater London Plan (1944). In the first plan one can see traces of the ideas of Steen Eiler Rasmussen and Alker Tripp, but on the whole the two plans for London represent a synthesis of developments in English urban planning from the beginning of the century and reveal the extent that it had moved away from the schemes of Ebenezer Howard. It was not the garden city that would transform the London metropolis but the satellite towns and intervening green belts proposed by Charles B. Purdom and Raymond Unwin from the 1920s. With this technical and methodological inheritance, Abercrombie approached such later plans as those for Plymouth (1945), Edinburgh (1949; with Derek Plumstead) and, finally, Addis Ababa (1956; with Gerald Dix): what had become a proven language of urban planning could be exported anywhere, duly amended, as a universal concept recognizing no frontiers. Abercrombie was knighted in 1945; he received gold medals from the RIBA (1946), AIA (1949) and the Town Planning Institute (1955).

WRITINGS

'The Era of Architectural Town Planning', *Town Planning Rev.*, v/3 (1914), pp. 195–213

'The Preservation of Rural England: The Control of Development by Means of Rural Planning', *Town Planning Rev.*, xii/1 (1926), pp. 5–56

Town and Country Planning (London, 1933, rev. 3/1959)

Planning in Town and Country: Difficulties and Possibilities (Liverpool and London, 1937)

BIBLIOGRAPHY

G. E. Cherry: *The Evolution of British Town Planning* (Plymouth, 1974)

A. Manno: *Patrick Abercrombie: A Chronological Bibliography, With Annotations and Biographical Details* [Brunswick Environmental Papers] (Leeds, 1980)

——: *Patrick Abercrombie: Storia della pianificazione urbane e rurale in Inghilterra, 1909–40* (diss., Venice, Ist. U. Archit., 1980)

G. Dix: 'Patrick Abercrombie, 1879–1957', *Pioneers in British Planning*, ed. G. E. Cherry (London, 1981), pp. 103–30

ANTONIO MANNO

Aberdeen. Scottish city situated on the east coast of the estuary of the River Dee and River Don, with a rich agricultural hinterland. The city centre is divided into two historic parts of distinct character: Old Aberdeen, dominated by St Machar's Cathedral and King's College (est. 1495), part of the University, which grew up near the Don around the seat of the bishop (the bishopric was established in 1137), and New Aberdeen, a royal burgh beside the Dee (est. ?early 12th century), which was extended in the Neo-classical style in the late 18th century and early 19th and which forms the heart of the present commercial centre.

In Old Aberdeen, well established by the time of the earliest surviving royal charter of 1179 and enhanced by the founding of a royal mint soon after, the High Street leads south from the cathedral, which was started by the Don in 1164, rebuilt from *c.* 1370 and is dominated by distinctive sandstone 16th-century spires. Nearby, King's College Chapel (completed 1505) is all that survives of Bishop Elphinstone's original foundation (1495). The centre of the royal burgh was, by the time of the first map (1661), concentrated around a castle and Castle Gate (now Street), and Broad Street and Gallowgate ran north. Rebuilding, though no major physical expansion, to house the growing population took place until improvements were made to roads and to the navigation of the Dee in the late 18th century; the docks and quays were built in the 19th and early 20th century.

Union Street, a major new route to the west, was laid out after 1800 and carried on arches across the River Denburn and the medieval streets below. Its success led to the development of streets and squares north and south of it, such as Golden Square (1817) and Bon Accord Square (1823–6). Union Street (see fig.) is particularly fine, lined with many handsome Neo-classical buildings by ARCHIBALD SIMPSON and John Smith (i), built with the sparkling local granite, which was both used in Aberdeen and exported. Union Street was extended later in the 19th century as Queen's Road, the catalyst for generously planned, smart suburban development with such villas as the Baronial-style No. 50 (1886) by the original and roguish John Bridgeford Pirie (1852–90). The quality of the granite imparted a crisp, hard character even to the most ornate Victorian and Edwardian buildings, such as the Perpendicular-style façade of Marischal College (1906) by A. Marshall Mackenzie (1848–1933). Although the inevitable suburban growth of speculative bungalows and local authority tower blocks occurred throughout the 20th century, commercial rebuilding did not destroy the essential character of the city centre.

Aberdeen Art Gallery was founded in 1884 and was greatly boosted by the bequest in 1900 of the collection of the granite merchant Alexander Macdonald. From 1880 he had commissioned a unique series of portraits of British artists and also collected the work of living artists. The gallery's strength is British art of the 18th, 19th and 20th centuries. It has an especially fine representation of most major groups, styles and movements of the first half of the 20th century, such as the New English Art Club, the Glasgow Boys, the Camden Town Group and the Scottish Colourists. Local artists are well represented with works by William Dyce, John Philip, James Cassie (1819–79), James McBey (1883–1959), James Cowie and Joan Eardley.

BIBLIOGRAPHY

R. E. H. Mellor and J. S. Smith: *A Visitor's Guide to Aberdeen* (Aberdeen, n.d.)

W. A. Brogden: *Aberdeen: An Illustrated Architectural Guide* (Edinburgh, 1986)

MALCOLM HIGGS

Abergen, Antonis van. *See* OBBERGHEN, ANTONIS VAN.

Aberdeen, view down Castle Street and Union Street; from a photograph by George Washington Wilson, *c.* 1880

Aberli, Johann Ludwig (*b* Winterthur, 14 Nov 1723; *d* Berne, 17 Oct 1786). Swiss painter, draughtsman and engraver. In 1741 he moved to Berne, where he took drawing lessons with Johann Grimm (1675–1747), whose school of drawing he took over in 1747. He visited the Bernese Oberland with Emanuel Handmann, Christian Georg Schütz (1718–91) and Friedrich Wilhelm Hirt (1721–72) in 1759 and in the same year travelled to Paris with Adrian Zingg (1734–86). This was his only trip abroad, but it determined him to work exclusively as a landscape painter. After nine months he returned to Berne, where his landscape views became popular, particularly with foreign travellers, enamoured of 'Nature' and keen to retain souvenirs of their travels. He was one of the first artists to portray the beauties of the Swiss countryside; his favourite subjects were the Aare Valley and views of Swiss lakes (e.g. *View of Erlach on the Lake of Biel*; Berne, Kstmus.). He invented a technique known as the 'Aberli style', which consisted of watercolour washes added to an image in which slightly smudged outlines were achieved through a combination of engraving and etching. The prints were made from drawings taken from nature and finished in the studio. His style was characterized by delicate execution, an intimate narrative approach, refined colours and the ability to convey a light and vaporous atmosphere. Aberli's success was such that he had to employ assistants and pupils to aid him in the coloration process; his pupils included Erasmus Ritter, Johann Jakob Biedermann, Marquard Wocher (1760–1830), Gabriel Ludwig Lory the elder (1763–1840) and Peter Birmann. From 1773 to 1775 Aberli also painted a series of costumes in response to tourist demand.

BIBLIOGRAPHY

SKL
Johann Ludwig Aberli, 1723–86 (exh. cat. by C. König-von Dach, Berne, Kstmus., 1987)

JEANNE-MARIE HORAT-WEBER

Abhānagari. *See* ABANERI.

ʿAbid [ʿĀbid] (*fl c.* 1615–58). Indian miniature painter, son of AQA RIZA (i) and brother of ABU'L-HASAN. Both his father and his brother worked for the Mughal emperor Jahangir (*reg* 1605–27). Although ʿAbid probably began working in the royal atelier *c.* 1615, all of his known signed works are datable to the reign of Shah Jahan (*reg* 1628–58). His style varied somewhat from that of his celebrated older brother, but ʿAbid's work also stayed within the strict formalism of the Persian-derived courtly concerns for symmetry, technical perfection and minute detail. Within these constraints, ʿAbid's portraits of court figures are injected with an animation that creates characterization of individual personalities and intensifies the narrative. ʿAbid was an accomplished colourist, whose vivid use of colour seems to contrast with the realism of his subjects, primarily battle and court scenes. His known paintings are relatively few; most are from the *Padshāhnāma* of *c.* 1636–58 (Windsor Castle, Royal Lib., MS. HB.149, fols 94*v* [signed], 192*v* and at least two dispersed leaves elsewhere).

See also INDIAN SUBCONTINENT, §V, 4(i)(c) and (d).

BIBLIOGRAPHY

The Art of Mughal India: Paintings and Precious Objects (exh. cat. by S. C. Welch, New York, Asia House Gals, 1964)
The Grand Moghul: Imperial Painting in India, 1600–1660 (exh. cat. by M. C. Beach, Williamstown, MA, Clark A. Inst.; Baltimore, MD, Walters A.G.; Boston, MA, Mus. F.A.; New York, Asia Soc. Gals; 1978–9)
W. Komala: *The Windsor Castle 'Badshah-Nama' and its Place in the Development of Historical Painting during the Reign of Shah Jahan, 1628–58* (diss., Iowa City, U. IA, 1982)

JEFFREY A. HUGHES

Abildgaard, Nicolai Abraham (*b* Copenhagen, 11 Sept 1743; *d* Frederiksdal, Copenhagen, 4 June 1809). Danish painter, designer and architect. His paintings reveal both Neo-classical and Romantic interests and include history paintings as well as literary and mythological works. The variety of his subject-matter reflects his wide learning, a feature further evidenced by the broad range of his creative output. In addition to painting, he produced decorative work, sculpture and furniture designs, as well as being engaged as an architect. Successfully combining both intellectual and imaginative powers, he came to be fully appreciated only in the 1980s.

1. Early life and painting, to 1790. 2. Painting and sculpture designs, 1790–1809. 3. Other activities.

1. EARLY LIFE AND PAINTING, TO 1790. He studied at the Kongelige Danske Kunstakademi in Copenhagen (1764–72), and in 1767 he assisted Johan Edvard Mandelberg (1730–86) in painting the domed hall of the Fredensborg Slot with scenes from the Homeric epic the *Iliad*. In 1772 he was granted a five-year travelling scholarship from the Kunstakademi to study in Rome. During his Roman sojourn he extensively copied works of art from the period of antiquity up to that of the Carracci family. His friendships with the Danish painter Jens Juel, the Swedish sculptor Johan Tobias Sergel and the Swiss painter Johann Heinrich Fuseli placed him among artists who were in the mainstream of a widespread upheaval in European art. In these years Abildgaard developed both Neo-classical and Romantic tastes; his masterpiece of the period is *Philoctetes Wounded* (1774–5; Copenhagen, Stat. Mus. Kst; see fig. 1), a highly personal interpretation of the Belvedere *Torso* (Rome, Vatican, Mus. Pio-Clementino) and Michelangelo's *ignudi* in the Sistine Chapel in the Vatican, Rome. The pains of the wounded man are passionately expressed, yet the pathos is balanced by the heroic idealism of the muscular body. A revealing instance of the artist's reinterpretation of an antique source is *Ymer Suckling the Cow Audhumla* (*c.* 1777; Copenhagen, Stat. Mus. Kst). In the famous fresco from the 'basilica' of Herculaneum, representing Hercules' first meeting with his son Telephos, the latter is suckling a deer (1st century AD; Naples, Mus. Archeol. N.). Abildgaard transferred this compositional idea to a subject from Norse mythology. In his first sketch, however, he had modelled the figure of Ymer after Sergel's sculpture *Resting Faun* (1770–74; Stockholm, Nmus.). The final painting was probably completed after Abildgaard's return to Denmark.

In 1777 Abildgaard was elected a member of the Kunstakademi and commissioned to produce a series of history paintings of the Danish kings of the house of Oldenburg for the Banqueting Hall of Christiansborg Slot in Copenhagen, then the royal residence. From 1778 to 1791 he made ten monumental paintings, of which only three survived the fire of 1794, when the whole palace

1. Nicolai Abraham Abildgaard: *Philoctetes Wounded*, oil on canvas, 1.23×1.74 m, 1774–5 (Copenhagen, Statens Museum for Kunst)

was ruined. The rest are known only from sketches (Copenhagen, Stat. Mus. Kst). Although Abildgaard adopted a realist approach, the large canvases rely strongly on European Renaissance and Baroque traditions. Thus, in terms of composition, *Christian I Raises Holstein to the State of Duchy* (1778–9; Copenhagen, Christiansborg Slot) is similar to Rubens's *Wisdom of Solomon* (Copenhagen, Stat. Mus. Kst), then in the royal collection, and more generally to 15th-century Italian ceremonial representations and the works of Raphael.

In 1778 Abildgaard had been appointed professor at the Kongelige Akademi, and the demands of this post together with those due to his royal commission left little time for small-scale paintings. Nevertheless, he did paint some, such as *Socrates in Prison* (*c.* 1784; Copenhagen, Ny Carlsberg Glyp.), whose subject-matter reflects his Neo-classical tastes. Though fully dressed, the pose of the philosopher is again inspired by the Belvedere *Torso.* Abildgaard was a man of extremely wide reading, as is witnessed by his copious private library (now part of the library of the Kunstakademi), and he also drew on themes from Ossian and Shakespeare, as well as from ancient Danish mythology and history in his work.

A most original and enigmatic work from the same period is the *Temple of Fortune* (1785; Hillerød, Frederiksborg Slot), which is actually a painted fire-screen. Iconographically, it is a complex work and is based on a satirical essay (1764) of the same title by the Danish poet Johannes Ewald (1743–81). In 1780 Abildgaard had made drawings to illustrate the text, which were engraved by Johan Frederik Clemens. In the fire-screen, people from all classes are grouped around the stairs leading to the Templum Fortunae, all of them playing a part in the representation of human folly. From 1785 to 1789 Abildgaard worked on a series of drawings and paintings inspired by the satirical novel *Niels Klim* (Latin edn, 1741; Danish edn, 1742) by Ludvig Holberg (1684–1754). They were eventually turned into copperplates by Clemens for a new Danish translation of the novel published in Copenhagen in 1789. From 1789 to 1791 Abildgaard was Director of the Kunstakademi.

2. PAINTING AND SCULPTURE DESIGNS, 1790–1809. In the last decade of the 18th century, and especially after the tragic fire at the Christiansborg Slot, besides teaching, Abildgaard largely dedicated himself to the realization of a public monument to commemorate the abolition of serfdom in Denmark in 1788. Popularly called the Liberty Memorial (1792–7; Copenhagen, Vesterbrogade), it consists of an inscribed obelisk surrounded at the base by the allegorical statues of Fidelity, Agriculture, Courage and Patriotism (or Civic Virtue), with other allegories carved in relief between them. Although Abildgaard probably contributed very little to the actual execution of the monument, he was responsible for the iconographical programme and the overall architectural design (the alle-

gorical statues were in fact carved by the sculptors Johannes Wiedewelt, Andreas Weidenhaupt (1738–1805) and Nicolai Dajon (1748–1823)). Through this work and the above-mentioned fire-screen Abildgaard stands out as characteristic of the idealistic artists that appeared in the wake of the European Enlightenment, a sort of *peintre-philosophe.* During the same period he also designed a series of tombstones and monuments to commemorate illustrious Danes. The sarcophagi for the heir-presumptive Frederik (*d* 1805) and his consort Sophie Frederikke (*d* 1794) were also made after Abildgaard's designs (Roskilde Cathedral, Frederik V Chapel).

From 1801 to 1809 Abildgaard was again Director of the Kunstakademi, and by the beginning of the 19th century he had entered into a second bloom as a painter. The monumental—in form if not in size—allegorical paintings from 1800 of *Theology, Justice* (Copenhagen, Stat. Mus. Kst) and *Philosophy* (priv. col., see Skovgaard, fig. 48) may be afterthoughts from his work on the Liberty Memorial. They have highly learned, somewhat unorthodox compositions (e.g. Theology holds out a Medusa head, thus opposing enlightenment with terror), and possibly Abildgaard's intentions were satirical. His interest in Voltaire's tragedy *Le Triumvirat* (1767) further indicates that he was deeply engaged in political thought at this time. He painted at least five scenes from the play, the first ones probably begun as early as 1796. Some formed wall decorations for the house he designed at 5, Nytorv in Copenhagen, such as that illustrating Act 4, Scene 4 (1800), which shows an instance of the struggle for power following the assassination of Julius Caesar. Two of the female protagonists, Fulvie and Julie, are engaged in violent action, as one, dagger in hand, eagerly seeks vengeance against the triumvirs, while the other urges for peace and reconciliation. The dramatic style of the figures harks back to his Roman years, and particularly to the influence of Fuseli. The compositional scheme is the same as used by Alexander Runciman in his etching *Landing of St Margaret* (*c.* 1774), a work Abildgaard may have known. In the painting of the two women Abildgaard characterized their moral standing by way of colour: Fulvie's fluttering cape is purple, suggesting blood and vengeance, while Julie wears a pale blue dress, indicating composure and continence.

From 1802 to 1804 Abildgaard executed four large canvases (Copenhagen, Stat. Mus. Kst) using episodes from Terence's play *Girl from Andros* (see fig. 2). Helped by Sebastiano Serlio's theories of perspective and his own reminiscences of Roman architecture, he created a vision of the ideal city of antiquity. These cityscapes bear little historical or topographical authenticity, and in their static austerity, clearly inspired by Nicolas Poussin, they form a sharp contrast to the lively movements of the 'actors'. Nevertheless, the artist achieved a perfect unity of composition and colour within each and between all four of the paintings, mostly due to a delicate, sometimes dramatic handling of light and shadow. The paintings were conceived as pendants and presented to his second wife, Juliane Marie, whom he married in 1803. They decorated the walls of their home at the Kunstakademi in the Charlottenborg Slot.

2. Nicolai Abraham Abildgaard: *Scene from Terence: Girl from Andros, 2, iii*, oil on canvas, 1.57×1.28 m, 1802 (Copenhagen, Statens Museum for Kunst)

Abildgaard's late work is thematically centred around literary and historical scenes from Greek and Roman antiquity. Thus in 1808–9 he painted 33 scenes from Apuleius' *Metamorphoses, or the Golden Ass*, a Roman novel in which the young hero Lucius is changed into an ass through the witchcraft of his lover, the maidservant Fotis. In *Fotis Appalled at the Sight of Lucius' Metamorphosis* (1809; Copenhagen, Stat. Mus. Kst) the girl strikes a dramatic pose in front of the youth, who has the head of an ass. His body, however, is still human and reveals the strong influence of the style found in work by the circle around the Carracci. A subdued, lyrical tone emanates from many of his late genre-like pictures, and the mature artist showed his ability to convey a universally human range of sentiment and feeling. Thus *Papirius and his Mother* (1809) is ironic, *Anacreon and Amaryllis* (1808) idyllic, and *Sappho and the Mytilene Woman* (1809; all Copenhagen, Stat. Mus. Kst) elegiac. The latter two form part of a series on ancient love poetry.

3. Other activities. Throughout his life Abildgaard was commissioned to produce work of a more decorative nature. He painted overdoors for the Potentate Apartment at Christiansborg Slot (*Allegories of the State of Things in Europe during Four Ages* and *Allegory of the Sound*, destr. 1794; studies in Copenhagen, Stat. Mus. Kst) and for Count Adam Gottlob Moltke's town house (*Allegories of the Three World Religions*, 1780s; Copenhagen, Håndværkerforen.). From 1794 he worked for the heir-presumptive Frederick on the decorations of the latter's apartments at the Amalienborg Palace in Copenhagen. The State Room is a work of great integrity and originality,

one of the first in the Neo-classicist style in Denmark. The originally yellow walls were divided by white and gilt Ionic pilasters resting on a violet-blue panel base. The frieze, with gilt garlands on a royal blue ground, corresponded to the colouring of the furniture and curtains. In niches flanking the main door there were sculptures of the muses *Euterpe* and *Terpsichore*, probably modelled by the young Bertel Thorvaldsen after Abildgaard's design. In the Throne Room the walls were decorated with allegorical oval paintings and overdoors by Abildgaard himself (the Continents and the Elements). On the whole, as an interior decorator Abildgaard avoided the neatness of the Empire style for the sake of a more grandiose vision of antiquity, preferring strong simplicity and striking colours. To complete the general effect he designed furniture that came to influence several generations of the Danish Golden Age era and fell within that peculiar field called 'artist's furniture' (i.e. that designed by painters to furnish their own homes). Abildgaard used and reinterpreted ancient Greek and Roman models. For his own home he designed, among other things, eight gilt chairs of the *klismos* type, with wickerwork seats and a palmetto frieze on the top rail, of exquisite taste and elegance, albeit hardly functional for the user (*see* DENMARK, fig. 16). He tried his hand in almost every field within the applied arts. In 1779 he made costume designs for a production of Johannes Ewald's *Balder's Death* at the Kongelige Teater in Copenhagen. He designed various medals, and in his *Apis Clock* (Copenhagen, Kstindustmus.) a Renaissance-style bronze bull is integrated in the work, wearing a round clock on its back.

Abildgaard's output as an architect is limited to only a few works, but they nonetheless show his versatility in this field also. From 1799 to 1803 he built a private house at 5, Nytorv in Copenhagen for which some of the above-mentioned Triumvirat scenes were painted as wall decorations. It is a simple, well proportioned Neo-classicist construction, which still contributes to the architectural harmony of the square, although the top floor is a later addition. After 1805 he built a country house for himself, called Spurveskjul (Sparrow's Hide) near Frederiksdal. For the English-style landscape gardens at the manor houses of Frederiksberg near Copenhagen and Sorgenfri he designed such follies as the Apis Temple (1802; Copenhagen, Frederiksborg Have). This was a small temple derived from Roman models, and the Dionysian bull in the fronton was copied from an ancient intaglio.

BIBLIOGRAPHY

L. Swane: *Abildgaard: Arkitektur og dekoration* (Copenhagen, 1926)

B. Skovgaard: *Maleren Abildgaard* (Copenhagen, 1961)

T. Holck Colding: *Akademiet og Guldalderen, 1750–1850* [The Academy and the Golden Age, 1750–1850], Dansk Kunsthistorie (Copenhagen, 1972), pp. 143–57

P. Kragelund: 'The Church, the Revolution and the "Peintre Philosophe": A Study in the Art of Nicolai Abildgaard', *Hafnia*, ix (1983), pp. 25–65

E. K. Sass: *Lykkens Tempel: Et maleri af Nicolai Abildgaard* [The Temple of Fortune: a painting by Nicolai Abildgaard] (Copenhagen, 1986)

P. Kragelund: 'Abildgaard around 1800: His Tragedy and Comedy', *Anlct. Romana Inst. Dan.*, xvi (1987), pp. 137–85

M. Gelfer-Jørgensen, ed.: *Herculanum paa Sjælland: Klassicisme og nyantik i dansk møbeltradition* [Herculaneum on Zealand: classicism and Neo-antiquity in the Danish tradition of furniture] (Copenhagen, 1988), pp. 33–60

J. Andersen: *De år i Rom: Abildgaard, Sergel, Füssli* [Those years in Rome: Abildgaard, Sergel, Fuseli] (Copenhagen, 1989)

JENS PETER MUNK

Abingdon, Alexander of. *See* ALEXANDER OF ABINGDON.

Abiseo. *See* GRAN PAJATÉN.

Åbo. *See* TURKU.

Aboba. *See* PLISKA.

Āboliņš, Valdis (*b* Liepāja, 14 April 1939; *d* West Berlin, 14 Feb 1984). Latvian performance artist. He arrived in Germany at the age of five as a refugee and later triumphed over geopolitical circumstances to help revitalize artistic culture in his occupied homeland. While pursuing architectural studies at the Technische Hochschule in Aachen (1961–71), he grew interested in the interplay of progressive politics and innovative art forms, which prompted early collaborations with Wolf Vostell and Joseph Beuys, such as their performance *20 July '64*. In 1966 Āboliņš and Gerd Vorhoff founded the Neue Galerie in Aachen, where they organized happenings and performances by Beuys, Jörg Immendorff, Nam June Paik, Tomas Schmit and other key members of FLUXUS, the movement instigated by another exiled Balt, the composer George Maciunas (1931–78). At the same time, inspired by the New Left, Āboliņš combated artistic provincialism within the conservative Latvian émigré community by proposing a cultural rapprochement with Soviet Latvia. Advocating an international—rather than a narrowly nationalist—Latvian identity, Āboliņš helped to organize in 1973 the first major exhibition of art from Latvia to reach the West since the Soviet annexation. One year later he became the executive secretary of the Neue Gesellschaft für Bildende Kunst in West Berlin, under the auspices of which he promoted the rediscovery of the avant-gardist Gustav Klucis and the Western European début of the contemporary realist MAIJA TABAKA. In turn, Āboliņš exhibited in Riga, where his irreverence, kitsch aesthetics and experiments with CORRESPONDENCE ART were revelatory to the local audience. Ironically, it was his leftist orientation that enabled him to alleviate the isolation of Latvian artists under Communism.

BIBLIOGRAPHY

Valdis Āboliņš, Miss Vietnam mit rohem Hering im Mund: Oder Fluxus, Berlin und die Riga-Konnekschen (exh. cat., W. Berlin, Staatl. Ksthalle, 1988)

MARK ALLEN SVEDE

Abondio. Italian family of medallists and wax modellers, active in Central Europe. (1) Antonio Abondio worked first in Italy and later for the imperial courts in Vienna and Prague. He worked in an eclectic style drawn from Italian and northern sources. His oeuvre consists principally of some 60 medals, though he also produced some wax portraits (13 of which survive) and a few plaquettes of religious and mythological themes. His son and pupil, (2) Alessandro Abondio, continued his father's work at the imperial court, developing the genre of portraiture in wax. He also made figure subjects. Alessandro's output was highly regarded by collectors.

BIBLIOGRAPHY
H. Stoecklein: 'Urkunden und Regesten: Alessandro Abondio', *Archv Medaillen- & Plakettenknd.*, i (1913–14), pp. 42–7

□

(1) Antonio Abondio (*b* Riva del Garda, Trento, 1538; *d* Vienna, 22 May 1591). He and Leone Leoni were the only Italian medallists to be highly successful as court artists north of the Alps. Abondio's earliest dated medal is of *Jacopo Antonio Buoncompagni-Sora* (1561; Vienna, Ksthist. Mus.). No stylistic development for his medals has been proposed. His eclectic style reflects Italian, German and Netherlandish sources. In Italy he followed the Milanese court style exemplified in the work of Leoni; he was influenced by medals of the Venetian Alessandro Vittoria, and, most surprisingly, early in his career he was influenced by the charming works of Alfonso Ruspagiari and the school of wax modellers and medallists centred on Reggio Emilia. Abondio's signed medal of *Caterina Riva* (1565; e.g. London, BM) presents her almost as a painting, three-quarter length and three-quarter facing, with the voluminous drapery used to make a Mannerist decoration.

Abondio appears to have left Italy first in 1565–6 for employment by the Holy Roman Emperor Ferdinand II in Innsbruck and Ambras. He was called to Vienna by the Emperor Maximilian II in 1566, was sent to the Netherlands in April of that year and appointed court medallist at Prague in December. His work at Vienna between 1567 and 1571 included a commission for a new series of imperial portraits, which was paid for in Prague in 1570. He was in Spain in 1571–2 in the retinue of the imperial ambassador Baron Johann von Khevenhüller, of whom three medals were made (e.g. Vienna, Ksthist. Mus.). In 1574 Abondio received confirmation from Emperor Maximilian II of a family patent of nobility, and in 1577 he was given a house by Emperor Rudolf II and was commissioned to produce the models for the coinage of the new reign. The medals Abondio produced after leaving Italy show the influence of the Netherlandish school of such medallists as Jacques Jonghelinck. Abondio combined the Netherlandish handling of the portrait with the court style of Leoni in a superb medal of the *Holy Roman Emperor Maximilian II* (1575; Dworschak, p. 62). His medal of the Emperor's wife, *Empress Marie* (1575; Dworschak, p. 63), is in the simpler style of Leoni.

Abondio's principal surviving portraits in wax depict *Emperor Maximilian II*, *Empress Marie* (Munich, Bayer. Nmus.) and the Emperor's brother *Charles, Archduke of Austria* (ex-Gould Collection, New York). A large wax of *Maximilian II* (1575; Vienna, Ksthist. Mus.) has as a reverse an *Allegory of Victory over the Turks* (Dworschak, pp. 84–5). Of the Spanish Habsburgs there are wax portraits of *Philip II, King of Spain*, his consort *Elizabeth of France* (*d* 1568) and son *Charles* (*d* 1568; all ex-Spitzer Collection, Paris). The reverses of Abondio's medals draw on the several Italian traditions represented by the work of Leoni, Vittoria and Pietro Paolo Galeotti, but they are less convincing than the prototypes. In Germany, Abondio adopted the local tradition of using elaborate coats of arms as reverse types. His plaquettes are entirely German in character. There is a set of single figures of *Mars*, *Mercury* and *Venus* (Weber, no. 646, 1–3), a *Virgin and Child* (Weber, no. 651) and a beautiful *Head of Christ* with reverse of *Christ at the Column* (Weber, no. 652). The most remarkable and original of the plaquettes is a *Toilet of Venus* (Weber, no. 650; see fig.), with both the figure composition and the monogram signature in the style of Dürer: a compliment from an Italian artist to his German patrons. His normal form of signature was AN.AB.

Antonio Abondio: *Toilet of Venus*, lead plaquette, 93×73 mm, 1587 (Cambridge, Fitzwilliam Museum)

The variety of portrait types in the medals and the establishment of the wax portrait as an independent form of court portraiture give Abondio an important place in the history of medalmaking both in Italy and in Germany. The style of the wax portraits, with an over-elaborate attention to detail (for example in the use of seed pearls as decoration), tends to deaden the vitality of his images. His imperial portraits are more interesting in the medals than in the waxes. His principal pupils were his son (2) Alessandro Abondio, Raffaello Ranghieri (*fl* 1567–87) and Pietro de Pomis.

BIBLIOGRAPHY
DBI; Meissner; Thieme–Becker
A. Fiala: *Antonio Abondio: Keroplastik a medajlér* [Antonio Abondio: wax modeller and medaller] (Prague, 1909)
G. Habich, ed.: *Die deutschen Schaumünzen des 16. Jahrhunderts*, II/ii (Munich, 1934), pp. 486–507
F. Dworschak: *Antonio Abondio: Medaglista e ceroplasta (1538–1591)*, Collana di artisti trentini (Trento, 1958)
J. Pope-Hennessy and R. W. Lightbown: *Catalogue of Italian Sculpture*, London, V&A cat. (London, 1964), ii, pp. 556–9, nos 582–7 [six wax portraits]
E. J. Pyke: *A Biographical Dictionary of Wax Modellers* (Oxford, 1973), p. 3; *Supplement* (London, 1981), p. 3; *Supplement II* (London, 1983), p. 3
I. Weber: *Deutsche, niederländische und französische Renaissanceplaketten, 1500–1650* (Munich, 1975), pp. 284–8
Antonio Abondio und seine Zeit (exh. cat. by K. Schulz, Vienna, Ksthist. Mus., 1988)

Prag um 1600: Kunst und Kultur am Hofe Rudolfs II (exh. cat., ed. J. J. W. Evans and J. Spicer; Essen, Villa Hügel, 1988), pp. 575–94 [entry by R.-A. Schütte]

J. G. POLLARD

(2) Alessandro Abondio (*b c.* 1580; *d* Munich, *bur* 29 April 1648). Son of (1) Antonio Abondio. He is recorded in the 1606 household register of Emperor Rudolf II as a 'sculptor and picture engraver' with a monthly salary of 20 gulden. It is difficult to follow his working career, which began a few years earlier, because, unlike his father, he did not sign his medals. In the inventory of Rudolf II's *Kunstkammer*, drawn up between 1607 and 1611, Alessandro Abondio is noted as the maker of a large number of embossed wax pieces, mainly of mythological subjects. After the death of Rudolf II, Abondio entered the service of Emperor Matthias II (*reg* 1612–19) and then worked for his successor, Emperor Ferdinand II. In 1619 Abondio married Regina von Aachen, the widow of the painter Hans von Aachen. In that same year he obtained Munich citizenship and from then on was largely resident there. At first Abondio worked for Duke Albrecht VI (*d* 1666); the surviving records attest to a long personal relationship between the artist and his ducal patron. Alessandro made wax portraits of the Duke, which were used by an Augsburg die-cutter as models for the dies for *Gnadenpfennige* ('charity pennies'); precious versions of these were produced by the Munich goldsmiths Christoph Ulrich Eberl (before 1580–1634) and Hans Osinger.

From 1630 Abondio was in the service of Elector Maximilian I. An annual maintenance payment of 150 gulden made to Abondio by the Elector documented from 1630 until Abondio's death suggests that Abondio also worked for other patrons. From 1630, or possibly earlier, Abondio collaborated with the die-cutter Paul Zeggin who cut his wax models in iron. Abondio made sculptures in wax as well as wax portraits. In 1639 a 'Hercules embossed in wax' by 'Alexander Abundi' is mentioned and also in that year an 'epitaph for the Duchess embossed from wax'. Both wax models were cast by the bell-founder Bernhard Ernst (*fl* 1633–68) and engraved by the goldsmith Melchior Epstein (*d* 1659); both are untraced. Abondio is documented as having produced an embossed wax *Entombment* dated 1640, which was identified by some writers with the *Pietà* (destr. during World War II) formerly in the Dreifaltigkeitskirche in Munich. Works by Abondio were included in numerous contemporary *Kunstkammern*; his friend Sandrart mentioned that the wax portraits of *Dr Paul Freher and his Wife* were regarded as a 'wonderful rarity' and 'shown to those who loved art'. Only one wax medal can be attributed to Abondio through an inscription: it shows *Johann Manlich* from Augsburg and was made in 1635 (Vienna, Ksthist. Mus.). Alessandro is linked stylistically in his medalmaking with his father—both men modelled in a similarly subtle and delicate way. While Antonio favoured cast medals, however, Alessandro preferred the struck medal, usually intended as a *Gnadenpfennig*, forming a transition from the Renaissance medal to that of the Baroque period.

BIBLIOGRAPHY

Meissner; *NDB*; Thieme–Becker

J. von Sandrart: *Teutsche Academie* (1675–9); ed. A. R. Peltzer (1925)

F. Kenner: 'Bildnissmedaillen der Spätrenaissance', *Jb. Ksthist. Samml. Allhöch. Ksrhaus.*, xii (1891), pp. 155ff

G. Habich: 'Wachsbildnis des *Johannes Manlich* von Alessandro Abondio', *Schwäb. Mus.* (1928), pp. 57–60

G. Habich, ed.: *Die deutschen Schaumünzen des 16. Jahrhunderts*, II/ii (Munich, 1934)

R. Bauer and H. Haupt, eds: 'Das Kunstkammerinventar Kaiser Rudolfs II., 1607–1611', *Jb. Ksthist. Samml. Wien*, lxxii (1976), pp. 1–191

L. Börner: *Deutsche Medaillenkleinode des 16. und 17. Jahrhunderts* (Würzburg, 1981)

D. Diemer: 'Bronzeplastik um 1600 in München: Neue Quellen und Forschungen, 2. Teil', *Jb. Zentinst. Kstgesch.*, iii (1987), p. 158, fig. 100

RUDOLF-ALEXANDER SCHÜTTE

Aboriginal Australia. Culture of the original inhabitants of Australia and their descendants. This survey covers the traditional art forms of the Australian Aborigines, such as rock art, sculpture in wood, clay and sand, body decoration and bark painting, both before and after European colonization took place at the end of the 18th century. It also examines the interrelationships between the art of Aboriginal groups living in different regions on the continent. Traditional art forms have continued to be produced in most regions well into the late 20th century, but at the same time some contemporary Aboriginal artists, influenced by the dominant white culture in which they now live, have begun to explore new forms and media; this art, produced mainly for external markets, is discussed separately.

I. Introduction. II. Traditional art forms. III. Regions. IV. Contemporary art. V. Collectors and dealers. VI. Museums and exhibitions. VII. Historiography.

I. Introduction.

1. Geography and early settlement history. 2. Religion. 3. Representational systems. 4. Role of the artist.

1. GEOGRAPHY AND EARLY SETTLEMENT HISTORY. Australia and New Guinea formed a single landmass, the prehistoric continent of Sahul, until *c.* 8000 years ago, when the rising sea-level separated them at the Torres Strait. This continent was first occupied at least 40,000 years ago, by people who arrived by boat from South-east Asia. By 30,000 BP people had spread across most of the continent, although the Central Desert remained largely unoccupied until 10,000 years ago (White and O'Connell). Until European colonization at the end of the 18th century Australian Aborigines were hunters and gatherers, even though they had been in contact with agriculturalists north of the Torres Strait for many thousands of years. According to the earliest European records, at the time of colonization in 1788 the population had reached a level variously estimated between 300,000 and 1,000,000 people, speaking some 200 separate languages with a great range of dialects (Dixon). Population density varied enormously according to environmental factors. Many of the well-watered coastal regions and the great inland river system of the Murray–Darling supported relatively dense populations for hunting and gathering societies, whereas the vast region of the Western Desert contained only a few thousand people in total (see fig. 1). Although there is considerable overlap in the environmental resources across the continent, populations in the richer tropical environments of the north and the well-watered temperate regions of the south-east were semi-sedentary with a predictable annual cycle of movement, whereas in some

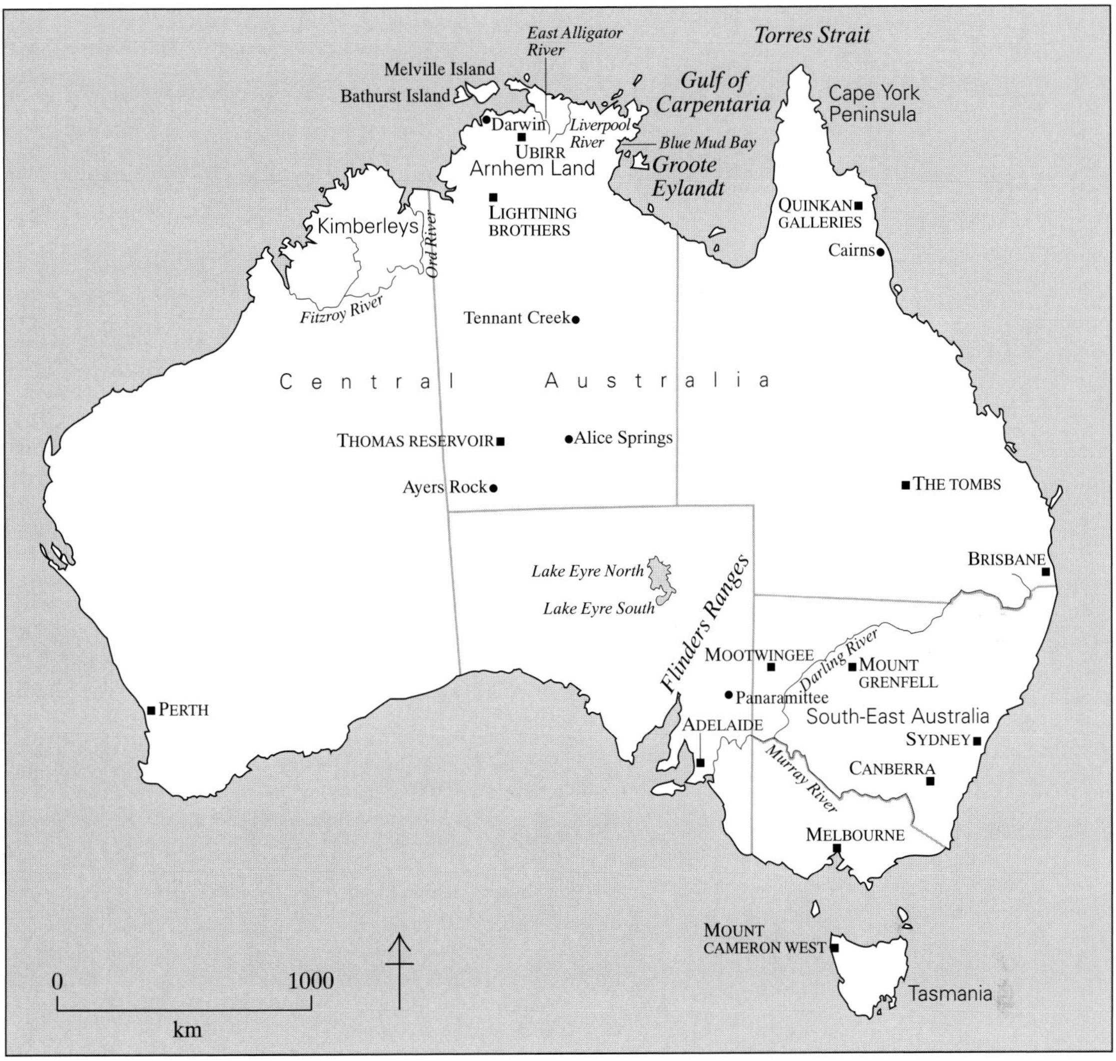

1. Map of Aboriginal Australia; those sites with separate entries in this dictionary are distinguished by CROSS-REFERENCE TYPE

of the less fertile and drier areas populations were nomadic and occupied vast tracts of land.

Aborigines have had a major impact on the Australian environment. Most profoundly, the use of fire both in hunting and in clearing the undergrowth has altered the flora and fauna of the continent in favour of a regime that tolerates, and in some cases benefits from, the regular burning of land. The archaeological record shows that changes occurred over time, including an increase in the systematic use of fire, the invention of polished stone axes *c.* 20,000 years ago, the introduction of the dog 4000 years ago and the general tendency towards the development of smaller stone tools and the production of composite hafted implements (Mulvaney; White and O'Connell). The correlation between social and technological changes is not precisely known, but by the time of European colonization Aborigines had developed a highly complex hunter–gatherer society involving the skilful management of land and resources, a predictable seasonal cycle and a system of social and religious organization centred on rights over land that ordered the relationship between people and the environment.

2. RELIGION. Despite considerable variation, Aboriginal religions throughout Australia share many common features. A central concept is the belief in a time of world-creation frequently referred to in English as the 'Dreaming' or 'Dreamtime' (Stanner). In the Dreaming, ancestral beings occupied the surface of the earth, emerging from beneath the ground or journeying from distant places. These ancestral beings varied in form, sometimes having the shape of animals or inanimate objects such as stones, at other times human characteristics. They travelled across the land, sometimes in groups, encountering others on the way and acting rather as humans do but on a grander scale. Through their actions they transformed the earth's surface, creating the form of the landscape: where they walked valleys were created, where they bled lakes were

formed and where they left their digging sticks in the ground, or splintered their spears against a rock, trees grew. Every action affected the landscape, which then took on mnemonic importance in their lives. At the end of the Dreaming, the ancestral beings withdrew from the surface of the earth, returning beneath the ground or simply transforming themselves into features of the landscape (Maddock; Charlesworth and others). They left behind human groups whom they had created and set in the landscape.

Although ancestral beings no longer occupied the earth, they continued to exist in another dimension necessary to the humans who succeeded them. They left behind a body of sacred law—songs, dances and paintings—that arose out of their world-creating acts and provided an account of them. The human groups used this sacred law to re-enact and preserve the memory of Dreamtime events in ritual, thus providing a source of spiritual power for subsequent generations. The songs and paintings, like the landscape itself, are considered to be not merely representations of the ancestral past but also manifestations of the ancestral beings themselves and a means of establishing contact with them.

People are linked with the ancestral past in a continuous cycle through the process of spirit conception, the performance of ritual and the return of the spirits of the dead to the ancestral domain. Within the landscape the ancestral beings created reservoirs of spiritual power, which provide the conception spirits that initiate each new existence. As people take part in ceremonies throughout their lives, they accumulate spiritual power progressively, moving closer to the ancestral domain towards the end of their lives. On death, their spirits return to the land or to certain lands of the dead, where they are reincorporated within the time-frame of the Dreaming, becoming a source of spiritual energy for subsequent generations. Religious practices are aimed at maintaining contact with the ancestral past and controlling the cyclical movement of spiritual power to ensure that the souls of the dead return to the land and that the fertility of people and land is maintained (Morphy, 1984).

There are important political dimensions to Aboriginal religion, in maintaining the relationship between groups of people, ancestral beings and land (Myers) and in reinforcing these relationships by means of a system of restricted knowledge. Through their journeys, ancestral beings are associated with particular areas of land, and in many parts of Australia rights to land are believed to have been entrusted by those ancestral beings to the founding human ancestors of patrilineal clans. The sacred law became a charter of rights for the continued ownership of the land by subsequent generations of the clan and a source of spiritual strength (Williams). Elsewhere, especially in the more sparsely populated desert regions, rights to land and membership of totemic cult groups are established on a wider basis, including kin ties through women and links to particular conception sites. Throughout Aboriginal Australia the system of restricted knowledge is associated with the segmentation of society based on age and gender. Religious knowledge is sometimes treated as secret, with certain objects and their meanings being revealed only within the closed context of the ceremonial ground to those who possess rights to such knowledge and have passed through previous stages of initiation. Usually it is the right to disseminate information and to be present in certain contexts that is controlled rather than the knowledge itself. In many parts of Australia, in particular towards the centre of the continent, ceremonies or phases of them may be restricted to men or women only. In general the authority of men and (to a lesser extent) women increases as they grow older and gain access to spiritual power by participating in ceremonies and acquiring knowledge.

3. Representational systems. Aboriginal art displays an enormous variety of styles, both regionally and over time. However, within this broad range of variation, it is possible to identify two contrasting systems of representation that each reflect formal similarities throughout the continent. One system consists mainly of figurative representations and has been referred to as 'iconic' or 'motivated', since there is a direct relationship between image and object. The other is characteristically geometric and has been called 'arbitrary' or 'unmotivated', since the same configuration can be attributed with various interpretations (Morphy, 1980, 1989; Munn). The distinction between the two systems is not an absolute one, and there are examples that do not fit neatly into either category; nevertheless it is a distinction that has proved useful. In most regions both systems are employed, often in different contexts, but sometimes in combination. For example, figurative representations in rock paintings are often thought to be the impressions of ancestral beings left behind on the rock surface, whereas geometric representations are believed to be designs that the ancestral beings painted on their bodies or that originated through ancestral action. The designs are both manifestations of ancestral beings, in that they are thought to be their creations or (like the landscape itself) an integral part of them, and representations of the ancestral past, in that they encode events that occurred in the Dreamtime.

In most cases the geometric art can be interpreted only by someone who already knows its meaning, as is appropriate for a system of restricted knowledge. Much of the sacred geometric art represents schematic relationships between topographic features, not entirely unlike maps. However these geometric configurations are multivalent and can encode a multiplicity of meanings, without giving priority to any single one. The same design can represent an area of land, marks on the body of an ancestral being or the 'crest' of a totemic cult group associated with that area of land. Thus geometric art can be used to encode the relationships and associations between particular places, the ancestral events that created them and the social groups that have rights in them.

4. Role of the artist. Since art mediates between the present and the ancestral past, the artist plays an important role in Aboriginal society and may possess significant status in ceremonial and political affairs. Paintings, sculptures, ground drawings and ceremonial constructions, like all other humanly produced expressions of the ancestral past, are forms of religious knowledge passed

on from one generation to the next. People can only reproduce works of art in which they have inherited rights. Moreover, art production is usually part of a ceremonial role that is defined by such factors as kinship relations to other participants, moiety affiliation and ritual status or seniority. Frequently only one or two people can perform the requisite act. On some occasions, however, when several individuals may be in the appropriate category, three factors are relevant in deciding who should produce the work: the right to produce it, knowledge of its correct form and the ability to produce it. Although there is no separate category of 'artists' in Aboriginal society, some people are recognized as being better at producing paintings and ceremonial objects than others; people who combine knowledge with skill are often given a major role in ceremonies.

With the exception of Tiwi artists of Melville and Bathurst Islands who produce *pukamani* funerary poles (*see* §II, 5 and fig. 8 below), artists seldom receive payment, but they may be fed and looked after while working. Although emphasis is placed on reproducing ancestral forms and there is a general denial of innovation, in reality considerable room for individual creativity exists. In rare cases, such as among the Tiwi, innovation is overtly encouraged in some contexts (Goodale and Koss), and throughout much of central Australia (*see* §III, 2 below) 'new' designs can enter the system through an individual's dreams, even though ideology will have it that this is simply the rediscovery of pre-existing forms.

BIBLIOGRAPHY

W. E. H. Stanner: *On Aboriginal Religion*, Oceania Monographs, 11 (Sydney, 1966/*R* 1990)
J. C. Goodale and J. D. Koss: 'The Cultural Context of Creativity among Tiwi', *Essays on the Verbal and Visual Arts: Proceedings of the Annual Spring Meeting of the American Ethnological Society: 1967*, pp. 175–91; also in *Anthropology and Art: Readings in Cross-Cultural Aesthetics*, ed. C. M. Otten (Garden City, NY, 1971), pp. 182–200
D. J. Mulvaney: *The Prehistory of Australia: Ancient People and Places* (London, 1969/*R* Ringwood, 1975)
K. Maddock: *The Australian Aborigines: A Portrait of their Society* (London, 1972)
N. D. Munn: *Walbiri Iconography: Graphic Representation and Cultural Symbolism in a Central Australian Society* (Ithaca, NY, 1973)
R. M. W. Dixon: *The Languages of Australia* (Cambridge, 1980)
H. Morphy: 'What Circles Look Like', *Canberra Anthropol.*, iii/1 (1980), pp. 17–36
J. P. White and J. F. O'Connell: *A Prehistory of Australia, New Guinea and Sahul* (Sydney, 1982)
M. Charlesworth and others: *Religion in Aboriginal Australia: An Anthology* (St Lucia, Queensland, London and New York, 1984)
H. Morphy: *Journey to the Crocodile's Nest* (Canberra, Washington, DC, and London, 1984)
F. R. Myers: *Pintubi Country, Pintubi Self: Sentiment, Place and Politics among Western Desert Aborigines* (Washington, DC, Canberra and London, 1986)
N. M. Williams: *The Yolngu and their Land: A System of Land Tenure and the Fight for its Recognition* (Canberra, 1986)
H. Morphy: 'On Representing Ancestral Beings', *Animals into Art*, ed. H. Morphy, One World Archaeology, 7 (London, 1989), pp. 144–60
W. Caruana: *Aboriginal Art*, World A. (London, 1993)
D. Horton, ed.: *Encyclopaedia of Aboriginal Australia*, 2 vols (Canberra, 1994)

II. Traditional art forms.

Aboriginal art is rich in the variety of its forms. The most durable art, and also that for which the earliest evidence exists, is rock art: examples of rock paintings and engravings, or petroglyphs (as they are also known), are found through the Australian continent. A wide variety of abstract and figurative sculptural forms is also produced across Australia, using a rich variety of materials—wood and stone, feathers, grasses and seeds, sand, clays and resins. Sand sculptures, though they sometimes occur separately, often provide the basis for more complex ceremonial constructions combining a variety of different media, such as painting, wooden objects and feather string, within the same overall creation. Perhaps the most widely used medium throughout Australia, however, is the human body. As with rock art, early evidence exists for ornaments and body decorations, both directly in the form of excavated artefacts and indirectly through representations on rock surfaces. Forms of art can also be defined according to their contexts of occurrence. Mortuary art is a particularly important category outside the desert regions. Architectural forms for the most part consisted of temporary constructions, occupied for part of the year only. But even so, bark huts, like most material culture objects, could become the subject or object of art. The use of bark and wood as supports for painting is now widely associated with Aboriginal art production, but it is a relatively recent development (since colonization) and occurs only in northern Australia.

1. INTRODUCTION. Aboriginal designs often exist independently of particular manifestations. The same design may be reproduced in such different art forms as body painting, sand sculpture and rock art. And because designs exist independently of particular objects and media, almost anything can be made into an art object. It may have a design produced on its surface, or it may be incorporated within a ceremonial construction. Producing the work of art often involves fitting the design to the shape of the surface and to the space available.

Most of the materials and techniques employed in the manufacture of everyday objects can be used in the production of art objects. Sculptures are frequently composite forms made from such naturally occurring materials as wood, plant fibres, animal fur, feathers, resins, seeds and beeswax. Numerous pigments are used, including mineral and vegetable dyes, which are combined with many different fixatives such as egg yolk, orchid juice and blood. Four colours (red, yellow, black and white) are most common, although the particular shade chosen may expand the range of variation. With mineral pigments, the source may be as significant as the colour, since particular ochre deposits are often transformations of the blood of specific ancestral beings.

Specialist equipment is limited to the woodworking tools available. Traditionally this would have included stone axes, shell or stone scrapers, engravers made from stone or teeth, and naturally occurring rasps such as the sharkskin employed in Arnhem Land. Pigments are applied by hand or sprayed on by mouth, although in many parts of Australia specialized brushes made from bark and various other fibres were and sometimes still are used.

HOWARD MORPHY

2. Rock art. Most regions of Australia have examples of rock art, which occur on outcrops or under the overhangs of rock shelters. Some regions, such as the Arnhem Land escarpment (*see* §III, 4–5 below) or the western Kimberleys (*see* §III, 3 below), are known for their high density of rock art sites and the distinctive character of the art. Images may be created by additive means, such as painting or drawing, or by extractive techniques, such as pecking, pounding or abrading the outer patinated layer of rock. Painting may be done in natural mineral pigments mixed with water; drawing, which occurs less frequently, uses lumps of dry pigment like crayons. Images created by extractive techniques are conventionally referred to as engravings, although the true engraving technique of incising the rock is uncommon in Aboriginal rock art. Engravings may be tens of millimetres deep or so shallow as to be imperceptible. Newly made engravings are visible due to colour differences between the freshly exposed rock and its patinated surround and in some cases due to the difference in depth. Many rock-engravings are difficult to see except in oblique light conditions, as the exposed rock has weathered back to the same patina as the original rock.

(i) Context and dating. (ii) Stylistic classification.

(i) Context and dating. Pigmented art is known only from rock shelters (usually sandstone or quartzite) where the walls are relatively well protected from rain and other destructive agents. Engravings may also be executed in rock shelters, but they are most abundant on other types of rock exposures. These range from broad, horizontal rock surfaces such as the ridge tops of the Sydney Basin region in south-east Australia to vertical walls of cliffs or boulders, such as those that characterize the massive screes of the Pilbara sites in Western Australia. Some rock art is closely associated with archaeological evidence of camping activities: stone artefacts, food debris and the ash of fires. Other rock art sites have clearly not been used for daily secular activities. In central Queensland, an extensive study of the relationship between paintings and other evidence of shelter use showed that in many cases these paintings were associated with burials (Morwood). There is, however, no consistent correlation between the visual characteristics of the art and the nature of related archaeological evidence.

Recent advances in radiocarbon dating provide new techniques for dating organic matter in pigments and in the patina formed on freshly exposed rock-engravings. Although results obtained to date are experimental, these techniques may eventually prove useful for dating rock art. The principal means of estimating the age of rock art in Australia remains to assess its relationship to other archaeological data. Only rarely has this been achieved by excavation of rock-engravings below archaeological deposits. More commonly, the postulated relationships are indirect, and only fairly broad estimates of the age of various rock art styles can be made. Excavated evidence from Cape York Peninsula (*see* §III, 6 below) suggests that the tradition of rock-engraving in Australia dates back to the late Pleistocene epoch (*c.* 13,000 BP; Rosenfeld, Horton and Winter; *see also* Quinkan galleries). Indirect evidence relating the fauna represented to past environments indicates that some rock paintings in Arnhem Land may be of similar age. Depictions relating to European contact, such as horses, ships or men with guns, show that both rock painting and engraving were carried out in early colonial times. At the end of the 20th century rock painting was still periodically, if rarely, practised in the Kimberleys and in areas in the Northern Territory.

(ii) Stylistic classification. In 1976 Lesley Maynard proposed a threefold classification for all Aboriginal rock art, which she believed showed its chronological development. Though later research has invalidated Maynard's chronological sequence her classifications have provided a framework for analysing the principal stylistic characteristics of Aboriginal rock art throughout the continent. She distinguished between Figurative styles, with images mainly of native fauna and humans (*see* §(b) below), and Non-figurative styles of circles, arcs and other motifs (*see* §(a) below), in which animals are indicated only by their tracks. She named the latter the Panaramittee style, after a locality in the Flinders Ranges. Panaramittee-style sites are most commonly found in the arid zones of the interior, where contemporary art in other media also relies heavily on Non-figurative patterns and tracks. The Figurative art styles are more widely distributed and these were classified by Maynard into the earlier Simple Figurative style and the more recent Complex Figurative style. This chronology was rejected when some of the art styles that she considered to be Complex Figurative were shown to be among the earliest known paintings. As a first guide to the geographical distribution of stylistic preferences, her schema still has value, but some rock art, notably the elaborate stencilled designs of the Carnarvon Ranges in central Queensland (*see* The Tombs), are excluded from this classification.

(a) Non-figurative styles. The arid-zone rock art sites comprise open rock exposures with engravings consisting of a fairly restricted range of motifs, principally circles, arcs, dots, meandering lines and the tracks of macropods, birds (probably emu) and humans, as well as rock shelters with similar motifs in paint. Distinctions between sites, however, can be established through a range of more complex designs, which tend to occur in relatively smaller numbers and vary significantly in form from area to area. Some of the most unusual are the elaborate but schematic, face-like designs of the Cleland Hills, 200 km west of Alice Springs (*see* Thomas Reservoir), the large feathery patterns and stick humans with huge headdresses at N'Dahla Gorge, 90 km east of Alice Springs, and the maze design at Panaramittee in the Flinders Ranges. Most of these engravings are heavily patinated despite their location in arid environments in which rock weathers slowly. This, together with the absence of dingo tracks and a supposed similarity to Tasmanian rock engravings, led R. Edwards to argue for a Pleistocene age for these arid-zone, Non-figurative, Panaramittee-style engravings. Since Tasmania was cut off from the mainland at the end of the Pleistocene epoch, *c.* 12,000 years ago, Edwards considered that this tradition of rock-engraving must have flourished and reached the island before that event. However, a re-evaluation of the Tasmanian engravings has shown that all the known sites (*see* Mt Cameron West) are located

on the present, post-glacial shoreline of the west coast and that they are associated with shell-middens dating no earlier than *c.* 1000 BC, making them a recent development in Tasmanian prehistory. Moreover, the similarity between Tasmanian and Panaramittee-style engravings is of such a generalized nature that an ontogenetic relationship is open to question and difficult to substantiate. The Tasmanian engravings consist almost exclusively of circles, dots and diffuse peck marks, and only at Mt Cameron West are more complex motifs found: some of the circles contain linear infill and are themselves contained within a larger enclosing outline. Similarities with the arid-zone engravings are limited to the shared use of circular motifs and the absence of figurative motifs.

An age of *c.* 10,000 years obtained by radiocarbon dating from calcrete covering the patina of Panaramittee-style engravings at Sturt's Meadow, western New South Wales (*see under* MOOTWINGEE), has confirmed a near-Pleistocene age for the site, although the duration of the tradition as a whole remains unresolved. There are, for instance, striking similarities between the feathery motifs engraved at the Panaramittee-style site of N'Dahla Gorge and recent paintings in one of the shelters at Ayers Rock (Uluru) in the same region. In general, the recent rock-shelter paintings and other art works of the arid zone tend to use complex arrangements with the same range of motifs as those found on the earlier engravings. This seems to indicate a long and continuous artistic tradition.

(b) Figurative styles. Figurative art styles appear to be much more varied than the Panaramittee styles but, to some extent, this diversity results from regional elaborations of a shared body of basic motifs. In most Figurative art styles essentially the same schemata are used for the most commonly depicted animals and for the human form. Larger animals, such as the emu (see fig. 2), are depicted in profile; short-legged or low animals, such as goannas and echidnas, are shown in bird's-eye view. Human figures are generally shown frontally. Female figures are commonly indicated by a lateral displacement of the breasts under the arms, while male figures are distinguished by their genitalia. Sexual exaggeration or overtly sexual themes, however, are rare, except in some sites of the Pilbara in Western Australia. Figures of humans and animals are usually static, and the compositional relationship between figures is often difficult to discern.

In some cases, the repetition of formal arrangements is suggestive of intentional and meaningful composition. For instance, the representation of a long snake superimposed by a number of diverse human and animal figures arranged in a frieze is repeated several times in shelters of the Laura region of Cape York Peninsula. More commonly, painted figures appear to have been placed more or less haphazardly over suitable rock surfaces. In the rock shelters of the Cobar Plain, in south-east Australia, small-scale paintings show groups of seemingly related figures in action (*see* MT GRENFELL). Here groups of men 'dancing', playing clapsticks or spearing game can be identified. Movement is suggested primarily by the angle and positioning of the limbs of the stick human figures and the silhouetted animals. In contrast to this lively style, the larger-scale paintings, such as those in the Laura area (*see* QUINKAN

2. Figurative-style rock painting of an emu with eggs, Laura region, Cape York Peninsula

GALLERIES), are striking in their anatomical and decorative elaboration and in the use of several colours, but their effect is static.

Essentially the same artistic devices as at Laura are reduced to simple outline in the large-scale engravings of the Sydney Basin. The multicoloured paintings of the LIGHTNING BROTHERS, in the north-west of the Northern Territory, are similar in style. In this case, the colourful elaboration is not mere embellishment: black, the colour of strength, highlights the backbone, feet, armpits, eyes and ears of the two mythological figures after whom the site is named, whose eyes must resist the brightness of lightning and whose ears resist the sound of thunder produced by the stamping of their feet.

Probably the most spectacular examples of Figurative rock art are the Wandjina-style paintings of the western Kimberley ranges (*see* §III, 3 and fig. 14 below) and the figures known as 'X-ray paintings' of Western Arnhem Land (*see* §III, 4 below). Both these types of rock paintings are relatively recent. They are still integral to the contemporary Aboriginal cultures of their respective regions. The most characteristic figures of the Kimberley paintings are large-scale human figures depicting ancestral heroes with large helmet-like headdresses that symbolize the storm clouds that herald the rainy season. The paintings are the transformations of the Wandjina spirits who created the land, the people and their laws. Wandjina paintings must be ritually maintained and repainted in order to ensure the continuance of the natural order, the seasons and the abundance of plants and animals. Many paintings in this region show evidence of superimposition, with variation in the details or even fairly substantial modification of the images.

In Western Arnhem Land a complex sequence of changing art styles has been uncovered. Authors differ on the details of the sequences identified but generally agree on the principal stages. The earliest is characterized by large-scale, but static, images of animals and humans painted in red. Some unusual figures among these have been identified as extinct animals and, on this basis, an antiquity of up to 25,000 years has been suggested (Murray and Chaloupka). These identifications, and hence the age of the paintings, are debated. The next recognized stage of paintings, known as the Dynamic style, constitutes the

3. X-ray style rock painting of a barramundi fish, Bala-uru, Deaf Adder Gorge, Western Arnhem Land, early 1900s

most detailed and controlled body of Aboriginal rock art known. The paintings are small-scale (200–300 mm high) and dominated by stylized, long-limbed human figures, whose exaggerated movements create an impression of frenetic activity (for illustration *see* UBIRR). They are adorned with huge headdresses, tassles, dancing skirts and other accessories and are shown carrying or using a range of weapons and other objects. The accompanying animal figures also show much detail of fur, feathers and other features, but their form and proportions are closer to reality. The absence of estuarine and wetlands animal species from this art style suggests that it pre-dates the establishment of the present environment following the post-glacial rise in sea-level *c.* 6500 years ago. The line-work is exceedingly delicate and must have required the use of a fine brush and thorough grinding of pigments to prepare the paints.

The Dynamic style gave way, through a series of less easily defined stages, to the style known as X-ray art. The distinguishing characteristic of this most recent rock art is the formalized depiction of internal organs and of skeletal traits in some animal figures (see fig. 3). Not all the figures in this style are shown with X-ray features. These paintings are considerably larger than those in the earlier Dynamic style, sometimes almost life-size. Fine line-work, intricate, almost geometric design for the X-ray features and the frequent use of a range of colours make this art visually very striking. This style appears to be the immediate precursor of contemporary bark paintings of Western Arnhem Land.

BIBLIOGRAPHY

F. D. McCarthy: *Australian Aboriginal Rock Art* (Sydney, 1958/*R* 1979)
I. M. Crawford: *The Art of the Wandjina: Aboriginal Cave Painting in Kimberley, Western Australia* (Melbourne, 1968)
R. Edwards: 'Art and Aboriginal Prehistory', *Aboriginal Man and Environment in Australia*, ed. D. J. Mulvaney and J. Golson (Canberra, 1972), pp. 356–67
E. J. Brandl: *Australian Aboriginal Paintings in Western and Central Arnhem Land* (Canberra, 1973)
V. Blundell: 'The Wandjina Cave Paintings of North-west Australia', *Arctic Anthropol.*, xi (1974), pp. 213–23
L. Maynard: 'Classification and Terminology of Australian Rock Art', *Australian Institute of Aboriginal Studies Biennial Conference: Canberra, 1974*
——: 'Classification and Terminology in Australian Rock Art', *Form in Indigenous Art: Schematisation in the Art of Aboriginal Australia and Prehistoric Europe*, ed. P. J. Ucko (Canberra, 1977), pp. 387–402
——: 'The Archaeology of Australian Aboriginal Art', *Exploring the Visual Art of Oceania*, ed. S. M. Mead (Honolulu, 1979), pp. 93–110
A. Rosenfeld, D. Horton and J. Winter: *Early Man in North Queensland: Art and Archaeology of the Laura Area* (Canberra, 1981)
E. Godden and J. Malnic: *Rock Paintings of Aboriginal Australia* (Sydney, 1982)
M. Morwood: 'The Prehistory of the Central Queensland Highlands', *Adv. World Archaeol.*, iii (1984), pp. 325–80
G. Chaloupka: 'Chronological Sequence in Arnhem Land Plateau Rock Art', *Archaeological Research in Kakadu National Park*, ed. R. Jones (Canberra, 1985), pp. 269–80
R. Layton: 'The Cultural Context of Hunter-Gatherer Rock Art', *Man*, xx/3 (1985), pp. 434–53
A. Rosenfeld: *Rock Art Conservation in Australia* (Canberra, 1985)
P. Murray and G. Chaloupka: 'The Dreamtime Animals: Extinct Megafauna in Arnhemland Rock Art', *Archaeol. Oceania*, xix (1986), pp. 105–16
R. Layton: *Australian Rock Art: A New Synthesis* (Cambridge, 1992)
G. L. Walsh: *Bradshaws: Ancient Rock Paintings of North-west Australia* (Geneva, 1994)
For earlier sources *see* the bibliography under §VII below.

ANDRÉE ROSENFELD

3. SCULPTURE. Using a broad definition of sculpture, most Aboriginal three-dimensional objects can be grouped into one of the following categories: carvings, moulded forms, constructions using several different media, assemblages and installations, and sand or ground sculpture. These categories should not be considered as exhaustive or closed: for example, a 'stuffed emu', recorded as having been used in an initiation ceremony in New South Wales in the 1870s, falls outside these groupings.

Most examples of Aboriginal sculpture found in permanent collections are sacred and depict ancestral beings, totemic heroes or mythological events. They thus refer either directly or obliquely to specific sites in Aboriginal religious geography and tend to express the association of specific groups of people with those places. Besides their mythological import, many also had ceremonial functions.

An increasing proportion of new Aboriginal sculpture, especially that produced since the 1950s, is non-sacred. The more secular works range widely, from those made for love magic to those that focus primarily on contemporary politics, for example *Maralinga* (1990; Perth, A.G. W. Australia; Crumlin, p. 106) by LIN ONUS. Many sculptures created specifically for the smaller artefact market have human or animal subjects, for example, the wooden figure of a *Darwin Policeman* (1964; Perth, U. W. Australia, Berndt Mus. Anthropol.) by MITHINARI (see Berndt, Berndt & Stanton, p. 130); a human-headed gypsum pipe bowl (*c.* 1920s; Adelaide, S. Austral. Mus.; see 1988–9 exh. cat., p. 198) by Jim Kite (*b c.* 1870s); birds made by Malangawa from buffalo horns (see Berndt and Phillips, p. 302); and the large number of wooden reptiles made in Central Australia and found widely in souvenir shops (see Brokensha).

(i) Carvings. (ii) Moulded forms. (iii) Constructions. (iv) Assemblages and installations. (v) Sand sculpture.

(i) Carvings. The most widespread category of Aboriginal sculpture is carving in wood. Such sculptures are frequently painted, incised or branded and sometimes complemented with fibre, feather or other symbolic attachments. Fragmentary records from the 19th century and the early 20th

indicate that wooden effigies of totemic and ancestral beings were used in ceremonies in both south-west and south-east Australia; carved sacred objects were also found in the latter region. But apart from the carved trees of New South Wales, with their highly varied geometric religious designs (*see* §III, 1(ii) below), and the cylindro-conical stones (or cylcons) of the Darling River area, few if any free-standing carved works survive from colonial or pre-colonial times in this region. Some affinity with sculpture in the round is exhibited by innovative relief-carving of implements, emu eggs and walking sticks from the Flinders Ranges, Adelaide and northern New South Wales, engraved pearl shells from the central and north-west regions and the extensive south-east Australian tradition of geometric incision of weapons (*see* §III, 1(i) and fig. 13 below).

Wooden figures of anthropomorphic ancestral beings, spirits, totemic animals and human beings are common in north-east Arnhem Land, as are sacred clan emblems (*rangga*), dancing-poles, memorial posts, representations of heads of deceased people and log bone-receptacles. Perhaps the most massive of all Aboriginal wooden sculptures are the poles used in the Kunapipi ceremonies of north-east Arnhem Land, which are up to 8 m high. The elongated Mimi figures of Western Arnhem Land are an energetic development in the adjacent region from the 1970s. Their impact is well matched by that of elaborately constructed ceremonial carvings from the Aurukun region in Cape York Peninsula, such as a totemic cult sculpture representing the culture hero Nhampa-Ngulpanh, which was photographed during a ceremonial performance in 1962 (Canberra, N. Mus.; see fig. 4; *see also* §III, 6 and fig. 17 below).

From Cape York in the east to the Kimberleys in the north-west, a basic commonality prevails of visual conventions, techniques and materials in wooden anthropomorphic sculpture. Somewhat culturally distinctive, the Tiwi of Bathurst and Melville Islands are noted for their tradition of monumental graveposts (see fig. 8 below), carved and painted in a vast variety of geometric and naturalistic designs, as well as for their powerful ironwood figures of people and animals and their elaborately serrated spears. Carved stone works were first produced in the Kimberleys in the 1960s and consist principally of human heads.

Anthropomorphic carvings in wood from desert Australia are far rarer than in the tropical north but include remarkable engraved spirit-child figures from Jigalong, unpainted and smooth human figures from Docker River and Yuendumu (e.g. Adelaide, S. Austral. Mus.) and powerful painted figures produced in Utopia in the 1980s. The Central and Western Desert areas are better known for the sacred, non-public slabs of stone and wood (*tjurunga*), which bear highly schematic and geometric engraved representations of ancestral beings, sites and mythic events, and also for the way-markers (*toas*) of the Lake Eyre area, which appear to have had a public role but a similar iconography to that of more restricted objects (see fig. 5). Small ritual icons of painted wood have also been recorded from Kununurra in the north-west, Victoria River in north-central Australia and Groote Eylandt in the Gulf of Carpentaria.

(ii) Moulded forms. These include the small beeswax figures of north-east Arnhem Land and Cape York Peninsula; clay heads used for sorcery in Western Arnhem Land;

4. Carved totemic cult sculpture representing the culture hero Nhampa-Ngulpanh, wood with paint and other materials, from Aurukun, Cape York Peninsula, 1962 (Canberra, National Museum of Australia); from a photograph by Fred McCarthy taken during a ceremonial performance, 1962

5. Carved way-markers (*toas*), wood with paint and other materials, h. 150–450 mm, from the area of Lake Eyre, central Australia, *c.* 1905 (Adelaide, South Australian Museum)

early works in mud by the Kimberleys artist Dodo (*b* 1910); gypsum grave-markers of far western New South Wales; and many of the gypsum forms moulded on to way-markers in southern central Australia. In the early 19th century, images of totemic animals and human figures in clay or grass were observed at an initiation ceremony in south-east Queensland. This suggests that such forms were not restricted to the arid and tropical zones. The work of Thancoupie (*b* 1937) of Cape York Peninsula is one of few forays into ceramic sculpture by an Aboriginal artist (*see* §IV below).

(iii) Constructions. Among the most spectacular of Aboriginal religious sculptures are constructions, usually consisting of a wooden base or frame to which hair-string, twine, feathers, moulded wax or gypsum and a wide variety of other objects may be attached. These were frequently worn fixed to the bodies of ceremonial performers or were carried by them, the boundary between ritual apparel and sculpture being thus blurred. In central Australia the most notable of such constructions are the *waninga* (or *wanigi*) string crosses and decorated *tnatantja* poles. Up to 5 m high, these sculptures are of astonishing beauty and variety but are largely kept hidden from public view. Trees, 'fantastically crowned at the summit', which from their description sound similar, were observed at a ceremonial ground in south-east Queensland in 1824; and inverted trees topped with bark lacework were seen at an initiation in the same region a few years later.

Like *waninga*, small public ritual icons in north-east Arnhem Land also combine wood with string and feathers in their construction. The ritual body-masks of Princess Charlotte Bay, Lockhart River and Pennefather River, all in Cape York Peninsula, and the complex tin, string and wood mythic emblems (or 'portable scenery') of ceremonies at Mowanjum, Western Australia, are among the most elaborate and arresting constructions borne by ceremonial performers in Australia. By contrast, a simple Tasmanian model raft collected in 1843 (Oxford U., Pitt Rivers Mus.) is at the humbler end of the construction scale.

(iv) Assemblages and installations. These normally combine a set of different sculptures of the categories already discussed. Tiwi graveposts, for example, are clustered at the grave, and a number of Aurukun installations consist of a dozen or more individual sculptures suspended from a rail resting on forked posts. Large sacred objects were observed *c.* 1812 in a bower construction on an island in the Gulf of Carpentaria. The assemblage of carved skulls, bones and implements, known both as *Violent Death* and *Carving of Bones* (1982; Darwin, Museums & A. Gals N. Territ.), by the innovative Arnhem Land artist Njinawanga (*b* 1947) has a powerful narrative structure.

BIBLIOGRAPHY

U. H. McConnell: 'Native Arts and Industries on the Archer, Kendall and Holroyd Rivers, Cape York Peninsula, North Queensland', *Rec. S. Austral. Mus.*, xi (1953), pp. 1–42
C. P. Mountford and R. Tonkinson: 'Carved and Engraved Human Figures from North Western Australia', *Anthropol. Forum*, ii/3 (1969), pp. 371–90
R. M. Berndt and E. S. Phillips, eds: *The Australian Aboriginal Heritage: An Introduction through the Arts* (Sydney, 1973)
P. Brokensha: *The Pitjantjatjara and their Crafts* (Sydney, 1975)
Aboriginal Australia (exh. cat. by C. Cooper and others, Sydney, Austral. Gal. Directors Council, 1981–2)
R. M. Berndt, C. H. Berndt and J. E. Stanton: *Aboriginal Australian Art: A Visual Perspective* (Sydney, 1982)
J. Isaacs: *Thancoupie the Potter* (Sydney, 1982)
K. Akerman and P. Bindon: 'Love Magic and Style Changes within One Class of Love Magic Objects', *Oceania*, lvii/1 (1986), pp. 22–32
P. Jones and P. Sutton: *Art and Land: Aboriginal Sculptures of the Lake Eyre Region* (Adelaide, 1986)
J. Hoff: *Tiwi Graveposts* (Melbourne, 1988)
Dreamings: The Art of Aboriginal Australia (exh. cat., ed. P. Sutton; New York, Asia Soc. Gals; U. Chicago, IL, Smart Mus. A.; Melbourne, Mus. Victoria; Adelaide, S. Austral. Mus.; 1988–90)
B. J. Dodo, K. Akerman and K. McKelson: *Kimberley Sculpture* (exh. cat., Perth, 1989)
R. Crumlin, ed.: *Aboriginal Art and Spirituality* (exh. cat., Canberra, High Court of Australia, 1991)

PETER SUTTON

(v) Sand sculpture. Sand sculptures generally consist of engraved lines or ridges of sand or earth on a flat area of ground, or of shaped mounds forming simple bas-reliefs. Intimately linked to places, terrestrial and celestial, they form a focus for ritual and dance, and as such are not primarily a mode of personal expression but an aspect of religious practice. They sometimes incorporate holes, leaves, rocks, sticks or carved objects, and even fire or water at a certain stage of the ritual. The term 'sand sculpture' is used to refer to three-dimensional designs in contrast to ground paintings, which are two-dimensional. Since both forms exploit the same materials and occur in similar contexts, this distinction is somewhat arbitrary for Aborigines. However, sand drawings, used by the Walpiri people in central Australia (*see* §III, 2 below), are considered to be different despite their visual resemblance, as they are an informal improvisational aspect of story-telling. Sand sculpture is also closely related to other media of expression, especially paintings in ochres on the body and on bark (*see* §§4 and 7 below), and in the south-east on carved trees (*see* §III, 1(ii) below).

Many sand sculptures made by the Yolngu people of north-east Arnhem Land are formed from simple geometric shapes, such as circles and semicircles, squares and rectangles, parallel lines, lenses, diamonds and triangles. While all are 'iconic', albeit schematized, some are more obviously figurative, such as a depiction of the dugout canoe belonging to Dingo Ancestor. They are employed primarily in mortuary ceremonies (*see* §5 below), especially water, fire and smoke purification rites (see fig. 6), as well as in ceremonies in which the disinterred bones of the dead are crushed and placed in a hollow-log coffin. For example, the Bukulup (washing) ceremony is performed for the purification of the close relatives of a person who has recently died. Men of a patrilineal clan sing throughout the day in the camp while a man of the clan or the son of a woman of the clan makes a sand sculpture in a cleared area, usually *c.* 5 m or more across. Near sunset others begin to gather; a few at a time stand in the sand sculpture, which depicts a lagoon or spring at the clan's country, while others pour water over them as a clan leader calls out names of the ancestors. In this way an ancestral waterhole is recreated wherever the ceremony is enacted, perhaps far from the country represented. In other ceremonies a simple sand sculpture forms the arena for dances.

The sand sculptures of the Yolngu are simplified, geometric versions of painted ancestral designs. As such, they have many possible interpretations, of varying degrees of secrecy. Each is a kind of map of the clan's country and a depiction of its ancestral beings and sacred objects, which are transformations of some attribute of an ancestor. The design is also specific to the clan that owns the country, while being similar in form to the designs of clans with the same ancestral being. The design thus encodes the connection between ancestor, place, the sacred object that the ancestor put into the country and the group that he or she created, as well as connections with other countries and clans related to the ancestral journey.

Sand engravings formerly used in the Burbung initiation ceremonies of the Wiradjuri people of New South Wales were both figurative and geometric. Some depicted anthropomorphic spirit beings, while others took the form of animals such as kangaroos and emus. The dominant geometric forms were meandering parallel lines, concentric circles and squares, and combinations and elaborations of these figures. The designs that depicted various aspects of ancestral beings, such as the Sky Being Biame, were revealed to male initiates and formed the focus of dances. One design, for example, represented the mounds in which mound-building birds incubated their eggs.

6. Sand sculpture made in connection with a Yolngu smoke purification ceremony by the Daygurrgurr Gupapuyungu clan at Ngangalala, Eastern Arnhem Land; from a photograph by Ian Keen, 1975

BIBLIOGRAPHY

R. H. Mathews: 'The Burbung of the Wiradthuri Tribes', *J. Anthropol. Inst. GB & Ireland*, xxv (1896), pp. 295–318, pls xxv–xxviii; xxvi (1897), pp. 272–85

R. M. Berndt: *Australian Aboriginal Religion* (Leiden, 1974)

M. Clunies Ross and L. R. Hiatt: 'Sand Sculptures at a Gidjingali Burial Rite', *Form in Indigenous Art: Schematisation in the Art of Aboriginal Australia and Prehistoric Europe*, ed. P. J. Ucko (Canberra, 1977), pp. 131–46

I. Keen: 'Yolngu Sand Sculptures in Context', *Form in Indigenous Art: Schematisation in the Art of Aboriginal Australia and Prehistoric Europe*, ed. P. J. Ucko (Canberra, 1977), pp. 165–83

H. Morphy: 'Yingapungapu: Ground Sculpture as Bark Painting', *Form in Indigenous Art: Schematisation in the Art of Aboriginal Australia and Prehistoric Europe*, ed. P. J. Ucko (Canberra, 1977), pp. 205–9

IAN KEEN

4. BODY DECORATION. Throughout Aboriginal Australia, adult men and women decorate their bodies and those of their children in many different ways. Decorative items that are worn include necklets, chaplets, waist- and armbands and pubic coverings. The naked body is a natural medium for painting. This is usually done by someone else for a particular reason, sometimes simply for enjoyment or enhancement of personal appearance, but more often it has some form of religious or magical significance, specifically identifying a person as a participant within a ritual or ceremony. Most parts of the body are decorated; designs cover the face, chest, thighs and upper legs and continue over the shoulders to the back.

A more permanent form of decoration, common in most Aboriginal areas, is scarring or cicatrization. Designs are usually arranged across the chest or arms and sometimes on the legs, to indicate the death of a close relative or spouse. On Melville and Bathurst Islands, for example, scarring called *miunga* covers both sides of the upper back as well as the upper and outer parts of the arms and thighs of men and women. Horizontal lines are also made across the chest and forehead. The V-shaped designs represent fronds of the zamia palm or barbs of spears. Such body decoration is apparently carried out in youth, but not as part of a formal rite. However, in north-central South Australia and some southern parts of the Western Desert, scarring constitutes part of the ritual process during the Wilyaru initiation of youths. Parallel cicatrices cut on the back of a novice are said to represent the marks on the mythic Lizard Man who instituted this ritual in the Dreaming.

Among the extensive range of body designs specific to any one region, each design or series of designs symbolizes particular mythic characters and relates to their activities in the creative era of the Dreaming. Moreover, the designs are usually linked directly to specific parts of the landscape. Often a highly stylized configuration is a shorthand statement of the topography associated with, or shaped by, these mythic beings. Men or women wearing these painted designs in ritual must be affiliated, by birth or in some other special way, to the body of myths concerned.

7. Body decoration of actors in the Djanba (mythical being) series of the Gadjari fertility ritual, Kalumburu, northern Kimberleys; from a photograph by J. E. Stanton, 1963

Since the aim of ritual is to bring about such events or conditions as the renewal of natural species, fertility of the land and the social well-being of the group, the actions of mythic beings must be replicated and the original scene of the Dreaming re-enacted as closely as possible. Actors, according to their ritual role and body painting, are believed to assume the character and quality of a Dreaming personage or natural species symbolizing that being. Body painting is therefore a means of ensuring the spiritual presence of these deities at a ritual.

In the secret–sacred rites the actual painting is part of the ritual itself, which is accompanied by songs or the retelling of the appropriate mythological accounts. The painting process can take several hours, especially in north-east Arnhem Land (see fig. 17 below) where the chest designs extend down the front of the legs to the knees. A person's body is prepared for painting by removing hair and smearing the skin with red ochre. The pigments used—red and yellow ochre, white pipeclay and black manganese or charcoal—are crushed on flat stones and mixed with water. They are applied with burred twigs, orchid roots or stems, sometimes with the fingers and, in Arnhem Land, with a brush made from human hair.

In central Australia and some other regions extensive use is made of birds' down, usually from eagle nestlings, although other white down and wild cotton are also used. Some of it is rubbed in red ochre while the rest is left in its natural colour (see fig. 7 for an illustration of this practice). After rubbing an initiate's body with red ochre, the basic design is lightly sketched, and the down or cotton is then superimposed, piece by piece, using human blood as an adhesive. The down covers the chest, back, shoulders and thighs. It often extends up the neck and the face and is integrated with an elaborate, usually conical headdress, decorated in the same way and tipped with feathers or a sacred object. In the central Australian area alone, thousands of patterns were used in the various ritual cycles, each clearly distinguishable and specifically related in meaning to a particular Dreaming character or place. For example, the design may refer to a Honey Ant place, the sun, or to some creature such as a bandicoot, emu or snake in the form of a human or natural species.

In northern Australia in the great Kunapipi fertility rituals feather down is also used in body designs together with elaborate extensions in the form of headdresses. The meanings of these relate to the great northern epic concerning the mythological travels of the two Wawilak Sisters, who were swallowed by the Yulunggul Snake, which eventually led to the onset of the monsoonal season. Among these designs, Yulunggul is referred to by cabbage trees associated with him as well as by lightning and by various creatures that became sacred by jumping into his watering-place. As the Kunapipi ritual spread south-westwards, it became known as Gadjari ('Old Woman' or 'Mother') and body painting resembling that of the Western Desert was incorporated (see fig. 7).

In Queensland, mainly in the Boulia area but also spreading into north-eastern South Australia, dancer–actors are painted to represent an unpredictable spirit, Molonga, in ceremonies witnessed by both men and women. They wear a bound and feathered conical headdress and their body designs consist of two red bands across the face and forehead with long bands down the body.

The body painting of women, although similar in many respects to men's, differs in meaning and sometimes in intention. Girls' puberty rites, while structurally comparable to the initiation of male youths, are shorter and generally less of a social occasion. The associated body painting is also less complex in most areas. In the Boulia area a girl is decorated with bands of charcoal and feather down: painted men and women dance to welcome her on her return to the main camp. Among the Aranda of central Australia, she is finally decorated with a headband, tips of bandicoot tails, necklets and string armlets, and her body is painted with a mixture of fat and red ochre. Actual body designs are apparently rare in female puberty rites: an example from Western Arnhem Land, however, is the painting of a crescent moon in white clay below the breasts, intended symbolically to regulate the girl's menstrual flow. On occasion, a naturalistic representation of Ngalyod, the Rainbow Serpent, is also used.

Body painting has particularly flourished within the sphere of women's secret–sacred rituals, especially in the west-central sector of the Northern Territory, west into the Kimberleys and throughout the Western Desert. In the Northern Territory there are two primary ritual–myth sequences: the Yawalyu and the Djarada (or Yilbindji). The Yawalyu, with wider connotations and more direct and powerful Dreaming implications, is concerned with the re-enactment and symbolic interpretation of mythological events and characters and with their territorial associations. In the Djarada the focus is on the supernatural powers of the two Dreaming Munga-munga women and on harnessing their powers for personal use (i.e. desirability to men, and healing). Indirectly, the concern is with fertility, since the Munga-munga are daughters of the great

8. Mortuary posts (*pukamani*) erected by the Tiwi, carved wood, h. *c.* 2–5.5 m, Snake Bay, Melville Island; from a photograph by M. Brandl, 1968

Gadjari (Kunapipi). In this ritual the bodies of participants are painted with ochre on a background of animal fat. Since the songs relevant to any Djarada ritual are arranged in series, distinctive sets of designs are correspondingly used. For example, rows of dots and bands with central, stylized configurations of genitalia represent the original patterns believed to have been worn by the Munga-munga. Other bands depict boomerangs and the grooves made by the Munga-munga's dancing feet. *Yawalyu* designs include representations of the Rainbow Serpent and the dangerous Djundagal snake; particular sites associated with mythic beings; clouds, water, rain and thunderbolts; red dust tossed about by a whirlwind; goanna tracks; stone spear-heads; and various creatures.

In almost all sacred ritual, whether for males or females, the most important of the mythic beings and the most elaborate and symbolically significant of these sacred designs are revealed only towards the end of a ritual sequence. Body painting and associated paraphernalia are essentially a kind of camouflage, intended to provide an extra dimension to the person painted, hiding his or her own human identity in the manifestation of a supernatural one—that of a Dreaming deity.

BIBLIOGRAPHY

W. E. Roth: *Ethnological Studies among the North-west-central Queensland Aborigines* (Brisbane, 1897)
W. B. Spencer and F. J. Gillen: *The Native Tribes of Central Australia* (London, 1899/*R* 1969)
T. G. H. Strehlow: *Aranda Traditions* (Melbourne, 1947)
C. H. Berndt: 'Women's Changing Ceremonies in Northern Australia', *L'Homme*, i (Paris, 1950)
C. P. Mountford: *The Tiwi: Their Art, Myth and Ceremony* (London, 1958)
R. M. Berndt, ed.: *Australian Aboriginal Art* (Sydney, 1964/*R* 1968)
R. M. Berndt and C. H. Berndt: *The World of the First Australians: An Introduction to the Traditional Life of the Australian Aborigines* (London and Canberra, 1964/*R* Canberra, 1988)
N. D. Munn: *Walbiri Iconography: Graphic Representation and Cultural Symbolism in a Central Australian Society* (Ithaca, NY, 1973, rev. Chicago, 1986)
R. M. Berndt: *Australian Aboriginal Religion* (Leiden, 1974)
H. Morphy: Ancestral Connections: Art and an Aboriginal System of Knowledge (Chicago, IL, 1991)

CATHERINE H. BERNDT

5. MORTUARY ART. In their concern about the fate of their dead, Aborigines generally believe that spirits eventually find their way to the land of the dead, where they are reunited with the Dreaming deities, or that they return to their own countries, perhaps to be reborn. Regional attitudes toward these beliefs and to related artistic expressions vary considerably. Highly developed and distinctive forms of mortuary art are characteristic of the northern coastal regions of Australia and to some extent the tablelands of New South Wales. In other areas, art forms clustered around the rites of death were and are less spectacular.

The Tiwi of Bathurst and Melville Islands prepare and erect wooden posts on and around a grave about two months after a death (see fig. 8). These posts, the rituals associated with them, the mourners and the corpse before burial are all termed *pukamani*, connoting a taboo condition. Rituals involving a wide range of dancing by men and women extend intermittently over three months or more. There is also ritual feeding of the 'workers' who cut, carve, decorate and erect the posts. Posts erected before the 1930s tend to be limited in their range of designs, with openings and projections at the apex. By the mid-1950s the designs had become more varied and innovative; many posts are surmounted by naturalistic human and spirit figures, as well as other creatures. Stylized designs are painted in ochres on their trunks. Apart from the more readily identifiable naturalistic representations, some of the upper parts of posts bear depictions such as limbs of trees, women's breasts, rocks, windows and doors. In their total conception most represent the deceased persons or their close relatives, while the designs, either carved or painted, refer to events in those persons' lives.

When the posts are brought to a graveside from the secluded places where they have been made, they are erected amid highly emotional scenes. Mourners throw themselves on the grave; men dance around the posts, while both men and women sing personal songs of grief. The posts are not only memorials to the dead, but are believed to house temporarily the dead person's spirit. Such spirits (*mopaditi*) are considered unpredictable. They remain at or near their graves both because they resent their death and are ready to blame the living for it and because they are attached to their relatives. On completion of the rituals, they leave for the land of the dead, or their particular countries. During the dancing, participants are decorated, some with ornate facial and body designs, and they wear various items, all of which are specifically named. Women wear chaplets of human-hair string with dog-tail tips. Men hold between their teeth a ball pendant of feathers, stained with mixed red and yellow ochres, and wear painted bark armlets with projecting decorations of feathers, sometimes ornamented with red seeds. Those dancing carry discs. Men also wave intricately carved and painted spears, made as gifts to the dead. At the conclusion of the rites the beards of the chief male mourners are plucked and the decorations are washed from their bodies, signifying that they are now released from their *pukamani* responsibilities and that the spirits of the dead have left the grave site. The posts are left to rot on the grave.

The mortuary art of the Yolngu of north-east Arnhem Land encompasses a wide variety of forms, easily differentiated from those of the Tiwi. They include decorated hollow logs, ground structures, wooden figures and flags. Although most corpses are now buried, traditionally a dead person was painted with his or her sacred clan designs and then exposed on a platform awaiting decomposition, so that the bones could be collected. After some months or even years, when the bones were ready for collection, they were covered in red ochre and placed temporarily in a painted bark coffin. The dead person's skull was cleaned and painted with its emblematic design and then worn as a shoulder-necklet by a widow or close female relative in memory of the dead person. Later, a tall hollow log (*laragidj*) was prepared and painted, and the bones broken up and placed inside. The log was then ritually erected in the main camp and left to disintegrate; finally its remains were scattered across the camp. The designs painted in ochre on the trunks of the logs represent the clan emblem of the dead man or woman. They vary according to the person's moiety affiliation and refer to his or her country and its mythological associations. Moreover, the logs themselves are often carved into highly conventionalized representations of a mythic creature such as a fish, an animal, a natural object or a feature related to the clan's mythology. Ground structures consisting of a complex patterning of sand mounds are topographic and mythological representations of the deceased's country.

Each of the two patrilineal intermarrying moieties, Dhuwa and Yirritja, has its own substantiating mythological repertory that sponsors not only the use of particular designs but also different objects. That relating to the Dhuwa moiety focuses mainly on the Banumbir 'Morning Star' song cycle in which spirits at Bralgu, the land of the dead, send out that star to their living relatives. In the actual mortuary rituals, long dancing-poles with lengths of feathered string and feather balls are used to signify this daily occurrence. The Yirritja moiety includes, among other things, a *wuramu* post figure representing either the deceased's image or a mythic or historical character. The *wuramu* tradition is usually associated with Indonesian ('Macassan') traders from the Celebes who visited the north Australian coast *c.* 1600–1900. During a delayed mortuary ritual, a carved wooden figure called a 'collection man', with feathered-string arms, is first carried through the camp and anything that is left lying around is collected to compensate the men responsible for making it. Afterwards it is erected near the deceased's camp to the accompaniment of songs and dancing relating to these early Indonesian visits. Masts and specially designed flags are used symbolically to bid farewell to the spirit of the dead. The figures represent Indonesians, the Dutch (*balanda*, now a general term for Europeans) or effigies of specific dead persons. The wide range of innovative designs of these sculpted figures often contrasted markedly with those produced by members of the Dhuwa moiety.

While in north-east Arnhem Land hollow logs are primarily of mortuary significance, in western and southern Arnhem Land their use in this context is combined with the initiation of young men. Mythologically, the ritual associated with this concerned Moon Man, who tried to persuade Red-Eyed Pigeon Man to do as he did—not to die permanently, but to return regularly to the world of the living; Pigeon Man was not convinced, and that is why human beings die physically. The Lorgun rites (the term refers to both the ritual and the actual hollow log) take place when the moon is waning, some time after a death. The log (*lorgun*) is relatively short compared with the north-east Arnhem Land variety; it has a V-shaped 'mouth' and is hung with lengths of feathered string. When people arrive for the rites, the deceased's mother or another close female relative prepares the dancing ground and then calls the men to paint themselves. Novices are brought forward to witness the dances and are told they must now observe a number of food taboos. Eventually the log is brought from its hiding place and the deceased person's bones are removed from their stringybark bundles and placed into the receptacle. As the last bones are put in, a song is sung whose words refer to the dead person's spirit diving into the sea. To the accompaniment of wailing, the log is erected in the main camp at sunrise and left there to disintegrate.

Among the people of the Wiradjuri and Kamilaroi language groups of the New South Wales tablelands carved trees feature in mortuary rites. Within a clearing where a grave has been dug, up to four adjacent trees are engraved boldly with geometrical, stylized designs arranged within a long oval of natural bark. These are said to be 'totemic' in significance, although their meanings have not been recorded. It seems that they symbolize the pathway that the spirit of the dead should take to its ultimate resting place in the Skyworld. According to reports, only important persons were given this form of burial and, like the Lorgun rites of the north, such rites were also relevant to male initiation.

Complex 'rituals of death' are observed in most areas of Aboriginal Australia, but they rarely involve the elaborate aesthetic manifestations common in northern Australia. This undoubtedly reflects the need felt in the north to retain an individual's personal identification after death, defining his or her role within the land of the dead. Aboriginal groups living in areas of northern Australia maintained complex forms of mortuary ritual into the late 20th century (*see* §III, 6 and fig. 17 below). In contrast, in New South Wales and other parts of Australia there is less emphasis on the aesthetic aspects and more on the social transformation, the depersonalization and merging of the deceased within the reservoir of the dead who are subject to being channelled back into the world of the living.

BIBLIOGRAPHY

H. Basedow: 'Anthropological Notes on the Western Coastal Tribes of the Northern Territory of South Australia', *Trans. Royal Soc. S. Australia*, xxxi (1907), pp. 1–62

W. B. Spencer: *Native Tribes of the Northern Territory of Australia* (London, 1914)

W. L. Warner: *A Black Civilization: A Social Study of an Australian Tribe* (New York and London, 1937, rev. 1958)

C. H. Berndt: 'Expressions of Grief among Aboriginal Women', *Oceania*, xx (1950), pp. 286–332

F. D. McCarthy: *Australia's Aborigines: Their Life and Culture* (Melbourne, 1957)

C. P. Mountford: *The Tiwi: Their Art, Myth and Ceremony* (London, 1958)

J. C. Goodale: 'The Tiwi Dance for the Dead', *Expedition*, ii/1 (autumn 1959), pp. 3–13

R. M. Berndt and C. H. Berndt: *The World of the First Australians: An Introduction to the Traditional Life of the Australian Aborigines* (London and Canberra, 1964/*R* Canberra, 1988)

——: *Man, Land and Myth in North Australia: The Gunwinggu People* (Sydney, 1970)

R. M. Berndt and E. S. Phillips, eds: *The Australian Aboriginal Heritage: An Introduction through the Arts* (Sydney, 1973, rev. 1978)

R. M. Berndt: *Australian Aboriginal Religion* (Leiden, 1974)

R. M. Berndt, C. H. Berndt and J. E. Stanton: *Aboriginal Australian Art: A Visual Perspective* (Sydney, 1982)

H. Morphy: *Journey to the Crocodile's Nest* (Canberra, 1984)

——: *Ancestral Connections: Art and an Aboriginal System of Knowledge* (Chicago, IL, 1991)

RONALD M. BERNDT

6. ARCHITECTURE. Indigenous Aboriginal architecture of north Australia has been well documented, but knowledge is sparse for the centre and the south. The dominant functional category was domestic shelter, the principal purpose of which was to protect against the weather. Separate shelters were used in settlements for diurnal activities, when men and women often congregated apart, and for nocturnal gatherings when nuclear families

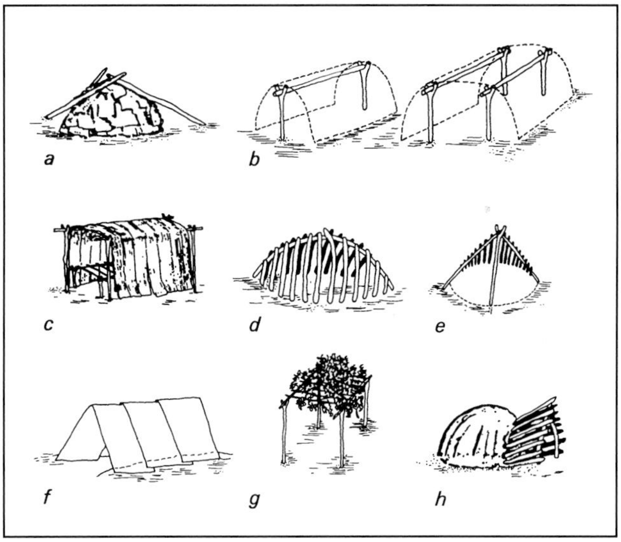

9. Types of Aboriginal shelter: (a) paperbark dome shelter; (b) single and double ridge vault types; (c) vaulted shelter with sleeping platform; (d) rigid bough structure for dome; (e) conical structure for dome; (f) folded plate shelter of stringybark; (g) shade shelter; (h) dome with porch

resided together. People either sat or lay inside shelters, so that these were consistently low (h. 1.2–1.5 m). There was also a wide distribution of common structural principles and forms, but materials and construction details were subject to regional variations. The mobile hunter–gatherer life style resulted in impermanent structures that were not technologically specialized and up to seven or eight shelter types might be employed during the changing seasons.

Two examples from the northern monsoonal coasts exemplify the influence of materials on form. The most suitable claddings were bark sheets from *Melaleuca leucadendron* (paperbark) and *Eucalyptus tetradontra* (stringybark). Paperbark is very flexible and thus suitable for making a dome over a structure of pliable saplings (see fig. 9a). At the start of the wet season, this coastal type was occupied with the opening sealed off and filled with smoke to repel mosquitoes. In contrast to paperbark, stringybark can bend in only one direction. As the wet season continued, the stringybark could be prised off its trunk and used in a range of vaulted forms supported on both single and double ridge-poles (9b). To avoid the boggy ground a further elaboration was a sleeping platform under which fires could be burnt to repel mosquitoes (9c).

In Arnhem Land the forked post and crosspole of this type of structure are still esteemed as religious objects rich in meaning. Their significance derives from the mythological activities of the Wawilak Sisters, ancestral heroines who built the first vaulted dwelling in the region. Among the many interpretations, one clan regards the horns of the fork as a personal totem representing red noses, fire, blood and the wet mud of a sacred well from which sacred objects emerged (Reser, 1977).

Domes covered either circular or elliptical ground-plans up to 3.6 m in diameter according to the size of the occupant group. A common type in the arid interior had a framework of rigid curved boughs (9d). Cladding was of thatched grass, foliage or reeds, sometimes with a coating of mud or clay, possibly for insulation against extremes of temperature or to keep off rain; examples have been recorded in all conditions. For the south-east of the continent there are reports of domes supported on low, circular stone walls. Conical forms were less common but nevertheless widely distributed (9e). A cubic wet-weather structure has been documented at two locations in the Gulf of Carpentaria (Biernoff; Memmott). A more complex architectural form was built by a sedentary group in the north Queensland rain-forest. Clusters of intersecting domes were clad with layers of palm-leaves plaited on to cane frames, covered with an outer skin of another type of leaf and overlaid with cane sticks for further stability. These domes were large enough to stand up in and were occupied by several families (Koettig).

Stringybark was also used for unsupported structures of both a folded plate (9f) and a barrel vault type. Other common seasonal shelters were windbreaks (linear and circular), open sleeping platforms and tree platforms for flood-prone areas. Shade was provided by implanting leafy boughs in the ground and erecting a horizontal roof structure (9g), or making a lean-to with a ridge-pole. Entry 'porches' were attached to some enclosed shelters (9h).

Apart from shelters, Aboriginal structures included rock-wall fisheries, hunting nets strung between posts, ground ovens, wells, storage platforms and posts, ceremonial stone arrangements and circular mounds, as well as foliage walls, trenches and pit traps for game. Various regional types of structure were used to house the dead: mounds, mounds inside huts, platforms, graves and cylindrical bark coffins (*see* §5 above). These were embellished by the various cultural groups with different types of symbolic markers and objects, including feathers, bones, painted wooden structures, cylindro-conical stones (cylcons), incised bark, carved tree trunks representing the dead person's chest cicatrices, the deceased's possessions and a fire laid ready for use at the time of reincarnation. Complex architectural symbolism was a product of the intellectual preoccupation with cosmology and cosmogony.

BIBLIOGRAPHY

R. B. Smyth: *The Aborigines of Victoria and Other Parts of Australia and Tasmania*, 2 vols (Melbourne and London, 1878)
W. E. Roth: *Ethnological Studies among the North-west-central Queensland Aborigines* (Brisbane, 1897)
T. Worsnop: *The Prehistoric Arts, Manufactures, Works, Weapons, etc. of the Aborigines of Australia* (Adelaide, 1897)
W. Roth: 'North Queensland Ethnography Bulletin No. 16: Huts and Shelters', *Rec. Austral. Mus.*, viii/1 (1910)
D. Thomson: 'The Seasonal Factor in Human Culture', *Proc. Prehist. Soc.*, n. s. 4 (1939), pp. 209–21 [West Cape York Peninsula]
P. Hamilton: 'Aspects of Interdependence between Aboriginal Social Behaviour and the Spatial and Physical Environment', *Aboriginal Housing*, ed. Royal Australian Institute of Architects (Canberra, 1972), pp. 1–13 [desert shelters and camps]
M. Koettig: *Rising Damp: Aboriginal Structures in Perspective* (diss., U. Sydney, 1976)
J. P. Reser: 'The Dwelling as Motif in Aboriginal Bark Painting', *Form in Indigenous Art: Schematisation in the Art of Aboriginal Australia and Prehistoric Europe*, ed. P. J. Ucko (Canberra, 1977), pp. 210–19 [Arnhem Land]
——: 'Values in Bark', *Hemisphere*, xxii/10 (1978), pp. 27–35 [Arnhem Land]
D. Biernoff: 'Traditional and Contemporary Structures and Settlement in Eastern Arnhem Land with Particular Reference to Nunggubuyu', *A Black Reality: Aboriginal Camps and Settlements in Remote Australia*, ed. M. Heppell (Canberra, 1979), pp. 153–79
P. Memmott: 'Lardil Artifacts and Shelters', *Occas. Pap. Anthropol.*, ix (1979), pp. 107–42

PAUL MEMMOTT

7. BARK PAINTING. Elaborately painted sheets of bark have gained appreciation in galleries, museums and private collections and for a while, in the 1960s and later, became almost synonymous with Aboriginal art. This type of bark painting, however, is relatively recent—the product of a gradually developing arts and crafts industry that began with European colonization—and the creation of such works is restricted to one main area, Arnhem Land (*see* §III, 4 and 5 below). In Arnhem Land bark painting is part of an active artistic tradition that continues to be expressed in other media such as body painting, sand sculpture and ceremonial carving, but bark has the advantage of being portable and therefore easily traded with Westerners. Before European colonization, bark painting was apparently carried out in varied traditional contexts over a more widespread area.

(i) Techniques. The bark for painting comes from the local species of stringybark tree and can be obtained most easily when the sap is flowing during the wet season and the following few months. The bark is removed by making two horizontal rings around the trunk with an axe, one close to the base, the second at the top of the trunk. A vertical line is then cut between the two and the sheet of bark is prised away using a pointed stick or lever. The bark is then straightened by laying its outer surface on a gently burning fire and allowing it to uncurl. Following this procedure the outer layer of stringybark is removed and the inner surface is sanded to a smooth finish in preparation for painting. The bark is then left flattened under heavy stones for a few weeks in order to be seasoned and to retain its shape.

Similar techniques are used for painting on bark as on other surfaces, although they vary somewhat according to area. Pigments are produced using natural ochres, pipe clay and charcoal, which are ground on stone palettes and applied with brushes of stringybark, human hair or palm fronds or with commercially made brushes. Natural fixatives, such as gulls' eggs or the juices of a tree orchid, are either added to the pigment or rubbed over the surface to preserve the painting and to add to its sheen. Since the 1960s, however, increasing use has been made of commercial wood glue for this purpose. In north-east Arnhem Land a split stick is fixed across the top and bottom and bound together at either end to keep the bark straight; while in Western Arnhem Land a series of holes are made at the top and bottom of the painting and sticks are bound to it using loops of string.

(ii) Early evidence. Early records for the colonial period suggest that bark may have been used for painting in parts of southern Australia, for example Tasmania, the eastern part of South Australia and Queensland, where there were suitable trees (Groger-Wurm). The reports refer to paintings or drawings on the inside of bark huts or, more rarely, to the use of bark painting in ceremonial contexts. François Péron (1775–1810) provided the earliest published reference (1807) to painted sheets of bark at the site of an

Aboriginal grave on Maria Island, off the east coast of Tasmania. There are other references to drawings in Tasmanian bark huts, including one depicting the bullock carts of an early European colonist, but no paintings survive and little detail has been recorded. Similarly only two works, both from Victoria, have survived from the rest of southern Australia (London, BM; Melbourne, Mus. Victoria). They depict scenes of Aboriginal life engraved on the fire-blackened inner surface of a bark sheet, but they may be atypical.

Traditional contexts for the use of bark painting are much better known from northern Australia. Painting on the inside of wet-season huts seems to have been a common practice in Western Arnhem Land, the region of Darwin and other parts of the tropical north. A few paintings survive from the 1870s and 1880s. The best known are those from the Port Essington region (collected before 1878; U. Sydney, Macleay Mus.) and those from the walls of a dismantled hut collected by Capt. James Carrington in 1887 (Adelaide, S. Austral. Mus.). In 1912 Sir W. Baldwin Spencer (1860–1929) started compiling a major collection of bark paintings from Oenpelli in Western Arnhem Land. He also dismantled wet-season huts but soon began commissioning paintings, resulting in the first commercial bark production. Painting on the inside of bark huts continues in those rare places where the huts are still made. In ceremonial contexts, bark paintings usually occurred on objects made from bark rather than on flattened bark 'canvases'. Among the main bark ceremonial objects in Arnhem Land were the cylindrical stringybark containers in which the remains of dead relatives were kept for several years until the final burial. The Tiwi of Melville and Bathurst Islands used elaborately painted baskets in burial ceremonies (*see* §5 above). There are, however, isolated accounts from as far apart as central Arnhem Land (Warner) and Victoria (Groger-Wurm) of painted bark sheets being used in initiation ceremonies.

(iii) Contemporary work. Bark paintings produced today reflect the range of stylistic characteristics of their region rather than, as formerly, the particular ceremonial context and set of subjects. Following European colonization, bark-painting imagery and styles became a product of the interaction between artists and purchasers. In Western Arnhem Land the emphasis has been on X-ray art (Taylor) with few geometric designs being produced other than those from the Port Keats region west of Darwin, which are predominantly geometric. In Eastern Arnhem Land the full range of regional art styles has been employed (Morphy), with a slight emphasis on the inclusion of a figurative component, as in the bark painting being completed by NARRITJIN MAYMURRU (see fig. 10). Groote Eylandt paintings are mainly figurative and often somewhat starkly outlined on a black background. Paintings from Melville and Bathurst Islands are often based on designs for the Pukamani mortuary ceremony (*see* §5 above).

Although Arnhem Land remains the main area for the production of contemporary bark paintings (see also fig. 15 below), works for sale are also produced by people living in the Kimberleys, where the figurative imagery is mainly of Wandjina ancestral beings (*see* §III, 3 below). The

10. Bark painting being completed by the Yolngu artist Narritjin Maymurru, Yirrkala, Eastern Arnhem Land; from a photograph by Howard Morphy, 1973 (Canberra, National Museum of Australia)

technique was briefly introduced on Mornington Island in north Queensland and in the Cape York Peninsula. In Arnhem Land, however, bark painting is an important economic activity, which also plays a vital role in the indigenous cultural system. It provides the main opportunity for the training of artists and for passing on knowledge about the artistic system. Also, since the imagery painted on bark and other surfaces can only be produced by those with an inherited right to it, bark paintings are used as a means of presenting Aboriginal culture to outsiders.

BIBLIOGRAPHY

F. A. Péron and C. L. de Freycinet: *Voyage de découvertes aux Terres Australes . . . pendant les années 1800, 1801, 1802, 1803 et 1804*, 2 vols (Paris, 1807–16)

W. B. Spencer: *Native Tribes of the Northern Territory of Australia* (London, 1914)

W. L. Warner: *A Black Civilization: A Social Study of an Australian Tribe* (New York and London, 1937, rev. 1958)

C. P. Mountford: *Art, Myth and Symbolism* (1956), i of *Records of the American-Australian Scientific Expedition to Arnhem Land, 1948* (Melbourne, 1956)

H. M. Groger-Wurm: *Eastern Arnhem Land*, i of *Australian Aboriginal Bark Paintings and their Mythological Interpretations*, Australian Aboriginal Studies, 30; Social Anthropology Series, 5 (Canberra, 1973)

H. Morphy: 'Schematisation to Conventionalisation: A Possible Trend in Yirrkala Bark Paintings', *Form in Indigenous Art: Schematisation in the Art of Aboriginal Australia and Palaeolithic Europe*, ed. P. J. Ucko (Canberra, 1977), pp. 198–204

L. Taylor: 'Seeing the "Inside": Kunwinjku Paintings and the Symbol of the Divided Body', *Animals into Art*, ed. H. Morphy, One World Archaeology, 7 (London, 1989), pp. 371–89

HOWARD MORPHY

8. OTHER ARTS. The beauty of other Aboriginal artefacts, such as containers, ornaments, pipes and weapons, is largely due to the way natural resources are used. Ochres, charcoal, clay, plant and hair fibres, root dyes, woods, resins, feathers, teeth, skin and shells are fashioned into objects of simple elegance that contrast sharply with the better-known, bolder and more highly coloured artefacts produced by the Maori people of New Zealand to the east (*see* MAORI, §1) and by the peoples of PAPUA NEW GUINEA to the north. Despite pronounced similarities in the approach to design, much variation occurred throughout Australia, partly as a result of the diverse materials available for the process of manufacture in different locations and also because of the distinct artistic traditions of the various social groupings.

(i) Containers. (ii) Ornaments. (iii) Pipes. (iv) Weapons.

(i) Containers. Aboriginal people manufactured many types of containers, including baskets woven from various plant fibres, bags made of string produced from the root bark of particular trees and a range of receptacles of different shapes and sizes made from bark, skin and shell. In Arnhem Land and parts of Cape York Peninsula, women make softened bark from the stringybark tree and fig tree into lengths of string. This handspun string is woven into rectangular 'dilly' or 'string' bags, using a variety of stitches (e.g. knotted netting, single loop, hour-glass and loop, and twist). Sometimes, before weaving, the string is dyed red or yellow with the roots of such plants as *Haemodorum coccineum* or *Ceolospernum reticulatum*. Dyed string is also used to add contrasting, horizontal bands of colour to the natural string bag. For special occasions, tiny, brightly coloured feathers from the necks of parakeets or the delicate white feathers from the breasts of magpie geese are rolled into the string, so as to give the bags a soft, fluffy, outer surface.

Baskets, either flat-based or conical in shape, are made from the young, green fronds of pandanus (especially *Pandanus spiralus*). These are split into strips, dried in the sun and then either left their natural colour or dyed and used as weft threads of the woven pattern. Some conical baskets are woven so tightly that honey from the hives of wild bees and water can be carried in them. Sometimes, especially since the emergence of a tourist industry, several split strands of pandanus fibre dyed bright orange, yellow, brown, pink or purple are bound into cylindrical lengths, which are then coiled into basket shape and held in place with blanket stitch to create a container resembling a European shopping basket.

Crescent-shaped baskets are made in the rain-forest regions of north Queensland from lengths of split lawyer cane (*Calamus caryotoides*), a prolific climbing plant. The basket is made using two continuous strands of cane, with several straight strands extending the length of the base. The distinctive shape is formed by stringing the ends of the split cane like a bow and attaching it by top-stitching to the inner surface. Sometimes men paint the outer surface with red and yellow ochres, white clay and charcoal. Coiled baskets of reeds were formerly made in eastern Australia. The reeds were wound on a continuous spiral starting from the centre of the base and ending at the rim. In Tasmania, women made delicately shaped, globular baskets from *Juncus* reeds for carrying personal items and food. These resembled the baskets of Aboriginal women in Victoria. Nowadays European materials are sometimes used in the manufacture of bags and baskets. For example, commercial dyes are used to colour plant fibres and strips of brightly printed cloth are used as decoration on small round-bottomed baskets made of pandanus. Some bags, such as those normally made from bark string, are crocheted from coloured wool or nylon string.

The Tiwi people of Bathurst and Melville Islands make large rectangular containers for use in mortuary ceremonies (*see* §5 above). These comprise a long sheet of flattened and cleaned stringybark folded in half lengthwise and sewn together at the sides with pandanus strips threaded through punched holes. Striking and bold geometric designs are painted on the outer surface.

In the Kimberleys region of Western Australia two types of elegant bark containers are made for utilitarian purposes. One, unique to the region, is shaped like a European bucket with the bark base attached to the cylinder by seams of handspun bark-fibre string. It is waterproofed with a thick layer of resin. String handles are added and the outer surface is decorated with traditional symbols, stencilled hands and Wandjina figures (*see* §III, 3 below), using white clay, sometimes blown on to the surface. The other type, similar to those found in northern Queensland and Arnhem Land, is long and cylindrical. Bark's tendency to curl back into the form of the original tree trunk is exploited by Aboriginal women, and rough bark at the ends of the rectangular strip is thinned to enable it to be pleated and bound into place with stick handles and twine. The outer surface is also sometimes decorated with designs using white clay, often on a red ochre background.

Elegantly carved, elongate wooden dishes are made in the desert region of central Australia. After chipping, shaping and hollowing, these multipurpose containers are usually left plain and smooth or they are finely chiselled with fluted decoration and covered with red ochre. For ceremonial purposes, Warlpiri, Pintupi and Luritja women painted Dreamtime designs on both the inner and outer surface of these wooden containers, using ochres to make circular and dotted motifs. Some bowls are now made for sale and these are often decorated with a wide range of acrylic paints. Pitjantjatjara women use hot wire to incise swirling linear designs of Dreamtime motifs on such bowls (see fig. 11).

In several areas of Australia, large gastropod shells are used to carry food and water. In Arnhem Land, for example, water is carried in the large *Syrinx aruanus* shell, to which is attached a fig-string handle.

(ii) Ornaments. Aboriginal people adorn their bodies with a variety of materials. In the Kimberleys, pearl shell pendants are highly prized and often traded far afield. String, handspun from human hair and sometimes greased and heavily laden with red ochre, is attached to the apex of the shell, so that the pendant can be hung around a

11. Wooden container being decorated with incised swirling lines by a Pitjantjatjara woman, central Australia

man's neck or waist. The beauty of this pendant lies in the interlocking key design, incised into the pearly inner surface and filled with red ochre to highlight the pattern.

During mortuary ceremonies, Tiwi men wear various special ornaments (*see* §5 above), and in Arnhem Land male dancers wear delicate handspun bark-fibre cords or tiny entwined parakeet feathers suspended from bark-fibre waist- and headbands. Finely plaited pandanus-fibre strips may be worn around the upper arm.

Throughout most of northern and central Australia, men often dance with bunches of fresh green leaves tied around their ankles. In Arnhem Land the practice is restricted to certain ceremonies such as initiation and mortuary rites. Human hairstring belts, greased and thickly covered with red ochre, are also worn. In the rain-forests of northern Queensland, white and yellow feathers from sulphur-crested cockatoos were used in the past for men's headdresses. These were either arranged as a radiating flat crown, with the central shaft of feather spines held together by beeswax, or they were clustered into small feather bunches stabilized with beeswax and affixed to separate locks of hair or beard. Forehead bands were made of handspun bark-fibre or possum-fur string, from which eel bones, kangaroo teeth or seeds were suspended so as to hang over the temple.

Women in the Western Desert regions of central Australia use bright red and yellow seeds from the bean tree (*Erythrina vespertilio*), threaded on string handspun from human hair. They wrap these strings of seeds across their breasts, over their shoulders and around their waists and wear them as armbands. Strips of white sheeting are also sometimes worn as a headband with a bunch of white feathers just above the centre of the forehead.

Delicate reed necklaces, threaded on vegetable-fibre string, are worn by Aborigines in eastern Australia. In Tasmania, striking necklaces are made from possum fur or kangaroo sinew, raddled with red ochre, and from iridescent trochus shell. Similar shell necklaces are still made by Aboriginal women on Cape Barren Island, but these are now threaded with European sewing cotton or nylon thread. As part of daily attire, incised kangaroo bone and reed ornaments were worn through the nasal septum by men in the rain-forest region of north Queensland. Many were decorated with tiny, incised parallel lines and short dashes and rubbed over with charcoal to highlight the pattern.

(iii) Pipes. Drone pipes (*didjeridu*) are found in Arnhem Land and more recently in the Kimberleys and Mornington Island in the Gulf of Carpentaria. They are made from small tree trunks or branches, the cores of which have been eaten out by termites. They are between 1.2 and 1.8 m long and vary considerably in diameter. In some areas the mouthpiece is shaped with beeswax to suit the player. In the Kimberleys these drone pipes are painted black or deep red-brown and then incised with images of Dreamtime figures and handprints so as to allow the natural colour of the timber to show through. In Arnhem Land the drone pipes are painted with earth ochres or acrylic paints in designs similar to those found on bark paintings from the region. Mornington Island pipes are coated with black or red-brown commercial paint, and bands of red, black and/or white often adorn part of the surface. Suitable lengths of metal or plastic piping are also occasionally used.

The smoking pipe was introduced to Arnhem Land by Indonesian ('Macassan') traders. Macassan pipes have a slender, cylindrical shaft of softwood, about 500–600 mm in length, with a metal bowl. The softwood barrel is decorated with finely incised, cross-hatched and geometric designs and painted with earth ochres or with yellow, black, white and red acrylic paints. These continue to be used in Arnhem Land together with European pipes and those made from the claw of the large mud crab.

(iv) Weapons. Aboriginal peoples from all over Australia used similar groups of weapons for both hunting and combat (see fig. 12). These included clubs, shields, spears, spear-throwers and boomerangs. However, boomerangs were not used in Arnhem Land or Cape York, and neither boomerangs, shields nor spear-throwers were used in Tasmania. In the Kimberleys, distinctive elongated hardwood shields are decorated on the outer surface with multiple incised zigzag designs. Some are covered with red ochre and others are infilled with alternate red and white bands. Arnhem Land spears and spear-throwers are sometimes painted with cross-hatched ochre designs similar to those of the region's bark paintings. Those from Port Essington are light and elegant with a beeswax knob at the handheld end decorated with an impressed linear design, and subtle red and white ochre motifs on the shaft. Bathurst and Melville Islands ceremonial spears and clubs are highly decorated, echoing the bold geometric designs of the islands' baskets, bark paintings, burial poles and body painting.

In the desert regions of central and north-western Australia, the thin, leaf-shaped spear-thrower made of mulga-wood (*Acacia aneura*) was a multipurpose object of

12. Weapons and other objects, painted wood, bark and vegetable fibre, at a rain-forest camp in northern Queensland, *c.* 1880

great elegance. Besides being used to propel a spear, it also doubled as an adze, as it had a stone blade embedded in resin at one end. Water, pigments or blood could be collected in its concave surface.

There are two distinctive central Australian hardwood boomerangs. The first type is fluted, coloured with red ochre, gently curved, and is either returning or non-returning. The other is the hook boomerang, sometimes known from its shape as a 'number 7'. These are left plain or decorated with parallel bands of incised lines filled with red ochre; some also have white bands painted on the hook as well as on the handheld end. Often a small band of dots and circles, reminiscent of the Dreamtime designs found in ground paintings from this region, is painted on one end or both.

Light, oval-shaped shields, made from bean-wood (*Erythrina vespertilio*), were similarly embellished with parallel grooves on both surfaces. They were usually red from ochre and sometimes a dot, circle and line design depicting Dreamtime events was painted on the outer surface in red, yellow, white and black. Today acrylic paints and a wider range of colours are often used.

In eastern Australia, extremely large, heavy boomerangs were decorated with delicate linear incisions. The natural grain of the wood sometimes enhanced the design. Narrow parrying shields had similar incised markings covering the outer surface. In the past these markings were engraved with a possum tooth or stone tool. The most common incised design was a diamond figure set in a field of herringbone patterns, parallel chevrons and diagonal fluting. A fine 19th-century shield from the Darling River, NSW, is illustrated at fig. 13 below.

A unique one-handed sword was used in the north Queensland rain-forest. Made of heavy hardwood, it had a small handgrip and a long blade with plain, polished, convex surfaces. The sword was used only with a highly decorated, kidney-shaped shield that was cut from the buttress of a fig-tree, the natural curve determining its shape. Ornate linear patterns were painted on the shield's outer surface, using red and yellow ochres, white pipeclay and ground charcoal. Blood, either human or animal, was used as a fixative. Designs were painted with the fingers, brushes made from lawyer cane chewed at one end, or with commercially produced brushes. It is thought that the designs probably related to totems.

BIBLIOGRAPHY

F. A. Péron and C. L. de S. de Freycinet: *Voyage de découvertes aux Terres Australes . . . pendant les années 1800, 1801, 1802, 1803 et 1804*, 2 vols (Paris, 1807–16)

W. B. Spencer and F. Gillen: *The Native Tribes of Central Australia* (London, 1899/*R* 1969)

W. E. Roth: *North Queensland Ethnography*, Queensland Government Printer, Bulletins nos 1–8 (1901–6); *Rec. Austral. Mus.*, vi–viii (1907–10) [Bulletins nos 9–18]

U. H. McConnel: 'Native Arts and Industries on the Archer, Kendall and Holroyd Rivers, Cape York Peninsula, North Queensland', *Rec. S. Austral. Mus.*, xi/1 (1953), pp. 1–42, pls i–xvii

F. D. McCarthy: *Australia's Aborigines: Their Life and Culture* (Melbourne, 1957)

C. P. Mountford: *The Tiwi: Their Art, Myth and Ceremony* (London, 1958)

P. Brokensha: *The Pitjantjatjara and their Crafts* (Sydney, 1975)

C. C. Macknight: *'The Voyage to Marege': Macassan Trepangers in Northern Australia* (Melbourne, 1976)

J. Clark: *The Aboriginal People of Tasmania* (Hobart, 1983)

J. Isaacs: *Arts of the Dreaming: Australia's Living Heritage* (Sydney, 1984)

K. Khan: 'North Queensland Aboriginal Baskets', *Craft Australia*, iv (1985), pp. 18–22

KATE KHAN, BETTY MEEHAN

III. Regions.

Australia is here divided into a number of geographical regions that reflect broad variations in the cultural and artistic systems of their Aboriginal populations (see fig. 1 above). The south and south-east was the first region to be colonized by Europeans, and knowledge of its art is less detailed than that of other areas. Nevertheless, the region does seem to have considerable unity, especially in the widespread tradition of finely engraved and incised wooden artefacts. The central region, stretching from south-east Queensland in the east across to the coast of Western Australia, is an arid zone with low population densities and considerable cultural continuities. Across the northern coastal region there is greater linguistic variation and art styles can differ markedly between adjacent areas, making it possible to define a number of more precisely demarcated regions. From west to east these comprise the Kimberleys, characterized by paintings of the legendary Wandjina heroes, Western Arnhem Land with its X-ray paintings, and Eastern Arnhem Land with its intricate clan designs. Cape York Peninsula on the eastern side of the Gulf of Carpentaria has distinctive art forms that show some continuities with works from the TORRES STRAIT ISLANDS. Within each region there is considerable variation and in some cases, such as Melville and Bathurst Islands, Groote Eylandt and Lake Eyre, sub-regions exist that have their own distinctive art styles.

□

1. South-east Australia and Tasmania. 2. Central Australia. 3. Kimberleys. 4. Western Arnhem Land. 5. Eastern Arnhem Land. 6. Cape York Peninsula.

1. SOUTH-EAST AUSTRALIA AND TASMANIA. This cultural and stylistic region can be defined as the area south and east of an arc drawn from near Adelaide in South Australia up through the great Murray–Darling River system of New South Wales and south-west Queensland to a point along the north-east coast just below Brisbane, together with the island of Tasmania. Over this entire area engraved linear designs display recognizable combinations of motif that typify the region's art. Within this overall style, variations on a theme have led to distinctive, localized designs. As in all Australian Aboriginal art, the designs are related to the land or country of their maker. They are primarily found incised on hunter's weapons, but variations occur on burial and ceremonial trees and on the richly decorated skin cloaks peculiar to some areas within the region. They even characterize the relatively sparse rock art of the region (*see* MOOTWINGEE). A number of significant rock art sites exist in south-eastern Australia. Among the most notable are the Sydney-Hawkesbury sandstone engravings at Cobar in central western New South Wales. Rock-engravings fit in with sequences found elsewhere in Australia. Paintings in rock shelters in New South Wales seem to be a more recent development, though the situation may have been distorted by differential preservation. Most extant specimens of traditional south-east Australian art were made, used, bartered and collected in the 19th century. Representative examples of small-scale works are found in museums throughout the world. Since the 1990s, Aboriginal people from the region have sought to strengthen their identity, resulting in a revival of interest in traditional arts and crafts. In such areas as the Lower Murray River replicas of 'traditional' weapons have been made based on 19th-century material preserved in museums.

As a result of the devastating impact of European colonization, little survives of the art of Tasmania. The early records suggest that rich and varied traditions similar to those in the rest of Australia also existed in Tasmania (see Ruhe for a summary). The paintings of Thomas Bock (1790–1855) and early photographs reveal traditions of elaborate hair decoration and body adornment (see Morphy and Edwards).

(i) Weapons. The formal and graphic elements that are combined to produce the recognizable 'South-eastern' style are relatively few and simple. The several varieties of weapons, shields, clubs, boomerangs and spear-throwers that were made throughout the region were decorated with designs formed from repeated crosshatch, herringbone, zigzag, chevron, diamond, interlocking diamond and rhombic elements. In some localities red, white and black pigments were used to accentuate areas of design. Discrete motifs were relatively uncommon, but when they do occur they usually take the form of curvilinear or geometric shapes enclosing smooth, recessed, raised, infilled or coloured areas. Human, animal and other representational figures are rare on artefacts, though their use was greatly stimulated when artefacts were produced for barter and sale outside Aboriginal society. One example,

13. South-east Australian shield, wood, 1125×240 mm, from Darling River, New South Wales, 19th century (London, British Museum)

a club collected by R. B. Smyth from the Aborigines of Victoria (Rome, Mus. N. Preist. & Etnog.), is decorated on both surfaces with finely incised representations of an emu and iguanas. Smyth thought such figures represented the totems of their maker's tribe. Another club (Melbourne, Mus. Victoria) possesses a linear design that Smyth claimed represented a lagoon and an anabranch of a river, the space enclosed by the lines showing the country occupied by the tribe of the weapon's owner.

The workmanship displayed in some of the old weapons, especially the shields traditionally carved by stone or animal-tooth tools, is striking, as is seen in a rare and superbly decorated specimen from the Darling River region (London, BM; see fig. 13). Made of hardwood rather than bark, its handle was cut into the solid wood at the back of the shield with a stone tool. The finely carved design was executed with an engraving tool made from a possum's jawbone. Broad shields of this type were about 1 m long on average and were used throughout south-east Australia to deflect spears in general fights between warring parties. The shields' designs stressed both individual and group identity. Like their owners, they were often 'painted up' for fights, as ethnographic accounts record, though this example has no traces of pigment and appears to have relied instead on the striking nature of its complex incised design for its effect. The unusual inclusion on the shield of circular motifs, which are uncommon for the south-east, link this design with those of the Lake Eyre region further west.

Stylistic variation between the internal groupings within the larger region is discernible. Just as the excellence of the work of individual craftsmen or artists stands out, so do particular styles that suggest specific provenances. For instance, in the early years of the 19th century Aborigines living in the upper Darling River area, more specifically along the tributaries of the Bogan and Macquarie rivers, seem to have possessed a special inventiveness in wood-carving, which is revealed in many particularly unusual and beautiful pieces.

(ii) Carved trees and decorated cloaks. The greatest concentration of dendroglyphs or carved trees (associated with either burial or ceremonial grounds) is also found to the east of the Darling, on the Bogan and Macquarie rivers, in Kamilaroi tribal lands. This area is noted for the greatest variety of motifs and greatest skill in their execution. One particular carved tree (Sydney, Austral. Mus.) was recorded by Etheridge (1918) as being one of two trees that marked 'the grave of a celebrated boomerang-thrower of the Macquarie tribe, killed in a fight with the Bogan blacks'. Though the design is cut with a metal tool, the deterioration in workmanship and design integrity often associated with the introduction of metal tools is not evident here. Indeed, the introduction of European woodworking tools into this area appears to have stimulated wood-carving skills, resulting in the production of some particularly fine carved weapons and trees.

Possum-skin cloaks, the other major vehicle for linear designs in the region, are extremely rare. While there are many records of these beautiful objects being collected, few survive in museums. Two outstanding examples come from the region's coastal area. One (Melbourne, Mus. Victoria) consisting of 50 engraved possum pelts, still bears traces of red-ochre decoration; it was obtained in 1872 from Lake Condah Aboriginal station in coastal Victoria and is remarkably similar in design to one collected in 1838–42 from the Hunter River in eastern New South Wales (Washington, DC, N. Mus. Nat. Hist.).

The exact relationship of the designs on the cloaks to those on the trees and weapons is obscure. Early commentators had difficulty in obtaining information from local Aborigines, who were hesitant to discuss their traditional practices with Europeans. There are, however, indications that there were associations between body cicatrice designs and those on the cloaks, trees and artefacts, as well as with ephemeral ceremonial-ground drawings.

BIBLIOGRAPHY

R. B. Smyth: *The Aborigines of Victoria*, 2 vols (London, 1878)
R. Etheridge: *The Dendroglyphs, or 'Carved Trees' of New South Wales*, Memoirs of the Geological Survey of New South Wales: Ethnological Series, 3 (Sydney, 1918)
N. Peterson: 'The Natural and Cultural Areas of Aboriginal Australia: A Preliminary Analysis of Population Groupings with Adaptive Significance', *Tribes and Boundaries in Australia*, ed. N. Peterson, Australian Institute of Aboriginal Studies Social Anthropology Series, 10 (Canberra, 1976), pp. 50–71
Aboriginal Australia (exh. cat. by C. Cooper and others, Sydney, Austral. Gal. Directors Council, 1981–2), pp. 29–42, 82–120
D. Bell: *Aboriginal Carved Trees of Southeastern Australia: A Research Report* (Sydney, 1982)
H. Morphy and E. Edwards, eds: *Australia in Oxford*, Pitt Rivers Museum Monograph 4 (Oxford, 1988)
P. Sutton, P. Jones and S. Hemming: 'Survival, Regeneration, and Impact', *Dreamings: The Art of Aboriginal Australia* (exh. cat., ed. P. Sutton; New York: Asia Soc. Gals; U. Chicago, IL, Smart Gal.; Melbourne, Mus. Victoria; Adelaide, S. Austral. Mus.; 1988–90), pp. 180–212
E. L. Ruhe: 'The Bark Art of Tasmania', *Art and Identity in Oceania*, ed. A. Hanson and L. Hanson (Honolulu, 1990), pp. 129–48
C. Cooper: *Designs in Wood* (diss., Canberra, Austral. N. U.) (in preparation)

CAROL COOPER

2. Central Australia. This extensive cultural region stretches from Tennant Creek in the north to the Flinders Ranges in the south, and from Queensland in the east to the west Australian coast. The main language groups are the Aranda, Warlpiri, Pintubi, Luritja and Pitjantjatjara. Most artists are based in the towns of Hooker Creek, Yuendumu, Papunya, Hermannsburg, Ayers Rock (Uluru), Ernabella, Utopia, Kintore and Balgo, although many live in smaller camps between these larger centres.

Throughout this vast area there is much stylistic continuity in the graphic designs used in sand drawings, body painting and the decoration of ceremonial objects. Patterns of circles, lines and dots characterize the designs, which are used in a variety of contexts to represent specific localities and events of ancestral importance. The indigenous symbolism and use of such designs has been thoroughly documented by Nancy Munn, who identified a set of 13 graphic elements regularly used in sand drawings; these include circles, arcs, dots, ovals and meandering or straight lines. Each element has a wide range of potential meanings: a simple circle can be used to indicate such varied items as a nest, water-hole, tree, hill or camp fire; a short, straight line may identify a spear, a digging stick, or an animal or person lying down or moving in a certain direction. The exact reference to each element is fixed within the accompanying narrative. The elements are combined into larger design units that build a broader picture of details about the daily activities of particular ancestral subjects.

While both men and women publicly engage in sand drawing to tell stories of ancestral times, they also control their own designs in different types of ceremonial contexts. Women's designs (*yawalyu*) are revealed to them in dreams by spirit children (*yinawuru*), acting as proxies for ancestral beings. The painting of such designs on the body in Yawalyu ceremonies is said to enhance the personal, sexual and procreative aims of the wearer. Although the accompanying stories are associated with specific ancestral figures and with a general locality, such locational references are not stressed by women (Munn). They tend rather to see in their dreams the ancestral precedent for their own hunting and gathering or food-consuming activities. *Yawalyu* body designs differ from those in sand drawings in that the basic elements are often outlined with one or more lines. Hence, circles become concentric and parallel lines are used instead of single straight lines.

Designs controlled exclusively by men (*guruwari*) are considered to be reproductions of marks originally created by the ancestral beings, although men also produce new designs from their dreams. They are painted on the body and on regalia such as shields and are incised on wooden or oval stone slabs known as *tjurunga*, as well as on waymarkers known as *toas* (see fig. 5 above). Larger and more elaborate designs may be constructed on the ground using white and ochred bird down or plant fibre. The ceremonies in which these designs are used include the Bulaba, a ritual that dramatizes ancestral events for the benefit of the whole camp, Guridji circumcision rituals and Banba or major fertility ceremonies that ensure the maintenance of different totemic species and of life sources as a whole. Since the standardized designs represent specific ancestral localities, their use during ceremonies is intended to tap the reserves of ancestral power left at these places and to communicate it to the participants and the objects. *Guruwari* designs are similar to women's *yawalyu* designs but generally larger. The concentric circle patterns are identified with sites created by ancestral beings when they stopped and the lines indicate the path of their travels. The designs help to create symbolic links between the hunting and ceremonial journeys undertaken by contemporary humans and the journeys and exploits of the ancestral beings. The prime underlying symbolic reference of concentric circles is to female sexuality, while parallel lines are associated with male sexuality.

For details concerning the Hermannsburg school of watercolourists, established in the area in the 1930s, and the contemporary production of acrylic paintings and batik textiles, *see* §IV below.

BIBLIOGRAPHY

W. B. Spencer and F. J. Gillen: *The Native Tribes of Central Australia* (London, 1899/*R* 1969)

C. P. Mountford: 'Aboriginal Crayon Drawings Relating to Totemic Places Belonging to the Northern Aranda Tribe of Central Australia', *Trans. Royal Soc. S. Australia*, lxi (1937), pp. 84–95

G. Roheim: *The Eternal Ones of the Dream: A Psychoanalytic Approach to Australian Myth and Ritual* (New York, 1945)

N. O. Munn: *Walbiri Iconography: Graphic Representation and Cultural Symbolism in a Central Australian Society* (Ithaca, NY, 1973, rev. Chicago, 1986)

G. Bardon: *Aboriginal Art of the Western Desert* (Adelaide, 1979)

L. Taylor: *Ancestors into Art: An Analysis of Pitjanjatjara Kulpidji Designs and Crayon Drawings* (diss., Canberra, Austral. N. U., 1979)

N. Peterson: 'Art of the Desert', *Aboriginal Australia* (exh. cat. by C. Cooper and others, Sydney, Austral. Gal. Directors Council, 1981–2), pp. 43–51

P. Jones and P. Sutton: *Art and Land: Aboriginal Sculptures of the Lake Eyre Region* (Adelaide, 1986)

LUKE TAYLOR

3. KIMBERLEYS. This cultural region between the Ord and Fitzroy rivers in Western Australia is occupied by speakers of a number of non-Pama-nyungan languages. The region is best known for its rock art (*see also* §II, 2 above), though Aboriginal communities have produced art in various media, including body painting (see fig. 7 above) and, in recent years, commercial paintings on board and bark. Two types of figures are characteristic of the region's rock paintings: Bradshaw and Wandjina figures. The first belong to a tradition that is no longer practised. They are known in the local languages as Giro-giro or Kiro-kiro but among archaeologists as 'Bradshaw figures', after their European discoverer, Joseph Bradshaw, who encountered them in 1892. These figures are caught in mid-action, often wear headdresses and other ornaments and sometimes occur in groups. Painted in red ochre, they are generally less than 300 mm high and in style are similar to the Mimi figures of the Oenpelli–Kakadu region of Western Arnhem Land (*see* §4 below). Bradshaw figures are found in both the western and eastern Kimberleys (though relatively little is known of the art of the eastern area). Welch (1993) considers that two phases can be detected within the 'Bradshaw' art, characterized by different headdresses, artefacts and poses. He tentatively equates the later Bradshaw art of the Kimberleys with the Lewis Stick period in the rock art of Western Arnhem Land.

Wandjina are legendary heroes depicted as mouthless human-like figures wearing semicircular headdresses (see fig. 14). The Wandjina are often accompanied by animals with which they are associated in legends; these are depicted in a twisted perspective: the body shown in

14. Kimberleys rock painting at Galvin's Gorge, head and shoulders of Wandjina (totemic clan hero) with two snakes depicted on right-hand side of head, red ochre on white background, diam. of head *c*. 400 mm

profile but the feet, anus and head seen from other angles. In the same caves as the Wandjina there are small, roughly drawn figures representing either malevolent and capricious beings that subvert the ancestral order established by the Wandjina, or the victims of sorcery. The latter were painted by people wishing to invoke the Wandjinas' power to cripple and kill their opponents (Layton). Indirect evidence suggests the Wandjina style is up to 3000 years old, since the earlier Dynamic 'Bradshaw' styles do not depict the use of stone-tipped spears, and Kimberley stone spear points are thought to appear *c.* 1000 BP (see Crawford, 1968, 1977; Welch, 1990). Confined to the western half of the Kimberleys, bounded roughly by the Drysdale River, the Wandjina tradition is later than that of the Bradshaw figures. It was first documented by Sir George Grey (1812–98) in 1838.

The Wandjina are seen as having established the Aboriginal social order by demarcating clan territories and instituting ceremonial exchanges (Blundell and Layton; Blundell). Each clan holds pre-eminent rights over an area containing one or more rock shelters bearing Wandjina and other paintings. The clans are totemic and in the western Kimberleys each is associated with a named Wandjina hero. Traditionally, the clan had a ritual responsibility for the increase of the particular animal species associated with its Wandjina, which was discharged at ceremonies in which the Wandjina paintings were retouched. This aspect of the cult ceased, probably during the 1930s, following the severe disruption caused by the attempts at white pastoral settlement and the relocation of Aboriginal groups on missions (Blundell). Senior men have nonetheless continued to repaint Wandjina whenever possible. A number of cases have been recorded between 1947 and 1986 (*see* WALL PAINTING, fig. 1). Rituals celebrating the Wandjina were being performed in the late 1980s–early 1990s, while commercial bark paintings of Wandjina heads are a popular modern art form. Pearl shell pendants, once exclusively produced for ceremonial exchange, are now also available commercially.

Little of the rock art in the eastern Kimberleys is directly associated with 'increase' ceremonies, although in one documented example the paintings are said to have been executed by an ancestral hero (Capell, 1972). Most paintings are placed in apparently random assemblages, not linked by the legendary associations of the site, and are more stereotyped than in the western zone. Only images of the spirits of unborn children are retouched, 'to replace a spirit-child born into the human world' (Kaberry, 1935, 1936; Capell, 1972).

Recent rock art styles are more static, and compositions are rarer. Figures are often more than 1 m high and are outlined and infilled in red, black and white on a white background. Among recent important contemporary developments in the region is the art from Turkey Creek in the East Kimberleys. The art developed as part of a renaissance of ritual that followed the death of a woman in a car accident, commemorated by the Krill Krill song cycle. Paintings on board made for rituals have become well known. The paintings of ROVER THOMAS with their stark geometricity have gained an international reputation (see 1994. exh. cat).

BIBLIOGRAPHY

A. P. Elkin: 'Rock-paintings of North-west Australia', *Oceania*, i (1930), pp. 257–79 [eye-witness accts of ptg tech.]
J. Love: 'Rock Paintings of the Worrora and their Mythological Interpretation', *J. Royal Soc. W. Australia*, xvi (1930), pp. 1–24
P. M. Kaberry: 'The Forrest River and Lyne River Tribes of North-west Australia', *Oceania*, v (1935), pp. 408–36
——: 'Spirit-children and Spirit-centres of the North Kimberley Division, West Australia', *Oceania*, vi (1936), pp. 392–400
J. Love: *Stone-age Bushmen of Today* (London, 1936) [eye-witness accts of ptg tech.]
A. Capell: 'Mythology in Northern Kimberley', *Oceania*, ix (1939), pp. 382–404
I. M. Crawford: *The Art of the Wandjina: Aboriginal Cave Paintings in Kimberley, Western Australia* (London and Melbourne, 1968) [colour photos]
A. Capell: *Cave Painting Myths: Northern Kimberley* (Sydney, 1972)
V. Blundell and R. Layton: 'Marriage, Myth and Models of Exchange in the Western Kimberleys', *Mankind*, xi (1978), pp. 231–45
V. Blundell: 'Symbolic Systems and Cultural Continuity in Northwest Australia: A Consideration of Aboriginal Cave Art', *Culture*, xi (1982), pp. 3–20
R. Layton: 'The Cultural Context of Hunter-gatherer Rock Art', *Man*, n. s., xx/3 (1985), pp. 434–53
D. Welch: 'The Bichrome Art Period in the Kimberley, Australia', *Rock A. Res.*, vii (1990), pp. 110–24
——: 'Early "Naturalistic" Human Figures in the Kimberley, Australia', *Rock A. R.*, x (1993), pp. 24–37
G. L. Walsh: *Bradshaws: Ancient Rock Paintings of North-west Australia* (Geneva, 1994)
Roads Cross: The Paintings of Rover Thomas (exh. cat. by R. Thomas, Canberra, N. G., 1994)
J. Schmiechen: *Survey of Aboriginal Rock Art and Cultural Sites: Drysdale River, East Kimberley, Western Australia: Report of Findings* (in preparation)

ROBERT LAYTON

4. WESTERN ARNHEM LAND. This cultural region is located in the Northern Territory of Australia and is bounded by the East Alligator and Liverpool rivers. Its landscape is dominated by spectacular escarpments, many containing caves decorated with rock paintings—among the most extensive and best-preserved of which are in the UBIRR complex in Kakadu National Park. The two other most important art forms are ceremonial body painting and bark paintings on stringybark produced for sale. Such bark paintings replaced the traditional painting of rock shelters and bark in wet-season huts as the arena for representing secular subjects, but in response to market demand, contemporary bark painters have been incorporating more sacred subject-matter relating to the creative actions of ancestral beings. Artists paint in recognizable local 'schools' or styles centred around the Aboriginal townships at Oenpelli, Maningrida and Bamyili, and at small bush camps throughout the region. Although the Aboriginal peoples of the region speak some ten different languages of the non-Pama-nyungan group, multilingualism is common, and this facilitates movement throughout the area and participation in major regional ceremonies. As a result artists share stylistic traits that emphasize their cultural distinctiveness from groups in Eastern Arnhem Land.

Among the large body of documented rock paintings in Western Arnhem Land, two characteristic styles are known: Dynamic Figurative, which was subsequently replaced by the X-ray style (*see* §II, 2(ii)(b) above). The term 'Dynamic Figurative' was introduced to describe the small, red, human-like figures (h. *c.* 200–300 mm) actively engaged in hunting, fighting and ceremonial scenes (for illustration *see* UBIRR). Neither the original meaning nor function of the Dynamic Figurative style paintings is known. Contemporary Aborigines describe them as representations of Mimi (rock country spirits), said to be long, thin, trickster spirits that live in the crevices of the rock caves. They also attribute the production of such paintings to the Mimi; hence some scholars refer to them as Mimi art. This type of painting has considerable antiquity, but direct evidence of its age is lacking. A Pleistocene date (*c.* 10,000 BP) has been suggested by relating the subject-matter of the paintings to geomorphological studies of environmental changes in the region (Chaloupka).

'X-ray' art, the term used to describe rock paintings of animals infilled with schematic representations of internal organs and skeletal features (see fig. 3 above), continued to be produced until recent times. The subject-matter reflects the changing economy of Aboriginal groups over a long period of environmental change, from pre-estuarine to estuarine (*c.* 7000–5000 BC) and finally to the present-day freshwater, wetland conditions (*c.* AD 1000). The region's Aborigines do not have a single term for all the different types of X-ray painting, although they acknowledge it as 'our way of painting' and its style is continuous with some paintings used in contemporary ceremonies.

The designs used in ceremonial body painting are believed to have been created by the ancestral beings and handed down through the generations. Figurative X-ray motifs are painted on the body during the most public stages of the Mardayin ceremony, performed to ensure the fertility of the natural world, to initiate young men and to settle the souls of the dead. During the more sacred stages of this ceremony, elaborate, geometric designs called *rarrk* are painted in natural ochres on the bodies of initiates and on sacred objects. *Rarrk* consist of geometric grids of dotted lines infilled with polychrome crosshatching patterns. These designs represent both features of the clan lands of the owner of the designs and the associated ancestral events. Since landscape is often conceived to be the transformed remains of ancestral beings, *rarrk* can also be interpreted as showing body parts. As ancestral creations, *rarrk* designs are considered to contain some of the power of the original beings, which can be transferred to the initiates who wear the designs. The Mardayin ceremony dramatizes the manner in which the power of the original ancestral beings is now controlled by the clan groups who own the designs.

Similar functions and interpretations are also ascribed to *buluk* designs, which are constructed from coloured cotton wool or kapok stuck to a dancer's torso. These designs are worn in the most important phases of the Kunapipi and Yabburdurrwa ceremonies, which are re-enactments of the Dreaming concerned with initiation and fertility. *Buluk* designs consist of either highly schematic figures or wholly geometric motifs.

Western Arnhem Land bark paintings are characterized by figurative subjects; the most common are representations of hunting scenes derived from stories of the Mimi spirits (see fig. 15). Such paintings generally show a relatively large X-ray representation of a common food species in combination with a much smaller Mimi figure in the act of spearing the animal. These paintings are associated with others that show the butchery or cooking

15. Western Arnhem Land bark painting by Robin Nganjmira: *Two Brolgas with Mimi Spirits*, natural ochres on bark, 1.20×0.67 m, 1981; from a photograph by Luke Taylor, 1981

of game. The characteristic body features that identify the distinct species of animal are carefully represented.

To indicate the particular creative and transformable characteristics of ancestral beings, the artist may elaborate either the internal infill or the outline of the figure. For example, the use of crosshatching infill, combined with X-ray motifs, identifies the painting with *rarrk* ceremonial designs. Since ancestral beings are also thought to have transformed themselves freely into different animal types or into composite animal and human body forms, artists may also modify the outline of the figures, combining figurative elements from a number of distinct species to create monstrous configurations that embody these mythical figures. A common example is seen in the paintings of Ngalyod (the First Mother) or Rainbow Serpent, the original mythical creator of Western Arnhem Land. The latter has been painted with a body form that combines

16. Eastern Arnhem Land body painting, the Yolngu artist Larrtjinga painting a boy's chest before circumcision, Yirrkala; from a photograph by Howard Morphy, July 1973

elements from such diverse species as kangaroo, crocodile, snake or barramundi to indicate its status as the creator of all subsequent beings.

BIBLIOGRAPHY

W. B. Spencer: *Native Tribes of the Northern Territory of Australia* (London, 1914)

A. P. Elkin, R. M. Berndt and C. H. Berndt: *Art in Arnhem Land* (Melbourne, 1950)

C. P. Mountford: *Art, Myth and Symbolism*, i of *Records of the American-Australian Scientific Expedition to Arnhem Land, 1948* (Melbourne, 1956)

R. M. Berndt, ed.: *Australian Aboriginal Art* (Sydney, 1964/*R* 1968)

K. Kupka: *Un Art à l'état brut: Peintures et sculptures aborigènes d'Australie* (Lausanne, 1962); Eng. trans. as *Dawn of Art: Painting and Sculpture of the Australian Aborigines* (Sydney, 1965)

R. M. Berndt and C. H. Berndt: *Man, Land and Myth in North Australia: The Gunwinggu People* (Sydney, 1970)

E. J. Brandl: *Australian Aboriginal Paintings in Western and Central Arnhem Land: Temporal Sequences and Elements of Style in Cadell River and Deaf Adder Creek Art* (Canberra, 1973)

P. J. Carroll: 'Mimi from Western Arnhem Land', *Form in Indigenous Art: Schematisation in the Art of Aboriginal Australia and Prehistoric Europe*, ed. P. J. Ucko (Canberra, 1977), pp. 119–230

Kunwinjku Bim: Western Arnhem Land Paintings from the Collection of the Aboriginal Arts Board (exh. cat. by A. Brody, Melbourne, N.G. Victoria, 1984)

G. Chaloupka: 'Chronological Sequence of Arnhem Land Plateau Rock Art', *Archaeological Research in Kakadu National Park*, ed. R. Jones (Canberra, 1985), pp. 269–80

L. Taylor: 'Seeing the "Inside": Kunwinjku Paintings and the Symbol of the Divided Body', *Animals into Art*, ed. H. Morphy, One World Archaeology, 7 (London, 1989), pp. 371–89

LUKE TAYLOR

5. Eastern Arnhem Land. This cultural region in the Northern Territory stretches from Cape Stewart in the west to the Gulf of Carpentaria in the east, and as far south as Blue Mud Bay. The area is occupied by some 5000 speakers of the Yolngu family of languages. Intensive European contact in the region began in the late 1920s with the establishment of the mission stations of Milingimbi, Elcho Island (Galiwinku) and Yirrkala. These have become the main centres for the Aboriginal population and are associated with minor variations in the regional art style.

People belong to patrilineal clans, which are divided between two moieties, Dhuwa and Yirritja. Each clan owns an area of land, the sacred law and objects associated with it and the ancestral designs on which all Yolngu art is based. Designs are produced in various media and on different objects according to the needs of the ceremonial context. For example, the same basic design can occur as a sand sculpture or body painting, or on a flat surface such as a coffin lid; it can be painted on a memorial post, woven into the pattern of a sacred basket or incised on to the wooden core of a sacred object.

The most characteristic features of this regional style are the geometric rendering of the clan designs and the elaborate crosshatching that covers much of a painted surface. Each design is unique in its details, although those associated with the same ancestral being often have common features. For example, the Wild Honey/Fire set of ancestral beings is associated with an overall diamond design. Alternate diamonds are infilled in varying ways to represent different attributes of the ancestral beings. Their meaning depends partly on focus, as the designs are multivalent: a red infilled diamond could represent flames or the honey-filled cell of a honeycomb. Each clan along a particular ancestral track has its own variant of the respective design: diamonds, for example, might be equilateral, elongated or in varying sizes.

Paintings are often divided into segments that represent different areas of land and sometimes adjacent segments may contain different clan designs, reflecting the association of different ancestral beings with the land. In addition to clan designs, paintings include other geometric elements representing features of the landscape and the ancestral events that resulted in their creation. Thus each painting has an underlying geometric structure, which relates to the area's totemic geography, serving both as a guide to its interpretation and as an active agent in the process of generating new paintings (Morphy, 1989). Figurative representations can be used to represent ancestral events and natural species associated with particular geographical features, and because of the multivalency of the geometric art many alternative figurative realizations of a geometric design are possible. The most sacred paintings (*mardayin miny'tji*) consist largely of clan designs and other geometric elements, although they may also include some figurative representations of associated totemic species. Paintings produced in public contexts tend to have greater figurative content than those produced in more restricted contexts.

Crosshatching, the last component of a painting to be completed, is produced by drawing a long brush of human hair across the surface of the painting to produce alternating colour sequences of fine parallel lines. The resulting shimmering effect is highly valued by the Yolngu, for it represents the ancestral power within the painting.

Some paintings and sacred objects are highly restricted forms, integrated within a hierarchical system of knowledge and revealed only to initiated adult men (Morphy, 1991). Moreover, knowledge of the meaning of designs is revealed to an individual only gradually; women are ostensibly denied access to the most restricted levels of knowledge. In ceremonies, designs are used as a means of contacting the ancestral being represented or creating a source of power that can be directed towards particular ends. In a circumcision ceremony, for example, initiates have their bodies painted with designs that belong to their own or a closely related clan (see fig. 16). The painting reinforces an initiate's position as a clan member and is thought to endow his body with spiritual power. Individuals are thought to accumulate power throughout their lives by participating in ceremonies and becoming associated with sacred objects. On the individual's death, paintings are used as a means to return that power, in the form of the dead person's soul, back to the ancestral clan lands. The designs are painted on the dead person's body, or in recent years more commonly on the coffin lid, to place the deceased in contact with ancestral powers who will assist the soul on its journey.

Since World War II Eastern Arnhem Land paintings on bark and other surfaces have taken on new functions. They have become an important commodity for sale to white Australians, with individual artists such as Mawalan Marika (*see* MARIKA, (1)), NARRITJIN MAYMURRU (see fig. 10 above) and DAVID MALANGI gaining widespread reputations. They have also acquired new significance in the political arena as symbols of Yolngu identity. One of the best-known events of the struggle for Aboriginal land rights occurred in 1963, when the people of Yirrkala sent a bark petition to the Australian Federal Parliament. Since then paintings have been used in many land right cases to demonstrate the religious basis for Aboriginal rights, for the art of Eastern Arnhem Land is rooted in the relationship between people, ancestral beings and land.

See also fig. 6 above.

BIBLIOGRAPHY

A. P. Elkin, R. M. Berndt and C. H. Berndt: *Art in Arnhem Land* (Melbourne, 1950)

H. M. Groger-Wurm: *Eastern Arnhem Land*, i of *Australian Aboriginal Bark Paintings and their Mythological Interpretations* (Canberra, 1973)

H. Morphy: '"Now you Understand": An Analysis of the Way Yolngu Have Used Sacred Knowledge to Retain their Autonomy', *Aborigines, Land and Landrights*, ed. N. Peterson and M. Langton (Canberra, 1983), pp. 110–33

——: 'Maintaining Cosmic Unity: Ideology and the Reproduction of Yolngu Clans', *Property, Power and Ideology in Hunting and Gathering Societies*, ed. T. Ingold, D. Riches and J. Woodburn (Oxford, 1988), pp. 141–63

——: 'On Representing Ancestral Beings', *Animals into Art*, ed. H. Morphy, One World Archaeology, 7 (London, 1989), pp. 144–60

——: *Ancestral Connections: Art and an Aboriginal System of Knowledge* (Chicago, 1991)

HOWARD MORPHY

6. CAPE YORK PENINSULA. This cultural region stretches from the Mitchell River drainage basin in the south to the tip of Cape York Peninsula in the north. It is an area of great linguistic diversity including many speakers of languages of the Wik group. The best known art forms of the region are the extensive paintings in the rock shelters of the Laura and Princess Charlotte Bay areas (*see* §II, 2 above). The galleries of the Laura region Caves, in particular, are spectacular, numerous and frequently on a large and imposing scale (*see* QUINKAN GALLERIES). The subjects most frequently depicted are the animals, plants and ancestral beings that comprised the main totemic and ceremonial symbols of the region's Aboriginal religion. Many of the human-like figures have been identified as images created during the practice of sorcery and sexual magic. Much of the rock art appears to be ancient, and engraved designs in one shelter have been assigned a minimum age of 13,000 years (Rosenfeld, Horton and Winter). Works from the colonial period are readily identified by their depiction of such subjects as armed horsemen and pearling boats.

Such rock art cannot, however, be taken as typical of the whole region, most of which lacks rock shelters or rocky country of any description. In fact, the Cape York Peninsula peoples concentrated greater artistic efforts on decorating bags, spears, throwing-sticks and other useful artefacts, and on ephemeral ceremonial objects and body painting. All portable works were made of local organic materials and, typically and intentionally, had a short life. Family resemblances among these objects identify them as coming from the Peninsula region. Such resemblances include the use of red abrus beads as decorative finishes to adhesives on throwing sticks, fire-stick holders and umbilical-cord pendants; the use of shell—for example trochus shell pendants and baler shell counterbalances on the handles of throwing-sticks; and the geometric, linear, painted designs on spears and ceremonial objects.

Melanesian influences are manifest in the region's ceremonial art and in the designs on Cairns rain-forest shields, traditions that were well entrenched in mainland Aboriginal culture at the time of colonization. Elaborate painted masks, drums and such features of painting styles as linear enclosures of colour fields and the use of triangular forms suggest, even more strongly, artistic influence from Torres Strait and New Guinea.

Ceremonial masks, some of which have entered public collections, were often highly detailed, painted constructions that covered not only the face or head but often the whole body. Normally, they were associated with esoteric rituals of the highest order and were not made for sale. By the 1990s they had all but disappeared from the living cultures of the region. With the introduction of steel woodworking tools to Aurukun in the 1940s, the production of carved wooden representations of mythic beings increased dramatically. These were still being made in the 1980s and 1990s, their basic carving and painterly conventions being the same as they were at the time of the earliest European contact. A good example is provided by two figures known as the *Two Young Women of Cape Keerweer* (Adelaide, S. Austral. Mus.; see fig. 17), which were carved for a ceremony held to release the spirit of a young man who had died in Aurukun gaol. A similar sculptural tradition existed in the south-east of the region, near Cooktown in the Starcke River area, where two highly decorated sculptures of Crocodile totemic beings were produced in the early 20th century (Adelaide, S. Austral. Mus.).

The art of Cape York Peninsula has never attained the same degree of fame as that of its counterparts in Arnhem Land or central Australia. This is partly because the destruction of ritual traditions has been greater but also because the Aboriginal people of the region have not been much involved in the production of art aimed at a non-Aboriginal cash market.

In the 1970s and 1980s, most of the traditional Aboriginal works leaving the region were utilitarian artefacts—woven bags, fire-sticks, throwing-sticks and spears, intended for sale at relatively low prices in the 'crafts' market. With reproductions based on photographs and examples preserved in museum collections, the production of Cairns

17. Cape York Peninsula mortuary sculpture by Angus Namponan, Peter Peemuggina and Nelson Wolmby: *Two Young Women of Cape Keerweer*, wood, nails, ochre and eucalyptus bark, h. 700 mm (left), 730 mm (right), 1987 (Adelaide, South Australian Museum)

rain-forest shields resumed. With the encouragement of art teachers at a local college, some artists in the town of Cairns began to apply designs adopted from the region's art to intaglio printmaking. At the same time, some attempts were made to enter the fine arts market. A small number of sacred carvings from Aurukun and bark paintings from Aurukun and elsewhere were sold. The bark paintings were experiments in the use of a new medium, influenced by the example of Arnhem Land and encouraged by non-Aboriginal entrepreneurs. Neither sacred carvings nor bark paintings became a major medium of production for the market, and by the early 1990s few works of significance were being made within the artistic traditions of Cape York Peninsula, apart from those meant for private use.

BIBLIOGRAPHY

D. Thomson: 'The Hero Cult, Initiation and Totemism on Cape York', *J. Royal Anthropol. Inst. GB & Ireland*, lxiii (1933), pp. 453–537 and pls xxvii–xxxvii

U. H. McConnel: 'Inspiration and Design in Aboriginal Art', *A. Australia*, n. s. 2, lix (1935), pp. 49–68

I. Dunlop: *Dances at Aurukun, 1962* (Sydney, 1964) [film]

F. D. McCarthy: 'The Dancers of Aurukun', *Austral. Nat. Hist.*, xiv (1964), pp. 296–300

P. Trezise: *Rock Art of South-east Cape York* (Canberra, 1971)

——: 'Aboriginal Rock Art of Cape York Peninsula', *The Australian Aboriginal Heritage: An Introduction through the Arts*, ed. R. M. Berndt and E. S. Phillips (Sydney, 1973), pp. 118–28

H. Morphy: 'The Art of Northern Australia', *Aboriginal Australia* (exh. cat. by C. Cooper and others, Sydney, Austral. Gal. Directors Council, 1981–2), pp. 52–65

A. Rosenfeld, D. Horton and J. Winter: *Early Man in North Queensland: Art and Archaeology in the Laura Area* (Canberra, 1981)

Cultural Exhibition of Queensland (exh. cat. by J. Bartlett, Omiya, Saitama Prefect. Mus., 1989) [well-illus. overview]

PETER SUTTON

IV. Contemporary art.

Much of 20th-century Aboriginal art is 'transitional' in a number of ways. It is the art of people overwhelmed by an alien culture within which they have had to learn to live. It has also accepted and used new media of expression learnt from the dominant culture. Most of the new forms are made for sale to white tourists, collectors, museums and public and private art galleries. Equally, many white teachers, missionaries, anthropologists, artists, crafts- and art-advisers have supported the emergence of new forms of Aboriginal art. Whether consciously or unconsciously, they have influenced Aboriginal artistic expression in both form and content. For many contemporary Aboriginal artists, the content of their art still provides a link to the Dreamtime past of their ancestors and in particular their connection with ancestral lands. Yet the forms their art now takes are often commercially motivated, and the proceeds of its sale provide the only non-Governmental income for many communities.

1. Painting and drawing. 2. Other arts.

1. Painting and drawing. In central Australia in the 1930s Aranda children on the Finke River Lutheran Mission at Hermannsburg produced drawings in a 'European' manner under the influence of Arthur Murch (1902–89) and Frances Derham (1894–1987). In the same decade Albert Namatjira decided to develop the foundations of the still continuing Hermannsburg school of Aranda watercolourists after some instruction from the Western artist Rex Battarbee (1893–1969) of Victoria. After decades of disdain by white art critics, Namatjira's work has recently been more sympathetically reassessed. In the 1940s lively genre pictures were executed at the Carrolup Aboriginal School in Western Australia, now an Aboriginal controlled settlement and a flourishing centre for 'new' arts and crafts including textile printing and potterymaking.

But even before that, from the late 1920s, the regular production for sale of bark paintings (*see* §II, 7 above) was actively sponsored by missionaries in north-east Arnhem Land. Barks are now produced mainly in Arnhem Land but also by the Tiwi of Bathurst and Melville Islands and in the Kimberleys region of Western Australia. This commercial production has encouraged new techniques to preserve both bark and pigments, and, although the use of designs for ritual purposes has continued (Berndt, Berndt and Stanton), new, non-secret, designs have been used by artists willing to indulge Western tastes for more representative imagery. Women, who until recently in Arnhem Land were confined to weaving baskets, bags and mats, are also beginning to paint barks, for example at Yirrkala, using both traditional designs and portrayals of their everyday life or even Christian iconography. Most recently, the all-pervading use of acrylic paints has been extended to the 'translation' of bark painting subjects to canvas.

The acrylic paintings—or 'dot paintings' as they are popularly referred to—of the various communities of central and Western Australia represent the most innovative and—again in Western terms—most successful contemporary art movement in Aboriginal Australia. They are based on the traditional iconography of largely curvilinear motifs which are still employed in ritual body painting and on sacred objects such as the flat oval stone or wooden slabs (*tjurunga*) and ground designs, as well as in less 'restricted' forms on shields, spears, carrying dishes and boomerangs, and in the illustrating of stories told to children. The translation into the modern, saleable medium of paint, canvas and artist's board came about in 1971 at the instigation of an art teacher, Geoffrey Bardon (*b* 1940), then working at the government-established Papunya settlement west of Alice Springs. Such paintings, like their prototypes, are generally a formalized mapping of a particular geographical location associated with a specific mythological happening or individual (see fig. 18). In the early days of the movement, many Papunya paintings incorporated clearly recognizable figures and even secret-sacred objects, but since 1971 there has been an increasing abstraction of motifs, a recodifying that renders impossible precise interpretation by the uninitiated. Certain artists have used a restricted palette corresponding to the traditional earth colours of body and ground painting. Others,

18. Paddy Jupurrurla Nelson, Paddy Japaljarri Sims and Larry Jungarrayi Spencer, advised by Jimmy Jungurrayi Spencer: *Star Dreaming*, acrylic on canvas, 3.72×1.71 m, 1985 (Canberra, Australian National Gallery)

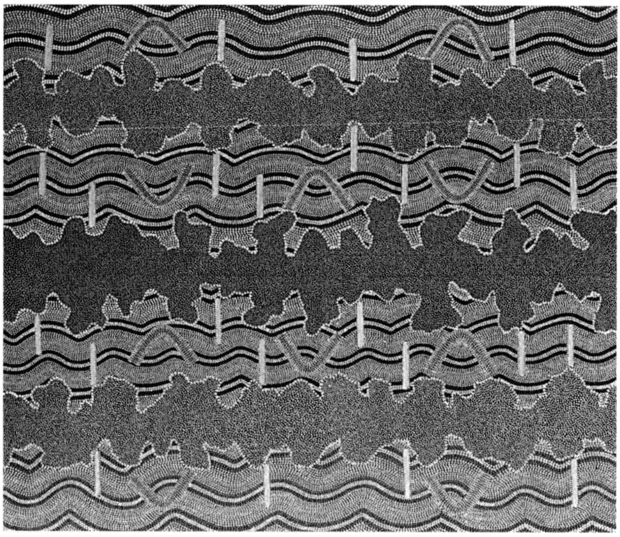

19. Clifford Possum Tjapaltjarri: *Water Dreaming*, acrylic on canvas, 1.52×1.83 m, 1983 (Bedford Park, Flinders University of South Australia, SA 150 Collection)

especially the newer artists in communities such as Balgo, Lajamanu and Utopia—who now include a significant number of women—continue to exploit the total chromatic freedom allowed by modern acrylic paints.

The success not only in Australia but also on the international art market of the work of such male artists as CLIFFORD POSSUM TJAPALTJARRI of the Anmatyerre/Aranda language group (see fig. 19), the Pintupi Charlie Tjaruru Tjungarrayi, the first Papunya artist to have been the subject of a retrospective exhibition, held in 1987, as well as the younger Warlpiri MICHAEL NELSON TJAKAMARRA, who has worked closely with the Sydney-based former conceptual artist Tim Johnson (*b* 1947), has led to an escalation of prices. In 1971 Papunya paintings sold for £A30–40; in the early 1990s they frequently fetched £A5000–10,000. This rise in individual acclaim has put strain on some communities since paintings are often collaborative works. Recognition has also encouraged the establishment of other acrylic painting centres, for example in the Warlpiri community at Yuendumu, west of Papunya, where women form 70% of the painters. This may have resulted from the fact that both the anthropologist and the teacher who encouraged the new art form were themselves women, while at Papunya, Bardon had found relations with the older men easier in a strictly gender-defined society. Yuendumu painting uses a wider range of colours than that from Papunya. In the same way that several Papunya artists have painted Hermannsburg-style watercolours, some Aranda painters, notably Wenten Rubuntja (*b* 1926), now work almost exclusively in the Papunya manner.

At Mt Allan (Yuelumu) in central Australia the elders of the Warlpiri and Anmatyerre community took a conscious decision in the 1980s to allow all members, men, women and children, to paint in acrylics. Some of the most accomplished work technically has been by girls as young as 12, though ownership of the stories, and the cash generated by their sale, remain with their parents. In Western Australia, the Balgo community has also turned to acrylic painting for external sale, while other groups have continued to prefer to use ochres on board or canvas. At Turkey Creek in the eastern Kimberley Ranges an artistic community has emerged around the painter ROVER THOMAS.

2. OTHER ARTS. While the Tiwi (both men and women) of Bathurst and Melville Islands continue to carve and paint *pukamani* poles as part of their own ceremonial life, they are also now producing them for sale as well as other carvings of birds and mythical beings. For the 1988 Bicentennial, the Aboriginal art adviser Djon Scott Mundine of Ramingining Arts in north-east Arnhem Land persuaded the Australian National Gallery to commission and purchase 200 log coffins, which their Aboriginal creators regarded as a proper commemoration of 200 years of white occupation.

In the north-west desert regions of South Australia dedicated white teachers introduced a whole range of new art forms to the women of the Pitjantjatjara (see fig. 11 above) and Yunkuntjatjara communities. From 1954, largely under the guidance of Winifred Hilliard at Ernabella, spinning and rug-weaving were introduced, but from *c.* 1971 these gave way to the less labour-intensive batik-printing for fashion fabrics. Anmatyerre/Aliawarra women at Utopia (in the central region) and Pitjantjatjara and Yunkuntjatjara women at Indulkana also turned to batik. Skills acquired from Indonesian textile-workers were used to produce a range of swirling foliate designs, which have also recently been translated by these and other communities into silkscreen or linocut prints. Women in the far west of Australia and at Yuendumu in central Australia as well as much further north on Bathurst Island and at Yirrkala have also taken up batik. Figures like those on the *pukamani* carvings are being repeated as motifs in the fabric printing of the Tiwi Designs Cooperative. Woodblock and silkscreen printing was begun in 1969 under the supervision of Madeline Clear as a partnership between two young Tiwi, Bede Tungutalum (*b* 1948) and Giovanni Tipungwuti. Other fabric production in more urban settings includes that of Jumbana Designs in Adelaide, Bronwyn Bancroft in Sydney and the aggressive marketing of the fabrics and prints of JIMMY PIKE, born in the Great Sandy Desert of Western Australia. Some fabrics, like some of the craft pottery now produced by various Aboriginal communities, including the Tiwi, have met with considerable white sales resistance for not looking 'Aboriginal' enough. Almost unique in gaining wide recognition and in achieving a freedom of expression in ceramics, both small pieces and murals, is the work of Thancoupie (*b* 1937), who is from Weipa on Cape York Peninsula but was trained in Sydney.

Though many Aborigines object to the use of the word 'urban'—an alternative Aboriginal term, 'Koori', is preferred in the south-east—the adjective does serve to describe the current residence of many Aboriginal artists living outside the communities of central or northern Australia. Like Thancoupie, many of these are working exclusively in non-traditional media. They are more likely to work without community support and to have to deal more directly with Western society and its art world. Among them is Banduk Marika (*see* MARIKA, (3)), who until the late 1980s spent most of her adult life in Darwin and Sydney. Sister of one famous bark painter and daughter of another, she has used traditional images, though for linocuts and prints, not barks and refers to her work as 'contemporary traditional'. Those without tribal upbringing or their own inherited traditional imagery include art school-trained TREVOR NICKOLLS from Port Adelaide, who in his search for roots has used a wide range of subject-matter and styles, including the dotting techniques of acrylic paintings from central Australia, yet has also expressed a wish to be recognized as an artist and not 'merely' as an Aboriginal artist (Beier). Sally Morgan (*b* 1951, active in Perth) and Robert Campbell jr (*b* Kempsey, NSW, 1944, *d* 1993) have also used the dotting or hatching techniques of traditional art to tell their own autobiographies or make political statements. Byron Pickett (*b* 1955) has used his silkscreen prints to show the different worlds of traditional Aborigines and Western culture, though even his grandparents did not live traditional Aboriginal lives. 'Koori' artists of Sydney and Melbourne, such as Gordon Syron (*b* 1941), LIN ONUS (see fig. 20), Jeffrey Samuels (*b* 1956), Arone Raymond Meeks (*b* 1957) and Fiona Foley (*b* 1964), have consciously sought out and borrowed from their Aboriginal heritage. Aboriginal photographers and film makers are also gaining recognition, such as Polly Sumner (*b* 1952) in Adelaide and Tracey Moffatt (*b* Brisbane, 1960) in Sydney. Much of the art of this group is nonetheless deeply concerned with the questions of Aboriginal identity and the problems of Aboriginal poverty and deprivation and is often more obviously political than that of groups still living in the communities of central and northern Australia.

20. Lin Onus: *Where to now?*, linocut on bone paper, 418×297 mm, 1986 (Bedford Park, Flinders University of South Australia)

BIBLIOGRAPHY

N. H. H. Graburn, ed.: *Ethnic and Tourist Arts: Cultural Expressions from the Fourth World* (Berkeley, 1976)
G. Bardon: *Aboriginal Art of the Western Desert* (Adelaide, 1978)
R. Edwards, ed.: *Aboriginal Art in Australia* (Adelaide, 1978)
A. Crocker: *Mr Sandman Bring Me a Dream* (Sydney, 1981)
R. M. Berndt, C. H. Berndt and J. E. Stanton: *Aboriginal Australian Art: A Visual Perspective* (Sydney, 1982, rev. 1989)
J. Isaacs: *Thancoupie the Potter* (Sydney, 1982)
——: *Australia's Living Heritage: Arts of the Dreaming* (Sydney, 1984)
Koori Art '84 (exh. cat., ed. T. Johnson and V. Johnson; Sydney Artspace, 1984)
U. Beier: *Dreamtime–Machine Time: The Art of Trevor Nickolls* (Bathurst, New South Wales, 1985)
W. Caruana: *Contemporary Australian Aboriginal Art* (Canberra, 1986)
Dot and Circle: A Retrospective Survey of the Aboriginal Acrylic Paintings of Central Australia (exh. cat., ed. J. Maughan and J. Zimmer; Bedford Park, Flinders U. S. Australia; Melbourne, Royal Inst. Technol. A.G.; 1986)
The Dreamtime Today: A Survey of Contemporary Aboriginal Arts and Crafts (exh. cat., ed. J. Maughan and J. V. S. Megaw; Bedford Park, Flinders U. S. Australia; Adelaide, Royal S. Austral. Soc. A., Kintore Gal.; 1986)
Aboriginal Australian Views in Print and Poster (exh. cat., ed. J. Samuels and C. Watson; Melbourne, Prt Council Australia, 1987)
Australia—Art and Aboriginality 1987: Portsmouth Festival U.K. (exh. cat., ed. V. Johnson; Portsmouth, Aspex Gal.; Sydney, Aboriginal A.; 1987)
Charlie Tjaruru Tjungarrayi (exh. cat., ed. A. Crocker; Orange, Reg. A. G., Hist. Soc. Mus., 1987)
J. Davila: 'Aboriginality: A Lugubrious Game?', *A. & Text*, xxv/4 (1987), pp. 53–7
KARNTA: Aboriginal Women's Art (exh. cat., ed. C. McGuignan, 1987)
Dreamings: The Art of Aboriginal Australia (exh. cat., ed. P. Sutton; New York, Asia Soc. Gals; U. Chicago, IL, Smart Gal.; Melbourne, Mus. Victoria; Adelaide, S. Austral. Mus.; 1988–90)
J. Altman, C. McGuigan and P. Yu: *The Aboriginal Arts and Crafts Industry: Report of the Review Committee*, Department of Aboriginal Affairs (Canberra, 1989)
J. Isaacs: *Aboriginality: Contemporary Aboriginal Paintings and Prints* (St Lucia, Queensland, 1989, rev. 1992)
Mythscapes: Aboriginal Art of the Desert (exh. cat., ed. J. Ryan; Melbourne, N.G. Victoria, 1989)
Nothing to Celebrate? Australian Aboriginal Political Art & the Bicentennial (exh. cat., ed. M. Ruth Megaw; Bedford Park, Flinders U. S. Australia, 1989)
S. Britton, L. Dauth and F. Wright, eds: 'Contemporary Australian Aboriginal Art', *Artlink*, x/1–2 (1990)
Balance 1990: Views, Visions, Influences (exh. cat., ed. M. Eather and Marlene Hall; Brisbane, Queensland A.G., 1990)
East to West: Land in Papunya Painting (exh. cat., ed. J. Kean; Adelaide, Tandamya Aboriginal Cult. Inst., 1990)
G. Bardon: *Papunya Tula: Art of the Western Desert* (Melbourne, 1991)
M. Boulter: *The Art of Utopia: A New Direction in Contemporary Aboriginal Art* (Tortola, BVI, 1991)
R. Crumlin, ed.: *Aboriginal Art and Spirituality* (North Blackburn, Victoria, 1991)
T. Smith: 'From the Desert: Aboriginal Painting, 1970–90', *Australian Painting, 1788–1990*, by B. Smith with T. Smith (Melbourne, 1991), pp. 495–517
Aboriginal Women's Exhibition (exh. cat., ed. H. Perkins; Sydney, A.G. NSW, 1991)
J. Hardy, J. V. S. Megaw and M. Ruth Megaw, eds: *The Heritage of Namatjira: The Watercolourists of Central Australia* (Melbourne, 1992)
G. Bennett: 'Aesthetics and Iconography: An Artist's Approach', *Aratjara: Art of the First Australians—Traditional and Contemporary Works by Aboriginal and Torres Strait Artists* (exh. cat., ed. B. Lüthi; Düsseldorf, Kstsamml. Nordrhein-Westfalen; London, Hayward Gal.;

Humlebæk, Louisiana Mus.; Sydney, Mus. Contemp. A.; 1993–4), pp. 85–91

J. V. S. MEGAW, M. RUTH MEGAW

V. Collectors and dealers.

Over two centuries of European colonization, interest in Aboriginal art has attracted the attention of different types of viewers and collectors. Aboriginal objects have been collected as art rather than as ethnographic curios only since World War II. They were first collected during such voyages as those from 1768 by James Cook (1728–79) and in 1800–04 by François Péron (1775–1810), but little of this survives. Until the mid-19th century, when well-documented collections began, artefacts were collected by individuals as mementoes of Australia: many found their way into European museums, but documentation on these objects and on their collectors is largely lost. Much of this material in Europe returned to Australia in the 1970s as part of the Christensen collection loaned to the National Gallery of Victoria, Melbourne.

From the 1850s a more systematic approach to collecting began with the acquisition of artefacts for private collections or for museums in Australia and overseas. One of the great collectors of this period was the amateur naturalist R. E. Johns, who formed two large collections from south-east Australia, one of which was given to the Robert O'Hara Bourke Memorial Museum in Beechworth, Victoria in 1868, while the other was acquired by the Museum (formerly National Museum) of Victoria in 1910. Operating on a smaller scale were people such as Mary Bundock, who spent most of her life at an isolated sheep station on the Richmond River, New South Wales, and used her contact with Aboriginal groups to collect for several museums during the 1870s, including the Rijksmuseum voor Volkenkunde in Leiden, Kew Gardens, London, and the Australian Museum in Sydney. The development of Australian anthropology in the 1890s owed much to the work of such collectors and recorders of Aboriginal artefacts and customs.

Until well after World War II missionaries and anthropologists were responsible for the major collections for the study of Aboriginal society, the former including Karl Strehlow and R. G. Reuther, and the latter Sir W. Baldwin Spencer (1860–1929) and W. E. Roth. T. T. Webb and Wilbur Chaseling made large collections from Milingimbi and Yirrkala respectively and sold them to museums in Brisbane, Sydney and Melbourne. In the 1930s and 1940s Donald Thomson of Melbourne University compiled one of the best-documented Arnhem Land collections, which was transferred on his death to the then National Museum of Victoria. Ronald Berndt and his wife Catherine collected from the 1940s onwards and their holdings became the basis of the Berndt Museum of Anthropology (formerly the Anthropology Research Museum) at the University of Western Australia, Perth. C. P. Mountford developed collections based on his expeditions to Arnhem Land, Melville and Bathurst Islands and central Australia. During this period museum ethnographers such as Norman Tindale of the South Australian Museum, Adelaide, and Fred McCarthy of the Australian Museum, Sydney, took active roles in acquisitions, and in the 1960s Helen Groger-Wurm acquired a superb collection for the National Museum of Australia in Canberra and the Museums and Art Galleries of the Northern Territory in Darwin.

The activities of anthropologists and missionaries stimulated private collecting in two ways: they gradually increased awareness of Aboriginal art and helped make art a commodity. From the late 1950s the market in Aboriginal art began to expand rapidly and, although it was still largely based on local community enterprises, a few major collector/dealers began to emerge. Jim Davidson, a Melbourne businessman, made annual journeys to the Northern Territory to purchase Aboriginal art and, in addition to dealing in the works, established a large personal collection. Dorothy Bennet began collecting and dealing in the early 1960s, organizing exhibitions in Australia and Japan and establishing a shop in Darwin. Sandra Holmes also built up large collections of Arnhem Land and Tiwi art in particular, concentrating on the work of YIRAWALA, whose art she did much to promote. Outside Australia major collections were developed by Ed Ruhe and Louis Allen in the USA and Karel Kupka in France. In the 1980s Aboriginal art was sold through specialist galleries in all the major cities in Australia, supported by a government marketing organization, and many private collections had begun to emerge, of which the most prominent were those of Robert Holmes à Court (1937–90), Lord McAlpine of West Green (*b* 1942), Margaret (Mrs Douglas) Carnegie and Sir Roderick Carnegie (*b* 1932) and John Kluge. By the 1990s there had been a dramatic increase in the number of dealers in contemporary Australian Aboriginal art. For example, in 1993 there were more than 20 galleries specializing in Aboriginal art in Alice Springs and two in central London.

BIBLIOGRAPHY

I. McBryde: 'Museum Collections from the Richmond River District', *Records of Times Past: Ethnohistorical Essays on the Culture and Ecology of New England Tribes*, ed. I. McBryde (Canberra, 1978)

Aboriginal Australia (exh. cat. by C. Cooper and others, Sydney, Austral. Gal. Directors Council, 1981–2)

J. Altman and L. Taylor: *Marketing Aboriginal Art in the 1990s: Papers Presented to a Workshop in Canberra, 12–13 June 1990* (Canberra, 1991)

VI. Museums and exhibitions.

The term 'Aboriginal art', as distinct from Aboriginal ethnographic objects, was hardly used as a category until the 20th century. Indeed, until the 1950s Aboriginal objects were not displayed in Australian art galleries but in museums of natural history. Even today the vast majority of Aboriginal art works are still housed in ethnographic departments of state and national museums.

Within Australia the largest collections of Aboriginal art are in museums in the state capitals: the Australian Museum in Sydney; the Museum of Victoria, Melbourne; the South Australian Museum, Adelaide; the Queensland Museum, Brisbane; and the Western Australian Museum, Perth. These museums all began to establish collections in the 19th century, beginning with the Australian Museum (1827) and the then National Museum of Victoria (1854). Much of the best 19th-century material, however, left Australia for museums in Europe. The British Museum, London, the Pitt Rivers Museum, Oxford, the Manchester Museum, the Museum of Archaeology and Anthropology at Cambridge University and the National Museum of

Ireland, Dublin all have large collections, as do most of the major ethnographic museums in Europe, for example the Staatliches Museum für Völkerkunde in Munich and the Museum für Völkerkunde in Hamburg. Missionaries, in particular, continued to supply large collections to museums in their home countries until the beginning of the 20th century: as late as 1913 Otto Liebler, a Lutheran missionary, presented a collection of 606 Arrente objects to the Staatliches Museum für Völkerkunde (now Linden-Museum) in Stuttgart.

As the 20th century progressed, the development of public collections shifted from overseas to Australian museums, which now house nearly all the major collections made during the first half of the century. In the 1960s major new collections were developed in Darwin through the Museums and Art Galleries of the Northern Territory and in the National Ethnographic Collection in Canberra (now part of the National Museum of Australia). After World War II, Aboriginal art began to gain a place in the state art galleries, beginning with the paintings collected by C. P. Mountford during the 1948 Australian–American Scientific Expedition to Arnhem Land. By 1988 the Australian National Gallery in Canberra had the fastest growing collection of Aboriginal art and had begun to devote considerable space to its exhibition. The first major exhibition of its holdings was launched in 1989. In the 1970s and 1980s overseas museums, especially the British Museum in London, the Musée de l'Homme in Paris and the National Museum of Ethnology in Osaka, began again to expand their holdings of Aboriginal work.

Major exhibitions of Aboriginal art were not held until about the mid-20th century, although Aboriginal artefacts were displayed as examples of Australian crafts at many 19th-century Great Exhibitions and they were housed in museum ethnographic galleries. The first generally recognized exhibition, *Australian Aboriginal Art*, took place in 1929 at the National Museum of Victoria. A second exhibition, *Primitive Art*, was organized in Melbourne in 1943 by Leonhard Adam. This exhibition stimulated Australian interest in Aboriginal art, according to Tony Tuckson, the artist and gallery director, who in 1960 organized the next major exhibition, *Australian Aboriginal Art*, which toured the major state capitals.

The first exhibition of an individual Aboriginal artist's work (apart from that of the watercolourist Albert Namatjira) was that of Yirawala, the Kunwinjku artist, at the University of Sydney in 1971. This was followed in 1978 by the joint exhibition in Canberra of work by Banapana Maymurru and NARRITJIN MAYMURRU. The first individual exhibition in a commercial gallery was that of Johny Bulunbulum at Sydney's Hogarth Galleries in 1981, followed shortly afterwards by a show devoted to works by Peter Marralwanga in the Creative Native Aboriginal Art Gallery in Perth. Also held in 1981 was *Aboriginal Australia*, which was circulated by the Australian Gallery Directors Council and which by the mid-1990s was the largest exhibition of Aboriginal art so far organized. The frequency of exhibitions increased greatly in the 1970s and 1980s, going from less than one per year in the 1960s to more than 20 a year by the mid-1980s; overseas exhibitions similarly increased during this period. The Australian bicentennial in 1988 further stimulated interest in Aboriginal art; this resulted in a series of major exhibitions in Australia and the USA, including *The Inspired Dream* and *Dreamings: The Art of Aboriginal Australia.* These were followed in Europe by *Aratjara: Art of the First Australians.*

BIBLIOGRAPHY

Australian Aboriginal Art (exh. cat. by C. Barrett and A. S. Kenyon, Melbourne, Mus. Victoria, 1929)
Primitive Art (exh. cat., intro. L. Adam; Melbourne, Mus. Victoria, 1943)
J. A. Tuckson: 'Aboriginal Art and the Western World', *Australian Aboriginal Art*, ed. R. M. Berndt (Sydney, 1964/*R* 1968), pp. 60–68
Aboriginal Australia (exh. cat. by C. Cooper and others, Sydney, Austral. Gal. Directors Council, 1981–2)
Koori Art '84 (exh. cat., ed. T. Johnson and V. Johnson; Sydney Artspace, 1984)
Dot and Circle: A Retrospective of the Aboriginal Paintings of Central Australia (exh. cat., ed. J. Maughan and J. Zimmer; Bedford Park, Flinders U. S. Australia; Melbourne, Royal Inst. Technol. A.G., 1986)
The Inspired Dream (exh. cat., ed. M. West; Brisbane, Queensland A.G., 1988)
Dreamings: The Art of Aboriginal Australia (exh. cat., ed. P. Sutton; New York, Asia Soc. Gals; U. Chicago, IL, Smart Gal.; Melbourne, Mus. Victoria; Adelaide, S. Austral. Mus.; 1988–90)
Aratjara: Art of the First Australians–Traditional and Contemporary Works by Aboriginal and Torres Strait Artists (exh. cat., ed. B. Lüthi; Düsseldorf, Kstsamml. Nordrhein-Westfalen; London, Hayward Gal.; Humlebæk, Louisiana Mus.; Sydney, Mus. Contemp. A.; 1993–4)
For further bibliography *see* §IV above.

VII. Historiography.

The authors of the early literature on the Australian Aborigines, such as Thomas Worsnop (1821–98), Robert Brough Smyth (1830–89) and Edward Curr (1820–89), occasionally referred to art but provided little detailed information. Indeed the prevailing attitude throughout most of the 19th century was that Aborigines did not produce 'art'. Evolutionary theorists placed Aborigines at the lowest level of human development and their paintings and carvings were dismissed cursorily: the anthropologist Sir Edward Burnett Tylor (1832–1917), for example, described them as 'rude frescoes'. This attitude may partly have arisen because much Aboriginal art, restricted to the ceremonial ground, was unknown to Europeans, while certain forms, such as body painting and sand sculpture, are ephemeral. Yet even when the art was recorded and admired, its Aboriginal roots were denied: Sir George Grey (1812–98) wrote in 1841 of the Wandjina paintings of the Kimberleys: '. . . whatever may have been the age of these paintings, it is scarcely probable that they could have been painted by a self-taught savage'.

Sir W. Baldwin Spencer, F. J. Gillen and, to a lesser extent, Alfred Howitt (1839–1908), Robert Mathews (1841–1918) and W. E. Roth produced the first detailed accounts of Aboriginal art at the end of the 19th century. Although Spencer and Gillen shared the prevailing evolutionary paradigm (Morphy, 1988), they wrote extensive ethnographic accounts of Aboriginal art and its ritual contexts: the rock art and bark paintings of Western Arnhem Land, for example, are referred to in positive terms (Spencer). Few other anthropologists wrote about Aboriginal art until after World War II, although references to art appear in general descriptive accounts (e.g. Tindale) and catalogues were produced to accompany the few exhibitions of Aboriginal art that were held during the period (*see* §VI above). The diffusionist anthropologist

Daniel Sutherland Davidson (1900–52) produced some comparative papers on Aboriginal art, and this work strongly influenced the prehistorian Fred McCarthy, who began his study of rock art. One of the few to write on Aboriginal art before World War II was Margaret Preston, who saw Aboriginal design as a possible source of inspiration in her desire to create a uniquely Australian art, although she tended to interpret its positive qualities as the accidental product of inadequate technique.

From the 1940s, writings on the subject increased with the publication of both substantial exhibition catalogues and monographs on the art of particular regions. C. P. Mountford, Ronald Berndt and Catherine Berndt discussed the ceremonial context of art, illustrating and documenting the meanings of paintings and objects. This provided invaluable data but did not attempt to analyse the systems of representation or the integration of art within Aboriginal knowledge. Nancy Munn filled this gap in the 1950s and 1960s by revealing the iconography and symbolism of art in the context of socialization in Warlpiri and Pitjantjantjara society. Building on Munn's work, Howard Morphy and Luke Taylor produced detailed semiological studies of the artistic systems of the Yolngu and Kunwinjku respectively, focusing on the role of art in the reproduction of systems of knowledge and structures of authority.

Two schools developed in the flourishing study of rock art: some scholars, such as John Clegg and Lesley Maynard, saw rock art as primarily archaeological data, while others, including Robert Layton, Michael Morwood and Andrée Rosenfeld, integrated rock art within general anthropological approaches to art. Ethnographic accounts of rock art began to appear just as the practice of painting on rocks was dying out (Chaloupka; Taçon; Blundell).

With the increased recognition and commercial success of Aboriginal art in the 1970s, and its prominence in Australian consciousness, it began to be written about from various different perspectives by art historians, artists and journalists as well as anthropologists. A more extensive range of art-historical problems began to be considered, including questions relating to aesthetics and audience creation (Morphy, 1987; Jones). Other major themes concerned the commercialization of art (Altman), the development of continuing traditions (Bardon; Megaw) and the effects on art of the dialogue between Aboriginal and European societies (e.g. Morphy, 1983; Jones and Sutton; Loveday and Cooke). Concerns with cultural heritage and conservation became important issues (Edwards, 1972; Edwards and Stewart; Rosenfeld) and interests extended to consideration of the art of urban Aboriginal people and the role of art in the creation of identity in the post-colonial context (e.g. Johnson). By 1990 Aboriginal art was liberated from its previous isolation in ethnographic museums, having gained increasing relevance to several academic disciplines and audiences, and it featured strongly in discourse on Australian art, its definitions and directions.

BIBLIOGRAPHY

EARLY STUDIES

G. Grey: *Journals of Two Expeditions of Discovery in North-west and Western Australia during the Years 1837, 38 and 39* (London, 1841)

R. B. Smyth: *The Aborigines of Victoria and Other Parts of Australia and Tasmania*, 2 vols (Melbourne and London, 1878)

E. M. Curr: *The Australian Race: Its Origins, Language, Customs*, 4 vols (Melbourne, 1886–7)

E. B. Tylor: *Anthropology: An Introduction to the Study of Man and Civilization* (London, 1892)

R. H. Mathews: 'Rock Carvings and Paintings of the Australian Aborigines', *Proc. Amer. Philos. Soc.*, xxxvii (1897), pp. 466–78

W. E. Roth: *Ethnological Studies among the North-west-central Queensland Aborigines* (Brisbane, 1897)

T. Worsnop: *The Prehistoric Arts, Manufactures, Works, Weapons, etc of the Aborigines of Australia* (Adelaide, 1897)

W. B. Spencer and F. J. Gillen: *The Native Tribes of Central Australia* (London, 1899/*R* 1969)

A. W. Howitt: *The Native Tribes of South-east Australia* (London, 1904)

W. B. Spencer and F. J. Gillen: *The Northern Tribes of Central Australia* (London, 1904/*R* 1969)

W. B. Spencer: *Native Tribes of the Northern Territory of Australia* (London, 1914)

M. Preston: 'The Indigenous Art of Australia', *A. Australia*, xi (1925), pp. 32–45

N. Tindale: 'Natives of Groote Eylandt and the West Coast of the Gulf of Carpentaria', *Rec. S. Austral. Mus.*, iii (1925), pp. 61–134

D. S. Davidson: *Aboriginal Australian and Tasmanian Rock Carvings and Paintings*, Memoirs of the American Philosophical Society, v (Philadelphia, 1936)

F. D. McCarthy: *Australian Aboriginal Decorative Art* (Sydney, 1938/*R* 1962)

GENERAL

C. P. Mountford: *Aboriginal Paintings from Australia* (London, 1954, rev. Milan, 1964)

F. D. McCarthy: *Australian Aboriginal Rock Art* (Sydney, 1958, rev. 1979)

R. M. Berndt, ed.: *Australian Aboriginal Art* (Sydney, 1964/*R* 1968)

R. Edwards, ed.: *The Preservation of Australia's Aboriginal Heritage* (Canberra, 1975)

L. Maynard: 'Classification and Terminology in Australian Rock Art', *Form in Indigenous Art: Schematisation in the Art of Aboriginal Australia and Prehistoric Europe*, ed. P. J. Ucko (Canberra, 1977), pp. 387–402

R. Edwards and J. Stewart: *Preserving of Indigenous Cultures: A New Role for Museums* (Canberra, 1980)

J. Clegg: *Notes towards Mathesis Art* (Balmain, 1979, rev. 1981)

P. Loveday and P. Cooke, eds: *Aboriginal Arts and Crafts and the Market* (Darwin, 1983)

R. Layton: 'The Cultural Context of Hunter-gatherer Rock Art', *Man*, xx/3 (1985), pp. 434–53

A. Rosenfeld: *Rock Art Conservation in Australia* (Canberra, 1985)

Australia—Art and Aboriginality 1987: Portsmouth Festival U.K. (exh. cat., ed. V. Johnson; Portsmouth, Apex Gal.; Sydney, Aboriginal A.; 1987)

H. Morphy: 'Audiences for Art', *Australians from 1939*, ed. A. Curthoys, A. W. Martin and T. Rowse (Sydney, 1987), pp. 167–75

——: 'The Original Australians and the Evolution of Anthropology', *Australia in Oxford*, ed. H. Morphy and E. Edwards, Pitt Rivers Museum Monograph 4 (Oxford, 1988), pp. 48–61

P. G. Jones: 'Perceptions of Aboriginal Art: A History', *Dreamings: The Art of Aboriginal Australia* (exh. cat., ed. P. Sutton; New York, Asia Soc. Gals; U. Chicago, IL, Smart Gal.; Melbourne, Mus. Victoria; Adelaide, S. Austral. Mus.; 1988–90), pp. 143–79

P. Sutton, P. Jones and S. Hemming: 'Survival, Regeneration, and Impact', *Dreamings: The Art of Aboriginal Australia* (exh. cat., ed. P. Sutton; New York, Asia Soc. Gals; U. Chicago, IL, Smart Gal.; Melbourne, Mus. Victoria; Adelaide, S. Austral. Mus.; 1988–90), pp. 180–212

J. Altman: *The Aboriginal Arts and Crafts Industry* (Canberra, 1989)

H. Morphy: 'On Representing Ancestral Beings', *Animals into Art*, ed. H. Morphy, One World Archaeology, 7 (London, 1989), pp. 144–60

S. Britton and F. Wright, eds: 'Aboriginal Arts in Australia', *Artlink* (1990) [special issue, 11]

SPECIALIST STUDIES

A. P. Elkin, R. M. Berndt and C. H. Berndt: *Art in Arnhem Land* (Melbourne, 1950)

R. M. Berndt: *Kunapipi: A Study of an Australian Aboriginal Religious Cult* (New York, 1951)

C. P. Mountford: *Art, Myth and Symbolism*, i of *Records of the American–Australian Expedition to Arnhem Land* (Melbourne, 1956)

——: *The Tiwi: Their Art, Myth and Ceremony* (London, 1958)

N. Munn: *Walbiri Iconography: Graphic Representation and Cultural Symbolism in a Central Australian Society* (Ithaca, NY, 1973, rev. Chicago, 1986)

V. J. Blundell: 'The Wandjina Cave Paintings of North-west Australia', *Arctic Anthropol.*, xi (1974), pp. 213–23
G. Bardon: *Aboriginal Art of the Western Desert* (Adelaide, 1979)
R. Edwards: *Australian Aboriginal Art: The Art of the Alligator River Region of the Northern Territory* (Canberra, 1979)
A. Rosenfeld, D. Horton and J. Winter: *Early Man in North Queensland: Art and Archaeology of the Laura Area* (Canberra, 1981)
J. V. S. Megaw: 'Western Desert Acrylic Painting: Artefact or Art?', *A. Hist.*, v (1982), pp. 205–18
H. Morphy: ' "Now You Understand": An Analysis of the Way Yolngu Have Used Sacred Knowledge to Retain their Autonomy', *Aborigines, Land and Landrights*, ed. N. Peterson and M. Langton (Canberra, 1983), pp. 110–33
M. Morwood: 'The Prehistory of the Central Queensland Highlands', *Adv. World Archaeol.*, iii (1984), pp. 325–80
G. Chaloupka: 'Chronological Sequence of Arnhem Land Plateau Rock Art', *Archaeological Research in Kakadu National Park*, ed. R. Jones (Canberra, 1985), pp. 269–80
N. Amadadio and others: *Albert Namatjira: The Life and Work of an Australian Artist* (Melbourne, 1986)
P. G. Jones and P. Sutton: *Art and Land: Aboriginal Sculptures of the Lake Eyre Region* (Adelaide, 1986)
Kuruwarri: Yuendemu Doors (Canberra, 1987) [works by Warlukurlangu artists]
H. Morphy: 'From Dull to Brilliant: The Aesthetics of Spiritual Power among the Yolngu', *Man*, xxiv/1 (1989), pp. 21–40; also in *Anthropology, Art and Aesthetics*, ed. J. Coote and A. Shelton, Oxford Studies in the Anthropology of Cultural Forms (Oxford, 1992/*R* 1994), pp. 181–208
P. Taçon: 'Art and the Essence of Being: Symbolic and Economic Aspects of Fish among the People of Western Arnhem Land', *Animals into Art*, ed. H. Morphy (London, 1989), pp. 236–50
L. Taylor: 'Seeing the "Inside": Kunwinjku Paintings and the Symbol of the Divided Body', *Animals into Art*, ed. H. Morphy (London, 1989), pp. 371–89
H. Morphy: *Ancestral Connections: Art and an Aboriginal System of Knowledge* (Chicago and London, 1991)

HOWARD MORPHY

About, Edmond(-François-Valentin) (*b* Dieuze, Meurthe, 14 Feb 1828; *d* Paris, 16 Jan 1885). French writer and critic. He had a brilliant scholastic career, and he was awarded a place at the Ecole Française d'Athènes in 1851, having shown, according to the jury, 'a strong appreciation of the great works of art'. He remained in Athens until 1853, when he returned to Paris to embark on a literary career. Although his first work, *La Grèce Contemporaine* (1855), was successful and was well received by the influential *Revue des Deux Mondes* (in which his novel *Tolla* was published in 1855), About was unsuccessful as a playwright. While he continued to write novels and political essays he contributed to several Parisian newspapers, such as *Le Figaro*, *L'Opinion Nationale*, *Le Constitutionnel*, *Le Gaulois* and *Le Soir*. Following the Franco-Prussian War of 1870, together with his friend Francisque Sarcey he founded his own newspaper, *XIXe Siècle*, a 'Conservative Republican' organ that was anticlerical and opposed to the restoration of the monarchy.

About quickly gained a reputation as an influential art critic. In 1855 he published his *Voyage à travers l'Exposition des Beaux-Arts*, a collection of apparently casual but extremely lively pieces on different sections of the Exposition Universelle of 1855 in Paris. In the following years he wrote a series of columns on the annual Salons in *Le Moniteur*, *Le Petit Journal*, *La Revue des Deux Mondes* and his own newspaper, which were sometimes collected in book form.

About was one of the last major French critics to uphold the supremacy of history painting and the hierarchy of the genres. He was particularly gripped by pictorial representation of dramatic historical events, to which he devoted long descriptions in his reviews, but he also appreciated paintings on contemporary social issues, for example *So That's What You Call Vagrancy* (exh. Salon 1855; Paris, Mus. d'Orsay) by Alfred Stevens (i). Violently hostile to Manet and dismissive of the Impressionists, he preferred to support young artists who expressed their originality within the French academic tradition, most notably Paul Baudry, whose Paris Opéra decorations he praised in several publications. About's newspaper columns reveal him as an articulate and brilliant journalist, eager to please the Parisian intelligentsia.

WRITINGS

Voyage à travers l'Exposition des Beaux-Arts (Paris, 1855)
Le Salon de 1864 (Paris, 1864)
Le Salon de 1866 (Paris, 1867)
Raphaël à l'exposition des Champs-Elysées (Paris, 1875)
Peintures décoratifs du grand foyer de l'Opéra par Paul Baudry (Paris, 1876)
Le Décameron du Salon de peinture pour l'année 1881 (Paris, 1881)
Quinze journées au Salon de peinture et de sculpture en 1883 (Paris, 1883)

For a full list of About's Salon criticism (1855–70), see M. Ward and C. Parsons: *A Bibliography of Second Empire Salon Criticism* (Cambridge, 1986).

BIBLIOGRAPHY

DBF
F. Sarcey: Obituary, *XIXe Siècle* (17 Jan 1885)
J. Barbey d'Aurevilley: *Journalistes et polémistes, chroniqueurs et pamphlétaires* (Paris, 1895)
'Edmond About: Ecrivain et critique d'art (1828–1885)', *Cah. Mus. A. & Essai*, 16 (Paris, 1985)

PAUL GERBOD

Abraham, Pol [Hippolyte] (*b* Nantes, 19 March 1891; *d* Paris, 20 Jan 1966). French architect and teacher. A student of Alfred-Henri Recoura (1864–1939), he graduated from the Ecole des Beaux-Arts, Paris, in 1920. He settled in Paris, and his first works were influenced by Art Deco. In 1923 he became one of the two architects of the new seaside resort of Sables-d'Or-les-Pins (Côtes-du-Nord). There, and in the nearby village of Val-André, Abraham began his analysis and rejection of the picturesque in such buildings as Villa Miramar (1928) and Villa Ramona (1929). In 1929, in partnership with Henry-Jacques Le Même (*b* 1897), he made his first design for a sanatorium, later executing three examples at Passy (Haute-Savoie), which are among his best works: Roc-de-Fiz (1931), Guébriant (1933) and Geoffroy de Martel de Janville (1939). Two blocks of flats built in Paris in 1931 (at 28 Boulevard Raspail and Square Albinoni) characterize the peak of his production in their precision and sobriety of composition, moderate use of the modernist vocabulary and use of new techniques and materials.

In 1934 at the Ecole du Louvre Abraham upheld a polemical thesis on Gothic contradicting Eugène Viollet-le-Duc. He subsequently undertook experiments on stone masonry. For several houses built in Brittany in 1939, he made use of a regionalism formerly despised, and in 1942 for the Etudes Provinciales competition, of which he was a prizewinner, he had recourse to historicism. Appointed architect-in-chief for the rebuilding of the Loiret, he returned to his former preoccupations there and in Orléans undertook remarkable works in which he tested his theories of the heavy wall and partial prefabrication. After World War II he was the consultant of numerous administrations, taught at the Ecole Spéciale d'Architecture, Paris, was on the jury of the Grand Prix de Rome and was nominated to the Inspection Générale des Bâtiments Civils et Palais Nationaux. He occupied himself by publishing designs and promoting his ideas, guided by the search for a constructive rationality, which, in his view, would transcend style.

WRITINGS

Quelques oeuvres réalisées, 1921–1923 (Strasbourg, n.d.)
Travaux d'architecture (Strasbourg, 1934)
Viollet-Le-Duc et le rationalisme médiéval (Paris, 1934)
Architecture préfabriquée (Paris, 1946)

BIBLIOGRAPHY

D. Le Couédic: 'Le Charme discret du mouvement moderne', *1919–1945: Bretagne, modernité et régionalisme* (Brussels, 1986), pp. 52–77

DANIEL LE COUÉDIC

Abraham ben Judah ibn Hayyim (*fl* 15th century). ?Portuguese writer of Jewish origin. A treatise on the preparation of colours and gold for use in manuscript illumination (Parma, Bib. Palatina, MS. De Rossi 945) has been attributed to him (for a contrary opinion see Metzger); it is the only extant book of this kind apparently written by a Jew. The Portuguese text is written in Hebrew characters. An ornate signature of Abraham ibn Hayyim appears on fol. 20*r*, and an inscription of fol. 1*r* states that the work was written by him in Loulé in 1262; the author was consequently believed to have lived in the 13th century, but the treatise is now generally accepted as being of the 15th century, when Portugal, especially Lisbon, was an important centre of Hebrew manuscript illumination. It has been suggested that JOSEPH IBN HAYYIM, the artist who illuminated the Kennicott Bible (1476; Oxford, Bodleian Lib., MS. Kenn. 1; *see* JEWISH ART, §IV, 1(ii)), was Abraham's son.

BIBLIOGRAPHY

D. S. Blondheim: 'An Old Portuguese Work on Manuscript Illumination', *Jew. Q. Rev.*, xix (1928–9), pp. 97–135
R. Vishnitzer: 'Note on "An Old Portuguese Work on Manuscript Illumination"', *Jew. Q. Rev.*, xx (1929–30), p. 89
T. Metzger: *Les Manuscrits hébreux copiés et décorés à Lisbonne dans les dernières décennies du XVe siècle* (Paris, 1977), pp. 4–6, note 5
H. J. Abrahams: 'A Thirteenth-century Portuguese Work on Manuscript Illumination', *Ambix*, xxvi/2 (1979), pp. 95–9
B. Narkiss: *The Kennicott Bible* (London, 1985), p. 79

EVELYN M. COHEN

Abrahams, Carl (*b* St Andrew, Jamaica, 1913). Jamaican painter. He began his career as a cartoonist for various local periodicals. In 1937 Augustus John, then working in Jamaica, encouraged him to begin painting. Unlike the majority of his contemporaries, he eschewed the 'official' classes of the Institute of Jamaica and virtually taught himself to paint through self-study courses and manuals and by copying masterpieces from art books. His cartoonist's wit and a sardonic humour became the most important ingredients in work that drew on numerous stylistic sources, from Renaissance painting to Cubism. He was a devout Christian, and produced a host of religious works of an undeniable sincerity, although he transformed many traditional Christian themes into witty contemporary parables. His *Last Supper* (1955; Kingston, Inst. Jamaica, N.G.) is the best known of these. Some of his finest work consists of ironic transformations of the great mythological themes of the past and intensely personal fantasies based on contemporary events. He was also one of the few painters to treat successfully historical Jamaican subjects, for example in paintings of the imagined daily lives of the extinct Arawaks, the landing of Columbus, and a series depicting the riotous living of 17th-century buccaneers in Port Royal. His *Destruction of Port Royal* (*c.* 1970; Kingston, Inst. Jamaica, N.G.) is a dramatic portrayal of that cataclysmic event. In 1985 he won a competition to create two murals for the Norman Manley Airport in Kingston. The murals successfully combine many of his thematic interests into a montage celebrating Jamaican life and history.

BIBLIOGRAPHY

Carl Abrahams: A Retrospective (exh. cat. by D. Boxer, Kingston, Inst. Jamaica, N.G., 1975)
Jamaican Art 1922–1982 (exh. cat. by D. Boxer, Washington, DC, Smithsonian Inst.; Kingston, Inst. Jamaica, N.G.; 1983)

DAVID BOXER

Abrahamstrup. *See* JÆGERSPRIS.

Abramo, Lívio (*b* Araraquara, 1903). Brazilian printmaker. He worked initially as a printmaker and painter until 1933 when, influenced by Lasar Segall's expressionism, he abandoned painting for wood-engraving, which he had first practised in São Paulo *c.* 1926. He initially treated social themes such as the São Paulo working class and between 1935 and 1938 produced a series of wood-engravings, *Spain*, based on the Spanish Civil War, for example *War* (1937; U. São Paulo, Inst. Estud. Bras.). In 1950 he won a trip abroad from the Salão Nacional de Belas Artes, Rio de Janeiro, and he visited Italy, Switzerland, France and the Netherlands. On his return he made the series of wood-engravings, *Rio*, with scenes and landscapes characterized by a frank lyricism. He was named best national engraver in the first São Paulo Bienal in 1951. His constant activity as a teacher influenced many younger engravers. In 1957 he founded the Julian de la Herreria engraving workshop in Asunción, Paraguay, and in 1960 the Estúdio Gravura in São Paulo. From 1962 he lived in Asunción, where he became director of the Centro de Estudos Brasileiros. In later years his work tended towards a geometrization of space as in the series on rain and on groups of Paraguayan houses, for instance *Paraguay* (1962; São Paulo, E. Wolf priv. col.; see exh. cat., pl. 112). He had a large retrospective in 1977 in the Museu de Arte Moderna in São Paulo.

BIBLIOGRAPHY

S. Milliet: *Pintores e pinturas* (São Paulo, 1940)
J. R. Teixeira Leite: *A gravura brasileira contemporânea* (Rio de Janeiro, 1965)
Art of Latin America since Independence (exh. cat. by S. L. Catlin and T. Grieder, New Haven, CT, Yale U. A.G.; Austin, U. TX, A. Mus.; San Francisco, CA, Mus. A.; La Jolla, CA, A. Cent.; 1966)

ROBERTO PONTUAL

Abramovitz, Max. *See under* HARRISON AND ABRAMOVITZ.

Abrams, Harry N(athan) (*b* London, 8 Dec 1904; *d* New York, 25 Nov 1979). American publisher and collector. He trained at the National Academy of Design and the Art Students League in New York before working in publishing. In 1950 he set up his own publishing company,

Harry N. Abrams Inc., one of the first American companies to specialize in art books. In 1968 he founded Abbeville Books. His collecting, which began in the mid-1930s, went through three distinct phases: his first interest was in such contemporary American painters as Milton Avery and Raphael Soyer. He continued to purchase such works into the 1950s, but from the mid-1940s his collecting began to be dominated by works by major 20th-century artists; he acquired, among other works, Marc Chagall's *Clock* (1948), Pablo Picasso's *Motherhood* (1921) and Georges Rouault's *Miserere* (1939).

Abrams's most notable period as a collector was the 1960s, when he became known as a major collector of new American art. His interest in this area was fuelled by the *New Realists* exhibition of 1962 at the Sidney Janis Gallery in New York, from which he acquired his first example of Pop art. He subsequently acquired such works as Morris Louis's *Pillar of Fire* (1961), a Robert Rauschenberg combine, *Third Time Painting* (1961), Lucas Samaras's *Chairs* (1965) and Wayne Thiebaud's *Football Player* (1963).

BIBLIOGRAPHY

Harry N. Abrams Family Collection (exh. cat., New York, Jew. Mus., 1966)

B. Kurtz: 'Interview with Harry N. Abrams', *Arts* [New York], xlvii/1 (Sept–Oct 1972)

A. DEIRDRE ROBSON

Abramtsevo. Russian estate near Sergiyev Posad, 57 km north of Moscow, and site of an artists' colony. It was first recorded in documents between 1584 and 1586 under the name Obramkovo. In the 18th century it became the village of Abramkovo, part of a private estate known by the mid-19th century as Abramtsevo. In 1843 the estate was acquired by the writer Sergey Aksakov (1791–1859). He wrote his most successful works there and had numerous artists and writers as visitors, including Taras Shevchenko and Vissarion Belinsky. In 1870 the estate was acquired by the prominent industrialist and patron SAVVA MAMONTOV, who made it a major Russian artistic colony from the 1870s to the 1890s. Here, as at Princess Tenisheva's estate at Talashkino, an interest in national culture and antiquities flourished, and there was a revival of Russian folk art. Various well-known Russian artists lived at Abramtsevo at that time, among them Il'ya Repin, Mikhail Vrubel', Valentin Serov, Konstantin Korovin, Mikhail Nesterov, Yelena Polenova, Vasily Polenov and Viktor Vasnetsov. They formed the Abramtsevo/Mamontov artistic circle—an association of representatives of the most advanced artistic intelligentsia, who were creatively involved in the construction and decoration of the estate.

A collection of items of everyday peasant life was started, and in 1884 a joiner's workshop was organized on the estate, soon headed by Yelena Polenova. It united local craftsmen from the villages of Kudrino, Akhtyrka and Mutovki and initiated the production at Abramtsevo of caskets, dishes and furniture, decorated primarily with bas-relief carving (Abramtsevo/Kudrinskaya carving), which employs vegetable and geometrical ornament with representations of birds and animals. A number of exceptional folk artists came from among the students in the workshop, including Vasily Vornoskov (1876–1940), who created his own original style of carving and who taught many other craftsmen. In 1890 a ceramics workshop was also set up at Abramtsevo, which instigated the production of maiolica, although this had never been traditional in Russia. Mikhail Vrubel' produced notable examples of maiolica at the Abramtsevo workshop.

Abramtsevo, main estate building, mid-18th century, rebuilt 1870–78

In what later became the Abramtsevo Museum-Estate are the main estate building, dating from the mid-18th century (rebuilt 1870–78; see fig.), buildings in the 'Russian style' by Viktor Gartman (e.g. the Studio, 1872), Ivan Ropet (e.g. the Terem, 'Tower Chamber', 1873), Viktor Vasnetsov (e.g. the Church, 1881–2, and the 'Hut on Hen's Legs', 1883). These contain exhibitions and information about the activities of the Abramtsevo circle. The nearby town of Khot'kovo contains a factory producing carved artistic items, its craftsmen continuing the traditions of Abramtsevo-Kudrinskaya carving. The wood-carvers are taught in the Vasnetsov Abramtsevo Art College in the same town.

BIBLIOGRAPHY

N. V. Polenova: *Abramtsevo* (Moscow, 1922)
N. Pakhomov: *Abramtsevo* (Moscow, 1969)
D. Z. Kogan: *Mamontovskiy kruzhok* [Mamontov's circle] (Moscow, 1970)
N. M. Beloglazova: *Abramtsevo* (Moscow, 1981)
O. I. Arzumanova and others: *Muzey-zapovednik v Abramtsevo* [The museum-estate at Abramtsevo] (Moscow, 1984)

ALEKSANDR U. GREKOV

Abrantes, Marquês de Fontes e. *See* FONTES E ABRANTES, Marquês de.

Abraq, Tell. *See under* ARABIA, PRE-ISLAMIC, §IV, 1, 3, 4, 6 and 8.

Abreu, José Francisco de (*b* Elvas, *fl* Elvas, 1753–9). Portuguese architect and master builder. His earliest known works are the six side altars (black-veined marble, 1753) in the small 15th-century chapel of S Bento in Vila Viçosa, where all his work is to be found. They are carved in a characteristic Late Baroque manner. In 1754 he designed and directed the installation of the high choir at the church of S Agostinho, with a baluster and handrail in white, black and pink marble. Also in 1754 he took charge of the reconstruction of the Paços do Concelho, fending off plans to open the work to public tender and undertaking to adhere to approved designs. He resumed work at S Agostinho in 1758, replacing the old retable of the high altar, thought unworthy by Joseph I, with a new design of coloured marble. He may also have directed work on the façade of the Matriz de Portel (1741–59). Abreu's chief work is the sanctuary of Nossa Senhora de Lapa (*c.* 1756). He probably designed its Latin-cross plan. A magnificent portico stands out from a building of great sobriety, which seems to herald Neo-classical taste in architecture.

BIBLIOGRAPHY

T. Espanca: *Inventário artístico do distrito de Evora, zonal sul*, i (Lisbon, 1978)

JOSÉ FERNANDES PEREIRA

Abreu, Mario (*b* Turmero, nr Maracay, 22 Aug 1919). Venezuelan painter and sculptor. From 1943 to 1947 he studied drawing and painting in the Escuela de Artes Plásticas y Aplicadas, Caracas. He was a founder-member of the Taller Libre de Arte, taking part in its activities from 1949 to 1952. His paintings, always within a figurative framework, are marked by a pursuit of the magical and of indigenous roots. In his early work he was interested in the themes of roosters and flowers, using the surrounding environment as a source of inspiration. He expressed human, animal and vegetable existence in strong, warm colours (e.g. *The Rooster*, 1951; Caracas, Gal. A. N.). In 1952 Abreu moved to Europe, visiting Spain and Italy and living in Paris until 1962, when he returned to Venezuela. In Europe his contact with the Musée de l'Homme in Paris and with Surrealism produced a profound transformation in his work. He created his first *Magical Objects* in 1960, and he continued to make these throughout the 1960s, in circular and rectangular forms, and with varied subject-matter made out of domestic and industrial materials, including refuse. The best-known of these objects are *Souvenir of Hiroshima* (*c.* 1965) and *I, Mario, the Planet Hopper* (1966; both Caracas, Gal. A. N.).

BIBLIOGRAPHY

A. Boulton: *Historia de la pintura en Venezuela*, ii (Caracas, 1972)
J. Calzadilla: *Pintura venezolana de los siglos XIX y XX* (Caracas, 1975)
Pinturas y objetos: Mario Abreu (exh. cat., ed. Binev; Maracay, Gal. Mun. A., 1990)

MARÍA ANTONIA GONZÁLEZ-ARNAL

Abreu do Ó. Portuguese family of wood-carvers. Manuel Abreu do Ó and his brother Sebastião Abreu do Ó (both *fl* Évora *c.* 1728–*c.* 1770) worked in collaboration, carving some of the finest and most influential Joanine and Rococo altarpieces in southern Portugal. They carved in delicate flat relief using patterns similar to those found in Spain, a style contrasting with the dramatic plastic effects seen in contemporary wood-carving in northern Portugal.

An example of the Abreu do Ó brothers' early work is the main retable of the Cartuxa, the Charterhouse, Évora, gilded in 1729. It is composed on one level, and a sense of movement is suggested by the projection of the outer columns. They created one of the finest ensembles of 18th-century carving in southern Portugal in the chancel and transept of the Carmelite church of Nossa Senhora dos Remédios, Évora (*c.* 1760–70). On the main retable the areas between the column shafts are decorated with leaves and roses scattered asymmetrically, creating the impression of a lace covering. The votive tablet crowning the arch of the retable is carved with great delicacy. The lateral retables have curving double pediments whose undulating movement is echoed by large canopies above. The design of the pulpit was important in southern Portugal, because although it was in the Joanine style and inspired by developments in Lisbon it was also Rococo in spirit. The interior of the church emphasizes the importance of the role that gilt wood-carving played in the decoration of Portuguese churches during the 18th century.

BIBLIOGRAPHY

T. Espanca: 'Artes e artistas em Évora no século XVIII', *Bol. Mun. Turismo*, vii (Évora, 1950), pp. 25, 128
R. C. Smith: *A talha em Portugal* [Wood-carving in Portugal] (Lisbon, 1963), pp. 74, 138, 162

NATALIA MARINHO FERREIRA ALVES

Abrugia, Niccolò di Bartolomeo dell'. *See* NICCOLÒ PISANO.

Absidiole [apsidiole]. Small apse-like chapel, usually projecting from the eastern side of a transept (*see* CHURCH, fig. 2).

Absolon, John de Mansfield (*b* London, *c.* 1843; *d* Perth, Western Australia, 8 May 1879). Australian watercolourist, soldier, colonist and businessman of English descent. The son of the watercolour painter John Absolon (1815–95), he served in the Queen's Rifles and exhibited paintings and sketches with the Society of British Artists before first visiting Western Australia in 1869. Shipboard watercolour sketches and many studies of the bushland environs of Perth, such as *From the Verandah at Northam*, (1869–70; see Kerr, p. 5) recorded this first journey. He returned to England to marry Sarah Bowles Habgood, the niece of Thomas Habgood, an influential colonist, and daughter of Robert Mace Habgood, who divided his business and shipping interests between London, Fremantle and Geraldton. The couple returned to Perth, Western Australia, where Absolon helped manage the family's mining and mercantile interests. The firm of R. W. Habgood & Co. of Fremantle and London was known thereafter as Habgood Absolon & Co. He adapted his painting methods to an impressionistic manner that captured the harsh light and sparsely vegetated antipodean landscape. He also represented the London Art Union in Western Australia from November 1871. Absolon's watercolour sketches of Western Australia demonstrate, like those of a former associate, the watercolourist John Skinner Prout, a keen eye and rare sensitivity to the appearance of his new surroundings. These he documented in a *plein-air* style that pre-dated works by members of Melbourne's Heidelberg school. His paintings depart, quite radically, from European prototypes. The handling of light, colour and atmosphere learnt during early painting trips with his father to the coast of Brittany probably assisted this process. He died, aged thirty-six, after only ten years in the colony.

BIBLIOGRAPHY

B. Chapman: *The Colonial Eye: A Topographical and Artistic Record of the Life and Landscape of Western Australia, 1798–1914* (exh. cat. by B. Chapman, Perth, A. G. W. Australia, 1979)

R. Erickson: *The Bicentennial History of Western Australia, Pre-1829–1888* (Nedlands, 1988)

J. Kerr: *The Dictionary of Australian Artists: Painters, Sketchers, Photographers and Engravers to 1870*, (Melbourne, 1992), pp. 4–5

□

Abstract art. Term applied in its strictest sense to forms of 20th-century Western art that reject representation and have no starting- or finishing-point in nature. As distinct from processes of abstraction from nature or from objects (a recurring tendency across many cultures and periods that can be traced as far back as Palaeolithic cave painting), abstract art as a conscious aesthetic based on assumptions of self-sufficiency is a wholly modern phenomenon. *See also* ABSTRACTION.

1. Origins and early experiments, to *c.* 1913. 2. Pioneers, 1912–20. 3. European movements of the 1920s. 4. Concrete art and geometric abstraction, 1930–45. 5. Abstract Expressionism, *Art informel* and related tendencies, mid- to late 1940s and 1950s. 6. Geometric and monochrome abstractions of the 1950s. 7. Post-painterly Abstraction, Op art, Minimalism and other objective forms of the 1960s. 8. Abstract art after the emergence of conceptual art, 1970s and after.

1. ORIGINS AND EARLY EXPERIMENTS, TO *c.* 1913. In the late 19th century, and particularly in Symbolist art and literature, attention was refocused from the object to the emotions aroused in the observer in such a way that suggestion and evocation took priority over direct description and explicit analogy. In France especially this tradition contributed to the increased interest in the formal values of paintings, independent of their descriptive function, that prepared the way for abstraction. In his article 'Définition du néo-traditionnisme', published in *L'Art et critique* in 1890, Maurice Denis proclaimed, in words that have since been much quoted, that 'It is well to remember that a picture, before being a battle horse, a nude woman or some anecdote, is essentially a flat surface covered with colours assembled in a certain order.' This definition of painting, which stresses the independence of form from its descriptive function while stopping short of a complete severing of links with perceived reality, continued to characterize the moves towards a more fully abstract art in France in the early 20th century.

A combination of circumstances helped lead a number of European artists towards abstract art in the years preceding World War I. The opening of ethnographic museums furthered an interest in art from other cultures and civilizations (*see* PRIMITIVISM, §2), which in turn encouraged artists to free themselves from conventional methods of representation. By looking to the arts of Africa and Oceania as much as to Cézanne, the major figures associated with CUBISM were among the first to rethink the approach both to figure and space. In Picasso's *Female Form* (1910; Washington, DC, N.G.A.), for example, multiple views of the figure are incorporated in such a way that forms are fractured, and the surface is fragmented to the point where any link to the subject is so tenuous that it can be reconstructed only with the aid of the title. Although Picasso, like Braque, retained his commitment to subject-matter, other artists took the formal implications of Cubism to an even more abstract conclusion: around 1913 Giacomo Balla in Italy and Mikhail Larionov and Natal'ya Goncharova in Russia combined Cubist fragmentation of form with a representation of movement derived from Futurism to create abstract paintings. Certain artists associated with Dada, notably Hans Arp and Kurt Schwitters, later applied Cubist collage techniques to abstract compositions.

The first abstract paintings in the strict sense, dating from *c.* 1910, were underpinned by a strong philosophical undercurrent derived from 19th-century German Idealist thought, which posited the supremacy of mind over matter. Such beliefs were especially important to two of the earliest practitioners of abstract art, Vasily Kandinsky and František Kupka, and to other influential figures of the period such as Piet Mondrian and Theo van Doesburg. Kupka, who as early as 1911 in France was producing abstract paintings such as *Nocturne* (Vienna, Pal. Liechtenstein), was also among the first to elaborate theories about abstract art; in unpublished notebooks written between 1910 and 1914, he expressed a belief in the capacity of abstract form and colour to embody an 'idea' of universal significance beneath the surface of appearance. In Munich by 1910, the contested date of his first abstract watercolour, Kandinsky was formulating the theoretical possibility of abstract art in a text published in 1912, *Über das Geistige in der Kunst.* This proved to be one of the most influential and widely read theoretical treatises on the subject over the next 30 years and beyond.

The ground for abstract art was also prepared by 19th-century scientific theories. The descriptions of optical and prismatic effects of pure, unmixed colour initiated by Johann Wolfgang von Goethe in his *Farbenlehre* (1810) and extended by colour theorists such as Michel-Eugène Chevreul and Ogden Rood had a direct impact on such artists as Robert Delaunay, who extended Chevreul's term 'simultaneous contrasts of colour' to suggest that colour could be the means by which not only form but also the illusion of movement could be created in abstract paintings. In *Simultaneous Windows on the City* (1912; Hamburg, Ksthalle; see fig. 1) and related works, and in the *Circular Form* series, for example *Circular Forms: Sun and Moon* (1913; Amsterdam, Stedel. Mus.), Delaunay reduced the emphasis on representing objects so as to increase the impact of colour and light; both his work and his writings, which were quickly made available in German translation, influenced the Blaue Reiter artists Franz Marc and August Macke. It was the Italian artists associated with FUTURISM, however, whose development of an abstract language was most clearly conditioned by the challenge of representing speed and motion. Gino Severini, for example, developed the associative power of abstraction by fusing remembered experience with current sensation in paintings such as *Dynamic Hieroglyphic of the Bal Tabarin* (1912; New York, MOMA; for illustration *see* SEVERINI, GINO). During the same period in England, similar ideas were explored within the movement known as VORTICISM. In his drawings and prints of 1912, for example, Wyndham Lewis transformed machine parts into cylindrical and geometric shapes in order to capitalize on the associations provoked by machinery independent of their forms. Around 1913 two American painters working in Paris, Stanton Macdonald-Wright and Morgan Russell, the instigators of a movement labelled SYNCHROMISM, created colour abstractions concerned with the twisting movement of form. Marcel Duchamp and Francis Picabia, two of the leading painters in a variation on Cubism christened ORPHISM by Guillaume Apollinaire, produced mechanomorphic paintings that transmuted vaguely mechanical and sexual parts into abstract forms. Duchamp's *The Bride* (1912; Philadelphia, PA, Mus. A.) and Picabia's *Udnie* (1913; Paris, Pompidou) invited the spectator to interpret the forms imaginatively from clues provided by their titles. During the same period another painter associated with Orphism, Fernand Léger, used abstract pictorial equivalents to capture the dissonant contrast of manmade machines set against the natural landscape. In spite of the central position of Paris in the development of a modernist avant-garde aesthetic, the continued devotion among French artists to recognizable subject-matter, combined with the absence of a firm metaphysical or theoretical basis for their experiments, ultimately restrained them from developing a full abstract language.

1. Robert Delaunay: *Simultaneous Windows on the City*, oil on canvas, 460×400 mm, 1912 (Hamburg, Hamburger Kunsthalle)

2. PIONEERS, 1912–20. By the end of World War I such artists as Kandinksy, Mondrian and Kazimir Malevich were creating paintings that were less reliant on appearances, perception and physical sensation and that instead obeyed their own laws of colour and form. Stylistically, this encompassed a wide range from a loose, free-form approach, as in Kandinsky's *Improvisations*, to a tight geometric abstraction as practised by Mondrian and the DE STIJL group. In spite of their differences, however, these artists shared an interest in esoteric doctrines that underpinned their commitment to abstract art.

Kandinsky's early writings were particularly influential for their analysis of colour, notably in *Über das Geistige in der Kunst*, and of form, which was the subject of an essay, 'Über die Formfrage', published in *Der Blaue Reiter Almanach* in 1912. Basing his approach to colour on the empirical theories of Goethe, Kandinsky went further in suggesting that colour, like music, can evoke certain emotional and psychological responses even when used non-representationally in a painting. Similarly, he argued that formal content was determined not by external appearances but by the 'inner necessity' of the artist's emotional response. In providing a theoretical justification for expressive abstraction, Kandinsky developed the notion of the affective purpose of art, basing this on the assumption that art must possess 'soul' in order to elicit a response from the spectator, and that this soul, manifested in the balance of colours and composition, is in turn dependent on the integrity of the artist. While Kandinsky's pictures of this period generally continued to combine apparently abstract forms with shapes suggestive of figures, animals and landscapes, in certain works, such as *Composition VII* (1913; Moscow, Tret'yakov Gal.), he approached pure abstraction.

The spiritual and moral dimensions of Kandinsky's art and theory, grounded in part on his understanding of THEOSOPHY, were shared by Mondrian even before World War I. It was not until 1917, however, that Mondrian developed the basis of his geometric abstraction and a theoretical justification for it. In his essay 'Natuurlijke en abstracte realiteit' (1919), Mondrian followed the mystic philosopher M. H. J. Schoenmaekers, whom he had met in 1916–17, in elaborating a theory of universal beauty by renouncing the 'particulars of appearance' and embracing the 'abstraction of form and colour' within the precise formulation of the 'straight line and the clearly defined primary colour'. For Mondrian, as for Schoenmaekers and the Theosophists, the orthogonal, in line with a long history of divine geometry, was cosmically pre-eminent, as it expressed the mystical concept of life and immortality in a harmonious relationship. By 1921 Mondrian had conceived the basis of a style that he termed NEO-PLASTICISM, which was based on the use of a black linear grid and on asymmetrically placed zones of primary colour. In such paintings as *Composition with Red, Yellow and Blue* (1921; The Hague, Gemeentemus.), 'dynamic equilibrium' is achieved by the juxtaposition of lines, planes and narrow bands of flat colour held in taut relation to each other.

The development by Malevich of a form of abstract painting known as SUPREMATISM was also stimulated by topical esoteric concerns. He first exhibited 35 such paintings, each consisting of flat shapes such as quadrangles against light grounds, at the exhibition *Poslednaya futuristicheskaya vystavka kartin: 0.10* ('The last Futurist exhibition of paintings: 0.10'), held at the Dobychina Gallery in Petrograd (now St Petersburg) in 1915. The titles of many of the works referred to the concept of the FOURTH DIMENSION, which was evolved partly in response to Russian mystical philosophy, as a new form of consciousness that provided an escape into the world of the spirit (for illustration *see* SUPREMATISM). To effect cosmic integration, Malevich, following the philosopher Pyotr Uspensky, affirmed the necessity of venturing into a new space–continuum by replacing the forms derived from nature with 'non-objective'—that is to say completely abstract—forms. The rectilinear planes featured in such paintings as *Untitled* (1915; Amsterdam, Stedel. Mus.) make no reference to things external to the picture, other than to mathematical figures such as parallelograms, yet despite this resolute flatness and expunction of associations, the disposition of overlapping forms against a white ground inevitably creates a sense of ebb and flow. In 1919, immediately after painting his *White on White* series of 1917–18 (*see* MALEVICH, KAZIMIR, fig. 2), Malevich wrote about the use of white in terms of space travel, and in 1920 he even suggested the possibility of building a Suprematist satellite. During this period other artists in Russia, such as Il'ya Chashnik (1902–29), El Lissitzky and Gustav Klucis, began to develop their own variants of Suprematism. After the Revolution of 1917, Suprematism quickly came to be regarded as one of the major new artistic tendencies to challenge the conservative traditionalism of the old Tsarist order, leading abstract art to gain official support, if only temporarily, for the first time in its history.

Other artists, especially those based in central Europe, sought to counter the barbaric realities of World War I through abstraction. Both Hans Arp and Sophie Taeuber (later Taeuber-Arp) sought to approach eternal values and to deny human egotism in a series of *Duo-collages* made as collaborations in 1918. They hoped that the impersonal technique employed in these works made with paper-cutters, together with the geometric rigour of presentation, would help to transcend human imperfections and in so doing 'cure' people of the frenzy of the period. In common with other Dadaists, such as Kurt Schwitters in the pictures and reliefs he called *Merzbilder*, from 1916 to 1919 Arp also produced more random arrangements that championed chance as the governing factor.

Artists working in France in the 1920s, such as Joan Miró and André Masson, came under the influence of Surrealism (and in particular its elevation of irrational forces) and began to explore 'pure psychic automatism', as defined in André Breton's *Manifeste du surréalisme* (Paris, 1924), employing such techniques as psychic improvisation, BIOMORPHISM and AUTOMATISM. Conceiving of their pictures as reflections of the workings of the subconscious mind, in works such as Miró's *Birth of the World* (1925; New York, MOMA) they created a form of improvised abstract painting that anticipated the gestural aspects of Abstract Expressionism referred to as action painting.

3. EUROPEAN MOVEMENTS OF THE 1920S. The dissemination of the theory and practice of abstract art in Europe after World War I was greatly aided by the banding together of artists into associations and by the establishment of schools and periodicals. Notable among them were De Stijl (1917–31) in the Netherlands, Vkhutemas (1920–30) and Inkhuk (1920–26) in Russia and the Bauhaus (1919–33) in Germany. Most of these were formed in a spirit of reconstruction after the devastation of war, with abstract art, like the machine, coming to be equated with both modernity and progress as a rejection of the old order and an embrace of a new future. The French periodical *L'Esprit nouveau* (1920–25), established by Le Corbusier and Amédée Ozenfant as the official organ of their movement, Purism (*see* PURISM, §1), conveyed a new aesthetic based on mathematics and geometry and inspired other artists to take up abstraction. In Europe, in response to debates concerning the role of art in effecting changes in society, abstract art came to be seen as an instrument with which to improve the quality of life. For artists who conveyed these views, including Theo van Doesburg in the Netherlands, Aleksandr Rodchenko in Russia and László Moholy-Nagy at the Bauhaus, abstract art became as important an issue for design as for painting. These developments, coupled with a concern for broadening their audience, led to an expanding of definitions of abstract art and to the introduction of new terms, such as CONSTRUCTIVISM and CONCRETE ART, to describe forms of abstract art based on the rigorous and non-referential use of geometric forms. Van Doesburg's insistence that the principles of De Stijl, also referred to as Neo-plasticism, be applied not only to easel painting, as exemplified by Mondrian, but also to architecture, furniture and interior design was symptomatic of this wider definition of abstract art. Van Doesburg urged collaboration between the practitioners of different disciplines in the hope of creating total environments capable of reaching a wide audience. However, the poor reception given to the Café de l'Aubette project in Strasbourg, on which van Doesburg collaborated in 1926–8 with Hans Arp and Sophie Taeuber-Arp, showed that the public was not to be easily persuaded.

Disagreements about how best to reach a general audience were vividly exemplified in Russia just after the

Revolution of 1917. Artists such as Malevich, Kandinsky (who had returned to Russia in 1914) and the sculptor Naum Gabo strongly believed that abstract art had a vital contribution to make to society in raising human consciousness and that this transformation could be effected in the traditional media of painting and sculpture. Gabo's work, for example, demonstrated that sculpture could be reinvented by using new materials to represent space and movement so as to concentrate attention on effects of light and on the apparent dissolution of solid mass. By contrast, Vladimir Tatlin and Rodchenko, both of whom had conducted important experiments with abstract forms in the pre-revolutionary period, came to regard the continuation of traditional fine art after the Revolution as contrary to the spirit of the urgent requirements of the day, judging that it should be replaced by self-evidently utilitarian forms of construction. By the time Tatlin exhibited his maquette for the *Monument to the Third International* (1919–20; destr.; *see* TATLIN, VLADIMIR, fig. 2) the notion of the 'artist' was giving way to that of the 'artist–technician' among Soviet Constructivists, with abstraction channelled largely through posters, textiles, ceramics and stage designs rather than through paintings. While the education system before the introduction of the first Five-year Plan in 1928 could allow the two factions to exist simultaneously for a time, increasing political opposition to what were deemed the obfuscations of abstract art led to arguments for a more easily understood and propagandistic realist art, culminating in the adoption of Socialist Realism as the official style in 1934.

In Germany an almost parallel sequence of events took place at the Bauhaus, albeit under different political circumstances. Paul Klee and Kandinsky, who had joined the teaching staff in 1920 and 1922 respectively, both rationalized further their theory and practice of abstract art. In *Punkt und Linie zu Fläche* (Munich, 1926) Kandinsky complemented his earlier theories about colour with an analysis of composition, retaining a belief in emotional expressiveness but acknowledging the need for intellectual control that was a major factor in his adoption at this time of a geometric idiom. Klee's *Pädagogisches Skizzenbuch* (1925) is a methodical study of compositional methods that reflects the increasingly 'scientific' bias of the Bauhaus at this stage; in the later 1920s his paintings became more overtly abstract, although he never fully severed his links with representational subject-matter. Kandinsky's affirmation in 1932 that both he and Klee were 'painters of spiritual essence', coupled with Klee's belief in intuition, were pitted against the cool rationalism of Hannes Meyer, who as the Bauhaus's director from 1927 introduced rigid Constructivist principles along Soviet lines; he asserted that form was a product of arithmetic and that no aesthetic factor was involved in design. In the event, neither view triumphed: with the ascendancy to power of the Nazis, the Bauhaus was closed in 1933, and abstract art in Germany came to be suppressed, if only temporarily, as 'degenerate art' (*see* ENTARTETE KUNST), while a largely neo-classicist-inspired realism became the officially promoted style.

4. CONCRETE ART AND GEOMETRIC ABSTRACTION, 1930–45. The ideological opposition to abstract art that developed in Germany and the USSR led many abstract artists to gravitate to Paris, which gradually became the most important centre for abstract art, despite the antipathy of the French art establishment to its stricter forms. Even before Kandinsky's arrival in 1933, a great range of Europeans had already established themselves in and around Paris, including the Russians Lissitzky, Gabo, Antoine Pevsner and Jean Pougny; Dutch artists associated with De Stijl, such as Mondrian, van Doesburg (who died in 1931), Georges Vantongerloo and César Domela; Hans Arp and Sophie Taeuber-Arp; the Poles Henryk Stażewski, Władysław Strzemiński and Katarzyna Kobro; and the Italian Enrico Prampolini. Most of these artists were among those who formed the nucleus of new groups and periodicals established in Paris during the 1930s to promote abstract art. Taeuber-Arp's *Composition with Rectangles and Circles on Black Ground* (1931; Basle, Kstmus.; see fig. 2) was typical of the geometric rigour of their work. One of the most important sculptors working in Paris during this period was Constantin Brancusi, who favoured forms of extreme simplicity abstracted from nature; although he was not identified with any movement, he had a lasting influence on the development of abstract sculpture well into the 20th century.

Arguments for the total autonomy of abstract art, which had gathered momentum during the 1920s, were vehemently expressed in a manifesto formulated by van Doesburg and published in April 1930 in the only issue of a new periodical based in Paris, *Art concret*. In it van Doesburg argued that a picture should be 'constructed entirely from purely plastic elements, that is to say planes and colours' and that as 'a pictorial element has no other significance than itself' the picture as a whole similarly has 'no other significance than itself'. This formalist emphasis reflected van Doesburg's familiarity with Constructivist tenets during the 1920s and illustrates the extent to which he had departed from Mondrian's mystical justifications. This rationale for Concrete art quickly gained followers, who used the term in preference to abstract because they agreed with van Doesburg that 'nothing is more real than a line, a colour, a surface'. Jean Hélion, who also signed the manifesto, sought in his *Equilibrium* series (1932–4) to express the effects of space and movement on geometric elements, while during the same decade Domela and Vantongerloo developed an impersonal, severe, mathematically based art; Arp, Strzeminski, Kobro and Max Bill were among those who proposed their own interpretations of Concrete art at this time, with Bill popularizing the concept in Switzerland and South America.

More catholic tendencies were embraced in the 1930s by an association based in Paris, ABSTRACTION-CRÉATION, which promoted its ideas through a magazine of the same name, and by another group and periodical, CERCLE ET CARRÉ, which flourished only briefly. The very diversity of Abstraction–Création, however—its members included Arp, Delaunay, Albert Gleizes, Hélion, Auguste Herbin, Kupka, van Doesburg and Vantongerloo—was also its weakness. Disagreements arose over exhibition policy: the dominant faction supported only 'pure' abstraction and would accept no painting containing any suggestion of an outside reference; those who resisted were eventually compelled to resign over what they considered

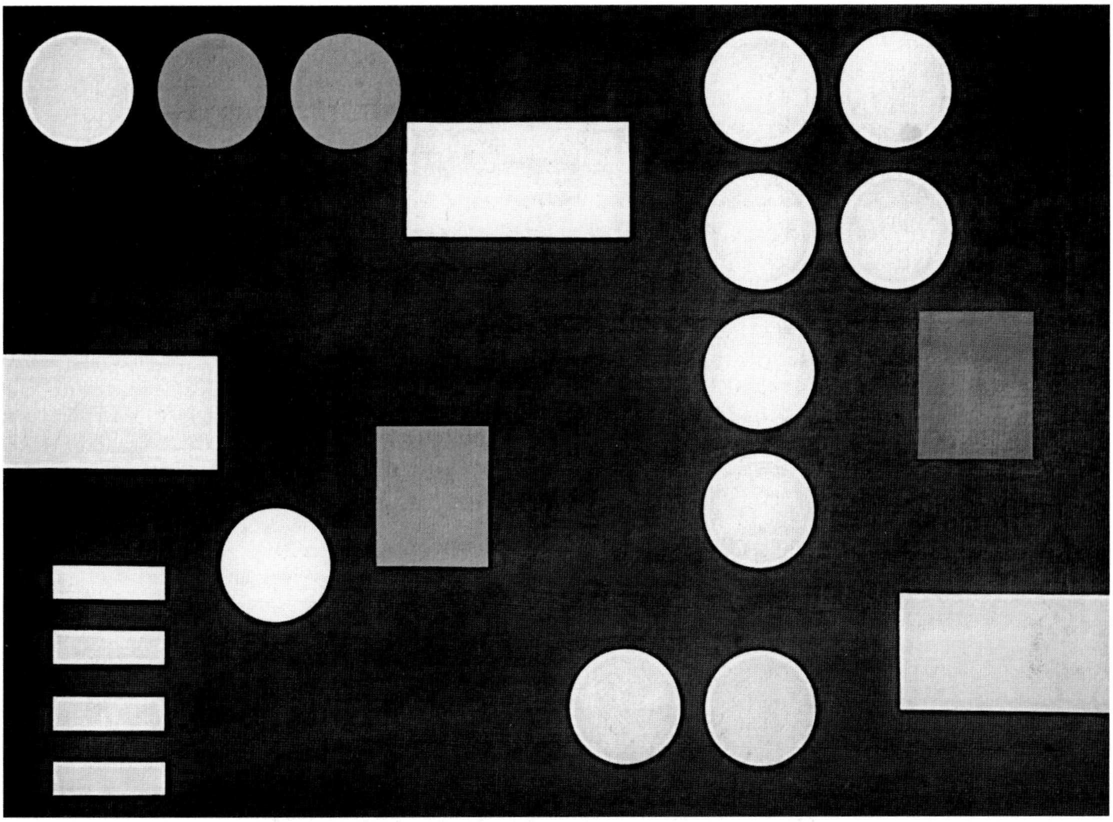

2. Sophie Taeuber-Arp: *Composition with Rectangles and Circles on Black Ground*, oil on canvas, 645×920 mm, 1931 (Basle, Kunstmuseum)

an excessively rigid approach. Debates also raged in their magazine over how abstract art could best serve society in the face of political events abroad. Some left-wing contributors argued that abstract art was too remote from the general population to succeed in such aims, while others argued for aesthetic freedom on the basis that the objective of Communism was to liberate the individual. If the two sides of the argument seemed irreconcilable, the editorial stance of the magazine at least promoted the view that commitment to abstract art represented independence and opposition to totalitarianism.

With the increasing threat of war in Europe, many European artists were forced to uproot themselves again. Towards the end of the 1930s England was perceived as a safer refuge. For a brief period after the arrival of Walter Gropius, Marcel Breuer, Moholy-Nagy, Gabo and Mondrian, the north London suburb of Hampstead and St Ives in Cornwall became centres of abstract and especially Constructivist art; English artists such as Ben Nicholson and Barbara Hepworth moved in their own work towards a greater degree of abstraction, while the cause of international abstract art was publicized through the touring exhibition *Abstract and Concrete Art* in 1936 and through the publication in 1937 of the collection of essays *Circle: International Survey of Constructive Art*. However, the British public showed little interest in abstract art, and with the outbreak of World War II many of the Europeans decided in any case to leave for the USA, where they continued to encourage the development of abstract art.

5. Abstract Expressionism, Art informel and related tendencies, mid- to late 1940s and 1950s. After World War II the geometric abstraction of artists such as Albers, Arp and Bill was shown widely in Europe, notably at the exhibition *Art concret* in 1945 (Paris, Gal. Denise René), organized with the help of Theo van Doesburg's widow, Nelly van Doesburg, and at the Salon des Réalités Nouvelles, which over the following ten years became the largest exhibiting forum in Paris. After the traumas of World War II, however, many other artists found the geometric order too limiting to reflect their particular psychological experiences; in their search for a more immediate expression, they turned to a looser and often more gestural form of abstract painting. Inspired partly by influential exhibitions at the Galerie René Drouin and the work of Jean Fautrier, Jean Dubuffet and Wols, the painting that resulted was exhibited and promoted in Paris under a plethora of names, including lyrical abstraction, Art informel, Matter painting and Tachism. Expressive abstraction soon became an international phenomenon, encompassing Zen 49 (founded 1949) and Quadriga (founded 1952) in Germany, the painters associated with Cobra (1948–51) and a group of younger English painters based primarily in St Ives, such as Patrick Heron and Peter Lanyon, while related developments also

took place in Italy, Spain, South America and in Japan with the GUTAI group. In the USA a separate but related phenomenon, ABSTRACT EXPRESSIONISM, flourished at this time.

These groups shared several characteristics: an emphasis on impulsiveness and spontaneity that rejected predetermined composition and that frequently equated drawing with painting; a concentration on the individual mark or 'tache', as opposed to the straight line or carefully circumscribed shape; a concern for the expressive potential of paint and its textured or optical effect; and a sense of immediacy in the execution. Qualities of freshness and urgency led to a physical awareness of the artist's contact with the picture surface and of the act of painting itself, manifested in the USA by ACTION PAINTING.

In spite of the common features, there were significant differences among the various post-war groups and problems even in naming them. For example the terms *Art informel* and Tachism are often used interchangeably, even though the painters associated with *Art informel*, such as Jean Fautrier, Jean-Paul Riopelle, Antoni Tàpies and Jean Dubuffet (who approached abstraction in his *Texturologies*), generally preferred to use thick accretions of layers of paint, hence the term matter painting (for illustration *see* TÀPIES, ANTONI); whereas the Tachists, such as Georges Mathieu (who coined the word), Hans Hartung and Henri Michaux, concentrated on the swift execution of the painted stroke or gesture. The degree or type of abstraction varied from group to group. Artists associated with St Ives, such as Lanyon and Terry Frost, produced atmospheric abstractions of the Cornish landscape, whereas many of the Cobra artists tended to create hybrid forms reminiscent of the mythological animals they admired in Nordic art and legend. Even within groups, the degree of abstraction was seldom clearcut, depending more on the individual proclivities of each artist. During this period, especially in Paris, tendencies were often named and promoted by critics and writers rather than by the artists themselves, thus helping to disseminate the work but also bracketing tendencies into a rather amorphous, international expansion of *Art informel* and Tachism from around 1956.

Confusion also arises from the application of the term Abstract Expressionism to American artists, as it has been used to encompass both the gestural action painting of artists such as Jackson Pollock, Willem de Kooning and Franz Kline and the COLOUR FIELD PAINTING of Mark Rothko, Barnett Newman and Ad Reinhardt; it is also used to describe paintings by artists who do not fit strictly into either category, such as Clyfford Still, Robert Motherwell and Hans Hofmann, or those whose work contains residual figuration, such as Adolph Gottlieb, William Baziotes and Arshile Gorky. Given this disparity, some critics and historians have preferred to refer to the New York school (as in the title of a major exhibition at Los Angeles, CA, Co. Mus. A., 1965), in response to the term Ecole de Paris, and to the role played by these American artists in transferring the centre of power from Paris to New York; even this term, however, is not wholly accurate, since most of the major painters originated from outside New York and in many cases continued to work in other places. Whatever name is given to these developments, the fact remains that they emerged not only as a reaction against dominant trends of realism within American painting but also from a knowledge and assimilation of European models, particularly Cubism and the Surrealist technique of automatism, and (in the case of Pollock and others) from Native American and Mexican art. The psychoanalytic theories of Sigmund Freud and Carl Gustav Jung provided an intellectual context for their search for a new subject-matter underpinning the raw and impressive physical presence of their paintings (*see* PSYCHOANALYSIS AND ART).

While the Abstract Expressionists made reference to shared influences and intentions, great formal differences nevertheless underlie such works as Pollock's *Autumn Rhythm* (1950; New York, Met.) and Newman's *Vir heroicus sublimis* (1950–51; New York, MOMA). Pollock placed his unstretched canvas on the floor and literally poured paint on to the surface to produce weaving, linear arabesques that create an 'all-over' effect. Newman and other artists associated with colour field painting, on the other hand, evenly covered the canvas with a flat application of paint so that the viewer's field of vision is saturated with colour; no allowance is made for individual 'gesture' within this unmodulated surface. Like the Surrealists, Pollock believed that the basic artistic impulse was grounded in the unconscious, and it was this concept, interpreted in Existentialist terms, that led the critic Harold Rosenberg to devise his definition of action painting. For Newman, as for Rothko, painting was a means of expressing the sublime, of creating a transcendent art that had its origins in Old Testament theology. Thus Rothko's zones of colour were conceived not as decoration but as a means of effecting a revelatory and emotional experience for the spectator. Such levels of meaning, however, were not taken into account by formalist criticism, especially as promoted by Clement Greenberg, who vaunted the new painting for its supercession of Cubist space. Abstract Expressionism came to be seen as essentially different from European painting because of its vitality, use of large scale, intense physicality and holistic quality, by which the entire picture surface pre-empted its segmentation into parts. A case was soon made by American critics for the superiority of this art, which was promoted internationally through exhibitions and publications in such a way that New York came to be generally recognized as the most important centre of artistic production after World War II.

6. GEOMETRIC AND MONOCHROME ABSTRACTIONS OF THE 1950S. Just as the various forms of expressive abstraction became established as an international style in the late 1950s, the weakening of the original impetus had led towards a certain mannerism. In New York, for example, de Kooning's many imitators, labelled the 10th Street school because of the preponderance of galleries representing them in that area, used the techniques of Abstract Expressionism more as surface embellishments than as signs of underlying content. Inevitably there was a reaction against this lapse of a once avant-garde style into a new kind of academicism. In its wake, artists developed styles that eschewed the personal touch, such as Minimalism,

hard-edge painting and Post-painterly Abstraction as well as Pop art.

In Europe geometric abstraction remained a force to be reckoned with. The Groupe Espace was formed in 1949 after the success of the *Art concret* exhibition of 1945 and the founding of the Salon des Réalités Nouvelles in Paris in 1946. The Groupe Espace sought to promote Constructivism as an influence on the urban environment. Their anti-expressive bias was shared by an international network of other groups such as MOVIMENTO ARTE CONCRETA (MAC) in Milan (1948), ART ABSTRAIT in Belgium (1952), LES PLASTICIENS (1955, from 1959 Les Nouveaux Plasticiens) in Canada and Equipo 57 in Spain (1957), all of which promoted alternatives to *Art informel* and pursued a programme of geometric abstraction. Josef Albers explored perception and the illusory aspects of colour from 1950 in his *Homages to the Squares* (for illustration *see* ALBERS, JOSEF), a series he worked on until his death. In Switzerland Karl Gerstner (*b* 1930) and Richard Paul Lohse continued the teachings of Max Bill in their investigation into the mathematical aspects of colour programming, which they called KALTE KUNST in 1954, while in Britain ties with Dutch Constructivism were established through the magazine *Structure* (1958–64) and through a shared interest in the theories of the American Charles Biederman.

During the 1950s a number of artists experimented with single-colour abstractions, including Lucio Fontana in his *Spatial Concepts* (from 1948), Piero Manzoni in his *Achromes* (exhibited from 1957), Yves Klein in blue monochromes (exhibited from 1956), Robert Rauschenberg in series of monochromes, including white paintings (exhibited in 1951) and Ad Reinhardt in his blue, red and ultimately 'black' paintings (*c.* 1954–67). Such works constituted the ultimate reduction of painting, but the artists' intentions were varied. To Rodchenko in 1921 the monochrome had represented the last venture in painting before he turned to Constructivism. By contrast, Rauschenberg wished to create an empty screen against which the moving shadows of spectators could be projected, while Fontana established the flat uniform surface only to pierce it spatially with holes and later slits; Manzoni seems to have been motivated by more purely nihilistic purposes; while for Klein blue was so potent and mysterious a hue that the canvas surface needed to be covered only in paint of that colour. Reinhardt's intention with his 'black' canvases was to make the 'first paintings which cannot be misunderstood'. Whatever the motive, the monochrome experiments of the 1950s offered a severe form of abstraction that both paved the way for Minimalism in the 1960s and for the ongoing critical debates concerning the 'end of painting'.

7. POST-PAINTERLY ABSTRACTION, OP ART, MINIMALISM AND OTHER OBJECTIVE FORMS OF THE 1960S. Abstract art enjoyed its greatest success in terms of support in the 1960s, in major exhibitions staged in Europe and the USA and through international art magazines. Broadly speaking, European artists explored scientific discoveries and experimentation, while Americans developed a more purely formal language. Both directions were characterized by a more objective and impersonal approach that transcended the individual imprint of the artist.

In Europe these new developments were encompassed largely by KINETIC ART, OP ART and art using electric light sources. All these were among the trends referred to as NOUVELLE TENDANCE, an umbrella term used in the early 1960s to describe the diverse Constructivist tendencies and movements that opposed expressive abstraction. Artists working with light, and kinetic and Op artists, all tended to depersonalize the art object, using materials and techniques borrowed from industrial science, exploiting direct stimuli such as light, sound and real movement, encouraging spectator involvement and generally subverting traditional aesthetic standards. Among the groups to develop these interests within *Nouvelle tendance* were the GROUPE DE RECHERCHE D'ART VISUEL (GRAV) in Paris, ARTE PROGRAMMATA, GRUPPO N and GRUPPO T in Italy, ZERO Group in Germany, NUL in the Netherlands and Equipo 57 in Spain. One of the most influential pioneers of Op art, however, was an English painter, Bridget Riley, and GRAV included Victor Vasarely as well as Jésus Soto and other South Americans among its members.

In the USA the direction towards a more objective abstract art was restricted largely to painting and sculpture, although there were also important American Op artists such as Richard Anuszkiewicz and at least one major artist working with light, Dan Flavin. Various exhibitions of American painting held in the USA during the 1960s, such as *Toward a New Abstraction* (1963), *Post-painterly Abstraction* (1964) and *Systemic Painting* (1966), brought together works that shared an ordered and structured composition, clearly defined edges and linear clarity. The two most commonly used terms for these developments are POST-PAINTERLY ABSTRACTION and HARD-EDGE PAINTING. Morris Louis, Kenneth Noland, Ellsworth Kelly and Frank Stella, who were included in all these exhibitions, may be taken as paradigms of this new direction (for illustrations *see* KELLY, ELLSWORTH and NOLAND, KENNETH).

Louis and Noland worked in Washington, DC (*see* WASHINGTON COLOR PAINTERS), not in New York, and they were inspired by the stain paintings of HELEN FRANKENTHALER rather than by Pollock. Both used acrylic paint for a kind of painting that allowed for no reworking. Louis, for example, in his *Unfurleds* series (1960–61), poured thinned paint on to unprimed or selectively sized canvas so that it sank into and stained the weave, making the image and its support inseparable and eliminating the gestural marks and tactile surface of action painting, thereby concentrating attention on the purely visual experience of colour. Similar techniques were employed by Noland but applied to more structured motifs of concentric circles or parallel bands of colour. Kelly, who had spent his formative years in Europe from 1948 to 1954, took his hard-edge shapes from nature or architecture and abstracted them to the point of unrecognizability. Stella was the most extreme of all in stressing the flatness of the picture plane, denying illusionism and other levels of meaning; he insisted that there were no suggestions in his paintings beyond the structure expressed on their surface. This emphasis on the work of art as a physical object was a reaction against the values of the previous generation but also part of a wider interest at the time in PHENOMENOLOGY.

MINIMALISM emerged in the 1960s as a highly influential development in abstract sculpture, especially in the USA. The *Primary Structures* exhibition (1966) brought together British and American artists, many of them trained as painters, who had begun to produce objects of extreme formal simplicity largely after the example of Brancusi. The Americans, notably Carl André and Donald Judd, used rigidly geometrical prefabricated industrial units often displayed according to serial principles; Judd's *Untitled* (1968; Toronto, A.G. Ont.; see fig. 3) is a characteristic example. They renounced what they considered to be a European preference for relational methods of composition, as Stella used in his paintings, favouring instead the use of regular grid structures or centralized formats so that the shape of the work as a whole could be apprehended at once. Along with Judd, Robert Morris (ii) provided a theoretical premise for Minimalist sculpture by stressing the presence or factuality of the work itself, the object's autonomy and the mind's powers of perception. In Britain a group of sculptors associated with the St Martin's School of Art, London, under the tutelage of Anthony Caro, explored new forms of abstract sculpture that were witty in conception and painted in bright colours. Phillip King, Tim Scott and William Tucker were among those who established their reputations at the exhibition *New Generation: 1965* (1965). Like the American Minimalists, they used industrially manufactured and synthetic materials, including sheet metal, glass, plastic and fibreglass, but unlike them they maintained a referential quality in their choice of both motifs and titles. In spite of the growing internationalism, national tendencies continued to be discernible.

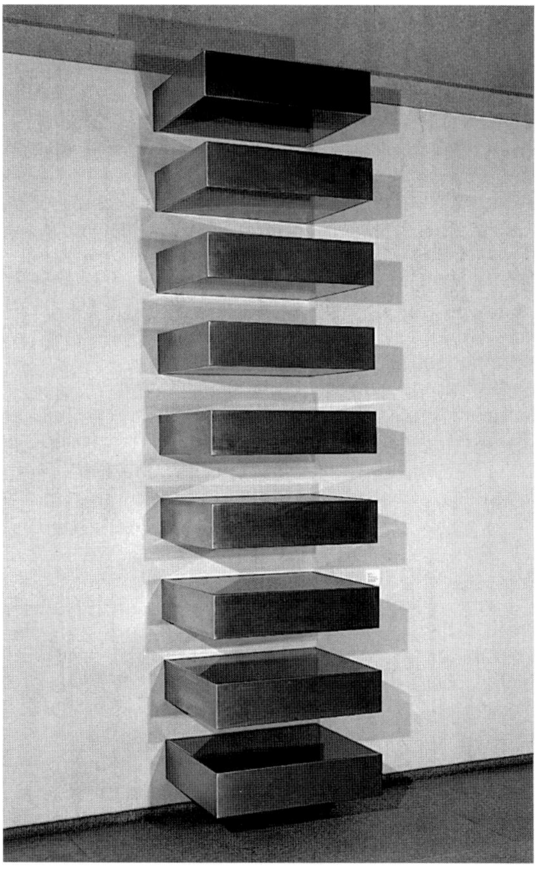

3. Donald Judd: *Untitled*, stainless steel and green perspex, nine of ten units, each 229×1016×788 mm, with 229 mm intervals, 1968 (Toronto, Art Gallery of Ontario)

8. ABSTRACT ART AFTER THE EMERGENCE OF CONCEPTUAL ART, 1970S AND AFTER. By the end of the 1960s the boundaries between abstract and representational art, as with so many other categories, began to break down. The international developments encompassed by the term CONCEPTUAL ART, which emerged in part as a reaction against the marketable art object, were closely related to movements important in the development of abstract art. LAND ART and ARTE POVERA, for example, drew attention to the environment and sought to transcend the distinction between sculpture and object and between abstraction and representation, while artists involved with PROCESS ART took as their main theme the methods by which their work was made. Land artists such as Robert Smithson, Richard Long and Jan Dibbets favoured abstract patterns or primary forms similar to those employed by the Minimalists, using nature as their raw material and often documenting their ephemeral or large-scale works in photographs. Smithson's *Spiral Jetty* (1970; for illustration *see* LAND ART)—a coil 457 m long of mud, salt crystals, rocks and water at the Great Salt Lake in Utah—is typical of this synthesis. The work was seen directly by few people other than the artist, but it was recorded in photographs and film, undercutting traditional expectations and resisting categorization. In Germany the most influential figure, both as an artist and teacher, was Joseph Beuys, who emphasized the largely personal associations of particular natural materials such as fat and felt, with form as their by-product rather than as a predetermined factor.

Conceptual attitudes, especially in the USA, revived in abstract art a concern for mental constructs and logic. As with artists of the *Nouvelle Tendance*, planning and programming became essential, and the work of art itself was frequently the fulfilment of a verbal construct or mathematical formula. Sol LeWitt, as a general principle, used written instructions as the starting-point of his art. In LeWitt's abstract *Wall Drawings*, for example, which consist of pencilled lines or coloured shapes, the impersonality of the idea logically entailed the collaboration of assistants for their execution. The client was often sold only the instructions, thus again calling into question the uniqueness of both the creator and the work itself. Although such strategies were not new to art, given the earlier example of artists such as Duchamp and Moholy-Nagy, their alliance in the 1970s with contemporary developments in critical theory and linguistics gave them a particular weight.

The challenge presented by conceptual art during the 1970s to traditional forms of painting and sculpture was met by a number of artists who continued to work in these media. In the context of these largely individual investigations, SUPPORTS-SURFACES, a group of painters based in France, was unusual in emerging as a cohesive movement; they were not alone, however, in their concern with material structure, physical attributes and use of decorative patterns, since these were shared by other Europeans such as Gillian Ayres and by Americans such as Miriam Schapiro and Robert Zakanitch (*b* 1936), loosely referred to as 'dekor' or 'pattern painters'. Agnes Martin, Robert Ryman and Brice Marden, three American abstract painters tangentially related to Minimalism, showed that formalism and metaphysical concerns could be intertwined, while a rearticulation of the compositional and relational tradition of Constructivism was to be found in the work of Beuys's pupils Blinky Palermo and Imi Knoebel.

The pluralism that increasingly dominated the evolution of art during the 1970s and 1980s created a climate in which abstract and representational forms were equally acceptable and sometimes even interchangeable. Many artists, such as Georg Baselitz, used referential imagery but conceived of their paintings as abstract, while others, such as the American sculptor Joel Shapiro (*b* 1941), took as their starting-point forms associated with abstract art but endowed them with suggestions of objects and of the human figure. Cy Twombly extended the language and meaning of gestural Abstract Expressionism by adding scrawled words embued with poetic and mythic associations to the other marks contained in his non-figurative canvases and drawings, while Gerhard Richter produced both figurative and abstract paintings, which by the particular nature of their painted surface and reference to the ambiguities of photography, seemed to call into question what is abstract and what is 'real': both lines of pursuit have since influenced and exercised many other artists. The pluralism of the period found numerous outlets even within the bounds of wholly non-referential work, and these could each be traced to earlier 20th-century movements as diverse as Constructivism and Abstract Expressionism. The relationship to earlier models could be as sincere as the emulation of Hans Hofmann by John Hoyland or as ironic in its appropriation of Op art and hard-edge painting as the parodies by American painters labelled Neo-Geo, such as Philip Taaffe (*b* 1955) or Peter Halley (*b* 1953). A widespread loss of faith in the concept of the avant-garde during this period brought with it a move away from the candour and utopian optimism that characterized abstraction in early modernism, to the extent that modernism itself was seen by some to have run its course and to have given way to the more eclectic impulses of Post-modernism. In this context, abstract art has generally changed both its meaning and its function while continuing to exploit the diverse forms and approaches associated with its history. Increasing access to information concerning art made outside western Europe and America prompts the need also for a greater awareness of other traditions and of new perspectives on abstraction that might be offered. In terms of the art discussed to date, it still remains to be resolved whether Post-modernism marked a moment of clear and decisive rupture in the history of abstract art, as proposed by much of the North American, English and French literature, or alternatively, whether the same moment was characteristic of a shift from a high to a late modernism in art, a position often argued for in German literature of the same period. While the Post-modern arguments of rupture lead to a discontinuous and variable problematization of abstract art and its history, the latter narrative offers the positive and diachronic advantages of an unfolding critical model and of continuous period histories into early–high–late types of abstract art production.

BIBLIOGRAPHY

PERIODICALS AND REVIEWS

De Stijl, i/1–viii/90 (1917–32)
Veshch–Gegenstand–Objet, 1–3 (1922)
Z. Elem. Gestalt (1923)
Bauhaus: Z. Bau & Gestalt. (1926–31)
A. Concr. (1930)
Cerc. & Carré (1930)
Abstraction, Création, A. Non-Fig., i–v (1932–6)
Axis, 1–8 (1935–7)
Réalités Nouv., 1–9 (1947–55)
Cobra: Rev. Int. A. Expermntl (1948–51)
Structure (1958–64)
Zero, 1–3 (1958–61)

ARTISTS' WRITINGS AND STATEMENTS

V. Kandinsky: *Über das Geistige in der Kunst* (Munich, 1912)
——: 'Über die Formfrage', *Der Blaue Reiter Almanach* (Munich, 1912, 2/1914), pp. 74–100
——: 'Rückblicke', *Kandinsky, 1901–1913* (Berlin, 1913), pp. iii–xxix
K. Malevich: *Ot kubizma i futurizma k suprematizmu: Novyy zhivopisnyy realizm* [From Cubism and Futurism to Suprematism: the new realism in painting] (St Petersburg, 1915, rev. Moscow, 3 and 4/1916)
P. Mondrian: 'Natuurlijke en abstracte realiteit', *De Stijl*, ii (1919), no. 8, pp. 85–9; no. 9, pp. 97–9; no. 10, pp. 109–13; no. 11, pp. 121–5; no. 12, pp. 133–7; iii (1919), no. 2, pp. 15–19; iii (1920), no. 3, pp. 27–31; no. 5, pp. 41–4; no. 6, pp. 54–6; no. 7, pp. 58–60; no. 8, pp. 65–9; no. 9, pp. 73–6; no. 10, pp. 81–4; repr. and Eng. trans. in *The New Art—The New Life: Collected Writings of Piet Mondrian* (London, 1987), pp. 82–123
Desyataya gosudarstvennaya vystavka: Bespredmetnoye tvorchestvo i suprematizm [Tenth state exhibition: non-objective creation and Suprematism] (exh. cat., essay by K. Malevich, Moscow, 1919)
P. Mondrian: *Le Néo-plasticisme: Principe général de l'équivalence plastique* (Paris, 1921); repr. in *The New Art—The New Life* (London, 1987), pp. 132–47
P. Klee: *Pädagogisches Skizzenbuch*, ed. W. Gropius and L. Moholy-Nagy (Munich, 1925; Eng. trans., New York, 1944, 2/1953)
V. Kandinsky: *Punkt und Linie zu Fläche* (Munich, 1926) [pubd as a Bauhaus bk]
P. Klee: 'Exakte Versuche im Bereich der Kunst', *Bauhaus: Z. Bau & Gestalt.*, ii/2–3 (1928)
N. Gabo: 'The Constructive Idea in Art', *Circle: International Survey of Constructive Art* (London, 1937), pp. 1–10
P. Mondrian: 'Plastic Art and Pure Plastic Art (Figurative Art and Non-Figurative Art)', *Circle: International Survey of Constructive Art* (London, 1937), pp. 41–56
G. Mathieu: 'La Liberté, c'est le vide' (exh. cat., Paris, Gal. Colette Allendy, 1947)
H. Arp: *Dadaland* (Paris, 1948)
A. Calder: 'What Abstract Art Means to Me', *MOMA Bull.*, xviii/3 (1951), p. 8
W. de Kooning: 'What Abstract Art Means to Me', *MOMA Bull.*, xviii/3 (1951), pp. 4–8
R. Motherwell: 'What Abstract Art Means to Me', *MOMA Bull.*, xviii/3 (1951), pp. 12–13
K. Gerstner: *Kalte Kunst* (Teufen, 1957)
J. Albers: *The Interaction of Color* (New Haven and London, 1963)
G. Mathieu: *Au-delà du tachisme* (Paris, 1963)
——: *Le Privilège d'être* (Paris, 1963)
'Conversation with A. Caro, K. Noland and J. Olitski', *Monad* (Jan 1964), pp. 18–22 [interview with D. Thompson]
'Questions to Stella and Judd', *ARTnews* [New York], lxv (1966), no. 5, pp. 55–61 [rev. transcript of original radio broadcast, New York, Feb 1964]
A. Hill, ed.: *Data-directions in Art, Theory and Aesthetics* (London, 1968)
G. Rickey: *Constructivism: Origins and Evolution* (London, 1968)
Art in Progress IV (exh. cat. by R. Ryman, New York, Finch Coll. Mus. A., 1969)
G. Mathieu: *De la révolte à la renaissance* (Paris, 1973)

G. de Vries, ed.: *Über Kunst/On Art: Artists' Writings on the Changed Notion of Art after 1965* (Cologne, 1974)
D. Judd: *Complete Writings, 1959–1975* (Halifax, NS, and New York, 1975)
A. Reinhardt: *Art as Art: The Selected Writings of Ad Reinhardt* (New York, 1975/*R* 1991) [intro. by B. Rose]
Fundamenteele schilderkunst/Fundamental Painting (exh. cat., Amsterdam, Stedel. Mus., 1975) [incl. statements by R. Mangold, B. Marden, A. Martin and R. Ryman, among others]
K. Noland: 'Color, Form and Abstract Art', *A. America*, lxv (1977), pp. 99–105 [interview with Diane Waldman]
N. Holt, ed.: *The Writings of Robert Smithson* (New York, 1979)
M. Poirier and J. Necol: 'The '60s in Abstract', *A. America*, lxxi (1983), no. 3, pp. 122–37 [13 statements and an essay]
P. Halley: *Collected Essays, 1981–1987* (Zurich and New York, 1987)
R. Weil, ed.: 'Talking Abstract', *A. America*, lxxv (1987), no. 7, pp. 80–97; no. 12, pp. 112–29 [interviews with American artists in two parts]
B. Newman: *Selected Writings and Interviews* (New York, 1990)
Collected Writings of Robert Motherwell (Oxford, 1993)

For further writings *see* individual biographies.

EXHIBITION CATALOGUES

Cubism and Abstract Art (exh. cat. by A. Barr, New York, MOMA, 1936)
Le Mouvement (exh. cat. by V. Vasarely, Paris, Gal. Denise René, 1955)
Situation (An Exhibition of British Abstract Painting) (exh. cat. by R. Coleman, London, RBA Gals, 1960)
American Abstract Expressionists and Imagists (exh. cat. by H. H. Arnason, New York, Guggenheim, 1961)
Toward a New Abstraction (exh. cat. by B. Heller, New York, Jew. Mus., 1963)
Post-painterly Abstraction (exh. cat. by C. Greenberg, Los Angeles, CA, Co. Mus. A., 1964)
The New Generation: 1965 (exh. cat., preface B. Robertson, intro. and notes I. Dunlop; London, Whitechapel A.G., 1965)
Primary Structures: Younger American and British Sculptors (exh. cat. by K. McShine, New York, Jew. Mus., 1966)
Systemic Painting (exh. cat. by L. Alloway, New York, Guggenheim, 1966)
Geometric Abstraction, 1926–1942 (exh. cat. by M. Seuphor and J. Elderfield, Dallas, TX, Mus. F.A., 1972)
Robert Ryman (exh. cat., London, Whitechapel A.G., 1977)
Abstraction–Création, 1931–1936 (exh. cat., Paris, Mus. A. Mod. Ville Paris; Münster, Westfäl. Landesmus.; 1978)
Origini dell'astrattismo: Verso altri orizzonti del reale (exh. cat. by G. Ballo and others, Milan, Pal. Reale, 1979)
Abstraction: Towards a New Art, Painting, 1910–1920 (exh. cat., London, Tate, 1980)
Arte astratta italiana, 1909–1959 (exh. cat., Rome, G.N.A. Mod., 1980)
The Avant-garde in Russia, 1910–1930: New Perspectives (exh. cat. by S. Barron and M. Tuchman, Los Angeles, CA, Co. Mus. A., 1980)
Brice Marden (exh. cat., London, Whitechapel A.G., 1981)
Abstract Painting and Sculpture in America, 1927–1944 (exh. cat., Pittsburgh, PA, Carnegie Inst., 1983)
Beyond the Plane: American Constructions, 1930–1965 (exh. cat., Trenton, NJ State Mus., 1983)
Kosmische Bilder in der Kunst des 20. Jahrhunderts (exh. cat., ed. S. Holsten; Baden-Baden, Staatl. Ksthalle, 1983)
Action Precision: The New Direction in New York, 1955–60 (exh. cat. by R. Rosenblum and others, Newport Beach, CA, Harbor A. Mus., 1984)
Carte Blanche to Denise René: Geometric and Kinetic Adventure (exh. cat. by A. Glibota and others, Paris, A. Cent., 1984)
Os grandes mestres do abstracionismo brasileiro (exh. cat. by M. R. Rathsam and A. F. Beuttenmuler, São Paulo, Sociedade de Amigos dos Museus do Brasil, [1984–5])
Contrasts of Form: Geometric Abstract Art, 1910–1980 (exh. cat. by M. Dabrowski, New York, MOMA, 1985)
Abstraction Abstraction (exh. cat. by E. A. King and D. Carrier, Pittsburgh, PA, Carnegie-Mellon U.A.G., 1986)
Arte astratta nelle Marche, 1935–1985 (exh. cat. by C. Melloni, Ascoli Piceno, Pin. Civ., 1986)
Konstruktion und Geste: Schweizer Kunst der 50er Jahre (exh. cat. by W. Rotzler and H. Walter-Dressler, Karlsruhe, Städt. Gal. Prinz-Max-Pal., 1986)
Neo-geometry (exh. cat., Munich, Kstver., 1986)
Nuove geometrie (exh. cat. by F. Caroli, Milan, Rotunda Besana, 1986)
The Spiritual in Art: Abstract Painting, 1890–1935 (exh. cat., Los Angeles, CA, Co. Mus. A., 1986)
L'Art en Europe: Les Années décisives, 1945–1953 (exh. cat., Saint-Etienne, Mus. A. Mod., 1987)
New York Art Now: The Saatchi Collection (exh. cat. by D. Cameron, London, Saatchi Col., 1987)
Astratta: Secessioni astratte in Italia dal dopoguerra al 1990 (exh. cat., Verona, Pal. Forti, 1988)
The Image of Abstraction (exh. cat. by K. Brougher, Los Angeles, CA, Co. Mus. A., 1988)
The Presence of Painting: Aspects of British Abstraction, 1957–1988 (exh. cat. by M. Tooby, Sheffield, Mappin A. G., and elsewhere; 1988)
Contemporary Perspectives I: Abstraction in Question (exh. cat. by R. Smith, J. Simm and W. Ferguson, Sarasota, FL, Ringling Mus. A., 1989)
Espagne arte abstracto, 1950–1965 (exh. cat. by J. M. Bonet, Paris, Artcurial, 1989)
The New Sculpture, 1965–75: Between Geometry and Gesture (exh. cat., ed. R. Armstrong and R. Marshall; New York, Whitney, 1990)
Paris 1930: Arte abstracto, arte concreto, Cercle et Carré (exh. cat. by G. Fabré and R. Stanislowski, Valencia, IVAM Cent. Julio González, 1990)
Aparición de lo invisibile: Pintura abstracta contemporánea en Mexico (exh. cat. by M. A. Alamilla and others, Mexico City, Mus. A. Mod., 1991)
Wille zur Form ungegenständliche Kunst, 1910–1938 in Österreich, Polen, Tschechoslowakei und Ungarn (exh. cat., Vienna, Messepalast, 1993)

GENERAL

W. Worringer: *Abstraktion und Einfühlung* (Munich, 1908; Eng. trans., London, 1948)
J. L. Martin, B. Nicholson and N. Gabo, eds: *Circle: International Survey of Constructive Art* (London, 1937)
S. Janis: *Abstract and Surrealist Art in America* (New York, 1944)
C. Estienne: *L'Art abstrait, est-il un académisme?* (Paris, 1950)
M. Seuphor: *L'Art abstrait, ses origines, ses premiers maîtres* (Paris, 1950)
T. B. Hess: *Abstract Painting: Background and American Phase* (New York, 1951)
H. Rosenberg: 'The American Action Painters', *ARTnews*, li/8 (1952), pp. 22–3, 48–50
M. Tapié: *Un Art autre, où il s'agit de nouveau d'évidages du réel* (Paris, 1952)
A. Heath: *Abstract Painting, its Origins and Meaning* (London, 1953)
M. Seuphor: *Dictionnaire de la peinture abstraite* (Paris, 1957)
P. Soulages: *Au-delà de l'informel* (Paris, 1959)
C. Greenberg: *Art and Culture* (Boston, MA, 1961)
J. MacTruitt: 'Art Arid, DC, Harbor's Touted "New" Painters', *Washington Post* (21 Dec 1961), p. 20
R. Rosenblum: 'The Abstract Sublime', *ARTnews*, lix/10 (1961), pp. 38–41, 56, 58
C. Gray: *The Russian Experiment in Art, 1863–1922* (London, 1962, rev. 1986)
C. Greenberg: 'After Abstract Expressionism', *A. Int.*, vi/8 (1962), pp. 24–32
J. Paulhan: *L'Art informel* (Paris, 1962)
D. Vallier: *L'Art abstrait* (Paris, 1967)
G. Battcock, ed.: *Minimal Art: A Critical Anthology* (New York, 1968)
G. Celant, ed.: *Arte Povera, Conceptual, Actual or Impossible Art?* (London and Milan, 1969)
S. Ringbom: *The Sounding Cosmos: A Study of the Spiritualism of Kandinsky and the Genesis of Abstract Painting* (Åbo, 1970)
I. Sandler: *The Triumph of American Painting: A History of Abstract Expressionism* (New York, 1970); repr. as *Abstract Expressionism: The Triumph of American Painting* (London, 1970)
M. Tuchman: *The New York School: Abstract Expressionism in the '40s and '50s* (London, [1970])
J. Leymarie and others: *Abstract Art since 1945* (London, 1971)
M. Ragon and M. Seuphor: *L'Art abstrait*, 4 vols (Paris, 1971–4)
C. Blok: *Geschichte der abstrakten Kunst, 1900–1960* (Cologne, 1975)
G. Levin: *Synchromism and American Color Abstraction, 1910–1925* (New York, 1978)
H. Osborne: *Abstraction and Artifice in Twentieth-century Art* (Oxford, 1979)
Towards a New Art: Essays on the Background to Abstract Art, 1910–20, preface M. Compton (London, 1980)
J. Gallego: *Arte abstracto español en la colección de la Fundación Juan March* (Madrid, 1983)
L. D. Henderson: *The Fourth Dimension and Non-Euclidean Geometry in Modern Art* (Princeton, 1983)
C. Lodder: *Russian Constructivism* (New Haven and London, 1983)

R. Pincus-Witten: *Entries (Maximilism): Art at the Turn of the Decade* (New York, 1983); rev. as *Postminimalism into Maximilism: American Art, 1966–1986* (Ann Arbor, 1987)
A. B. Nakov: *Abstrait/Concret: Art non-objectif russe et polonais* (Paris, 1984)
M. A. Prat: *L'Abstraction en France, 1919–1939* (Paris, 1984)
D. Vallier: *L'arte astratta* (Milan, 1984)
R. Krauss: *The Originality of the Avantgarede and other Modernist Myths* (Cambridge, MA, and London, 1986)
J. O'Brian: *The Collected Essays and Criticism*, 4 vols (Chicago and London, 1986, rev. 1993) [Clement Greenberg]
M. Ragon: *25 ans d'art vivant: Chronique vécue de l'art contemporain de l'abstraction au Pop art, 1944–1969* (Paris, 1986)
F. Whitford: *Understanding Abstract Art* (London, 1987)
D. J. Clarke: *The Influence of Oriental Thought on Postwar American Painting and Sculpture* (New York and London, 1988)
J. L. Duval: *Histoire de la peinture abstraite* (Paris, 1988; Eng. trans., London, 1989)
D. Kuspit and others: *Abstrakte Malerei aus Amerika und Europa/Abstract Painting from America and Europe* (Vienna, 1988)
M. Pleynet and M. Ragon: *Art abstrait, 1970–1987* (Paris, 1988)
M. Auping: *Abstraction, Geometry, Painting: Selected Geometric Abstract Painting in America since 1945* (New York, 1989)
D. Anfam: *Abstract Expressionism* (London, 1990)
Y. A. Bois: *Painting as Model* (New Haven, 1990)
G. Boudaille and P. Javault: *L'Art abstrait* (Paris, 1990)
A. E. Gibson: *Issues in Abstract Expressionism: The Artist-run Periodicals* (Ann Arbor and London, 1990)
S. Guilbaut, ed.: *Reconstructing Modernism: Art in New York, Paris and Montreal, 1945–1964* (Cambridge, MA, and London, 1990) [esp. essay by T. de Duve]
A. Moszynska: *Abstract Art* (London, 1990)
R. Paulson: *Figure and Abstraction in Contemporary Painting* (New Brunswick, 1990)
D. Shapiro: *Abstract Expressionism: A Critical Record* (Cambridge, 1990)
A. C. Chave: 'Minimalism and the Rhetoric of Power', *Power: Its Myths and Mores* (exh. cat., Indianapolis, IN, Mus. A., 1991)
M. Cheetham: *The Rhetoric of Purity: Essentialist Theory and the Advent of Abstract Painting* (Cambridge, 1991)
C. Millet: *Conversations avec Denise René* (Paris, 1991)
S. Polcari: *Abstract Expressionism and the Modern Experience* (Cambridge, 1991)
U. Ruberti: *Il post-informale in Europa* (Rome, 1991)
D. Leclerc and M. H. Barclay: *The Crisis of Abstraction in Canada: The 1950s* (Ottawa, 1992)
M. Ragon: *Journal de l'art abstrait* (Geneva, 1992)
C. Harrison, F. Frascina and G. Perry: *Primitivism, Cubism, Abstraction: The Early Twentieth Century* (New Haven and London, 1993)
E. Strickland: *Minimalism: Origins* (Indianapolis, 1993)
A. Kagan: *Absolute Art* (St Louis, 1995)

ANNA MOSZYNSKA

Abstract Expressionism. Term applied to a movement in American painting that flourished in the 1940s and 1950s, sometimes referred to as the New York School or, very narrowly, as ACTION PAINTING, although it was first coined in relation to the work of Vasily Kandinsky in 1929. The works of the generation of artists active in New York from the 1940s and regarded as Abstract Expressionists resist definition as a cohesive style; they range from Barnett Newman's unbroken fields of colour to Willem de Kooning's violent handling of the figure. They were linked by a concern with varying degrees of abstraction used to convey strong emotional or expressive content. Although the term primarily denotes a small nucleus of painters, Abstract Expressionist qualities can also be seen in the sculpture of David Smith, Ibram Lassaw and others, the photography of Aaron Siskind and the painting of Mark Tobey, as well as in the work of less renowned artists such as Bradley Walker Tomlin and Lee Krasner. However, the majority of Abstract Expressionists rejected critical labels and shared, if anything, only a common sense of moral purpose and alienation from American society. Abstract Expressionism has nonetheless been interpreted as an especially 'American' style because of its attention to the physical immediacy of paint; it has also been seen as a continuation of the Romantic tradition of the Sublime. It undeniably became the first American visual art to attain international status and influence.

1. Background, origins and early phase. 2. The 1940s: paths to abstraction. 3. The 1950s: climax, reaction and later work.

1. BACKGROUND, ORIGINS AND EARLY PHASE. The roots of Abstract Expressionism lie in the social and artistic climate of the 1920s and early 1930s. Apart from Hans Hofmann, all its major exponents were born between 1903 and 1915 and grew up during a period of American isolationism. Although Europe remained the traditional source of advanced culture, American efforts during the 1920s to develop an aesthetic independence culminated in the direct, homespun realism of Regionalism. Consequently, the development of the art of Willem de Kooning, Arshile Gorky, Jackson Pollock and Clyfford Still, for example, illustrates a complex interaction between tradition, rebellion and the individual talent. European modernism stimulated them deeply, while their desire to retain the impact of personal experience recalled the aims of American Scene painting. Pollock, Still, Smith and Franz Kline were all affected by their native backgrounds in the rural West and in the steel- and coal-producing regions respectively. In other cases Jewish or European origins contributed to an unusual gamut of ethnic, intellectual and private sources of inspiration.

Between the wars New York offered some notable opportunities to assimilate comparatively recent artistic developments. Its galleries included the Museum of Non-objective Art, which housed the impressive Kandinsky collection, and the Museum of Modern Art, which mounted exhibitions throughout the 1930s and 1940s covering many aspects of 20th-century painting.

Much of the creative intellectual ferment of the time was focused in the theories of the Russian émigré painter and writer John Graham who befriended Gorky, Pollock and others. His book *Systems and Dialectics of Art* (1937) justified abstraction as distilling the essence of reality and traced its roots to primitivism, the unconscious and the painter's empathy with the brushstroke. The younger American artists thus seem to have become highly conscious of their historical position and dictates. Most felt that they had to reconcile Cubist spatial organization with the poetic subject-matter of Surrealism and realized that original art would then need to go beyond both.

The development of Arshile Gorky's art from the late 1920s exemplified the cross-currents in the matrix of Abstract Expressionism. He progressively assimilated the main phases of modern European painting in order to explore his own identity until in *The Artist and his Mother* (*c.* 1926–34; New York, Whitney) the private world of Gorky's Armenian origins merged with his contemporary stance as heir to the space and forms of Synthetic Cubism, Picasso and Miró. This mood of transition is especially apparent in technical paradoxes, such as the strange contrasts of carefully finished areas with unresolved passages of paintwork that make this double portrait appear as if it were suspended in a process of change. By the early 1940s this tendency (which can be traced back to Paul Cézanne and to Futurism) provided new means of incorporating the tensions of the artist's immediate circumstances into the actual picture. De Kooning, for example, deliberately allowed successive efforts to capture volume and contour to overtake the stability of his figures, as in *Queen of Hearts* (*c.* 1943; Washington, DC, Hirshhorn); such figures typify one aspect of early Abstract Expressionism in retreating into a dense, ambiguous visual fabric.

At an early stage Pollock, Still and Mark Rothko established a similar polarity between the figure (or other signs of existence) and external forces. The 'realism' of their early landscapes, interiors and urban scenes undoubtedly reflected the emphasis on locale in American Scene painting, but the expressive symbolism was prophetic. A sense of isolation and gloom probably derived in part from the context of the Depression allied with personal factors. They combined highly sensitive, romantic temperaments with left-wing or radical views so that the social circumstances of the period naturally suggested an approach to art that explored the human predicament. This had already been anticipated by some literature of the 1920s and 1930s, notably the novels of William Faulkner (1897–1962), that placed the self against an inimical environment; contemporary American art, however, offered few successful precedents. On the contrary, the weaknesses of depicting human themes literally had already surfaced in Thomas Hart Benton's anecdotal brand of Regionalism that Pollock, a former pupil of Benton, later described as 'something against which to react very strongly'. Despite the wagons, cowboy and mules in Pollock's *Going West* (*c.* 1934–5; Washington, DC, N. Mus. Amer. A.), it remains more elemental than anything by Benton. A feeling of almost cosmic tumult is countered by an overall vortex-like unity.

As Pollock's work became more abstract during the 1930s it nonetheless retained an underlying conflict between impulsive chaos and the need to impose some overall sense of order. Yet the common problem of the 1930s was not just evolving a formal language for what Rothko subsequently termed 'pictures of the human figure—alone in a moment of utter immobility' ('The Romantics were prompted': *Possibilities*, 1, winter 1947–8, p. 84) and other contrasting psychological states; the controversy in the USA focused instead upon the definition and priorities of an authentic avant-garde art.

Several future Abstract Expressionists were employed on the Works Progress Administration's Federal Art Project (WPA/FAP). Alongside the practical benefits of financial support and official endorsement, the WPA/FAP allowed opportunities to experiment with new techniques and to tackle the problems of working on a large scale. It also acted as a catalyst for a more cohesive New York community. But the advocacy of Social Realism on the project alerted many to its academic nature, which Gorky summarized as 'poor art for poor people'. From a visual rather than literary standpoint, the humanitarian imagery of a leading Social Realist such as Ben Shahn seemed as barren as the reactionary equivalents in Regionalism. David Smith's *Medals for Dishonor* series (15 plaster models, 1939; e.g. *No. 9—Bombing Civilian Populations*, ex-artist's priv. col., see G. McCoy, ed.: *David Smith*, New York, 1973, fig. 15) and the early paintings of Philip Guston not only engaged anti-Fascist ideas but also revealed a legacy of the radicalism of the 1930s that was never abandoned, despite largely unfounded claims that later the movement was on the whole 'de-politicized'. Smith and Guston, rather, subsequently sought to show how their respective media could signify and not merely illustrate their beliefs about freedom, aggression and constraint. Similarly, Pollock drew almost nothing from the overt Socialism of the Mexican José Clemente Orozco's murals but a great deal from their capacity to embody human strife in the objective pictorial terms of rhythm and surface pattern.

Another alternative in the 1930s was the tradition of 'pure' abstraction, stemming from Piet Mondrian and upheld by the AMERICAN ABSTRACT ARTISTS group (AAA) to which Ad Reinhardt belonged. Reinhardt's eventual divergence from mainstream Abstract Expressionism can be traced to this initial assumption that the liberating potential of non-objective and specifically geometric art lay in its very independence from the social sphere. A more moderate approach was adopted by the painters Hans Hofmann and Milton Avery. Hofmann, born in Bavaria in 1880, provided a link with an earlier phase of European modernism and, through his own school, which he founded in New York in 1934, taught the synthesis of Cubist structure (emphasizing the unity of the picture plane) with the brilliant colours of Fauvism. Avery's more lyrical approach suffused a simple, flat handling of space with light and atmosphere. This inspired Rothko and Adolph Gottlieb, with its Matisse-like balance between observation and the artist's feelings. Moreover, the growing popularity among an emergent New York avant-garde of theories originated by Leon Trotsky tended to discourage strict orthodoxy by stressing the autonomy of art over social and political restrictions. Out of this amalgam of diverse sources and beginnings, Abstract Expressionism during the 1940s sought to integrate the inner world of emotions with the realities of the picture-making process.

2. THE 1940S: PATHS TO ABSTRACTION. The exhibition *Fantastic Art, Dada, Surrealism* (1936–7; New York, MOMA) heralded a phase when Surrealism and its affinities changed the course of American painting. Furthermore, the arrival of several leading European Surrealists including André Breton, André Masson and Max Ernst in the USA after the outbreak of World War II allowed stimulating personal contacts, Robert Motherwell being one of the first to benefit in this way. This brought an international note to the art scene and reinforced a sense of historical moment: the hegemony of the Ecole de Paris had shifted to New York. As the war continued it also seemed that new subject-matter and accompanying techniques were necessary to confront what was perceived as the tragic and chaotic zeitgeist. Surrealism had partly satisfied such needs by unleashing the disruptive forces of the unconscious, but its tendency towards pure fantasy now appeared irrelevant. In a statement made in 1943 in the *New York Times* (13 June, p. 9), Rothko and Gottlieb declared the new gravity of intent: 'There is no such thing as good painting about nothing. We assert that the subject

is crucial and only that subject-matter is valid which is tragic and timeless.'

The pursuit of universal themes continued Surrealist artists' fascination with the omnipotent force of sexuality and explained much apparently Freudian imagery in paintings of the earlier 1940s. Erotic motifs occur in Gorky's *The Liver is the Cock's Comb* (1944; Buffalo, NY, Albright–Knox A.G.). Interpenetrating or phallic elements characterized Smith's sculptures at times, as well as the paintings of Pollock, Rothko, Still and Theodoros Stamos; the living figure in Motherwell's *Pancho Villa Dead and Alive* (1943; New York, MOMA) is distinguished by his genitalia. Such inconography in fact derived less from Freud than from a more universal symbolism invoking regeneration, fertility and primitive impulses. These themes in twin stemmed from the Abstract Expressionist's overriding concern with subjectivity. To this end the Surrealist use of biomorphism, a formal language of organic curves and similar motifs, was variously exploited. For Gorky it evolved into a metamorphic realm where tendrils, spikes and softer masses referred simultaneously to nature and to human anatomy. Pollock's version was less specific, and in *Pasiphaë* (1943; New York, Met.) it implied womb-like enclosure versus whirling activity. Even de Kooning, the least sympathetic towards Surrealism, reiterated organic contours in his claustrophobic canvases of the mid-1940s as reminders of a strong yet cryptic eroticism. Thus biomorphism served to bridge the figurative modes of the 1940s with a manifold path to abstraction.

Another catalyst in the 1940s was a preoccupation with the concept of myth, especially as interpreted by the Swiss psychologist Carl Gustav Jung, whose writings had gradually gained an American readership. According to Jung, myths gave universal form to basic human truths and related to a profound level of experience that he identified as the 'collective unconscious'. These theories helped several Abstract Expressionists attain more reductive styles because myth, Jung claimed, had a dramatic simplicity expressed through 'archetypes', that is, primal figures and symbols. Primitive art often dealt with myth and became a secondary source at this stage, particularly in the aftermath of exhibitions at the Museum of Modern Art in New York, ranging from prehistoric rock pictures in Europe and Africa (1937) to American Indian art (1941). The totem was a frequently used primitive motif, aptly fitted to personify the Jungian archetype in the guise of a mysterious, upright entity. In Pollock's *Guardians of the Secret* (1943; San Francisco, CA, MOMA) sentinels at either side of the picture seem to guard a central maze of lines and markings that suggests the chaotic recesses of the collective unconscious. Similarly, Still, Smith and others turned the totem into a visual cipher halfway between a figure and a non-representational emblem.

The great potential of the abstract sign soon became clear: it embodied a kind of terse pictorial shorthand, provocative in itself or, rather like individual script, imbued with the physical impetus of its creator. In 1941 Gottlieb began a series known collectively as *Pictographs* (e.g. *Voyager's Return*, 1946; New York, MOMA). Enigmatic details, including body parts and geometric motifs, were set within a rough gridwork that recalled an archaic sign system or petroglyph. By 1947 Rothko, Stamos and others had created sparse schematic images marked by a shallow, post-Cubist space, and defined in the *Ideographic Picture* exhibition, organized by Barnett Newman for the Betty Parsons Gallery, New York, in 1947, as 'a symbol or character painted, written or inscribed representing ideas'.

Newman's own works of this period reflected the theory that abstraction could convey awesome meanings. Their breakthrough was analogous to that in Aaron Siskind's contemporary photographs, such as *Iron Work I* (1947; see C. Chiarenza: *Aaron Siskind: Pleasures and Terrors*, Boston, 1982, fig. 77), which gained impact from a calculated ambiguity. Their syntax of vertical elements, quivering edges and voids retained the dramatic aura associated with figuration but no longer conformed to either a biomorphic style or to the geometry of Mondrian. Rothko's paintings also progressed in a similar direction already anticipated in 1943 when he wrote, 'We favor the simple expression of the complex thought' (letter to the *New York Times* Art Editor, Edward Alden, 7 June 1943), which was to be achieved through the 'large shape' that could impose its monumentality upon the viewer.

This reduction to essentials had widespread consequences during the 1940s. It shifted attention away from relatively graphic symbolism towards the capacities of colour and space to acquire an absolute intensity, not bound to describe events and forms within the picture but free to embody extremes of light and darkness, enclosure, liberation and so on. The dynamics of the act of painting assumed a central role. Gorky's use of very fluid washes of pigment in 1942, under the influence of the Chilean Surrealist Matta (Echaurren), foreshadowed both tendencies. The resultant veils, billows and liquid runs of colour created an unusually complex space, as in *Water of the Flowery Mill* (1944; New York, Met.) that changed from one area to another with the same spontaneity that had previously been limited to Gorky's organic shapes.

Still, Gottlieb, Stamos and Richard Pousette-Dart pursued a different course in the 1940s by stressing tangible paint layers with heavy or unconventional textures. These methods altered their works from the traditional concept of a discrete easel picture to more palpable images whose presence confronted the actual world of the spectator. Dimensions grew in order to accentuate psychological and physical rapport with the viewer. Inevitably, the search for heightened immediacy, for a charged relationship between surface and viewer, meant that a number of artists would regard the painting as an incarnation of the process—the energy, tensions and gestures—that had created it.

The Surrealist technique AUTOMATISM again unlocked possibilities for incorporating immediacy with a vivid record of manual activity, and the impulses behind it, into the final work. Automatism had supposedly allowed Surrealists like Miró and Masson to paint without full conscious control and so essentially stimulated the discovery of unorthodox forms. In contrast, Abstract Expressionism elevated Automatist procedures into a means of reorganizing the entire composition. Hofmann was among the first to pour and drip paint in the early 1940s in order to achieve increased liveliness, but Pollock took the technique to revolutionary limits. By the mid-1940s he painted with such urgency that the remnants of figures and other symbolic details were almost dismembered and lost within the great arcs and whorls formed by his sweeping gestures, for example *There were Seven in Eight* (1945; New York, MOMA). A climax came in 1947 when the restrictions of brushes and the upright format of the easel picture were abandoned as Pollock took to working directly on the floor, dripping paint either straight from the can or with the aid of an implement such as a stick or a trowel. Consequently, in works of this period an astonishing labyrinth of paint traces expand, oscillate and hurtle back upon themselves resembling, as the artist described it, 'energy and motion made visible'. Pollock had reconciled two long-standing though divergent impulses, an obsession with chaotic force and the desire for order, into the vibrant unity of a field, for example *Number 2, 1949* (Utica, NY, Munson–Williams–Proctor Inst.; see fig. 1).

This synthesis was unique at the time, but Abstract Expressionist painting in the late 1940s generally approached a threshold where restlessness and flux predominated. The composition dissolved into a seething field of fragments dispersed with almost equal intensity throughout the picture, hence the term 'all-over' was sometimes used to describe this tendency. A type of space evolved that was dense and unstable beyond even that of Analytical Cubism, as in de Kooning's *Painting* (1948; New York, MOMA). This probably owed something to the doubt-ridden anxieties of the post-war years and perhaps the pressures of fast-moving urban life. It certainly also stemmed from the consequences of Automatism, which took even less overtly Abstract Expressionist painters like Reinhardt and Tobey to the stage where a teeming, calligraphic field of brushstrokes predominated. By the end of the decade the need to reassert meaningful content in unprecedented ways had again become imperative.

3. THE 1950S: CLIMAX, REACTION AND LATER WORK. Newman's essay 'The Sublime is Now', published in the *Tiger's Eye* (i/6, 1948), called for a new art stripped to its formal essentials that still dealt with 'absolute emotions'. He concluded, 'The image we produce is the self-evident one of revelation, real and concrete.' Within two years Newman, Rothko and Still fulfilled these aims, primarily through a total concentration on colour, a pictorial element loaded with dramatic connotations, simultaneously palpable and metaphysical insofar as its total effect transcends analysis. The deep redness of Newman's *Onement I* (1948; New York, MOMA) no longer describes forms since it comprises an absolute continuum, punctuated, though not broken, by a central vertical band of a brighter hue. Encompassing fields of colour tended to minimize internal pictorial relations and so invite the onlooker's participation, especially when enlarged to the mural scale sometimes adopted in the early 1950s. Small incidents acquired an uncanny prominence; the luminous rifts that escaped from Still's essays in black or the slight haloes around Rothko's rectangles implied the numinous behind the apparently monolithic façades. By 'telling little', as Rothko described it in 1958, these works in fact managed to express more.

COLOUR FIELD PAINTING was championed, using narrow stylistic criteria, by the critic Clement Greenberg as a breakthrough in modernist painting's attitude to space because it superseded the shallow figure-ground relationships found in Cubism. Another interpretation has concentrated upon its elemental conflicts of light and scale, and of void and presence, as extending the Romantic tradition of the Sublime with its predilection for epic revelations. Both readings are valid but overlook the fact that the artists had essentially lifted the symbolic extremes and states of consciousness depicted in their earlier works on to an abstract plane. Moreover, the primal field of colour, accentuating the viewer's isolation and sense of self, may equally have reflected a need for strong emotional experience in the barrenness of the Cold War during the late 1940s and the 1950s in the USA. Indeed its imagery was not confined to Abstract Expressionist painting and recurred in the photographs of Siskind and Harry Callahan as well as in the expanses of space that engulfed the solitary figures painted by Ben Shahn and Andrew Wyeth.

In 1950 de Kooning abruptly abandoned his increasingly hermetic all-over compositions, such as *Excavation* (1950; Chicago, IL, A. Inst.; see fig. 2), to begin a number of female subjects, the first being *Woman I* (1950–52; New York, MOMA). Paradoxically, this return to the figure vied with de Kooning's painting style, where the furious tumult of brushstrokes seemed to possess independence and velocity. The poet and critic Harold Rosenberg traced similarities in the work of Pollock, de Kooning and Franz Kline, who had begun black-and-white abstractions *c.* 1949 that aggrandize the individual brushstroke into enormous vectors appearing to continue beyond the picture's edges (for illustration *see* KLINE, FRANZ). Rosenberg had assimilated the existentialism popular among the New York intelligentsia of the late 1940s and claimed that this art represented the physical traces of its creator's spontaneous working methods. He characterized it as Action painting. Subsequent histories have tended to maintain the consequent division into 'action' or 'gestural' styles and 'colour field painting', although these rather

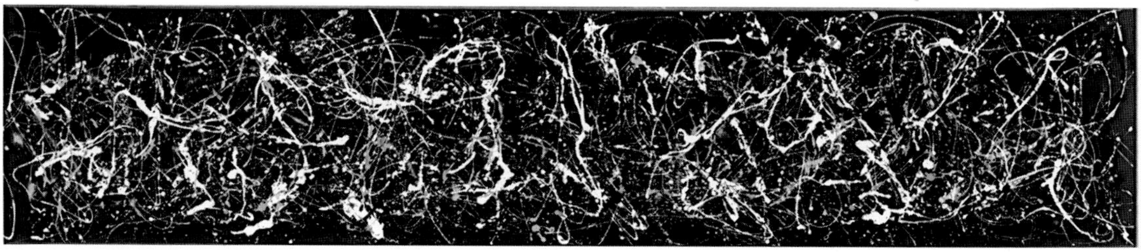

1. Jackson Pollock: *Number 2, 1949*, oil, duco and aluminium paint on unsized canvas, 375×1950 mm (Utica, NY, Munson–Williams–Proctor Institute)

2. Willem de Kooning: *Excavation*, oil and enamel on canvas, 2.03×2.54 m, 1950 (Chicago, IL, Art Institute of Chicago)

simplistic critical categories were disowned by the artists and overrode many subtle connections.

Newman's *Onement* paintings (which date from *c.* 1948 to 1953) and de Kooning's *Woman* paintings, a theme to which he repeatedly returned, stand at opposite poles of technique and mood, ranging from the exalted to the grotesque. Both nonetheless juxtapose a centralized presence against an ambience, whether of colour or urban chaos. Still's *1957-D-No1* (1957; Buffalo, NY, Albright-Knox A.G.; for illustration *see* STILL, CLYFFORD) further demonstrates the shortcomings of critical categories by conferring the graphic contours and energy associated with gestural painting upon grandiose and otherwise almost homogeneous walls of pigment. Alongside Pollock's 'drip' paintings and the large, linear steel sculptures by Smith of the late 1940s onwards, it established a radical type of Abstract Expressionist work where any static or conventional background ceased to exist and all parts interacted as if galvanized into a network of forces. The viewer's perceptual process had to integrate the pictorial incidents actively, the far-flung extremes of scale, colour and focus and, in Smith's sculptures, the great disparities when seen from different viewpoints. This meant that they had a 'life' beyond what was contained in any one aspect. The dynamic encounter between the work and its audience became a hallmark of Abstract Expressionism.

National recognition increased during the 1950s. The role of dealers, critics and institutions such as the Museum of Modern Art, New York, in this development encouraged the theory that the movement was promoted at home and abroad as a weapon of Cold War ideology to stress the USA's superior freedom of expression. While the claim may be just, the artists themselves were not actively responsible. In fact several challenged such control by avoiding contact with the art establishment or taking their work to conclusions that almost defied critical commentary, such as the progression towards hypnotic monochrome painting by Reinhardt and Rothko in the 1960s.

While Abstract Expressionism's intensity depended partly on its very stylistic terseness, as in Newman's work, or singularity, as in Pollock's, its latter phases tended to pivot around a search to avoid defined limits or to extract the greatest range of meanings from a strictly limited idiom. The notion of working in series allowed nuances and variations to register most forcefully against a fairly constant visual syntax: Newman's group of 14 paintings, *Stations of the Cross* (1958–66; *see* NEWMAN, BARNETT, fig. 1), or Smith's *Cubi* series (1961–5) show a creative impulse transcending the parameters of a single act. Themes and images from the 1940s also returned on a grandiose scale. Thus Gottlieb's *Bursts* (which he painted from 1957) refashioned pictograph symbols into newfound explosive gestures and calmer fields of colour. It was Pollock's last period, however, that encapsulated the movement's overall dilemma. At best he summoned earlier mythic imagery, through methods such as black paint soaked into bare canvas in the remarkable, nightmarish compositions of 1951 and 1952. More often the sheer fusion of audacity and control attained in the 'drip' paintings pre-empted further innovation, and Pollock's death in 1956 reinforced suspicions that a vanguard was now in decline.

In this later phase a community of younger artists emerged to adopt the tenets of spontaneity, improvisation and the importance of process. They included the painters Helen Frankenthaler and Joan Mitchell, poet Frank O'Hara (1926–66) and the sculptors associated with assemblage. However, they replaced the basic urgency and existential vision of their models with a more lyrical and relatively decorative stance, (that could indeed suggest a feminist revision of 'masculine' premises), characterized for example by Frankenthaler's *Mountains and Sea* (1952; artist's col., on loan to Washington, DC, N.G.A.; for illustration *see* FRANKENTHALER, HELEN). By then Abstract Expressionism had nonetheless transformed the fundamentals of painting and sculpture in the mid-20th century, and its influence in terms of style and aesthetics extended over a vast spectrum of subsequent art.

BIBLIOGRAPHY

C. Greenberg: *Art and Culture* (Boston, 1961)
H. Rosenberg: *The Tradition of the New* (New York, 1961)
Artforum, iv/1 (1965) [issue ded. to Abstract Expressionism]
M. Tuchman, ed.: *New York School* (Greenwich, NY, 1965)
B. Rose: *Readings in American Art Since 1900* (New York, 1968)
W. Rubin: *Dada and Surrealist Art* (London, 1969), pp. 342–410
I. Sandler: *The Triumph of American Painting: A History of Abstract Expressionism* (New York, 1970)
D. Ashton: *The Life and Times of the New York School* (Bath, 1972)
S. Hunter: *American Art of the Twentieth Century* (New York, 1972)
C. Harrison: 'Abstract Expressionism', *Concepts of Modern Art* (London, 1974/1988, ed. N. Stangos), pp. 169–211
W. Andersen: *American Sculpture in Process: 1930–1970* (Boston, MA, 1975)
R. Rosenblum: *Modern Painting and the Northern Romantic Tradition* (London, 1975)
K. McShine, ed.: *The Natural Paradise* (New York, 1976)
J. Wechsler: *Surrealism and American Painting* (New Brunswick, 1977)
E. Carmean jr: *The Subjects of the Artist* (Washington, DC, 1978)
R. Hobbs and G. Levin: *Abstract Expressionism, the Formative Years* (New York, 1978)
I. Sandler: *The New York School* (New York, 1978)
B. Rose: *American Painting* (London, 1980)
A. Cox: *Art-as-politics: The Abstract Expressionist Avant-garde and Society* (Ann Arbor, 1982)
S. Guilbaut: *How New York Stole the Idea of Modern Art* (Chicago, 1983)
W. Seitz: *Abstract Expressionist Painting in America* (Cambridge, MA, 1983)
M. Baigell: *A Concise History of American Painting and Sculpture* (New York, 1984)
P. Turner, ed.: *American Images: Photography, 1945–80* (London, 1985)
M. Auping, ed.: *Abstract Expressionism: The Critical Developments* (New York, 1987)
D. Shapiro and C. Shapiro, eds: *Abstract Expressionism: A Critical Record* (Cambridge, 1989)
D. Anfam: *Abstract Expressionism* (London, 1990)
C. Ross: *Abstract Expressionism: Creators and Critics* (New York, 1990)
S. Polcari: *Abstract Expressionism and the Modern Experience*, (Cambridge, 1991)
D. Thistlewood, ed.: *American Abstract Expressionism* (Liverpool, 1993)

DAVID ANFAM

Abstraction. Term used in an art context in several ways: in general for processes of imagemaking in which only some of the visual elements usually ascribed to 'the natural world' are extracted (i.e. 'to abstract'), and also for the description of certain works that fall only partially, if at all, into what is commonly understood to be representational. Differing ideas and manifestations of abstraction appeared in artists' works in the successive modern movements of the 20th century (*see* ABSTRACT ART). As the notion of abstraction in the second sense is always dependent on what the parameters of representation are thought to be, the two terms can be contiguous in definition, raising interesting points for the general theory of reference. For instance, an abstract work is often defined as one that does not represent anything, but not every work that does not represent anything is necessarily abstract. A painting that has a fictitious subject, for example a painting of Don Quixote or Camelot, does not represent anything (for there is no such person or place) but is not therefore abstract. A Zeus-picture or a Paradise-picture is no more abstract than a Napoleon-picture or a Paris-picture. An abstract work neither represents anything nor is representational.

This runs close to paradox. Does it amount to saying that an abstract picture pictures nothing and indeed is not a picture? It is perhaps better to speak of works rather than pictures. Still, to say that a work is abstract if it is non-representational does not hold in general. Most architectural and musical works are non-representational, yet are not thereby classed as abstract. Something is missing in the equation of 'abstract' with 'non-representational'.

What is missing in such qualifications is that 'abstract' as applied to works of art is not a merely passive negative characterization, but has a further privative force. A non-representational painting is abstract in that it lacks a certain function or feature that is usual for and expected of paintings in general, while representationality (or more generally, denotationality) is not usual in or expected of architectural or musical works, and its absence in such a work does not constitute a lack or deprivation, or the classification of the work as abstract. Likewise, while it seems feasible to call a fish without fins 'finless', and a dog that doesn't bark 'barkless', it would seem odd to call fish 'barkless' or dogs 'finless', or birds and horses either 'finless' or 'barkless'. In spirited discussion among artists and critics, abstraction, that is, absence of representation, is sometimes presented in a more positive light—not as a lack or deprivation but as a purification. Not only does representation, incessantly before us in practical and commercial contexts on postcards, billboards and screens, come to be disparaged as having little or no aesthetic import, but furthermore, the argument runs, representation relates a work to something outside it, whereas an abstract work keeps entirely to itself with no distraction or detraction from its own functions and features.

It still remains, however, that abstraction, whether deprivation or purification, is a matter of what a work does not do or what features it does not have. To say that a work is abstract is to say only that it does not represent and is not even representational, so 'Abstract' is often combined with another term that indicates a primary function or feature of a work, as for example in 'Abstract

Expressionist'. Other combinations may be contemplated, such as 'abstract allusionist'. 'Abstract representational' would, of course, be self-cancelling, and, strictly, so would 'abstract portrait' and 'abstract landscape'. These latter terms, however, can be regarded as indicating that representation, though not altogether absent from the work, is subordinated to other symbolic functions such as exemplification, expression or allusion.

Since an abstract work is one without representation, or more generally denotation, the question naturally arises what an abstract verbal or linguistic work may be, a text that says nothing, a story that does not tell a story, a poem that does not speak of anything. Like a picture that does not picture, these works are deprived of a normal denotative function and refer directly by showing rather than saying, as by exemplifying patterns or expressing feelings. A curious anomaly arises here. Through the ambiguity in the use of 'abstract', extreme cases of this kind, such as a page of miscellaneous and irregularly distributed words, are sometimes called not 'abstract' but 'concrete'! For example, in CONCRETE POETRY, 'concrete' is used as opposed not to 'abstract' as 'non-representational' but to 'abstract' as 'repeatable' or 'universal'. For a normal denotative text, whatever is spelt the same way in the same language, regardless of differences in fount, hand, size, colour etc, is another instance of the same work. On the other hand, a Concrete poem, an alphabet painting by Jasper Johns or an example of Chinese calligraphy is unrepeatable—the particular concrete object is the functioning symbol. Other objects, even if spelt the same way (where that term is applicable), are not instances of the same work but are different works.

See also REPRESENTATION.

BIBLIOGRAPHY

N. Goodman: *Languages of Art* (Indianapolis, 1968, 2/1976)

C. Z. Elgin: *With Reference to Reference* (Indianapolis, 1983)

N. Goodman: *Of Mind and Other Matters* (Indianapolis, 1984) [esp. chap. 3]

N. Goodman and C. Z. Elgin: *Reconceptions in Philosophy and Other Arts and Sciences* (Cambridge, MA, 1988)

NELSON GOODMAN

Abstraction-Création. International group of painters and sculptors, founded in Paris in February 1931 and active until 1936. It succeeded another short-lived group, CERCLE ET CARRÉ, which had been formed in 1929 with similar intentions of promoting and exhibiting abstract art. Its full official title was Abstraction-Création: Art non-figuratif. The founding committee included AUGUSTE HERBIN (president), Georges Vantongerloo (vice-president), Hans Arp, Albert Gleizes, Jean Hélion, Georges Valmier and František Kupka.

Membership of Abstraction-Création was in principle open to all abstract artists, but the dominant tendency within the group was towards the geometric formality championed by Theo van Doesburg and by other artists

Jean Hélion: *Ile-de-France*, oil on canvas, 1454×2000 m, 1935 (London, Tate Gallery)

associated with De Stijl. Works such as Jean Hélion's *Ile-de-France* (1935; London, Tate; see fig.), which came to typify the group's stance, owed more to the post-war 'rappel à l'ordre' interpreted by the Purists in terms of a 'classic' and 'architectonic' ordering of art, design and architecture, than to the biomorphic abstraction derived from Surrealism. During its brief existence the group published annual *cahiers*. The first issue, edited by Hélion and published in 1932, offered some definitions:

> Non-figuration, that is to say cultivation of pure plasticity, to the exclusion of any explanatory, anecdotal, literary or naturalistic element . . . ; abstraction because certain artists have arrived at the conception of non-figuration through progressive abstraction from the forms of nature; creation because artists have achieved non-figuration directly through a conception of purely geometric order.

Over 40 artist-members, including the members of the committee, were represented by reproductions of their non-figurative works, in some cases with accompanying statements. Among them were Willi Baumeister, Alexander Calder, Robert Delaunay and Sonia Delaunay, Otto Freundlich, Naum Gabo, Jean Gorin, László Moholy-Nagy, Piet Mondrian, Antoine Pevsner, Kurt Schwitters, Henryk Stazewski, Theo van Doesburg, Jacques Villon and Edward Wadsworth. It was acknowledged that the Russian artists El Lissitzky, Malevich and Tatlin were 'unable to join'.

If Abstraction-Création had a dominant theme at the outset, this was the idealist tendency in late Cubism (represented by Gleizes, Hélion and Herbin). To this was added the geometrical tendency of De Stijl, represented by Mondrian, van Doesburg and Vantongerloo, and an émigré version of Constructivism (represented by the expatriates Gabo and Pevsner). A commitment to the rationalization of design went hand in hand with a tendency to spiritualize geometry.

By 1935 the association had 'about 50' members, of whom 32 contributed to the annual *cahier*. In the same year a broader category of 'Members and Friends' numbered 410. A breakdown of these by countries was published in the fourth *cahier*. The majority were resident in France, with 209 based in Paris; Switzerland, the Netherlands, Great Britain, Germany, Poland and Italy and a further 10 countries provided the remaining members. Among those who had joined by this time were Josef Albers, Lucio Fontana, Julio González, Arshile Gorky, Barbara Hepworth, Vasily Kandinsky and Ben Nicholson. From December 1933 an exhibition of members' work was held for about a year at an address on the Avenue de Wagram, Paris.

The diverse members of Abstraction-Création were united by their commitment to the identification of abstract art with liberation. Although the association between aesthetic and political freedom was generally idealistic in character, it gained significance from the suppression of modern artistic practice under various totalitarian governments during the 1930s. The following editorial statement was published in 1933:

> The second issue of *Abstraction-Création* appears at a time when, under all régimes, in some countries more effectively than others, but everywhere, free thought is fiercely opposed. . . . We place this issue under the banner of a total opposition to all oppression, of whatever kind it may be.

The last *cahier* appeared in 1936 after much deliberation. It must by then have been clear to many of the contributors that abstract art was not the means of saving the world from the forces of oppression. During the prelude to World War II, many of those who had gathered in Paris in the late 1920s and early 1930s travelled to the USA in pursuit of security, their migrations partly encouraged by the network of contacts that Abstraction-Création had established.

WRITINGS

Abstraction-Création: Art non-figuratif, 1–5 (1932–6)

BIBLIOGRAPHY

Abstraction-Création, 1931–36 (exh. cat., Paris, Mus. A. Mod. Ville Paris, 1978)

□

Abu (i). *See* MT ABU.

Abu (ii). *See* ASWAN.

Abu ʿAli Muhammad ibn ʿAli ibn Muqla. *See* IBN MUQLA.

Abu Dhabi. *See under* UNITED ARAB EMIRATES.

Abu Ghurab. Site of the ancient Egyptian sun temple of King Neuserre (*reg c.* 2416–*c.* 2392 BC), on the western bank of the Nile north-west of Abusir, almost opposite the southernmost suburbs of modern Cairo. The temple, called Shesepib re ('joy of the sun god Re'), is situated at the edge of the Libyan Desert, in the area of the Memphite necropolis.

Six sun temples were built for the state sun god Re-Horakhty by the kings of the 5th Dynasty, but by the late 20th century only two had so far been located. The sun temple of Neuserre was excavated by Friedrich Wilhelm von Bissing in 1898–1901. Nearly all the reliefs were removed, mostly to German collections, and many perished during World War II. The temple was built mainly of limestone. It consists, from east to west, of the valley temple, causeway and upper temple. This arrangement is similar to that of pyramid complexes and suggests a generally accepted concept of a purpose-built temple during the Old Kingdom. A brick-built bark of the sun god was discovered near by.

The main features of the upper temple (about 110×80 m; see fig.) are an entrance passage; a large court open to the sun with a covered corridor round its three sides; a massive platform on which stood a masonry-built obelisk symbolizing the sun god; a one-room chapel; and the Room of the Seasons connected with an ascending corridor leading on to the obelisk-platform. A large alabaster altar stands in the centre of the court.

The painted raised reliefs (bas-reliefs) are skilfully designed but less carefully executed than those of the 4th and early 5th dynasties. Some of the reliefs show the sun god's beneficent attitude towards the king's reign through episodes of the *sed*-festival (a celebration of the royal jubilee) and represent the most detailed treatment of this theme known from the Old Kingdom. The reliefs from the Room of the Seasons illustrate the sun's life-giving influence in nature. The panorama of Egyptian country

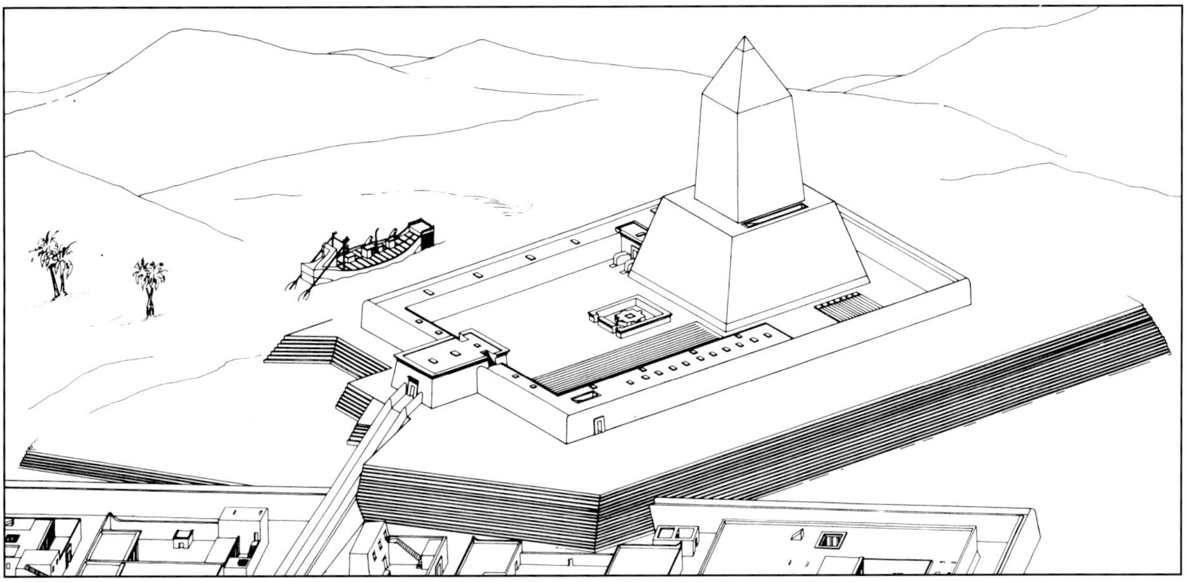

Abu Ghurab, upper temple of the sun temple of King Neuserre (*reg c.* 2416–*c.* 2392 BC); reconstruction drawing

scenes is divided into two periods, *akhet* (inundation, or autumn/winter) and *shemu* (spring/summer). The most characteristic images of animal, bird and plant life are represented, as well as man's typical outdoor activities. This is the earliest extensive corpus of such scenes, accurately observed and realistically portrayed, from Egypt.

BIBLIOGRAPHY

LÄ

F. W. von Bissing, ed.: *Das Re-Heiligtum des Königs Ne-woser-re (Rathures)*, i, L. Borchardt: *Der Bau* (Berlin, 1905); ii, F. W. von Bissing and H. Kees: *Die kleine Festdarstellung* (Leipzig, 1923); iii, H. Kees: *Die grosse Festdarstellung* (Leipzig, 1928)

E. Edel and S. Wenig: *Die Jahreszeitenreliefs aus dem Sonnenheiligtum des Königs Ne-user-re* (Berlin, 1974)

JAROMIR MALEK

Abu Habba. *See* SIPPAR.

Abularach, Rodolfo (*b* Guatemala, 7 Jan 1933). Guatemalan painter and printmaker. From 1954 to 1957 he studied at the Escuela Nacional de Artes Plásticas in Guatemala City while researching folk art for the Dirección de Bellas Artes, but he was virtually self-taught and began as a draughtsman and painter of bullfighting scenes. In 1958 he travelled to New York on a Guatemalan government grant, prolonging his stay there with further grants, studying at the Arts Students League and Graphic Art Center and finally settling there permanently. He was influential in Guatemala until *c.* 1960, but because of his long residence abroad his work did not fit easily in the context of Central American art. Before leaving Guatemala he had painted landscapes and nudes in a naturalistic style, but he soon adopted a more modern idiom partly inspired by aboriginal Guatemalan subjects. After moving to New York, and especially from 1958 to 1961, his art underwent a profound transformation as he sought to bring together elements of abstract art and Surrealism and experimented with textures, for example in cross-hatched pen-and-ink drawings such as *Fugitive from a Maya Lintel* (1958; Washington, DC, MOMA Latin America). Later he simplified his art and turned his attention to light as a substance emanating from within his works. In the 1980s he began to paint large landscapes characterized by a magical symbolism.

BIBLIOGRAPHY

L. Méndez Dávila: *Arte vanguardia Guatemala* (Guatemala City, 1969), pp. vii–viii

R. Cabrera: *Rodolfo Abularach: Artista testimonial* (Guatemala City, 1971)

JORGE LUJÁN MUÑOZ

Abu'l-Hasan (*b* 1588; *fl* 1600–30). Indian painter. In 1618 the Mughal emperor Jahangir (*reg* 1605–27) wrote in his memoirs that Abu'l-Hasan's 'work was perfect...At the present time he has no rival or equal... Truly he has become *Nadir al-Zaman* ("Wonder of the age")'. Some of this artist's paintings are among the greatest in Mughal art. He was born in Jahangir's household in 1588, the son of the erstwhile Safavid artist AQA RIZA (i). Abu'l-Hasan's earliest known work, a drawing based on Albrecht Dürer's *St John* and executed when he was only 12 (Oxford, Ashmolean), already shows in its naturalism the trend of his mature work. A single painting in a manuscript of the fable-book *Anvār-i Suhaylī* ('Lights of Canopus'), probably done in 1604 (London, BL), develops the naturalism of his portraiture but still contains a Safavid landscape based on his father's work; his sense of respect for the latter is indicated by his signing himself here 'the dust of Riza's threshold'. He maintained throughout his career the meticulous finish of the Safavid style.

The most famous painting of his youthful maturity is his *Squirrels in a Plane Tree* (1605-7; London, India Office Lib.), depicting 12 squirrels gambolling in a plane tree while a hunter below tries to climb the trunk. The painting combines his new mastery of volume, shown in the squirrels, the hunter and the tree trunk, with homage to the Safavid masters in the landscape background with its gold sky and mauve hills. The general composition seems to have been based on a page executed by ʿAbd al-Samad in 1555–6 in the *Muraqqaʿ-i gulshan* or Gulshan Album (Tehran, Gulistan Pal. Lib.). This youthful masterpiece seems to have earned Abu'l-Hasan the privilege of being portrayed before 1608 with a select group of other masters on a page by Daulat in the Gulshan Album.

There are few pictures attributable to Abu'l-Hasan between the *Squirrels* and the remarkable group of paintings produced in the ten years after 1615, which shows his powers at their height. Some of these were intended for the *Jahāngīrnāma*, the imperial copy of Jahangir's memoirs. It was Abu'l-Hasan's presentation in 1618 of the *Celebrations at Jahangir's Accession* (St Petersburg, Acad. Sci.) that induced Jahangir to write so fulsomely about his favourite artist. It was also to Abu'l-Hasan that Jahangir turned for pictorial expression of his moods, whether political wish-fulfilment or his preoccupation with the poet Saʿdi's idea of a 'dervish-oriented kingship' in which the king put away from himself the cares of state but came to Paradise because of his love for holy men: the Emperor may have been seduced by Abu'l-Hasan's increasing powers of realism into attributing to these fantasies power to heal what he thought of as his wounded spirit. Two of Abu'l-Hasan's finest paintings illustrate Jahangir's regard for dervishes and increasing contempt for kingship. A double page (one half 1615, the other possibly slightly later; Washington, DC, Freer, and Baltimore, MD, Walters A.G.) shows Jahangir with his sons and surrounded by his chief noblemen, his feet resting on a globe; court officials usher into his presence the long-dead Saʿdi and other mystics while the Ottoman and Persian emperors stand rejected. In another painting (1619; Geneva, Prince Sadruddin Aga Khan priv. col.) Jahangir shows himself to his people at the *jharokā* window in the Agra Fort from which early in his reign he had let down a golden chain hung with bells to be rung by those seeking justice; however, in the painting officials drive suppliants away while the Emperor gazes at a holy man who has taken up residence in a hut below.

Abu'l-Hasan also painted the most important political paintings of Jahangir's reign. In one example (1616–17; Dublin, Chester Beatty Lib.) Jahangir is depicted as an archer standing on a globe shooting an arrow at the severed head of the black Malik ʿAmbar, the general of the Ahmadnagar army. Since Malik ʿAmbar lived until 1626, this painting is pure wish-fulfilment, as is Abu'l-Hasan's painting of 1618–20 showing *Jahangir Embracing Shah ʿAbbas I of Iran* (Washington, DC, Freer; see fig.). This is Abu'l-Hasan's supreme representation of his master and one of the greatest of political pictures. Whereas *Jahangir Shooting the Head of Malik ʿAmbar* is weighed down by symbolism and quotation, the new picture speaks for itself. Ostensibly a representation of the friendship between Jahangir and Shah ʿAbbas, it shows the two rulers standing on a globe on their respective countries; in fact the powerful Jahangir is pushing the deferential figure of Shah ʿAbbas off into the Mediterranean. Jahangir's head is encircled by the sun and moon, a reference to his title of Nur al-Din ('Light of religion'). A later picture (1623; Washington, DC, Freer) adds yet another dimension to imperial iconography: Jahangir, fully armed, stands on top of a segment of the globe in remote, godlike isolation from a battle being fought between his forces and those of his rebellious son Shah Jahan (*reg* 1628–58) represented by tiny figures in the vast green plain below.

Abu'l-Hasan: *Jahangir Embracing Shah ʿAbbas I of Iran*, colour and gold on paper, 238×154 mm, *c.* 1618–20 (Washington, DC, Freer Gallery of Art)

There is no further evidence of Abu'l-Hasan's work apart from a few accession portraits executed early in the reign of Shah Jahan. As he was so closely identified with Jahangir, he is unlikely to have found much favour with the new ruler. Abu'l-Hasan remained in many respects a deeply conservative artist. Although he consciously adopted European naturalism in portraiture, he refrained from experimenting with expanding the background of his pictures, which are remarkable for their flatness. This seems to have been a conscious decision, since it serves to highlight his powers of realistic portraiture. More than any other Mughal artist, his fame rests on his status as a portrait painter to Jahangir, the portrayer of the Emperor's moods and innermost desires. In this he was unequalled, both in his portrayal of Jahangir's gradual imaginative withdrawal from the world and in the iconographic imagery that accompanied this spiritual progress.

BIBLIOGRAPHY

A. Rogers, trans.: *The Tūzuk-i-Jahāngīrī or Memoirs of Jahāngīr*, ed. H. Beveridge (London, 1909–14)

R. Ettinghausen: 'The Emperor's Choice', *De artibus opuscula XL: Essays in Honor of Erwin Panofsky*, ed. M. Meiss (New York, 1961), pp. 98–107

——: *Paintings of the Sultans and Emperors of India in American Collections* (New Delhi, 1961)
A. K. Das: *Mughal Painting during Jahangir's Time* (Calcutta, 1978)
The Grand Moghul: Imperial Painting in India, 1600–1660 (exh. cat. by M. C. Beach, Williamstown, MA, Clark A. Inst., 1978)
The Imperial Image: Paintings for the Mughal Court (exh. cat. by M. C. Beach, Washington, DC, Freer, 1981)
J. P. Losty: 'Abu' l Hasan', *Master Artists of the Imperial Mughal Court*, ed. P. Pal (Bombay, 1991), pp. 69–86

J. P. LOSTY

Abu'l-Hasan ʿAli ibn Hilal al-bawwab. *See* IBN AL-BAWWAB.

Abu'l-Hasan Ghaffari. *See* GHAFFARI, (2).

Abu'l-Hasan Mustawfi Ghaffari. *See* GHAFFARI, (1).

Abu'l-Qasim [Abū'l-Qāsim] (*fl c.* 1816). Persian painter. His only known work is a long composition depicting the Qajar monarch *Fath ʿAli Shah* (*reg* 1797–1834) entertained by female musicians and dancers. The only surviving fragments of it are a painting of the Shah (London, B. W. Robinson priv. col.) and three paintings of the entertainers (Tehran, Nigaristan Mus., ex-Amery priv. col.). The paintings of a woman playing a drum and of a woman playing a stringed instrument are signed *raqam-i kamtarīn Abū'l-Qāsim* ('painted by the most humble Abu'l-Qasim') and dated 1816, but the third painting showing a woman dancing is half-length and damaged. All the fragments share the same continuous architectural background and scale (a little less than life-size). Robinson has suggested that this mural might be the one described in the mid-19th century by the traveller Robert Binning, who reported that the house he occupied in Shiraz contained a painting of Fath ʿAli Shah seated in state attended by ten women. The composition extended around three sides of the room and the figures were almost life-size. This identification suggests that Abu'l-Qasim might have been a native of Shiraz.

BIBLIOGRAPHY

B. W. Robinson: 'The Court Painters of Fatḥ ʿAlī Shāh', *Eretz-Israel*, vii (1964), pp. 94–105
S. J. Falk: *Qajar Paintings: Persian Oil Paintings of the 18th and 19th Centuries* (London, 1972)
B. W. Robinson: 'The Amery Collection of Persian Oil Paintings', *Stud. Iran.*, i (1972), pp. 43–53
——: 'Persian Painting in the Qajar Period', *Highlights of Persian Art*, ed. R. Ettinghausen and E. Yarshater (Boulder, 1979), pp. 331–62
M. A. Karimzada Tabrizi: *Aḥvāl u āthār-i naqqāshān-i qadīm-i īrān* [The lives and art of old painters of Iran] (London, 1985), no. 66
B. W. Robinson: 'Persian Painting under the Zand and Qājār Dynasties', *From Nadir Shah to the Islamic Republic* (1991), vii of *The Cambridge History of Iran* (Cambridge, 1968–91), pp. 870–90

S. J. VERNOIT

Abu Mina [Abū Mīnā]. Site of a Christian city and pilgrimage centre in the Maryūt Desert, *c.* 45 km south-west of Alexandria, Egypt. It grew up around the shrine of St Menas, who was martyred during the persecution of the Christians instigated by Diocletian (*reg* 285–305). The ancient name of the site is not known, and the position of the saint's grave had been long forgotten until, according to legend, several miracle cures led to its rediscovery. The place then quickly developed into an increasingly major centre of pilgrimage where, among other things, the so-called Menas ampules were manufactured as pilgrim flasks and achieved particular renown. The first excavations of the site were undertaken by Kaufmann in 1905–7. Further excavations have been directed successively by the Coptic Museum in Cairo (1951), Schläger (1963 and 1964), Wolfgang Müller-Wiener (1965–7) and Peter Grossmann (since 1969).

The earliest archaeological remains date to the late 4th century, although the grave itself was in an older hypogeum. The first martyrium basilica erected over the grave dates to the first half of the 5th century and was rapidly enlarged by various reconstructions and extensions. Around the turn of the 5th and 6th centuries, the Great Basilica was added to the east in the form of a transept-basilica, making it the largest church in Egypt (see fig.). Some decades later a small baptistery was replaced by an octagonal baptistery with niches, a dome and a large piscina, suitable for mass baptisms (a).

During the reign of Justinian I (*reg* 528–65), the first basilica was replaced by a double-shell tetraconch church similar to a type current in Syria (*see* EARLY CHRISTIAN AND BYZANTINE ART, §II, 2(i)(d)) but with a slightly elongated east–west axis and with straight outer walls that do not follow the curves of the conches (b). Only the eastern conch, because of its significantly firmer foundation, appears to have had a semi-dome, while the remaining conches were covered by half-vaulted wooden roofs. A bi-apsidal narthex (c) was also constructed between the tetraconch church and the Great Basilica (d).

From the last quarter of the 5th century onwards, the site became a pilgrimage centre. An ecclesiastical district developed around the sanctuary area with colonnaded streets, courtyards and squares, as well as pilgrims' hostels, baths, church administration buildings and storage structures. It was enclosed by a surrounding wall with its own gates. Beyond lay the civilian settlement, with housing distributed in a markedly disorganized fashion. Interpersed among the houses were a few small burial areas that most likely belonged to individual, probably Alexandrian, families. In the late 6th century, the whole area was surrounded by a defensive wall, of which *c.* 600 m, including two gates, survived in the north-west of the city. The North Gate, situated on the main urban thoroughfare, was constructed as a gate of state with three passageways and a portico positioned on the city side. A colonnaded street, which was never completed, connected this gate with the inner ecclesiastical district. It intersected an older residential area.

Of the two ecclesiastical complexes that lie outside the city, the one to the north comprises a well-proportioned basilica with a narthex and an atrium-like courtyard, surrounded by a triclinium and several lodging rooms. There is also a baptistery to the south of the church. Presumably this complex was used by Monophysites, who were regarded as heretics by the city's inhabitants. About 1.5 km east of the city is a community of *c.* 100 small hermitages, in the middle of which stands the Eastern Church, a double-shell tetraconch structure of the 6th century, which replaced a small basilica built of unfired bricks. The outer walls of the later structure also have a tetraconch shape, which is more in keeping with the Syrian model for this building type.

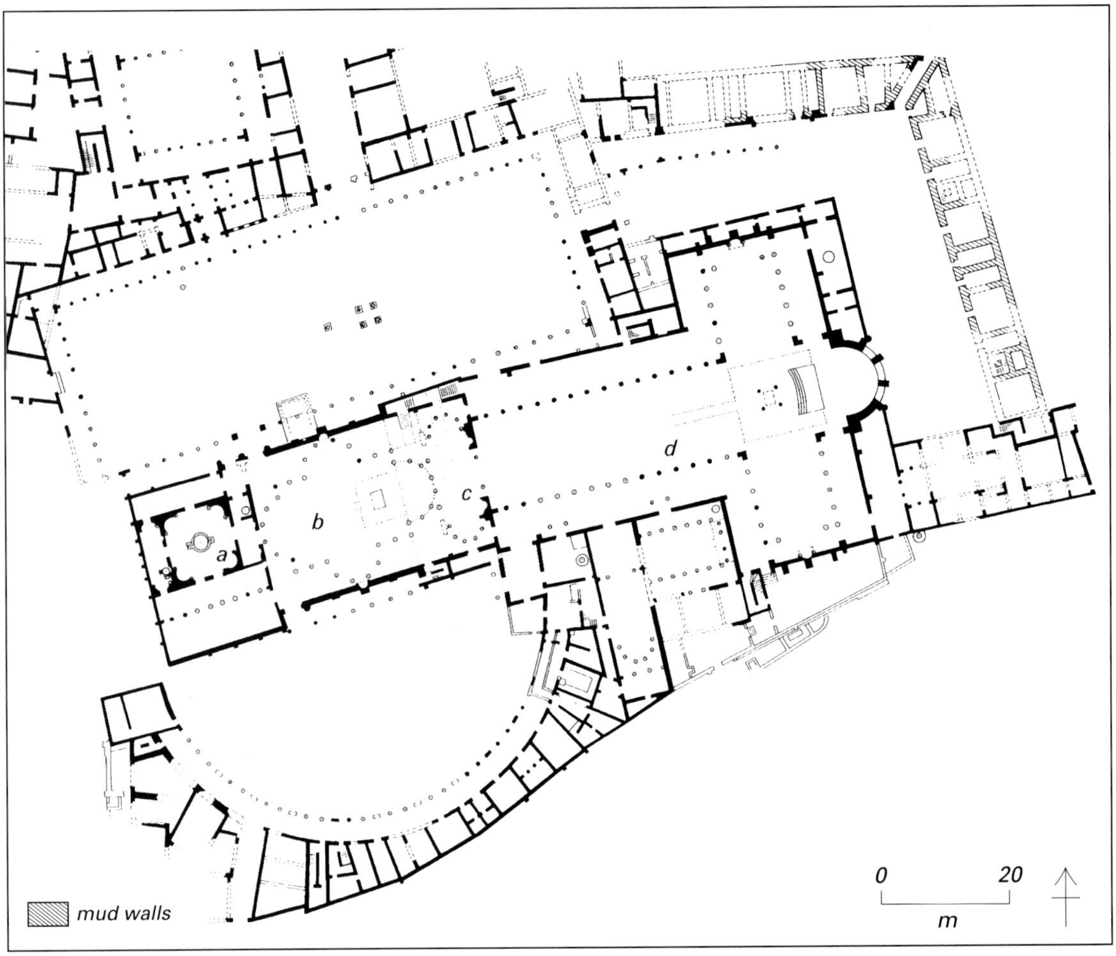

Abu Mina, church complex, remodelled late 5th century AD to mid-6th, ground-plan: (a) octagonal baptistery; (b) martyr's tetraconch church; (c) bi-apsidal narthex; (d) cross-transept basilica

In AD 619, the city was destroyed by the Persians. After only perfunctory reconstruction, it was conquered by the Arabs in 639–41, and it fell into the hands of the Coptic Church, which presumably led to the emigration of a large proportion of the original Greek population. The subsequent inhabitants had a totally different understanding of architecture, and only rubble was used for the newly constructed areas. Streets and courtyards were built over, and the formerly large rooms of the hostels were subdivided into smaller units. Several small commercial winepresses and pottery kilns were established.

In the 8th century, only the tetraconch martyr's church was renovated and transformed into a five-aisled basilica. The city flourished briefly, and the quantity of discernible housing indicates a considerable population; select people were entrusted with its administration. By the early 9th century, however, the nomads had begun to attack the city, forcing its inhabitants to leave.

BIBLIOGRAPHY

K. M. Kaufmann: *Die Menasstadt*, i (Leipzig, 1910)

F. W. Deichmann: 'Zu den Bauten der Menas-Stadt', *Archäol. Anz.* (1937), pp. 75–86

J. Drescher: *Apa Mena: A Selection of Coptic Texts Relating to St Menas* (Cairo, 1946)

J. B. Ward-Perkins: 'The Shrine of St Menas in the Maryût', *Pap. Brit. Sch. Rome*, xvii (1949), pp. 26–71

P. Labib: 'Fouilles du Musée Copte à Saint Ménas', *Bull. Inst. Egypte*, xxxiv (1951/2), pp. 133–8

P. Grossmann: *Abu Mina: A Guide to the Ancient Pilgrimage Center* (Cairo, 1986)

G. Severin and H.-G. Severin: *Marmor vom heiligen Menas*, Liebieghaus Monographie, x (Frankfurt am Main, 1987)

P. Grossmann: *Die Gruftkirche und die Gruft* (1989), i of *Abū Mīnā* (Mainz, 1989–)

PETER GROSSMANN

Abu Rawash [now Abū Ruwāsh]. Site of necropolis in Egypt, 9 km north of Giza, which flourished *c.* 2925–*c.* 2450 BC. Mud-brick mastaba tombs of 1st Dynasty nobles are the earliest buildings at Abu Rawash. The largest mastaba (26×14 m) has eight large recesses in its long walls and is flanked by eight servants' burials on its eastern side. Two funerary boats are associated with Tomb M25. The pyramid of King Radjedef of the 4th Dynasty dominates the site. Reached by a gigantic causeway, it is spectacularly situated at a height of *c.* 157 m above the level of the Nile Valley. It was originally *c.* 67 m high and

105 m square. The 1500 m causeway originally supported a stone corridor, which, with its side walls, measured 14 m wide, while the embankment below widened to 31.5 m at its base and reached a height of 12 m in places. Most of the stone has been quarried away, but the burial-chamber pit (now open to the sky) gives a good impression of the pyramid's former splendour. The pyramid stood in a large enclosure (267×217 m) on levelled rock. The funerary temple was never completed as designed, but a boat trench (37×9 m) lies beside the pyramid, and a smaller ritual pyramid stood near by. The easternmost promontory of the mountain range was thought by the German Egyptologist Karl Richard Lepsius to be the rock core of an enormous mud-brick pyramid.

Over 20 fragments of fine statues of Radjedef and his family were found at Abu Rawash, including red quartzite heads of the King (Cairo, Egyp. Mus., and Paris, Louvre), a limestone bust of his daughter Neferhetepes and a pink granite statuette of his son Sitka (both Paris, Louvre).

BIBLIOGRAPHY

F. Bisson de La Roque: *Rapport sur les fouilles d'Abu-Roasch*, 3 vols (Cairo, 1924–5)

B. Porter and R. L. B. Moss: *Topographical Bibliography* (1927–), III/i pp. 1–10

P. Montet: 'Tombeaux de la Ière et de la IVe dynasties à Abu-Roach', *Kêmi: Rev. Philol. Archéol. Egyp. & Copt.*, vii (1938), pp. 11–69

A. Klasens: 'The Excavations of the Leiden Museum of Antiquities of Abu-Roash', *Oudhdknd. Meded. Rijksmus. Ouden Leiden*, xxxviii (1957), pp. 58–68

V. Maragioglio and C. Rinaldi: *L'architettura della piramidi Menfite*, v (Rapallo, 1966), pp. 7–41

E. P. UPHILL

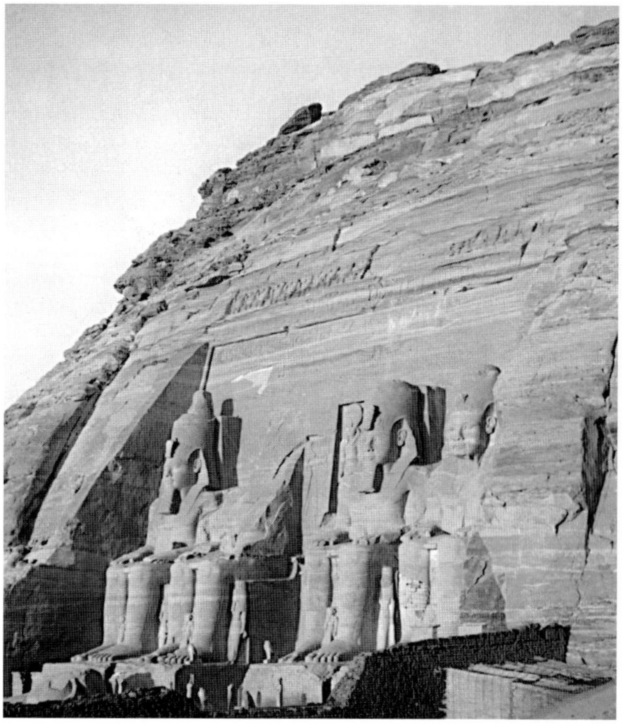

Abu Simbel, the Great Temple of Ramesses II (*reg c.* 1279–*c.* 1213 BC), before its removal to higher ground

Abu Simbel. Site in Egypt, on the west bank of the Nile in Lower Nubia, 280 km south of Aswan. With the construction of the Aswan Dam in the early 1960s, the temple complex was one of a number of ancient monuments saved by being moved to a new site. Having been cut into pieces and reassembled, it now stands on the shores of Lake Nasser, 64 m higher and 180 m west of its ancient site. It is not known whether any small rock-cut chapels already existed at Abu Simbel, but inscriptions from the Middle Kingdom show that it was already an ancient sacred site when Ramesses II (*reg c.* 1279–*c.* 1213 BC) chose it for his most grandiose, and most famous, Nubian monument.

The construction of the Great and Small Temples of Abu Simbel began in the early years of Ramesses II, and they were completed by around the 25th year of his reign. The Great Temple (see fig. and §1 below) is the first of four temples that were dedicated to the King himself in association with the chief gods of Egypt, Amun-re, Re-Horakhty and Ptah. The other temples, at Wadi es-Sebua, ed-Derr and Gerf Hussein, were completed in the middle and later years of the reign (*see* NUBIA, §III). The Small Temple (see §2 below) is situated a little way to the north of the Great Temple. The temples were rediscovered by Jean-Louis Burckhardt, who, in 1813, was the first European to visit and describe them in modern times.

1. THE GREAT TEMPLE. Any forecourt preceding the temple has disappeared, although, by analogy with others, a dromos and perhaps brick pylon would be expected. All that survives in front of it is a brick wall with a gateway leading towards the Small Temple. Flanking the ramp-stairway leading to the terrace are two stelae mounted in stone niches. The terrace is lined with statues of falcons alternating with statues of the King as Osiris and as living ruler. These statues, although on a large scale, are dwarfed by the rock-cut façade of the temple (30 m high and 35 m long). At the northern end of the terrace is a solar chapel with an altar. The altar originally incorporated four statues of baboons and had obelisks on its north and south sides, but these are now in the Egyptian Museum, Cairo. At the southern end of the terrace is a copy of the 'Marriage Stele' of the 34th Year of Ramesses II's reign, recording his marriage with a Hittite princess.

South of the terrace is a small rock-cut chapel, the function of which is not clear, although it may be a MAMMISI or 'birth house'. The main façade is carved in the form of a single pylon, the cavetto cornice of which is crowned with a frieze of baboons in the attitude of adoration. The whole is dominated by four colossi of Ramesses II, each 22 m high (*see* PHOTOGRAPHY, fig. 11). The King is seated, wearing the *nemes* headcloth and double crown. Smaller figures, representing his chief wife, his mother and some of his children, are carved in front of the throne and between his legs (as in the case of the Colossi of Memnon; *see* THEBES (i), §V). The bases of the statues are carved with the King's name and figures of a religious official known as the iun-mwt.f (Egyp.: 'pillar of his mother') priest.

Over the doorway, in a large rectangular niche, a figure of the King as the hawk-headed god Re-Horakhty emerges. This large image is flanked by smaller figures of the goddess Maat and the *was* sceptre, thus creating a rebus of the King's throne name, User-maat-Re. Two sunk-relief figures of the King (possibly added at a later stage) make offerings to the rebus within the niche.

The temple is entirely hewn from the rock; therefore the conventional Egyptian temple plan has been adjusted. The first hall is analogous with the statue-lined courtyards of the royal mortuary temples at Thebes (*see* THEBES (i), §§VI and VII) and the small temple of Ramesses III in the first courtyard at Karnak. It consists of a central nave and two aisles rather than an open peristyle court. The hall (h. 8 m) is supported by eight square piers, each accompanied by a colossus of the King (of the 'Osirid' or mummiform type) wearing the *shendyt* kilt (the 'royal pleated kilt'), with arms crossed on the chest holding crook and flail. The colossi on the northern side wear the double crown, and those on the southern side wear the white crown. Two chambers open from the northern side of the hall, while two suites (consisting of three rooms each) are entered through doors flanking the central axis of the hall. These were temple storerooms and possibly the resting places of certain cult images.

A second hall supported by four square piers precedes the sanctuary. The dominant feature of the sanctuary, occupying the whole of the back wall, is a statue group of the presiding deities, which is designed to be illuminated by the rising sun on two days each year. Ptah and Re-Horakhty flank the King and Amun-Re in the centre. When the sun enters the sanctuary, it completely illuminates only the image of the King. These statues and the altar in front are carved from the rock. The decoration of the temple interior is in sunk relief of quite good workmanship, with paint surviving in many places. Among the most important reliefs is the large scene of the Battle of Qadesh (between Ramesses II and the Hittite king Muwatallis), on the north wall of the first hall. This relief, unusually, has been signed by the chief sculptor, Piaay, son of Khanefer. The temple contained other statuary, including two hawk-headed sphinxes (London, BM) and a statue dedicated by the Viceroy of Nubia, Paser II (London, BM).

2. THE SMALL TEMPLE. Its façade is dominated by six colossi (h. 10 m), four of Ramesses II and two of his chief wife Nefertari, to whom the temple is dedicated. Smaller statues of the royal children (princes with the King, princesses with the Queen) flank the larger ones. The doorway leads into a square hall supported by six square piers. The sides of the piers facing inwards towards the aisle have been carved into the form of sistra with heads of the goddess Hathor. The entrance hall is decorated with two scenes of Ramesses II smiting his enemies, accompanied by Nefertari. This type of scene is usually found as decoration of the façade, but due to the unusual nature of the temple has here been placed inside (as also in the Great Temple). The remainder of the scenes in this hall are well-executed depictions of standard types of offering and ritual. Three doors give access to a narrow hall. An unusual scene depicts the coronation of Nefertari by the goddesses Hathor and Isis. Two statue groups may originally have been placed in this room. The sanctuary has a large statue of Hathor in the form of a cow emerging from the wall, protecting a small figure of the King in front of her (as in the Hathor chapel of Tuthmosis III at Deir el-Bahri). The wall reliefs show Ramesses II worshipping himself and Nefertari (who in this temple was identified with a local form of Hathor). The relief work throughout the temple is of good quality (considering the poor sandstone) with rather attenuated figures. The colouring used is predominantly yellow, which adds to the delicate effect.

BIBLIOGRAPHY

LÄ
L. Christophe: *Abou-Simbel et l'épopée de la découverte* (Brussels, 1965) [a history of the temple since the earliest European visitors]
C. Desroches-Noblecourt and C. Kuentz: *Le Petit Temple d'Abou Simbel*, 2 vols (Cairo, 1968)
T. Säve-Söderbergh, ed.: *Temples and Tombs of Ancient Nubia* (London, 1987) [account of the campaign for the salvage of Abu Simbel and other Nubian monuments]

R. G. MORKOT

Abusir [Egyp. Per-Usir; Gr. Busiris]. Ancient Egyptian royal necropolis that flourished during the 5th Dynasty (*c.* 2465–*c.* 2325 BC). The site is 25 km south-west of the centre of Cairo and has been intermittently excavated since the beginning of the 19th century by teams of English, French, German, Egyptian and Czech archaeologists.

In the 5th Dynasty the sun cult reached its climax, and, according to legend, the first kings of that dynasty were considered the direct descendants of the sun god Re. Sahure (*reg c.* 2458–*c.* 2446 BC), the first king who established his pyramid complex at Abusir, presumably wished to be buried in the vicinity of the sun temple of his predecessor, Userkaf, which stood at the northern outskirts of the necropolis. Sahure's pyramid was small, and its core was built of poor quality limestone. His pyramid temple, however, was carefully executed in different kinds of stone and richly decorated with reliefs, the whole representing a new stage in the evolution of this type of monument. A small subsidiary pyramid, an enclosure wall, a causeway and a valley temple also originally belonged to the pyramid complex.

Sahure's brother, Neferirkare (*reg c.* 2446–*c.* 2426 BC), started to build his pyramid complex a little further to the south and at a higher level than Sahure's. His pyramid, initially *c.* 74 m high, still dominates the necropolis. In the pyramid temple, which was hastily finished in mud-brick, were found remains of papyrus archives with invaluable data about the function of the pyramid complex, the organization of the royal mortuary cult and the state administration in general. Raneferef (*reg c.* 2419–*c.* 2416 BC), the elder son of Neferirkare, died at the very beginning of the construction of his pyramid, which was hastily changed into a *mastaba* and completed by his younger brother Neuserre. The mortuary temple attached to the *mastaba* included a columned hall (unique in the 5th Dynasty), another papyrus archive (similar to that of Neferirkare) and rare royal sculptures (Cairo, Egyp. Mus.) that constitute the richest collection of such statuary from the 5th Dynasty. A ritual slaughterhouse was built in front of the unfinished pyramid of Raneferef.

Neuserre (*reg c.* 2416–*c.* 2392 BC) also completed a third pyramid complex, adjacent to the south side of his father's pyramid (*see* PYRAMID, fig. 1(d)). This small but very important structure was begun for Khentkaus, the 'king's wife' to Neferirkare, who was buried at Giza; Neuserre completed it as a cenotaph where she was worshipped as 'the King's mother'. Despite the lack of a convenient building site on the desert plateau, Neuserre decided to construct his burial complex there. He took over a part of his father's causeway, modified the standard form of his mortuary temple and built his pyramid next to the north wall of his father's pyramid temple.

The foundations of a second unfinished pyramid on the Abusir plateau can be seen to the north-west of the pyramid of Sahure. This tomb can be tentatively attributed to Shepseskare (*reg c.* 2426–*c.* 2419 BC). The tombs of the members of royal families and high state officials of that time are clustered around the pyramids. Of the few tombs unearthed to date, the *mastaba* of Ptahshepses (*c.* 2400 BC), the vizier and son-in-law of Neuserre, ranks highest. Approximately 1 km north of the pyramid of Sahure, the remains of two sun temples out of six known to have been built by the 5th Dynasty kings have been found: those of Userkaf and Neuserre (*see* ABU GHURAB). From the papyrus archives found in the Abusir mortuary temples, the sun temples, which were dominated by an obelisk, were closely connected both in their religious cult and economically with the pyramid complexes of their builders.

On the south-western outskirts of the site, large and very sophisticated complexes of shafts dating from the end of the Late Period have been discovered. The necropolis was abandoned by the last kings of the 5th Dynasty, presumably because of the lack of a suitable building site. From the Middle Kingdom, it became a cemetery for common people that flourished particularly in the Late Period, under the influence of the cults in nearby North Saqqara. In the New Kingdom, the pyramid temple of Sahure became the centre of the cult of the goddess Sakhmet.

BIBLIOGRAPHY

L. Borchardt: *Das Grabdenkmal des Königs Ne-user-rʿ* (Leipzig, 1907)
——: *Das Grabdenkmal des Königs Nefer-ír-ke'-re* (Leipzig, 1909)
——: *Das Grabdenkmal des Königs Sa'ḥu-rʿ*, 2 vols (Leipzig, 1910–13)
F. W. von Bissing: *Das Re-Heiligtum des Königs Ne-woser-re (Rathures)*, 3 vols (Leipzig, 1905–28)
B. Porter and R. L. B. Moss, eds: *Topographical Bibliography* (1927–), III/i, pp. 314–48
H. Ricke and others: *Das Sonnenheiligtum des Königs Userkaf*, 2 vols (Cairo, 1965, 2/Wiesbaden, 1969)

MIROSLAV VERNER

Abu Tahir [Abu Ṭāhir]. Persian family of potters. The family is sometimes known, somewhat improperly, by the epithet Kashani [al-Kashani, Qashani], which refers to their home town, Kashan. It was a major centre for the production of lustre pottery in medieval Iran, and they were among the leading potters there, working in both the Monumental and the Miniature styles (*see* ISLAMIC ART, §V, 3(iii)). As well as the lustre tiles for many Shiʿite shrines at QUM, MASHHAD, Najaf and elsewhere, they made enamelled and lustred vessels. Three other families of Persian lustre potters are known, but none had such a long period of production. At least four generations of the Abu Tahir family are known from signatures on vessels and tiles, including dados, large mihrabs and grave covers. The family may be traced to Abu Tahir ibn Abi Husayn, who signed an enamelled bowl (Cairo, Mus. Islam. A.). A lustre bowl in the Monumental style (London, N.D. Khalili priv. col.), signed by Abu Tahir ibn Muhammad Hamza ibn al-Hasan, may also be his work, but the genealogy is slightly different. The first clearly documented member of the family is (1) Muhammad ibn Abi Tahir, who worked with another potter ABU ZAYD on the most important projects of the pre-Mongol period. Muhammad ibn Abi Tahir's son (2) ʿAli worked in the mid-13th century and ʿAli's son (3) Yusuf in the early 14th. Dated works by these three thus span more than a century (1205–1334), although there are surprisingly long gaps between generations. In the 14th century the family turned to other professions, for one of Yusuf's brothers, (4) Abu'l-Qasim, became a scribe and accountant in the Ilkhanid bureaucracy, and another brother, 'Izz al-Din Mahmud, became a Sufi who entered the Suhrawardi *khānaqāh* at Natanz and wrote a spiritual guide, the *Miṣbāh al-Hidāya wa Miftāḥ al-Kifāya* ('Light of Divine Guidance and Key to Completeness').

BIBLIOGRAPHY

O. Watson: *Persian Lustre Ware* (London and Boston, 1985)
S. S. Blair: 'A Medieval Persian Builder', *J. Soc. Archit. Historians*, xlv (1986), pp. 389–95

(1) Muhammad ibn Abi Tahir [Muḥammad ibn Abī Ṭāhir] (*fl* 1206–15). His earliest work is a large (2.9×1.2 m) panel of 15 tiles that covers the top of the cenotaph of Fatima in the shrine at Qum. It is composed of large central panels enclosing arch motifs filled with the finest of arabesques in relief, framed by multiple borders of blue-glazed relief inscriptions; all these relief elements are set against a background of lustre scrolls. The narrow inscription bands, fine detail and flat modelling distinguish this piece from later works and show its somewhat experimental style. Muhammad apparently collaborated on the project with Abu Zayd, who signed the frieze dated 1206 around the sides of the cenotaph. A decade later Muhammad again collaborated with Abu Zayd on a more ambitious programme of lustre decoration for the shrine of Imam Riza at Mashad (*see* SHRINE, colour pl. IV, fig. 1). Muhammad was responsible for the framing around the entrance and perhaps for an unsigned mihrab and the dado frieze tiles, while Abu Zayd signed a mihrab dated 1215 and a number of star and octagonal tiles. Muhammad must have worked on other large-scale projects, for his signature is found on other high-quality pieces, such as a fragment from a large mihrab (ex-Kelekian priv. col.; see Ettinghausen, fig. 25). His work represents the artistic and technical peak achieved by the Kashan lustre potters, in which calligraphy and background decoration are carefully balanced and arabesque mouldings are elaborate yet lively and uncluttered.

(2) ʿAli [ʿAlī ibn Muḥammad ibn Abī Ṭāhir] (*fl* 1242–65). Son of (1) Muhammad ibn Abi Tahir. His earliest work is a large mihrab (1242) in the shrine at Meshed. It uses the same types of decoration seen in the work of his father but is more coarsely executed. Within a few years ʿAli made another large mihrab, fragments of which have been found in a tomb tower at Gurgan. He apparently used the same mould for his signature tile as he had in the earlier mihrab, although the other sections are different. In the 1260s, when the Kashan potteries revived after half a century of stagnation, ʿAli's virtuosity was revealed. He made a series of stars and crosses (Oct–Dec 1262; see fig.) set in dado panels and a large mihrab (May 1265) for the Imamzada Yahya in Varamin. He also signed the mihrab dated November 1264 in the Imamzada Ahmad Qasim at Qum. By stylistic analogy, the large mihrab in the shrine at Najaf must be his work of the same period. He is the only lustre potter in this period to sign his wares, and, although his work is not as sophisticated as the best work done earlier in the century, the quality of design and drawing remains high.

(3) Yusuf [Yūsuf ibn ʿAlī ibn Muḥammad ibn Abī Ṭāhir] (*fl* 1305–34). Son of (2) ʿAli. In 1305 he finished his father's work in the Imamzada Yahya at Varamin, collaborating with ʿAli ibn Ahmad ibn ʿAli al-Husayni on a medium-sized arched tile (St Petersburg, Hermitage). In the following years he produced several sets of frieze tiles. One dated January 1310 is remarkable for its high technical quality and clean drawing; another is dated January 1311. His work soon declined in quality, for his modest (460×760 mm) moulded tile recording repairs undertaken some time between 1316 and 1327 to the Qalʿa Mosque in the nearby village of Quhrud is mediocre. Its importance lies in its technique (it is underglaze painted in blue and black), for it shows that in the 14th century the family worked in cheaper techniques as well as lustre. The final lustre piece produced by the family (Tehran, Archaeol. Mus., 3270) is a large (1.29×2.12 m) mihrab made in May 1334 for the Imamzada ʿAli ibn Jaʿfar at Qum. Although it is larger than any other mihrab, the moulded decoration is clumsy and the painting sketchy. Its poor quality was a harbinger of the demise of Kashan lustre potteries, which apparently ceased production by 1340.

ʿAlī ibn Muhammad ibn Abī Tāhir: panel of star-shaped tiles from the Imamzada Yahya, Varamin, 2.9×1.2 m, each tile diam. 310 mm, 1262 (London, Victoria and Albert Museum)

(4) Abu'l-Qasim Jamal al-Din ʿAbdallah (*d* 1337–8). Brother of (3) Yusuf. On the orders of the Ilkhanid vizier Rashid al-Din (*reg* 1295–1316), Abu'l-Qasim wrote a biography of the sultan entitled *Tārīkh-i Uljaytū* ('History of Uljaytu'). His treatise on minerals and precious substances, including precious stones, composed in 1303, belongs to a recognized genre of Islamic scientific literature descending from classical prototypes, but Abu'l-Qasim appended a technical description of pottery manufacture. This appendix is perhaps the only document of its sort to survive from the pre-modern Islamic world. In it Abu'l-Qasim described the potter's raw materials, where they might be found in the Kashan area and their properties. They included various stones, clay and metals in mineral form. He discussed the processing of these materials by means of grinding, sifting and smelting, as well as the proportions in which they should be compounded to produce the frit body of ceramic vessels and tiles and to make the glazes and colourings applied to the frit body. He also described the firing of fine ceramic vessels in clay cases provided with lids (saggars), the design and furnishing of the kiln in which the firing occurred, and the sorts of wood used to fire kilns in Kashan, Baghdad and Tabriz. Finally he discussed the application of 'enamel' glazes and gilding, for which a special gilding kiln was required.

WRITINGS

ʿArāʾis al-Jawāhir wa Nafāʾis al-Aṭāʾib [Brides of gems and delicacies of amenities], (1303); ed. I. Afshar (Tehran, 1967); part. ed. and German trans. by H. Ritter, J. Ruska and R. Winderlich as 'Orientalische Steinbücher und persische Fayencetechnik', *Istanbul. Mitt.*, iii (1935) [whole issue]; Eng. trans. by J. W. Allen as 'Abū'l-Qāsim's Treatise on Ceramics', *Iran*, xi (1973), pp. 111–20

BIBLIOGRAPHY

R. Ettinghausen: 'Evidence for the Identification of Kashan Pottery', *A. Islam.*, iii (1936), pp. 44–70

SHEILA S. BLAIR

Abu Zayd [Abū Zayd ibn Muḥammad ibn Abī Zayd] (*fl* Kashan, 1186–1219). Persian potter. At least 15 tiles and vessels signed by Abu Zayd are known, more signed works than are known for any other medieval Iranian potter. He frequently added the phrase 'in his own hand' (*bi-khāṭṭihi*) after his name, so that it has been misread as Abu Zayd-i Bazi or Abu Rufaza. His earliest piece is an enamelled (Pers. *mīnāʾī*) bowl dated 4 Muharram 583 (26 March 1186; ex-Tabbagh priv. col.), but he is best known for his lustrewares. A fragment of a vase dated 1191 (ex-Bahrami priv. col., see Watson, pl. 53) is in the Miniature style, but most of his later pieces, such as a bowl dated 1202 (Tehran, priv. col., see Bahrami, pl. 16a) and a dish dated 1219 (The Hague, Gemeentemus.), are in the Kashan style, which he is credited with developing (*see* ISLAMIC ART, §V, 3(iii)). He collaborated with Muhammad ibn Abi Tahir (*see* ABU TAHIR, (1)) on the two most important lustreware projects of the period, the decoration of the tomb chambers in the

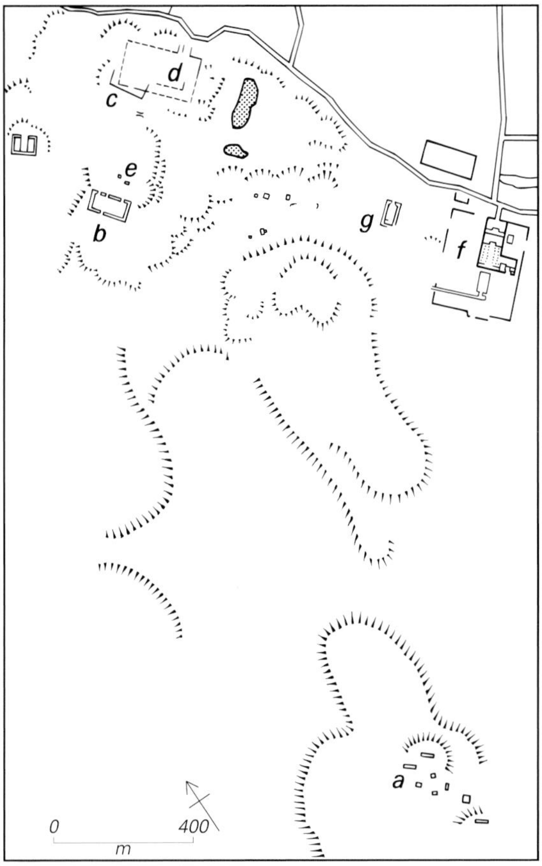

1. Abydos, general plan: (a) Umm el-Qaab; (b) Shunet el-Zebib; (c) Kom el-Sultan; (d) Temple of Osiris; (e) Middle Kingdom tombs and cenotaphs; (f) temple of Sethos I; (g) temple of Ramesses II

shrines of Fatima at Qum and Imam Riza at Mashhad. Abu Zayd's signature on pieces in the two most important techniques of overglaze luxury ceramics is one of the main reasons that enamelled ware, like lustreware, can be attributed to Kashan.

BIBLIOGRAPHY

M. Bahrami: 'A Master Potter of Kashan', *Trans. Orient. Cer. Soc.* (1944–5), pp. 35–40

O. Watson: *Persian Lustre Ware* (London and Boston, 1985)

——: 'Documentary Mīnā'ī and Abū Zaid' Bowls', *The Art of the Saljūqs in Iran and Anatolia: Proceedings of a Symposium Held in Edinburgh in 1982*, ed. R. Hillenbrand (Cosa Mesa, 1994), pp. 170–80

□

Abydos [anc. Egyp. Abdjw]. Egyptian site, *c.* 50 km south of Sohag, and necropolis of the ancient city of This (perhaps modern Girga), which was briefly the capital of the newly united Egypt in the Late Predynastic period (*c.* 3000–*c.* 2925 BC). As the country's most ancient capital, it remained significant throughout Egyptian history, becoming the principal cult centre of Osiris, a funerary deity who embodied the tradition of kingship. From the later Middle Kingdom (*c.* 1750 BC), the Early Dynastic period (*c.* 2925–*c.* 2575 BC) royal necropolis was believed to contain the tomb of Osiris; because of this, it was visited by pilgrims until Roman times (30 BC–AD 395). Large cemeteries continued to accumulate, and they were characterized in the latest period by a distinctive Greco-Egyptian type of stele. These merged Egyptian and Classical styles with a largely Egyptian decorative repertory and were increasingly inscribed in Greek. Thus for two millennia Abydos was an important centre of non-royal art, as well as the location of major temples.

1. EARLY DYNASTIC PERIOD–MIDDLE KINGDOM (*c.* 2925–*c.* 1630 BC). Many kings of the 1st and 2nd dynasties (*c.* 2925–*c.* 2650 BC) were buried in the cemetery of Umm el-Qaab (see fig.1a), set in the low desert near a cleft in the rock escarpment, which contained the cemetery of the latest Predynastic kings of Egypt. These tombs had little, if any, superstructure, but their occupants were buried with abundant grave goods of high quality, such as stone vases, ivory furniture and jewellery (e.g. Paris, Louvre; Oxford, Ashmolean). They were marked by mortuary stelae giving the kings' Horus names (the first part of the royal titulary); the limestone stele of Wadj (Paris, Louvre, E 11007; see fig. 2) is a masterpiece of carving. The tombs were complemented by sacred areas, surrounded by élite graves that were located near the cultivation. The later areas were enclosed by massive, richly decorated mud-brick walls: one, the Shunet el-Zebib (1b), stands more than 6 m high. These structures were

2. Abydos, stele of Wadj, limestone, Early Dynastic period, 1st Dynasty, *c.* 2925–*c.* 2775 BC (Paris, Musée du Louvre)

3. Abydos, temple of Sethos I, relief carving of Sethos I offering to Nefertem and Sakhmet on the south wall of the hall of Ptah-Sokar and Nefertum, *c.* 1290–*c.* 1279 BC

probably the forerunners of the step-pyramid enclosures at Saqqara.

Kom el-Sultan (1c), near the Shunet el-Zebib, is the site of the early town of Abydos. Its temple was probably dedicated originally to the local funerary gods Khentiamentiu and Wepwawet; later it became the Temple of Osiris (1d). The temple may have been founded before the 1st Dynasty, and early votive objects have been recovered from the site; most later periods are attested by fragments of architecture and sculpture, including a tiny ivory statuette of Cheops (h. 75 mm; Cairo, Egyp. Mus., JE 36143), which may be archaistic. Little of the temple's structure has been preserved. In the Middle Kingdom the area became a focus of pilgrimage: extensive cemeteries grew up (1e), while near the temple were cenotaphs in the form of chapels with mortuary stelae, offering tables and statues, but without burials. The cenotaphs, which were set up for individuals or groups, secured for the deceased perpetual participation in the festivals of Osiris. The site has yielded *c.* 2000 Middle Kingdom private stelae, ranging from excellent works to crude objects resembling ostraca, but very few belonged to members of the core élite. The larger cenotaphs were vaulted mud-brick chambers set in small enclosures and flanked by trees; they imitated the form and context of temple sanctuaries and are therefore significant as evidence for lost architectural types, while their massive construction has parallels among other Middle Kingdom tombs. The small temple of Ramesses II (*see* §2 below) later covered part of the cenotaph area.

2. New Kingdom (*c.* 1540–*c.* 1075 BC). From the 12th Dynasty (*c.* 1938–*c.* 1756 BC) some rulers built cenotaph or temple complexes in the low desert south of Kom el-Sultan. A chapel of Queen Tetisheri of the 17th Dynasty (*c.* 1630–*c.* 1540) has yielded a fine stele (Cairo, Egyp. Mus., CG 34002), and fragmentery reliefs of Ahmose (*c.* 1540–1514), the founder of the New Kingdom, were discovered in the early 1990s. The only substantial standing remains, however, are from early 19th Dynasty temples: a chapel of Ramesses I (*reg c.* 1292–*c.* 1290 BC), dedicated after his death and known only from superb relief blocks (New York, Metropolitan); a temple and cenotaph of Sethos I (*reg c.* 1290–*c.* 1279 BC); and a temple of Ramesses II (*reg c.* 1279–*c.* 1213 BC). These monuments display a striking unity of style.

The complex of Sethos I (see fig. 1f) is an unfinished architectural and artistic masterpiece constructed on a broad, uneven site. The limestone temple is approached from a quay with an 'esplanade' through two ruined open courts; the portico of the second court had seven doorways, four of which were subsequently blocked by Ramesses II, leading through two hypostyle halls to seven chapels roofed with false vaults and respectively dedicated to Sethos himself, Ptah, Re-Harakhty, Amun-Re, Osiris, Isis and Horus. Behind these chapels is a suite of rooms dedicated to the local divine triad of Osiris, Isis and Horus, while to the south of them is a unique extension incorporating chapels for the Memphite gods Ptah-Sokar and Nefertum, along with corridors, stairways, a repository for divine barks and suites of service rooms. Parallel to the first two courts is a complex of mud-brick storage magazines surrounding a central stone hall. The entire area was surrounded by an enclosure wall, with a brick pylon on the desert side pointing towards the supposed tomb of Osiris.

In its architecture and dedication, the temple forms a national cult centre with an emphasis on Osiris and Sethos. Apart from its grand yet compact conception, it is outstanding for its sophisticated articulation of space and light, especially in the second hypostyle hall, where a change in levels and column forms signals a change in context. Subtle distinctions in the design of doorways indicate their relative importance, while niches provide transitions between each deity's axis and the next. The wall reliefs of Sethos I, which fill the rear portion and part of the southern extension, are 'classicizing', perhaps looking back to the mid-18th Dynasty (*c.* 1400 BC), and are relatively stiff and formal (see fig. 3). The quality of line and detail is remarkable, and the composition of larger areas is free and inventive. The texts are fuller than in most temples, and the space around the figures is elegantly arranged to allow for this. Text and relief complement and comment on each other in rich patterns. The excellent preservation of colour in a number of places demonstrates an extra dimension of decoration and meaning. The unpainted reliefs in the southern extension, which are among the finest, date to the end of Sethos' reign. Further south are faded paintings in a restricted range of colours, which demonstrate that much of the temple was completely decorated in paint before carving; in the hall of barks, most of the paintings were later used as drafts for carving reliefs. The adjacent corridor was carved in the early reign of Ramesses II with a vigorous relief of the King and his heir lassoing a bull. All the reliefs in the first hypostyle hall and courts are also from the time of

Ramesses II, but many of these, some of inferior quality, may represent designs of Sethos I executed during his son's reign.

The underground cenotaph of Sethos I at the rear of the temple is commonly known as the Osireion. It was constructed by Sethos, but most of its decoration dates to the reign of his grandson Merneptah (*reg c.* 1213–*c.* 1204 BC). It is approached from the north by a descending corridor leading into a sequence of rooms. Its central hall consists of an open space with eight square granite pillars surrounded by a water-filled moat and enclosed by an outer wall with seventeen niches. Beyond this hall is a transverse room with a pitched ceiling, which seems to have been inaccessible when complete; it had been decorated with underworld and astronomical scenes in the reign of Sethos. The style of the granite pillars in the cenotaph recalls the architecture of the 4th Dynasty (*c.* 2575–*c.* 2465 BC), but analogies for most of its features are nearer at hand in the royal tombs of the Valley of the Kings (*see* THEBES (i), §IX), on which the general design of this remarkable structure is based. The choice of granite and sandstone (not local stones) for its construction is probably symbolic. The central hall was open to the sky, and rites of the resurrection of Osiris may have been performed there.

The limestone temple of Ramesses II (see fig. 1g), which dates to the earliest years of his reign, is smaller than his father's; only the lower parts of the walls are preserved. It is less original in design and has a single axis. The first court is lost; the second retains a fine register of reliefs showing the presentation of offerings. The inner areas are unusual in having pillared octostyle halls, as well as two corner rooms, each with a pair of pillars, surrounding benches and wall niches. In its present unroofed state, the most striking feature of the temple is the preservation of the brilliant polychromy of the reliefs, which are sunk as far as the first octostyle hall and raised beyond. Complex patterns of colour symbolism can be identified, for example on the fecundity figures in the first octostyle hall. The reliefs are probably the finest non-military carvings of Ramesses II; they are close to those of the temple of Sethos I in technique and quality, but livelier and denser, and were perhaps executed by the same sculptors.

BIBLIOGRAPHY

LÄ

A. Mariette: *Abydos: Description des fouilles exécutées sur l'emplacement de cette ville*, 2 vols (Paris, 1869–80)

W. M. F. Petrie: *The Royal Tombs of the Earliest Dynasties*, 2 vols (London, 1900–01)

A. M. Calverley and others: *The Temple of King Sethos I at Abydos* (London and Chicago, 1933–)

H. E. Winlock: *The Temple of Ramesses I at Abydos* (New York, 1937)

B. J. Kemp: 'The Egyptian 1st Dynasty Royal Cemetery', *Antiquity*, xli (1967), pp. 22–32

——: 'The Osiris Temple at Abydos', *Mitt. Dt. Archäol. Inst.: Abt. Kairo*, xxiii (1968), pp. 138–55

W. Kaiser: 'Zu den königlichen Tabelzirken der 1. und 2. Dynastie in Abydos und zur Baugeschichte des Djoser-Grabmals', *Mitt. Dt. Archäol. Inst.: Abt. Kairo*, xxv (1969), pp. 1–21

W. K. Simpson: *The Terrace of the Great God at Abydos: The Offering Chapels of Dynasties 12 and 13* (New Haven and London, 1974)

K. P. Kuhlmann: 'Der Tempel Ramses II in Abydos: Vorbericht über eine Neuaufnahme', *Mitt. Dt. Archäol. Inst.: Abt. Kairo*, xxxv (1979), pp. 189–93

A. R. David: *A Guide to Religious Ritual at Abydos* (Warminster, 1981)

W. Kaiser and G. Dreyer: 'Umm el Qaab: Nachuntersuchungen im frühzeitlichen Königsfriedhof, 2. Vorbericht', *Mitt. Dt. Archäol. Inst.: Abt. Kairo*, xxxviii (1982), pp. 211–69

Z. Hawass: 'The Khufu Statuette: Is it an Old Kingdom Sculpture?', *Mélanges Gamal eddin Mokhtar*, i (Cairo, 1985), pp. 379–94

D. O'Connor: 'The "Cenotaphs" of the Middle Kingdom at Abydos', *Mélanges Gamal eddin Mokhtar*, ii (Cairo, 1985), pp. 161–77

A. Abdalla: *Graeco-Roman Funerary Stelae from Upper Egypt*, Liverpool Monographs in Archaeology and Oriental Studies (Liverpool, 1992)

JOHN BAINES

Academy. Association or school of artists organized as a professional institution with a view to providing training, theoretical debate and exhibiting opportunities, and to mediate between its members and patrons or public. The word 'academy' derives from the ancient Greek 'akademeia', the name of the grove near Athens where Plato taught his pupils philosophy. In early modern times the term was first used in 15th-century Italy to describe meetings of literati, but from the 16th century it was adopted by those artists' corporations that included teaching as one of their main purposes, particularly teaching with an intellectual as opposed to a purely manual content. Drawing after antique statuary and from the live model (*see* ACADEMY FIGURE) played a preponderant part in this teaching, although anatomy, geometry, perspective, history and other disciplines were variously included in the curricula of academies. From around 1600 the academic idea spread from Italy to France, Spain and the Netherlands. It was in France under Louis XIV, however, that an artists' academy first became an effective and integral part of state arts policy and commanded sufficient authority to affect materially the training, aspirations and career structure of artists (*see* FRANCE, §XV, 2). Many academies of art established in the 18th century took the Académie Royale de Peinture et de Sculpture (founded 1648), Paris, as a model, and its teaching methods remained current in most art schools until the middle of the 20th century. With the decline in the 20th century of the prestige of the academic idea and the concomitant growth of alternative institutions devoted to art education, some academies dropped their teaching function and concentrated on their honorific, administrative and exhibiting roles.

This article is concerned primarily with the history and development of the academy in the Western tradition. Further information on specific academies is given in this dictionary within the relevant articles on cities (where subdivided, under the headings 'Art life and organization' or 'Institutions') and on countries (under 'Art education').

See also EDUCATION.

1. Origins and early development. 2. The first official academies. 3. The spread of the academic idea. 4. The influence of the Académie Royale de Peinture et de Sculpture. 5. Academic ideals versus practical concerns. 6. 20th-century developments.

1. ORIGINS AND EARLY DEVELOPMENT. The earliest known Renaissance use of the word 'academy' occurs in a letter of 1427 from the humanist scholar Poggio Bracciolini (Eng. trans. in P. W. G. Gordan: *Two Renaissance Book Hunters*, New York, 1947, p. 118). This recounts his wish to decorate his villa near Florence with a collection of Antique sculpture, which he described figuratively as 'my "Academy" in Val d'Arno'. It is clear from the context

that he intended the word to be taken as meaning a place for contemplation and discussion away from the everyday business of the world. It was this usage that was applied in the 15th century to informal gatherings of literati for discussion of literary or philosophical topics. There is evidence of the existence, but not of the nature, of an 'Academia Leonardi Vincii' run by Leonardo in Milan around 1490; this may have been an informal group discussing questions of art theory rather than an institution with a clear didactic intention. Nevertheless, the fact that such philosophical enquiries could take place would have supported the arguments aimed at raising painting from the status of craft to that of a liberal art presented in Leonardo's writings. In these Leonardo advised beginners first to acquire knowledge and only then to practise painting, and he suggested that perspective and proportion be taught, and that drawing be mastered before undertaking (the more material procedures of) painting. Such an intellectualization of the processes of painting, which emphasized conceptual over manual skills, is connected with artists' attempts to promote their status. Thus, though Leonardo's Academia was probably not a teaching institution, the link between the idea of 'academy' and a more intellectual approach to painting was significant in the light of later developments.

In Florence at about the same time Lorenzo de' Medici appointed the sculptor Bertoldo di Giovanni as head of a 'school and academy' for the education of painters and sculptors. The exact nature of this institution (*see* FLORENCE, §V, 2) is not clear. According to Vasari, writing 70 years later (*Vite*, 2/1568), Lorenzo's purpose was to remedy the shortage of sculptors in Florence, and he offered to educate Domenico Ghirlandaio's apprentices 'in such a way that it would do credit to himself and Ghirlandaio and the city of Florence'. It would seem that the 'students' had access to the Medici collection of antiquities in a garden opposite the convent of S Marco. If Vasari's account is accurate, Bertololo's school was independent of the craft guilds. It also pursued educational methods (drawing after the Antique) that, if Ghirlandaio was representative, Florentine artists could not offer in their workshops; in so doing they enhanced the prestige of a supportive political authority.

Another similarly ambiguous piece of evidence in the early history of the art academy is Agostino dei Musi's engraving of 1531 inscribed *Academia di Bacchio Bandin in Roma in luogo detto Belvedere*, which shows a group of artists drawing a small statue in the studio of the sculptor Baccio Bandinelli. Apart from the inscription itself, there is no evidence to suggest that it represents more than a group of friends gathered to draw from the Antique and to discuss questions of art.

2. THE FIRST OFFICIAL ACADEMIES. Vasari's account of the Medici academy occurs in his *Vite* (2/1568) of Michelangelo and of Pietro Torrigiani. Michelangelo considered sculpture to be a 'scienza studiosa', and he also said that 'One paints with the brain and not with the hand'. Although Vasari recognized the need for practical training, he endorsed this image of the learned artist not only in his *Vite* but also in his promotion of the Accademia del Disegno (*see* FLORENCE, §V, 1), the constitution of which was formally granted in 1563. It is, perhaps, in this context that his description should be read. At all events, the Accademia del Disegno shared certain important characteristics with Lorenzo's academy as it appears in Vasari's account. First it enjoyed political protection and control in that the Grand Duke Cosimo I de' Medici was (with Michelangelo) joint head of the institution; effective control was vested in Cosimo's representative, Vincenzo Borghini. Second, and related to this, the Accademia itself was independent of the trade guilds, albeit that its members who were practising artists were not released from the obligation to join the appropriate guild until 1571. Thereafter the Accademia began to assume guild functions, becoming itself officially incorporated as a guild in 1584. Third, the Accademia's regulations of 1563 contained mandatory provisions for the education of young artists: arithmetic, geometry and anatomy lectures were envisaged; masters were to be elected to teach the art of *disegno* and to visit artists' workshops to correct students' work before it was allowed to leave the shop. While the last regulation may imply a continuing guild-like concern with quality control, it can be interpreted as an attempt to substitute criteria for judging art that acknowledged intellect as superior to craft.

Borghini instituted discourses on artistic matters in 1563. Such discourses are recorded as still occurring in 1591. However, the Accademia del Disegno's educational programme as a whole seems never to have been carried out with any degree of continuity. In the later 1570s the painter Federico Zuccaro drafted proposals intended to revitalize the programme, including the teaching of mathematics, henceforth taught more or less continuously for the rest of the century and through that following. The incorporation of mathematics reflected the belief that the external world was to be understood in terms of mathematical structures. In his other reform proposals, Zuccaro made two suggestions that would become significant features of later academies—a room for life drawing and students' prizes. Life classes may have been held at the Accademia in the 1590s and it seems likely that during the same period there were classes in physiognomy and other branches of natural philosophy. The proposals for life drawing and prizes were incorporated into the rules of the Accademia di S Luca (*see* ROME, §VI), founded in 1593 under Zuccaro's presidency. (In 1577 and 1588 Gregory XIII and Sixtus V had failed in their attempts to establish an academy with an education programme for young artists that would have regard to Tridentine dogma.) Rules in the statutes of the new institution provided for regular debates on art-theoretical matters, and for twelve visiting teachers annually (one per month) to decide from among the students who should draw from casts, who from life. All these proposed features of the Accademia di S Luca—a rotating academic staff, prizes, life drawing, debates on questions of art—would in due course be adopted by the Académie Royale de Peinture et de Sculpture in Paris, as would the rule that no academician was to sell his work from an open shop because this was not an 'opera intellettuale'. Zuccaro's fellow artists seem to have found the theoretical debates tedious, and the Accademia's teaching programme foundered after only a few years, not to be securely revived until after Carlo Maratti became its

1. Bartolomeo Passarotti: *Anatomy Lesson*, ink and wash, 385×540 mm, late 16th century (Paris, Musée du Louvre)

principal in 1664 and Giovanni Pietro Bellori its secretary in 1671; although there was no regular life class in Rome outside the Académie de France (*see* §4 below), established in 1666, until the Accademia's affiliate, the Accademia del Nudo, opened in 1754.

Besides the officially recognized academies of Florence and Rome, the other notable 16th-century academy was that established privately by the artists Ludovico Carracci and his cousins Agostino Carracci and Annibale Carracci (*see* CARRACCI) in Bologna, probably in 1582; it soon became known as the Accademia degli Incamminati, where, according to Malvasia (*Felsina pittrice*, 1678, i, pt 3), it was 'expected ... with admirable frequency to draw living persons, nude entirely or in part, weapons, animals, fruits, and, in short, all things in Creation'. Besides the stress on drawing after nature, in conscious reaction to the prevailing Mannerist style, which the Carracci saw as too much based on imagination rather than observation, lectures on perspective, architecture and anatomy were held and drawing competitions organized. By combining the programme of an academy with that of an active studio, the Carracci were better able to promote their aesthetic ideals, which sought to create a synthesis of the draughtsmanship of the Roman school, exemplified by Raphael and Michelangelo, with the colourism of northern Italian art, exemplified by Titian and Correggio. Just as the Carracci took as models different masters of the past, they seem also to have encouraged their pupils to learn from Bolognese artists other than themselves. Following the departure of Annibale and Agostino for Rome in the mid-1590s, Ludovico tried to have the Incamminati put on a more official footing and it seems that around 1603 they became associated with Bologna's Company of Painters. The Carracci academy closed in 1620, the year following the death of Lodovico: it had included among its pupils Francesco Albani, Guido Reni and Domenichino, painters widely admired in 18th-century artistic academies.

3. THE SPREAD OF THE ACADEMIC IDEA. Few further public academies were founded before the 18th century. An academy modelled on that of Florence was opened at Perugia in 1573, but by 1600 it seems to have stopped operating. In 1637 the city of Modena assigned rooms for an academy, which, however, ceased operating in 1646 with the death of its principal, Lodovico Lana. In Milan the archbishop Federico Borromeo (*see* BORROMEO, (2)), who had been the first Cardinal Protector of the Accademia di S Luca in Rome, founded an academy in 1620 with a view to revitalizing religious art. He donated to the academy paintings and sculptures from his own collection for the students to use as models. The Accademia Ambrosiana ceased operating in 1625, but was reactivated between 1669 and 1690. In 1678 an academy was successfully founded in Turin with rules modelled on those of Rome and under the protection of Mary Joanna, Duchess and Regent of Savoy, widow of Charles-Emanuel II. A class at a late 16th-century Italian academy is depicted in *Anatomy*

Lesson (Paris, Louvre; see fig. 1) by the 16th-century artist Bartolomeo Passarotti.

From around 1600 some private patrons made rooms available in their residences and provided models for artists to draw from. An example of such a life class is that of Prince Gian Carlo Doria in Genoa in the second decade of the century. Other private academies were run by artists in their own studios: Pietro Paolini ran an academy at Lucca, as did Camillo Procaccini and Giulio Cesare Procaccini in Milan. The main activity of these 17th-century academies seems to have been life drawing, thus enabling a number of artists to share the costs of the model, light and heating, but it is not clear how much teaching was done. Paolini is said to have given instruction in life drawing and drawing after casts, but Malvasia's description (*Felsina pittrice*, 1678, ii, pt 4) of a number of painters in the Ghislieri academy in Bologna as 'maestri' is ambiguous.

Outside Italy public academies were rare in the 17th century. In Seville the house of the painter and writer Francisco Pacheco was referred to as an academy, but it seems to have been more in the nature of an informal, literary academy that included artists and amateurs among its members. The activities of the academy which existed in Seville during the years 1660–74 were limited to life drawing. In 1606 a group of painters in Madrid agreed to rent premises for 'an academy of the art of painting', but this may have been to conduct no more than life drawing in common. A more ambitious plan of around 1600 for a teaching academy that would include not just life drawing-classes but also lectures on perspective, anatomy, physiognomy and mathematics was not realized in Madrid until 1744. Such efforts were connected with the concern of Spanish artists to raise the status of their profession and with a desire to avoid tax and military service by being practitioners of a recognized liberal art.

In Haarlem around 1600 Karel van Mander I set up a private academy for life drawing in conjunction with Hendrick Goltzius and Cornelis Cornelisz. van Haarlem. Van Mander's concern with painting as a liberal profession is indicated in his *Schilder-boek* (Haarlem, [1603]–1604), in which he wrote of the 'shameful laws and narrow rules' by which in nearly all cities save Rome 'the noble art of painting has been turned into a guild'. The concern with status was transformed into more concrete terms in 1631, when the Haarlem guild's rules were altered to give artist painters (as opposed to house painters and gilders who were also members) the highest rank within the corporation. At the same time a rule was adopted providing joint sessions in drawing and anatomy, and public lectures. Life drawing was not, however, referred to explicitly.

Elsewhere in the Netherlands the pattern was for painters to establish their own life classes and there is no record of a guild life class being held before that introduced in 1682 at the guild of painters and sculptors of The Hague founded 26 years previously. Probably most life drawing and related instruction was conducted in artists' studios. Rembrandt, for example, corrected his pupils' drawings, and Joachim von Sandrart called Gerrit van Honthorst's studio at Utrecht an academy (*Teutsche academie*, Nuremberg, 1675). Sandrart himself was involved in an academy in Nuremberg in the mid-1670s, in which for a short time architecture lessons were also given. In Antwerp an academy was founded by royal decree in 1663 and put under the direction of David Teniers II. The Antwerp academy, however, remained under the control of the painters' guild. In England some kind of academy for the study of the nude model existed in 1673; in 1692 a drawing-class was established at Christ's Hospital attached to the Writing School; and in 1697 a school of drawing started under the direction of Bernard Lens (ii). Elsewhere in northern Europe the guild remained the dominant social and economic group structure for artists until well into the 18th century. The major exception to this situation was in Paris, where the Académie Royale de Peinture et de Sculpture had been established in 1648 (*see* PARIS, §VI, 1).

4. THE INFLUENCE OF THE ACADÉMIE ROYALE DE PEINTURE ET DE SCULPTURE. The foundation document of Teniers's life class referred to an 'academy . . . like those of Rome and Paris'. This provides evidence of the early influence abroad of the Académie Royale and acknowledges its similarity to that of Rome. The Académie Royale's regulations and its aim of raising the status of painting and painters followed Zuccaro's original conception for the Roman academy. Thus, provision was made for professors rotating on a monthly basis to supervise the life class, for prizes for students, and for members' debates on all questions of art, which students could attend. Additionally, regular lectures on perspective, anatomy and geometry were conducted, developing the rules of the Académie's other model, Vasari's Accademia. Such an ambitious programme was not always followed consistently. By 1662 the students were complaining of a lack of teaching—evidence that the academic idea had taken firm hold among the rising generation. Nevertheless, the Académie Royale's educational programme was the most consistently applied hitherto and the most widely followed henceforth, in both its curriculum and its method. The prescribed progress of drawing from drawings, drawing from casts and drawing from life (as depicted by Charles-Nicolas Cochin II; see fig. 2) formed, with local variations, the basis of the training of artists in the European tradition until well into the 20th century.

Further regulations promulgated in 1663 and adopted by the Académie Royale in 1664 contained certain features that contributed to the nature of academies in general. First, provision was made for members' works to be exhibited annually—this was complied with only intermittently until 1737 and shortly thereafter changed to a biennial privilege rather than an annual obligation. The regular exhibitions organized by the Académie Royale in the 18th century quickly became major artistic and social events, and they were widely copied, notably by the Royal Academy in London, which continued to exhibit members' works into the late 20th century. Second, the Académie Royale's regulations provided in effect that no one could be appointed a professor who had not been received as a history painter or sculptor. It was this rule that institutionalized the precedence of history painting and that created a self-perpetuating oligarchy within the academic membership, because the higher officers of the institution could come only from the professorate. Hence the precedence

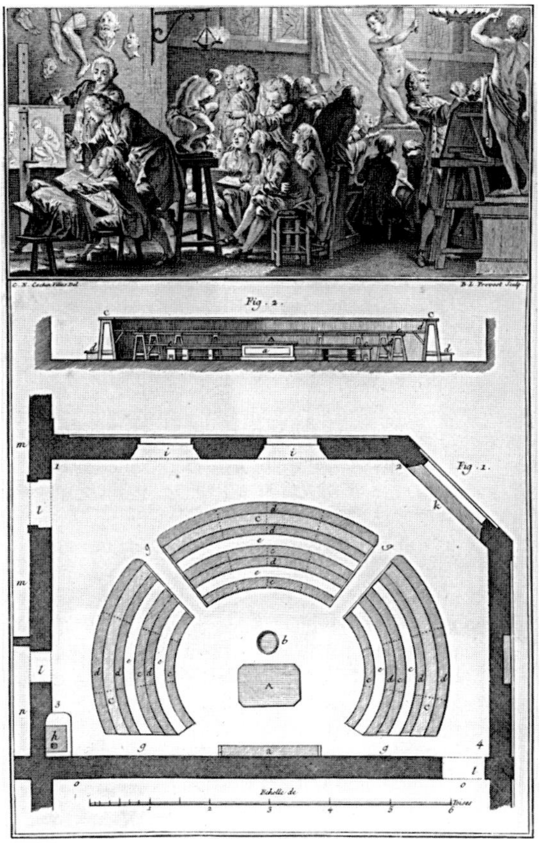

2. Charles-Nicolas Cochin II: *School of Drawing*, engraving, pl. 1 for the article 'Dessein' in Diderot's *Encyclopédie*, iii (Paris, 1763), showing the stages of academic instruction rather than an actual drawing school (London, British Library)

of history painting and of history painters became mutually reinforcing, a concept that was scarcely questioned for the next 200 years wherever the academic idea had been adopted. Third, although the regulations did not expressly refer to a PRIX DE ROME, in practice (funds permitting) the top prizes for students in painting and sculpture were scholarships to study in Rome. With the opening of the Académie de France in Rome in 1666 (*see* PARIS, §VI, 1) the prevalent view of the superiority of the art of ancient Rome and of the masters of the Renaissance as models for the young artist was institutionalized in a form broadly accepted throughout Europe until the later 19th century. Fourth, in granting to the Académie Royale a state grant to cover its costs and (until 1705) a monopoly in holding life classes, and to academicians a monopoly of royal commissions, as well as in the designation of the Académie as 'Royale', the idea that the state had a role in art education and production became firmly established.

One characteristic of the Académie Royale that was less often followed elsewhere was the separation of painting and sculpture from architecture. In Paris the latter had a separate academy founded in 1671, the Académie Royale d'Architecture (*see* PARIS, §VI, 1). Nevertheless, in many material respects the academies established outside France modelled themselves on that of Paris, with which they often had a personal connection. The Accademia di S Luca in Rome formally amalgamated with the Académie Royale in 1676, although the merger did not last long; and a French painter on occasion became principal of the Accademia, for example Charles Errard in 1672 and Jean-François de Troy in 1744. In 1726 Jacob van Schuppen (1670–1751), who had belonged to the Académie Royale, introduced rules closely modelled on those of Paris for the academy in Vienna, now known as the Akademie der Bildenden Künste, which had been first established in 1692. The rules provisionally adopted by the academy in Madrid in 1744 were modelled on those of Paris and Rome—most of its founder-members were French or Italian, or, if Spanish, trained in France or Italy, and its professor of painting was Louis-Michel van Loo, the Paris academician. In 1762, inspired by the model of the Académie Royale, the students of the Brussels academy, founded in 1711 by the municipality and now the Académie Royale des Beaux-Arts, successfully petitioned Duke Charles of Lorraine to become its protector. In Copenhagen, Stockholm and St Petersburg rules that followed the Paris model were adopted (in 1754, 1768 and 1757 respectively) when the academies were directed by the Paris academicians Jacques Saly, Pierre-Hubert L'Archevêque (1721–78) and Louis-Joseph Le Lorrain. These examples indicate the geographic spread of academies, which extended to Mexico in 1785. Their quantitative expansion also accelerated in the later 18th century so that by 1800 over 100 public academies existed, including those at Berlin (founded 1697, reorganized 1786), Dresden (founded 1705, reorganized 1762), Naples (1755) and Venice (1756). This number also includes provincial academies in Spain and France, such as those at Valencia (1768) and Dijon (1767), dependent on their respective central institutions in Madrid and Paris.

No single factor explains this growth. The conviction of artists that art was subject to teachable rules, albeit then mutable by individual genius, was not new, nor was their concern with their status as artists as opposed to craftsmen. Further, the artists of Madrid had invoked a mercantilist argument (unsuccessfully) to persuade Philip IV to open an academy in 1620: it would, they said, train Spanish artists and so avoid the employment of foreigners. As befitted the optimism of the 18th century, that argument was later put more positively. Thus Christian Ludwig von Hagedorn, who reorganized the Dresden Kunstakademie in 1762, wrote, 'Art can be looked at from a commercial point of view . . . while it redounds to the honour of a country to produce excellent artists, it is no less useful to raise the demand abroad for one's industrial products.' In Prussia, Friedrich Anton von Heinitz, who reorganized the Berlin Akademie der Künste, said in 1788, 'We pursue no other aim than to enhance national industry', and he cited art as an important source of income in France, England and Italy. Similar arguments were used in connection with the reorganization of the academies in Copenhagen in 1771 and The Hague and Stockholm in 1779, and all envisaged that the teaching of drawing would have a beneficial effect on the craft industries. Increasing nationalism and positive assessment of art's role in commerce, and of the State's role in art, combined with artists' aspirations to produce the enormous growth in the number of academies.

The corollary of state subvention for the academies was state control to a greater or lesser degree. The academies at St Petersburg and (under its 1757 rules) Madrid were seen as organs of state. The position of the Royal Academy of Arts (*see* LONDON, §VI), founded in 1768, was different. It had evolved from the wish of artists to have a state-sponsored, formally run academy on the continental model in contrast to the St Martin's Lane Academy, which was the main training ground for artists in England from 1720 to 1768, and which had been run on informal, democratic lines. (Sir Godfrey Kneller had earlier run a private academy in London, which operated from 1711 to *c*. 1720, also on democratic lines.) The Royal Academy's declared aims were to conduct a free school for students and annual exhibitions of contemporary art, the profits of the latter to be used mainly to pay the costs of the former. These aims were soon realized, resulting in financial independence and freedom from overt political pressure and in this respect providing a model for Edinburgh's Royal Scottish Academy (1826) and New York's National Academy of Design (1825). By the time of the foundation of the Royal Academy, the exhibition of members' works had a well-established precedent in the biennial Salons of the Académie Royale; its training curriculum and methods were also similar to those of Paris, complete with prizes and travelling scholarships to Rome.

Unlike the Académie Royale, the London academy included architects. In Paris the teaching of architects was not combined with that of painters and sculptors until 1795. The Académie Royale d'Architecture was founded in 1671 essentially as a school, but without the monopoly of teaching enjoyed by the painter and sculptor academicians. The curriculum included lectures on architecture, mathematics and mechanics. In the middle years of the 18th century students registered at the Académie only to enter the annual competition, the winning of which usually, but not automatically, conferred a scholarship for study in Rome; many trained at the private school run by Jacques-François Blondel (*see* BLONDEL, (2)) from 1740 until he became a professor at the Académie in 1762. Although recommended styles of architecture changed with changes of teacher and the times, the Académie's programme was geared to producing highly finished drawings of grand architectural projects. From the end of the 18th century its curriculum began to be criticized for producing architects who could invent designs but did not know how to build, and, notwithstanding numerous institutional changes, the teaching of architecture remained broadly the same in France for another 150 years, and in most other centres for almost as long.

5. ACADEMIC IDEALS VERSUS PRACTICAL CONCERNS. Architectural academic training was not alone in being criticized. From around the end of the 18th century the existing academic method was increasingly challenged. Some Romantic writers, and then artists, questioned whether art could be taught at all, since, as Johann Wolfgang von Goethe put it in 1772 in his essay *Von deutscher Baukunst* (published in 1773 in J. G. Herder's *Von deutscher Art und Kunst*), a good work of art should be more experienced than calculated. Some German artists in particular reacted against what they saw as neglectful teachers, and against mechanical copying exercises of parts of bodies, or of schematically rendered gestures and expressions. The engravings of facial expressions in Charles Le Brun's *Conférence sur l'expression générale* (numerous posthumous editions; the most complete being that of Etienne Picart, Amsterdam and Paris, 1698), which must have seemed a great pedagogic advance to artists concerned with differentiating states of emotion, would a century later appear tyrannical to artists concerned with invention, individual genius and self-expression. Hence in place of rules these artists proposed advice, and in place of formal teaching they proposed a more friendly relationship between master and pupil. In 1818 the Prussian architect Karl Friedrich Schinkel recommended replacing academic classes with workshops. Ten years earlier the revived constitution of the Munich Akademie der Bildenden Künste had declared: 'The teacher shall not suffer any uniform mechanism, but leave to the pupil as much freedom as possible to show his particular talent and the special qualities of his manner of looking at objects and imitating them.' In practice, however, copying from drawings and casts was usually retained in German academies in the elementary classes. Only from the 1840s did the most advanced students enjoy relative freedom in master classes where they could work on their own projects with the benefit of guidance.

In the 19th century, German academies also adopted from the French ateliers the inclusion of the teaching of painting, in addition to drawing. These ateliers were artists' studios with a stock of casts and models for life drawing and painting, in effect private academies. The best known was that of Jacques-Louis David, which was taken over by Antoine-Jean Gros when David fled Paris in 1816. It was subsequently run by Paul Delaroche and then by CHARLES GLEYRE. Artists trained in such establishments, which were separate from the proprietor's working studio, followed a curriculum that revolved around the requirements of the Prix de Rome competition and its qualifying competitions. Michel-Martin Drolling and Delaroche, for example, ran competitions for painted compositional sketches (*esquisses*) probably because the Académie des Beaux-Arts (*see* PARIS, §VI, 3), administrative successor of the *ancien régime* academies, had decided in 1817 on the oil sketch as a means of weeding out entrants for the Prix de Rome competition. Painting was not taught at the Ecole des Beaux-Arts (which had taken over the teaching functions of the old academies) before 1863. On the other hand, formal lectures on anatomy, perspective and, from 1819, ancient history (and for architectural students mathematics and descriptive geometry) were available only at the Ecole, whose curriculum, except for a few years after the reforms of 1863, stayed largely unchanged until 1968. The ateliers were therefore providing teaching supplementary to that available at the Ecole, but whereas artists had always learnt to paint in artists' studios, previously this had been in the course of helping the master on actual commissions. Now the great majority of pupils did not assist the master in any way but devoted their time to academic exercises. Although the Académie Julian (*see* FRANCE, §XV), founded in 1868, made much of its undogmatic teaching methods, its teaching was geared to Ecole des Beaux-Arts requirements, its visiting professors included many Prix de Rome winners, and its publicity (it was a commercially run art school) advertised student successes in terms of the academic system. It did, however, provide tuition for women, who were excluded from the Ecole until 1897.

There was one major change in the academic curriculum in France in the 19th century, namely the recognition of landscape as an academic subject, with the first Prix de Rome for historic landscape taking place in 1817. Initially, however, entries were judged by reference to the execution of the figures within the landscape and the depiction of the character of the site in relation to the given, Classical, theme. Furthermore, from 1839 candidates had to pass a perspective test to be eligible to compete. All this reflected the traditional concerns of history painters. Nevertheless, the criteria for judging entries changed over the decades, the overall effect becoming important from the 1830s, and, significantly, neither historical theme nor figure was required in the subject for the Prix Troyon of 1869 (the landscape prize administered by the Académie des Beaux-Arts in place of the Prix de Rome for historic landscape). Landscape painting was not, however, taught at the Ecole, although it was introduced at the Düsseldorf Kunstakademie in 1830 and a few other academies subsequently.

Thus, in spite of the Romantic attack on the academies, the academic system remained intact and the curriculum almost unchanged conceptually. Another potential agent for change had, however, been developing, namely discussions of the relationship between the fine arts and design for commercial purposes. Many late 18th-century academies were established or, like those at Dresden (1762), Stockholm (1779) and Berlin (1786), reorganized, in part to raise standards of draughtsmanship within craft industries. Since the previous century academic artists had been put in charge of the French national tapestry works, the Gobelins, where, moreover, some apprentices were given drawing-lessons by members of the Académie Royale. Elsewhere art schools were established for craftsmen, as at Naples in 1741 and Geneva ten years later, a Manufakturschule in Vienna in 1758 and the Trustees' Academy of Design in Edinburgh in 1760. In 1767 the Ecole Royale Gratuite de Dessin opened in Paris under the flower painter Jean-Jacques Bachelier. Its 1500 pupils copied drawings and prints of figures, animals, flowers and ornament, and they took lessons in geometry and architecture. The trend in central Europe, however, was for trades classes to be incorporated as elementary classes within fine arts academies. In the 19th century this trend was reversed by the establishment of separate trade schools, for example the Berlin Gewerkschule in 1809, a trade school in Augsburg in 1836 and in Copenhagen in 1857. The courses they offered were, however, drawing courses, without teaching of working processes, and their function was to enable craftsmen to translate the designs provided by academically trained artists into their particular media more accurately. Both the trade schools and the trades classes can be distinguished from the academies by their lack of provision for training of the intellect, which, at least in theory, was what gave academies their particular status. Implicit in this distinction was a view of a clear demarcation between the fine arts and the applied arts, with the academies, or at least the 'advanced' classes within them, catering only for the former.

This divorce between conception and execution, between art and craft, was especially marked in Great Britain, where in the early 19th century machines were increasingly taking over working processes, and where, save in Edinburgh, no drawing schools for craftsmen had been set up. By mid-century criticism of the standards of industrial design was being voiced in France and England. The solution adopted was the setting up of more drawing schools, this time, however, in conjunction with museums of applied art, notably the South Kensington Museum (later the Victoria and Albert Museum), London, founded after the Great Exhibition of 1851, which would furnish models of taste to copy. Workshop practice remained outside the curriculum. It was William Morris who from 1861 cooperated with major British artists to design and produce articles for everyday use in a practical demonstration of his belief in the unity between the material, working process, function and aesthetic form (*see* ARTS AND CRAFTS MOVEMENT). In questioning the functioning of the fine arts Morris was also questioning the special, and exclusive, role of the academies of art as teaching institutions. By the end of the 19th century craft instruction was being taught in a few British art schools.

Around the beginning of the 20th century there appeared in German art schools a new emphasis on making, rather than just designing. The inspiration derived indirectly from Morris, but with the difference that in Germany the aim was unity between art and industrial production, not art and craft. With this aim in mind some German academies established craft workshops, such as that at the academy at Breslau (now Wrocław in Poland), around 1903. The Leipzig academy, founded in 1764 as a traditional fine arts institution, became an academy of the art of printing. On the other hand, the trade school, the Kunstgewerbeschule, in Hamburg began to include fine arts courses. Such an amalgamation between conception and production was alien to the traditional concept of the academy of arts, in which the only material process of painting, sculpture and architecture that was taught was drawing, a process that was, moreover, intellectualized by reference to the Antique. It is with this 'clean hands' approach of the academies that the programme of the BAUHAUS, founded by Walter Gropius at Weimar in 1919, may be contrasted.

Gropius's central concern was 'the unified work of art . . . in which there is no distinction between monumental and decorative art'. Thus craft training was seen as essential for architects, painters and sculptors. Moreover, Gropius was concerned that art should have a practical end: from 1923 the Bauhaus was directed towards marrying art with the technology of the machine age. It aimed at a thorough craft, technical and formal training with the aim of collaboration in building, practical research into problems of house construction and furnishing, and the development of standard prototypes for industry and the crafts. The later Bauhaus thus operated as a quasi-commercial organization selling an increasing number of licences to industry to manufacture Bauhaus-designed products. Although the Bauhaus included fine arts courses within its programme, it was totally different in concept from the traditional fine arts academy, first because of its commerciality, second because it produced actual items for use, albeit prototypes, and third because, in producing prototypes, it acknowledged that the ultimate product of its teaching was not the unique result of individual genius, but the machine-made, and so repeatable, result of collective ideas and practical design.

6. 20TH-CENTURY DEVELOPMENTS. By the middle of the 20th century the ossification of the academic system was complete. The Accademia di S Luca had ceased to be responsible for teaching in 1873, and erosion of the financial value of legacies intended for student prizes resulted in its administering only one important competition. Its continuing prestige resides in its archives and its collection of works of art by past members. The Royal Scottish Academy's school, started in 1839, closed in 1931. The Royal Academy in London became associated for a long period with conservative opposition to avant-garde art. Sir Alfred Munnings, appointed President in 1944, used his office as a platform for his reactionary views on modern art, causing embarrassment and controversy in a broadcast speech in 1949. In Paris the academic courses of the Ecole des Beaux-Arts were modernized only after the student protests of 1968.

Elsewhere, art schools have increasingly become part of larger educational institutions offering degree courses. This is the case in the USA and to some extent in Britain, for example with the Slade School of Fine Art, which is part of University College in the University of London. The role of the academies of art in the education of artists has thus become marginalized. In 1977 the Royal Academy in London began charging fees to students, contrary to its original purpose; the National Academy of Design, New York, had done so 100 years earlier. The Royal Academy's better known functions are as a venue for loan exhibitions and retrospectives, as well as for the annual exhibition of the works of members and others. All these developments reflect particular historical, political and social circumstances, although the separation of the teaching of architecture from that of painting and sculpture, now standard, additionally reflects a late 20th-century perception that the teaching of architecture should be as much concerned with function and technical problems as with form.

BIBLIOGRAPHY

G. Vasari: *Vite* (1550, rev. 2/1568); ed. G. Milanesi (1878–85), iv, p. 256; vii, pp. 141–2
C. C. Malvasia: *Felsina pittrice* (1678); ed. M. Brascaglia (1971)
A. de Montaiglon, ed.: *Procès-verbaux de l'Académie Royale de Peinture et de Sculpture, 1648–1793*, 10 vols (Paris, 1875–92)
J. Guiffrey: 'L'Histoire de l'Académie de St Luc', *Archv A. Fr.*, n. s., ix (1915) [whole vol.]
N. Pevsner: *Academies of Art Past and Present* (Cambridge, 1940/*R* New York, 1973)
D. Mahon: *Studies in Seicento Art and Theory* (London, 1947)
H. M. Wingler: *The Bauhaus: Weimar, Dessau, Berlin, Chicago* (Cambridge, MA, and London, 1969)
A. Boime: *The Academy and French Painting in the Nineteenth Century* (Oxford, 1971)
E. Taverne: 'Salomon de Bray and the Reorganization of the Haarlem Guild of St Luke in 1631', *Simiolus*, vi/1 (1972–3), pp. 50–59
C. Bédat: *L'Académie des Beaux-Arts de Madrid, 1744–1808* (Toulouse, 1974)
A. Blaugrund: *The National Academy of Design: A Brief History* (New York, n. d.) [after 1975]
J. Brown: *Murillo & his Drawings* (Princeton, 1976)
E. Gordon: *The Royal Scottish Academy of Painting, Sculpture and Architecture, 1826–1976* (Edinburgh, 1976)
R. Chafee: 'The Teaching of Architecture at the Ecole des Beaux-Arts', *The Architecture of the Ecole des Beaux-Arts*, ed. A. Drexler (London, 1977), pp. 61–109
A. Sutherland Harris: *Andrea Sacchi* (Oxford, 1977)
R. A. Moore: 'Academic *Dessin* Theory in France after the Reorganization of 1863', *J. Soc. Archit. Hist.*, xxxvi/3 (1977), pp. 144–74
J. H. Rubin: *Eighteenth-century French Life Drawing* (Princeton, 1977)
J. Brown: *Images and Ideas in Seventeenth-century Spanish Painting* (Princeton, 1978)
M. Crawford Volk: 'On Velázquez and the Liberal Arts', *A. Bull.*, lx (1978), pp. 69–86
——: 'The Madrid Academy', *A. Bull.*, lxi (1979), p. 627
C. Dempsey: 'Some Observations on the Education of Artists in Florence and Bologna during the Later Sixteenth Century', *A. Bull.*, lxii (1980), pp. 552–69
V. Kemenov: *The USSR Academy of Arts* (Leningrad, 1982)
C. Fehrer: 'New Light on the Académie Julian and its Founder (Rodolphe Julian)', *Gaz. B.-A.*, 6th ser., ciii (1984), pp. 207–16
'France's New Design School', *Indust. Des.*, xxxi/3 (May–June 1984), p. 80
E. Levy: 'Ideal and Reality of the Learned Artist: The Schooling of Italian and Netherlandish Artists', *Children of Mercury: The Education of Artists in the Sixteenth and Seventeenth Centuries*, ed. J. M. Muller (Providence, RI, 1984), pp. 20–27
J.-M. Pérouse de Montclos: *'Les Prix de Rome': Concours de l'Académie Royale d'Architecture au XVIIIe siècle* (Paris, 1984)
L. Olmstead Torelli: 'Academic Practice in the Sixteenth and Seventeenth Centuries', *Children of Mercury: The Education of Artists in the Sixteenth and Seventeenth Centuries* (Providence, RI, 1984)
L. Richard: *Encyclopédie du Bauhaus* (Paris, 1985)
P. Grunchec: *Les Concours d'esquisses peintes, 1816–1863* (Paris, 1986)
S. C. Hutchison: *The History of the Royal Academy, 1768–1986* (London, 1986)
C. Dempsey: 'The Carracci Reform of Painting', *The Age of Correggio and the Carracci* (exh. cat., Washington, DC, N.G.A.; New York, Met.; Bologna, Pin. N.; 1986–7), pp. 237–54
G. Mayer and others: *Académie Royale des Beaux-Arts de Bruxelles: 275 ans d'enseignement* (Brussels, 1987)
A. W. Boschloo and others, eds: *Academies of Art between Renaissance and Romanticism* (The Hague, 1989), pp. 14–60, 77–104, 302–19, 434–50
G. Feigenbaum: 'Practice in the Carracci Academy', *The Artist's Workshop*, ed. P. M. Lukehart, Stud. Hist. A., xxxviii (Washington, DC, 1993), pp. 58–76

HUMPHREY WINE

Academy figure. Term applied to a drawn or painted representation of the human figure, most commonly made as part of the instruction in an academy or art school. Although the practice of making drawings from nude models had developed during the Renaissance and was commended by such theorists as Alberti, it was only with the foundation of academies of painting in the 17th century that such drawing became formalized as part of a rigorous programme of training. Indeed, by the mid-18th century, the word 'académie' was defined in Diderot's *Encyclopédie* as 'a public school where painters go to draw or paint, and sculptors to model, after a nude man called the model'. In France one of the principal means by which the Académie Royale de Peinture et de Sculpture asserted its predominance was by maintaining a monopoly on life classes. After the student had mastered the difficulties of copying engravings and plaster casts, he was set to draw from the nude figure under the supervision of the professor. The model was almost invariably male because female models were forbidden at the Académie Royale, and elsewhere they were extremely expensive to hire. Classes lasted two hours, and the pose was usually changed twice a week. The student began by drawing with red chalk on white paper and later progressed to black chalk on tinted papers, applying white chalk for highlights. Such drawing was an exercise in shading, hatching, graining and stumping, and increasingly the results became so homogeneous in style that unsigned examples are almost impossible to attribute. Painted academy figures (*académies*) were made by more advanced students and were sent to Paris by *pensionnaires* at the Académie de France in Rome as indicators of their progress. As the art academies gradually lost their prestige towards the end of the 19th century, their mainstay also fell into disrepute, although the practice of making academy figures has never been entirely abandoned.

See also ACADEMY; FRANCE, §XV; and PARIS, §VI, 1.

BIBLIOGRAPHY

A. Boime: *The Academy and French Painting in the Nineteenth Century* (New Haven and London, 1971)

Eighteenth-century French Life-drawing: Selections from the Collection of Mathias Polakovits (exh. cat. by J. H. Rubin, Princeton U., NJ, A. Mus., 1977)

M. Roland Michel: *Le Dessin français au XVIIIe siècle* (Paris, 1987), pp. 47–76

The Artist's Model: Its Role in British Art from Lely to Etty (exh. cat. by I. Bignamini and M. Postle, U. Nottingham, A.G.; London, Kenwood House; 1991)

□

Acanthus. Ornamental motif based on the leaves of the acanthus plant, an evergreen shrub native to the Mediterranean area. Two species have been proposed as likely models for different forms of decorative leaf motifs: *Acanthus mollis*, with broad, blunt tips to the leaves, and *Acanthus spinosus*, with comparatively narrow leaves and pointed lobes terminating in spines. Acanthus leaves added to a lotus and palmette border gave rise to a motif known as ANTHEMOIN. The acanthus was described by ALOIS RIEGEL as a variant of the palmette motif (for discussion and illustration *see* PALMETTE). The acanthus leaf's spiky form and scrolling growth made it highly suitable for both ornamental and architectonic use, although, after its initial introduction in Greek art and architecture, the motif rarely corresponded closely to a particular species of plant; throughout its long history the leaf ornaments known as acanthus were imaginary designs adapted variously with no reference to any living plant. In various forms, it was one of the most widely used types of foliage motif from antiquity until the late 19th century.

1. EARLY DEVELOPMENT, BEFORE *c.* 1600. The earliest, most notable and most enduring use of the acanthus is in the capital of the Corinthian order (*see* ORDERS, ARCHITECTURAL, §I, 1(iii), 2(i)(a) and fig. 4), first adopted in Greece in the late 5th century BC as a variation on capitals of the Ionic order, the earliest example being a free-standing column (untraced) from the interior of the Temple of Apollo at Bassai (*c.* 430–*c.* 400 BC; for a later example see fig. 1a). The Roman architect Vitruvius, writing in the 1st century BC, attributed the origins of the Corinthian capital to acanthus leaves growing round a basket of toys left in a cemetery (*On Architecture* IV.i.9–10). The story, though clearly an invention, shows the early connection between the ornamental leaf and this plant. The essentially ornamental nature of the Corinthian order was further developed by the Romans in the ornate Composite order (*see* ORDERS, ARCHITECTURAL, §I, 1(iv)), with elaborate, heavily foliate capitals using fleshy, florid

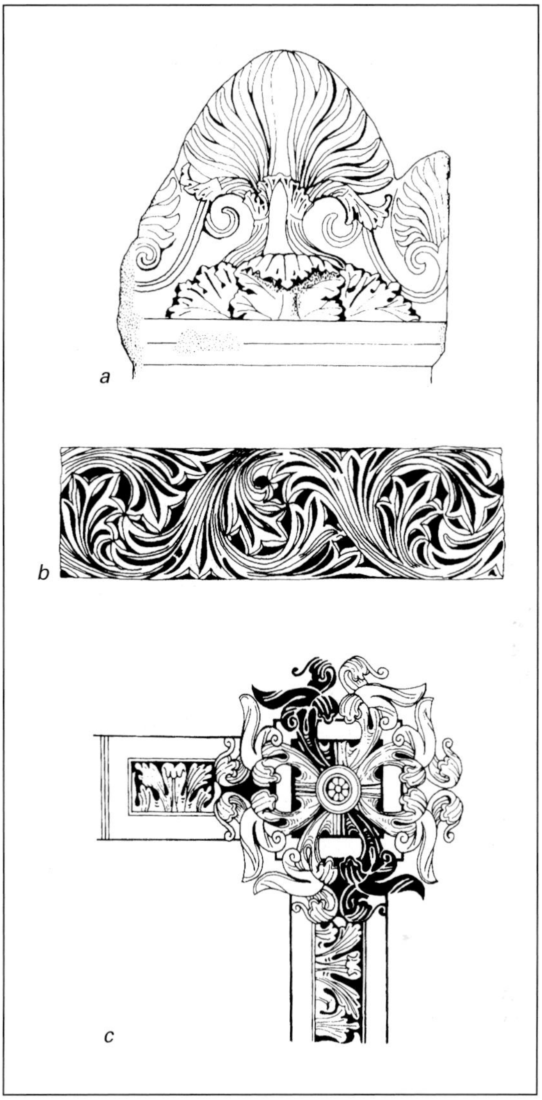

1. Acanthus motifs (from top to bottom): (a) carved ornament at the top of a marble stele, from Athens, *c.* 390–*c.* 365 BC (London, British Museum, Sculpture 605); (b) stone relief from the church of SS Sergios and Bakchos, Istanbul, AD 527–36; (c) detail of a border and corner rosette from the Benedictional of St Aethelwold, Winchester, Old Minster, *c.* AD 980 (London, British Library, Add. MS. 49598, fol. 25)

acanthus leaves with looser, bolder curves and blunter tips. The richer, scrolling form of the Roman acanthus provided an adaptable motif that was used throughout the Greco-Roman world. Acanthus, ivy and vine scrolls were disseminated as enrichments on buildings and in designs on wall paintings and mosaics (for scrollwork on the frieze of the Ara Pacis *see* ROME, ANCIENT, fig. 23).

In Byzantine art the acanthus became a supporting decorative motif apparently without any specific symbolic associations. It developed away from Classical realism to a linear style, in which it took on a spiky, highly stylized form that owes nothing to the acanthus plant in nature

2. Byzantine acanthus leaf motif on a capital, AD 532–7, Hagia Sophia, Istanbul

(see fig. 1b and fig. 2; *see also* EARLY CHRISTIAN AND BYZANTINE ART, fig. 49). In the course of the 6th and 7th centuries, in those areas of Europe where animal ornament had dominated, the Church introduced plant ornament, one element of which was the acanthus leaf in its Byzantine form.

In Carolingian art the acanthus was part of the classical revivals initiated by Charlemagne (*see* ORNAMENT AND PATTERN, §III, 2). Byzantium rather than Rome was the source for the re-introduction of the motif, which was employed in such buildings as the palatine chapel at Aachen (late 8th–early 9th century; *see* AACHEN, §2(ii) and fig. 2), which had Corinthian capitals. In secular and religious metalwork the acanthus ranged from classical forms and spikier, harsher Byzantine forms to richer and more elaborate designs that were combined with other motifs (e.g. baldric mounts with acanthus design, 9th century; Stockholm, Stat. Hist. Mus.; *see* ORNAMENT AND PATTERN, fig. 4). In the 10th century the acanthus scroll was introduced to Scandinavian art, where animals were depicted entwined in its leafy scrolls, particularly in the Ringerike style (*see* VIKING ART, §II, 1(vii)). In northern Europe the acanthus, in a modified and more naturalistic form, was one of the most commonly used motifs in the Romanesque style. It is used prolifically in the west façade (early 12th century) of Notre-Dame-La-Grande, Poitiers (11th century; *see* POITIERS, §2(iii)). The lobed leaf, the half leaf and the leaf collar served many purposes, such as supporting or repeat patterns. These motifs remain stylized and non-specific alongside the naturalistic leaves that were introduced in later Gothic architecture. The acanthus played a prominent part in manuscript illumination, in particular the art of the Winchester school (e.g. Benedictional of St Aethelwold, see fig. 1c; *see also* WINCHESTER, §II and ANGLO-SAXON ART, fig. 9), and appears on such objects as manuscript covers (e.g. whalebone manuscript cover, early 12th century; London, V&A; *see* ORNAMENT AND PATTERN, fig. 5).

During the early Renaissance in Florence the Classical acanthus was used in both architectural and non-architectural contexts. Several of the trade guild statue niches on the Orsanmichele, Florence, have columns with acanthus capitals, notably those for Nanni di Banco's *Four Crowned Saints* (1416; *in situ*; for discussion and illustration *see* NANNI DI BANCO) and Donatello's *St Mark* (1411–13; *in situ*) and *St George* (*c.* 1414; Florence, Bargello). Brunelleschi employed the archaeologically accurate Corinthian order in the church of S Lorenzo, Florence, where the tomb of *Piero I and Giovanni de' Medici* (completed 1472; Florence, S Lorenzo, Old Sacristy; *see* VERROCHIO, ANDREA DEL, fig. 2) by Andrea del Verrochio is decorated with large bronze acanthus leaves on the lid of the sarcophagus. As a non-architectural motif, the acanthus was applied to furniture, woodwork and ceramics, frequently in a hybrid acanthus/palmette form (e.g. Faienza maiolica dish, showing the *Arrival of Aeneas at Delos*, 1497; Sèvres, Mus. N. Cér.). The invention of printing radically changed the means by which patterns and motifs were dispersed in Europe. From the late 15th century onwards individual decorative motifs were transmitted through engravings and pattern books, which were published in large numbers in Italy, Germany, France and the Netherlands (*see* PATTERN BOOK, §I, 2). In these designs, which generally originated in Italy, ornamental foliage of all kinds was prominent, drawn from naturalistic Gothic and classicizing Renaissance as well as Islamic forms, and variations on the acanthus were numerous. Alessandro Vittoria (1525–1608) used the acanthus in the stucco fireplace (1552–3) in the Palazzo Thiene, Vicenza, and WENDEL DIETTERLIN in his book *Architectura* (Stuttgart, 1593, rev. ed. 1598) used the motif in a purely decorative way, with only brief consideration for its Classical architectural function.

2. *c.* 1600 AND AFTER. Drawing the acanthus was an essential skill for 17th- and 18th-century craftsmen, as the motif was one of the leading decorative elements in the Baroque style. It was used extensively on mouldings and cornices by such designers as Daniel Marot (*see* ORNAMENT AND PATTERN, fig. 7); on *boiseries*; in ormolu furniture decoration by the workshop of André-Charles Boulle in such pieces as the two commodes (1708–9; Versailles, Château; *see* FRANCE, fig. 54) commissioned by Louis XIV; and in the marquetry commode (1739; London, Wallace; for illustration *see* COMMODE) designed by Antoine-Robert Gaudreaus for the bedroom of Louis XV at Versailles, Jacques Caffiéri used acanthus decoration in heavily cast and chased bronze mounts. In England from the 1660s until the early 18th century it appeared on silverware in many forms: embossed in bands, chased and engraved, used in running scrolls and applied to handles, candlesticks and church plate (e.g. silver-gilt ewer and communion cup, 1683; London, V&A). It was often used to hide joins in metalwork (e.g. candle sconces, mid-18th century; London, V&A). *Eléments d'orfèvrerie* (1748) by Pierre Germain II (1703–83), a collection of engraved designs for metalwork, helped to popularize a form of the motif that was used in metalwork and also adapted for ceramics, such as Sèvres porcelain (e.g. pair of vases, *c.* 1761; London, Wallace) and Josiah Wedgwood's Queen's ware (e.g. vase, *c.* 1785–7; London, V&A).

The acanthus was employed as a motif in Neo-classical interiors in France by Charles Percier and Pierre-François-Léonard Fontaine, in England by Thomas Hope and

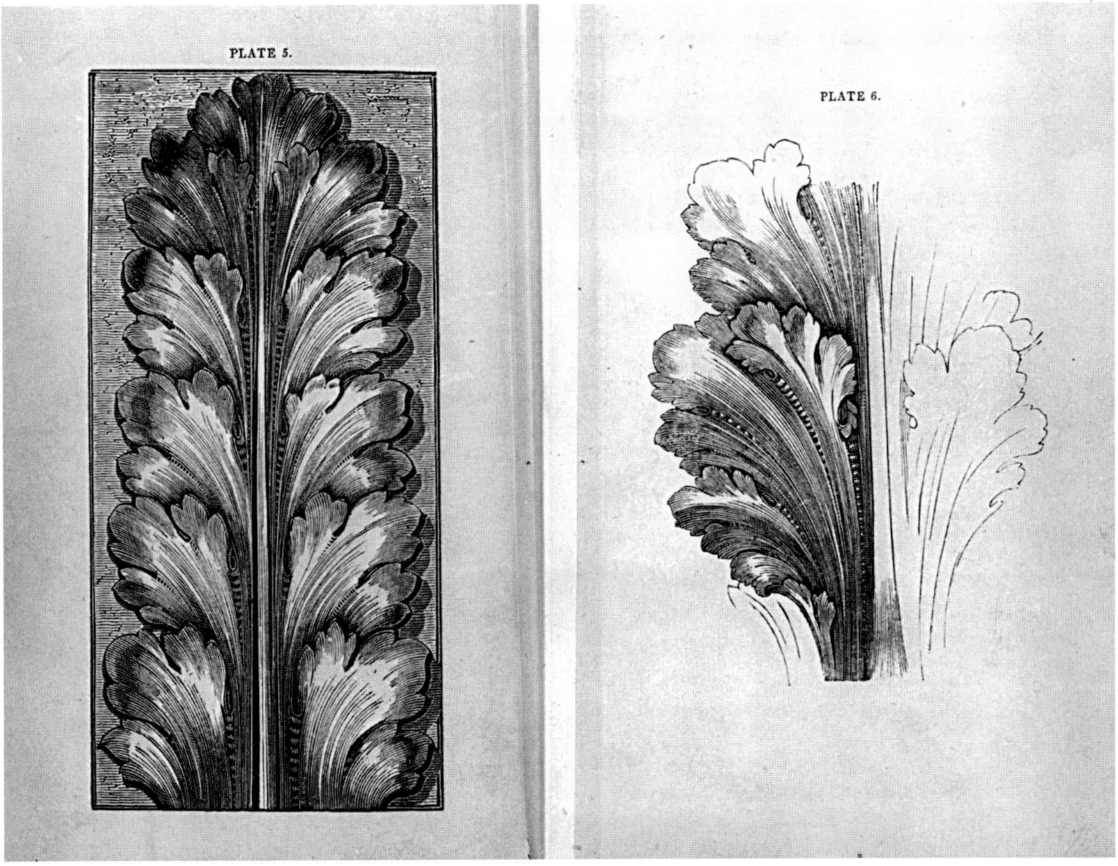

3. James Pope: *A Guide for Drawing the Acanthus and Every Description of Ornamental Foliage* (London, 1850), pls 1 and 6

Robert Adam (for example at Kenwood House, London) and in Russia by Charles Cameron, for example at the Roman Baths in the garden of the summer palace of Catherine II at Tsarskoye Selo (1749–56; now Pushkin Palace-Museum). A series of influential designs that made extensive use of the acanthus were published by Michelangelo Pergolesi (*d* 1801), who may have come to England at the invitation of Robert Adam, in his *Designs for Various Ornaments* (London, 1777–1801). In furniture and metalwork the motif was used in an upright rather than a curved form, in keeping with the restraint of the Neo-classical style (e.g. console table designed by William Kent, 1727–32; London, V&A). In late Regency England the acanthus motif had become commonplace and unrestrained and was used indiscriminately, without regard for its classical associations (e.g. porcelain teapot, Spode, *c.* 1830; London, V&A). In the USA it was applied to furniture both as a decorative motif, for example as freehand painted scrolling leaves (e.g. couch, 1810–25), and with an acknowledgement of its classical origins, for example on the capitals of columns used as supports for a pier table (1820–35; both Winterthur, DE, Du Pont Mus.). Throughout the 19th century pattern books were produced devoted solely to varieties of the representation of the acanthus leaf and stalk, a notable example being James Page's *A Guide for Drawing the Acanthus and Every Description of Ornamental Foliage*, which appeared in several editions, including one of 1850 (see fig. 3). By the mid-19th century A. W. N. Pugin was railing against its debasement in such publications as *The True Principles of Pointed or Christian Architecture* (London, 1841) and *Contrasts* (London, 1856). Although it was included in Owen Jones's *Grammar of Ornament* (London, 1856) in both its natural and stylized form, Jones complained of acanthus leaves being applied 'to any form and in any direction'. William Morris, however, revitalized the motif by studying early examples and the behaviour of real plants (e.g. 'Acanthus' wallpaper, 1875; London, V&A), and Christopher Dresser, a botanist and designer, not only studied the growth patterns of the acanthus but also formalized it into a design called 'Power', which was applied to a number of Wedgwood cane-ware vases and wine-coolers (e.g. pair, *c.* 1880; Barlaston, Wedgwood Mus.).

Although the scrolling foliage motif was an important component in Art Nouveau, the acanthus rarely appears in a recognizable form. Notable exceptions are the decorative plasterwork in the Karlsplatz Underground Station (1898) designed by Otto Wagner and the architecture of Louis Sullivan, who used the motif in stuccowork on the Auditorium Building (inaugurated 1889), Chicago, and decorated the Getty tomb (1890) in Graceland Cemetery, Chicago, with bronze acanthus leaves that may have been influenced by Verrochio's Medici Tomb. In the early 20th century René Lalique employed the acanthus motif on such pieces as the Amiens vase, a rhomboidal frosted vase in which four stylized coiled acanthus leaves protrude from each side (e.g. Paris, Mus. A. Déc.), and Jacques-Emile Ruhlmann used acanthus-derived motifs, often in delicate fillets of ivory, on a small roll-top desk (Paris, Mus. A. Déc.) exhibited in 1923 and on furniture exhibited at the Exposition International des Arts Décoratifs et Industriels Modernes in Paris in 1925. With the advent of modernism and the consequent reduction in ornament and decoration, the acanthus motif was little used in the mid- and late 20th century.

BIBLIOGRAPHY

H. Shaw: *The Encyclopedia of Ornament* (London, 1842)
G. Ebe: *Akanthus* (Berlin, 1883)
A. Riegl: *Stilfragen: Grundlegungen zu einer Geschichte der Ornemantik* (Berlin, 1893)
J. Evans: *A Study of Ornament in Western Europe* (New York, 1975)
E. Temple: *Anglo-Saxon Manuscripts, 900–1066: A Survey of Manuscripts Illuminated in the British Isles* (London, 1976)
E. H. Gombrich: *The Sense of Order: A Study of the Psychology of Decorative Art* (Oxford, 1979)
R. Peesch: *The Ornament in European Folk Art* (New York, 1983)
J. Rawson: *Chinese Ornament: The Lotus and the Dragon* (London, 1984), pp. 9–89
J. Onians: *Bearers of Meaning: The Classical Orders in Antiquity, the Middle Ages and the Renaissance* (Princeton, NJ, 1988)
L. Burn: *The British Museum Book of Greek and Roman Art* (London, 1991)
E. Wilson: *8000 Years of Ornament: An Illustrated Handbook of Motifs* (London, 1994), pp. 125–41

BRUCE TATTERSALL, EVA WILSON

Accardi, Carla (*b* Trápani, 9 Oct 1924). Italian painter. After training at the Accademie di Belle Arte in Palermo and Florence, she moved to Rome in 1946, where she met the Sicilian artists Pietro Consagra, Ugo Attardi (*b* 1923) and Antonio Sanfilippo (1923–80), the last of whom she married in 1949. Together with Giulio Turcato, Mino Guerrini (*b* 1927), Piero Dorazio and Achille Perilli (*b* 1927), the group established FORMA in 1947 to promote an abstract Marxist art distinct from social realism. Accardi participated in the *Forma* exhibition (October 1947; Rome, A. Club) with work still indebted to post-Cubism (e.g. *Decomposition*, 1947; U. Parma, Cent. Studi & Archv Communic.). After one-woman shows in Rome (Lib. Age Or, 1950) and Milan (Lib. Salto, 1951), and having established contact with the Movimento Arte Concreta, Accardi visited Paris. There the contrasting static and energetic work of Alberto Magnelli and Hans Hartung initiated a crisis of direction, and she abandoned painting in 1952–3. On resuming, her dynamic and calligraphic marks in the largely black-and-white *Integrazione* series (e.g. *Negative-Positive*, 1956; artist's col., see 1986–7 exh. cat., p. 28) achieved a balance between sign and ground, surface and space. Their spontaneity as traces of existential experience brought her wide recognition in Italy and France. After joining the Continuità group in 1961 in reaction to *Art informel*, she reintroduced colour, applying repeated rhythmic strokes to transparent plastic, which afforded an open ground (e.g. *Red–Black*, 1967; artist's col., see 1986–7 exh. cat., p. 44). In the 1970s she mounted plastic on shaped stretchers with which she created fragile environments that influenced the practitioners of Arte Povera. When she subsequently reverted to painting on canvas, she adopted greater variety in her mark-making.

BIBLIOGRAPHY

Carla Accardi (exh. cat. by C. Levi, Milan, Padiglione A. Contemp., 1983)
Accardi: Il campo del togliere (exh. cat. by A. Bonito Oliva, Acireale, Pal. Città, 1986–7)

MATTHEW GALE

Acceptus (*fl* Apulia, *c.* 1039–41). Italian sculptor. His name occurs in inscriptions on a marble pulpit in Canosa Cathedral and on the beams of similar pulpits at S Maria, Siponto, and the Sanctuary of S Michele at Monte Sant'Angelo. The inscription on the Canosa pulpit (PER IUSSIONEM DOMINI MEI GUITBERTI VENERABILIS PRESBITERI, EGO ACCEPTUS PECCATOR ARCHIDIACONUS FECI[?T] HOC OPUS) identifies Acceptus as an archdeacon who made the pulpit on the orders of the priest Guitbertus. The inscription on the beam at Siponto refers to Acceptus (DMITTE CRIMINA ACCEPTO) and gives the date 1039; the lectern at Monte Sant'Angelo is dated 1041, and the inscription on one of the beams identifies Acceptus as sculptor ([SC]ULPTOR ET ACCEPTUS BULGO). The workshop evidently included more than one sculptor, since another beam at Siponto is signed DAVID MAGISTER. Fragments of choir screens at Monte Sant'Angelo and Siponto, and the lion support and crossbeam of a throne at Siponto, indicate that the Acceptus workshop made several kinds of liturgical furniture.

The original form of the pulpits at Siponto and Monte Sant'Angelo can be reconstructed on the basis of the Canosa pulpit (total h. 2.74 m), which consists of a rectangular box raised on columns and archivolts, with a semicircular projection for the lectern, which is in the form of an open book decorated with a lion mask, supported by a displayed eagle resting on a human head. The pulpit box is constructed of panels of marble slotted into beams and uprights, suggesting origins in wooden furniture. The beams are decorated with foliage scrolls and the uprights with geometric motifs and terminal knobs. The remains at Monte Sant'Angelo include the lectern, eagle support, three beams with inscriptions and foliage scrolls, two uprights and three capitals; those from Siponto include the eagle and two uprights of a pulpit, as well as seven beams with foliage scrolls and inscriptions, some from the pulpit and some probably from a ciborium.

The sculpture is stylized but of high quality. There is some difference between the smoother and more simplified forms of the Canosa pulpit and the more finely detailed carving of the Siponto and Monte Sant'Angelo fragments, suggesting either a difference in date or that the Canosa pulpit may have been carved by assistants. It is also possible that the rigid style of the Canosa pulpit was influenced by a local metalworking tradition. Acceptus's workshop may have carved the upper parts of the archbishop's throne in Canosa Cathedral (*see* ROMOALDUS), which are very like the pulpit box; there are also similar lion and human masks on the transept capitals of the cathedral. The workshop was also active in Bari, where the door jambs of Bari Cathedral (begun under Archbishop Bisantius, 1025–35) are decorated with foliage scrolls identical to those on some of the Siponto beams. Bari, which formed a joint see with Canosa, may have been the main centre of production.

The sculpture of Acceptus represents the earliest phase of Romanesque sculpture in Apulia and formed the basis of its subsequent development. Influenced by Byzantine and Islamic art, and by small-scale objects in precious materials, it established a distinctive style and iconography.

BIBLIOGRAPHY

E. Bertaux: *L'Art dans l'Italie méridionale*, 3 vols (Paris, 1904/*R* Rome, 1968)
M. Wackernagel: 'La bottega dell'arcidiacono Acceptus, scultore pugliese dell'XI secolo', *Boll. A.*, ii/4 (1908), pp. 143–50
——: *Die Plastik des XI. und XII. Jahrhunderts in Apulien* (Leipzig, 1911)
F. Schettini: *La scultura pugliese dall'XI al XII secolo* (Bari, 1946)
J. R. Gaborit: 'L'Ambon de Sainte Marie de Siponte et les origines de la sculpture romane en Pouille', *Mélanges offerts à René Crozet*, i (Poitiers, 1966), pp. 253–8
H. Schäfer-Schuchardt: *Die Kanzeln des 11. bis 13. Jahrhunderts in Apulien* (Wurzburg, 1972)
Alle sorgenti del romanico: Puglia XI secolo (exh. cat., ed. P. Belli D'Elia; Bari, Pin. Prov., 1975)
A. Prandi, ed.: *Aggiornamento dell'opera di Emile Bertaux*, v (Rome, 1978), pp. 644–7, 649, 694–5, 795, 803, 991
P. Belli D'Elia: 'Il Romanico', *La Puglia fra Bisanzio e l'occidente* (Milan, 1980), pp. 117–253
T. Garton: *Early Romanesque Sculpture in Apulia*, Outstanding Diss. F.A. (New York, 1984)
P. Belli D'Elia: *La Puglia* (Milan, 1986)

TESSA GARTON

Accolti, Pietro (di Fabrizio) (*b* ?Arezzo, 1579; *d* Florence, 1642). Italian writer, painter and architect. He was descended from an illustrious Aretine family (his grandfather was Cardinal Benedetto Accolti (1497–1549), Archbishop of Ravenna and Secretary to Pope Clement VII). He was librarian and architect in the service of Cardinal Carlo Medici, and a member of the Florence Accademia and the Accademia di Disegno. He is known for *Lo inganno degli occhi* (1625), a three-part treatise (on plane figures, solids and shading) in which he showed how perspective practice derived from principles of visual perception. In this he examined classical and modern theories of vision, including those by Euclid (*fl c.* 300 BC), Witelo (*c.* 1230–80), Franciscus Aguilonius (1567–1617) and Guidobaldo del Monte, and criticized contemporary writers on perspective for underestimating the importance of light and shadow. He emphasized the need to distinguish parallel solar rays from diverging point sources of light, such as candlelight, and presented some original ideas on arranging compositions with multiple vanishing points and on foreshortening pictures within pictures. Chapters on anamorphosis and *quadratura* ceiling painting represent contemporary interest in these topics. Accolti's attitude towards perspective rules was remarkably flexible; he cited them only to 'open the eyes and minds' of students without intending to set restrictions. Cropper compares his ideas on *unione* and *sfumamento* (the transitions between light and shadow) to those of Pietro Testa and interpreted them as a product of the Carracci reform of colour and chiaroscuro. As with Matteo Zaccolini's four-volume treatise on perspective (1618–22), his writings testify to the 17th-century revival of Leonardo's ideal of scientific painting. In fact, the 'Discorso intorno al disegno', dedicated to young academicians, in *Lo inganno* is a paraphrase of the latter's *Trattato della pittura.* None of Accolti's painted or architectural works has been identified.

UNPUBLISHED SOURCES

Florence, Bib. N., MS. Passerini 158 bis (Accolti)
Arezzo, Biblioteca Consortile, MS. 34, fol. 92*v*, 103, 118*v* ['Memorie di casa Accolti', 1623–1628, by Lionardo di Jacopo Accolti]

WRITINGS

Lo inganno degli occhi (Florence, 1625)
'Delle lodi di Cosimo II, Granduca di Toscana' [oration to the Accademia di S Luca, 1621], *Prose fiorentine raccolte dallo Smarrito accademico della Crusca*, ed. C. Dati and G. G. Bottari (Florence, 1661 and 1716–45), vi (1716), pp. 111–33

BIBLIOGRAPHY

C. Pedretti: 'Il *Trattato della pittura* di Leonardo plagiato da Pietro Accolti nel 1625', *Rac. Vinc.*, xix (1962), pp. 292–4
E. Cropper: *Ideal of Painting: Pietro Testa's Düsseldorf Notebook* (Princeton, 1984)
M. Kemp: *Science of Art* (New Haven and London, 1990)

JANIS CALLEN BELL

Acconci, Vito (Hannibal) (*b* New York, 24 Jan 1940). American sculptor, performance artist and video artist. He worked for an MFA degree at the University of Iowa from 1962 to 1964. He initially devoted himself to poetry and writing but began to produce visual work in 1969, most of which incorporates subversive social comment. The works of 1969 were photographic records of actions such as bending and throwing, as in *Toe-Touch* (1969; see 1980 exh. cat., p. 12). From 1970 until 1974 he staged a series of activities and performances, such as *Broad Jump '71.* This took place at the Convention Hall in Atlantic City, NJ, and was a jumping competition for men, with a woman as the prize: the work was designed to expose the conventions of male ownership of women.

After 1974 and for the remainder of the 1970s Acconci's presence was only registered at most through recorded tapes of his voice. In *Tonight We Escape from New York* (1977) he installed a rope ladder in the Whitney Museum; alongside this were four loudspeakers, through which fragments of a racist dialogue were played, sounding as if they rose and fell along the ladder. He also used video and film in his work, as in the installation *VD Lives/TV Must Die* (1978) at the Kitchen in New York. This consisted of two TV monitors through which erotic images and sounds were played and in front of which were metal balls on stretched elastic bands, poised to smash the monitors. In the 1980s Acconci turned to permanent sculptures and installations, as in *Instant House* (1980; La Jolla, CA, Mus. Contemp. A.), in which the four sides of a house were pulled together by ropes by the viewer inside. He also produced sculpture and furniture made from natural and incongruous mass-produced objects, as in *Garbage Seating* (1986; see 1987 exh. cat., p. 39), made from dustbins, earth and tree branches.

BIBLIOGRAPHY

Vito Acconci: A Retrospective, 1969–1980 (exh. cat. by J. R. Kirshner, Chicago, IL, Mus. Contemp. A., 1980)
Vito Acconci: Domestic Trappings (exh. cat. by R. J. Onorato, La Jolla, CA, Mus. Contemp. A., 1987)

□

Acemhöyük. Site in central Turkey that flourished in the first half of the 2nd millennium BC, in a fertile plain watered by the River Karasu. The oval mound of Acemhöyük, measuring 700×600 m, and 20 m high, rises in the

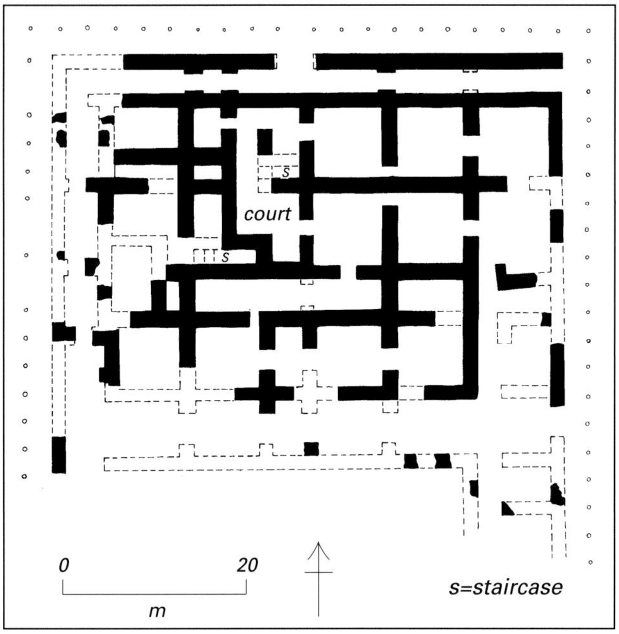

Acemhöyük, plan of central building of the Sarıkaya Palace, first quarter of the 2nd millennium BC

centre of the town of Yeşilova, 18 km north-west of Aksaray; it was surrounded by a lower city 600 m wide, now covered by the modern town. Acemhöyük was thus the largest ancient settlement in this agricultural region, and excavations were begun in 1962 by a Turkish team led by Nimet Özgüç. Some of the objects from the excavations are in the Museum of Anatolian Civilizations, Ankara; most are in the archaeological museums at Niğde and Aksaray; and a fine collection of ivories from the site is in the Metropolitan Museum of Art, New York.

Occupation of the mound began at least as early as 3000 BC and the surviving architectural remains and artefacts from the Early Bronze Age settlements (levels IX–VI) testify to the existence of a distinctive local culture that nevertheless maintained close links with contemporary settlements in central Anatolia and Cilicia. The lower town was first occupied in *c.* 2000 BC, and during the first quarter of the 2nd millennium BC Acemhöyük developed into a great city, and the mound and lower town were occupied to their fullest extent. This city is probably to be identified as ancient Burushhanda, the capital of one of the great kingdoms of Anatolia during the period of the Old Assyrian trade colonies, mentioned in cuneiform texts of the first quarter of the 2nd millennium BC (*see* ANATOLIA, §I, 2(ii)(a)), and celebrated for copper-working and trade. Large areas of level III (19th and 18th centuries BC) were investigated, and private and public buildings have been uncovered. Although the rectangular plans of the private dwellings resemble those of Kültepe, the building techniques were not the same. Because of the scarcity of stone in this area, mud-brick and wood formed the basic construction materials, generally on stone foundations. Houses each contained a kitchen, storerooms and a large room, with a hearth in the form of a wide platform in the middle.

Three public buildings have been investigated: two are referred to for convenience as the Sarıkaya Palace, at the highest point on the south side of the mound, and the Hatipler Palace, on the eminence on the north side of the city, while the third is a large but heavily damaged structure on the west side of the mound. Identical construction techniques and similar artefacts show that these buildings all belong to level III, which was destroyed by an extremely fierce conflagration *c.* 1700 BC. The Acemhöyük palaces were constructed on 4 m-wide foundations of huge stones laid on level ground. Across these stones 4 m wooden cross beams were set side by side to cover the entire surface. A second layer of thick wooden beams was laid at right angles to the first (i.e. along the line of the stone foundations) to act as bonding beams. Mud-brick walls 1.5 m thick were placed in the centre of this composite foundation. Since mud-brick walls are not very durable, vertical wooden posts were placed at 0.9 m intervals within the thickness of the wall. The wall intersections and the doorways were further reinforced with a lattice of timber poles cut to the thickness of the mud-brick walls and laid horizontally one on top of the other for the entire height of the wall. The lowest layer of this reinforcing lattice was extended across the bottom of the doorways to form a threshold. This building technique differs significantly from those found in contemporary palaces elsewhere in Anatolia, although wood was frequently used in buildings (e.g. at BEYCESULTAN) to give added elasticity in the event of an earthquake.

The central building of the Sarıkaya Palace (see fig.) has a portico of wooden columns, set on stone bases that supported a roof on its north façade. The east and west sides of the palace were probably surrounded by the same construction, while the south façade looked out on to the River Karasu. It is assumed that subsidiary buildings, such as the kitchen and archive, were situated around adjacent courtyards that have not been excavated. The ground floor of the central building survives, but the massive foundations and the collapsed remains of upper floors suggest that the building had two storeys. A depiction of the building found on the walls of a large bathtub from the palace implies that the second storey had balconies. The area covered by ruins makes it probable that the ground floor of the palace consisted of at least 50 rooms. By the 1990s the Hatipler Palace had not been fully excavated, but it had at least 76 rooms. Only its south-east façade had a portico, supported on six mud-brick piers 3.0×0.5 m.

Although much was lost in the fire that destroyed the city, Acemhöyük has proved one of the richest sites in Anatolia, both for luxury goods and everyday artefacts. Ivory was used for figurines to adorn furniture, for relief plaques decorated with figures or geometric designs and covered with gold leaf, and for other ornaments; there are gaming boards, the bead decoration from items of dress, vessels made of obsidian and rock crystal, bronze weapons, a large number of copper ingots, the remains of a four-wheeled chariot and pottery. Clay bullae, impressed with the designs from cylinder and stamp seals, have been found in private storerooms and in all the rooms of the palaces. The designs illustrate the contemporary styles of

Assyria, Babylonia and Syria, as well as Anatolia. Seal impressions on some of the bullae are identified by their cuneiform inscriptions as belonging to Shamshi-Adad I, King of Assyria (*reg* 1813–1781 BC), the daughter of Iahdun-Lim, King of Mari, and Aplahanda, King of Carchemish in the early 18th century BC.

After the destruction of level III, there was some reoccupation of the site until *c*. 1650 BC (level II). Much later, in the Hellenistic period (level I, 4th century BC), a village was founded on the southern and western parts of the site with houses, some of them two storeys high, constructed according to central Anatolian architectural traditions. Earlier strata were levelled and built over, stones quarried from older structures were broken up and used to prepare the foundations, and, upon these, walls of sun-dried brick were erected. Among the artefacts found in these houses were figurines, rhyta, moulds for decorated clay plaques, and pottery, both Hellenistic and local.

BIBLIOGRAPHY

K. Emre: 'The Pottery from Acemhöyük', *Anatolia*, x (1966), pp. 99–153
N. Özgüç: 'Excavations at Acemhöyük', *Anatolia*, x (1966), pp. 38–52
——: 'An Ivory Box and a Stone Mould from Acemhöyük', *Turk Tarih Kurumu: Belleten*, xl/160 (1976), pp. 555–60
——: 'Some Contributions to Early Anatolian Art from Acemhöyük', *Belleten*, xliii/170 (1979), pp. 289–305
A. Özten: 'Two Stone Plates from the Sarıkaya Palace at Acemhöyük', *Belleten*, xliii/170 (1979), pp. 385–8
N. Özgüç: 'Seal Impressions from the Palaces at Acemhöyük', *Ancient Art in Seals*, ed. E. Porada (Princeton, NJ, 1980), pp. 61–80
——: 'Seals of the Old Assyrian Colony Period and Some Observations on the Seal Impressions', *Ancient Anatolia: Aspects of Change and Cultural Development. Essays in Honor of Machteld J. Mellink* (Wisconsin, 1986), pp. 48–53
A. Özten: 'Acemhöyük taş kapları' [Stone vessels from Acemhöyük], *Belleten*, lii/203 (1988), pp. 393–406
N. Özgüç: 'An Early Bronze Age Pot Grave of a Child from Acemhöyük', *Between the Rivers and Over the Mountains*, ed. M. Frangipane and others (Rome, 1993), pp. 517–20

NIMET ÖZGÜÇ

Acevedo, Alonso de Fonseca y, Archbishop of Toledo. *See* FONSECA Y ACEVEDO, ALONSO DE.

Acevedo y Zúñiga, Manuel de. *See* MONTERREY, 6th Conde de.

Aceves Navarro, Gilberto (*b* Mexico City, 24 Sept 1931). Mexican painter. He studied at the Escuela Nacional de Pintura y Escultura 'La Esmeralda' under Enrique Assad Lara and Carlos Orozco Romero. His work reflects a concern for the negative effects of industrialization and modernization on cities and displays a nostalgia for more humane urban conditions. His large-scale paintings, for example the *Boots of the Gran Solar* (oil on canvas, 1.60×1.80 m, 1982; artist's col.), convey a sense of urgency through the use of light and colour, with broad lines and chromatic tones creating dynamic forms that show the influence of Abstract Expressionism.

BIBLIOGRAPHY

Siete pintores contemporáneos: Gilberto Aceves Navarro, Luis López Loza, Rodolfo Nieto, Brian Nissen, Tomás Parra, Vlady, Roger von Gunten (exh. cat., Mexico City, Pal. B.A., 1977)
R. Tibol: *Aceves Navarro, Durero y las variaciones* (Mexico City, 1978)
M. Idalia: 'Más libertad y menos barroquismo en la nueva pintura de Aceves Navarro' [Greater freedom and less extravagance in the new painting of Aceves Navarro], *Excelsior* (13 Sept 1979), p. 1-B
S. Alatriste: *La intuición primitiva* (Mexico City, 1986)

JULIETA ORTIZ GAITÁN

Achaemenid. Name given to a people of Persian origin, who founded an empire that flourished *c*. 550–331 BC.

1. Introduction. 2. Official art. 3. Private art. 4. Regional styles.

1. INTRODUCTION. The Achaemenid Persian empire was founded *c*. 550 BC by Cyrus the Great. At its greatest extent under Darius the Great (*reg* 522–486 BC), it stretched from the Indus into northern Greece and across Egypt. The Macedonian Alexander the Great (*reg* 336–323 BC) was able to defeat the Achaemenids in 331 BC only after prolonged military campaigns.

This vast Persian hegemony was rich in legacies of administrative expertise and cultural heritage. Its dynastic name was derived from an 8th-century BC ancestor who ruled as a Persian vassal of the Iranian kingdom of the Medes, who were to inherit great power by conquering the Assyrians in the late 7th century BC. Both the Median overlords and Persian vassals enjoyed access to the Mesopotamian/Iranian artistic heritage. Annals of the Assyrian kings describe the Medes and the Persians living in fortified cities as early as the 9th century BC, while 7th-century BC paylists state that Persians worked alongside Egyptians, Ionians, Lydians, Medes and Elamites at the court of Nebuchadnezzar II of Babylon (*reg* 604–562 BC).

The artistic traditions fostered within the Achaemenid empire cover a complex system of influences presented in a full range of media: monumental stone and brick architecture, applied and free-standing sculpture in stone, moulded brick and metal, wall painting, coins, seals, vessels of glass, alabaster and metal, metal jewellery, horse trappings and decorated weaponry, ornamental woodwork, ivory carving and textiles. An official court art was created under the patronage of the early Achaemenid kings that was acutely aware of the propaganda value of reflecting the geographical diversity of the realm as well as the ancient artistic heritage that persisted in these locales. At the same time, art was also created for private use both within and outside the court circle. In order to understand the art of the Achaemenid empire it is necessary to distinguish between official and private art, both within the Persian heartland of south-west Iran and in the far-flung administrative provinces, with their strongly individual traditions.

Textual documentation on Achaemenid society is very limited. The surviving official imperial texts need careful interpretation. They do not, for example, contain explicit narrative accounts of court ceremonies that might explain some of the iconographical intricacies of official representations. Similarly there are no anecdotal, religious or poetic texts from which to gather information relevant to the interpretation of Achaemenid art. Commentary on monuments, which is available for ancient Greece, for example, through the travelogues of Pausanias, is lacking. Much of the textual documentation on the Achaemenids actually derives from the Greek world, notably the *Histories* of Herodotus (5th century BC) and the *Anabasis* of Xenophon (4th century BC), but these sources, as well as the later ones describing Alexander's conquests, provide only an external view of the Persian empire. An understanding of Achaemenid art has been further hampered by the fact that much historical discussion on the Persians has

1. Rock relief and inscription of Darius the Great, w. *c.* 6 m, Bisitun, Iran, *c.* 520–519 BC

emerged from analysis of Greek texts by scholars steeped in Classical rather than Near Eastern traditions.

Most of the surviving art is derived from the imperial cities of Pasargadae, Persepolis and Susa in south-west Iran. Elsewhere in the empire there is little evidence that has been systematically excavated, partly because only recently has interest been shown in the later levels of long-inhabited sites. The ephemeral natures of wall painting, metalwork and textiles have led to few examples surviving.

2. OFFICIAL ART. Official Achaemenid art was produced under the king's direct authority. This applies to the palatial architecture and monumental sculpture commissioned by the Persian rulers in their capitals and to the series of imperial coins of royal issue. Less straightforward, but of prime importance, are the many seals used by court officials, which provide a bridge between the public and private spheres of artistic production. The Persian kings were informed patrons, selectively adapting antique and foreign images and styles of architecture and sculpture to serve specific new purposes. This may be seen most clearly in the two newly founded Achaemenid capitals, PASARGADAE and PERSEPOLIS. Pasargadae was founded by Cyrus the Great, probably after his victory over Croesus of Lydia in 547 BC, and its buildings exhibit a blend of Near Eastern and Western techniques and forms. The palaces display characteristic Lydian and Ionian stone-working techniques and styles, such as the methods of joining masonry and column drums and the profiles of column base mouldings. However, they also display decidedly Eastern architectural decoration, as in the colossal Assyrianizing guardian bulls at the main doors of the Gatehouse. This mixture of approaches reflects both the use of craftsmen from throughout the empire and the harmonious assimilation of rituals and visual ideas from the conquered lands.

One relief, carved on the sole preserved doorjamb of the twin secondary entrances to the Gatehouse (for illustration *see* PASARGADAE), indicates the importance of viewing Achaemenid art against earlier Near Eastern traditions of kingship, diplomacy and art. It depicts a composite creature wearing the quadripartite wings commonly associated with Assyrian guardian genii, the 'atef' war crown of Egypt and an elaborate Elamite royal robe. The figure faces into the Gatehouse and seems to symbolize access to the interior by privileged invitation rather than its defence. The relief reflects Cyrus's ideological embracing and acquisition of critical Near Eastern traditions, joining together the cultural and administrative traditions of the Elamite civilization and his aspirations towards Egypt, although the actual conquest of Egypt was not effected until after his death. In the context of the Pasargadae Gatehouse, the Elamite robe and the Egyptian crown suggest eastern and western limits of civilization brought together into a new union. The wings evoke the rich legacy of Mesopotamian palatial art. In the Achaemenid context they may also have alluded allegorically to the four quarters of the empire. Herodotus reports that Cyrus had a prophetic dream in which Darius had wings shadowing both Asia and Europe. This story may preserve a vestige of a Persian interpretation of the winged figure as symbol of defined domain.

The ideological and stylistic roots of official Achaemenid art were refined under Darius the Great. The city of Persepolis, which he founded in the last quarter of the 6th century BC, epitomized an international expression of imperialism. Its architecture was laden with symbolism, drawing upon Egyptian, Mesopotamian/Iranian and East Greek traditions to produce an elaborate syncretism of style and iconography. The overall message is of a harmonious world order in which the virtues of kingship have resolved all conflict. Significantly, official Achaemenid art is not historical in the annalistic sense, for representations of the king stress dynastic identity rather than the individual.

One monument alone is a historical record in the usual sense: the rock relief and text (see fig. 1) carved at the beginning of Darius's reign high up on the cliff face of Mount BISITUN in western Iran. The main text describes a series of battles fought by various generals, while the relief presents the ideological basis of these historical victories. Darius stands with his foot upon the squirming figure of one rival claimant to the throne (Gaumata), while the bound figures of other rebels are lined up before him. Two Persian weapon-bearers stand behind the king. Hovering over the scene is the image of Ahura Mazda, the patron deity of the Achaemenids, who is constantly invoked in imperial texts as the divine collaborator of the king in all things. Ahura Mazda wears a crown of divinity and holds the ring, an ancient Mesopotamian symbol of divine authority. His torso emerges from a winged disc. The human figures on the relief are rendered according to the principles of social perspective, clearly establishing the relative status of the king, his helpers and his foes. The basic composition is directly modelled upon a rock relief of the late 3rd millennium BC at Sar-i Pul-Zuhab, *c.* 100 km east of Bisitun on the same ancient road to Babylon, that is itself a somewhat provincial version of an Akkadian royal relief. Stylistically, however, the Bisitun monument reflects a conscious reworking of Assyrian art of the reign of Assurbanipal (*reg* 668–627 BC). The selection of these prototypes was not fortuitous, for both possess different but compatible formal elements. The Achaemenid synthesis reveals a preference for the visual experience rather than episodic narrative. In this aspect it draws upon a whole category of Akkadian period monuments such as the Victory stele of Naram-Sin (*reg* 2254–2218 BC; Paris, Louvre; *see* AKKADIAN, fig. 1).

Such conscious evocations may seem too elaborate for Achaemenid Persia, yet similar forms of intricate allusion are documented in literary construction. In a famous edict recovered at Babylon, Cyrus the Great had himself cast in the role of pious king, preserver of the ancient line of worthy rulers. The edict specifically describes Cyrus as a follower in the tradition of the Assyrian king Assurbanipal, who had conquered Babylon, rebuilt the temples and restored its institutions. Cyrus deliberately echoed the archaizing phraseology of Assurbanipal's pronouncements in Babylon. Achaemenid official art was thus the visual expression of this well-informed, adaptive emulation of earlier expressive modes.

Under the patronage of Darius a distinctly Achaemenid sculptural style developed, best seen in the extensive architectural reliefs at Persepolis, though it is also apparent in other media, particularly seals and metalwork. On the natural forms of men and animals this style contrasts flowing contours with intricate and often abstract patterned elements of coiffure, dress and ornament. The Achaemenid court style has often been described as cold or even deadly, but viewed positively it achieves a formal harmony and discretion, which complements an iconographic programme describing dynastic control and world order.

Official representations of the king have been found in stone reliefs at Pasargadae, Persepolis and neighbouring Naqsh-i Rustam, the site of several of the royal tombs. At Susa, due to the scarcity of local stone, the palaces were mainly decorated with moulded-brick relief. Fragments of palace wall paintings have also been discovered there. A colossal gateway statue of Darius the Great was excavated by the French mission at Susa in 1972. This is made of Egyptian stone and was originally intended to stand before a temple in Egypt; its secondary usage at Susa emphasizes the ability of ancient monarchs to harness manpower and transport technology to royal demand. In all the extant representations of the king (except the Bisitun relief and a copy set up in Babylon) the dynastic image is presented in static, timeless mode. The king appears in audience, stands (bow in hand) before Ahura Mazda and a blazing fire altar, or passes in stately splendour with servants close behind. In each case the figure is crowned and wears royal shoes without straps. Interestingly, in the numerous representations of a heroic figure slaying lions, bulls and fantastic creatures, the personage wears a headdress and strapped shoes, which are characteristic of non-royal figures on other reliefs. For this reason the heroic figure is often called a Royal Hero—as distinct from a king *per se*. Although he surely represents the king in some sense, he is best understood as depicting the king in his aspect as the archetypal embodiment of 'a Persian man'.

The image of kingship preserved on Achaemenid coins of centralized royal issue offers yet another aspect of dynastic identity. Darius the Great commissioned the development of a distinctive coinage in gold and silver (*see* ANCIENT NEAR EAST, §II, 8(i)). Four types are known, all variations on the theme of the crowned king as warrior/hunter. On the first two types the royal figure is either half-length holding his bow and arrows (type I), or full-length and drawing his bow (type II). The coins bear no inscriptions, and the dating of individual issues has relied upon the evidence of hoard contexts and presumed stylistic development. The use of a type II archer coin as a stamp seal on a dated administrative tablet from Persepolis has proved that this type, at least, had been issued by 500 BC.

Achaemenid coins provide the earliest known types bearing representations of a personage rather than a divinity. The depictions of the ruler are not likenesses in any naturalistic sense, but idealized visions, and present a dynastic portrayal of the ruler as warrior and hunter. Individualized portraiture developed on coins produced by satraps within the western reaches of the empire, and these early ruler portraits are generally considered part of the Greek tradition. Formally they certainly reflect Greek style, but they emulated an idea devised originally by Darius of using coins as a vehicle for representation of the ruler.

Official Achaemenid coinage was minted mainly for use in the western parts of the empire, where payment in coin (especially to engage mercenaries) was expected, and the image chosen for this coinage was designed to advertise the Persian king in a quintessentially Persian mode. Commentary on Achaemenid art frequently presumes a rigid division in the system of workshop production and market destination of portable goods. Items which look predominantly Greek are presumed to have been made for a Hellenic or Hellenized clientele, while items that look essentially Persian or eastern are presumed to have been made for an eastern market. In fact, the imperial coins relate in style and iconography to well-documented schools of seal production in the heartland of the empire. It is likely that the coin dies were made in the busy seal workshops at the Persian court, even though they were used to mint currency to pay westerners far from the imperial centre.

The Achaemenid empire inspired the culmination of a great Near Eastern heritage in the art of seals. During this period the cylinder seal enjoyed a revival, alongside the continued use of the stamp. Analysis of several thousand seals known through their impressions on imperial administrative documents from Persepolis (the Treasury and the Fortification Tablets) has provided much information on the complexities of seal production within the empire. Many of the documents are dated and give extensive information on the users of the seals. It is thus possible to distinguish between official and private seal art. The court style was formulated in an official workshop near Persepolis. Evidence from the Fortification Tablets indicates that, for example, the rendering of the Achaemenid court robe had reached a standard style several years before the end of the 6th century BC. An important group of seals, some known through actual seals and more through impressions, are cylinders bearing an inscription panel with the name and titles of the Persian king. All bear representations of a royal figure in court robe, royal beard and crown, and include framing palm trees that may have alluded to royal authority through reference to a specific royal grove of palms. The Persians were famous for their

2. Lobed phiale inscribed with name and titles of Artaxerxes I, silver, diam. 295 mm, *c.* 464–424 BC (Washington, DC, Freer Gallery of Art)

'paradise' gardens, and architectural remains at Persepolis and Susa have revealed hypostyle audience halls designed to symbolize groves in which the soaring columns resembled stylized palm trees. The seals bearing royal names seem to have been official seals owned by specific court offices rather than by persons holding those offices, and they may have been commissioned directly by the named king. These official seals offer a restricted range of imagery: the king before an altar; the king hunting lions from a chariot; the king as heroic vanquisher of beasts; and the king with defeated enemies.

3. PRIVATE ART. Many seals that are known to have been owned by specific court individuals may be considered examples of private art, and the Fortification Tablet seal impressions from the reign of Darius display the richness of artistic vocabulary available to high-status patrons at the Persian court (*see* ANCIENT NEAR EAST, fig. 23). Sometimes this was closely linked to the established court style, but very often it was responsive to other influences. A superb example is the seal of Parnaka, the most powerful man in the Persepolis bureaucracy under Darius. After losing his seal, he had a new one made in the 22nd regnal year of the king (500 BC). This new seal, commissioned after the Achaemenid court style was well established, is a blatant return to the modelled style of Neo-Assyrian seals, but the archaizing element must be understood as being a positive quality rather than a sign of creative poverty.

Vessels and jewellery are an important, if problematic, source of information on the Achaemenid court style and the social and economic functions of its relations to private art. Few of these objects have been found in context, making precise dating and workshop relationships elusive. Nevertheless, the extant examples can be compared with representations on architectural reliefs and wall paintings. Those made of precious metals (*see* METAL, colour pl. II, fig. 1) conform to the court-style preference for graceful animal forms and abstract ornamental refinement, confirming Greek accounts of the lavish use of gold and silver plate and jewellery by the Persian court. A characteristic vessel form, both in silver and bronze, was the phiale (a shallow bowl with offset rim and lobed patterns hammered out in full relief). Several examples incorporate a royal-name inscription (see fig. 2), suggesting, coupled with a remark by Aelianus (*Varia Historia* 1.22), that such inscribed silver phialai may have been given as gifts of state to ambassadors. Beautifully crafted as these objects were, they seem to have been assessed by weight rather than by aesthetic criteria and were an important means of accumulating and dispersing wealth within the empire.

4. REGIONAL STYLES. A large category of art produced within the Persian empire—so-called 'Greco-Persian' art—is familiar mainly from hundreds of unprovenanced stamp seals. It seems to blend the characteristics of Greek and Persian court style and imagery in a distinctive way, and presumably emerged in regional workshops of the western empire. The Greek contribution may be seen in elements such as smooth, fully modelled forms, free-field compositions, the depiction of women and of genre scenes (e.g. non-heroic hunts); but in order to assess the Achaemenid contribution a wider knowledge of the Persepolis seal impressions must be awaited.

In the 5th and 4th centuries BC the impact of internationalism had a major effect upon expressive interchange. Greco-Persian art is but one manifestation of this environment. Imported Persian textiles found in the Siberian tombs of Scythian chieftains on the eastern fringe of the empire suggest a largely lost medium that must have played a major part in the transmission of visual ideas across the empire and beyond its borders. The wealth of gold objects from the OXUS TREASURE and the BLACK SEA COLONIES demonstrates another area within the greater empire that was attuned to a creative blend of local and exotic traditions. The tomb paintings discovered at Karaburun in Anatolia (for illustration *see* ELMALI) are yet more examples of regional art in the empire; they combined local modes of representation and funeral custom with elements of the court style from the heart of the empire.

While discussion of Achaemenid art ought perhaps to be confined to manifestly official examples, it is becoming apparent that it possessed different styles and levels of execution, which made it a fertile ground for creative encounters between Western and Eastern artistic traditions.

BIBLIOGRAPHY

E. Porada: *Alt-Iran: Die Kunst in vorislamischer Zeit* (Baden-Baden, 1962); Eng. trans. as *Ancient Iran: The Art of Pre-Islamic Times*, A. World (London, 1965); *The Art of Ancient Iran: Pre-Islamic Cultures*, A. World (New York, 1965)

R. Ghirshman: *Perse: Proto-Iraniens, Mèdes, Achéménides*, A. Mankind (Paris, 1963); Eng. trans. as *The Art of Ancient Iran from its Origins to the Time of Alexander the Great* (London, 1964)

J. Boardman: *Greek Gems and Finger Rings* (London, 1970), pp. 303–57

C. Nylander: *Ionians in Pasargadae: Studies in Old Persian Architecture* (Uppsala, 1970)

P. Amiet: 'La Glyptique de la fin d'Elam', *A. Asiat.*, xxviii (1973), pp. 3–32
C. Starr: 'Greeks and Persians in the Fourth Century BC', *Iran. Antiq.*, xii (1977), pp. 49–115
M. C. Root: *The King and Kingship in Achaemenid Art: Essays on the Creation of an Iconography of Empire*, Acta Iranica, 19 (Leiden, 1979)
P. R. S. Moorey: 'Deve Hüyük II in Context: The Archaeological Evidence for Persian Occupation of the Near East *c.* 550–330 BC', *Cemeteries of the First Millennium BC at Deve Hüyük*, Brit. Archaeol. Rep., Int. Ser., 87 (1980), pp. 128–42
M. C. Root: 'The Parthenon Frieze and the Apadana Reliefs at Persepolis: Reassessing a Programmatic Relationship', *Amer. J. Archaeol.*, lxxxix (1985), pp. 103–20
M. B. Garrison: *Seal Workshops and Artists in Persepolis: A Study of Seal Impressions Preserving the Theme of Heroic Encounter on the Fortification and Treasury Tablets* (diss., U. Michigan, 1988)
M. C. Root: 'Evidence from Persepolis for the Dating of Persian and Archaic Greek Coinage', *Numi. Chron.*, cxlviii (1988), pp. 1–12
H. Sancisi-Weerdenburg and A. Kuhrt, eds: *Achaemenid History*, 4 vols (Leiden, 1988–)
M. C. Root and M. B. Garrison: *Seal Impressions on the Persepolis Fortification Tablets: A Catalogue Raisonné* (Chicago, in preparation)

MARGARET COOL ROOT

Achenbach, Oswald (*b* Düsseldorf, 2 Feb 1827; *d* Düsseldorf, 1 Feb 1910). German painter. He studied at the Kunstakademie in Düsseldorf, as did his elder brother, the painter Andreas Achenbach (1815–1910), who was the main influence on him other than his teacher, Johann Wilhelm Schirmer. At a very early stage he began to prepare studies for landscapes in the area around Düsseldorf, sketching boulders, rocks, bushes, trees and people. From 1843 he went on many study tours, visiting Bavaria in 1843 and northern Italy and Switzerland in 1845. The Bavarian and Italian Alps stimulated him to create a unified approach to landscape painting. In such early works as *Landscape* (1846; Düsseldorf, Kstmus.) his receptiveness to atmospheric values can be seen, even if the precise detail and clear articulation into foreground, middle ground and background still clearly show his debt to Schirmer.

In 1850 Achenbach travelled to Rome and the Campagna, where he met Arnold Böcklin, who was also studying in Düsseldorf, and Heinrich Dreber. This journey was very significant for Achenbach; from then on Italian landscape and the southern way of life became his main subjects. Numerous drawings and oil sketches bear witness to his intensive study of nature. The warm ochre tones, attention to detail and the severe form of his works at this period still show Schirmer's influence, but after another journey to Italy in 1857, when he visited Rome, Naples and Capri, these traits were almost completely eliminated. In contrast to Schirmer's rational compositional methods, atmospheric elements became crucial to Achenbach's work. His study of light and colour had shown him that the best way of conveying the sensation of a *plein-air* landscape was by blending one area of the picture into the next to create an atmospheric haze of colour, as in *Landscape in the Campagna* (1855; Düsseldorf, Kstmus.). Achenbach's taste for the picturesque and his ability as a colourist enabled him to depict landscapes with conviction and unity. His liking for using his fingers and palette knife to distribute colour and model form was typical of his method of painting, with its broad outlines and wide variety of approaches.

Achenbach achieved international recognition early in his career: in 1852 he was made a member of the Rijksakademie van Beeldende Kunsten in Amsterdam. In 1863 he succeeded Schirmer as professor of landscape painting at the Kunstakademie in Düsseldorf. He used the local Rhine scenery as the basis of his teaching, and also increasingly devoted his own work to it. He travelled to Paris and Normandy in 1859, and to Kissingen, Marienbad and Heidelberg in 1866 and 1870, but neither these journeys nor subsequent visits to Belgium and the Netherlands in 1873 made a deep impact on his work. A further stay in Rome and Naples in 1871 did produce changes. If his earlier drawings and oil sketches had enabled him to familiarize himself with the details of a particular locale, the studies he made at this time were aimed increasingly at clarifying composition.

Achenbach also became more intensively concerned with architecture. As well as paintings of Roman monuments and the colourful city life of Rome and Naples, such as *By the Porta Capuana in Naples* (1875; Munich, Neue Pin.), he continued to produce landscapes, but in the following decade his interest was concentrated less on the Campagna and more on the area round Naples, Sorrento and Capri. His liking for architecture led him to paint architectural views, but this resulted in a repetitious over-use of certain motifs. In his later pictures he quite often enhanced genre scenes by adding figures in fashionable dress, as in *Social Gathering on a Garden Terrace* (1889; Berlin, Neue N.G.). Achenbach attempted to depict landscape naturalistically in all its possible manifestations; colour effects and light phenomena were of particular importance to him in his work, although this often gives his pictures a theatrical effect. He was one of the most important landscape painters of the Düsseldorf school.

BIBLIOGRAPHY

Meissner
J. H. Schmidt: *Oswald Achenbach* (Düsseldorf, 1944)
W. Hütt: *Die Düsseldorfer Malerschule, 1819–1869* (Leipzig, 1964), pp. 136–8
J. Markowitz: *Die Düsseldorfer Malerschule*, ii, Düsseldorf, Kstmus. cat. (Düsseldorf, 1969), pp. 28–40
Die Düsseldorfer Malerschule (exh. cat., ed. W. von Kalnein; Düsseldorf, Kstmus., 1979), pp. 247–56

JOSEF STRASSER

Achilles Painter. *See* VASE PAINTERS, §II.

Achmim. *See* AKHMIM.

Achtermann, (Theodor) Wilhelm (*b* Münster, Westphalia, 15 Aug 1799; *d* Rome, 26 May 1884). German sculptor. He first trained with his father as a joiner, and in 1829 he won a scholarship to Berlin. From 1830 to 1836 he studied at the Akademie der Künste, Berlin, with the sculptors Friedrich Tieck and Christian Daniel Rauch. He was deeply religious and during these years he concentrated almost exclusively on religious themes, for example a *Christ on the Cross* (1830), a *Hovering Angel* for a font (1831), a *Resurrection* relief (1834) and a *Virgin and Child* (1836). In 1838 the Prussian Minister of Culture, Bethmann Hollweg, commissioned Achtermann to make a marble crucifix for Burg Rheineck bei Niederbreisig (*in situ*) and this enabled Achtermann to travel to Italy, initially to Carrara for marble for his work, and subsequently to

Rome, where he later settled. In Rome the main influences on his work derived from artists in the circles around Bertel Thorvaldsen and Friedrich Overbeck. Affinities with the work of the Lukasbrüder characterized his principal sculpture for Münster Cathedral: an over life-size *Pietà* (1843–9; destr. World War II; small marble version in Rome, S Prassede) and a large-scale *Deposition* group (1850–58; destr. World War II; plaster cast in Rome, Trinità dei Monti). Achtermann's preoccupation with the theme of the Crucifixion continued throughout his life with, for example, a work of *c.* 1821 in the Mausoleum, Charlottenburg, Berlin, and in 1857 a work for Achtermann's tomb in the Campo Santo Teutonico, Rome. Although his work was limited stylistically and veered between self-quotation and sentimentality, Achtermann was one of the most consistent representatives of 19th-century German religious sculpture. His work, however, derived from his training as a craftsman and his deeply felt Catholicism, and Achtermann thus remained an outsider within the Rauch school.

BIBLIOGRAPHY

J. M. Strunk: *Wilhelm Achtermann: Ein westfälisches Künstlerleben* (Vechta, 1931)

P. Bloch and W. Grzimek: *Das klassische Berlin: Die Berliner Bildhauerschule im 19. Jahrhundert* (Frankfurt am Main, Berlin and Vienna, 1978, 2/1994)

Abbilder—Leitbilder: Berliner Skulptur von Schadow bis heute (exh. cat., ed. H. Börsch-Supan; W. Berlin, Schloss Charlottenburg, 1978)

H. Börsch-Supan: *Die Kunst in Brandenburg-Preussen* (Berlin, 1980)

Rheinland Westfalen und die Berliner Bildhauerschule des 19. Jahrhunderts (exh. cat., ed. P. Bloch; Bottrop, Mod. Gal.; Cappenberg-Salm, Schloss Cappenberg; Aachen, Suermondt-Ludwig-Mus.; 1984)

D. Kaiser-Strohmann: *Theodor Wilhelm Achtermann (1799–1884) und Carl Johann Steinhäuser (1813–1879): Ein Beitrag zu Problemen des Nazarenischen in der deutschen Skulptur des 19. Jahrhunderts* (Frankfurt am Main, Berne and New York, 1985)

R. Thiele: 'Achtermann', *Allgemeines Künstlerlexikon*, i (Munich and Leipzig, 1992)

PETER SPRINGER

Acker, Hans [Hans von Ulm] (*fl* Ulm, 1413–61). German painter. He belonged to an artist family of which several generations were documented in 15th-century Ulm. According to municipal tax lists, 'Ackerlin, painter' was a master by 1413. He received payments from the masons' lodge of Ulm Cathedral from 1415. In 1441 the cathedral lodge in Berne paid 'Master Hans of Ulm' for the production and delivery of stained-glass windows: this Hans is identified with Acker (*see also* GOTHIC, §VIII, 5). The Berne *Passion* window (1441; Berne Cathedral, chancel), his only surviving documented work, demonstrates the capabilities of mid-15th-century German glass painting in dealing with box-shaped hall-church interiors. Its Apostle figures still belong to the tradition of the 'Soft style', inspired by Bohemian art, while the style of their robes is reminiscent of those in the chancel windows of Ulm Cathedral. The appearance of a landscape background reveals the influence of the glass paintings (*c.* 1420) in the cathedral's Besserer Chapel.

However, as the latter are no longer assumed to be the product of Acker's workshop, related windows in Ulm Cathedral (Kuttel window, *c.* 1413; *Day of Judgement* window, 1431; *Passion* cycle windows, 1440) must be removed from the workshop's oeuvre. Nor can the former upper windows of the Margarethenkapelle of Konstanz Cathedral (1430; Freiburg im Breisgau Cathedral since 1820) be definitely identified as a product of the workshop. It is fairly certain that there was an Acker workshop, though not that Lukas Moser was a member of it or even Acker's teacher. However, stylistic similarities between figures in the Berne *Passion* windows and a *St Jerome* window (*c.* 1447–50; Ulm Cathedral, Neithardt Chapel), as well as the direct transposition of facial features, affirm workshop attribution, and a payment made by the Ulm Cathedral lodge in 1449 is generally connected with the workshop's repairs on the chancel windows. It cannot be conclusively proved that Acker worked as a panel painter.

BIBLIOGRAPHY

W. Lehmbruck: *Hans Acker: Maler und Glasmaler von Ulm* (Ulm, 1968)

N. Werner: 'Zu den Glasgemälden der Bessererkapelle des Münsters zu Ulm', *Giessen. Beitr. Kstgesch.*, i (1970), pp. 29–49

R. Becksmann: Corp. Vitrearum Med. Aevi: Deutschland, ii/1 (Berlin, 1979), pp. 102–10

C. Reisinger: *Flandern in Ulm: Glasmalerei und Buchmalerei—Die Verglasung der Bessererkapelle am Ulmer Münster* (Worms, 1985)

R. Becksmann: 'Der Mann aus Brügge: Eine Fiktion', *Kstchronik*, xliv (1988), pp. 315–21

WERNER BRODA

Ackermann, Max (*b* Berlin, 5 Oct 1887; *d* Bad Liebenzell, nr Stuttgart, 14 Nov 1975). German painter. He studied under Henry Van de Velde at the School of the Fine Arts and Arts and Crafts of the Grand Duchy of Saxony (later the Bauhaus, Weimar) (1906–7), and under Franz von Stuck at the Akademie der Bildenden Künste, Munich (1909–10). He worked under Adolf Hölzel at the Staatliche Akademie der Bildenden Künste in Stuttgart from 1912, and by 1918 he had produced his first non-objective works under the influence of the latter. Although primarily an abstract painter he was briefly involved with Magic Realism in the 1920s. He devised a type of colour abstraction, which he called 'Absolute Painting', and in 1930 he founded a 'Seminar for Absolute Painting' at the Volkshochschule in Stuttgart. Works such as *Painting XII* (1949; Berlin, Alte N.G.) relied heavily on a body of theory derived mainly from Hölzel and the colour theories of Goethe.

BIBLIOGRAPHY

L. Langenfeld, ed.: *Max Ackermann: Aspekte seines Gesamtwerkes* (Stuttgart, 1972)

COLIN RHODES

Ackermann, Rudolph [Rudolf] (*b* Stollberg, Saxony, 20 April 1764; *d* Finchley, London, 30 March 1834). English publisher and patron of German birth. He trained as a carriage designer in Paris and moved to England between 1783 and 1786. He established his own business as a carriage maker, undertaking major commissions in London and Dublin. In 1804 he designed Pius VII's carriage for the coronation of Napoleon and in 1805 the funeral carriage of Horatio, Viscount Nelson. By 1800 Ackermann had built up a unique business at 101 The Strand, London, known as 'The Repository of Arts'. This encompassed a drawing school with 80 pupils, the sale and loan of Old Master paintings and watercolour drawings, the publication of decorative prints and illustrated books and the manufacture of watercolour paints including a number of new chemical pigments.

In the early 19th century, Ackermann was an important and regular patron of English watercolour painters, employing William Henry Pyne, Augustus Charles Pugin, Thomas Heaphy, Frederick Mackenzie (1787–1854), Thomas Uwins and John Gendall. Much of the later work of Thomas Rowlandson was commissioned by Ackermann; the prolific association of the author William Combe and Rowlandson began in 1810 in the third volume of Ackermann's *The Microcosm of London* and flourished in the three *Tours of Doctor Syntax* (1811, 1820, 1821), *The Dance of Life* (1817), *The English Dance of Death*, 2 vols (1815–16) and *The History of Johnny Quae Genus* (1821–2).

Ackermann was fascinated by scientific and technological advances as they related to the fine and decorative arts. He published many of the first backlit transparencies (1796–8), patented a waterproof paper (1801) and was the first to employ gas lighting in a manufactory (1811). In 1817 he patented Alois Senefelder's process of lithography in England, operating his own lithographic press until 1822. He was active in the search for an unforgeable note for the Bank of England (1819) and recommended a new steel plate engraved on a cylindrical die.

Between 1794 and 1832 Ackermann published over 300 books, many with hand-coloured plates, and tens of thousands of copies of decorative prints in aquatint, mezzotint, stipple, lithography, steel plate engraving and soft-ground etching, all produced to the highest technical standards. His principal publications included: *The Microcosm of London*, 3 vols (1808–10; 104 aquatints); *The History of the Abbey Church of St Peter's Westminster*, 2 vols (1812; 80 aquatints); *A History of the University of Oxford* (1814; 64 aquatints); *A History of the University of Cambridge* (1815; 80 aquatints); *The History of the Colleges* (1816; 44 aquatints); and *The Repository of Arts*, a monthly magazine published from 1809 to 1828 (1432 coloured plates). His younger sons succeeded him in 1830 as Ackermann & Co., and the business of his eldest son, Rudolph Ackermann jr, established in 191 Regent Street in 1822, continues as Arthur Ackermann & Son Ltd at 33 New Bond Street, London.

BIBLIOGRAPHY

DNB

J. Ford: *Ackermann, 1783–1983: The Business of Art* (London, 1983)

S. Jervis: 'Rudolph Ackermann', *London, World City, 1800–1840* (exh. cat., ed. C. Fox; Essen, 1992)

R. Hill: 'Bankers Boards & Beau Monde', *Country Life*, clxxxviii (1994), pp. 64–7

JOHN FORD

Ackersloot [Akersloot], **Willem (Outgertsz.)** (*b* Haarlem, *fl* 1620–34; *d* The Hague, ?1634). Dutch engraver. He was the son of Outgert Arisz. Ackersloot (*fl* 1631). In 1624 he became the brother-in-law of the artist Cornelis van Kittensteyn (1600–38). After a stay in Paris in 1620, he was back in his native Haarlem by 1624. His oeuvre comprises 18 engravings, dating from 1624 to 1633. He eventually became a skilful reproductive engraver; among his best works are the portraits of *Frederik Hendrik* and *Amalia van Solms* after Adriaan van de Venne (both 1628), the *Ceres Changing Stellio into a Lizard* after Jan II van de Velde (i) and the book illustrations after Pieter Jansz. Saenredam's early drawings for Samuel Ampzing's *Beschryvinge en de lof der stad Haerlem* ('Description and praise of the city of Haarlem'; Haarlem, 1628). He is last documented in The Hague in 1634.

BIBLIOGRAPHY

Hollstein: *Dut. & Flem.*; *NKL*; Thieme–Becker

F. G. Waller: *Biographisch woordenboek van Noord Nederlandsche graveurs* (The Hague, 1938), p. 2

CHRISTIAAN SCHUCKMAN

Acmeism [Rus. Akmeizm, from Gr. akmē: 'perfection']. Russian poetic movement established in St Petersburg in 1913, which flourished until the early 1920s and was associated with the journal *Apollon*. The leaders and theoreticians of this movement were Nikolay Gumilyov (1886–1921) and Sergey Gorodetsky (1884–1967), and the movement's poets included Anna Akhmatova (1888–1966) and Osip Mandel'shtam (1891–1938). In general terms Acmeism professed a conservatism and a dedication to 'world art' and its preservation in the turbulent period of the October Revolution of 1917, when other literary trends, such as Futurism, were denouncing the past. The primary links between this literary movement and art were forged through Gumilyov and his relationship with Natal'ya Goncharova and Mikhail Larionov. Both artists made portraits of him as well as illustrating his poems.

In the early part of his career Gumilyov wrote three pieces of art criticism for Russian journals, discussing the work of Paul Gauguin and Paul Cézanne, among others. He also wrote an article (unfinished) on African art. During visits to London and Paris, Gumilyov met Roger Fry, worked with the Russian sculptor Boris Anrep (1883–1969) and discussed collaborations with Larionov and Goncharova on a production for Diaghilev. Gumilyov's late Acmeist work shows the probable influence of Rayism. The enthusiasm shared by Gumilyov, Goncharova and Larionov for ethnography and Eastern art forms is felt in their work from the period of their friendship in 1917.

Acmeism also had much in common with the poetic movement Imagism, which rejected Romanticism. The Acmeists were opposed to the mystical vagueness of the Russian Symbolists, and they emphasized craftsmanship and earthly reality. Their poetry was characterized by clarity of language and a visual orientation, some of the best describing objects from the natural world or timeless objects of man's creativity. More concerned with grounding their work in the systems of art and verbal culture than in social reality, the Acmeists filled their verse with allusions to other artistic systems, justifying Mandel'shtam's definition of the movement as 'the yearning for world culture'.

BIBLIOGRAPHY

S. Driver: 'Acmeism', *Slav. and E. Eur. Rev.*, xii (1968), pp. 141–56

D. Mickiewicz: 'The Problem of Defining Acmeism', *Rus. Lang. J.*, suppl. (Spring 1975), pp. 1–20

E. Rusinko: 'Russian Acmeism and Anglo-American Imagism', *Ulbandus Rev.*, i (1978), pp. 37–49

——: 'Acmeism, Post-symbolism and Henri Bergson', *Slav. Rev.*, xli (1982), pp. 494–510

A. Parton: 'Goncharova and Larionov—Gumilev's Pantum to Art', *Nikdaj Gumilev, 1886–1986: Papers from the Gumilev Centenary Symposium* (Berkeley, 1987), pp. 225–42

ELAINE RUSINKO

Acosta, Wladimiro [Konstantinovsky, Wladimir] (*b* Odessa, Russia, 23 June 1900; *d* Buenos Aires, 11 July 1967). Argentine architect. He studied architecture at the

Istituto di Belle Arti in Rome, graduating in 1919. From 1922 he worked in Germany, gaining experience in building engineering and urban design, before moving to Argentina in 1928. He worked in Chile, Uruguay, Brazil, Venezuela, Guatemala and, from 1954 to 1957, in the USA, where he taught (1956) at Cornell University, Ithaca, NY. On his return to Argentina he was appointed Professor of Architectural Composition (1957–66) at the Universidad de Buenos Aires. Acosta was an early exponent of an approach to architecture through environmental design and engineering, which he promoted through his book *Vivienda y clima* (1937) and his 'Helios' buildings. These were based upon correct orientation, cross-ventilation, and the control of solar radiation by means of *brises-soleil*, with a minimum of mechanical inputs. Like the architects of the Modern Movement in Europe, he saw architecture as a social phenomenon and became dedicated to the provision of mass housing for rapidly growing urban populations. His early work included individual houses in Buenos Aires, for example the Casa Stern, Ramos Mejia (1939), the 'Helios' villa (1943) at La Falda and others elsewhere in Argentina, at Rosario, Córdoba, Bahia Bianca and Bariloche. He also designed a psychiatric hospital (1942) at Santa Fé, but he is principally known for his multi-storey 'Helios': Departmentos de Figueroa Alcorta y Tagle (1942–3) and Co-operativa El Hogar Obrero workers' housing (1954; with Fermin Bereterbide and A. Felici), Avenida Rivadavia y Riglos, Buenos Aires, a slim 24-storey slab block on a two-storey podium. Acosta's buildings are simple and astylar in the early Modern Movement genre, although expressive of the principles of solar control.

WRITINGS

Vivienda y clima (Buenos Aires, 1937)
Vivienda y ciudad (Buenos Aires, 1947)
'Villa à La Falda', *Archit. Aujourd'hui* (Sept 1948), pp. 62–3

BIBLIOGRAPHY

F. Bullrich: *Arquitectura Argentina contemporánea* (Buenos Aires, 1963)
S. Borghini, H. Salama and J. Solsona: *1930–1950: Arquitectura moderna en Buenos Aires* (Buenos Aires, 1987), pp. 30–37, 99–101

LUDOVICO C. KOPPMANN

Acoustics. Sound can be defined as audible vibrations within a relatively steady medium, and in buildings sound may be air-borne or structure-borne. The science of architectural acoustics is divisible into noise control and room acoustics. The following article is mainly concerned with the latter and the 'desired' sound generated within a space, because its design has had a significant impact on architectural form; it concentrates on examples of Western architecture.

For an extended discussion of acoustics see *Grove 6*.

1. The science of room acoustics. 2. Types of acoustic space.

1. THE SCIENCE OF ROOM ACOUSTICS. Different acoustical conditions are preferable for listening to the spoken word as compared with different types of music. The shape, size and construction of halls and theatres—and to some extent other building types, including churches—developed historically in response to acoustical requirements. Room-acoustic design, however, is a relatively recent subject of study. Until the 20th century this relationship between acoustical requirements and the building form resulted from trial and error, involving the architect's intuition and awareness of precedent rather than scientific knowledge. Acoustically inadequate halls were usually demolished within about 50 years, so that most surviving older halls are probably among the best that were built.

From 1895 the American physicist Wallace Clement Sabine (1868–1919) carried out experiments on reverberation time. Three years later he was asked to apply his knowledge of room acoustics to the planning of the auditorium at Symphony Hall (opened 1900–01), Boston, MA, designed by McKim, Mead & White. Reverberation is the sound that lingers in a space when the sound source has stopped, as the sound energy reflects off the enclosing surfaces of the room before gradually escaping from the room or becoming absorbed; the time taken for the reverberant sound to disappear beyond audibility was standardized for scientific purposes as a reduction in sound level of 60 decibels. Reverberation time depends on the cubic volume of the room and the amount of sound-absorption present. Sabine evolved a simple formula for its calculation, and for many years this remained practically the only easily measurable aspect of room acoustics. Accordingly until *c.* 1960 much effort was focused on prescribing an exact reverberation time for various types of room.

The reverberation-time calculation, however, is independent of a room's shape. Sound is assumed to be analogous to a gas filling a room and then gradually escaping: for a room of given cubic volume the rate of escape of gas remains the same regardless of its shape. For several decades halls were constructed with reverberation characteristics that were similar to the admired historic halls, yet their acoustics were invariably inferior. It became apparent that the shape of a room—or, more precisely, the position of sound-reflecting surfaces—is important in determining its acoustical character, especially the clarity and loudness of music played in the room, and the acoustical 'scale' of the space.

When a musical sound is produced in a hall, the sound arriving at the listener's ears is a combination of sound direct from the musicians' instruments and sound reflected off the wall, balcony and ceiling surfaces. The sound continues to reflect many times, and the same acoustic information continues to reach the ear in sequence according to the number of times the sound has reflected. The sound strength and tonal fullness are determined by the density and arrival time of these reflections, especially with regard to those arriving within about 200 milliseconds of the direct sound. It is the shape of the room that determines this pattern and the degree to which the reflections are sustained and guided to the listener.

Sound that is reflected laterally is particularly important in a concert hall, since the listener feels enveloped by the music and involved in the performance when sound arrives from different directions. This effect is especially exciting when the orchestra plays forte and reflections from the surfaces of the room are strong. Tall, narrow room proportions—as in the traditional 19th century, rectangular concert halls—are more desirable than the low, wide proportions of most 20th-century auditoria. In the former, multiple cross-reflections of sound are generated, so that sound energy is retained as long as possible, and music played in the hall has great fullness and strength.

Each element of the hall can be studied and made optimal using the modelling techniques available to the acoustician. The pattern of sound distribution in a hall is affected by the angle in three dimensions of each section of wall, ceiling and floor, together with its position in space. The angle and position in plan of the side walls are particularly critical at the mid-section of the hall for encouraging the lateral reflection of sound. Various methods may be adopted to simulate the pattern of sound distribution in a room. Light-reflection, or sound of a suitably scaled pitch, may be used with an architectural model, or sound reflections may be simulated graphically by computer. Modelling is especially useful for identifying potential acoustical faults, such as long-delayed echoes.

2. TYPES OF ACOUSTIC SPACE. The history of auditoria may be divided into those buildings where speech intelligibility should not be obscured by late-arriving reflected sound, and concert halls for the performance of instrumental music, where fullness of tone and a longer reverberation time are desirable. Leonardo da Vinci projected these acoustic criteria into sketches depicting two buildings of contrasting form, one containing 'theatres for hearing mass' (Paris, Inst. France, Codex B, fol. 55*v*) and another labelled 'place for preaching' (Paris, Inst. France, MS. B.N. 2037, fol. 5*v*; see fig. 1).

(i) Churches. (ii) Theatres. (iii) Opera houses. (iv) Rooms for speech. (v) Concert halls.

(i) Churches. In the Middle Ages churches were the first large-scale enclosures for public assembly. The stone walls and vaults, and the large cubic volume relative to the number of occupants, resulted in a relatively long reverberation time—some 12 seconds in the largest cathedrals, much less in village churches. The strength of long-delayed reflected sound is increased by the extreme height-to-width ratio of many Gothic churches. The reverberation is predominantly of low frequency because there are no bass absorbers except the windows, and stonework can absorb high-frequency sound. The acoustics of these buildings did much to encourage the development of Western music, especially the choral tradition. Music drama was also much performed, and, although speech intelligibility was poor, this was overcome by the audience following the performers around the building as the scene of the action changed. In Baroque churches, however, the ample wooden furnishings are efficient bass absorbers, and the reverberation tends to be strongest at middle frequencies. Such acoustic conditions are excellent for the instrumental music that developed during the Baroque era.

Church design after the Reformation illustrates a conscious adaptation from one type of acoustic environment to the other. When the sermon became a major element in Protestant services, Gothic churches in northern Europe—for instance the Thomaskirche, Leipzig, where Johann Sebastian Bach (1685–1750) was Cantor—were remodelled by hanging curtains and by inserting new galleries near the pulpit. This reduced reverberance and increased speech clarity. When designing the 50 new parish churches for the City of London, Christopher Wren (in a letter of 1711) emphasized that they should be small enough for everyone to see and hear the preacher.

(ii) Theatres. According to Vitruvius, however, the earliest attempt at acoustic control in buildings was in Classical theatres. In *On Architecture* (V.5) he claimed that bronze acoustic vases were commonly built into seating risers to act as resonators for amplifying the sound; yet their actual effect must have been negligible. (Many similar vessels can be seen built into the walls of such widely scattered churches as the parish church (12th century), Bjäresjö, near Ystad, Sweden; St Nicholas (13th century), Leeds,

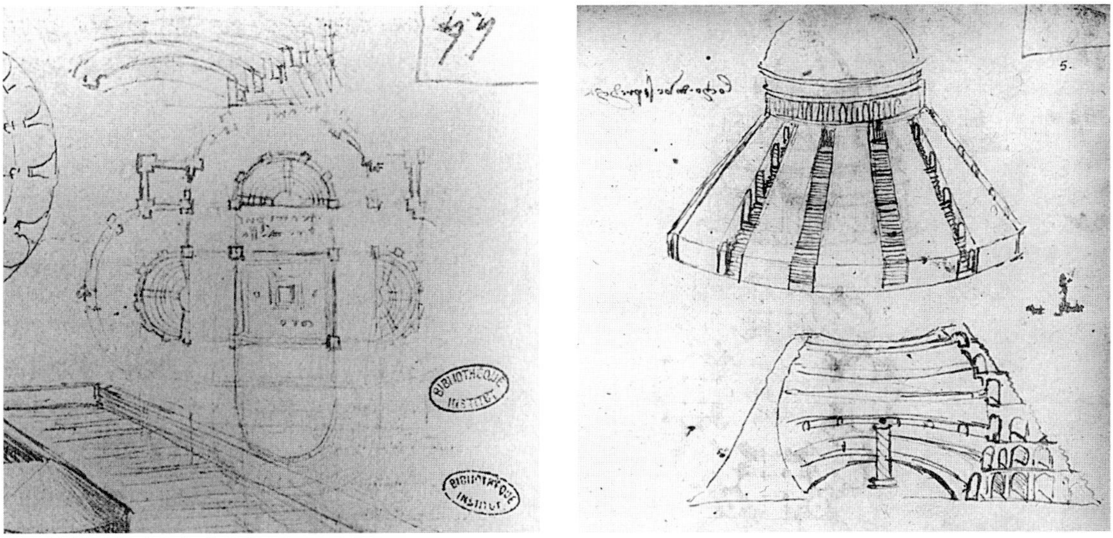

1. Acoustic designs by Leonardo da Vinci, pen and ink, *c.* 1488: (left) 'theatre for hearing mass', Cod. B, fol. 55*v*; (right) 'place for preaching', MS. B.N. 2037, fol. 5*v* (Paris, Institut de France)

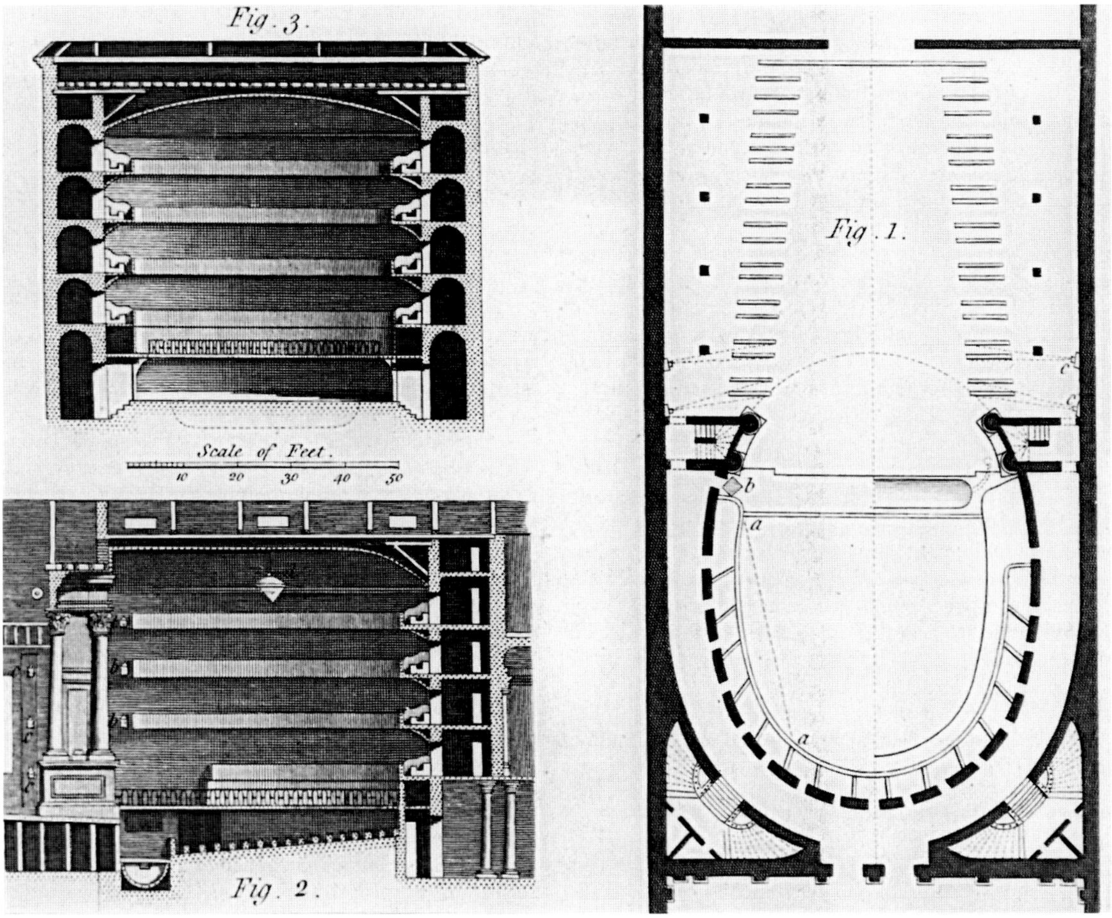

2. Acoustic theatre design of truncated elliptical plan by Pierre Patte, engraving, 1782; from George Saunders: *A Treatise on Theatres* (London, 1790)

Kent; and Hagios Mamas (17th century), Korakov, Cyprus. These were presumably intended for the opposite purpose, that of absorbing sound, like the modern Helmholtz resonator.)

Following the Renaissance revival of the Classical theatre, for example at Andrea Palladio's Teatro Olimpico (1580) at Vicenza, the enclosing colonnade around the auditorium gradually evolved into tiers of boxes, developing by the later 17th century into the Italian Baroque form of theatre (*see* THEATRE, §III, 2(i)(a) and 3(i)(a)). Although designed principally around social and theatrical rather than acoustical needs, such theatres proved acoustically suited to their purpose. The boxes around the walls, crowded with an audience in full costume, would have reduced the reverberation time, helping to provide the acoustical clarity necessary for revealing the detail of both the elaborate aria and *recitativo secco.* The ceiling and box fronts at the same time provided the sound-reflecting surfaces essential for tonal liveliness and strength. The interior surfaces were frequently lined with thin wood panelling, which absorbed the bass frequencies but reflected the middle and upper frequencies, further enhancing speech clarity. Contemporary writers, such as Fabrizio Carini Motta, Francesco Algarotti, Pierre Patte and George Saunders, stressed the importance of wood, though invariably stating wrongly that it acts as a resonator analogous to a musical instrument, rather than as a low-frequency sound-absorber.

(iii) Opera houses. The truncated ellipse was a common plan shape for opera houses, favoured on acoustical grounds by contemporary architectural theorists. Patte recommended concave surfaces in general, especially the double-focus ellipse, for 'concentrating' the sound (see fig. 2). He considered the ellipse especially appropriate for theatres, believing that speech propagates in ellipsoidal waves. (In reality convex, diffusing surfaces are preferable, and the relief surface decoration used in Baroque-style theatres and concert halls helps to achieve a diffuse, or evenly scattered, sound field.) The hallmark of theatres decorated by the Galli-Bibiena family was their bell- or trumpet-shaped plan, for example the Markgräfliches Opernhaus (1744–8), Bayreuth. This shape was also traditionally supposed to have been adopted for acoustic reasons, but unfortunately there is no surviving statement by the Galli-Bibienas on acoustics. Many 18th-century opera houses were designed with curious acoustic devices

to help amplify and project the orchestra's sound. In Italian theatres an airspace was often incorporated below the orchestra pit to help the wooden floor resonate, for example at the Teatro Regio (1738–40; destr.), Turin, designed by Benedetto Innocente Alfieri, while at the Teatro Nuovo in Parma the entire parterre was built over a great semi-elliptical masonry saucer connected with passages from the orchestra pit.

An important acoustical advantage of 18th-century theatres and playhouses was that with the projecting forestage the relationship of actor and audience was acoustically intimate. Advances in theatre lighting in the 19th century and the consequent exploitation of spectacular theatre, however, caused the actor to retreat behind the proscenium arch, which placed him, acoustically speaking, in a different space from the audience. At the Festspielhaus (1872–6), Bayreuth, Richard Wagner further distanced his performers by creating a sunken and hooded orchestra pit. Although intended for visual rather than acoustic reasons, the sound reaching the audience is entirely reflected, giving a mysterious distant quality. In the 20th century reaction away from the proscenium stage towards various forms of open stage, for example in the auditorium designed by Tanya Moiseiwitsch (*b* 1914) for the Shakespeare Festival Theater (1957) at Stratford, Ont., enabled a more intimate style of performance suited to the age of radio and television.

(iv) Rooms for speech. Several other building types require clear acoustics for speech, including parliament buildings, debating chambers, lecture and conference halls and courtrooms. Historically, acoustical considerations usually influenced their architectural form and layout, although, even in the present day, rooms with up to about 100 seats may be satisfactory for natural speech without the use of electronic sound reinforcement. The distance from the chairman to the farthest speaker should be minimal. Also, because sound is attenuated as it passes across successive rows of seats, audibility is improved when the seating is raked. The press galleries in such debating chambers as the House of Commons, Westminster, are often located high up to gain sound reflection from the walls and ceiling surfaces, while in churches the traditional canopy over the pulpit is useful for projecting the voice of the preacher. Before the invention of the electroacoustic public-address system, acoustical considerations occasionally resulted in elegantly expressive interior forms. For example, Le Corbusier's competition design (1926–7; unexecuted) for the Palace of the League of Nations, Geneva, contains a parabolic ceiling in the assembly hall for projecting speech from the stage, while Alvar Aalto's lecture hall at the Viipuri (now Vyborg) City Library, built in 1934–5 (destr. 1940–41), had an undulating, sound-reflective timber ceiling intended to diffuse sound as it travelled from either end of the hall, so that during debates audience members could be heard equally as well as speakers on the platform.

(v) Concert halls.

(a) Before the 20th century. Unlike theatres, only a few purpose-built concert halls were built before the mid-19th century (*see* CONCERT HALL). The earliest, such as the elliptical St Cecilia's Hall (1762), Edinburgh, designed by Robert Mylne the younger, the concert hall at the Hanover Square Rooms (1774–5), London, which were sponsored by Giovanni Andrea Battista Gallini (1728–1805), Johann Christian Bach (1735–82) and Carl Friedrich Abel (1723–87), and the Altes Gewandhaus (1794; destr. 1894), Leipzig, designed by Johann Friedrich Carl Dauthe (1749–1816), must have had clear, intimate acoustics on account of their small size; with a full audience crowded within, however, they would have been much less reverberant than is now regarded as optimal.

The numerous larger symphony halls that were built in the second half of the 19th century were based on the form of the palace ballroom, being rectangular in shape and roughly a double cube in volume. These (the Musikvereinsgebäude, 1867–9, Vienna, by Theophilus Hansen being the most celebrated) remain acoustically the most admired concert halls in the world. Their excellence is due to several factors. They are still relatively small, containing typically 1500–2000 seats within a floor area that, if replanned to present-day standards of safety and comfort, would accommodate about 1100. They are constructed of hard, dense materials (masonry, plaster or occasionally thick, closely fastened wood panels), which sustain strong, multiple reflections of sound from the enclosing surfaces. The tall, narrow shape encloses a large cubic volume relative to the sound-absorptive audience area, providing substantial reverberance. The parallel side walls ensure that strong, lateral sound reflections (from the junction of the wall with the balcony and ceiling soffits) are directed into the centre of the main floor. Their narrow width provides a short travel path for reflected sound, with a consequently small 'time delay gap' between the direct and early reflected sound, so that the reverberance is combined with a clear, strong sound in the hall.

(b) 20th century. These attributes were not understood at the time, and with the early 20th-century demand for greatly increased audience capacities, architects and acousticians sought principally to direct the sound efficiently towards the rear of the hall. (In reality, the rear seats are seldom problematic in this respect, even in very large halls.) Designs were modelled around graphic 'ray diagrams' of sound distribution, but the resulting flared profile ensured that the sound, directed into the seating area, is quickly absorbed by the audience. Music produced in such halls, most notoriously the Salle Pleyel (opened 1927), Paris, designed by Aubertin, Granel and Mathon, with Gustave Lyon, has a thin, directional quality.

The fan-shaped plan introduced at this time to accommodate ever-larger audiences caused reflected sound to be channelled along the side to the rear of the hall, leaving most of the main floor without the benefit of reflected sound. To compensate, the ceiling was lowered to become the principal sound-reflecting element, but the smaller cubic volume relative to the sound-absorptive area of audience renders such halls acoustically 'dead'. Music played in many 20th-century halls was further weakened because of the use of thin wood panelling, owing to the myth that the walls of a hall could be made to vibrate and strengthen (rather than in reality absorbing) low-frequency reflected sound.

The acoustics of numerous auditoria of the early- to mid-20th century, especially in North America, were also compromised by their intended use for both speech events and music, with the result that the halls were seldom acoustically optimal for either purpose. Several techniques for varying a hall's suitability for different types of performance have since been developed. Chamber music, for example, and music of the classical period require more intimate, less reverberant acoustics, and large-scale choral and symphonic music of the Romantic period may require near church-like acoustics. Motorized fabric banners may be introduced into a basically reverberant space, either to reduce the reverberation time, as at Roy Thomson Hall (1976–82), Toronto, by Arthur Erickson, or to reduce side wall reflections when used in conjunction with electronic sound amplification, for example at Pikes Peake Center (1980), Colorado Springs, CO, by Artec Consultants Inc. The reverberation time of an auditorium may be varied by altering the cubic volume, either by means of openable 'reverberation chambers', such as one used at the International Convention Centre Concert Hall (1991), Birmingham, by Percy Thomas Partnership and Artec Consultants Inc., or, less usually, a movable ceiling, for example at IRCAM (1977), Paris, by Piano and Rogers. The position of sound-reflective surfaces may be varied, by the use of a motorized suspended canopy, for example at the Royal Concert Hall (1982), Nottingham, by the Renton Howard Wood Levin Partnership. Alternatively, the impression of added sound reflections and increased reverberation time can be created electronically. Electronic 'assisted resonance' was developed in the 1960s as a remedial measure at London's Royal Festival Hall (1948–51), designed by Leslie Martin and Robert Matthew (1906–75), but it has since been applied by design at various halls, for example the Kremlin Palace of Congresses (1959–61), Moscow, designed by a team headed by Mikhail Posokhin and Ashot Mndoyants, and the Hult Center for the Performing Arts (1978–82), Eugene, OR, by Hardy Holzman Pfeiffer Associates.

The positioning of sound-reflective surfaces (as against the simple calculation of reverberation time) became especially important in Hans Scharoun's design for the Philharmonie (1956–63), Berlin (for illustration *see* SCHAROUN, HANS). With its centralized concert platform, the lack of sound-reflective side walls is overcome by stepping the seating into terraces, providing a successful mixture of sound-reflective and sound-absorptive surfaces. Studies made since the 1960s have provided a clearer understanding of the attributes of the traditional rectangular hall, in particular on the value of lateral sound reflection to the sensation of acoustic envelopment. This has been applied in, for example, Christchurch Town Hall (1972), New Zealand, by Warren and Mahoney; the National Theatre and Concert Hall (1987), Taipei, by Yang Chüeh-cheng; the Dr Anton Philips Concert Hall (1987), The Hague, by D. van Mourik; and the Eugene McDermott Concert Hall (1989) of the Morton H. Meyerson Symphony Center, Dallas, designed by I. M. Pei.

BIBLIOGRAPHY

Grove 6

F. Carini Motta: *Trattato sopra la struttura de' theatri e scene che a nostri tempi si costumano* (Guastalla, 1676/*R* Milan, 1972)

C. Wren: *Parentalia, or Memoirs of the Family of the Wrens: Viz. of Mathew Bishop of Ely, Christopher Dean of Windsor, etc, But Chiefly of Sir Christopher Wren, in which is Contained, besides his Works, a Great Number of Original Papers and Records* (London, 1750), p. 130

F. Algarotti: *Saggio sopra l'opera in musica* (Livorno, 1763; Eng. trans., London, 1917)

P. Patte: *Essai sur l'architecture théâtrale* (Paris, 1782); ed. C.-N. Cochin in *Projet d'une salle de spectacle pour un théâtre de comédie* (Geneva, 1974)

G. Saunders: *A Treatise on Theatres* (London, 1790/*R* 1968)

W. C. Sabine: *Collected Papers on Acoustics* (Cambridge, MA, 1924/*R* New York, 1964)

L. L. Beranek: *Music, Acoustics and Architecture* (New York, 1962/*R* Huntingdon, NY, 1979)

V. L. Jordan: *Acoustical Design of Concert Halls and Theatres: A Personal Account* (London, 1980)

L. Cremer and H. A. Muller: *Principles and Applications of Room Acoustics*, 2 vols (London and New York, 1982)

M. Forsyth: *Buildings for Music: The Architect, the Musician, and the Listener from the Seventeenth Century to the Present Day* (Cambridge, MA, 1985)

P. Lord and D. Templeton: *The Architecture of Sound* (London, 1986)

M. Forsyth: *Auditoria: Designing for the Performing Arts* (London, 1987)

MICHAEL FORSYTH

Acquarossa, painted roof-tile from a house, terracotta, 595×530 mm, 6th century BC (Viterbo, Museo Civico)

Acquarossa [It.: 'red water']. Modern name of an Etruscan settlement near Viterbo, Italy. It is situated on a small tufa plateau bounded on three sides by streams, one of which runs red. Excavations conducted by the Swedish Institute of Classical Studies during the 1960s and 1970s uncovered the tufa foundations of buildings that comprised various sectors of an ancient town. These provide some of the most extensive archaeological evidence relating to Etruscan domestic architecture and urban organization. The site was already inhabited in the 8th century BC and grew considerably during the following two centuries. Its main economic activity was apparently agriculture. Throughout its history the settlement had close links both with the coastal Etruscan cities and with those inland, in particular Tarquinia and Volsinii Veteres (Orvieto). It was permanently abandoned at the beginning of the 5th century BC, and the absence of any overlay of Roman or later material contributes to its archaeological importance.

Acquarossa does not display a regular overall plan, although in the area considered to have been the centre of political and social life the buildings seem to have been arranged according to a rational system. The remains of 6th-century BC houses reveal the use of several different standard plans, notably the 'broad house' type, which consists of two or three parallel rooms fronted by an elongated vestibule with a fireplace (*see* ETRUSCAN, fig. 8c); they show close similarities with some contemporary rock-cut tombs at Cerveteri (Caere). The final phase of a later, complex structure in Zone F may have been the religious or administrative centre of the settlement (*see* ETRUSCAN, fig. 8d). Its L-shaped plan shows two wings, each comprising several rooms and facing a colonnaded courtyard, apparently with both private and public areas. In addition to foundations, finds at Acquarossa include many architectural terracottas, some with white painted designs (see fig.). With the terracottas from Poggio Civitate (Murlo), they are among the earliest Etruscan examples of this kind of roof decoration in a domestic, rather than religious, context.

BIBLIOGRAPHY

E. Wetter, M. Moretti and C. E. Östenberg: *Med kungen på Acquarossa* [With the king at Acquarossa] (Malmö, 1972)

C. E. Östenberg: *Case etrusche di Acquarossa* (Rome, 1975)

MARCO RENDELI

Acquaviva d'Aragona, Andrea Matteo III, Duca d'Atri (*b* Conversano, Puglia, Jan 1458; *d* Conversano, 9 Jan 1529). Italian patron. He was the son of Giulio, Duca d'Atri (*d* 1481), and Caterina Orsini, Contessa di Conversano (Apulia), a cousin of Queen Isabella of Castile; in 1477 he married Isabella Piccolomini of Aragon (*d* 1504). His extensive territories included much of the Abruzzo and Apulia, and through his second marriage to Caterina della Ratta, Contessa di Caserta, he gained lands in Campania, Lucania and Calabria. Andrea Matteo led a tumultuous political and military career, alternately supporting the Aragonese and the Angevins and losing and regaining his lands several times. From 1505, however, he settled in Naples, devoting himself increasingly to cultural activities. He was one of the most important humanist princes in southern Italy, and a member of Giovanni Pontano's Neapolitan academy; Pontano (1422–1503) dedicated his *De magnanimitate* to the Duca, whom he saw as the incarnation of Renaissance man, while Paolo Giovio praised him as '*heros antiquae virtutis*'.

Andrea Matteo had a thorough knowledge of Greek literature, writing a commentary on Plutarch's *De virtute morali* (1526), which he published in his own press, installed in 1518–19. He also took an interest in astrology and music. His rich library (MSS in Vienna, Österreich. Nbib.; Naples, Bib. Girolamini, and various European and North American collections) must have possessed the most important Classical works. He collected manuscripts from his early youth and commissioned such illuminators as Cola Rapicano, CRISTOFORO MAJORANA, Gioacchino di Gigantibus de Rottenburg and REGINALDO PIRAMO DA MONOPOLI to decorate his books. He also employed illuminators from Ferrara and Siena, as well as some showing the influence of Antonello da Messina and Bramante. His manuscripts have complex iconographic schemes, revealing Andrea Matteo to have been a man of broad culture, and they also illustrate the evolution of taste during the period. The earliest examples, illuminated during the 1470s and 1480s, contain the popular white-scroll decoration. These are followed by books with classicizing architectural frontispieces in the Paduan style, while the later manuscripts bear elegant frames with grotesque decoration. In 1506–7 Andrea Matteo had a votive chapel built in Atri Cathedral, for which he commissioned panels of the *Nativity* and *Flagellation*. The artist, Pedro de Aponte, a Spaniard in the entourage of Ferdinand II, also illuminated a copy of Pliny for the Duca (Naples, Bib. Girolamini, MS. C FIII 6).

BIBLIOGRAPHY

DBI

A. Putaturo Murano: *Miniature napoletane del rinascimento* (Benevento, 1973)

M. Santoro: 'La cultura umanistica', *Storia di Napoli*, iv/2 (Naples, 1974), pp. 317–400

F. Bologna: *Napoli e le rotte mediterranee della cultura da Alfonso il Magnanimo a Ferdinando il Cattolico* (Naples, 1977), pp. 215–36

F. Tateo: *Chierici e feudatari del Mezzogiorno* (Bari, 1984)

E. Cassec: 'La miniatura italiana in Olanda: Risultati di ricerche nella collezione della Biblioteca dell'Università di Leida', *La miniatura italiana tra gotico e rinascimento. Atti del II congresso di storia della miniatura: Firenze, 1985*, pp. 155–74

P. Giusti and P. Leone de Castris: *'Forastieri e regnicoli': La pittura moderna a Napoli nel primo cinquecento* (Naples, 1985), pp. 103–4

A. Putaturo Murano, A. Perriccioli Saggese and A. Locci: 'Reginaldo Piramo da Monopoli e i miniatori attivi per Andrea III Acquaviva', *Monopoli nell'età del rinascimento. Atti del convegno internazionale di studio: Monopoli, 1985*, pp. 1102–68

GIOVANNA CASSESE

Acrocorinth. *See* CORINTH.

Acrolith [Gr.: 'high stone']. Ancient Greek statue with the limbs and head made of marble or stone and the body of wood, sometimes covered with a layer of gold.

□

Acropolis, Athenian. *See* ATHENS, §II, 1.

Acropolis 606, Painter of. *See* VASE PAINTERS, §II.

Acroterion. Decorative finial crowning the apex and lower angles of the pediments of ancient Greek and Roman buildings. Acroteria were normally made of terracotta, poros, limestone or marble, although bronze acroteria are mentioned in the literary sources: Pausanias (*Guide to Greece* V.x.4) noted gilded Victories framed by bronze cauldrons at the lower angles of the pediments of the Temple of Zeus at Olympia. The bronze Victories framing *Bellerophon and the Chimaera* on the Temple of Athena Nike on the Acropolis at Athens are recorded in inscriptions, and traces of their bases survive.

The stylistic development of acroteria begins in the 7th century BC. The earliest surviving examples are the frequently enormous terracotta discs that crowned Lakonian-tiled roofs, such as that from the Temple of Hera at Olympia (Archaeol. Mus.; *c.* 600 BC; *see* OLYMPIA, fig. 3). This type continued in the 6th century BC, and it was also sculpted in marble with relief decoration—rosettes, gorgoneia and gorgons—mainly in regions under Lakonian influence. Terracotta acroteria became highly decorative in the course of the 6th century, thanks to the potential of the more flexible Corinthian system of tiling and the advanced coroplastic tradition of the Corinthian workshops. The evolution of acroteria into increasingly sophisticated compositions based on floral, animal and mythological themes and the development of great plasticity and spectacular polychromy are recorded in a series of fragmentary examples from Greece, Magna Graecia and Sicily. Floral elements appear quite early on in variations of the palmette motif and predominate as central acroteria even after the establishment of marble as the standard sculptural material. Hybrid figures of fantastic beasts, such as sphinxes and griffins, were popular as lateral acroteria, initially in terracotta and later in marble; these did not persist after the 6th century BC, however, except in certain 4th-century BC funerary reliefs, which included depictions of Sirens and birds. Acroteria with mythological themes that included groups of figures usually crowned small buildings and expressed the same anthropocentric spirit as that found in the pedimental compositions.

Terracotta acroteria continued to be produced until the end of the 5th century BC, although because of the fragility of the clay, complete groups have not survived. Thus the central subject framed by the fragmentary sphinxes at the lower pedimental angles on the Temple of Artemis Laphria at Kalydon (*c.* 580–570 BC) remains elusive. Nevertheless, it is possible in many instances to form a very general picture of the impressive acroteria of the Archaic and Classical periods (*c.* 750–323 BC). At Olympia, for example, the central group of *Silenus Attacking a Maenad* is framed by fleeing Maenads (*c.* 530 BC), and the central acroterion showing *Athena Fighting a Giant* is framed by Victories (*c.* 490 BC). Later examples include the group of *Zeus Abducting Ganymede* (Olympia, Archaeol. Mus.; *c.* 480–470 BC; *see* OLYMPIA, §2(ii) and fig. 6), although there is no evidence for the framing acroteria. Also unknown are the lateral acroteria that complemented the central compositions of *Theseus with Skiron* and the *Abduction of Kephalus by Eos* on the Stoa Basileios in the Athenian Agora (Pausanius, *Guide to Greece* I.iii.1), of which only sparse fragments have been recovered.

Marble acroteria, which began replacing terracotta ones from the 6th century BC, are better preserved. This does not mean, however, that the reconstruction of complete compositions is always possible. It is certain that the Siphnian Treasury at Delphi (*c.* 525 BC) was crowned by flying Victories framed by sphinxes in the lower angles, as was the Alkmaionid Temple of Apollo (*c.* 520 BC). On the other hand, the context of the Victories associated with the Giantomachy pediment on the Athenian Acropolis is still uncertain, as is that of the remnants of a battle scene that surmounted the Amazonomachy pediment on the Temple of Apollo Daphnephoros at Eretria (*c.* 500–490 BC).

The central acroteria above both pediments on the Temple of Aphaia on Aigina (*c.* 500–*c.* 490 BC) were large floral compositions with palmettes and lyre-shaped volute motifs, flanked heraldically by two female figures; the acroteria in the lower angles were sphinxes. An evolved version of this scheme appeared on the Temple of Poseidon at Sounion towards the middle of the 5th century BC, where a single anthemion dominated the apex, framed by two probably female figures as lower-angle acroteria. Compositions with central anthemion elements framed by, as a rule, female figures at the lower angles crowned both the Parthenon at Athens and the Temple of Hera at Argos, as well as the Temple of Athena Alea at Tegea, the Temple of Artemis at Epidauros and Temple of the Sanctuary at Samothrace.

In the Ionic temple at Lokroi Epizephyrioi in southern Italy (last quarter of the 5th century BC) the central floral acroterion evidently enveloped a female figure in its tendrils, while the lateral acroteria depicted the Dioskuroi slipping on to the backs of their horses, supported on Tritons. The precursors of these are the early 5th-century BC mounted Amazons that crowned the Athenian Treasury at Delphi (*c.* 490 BC). Other elaborate groups appear as lateral acroteria in the closing years of the 5th century BC: *Nereids Riding Dolphins* on the Athenian Temple of Ares, *Nereids Riding Whales* (from Formia, *c.* 400 BC) and the equestrian female figures on the west pediment of the Temple of Asklepios at Epidauros (first quarter of the 4th century BC; *see* EPIDAUROS, fig. 2). In the last case the central element of the composition represented an abduction. There are also depictions of abductions framed by running female figures, such as the representations of *Boreas and Orithyia* and of *Eos and Kephalos*, which surmounted the Temple of the Athenians on Delos (*c.* 425–420 BC), or the two comparable representations on the Nereid Monument from Xanthos (London, BM; *c.* 400 BC; for illustration *see* XANTHOS).

Acroterial figures that are frequently thought to personify forces of nature probably represent specific mythological figures whose identity may be deciphered only when evidence of the representations they frame (undoubtedly mythological) is brought to light. Nevertheless, it is reasonably certain that a more or less direct thematic correspondence between the compositions of the acroteria and those of the pediments always existed. It is virtually impossible to distinguish acroterial sculptures from pedimental figures, except that the former tend to be larger.

Floral acroteria, often in impressively elaborate compositions, also crowned funerary monuments in the 4th century BC, although from Hellenistic times (331–23 BC) onwards these gradually degenerated into conventional ornaments. The Temple of Artemis Leukophryene at Magnesia on the Maeander (2nd century BC), as well as that of Despoina at Arcadian Lykosoura (2nd century BC), had tripartite compositions in which both the lateral and apex elements were floral, a pattern that dominated the architecture of the Roman period.

BIBLIOGRAPHY

H. Gropengiesser: *Die pflanzlichen Akrotere klassischer Tempel* (Mainz, 1961)

A. Delivorrias: *Attische Giebelskulpturen und Akrotere des 5. Jhs. v. Chr.* (diss., U. Tübingen, 1974)

M. Y. Goldberg: *Types and Distribution of Archaic Greek Akroteria* (diss., Bryn Mawr Coll., PA, 1977; microfilm, Ann Arbor, 1980)

A. Gulaki: *Klassische und klassizistische Nikedarstellungen: Untersuchungen zur Typologie und Bedeutungswandel* (diss., U. Bonn, 1981)

P. Danner: 'Westgriechische Akrotere', *Röm. Hist. Mitt.*, xxx (1988), pp. 17–40

——: 'Griechische Akrotere der archaischen und klassischen Zeit', *Riv. A.* (1989) [suppl. 5]

A. DELIVORRIAS

Acrylic painting. Although 'acrylic' has become a generic term for any synthetic paint medium, acrylics are a specific type of manmade polymer that has become standard in the commercial paint industry as well as widely used by artists from the mid-20th century; most synthetic paint media in contemporary artistic use are based on acrylic emulsions. Acrylics are thermoplastic, have great optical clarity and excellent light stability, good adhesion and elasticity and resist ultraviolet and chemical degradation. Their unique surface properties, transparency and brilliance of colour, together with the possibilities they offer for indeterminacy, immediacy, randomness and the ability to rework immediately and to achieve extremely thin or thick surfaces, are qualities that have been exploited fully by such painting movements as Abstract Expressionism in the 1950s, and, subsequently, colour field painting, hard-edge painting and Pop art.

See also PAINT, §§I and II; POLYMER COLOUR; and PLASTIC, §2(ii).

1. HISTORY AND USES. Acrylics were first prepared in 1880 as acrylate by Otto Rohm. He patented it in 1915, and its suggested use was as a substitute for drying oils in industrial paints and lacquers. Polymethyl methacrylate, a rigid form of acrylic, was first marketed in Germany in 1927, but large-scale production of it in the form of Plexiglass (Perspex) began in 1936 in the USA, where acryloid—an acrylic resin surface coating—was first marketed in 1931. Thus the early development of acrylics was for industrial purposes. In the 1920s, however, the Mexican muralists experimented with synthetic media developed for industrial use, including pyroxylin (nitro-cellulose) automobile lacquers and ethyl silicate (an organic/silicon compound) when looking for a durable material for outdoor use (*see* WALL PAINTING, §I). In 1936 David Alfaro Siqueiros held an experimental workshop in New York City, where artists, among them Jackson Pollock, experimented with the latest synthetics and paints, trying new methods of application such as spray-guns. Subsequently Siqueiros used pyroxylin for *Echo of a Scream* (1937; New York, MOMA; *see* SIQUEIROS, DAVID ALFARO, fig. 1) and for *Portrait of the Bourgeoisie* (1939; *see* SIQUEIROS, DAVID ALFARO, fig. 2) in the stairwell of the Electricians' Union Building in Mexico City; and from the late 1940s Jackson Pollock used a pyroxylin lacquer tradenamed Duco in many of his works (e.g. *Number 2, 1949*; Utica, NY, Munson–Williams–Proctor Inst.; *see* ABSTRACT EXPRESSIONISM, fig. 1). The disadvantage of Duco and lacquer-based paints, however, is their toxic solvent base which may be damaging to the artist's health.

The alkyd resins (a type of polyester) were discovered in 1902 and marketed as Glyptal from 1926. Many WPA artists experimented with alkyd-based paints in the 1930s. (In the late 20th century they have been used to manufacture artists' paints that have faster drying properties and a higher gloss than oil paints; *see* PAINT, §I). In 1946 Bocour Artists Colours Inc. first marketed Magna, an oil-like painting medium comprising acrylic resin (n-butyl methacrylate) dissolved in an organic solvent, which could be thinned with turpentine or mineral spirits and combined with oil paints. Magna colours were used in the 1950s by Morris Louis, Helen Frankenthaler and later by Roy Lichtenstein (e.g. *Whaam!*, 1963; London, Tate; see fig.). They were also used extensively by Mark Rothko, who employed them to originate a form of colour field painting that strongly resembled the effect of watercolour stain.

After World War II the vinyl polymers—polyvinyl acetate (PVA) and polyvinyl chloride (PVC)—superseded the alkyd-based paints in industrial use but were never widely used by artists. Acrylics and vinyls were developed simultaneously, but the former superseded the latter because of their extensive handling and colour properties. There was a major breakthrough in the 1950s with the introduction of aqueous emulsion acrylics or latex paints. In 1953 Rohm and Haas Co. introduced Rhoplex, the first acrylic emulsion specially designed for paint. Rhoplex

Roy Lichtenstein: *Whaam!*, acrylic on canvas, 1.73×4.06 m, 1963 (London, Tate Gallery)

resists aging, is exceptionally fast drying and has good adhesion and intermixing properties, including a tolerance for a wide variety of pigments; it is also alkaline, non-yellowing and resistant to ultraviolet and most mild acids. It has become the base for all contemporary artists' acrylic emulsions and was instrumental in the development of HARD-EDGE PAINTING, COLOUR FIELD PAINTING and stain painting. Notable exponents of acrylic painting in the USA include Helen Frankenthaler (e.g. *Cape (Provincetown),* 1964; Melbourne, N.G. Victoria; *see* UNITED STATES OF AMERICA, fig. 18), Kenneth Noland (e.g. *Trans West*, 1965; Amsterdam, Stedel. Mus.; for illustration *see* NOLAND, KENNETH), Morris Louis (*see* LOUIS, MORRIS and fig.), Sam Francis, Jules Olitski, who used a spray-gun to create subtle variations of colour, and Larry Poons, who at first used acrylics to produce dot Op art paintings and later poured layers of acrylic into one another to create a heavy, craggy surface.

Acrylic painting was an integral part of Pop art, where its adhesive qualities and brilliant colour were exploited in such collage paintings as Peter Blake's *Got a Girl* (1960–61; Manchester, Whitworth A.G.; for illustration *see* BLAKE, PETER). By the mid-1970s there had been a thorough investigation of acrylic painting media, in particular thickeners, gels, dispersants (to ensure uniform pigment dispersion), wetting agents and preservatives to prevent bacterial contamination through water or other additives (*see* PAINTING MEDIUM). Acrylic paint could be used in a wider variety of techniques than oil paint and with much more primitive tools, for example brooms and razors, as it tends to retain the integrity of the colour with manipulation. Such techniques as pouring, splashing, blowing and adding other materials to the paint made the entire painting process more fluid and accelerated painterly experimentation from the mid-1970s. In the late 1970s and early 1980s fluorescent colours (Day-glo paints) became popular but proved ephemeral as the dyes fade in a few years. They were used by Frank Stella in such paintings as *Darajerd III* (1967; Washington, DC, Hirshhorn). More recently, painters such as Paula Rego have abandoned oil in favour of acrylic, partly because of its quick drying properties but also because of an aversion to the smell of turpentine.

2. PROPERTIES. The properties of acrylic paints include durability, good flexibility and brushing properties, and a range of transparent to opaque covering qualities. The advantages include ease of use, quick drying time, easy mixture with other media and with elements to create body and texture (e.g. sand, plaster, twigs, diatomaceous earth, glitter, modelling paste and spackling paste). Their good adhesive qualities allow the medium to be used as a glue in collage and permit much more flexibility than the brittle surface of an oil painting. They can be thinned with water or with an acrylic base painting medium such as gloss, matt, or gel, without becoming granulated. In hard-edge, colour field and stain painting, acrylic paint (unlike oil paint) produces no halo and is therefore ideal for the fresh watercolour effect and matt surface of these styles. Alternatively, acrylic may be thickened with additives to make a 'stiffer' paint that can be used to imitate oil techniques. Other advantages include easy cleaning (soap and water as opposed to thinner and soap and water with oils) and the absence of hazardous (or simply unpleasant) fumes. Large amounts of acrylic mixed colour may be combined with water, or medium or texture, and stored in a tightly closed container for long periods of time for later use.

Acrylics can be used with wax or oil crayons in a resist technique or mixed with chalk, which will partially resist and partially blend with the acrylic, causing unpredictable results, a combination used in situations where the artist wishes to work with little control of the medium for 'fresh' results. These methods are too new to permit proper assessment for longevity and colourfastness by conservators, however, and for conservation purposes the artist should employ only the family of acrylic paints and gels developed for artists' use; it is also helpful if all the materials used, along with brand names, are recorded on the reverse of the support. Although conservators discourage the use of oil over an acrylic underpainting as a more rapid way of building a painting, suggesting that mixtures of oils and acrylics are probably not permanent, many artists do use acrylic in combination with oils for underpainting (*see* GROUND). Acrylic paint can be glazed over with oils, allowing the saturated acrylic colour to 'glow' through. This method has been employed by photorealist artists such as Richard Estes and Audrey Flack. As acrylic paint is easily soluble in relatively weak solvents, acrylic paintings should not be varnished with a traditional varnish; even 'Soluvar' varnish, formulated specifically to address this problem, is not safe in all cases. Acrylic is useful in multimedia art objects such as painted sculpture, ceramics or wood because, if a medium other than water is used, acrylic paint does not sink into the material or damage it as oil would.

Acrylics can be used with multiple supports of varying texture as they are not abrasive or deleterious to either raw canvas or paper. Rigid supports, such as masonite, can be used and are preferable for thickly applied paint or a heavily laden mixed-media work. The high flexibility of acrylics makes them particularly suitable for use on fabrics, as the fabric can be stretched and pulled without cracking the paint; it also enables their use with heavy texturizing elements and allows scraping, scratching and modelling into the surface.

BIBLIOGRAPHY

H. T. Neher: 'Acrylic Resins', *Indust. & Engin. Chem.*, xxviii (1936), pp. 267–71

'Methacrylate Resins', *Indust. & Engin. Chem.*, xxviii (1936), pp. 1160–63

R. L. Wakeman: *The Chemistry of Commercial Plastics* (New York, 1947)

G. Allyn: *Basic Concepts of Acrylic Resin Emulsion Technology* (Philadelphia, 1956)

A. Duca: *Polymer Tempera Handbook* (Somerville, MA, 1956)

J. Gutierrez: *From Fresco to Plastics, New Materials for Easel and Mural Painting* (Ottawa, 1956)

B. Chaet: *Artists at Work* (New York, 1960)

A. M. Reed: *The Mexican Muralists* (New York, 1960)

Amer. Artist (1962–77) [technical page]

J. Charlot: *The Mexican Mural Renaissance, 1920–25* (New Haven, 1963)

L. N. Jensen: *Synthetic Painting Media* (Englewood Cliffs, NJ, 1964)

C. R. Martens: *Emulsions and Water-soluble Paints and Coatings* (New York, 1964)

J. Gutierrez and N. Roukes: *Painting with Acrylics* (New York, 1965)

R. O. Woody: *Painting with Synthetic Media* (1965)

J. A. Brydson: *Plastics Materials* (London and New Jersey, 1966/*R* London, 1975)

R. J. Gettens and G. L. Stout: *Painting Materials* (Dover, 1966)

A. Rodriguez: *A History of Mexican Mural Painting* (London, 1969)
R. Mayer: *The Artists' Handbook* (New York, 1970)
R. O. Woody: *Polymer Painting* (New York, *c.* 1970)
R. Kay: *The Painter's Guide to Studio Methods and Materials* (New York, 1972)
C. R. Martens: *Technology of Paints, Varnishes and Lacquers* (New York, 1974)
B. Chaet: *An Artist's Notebook: Materials and Techniques* (London and New Jersey, 1979)
R. Mayer: 'The Alkyd Generation', *Amer. Artist* (1979)

CARMEN BRIA, CELIA RABINOVITCH, with MICHAEL SICKLER

Action painting. Term applied to the work of American Abstract Expressionists such as Jackson Pollock and Willem de Kooning and, by extension, to the art of their followers at home and abroad during the 1950s. An alternative but slightly more general term is gestural painting; the other division within ABSTRACT EXPRESSIONISM was colour field painting.

The critic Harold Rosenberg defined action painting in an article, 'The American Action Painters' (1952), where he wrote: 'At a certain moment the canvas began to appear to one American painter after another as an arena in which to act. . . . What was to go on canvas was not a picture but an event'. This proposition drew heavily, and perhaps crudely, upon ideas then current in intellectual circles, especially in the wake of Jean-Paul Sartre's essay *L'Existentialisme est un humanisme* (Paris, 1946; Eng. trans., 1948), which claimed that 'there is no reality except in action'. In the 1940s Herbert Ferber, Barnett Newman and others had already characterized their creative process in similar terms; Rosenberg was probably also inspired by photographs of Pollock at work (rather than the actual paintings) that emphasized his apparent psychological freedom and physical engagement with materials. 'Action painting' became a common critical term to describe styles marked by impulsive brushwork, visible pentiments and unstable or energetic composition (for illustration *see* ABSTRACT EXPRESSIONISM, fig. 1), which seemed to express the state of consciousness held by the artist in the heat of creation. Action painting thereby shared the spontaneity of Automatism. Although this implicit, direct synthesis of art and consciousness is questionable, the spontaneous methods associated with the concept were paralleled in European movements such as TACHISM and ART INFORMEL.

BIBLIOGRAPHY

H. Rosenberg: 'The American Action Painters', *ARTnews*, li/8 (1952), pp. 22–3, 48–50
——: 'The Concept of Action in Painting', *New Yorker*, xliv (25 May 1968), pp. 116–28
F. Orton: 'Action, Revolution and Painting', *Oxford A. J.*, xiv/2 (1991), pp. 3–17
For further bibliography *see* ABSTRACT EXPRESSIONISM.

DAVID ANFAM

Activists [Hung. Aktivizmus]. Hungarian artistic, literary and political group that emerged *c.* 1914, after the disintegration of the group THE EIGHT (iii) in 1912. Though not a cohesive group, the Activists were stylistically united by their reaction to the predominantly Post-Impressionist aesthetic of the Eight. Instead they turned for inspiration to Cubism, Expressionism, Futurism, Dada and Constructivism, and although some of these had previously influenced the Eight, the Activists made most consistent and profound use of these modern movements. The most notable Activists were Sándor Bortnyik, Péter Dobrović (*b* 1890), János Kmetty, János Máttis Teutsch, László Moholy-Nagy, Jószef Nemes Lampérth, Lajos Tihanyi and Béla Uitz, of whom only Tihanyi had previously been a member of the Eight. Many Activists were at some time members of the MA GROUP, which revolved around the writer and artist Lajos Kassák, the main theoretical, and later artistic, driving force behind Hungarian Activism.

Both artistically and politically the Activists were more radical and international than the Eight, a reflection of both the turbulent atmosphere caused by World War I and the revolutionary fervour within Hungary itself. The Activists saw themselves as giving a voice to the working classes and, like the Eight, as agitators for a Utopian, Socialist society. Unlike the members of the Eight, however, many of the Activists were of working-class origin, and while not intellectuals themselves, they received many of their ideas from the Galilei Circle of young Hungarian intellectuals, which organized debates and lectures in Budapest. One of the earliest artistic stimuli on the Activists was the exhibition of Expressionist and Futurist art in the Nemzeti Szalon (National Salon) in Budapest at the beginning of 1913. This show had previously been in Berlin and included work by the Expressionists Oskar Kokoschka, Alexei Jawlenski and Ludwig Meidner, as well as Futurist works by Umberto Boccioni, Carlo Carrà, Luigi Russolo and Gino Severini. This affected both the style and aesthetic of the Activists and, in place of the Eight's call for order and harmony, they posited the tortured, emotional disorder of Expressionism.

On 1 November 1915 the first issue of Kassák's periodical *A tett* ('The deed') appeared in Budapest, modelled on Franz Pfemfert's *Die Aktion*. *A tett* included works by Uitz and Dobrović among others, and in such works as Dobrović's linocut *The Lamentation* (1915; see Szabó, 1971, pl. 13) the rough angularity, medium and subject-matter reveal the debt to German Expressionism. The same influence in painting can be found in such works by Tihanyi as the portrait of *Lajos Kassák* (1918; see 1973 exh. cat., pl. 168). *A tett* also had a strong social message and, as its name suggests, called for individual action as a means of broad social change. This attitude contrasted with the passive nostalgia that marked *Nyugat*, the formerly radical literary forum of the Eight. The subversive, outspoken tone of *A tett* ensured the confiscation of several editions by the authorities; it was banned after 17 issues, on 20 September 1916, accused of publishing 'propaganda hostile to the nation'. Soon after this, Kassák founded the journal *MA* ('Today'), which became the central forum and organizing body for most of the Activists even after its move to Vienna in 1920.

In April 1916 and again in June 1917 a group of Activists called the Fiatalok ('The young'), including Dobrović, Kmetty, Nemes Lampérth and Uitz, exhibited in the Nemzeti Szalon in Budapest. The catalogue for the second exhibition stated that, while starting from Cubism, they aimed at a 'great monumental art of the 20th century'. Nemes Lampérth, for example, was at this time painting highly coloured, near abstract works such as *Landscape* (1917; Pécs, Pannonius Mus.), which, while using Fauvist colour, showed a Cubist-influenced composition from flat planes. During the brief Communist regime of Béla Kun in 1919, the Activists assumed a central role in the country's culture, in particular as teachers of art: Uitz, for example, was made head of the Proletarian Fine Arts workshop. They also produced posters to propagate government messages, as in Uitz's *Red Soldiers, Forward!* (1919; Budapest, N.G.), designed to rouse the army in defence of the unstable Communist regime. On 25 March 1919 some Activists signed a manifesto calling for the establishment of a mass Communist culture. Following the fall of the Kun government, the aesthetic of the Activists began to be subsumed under the Constructivist aesthetic of *MA*, by then exiled in Vienna. Uitz, for example, visited Moscow in 1921 and after leaving the MA group, in autumn 1922 founded, with Aladár Komját, the journal *Egység* ('Unity'), which published Naum Gabo and Antoine Pevsner's *Realistic Manifesto* and other important documents on avant-garde Soviet art.

BIBLIOGRAPHY
L. Neméth: *Modern Art in Hungary* (Budapest, 1969)
J. Szabó: *A magyar Aktivizmus története* [History of Hungarian Activism] (Budapest, 1971) [with Fr. summary]
Magyar Aktivizmus (exh. cat. by J. Szabó, Pécs, Pannonius Mus., 1973)
K. Passuth: *Magyar művészek az európai avantgarde-ban, 1919–1925* [Hungarian artists in the European avant-garde, 1919–25] (Budapest, 1974)
The Hungarian Avant Garde: The Eight and the Activists (exh. cat. by J. Szabó and others, London, Hayward Gal., 1980)
J. Szabó: *A magyar Aktivizmus művészete, 1915–1927* [Hungarian Activist art] (Budapest, 1981)
S. A. Mansbach: 'Revolutionary Events, Revolutionary Artists: The Hungarian Avant-Garde until 1920', *'Event' Arts and Art Events*, ed. S. C. Foster (Ann Arbor, 1988), pp. 31–60

□

Acudoğu [Acudoğlu], **Ratip Aşir** (*b* Istanbul, 1898; *d* Istanbul, 1957). Turkish sculptor. After military service in World War I he went in 1918 to the Fine Arts Academy in Istanbul, where he studied under the sculptor Ihsan Özsoy (1867–1944). With the help of his father he then went to Germany, where he studied at the Akademie der Bildenden Künste in Munich. From Munich he went to Paris, where, after failing to get lessons from Aristide Maillol, he worked independently, inspired by the work of Maillol and Emile-Antoine Bourdelle. After returning to Turkey in 1925 and passing an examination he was able to go back to Paris, where he entered the Académie Julian and worked under the sculptors Henri Bouchard (1875–1960) and Paul Landowski (1875–1961). He returned to Turkey in 1928 and worked first as an art teacher at Edirne Teachers' College and then at various middle schools in Istanbul until his death. His principal works included the monument in Menemen to *Mustafa Fehmi Kubilây*, a young officer who was shot in the city in 1930 while ordering crowds to disperse; the monument to *Ismet Inönü* in Erzincan; and the monument to *Atatürk* at the Faculty of Agriculture in Ankara. He also worked on portrait busts, that of *Fahriye Yen* (Istanbul, Mimar Sinan U., Mus. Ptg & Sculp) being particularly successful.

BIBLIOGRAPHY
S. Tansuğ: *Çağdaş Türk sanatı* [Contemporary Turkish art] (Istanbul, 1986)

□

Adalbertus. *See* TYLKOWSKI, WOJCIECH.

Adam (i). French family of sculptors. Originally from Lorraine, the earliest known members of the family to be involved with the arts were Sigisbert Adam, a sculptor, and Lambert Adam, a metal-founder (both *fl* late 17th century). Lambert's son (1) Jacob-Sigisbert Adam spent most of his working life in Nancy, where he undertook the early training of his sons (2) Lambert-Sigisbert Adam, (3) Nicolas-Sébastien Adam and (4) François-Gaspard-Balthazar Adam. His daughter Anne married Thomas Michel (*d* before 15 May 1751), a sculptor from Metz; among their children were the sculptors Sigisbert-François Michel (1727–after 1785) and Claude Michel (known as CLODION). The three Adam brothers went to Rome at the start of their careers, Lambert-Sigisbert and Nicolas-Sébastien returning to France to work on the outdoor sculpture at Versailles, among other projects, and François-Gaspard-Balthazar going on to Sanssouci, Potsdam.

(1) Jacob-Sigisbert Adam (*b* Nancy, 28 Oct 1670; *d* Nancy, 6 May 1747). He is said to have been a pupil of César Bagard. He worked for Leopold, Duke of Lorraine, both on the decorative sculpture at the Palais Ducal at Nancy and at the château of Lunéville, and his small bronzes and terracottas were much admired by contemporary collectors. Typical of his small-scale work are the terracotta statuettes of *Bacchus* and *Jupiter* (Nancy, Mus. B.-A.). They are attractive but without marked character.

(2) Lambert-Sigisbert Adam [Adam *l'aîné*] (*b* Nancy, 10 Oct 1700; *d* Paris, 12 May 1759). Son of (1) Jacob-Sigisbert Adam. He was a pupil of his father and finished his training in the Paris workshop of François Dumont. In 1723 he won the Prix de Rome. During his period in Rome, at the Académie de France, he was patronized by the influential Cardinal Melchior de Polignac, the French Ambassador to the Holy See, for whom he restored and copied antique sculpture. He contributed a relief of the *Virgin Appearing to St Andrew Corsini* to Clement XII's Corsini Chapel at S Giovanni in Laterano (marble, *c.* 1732; *in situ*) and became a member of the Accademia di S Luca, presenting a bust of *Sorrow* (marble, 1732; *in situ*). He also entered the competition for the Trevi Fountain, but although his elaborate Baroque design (1731) was selected as the winner, Clement XII eventually commissioned the fountain from Nicola Salvi. After his return to Paris in 1733, Adam produced reclining statues personifying *The Seine* and *The Marne* rivers for the cascade at Saint-Cloud (1733–4; *in situ*). In 1737 he was received (*reçu*) as a member of the Académie Royale de Peinture et de Sculpture in Paris on presentation of the marble group *Neptune Calming the Waves* (1737; Paris, Louvre), sculpted in the manner of Bernini. In collaboration with his brother Nicolas-Sébastien he created the vast and riotous lead group the *Triumph of Neptune and Amphitrite* for the Bassin de Neptune in the park at Versailles (1735–40; *in situ*; see fig.); this is considered the most flamboyant Baroque sculpture to have been executed in 18th-century France, and it represents an eloquent testimony to Lambert-Sigisbert Adam's interest in the art of Bernini.

In spite of difficulties caused by his rebarbative personality, Adam's official career was brilliant and productive.

In 1752 his large groups representing *Fishing* and *Hunting* (marble; Potsdam, Schloss Sanssouci) were given by Louis XV to Frederick II of Prussia; he received many other state commissions, including those for statues of *Plenty* for the Château de Choisy, Val-de-Marne (now priv. col.), *Lyric Poetry* for Mme de Pompadour's château at Bellevue (marble, 1752; now Paris, Louvre) and *St Jerome* for the Dôme des Invalides, Paris (marble, 1752; now Paris, St Roch). Among his works for private clients were busts of *Neptune* and *Amphitrite* (marble, 1724; Berlin, Schloss Charlottenburg) for Cardinal de Polignac, and bas-reliefs at the Hôtel de Soubise, Paris (1735–6; *in situ*) for the Rohan family. He also produced some portrait busts (most destr.) and groups with light-hearted themes, including *Child with its Hand Gripped by a Lobster* (plaster, exh. Salon 1740; bronze reductions, Detroit, MI, Inst. A., and London, V&A).

In his attempt to introduce the pathos of Italian Baroque art into French sculpture in the 18th century, Adam became an increasingly isolated figure, clinging to the style of his youth and already criticized in his lifetime for the rhetorical extravagance of his work. Nevertheless, much of his sculpture demonstrates his virtuosity as a marble carver. He exercised an influence not only over his two younger brothers, Nicolas-Sébastien and François-Gaspard-Balthazar, but also over his nephews Sigisbert-François Michel and Clodion.

(3) Nicolas-Sébastien Adam (*b* Nancy, 22 March 1705; *d* Paris, 27 March 1778). Son of (1) Jacob-Sigisbert Adam. He was trained by his father and then joined his eldest brother (2) Lambert-Sigisbert in Paris. Failing to win the Prix de Rome, he travelled to Italy at his own expense, working on the way in the Château de La Mosson, near Montpellier, and arriving in Rome in 1726. There he was introduced by Lambert-Sigisbert to Cardinal Melchior de Polignac, for whom he restored a number of antique marbles. He returned to Paris in 1734 and pursued what was to be a busy career. Although he was not received (*reçu*) as a member of the Académie Royale de Peinture et de Sculpture in Paris until 1762, his reception piece, a marble statue of *Prometheus* (Paris, Louvre), is one of the best of the century. He collaborated with Lambert-Sigisbert on the flamboyant lead group of the *Triumph of Neptune and Amphitrite* for the Bassin de Neptune in the park at Versailles (1735–40; *in situ*; see fig.) and also worked for the Rohan family at the Hôtel de Soubise, Paris, executing bas-reliefs of the *Loves of the Gods* (1736) in the Salon de la Princesse. He was employed by the Bâtiments du Roi at the Chambre des Comptes in Paris, at the abbey of St Denis and at Versailles, where he produced a bronze relief of the *Martyrdom of Ste Victoire* for the chapel (1747; *in situ*). Among his other works were a marble vase with the attributes of *Autumn* for the park at the Château de Choisy, Val-de-Marne (1745; now New York, Met.); a statue of *Iris Attaching her Wings* (marble, 1775–6; Versailles, Château), finished after his death by his nephew Clodion; *Religion Welcoming a Convert* (plaster, 1745; Paris, St Paul-St-Louis); and bas-reliefs of the *History of Apollo* for the Hôtel de la Boexière, Paris (*c.* 1753; now Paris, Château de Bagatelle). However, his most accomplished work is the funerary monument to

Lambert-Sigisbert Adam and Nicolas-Sébastien Adam: *Triumph of Neptune and Amphitrite*, lead group for the Bassin de Neptune, château of Versailles, 1735–40

Catharina Opalinska, wife of Stanislav I Leszczyński, Grand Duke of Lorraine (coloured and white marbles and bronze, 1749; Nancy, Notre-Dame-de-Bon-Secours). This white marble group shows the deceased being guided heavenwards by an angel silhouetted against a pyramid of dark marble; executed with great technical refinement, it is considered one of the finest and most genuinely pathetic French funerary monuments of the 18th century. The art of Nicolas-Sébastien, though equally influenced by the Roman Baroque and just as versatile and polished, is more delicate and subtle than that of Lambert-Sigisbert. It was to have a marked influence on the work of Clodion.

(4) François-Gaspard-Balthazar Adam (*b* Nancy, 23 May 1710; *d* Paris, 18 Aug 1761). Son of (1) Jacob-Sigisbert Adam. He was a pupil of his father and followed his brothers (2) Lambert-Sigisbert and (3) Nicolas-Sébastien to Rome in 1730, later establishing himself in Paris. In 1740 he won second place in the Prix de Rome competition and returned to Rome in 1742, to the Académie de France. From 1747 to 1760 he was in the service of Frederick II of Prussia, who made him his principal sculptor. He executed numerous sculptures for the decoration of the park of Sanssouci at Potsdam, including marble statues of *Apollo* (1748), *Urania* (1748), *Zephyrus and Flora* (1749), *Cleopatra and the Asp* (1750), *Vulcan* (1756) and *Cybele* (1758; all *in situ*). He was succeeded at Sanssouci by his nephew Sigisbert-François Michel. His work, though unoriginal, helped to spread the French Rococo style in northern Europe.

BIBLIOGRAPHY

Lami; Meissner

A.-N. Dezallier d'Argenville: *Vie des fameux sculpteurs depuis la renaissance des arts* (Paris, 1787/*R* Geneva, 1972), pp. 339–52
P.-J. Mariette: 'Abecedario', *Archvs A. Fr.*, ii (1851–3), pp. 7–8
H. Thirion: *Les Adam et Clodion* (Paris, 1885)
F. Souchal: *Les Artistes à la cour des ducs de Lorraine Léopold et François III* (diss., Paris, Ecole Chartes, 1950)
M. Levey: *Art and Architecture of the 18th Century in France*, Pelican Hist. A. (Harmondsworth, 1972), pp. 62–7
F. Souchal: 'L'Inventaire après le décès du sculpteur Lambert-Sigisbert Adam', *Bull. Soc. Hist. A. Fr.* (1974), pp. 181–91
P. Fusco: 'Lambert-Sigisbert Adam's "Bust of Neptune"', *Bull. LA Co. Mus. A.*, xxi (1975), pp. 13–24
L. Seelig: 'François-Gaspard Adam Standbild des Feldmarschalls Schwerin', *Münchn. Jb. Bild. Kst*, xxvii (1976), pp. 155–98

FRANÇOIS SOUCHAL

Adam (ii). Scottish family of architects and designers. (1) William Adam had four sons, three of whom, (2) John Adam, (3) Robert Adam and (4) James Adam, were also architects. On William's death, John assumed control of his father's practice in Scotland; he took first Robert and then James into partnership, and together they completed some of their father's projects as well as taking on new commissions. In 1758 Robert, who was among the leading architects and designers in Europe in the second half of the 18th century, opened his own practice in London, where James joined him in partnership in 1763. William's fourth son, also called William Adam (1738–1822), was active in the London partnership from 1763, but his concern was primarily with its business dealings.

(1) William Adam (*b* Kirkcaldy, Fife, 30 Oct 1689; *d* Edinburgh, 24 June 1748). Architect and landscape designer. He was the leading architect in Scotland during the second quarter of the 18th century and had an extensive practice. An important contractor for the Government, serving from 1730 to his death as Master Mason to the Board of Ordnance for North Britain, he also pursued various business enterprises, including ownership of a brickworks. Apparently self-taught as an architect, he was involved with building country houses from the early 1720s. His early patron, Sir John Clerk, 2nd Baronet of Penicuik, made his own library available to Adam, and in 1727 they made a joint trip to England. Adam developed a style that was influenced by Sir John Vanbrugh, James Gibbs and the English Palladianism of Richard Boyle, 3rd Earl of Burlington and 4th Earl of Cork, and his circle. Thus, Baroque and Palladian forms co-existed in his work, although he handled them in a very personal and inventive way.

Among Adam's country houses were such villas and smaller houses as Mavisbank (1723–39; gutted 1973), Clerk's own house on which the two collaborated; The Drum (begun *c.* 1724); and Arniston (begun *c.* 1726), all in Lothian. His larger houses included Hopetoun House, Lothian (begun 1721; completed by his sons, *c.* 1750–60), and Duff House, Grampian (*c.* 1730–43). At Duff House he was involved in a law suit with William Duff, Lord Braco, afterwards 1st Earl of Fife (*d* 1763), over costs and his fee, but otherwise his relations with clients appear to have been good. His public buildings included Robert Gordon's Hospital, Aberdeen (1730–32); the Town House, Dundee (1731–4; destr.); the University Library, Glasgow (1732–45; destr.); and the Royal Infirmary, Edinburgh (1738–48; partially destr. 1884). He was involved as a landscape designer at several estates (e.g. Newliston, Lothian, 1731), had responsibility for constructing forts in the Highlands and supervised initial building work at Inveraray Castle, Strathclyde, begun in 1745 to Roger Morris's designs.

As early as 1727 Adam conceived the idea of producing a volume of engraved illustrations depicting his own as well as earlier Scottish architecture. A number of plates were engraved and subscriptions sold, but this project was brought to fruition only in 1810 with the publication of *Vitruvius Scoticus* by his grandson, William Adam (1751–1839), the son of John Adam.

UNPUBLISHED SOURCES

Edinburgh, Register House, Clerk of Penicuik Papers, GD 18/4981 [J. Clerk of Eldin: 'Draft Notes of a Life of Robert Adam' (?1790s)]

BIBLIOGRAPHY

W. Adam: *Vitruvius Scoticus* (Edinburgh, 1810); repr. with intro. by J. Simpson (Edinburgh, 1980)
R. Fleming: *Robert Adam and his Circle in Edinburgh and Rome* (London, 1962)
J. Gifford: *William Adam, 1689–1748* (Edinburgh, 1989)

(2) John Adam (*b* Kirkcaldy, Fife, *bapt* 5 March 1721; *d* Blair Adam, Tayside, 25 June 1792). Architect, son of (1) William Adam. He was trained by his father and worked with him until the latter's death in 1748. He succeeded to the family's architectural practice and contracting business, including the post of Master Mason to the Board of Ordnance for North Britain. He brought his brother Robert into partnership immediately, and James shortly after. During the late 1740s and the 1750s all three brothers were active as contractors on the Highland forts, especially Fort William, and at Inveraray Castle, Strathclyde, as well; but they also continued their father's architectural projects, for example Hopetoun House, Lothian (*c.* 1750–60), and took on new commissions, including Dumfries House, Strathclyde (1753–9), and Arniston, Lothian (1753–8). Since his partnership with Robert was dissolved in 1758, and that with James two years later, during the 1760s Adam practised alone in Edinburgh, though he was increasingly active in other business interests. After *c.* 1770 he seems to have ceased working as an architect, though he retained a strong interest in the London activities of his two brothers.

BIBLIOGRAPHY

W. Adam: *Vitruvius Scoticus* (Edinburgh, 1810); repr. with intro. by J. Simpson (Edinburgh, 1980)
R. Fleming: *Robert Adam and his Circle in Edinburgh and Rome* (London, 1962)
I. Lindsay and M. Cosh: *Inveraray and the Dukes of Argyll* (Edinburgh, 1973)

(3) Robert Adam (*b* Kirkcaldy, Fife, 3 July 1728; *d* London, 3 March 1792). Architect and designer, son of (1) William Adam. He and his rival William Chambers were the leading British architects in the second half of the 18th century. After training under his father, he embarked on a Grand Tour in 1754; this ended early in 1758 when he settled in London rather than Edinburgh. There he established a practice that was transformed into a partnership with his younger brother James after the latter's return in 1763 from his own Grand Tour. By then, however, the Adam style was formed, and Robert remained the partnership's driving force and principal designer until his death. He not only developed a distinctive and highly influential style but further refined it through his large number of commissions, earning fame and a certain amount of fortune along the way. Eminently successful, he left an indelible stamp on British architecture and interior decoration and on international Neo-classicism.

1. Life and work. 2. Working methods. 3. Sources and influence.

1. Life and work.

(i) Early work in Scotland, to mid-1754. (ii) Grand Tour, mid-1754–1757. (iii) Early work in London, 1758–mid-1760s. (iv) Mature work, mid-1760s–mid-1780s. (v) Late work, late 1780s and after.

(i) Early work in Scotland, to mid-1754. Born into a close-knit Lowlands family, Adam grew up in Edinburgh surrounded by intellectuals and the architectural and building affairs of his father, from whom he learnt both the art and business of his future profession. He attended the High School in Edinburgh and matriculated in 1743 at Edinburgh University, though he does not appear to have graduated. Joining his father's architectural office, where his older brother, John, was already at work, he participated in the activities then underway. These included not only buildings designed by his father but also very profitable contracting work, both for the Board of Ordnance and for private individuals. In this latter category was Inveraray Castle, Strathclyde, begun in 1745 in the Gothic Revival style to Roger Morris's designs. Following the death of their father in 1748, John took over both sides of the work and established a partnership with Robert. In addition to Inveraray, their contracting work included a number of forts, including Fort George, Highland, built after the failed Jacobite rising of 1745; this aspect of their business was supplemented by various other commercial enterprises, all of which contributed to the family's wealth and enabled both Robert and James to make the Grand Tour to Italy.

In the 1750s the partnership—which by now included James—gradually increased the number of its commissions. Among them were Hopetoun House, Lothian (*c.* 1750–60), where they completed the exterior their father had begun and designed and executed the interiors; a new wing at Arniston, Lothian (1753–8), where their father had worked earlier; and a totally new building, Dumfries House, Strathclyde (1753–9). At all three they followed current English fashion. Thus on, and to a substantial extent in place of, their father's robust Anglo-Baroque manner, the brothers (but primarily Robert, who seems to have been the chief designer) introduced Rococo and even chinoiserie decorative details along with Palladian formats their father had employed. Adam learnt these styles from engravings and books but also from a trip to England that he made in 1749–50. He recorded the things that interested him on this tour in a sketchbook (London, RIBA); these include fanciful Gothick buildings and landscaped parks and gardens, as well as Palladian structures.

(ii) Grand Tour, mid-1754–1757. In October 1754 Adam left Edinburgh for a tour in Italy, an experience that was to alter radically not only his style but also his career, though aspects of his Scottish experiences were to colour both. Stopping briefly in London, he met the painter and archaeologist Gavin Hamilton. He then travelled to Brussels to join up with Charles Hope, the younger brother of John Hope, 2nd Earl of Hopetoun (*d* 1781), who was to share expenses and, hopefully, introduce Adam to various aristocrats. Travelling via Paris and southern France, they reached Florence in February 1755, where Adam met Charles-Louis Clérisseau, a French architect and draughtsman of ruins. Clérisseau was a former *pensionnaire* at the Académie de France in Rome and had, in Adam's words (letter to James Adam, 19 Feb 1755; Edinburgh, Register House):

> the utmost knowledge of Architecture of perspective & of Designing & Colouring I ever saw, or had any Conception of; He rais[e]d my Ideas, He created emulation and fire in my Breast. I wish[e]d above all things to learn his manner, to have him with me at Rome, to Study close with him & to purchase of his works. what I wish[e]d for I obtain[e]d.

Clérisseau agreed to accompany him to Rome, to live with him there and to teach him 'all these Knacks, so necessary to us Architects'. He became, in effect, Adam's instructor, friend, employee and guide to the marvels of antiquity and techniques of drawing. From him, from the painter Laurent Pécheux (1729–1821) and from Giovanni Battista Piranesi, whom he met shortly after his arrival in Rome, Adam imbibed the excitement and variety of antique sources, a sense of scale and a manner of rendering them in drawings. These influences mingled with and overlaid those he had brought with him from Scotland, and together they formed the seeds of the Adam style.

During his two-year sojourn in Rome (Feb 1755 to May 1757), Adam sketched antique ruins, as well as Renaissance and Baroque buildings. He developed his skill at drawing and prepared for a career in London. For by now his aim had changed, and he was determined to play a central role in British architecture. He set about meeting important noblemen who might further his career and planned a variety of publications that would ensure his fame and success. Among them was a revision of Antoine Desgodetz's *Les Edifices antiques de Rome* of 1682, which he proposed to correct by underlining in red the author's errors, in order to demonstrate his own knowledge of 'Antiquitys to an Inch'. Although this particular scheme was not realized, Adam did manage to initiate work on the *Ruins of the Palace of the Emperor Diocletian at Spalatro in Dalmatia*, a grand folio volume that commemorated his five-week trip to Spalato (now Split). The drawings were executed by Clérisseau and two Italian draughtsmen, the plates were produced by various English and Italian engravers (including Francesco Bartolozzi), and the text was written anonymously by his cousin, the Edinburgh University principal William Robertson. Published in London in 1764, this impressive volume certainly demonstrated to the world Adam's familiarity with the monuments of antiquity. By the time it appeared, however, he had already established himself as one of the leading figures in London's architectural scene.

(iii) Early work in London, 1758–mid-1760s. Arriving in London on 17 January 1758, Adam set about the development of his career. In this he was enormously successful. Within two weeks he was elected a member of the Society of Arts, and he soon began to meet potential clients. In 1761 he was elected a fellow of the Royal Society and was appointed, with William Chambers, joint Architect of the

King's Works. Although obtaining commissions was initially perhaps slower than he had hoped, in his first three years in London he was engaged on 25 projects, the majority of which were executed; in January 1763 he informed Henry Home, Lord Kames, that he had 'business all over England, which I am with difficulty able to get managed with Honour to myself & Satisfaction to my Employers' (Abercairny Papers; Edinburgh, Register House). His brothers James and William joined him in London that year, and during the 1760s and into the 1770s Adam and Chambers were the leading architects in Britain.

In his early work (i.e. to *c.* 1765), Adam was assimilating a variety of sources, though from the first he was introducing into Britain new Neo-classical ideas and stylistic effects from Italy. These turn up in the series of country houses he remodelled or completed and in his occasional commissions for original undertakings. These included garden buildings, London town houses and small public edifices, such as the Admiralty Screen, Whitehall, London (1759–60). In his earliest projects (e.g. the interiors for Hatchlands, Surrey, NT, 1758–61), the mélange of sources is still quite evident, as is the relative heaviness of the relief; but, shortly after, he began to blend the elements and soften the relief. From the beginning, the results of his Roman studies were displayed. Thus, his ceilings at Hatchlands show the influence of 17th-century decoration at the Villa Pamphili (now Doria-Pamphili), Rome, and he had planned to introduce grotesque panels there derived from antique decorations recovered during excavations and from Renaissance adaptations of them. Although these were not carried out, they were at Shardeloes, Bucks (1761–4), and at a host of later houses, but flatter and more refined in form than those intended for Hatchlands. For the garden façade (see fig. 1) at Kedleston Hall, Derbys (a house completed by him *c.* 1760–71), he drew on two Roman monuments—the Arch of Constantine and the Pantheon (for its low saucer dome)—to transform a typical Palladian composition, but again cleaning up, flattening and refining his sources.

At Syon House, London, between 1760 and 1769, Adam took a quadrangular Tudor nunnery with a later Jacobean long gallery, which had been somewhat adapted for greater aristocratic comfort, and transformed it into what Horace Walpole was to describe as 'another Mount Palatine' (see fig. 2). He created a series of rooms of varied and unusual shapes, partially derived from Roman Baths; these he ornamented with lively decoration, also reflecting Classical influences, ranging from apses screened by columns to statuary, grotesques and trophy panels. Responding to the demands of fashionable society, these were spaces intended for various functions that not only were appropriate for those functions but delighted the eye by their variation and ornamentation. This would have been carried even further had he been allowed to fill Syon's interior courtyard with a great circular saloon, as he had intended.

Adam's remodellings, interior decoration and completion of projects begun by others was only partly the result of an enormous amount of recent country-house building in England. In the first volume to appear of their *Works in Architecture* (1773), Robert and his brother James not only claimed to have brought about 'a kind of revolution in the whole system of this useful and elegant art' but cited specifically their accomplishments in interior decoration: 'We have introduced a great diversity of ceilings, freezes, and decorated pilasters, and have added grace and beauty to the whole, by a mixture of grotesque stucco, and painted ornaments, together with the flowing rainceau, with its fanciful figures and winding foliage' (i/1, pp. 3, 5-6). Nevertheless, Robert yearned to build grand external elevations and made many designs, though relatively few were carried out. When they were, as at Kedleston, they

1. Robert Adam: Kedleston Hall, Derbyshire, south (garden) façade, *c.* 1760–61

too left their mark. Even there, however, he was unable fully to execute his plans, for the absence of the wings he had wished to add partially deprives the elevation of that sense of movement both brothers cherished, derived ultimately from Vanbrugh. They defined this in the *Works* as 'the rise and fall, the advance and recess, with other diversity of form, in the different parts of a building, so as to add greatly to the picturesque of the composition' (i/1, p. 3).

(iv) Mature work, mid-1760s–mid-1780s. By the middle of the 1760s Adam had realized his mature manner, having synthesized his various sources into an effective personal style. Although he further refined that manner over the next three decades, flattening and attenuating its decorative components and making the style ever more elegant, the basic ingredients and their compositional effects were by now established. There were some new influences, especially the ETRUSCAN STYLE for interiors and the use of broad, complex chimney-pieces, both inspired by Piranesi's *Diverse maniere d'adornare i cammini* (1769); but these contributed to those general tendencies evident from the 1770s on, and they did not materially alter the basic style that was set within the first seven or eight years of his London career.

In 1765 Adam became Surveyor of Chelsea Hospital and in 1769 MP for Kinross-shire, at which time he resigned his position as joint Architect of the King's Works, which passed to his brother James. He never became a member of the Royal Academy, no doubt because of the enmity of Chambers, who was then Treasurer and the institution's dominating force.

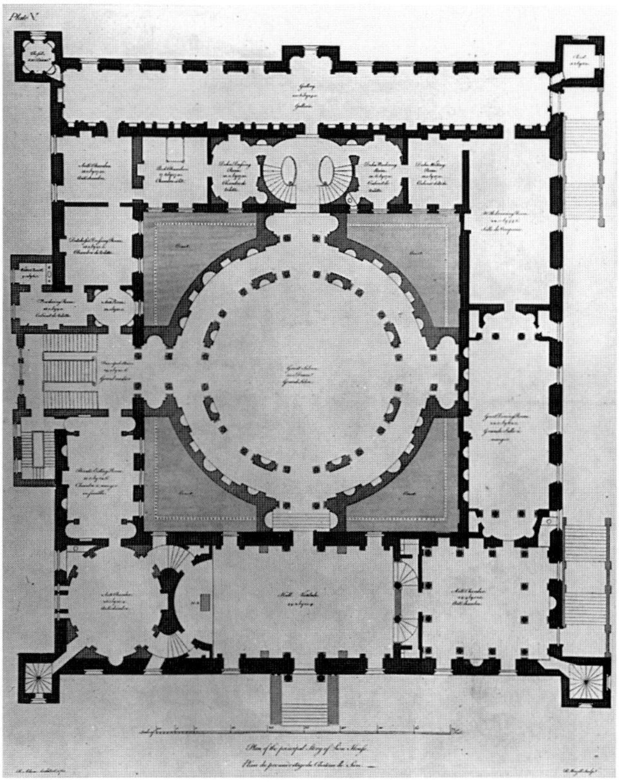

2. Robert Adam: plan of Syon House, London, 1760–69; from Robert and James Adam: *Works in Architecture*, ii (London, 1778)

(a) Country houses. These continued to provide a highly important source of work. Adam built some major new houses of this type, from Luton Hoo, Beds (1766–74), to Gosford House, Lothian (1790–*c.* 1800), as well as a number of smaller villas, among them Brasted Place, Kent (1784–5), and Walkinshaw House, Strathclyde (*c.* 1791–3). But, as before, some of his greatest accomplishments involved remodelling existing houses and completing others. Of these, perhaps the most impressive are Osterley Park House, Middx (1765–80); Kenwood House, London (1767–9); Harewood House (1759–71) and Nostell Priory (1765–85), both W. Yorks; Newby Hall, N. Yorks (1767–*c.* 1780); and Saltram, Devon (1768–79) (*see also* SCOTLAND, fig. 15).

At Osterley Park, Adam again took a quadrangular Tudor house and transformed it, this time by breaking through one of the sides with a dramatic double-columned portico, raising the level of the courtyard and ornamenting the rooms in spectacular fashion. The entrance hall is dominated by designs based on Roman sources, featuring coffered apses, trophy panels and pilasters, the capitals of which were derived from the relatively unusual ones Adam had seen in the peristyle at Spalato. He decorated the dining-room with his mature grotesque panels, here complex, refined and flat. The Etruscan Dressing-room (for illustrations *see* ETRUSCAN STYLE) is the finest surviving example of this style, inspired by Piranesi and 'Etruscan' vases (they were probably Greek), but developed by Adam into the height of elegant, brittle and flat Neo-classical decoration. At Kenwood House, Adam ornamented his flat garden façade with delicate attenuated pilasters, their shafts converted into decorative panels using Liardet's cement, a newly invented patent stucco, of which the Adams bought the patent; he also designed a grand tunnel-vaulted library (see fig. 3). In this space, intended for fashionable entertaining as well as for the books of his patron, William Murray, 1st Earl of Mansfield (*d* 1793), Adam produced perhaps his finest room. Inserting the bookshelves within screened apses at either end, he employed large columns, grotesque panels and a variety of ornaments on the ceiling and walls and in the frieze. In the last, he combined the insignia of his client with a motif derived from the Temple of Antoninus and Faustina in Rome, an imaginative adaptation of antiquity characteristic of Adam's approach.

In addition to the smaller classical villas that Adam designed in the last two decades of his career, he also built a number of castellar houses, especially in Scotland. Among these are Wedderburn Castle, Borders (1771–5); Culzean Castle, Strathclyde (1777–92); and Seton Castle, Lothian (1789–91). Although he employed turrets and battlements for these, he also drew on Roman, Early Christian and later buildings which he had seen in Italy and Germany. He arrived at a picturesque synthesis, rather than a nostalgic re-creation of a long-lost era; a generally symmetrical composition; and interiors that were as classical as those of his other country houses.

3. Robert Adam: library, Kenwood House, London, 1767–9

(b) Town houses. From the outset of his career in London, Adam received commissions for town residences, but these increased substantially from the later 1760s. Among the earliest were Coventry House, Piccadilly (1764–6), and Shelburne (later Lansdowne) House, Berkeley Square (1761–8), the former involving interior remodelling, where the latter was a large new house. In the early to mid-1770s his London houses provided perhaps the most striking demonstration of his talent; these included Wynn House, 20 St James's Square (1772–6); Derby House, 23 Grosvenor Square (1773–4; destr.); and Home House, 20 Portman Square (1773–7). This continued into the early 1780s, typified by Cumberland House, Pall Mall (1780–82, 1785–8). As with the country houses, Adam moved from his early mature synthesis, as at Lansdowne House, to the elegant attenuation and refinement of Derby House or Home House. In some ways his accomplishment is even more marked here, because he was creating appropriate settings for fashionable society within the tight confinements of relatively narrow terrace houses. At Derby House the variety of spaces and their juxtaposition vied with the refined delicacy of the ornamentation to achieve Adam's most brittle and rarefied manner. The splendour of the Great Drawing-room was complemented by the novel motifs and colouring of Etruscan decoration elsewhere.

(c) Urban planning. In addition to individual town houses, Adam engaged in a number of urban-planning schemes. He often introduced varied shapes, including squares, crescents and circuses, although his long terraces of juxtaposed houses or unified façades on the sides of a square were more common. As early as his stay in Italy he drew up designs for rebuilding Lisbon, a city devastated by earthquake in 1755. This was not taken up; nor were his later schemes for the expansion of Bath beyond the River Avon (1777–82) and of Edinburgh beyond the Cowgate across a new South Bridge (*c.* 1785–6). He was, however, able to carry out such London developments as the Adelphi (1768–72), Mansfield Street (1770–75), Portland Place (1776–*c.* 1780 and later) and Fitzroy Square (1790–94), as well as Charlotte Square in Edinburgh (1791–1807). For these, he took the principles of his individual town-house compositions and adapted them to large and more complex groupings, often applying the delicate ornamentation in Liardet's cement.

The grandest of Adam's schemes was the Adelphi, built on leased land between the Strand and the Thames. He embanked the Thames, raising the Royal Terrace's houses (destr.) above vaulted warehouses that he hoped the Government would lease. For this, and for the rest of this H-shaped development, he employed his favourite decorative elements, but in a composition without an obvious central emphasis. Though aesthetically satisfying, the Adelphi was a failure financially. The Government declined to lease the warehouses, and the troubles of the Adam brothers were compounded by a run on Scottish banks. Placed thus in dire financial straits, they were forced to dispose of the Adelphi by lottery.

(d) Public buildings. Adam never ceased to yearn for grand commissions, and his unexecuted projects include major buildings designed for Lincoln's Inn, London (1771–2), and King's College (1784–7) and the University (1788–9) at Cambridge (designs for all three, London, Soane Mus.). In Edinburgh he was able to erect the Register House (1774–92) and at least the beginning of the University (1789–93), though it was completed long after his death and to a different design. These buildings characteristically relate to his country houses in composition and exterior decoration, with rusticated lower floors, shallow domes, emphasis on the centres and ends of buildings, and such recurring motifs as Palladian windows within relieving arches and modified triumphal arches.

Two especially interesting examples of Adam's small semi-public buildings are the Society of Arts (1772–6) and the Theatre Royal, Drury Lane (1775–6; destr.), both in London. The Society of Arts was incorporated within his Adelphi development and, as with the central pavilion of his Edinburgh Register House, employed a temple-front arrangement of large attached columns supporting a pediment (see fig. 4). Once again Adam departed from traditional rules; he combined the Ionic order with a Doric frieze and incorporated both Classical roundels and a Palladian window within a relieving arch, the latter featuring a delicate velarium filled with bell-flower ornamentation. The overall effect refashioned a variety of sources into a flat, refined and attenuated style. For the Theatre Royal, remodelled for the actor-manager David Garrick, he combined a temple-front façade with a refined and elegant interior. Ornamented by arabesque pilasters whose gilded decoration was set on glass, behind which was red and green foil, this was an effect Adam had employed a few years earlier in the Glass Drawing-room at Northumberland House, London (1773–5; destr.).

(e) Churches, mausolea and monuments. The largest and most impressive of Adam's churches was St Mary, Mistley,

Essex (1775; partially destr.). There he transformed an early 18th-century church into one that echoed his own spatial and decorative manner—dramatically accentuated by the twin towers, which are all that survive. He made a number of designs for small churches, a few of which were executed, including St Andrew, Gunton, Norfolk (completed 1769), the façade of which was conceived as a Classical pedimented temple.

The mausoleum thrived as a building type during the second half of the 18th century, providing another form of building in which Adam could experiment. Among his earliest mausolea was that for Bowood, Wilts (1761–4), which devolved from a cylindrical design to a square. Others included the cylindrical tomb for his friend, the philosopher David Hume, in Edinburgh's Old Calton Burying Ground (1777–8), and one on a square plan at Castle Upton, Co. Antrim, Ireland (1789–91). Related to these mausolea, though not independent structures, are church memorials, and Adam designed a number of them during his career. Among the earliest is the *Lt-Col. Roger Townshend* monument in Westminster Abbey, London (designed 1759); a later example is that in Warkton, Northants (1775), dedicated to *Mary, Duchess of Montagu*.

(f) Furniture and decorative objects. Adam designed a multitude of decorative objects for his domestic interiors, from furniture, carpets, door-knobs and escutcheons to stove-grates (for illustration *see* FIREPLACE FURNISHINGS), candelabra, silverware, ink wells and (even) sedan chairs. This is not to say he designed everything that was included in any one commission or that Neo-classical furniture made for an Adam house was necessarily made to his designs. For many clients he designed only wall furniture—pier-tables, mirrors, bookcases—or a decorative object or two. In some cases he did design a great deal. For Robert Child (*d* 1782) at Osterley Park House, for example, this included chairs for the dining-room, a commode and carpet for the drawing-room, a bed for the State Bedroom (*see* ENGLAND, fig. 92) and chairs and a chimney-board for the Etruscan Dressing-room. But even there, most of the furniture was designed and executed by such professional cabinetmakers as John Linnell (i); this was also true of Adam's other commissions. Those pieces that he did design—delicate, refined and ornamented with elegantly flattened Classical motifs in relief—were all in the Adam style.

(g) Gothic Revival. Although his architectural and decorative style was predominantly Neo-classical, Adam occasionally produced Gothic Revival designs if clients insisted. This differed from his castellar manner, which conveyed a picturesque impression by effects of massing drawn from a variety of sources, for his Gothic Revival buildings emulated a more playful and frivolous Gothick. Examples include the exterior of St Mary Magdalene at Croome d'Abitot, Hereford & Worcs (1763), and Brizlee Tower at Alnwick Castle, Northumb. (1777–83). But his Gothic Revival work was primarily for interiors, as at Strawberry Hill, Middx (1766–8), and Alnwick Castle itself (late 1760s–*c*. 1780). At Strawberry Hill, Horace Walpole, the revival's leading promoter, not only commissioned a chimney-piece and ceiling for the Round Tower there, but

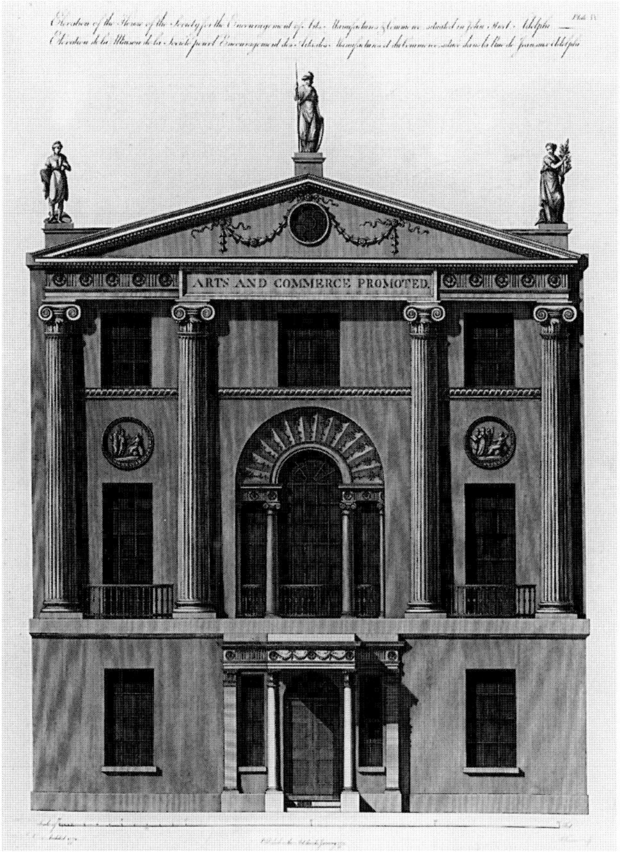

4. Robert Adam: elevation of the Society of Arts, London, 1772–6; from Robert and James Adam: *Works in Architecture*, ii (London, 1778)

supplied Adam with medieval models from which to design. Nevertheless, the result was as delicate and refined as Adam's Neo-classical decoration. At Alnwick the result was apparently similar (his work there has since been obliterated). His Gothic Revival decorations for the interiors of Hulne Abbey on the Alnwick estate survive (1778); these reveal how delightful, if fanciful and unauthentic, Adam's essays in this manner were.

(v) Late work in Scotland, late 1780s and after. In the early and mid-1780s Adam was less busy, perhaps due to the building recession brought about by the American Revolution. But at the end of the decade and in the early 1790s, during which there was a phenomenal building boom, he was once again very active, especially in Scotland. At Gosford (1790–*c*. 1800) and Archerfield (1789–91), two Lothian houses, Edinburgh University (1789–93) and Glasgow's Royal Infirmary (1791–5; destr.), his powers and his style continued unabated. The exteriors retained the attenuated proportions and staccato emphases, and the interiors, though sometimes employing certain plainer passages, displayed the delicate and elegant refinement of his most rarefied manner.

2. WORKING METHODS. Adam was the dominating figure in the partnership with his brother James. It was he who generally met with clients, created the initial sketches

and retained ultimate control over the commissioned work. This can be seen in the large collection of almost 9000 drawings, both sketches and renderings, preserved in Sir John Soane's Museum in London. Even the drawings made for clients by the office staff can often be related to sketches in Adam's hand. His initial effort for an interior was often directed to its ceiling, with the design for a carpet or pavement frequently related to, yet different from, its counterpart above. He worked quickly, as can be seen from the quantity of designs that issued from his office. In 1762 James commented that 'I think from what I can perceive he makes plans much faster than I can make Cornishes.'

Adam's speed in designing was materially assisted by a number of draughtsmen or office assistants and a 'regiment of artificers', as Elizabeth Montagu called his craftsmen in 1779. In Italy he had assembled a group of draughtsmen to help him; on his return to England, Augustin Brunais (1730–96) and one other (most probably Laurent-Benoît Dewez) accompanied him. George Richardson, who had accompanied James on his Grand Tour, also joined the office. Other Italians arrived subsequently, among them Giuseppe Manocchi (*d* 1782) and Joseph Bonomi. The latter (after four years measuring and drawing antiquities for the Adam brothers in Rome) was employed from 1767 to 1781 as a draughtsman, during which time he was prohibited by contract from doing any other drawings, even for himself, under a penalty of £200. Robert's fame was such that even after his death architects continued to identify themselves in advertisements as his former draughtsmen.

Those craftsmen responsible for executing Adam's designs included plasterers, decorative painters, wood- and stone-carvers, metalworkers (notably Matthew Boulton), locksmiths, cabinetmakers, carpet manufacturers and every type of artisan from bricklayers to glaziers. The principal stuccoists were Joseph Rose (*c.* 1723–80) and his nephew, also called Joseph Rose (1746–99). Adam's decorative painters included Antonio Zucchi, who arrived about 1766 and remained until 1781, when he returned to Italy. Although Zucchi was relied upon to supply inset decorative paintings that were independent of specific designs by Adam, in almost all other cases craftsmen followed his designs extremely closely.

3. SOURCES AND INFLUENCE. The most significant source for the Adam style was Roman antiquity. A good part of this was the result of Adam's years spent in Italy, but it was supplemented by studying books, engravings and drawings. Through them he learnt of such Roman monuments as those at Palmyra. They also provided sources for his occasional use of Greek motifs. Complementing these ancient sources were those of the Renaissance and Baroque eras. Although the Adam brothers claimed these were employed primarily as a means of elucidating ancient ones, in fact they had significant influence in their own right, providing, for example, inspiration for Robert's grotesque decoration (e.g. his design for the Breakfast Room at Kedleston Hall, 1768).

Three aspects of 18th-century architectural design were also influential. Most significant was the Palladian style of the Burlington circle, inherited by Adam from his father and used by the brothers in their early work in Scotland. It remained important throughout Robert's career for compositional effects and for a variety of detailing, ranging from rustication and modillion cornices to the ubiquitous Palladian-window motif within a relieving arch. Second was Piranesi, who, from his formative influence during Robert's Grand Tour and through his *Diverse maniere d'adornare i cammini* (1769), left an indelible mark on the Adam manner. Finally, there was a French influence that can be seen in Adam's planning, as in his use of the *enfilade* and in his courtyard screens.

Although Adam had an army of assistants, he took no pupils. Nevertheless, his influence was enormously widespread. This he accomplished through both his executed work and published designs. By the 1760s such older architects as Robert Taylor and James Paine were beginning to change or at least modify their styles in response to Adam's innovations. In addition, from the later 1760s on, a whole host of younger architects, including George Dance (ii), Thomas Leverton, Henry Holland, James Wyatt and John Soane, began their careers in the Adam mould. Though some, for example Wyatt, were to retain this style while others changed dramatically, Adam's influence was an important aspect of their early development. Lesser architects were even more influenced by his work, as were scores of pattern-book authors. Among these was William Pain, whose conversion can be seen by comparing his early *Builder's Companion and Workman's General Assistant* (1758) with his Adam-influenced *Practical Builder* of 1774. Adam's effect was also strong in the decorative arts, and Thomas Chippendale's Neo-classical furniture after *c.* 1763 is one excellent example of this.

The Adam influence extended far beyond Britain. In Russia it can be seen in the work of Charles Cameron at the palaces of Tsarskoye Selo (1779–84) and Pavlovsk (1782–5), both near St Petersburg. In the USA examples range from the work of such established architects as Charles Bulfinch and Samuel McIntire in Massachusetts to numerous anonymous buildings as far south as Georgia, as far west as Indiana, and as late as the 1820s.

UNPUBLISHED SOURCES

Edinburgh, Register House [family letters from Robert and James Adam, from the 1740s on; Clerk of Penicuik Papers]

WRITINGS

Ruins of the Palace of the Emperor Diocletian at Spalatro in Dalmatia (London, 1764)

with J. Adam: *The Works in Architecture of Robert and James Adam*, i–ii (London, 1773–8), iii (London, 1822); repr. in 1 vol. (London, 1975)

BIBLIOGRAPHY

J. Swarbrick: *Robert Adam and his Brothers* (London, 1915)
A. T. Bolton: *The Architecture of Robert and James Adam*, 2 vols (London, 1922)
J. Lees-Milne: *The Age of Adam* (London, 1947)
J. Fleming: 'Robert Adam, the Grand Tourist', *Cornhill Mag.*, clxviii/1004 (1955), pp. 118–37
G. Beard: 'Robert Adam's Craftsmen', *Connoisseur Yb.* (1958), pp. 26–32
D. Stillman: *The Genesis of the Adam Style* (diss., New York, Columbia U., 1961)
G. Beard: 'New Light on Adam's Craftsmen', *Country Life*, cxxxi (10 May 1962), pp. 1098–1100
J. Fleming: *Robert Adam and his Circle in Edinburgh and Rome* (London, 1962)

E. Harris: 'Robert Adam and the Gobelins', *Apollo*, lxxvi (1962), pp. 100–06
——: *The Furniture of Robert Adam* (London, 1963)
A. Rowan: *The Castle Style in British Domestic Architecture in the 18th and Early 19th Century* (diss., U. Cambridge, 1965)
R. Rowe: *Adam Silver* (London, 1965)
G. Beard: *Georgian Craftsmen and their Work* (London, 1966)
D. Stillman: *The Decorative Work of Robert Adam* (London, 1966)
——: 'Robert Adam and Piranesi', *Essays in the History of Architecture Presented to Rudolf Wittkower* (London, 1967), pp. 197–206
J. Fleming: '"Retrospective View" by John Clerk of Eldin with Some Comments on Adam's Castle Style', *Concerning Architecture*, ed. J. Summerson (London, 1968), pp. 75–84
——: 'Robert Adam's Castle Style', *Country Life*, cxliii (23 May 1968), pp. 1356–9; (30 May 1968), pp. 1443–7
E. Croft-Murray: *Decorative Painting in England, 1537–1837*, ii (London, 1971)
M. Tomlin: *Catalogue of Adam Period Furniture* (London, 1972)
A. Rowan: 'After the Adelphi: Forgotten Years in the Adam Brothers' Practice', *J. Royal Soc. A.*, cxxii (1973–4), pp. 659–78
G. Beard: *Decorative Plasterwork in Great Britain* (London, 1975)
——: *The Work of Robert Adam* (New York, 1978)
——: *Craftsmen and Interior Decoration in England, 1660–1820* (Edinburgh, 1981)
M. Sanderson: 'Robert Adam's Last Visit to Scotland', *Archit. Hist.*, xxv (1982), pp. 33–46
City Dwellings and Country Houses: Robert Adam and his Style (exh. cat., New York, Cooper-Hewitt Mus., 1982)
A. A. Tait: 'Reading the Ruins: Robert Adam and Piranesi in Rome', *Archit. Hist.*, xxvii (1984), pp. 524–33
A. Rowan: *A Catalogue of the Architectural Drawings of Robert Adam in the Victoria and Albert Museum* (London, 1985)
——: *Designs for Castles and Country Villas by Robert and James Adam* (Oxford, 1985)
J. Rykwert and A. Rykwert: *Robert and James Adam: The Men and the Style* (London, 1985)
I. Bristow: 'The Room in the Context of Robert Adam's Work', *Philadelphia Mus. A.: Bull.*, lxxxii (1986), pp. 13–19
D. Stillman: *English Neo-classical Architecture*, 2 vols (London, 1988)
——: 'The Neo-classical Transformation of the English Country House', *Stud. Hist. A.*, xxv (1989), pp. 75–93
D. N. King: *The Complete Works of Robert and James Adam* (Boston, 1991)
J. Bryant: *Robert Adam, 1728–92: Architect of Genius* (London, 1992)
S. Parissien: *Adam Style* (Washington, DC, 1992)
A. A. Tait: *Robert Adam: Drawings and Imagination* (New York, 1993)

(4) James Adam (*b* Edinburgh, 21 July 1732; *d* London, 20 Oct 1794). Architect, son of (1) William Adam. In the 1750s he was taken into partnership in Edinburgh with his older brothers John and Robert, and from 1760 to 1763 he was on a Grand Tour in Italy. Accompanied by an architectural draughtsman, George Richardson, James was guided by Charles-Louis Clérisseau, Robert's teacher, employee and friend during his time in Italy. In 1763 James joined Robert in a London partnership, remaining his brother's associate and subsidiary designer until Robert's death in 1792. He then continued alone until his own death two years later.

In 1769 James succeeded Robert as joint Architect of the King's Works, remaining in that post until its dissolution in 1782. Most of his architectural work was subsumed within the Adam partnership, whose chief designer was Robert, but James executed a few independent designs, among them the Shire Hall at Hertford, Herts (1767–71); façades for Portland Place, London (1776); and late works in Scotland in the two years between Robert's death and his own. These included St George's Episcopal Church, Edinburgh (1792–4), and College Houses (1793) and the Tron Church (1794) in Glasgow.

WRITINGS

with R. Adam: *The Works in Architecture of Robert and James Adam*, i–ii (London, 1773–8), iii (London, 1822); repr. in 1 vol. (London, 1975)
Practical Essays on Agriculture, 2 vols (London, 1789, 2/1794)

BIBLIOGRAPHY

A. T. Bolton: 'The Shire Hall, Hertford', *Archit. Rev.* [London], xliii (1918), pp. 68–73
——: *The Architecture of Robert and James Adam*, 2 vols (London, 1922)
J. Fleming: *Robert Adam and his Circle in Edinburgh and Rome* (London, 1962)
A. Rowan: 'After the Adelphi: Forgotten Years in the Adam Brothers' Practice', *J. Royal Soc. A.*, cxxii (1973–4), pp. 659–78

DAMIE STILLMAN

Adam (iii). German family of painters. (1) Albrecht Adam had four sons who were artists: Benno Adam (1812–1892), Franz Adam (1815–1886), Eugen Adam (1817–1880), and Julius Adam (1826–1874). Albrecht's brother Heinrich Adam (1787–1862) was also an artist. (2) Richard Benno Adam was the grandson of Benno Adam.

(1) Albrecht Adam (*b* Nördlingen, 16 April 1786; *d* Munich, 28 Aug 1862). He trained under Christoph Zwinger (1744–1813) in Nuremberg, and in 1807 he moved to Munich to continue his studies. From 1809 he worked in Milan, following his appointment as court painter to Eugène de Beauharnais, viceroy of Italy, whom he accompanied to Russia in 1812. After returning to Munich in 1815, he executed a series of 83 small battle-pieces in oil on paper, based on sketches made in 1812. His Russian exploits also provided the material for a set of 100 lithographs entitled *Voyage pittoresque et militaire de Willenberg en Prusse jusqu'à Moscou* (1827–33), produced with the assistance of his sons Franz and Benno, which helped to establish his contemporary reputation. In Munich, Albrecht's patrons included Maximilian I and his successor, Ludwig I of Bavaria, at whose behest Albrecht painted the *Battle of Borodino* for the Munich Residenz. For the palace in St Petersburg of Maximilian, Duc de Leuchtenberg, he executed 12 large battle-pieces. Other commissions took him to Stuttgart in 1829 and to Mecklenburg in 1838. After 1848 he was employed as a battle painter by Marshal Radetzky and by Emperor Francis Joseph of Austria, of whom he also produced several portraits during his residence in Vienna from 1855 to 1857. In 1859 he followed the army of Napoleon III during the Italian campaign against the Austrians, which he recorded in a series of drawings and sketches. On his return to Munich he painted the *Battle of Landshut* (1858–9) for Archduke Charles Ludwig and the *Battle of Zorndorf* (1859–62; Munich, Maximilianum) for King Maximilian II. In his later years, many of his pictures were painted in collaboration with his sons.

WRITINGS

H. Holland, ed.: *Aus dem Leben eines Schlachtenmalers: Selbstbiographie* (Stuttgart, 1886)

COLIN J. BAILEY

(2) Richard Benno Adam (*b* Munich, 5 March 1873; *d* Munich, 20 Jan 1937). Great-grandson of (1) Albrecht Adam. He studied in Munich with Nicolas Gysis at the Akademie der Bildenden Künste, with Sigmund Strähuber and Ludwig von Langenmantel (1854–1922), and in the private school run by Heinrich Knirr (*b* 1862). Between

1892 and 1894 he studied at the Staatliche Akademie der Bildenden Künste in Karlsruhe. From 1896 he painted his first equestrian portraits of the German, Austrian, Bohemian and Hungarian nobility. In 1899 he painted the *Budapest Hunting Society*, which included 47 equestrian portraits. He was a war artist during World War I in Galicia and in the Imperial Headquarters in France. Between 1928 and 1931 he made several commission-related journeys to the USA, producing such works as the *American Sportsmen*.

UNPUBLISHED SOURCES

Munich Stadtarchv [letters and diaries]

BIBLIOGRAPHY

Albrecht Adam und seine Familie: Zur Geschichte einer Münchner Künstlerdynastie im 19. und 20. Jahrhundert (exh. cat. by U. v. Hase-Schmundt and others, Munich, Stadtmus., 1987)

U. V. HASE-SCHMUNDT

Adam, Henri-Georges (*b* Paris, 14 Jan 1904; *d* La Clarté, Brittany, 27 Aug 1967). French sculptor, printmaker and tapestry designer. His father was a jeweller, and after his return from World War I in 1918 Adam worked in his studio and learnt how to engrave. At the same time he studied drawing at the Ecole Germain-Pilon and read Charles Baudelaire's *Les Fleurs du mal*, which was to have a great influence on him. In 1925 he attended evening classes at a school of drawing in Montparnasse. From 1928 to 1934 he started to produce prints and became associated with André Breton, Louis Aragon and Paul Eluard, although he was never greatly influenced by them. His early prints, reminiscent of the work of George Grosz, were mostly designed as social satire, mocking the myths surrounding patriotism, the family and religion, as in *When Papa is Patriotic* (1935). In 1933 he designed the costumes and scenery for Hans Schlumberg's *Miracle à Verdun* performed at the Théâtre des Bouffes du Nord in Paris. His first exhibition of prints was held in 1934 at the Galerie Billiet-Vorms in Paris.

The Spanish Civil War (1936–9) prompted Adam to create a cycle of engravings entitled *Disasters of War*, which included such works as the *Horse and the Plough* (1941; Y. Adam priv. col., see 1968 exh. cat., p. 106). In 1937 he participated in the exhibition *Artistes de ce temps* at the Petit Palais in Paris, and the following year he was awarded the Blumenthal prize for engraving. After being mobilized in 1939 and taken prisoner in 1940, he then worked as a hospital attendant in Besançon. His experiences led to a series of 120 drawings evoking the horrors of war. In 1943 he produced costume and stage designs for Jean-Paul Sartre's *Les Mouches*, performed at the Théâtre de la Cité in Paris. He began producing sculpture in 1942 and the following year executed his first important work *The Effigy* (Y. Adam priv. col., see 1966 exh. cat., p. 7), based on medieval tomb figures. It was exhibited at the Salon de la Libération, Paris, in 1944 through the intervention of Picasso and caused a considerable stir at the exhibition, André Lhote being its strongest defender. Adam's friendship with Picasso led to the latter offering him his studio in the Rue des Grands-Augustins, where Adam worked for the next seven years. In 1945 he was one of the co-founders of the Salon de Mai in Paris, at which he exhibited his *Burnt Man* (1945; Y. Adam priv. col.). In 1947 he engraved a series of plates to illustrate Gérard de Nerval's *Les Chimères*, although they were never published (see Gheerbrant, pls 52–61, 70–83). The same year he produced the first of many tapestry cartoons, for *Danae*, which was woven at Aubusson. His tapestry *Meridian* was hung in the UNESCO Palace in Paris in 1958.

In 1956 Adam began his series of sculptures *Vegetable and Marine Mutations*, which were designed to expand the subject-matter of sculpture beyond the tradition of the human form, as in *Large Shell* (1956; Y. Adam priv. col., see George, pl. 31). The same year he began the series of engravings *Flagstones, Sand and Water*, which included such works as *Flagstone, Sand and Water, No. 1* (1956; Y. Adam priv. col., see Gheerbrant, pl. 109). He produced a number of large public sculptures, the first of which was *The Signal* (1959–61; Le Havre, Mus. B.-A.), a vast geometric work whose aspect radically alters from different viewpoints. One of his most impressive public works is *The Wall* (1965–6; Chantilly, Lycée), a series of unevenly sized and shaped stones with a network of deep incisions. From 1963 to 1967 he provided sculptural decoration for the church at Moutier in Switzerland.

BIBLIOGRAPHY

B. Gheerbrant: *Henri-George Adam: Oeuvre gravé, 1939–1957* (Paris, 1957)
Adam (exh. cat. by B. Dorival and others, Paris, Mus. N. A. Mod., 1966)
W. George and I. Jianou: *Adam* (Paris, 1968)
A la rencontre d'Adam (exh. cat. by Y. Goldenberg, Paris, Hôtel de la Monnaie, 1968)

□

Adam, Paul (*b* Paris, 7 Dec 1862; *d* Paris, 1 Jan 1920). French writer and critic. His fictional work developed rapidly from a naturalist concept of the novel (e.g. *Chair molle*, Paris, 1885) to a symbolist one (e.g. *Etre*, Paris, 1888). As an art critic, he played an important role in the first years of Neo-Impressionism. The few pieces that he wrote between 1886 and 1889 placed him in the top rank of contemporary critics and were of considerable influence. He was less interested in analysing the theoretical bases of Neo-Impressionism than in deciphering their implications, stressing the relationship of this new method of painting to Symbolism. He felt that the use by Seurat and his followers of a body of scientific theories on which to base their art was not only an indication of their adherence to the modernity that pervaded the century but also revealed an underlying tendency towards abstraction. At the same time fundamental visual concepts or 'preconceived sensorial notions' that had served as the basis of western art were called into question. In this regard, the 'pictorial concern to interpret the pure phenomenon' corresponded to the aspiration towards synthesis that marked Symbolism and was 'in close correlation to contemporary philosophy, biology and physics in denying the existence of objects, declaring matter to be the mere appearance of vibratory movement that is the source of our impressions, our sensations, our ideas' (*Dix ans d'art français*, p. 38). In this collection of his articles that had appeared between 1896 and 1907, his opinions evolve from the intransigent approach he took during the years when Symbolist art was prominent, to a more eclectic one. He continued, however, to see Seurat as the dominant artist of his time.

WRITINGS
'Peintres impressionnistes', *Rev. Contemp.* (April–May 1886)
'Les Artistes indépendants', *La Vogue*, viii (Sept 1886)
'Les Impressionnistes à l'exposition des Indépendants', *Vie Mod.*, x (15 April 1888)
preface: G. Vanor: *L'Art symboliste* (Paris, 1889)
Dix ans d'art français (Paris, 1909)

BIBLIOGRAPHY
J. Huret: *Enquête sur l'évolution littéraire* (Paris, 1891, rev. Vanves, 1982)
C. Mauclair: *Paul Adam* (Paris, [1921])
F. Jean-Desthieux: *Le Dernier des encyclopédistes, Paul Adam* (Paris, 1928)
P. Smith: 'Paul Adam, "Soi" et les "Peintres impressionnistes": La Genèse d'un discours moderniste', *Rev. A.* [Paris], 82 (1988)
R. Rapetti: '"Ce mode neuf de voir": Neo-impressionismo e simbolismo in Francia', *L'età del divisionismo* (exh. cat., ed. G. Belli and F. Rella; Trent, Mus. A. Mod. & Contemp. Trento & Rovereto, 1990), pp. 56–74
M. F. Zimmermann: *Les Mondes de Seurat* (Anvers-Paris, 1991)

RODOLPHE RAPETTI

Adami, Valerio (*b* Bologna, 17 March 1935). Italian painter, draughtsman and printmaker. He was given a rigorous training as a draughtsman between 1951 and 1954 in Achille Funi's studio at the Accademia di Belle Arti di Brera, Milan, which provided the basis for his mature work. Before developing his characteristic contour line and flat surfaces, he experimented briefly with an expressionistic style that combined violent and humorous imagery inspired by the explosive forms in space favoured by Roberto Matta and by strip cartoons; typical of this phase is one of his earliest large canvases, *L'ora del sandwiche* (1963; Camilla Adami priv. col., see Damisch and Martin, pl. 42). He settled in Paris in 1957 but divided his time between France and Italy. In such paintings as *Stanze a cannocchiale* ('Telescoped rooms', 1965; Pittsburgh, PA, Carnegie Mus. A.) he began to develop a highly decorative idiom of stylized images outlined in black on a surface of interlocking areas of intense, unmodulated colour. His usual starting-point was a photograph or several associated images, which he reworked, fragmented and presented in a schematic form. This remained Adami's system of working in later years, although his subject-matter changed.

From 1968 to 1970 he favoured everyday themes, such as shop-windows, hotel rooms or bathroom interiors of a clinical and disturbing cleanliness. In the early 1970s he turned to recent political events and to literary and philosophical themes for inspiration. He produced paintings of representatives of modern European culture, such as *Sigmund Freud Journeying to London* (1973; Saint-Paul-de-Vence, Fond. Maeght). In the mid-1970s he introduced mythological and metaphysical themes. Adami conceived of his painting as a synthesis of Western memory, a humanist quest infused with nostalgia.

BIBLIOGRAPHY
H. Damisch and H. Martin: *Adami* (Paris, 1974)
M. Le Bot: *Valerio Adami, essai sur le formalisme critique* (Auvers-sur-Oise, 1975)
Adami (exh. cat., Paris, Pompidou, 1985)

ALFRED PACQUEMENT

Adams, Ansel (Easton) (*b* San Francisco, CA, 20 Feb 1902; *d* Carmel, CA, 22 April 1984). American photographer. He trained as a musician and supported himself by teaching the piano until 1930. He became involved with photography in 1916 when his parents presented him with a Kodak Box Brownie camera during a summer vacation in Yosemite National Park. In 1917–18 he worked part-time in a photo-finishing business. From 1920 to 1927 he served as custodian of the LeConte Memorial in Yosemite, the Sierra Club's headquarters. His duties included leading weekly expeditions through the valley and rims, during which he continued to photograph the landscape. He considered his snapshots of Yosemite and the Sierra Nevada Mountains, taken during the early 1920s, to be a visual diary, the work of an ardent hobbyist. By 1923 he used a $6\frac{1}{2}\times8\frac{1}{2}$-inch Korona view camera on his pack trips, and in 1927 he spent an afternoon making one of his most famous images, *Monolith, the Face of Half Dome, Yosemite National Park* (Chicago, IL, A. Inst.; see fig.). Adams planned his photograph, waited for the exact sunlight he desired and used a red filter to darken the sky against the monumental cliff. He later referred to this image as his 'first true visualization' of the subject, not as it appeared 'in reality but how it *felt* to me and how it must appear in the finished print' (*Ansel Adams: An Autobiography*, p. 76).

With the assistance of Albert Bender (1866–1941), one of San Francisco's foremost patrons of the arts, Adams published his first portfolio, *Parmelian Prints of the High Sierras* (San Francisco, 1927), and his first illustrated book, *Taos pueblo* (San Francisco, 1930). In 1930 he met Paul Strand and decided to devote himself to photography. Strand's photographic vision made Adams realize the potential of the medium as an expressive art form. Adams abandoned textured photographic paper, his last vestige of Pictorialism, for glossy stock and experienced a liberation in his creative direction as well. In 1932 he and several San Francisco Bay Area photographers formed GROUP f.64 to promote 'straight' unmanipulated photography.

Adams visited Alfred Stieglitz at his New York gallery, An American Place, in 1933 and exhibited there in 1936, his contact with Stieglitz giving him more confidence in the medium. He wrote his first technical manual, *Making a Photograph* (London & New York, 1935), and subsequently published several others, along with collections of photographs.

Adams used all types of camera and experimented constantly with new techniques. He developed a 'zone system', which divided the gradations of light into ten zones from black to white, allowing the photographer, with the help of an exposure meter, to correlate areas of different luminosity in the subject with the approximate value of grey in the final print. Adams's technical mastery, his complete control of the final image, was a necessary stage of development in achieving his full creative vision. His photographs transcend the simple description of objects and landscape: they depict transient aspects of light, atmosphere and natural phenomena.

In 1940 Adams helped to establish the Department of Photography at the Museum of Modern Art in New York and co-curated its first exhibition. He also established the Department of Photography at the California School of Fine Arts (now the San Francisco Art Institute) in 1946. He moved to Carmel, CA, in 1961 and was one of the founders of the Friends of Photography in 1966.

Ansel Adams: *Monolith, the Face of Half Dome, Yosemite National Park*, 1927 (Chicago, IL, Art Institute of Chicago)

WRITINGS

with V. Adams: *Illustrated Guide to Yosemite Valley* (San Francisco, 1946, rev. 2/1963)
with E. Land, D. McAlpin and J. Holmes: *Ansel Adams: Singular Images* (New York, 1974)
Ansel Adams: An Autobiography (Boston, 1985)

PHOTOGRAPHIC PUBLICATIONS

Sierra Nevada: The John Muir Trail (Berkeley, CA, 1938)
Born Free and Equal: Photographs of the Loyal Japanese-Americans at Manzanar Relocation Center, Inyo County, California (New York, 1944)
Camera and Lens (New York, 1948)
The Negative (New York, 1948)
My Camera in Yosemite Valley (Yosemite, CA, 1949)
My Camera in the National Parks (Yosemite, CA, 1950)
The Print (New York, 1950)
Natural Light Photography (New York, 1952)
Artificial-Light Photography (New York, 1956)
These we Inherit (San Francisco, 1962)
Polaroid Land Photography Manual (New York, 1963, rev. 1978)
Examples: The Making of 40 Photographs (Boston, 1983)

BIBLIOGRAPHY

J. Muir: *Yosemite and the High Sierra* (Boston, 1948)
M. Austin: *The Land of Little Rain* (Boston, 1950)
N. Newhall: *Death Valley* (Redwood City, CA, 1954)
——: *Mission San Xavier del Bac* (Redwood City, CA, 1954)
——: *The Pageant of History in Northern California* (San Francisco, 1954)
N. Newhall, ed.: *Yosemite Valley* (San Francisco, 1959)
E. Corle: *Death Valley and the Creek Called Furnace* (Los Angeles, 1962)
N. Newhall: *The Eloquent Light*, i of *Ansel Adams* (San Francisco, 1963) [only vol.]
E. Joesting: *An Introduction to Hawaii* (Redwood City, CA, 1964)
N. Newhall: *Fiat Lux: The University of California* (New York, 1967)
——: *The Tetons and the Yellowstone* (Redwood City, CA, 1970)
L. de Cock, ed.: *Ansel Adams* (New York, 1972)
W. Stegner: *Ansel Adams: Images, 1923–1974* (Boston, 1974)
L. C. Powell: *Photographs of the Southwest* (Boston, 1976)
J. Szarkowski: *The Portfolios of Ansel Adams* (Boston, 1977)
J. Alinder and M. S. Alinder: *Ansel Adams: A San Francisco Heritage* (San Francisco, 1978)
P. Brooks: *Yosemite and the Range of Light* (Boston, 1979)
J. Alinder: *The Unknown Ansel Adams* (Carmel, 1982)
A. Gray: *Ansel Adams: An American Place, 1936* (Tucson, 1982)
H. M. Callahan, ed.: *Ansel Adams in Color* (Boston and London, 1993)

RICHARD LORENZ

Adams, Clinton (*b* Glendale, CA, 11 Dec 1918). American painter, printmaker, art historian, writer and teacher. His appointment to the art faculty of the University of California, Los Angeles, in 1942 was interrupted by military service, and it was not until 1946 that he resumed his career as a teacher of the practice and theory of art. This took him to the universities of Kentucky (Lexington), Florida (Gainesville) and finally New Mexico (Albuquerque), where he served as Dean (1961–76). Despite academic demands, Adams always found time to paint and showed his work in over 50 solo exhibitions. Equally at home in oil, acrylic, watercolour and egg tempera, he was initially inspired by the abstracted cityscapes of Stuart Davis. Later he absorbed the lessons of Matisse, achieving particularly radiant paintings during the 1980s. In 1993 he was elected an Academician by the National Academy of Design.

In 1948, at Stanton Macdonald-Wright's suggestion, Adams began to make lithographs with the Los Angeles printer, Lynton Kistler. Early in his use of colour, he exhibited at the *1st International Biennial of Color Lithography* (1950) in Cincinnati, OH. During 1960 Adams helped JUNE WAYNE set up the Tamarind Lithography Workshop, which transformed printmaking in the USA. When the Workshop moved to Albuquerque as the Tamarind Institute, Adams became its Director (1970–85; *see* LITHOGRAPHY, §II, 2(ii)(c)).

During the 1970s Adams entered an intensive period as a writer, founding the exemplary research journal *The Tamarind Papers* in 1974, and editing and contributing to it until 1996. The author of more than 100 articles about lithography, he co-authored the 'bible' of the process in 1971 and went on to write an outstanding history (1983) of lithography in America. In 1985, Adams received the Governor's Award for 'Outstanding Contributions to the Arts of New Mexico'. In fact, through his many activities, his impact on the knowledge and practice of lithography has been world-wide.

WRITINGS

with G. Antreasian: *The Tamarind Book of Lithography: Art and Techniques* (New York, 1971)
Fritz Scholder Lithographs (Boston, 1975)
'The Prints of Andrew Dasburg: A Complete Catalogue', *Tamarind Pap.*, iv (1980–81), pp. 18–25
American Lithographers, 1900–1960: The Artists and their Printers (Albuquerque, 1983)
'Adolf Dehn: The Lithographs', *The Prints of Adolf Dehn: A Catalogue Raisonné* (St Paul, 1987), pp. 26–42
'The Nature of Lithography', *Lasting Impressions: Lithography as Art*, ed. P. Gilmour (Canberra, London, Philadelphia, 1988), pp. 24–41
Printmaking in New Mexico, 1880–1890 (Albuquerque, 1991)
Crayonstone: The Life and Work of Bolton Coit Brown, with a Catalogue of his Lithographs (Albuquerque, 1993)
Regular contributions to *Tamarind Pap.* (1974–95)

BIBLIOGRAPHY

Tamarind: Homage to Lithography (exh. cat. by V. Allen, New York, MOMA, 1969), pp. 10, 13, 27, 60
Clinton Adams (exh. cat. by V. D. Coke, Albuquerque, U. NM, A. Mus., 1971)
J. Watrous: *A Century of American Printmaking, 1880–1980* (Madison, WI, 1984)
Clinton Adams: Paintings and Watercolours, 1945–1987 (exh. cat. by V. D. Coke and P. Walch, Albuquerque, U. NM, A. Mus., 1987)
P. Gilmour: 'Lithographic Collaboration: The Hand, the Head, the Heart', *Lasting Impressions: Lithography as Art*, ed. P. Gilmour (Canberra, London and Philadelphia, 1988), pp. 264, 344–5, 347–9, 358
Spectrum of Innovation: Color in American Printmaking, 1890–1960 (exh. cat. by D. Acton, Worcester, MA, A. Mus., 1990–91), pp. 33–9, 246–8

PAT GILMOUR

Adams, Mark (*b* Fort Plain, NY, 27 Oct 1925). American tapestry artist, painter and stained-glass designer. He studied painting at Syracuse University and with Hans Hoffmann in New York, where he was influenced by the medieval tapestries in the Cloisters and also by the work of Matisse. In the 1950s Adams was apprenticed to the influential French tapestry designer Jean Lurçat, from whom he learnt the bold colours and clear imagery that characterize his work. He also studied at the Ecole Nationale d'Art Décoratif in Aubusson before beginning to use a series of workshops, notably that of Marguerite and Paul Avignon, who wove his first nationally acclaimed tapestry, *Phoenix and the Golden Gate* (1957). *Flight of Angels* (1962) was exhibited at the first Biennale Internationale de la Tapisserie in Lausanne. In 1976 his cartoon of *California Poppies* (San Francisco, CA Pal. Legion of Honor; see fig.) was woven for the *Five Centuries of Tapestry* exhibition at the California Palace of the Legion of Honor, San Francisco, as a demonstration piece. Later tapestries, for example *White Block* (1977) and *Sunset with Palms* (1979), were woven by the San Francisco Tapestry Workshop, with which he was associated. Public

Mark Adams: *California Poppies*, cotton and wool, 1.37×0.86 m, 1976 (San Francisco, CA, California Palace of the Legion of Honor); woven by graduate students of the Fine Arts department of San Francisco State University under the direction of Jean-Pierre Larochette

commissions included a series of panels depicting garden scenes for the San Francisco International Airport (1981–3) as well as designs for stained-glass windows, notably two for the Temple Emanu-El in San Francisco (*Fire* and *Water*, 1971–4). He painted a self-portrait in 1982 (artist's col., see Johnson, Mills and Price, p. 25).

BIBLIOGRAPHY

Mark Adams: An Exhibition of Tapestries, Paintings, Stained Glass Windows and Architectural Designs (exh. cat. by W. H. Elsner, San Francisco, CA Pal. Legion of Honor, 1970)
Mark Adams (exh. cat. by H. T. Hopkins, San Francisco, CA, John Berggruen Gal., 1980)
R. F. Johnson, P. Mills and L. Price: *Mark Adams* (San Francisco, 1985)

COURTNEY ANN SHAW

Adams, Maurice B(ingham) (*b* Burgess Hill, Sussex, 1849; *d* London, 17 Aug 1933). English architect, editor and draughtsman. After completing his articles with H. N. Goulty of Brighton, he became assistant to William Ralph Emerson, and Architect to Brighton Council. Between 1872 and 1923 he was Editor of *Building News*. He instituted the Building News Designing Club, which enabled young architects to submit designs for his criticism. He contributed largely to the paper's illustrations, redrawing designs for lithographic reproduction, and covered a wide range of subjects in a skilful and accurate, if somewhat dull, linear style. He also published several architectural books. Through the owner of *Building News* he obtained his major architectural commissions, notably Camberwell Polytechnic and Art Gallery (1902). He also designed country houses near London, for example Queensmead Cottage, Kings Road, Windsor, Berks (1883), for Reginald Talbot, as well as in Australia (e.g. Bellevue Hill, Double Bay, for Charles B. Fairfax in the mid-1880s) and America, where he designed timber houses in New Jersey for E. S. Wilde in *c.* 1890. By 1878 he had settled in Bedford Park, the pioneering London garden suburb, which he helped to publicize. There he completed R. Norman Shaw's church of St Michael and All Angels, adding the north aisle and parish hall (1887), and the chapel of All Souls (1909). He also designed the School of Art in 1882 (destr.) and two houses with a studio for the artist J. C. Dollmann (1851–1934) in 1880. Adams was a practical planner and his style varied from domestic QUEEN ANNE REVIVAL to a cheerfully inventive Jacobean eclecticism.

WRITINGS

with R. N. Shaw: *Sketches for Cottages* (London, 1878)
Artists' Homes (London, 1883)
Modern Cottage Architecture (London, 1904)
Cottage Housing (London, 1914)

BIBLIOGRAPHY

T. A. Greeves: 'London's First Garden Suburb', *Country Life*, cxlii (7 Dec 1967), pp. 1524–9
——: 'The Making of a Community', *Country Life*, cxlii (14 Dec 1967), pp. 1600–02
——: *Bedford Park: The First Garden Suburb* (London, 1975)
——: 'London's First Garden Suburb: 100 Years of Bedford Park', *Country Life*, clviii (27 Nov 1975), pp. 1446–8
A. S. Gray: *Edwardian Architecture: A Biographical Dictionary* (London, 1985)

T. AFFLECK GREEVES

Adams, Robert (i) (*b* Northampton, 5 Oct 1917; *d* Gt Maplestead, Essex, 5 April 1984). English sculptor and painter. He studied at the Northampton School of Art from 1933 to 1944. During World War II he was employed as an engineer, and after the war he spent two years teaching himself to sculpt in wood. Though he had participated in various group exhibitions during the war, it was not until 1947 that he had his first one-man show, of sculpture, at the Gimpel Fils Gallery in London. He also produced abstract paintings, but soon came to specialize in sculpture. His early sculpture of this period, such as *Figure* (1949–51; London, Tate), showed the influence of Henry Moore, whose works he knew from photographs. These comprised forms abstracted from natural objects, executed in wood, plaster and stone. After his one-man show he made several extended trips to Paris, where he became interested in the work of Brancusi and Julio González. In 1950 he received a Rockefeller award from the Institute of International Education to visit the USA. Having by then an established reputation, he was also commissioned to produce a 3-m high carving for the Festival of Britain in 1951.

In 1949 Adams had begun to work with metal and the same year was given a teaching post in industrial design at the Central School of Art and Design in London, which he held until 1960. While there he came into contact with Victor Pasmore and with the group of artists around him, which included Adrian Heath (*b* 1920), Anthony Hill, Kenneth Martin and Mary Martin. The group acted as a forum for Constructivist ideas in Britain and Adams exhibited with them from 1951 to 1956. Unlike the rest of the group, however, he rejected both mathematical formulae and new materials in sculpture. Many of his works were in wood and were based on organic forms, as in *Growing Forms* (1954; see 1962 exh. cat., pl. D). He was nevertheless sympathetic to the group's aim of forging a link between art and architecture, and this was reflected in his vast mural relief for the Municipal Theatre at Gelsenkirchen in Germany, constructed in 1959 from reinforced concrete.

While teaching at the Central School Adams learnt how to weld and in 1955 began to produce constructions of sheet and rod elements, as in *Tall Spike Forms* (1956; see 1962 exh. cat., pl. L), which showed the influence of González and a move towards non-figuration. In 1962, together with Hubert Dalwood (1924–76), Adams represented British sculpture at the Venice Biennale. His work of the 1960s often used welded steel sheets, sometimes perforated, as in *Large Screen Form* (1962; London, Tate). These were ideally to be displayed against a well-lit background so as to allow light to shine through. In 1966 he produced a large steel sculpture for the British Petroleum building in London, made from welded geometrical elements formed into a relief arrangement.

In the 1970s and until his death Adams concentrated on bronze casts, which though still non-figurative were softer and less geometrical than before, as in *Ovoid Variations* (1980; see 1988 exh. cat., pl. 27). Among his later public works was the large steel sculpture for Kingswell in Hampstead (1973), designed from a simple, Minimalist form.

BIBLIOGRAPHY

Robert Adams (exh. cat. by A. Hill, London, Gimpel Fils, 1951)
L. Alloway: *Nine Abstract Artists* (London, 1954), pp. 21–2
Ceri Richards, Robert Adams, Hubert Dalwood: British Pavilion (exh. cat. by J. P. Hodin, Venice Biennale, 1962)
Robert Adams, Retrospective Exhibition (exh. cat. by C. Spencer, London, Camden A. Cent., 1971)
P. Curtis: *Modern British Sculpture from the Collection* (Liverpool, Tate, 1982)
Robert Adams: Late Bronzes (exh. cat., London, Gimpel Fils, 1988)

□

Adams, Robert (ii) (*b* Orange, NJ, 8 May 1937). American photographer. After teaching English literature for several years, Adams turned to photography in the late 1960s, studying with Minor White. In his black-and-white photographs of the American West, such as his series *From the Missouri West* (1980), he emphasized man's presence in nature and the tension between the beauty of the landscape and man's effect upon it. His landscapes include such features as telephone poles and wires, mountains edged by highway guard-rails, parking lots and housing complexes. In 1975 Adams took part in the group exhibition *New Topographics: Photographs of a Man-altered Landscape* (*see* NEW TOPOGRAPHICS). As a photographer and an articulate writer on photography, he has published *Summer Nights* (1985) and important essays on 19th- and 20th-century photography.

BIBLIOGRAPHY

Mirrors and Windows: American Photography since 1960 (exh. cat., ed. J. Szarkowski; New York, MOMA, 1978)
J. Z. Grover: 'The Sublime and the Anachronistic: Robert Adams' American Landscape', *After image* (1981), pp. 6–7

MARY CHRISTIAN

Adams, Tate (*b* Holywood, County Down, Ireland, 26 Jan 1922). Australian painter, printmaker, book designer, lecturer, collector, gallery director and publisher of limited edition artists' books, of Irish decent. He worked as a draughtsman before entering war service in the British Admiralty from 1940 to 1949, including five years in Colombo, where he made sketching trips to jungle temples with the Buddhist monk and artist Manjsiro Thero. Between 1949 and 1951 Adams worked as an exhibition designer in London and studied wood-engraving with Gertrude Hermes in her evening class at the Central School of Arts and Crafts (now Central St Martin's College of Art and Design). In 1951, after moving to Melbourne, Adams began a 30-year teaching commitment at the Royal Melbourne Institute of Technology (RMIT), where he instructed many of the younger generation of Australian printmakers, including George Baldessin and Jan Senbergs. A brief return to Britain and Ireland in 1957–8 provided experience with Dolmen Press, Dublin, which published his first book of engravings, *The Soul Cages* (1958). Returning to Melbourne, Adams established a specialized printmaking diploma at the RMIT and, from 1959, undertook nine journeys to Japan, making contact with contemporary printmakers there. His Crossley Gallery, the first in Australia devoted exclusively to prints, opened in 1966. Located in Melbourne, it became the active hub of Australian contemporary printmaking, showing such artists as Fred Williams, Roger Kemp, Leonard French and John Brack. In 1974 Adams and Baldessin opened the Crossley Print Workshop to publish artists' prints. Subsequently the Lyre Bird Press, established in 1977, published fine-quality limited-edition books, among them the award-winning *John Brack Nudes* (1982). In 1989, shortly before his election to Fellowship of the Royal Society of Painter-Etchers and Engravers, Adams moved to northern Queensland, re-establishing the Lyre Bird Press at James Cook University of North Queensland, Townsville, where it continues to publish.

WRITINGS

The Lyre Bird Speaks (Townsville, 1994)

BIBLIOGRAPHY

J. Zimmer: *Recent Australian Prints* (Melbourne, 1984)
A. McCulloch and S. McCulloch: *The Encyclopedia of Australian Art* (Sydney, 1994), pp. 27–8

□

Adam-Salomon, Antoine-Samuel (*b* La Ferté-sous-Jouarre, Seine-et-Marne, 9 Jan 1818; *d* Paris, 1881). French photographer and sculptor. He originally worked as a sculptor, and he turned to portrait photography under the influence of the Munich photographer Franz Hanfstaengel. Adam-Salomon's antique poses, making much use of light and shade to give painterly effects, were inspired by Classical sculpture and painting and incorporated expensive fabrics and settings. He also favoured heavy retouching of the negatives, for which he was criticized by some contemporaries. He was, however, much admired for the imposing character of many of his portraits (e.g. *Portrait of a Man*, *c*. 1865; see Berger and Levrault, no. 1). He continued his sculpture as well, producing portrait busts (many still extant), generally based on photographs. Subjects included Rossini and the poet Lamartine, as well as a monument in Les Invalides, Paris, to the Duke of Padua. Some of those hostile to photography, such as Lamartine, were persuaded to consider it as an art by the work of Adam-Salomon. He founded his studio in Paris in 1859, working on reproductions of works of art as well as portraits of the rich bourgeoisie, and he proposed working on a portrait gallery of European notables. He was made a member of the Société Française de Photographie in 1870 and received the Légion d'honneur the same year. He held exhibitions of his work in Paris in 1859, 1867 and 1869, in London in 1867 and in Boston, MA, in 1869. His style is typified by the late *Self-portrait as Dr Faust*, where he portrays himself in velvet robe, seated on a carved throne with his hand resting on a skull.

BIBLIOGRAPHY

A. de Lamartine: *Cours familier de littérature* (Paris, 1859) [interview]

R. Lecuyer: *Histoire de la photographie* (Paris, 1945), pp. 99–100

Berger and Levrault, eds: *Regards sur la photographie en France au XIXe siècle* (Paris, 1980)

PATRICIA STRATHERN

Adamson, Amandus [Amand (Ivanovich)] (*b* Uuga Rätsepa, nr Paldiski, 12 Nov 1855; *d* Paldiski, 26 June 1929). Estonian sculptor. From childhood he excelled in wood-carving. His first serious work after graduating from the St Petersburg Academy of Arts, where he studied (1876–81) under Alexander Bock (1829–95), was a carved frame for Johann Köler's painting *Tribute to Caesar* (1883; Tallinn, A. Mus.), commissioned by several Estonian art associations on the occasion of the coronation of Alexander III (*reg* 1881–94). This work was inspired by Adamson's impressions of altars in 17th-century churches in Tallinn. Baroque motifs became an important feature of his work, as in his allegorical miniatures *Dawn* and *Dusk* (1895; Tallinn, A. Mus.), carved from pear wood. Adamson completed his studies in Paris, where he was influenced by the works of Jean-Baptiste Carpeaux and Jules Dalou. A theme that runs through his smaller works is the sea, as in the *Boat's Last Breath* (wax, 1899; biscuit, 1901, executed at the Imperial Porcelain Factory, St Petersburg, Rus. Mus.; marble, 1926, Tallinn, Salme Cult. Cent.). He also sculpted monumental works on the Baltic and Black Seas, such as the monument to the *Sailors of the Battleship Rusalka* (1902; Tallinn) and a monument to *Boats Lost at Sea* (1904; Sevastopol'). Alongside his romantic interpretation of the sea, Adamson also depicted the sea as a workplace, as in *Fisherman from the Island of Muhu* (plaster, 1892) and *In Anxious Expectation* (bronze, 1897; both Tallinn, A. Mus.).

In 1907 Adamson became an academician of the Academy of Arts in St Petersburg. He created models for several multifigural monuments that can be compared with works by Mikhail Mikeshin. Adamson sculpted a composition for the 300th anniversary of the Romanovs in Kostroma (1911–17; destr.) and was also involved in the decoration of several important buildings in St Petersburg, including a frieze for the Russian Museum of Alexander III (1900–1911; now the Museum of Ethnography) and ornamentation for the Singer Company building (1902–4; architect Pavel Syuzor) and the Yeliseyev trading house (1902–6; architect Gavriil Baranovsky), both on Nevsky Prospect.

After Estonia proclaimed its independence in 1917, Adamson lived in Paldiski. His allegorical works of this period show the drama of post-war life, as in *Hunger, 1918–20* (Tallinn, City Mus.). In 1922–3 in Italy, he reworked many of his earlier creations in marble and sculpted a group for the altar of St Paul's, Tartu. He had earlier taken up painting, as in *Women from the Island of Capri Repairing Nets* (1896; Tallinn, priv. col.). He also taught at the Baron Stieglitz Institute of Technical Drawing (1901–4) and the drawing school of the Society for the Encouragement of the Arts (1881–7) in St Petersburg.

BIBLIOGRAPHY

T. Nurk: *Amandus Adamson, 1855–1929* (Tallinn, 1960)

SERGEY KUZNETSOV

Adamson, John (*b* Fife, 1809; *d* St Andrews, Fife, 1870). Scottish photographer. He studied medicine in Edinburgh (1829) and Paris, but returned to St Andrews in the 1830s. A member of the St Andrews Literary and Philosophical Society, he associated with the circle interested in photographic experimentation and theory. Adamson experimented with Talbot's calotype process, introduced to Scotland by Sir David Brewster (1781–1868), and made the first calotype portrait in Scotland, of *Miss Melville Adamson* (*c*. 1842; Edinburgh, Royal Mus. Scotland; see Morrison-Low, p. 20). He taught several of the early Scottish photographers, including his younger brother, Robert (*see* HILL AND ADAMSON), and Thomas Rodger (1833–83) of St Andrews. Most of Adamson's surviving work is in the Royal Museum of Scotland, Edinburgh, and St Andrews University Library.

BIBLIOGRAPHY

A. D. Morrison-Low: 'Dr John and Robert Adamson: An Early Partnership in Scottish Photography', *Phot. Col*, iv/2 (1983), pp. 198–214

JULIE LAWSON

Adamson, Robert. *See under* HILL AND ADAMSON.

Adamson Associates. Canadian architectural partnership established in 1934 in Toronto by Gordon Sinclair Adamson (1904–86), who practised in the city for 20 years. The firm has been prominent internationally for many decades, and responsible for major, multi-complex modern building projects in Canada, North America and England. In 1949 Adamson Associates was the first architectural group in Ontario to establish an in-house consultancy for the interior design and furnishing of their buildings. In 1962 the company expanded into large-scale structural and site planning. By the 1970s the firm was recognized for its expertise in curtain-wall and cladding techniques, and for state-of-the-art, energy-saving heating and cooling systems. The company's notable projects include the North York Municipal Building (1974–8), Toronto, Gulf Canada Square (1977–9; now Canada Crescent Corporation; associate architects), Calgary, Alta, and North American Life Centre (1986–8), North York, Ont. Adamson Associates was the architectural company responsible for coordinating all the buildings that comprise New York's World Financial Center, and architects for the pyramidal-roofed Three World building (1985) and the Winter Garden (1988), both designed by Cesar Pelli. The latter is a glazed, barrel-vaulted public promenade, lined with shops and cafés and decorated with tall palm trees brought from California. The company also acted as executive architects for the Canary Wharf scheme in London's docklands (from 1987) in association with Cesar Pelli and others. Adamson Associates built the 50-storey Canary Wharf tower, which is clad in stainless steel, and designed the Docklands Light Railway Station there.

BIBLIOGRAPHY
'Hydro Place, Toronto', *Can. Architect*, xxi (April 1976), pp. 26–9
J. Hix: 'Learning from Hydro Place', *Can. Architect*, xxi (April 1976), pp. 30–38
'C. D. Howe Building, Ottawa', *Can. Architect*, xxv (March 1980), pp. 19–27
L. Whiteson: *Modern Canadian Architecture* (Edmonton, Alta, 1983), pp. 188–91, 270

□

Adam van Düren. *See* DÜREN, ADAM VAN.

Adán, Juan (*b* Tarazona, 1741; *d* Madrid, 1816). Spanish sculptor. He was trained in Saragossa with José Ramirez. In 1765 he went to Rome, where he won a scholarship from the Spanish Academia de Bellas Artes and was appointed Director of the Accademia di S Luca, Rome. Adán's early work became known in Spain through the drawings and sculptures he sent from Rome, the finest being a *Lamentation.* He returned to Spain in 1776 and worked in Lérida, Granada and Jaen, finally settling in Madrid in 1786. In 1793 he was appointed court sculptor (Escultor de Cámara) by Charles IV (*reg* 1788–1808). He made many carvings in wood, such as a *St Joseph* and a *Virgin of the Sorrows*, for churches in Madrid. Other characteristic works are the portrait busts of leading contemporary figures such as *Manuel Godoy, the Prince de la Paz*, and *José Monino, the Conde de Floridablanca.* The busts of *Charles IV* and *Queen Maria Luisa* (Madrid, Pal. Real) recall their portraits by Goya. Adán's *Venus* (1793) at the Alameda, Osuna, is one of the finest works of Spanish Neo-classicism. During the French invasion of 1808 he refused to cooperate with the enemy, and after the war he was elected Director of Sculpture at the Real Academia de S Fernando, Madrid.

BIBLIOGRAPHY
E. Pardo Canalís: *Escultores del siglo XIX* (Madrid, 1951)
F. J. Sánchez Cantón: *Escultura y pintura del siglo XVIII*, A. Hisp., xvii (Madrid, 1965)

JUAN NICOLAU

Adaro Magro, Eduardo (*b* Madrid, 6 Feb 1848; *d* Madrid, 27 March 1906). Spanish architect. In 1872 he graduated from the Escuela de Arquitectura of the Real Academia de Bellas Artes de S Fernando, Madrid, and began his long service with the Banco de España. He belonged to the generation of Spanish architects active after the restoration of Alfonso XII in 1874. Adaro Magro favoured a variant of eclectic classicism, embellishing the academic designs of his façades with ornament drawn from Renaissance models and in a style not far removed from that of the Beaux-Arts. He was elected a member of the Real Academia de Bellas Artes de S Fernando in 1903 but was unable to take his place there.

Adaro Magro's principal work was the Banco de España (begun 1884; inaugurated 1891) in the Paseo del Prado, Madrid. He received the commission after a national competition failed to produce an entry. Severiano Sáinz de la Lastra (*d* 1884) contributed to the plans, Lorenzo Alvarez Capra (1836–1901) and José María Aguilar collaborated on its execution, while Alejandro Herrero, José Amador de los Ríos and Aníbal Alvarez (1806–70) were engaged in the decoration. The building is designed in a classicist aesthetic, in which Italian and French influences are intermingled. Adaro Magro was also active in the construction of elegant country houses, luxury residences and penitentiary buildings. He designed memorial monuments and took part in the reconstruction of buildings destroyed by the earthquake in Upper Andalusia in 1884.

BIBLIOGRAPHY
P. Navascués: *Arquitectura y arquitectos madrileños del siglo XIX* (Madrid, 1973)
Guía de arquitectura y urbanismo de Madrid, Colegio Oficial de Arquitectos de Madrid, 2 vols (Madrid, 1982–3)

ALBERTO VILLAR MOVELLÁN

Addaura. Cave site in the northern slope of Monte Pellegrino 8 km north of Palermo on the north coast of

Addaura, engraved figures on the cave wall, *c.* 12,000 BP

Sicily. It contains a number of prehistoric figures engraved in the surface of a smooth slab of rock on the left-hand side (see fig.), which were revealed when a layer of stalagmite was detached by exploding ammunition in the 1940s. The earliest, lightly incised group includes horses, cattle, a hind and a woman carrying a bundle. The main group consists of ten male figures, each about 250 mm high, and a larger figure of a deer. The outlines of the former are bold and assured, though the heads are invariably crude, often animal- or bird-like; hands and feet were simply omitted. Later two bovids were added; these are much more roughly drawn. All had been covered by the stalagmite, which must have taken many centuries, if not millennia, to form. A date of *c.* 12,000 BP seems likely, since flints of this period were found in an adjacent cave. However, the scenes cannot be matched closely in comparable painted and engraved caves of France and Spain (*see* PREHISTORIC EUROPE, §II, 2). Even the rarer Italian examples, such as those at Romanelli, near Lecce, and Genovesi, Levanzo, contain nothing quite like them. The interpretation of the figures at Addaura is particularly controversial. The human figures stand, walk, crouch or lie on their faces, apparently painfully trussed; but it is not clear whether the artist intended them to be viewed as a single scene, perhaps of dancing or sacrifice, or as individual unrelated figures. The effect is powerful, but nevertheless it remains puzzling.

BIBLIOGRAPHY

I. Marconi Bovio: 'Incisioni rupestri all' Addaura (Palermo)', *Bull. Paletnol. It.*, viii/5 (1953), pp. 5–22
L. Bernabò Brea: *Sicily* (London, 1957), pp. 32–3
J. Hawkes: *Atlas of Ancient Archaeology* (London, 1974), p. 98

DAVID TRUMP

Addis, Sir **John M(ansfield)** (*b* London, 11 June 1914; *d* Pembury, Kent, 31 July 1983). English diplomat, collector and art historian. In 1947, as a member of the British Diplomatic Service, he was posted to Nanjing, Jiangsu Province, then the capital of the Nationalist Chinese government. He became interested in Chinese art and history and began a collection of porcelain, furniture and textiles at a time of political and economic uncertainty, when Chinese collectors were forced to sell. When he moved to the British embassy in Beijing in 1954 he continued his research into Chinese ceramic history with the help of specialists from the Palace Museum. In 1963 he became British ambassador to the Philippines and was largely responsible for organizing the Manila Trade Pottery Seminar (1968), to which he also contributed five of the nine discussion monographs. From 1972 to 1974, as British ambassador to China, he played an important part in promoting the Chinese archaeological exhibition *The Genius of China*, held in London at the Royal Academy in 1973–4, the first comprehensive exhibition of Chinese archaeological discoveries to be held in Europe. He contributed a number of valuable papers on underglaze copper red decorated wares to the Oriental Ceramic Society, London, of which he was president from 1974 to 1977. He gave most of his important collection of Chinese blue-and-white porcelain to the British Museum, London, together with a bequest that was used to establish the John Addis Islamic Gallery, and bequeathed his valuable textile collection and unique pieces of Chinese furniture to the Victoria and Albert Museum, London. He was a trustee of both the British Museum and the Victoria and Albert Museum, where he also served on the advisory council.

WRITINGS

'Some Buddhist Motifs as a Clue to Dating', 'Shu fu Type Wares Excavated in the Philippines', 'Some Ch'ing pai and White Wares Found in the Philippines', 'Early Blue and White Excavated in the Philippines', 'Underglaze Red Discovered in the Philippines', *Manila Trade Pottery Seminar: Manila, 1968*, nos 1–5
Exhibition of Chinese Blue and White Porcelain and Related Underglaze Red (exh. cat., Hong Kong, City A. Mus. & Gal., 1975)
Chinese Ceramics from Datable Tombs and some other Dated Material (London, 1978)
Chinese Porcelain From the Addis Collection: 22 Pieces of Jingdezhen (Chingtechen) Porcelain Presented to the British Museum (London, 1979)

MARGARET MEDLEY

Addison, Joseph (*b* Milston, Wilts, 1 May 1672; *d* London, 17 June 1719). English writer and politician. He was educated at Charterhouse School and Queen's College, Oxford, receiving his MA in 1693. Between 1699 and 1703 he travelled on the Continent; in his *Remarks upon Several Parts of Italy* (1705) he noted that Italy was 'the great school of Musick and Painting', and a primary purpose of his tour was 'to compare the natural face of the country with the Landskips the [classical] Poets have given us of it'. His *Remarks* became a *vade-mecum* on artistic matters for 18th-century British travellers.

Although he was active as a politician (he was appointed Under-Secretary of State in 1706 and was an MP, 1708–19), Addison's greatest influence was as an educator and popularizer of ideas on taste and culture, which he achieved through the periodical essay. He contributed to *The Tatler*, a thrice-weekly half-sheet founded by his friend Richard Steele (1672–1729), which ran from 1709 to 1711. Its successor, *The Spectator* (1711–12, 1714), was largely co-written with Steele; although first published as a daily periodical essay, it appeared soon after in book form and remained in print throughout the 18th century. As an arbiter of English taste in manners, literature and the arts for the age that followed him, Addison was without rival. His influence on aesthetic theory derives from such essays in *The Spectator* as the one on English gardens (no. 477), another on literature and art (no. 166) and, most importantly, from a series of 11 essays on the 'Pleasures of the Imagination' (nos 411–21), loosely indebted to John Locke's *An Essay Concerning Human Understanding* (1690). Though lacking complexity, Addison's judgements were frequently based on the pragmatic assumption that the arts should 'deduce their Laws and Rules from the general Sense and Taste of Mankind, and not from the Principles of those Arts themselves' (no. 29). The short fictional tales with which his essays abound can be seen as literary prototypes for the engraved moral tableaux of William Hogarth. Around 1712 Addison's kit-cat portrait was painted by Sir Godfrey Kneller (London, N.P.G.).

WRITINGS

Remarks upon Several Parts of Italy (London, 1705)
essays in *The Tatler* (1709–11); ed. D. F. Bond, 3 vols (Oxford, 1987)
essays in *The Spectator* (1711–12, 1714); ed. D. F. Bond, 5 vols (Oxford, 1965/*R* 1987)
Dialogues upon the Usefulness of Ancient Medals (London, 1721)

BIBLIOGRAPHY
S. Johnson: 'Addison' [1779], *Lives of the English Poets*, ed. G. B. Hill, 3 vols (Oxford, 1905), ii, pp. 79–158
P. Smithers: *The Life of Joseph Addison* (Oxford, 1954)
M. G. Ketcham: 'The Arts of Gesture: The *Spectator* and its Relationship to Physiognomy, Painting, and the Theater', *Mod. Lang. Q.*, xlii (1981), pp. 137–52
W. H. Youngren: 'Addison and the Birth of Eighteenth-century Aesthetics', *Mod. Philol.*, lxxix (1982), pp. 267–83

FRANK FELSENSTEIN

Adelaide. Australian city and capital of the state of South Australia. It is situated on the banks of the River Torrens, between the Mt Lofty Ranges and Gulf St Vincent in the south-eastern part of the continent. The city (population *c*. 1 million) is noted for its fine colonial urban plan. Adelaide was founded in 1836 as an exercise in planned settlement, jointly controlled by the British Government and a London committee whose members were influenced by Edward Gibbon Wakefield's ideas on systematic colonization. The final site for the city, *c*. 8 km from the sea, with a suitable inlet for a harbour (Port Adelaide) *c*. 11 km to the north-west, was selected amid considerable controversy by Surveyor-General Colonel William Light (1786–1839). Light's urban plan (see fig.) is remarkable for its public squares and parkland, features not included in Governor Darling's regulations (1829) for New South Wales, which dominated 19th-century urban planning in most parts of Australia. Light planned Adelaide in two parts, north and south of the river. The grid of the southern part, the principal commercial area, was orientated to the cardinal directions, with two main streets (King William Street and Grote/Wakefield streets) intersecting at a central square (Victoria Square). Four smaller squares were also included, and the outer streets on all four sides were planned as broad terraces, with North Terrace, bordering the river, intended for the best residences: Government House, a stuccoed Regency villa by GEORGE KINGSTON, was built there in 1838–9 (extended 1855 by E. A. Hamilton). A wide belt of parkland bisects the city along the river and surrounds it on all sides, separating it from its suburbs. North Adelaide, also with a public square, was orientated to the contours of the sloping land north of the river and was designed as the city's principal residential area.

A Board of Commissioners supervised the sale of land in the colony, cash purchasers receiving a town allotment of one acre (0.405 ha) and another 80 acres (*c*. 35.5 ha) in the country. By 1850 the growth of wheat production and the discovery of silver, lead and copper in the surrounding region had provided an influx of wealth and new migrants to Adelaide, among them German settlers who established the wine industry in the Barossa Valley, north of the city. South Australia received self-government in 1856, and its first parliament house was built in North Terrace, Adelaide, in the 1850s (rebuilt 1883–1939 by Edmund Wright and Lloyd Taylor). North Terrace subsequently became the cultural centre of the city and the site of such institutions as the South Australian Museum (founded 1856), which has the world's largest collection of Aboriginal artefacts, the University of Adelaide (1874) and the State Library (1879). In the vicinity of Victoria Square are the principal government buildings, including the Greek Revival Magistrates' Court (1847–50; by Richard Lambeth) and several Renaissance Revival buildings: the Treasury (1858–76, by E. A. Hamilton), Town Hall (1863–6; by EDMUND WRIGHT and E. J. Woods), General Post Office (1867–72; by Wright and Hamilton) and Supreme Court (1869; by R. G. Thomas). Nearby is the Roman Catholic cathedral of St Francis Xavier (begun 1856 by Charles Hansom, completed 1889 by Edward Pugin), in Spanish Gothic style, while the Anglican cathedral of St Peter (begun 1869; by William Butterfield) was built in North Adelaide in a French Gothic style. Suburban development around the city centre was greatly stimulated by a speculative land boom in the 1870s and early 1880s, leading to large-scale construction of single-storey houses and some fine mansions built in fashionable styles.

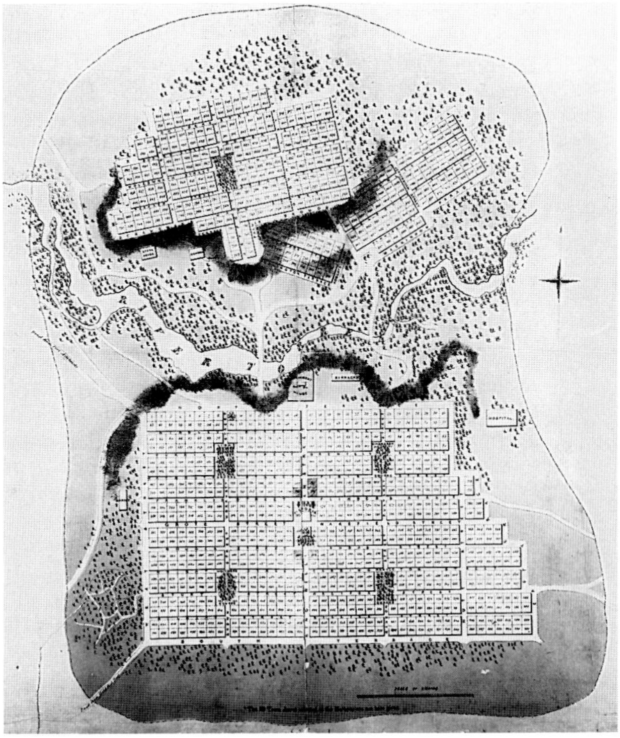

Adelaide, city plan by Colonel William Light, 1837 (Adelaide, South Australian State Archives)

Modern planning techniques were introduced to Adelaide with the Town Planning and Development Act of 1920, when garden suburbs (e.g. Colonel Light Gardens) were established to help meet the housing shortage created by a new influx of migrants after World War I. Expansion continued after World War II, when the satellite city of Elizabeth, north of Adelaide, was founded (1954–5), accompanied by the development of regional shopping and administrative centres. Population growth had slowed by the 1970s, however, and the following decades were marked by urban consolidation and inner-city renewal. Significant, mainly medium-rise commercial construction cycles took place in the city centre in the 1960s and 1980s, the latter including the development of a casino, hotel and conference centre over the railway station in North Terrace.

Notable artists active in Adelaide included George French Angas (1822–86), who recorded early views of the city, and HANS HEYSEN, who later rendered the landscape of the Adelaide Hills with great intensity (*see* AUSTRALIA, fig. 10). Adelaide boasts Australia's oldest art society, the Royal South Australian Society of Arts (1856), initiated by painter and teacher Charles Hill (1824–1916). In 1861 the School of Design (now Adelaide College of Arts and Education) was founded, laying the foundations for public art teaching in South Australia. Adelaide's principal gallery is the Art Gallery of South Australia (founded 1881), while Flinders University Art Museum (founded 1966) was one of the first in Australia to function in conjunction with art-historical studies. The Adelaide Festival Centre (1970–77; by Hassell & Partners) in the North Terrace parklands provides a focus for the prestigious biennial Adelaide Arts Festival (initiated 1960).

See also AUSTRALIA, especially §§II, III and XI–XIII.

BIBLIOGRAPHY

A. Grenfell Price: *Foundation and Settlement of South Australia* (Adelaide, 1924)
E. J. R. Morgan and S. H. Gilbert: *Early Adelaide Architecture, 1836–1886* (Melbourne, 1969)
C. Bond, ed.: *Preserving Historic Adelaide* (Adelaide, 1978)
E. Jensen and R. Jensen: *Colonial Architecture in South Australia* (Adelaide, 1980)
D. L. Johnson and D. Langmead: *The Adelaide City Plan* (Adelaide, 1986)
D. Whitelock: *Adelaide, 1836–1986: A History of Difference* (Adelaide, 1986)
G. Dutton and D. Elder: *Colonel William Light: Founder of a City* (Melbourne, 1991), pp. 137–276

VALERIE A. CLACK

Adelcrantz, C(arl) F(redrik) (*b* Stockholm, 3 Jan 1716; *d* Stockholm, 26 Feb 1796). Swedish architect. His father, Göran Josuae Adelcrantz (1668–1739), was a pupil and associate of Nicodemus Tessin (ii) and had studied in France and Italy before assisting in the building of the Kungliga Slott in Stockholm. He became City Architect of Stockholm and created the splendid Baroque cupola (1724–44) on Jean De la Vallée's Katarinakyrka, but he had been pushed aside during the political crisis that followed the death of Charles XII in 1718. He advised his son not to become an architect but nevertheless let him attend the drawing school at the palace. After his father's death, Adelcrantz went abroad for architectural study in Paris and Italy, returning in 1743 to assist Carl Hårleman in the interior work on the Kungliga Slott. In 1757 he became Superintendent and in 1767 President of the Royal Academy of Arts, which he reorganized by instituting schools of drawing and painting, sculpture and architecture. He was made a baron in 1766.

The Kina Slott (1763) in the gardens of Drottningholm Slott, near Stockholm, is the major work of Adelcrantz's Rococo period and a gem of sophisticated chinoiserie. The façades are in oxblood and ochre rendering, under gently curved, green copper roofs with bells and dragons on the corners. The interiors combine original Chinese material with painted pastiche ornaments of Rococo character and wainscoting painted in strong blue, green and red. Also at Drottningholm, Adelcrantz was responsible for the Court Theatre (1764–6; *see* THEATRE, fig. 16), which survives in its original state, as do the 18th-century costumes and stage machinery (*see* STOCKHOLM, §4(ii)). His main work as a theatre architect was the Royal Opera House (1775–82; destr. 1892) in Gustav Adolfs Torg, Stockholm, which had a horseshoe auditorium with balconies and a sloping stage incorporating machinery of the type established by Jacques-Germain Soufflot in Lyon. The interiors, like his contemporary palace interiors, were in the Swedish variant of the Louis XVI style, known as Gustavian, after Gustav III (who was assassinated in this opera house in 1792). The exterior (whose identical counterpart is mirrored in Erik Palmstedt's Sophia Albertina Palace on the opposite site) was Neo-classical with a giant order of Corinthian pilasters. This vocabulary was also used in Adelcrantz's Court of Appeal (1776) at Vaasa in Finland.

As Superintendent for almost 40 years, Adelcrantz strengthened his office's control of ecclesiastical and civic building. Among his own church projects, the Adolf Fredrikskyrka (1767–83) in Stockholm is of a centralized type on a slightly elongated Greek-cross plan and with a tower surmounted by a cupola over the crossing. For parish churches he preferred a longitudinal type with a simple, rectangular layout. In his mansions and country houses, he developed Hårleman's model, with simple, rectangular layouts and symmetrical arrangements of detached wings, as at Sturehof (1778) near Stockholm. Adelcrantz's work continued the French influence favoured by Hårleman, developing from Rococo into Neoclassicism. Later works demonstrate his awareness of the archaeologically severe early Greek revivalism that was coming into fashion at the end of his life.

BIBLIOGRAPHY

S. Fogelmarck: *Carl Fredrik Adelcrantz, arkitekt* (diss., Stockholm U., 1957)
H. O. Andersson and F. Bedoire: *Swedish Architecture: Drawings, 1640–1970* (Stockholm, 1986)

□

Ademollo, Carlo (*b* Florence, 9 Oct 1824; *d* Florence, 15 July 1911). Italian painter. He was the nephew of the painter Luigi Ademollo (1764–1849) and studied under Giuseppe Bezzuoli at the Accademia dei Belle Arti in Florence. He initially specialized in history painting, turning to genre painting and *vedute* in the 1850s. In about 1854 he joined the Scuola di Staggia, a group of painters who painted *en plein air* in the Sienese countryside near Staggia. He also frequented the Caffè Michelangelo in Florence, an important centre of artistic life at the time.

Ademollo was a volunteer in the campaigns of the Risorgimento in 1859 and 1866 and made many sketches and drawings of them, finally being appointed official painter to Garibaldi's army. He thus established himself as a popular painter of patriotic scenes, such as the monumental *Last Onslaught at the Battle of San Martino* (Florence, Pitti), the *Death of the Cairoli Brothers* (Pavia, Mus. Risorgimento) and the *Breach of Porta Pia* (Milan, Mus. Risorgimento). As well as these quasi-official activities, he produced successful portraits of contemporary politicians and the Florentine nobility, such as *Benedetto Cairoli* (1890; Pavia, Mus. Risorgimento).

BIBLIOGRAPHY
Thieme–Becker
A. De Gubernatis: *Dizionario degli artisti italiani viventi* (Florence, 1889)
ETTORE SPALLETTI

Adena Mound. Prehistoric site in North America. It is the largest of several mounds along the Scioto River north of Chillicothe, OH. Although it is the eponym of the Early Woodland-period Adena culture of the Upper Ohio River Valley (*c.* 1000–*c.* 100 BC), the date of the mound itself is unknown. No stylized engraved palettes, characteristic of Adena culture, were found. The mound comprises a penannular earthwork built in several stages to a height of 8 m. A circular structure with sloping sides and double-set wooden post walls was constructed on a floor from which numerous fires had been cleared. Next, burials were placed centrally in rectangular tombs dug into the floor of the structure, a low mound was heaped over them and the funerary structure was burned. The entire area was then covered by layers of black sand incorporating several new cremations and burials outside the central tombs. For some considerable time after this, additional cremated human remains and extended burials were placed in further layers of sand and gravel. The cremation and inhumation burials, and occasionally clay-covered bundles of bones, were accompanied by annular and penannular copper bracelets and rings; cut river mussel shell animal effigies; cut mica headbands; expanded centre gorgets, ground, polished and drilled, of schist and chlorite; and a human effigy carved in the round on an Ohio pipestone tube (see fig.).

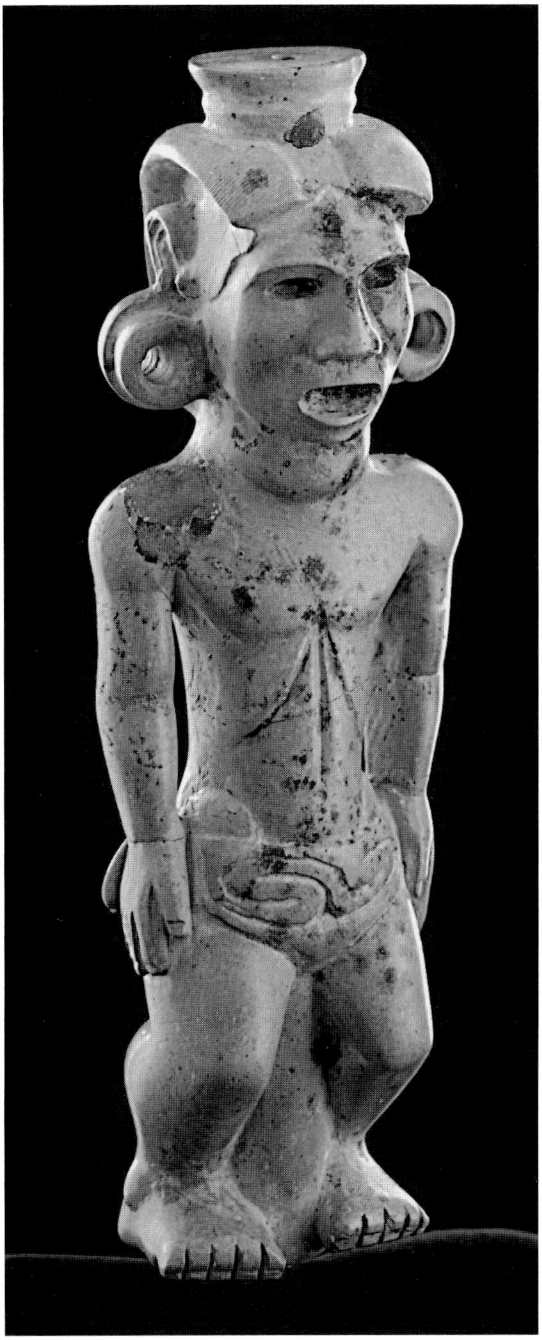

Adena Mound, human effigy, Ohio pipestone, late 1st millennium BC

BIBLIOGRAPHY
W. C. Mills: 'Excavation of the Adena Mound', *OH State Archaeol. Hist. Q.*, x (1902), pp. 451–79
W. S. Webb and C. E. Snow: *The Adena People*, University of Kentucky Reports in Anthropology and Archaeology, vi (Lexington, KY, 1945)
W. S. Webb and R. S. Baby: *The Adena People 2* (Columbus, OH, 1957)
D. S. Brose, J. A. Brown and D. W. Penney: *Ancient Art of the American Woodland Indians* (New York, 1985)
K. B. Farnsworth and T. E. Emerson: *Early Woodland Archaeology*, Center for American Archaeology, Kampsville Seminars in Archaeology, ii (Kampsville, IL, 1986)
DAVID S. BROSE

Adeodato. *See under* GRUAMONTE.

Aders, Carl (*b* Elberfeld, nr Wuppertal, 1780; *d* Italy, before 10 July 1846). German merchant and collector. He played a key role in the introduction of early Netherlandish art to British writers and artists during the reign of George IV. In 1806, Aders and an Englishman, William Jameson, co-founded a counting house—sources suggest it was an accounting firm serving the shipping industry—in Elberfeld, Germany. Business often called him to the commercial centres of Europe, and in the 1810s he began to frequent art dealers and to make purchases. His only adviser in this appears to have been his fiancée (later his wife), Elizabeth Smith, whom he met *c.* 1816. She was the daughter of the mezzotint engraver John Raphael Smith and was herself an amateur artist.

Aders bought prints and paintings of the Italian and Dutch schools, but the core of his collection was early Netherlandish painting. Few northern artists were known at the time, and little attempt had been made by scholars to sort out and identify various oeuvres. Art dealers attached a few recognizable names, such as Dürer, van Eyck and Memling, to almost any work that came into their possession, and many of Aders's paintings were falsely attributed to these artists. His collection, mainly purchased by the mid-1820s, was divided between his London house in Euston Square and a summer retreat in Godesberg, Germany. Alexander Gilchrist described the London establishment: 'The walls of drawing-room, bedroom, and even staircase, were all closely covered; with gallery railings in front to protect the pictures from injury.'

Aders owned a copy of Hubert and Jan van Eyck's *Adoration of the Lamb* (attributed to a 17th-century Netherlandish master and now in Antwerp, Kon. Mus. S. Kst.) that was celebrated during the 19th century as the only intact version of the altarpiece, the original having been dismantled and dispersed. (It is now reunited in Ghent, St Bavo's Cathedral; for illustration *see* EYCK, VAN, (1).) He also owned an exquisite *Virgin and Child* by Rogier van der Weyden (Lugano, Col. Thyssen-Bornemisza), believed to be part of a diptych with *St George and the Dragon* (Washington, DC, N.G.A.); a *Rest on the Flight into Egypt* by Memling (Paris, Baron Guy de Rothschild priv. col.); the *Virgin and Child with SS Jerome and Francis* by Petrus Christus (Frankfurt am Main, Städel. Kstinst. & Städt. Gal.); and many paintings now in the National Gallery, London, among them *Portrait of a Man* by Dieric Bouts I and a *Deposition* and *Adoration of the Magi* from an altarpiece by Gerard David.

Word of Aders's collection spread among contemporary artists, and many were invited to view it, including William Blake, Thomas Lawrence, George Beaumont, John Linnell, Francis Danby, Samuel Palmer, James Ward, Thomas Stothard, John Flaxman and the German Jakob Götzenberger. Samuel Coleridge, William Wordsworth and Charles Lamb were also friends of the Aderses; Lamb dedicated a charming poem to the collection, 'To C. Aders, Esq. On his collection of paintings by the Old German masters'. Three art critics, Johanna Schopenhauer, Johann David Passavant and Gustav Waagen, wrote about the paintings. Around 1830, 'a terrible reverse in trade' (Gilchrist) forced Aders to dissolve his business partnership and to sell the collection. First to go were books and engravings, including copies of Blake's *Canterbury Pilgrims* and *Songs of Innocence* bought from the artist. In May 1833 the barrister Henry Crabb Robinson reported that the prints were sold 'very, very cheap'. The next year the paintings were shown at the Gallery of British Artists, Pall Mall East, and on 1 August 1835 they were auctioned by E. Foster & Son, Pall Mall. Records indicate all lots were sold; but more than half, having been bid on by friends, reappeared in the Christie and Manson sale on 26 April 1839. A great portion of the Netherlandish collection was bought by the surgeon, Joseph H. Green, and donated to the National Gallery, London, by his family in 1880. Proceeds from the sale amounted to less than £650.

UNPUBLISHED SOURCES

Cambridge, MA, Harvard U., Houghton Lib. [album of Elizabeth Aders]

BIBLIOGRAPHY

J. Schopenhaeur: *Ausflug an den Niederrhein und nach Belgien* (Leipzig, 1830)
J. D. Passavant: *Tour of a German Artist in England*, 2 vols (London, 1836)
G. Waagen: *Works of Art and Artists in England*, 2 vols (London, 1838/R 1970)
A. Jameson: *Companion to the Most Celebrated Private Galleries of Art in London* (London, 1844)
G. Waagen: *Treasures of Art in Great Britain*, 3 vols (London, 1854)
A. Gilchrist: *Life of William Blake*, 2 vols (London, 1863)
H. C. Robinson: *Diary, Reminiscences, and Correspondence*, ed. T. Sadler (London, 1869)
M. K. Joseph: 'Charles Aders', *Auckland U. Coll. Bull.*, xliii/6 (1953)
S. Sulzberger: 'La Réhabilitation des primitifs flamands, 1802–1867', *Bull. Cl. B.-A., Acad. Royale Sci., Lett. & B.-A. Belgique*, xii/3 (1959)
K. Bonomi: *The Karl and Eliza Aders Collection of Early Netherlandish Paintings* (MA thesis, New York U., Inst. F.A., 1987)

KATHRYN BONOMI

Adharbayjan. *See* AZERBAIJAN.

Adhémar, Jean (*b* Paris, 1908; *d* Paris, 20 June 1987). French art historian. He came from a distinguished Provençal family and studied art history first at the Ecole des Chartes, Paris, under Marcel Aubert and then at the Sorbonne, Paris, under Henri Focillon. At the invitation of Julien Cain (*d* 1974), in 1932 he joined the staff of the Cabinet des Estampes et de Photographie in the Bibliothèque Nationale, Paris. As Director of the department (1961–77) he made a significant contribution to the collection, acquiring numerous old and contemporary works. He also recognized the importance of the photographic collection and oversaw its expansion. Adhémar was involved in organizing over 20 exhibitions at the library; in 1935 he organized a major exhibition of the prints of Francisco de Goya. During the 1930s Adhémar was the Paris correspondent for Fritz Saxl and the Warburg Institute in London. His first book (1939) showed the inspiration of the Warburg on his approach. His principal interest was the arts and patronage of the French Renaissance. He edited important catalogues on 16th-century engravers (1938) and the drawings of François Clouet (1970). Adhémar was equally familiar with the 19th century and published important contributions to the study of the graphic work of Honoré Daumier, Edgar Degas and Henri de Toulouse-Lautrec. He became increasingly interested in the relationship between the arts and literature. He studied the writings of Diderot, Baudelaire, Flaubert and Zola and arranged exhibitions devoted to, among others, Racine, Rousseau and Balzac. From 1956 Adhémar was editor of the *Gazette des Beaux-Arts*. He expanded the scope of the journal to include such topics as the history of caricature and collecting. During his long career, he was involved with over 100 exhibitions, covering the works of such diverse artists as Pablo Picasso, Max Ernst, Brassaï, Man Ray, Robert Doisneau and Roger Vieillard (1907–89). His wide-ranging interests are attested to in his prolific list of publications, which appeared in *Nouvelles de l'estampe* (1978), which he had founded in 1965.

WRITINGS

Goya: L'Oeuvre gravé, les peintures, les tapisseries et 110 dessins du Musée du Prado (exh. cat., Paris, Bib. N., 1935)
Inventaire du fonds français: Graveurs du XVIe siècle, Bib. N. cat. (Paris, 1938)
Influences antiques dans l'art du moyen âge français (London, 1939/R Liechtenstein, 1968)
ed., with J. Seznec: D. Diderot: *Salons, 1759–81*, 4 vols (Oxford, 1957–67, rev. 1983)

BIBLIOGRAPHY

'Essai de bibliographie des travaux de Jean Adhémar', *Nouv. Est.*, xxxvii (1978), pp. 20–35
'Hommage à Jean Adhémar', *Gaz. B.-A.*, cxi (1988) [whole issue; with full bibliog.]

See also bibliographies of the articles on the individual artists cited.

□

Adhesives. Substances used to bond two surfaces. The surfaces may consist of the same material, as when mending a broken object, or of different materials, for example a collage. When applied to pigments the adhesive is called a FIXATIVE, when applied to a crumbling solid a CONSOLIDANT.

1. Types. 2. Uses.

1. TYPES. The earliest adhesives used in the making of works of art and decorative objects were such natural products as proteins, resins, juices of plants, waxes and fats. In the 20th century the development of synthetic polymer adhesives has made it possible to join any two materials.

(i) Natural.

(a) Animal-derived adhesives. 'Glue' is a general term for adhesives based on gelatine, that is degraded collagen (the major connective protein in animals). Skin and bone waste products are the most generally used source of collagen but yield contaminated products, for example glue made from tannery waste is likely to contain both metal and organic tanning agents and be of low quality. Purer forms of collagen provide better products, for example the swim-bladders of fish, especially sturgeon, yield isinglass, while parchment yields parchment glue. The glue is made by slow cooking of the source-material in water, then clarifying the resulting solution and concentrating or drying the gelatine. Mammal-derived glues are soluble only in hot water, while fish glues dissolve to form liquids at room temperature. Skin glues tend to be stronger than other types. Terms such as 'rabbit-skin glue' (Europe) and 'deer-skin glue' (Japan) do not now define the source-material but indicate the grade. CASEIN, a protein obtained from milk, can be converted to very strong adhesive by mixing with lime (calcium hydroxide) suspension; the calcium cross-links the protein to form a strong, water-resistant film. Albumin, a protein derived from egg white or blood, has been used in the same way as casein or by hot pressing to denature and cross-link the molecules while drying the adhesive to a film. All proteins are susceptible to bacterial attack in damp conditions. Two other animal-derived adhesives are beeswax (*see* WAX) and shellac (*see* RESIN, §1).

(b) Plant-derived adhesives. Starch pastes are some of the oldest adhesives. Starch occurs in roots or seeds as granules, which can be separated and purified by milling. Pastes can be made from the purified starch or the crude flour, which contain proteins and oils. The granules must be heated in water to break down their structure and dissolve the starch. Starch occurs in two main forms: branched amylopectin and straight-chained amylose. The amylopectin is soluble in cold water, but an amylose solution will gel or precipitate on standing. The composition and proportions of the two components in different starches determines the resultant working and adhesive properties of the paste. Starch is a polysaccharide and can be degraded to make semi-synthetic gums. In Mexico, after the Spanish conquest of 1519, Christian 'stalk' sculptures were constructed from plant stems, held together by the mucilage extracted from an orchid root (*Sobralia citrina*). The alginates obtained by heating seaweeds in water are a different class of polysaccharide. Polysaccharides are susceptible to fungal attack in damp conditions. Tree exudations, resins such as rosin, dammar and rubber, and GUM, such as gum arabic, are also used in adhesives.

(c) Mineral-derived adhesives. The major natural mineral adhesive is bitumen, a mixture of solid and semi-solid hydrocarbons derived from crude oil; it is soluble in solvents but was mostly applied molten. Hydrocarbon waxes purified from bitumen can be classified as micro-crystalline (branched molecules) and paraffin (straight chain molecules) waxes (*see* PIGMENT, §IV, 2)

C. V. HORIE

(ii) Synthetic.

(a) Solvents. Materials that dissolve in organic solvents can be stuck by applying the appropriate SOLVENT to the surfaces to be joined. The material will then swell or even dissolve, and when the surfaces are pressed together the molecules of one surface will merge with those of the other, leaving a strong bond once the solvent has evaporated. The strength of the bond depends primarily on the polarity of the materials: if the materials are of identical polarity the surfaces will merge completely and it is hardly appropriate to speak of a glued joint. If, however, different materials are joined, polarity and solubility will have a crucial influence on the final result—for example, in the bonding of polymethyl methacrylate (perspex) with toluene.

(b) Polymer solutions. The most frequently used adhesives are made by dissolving polymers in a highly volatile solvent. In this way the polymer can be applied as a liquid film. The solvent evaporates, leaving a polymer film that bonds the two surfaces. Because the evaporation is accompanied by a reduction of volume, air bubbles may appear between the adhesive and the surface to which it is applied. This will weaken the adhesion. The bonding is chiefly brought about by electrostatic attractions and by the mechanical adhesion of the glue to the irregularities of the surface. In order to get the highest possible concentration of solid material, low-molecular polymers are used. In many cases the temperature at which these polymers will turn into glass lies below room temperature, which may cause problems with cohesion. Typical adhesives of this kind are contact adhesives such as polyvinyl acetate (PVA), nitrocellulose and chloroprene.

(c) Dispersants. A high-molecular substance (i.e. one with a high relative molecular mass) can be combined with a larger volume of solid material and given lower viscosity by using dispersants. This means that the monomer is dispersed in a non-solvent. After polymerization the viscosity of the mixture is determined primarily by the size of the polymers and no longer by their molecular volume. Water is invariably the vehicle used for these glues so that the adhesion is mostly of a mechanical nature. Nevertheless they contain another 40% to 50% water, which has to evaporate after the surfaces have been pressed together. This means that they are suitable only for joining porous materials. Typical adhesives of this kind include white-wood glues and acrylate dispersants.

(d) Heat sealing. Thermoplastics can sometimes be used as adhesives without the need for a solvent. The solid polymer is applied between two surfaces and then heated to above its melting point. When liquid, the polymer flows into the irregularities of the surfaces to be joined and holds these together mechanically once it has solidified again. Because melted polymers have a high viscosity and surface tension it may be difficult to achieve good adhesion. This can be remedied by using a mixture of high-molecular and low-molecular polymers: when heated the low-molecular polymer will melt and the high-molecular polymer will then dissolve in it. After solidification the low-molecular polymer secures adhesion and the high-molecular polymer cohesion. A typical example of this type of adhesive is polyvinyl acetate (PVA).

(e) Reactive adhesives. Liquid substances consisting of monomers and pre-polymerized monomers can be polymerized into thermosetting or thermoplastic polymers after they have been applied between two surfaces. Because this involves no evaporation of solvents, and shrinkage tends to be limited with polymerization, good adhesion can be achieved. By adjusting the viscosity of the basic liquid it is possible to join smooth as well as rough surfaces. Typical adhesives are epoxy resins and polyesters.

See also PLASTIC, §I, and RESIN, §2.

EDDY DE WITTE

2. USES.

(i) Natural adhesives. All the water-soluble adhesives (glue, albumin, starch and alginates) have been used more or less interchangeably in lightweight, non-critical applications. Glue is an excellent adhesive for wood, and its use in furniture production has been documented from the earliest records over 3000 years ago (*see* WOOD (i), §III, and MARQUETRY, §1). The solution is applied hot to warmed surfaces and the parts are closed quickly. A join that can be handled forms rapidly by the cooling and jelling of the glue, which dries to create a joint frequently stronger than the wood itself, although over time, and particularly in damp conditions, the join deteriorates. This defect ensures that gluing wood is reversible and that the process has as a result been retained as the major technique in conservation of both structural and decorative repairs. Glue is the binding agent in GESSO, a coating used as a ground for painting and gilding since antiquity. Glue has long been used for sizing fibres for textiles and paper (*see* SIZE). The drying of glue from a jelly causes considerable shrinkage, and glass can be decorated by glue etching in which the surface is pulled off in the required design and texture by the shrinking film (*see* GLASS, §III). Glue is widely used as a paper adhesive, for instance in COLLAGE, paper tapes and cardboard. Shrinkage damages objects by detaching surfaces or disturbing shapes, and the gradual delamination of aging ephemeral paper objects is a considerable problem (*see* PAPER, §VI). Both parchment glue and egg white have been used traditionally as the adhesive for gold leaf (*see* GILDING, §I, 1(i)).

Casein adhesives have similarly been used for millennia, primarily for wood where some water resistance was required. Until the late 20th century much plywood was constructed using casein. Beeswax was used as a medium in encaustic painting (*see* ENCAUSTIC PAINTING, §1), and shellac is widely used as a heat-set adhesive for photographs but may prove impossible to detach. Starch pastes are the traditional adhesives for paper and generally facilitate conservation (*see* PAPER, §VI). Resin and bitumen have been used since antiquity as adhesives and waterproofing agents for masonry constructions. Genesis (11:3) states that bitumen was employed as a mortar and adhesive in the construction of the Tower of Babel. Molten sulphur, which sets to a rigid solid, holds interlocking parts together, in a similar fashion to the use of molten lead for securing iron clamps in stonework, and has been used both for constructing and repairing ceramics. The technique was used as porcelain increasingly became more sculptural. An example is the Sèvres centrepiece presented to the Duke of Wellington.

C. V. HORIE

(ii) Synthetic adhesives. With the development of synthetic adhesives it is now possible to join any two materials. Two major factors are the choice of the right type of glue—one that is adapted to the chemical composition of the materials to be joined—and the preparatory treatment of the surfaces. The actual adhesion of the glue and the surface to be bonded takes place at a molecular level, and every alteration in the surface condition, no matter how small, has an influence on the final result. Metal surfaces, for example, may be covered with a thin layer of grease or rust, or with inhibitors, used to prevent corrosion during storage, which change the surface structure. Plastic surfaces may be contaminated with the remains of stripping agents or by the diffusion of softeners. Any surface to be bonded should therefore be degreased with a suitable solvent. In order to improve the mechanical aspects of the adhesion the surface may be roughened with sandpaper or a sandblaster, by etching with acids or alkalis, or by means of a bombardment of ions or electric discharge. Immediately after the preparatory treatment the surfaces must be covered with a film of glue to avoid new corrosion or the deposition of contaminants.

The physical characteristics of commercial glues can be adapted to specific needs, bearing in mind the following basic principles. In order to avoid the evaporation of solvents and to slow down chemical reactions, adhesives are best stored at a low temperature. Before use, however, they must be brought up to room temperature in their sealed container, as opening the container at a low temperature causes condensation of water on the adhesive. The viscosity of adhesives dissolved in organic solvents can be reduced by adding quick solvents. Slow-evaporating solvents will sometimes improve the penetration and can increase the flexibility of the glued joint for a long time. In the case of soluble adhesives both surfaces are covered with a thin film of glue. Before pressing the surfaces together time should be allowed for most of the solvent to evaporate, thus achieving almost instant bonding. The optimal adhesive power, however, will not occur until after several hours or days, depending on the nature of the solvents and the porosity of the materials joined. The viscosity of dispersants can be either increased or reduced. It is increased by adding small quantities of water-soluble polymers (carboxymethyl cellulose, polyvinyl alcohol) of an aromatic hydrocarbon (toluene, xylene) or of an acrylic acid dispersant. To improve the moistness of the surfaces to be joined, small quantities of tensioactive substances may be added. These are also necessary when fillers (sawdust, stone dust, pigments) are added to dispersants in order to fill bigger gaps or to colour the glued joint. Dispersants contain a high proportion of water, which makes them suitable only for joining porous materials.

A slightly raised temperature can help to accelerate the evaporation of water or solvents. When using reactive adhesives (epoxys, polyesters) it is important to measure the various components carefully before mixing them. In the case of polyesters an increased quantity of initiator will influence the setting time. With epoxy resins, however, the setting time is influenced not by the mixture but by the chemical composition of the hardener. Because of the reaction mechanism, an incorrect mixture will in this case invariably result in weaker adhesion. The adhesive powers of reactive glues can be strongly increased by using linking agents. These are products that combine various reactive groups in one molecule (vinyl and epoxy materials). One of the reactive groups will react chemically with the surface to be bonded while the other will react with the adhesive. Pressure-sensitive adhesives are used to join close-fitting surfaces quite rapidly. The glue consists of a highly reactive monomer (cyanoacrylate), which is stabilized with an acid. When the adhesive is spread out over a large surface the acid is neutralized and the glue polymerizes instantly. Because the inhibitor is destroyed at the contact surface only, and because the monomer is highly liquid, these adhesives are suitable only for joining tightly fitting, non-porous materials.

(iii) Conservation. In conservation it is never the intention to bring about an adhesion that is stronger than the original materials; thus when a glued joint is exposed to pressure or stretched or bent, the bond must break first to avoid damage to the original. Another fundamental rule is the principle of reversibility; when choosing an adhesive it is again necessary to be able to break the seal without damaging the original. This may cause problems, especially when liquid glue flows into porous surfaces. The choice of adhesive for a specific conservation task depends primarily on the object to be treated. Further information on the use of adhesives in the conservation of a specific material will be found in the relevant section of that article.

EDDY DE WITTE

BIBLIOGRAPHY

A. Lucas and J. R. Harris: *Ancient Egyptian Materials and Industries* (London, 1962)
H. Lee and K. Neville: *Epoxy Resins* (London, 1967)
J. T. Martin: *Adhesion and Adhesives* (Amsterdam, 1967)
B. Parkyn, F. Lamb and B. V. Clifton: *Polyesters* (New York, 1967)
C. V. Cagle: *Adhesive Bonding: Techniques and Application* (New York, 1968)
Hoechst, ed.: *Manuel sur la Mowilith* (Frankfurt, 1970)
J. Shields: *Adhesives Handbook* (London, 1970)
J. F. Kohlwey: *Kunststoffen* [Artificial materials] (Amsterdam, 1971)
W. J. Roff and J. R. Scott: *Fibres, Film, Plastics and Rubbers* (London, 1971)
E. De Witte and M. Goessens-Landries: 'The Use of Synthetic Resins in Conservation: An Annotated Bibliography, 1932–1974', *A. & Archeol. Tech. Abstr.*, xiii/2 (1976), supplement, pp. 279–354
N. S. Brommelle and G. Thomson: *Science and Technology in the Service of Conservation* (London, 1982)
Science for Conservators Book 3: Adhesives and Coatings, Crafts Council Conservation Science Teaching Series, ed. H. Wilks (London, 1983)
Adhesives and Consolidants, Paris Congress 1984, Reprints, International Institute for Conservation of Historical and Artistic Works [IIC]
P. Mora, L. Mora and P. Philippot: *Conservation of Wall Paintings* (London, 1984)
L. Masschelein-Kleiner: *Ancient Binding Media, Varnishes and Adhesives*, International Centre for the Study of the Preservation and Restoration of Cultural Property, Rome (ICCROM), Technical Notes Series (Rome, 1985)
C. V. Horie: *Materials for Conservation: Organic Consolidants, Adhesives and Coatings* (London, 1990)

C. V. HORIE, EDDY DE WITTE

Adhicchatra. *See* AHICHCHHATRA.

Adılcevaz. *See* KEFKALESI.

ʿAdil Shahi [ʿĀdil Shāhī]. Dynasty that ruled portions of southern India from 1489 to 1686. Its founder, Yusuf ʿAdil Shah (*reg* 1489–1509), had come to India from Persia and was appointed governor of BIJAPUR under the BAHMANI rulers. He declared his independence when that dynasty declined. Yusuf had a prolonged conflict with the Portuguese, who were able to secure Goa in 1510. The ʿAdil Shahis and their rival states in the Deccan formed a series of alliances and counter-alliances in the struggle for hegemony. For example, in 1543 a confederacy of Ahmadnagar, Golconda and Vijayanagara attacked the ʿAdil Shahi capital Bijapur, but Ibrahim ʿAdil Shah (*reg* 1534–57) maintained control. His successor ʿAli ʿAdil Shah (*reg* 1557–79) joined an alliance that destroyed Vijayanagara in 1565. ʿAli ʿAdil Shah was an enlightened prince who built a large number of public works, including the Jamiʿ Mosque at Bijapur. The dynasty reached its zenith under Ibrahim ʿAdil Shah II (*reg* 1579–1627), a great patron of art, music and letters; fine surviving paintings include a number of his portraits. One of the most outstanding architectural achievements of his reign is the Ibrahim Rauza, the mausoleum of Ibrahim II and his family, which is set in a walled garden with tomb and mosque on a common plinth. While Ibrahim was able to avert confrontation with the MUGHAL rulers, who were slowly expanding into the Deccan, his successor Muhammad ʿAdil Shah (*reg* 1627–56) was forced to agree to a 'Deed of Submission' in 1636. Muhammad's tomb, the Gol Gumbaz, is a gigantic domed structure (*see* INDIAN SUBCONTINENT, fig. 110). In the reign of Sikandar ʿAdil Shah (*reg* 1672–86) Bijapur fell to the Mughal emperor Aurangzeb.

See also INDIAN SUBCONTINENT, §§III, 7(ii)(a) and V, 4(vi)(b).

BIBLIOGRAPHY

W. Haig: 'The Five Kingdoms of the Deccan, 1527–1599', *The Cambridge History of India*, iii (Cambridge, 1928/*R* Delhi, 1965), pp. 433–66
H. K. Sherwani and P. M. Joshi, eds: *History of the Medieval Deccan (1295–1724)*, 2 vols (Hyderabad, 1973)
D. C. Varma: *History of Bijapur* (New Delhi, 1974)

R. NATH

Adler, Dankmar (*b* Stadtlengsfeld, nr Eisenach, 3 July 1844; *d* Chicago, 16 April 1900). American architect and engineer of German birth. His family moved to the USA in 1854, and he trained in Detroit, in the architectural offices of John Schaefer, E. Willard Smith and others. After his family moved from Detroit to Chicago, Adler

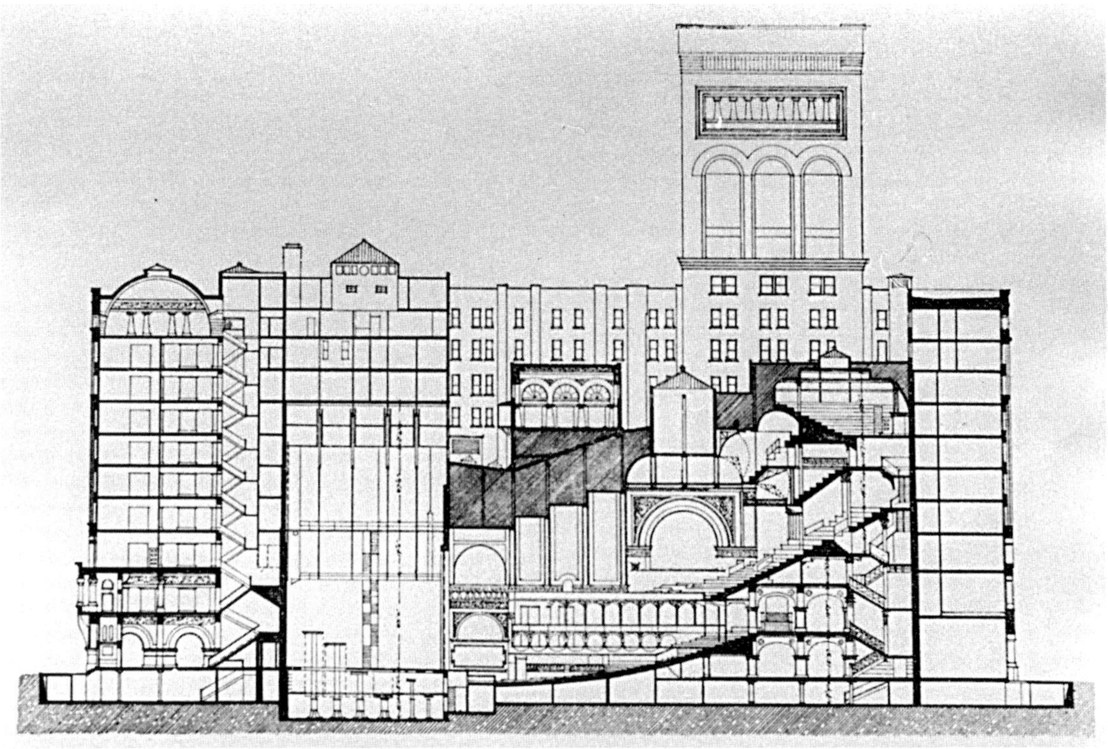

Adler & Sullivan: longitudinal section of the Auditorium Building, Chicago, 1886–9

worked under a German émigré architect, Augustus Bauer (1827–94), and gained valuable training in an engineering company during his military service in the American Civil War. After the war, he worked with O. S. Kinney (*d* 1868), and later Ashley Kinney, building educational and civic structures in the Midwest. Adler's ability soon brought him to the attention of an established practitioner, Edward Burling (1818–92), who needed assistance in the aftermath of the Chicago fire of 1871. Burling & Adler's many buildings include the First National Bank (1871) and Mercantile (1873) buildings and the Methodist Church Block (1872), all designed in Chicago by Adler and all demolished. In 1879 he and Burling parted.

Adler's first independent commission was the Central Music Hall (1879; destr. 1900), Chicago, which integrated an office-block, a multipurpose auditorium and shops, a successful formula that Adler later repeated. Other early commissions in Chicago were houses for John Borden (1880; destr. 1955) and Henry Leopold (1882; destr. before 1932), and a number of commercial buildings: the Borden Block (1881; destr. 1916), Jewelers' Building (1882), the Brunswick and Balke Factory (1882–91; destr. 1989) and the Crilly & Blair Complex (1881; destr. *c.* 1970). By 1881 Adler's employees included Louis Sullivan, as is evident from the style and placement of the ornament on the Borden Block. Adler made Sullivan a full partner in 1883, by which time the office was designing factories, stores, houses, office-blocks and especially theatres. The early success of Adler & Sullivan was due to Adler's planning and engineering innovations and his reputation as a careful builder and businessman of integrity. He could recognize and guide talent in others, and the firm also benefited from his many social connections. A founder of the Western Association of Architects, he led its merger into the American Institute of Architects, of which he was secretary in 1892.

Between 1879 and 1889 Adler executed many commissions for theatres and concert halls, ranging from remodellings to enormous multipurpose complexes. He was recognized as a leading expert in acoustics and served as acoustics consultant during the construction (1890–91) of Carnegie Hall, New York. Adler & Sullivan's records do not survive, and the contribution of the partners and their employees can only be inferred; for the Auditorium Building, Chicago (1886–9; see fig.), Sullivan, Paul Mueller and Frank Lloyd Wright, who was employed as a draughtsman, all contributed to the building complex, but the commission and the overall design were Adler's. Among the innovations Adler adapted for the Auditorium Building were caisson foundations (*see* SKYSCRAPER), huge trusses to support the rooms above the theatre space and hydraulic machinery to raise and lower sections of the stage. The plan of the concert hall, with its excellent provision for sight and sound, evolved from early Adler designs; Sullivan was engaged on the ornamental decoration, and Mueller contributed to the engineering. The result was a true synthesis of acoustics, aesthetics and technical innovation, with colour and ornament, science and technology harnessed in the service of art. Wright called it 'the greatest room for music and opera in the world'. Other theatre commissions carried out by Adler & Sullivan include the Schiller Theatre (1891–3; destr. 1961), Chicago, which—

like the Auditorium Theatre—was part of a tall office building. Several influential early skyscrapers were also produced by the firm, notably the Wainwright Building, St Louis (1890–91; *see* UNITED STATES OF AMERICA, fig. 7), the Chicago Stock Exchange (1893; destr. 1971) and the Guaranty Building, Buffalo (1894–6; *see* SULLIVAN, LOUIS, fig. 1).

The financial crash of 1893–4, a shift in architectural taste and irreconcilable aesthetic and economic arguments between Adler and Sullivan led to the partnership being acrimoniously dissolved in 1895. That year Adler became a consultant for a company manufacturing lifts for new skyscrapers, mostly in New York. He left after six months, returning to architecture and to Chicago, taking his son Abraham (1876–1914) into partnership. Adler and Sullivan now became competitors—but not implacable enemies—in a shrinking market. Between 1896 and 1900 Adler's offices in Chicago and New York had fewer than a dozen commissions, whereas in 1886 Adler & Sullivan had had 18 jobs in addition to the Auditorium. Of the edifices built after the split with Sullivan, Adler's Morgan Park Academy dormitories (1896; destr. *c.* 1970) for a college preparatory school and Isaiah Temple (1898), both in Chicago, were architecturally the most interesting. The temple contains many elements he had used in the Central Music Hall, but the overall style is more historically derived than any Adler & Sullivan designs.

Adler spent much of his later life writing and working successfully for state licensing of architects. He was particularly interested in two causes: recognition for architecture as a learned profession and the education of both the public and the practitioners on how to design for modern society. There were some unbuilt projects, but after his death the firm he left behind did not flourish. A brilliant and conscientious architect and engineer, Adler's work was dominated by the idea of the building as a synthesis, in which 'form and function are one' and in which 'there must be throughout, from foundation to roof, in the arrangement of all the parts, in the design of every line, the imprint and all-pervading influence of one master mind'. He solved practical problems creatively and literally put a firm foundation under the skyscraper and a solid skeleton under its skin. Adler opposed height limitations and slavish obedience to historical precedents, and he was unusual in his willingness to experiment with new materials and relatively untried structural and foundation techniques, as well as in the breadth of building type undertaken. With Sullivan he provided a model for the modern, multi-specialist architectural office, providing also a creative and productive milieu, in which some of the 20th century's leading architects began their careers.

UNPUBLISHED SOURCES

Chicago, IL, Newberry Lib., Dankmar Adler Archv [journals, letters, autobiography]

Chicago, IL, Richard Nickel Cttee [architectural photographs and archv, 1972]

WRITINGS

'Foundations of the Auditorium Building', *Inland Architect & News Rec.*, xi (1888), pp. 31–2

'The Auditorium Tower', *Amer. Architect & Bldg News*, xxxi (1891), pp. 15–16

'Tall Office Buildings—Past and Future', *Engin. Mag.*, iii (1892), pp. 765–73

'Theater-Building for American Cities', *Engin. Mag.*, vii (1894), pp. 717–30; viii, pp. 814–29

'The Influence of Steel Construction and of Plate Glass upon the Development of Modern Style', *Inland Architect & News Rec.*, xxviii (1896), pp. 34–7

BIBLIOGRAPHY

M. Schuyler: 'Architecture in Chicago: Adler & Sullivan', *Archit. Rec. Suppl.*, 3 (1895), pp. 3–48

L. Sullivan: *Autobiography of an Idea* (New York, 1924)

F. Lloyd Wright: *Genius and the Mobocracy* (New York, 1949)

C. Condit: *American Building Art: Nineteenth and Twentieth Century* (New York, 1961)

R. Elstein: *The Architectural Style of Dankmar Adler* (MA thesis, U. Chicago, 1963)

R. Baron: 'Forgotten Facets of Dankmar Adler', *Inland Architect & News Rec.*, vii (1964), pp. 14–16

C. Condit: *The Chicago School of Architecture* (Chicago, 1964)

R. Elstein: 'The Architecture of Dankmar Adler', *J. Soc. Archit. Historians*, xxvi (1967), pp. 242–9

J. Saltzstein: 'Dankmar Adler: The Man, the Architect, the Author', *Wisconsin Architect*, xxxviii (1967): (July), pp. 15–19; (Sept), pp. 10–14; (Nov), pp. 16–19

N. Menocal: *Architecture as Nature: The Transcendentalist Idea of Louis Sullivan* (Madison, 1981) [with complete list of Adler's pubd writings, pp. 206–07]

C. Grimsley: *A Study of the Contributions of Dankmar Adler to the Theater Building Practices of the Late Nineteenth Century* (diss., Evanston, IL, Northwestern U., 1984)

L. Doumato: *Dankmar Adler, 1844–1900* (Monticello, IL, 1985)

R. Twombly: *Louis Sullivan: His Life and Work* (New York, 1986) [with full list of Adler & Sullivan commissions]

C. Gregersen: *Dankmar Adler: His Theatres and Auditoriums* (Athens, OH, 1990)

ROCHELLE BERGER ELSTEIN

Adler, (Johann Heinrich) Friedrich (*b* Berlin, 15 Oct 1827; *d* Berlin, 15 Sept 1908). German architect, archaeologist and writer. He was one of the leading figures of Berlin's architectural establishment in the latter half of the 19th century. On completion of his studies in 1852, he was given the prestigious post of Bauleiter at the Neues Museum in Berlin, designed by Friedrich August Stüler. He subsequently became a lecturer and in 1861 a professor of architectural history at the Bauakademie in Berlin. Many of his church buildings used medieval motifs and elements, for example the Christuskirche (1862–8) in Berlin and the Elisabethkirche (1869–72) in Wilhelmshafen. He followed Karl Bötticher in his attempts to merge medieval and classical elements, best illustrated in his design for the Thomaskirche (competition 1862; built 1865–70), Berlin. There, Adler used Gothic structural devices embellished with rich Renaissance detail, a tendency that was also present in many of the entries for the Berlin Cathedral competition (1869). The Thomaskirche became something of a prototype for Protestant churches in Germany. A keen archaeologist, Adler participated in the excavations by Ernst Curtius (1814–96) in Olympia (1875–81). He also designed the Archaeological Museum at Olympia in 1883. After entering the civil service in 1877, he quickly rose to an influential position in the Ministerium für Öffentliche Arbeiten, where he was responsible for church building until his retirement in 1903. He also restored Schleswig Cathedral (1888–94), and the Schlosskirche at Wittenberg in 1892 as a monument to the Reformation. Adler was a member of several national and foreign academic institutes and scholarly societies. He travelled widely in Greece, Palestine and Asia Minor and published numerous articles and books on archaeology and architectural history.

WRITINGS

Die mittelalterlichen Backstein-Bauwerke des preussischen Staates, 2 vols (Berlin, 1859–69)

Baugeschichtlichen Forschungen in Deutschland, 2 vols (Berlin, 1870–79)

with E. Curtius: *Olympia: Die Ergebnisse*, 5 vols (Berlin, 1890–97/R 1966)

[autobiographical contrib. to] *Das geistige Deutschland am Ende des XIX. Jahrhunderts*, i (Leipzig and Berlin, 1898), p. 8

BIBLIOGRAPHY

Thieme-Becker; Wasmuth

V. Hammerschmidt: *Anspruch und Ausdruck in der Architektur des späten Historismus in Deutschland, 1860–1914* (Frankfurt am Main, 1985)

□

Adler, Jankel (*b* Tuszyn, nr Łódź, 26 July 1895; *d* Aldbourne, Wilts, 25 April 1949). Polish painter. He underwent an apprenticeship in engraving in 1912 and in 1913 moved to Barmen (now Wuppertal) in Germany, where he studied under Gustav Wiethüchter at the Kunstgewerbeschule during World War I. In 1918 he came into contact with Das Junge Rheinland, a group of artists based in Düsseldorf. In the same year he visited Poland, where he was one of the founders of the Ing Idisz (Young Yiddish) group, an association of painters and writers in Łódź dedicated to the expression of their Jewish identity. The few surviving works produced by Adler during this period, all in an Expressionist style, with the human figure subjected to elongated and distorted proportions, reveal his own response to these concerns. *The Rabbi's Last Hour* (1919; Łódź, Mus. A.), in which the influence of El Greco has been discerned, is a good example. His inventory of images included motifs from Jewish folk art and Hebrew calligraphy.

In 1920 Adler returned to Barmen, moving later to Düsseldorf, where he remained in contact with the Junge Rheinland group. He played a major role in the Rheinische Sezession, joined the Rheingruppe and the Gruppe Progressiver Künstler in Cologne and in 1922 helped organize a congress of the Union of Progressive International Artists. From 1922 to 1933 he participated in major German and international exhibitions of progressive art; in 1926 he was awarded first prize for *Wall Painting* (mixed media on canvas, 3.08×4.6 m, 1926; Düsseldorf, Tonhalle), representing three women against an abstract faceted background, and in 1928 he won a gold medal for his painting *Cats* (1927; Cologne, Mus. Ludwig). Adler's paintings of this period, such as *Three Women* (1926; Düsseldorf, Kstmus.), dominated by static human figures with an overpowering presence and heavy facial features and limbs, are restrained and monumental. They incorporate formal, stylistic and technical elements derived from a variety of sources including German Expressionism, Picasso and Cubism, and Constructivism. In order to explore the tension between abstraction and naturalism he borrowed Cubist devices such as multiple viewpoints, the tilting of the picture plane and the isolation and reintegration of decorative elements and details. Unlike the Cubists, however, he used these elements in pictures such as *Still-life (Tea)* (oil, ink and sand on paper, 1928; Düsseldorf, Kstmus.) to add a mystical dimension to his work. His concern with the formal design of his compositions, with their carefully balanced tonal contrasts, and the variations of texture achieved by mixing sand and other substances into the paints, can be linked to Constructivism. His approach to imagery in the early 1930s, on the other hand, indicates an affinity with Neue Sachlichkeit.

Adler was forced to leave Germany in 1933, at the height of his success there, because of the rise to power of the Nazis. His paintings were removed from German museums and appeared on the lists of 'degenerate art' (*see* ENTARTETE KUNST). He settled in France in 1934, living first in Paris and later in Argèles-sur-Mer and Cagnes-sur-Mer. In 1940 he joined the Polish Army, with which he travelled in 1941 to Glasgow, where he had a strong influence on young painters such as Robert Colquhoun and Robert MacBryde. He made direct reference to the suffering occasioned by World War II in *The Mutilated* (1942; London, Tate) and continued to explore his Jewish identity, for example in *Two Rabbis* (1942; New York, MOMA). He settled permanently in London in 1943, taking an active role in the circle of European refugee artists and also making contact with British painters and poets. The images in his paintings became more ambiguous, turning into ideograms or abstract symbols, and his figures became more abstract and geometrical, more delicate and refined in their proportions and at the same time more expressive of movement and vitality. In these works, such as *Woman with Raised Hands* (1948–9; Jerusalem, Israel Mus.), abstract symbolism merges with a sense of impending destiny and respect for the human experience.

BIBLIOGRAPHY

P. Fierens: *Jankel Adler* (London, 1948)

S. W. Hayter: *Jankel Adler* (London, 1948)

A. Klapheck: *Jankel Adler* (Recklinghausen, 1966)

N. Guralnik: 'Jankel Adler's "Purim Spiel": An Encounter between Picasso and Chassidism', *Ann. Rev.: Tel Aviv Mus.*, 2–3 (1984), pp. 20–29

Jankel Adler (exh. cat., ed. N. Guralnik; Tel Aviv Mus., 1985) [retro.]

Jankel Adler (exh. cat., ed. U. Krempel and K. Thomas; Düsseldorf, Städt. Ksthalle, 1985) [retro.]

NEHAMA GURALNIK

Admont Abbey. Benedictine abbey in Styria, Austria. It was founded in the mid-11th century by Bishop Gebhard from Salzburg, endowed by Saint Henna von Gurk, Gräfin von Friessach (*d* 1045), and settled by Benedictine monks from St Peter's, Salzburg. The Romanesque minster (consecrated 1074), which was famous for its marble columns, was rebuilt after a fire in 1152; a Gothic choir was added in 1276–86. The abbey became an important cultural centre with a renowned scriptorium. From 1121 to the 16th century a convent was attached to the abbey. Under the abbots Mathias Preininger (1615–28) and Urban Weber (1628–59) the whole establishment was transformed in the Baroque style, and the church was rebuilt (1615–26). In 1742 Gotthard Hayberger submitted to Abbot Anton II von Mainersberg (1718–51) a huge plan for the rebuilding of the complex, although only a fraction was undertaken owing to its cost. Hayberger's most important building was the library in the east wing, which was completed in 1776 by Josef Hueber (*d* 1787). The room is two storeys high and 70 m long, with a domed, longitudinal ellipse in the centre, bounded by piers faced with pairs of colossal half columns. At either side is a three-bay wing, each bay sail-vaulted. The main impact is made by the

Rococo bookcases, with gilt decoration sparingly applied, and by the galleries that run along the wings at first-floor level. In 1774–6 Bartolomeo Altomonte painted allegories of the *Arts and Sciences under the Patronage of the Church and Religion* on the side and central vaults. The library contains 14 bronzed limewood sculptures by JOSEF STAMMEL, of which the most important are the 'Four Last Things' (*Death, Judgement, Hell, Heaven*) under the central dome. Except for the library, the abbey buildings burnt down in 1865 and were rebuilt (1866–9) in a Gothic Revival style by Wilhelm Bücher (1824–88).

BIBLIOGRAPHY

K. Woisetschlager: *Steiermark (ohne Graz)*, Dehio-Handbuch, iv (Vienna, 1982), pp. 3–6

M. Mannewitz: *Stift Admont* (Freiburg im Breisgau, 1987)

Kunstschatten uit de Benediktijnerabdij Admont (exh. cat., Europalia; Tienen, 1987)

A. GERHARDT

Adoian, Vosdanig Manoog. *See* GORKY, ARSHILE.

Adriaenssen [Adrieanssen], **Alex(ander)** (*bapt* Antwerp, 16 Jan 1587; *d* Antwerp, 30 Oct 1661). Flemish painter. He was the son of the composer Emanuel Adriaenssen and brother to the painters Vincent Adriaenssen (1595–1675) and Niclaes Adriaenssen (1598–1648/9). In 1597 he was apprenticed to Artus van Laeck (*d* 1616) and in 1610 became a master in the painters' guild. In 1632 he took on Philips Milcx as apprentice, and in 1635 he painted the coats of arms of the 17 provinces on the triumphal arches in honour of the new governor. Adriaenssen's many signed and often dated oil paintings on wood and canvas are all still-lifes, mainly of food on tables with copper- and tinware, glass and pottery (e.g. *Still-life with Fish*, 1660; Amsterdam, Rijksmus.). There are four paintings of vases of flowers, but vases of flowers, as well as single flowers on the table, also appear in other still-life combinations. Only two canvases are known in which he worked with figure painters: a garland of flowers around a painting of the *Holy Family* (Ghent, Paul Boterdaele priv. col.) by Simon de Vos and a porcelain bowl of fruit beside a *Virgin and Child* (ex-Gal. 'Den Tijd', Antwerp, 1982) attributed to a follower of Rubens. His compositions are graceful and balanced but somewhat stereotyped, and they are bathed in a soft chiaroscuro. Adriaenssen depicted with great skill the moist waxiness of fish and oysters, the luminous transparency of drops of water and glasses filled with liquid, as well as crisp, juicy fruit, downy feathers and velvety fur.

BIBLIOGRAPHY

Bénézit; *BNB*; *NBW*; Thieme–Becker; Wurzbach

P. Rombouts and T. van Lerius: *De Liggeren (1453–1794) en andere historische archieven der Antwerpsche Sint Lucasgilde* (Antwerp, 1864–76/*R* Amsterdam, 1961), i, pp. 399, 460, 471; ii, pp. 41, 44, 58

T. van Lerius: *Biographies d'artistes anversois* (Antwerp, 1880), i, pp. 12–24

M. L. Hairs: *Les Peintres flamands de fleurs au XVIIe siècle* (Brussels, 1955, rev. 3/1985), pp. 361, 364–6

E. Greindl: *Les Peintres flamands de nature morte au XVIIe siècle* (Brussels, 1956, rev. 2/1983), pp. 55–7, 178–9, 333–4

E. Duverger: *Antwerpse kunstinventarissen uit de zeventiende eeuw*, I/ii (Brussels, 1985), p. 153; I/iv (Brussels, 1989), nos 899, 1031; I/v (Brussels, 1991), p. 79; I/vi (Brussels, 1992), no. 1719, pp. 268, 297, 343, 348, 351, 354; I/vii (Brussels, 1993), p. 163

G. Spiessens: *Leven en werk van de Antwerpse schilder Alexander Adriaenssen (1587–1661)* (Brussels, 1990)

J. de Maere and M. Wabbes: *Illustrated Dictionary of 17th-century Flemish Painters* (Brussels, 1994), i, p. 28; ii, pp. 14–16

G. SPIESSENS

Adrian-Nilsson, Gösta [GAN] (*b* Lund, 2 April 1884; *d* Stockholm, 29 March 1965). Swedish painter. After studying at Zahrtmanns Skole, Copenhagen, in 1914 he went to Berlin; both Kandinsky and Franz Marc were of great importance to his development at this time of a semi-abstract style with deep, glowing colours. He developed his own style of expressive Cubism (e.g. *Sailors' War Dream*, 1917; Malmö, Kstmus.). He was captivated by modern technology and masculine strength, and this was often reflected in his work. In 1919 he began producing purely non-objective work, and he made numerous collages *c.* 1920 in a Dadaist spirit. Between 1920 and 1925 he lived in Paris, coming into contact with Alexander Archipenko and Fernand Léger. Léger's influence can partly be seen in his depiction of figures as robotic human shapes in the form of sportsmen, seamen and soldiers. Adrian-Nilsson also produced geometric abstract work in the late 1920s. In the 1930s he developed a personal approach to Surrealism, participating in exhibitions such as Kubisme-Surrealisme in Copenhagen (1935). During the 1940s his work again became purely abstract. He was influential to the members of the Halmstad group, particularly during their Surrealist phase. His later work was nearer to Romantic painting, inspired by the Swedish landscape painter Marcus Larson. He signed his works 'GAN'.

WRITINGS

Den gudomliga geometrien [The divine geometry] (Stockholm, 1922)

BIBLIOGRAPHY

N. Lindgren: *GAN* (Halmstad, 1949)

GAN (exh. cat.; Stockholm, Liljevalchs Ksthall; Malmö, Ksthall; 1984)

J. T. Ahlstrand: *GAN: Gösta Adrian-Nilsson* (Arlöv, 1985)

JACQUELINE STARE

Adriano Fiorentino [Adriano di Giovanni de' Maestri] (*b* ?Florence, *c.* 1450–60; *d* Florence, before 12 June 1499). Italian sculptor. Like his collaborator Bertoldo di Giovanni, he may have started his working life as a servant in the house of Lorenzo de' Medici. An 'Adriano nostro' is recorded delivering letters for Lorenzo in 1483 and again in March 1484, when Lorenzo referred to him as 'Adriano formerly our groom' (*staffiere*).

Adriano's best-known enterprise is the bronze statuette of *Bellerophon and Pegasus* (Vienna, Ksthist. Mus.; *see* BERTOLDO DI GIOVANNI, fig. 2), which he cast after a model of Bertoldo's. Its underside is signed *Expressit me Bertholdus. Conflavit Hadrianus.* Marcantonio Michiel, who saw the piece in a Paduan collection, took this to mean that Adriano was Bertoldo's assistant in casting. Bertoldo's influence is certainly apparent in Adriano's signed bronze statuette of *Venus* (Philadelphia, PA, Mus. A.; see fig.). The nude *Hercules* (J. W. Frederiks priv. col., on loan to Rotterdam, Mus. Boymans–van Beuningen), formerly attributed to Bertoldo, matches the *Venus* in both its facture and its stance. A signed *Venus and Cupid*, reproduced by Fabriczy (1886), has since disappeared. Important evidence of Adriano's activity in the production of small bronzes was provided by the discovery of his signature

Adriano Fiorentino: *Venus*, bronze, h. 422 mm, *c.* 1490 (Philadelphia, PA, Museum of Art)

beneath a leering *Pan* with tautly flexed legs (Vienna, Ksthist. Mus.); this is the finest example in the group of statuettes attributed to him and the one most likely to have been made in Florence. He also signed a marble statuette of a *Sleeping Satyr* (Berlin, Skulpgal.).

According to a deposition of May 1499, Adriano served for a time with Buonaccorso Ghiberti, a fortifications expert and founder of artillery who worked for over two years under Virginio Orsini, the condottiere commander of the Aragonese army. Buonaccorso's service ended in June 1488. The hardy simplicity of Adriano's *Venus* and *Hercules* statuettes perhaps reflects his experiences with the casting of cannonry during this period.

In 1493 Adriano is recorded living in the household of King Ferdinand in Naples and the following year in the house of the Duke of Calabria, where his brother Amadeo wrote to him with the news of Michelangelo's flight from Florence. The three medals of *Ferdinand II* (Hill, *Corpus*, nos 335–7) and the portrait medals of the Neapolitan writers *Pietro Compatre*, *Giovanni Pontano* and *Jacopo Sannazaro* (Hill, *Corpus*, nos 339–43) probably date from this time. The heads of the writers are shown in striking, classical profile, while the faintly sketched figures on the reverses are reminiscent of antique encaustic painting. The *Pontano* medal prompted the attribution to Adriano of a bronze bust of that humanist (Genoa, Gal. Pal. Bianco), a balding, staring head set at an ungainly angle in a Roman tunic. The medal and bust in turn determined his authorship of a slightly more classical marble relief portrait of *Pontano* (New York, Met., since 1991).

Adriano's search for work took him northward; in a letter of May 1495 Elisabetta Gonzaga, Duchess of Urbino, urged her brother Francesco II, Marquis of Mantua, to employ Adriano. She had been sufficiently impressed by his talents during his three-month stay in Urbino to praise him as 'a good sculptor' who 'has made here some very beautiful medals', adding that he was 'a good composer of sonnets, a good player of the lyre, and he also improvises rather outstandingly'. Adriano's medal of the *Duchess of Urbino* (Hill, *Corpus*, no. 344) dates from this time. He then worked in Germany, where he made a bust of *Frederick the Wise of Saxony* in bell-metal, signed and dated 1498 (Dresden, Grünes Gewölbe). This owlish portrait with carefully studied details of costume has more in common with the spirit of contemporary German painting than with Italian sculpture.

BIBLIOGRAPHY

Thieme–Becker

C. von Fabriczy: 'Ein bisher unbeachtetes Werk des Adriano Fiorentino', *Kst & Gew.*, xx (1886), p. 7

——: 'Adriano Fiorentino', *Jb. Kön.-Preuss. Kstsamml.*, xxiv (1903), pp. 71–98

G. F. Hill: *Corpus* (1930), pp. 82–7

G. L. Hersey: *Alfonso II and the Artistic Renewal of Naples, 1485–1495* (New Haven, 1969), pp. 29–30

J. D. Draper: *Bertoldo di Giovanni, Sculptor of the Medici Household* (Columbia, MO, 1992), pp. 44–52, 69, 181

The Currency of Fame: Portrait Medals of the Renaissance (exh. cat., ed. S. K. Scher; New York, Frick, 1994)

JAMES DAVID DRAPER

Adrianople. *See* EDIRNE.

Adsett, Sandy (*b* Wairoa, Hawke's Bay, NZ, 27 Aug 1939). Maori painter, carver, weaver, costume and stage designer. His involvement with art began at Te Aute Maori Boys' College (1954–7), Hawke's Bay, Waipawa County, and continued with formal art training at Ardmore Teachers' College (1958–9) and at Dunedin Teachers' College (1960), where he trained as an art specialist. He subsequently worked for the Department of Education as an arts and crafts adviser and served on committees for national art education policies, the Historic Places Trust (with particular reference to Maori sites), art museums and tribal committees (dealing with traditional and customary art forms and architecture). He helped to promote contemporary developments in Maori arts for community buildings, meeting houses, churches and public sites, serving on private and governmental commissions. In his own work he maintains a balance between the conservation of older traditional materials and forms of Maori arts and the experimental use of new materials, such as composite chipboard, synthetic dyes, plastic-coated basketry fibres and composite, laminated board. His painted and woven-fibre works are notable for their rich but subtle colours and controlled sense of line. They vary in size from complex architectural installations or stage designs for the Royal New Zealand Ballet to designs for postage stamps. At Te Huki Meeting House (1982), for example, the carved figures supporting the walls and the house-posts, as well as the painted rafter patterns of the ceiling and woven wall panels are all linked by style, motif and colour to relate intricate tribal narratives.

JOHN HOVELL

BIBLIOGRAPHY

D. Nicholas and K. Kaa: *Seven Maori Artists* (Wellington, 1986), pp. 16–19 and pls 6–10 [interviews]

Adshead, S(tanley) D(avenport) (*b* Bowdon, Cheshire, 1868; *d* London, 11 April 1946). English architect and urban planner. The son of a landscape painter, he was apprenticed to an architect in Manchester in 1885. He went to London in 1890, where he built up experience in well-known architectural offices, notably with George Sherrin (*d* 1909) and William Flockhart (*d* 1913). His brief and shrewd recollections of these years are a valuable record of prosperous London practice in the 1890s. He gradually gained a reputation as a perspectivist but his architectural career was slow to develop. The library and assembly rooms at Ramsgate, Kent (1904), and offices for the Bennett Steamship Co., Southwark, London (1908), show his preference for an individual, refined Georgian-revival style.

In 1909 Adshead became Professor of Town Planning at Liverpool University and inaugurated the Department of Civic Design, the first town-planning school in Britain, with Patrick Abercrombie as his deputy. In 1910 they founded the *Town Planning Review*, which called for a crisper, more formalized and more internationally conscious approach to urban design than that which had hitherto found favour with Raymond Unwin and the pioneers of the garden city. Adshead became Professor of Town Planning at University College, London, in 1914 but remained loyal to the tenets of 'Liverpool-school' planning. After Unwin's, his was the most articulate architectural voice in the implementation of the national housing programmes of the 1920s. Between 1911 and 1931 Adshead was in partnership with Stanley C. Ramsey (1882–1968) and their projects included housing on the Duchy of Cornwall Estate, Kennington, London (from 1911), a wartime housing scheme for Dormanstown, Middlesbrough, and a series of consultancies for British local authorities in the 1920s. In due course Adshead moved on to develop a number of regional planning schemes of which the earliest and most important was for the Middlesbrough area, made with Abercrombie in 1925. A later scheme of significance was his layout for Lusaka, Zambia (1930–31), developed and carried out by others.

Adshead's approach to urban planning remained that of the artist rather than the social scientist, but he was always open to ideas. His passion for orderly, simplified appearances helped to curb the more picturesque tendencies in British planning and national housing programmes of the 1920s. Although none of his great projects was carried out *in toto*, the Duchy of Cornwall Estate admirably shows the refinement of his sober, neo-Georgian style, which influenced the plans of others, notably Louis de Soissons's layout for Welwyn Garden City.

BIBLIOGRAPHY

C. H. Reilly: *Representative British Architects of the Present Day* (London, 1931), pp. 15–27
S. Pepper and M. Swenarton: 'Neo-Georgian Maison-type', *Archit. Rev.* [London], clxviii (1980), pp. 87–92
A. Powers, ed.: '"Architects I have known": The Architectural Career of S. D. Adshead', *Archit. Hist.*, xxiv (1981), pp. 103–23
M. Swenarton: *Homes Fit for Heroes* (London, 1981)

□

Adygey region. *See under* RUSSIA, §XII, 1.

Adyton [Gr. 'not to be entered'; Lat. *adytum*]. Most sacred inner part of a temple, accessible only to the priests (*see* GREECE, ANCIENT, fig. 7g).

□

Adzhina Tepe. Buddhist monastery of the 7th century AD to first half of the 8th, in the valley of the Vakhsh River, 12 km east of Kurgan-Tyube, southern Tajikistan. During this early medieval period it belonged to Vakhsh (U-sha in Chinese sources), one of the 27 domains of Tokharistan. Excavations between 1960 and 1975 by the Academy of Sciences, Tajikistan, and the Hermitage Museum, St Petersburg, exposed the entire site; most of the finds are on loan to the Hermitage Museum, St Petersburg. The buildings, which covered an area of 100×50 m, were constructed of mud-bricks (*c*. 490×250×110 mm) and rammed earth, with walls surviving to a height of 5.5 to 6.0 m. The site comprised two square complexes linked by an enfilade of three rooms (see fig. (a)). The south-eastern complex or monastery (b) had domed cells (c) for monks, a hall or refectory (d), service quarters, store-rooms and a small sanctuary (e). An open courtyard in the centre had a fired brick path across it, linking the enfilade to the sanctuary. A corridor around the perimeter of the courtyard was divided into four right-angled sections by a deep iwan, or vestibule, in the middle of each side. One of these vestibules led into the sanctuary, the second into the meeting-hall, the third into the enfilade and the fourth to the monastery exit (j) and also on to a vaulted ramp (k) that originally gave access to the roof and the now lost second storey.

The north-western or main stupa complex had a similar plan. In the centre of the courtyard was a large terraced cruciform stupa (f). Subsidiary stupas (g) were located in the corners of the courtyard. Small platforms or pedestals with sculpture were found in small domed sanctuaries (h) facing the main stupa. Sculpture (e.g. a *parinirvāṇa* scene (i) with a 12 m reclining Buddha) was also found in the right-angled corridors, either in specially built niches or on pedestals. Polychrome clay images of the Buddha, *bodhisattvas*, various divinities and demonic beings were used in compositions juxtaposing statues in the round on pedestals with wall reliefs of images, leaves, flowers,

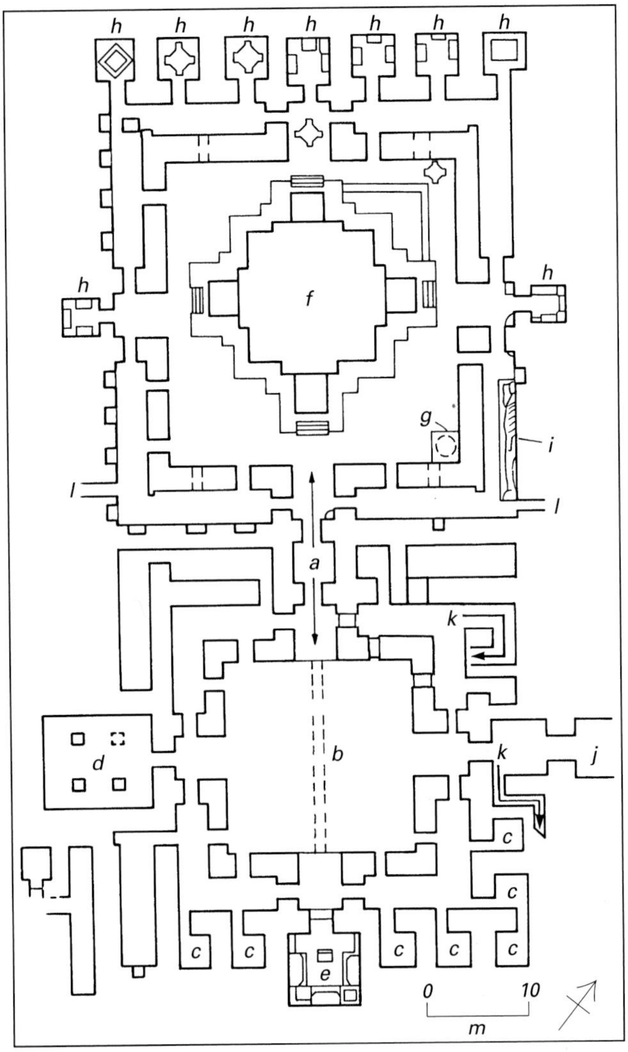

Adzhina Tepe, 7th century AD–first half of the 8th, plan: (a) enfilade of three rooms; (b) monastery courtyard; (c) domed cells; (d) hall or refectory; (e) sanctuary; (f) stupa; (g) subsidiary stupas; (h) small domed sanctuaries; (i) statue of Buddha in *parinirvāṇa*; (j) entrance to monastery; (k) ramp to first floor; (l) gates

tendrils and intertwining patterns. When any damaged sculpture had to be replaced, the remains were carefully bricked up in the walls, pedestals, floors and courtyard around the main stupa (*see also* CENTRAL ASIA, §I, 3(iii)(b)).

The main stupa complex and the sanctuary in the monastery were also richly painted. The paintings in the vaulted corridors of the stupa complex, as reconstructed, seem to illustrate the 'Thousand Buddhas', with rows of seated Buddhas, each differing in pose and gesture, and in the colour of their robes, haloes and mandorlas. There were probably several versions of the 'Preaching Buddha' and also scenes of local Tokharistan nobles bearing gifts and flowers (*see* CENTRAL ASIA, fig. 34).

During the spread of Islam to Tokharistan (*c*. 750 onwards), the sculpture and murals were destroyed. In several rooms the resulting rubble was *c*. 1 m in depth, and it is thus impossible to reconstruct fully the original scheme. Chinese authors related that in the Vakhsh region Hinayana teachings were followed, but archaeological data are not sufficient to determine whether Adzhina Tepe was a Hinayanist or Mahayanist monastery.

BIBLIOGRAPHY

B. A. Litvinsky and T. I. Zeymal': *Adzhina-tepe: Arkhitektura, zhivopis', skul'ptura* [Adzhina Tepe: architecture, painting, sculpture] (Moscow, 1971)

T. I. Zeymal': 'Raskopki na Adzhina-tepe v 1975' [Excavations at Adzhina Tepe in 1975], *Arkheol. Raboty Tadzhikistane*, xv (1975), pp. 147–56

T. I. ZEYMAL'

Aech'un. *See* SIN, (2).

Aedicula. Columnar niche or shrine applied decoratively to a larger building. The word is a diminutive from the Latin word *aedes* ('temple'). Summerson traced its application to Gothic architecture and drew attention to the importance of playing at being in a house for all small children; he claimed that this kind of play has much to do with the aesthetics of architecture and leads ultimately to the use of the aedicula. The earliest surviving examples of aediculae are shop-signs from Pompeii, such as that showing Mercury or Hermes emerging from a small building. Later aediculae appear extensively in wall paintings of the Fourth Style (*c*. AD 20–*c*. 90; *see* ROME, ANCIENT, §V, 2). Later still, aediculae were often used in the architecture of the eastern provinces of the Roman Empire; they consisted of columns or pilasters flanking a niche for statuary, with a pediment above, as in the stage-building of the theatre at ASPENDOS (later 2nd century AD). Aediculae were also used in the interior of the 'Temple of Bacchus' at BAALBEK (2nd century AD) and the nymphaeum and propylaea at Gerasa (later 2nd century AD). The aediculae of the 'Temple of Bacchus' consist of alternating triangular and segmental pediments framing the statues that articulate the upper part of the walls, between the giant order of engaged columns. An aedicula at the far end of the temple has been restored as a broken pediment supported on small columns; this example may be over-ripe and complex, reflecting a late stage in a long tradition.

The term is also applied to the architectural framing of doors and windows with columns or pilasters supporting a lintel or an entablature and pediment. This type of aedicular opening was adapted from Roman use and became a common feature of classical architecture in the Renaissance and after, as seen, for example, in the interior of the Old Sacristy (commissioned 1419), S Lorenzo, Florence (*see* BRUNELLESCHI, FILIPPO, fig. 2). It was also used as a design element on façades, as at S Giuseppe, Milan, where the façade (1629–30; *see* RICCHINI, FRANCESCO MARIA, fig. 1) is composed of two tall aediculae, one superimposed on the other. This type of 'aedicular façade' became the most popular type for churches in the Italian Baroque. Another well-known example of the use of the aedicula in the Renaissance can be seen in the vestibule of the Biblioteca Laurenziana (commissioned 1523), S Lorenzo, Florence (*see* MICHELANGELO, fig. 10).

BIBLIOGRAPHY
J. Summerson: *Heavenly Mansions: An Interpretation of Gothic* (London, 1949), pp. 1–28
R. Wittkower: *Art and Architecture in Italy, 1600–1750*, Pelican Hist. A. (Harmondsworth, 1958, rev. 2/1973)
MARGARET LYTTELTON

Aegean Bronze Age civilizations. For the art produced during the Greek Bronze Age (*c.* 3600–*c.* 1100 BC) on Crete *see* MINOAN, in the Cyclades *see* CYCLADIC, and on the Greek mainland *see* HELLADIC. The Mycenaean civilization is covered under the last phase of Helladic. □

Aegeri, Carl. *See* EGERI, CARL VON.

Aegina. *See* AIGINA.

Aelst, Pieter Coecke van, I. *See* COECKE VAN AELST, PIETER, I.

Aelst, Pieter van (*b* ?Alost; *fl* 1509–55). Flemish tapestry-maker. He was the son of Pieter van Edingen Aelst, also a weaver of tapestries, and a member of his father's workshop in Brussels. In 1509 he was cited as a restorer of Margaret of Austria's collection of tapestries. In 1517 he was paid for tapestries of David and John the Baptist made for Henry VIII, and in 1547 and 1548 he was still listed as a tapestry maker for the court of Charles V. His mark, PVA, has been found on four tapestry series, all made in collaboration with others: on five of eight *History of Noah* tapestries (Kraków, N.A. Cols), part of a series made by six Brussels workshops for the King of Poland; on seven of ten *History of Abraham* tapestries, after Bernard van Orley (Vienna, Ksthist. Mus.); on two of eight *History of Odysseus* tapestries (Hardwick Hall, Derbys, NT); and on three of six *History of Moses* tapestries (San Francisco, CA Pal. Legion of Honor).

BIBLIOGRAPHY
Thieme–Becker
L. Baldass: *Die Wiener Gobelinssammlung* (Vienna, 1920)
M. Roethlisberger: 'Deux tentures bruxelloises du milieu du XVIe siècle', *Oud-Holland*, lxxxvi (1971), pp. 88–115
——: 'The Ulysses Tapestries at Hardwick Hall', *Gaz. B.-A.*, lxxix (1972), pp. 111–25
J. Szablowski, ed.: *The Flemish Tapestries at Wawel Castle in Cracow* (Antwerp, 1972)
A. Bennett: *Five Centuries of Tapestry from the Fine Arts Museum of San Francisco* (San Francisco, 1976)
ELISE L. SMITH

Aelst, Willem van (*b* Delft, 1627; *d* ?Amsterdam, after 1687). Dutch painter. He specialized in still-lifes, as did his uncle and teacher Evert van Aelst of Delft (1602–57), whose name survives only in inventories and who died in poverty. Willem's earliest known work, a *Still-life with Fruit* (1642; destr., ex-Suermondt-Ludwig-Mus., Aachen), is likely to have been influenced by his uncle's style. On 9 November 1643 he enrolled in the Delft painters' guild and from 1645 to 1649 was in France, where he painted the *Still-life with Fruit* (1646; Stockholm, E. Perman priv. col.). From 1649 to 1656 he worked in Florence as court painter to Ferdinando II de' Medici, Grand Duke of Tuscany. There he met his fellow countrymen Matthias Withoos and Otto Marseus van Schrieck, the latter also a still-life painter, who probably influenced van Aelst's detailed and smooth style, and with whom van Aelst returned to the Netherlands in 1656—first briefly to Delft before settling in Amsterdam in 1657. Van Aelst's usual signature on paintings, *Guill*[er]*mo van Aelst*, recalls his stay in Italy, as does the (occasional) use of his bent-name 'Vogelverschrikker' (scarecrow), which appears, for example, on a *Still-life with Poultry* (1658; Amsterdam, Rijksmus.).

Van Aelst became famous for his ornate still-lifes with fine glassware, precious silver goblets, fruit and flowers. They are unparalleled in the rendering of surfaces and characterized by a bright, sometimes rather harsh colour scheme. His *Still-life with Shell* (1659; Berlin, Bodemus.) demonstrates that, although he was influenced by Willem Kalf, he preferred sharply outlined forms and more striking colour contrasts. His connection with Amsterdam is especially evident in the flower still-lifes painted between 1659 and 1663, such as *Still-life with Flowers in a Niche* (1662; Rotterdam, Boymans–van Beuningen) and *Still-life with Flowers and a Watch* (1663; The Hague, Mauritshuis; see fig.), in which the ear-shaped vases can be recognized as the work of Johannes Lutma (i), a famous Amsterdam silversmith. As well as a subtle combination of bright colours and the use of striking light effects, the Mauritshuis painting is remarkable for its asymmetrical arrangement of the bouquet, a new idea in flower painting, and one soon taken up by many other painters.

Van Aelst also specialized in still-lifes with game, at least 60 of which survive, painted between 1652 and 1681. A comparison between one of the earliest dated examples

Willem van Aelst: *Still-life with Flowers and a Watch*, oil on canvas, 625×490 mm, 1663 (The Hague, Koninklijk Kabinet van Schilderijen 'Mauritshuis')

(1653; destr. World War II, ex-Kaiser-Friedrich Mus., Berlin, see Sullivan, fig. 100) and his latest known work, *Still-life with Dead Cocks* (1681; sold The Hague, Van Marne & Bignall, 27 Jan 1942, lot 2; see Sullivan, fig. 105), shows that his successful formula was established early and remained virtually unchanged for over 30 years. At the centre of both is a marble tabletop on which birds and hunting accessories are displayed, the vertical element provided by a bird hanging down over the table. Certain items associated with hunting (game bag, bird net, hunting horn, falcon's hoods and quail pipes) are always included, yet the compositions are individually varied, and the skilful style of painting makes each one a pleasure to look at (e.g., 1664, Stockholm, Nmus.; 1668, Karlsruhe, Staatl. Ksthalle; 1671, The Hague, Mauritshuis). His pupils included Maria van Oosterwijck in Delft and Rachel Ruysch in Amsterdam.

BIBLIOGRAPHY

S. A. Sullivan: *The Dutch Gamepiece* (Totowa and Montclair, NJ, 1984), pp. 52–4, 97

Great Dutch Paintings from America (exh. cat.; The Hague, Mauritshuis; San Francisco, F.A. Museums; 1990–91), pp. 130–33, no. 1

B. P. J. BROOS

Aerial perspective. *See under* PERSPECTIVE, §III.

Aerograph. *See* AIRBRUSH.

Aeropittura. Italian movement that emerged in the late 1920s from the second wave of Futurism (*see* FUTURISM, §1), which it eventually supplanted. It was announced by the publication on 22 September 1929 of the *Manifesto dell'Aeropittura*, signed by Giacomo Balla, Benedetta (Marinetti's wife, the painter and writer Benedetta Cappa, 1897–1977), Fortunato Depero, Gerardo Dottori, Fillia, Filippo Tommaso Marinetti, Enrico Prampolini, the painter and sculptor Mino Somenzi (1899–1948) and the painter Tato (pseud. of Guglielmo Sansoni, 1896–1974). This text became the key document for the new adherents of Futurism in the 1930s. Although Marinetti had written the first Futurist manifestos, and Balla, Depero and Prampolini were senior figures within the movement, it was Dottori and younger painters who developed the new form most impressively. Building on earlier concerns with the speeding automobile, both Marinetti and the Fascist government gave particular importance to aeronautics in the 1920s, extolling the pilot as a type of Nietzschean 'Superman'.

There were various applications of the new tendency. Painters such as Tato, Ugo Pozzo (1900–1981), Tullio Crali (*b* 1910) and Renato Di Bosso (*b* 1905), who was also active as a sculptor, engaged in a naturalistic representation of the pilot's new perceptions of landscape seen from extreme angles of perspective. Other painters, such as Prampolini in *The Cloud Diver* (1930; Grenoble, Mus. Peint. & Sculp.), evolved a more abstract language of circles, spirals and intersecting shapes to evoke mood and the symbolism of flight. Other exponents of this approach included Fillia, Benedetta and Pippo Oriani (1909–72). Dottori also tended to abstract from reality, while Bruno Munari favoured geometrical abstraction. A third aspect of Aeropittura involved the movement of the pencil, brush or spray as an analogy for the movement of the aeroplane, as in Di Bosso's *Spiralling towards the Island of Garda* (1934; see G. Lista, *Futurismo*, Paris, 1985, p. 96), in which the giddy plunge to earth is represented by rotating circular forms.

The first exhibition of Aeropittura, held in 1931 at the Galleria Pesaro in Milan, included works by Dottori, Tato, Munari and Fillia. It was followed by an exhibition in Paris in 1932 and in 1934 by one in Berlin sponsored by Joseph Goebbels. By the late 1930s there were manifestos of Aeropoesia and Aeromusica, Prampolini had created Aerodanza Futurista, and manifestations related to Aeropittura had been proposed even for photography, sculpture and architecture. The movement fragmented on Marinetti's death in 1944 and dissolved completely with the collapse of Fascism at the end of World War II.

BIBLIOGRAPHY

E. Crispotti: *Il mito della macchina e altri temi del Futurismo* (Trapani, 1969; rev. 1971)

Aeropittura futurista (exh. cat., Milan, 1970)

Aeropittura (exh. cat., London, Accad. It. A. & A. Applic., 1990)

For further bibliography *see* FUTURISM, §1.

KENNETH G. HAY

Aertgen van Leyden [Aert Claessoon; Aernt Claesz.] (*b* Leiden, 1498; *d* Leiden, 1564). Dutch painter, draughtsman and designer of stained glass. Van Mander's extensive biographical account forms the basis of knowledge of the life and work of this otherwise elusive artist. According to him, Aertgen was the son of a Leiden 'fuller' or cloth finisher, but in 1516 he chose to become a painter and apprenticed himself to Cornelis Engebrechtsz. Van Mander describes the uneven quality and vast stylistic changes within Aertgen's work: at first he painted in the style of his master, then he was influenced by Jan van Scorel and later by Maarten van Heemskerck. Van Mander further reports that Aertgen's paintings represented mainly biblical stories from the Old and New Testament and that they were often beautifully composed, though painted in a 'loose and unpleasant manner'. Leiden city records confirm that a painter called Aert Claesz. was working in Leiden between 1521 and 1564 and living, as van Mander states, on the Zijdegracht (at least in 1561 and 1564). Van Mander also mentions that he made hundreds of designs for 'glass engravers' and lists a number of his paintings. One of these was rediscovered in 1969: a late triptych with the *Last Judgement* including donor portraits of the Montfoort family (1555; Valenciennes, Mus. B.-A.). This has proved the only undisputed work by Aertgen van Leyden, to whom a good many anonymous early 16th-century Leiden school drawings and paintings have been ascribed.

Attributions to Aertgen were made partly on the basis of old inscriptions on drawings and partly from references to paintings in 17th-century inventories. Relying on van Mander's description of the artist's eclectic style, scholars have tended to emphasize the stylistic differences between the works making up Aertgen's hypothetical oeuvre, notwithstanding the improbability that one artist made all the work. Taking Aertgen's rediscovered late triptych as a starting point, it is not easy to determine which of the paintings and drawings attributed to Aertgen in the past might be regarded as works from an earlier period. There is a small group of paintings grouped around the *Church Sermon* (*c.* 1530–35; Amsterdam, Rijksmus.), which, with

Aertgen van Leyden (attrib.): *Christmas Night*, oil on panel, 450×580 mm, *c.* 1511 (Paris, Musée du Louvre)

its cool palette, Italian Renaissance ornamental details in the architecture and fine portrait heads among the members of the congregation, suggests the influence of Lucas van Leyden (to whom it was long attributed, later being given to the eponymous Master of the Church Sermon).

Another group is centred around a triptych with the *Raising of Lazarus* (*c.* 1530–35; Amsterdam, Rijksmus.), which shows a completely different style and manner of painting: the figures are more stylized and elongated, but better organized within an attractive landscape. The underdrawing in the triptych reveals similarities with the exaggerated figure types in a group of drawings in chalk and ink, some of which are designs for stained-glass windows. These were attributed by Wescher to the Master of the Miracle of the Apostles after the drawing of *SS Peter and John Healing the Lame Man* (Berlin, Kupferstichkab.). The style of the figures in this last group is most closely related to that of the *Last Judgement* from 1555.

A third group of works attributable to Aertgen comprises primarily drawings in pen and ink and wash, some of which were also intended as designs for stained-glass windows. Distinguished by thick parallel brushstrokes for shading, these were assigned by Wescher to the Master of 1527, after the drawing of *Christ among the Children* (Paris, Louvre) bearing that date. With their more crowded compositions of sturdy figures placed close to the picture plane, these drawings resemble the painting *Christmas Night* (various copies, e.g. Paris, Louvre, see fig.; and Cologne, Wallraf-Richartz-Mus.), which as early as the beginning of the 17th century was thought to be by Aertgen van Leyden.

The two separate groups of drawings assembled by Wescher were discussed together for the first time under Aertgen's name by van Regteren Altena, who used the painting of *Christmas Night* as one of the starting points for the proposed reconstruction of the artist's work. Bruyn added substantially to this assembled oeuvre, but in the 1986 Amsterdam exhibition Wescher's division of the drawings was reinstated and the attributions of the paintings left open to question. Despite certain resemblances between the various groups, it seems reasonable to assume that more than one artist lies behind the works provisionally assigned to Aertgen van Leyden, especially since dozens of other painters are recorded working in Leiden at that time.

BIBLIOGRAPHY

C. van Mander: *Schilder-boeck* ([1603]–1604), fols 236v–238r

P. Wescher: 'Höllandische Zeichner zur Zeit des Lucas van Leiden', *Oud-Holland*, xlv (1928), pp. 245–54

I. Q. van Regteren Altena: 'Aertgen van Leyden', *Oud-Holland*, lvi (1939), pp. 17–25, 74–87, 129–38, 222–35

J. Bruyn: 'Twee St Antonius-panelen en andere werken van Aertgen van Leyden' [Two panels of St Anthony and other works by Aertgen van Leyden], *Ned. Ksthist. Jb.*, xi (1960), pp. 36–119

J. D. Bangs: *Cornelis Engebrechtsz.'s Leiden: Studies in Cultural History* (Assen 1979), pp. 128–43

F. Scholten: 'Technische aspecten van de *Kerkprediking* en twee andere werken uit de Aertgen van Leyden-groep' [Technical aspects of the *Church Sermon* and two other works from the Aertgen van Leyden group], *Ned. Ksthist. Jb.*, xxxvii (1986), pp. 53–74

Kunst voor de beeldenstorm [Art before the iconoclasm] (exh. cat., ed. J. P. Filedt Kok, W. Halsema-Kubes and W. Th. Kloek; Amsterdam, Rijksmus., 1986), pp. 153–72, 328–30

J. P. FILEDT KOK

Aert Ortkens [Aert de Glaesmakere]. *See* ARNOULT DE NIMÈGUE.

Aertsen [Aertsz.], **Pieter** [Lange Pier] (*b* Amsterdam, 1507/8; *d* Amsterdam, *bur* 3 June 1575). Dutch painter and draughtsman, active also in the southern Netherlands. He probably trained in his native Amsterdam but early on moved to Antwerp, where he enrolled in the Guild of St Luke as a master in 1535. In 1542 he was granted citizenship of the city. Among his pupils in Antwerp were Johannes Stradanus and later Joachim Beuckelaer, a cousin of the artist's wife and his most loyal follower. The earliest known work by Aertsen is a triptych with the *Crucifixion* (*c.* 1545–6; Antwerp, Maagdenhuismus.) for the van den Biest Almshouse in Antwerp. From 1550 Aertsen's development can be traced through a large number of signed and dated paintings. Religious works, mostly intended for churches, must have formed an important part of Aertsen's output. His early paintings seem to have been strongly influenced by other Antwerp artists, as can be seen in the van den Biest triptych, where the figures are close to those in Jan Sanders van Hemessen's background scenes. Van Hemessen's influence is also strong in the pair of triptychs showing the *Seven Sorrows of the Virgin* and the *Seven Joys of the Virgin* (the latter dated 1554; both Zoutleeuw, St Leonard).

Aertsen returned to Amsterdam in or shortly before 1557, probably in connection with important commissions for churches there. He took up residence permanently in the city and repurchased his burghership in 1563. The paintings from his Amsterdam period show a more personal character, although they form a highly fragmented group since all the large altarpieces were destroyed during the subsequent religious iconoclasm. The inner panels of a triptych showing the *Adoration of the Magi*, which was probably made for a church in Delft and of which only two wings survive (Amsterdam, Rijksmus.), form a continuous scene with a monumental figure group, which is close to the powerful naturalism of Aertsen's secular work. Other fragments surviving from this period are also large in scale and their subjects are executed in a similarly direct manner, for example the fragment from the *Adoration of the Shepherds* (Amsterdam, Hist. Mus.), which presumably formed part of Aertsen's altarpiece (finished 1559) for the Nieuwe Kerk in Amsterdam. The same is true of a number of religious pieces apparently intended for domestic interiors rather than churches (e.g. *Adoration of the Shepherds*, 1559; Rouen, Mus. B.-A.).

Aertsen's fame, however, is primarily based on his monumental genre paintings, which introduced a number of new themes into Dutch painting. The earliest examples date from the beginning of the 1550s. The *Country Feast* (1550; Vienna, Ksthist. Mus.) is the first in an extensive series of scenes of country life, mainly festivals, scenes of social gatherings (e.g. *Country Gathering*, 1557; Antwerp, Mus. Mayer van den Bergh) and popular customs (the *Egg Dance*, 1552; Amsterdam, Rijksmus.); these themes had previously been restricted to prints and drawings before Aertsen introduced them as suitable subject-matter for paintings. There were no precedents at all for his kitchen scenes (e.g. *Kitchen Scene with Christ in the House of Martha and Mary*, 1553; Rotterdam, Mus. Boymans–van Beuningen; see fig.) nor for his market scenes in which peasants offer their goods for sale (e.g. *Market Scene with Christ and the Adulteress*, 1559; Frankfurt am Main, Städel. Kstinst. & Städt Gal.). All these works are closely related in style and composition. Large half-length or full-length figures, surprisingly naturalistic in appearance, fill the canvas, while much importance is attached to still-life elements, which are rendered with unusual precision. These images are also related thematically; the frivolous, at times overtly erotic, character of the gatherings suggests that the country scenes were probably intended as a warning against excess and voluptuousness. In the kitchen and market scenes Aertsen made his intentions explicit by adding biblical scenes in the background, which form an appropriate contrast to the abundance of the main scene. Aertsen continued to make monumental genre paintings throughout his career. During his Amsterdam period he extended his repertory to include the single full-length figure (e.g. the *Kitchen Maid*, 1559; Genoa, Pal. Bianco) and the harvest scene, which he seems to have favoured in the 1560s (e.g. *Harvest Scene*; Stockholm, Hallwylska Mus.).

A special group within Aertsen's oeuvre is formed by a small group of paintings from the early 1550s that have no large foreground figures so that they resemble more closely a still-life (e.g. the *Butcher's Stall*, 1551; Uppsala, U. Kstsaml.; *see* THE NETHERLANDS, fig. 15; and the *Still-Life with Christ Visiting Martha and Mary*, 1552; Vienna, Ksthist. Mus.). Although these scenes were important for the development of the still-life as a form in itself, it must be emphasized that their significance was still determined by small biblical scenes in the background.

An important example for Aertsen must have been the scenes in brothels or in notaries' offices painted by van Hemessen during the 1530s and 1540s; these are similar to Aertsen's genre paintings in composition as well as their extremely naturalistic style. However, compared with van Hemessen, who painted in a satirical manner typical of early 16th-century Flemish genre painting, Aertsen was much more restrained in his approach. His combination of biblical and genre motifs is prefigured in the work of landscape painters such as Herri met de Bles and the Brunswick Monogrammist, whose compositions and subjects were copied by Aertsen in a number of smaller, more traditional scenes, with a high viewpoint and large numbers of small figures; these are undated, but it is possible some may have been executed in the 1540s (e.g. *Market Square with Ecce homo*; Utrecht, Catharijneconvent). Aertsen also painted several images of this type during the last year of his life, achieving a more striking structure and composition by setting his biblical subjects in idealized townscapes based on illustrations from Sebastiano Serlio's treatise on architecture (Dut. trans. by Pieter Coecke van Aelst, 1539–50).

Pieter Aertsen: *Kitchen Scene with Christ in the House of Martha and Mary*, oil on panel, 1.26×2.00 m, 1553 (Rotterdam, Museum Boymans–van Beuningen)

A number of Aertsen's drawings have been preserved, some showing designs for altarpieces or parts of altarpieces, for instance *St Martin and the Beggar* (Munich, Staatl. Graph. Samml.), a design for one of the outer panels of the triptych with the *Seven Sorrows of the Virgin*. Others show idiosyncratic designs for monumental church windows, the compositions of which seem barely restricted by the patterns of the window tracery, as in *Christ Washing the Disciples' Feet* (Bergues, Mus. Mun. Mont-de-Piété).

Initially the new possibilities introduced by Aertsen for genre and still-life painting as independent forms were not followed up by other artists in Antwerp, with the exception of Joachim de Beuckelaer. In the northern Netherlands the artist's sons Pieter Pietersz. (1540–1603) and Aert Pietersz. (1550–1612) remained strongly indebted to their father's style and imagery. It was not until about 1600 that a younger generation of Netherlandish painters developed an interest in market and kitchen scenes. By that time the genre had also become popular in Italy, Spain and the German-speaking countries, so it must really be considered a European phenomenon.

BIBLIOGRAPHY

Thieme–Becker; Wurzbach

van Mander: *Schilder-boeck* ([1603]–1604), ii, fols 238*r*, 243*r*–4*v*

F. J. van den Branden: *Geschiedenis der Antwerpsche schilderschool* (Antwerp, 1883), pp. 163–72

G. J. Hoogewerff: *De Noord-Nederlandsche schilderkunst*, iv (The Hague, 1941–2), pp. 488–580

T. H. Lunsingh Scheurleer: 'Pieter Aertsen en Joachim Beuckelaer en hun ontleeningen aan Serlio's architectuurprenten' [Pieter Aertsen and Joachim Beuckelaer and their borrowing from Serlio's architectural prints], *Oud-Holland*, lxii (1947), pp. 123–34

J. Bruyn: 'Some Drawings by Pieter Aertsen', *Master Drgs*, iii (1965), pp. 355–68

D. Kreidl: 'Die religiöse Malerei Pieter Aertsens als Grundlage seiner künstlerischen Entwicklung', *Jb. Kstwiss.*, lxviii (1972), pp. 43–108

J. A. Emmens: '"Eins aber ist nötig": Zu Inhalt und Bedeutung von Markt- und Küchenstücken des 16. Jahrhunderts', *Album amicorum J. G. van Gelder* (The Hague, 1973), pp. 93–101

A. Grosjean: 'Toward an Interpretation of Pieter Aertsen's Profane Iconography', *Kstbist. Tidskr.*, xliii (1974), pp. 121–43

M. Braman Buchan: *The Paintings of Pieter Aertsen*, 2 vols (diss., New York U., Inst. F.A., 1975) [with further bibliog.]

R. Genaille: 'Pieter Aertsen: Précurseur de l'art rubénsien', *Jb.: Kon. Mus. S. Kst.* (1977), pp. 7–96

K. P. F. Moxey: *Pieter Aertsen, Joachim Beuckelaer, and the Rise of Secular Painting in the Context of the Reformation* (New York, 1977) [with further bibliog.]

K. M. Craig: 'Pieter Aertsen and *The Meat Stall*', *Oud-Holland*, xcvi (1982), pp. 1–15

——: '*Pars ergo Marthae transit*: Pieter Aertsen's "Inverted" Paintings of *Christ in the House of Martha and Mary*', *Oud-Holland*, xcvii (1983), pp. 25–39

J. Bruyn: 'De Meester van Paulus en Barnabas (Jan Mandijn ?) en een vroeg werk van Pieter Aertsen', *Rubens and his World: Bijdragen opgedragen aan prof. dr. ir. R.-A. d'Hulst* (Antwerp, 1985), pp. 17–29

G. Irmscher: '*Ministrae voluptatum*: Stoicizing Ethics in the Market and Kitchen Scenes of Pieter Aertsen and Joachim Beuckelaer', *Simiolus*, xvi (1986), pp. 219–32

H.-J. Raupp: *Bauernsatiren: Entstehung und Entwicklung des bäuerlichen Genres in der deutschen und niederländischen Kunst, ca. 1470–1570* (Niederzier, 1986), pp. 214–23

Art before the Iconoclasm: North Netherlandish Art, 1525–1580, 2 vols (exh. cat., ed. J. P. Filedt Kok, W. Halsema-Kubes and W. Th. Kloek; Amsterdam, Rijksmus., 1986)

R. L. Falkenburg: 'Iconographical Connections between Antwerp Landscapes, Market Scenes and Kitchen Pieces', *Oud-Holland*, cii (1988), pp. 114–26

Ned. Kstbist. Jb., xl (1989) [whole issue]

HANS BUIJS

Aertsz., Jan. *See* AMSTEL, JAN VAN.

Aeschbacher, Hans (*b* Zurich, 18 Jan 1906; *d* Russikon, Zurich, 27 Jan 1980). Swiss sculptor, painter and draughtsman. He was self-taught as a draughtsman and only turned to sculpture in 1936. His early sculptural work (1936–45) mainly comprises heads and torsos in addition to heavy, life-size female nudes. These works, mainly in marble and bronze, emphasize volume and were influenced by Aristide Maillol, Charles Despiau and Wilhelm Lehmbruck. During the 1940s Aeschbacher gradually subordinated the human form to a study of the stone's own biomorphic structure. A series of amorphous *Bumps* heralded the final departure from naturalism. In 1952–3 Aeschbacher started to produce *Stelae*, a series of colossal but slender vertical structures that were influenced by the tectonic quality of Archaic Greek masonry. This new emphasis on verticality led after 1960 to the production of lighter, more airy works. Notable examples of work from this period are *Figure IV* (granite, h. 3.92 m, 1967; Bregenz, Kultzent. Schendlingen); *Figure I* (granite, h. 3.05 m, 1969; Hakone-machi, Hakone Open Air Mus.); *Figure I* (granite, h. 3.60 m, 1970; Zurich, Spital Triemli); and *Figure I* (concrete, h. 5.89 m, 1973; Zurich, Überbauung Utohof). In 1975 Aeschbacher returned to earlier themes by producing compositions using parabolic curves and concentric circles. On the other hand, however, he turned to new materials such as concrete, lava and acrylic glass. During his career Aeschbacher also executed a large number of paintings and drawings, which illustrate the same development from naturalism to abstraction.

BIBLIOGRAPHY

H. H. Holz, ed.: *Hans Aeschbacher* (Zurich, 1976) [excellent bibliog.]
B. A. Miesch-Müller: *Hans Aeschbacher (1906–1980): Eine Studie zum Gesamtwerk eines aussergewöhnlichen Schweizer Plastikers* (Zurich, 1990)

CHRISTINA MAURER

Aesslinger, Hans (*b* ?Munich, *fl* 1535; *d* Munich, 1567). German sculptor, mason and medallist. In 1536 he became a master sculptor in Munich and shortly afterwards entered the service of Ludwig X, Duke of Bavaria. He moved to Landshut in 1537 to work on the construction of the Italian wing of the ducal Stadtresidenz. In 1555 he travelled to Neuburg an der Donau to oversee the shipment of stone for the palace's chimneys. He was influenced by and may have assisted Thomas Hering, the sculptor of these chimneys. Also in 1555 he reverted to Munich citizenship.

The few surviving examples of his sculpture show him to have been an accomplished if somewhat derivative artist. Many seem to have been commissioned by Duke Albrecht V of Bavaria, who paid him an annual salary from 1558 (and perhaps as early as 1551) to 1567. Aesslinger's limestone reliefs (both 1550) of the *Massacre of the Innocents* (Berlin, Skulpgal.) and the *Judgement of Paris* (Munich, Bayer. Nmus.) are based on prints by Marcantonio Raimondi after Raphael. In addition to his carving of reliefs, Aessingler's activities as a court artist were varied. He also worked as a portraitist, identified by Habich (1932) as the Monogrammist HA of the *Albrecht V* medals of 1554 and 1558, and as the sculptor of the related life-size limestone portrait relief of *Albrecht V* (ex-Munich, Staatl. Münzsamml.). Aesslinger also worked for the Archiepiscopate of Salzburg. Between 1559 and 1561 he carved the *Resurrection* relief for the epitaph of *Archbishop Michael von Kuenburg* (Franziskanerkirche). A portrait medal (*c.* 1562) of Archbishop Johann Jakob Khnen von Belasi is attributed to Aesslinger.

BIBLIOGRAPHY

NDB; Thieme–Becker
W. Vöge: *Königliche Museen zu Berlin: Beschreibung der Bildwerke der christlichen Epochen*, iv (Berlin, 1910), pp. 167–8
E. F. Bange: *Die Kleinplastik der deutschen Renaissance in Holz und Stein* (Leipzig, 1928), pp. 94–5
O. Hartig: 'Münchner Künstler und Kunstsachen', *Münchn. Jb. Bild. Kst*, n. s. 1, vii (1930), pp. 365, 367–71; viii (1931), pp. 322–4, 327, 329, 331, 333–4, 336–7, 340, 343
G. Habich: *Die deutschen Schaumünzen des XVI. Jahrhunderts*, ii (Munich, 1932), pp. 457–60
V. Liedke: 'Die Landshuter Maler- und Bildhauerwerkstätten von der Mitte des 16. bis zum Ende des 18. Jahrhunderts', *A. Bavar.*, xxvii/xxviii (1982), pp. 34–5, 96–7
J. C. Smith: *German Sculpture of the Later Renaissance, c. 1520–1580: Art in an Age of Uncertainty* (Princeton, 1994), pp. 51–2, 288, 312, 334–5, 360, 363–4

JEFFREY CHIPPS SMITH

Aesthetic Movement. Term used to describe a movement of the 1870s and 1880s that manifested itself in the fine and decorative arts and architecture in Britain and subsequently in the USA. Reacting to what was seen as evidence of philistinism in art and design, it was characterized by the cult of the beautiful and an emphasis on the sheer pleasure to be derived from it. In painting there was a belief in the autonomy of art, the concept of ART FOR ART'S SAKE, which originated in France as a literary movement and was introduced into Britain around 1860.

The Aesthetic Movement was championed by the writers and critics WALTER PATER, Algernon Charles Swinburne and Oscar Wilde. In keeping with Pater's theories, the artists associated with it painted pictures without narrative or significant subject-matter. Dante Gabriel Rossetti took his inspiration from Venetian art because of its emphasis on colour and the decorative. This resulted in a number of half-length paintings of female figures, such as the *Blue Bower* (1865; U. Birmingham, Barber Inst.). James McNeill Whistler came closest to the ideals of the Aesthetic Movement. In such paintings as *Nocturne in Blue and Gold: Old Battersea Bridge* (*c.* 1872–5; London, Tate), he did not intend to achieve topographical accuracy: truth to nature was not one of the aims of the Aesthetic Movement. At the famous libel trial between John Ruskin and Whistler in 1878, Whistler said of this work, 'The thing is intended simply as a representation of moonlight. My whole scheme was only to bring about a certain harmony of colour' (Spencer, p. 85). Albert Joseph Moore used formalized Classical settings for his languorous female figures, which seduce the viewer by the harmonies of colour and form as well as the latent eroticism, as in *A Venus* (York, C.A.G.; for illustration *see* MOORE, (1)). The neutral titles of his pictures serve to distract from the content and discourage narrative readings. Frederic Leighton leaned even more heavily on the Classical past, and he often adopted mythological figures (e.g. *Bath of Psyche*, exh. 1890; London, Tate).

The formal arrangement of Whistler's *Nocturne in Blue and Gold* was derived from Japanese art (*see* JAPONISME), which was an important influence on designers (see fig.) as well as painters. The furniture of E. W. Godwin, for

Aesthetic Movement interior by Walter Crane; from C. Cook: *The House Beautiful* (New York, 1881) (London, Victoria and Albert Museum)

example, is simple and elegant—solid balanced by void—occasionally with painted decoration. His preferred material was ebonized mahogany, which he used for the buffet that he designed originally for himself in 1867 (e.g. London, V&A), inset with panels of embossed Japanese leather paper. In the house in London that he decorated for himself there were Japanese fans on the ceiling and skirting, and Japanese vases. Such items were imported and sold at Liberty & Co. in London and could be found in fashionable 'Aesthetic' interiors of the 1870s and 1880s.

In 1876 F. R. Leyland commissioned Thomas Jeckyll to design the dining-room (now in Washington, DC, Freer) of 49 Princes Gate, London, which was to be the setting for his collection of porcelain and Whistler's painting *La Princesse du pays de la porcelaine* (1863–4). The walls behind Jeckyll's elaborate shelving were covered with Spanish leather, which Whistler overpainted in 1877 in gold on a blue ground with motifs based on the eye and tail-feathers of the peacock; opposite his picture, which hung over the fireplace, he painted two peacocks in full plumage. In the fireplace stands a pair of wrought-iron fire-dogs designed by Jeckyll in the form of sunflowers. With the peacock, the sunflower was a characteristic motif of the Aesthetic Movement, appearing in tiles painted by William De Morgan, embroidery designed by C. R. Ashbee, chintz and wallpaper designed by Bruce J. Talbert and in the painted face of a clock (1880; London, V&A) that was probably designed by Lewis Foreman Day.

The principal link between 'art' furniture, ceramics, metalwork and textiles of the Aesthetic Movement and the QUEEN ANNE REVIVAL style of architecture favoured by Godwin (for illustration *see* GODWIN, E. W.) and Richard Norman Shaw, among others, is the fact that their creators were, in the sophistication of their designs, elevating the form of their work to the status of fine art. They were creating 'artistic' objects and buildings. They were both reforming and informing taste, a matter that was of great concern to William Morris, who, though at odds with much of the philosophy of the Aesthetic Movement, helped to extend its influence to the USA. By 1870 Morris's wallpapers were on sale in Boston, and two years later *Hints on Household Taste* (1868) by Charles Locke Eastlake was produced in an American edition. This was important to the dissemination of the notion that art should be applied to all types of decoration. In 1876 the Centennial Exposition in Philadelphia did much to familiarize Americans with reformed taste in England, and in 1882–3 Wilde made a lecture tour of the USA. Though satirized for his effeteness and posturing, he increased awareness of the Aesthetic Movement.

In the USA Christian Herter produced his own version of Godwin's 'Anglo-Japanese' style (e.g. wardrobe, 1880–85; New York, Met.), and Ott & Brewer of Trenton, NJ, made ceramics in the Japanese taste. Louis Comfort Tiffany designed jewellery and silver (e.g. vase, 1873–5; New York, Met.), as well as glass and interiors, and must be regarded as one of the principal American exponents of the Aesthetic Movement, as he was to be of Art Nouveau. John La Farge contributed decorations to the Japanese Parlor (1883–4) of the house (destr.) of William Henry Vanderbilt in New York, which was the epitome of fashionable taste. In the fine arts Whistler's influence made a brief impact on the work of Winslow Homer (e.g. *Promenade on the Beach*, 1880; Springfield, MA, Mus. F.A.) and Elihu Vedder.

BIBLIOGRAPHY

W. Pater: *Studies in the History of the Renaissance* (London, 1873, rev. 4/1893); rev. as *The Renaissance: Studies in Art and Poetry* (Berkeley, 1980)

W. Gaunt: *The Aesthetic Adventure* (London, 1945)

E. Aslin: *The Aesthetic Movement: Prelude to Art Nouveau* (London, 1969)

R. V. Johnson: *Aestheticism* (London, 1969)

R. Spencer: *The Aesthetic Movement* (London, 1972)

M. Gironard: *Sweetness and Light: The Queen Anne Movement, 1860–1900* (Oxford, 1977/*R* New Haven and London, 1984)

I. Small, ed.: *The Aesthetes: A Sourcebook* (London, 1979) [excellent intro. and reprints of texts]

In Pursuit of Beauty: Americans and the Aesthetic Movement (exh. cat., New York, Met., 1986)

□

Aesthetics. Branch of Western philosophy concerned primarily with the arts, especially the fine arts, although it often treats the concepts of natural beauty and appreciation of nature as well. The notion of fine art and that of a corresponding branch of philosophy are of relatively recent origin, dating from the 18th century, although historical antecedents of many of the particular issues now recognized as belonging to aesthetics go back to antiquity. The present usage of the term stems from its adoption in 1735 by Alexander Gottlieb Baumgarten, who employed the Greek *aisthesis* (perception) to distinguish the study of sensory, perceptual concerns, such as beauty, from logic, the study of reason and intellect.

I. Introduction. II. Western survey.

I. Introduction.

The primary subject-matter of aesthetics is the complex cultural institution in which works of art are embedded, including artistic creation, performance, appreciation, interpretation, criticism, judgement, and the various roles the arts play in people's lives and in society. The aesthetician steps back from this institution and examines it from the outside (although the line between participating in the institution and studying it is somewhat arbitrary). In the 20th century the term has come to embrace an enormously diverse collection of particular issues, with no very definite central core. However, several frequently occurring themes can be identified.

1. Defining art. 2. Objectivity and subjectivity. 3. Values. 4. Art and art-making. 5. Aesthetics and practice.

1. DEFINING ART. The central question of aesthetics, according to some, is what art is, what works of art have in common and how they differ from non-art (*see* ART). Plato and Aristotle have inspired definitions in terms of mimesis or imitation. Benedetto Croce and R. G. Collingwood took art to be essentially expression of a certain sort. Tolstoy emphasized the communication of emotion. Clive Bell and others focused on formal properties. Some definitions are based on intrinsic features of works of art themselves (*see* ART, WORK OF). According to others, whether something is art depends rather on how it was created, the effects it does, or might, have on those who experience it, how people use it or think of it, or its role or status in society. Some aestheticians understand a concept of aesthetic experience, aesthetic emotion, aesthetic attitude, artistic creation or aesthetic objects (including natural objects) to be more fundamental than that of works of art and define the latter in terms of one or another of the former.

There has been considerable scepticism about the possibility of defining art, or of defining it in a useful and illuminating way. The diversity of what is commonly called art, as well as the variety of definitions that have been suggested, the often striking similarities between some kinds of art and some things, or activities, that are not usually considered art, the absence of a clear correlation between the notion of art in non-Western and pre-18th-century cultures, and also the dramatic shifts in uses of the term in recent Western culture, can easily make it seem that any definition will be arbitrary and pointless. Whether it is worth worrying about what art means rests in large part on how important that notion is within the cultural practices being investigated. If the creation, appreciation, understanding or value of such things as paintings, novels and musical works essentially involves thinking of them as instances of art, aestheticians will want to explain what it is to think of them in that way; but if art is a category imposed on these practices from above in an attempt to understand them, there is always the possibility that another way of understanding them might be more perspicuous, one that does not classify certain things as art or certain objects, activities, emotions or attitudes as aesthetic. If the notion of art is intrinsic to the practices of one particular society but not to others, examining it will be necessary in order to understand that society; but the fact that the notion is merely a local one may suggest that it is not very fundamental, even in that society.

Uncertainties about how to define art translate into uncertainties about the scope of aesthetics. But many issues traditionally classified under that heading can be pursued independently of a definition. Rather than making and defending generalizations about art, the nature and importance of works of specific media, periods, genres or styles can be investigated. Concepts of imitation, expression and communication can be examined without troubling over whether they apply to everything properly called art. Pictorial representation, metaphor, fiction and other notions, which appear to be important outside the realm of art as well as within it, can be explored without deciding where to draw the line.

2. OBJECTIVITY AND SUBJECTIVITY. Much discussion has focused on questions about the objectivity or subjectivity of aesthetic judgements. Some speak of a 'science' of criticism whose task is to ascertain objective facts about works of art and regard aesthetic judgements, when true, as expressing such facts. There are, in contrast, various more subjective conceptions of aesthetic judgement, some of them encapsulated in the idea that 'beauty is in the eye of the beholder'. Such judgements are said to be descriptions not of the work but of the speaker's response to it, or claims about how the work does or would affect people of certain sorts, or projections on to the work of the ideas or feelings of the person who judges it. Some take judgements to be mere expressions of the speaker's feelings or responses, not allowing for truth or falsity at all. Criticism is sometimes regarded as a creative enterprise, not unlike that of an artist, rather than anything like a search for knowledge or truth.

David Hume articulated a dilemma that vexed Immanuel Kant and many others: aesthetic judgements seem to be mere matters of taste, there being nothing in the object to make them correct or incorrect; so no-one has a right to demand the agreement of others. Nevertheless, in some particular instances it seems entirely reasonable to demand agreement—it may simply seem obvious that works by Rembrandt (or Homer or Bach) are superior to those of many 'lesser' artists. More recently some have argued that multiple incompatible interpretations of a work may be equally reasonable and hence that no interpretation can be considered correct or true (even if some can be ruled out as definitely incorrect); the best that can be said about an interpretation, it is argued, is that it is 'valid', or 'interesting', or more plausible than various alternatives (*see* HERMENEUTICS). These issues are analogous to ones about the objectivity or subjectivity of moral judgements, of judgements about colours and other secondary properties, and even of hardcore scientific propositions. The status of aesthetic judgements needs to be investigated in the context of more general theories of language and truth.

3. VALUES. Aesthetics is sometimes classified as a branch of value theory, along with ethics. This ignores the

many significant issues of aesthetics that are related only indirectly, if at all, to questions of value, and it begs questions about how fundamental judgements of value are. It may be more important to understand a work than to decide how good it is. Nevertheless, questions about value have been central in the work of many aestheticians.

The most obvious ones concern evaluative judgements of particular works: judgements that a work is good, great, successful, mediocre, or better or worse than another. There are discussions of the grounds on which such evaluations are made and, of course, disputes about their objectivity or subjectivity. Some have attempted to formulate general criteria of aesthetic value, to specify what characteristics of a work or natural object constitute aesthetic merits. Some definitions of art are in effect specifications of such criteria. Only good art counts as art at all, on some accounts, and to be good art is, for instance, to be expressive or to possess 'significant form'. Those who distrust generalizations about the arts may deny that there is a single kind of value that might be called aesthetic. The fact that questions of comparative value seem so often to make little sense (e.g. which is better, the Sistine Chapel or the Taj Mahal?) may suggest that works of different kinds are valuable in very different and incommensurable ways. Some argue that no useful rules or criteria can be given for judging aesthetic value, and some consider the whole enterprise of assessing the value of a work irredeemably subjective and pointless. There are fundamental questions about how aesthetic value is related to other kinds of value, especially moral value: do moral virtues or defects in a work have any bearing on its aesthetic value or are the two entirely independent? Is there an aesthetic component to moral values—do or should distinctively aesthetic considerations play a part in determining whether someone is a good or a virtuous person or lives a good life?

In addition to questions about the merit of particular works, one can ask about the value of the institution of art as a whole, the reasons why people engage in it and the benefits they derive from it—or the ills that it is responsible for. Questions about the importance of the institution in people's lives and in society remain even for those who reject estimations of the value of particular works (*see also* PSYCHOANALYSIS AND ART; PSYCHOLOGY AND ART; and SOCIAL HISTORY OF ART).

Some consider the values of the arts—either of particular works or of the institution—to be primarily cognitive; others consider them primarily emotive. The former emphasize the role of art in expressing or communicating knowledge, understanding or insight, in its capacity to edify or instruct; the latter focus on the evocation of emotional experiences in appreciators or the expression of emotions by artists, or simply the pleasure of appreciating and creating art. However, the distinction between emotive and cognitive conceptions of art is not very clearcut. A cognitivist may hold that the insights art provides are primarily about emotions or that art promotes understanding of a special intuitive or emotive kind, perhaps one involving empathy. Appreciators' emotional experiences may be important because of their contributions to understanding—understanding either of emotions or of their objects. Emotions themselves, on some accounts, are partly cognitive or even constitute ways of knowing.

There are sharp differences among aestheticians about how special the arts are, how closely they are linked to other interests and integrated into the rest of life. For theorists influenced by Plato, Aristotle, Freud, Darwin and Marx, for instance, the importance of the arts consists in their bearing on other aspects of our lives. Art is said to provide a safe outlet for dangerous emotions, to contribute to emotional catharsis, to promote understanding and empathy. It is praised for its capacity to reveal truths about ourselves and the human condition or to improve people morally—or it is damned for obscuring the true nature of reality or for its contributions to moral depravity (*see also* IDEOLOGY). It is an effective tool of PROPAGANDA, some say, a means of achieving political domination or fomenting revolution, or a means of deepening religious faith (*see also* CENSORSHIP and RELIGION AND ART). Even when art serves as an escape from the cares of life, its benefits may be thought to consist in its capacity for psychic renewal.

There has been a strong tendency, however, deriving partly from Kant but especially prominent in the late 19th century and early 20th, to regard art as essentially autonomous from the rest of life, to think of the arts as inhabiting a separate domain with its own distinctive intrinsic values. Some recognize a special 'aesthetic emotion', stressing the disparity between it and the emotions of life (Clive Bell and Roger Fry). Some regard the representational content of visual art as being not truly aesthetic and resist works with messages or morals, or ones that are 'merely' informative or interesting. The notions of 'disinterest' as a crucial ingredient of the aesthetic attitude (Kant), of the advisability of 'distancing' works from personal needs and ends (Edward Bullough) and of 'art for art's sake' emphasize what is distinctive about the arts or the aesthetic and their separation from other aspects of life.

4. ART AND ART-MAKING. There is a nest of traditional problems concerning whether and to what extent what is important about art is located in works of art themselves, whether the artist and his act of creation, or more broadly the manner and circumstances in which the work came about, come into play, and in what ways they do. Some of these problems are discussed under the rubric of the 'intentional fallacy', but the issues are much larger than that of the relevance of artists' intentions. According to Monroe Beardsley and the 'New Critics', all that matters aesthetically about a work are its intrinsic properties, what is perceptible in it and the effects its perceptible properties have on appreciators; the artist is important only as a means whereby the work is produced.

Contrary views take many forms. Some have regarded art as essentially a matter of communication between the artist and appreciators, with the work serving as a vehicle of such communication. The appreciator's primary interest is in the person who made the work, in something like what he meant by it, rather than in properties of the work itself. The communication theorist (*see* COMMUNICATION THEORY) recognizes a fundamental difference between works of art and aesthetically regarded natural objects, since the latter seem not to be vehicles of anyone's acts of communication. According to Richard Wollheim, the task of the critic is to reconstruct the artist's creative process as it appears in the work. Some recognized fictive or apparent communicators (which arguably are to be found in the work itself)—what Wayne Booth called 'postulated authors', for instance—rather than actual ones. Nietzsche, Benedetto Croce and R. G. Collingwood emphasized the artist's creative act rather than the product of his action but did not think of it especially as an act of communicating with appreciators.

Ernst Gombrich and Nelson Goodman, among others, contend that a work of art is to be understood in a certain language or in terms of certain conventions, and that identifying the relevant language or conventions requires going beyond a work's intrinsic properties (*see also* ICONOGRAPHY AND ICONOLOGY; SEMIOTICS; and SYMBOL). Communication may involve such conventions, but in some views what an appreciator is primarily interested in is what the work itself means, given the relevant conventions, rather than what the artist meant by it or communicated by means of it. Others have claimed that works need to be understood against the background of the circumstances in which they were produced but in ways that may not involve conventions; Michael Baxandall, for instance, argued that appreciation requires awareness of the problems the work was designed to solve.

5. AESTHETICS AND PRACTICE. Many important questions of aesthetics are specific to particular genres, media or styles of art, and many of them grow naturally out of the concerns of artists and critics. In some cases aestheticians aim to provide theoretical backing for one or another side of a critical dispute or attempt to justify a particular kind of art. Assessing the significance of various techniques for representing reality in the visual arts requires consideration of what may be meant by realism and the ways in which realism of various sorts may be desirable or undesirable. These interests—and also disputes about non-objective or abstract art—lead quickly to fundamental questions about the very notion of REPRESENTATION: questions about what it is to represent something and how pictorial representation differs from verbal description; about the point or purpose of pictorial representation or of the portrayal of reality by any means. There are lively disputes concerning what might be special about the medium of photography: whether the supposedly automatic manner of their genesis makes photographs inherently more realistic than paintings and drawings; whether photographs are merely mechanical reproductions of reality lacking in artistic value. Many aestheticians have been especially intrigued by the Dadaists and Surrealists and avant-garde figures such as John Cage, Marcel Duchamp and Robert Rauschenberg—by their ready-mades, happenings, Minimalism, performance art and conceptual art. Some worried whether, for example, Duchamp's *Fountain* (1917; editioned replica, 1964; Ottawa, N.G.; for illustration *see* READY-MADE) qualifies as art, but many issues are independent of this one. Critical disputes about whether to regard such works, events or activities as frauds perpetrated on a gullible public or as refreshing escapes from stodgy tradition, or something in between, need to be adjudicated. What is the point of using indeterminate or aleatoric means in the production of works of art? What significance is there in the breakdown of traditional genre, in the extreme emphasis on newness and originality, in the blurring of the lines between artist, performer, work and audience and in the apparent disdain for value judgements and the lack of interest in 'greatness'? Avant-garde works are sometimes said to be about art itself, and many of them inevitably raise fundamental issues of aesthetics.

Other practical matters that lead quickly to larger theoretical concerns for aestheticians include questions about AUTHENTICITY and FORGERY. If it is only a work's intrinsic properties that are important aesthetically, a forgery indistinguishable from the original will be no different from it aesthetically. The communication theorist, however, can argue that the forgery and the original are vehicles of very different acts of communication, even if they are indistinguishable. There are related questions about how, and whether, to repair or reconstruct damaged works and archaeological sites—whether the aim should be to restore the appearance of the original as nearly as possible or to avoid disturbing the remains.

Other practical matters that lead quickly to larger theoretical concerns include questions about relations between form and function in architecture and design, about pornography and censorship, about public support for the arts, about choices between 'high art' and popular art, and about the nature and validity of the 'test of time' for greatness in art.

BIBLIOGRAPHY

A. G. Baumgarten: *Meditatione philosophicae de nonnulis ad poema pertinentilous* (Halle, 1735); trans. by K. Aschenbrenner and W. Holther as *Reflections on Poetry* (Berkeley, 1954)
K. Gilbert and H. Kuhn: *A History of Aesthetics* (New York, 1939)
E. Cassirer: *The Philosophy of the Enlightenment* (Princeton, 1951)
P. O. Kristeller: 'The Modern System of the Arts', *J. Hist. Ideas*, xii (1951), pp. 465–527; xii (1952), pp. 17–46
M. H. Abrams: *The Mirror and the Lamp* (Oxford, 1953)
R. Arnheim: *Art and Visual Perception: A Psychology of the Creative Eye* (Berkeley, 1966)
G. Dickie: *Art and the Aesthetic* (Ithaca, 1974)
G. Dickie and R. Sclafani, eds: *Aesthetics: A Critical Anthology* (New York, 1977, 3/1989)
R. Scruton: *The Aesthetics of Architecture* (Princeton, 1979)
J. Margolis: *Art and Philosophy* (Brighton, 1980)
N. Wolterstorff: *Works and Worlds of Art* (Oxford, 1980)
A. Savile: *The Test of Time: An Essay in Philosophical Aesthetics* (Oxford, 1982)
F. Sparshott: *The Theory of the Arts* (Princeton, 1982)
M. Baxandall: *Patterns of Intention: On the Historical Explanation of Pictures* (New Haven and London, 1985)
R. Wollheim: *Painting as an Art* (Princeton, 1987)
K. L. Walton: *Mimesis as Make-believe: On the Foundations of the Representational Arts* (Cambridge, MA, 1990)

For further bibliography *see* §II below.

KENDALL L. WALTON

II. Western survey.

Certain Classical, medieval and Renaissance concepts related to visual culture have sometimes been characterized as being part of the history of aesthetics, but this notion of aesthetic history is argued by some historians to be misleading. However, as some of the major issues of aesthetics, particularly beauty, were also discussed in earlier periods, it is reasonable at least to examine these antecedents as well as modern developments.

1. Classical. 2. Medieval. 3. Renaissance and Baroque. 4. Modern.

1. CLASSICAL. Any approach to ancient Greek thought about the arts must begin by stressing how different Greek conceptions of the aesthetic were from some influential modern conceptions. In modern aesthetics it is common to think of the aesthetic as a domain clearly bounded off from the ethical and practical, aesthetic interest as clearly distinct from practical interest. For the ancient Greeks, this was not the case. Poetry, visual art and music were all taken to have an ethical role, in virtue of their form as well as in virtue of their content, and a citizen's interest in them was understood to be an interest in pursuing questions about how best to live. Aesthetic innovations were to be assessed for their contribution to human action and practical (usually communal) self-understanding. This attitude was reinforced by the civic institutions in which the arts were embedded; the major dramatic festivals of Athens were civic religious festivals at which citizens gathered together. Looking at the staged action and across the amphitheatre at one another, they characteristically saw in the performance an occasion both for the moral education of the young and the communal exploration of tensions and complexities in civic norms of excellence. Because of this view of the goal of art, aesthetic assessment was, like Athenian social assessment, a democratic business; every citizen was encouraged to engage in aesthetic/ethical reflection.

One sign of the thoroughgoing unity of the aesthetic with the ethical can be seen in the Greek word *kalon*. Usually translated as 'beautiful' in some contexts, as 'noble' or 'fine' in others, it is in reality a univocal word, giving evidence of the Greek belief that only what is ethically fine is pleasing to behold and that visible beauty is a sign of excellence.

The ancient Greeks are frequently described as coolly contemplative, devoted to ideals of perfect symmetry and proportion. Although there is an element of truth in this portrayal, as the Pythagorean theories of cosmic mathematical harmony did have influence on Greek thought about the arts, far more central to the Greek experience of the arts was the activity of the emotions. Most Greek thinkers about art emphasized the powerfully emotive effects of music, dance, drama, even painting and sculpture. They did not, however, hold that emotions are unintelligent, mere bodily drives or surges of affect. They tended to think of grief, fear, anger, love etc as involving (or even as being) value judgements, and as educable through the alteration of those judgements. This is one reason why they believed that works that arouse and shape emotion can have such a profound effect on moral development.

A central concept in ancient Greek aesthetic thought has often been seriously misunderstood. The crucial word *mimesis* has frequently been translated as 'imitation', and it has been assumed that a thinker who described the function of art as *mimesis* meant that the goal of art is the literal copying of natural reality through the production of objects that are as similar as possible, in all respects, to some concrete model. In fact an interest in *mimesis* implies no such view. The word is closely linked to the verb *mimeisthai*, which denoted the behaviour of actors in the dramatic performance of the mimes and meant simply 'to behave like a mime actor'. A study of the early evidence shows that, through this comparison, *mimeisthai* came to mean 'to represent something by conveying some of its characteristic traits'. *Mimesis*, then, is usually better translated as 'representation', and in the context of a view of representation that does not insist on literal naturalistic similarity. In no case was there an interest in the literal copying of all characteristics or on the use of a particular, rather than a generic, model. The emphasis was on the (usually very stylized) displaying of some features that were conventionally allowed to signify the sort of thing that the artist wished to represent, and the object was almost always a type of thing rather than a concrete particular.

Aesthetic thought in the Greek world began with the Homeric poems, in which the poet/speaker ascribes the origins of his art to the Muses, claiming that his art can educate because it embodies divine knowledge. The didactic poet Hesiod (*fl c.* 8th century BC) told a more complex story. His poet/speaker draws attention to the elusive character of poetic information by ascribing to his Muses the claim that they can make lies look like truth, but they can also tell the truth, if they so choose. These influential passages set the stage for a debate about the reliability of the poets as educators that continued throughout the history of Greek aesthetic theory and was broadened to take in mimetic art as a whole.

A particularly rich source of early reflection about art and education is the work of the comic poet Aristophanes (*c.* 450–385 BC), who commented at length on his own art and poetic art in general. His work *Frogs*, produced in 405 BC, shows a competition in the underworld between the shades of the poets Aeschylus and Euripides; the winner will return to help the city in its political crisis. Poetic statements, formal and metrical devices, and even musical choices—all arts are assessed for their ethical contribution, as all participants agree that poets are the city's primary teachers and guides. The play's defence of the morality of poetry gains force from the fact that sophists and rhetoricians had recently been drawing attention to the subversive and potentially deceptive powers of literary speech. The Aristophanic victor, Aeschylus, argued successfully that the poet is a much needed source of ethical truth and that the emotionally stirring features of poetic art are themselves ethically valuable.

Philosophers of the 4th century BC undertook a newly detailed examination of artistic techniques, always with a view to art's ethical and social role. The popular thought of the early 4th century on these subjects is probably well exemplified in a passage from the *Memorabilia* of XENOPHON, in which Socrates is shown advising painters and sculptors how to render visually the characteristic signs of different sorts of souls. As usual, it is stressed that the artist will truly please only if he represents what is admirable. The passage gives a good example of the concept of *mimesis* at work.

The two greatest aesthetic thinkers of ancient Greece, PLATO and ARISTOTLE, agreed with their tradition that the function of art is to promote the ethical education of citizens and that formal and stylistic devices should be assessed with that end in view. They also agreed that most great art, and especially dramatic poetry, reveals a passionate interest in the mutable and undependable things of this world, teaching the beholder to cultivate such attachments. They differed sharply, however, in their assessment of the value of these attachments and therefore concerning their judgement on art. Plato's *Republic* argues that, since we wish citizens to believe that the good person is sufficient unto him or herself for good living, we should rule out works that represent or arouse emotions such as grief, fear and pity, which presuppose that things beyond our control do matter greatly. Aristotle's *Poetics* replies, arguing that the reversals displayed in the great tragic plots, and the pity and fear they arouse in their audience, are educational in a good sense, conducive to a true understanding of the relationship between the good human life and the goods of fortune.

The Hellenistic era in both Greece and Rome was especially rich in high-level aesthetic reflection. The two major philosophical schools, Epicureans and Stoics (*see* STOICISM), agreed that philosophers concerned with the 'therapeutic' education of the passions of the soul must also be concerned with the aesthetic form in which philosophical teaching is expressed. They reflected in complex ways about the contribution of visual art, music and, above all, literary forms to that education. Although Epicurus preferred to write in a plain non-literary style, the great Epicurean poet Lucretius (*c.* 99–55 BC) defended the importance of a certain type of poetry in education. The Stoics found in all the arts signs of nature's purpose, praising tragic poetry above all for its insight into the violence of passion. Meanwhile, literary and rhetorical theorists of many types, writing in both Greek and Latin, advanced the detailed study of literary form and style; and specialized works such as *De architectura* by VITRUVIUS promoted the understanding of aesthetic structure in the plastic arts.

See also NEO-PLATONISM.

BIBLIOGRAPHY

H. Koller: *Die Mimesis in der Antike* (diss., U. Berne, 1954)
G. Sörbom: *Mimesis and Art* (Uppsala, 1966)
J. Pollitt: *Art and Experience in Classical Athens* (Cambridge, 1972)
D. Russell and M. Winterbottom, eds: *Ancient Literary Criticism* (Oxford, 1972)
D. Russell: *Criticism in Antiquity* (London, 1981)
M. C. Nussbaum and S. Halliwell: *The Fragility of Goodness: Luck and Ethics in Greek Tragedy and Philosophy* (Cambridge, 1985)
S. Halliwell: *Aristotle's Poetics* (Chapel Hill, 1986)

MARTHA C. NUSSBAUM

2. MEDIEVAL. Evidence for medieval aesthetics may arguably be sought in the sophisticated, reflective discussions, mostly of theologians, about the concept of beauty. These formed a minor part of investigations into God's attributes and his relation to the created world. They were stimulated by one particular text, *De divinis nominibus* by Pseudo-Dionysius (*c.* AD 500), which included 'Beauty' and 'Beautiful' among the various names denoting God's attributes (chapter 4). Medieval readers believed Pseudo-Dionysius' works were the products of Dionysius, the Areopagite converted by St Paul (Acts xvii.34). As such, they had enormous prestige and were discussed in great detail by 13th-century theologians. Pseudo-Dionysius stated that not only does all beauty derive from God but also that, like goodness, beauty is a quality possessed by all things that exist. This presented the commentators with two main problems—in what way can all things be said to be beautiful and what is the relationship between this universal sense of 'beautiful' and the normal meaning of the word, by which some things are described as 'beautiful' and some not? Among the four medieval theologians who discussed the concept of beauty most acutely, Robert Grosseteste (*c.* 1170–1253) and Albert the Great (*c.* 1200–80) attempted to answer only the first of these questions, whereas Ulrich of Strasbourg (*d* ?1278) and THOMAS AQUINAS tried also to answer the second.

In order to explain Pseudo-Dionysius' text, the theologians turned to an ancient Greek definition, according to which beauty results from symmetry together with colour. They found this definition in Cicero and Augustine (AD 345–430), but whereas Cicero and Augustine saw it as a criterion for deciding which particular things are beautiful or not, Grosseteste and Albert turned it into a way of explaining how all things are beautiful. Grosseteste's metaphysics made it easy for him to assert that all things possess colour and symmetry. Colour, most medieval thinkers held, is an effect of light, and Grosseteste saw the whole universe in terms of the irradiation of light from its primal source. Grosseteste also considered that the universe is designed according to the laws of geometry and so was happy to allow that everything in it is symmetrically proportioned. In his view light and symmetry are not different, contrasting requirements for beauty; light, he explained, is 'the most unitary of things and, by its equality to itself, the most fittingly proportioned'.

Grosseteste's metaphysics of light found few adherents. Albert the Great chose rather to use the Aristotelian concepts of matter and form to explain how all things combine colour or, more generally, the resplendence of light, with proportion and so are beautiful. Commenting (*c.* 1250) on *De divinis nominibus* , he proposed that the beautiful is 'the resplendence of a substantial or accidental form over proportioned and bounded parts of matter'. A well-proportioned, coloured body provides an obvious example of beauty: it is beautiful by the 'resplendence' of its colour, an accidental form, over its proportionate parts. Less obviously, everything made of matter and form must be beautiful. Matter is pure potentiality; a substantial form makes it actual by delimiting it and proportioning it to itself. For example, it is the form of a table that delimits matter into the proportions of a table. The form could be said, in Albert's terms, to be 'resplendent' over the parts of the table proportioned and delimited by it, and the table therefore to be beautiful.

Ulrich of Strasbourg was Albert's pupil and, in explaining how all things are beautiful, he followed his master closely. In his *De summo bono* (*c.* 1262–72)—a commentary on Pseudo-Dionysius in the form of a treatise—he devoted a section (ii/4) to the concept of beauty. Like Albert, he defined beauty as 'form . . . resplendent like light over that which is formed', and argued that, in one sense, matter is always proportioned to its form. All things, therefore, are beautiful. Unlike his teacher, however, Ulrich went on to explain the way in which 'beautiful' is said of some things but not of others. There are a number of senses in which matter can be more or less well-proportioned to its form: by its disposition, its quantity, the number of its parts and the relation of each part's size to that of the whole. It is this variation that accounts for differences in bodily beauty. So, for example, a man whose humours are well-balanced is more beautiful than one in whom a particular humour, such as melancholy, prevails; a body that is too small is not beautiful, nor is a man who has lost a limb, nor someone whose head is disproportionate to his body.

Unlike Ulrich, Aquinas did not devote a whole chapter or article to the concept of beauty, and his views must be gathered from a passage in his commentary (*c.* 1267) on *De divinis nominibus* and from isolated remarks in his *Summa theologiae* (I and IaIIae). Sometimes when Aquinas referred to beauty he was following the tradition of Pseudo-Dionysius and meaning the beauty that all things possess. For him, as for Albert and Ulrich, this beauty results from the combination of form with matter proportionate to it. More often, however, the context shows that he was speaking about the beauty that belongs only to some things, which, according to him, 'are pleasing when they are seen' or 'heard'. He explained that beauty is like goodness in that both attributes make things desirable, but whereas the desire towards something good is to obtain it, the desire for something beautiful is to see or know it. Beauty gives pleasure just by the disinterested awareness of it. Yet, although beauty is connected with cognition, there are objective criteria for it. At one point (ST I.q.39, a.8), Aquinas listed wholeness, proportion and brightness, although initially (ST I.q.5,a.4ad 1) he mentioned only proportion and explained that our senses, being themselves (according to Aristotle) 'a sort of proportion', take delight in proportioned things.

An interesting, but isolated, contrast to all these theories of beauty is found in the work of the Polish writer Witelo (or Erazm Ciołek; *c.* 1233–78), who discussed beauty not in the context of theology but in the course of his treatise on optics, the *Perspectiva* (early 1270s; IV. 148–50). He considered only visual beauty and took it for granted that some things are beautiful and some ugly. Instead of trying to provide a single definition for beauty, he set about listing some of the aspects that, individually or in appropriate combination, make an object's beauty manifest to the sight. He included colour, size and setting but also a number of pairs of contraries, such as continuity and discontinuity, transparency and opacity, similarity and dissimilarity. For, as he explained, the continuity of a green meadow is pleasing to the eyes, but stars that are separate and distinct are more beautiful than those very close together. Witelo also allowed that often 'custom makes beauty': for example, the shape and colour of the human body that the Moors might find pleasing are different from those that would please a Dane. However, although he considered beauty to be multiform and relative to the perceiver, Witelo nonetheless treated it as an objective feature of things—for example, beautifully painted workmanship is beautiful even when the onlooker, hindered by darkness, fails to see the painting and recognize its beauty.

It is open to question, however, whether these medieval theories about beauty were, as many historians believe, aesthetic theories. Although many aestheticians, especially in the 19th century, made beauty a central concept in their theories, there is an important difference between such philosophers and the medieval thinkers. Nineteenth-century aestheticians argued or assumed that there is a close relation between the concept of beauty and the products of such arts as music, painting, sculpture, architecture and literature. By contrast, no such relation was envisaged by medieval thinkers. Some were concerned only with beauty as an attribute of all things; for others, who examined beauty as an attribute that some things have and some lack, there was no special connection between beauty and human artifice. Ulrich of Strasbourg thought of visible beauty solely in terms of the human body, while Aquinas's only illustration of a beautiful thing is the Son of God. Even Witelo, who included among his examples of beautiful objects such products of artifice as smooth silks, regular handwriting and rounded columns, declared that while well-painted or well-sculpted figures are beautiful, 'the works of nature are more so'.

In the Middle Ages 'art' (Lat. *ars*) was a term with a very wide range of meaning: any productive skill from making shoes to making cathedrals was an 'art', and a number of non-productive intellectual disciplines such as grammar, arithmetic, physics and biology were also sometimes called 'arts'. Medieval treatises on some of these individual arts exist, including those arts that now interest aestheticians, but these were designed to be strictly practical handbooks, and conceptual reflection on their subjects is almost entirely absent. It is therefore still debatable whether a concept of art close to the modern one was implicit within medieval culture and can be discerned from the artefacts of the period. Although historians have combined theories derived from medieval artefacts with the theories about beauty that medieval scholars developed, often including medieval comments and technical discussion about various arts, the resulting mixture, presented to the reader as a homogeneous 'medieval aesthetics', can mislead rather than enlighten.

BIBLIOGRAPHY

Pseudo-Dionysius: *De divinis nominibus* (early 6th century AD), iii of *Patrologia Graeca*, ed. J.-P. Migne (Paris, 1857; Eng. trans., 1920)

Albert the Great: *Super Dionysium de divinis nominibus* (*c.* 1250), ed. P. Simon (Münster, 1972)

Ulrich of Strasbourg: *De summo bono* (*c.* 1262–72), II.1–4, ed. A. de Libera (Hamburg, 1987)

T. Aquinas: *In librum beati Dionysii de divinis nominibus expositio* (*c.* 1267), ed. C. Pera (Turin and Rome, 1950)

——: *Summa theologiae* (1268–72); Eng. trans., ed. T. Gilby and others (London and New York, 1964–80)

C. Baumker, ed.: *Witelo: Ein Philosoph und Naturforscher des XIII. Jahrhunderts* (Münster, 1908) [with extracts of *Perspectiva*]

E. de Bruyne: *Etudes d'esthétique médiévale*, 3 vols (Bruges, 1946)

H. Pouillon: 'La Beauté, propriété transcendentale chez les scolastiques (1220-1270)', *Archives d'histoire doctrinale et littéraire du moyen âge*, xv (1946), pp. 263–329 [with extracts of R. Grosseteste]

E. de Bruyne: *L'Esthétique du moyen âge* (Leuven, 1947; Eng. trans., New York, 1969)

U. Eco: *Il problema estetico in Tommaso d'Aquino* (Milan, 1954); Eng. trans. as *The Aesthetics of Thomas Aquinas* (London and Cambridge, MA, 1988)

——: 'Sviluppo dell'estetica medievale', *Momenti e problemi di storia dell'estetica* (Milan, 1959); Eng. trans. as *Art and Beauty in the Middle Ages* (New Haven and London, 1986)

W. Czapiewski: *Die Schöne bei Thomas von Aquin* (Freiburg, Basle and Vienna, 1964)
W. Tatarkiewicz: *History of Aesthetics*, ii (The Hague and Paris, 1970)

JOHN MARENBON

3. RENAISSANCE AND BAROQUE. Three main themes were developed and repeated in aesthetic thought between 1400 and 1600: synthetic beauty, a theme with literary origins; spiritual beauty, a notion ultimately derived from NEO-PLATONISM; and physical beauty, a type based on measurements and proportions that stem from Aristotelian philosophy. To these should be added the feminine ideal of the Renaissance, as exemplified in Petrarchan poetry. These ideas, formulated in the 16th century, remained the main basis for discussion until the end of the 17th.

(i) Synthetic beauty. Pliny relates that the painter Zeuxis, in order to represent Helen of Troy, selected the five most beautiful maidens of the town of Crotona and synthesized their most striking features into a perfect image. This idea that in order to produce a perfect image the artist must select and combine the best parts of everything belongs to a topos that permeated other disciplines such as rhetoric and ethics. In Renaissance art theory the notion appears in Leon Battista Alberti's treatise *De pittura* (1435) and it was repeated in every art treatise of the 16th century. Indeed, it affected art education, as the young artist was expected to distil his own style from the study of nature and the great masters, as well as the Antique. The notion of synthetic imitation developed further, giving rise to what was later called eclecticism. This doctrine is prefigured by Giulio Camillo in his treatise on imitation (1544), which suggests that, since the best art has already synthesized the best of nature, artists need only look at other works of art to gather a synthesis of the perfect visible. A few years later Paolo Pino in his *Dialogo di pittura* (1548) wrote that the best painting would be drawn by Michelangelo and coloured by Titian; but the culmination of this view is to be found in a sonnet attributed to Agostino Carracci, describing the best art as a synthesis of the talents of the best painters.

(ii) Spiritual beauty. It is through Marsilio Ficino's commentary (1469) on Plato's *Symposium*, rather than the original text, that Plato's doctrine of love became increasingly popular in the 16th century. Platonic love is a spiritual journey. It begins with the visual or auditory perception of beauty and ends with the ecstatic vision of God (Ficino, *Commentary*, VII, 14). Given the incorporeal nature of true beauty, it can only be perceived by incorporeal senses—sight and hearing (V. 2). In Baldassare Castiglione's *Il libro del Cortegiano*, Pietro Bembo speaks of this type of love whose strength 'guides the soul from the particular beauty of one body to the universal beauty common to all bodies' (IV, 68). This spiritual ascent begins with visual perception. These texts were influential, in so far as they led to an emphasis on spiritual love at the expense of physical love and beauty. They explain the emergence of an aesthetics based on the appreciation of incorporeal qualities perceived through the eye or the ear. From this emerged a vocabulary suited to describe purely visual qualities, which, in turn, were easily transferable to works of art.

Agnolo Firenzuola in his *Dialogo delle bellezze delle donne* (Florence, 1548) offers a good example of this phenomenon of transposition. This author fully agreed with Ficino on the effect of beauty, as a reflection of divine beauty, although he limited its field to beautiful women. While he defined physical *bellezza* (beauty) in terms of measurements and proportions (fols 73ff), he opposed it to spiritual *bellezza*, of which he identified six qualities: *leggiadria*, *venustà*, *grazia*, *vaghezza*, *aria* and *maestà*. English approximations to these are, consecutively, 'prettiness', 'beauty', 'grace', 'charm', 'demeanour' and 'dignity', but they remain beyond the reach of any verbal definition. Blended in ideal proportions, these features will produce a likeness of the idea of the perfect woman, capable of plunging man into a mystic state of divine ecstasy.

In the field of the visual arts, where categories such as *venustà*, *grazia* and *aria* were currently applied, these notions never implied that images could lead the soul to the contemplation of God through the graphic expression of divine beauty. Notions such as *bellezza* and *grazia*, however, became the mundane criteria through which writers spoke about the style and qualities of painting in an empirical, if not intuitive, fashion. Their use is connected to another theme, introduced by Castiglione, the concept of *sprezzatura*, i.e. the specific quality emerging from something difficult done with ease and elegance. It is precisely this criterion, used in conjunction with the notion of grace, that Lodovico Dolce, in his *Dialogo della pittura* (1557), invoked in order to praise Raphael and Titian and to attack Michelangelo's *Last Judgement* (1536–41; Rome, Vatican, Sistine Chapel), not only for its lack of decency but also, from a stylistic point of view, for the affectation and absence of grace of the figures that 'display all the difficulty of the art'.

(iii) Physical beauty and the Petrarchan ideal. The Renaissance ideal of feminine beauty is inspired by the love poetry of Petrarch. The physical features of Laura, Petrarch's mistress and muse—long blond hair, fine eyebrows, dark sparkling eyes, slightly rosy cheeks, long and slender neck, firm and white breasts, well-proportioned arms on which no veins can be seen and small, delicate white hands, together with perfect proportions—were paired with spiritual qualities in the appreciation of paintings of beautiful women. Pino confirmed this when referring to the 'true beauty' (*vaghezza*) of his art in his *Dialogo di pittura*: 'The painter is not worthy of praise for depicting all his [feminine] figures with pink cheeks and blond hair . . . but true beauty is nothing else than *venustà* and *gratia*; it is generated through a deep understanding of things as well as a proportion in things.' The opposition set by Pino between physical characteristics and painterly qualities is exemplified in Benedetto Varchi's *Della beltà e grazia* (*c.* 1550), which opposes a 'spiritual and platonic beauty' (*grazia*) to an Aristotelian beauty 'which consists in the proportion of the limbs'. This notion is further developed by the sculptor Vincenzio Danti, in his *Trattato delle perfette proporzioni* (1567), with the Aristotelian addition that beauty lies not only in perfect proportions but

also in the harmony between the shape of an object or a limb and the function it is intended to fulfil.

(iv) Later modifications. Towards the end of the 16th century there is a slight shift in ecclesiastical writers such as Gabriele Paleotti, writing in 1582, or Gregorio Comanini in 1592, who seem to favour naturalism. This coincides with the Counter-Reformation belief that more realistic representation in religious art, especially in scenes of martyrdom, would inspire strong religious emotions in the viewer. The naturalistic ideal, adopted by painters such as Caravaggio—who pointed to Nature as his only master—was severely criticized by most 17th-century writers on both sides of the Alps. They favoured instead a careful and discerning blend of naturalism and idealism. This is, in Italy, Giovanni Pietro Bellori's conception, expressed in his *L'idea del pittore, dello scultore e dell'architetto* (Rome, 1672; preface to his *Vite*), or in France the theory of the *beau idéal* expressed by writers such as Roland Fréart (*Idée de la perfection de la peinture . . .*, Le Mans, 1672) or André Félibien (*Entretiens*, 1666–88), both of whom shared an intense admiration for Raphael and Poussin. They defined *le beau idéal* as a golden mean between visual appearances and conceptual beauty.

The main problem for Renaissance and Baroque aesthetics is that its basis in a philosophical, if not theological, conception of beauty—a divine beauty, originally meant to induce divine ecstasy—was treated in a purely rhetorical way to express intuitions and empirical perceptions. As a result aesthetic thought always oscillated between fictively invoking painting as a representation of divine ideas and conceiving representation as a synthetic transcription of visual perceptions. In the late 17th century Roger de Piles addressed this dilemma in writings given final expression in the *Cours de peinture par principes* (Paris, 1708). His notions of 'truth in painting' led him to explore the link between the state of mind of the artist—the *enthousiasme*—transposed in the work and that felt by the viewer: a new kind of aesthetic, based on the work of art itself.

BIBLIOGRAPHY

D. Mahon: *Studies in Seicento Art and Theory* (London, 1947)
E. Panofsky: *Idea* (Eng. trans. by J. S. Peake, New York, 1968)
E. Cropper: 'On Beautiful Women, Parmigianino, *Petrarchismo* and the Vernacular Style', *A. Bull.*, 58 (1976), pp. 374–94
C. Dempsey: *Annibale Carracci and the Beginnings of Baroque Style* (Munich, 1977) [on the notion of eclecticism]
D. Summers: *Michelangelo and the Language of Art* (Princeton, 1981)
T. Puttfarken: *Roger de Piles' Theory of Art* (London, 1985)

FRANÇOIS QUIVIGER

4. MODERN. Aesthetics was conceived as a philosophical discipline within European rationalist and empiricist thought of the 17th and 18th centuries, the term being invented by the German philosopher Alexander Gottlieb Baumgarten. In the late 18th century Immanuel Kant formulated a highly influential, rigorous aesthetic theory about judgements of beauty and the sublime. In the 19th century Georg Wilhelm Friedrich Hegel's important writings were instrumental in moving aesthetic theories away from a concern with beauty to an emphasis on art and its cognitive significance. In the 20th century aesthetic theories of many different kinds were developed by American and European thinkers as diverse as John Dewey, Benedetto Croce and Martin Heidegger, and within such different intellectual traditions as phenomenology, semiotics, structuralism and hermeneutics.

(i) 17th–18th centuries. (ii) 19th century. (iii) 20th century.

(i) 17th–18th centuries.

(a) The Cartesian rationalist tradition. Although RENÉ DESCARTES himself wrote very little about the arts, the spirit of Cartesian rationalism pervaded classical writing on poetry and painting in France and England in the 17th and early 18th centuries, with its emphasis on system and rules and its praise of reason. The actual rules of poetry and painting defended, however, derived from Aristotle, Horace (65–8 BC) and other Classical sources. In such treatises as *De arte graphica* (1668) by CHARLES-ALPHONSE DU FRESNOY and *Cours de peinture par principes avec une balance des peintres* (1708) by ROGER DE PILES, the central idea is that the aim of painting is to please and instruct by means of the imitation of nature. These theorists distinguished different genres of painting and established canonical styles for each, the 'firm' style for heroic painting, the 'polished' for pastoral and so on. The greatest exponent of this type of art theory was JOSHUA REYNOLDS, whose *Discourses* to the Royal Academy (delivered between 1769 and 1790) summarize the Classical ideal with elegance, clarity and authority. Reynolds formulated a hierarchy of styles and genres, each with its own rules of composition, the 'grand style' of Raphael and Michelangelo being the highest. He urged the painter to imitate Nature, by which he meant Nature under the influence of great painters. Being true to nature meant representing the general rather than the particular, the ideal rather than the actual. When, in *Les Beaux Arts réduits à un même principe* (1746), Abbé CHARLES BATTEUX first articulated the modern system of the fine arts, he united poetry, painting and the other arts under the principle of the imitation of beautiful nature.

In Germany rationalism had a further, different effect on the development of thought about art. ALEXANDER GOTTLIEB BAUMGARTEN, writing in 1735, distinguished two spheres of cognition, that of thought or intellect and that of perception. Just as logic is the science of intellect, so, Baumgarten proposed, there should be a science of sensory perception or *Ästhetik*, a term he coined from the Greek *aisthesis* (perception), which would establish rules governing 'concrete sensory discourse' in general (i.e. the realm of paintings, poetry, music etc). Among Baumgarten's successors in the rationalist tradition was GOTTHOLD EPHRAIM LESSING, who argued in his celebrated essay *Laokoon* (1766) that poetry and painting are not analogous as the UT PICTURA POESIS doctrine had suggested, because the 'signs' utilized in poetry and painting are of radically different sorts. Since the medium of poetry is a temporal sequence of sounds, it can express only temporal objects, namely actions, whereas the medium of painting is spatial and can therefore express only spatial objects, namely bodies. Like Baumgarten, Lessing used a deductive method to establish his conclusions.

(b) The British empiricists. While the rationalists provided the term 'aesthetics' as well as the method and some of the assumptions governing classical criticism, it was the British empiricists who established aesthetics as an

independent philosophical field. The empiricists by and large accepted the Classical doctrines that art is an imitation of nature, that it pleases us by instructing us, and that it should imitate the general rather than the particular. The questions they asked concerned not the work of art itself but the experience of the spectator or critic of art, in particular the nature of good taste and aesthetic pleasure. ANTHONY ASHLEY COOPER, 3rd Earl of Shaftesbury, thought that we have a special intuitive insight or 'inward eye' that enables us to distinguish in an immediate way between the good and the bad, the beautiful and the ugly. In his *Inquiry Concerning Beauty, Order, Harmony, Design* (1725) FRANCIS HUTCHESON echoed this idea but reconstructed the 'inward eye' in empiricist terms as a type of sense perception: we have an internal sense of beauty much like the external senses of sight, hearing and so on. Moreover, while for Shaftesbury beauty is a property actually inhering in things, for Hutcheson it is a pleasant experience or feeling, which he called a pleasant 'idea', and the sense of beauty is 'our power of receiving this idea'. By contrast, other theorists such as Archibald Alison (1757–1839), in his *Essays on the Nature and Principles of Taste* (1790), explained beauty as arising from the pleasant associations an object or a scene may evoke in us.

In general, the empiricists recognized two kinds of beauty or 'pleasures of the imagination': the beauty of nature, often identified in terms of proportion and symmetry, and the beauty of imitations in literature, painting and the other 'imitative' arts. Beauty, however, is not the only recognized source of aesthetic pleasure. The category of the PICTURESQUE applies to landscapes and pictures exhibiting intricacy, roughness, variety and irregularity, and in his *Philosophical Inquiry into the Origin of our Ideas of the Sublime and Beautiful* (1757) EDMUND BURKE identified THE SUBLIME as whatever delights us yet is associated with pain and danger, such as the obscure, the powerful or the infinite. Burke's treatise influenced DENIS DIDEROT, whose *Salon* writings from 1759 to 1781 stress emotional effect rather than imitative accuracy and foreshadow Romanticism.

The empiricist view that aesthetic experience is a subjective feeling of pleasure caused by our perception of certain qualities in things raised the problem of how there can be an objective standard of taste. This problem was particularly acute for associationist theories of beauty. By contrast, Hutcheson and Burke thought that a standard of taste was assured because we are so constituted biologically that we naturally perceive all the same things as beautiful. For DAVID HUME, taste, or the faculty whereby we discriminate beauty, is simply the sophisticated exercise of our ordinary faculties of judgement and sensitivity. In his essay 'Of the Standard of Taste' (1757), Hume argued that the standard of taste is set by a particular group of people, the 'true judges', who are characterized as those who are particularly sensitive, disinterested and experienced in judging. Ultimately, however, Hume was sceptical about how absolute the standard would turn out to be.

(c) Kant and Romanticism. The aesthetic theory of the late 18th century and the early 19th was largely conditioned by two influences: one was the philosophy of the German philosopher IMMANUEL KANT and the other was the rather amorphous body of ideas and attitudes that constituted ROMANTICISM. Kant gave a new and more sophisticated answer to Hume's questions concerning the aesthetic judgement, the beautiful and the standard of taste and thereby furthered Baumgarten's project of founding a rational science of aesthetics. In his *Kritik der Urteilskraft* (1790) Kant argued that the judgement of taste is subjective, since it is a feeling of pleasure, but that nevertheless it can justifiably lay claim to universal acceptance, since the pleasure is both disinterested, i.e. unconcerned with personal practical goals, and also derived from the harmonious interaction of the imagination and the understanding, which are faculties shared by all knowing subjects. However, since to ascribe beauty to something is not to ascribe a concept to it, there can be no objective canons of beauty as envisaged by the rationalists. In his discussion of the aesthetic judgement, Kant, like his predecessors, took his examples as readily from nature as from art, and his emphasis on harmony of design ('purposiveness without purpose') as the source of a disinterested aesthetic delight tended to demote the importance of subject-matter in art as opposed to form. However, in his discussion of fine art, Kant gave a central place to 'aesthetic ideas': the artist tries to communicate through sensuous representations something that goes beyond the world of sense.

Romantic artists exalted the importance of art, seeing it as a source of insight and a means of self-expression. Art was no longer thought of as the mere imitation of an inert nature but as the expression of feeling and imagination. The mind has creative powers beyond both sensuous perception and reason; the imagination in particular is a source of intuitive insight into the true nature of reality. Furthermore, this insight into reality is possible because nature is an organic whole, imbued with spirit, and Man is a part of that whole. For the Romantics the artistic genius is the man of insight who can effect the union of real and ideal, nature and freedom, conscious and unconscious.

Some of these Romantic ideas had their source in Kant's philosophy, in particular the emphasis on the constructive powers of the mind and the importance attributed to the imagination as a source of human knowledge. However, the Romantics were critical of several elements in Kant's philosophy. JOHANN GOTTFRIED HERDER and FRIEDRICH SCHILLER, for example, criticized Kant's sharp division between reason and sense, thought and feeling. For Schiller, man arrives at a true 'harmony of the faculties' through a synthesis of impulses that is achieved in aesthetic experience. JOHANN WOLFGANG VON GOETHE and the English poet and essayist Samuel Taylor Coleridge (1772–1834), among others, objected to Kant's conception of man as rational and free in opposition to brute nature, which is governed by the categories of space, time and causality: instead they conceived of nature as an organic unity, with man expressing his sense of this unity through the creation of organically unified works of art.

(ii) 19th century. For the post-Kantian idealists, GEORG WILHELM FRIEDRICH HEGEL and FRIEDRICH SCHELLING, art was capable of revealing important insights about man and his relation to the universe. According to Hegel, art, religion and philosophy are three different modes of

consciousness whereby man arrives at an awareness of Absolute Spirit, i.e. of the rational necessity that governs the universe. For Hegel art, religion and philosophy are different ways in which Absolute Spirit reflects upon and becomes aware of its own activity. Individual human minds are the vehicle of self-awareness for Absolute Spirit. Hegel had much in common with the Romantics: both thought of nature and spirit as one, of art as a mode of self-expression and self-realization, and of the artist as one who seeks the infinite through the finite. However, in one crucial respect Hegel was a successor to Kant rather than the Romantics, for his entire system is based on the idea of reason, of the way in which rational necessity comes to self-awareness.

According to Hegel's *Vorlesungen über die Ästhetik* delivered in the 1820s (pubd posthumously, 1835), art is that particular mode of consciousness whereby ideas are presented in a 'sensuous' form rather than through myth or theology (religion) or through conceptual thought (philosophy). Like Schelling and the Romantic theorists, Hegel argued forcefully that art is not the mere imitation of an inert nature. Instead he adopted Kant's idea that the fine arts express 'aesthetic ideas', arguing that 'the work of art stands in the middle between immediate sensuousness and ideal thought'. Hegel's discussion of fine art powerfully asserts the cognitive importance of art, the importance of theme or subject-matter, and the way in which theme cannot be abstracted from the sensuous medium that conveys it. Hegel also emphasized art's historicity; his idea that art develops teleologically influenced several generations of art historians such as ALOIS RIEGL, HEINRICH WÖLFFLIN and ERWIN PANOFSKY.

Although ARTHUR SCHOPENHAUER was a contemporary of Hegel, his influence was not felt until much later. In *Die Welt als Wille und Vorstellung* (1819) Schopenhauer argued that underlying the world of appearances or 'representations' is a terrible, aimless force or energy, which he called the 'Will' and which is the basis of reality. Art is one of the few ways in which we can achieve temporary release from our subjection to the Will. When we experience a work of art (with the exception of music, which is the direct manifestation of the Will), we are contemplating the Platonic Ideas instantiated in that work of art, such as mass and extension in architecture. In Schopenhauer the disinterested Kantian aesthetic judgement becomes an aesthetic experience, in which we are 'outside' ordinary experience, lost in rapt contemplation of the art object. Schopenhauer's ideas influenced FRIEDRICH NIETZSCHE, writing in the 1870s and 1880s, who, however, thought that art is an affirmation of life rather than a means of withdrawing from it.

Hegel's emphasis on history gave support to the contemporary rediscovery of the art of the past, particularly that of the Middle Ages. In *The Stones of Venice* (1851) and elsewhere, the Victorian art critic JOHN RUSKIN glorified the Middle Ages as a period in which Christian faith and morality were expressed in both art and social arrangements. Ruskin saw in art a means of moral salvation in a mechanistic, scientific age dominated by the crisis in faith, the philosophy of utilitarianism, Darwin's evolutionary theory and the overwhelming social changes brought about by the Industrial Revolution. WILLIAM MORRIS and the ARTS AND CRAFTS MOVEMENT were greatly indebted to Ruskin, as were the Pre-Raphaelite painters whom he defended (*see* PRE-RAPHAELITISM). A similarly idealized view of art as a means of moral salvation and a way of promoting Christianity and human brotherhood is to be found in *Chto takoye isskustvo?* ('What is art?'; 1898), by LEO TOLSTOY.

The ART FOR ART'S SAKE movement, initiated by JAMES MCNEILL WHISTLER and OSCAR WILDE and taking its inspiration from WALTER PATER, together with the closely linked AESTHETIC MOVEMENT, expressed the reaction to the scientific spirit of the age in a different form. By contrast, the scientific spirit in aesthetics itself can be seen in the birth of experimental aesthetics, in the psychological theory of empathy of THEODOR LIPPS, which influenced Wölfflin and BERNARD BERENSON, and in evolutionary aesthetic theories such as that of Herbert Spencer (1820–1903), which claimed that art is a form of play resulting from excess energy generated in the human struggle for survival.

(iii) 20th century.

(a) Early 20th-century aesthetic theories. *The Sense of Beauty* (1896) by GEORGE SANTAYANA is a naturalistic, psychological theory of aesthetics that studies the aesthetic experience of spectators as they contemplate beautiful art or nature. Beauty itself is defined as 'pleasure regarded as a quality' of the object contemplated. Beauty of expression occurs when the associations we have to an object are experienced as one of its pleasant qualities. For Edward Bullough, writing in 1912, the aesthetic experience is no longer mere pleasure but a special psychic act of 'distancing'. To adopt the aesthetic attitude to a fog at sea, for example, is to ignore its practical implications and to focus on its 'aesthetic qualities'. These turn out to be not Schopenhauerian essences but qualities of the sensuous surface before us. Thus began a new empiricist tradition, in which aesthetic experience was analysed as awareness of qualities in their sensuous immediacy together with their sensuously grasped formal relations, and in which expression was reduced to immediately experienced expressive qualities (*see* FORMALISM). These ideas owed much to the art critics ROGER FRY and CLIVE BELL, the heirs of the Art for Art's Sake movement and propagandists for Cézanne and the Post-Impressionists. Fry and Bell argued that representational content in painting is of aesthetic interest only as form and that only form can produce the 'aesthetic emotion'.

The Italian idealist philosopher BENEDETTO CROCE had a very different view. In his *Estetica come scienza dell'espressione e linguistica generale* (1902) Croce defended the view that art is 'intuition', by which he meant a type of non-conceptual knowledge that contrasts with 'logic' understood as knowledge of general concepts. According to Croce, intuition is identical to expression, since the articulation of a cognition is its expression. However, expression does not entail embodiment in a medium; as soon as the artist has formulated the intuition completely in his mind the work of art is complete. The audience can grasp the work only by imaginatively recreating the artist's intuition for themselves. R. G. Collingwood (*see*

COLLINGWOOD, (2)) adopted many of Croce's ideas and developed them into his own theory of art (1938) as the expression of emotion, in which expression is defined as a cognitive process of clarifying and articulating a hitherto inchoate emotion.

Others also argued that art gives us a special intuitive insight into reality: both HENRI BERGSON and the later Santayana followed Schopenhauer in claiming that the artist can penetrate essences in a way that the discursive intellect cannot, while for JACQUES MARITAIN, who based his theories on Aristotle and Thomas Aquinas, the artist's non-conceptual knowledge is to be achieved through a type of mystical 'affective union' between artist and world.

By contrast, *Art as Experience* (1934) by the American philosopher JOHN DEWEY is a materialist, instrumental theory of art that emphasizes the important role of art in any good, productive life and condemns the rigid separation between art and life characteristic of formalism. In making a work of art the artist expresses an emotional experience in a medium. To understand the work, the audience recreates this experience. However, for Dewey, unlike Croce, the art object is a sensuous thing, imbued with meanings and values. Monroe Beardsley's *Aesthetics: Problems in the Philosophy of Criticism* (1958) combines an empiricist view of the aesthetic object as essentially perceptual with a Deweyan conception of aesthetic quality.

(b) The influence of linguistics. New developments in logic and linguistics in the 20th century led Charles Morris and SUSANNE K. LANGER to articulate different versions of a semiotic aesthetics. Following the work of Charles Sanders Peirce (*see* SEMIOTICS), Morris described the situation of signification or communication as one in which an 'interpreter' takes a 'sign' or 'sign vehicle' to refer to a 'referent' or 'designatum'. Morris followed Dewey in claiming that the expressive art object has what Peirce called 'iconic' meaning, since the expressive work of art displays its values and meanings in the medium itself. Susanne Langer distinguished between 'discursive' symbolic forms such as language, which have a syntax, a vocabulary and semantic rules for combining meaningful elements into meaningful wholes, with 'presentational' forms that lack these features but instead refer in a global way like Morris's iconic signs. In *Feeling and Form* (1953) she claimed that the forms in a work of visual art, considered abstractly, present an image or 'virtual object' that is apparent only to sensory perception and which symbolizes virtual space (pictures), virtual kinetic volume (sculpture) or virtual place (architecture).

Whereas Langer assumed that pictures symbolize iconically or presentationally, the art historian Ernst Gombrich argued that even the literal representational content of a picture is not entirely iconic but that art is in part, like language, a conventional symbol system. Gombrich argued in *Art and Illusion* (1960) that representation always begins with the making of a more or less conventional 'schema', which is then matched against reality. The most rigorous and systematic investigation of the idea that art is a language is Nelson Goodman's *Languages of Art* (1968), which considers each art form as a type of symbol system. Goodman attacked the notion that pictures are iconic and claimed that what counts as a picture is a function of the kind of symbol system to which it belongs. Thus pictures are symbols in systems that are syntactically and semantically dense and relatively replete.

The French structuralists, beginning with the work of the Swiss linguist Ferdinand de Saussure (1857–1913), also thought of works of art as operating like a language in the sense that their meaning is a function of the symbol system or 'langue' to which they belong (*see* STRUCTURALISM). According to Saussure, different sign systems or 'langues' carve up the set of 'signifiers' (sound patterns) and 'signifieds' (concepts) in quite different ways, so that different 'langues' define different systems of sound patterns and different systems of concepts that can only be understood in terms of other concepts in the system. JACQUES DERRIDA took this idea of language as a 'system of differences' and maintained that, consistently pursued, it leads to the 'post-structuralist' conclusion that meaning is never stable and that the 'fixed centres' or central concepts used to anchor a philosophical system or the meaning of a work of art can always be 'deconstructed' or shown to undermine themselves. There have been some attempts at 'deconstructivist' architecture in which the building is viewed as a palimpsest, a multi-layered collage of meanings with no central 'truth', and in which even the most basic architectural assumptions (such as that buildings exist for human use) are deconstructed (*see* DECONSTRUCTION and POST-STRUCTURALISM).

(c) The influence of phenomenology and Existentialism. In continental Europe PHENOMENOLOGY produced theories about the nature of the aesthetic object. According to the Polish philosopher Roman Ingarden, there is a distinction between the physical work of art and the phenomenological, intentional aesthetic object, which has no physical properties, only qualities directly given to sense perception. JEAN-PAUL SARTRE had a somewhat different view according to which the aesthetic object is an unreal object, which is both constituted and apprehended by the imagination (*see* EXISTENTIALISM). By contrast, Mikel Dufrenne's *Phénomenologie de l'expérience esthétique* (1953) argues that the aesthetic object is a phenomenal object, rather like Langer's 'virtual' image, which nevertheless has 'worlds': a represented world of persons, places and things and an expressed world of qualities that give the work its unified, person-like character.

For MARTIN HEIDEGGER and MAURICE MERLEAU-PONTY art had a metaphysical significance. For Heidegger, as for Derrida, there are no fixed centres or concepts such as 'self' or 'world' to which we can anchor our philosophical systems. *Dasein* (literally: 'being-there') consists in an active engagement in the world conceived of as primarily a world of equipment or tools to use rather than a world of objects to know. Throughout his career Heidegger attacked the notion of truth as correspondence between an inner and an outer world, claiming that the dichotomy made no sense, as we are necessarily 'in-the-world'. In his later essays on aesthetics Heidegger talked of truth as 'disclosure' or 'revelation' and claimed that this is the primary function of works of art. Thus van Gogh's picture *Old Boots with Laces* (Amsterdam, Rijksmus.), of peasant boots, discloses what the boots are in truth: there is a 'happening of truth at work', the revelation of a 'world' (the peasant's mode of being).

Like Heidegger, Merleau-Ponty saw no dichotomy between self and object, only a world of tools and tasks, but he differed from the other phenomenologists in thinking of consciousness as necessarily embodied: the body is the 'in-between realm' through which consciousness interacts with the world. Merleau-Ponty claimed that paintings function as emanations from this perceiving body.

(d) Other developments. The idea that a work of art is a cultural artefact whose meaning is determined by its role in society and history is implicit in Heidegger and also appears in the work of the analytic philosophers Arthur Danto and Richard Wollheim. In *The Transfiguration of the Commonplace* (1981) Danto argued that a work of art cannot be identified independently of an 'artworld', that is, independently of a historical context of art theory through which it achieves meaning. Wollheim borrowed the notion from the later writings of Ludwig Wittgenstein (*see* WITTGENSTEIN, (2)) of a 'form of life' and in *Art and its Objects* (1968) claimed that art itself is a form of life essentially embedded in institutions and practices. This view is to be sharply distinguished from the idea that art should serve as a means of promoting a particular form of society, as is suggested, for example, by the Marxist critics György Lukács (1885–1971) and WALTER BENJAMIN (*see also* MARXISM). It should also be distinguished from the Institutional Theory of art, which claims that what counts as an artwork is determined not by its having a meaning or by formal or expressive qualities, but solely by its playing the right kind of role in the right kind of social and artistic institutions.

Interest in the somewhat passive idea of 'aesthetic experience' has given way to a focus on the concept of interpretation, conceived of as an active search for the meaning of a work of art. HERMENEUTICS, the tradition stemming from Heidegger and his pupil Hans-Georg Gadamer (*b* 1900) treats interpretation as a linguistic process of translation from the author's 'language' to that of the audience. However, since a work of art cannot transcend its historical context, the artist's original intentions can never be fully recovered. The art object necessarily has 'gaps' that need to be filled in by the interpreter. By contrast, for semiotic and structuralist theories, interpretation is not a process of recovering artists' intentions but a matter of focusing on the work of art itself and the structures to which it belongs.

BIBLIOGRAPHY

A. A. Cooper (Shaftesbury): *Characteristics of Men, Manners, Opinions, Times*, 3 vols (London, 1711); ed. J. M. Robertson, 2 vols (New York, 1900)
F. Hutcheson: *An Inquiry concerning Beauty, Order, Harmony, Design* (London, 1725); ed. P. Kivy (The Hague, 1973)
A. G. Baumgarten: *Meditationes philosophicae de nonnulis ad poema pertinentilous* (Halle, 1735); trans. by K. Aschenbrenner and W. Holther as *Reflections on Poetry* (Berkeley, 1954)
E. Burke: *A Philosophical Inquiry into the Origin of our Ideas of the Sublime and Beautiful* (London, 1757); ed. J. Boulton (Notre Dame, IN, 1968)
D. Hume: *Of the Standard of Taste* (Edinburgh, 1757); ed. J. Lenz in *Of the Standard of Taste and Other Essays* (Indianapolis, 1965)
G. E. Lessing: *Laokoon: Oder über die Grenzen der Malerei und Poesie* (Berlin, 1766); Eng. trans. as *Laocoon*, ed. E. A. McCormick (Indianapolis, 1962)
J. Reynolds: *Discourses on Painting and the Fine Arts Delivered at the Royal Academy* (London, 1778); ed. S. Mitchell as *Discourses on Art* (Indianapolis, 1965)
I. Kant: *Kritik der Urteilskraft* (Berlin, 1790); Eng. trans. by J. C. Meredith (Oxford, 1952)
F. Schiller: *Über die ästhetische Erziehung des Menschen—in einer Reihe von Briefen* (Stuttgart, 1793); Eng. trans. by E. M. Willoughby and L. A. Willoughby as *On the Aesthetic Education of Man* (Oxford, 1967)
F. W. J. Schelling: *Über das Verhältniss der bildenden Künste zu der Natur* (Munich, 1807); Eng. trans. by D. Stott (Minneapolis, 1989)
A. Schopenhauer: *Die Welt als Wille und Vorstellung* (Leipzig, 1818, rev. 1844); Eng. trans. by E. F. J. Payne, 2 vols (Colorado, 1958)
G. W. F. Hegel: *Vorlesungen über die Ästhetik* (Berlin, 1835, rev. 1842); Eng. trans. by T. M. Knox as *Lectures on Fine Art*, 2 vols (Oxford, 1975)
F. Nietzsche: *Die Geburt der Tragödie aus dem Geiste der Musik* (Leipzig, 1872; Eng. trans., New York, 1968)
G. Santayana: *The Sense of Beauty* (New York, 1896/*R* 1955)
L. Tolstoy: *Chto takoye isskustvo?* (Moscow, 1898); Eng. trans. by A. Maude (Indianapolis, 1960)
B. Croce: *Estetica come scienza dell'espressione e linguistica generale* (Bari, 1902); Eng. trans. by D. Ainslie (London, 1922; rev. 3/Boston, MA, 1978)
G. Santayana: *Reason in Art* (New York, 1905)
E. Bullough: '"Psychical Distance" as a Factor in Art and as an Aesthetic Principle', *Brit. J. Psychol.*, v (1912), pp. 87–98
J. Maritain: *Art et scolastique* (Paris, 1920)
R. Ingarden: *Das literarische Kunstwerk: Eine Untersuchung aus dem Grenzgebeit der Ontologie, Logik und Literaturwissenschaft* (Halle, 1931; Eng. trans., 1973)
J. Dewey: *Art as Experience* (New York, 1934)
R. G. Collingwood: *The Principles of Art* (Oxford, 1938)
M. Dufrenne: *Phénoménologie de l'expérience esthétique*, 2 vols (Paris, 1953; Eng. trans., Evanston, 1973)
S. K. Langer: *Feeling and Form* (New York, 1953)
M. Beardsley: *Aesthetics: Problems in the Philosophy of Criticism* (New York, 1958, Indianapolis, 2/1981)
H.-G. Gadamer: *Wahrheit und Methode* (Tübingen, 1960; Eng. trans. rev. 2/New York, 1989)
E. H. Gombrich: *Art and Illusion* (London, 1960)
J. Derrida: *De la grammatologie* (Paris, 1967); Eng. trans. by G. C. Spivak (Baltimore, 1976)
N. Goodman: *Languages of Art* (Indianapolis, 1968)
R. Wollheim: *Art and its Objects* (New York, 1968, rev. 1980)
M. Heidegger: *Poetry, Language, Thought*, trans. and ed. by A. Hofstadter (New York, 1971) [selection of writings]
A. Danto: *The Transfiguration of the Commonplace* (Cambridge, MA, 1981)

For general bibliography *see* §I above.

JENEFER ROBINSON

Aethelwold [Æthelwold; Ethelwold], Bishop of Winchester (*b* Winchester, *c.* AD 908; *d* Beddington, Surrey, 1 Aug 984; *fd* 1 Aug). Anglo-Saxon saint, Church leader and patron. With Dunstan, Archbishop of Canterbury (*reg* 959–88), and Oswald, Archbishop of York (*reg* 972–92), he was the moving spirit behind the English monastic revival of the late 10th century.

Aethelwold's career began at the court of King Athelstan (*reg* 924–39). After ordination he joined Dunstan's reformed monastic community at Glastonbury. About 954 he established his own monastic house at Abingdon. According to later tradition, he was a skilled worker in metals and personally contributed to the embellishment of the abbey church. Appointed Bishop of Winchester in 963, he introduced reformed communities into both Old and New Minsters and established a regular monastic life in several other centres, notably Ely, Peterborough and Thorney. He was an enthusiastic patron: the masterpiece of the Winchester School of illumination, the Benedictional of St Aethelwold (London, BL, Add. MS. 49598; *see* ANGLO-SAXON ART, fig. 9), was made for his personal use

by his chaplain, the monk Godeman, later Abbot of Thorney. He ordered major additions to his cathedral church, consecrated with great splendour in 980. He was also responsible for the translation of the relics of St Swithin to a new shrine within the cathedral in 971.
See also WINCHESTER, §§II and III, 1(i).

BIBLIOGRAPHY
F. Wormald: *The Benedictional of St Ethelwold*, Faber Library of Illuminated Manuscripts (London, 1959)
M. Winterbottom, ed.: *Three Lives of English Saints* (Toronto, 1972)
B. Yorke, ed.: *Bishop Æthelwold: His Career and Influence* (Woodbridge, 1988)

JANET BACKHOUSE

Aetion (*fl* late 4th century BC). Greek painter. Pliny (*Natural History*, XXXV.78) placed Aetion in the 107th Olympiad (352–349 BC) and (XXXV.50) included him in a list of painters who used a palette restricted to four colours: white, yellow, red and black. Cicero (*Brutus* xviii.70), however, listed him among those painters who used a wider palette. It is likely that the four-colour palette was a restriction adopted occasionally by many artists who, in other works, used more than four colours. None of Aetion's work survives, but Pliny ascribed to him pictures of *Dionysos*, *Tragedy and Comedy*, *Semiramis Rising from Slavery to Royal Power* and an *Old Woman Carrying Lamps and Attending a Bride*, whose modesty was apparent. His most famous painting depicted the *Wedding of Alexander the Great and Roxane*, and it was perhaps painted to celebrate it (327 BC). It was described by Lucian of Samosata (*Aetion* iv–vi), who saw it in Italy. Lucian added that when the painting was shown at Olympia, Proxenides, one of the chief judges of the games, was so impressed by it that he gave his daughter to Aetion in marriage. Alexander the Great stood best man. The painting included erotes playing with Alexander's armour, a motif repeated in several Roman wall paintings with reference to Mars and Hercules. Another Aetion, also assigned to the 107th Olympiad, appears in a list of bronze sculptors drawn up by Pliny (XXXIV.50); this is probably an interpolation from XXXV.78.

BIBLIOGRAPHY
W. Helbig: *Wandgemälde der vom Vesuv verschütterten Städte Campaniens* (Leipzig, 1868), nos 320 and 1137–9
J. Overbeck: *Die antiken Schriftquellen zur Geschichte der bildenden Künste bei den Griechen* (Leipzig, 1868/R Hildesheim, 1959), nos 1067, 1073, 1728(2), 1754, 1937–41
O. Elia: *Pitture murali e mosaici nel Museo Nazionali di Napoli* (Rome, 1932), no. 121

C. HOBEY-HAMSHER

Afạmiya. *See* APAMEIA.

Affecter. *See* VASE PAINTERS, §II.

Affleck, Ray(mond Tait) (*b* Penticton, BC, 20 Nov 1922; *d* Montreal, 16 March 1989). Canadian architect. He graduated in architecture from McGill University, Montreal, and began post-graduate studies at the Eidgenössische Technische Hochschule in Zurich. Between 1949 and 1953 he worked for various Montreal-based architectural firms before setting up his own practice in the city in 1953; it later became Affleck, Desbarats, Dimakopoulos, Lebensold, Sise (1955–69). The group worked with I. M. Pei and Partners on Place Ville Marie (1958–63), then, with Affleck as principal designer, on the Stephen Leacock Building (1961–5) and the Place Bonaventure (1964–8), all in Montreal. Another notable work was the National Arts Centre complex, Ottawa (completed 1969), in which Affleck and company devised a handsome, low-rise group of buildings, including a 2300-seat opera house, an 800-seat theatre and a 300-seat studio workshop. Affleck also taught for many years at the School of Architecture, McGill University (1954–8; Visiting Professor from 1965). Affleck is judged to be one of the few major Canadian architects to establish a reputation abroad. His concerns were tied less to a building's ultimate appearance than to people's experience of and movement through its internal spaces. His ideas for internal 'streets' were emulated by a generation of Canadian architects: he thought that indoor and outdoor systems should be interconnected and punctuated by 'events', which could take the form of garden areas or terrace restaurants, with shopping and office levels adjacent, all woven together with easy pedestrian access up, down or through the complex. His schemes were often gigantic, multipurpose buildings, and from the late 1960s Affleck and his partners (reorganized as Arcop Associates in 1969–70) were responsible for many substantial projects in Canada. In later years Affleck, sensitive to conservation movements, designed Maison Alcan (1980–83), Montreal, in which he preserved *in toto* a venerable 19th-century residence and two commercial buildings (1894 and 1928), all of differing heights, linking them at the rear with a full-length modern atrium; its long, pedestrian mall is lined with cosmopolitan-style cafés and boutiques.

BIBLIOGRAPHY
A. Schouvaloff: *Place for the Arts* (Liverpool, 1970)
'Centre National des Arts, Ottawa, Canada', *L'Archit. Aujourd'hui*, 169 (Sept–Oct 1973), p. 31
L. Whiteson: *Modern Canadian Architecture* (Edmonton, Alta, 1983), pp. 214–17, 254–7, 270

□

Affleck, Thomas (*b* Aberdeen, 1740; *d* Philadelphia, PA, 5 March 1795). American cabinetmaker of Scottish birth. He trained as a cabinetmaker in London. In 1763 John Penn, Governor of Pennsylvania, invited Affleck to Philadelphia, where the latter opened a shop on Second Street in the Society Hill area. He made stylish mahogany furniture (sold 1788; e.g. Philadelphia, PA, Cliveden Mus.; armchair, Winterthur, DE, Mus. & Gdns) for the governor's mansion at Lansdowne, PA, and for many of the most prominent families in the city, including the Mifflins, the Whartons and the Chew family at Cliveden.

A Quaker and Loyalist, Affleck refused to participate in the Revolution (1775–83), and he was banished for several months to Virginia in 1777. By the end of the war, however, he was the most prosperous cabinetmaker in the city. His Loyalist sympathies seem to have been forgiven because he was given a number of important commissions, including furniture, for the Pennsylvania Hospital, Congress Hall and the first Supreme Court Chamber in the City Hall, all in Philadelphia.

The large body of surviving furniture attributed to Affleck, which includes wall-brackets, chairs (New York, Met.), grand chest-on-chests and elaborately carved tallboys or high chests-of-drawers, confirms his reputation as the leading cabinetmaker in Philadelphia in the 18th century. Much of his furniture was derived from designs in his personal copy of *Gentleman and Cabinet-maker's Director* by Thomas Chippendale (i). He also made furniture in the Neo-classical style. After his death his son Lewis G. Affleck carried on the business for a short time until he went bankrupt.

BIBLIOGRAPHY

W. Hornor: *Blue Book, Philadelphia Furniture: William Penn to George Washington* (Philadelphia, 1935/*R* Washington, DC, 1977)

OSCAR P. FITZGERALD

Affry, Adèle d'. *See* MARCELLO.

Afghanistan. Country of some 647,500 sq. km in the middle of the steppe and desert zone of Eurasia. It is bounded on the north by the Amu (Oxus) River and the republics of Central Asia, on the west by Iran and on the south and east by the Indian subcontinent. In the Pamir Mountains to the north-east, a narrow tongue of land known as the Wakhan corridor links the country with China (see fig. 1). Located at the crossroads of major trade and migration routes between the Mediterranean, Central Asia, India and China, the region has been subjected to diverse cultural influences throughout its history.

I. Introduction. II. Historical survey. III. Historiography. IV. Museums and collections.

I. Introduction.

1. Geography and climate. 2. History. 3. Language and ethnic groups. 4. Religion and iconography.

1. GEOGRAPHY AND CLIMATE. The physical geography of Afghanistan is very varied and includes formidable mountain ranges, fertile valleys and barren deserts. The dominant mountainous core is the Hindu Kush, an extension of the Karakoram and Pamir mountains that stretches south-west for some 965 km and has peaks rising to some 5180 m in height. To the north, between the Hindu Kush and the Amu River lie the semi-desert plains of Turkestan. South of the Hindu Kush is a transitional zone of plateaux with broad mountain valleys. To the west and south-west the mountains gradually descend to the stony and sandy deserts of the Iranian plateau. North of Kabul the Kuh-e-Baba range ('Grandfather Mountains') of the Hindu Kush is the watershed for four great Afghan rivers: the Kabul River flowing east to the Indus, the Kunduz flowing north into the Amu River, the Hari Rud flowing west to Herat and the Helmand, which flows southwards into the marshy lake of Hamun Helmand in Sistan. There are several passes through the mountainous core of the country linking north to south and east to west, and traffic is also channelled along the rivers or round the mountain mass. The low-lying plains and deserts between Herat and Kandahar provide an easy route for traders and invaders travelling eastwards into the Indus Valley.

The climate is generally dry, with wide variations in temperature. Snow falls in the mountainous areas above *c.* 1830 m from October onwards and blocks the passes for much of the winter. In the plains of Turkestan most of the rain falls as spring thunderstorms, and there are sometimes disastrous floods when this water combines with melting snow from the mountains. In winter there is rain in the Herat area and the rivers are swollen with melt water in the spring, but in the Helmand basin there is virtually no rainfall in any season. The Jalalabad Valley has a winter rainfall and can, with irrigation, grow rich crops.

2. HISTORY. The limited documentation of prehistoric sites in Afghanistan has produced evidence of a small Palaeolithic hunter–gatherer population, part of which was established by about 20,000–15,000 BP in the northern foothills of the Hindu Kush at cave sites such as Aq Kupruk II (Ghar-i Mar). The domestication of sheep, goats and possibly cattle seems to have taken place by about the 9th millennium BC. Some of the Neolithic sites produced pottery, but there are no architectural remains associated with this phase of the transition from hunter-gathering to food production. Knowledge of bronze technology and embossing by the late 6th millennium BC is indicated by finds of sheet metal from Aq Kupruk II. From about 3500 BC onwards there is evidence of trade links associated with the export of lapis lazuli, particularly at Shahr-i Sokhta in Sistan. The lapis lazuli, which seems to have derived from the Badakhshan region in north-east Afghanistan, especially the Kokcha Valley, was exported all over the Near East. Mundigak and the related sites of Deh Morasi and Said Qala in southern Afghanistan show the development of urbanization from around the early 4th millennium BC to the 2nd.

From the *Ṛg veda* (*see* INDIAN SUBCONTINENT, §I, 2(i)), it appears that the Aryans passed through Afghanistan *c.* 1500 BC. Later Aryan migrants from Transoxania settled on the Iranian plateau and established the Achaemenid empire in the regions between the Mediterranean and the Indus River by the 6th century BC. In 330 BC the last Achaemenid, Darius III (*reg c.* 336–330 BC), was defeated by Alexander the Great, who went on to conquer the eastern satrapies in Afghanistan, bringing them into direct contact with Hellenism from the west. Alexander's successors, the SELEUCIDS, retained control in Bactria (the Amu River region north of the Hindu Kush and east of Merv and Herat) but lost the territories of Kabul and Kandahar *c.* 305 BC to the Mauryans from India.

About 250 BC Diodotus, the governor of Bactria, declared independence from the Seleucids. Subsequent Greco-Bactrian kings extended their territory south of the Hindu Kush to Kabul and Kandahar and invaded India (*see* BACTRIAN AND INDO-GREEK MONARCHIES). After the initial successes of Menander (*reg c.* 170 BC), the kingdom became fragmented under several rulers, partly as a result of increasing pressure from nomadic Sakas or Scythians migrating southwards from Central Asia. One group, the Yueh-chih, occupied Bactria *c.* 130 BC. The remaining Indo-Greek kings to the south were replaced by Indo-Scythian rulers of the house of Azes in the 1st century BC and by INDO-PARTHIANS under Gondophares (*reg c.* AD 20–50) in the 1st century AD.

In the 1st century AD the KUSHANA tribe united the Yueh-chih confederacy and established a powerful empire that expanded from Central Asia across Afghanistan to north-west India. The extent and stability of this empire

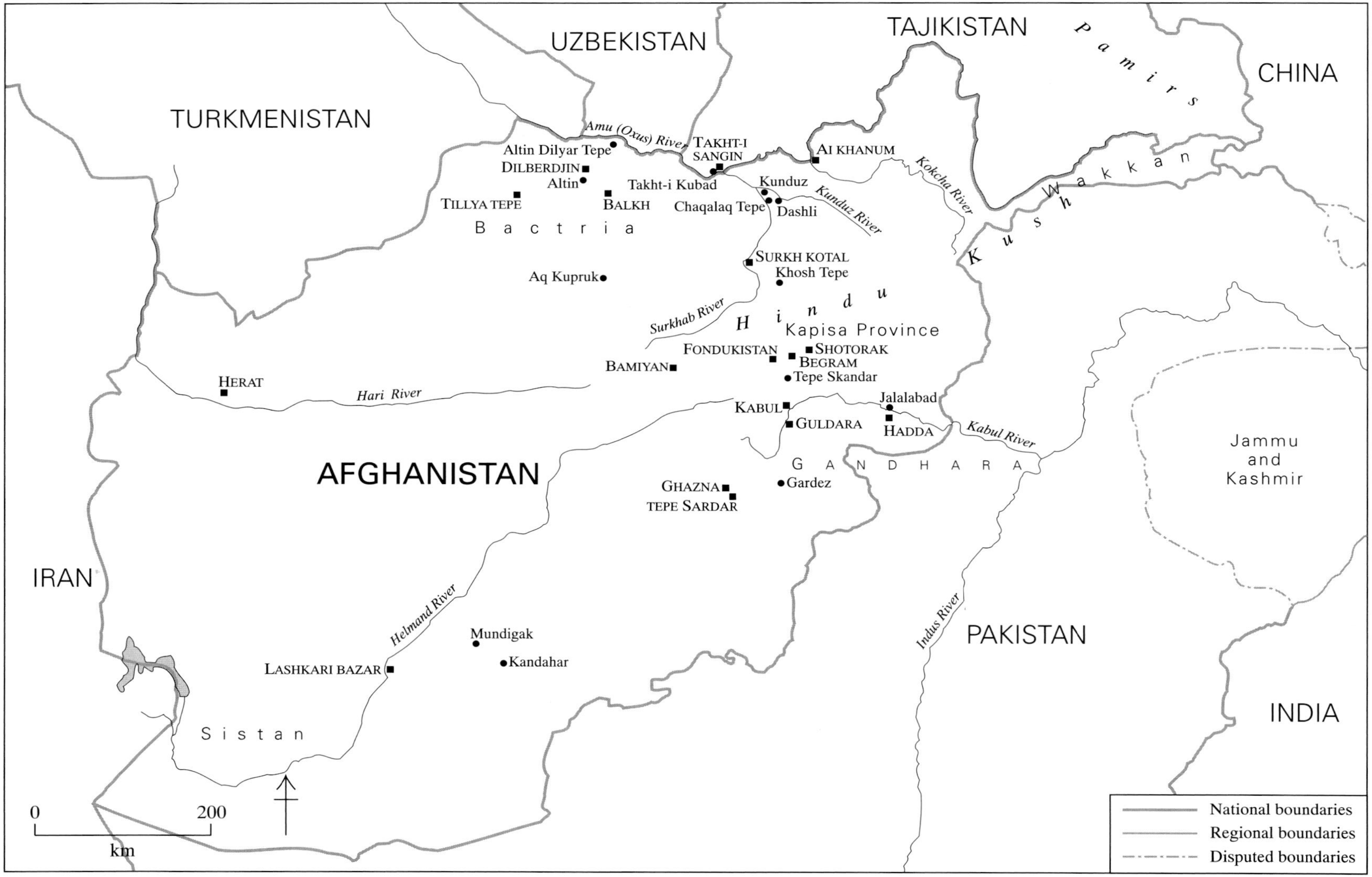

1. Map of Afghanistan; those areas with separate entries in this dictionary are distinguished by CROSS-REFERENCE TYPE

encouraged the growth of international trade along the silk route from China across Afghanistan to the Indus River ports and thence by sea to Alexandria and Rome. Under the third king, Kanishka I, the Kushanas patronized Buddhism, stupas and monasteries were established throughout Afghanistan, and missionaries followed Kushana traders across Central Asia to China. The chronology of this period is still disputed, the era of Kanishka being attributed to various dates between AD 78 and the 3rd century (*see also* INDIAN SUBCONTINENT, §IV, 5(ii)). What is clear is that the Kushanas were defeated by the rising power of the SASANIANS (*c.* 224–651) in the 3rd century. Afghanistan suffered again in the 5th century from the invasions of the Hephthalites (White Huns), who in turn were overthrown in the mid-6th century by the Turki Shahis, allied to the Sasanians. Raids into western Afghanistan in the late 7th century gave the Arabs control of Sistan and HERAT. From the 9th century, western Afghanistan was ruled by local Islamic dynasties: the SAMANIDS (*reg* 874–999) based in Bukhara and the Saffarids (*reg* 867–1495) based in Sistan. Eastern Afghanistan remained an independent non-Muslim kingdom, centred at Kabul, under the Turki Shahis and their successors the Hindu Shahis, until conflicts with the GHAZNAVIDS (*reg* 977–1186), an Islamic dynasty originating from GHAZNA, forced a transfer of the Hindu Shahi capital to Hund, on the Indus River east of Peshawar.

The first Ghaznavid, Sebüktigin (*reg* AD 977–97), governed on behalf of the Samanids, but his son Mahmud (*reg* 998–1030) established an independent empire over Samanid territories south of the Amu River and expanded eastwards into India. By the mid-11th century, western Afghanistan had been relinquished to the Saljuqs (*see* SALJUQ, §1), Turkish nomads originating from the steppelands north of the Caspian and Aral seas, but the Ghaznavids retained control of eastern Afghanistan and northern India. In 1151 Ghazna was sacked by GHURID chieftains from the inaccessible mountainous region east of Herat. Turkish tribes from the lower Syr (Jaxartes) River region overthrew the Saljuqs in 1153 and occupied Ghazna in 1163. In the next decades, the Ghurids gained control of Afghanistan and finally defeated the last Ghaznavid principality at Lahore in 1186.

Internal dynastic struggles and confrontation on the northern borders with the Khwarazmshahs resulted in the breakup of the Ghurid empire. From 1215–16 Ghurid territories were ruled by the Khwarazmshah Muhammad b. Takash (*reg* 1200–21), until the entire region was overrun in 1221 by the Mongols under Genghis Khan (*reg* 1206–27). Herat was restored in 1236 by his third son Ogedey (*reg* 1227–41), while Ghazna and Kabul became military bases for Mongol raids into India. From 1250 onwards the different Afghanistan regions were controlled by independent Mongol rulers, such as the Neguderis at Ghazna.

Timur extended his Transoxanian steppe empire southwards into Afghanistan with the capture of Herat in 1380. Under his son Shahrukh, Herat became the TIMURID capital. From 1469 Afghanistan was divided into two Timurid principalities, one based at Herat, the other at Kabul. In the 16th century incursions by the Uzbek tribal confederacy of the Amu River region meant that frontier towns such as Herat frequently changed hands.

Following the loss of his Central Asian Timurid principality of Ferghana to the Uzbeks, Babur (*reg* 1526–30), the founder of the MUGHAL dynasty, occupied Kabul in 1504. He began raids into India and captured Delhi in 1526. Afghan chiefs led by Sher Shah Sur (*reg* 1540–45; *see* SUR (ii)) forced Babur's son Humayun (*reg* 1530–40, 1555–6) into exile in 1540. The capture of Kabul in 1545 gave Humayun a base from which to reconquer India in 1555. During the reign of Akbar (*reg* 1556–1605) boundaries between Afghanistan and the Uzbek territories to the north were demarcated, but control of Kandahar remained disputed with the Safavid dynasty (*reg* 1501–1732; *see* SAFAVID, §1) to the west. Succeeding Mughals retained Kabul, but western Afghanistan came increasingly under Safavid control. In the early 18th century the Safavid governor, Mir Ways, declared independence. The Afghans occupied most of Iran from 1722 until expelled in 1727 by Nadir Shah (*reg* 1736–47), a Turkoman chieftain from Khurasan in service with the Safavids, who subsequently founded the Afsharid dynasty (*reg* 1736–95) of Iran. When Nadir was assassinated in 1747, Afghan soldiers in his army elected one of his leading commanders, Ahmad Khan of the Afghan Sardozay tribe, as Shah (*reg* 1747–73). The Durrani dynasty (*reg* 1747–1842), which Ahmad Shah founded, derived its name from his title *Dur-i Durrān* ('Pearl of pearls'). He established an empire comprising Afghanistan and north-west India, including Sind, Baluchistan, part of the Punjab and Kashmir, but most of the Indian territories were lost during the reign of Zaman Shah (*reg* 1793–1800).

In 1819 Dost Muhammad of the Barakzay tribe (*reg* 1819–62) took Kabul and retained control of Afghanistan despite pressures from Iran, Russia and the British. The kingdom of Afghanistan survived as a political entity until overthrown by leftist urban groups in 1978. The ensuing civil war was not halted by Soviet military intervention in 1979 or by the withdrawal of Soviet troops in 1987–9.

BIBLIOGRAPHY

C. E. Bosworth: *The Islamic Dynasties: A Chronological and Genealogical Handbook* (Edinburgh, 1967, rev. 1980)

F. R. Allchin and N. Hammond, eds: *The Archaeology of Afghanistan: From Earliest Times to the Timurid Period* (London and New York, 1978)

L. Dupree: *Afghanistan* (Princeton, 1980)

A. B. Delmas and M. Casanova: 'The Lapis Lazuli Sources in the Ancient East', *South Asian Archaeology, 1987*, ed. M. Taddei (Rome, 1990), pp. 493–505

3. LANGUAGE AND ETHNIC GROUPS. The earliest official inscriptions date from the Mauryan period. These comprise Aramaic inscriptions from Laghman and two bilingual inscriptions of Ashoka (*reg c.* 269–*c.* 232 BC) from Kandahar, one combining Aramaic with Greek and the other Aramaic with Indian Prakrit. Under the Greco-Bactrians at AI KHANUM, official inscriptions were in good Classical Greek. Under the Kushanas, inscriptions at Surkh Kotal, north of the Hindu Kush, were in Bactrian; inscriptions at Dasht-i-Nawar, 60 km west of Ghazna, were in Bactrian, Prakrit and an undeciphered local language, while the inscriptions of south-eastern Afghanistan were in Prakrit.

Afghanistan is not a single ethnic unit. In the pre-Muslim period, the Hindu Kush ('Death to the Hindu') Mountains formed a natural divide between the Hindu-dominated areas of the south and the Zoroastrian peoples of the north. The largest racial group in modern Afghanistan consists of the Pathans, a people of Turko-Iranian origin who speak Pushtu and are probably the descendants of the original inhabitants of the south. The Tajiks, who live north and east of Kabul, are of Iranian origin, speak Farsi and are thought to be descendants of the original northern inhabitants. The Hazaras who inhabit the central massif are thought to be descendants of the Mongols. There are also many minority groups, such as the Turkomans, Uzbeks and Nuristanis, who all speak their own dialects.

4. RELIGION AND ICONOGRAPHY. The terracotta female figures from Mundigak (*see* §II, 1(ii)(a) below) suggest that a fertility goddess resembling the great mother goddess of Mesopotamia was worshipped in the prehistoric period (*c*. 2000 BC). Zoroastrianism played an important role in Iranian lands such as Bactria before the conquest of Alexander the Great in 330 BC, but many remains of a pre-Zoroastrian religion also survived. The Sakas and Yueh-chih in Central Asia probably worshipped the sun and regarded Ahuramazda (the Zoroastrian supreme Good Spirit) as a god with a strong solar function (*see also* CENTRAL ASIA, §I, 1(v)(a)).

The coins of the Greek rulers of Bactria showed a typical range of Greek divinities, with the same attributes and iconography as found throughout the Hellenistic world: Zeus with his thunderbolt, Artemis with her bow and Pallas Athena with her shield. According to Herodotus (*Histories* IV.lviii–lxix), the Scythians worshipped Greek gods but called them by Scythian names, and this also reflects the Greek approach to foreign deities. Native divinities were syncretized with Greek gods and represented in Greek iconographic forms. The votive pedestal at TAKHT-I SANGIN, dedicated by the Iranian priest Atrosokes to the deity of the Oxus (Amu River) in the 2nd century BC, supported a statue of the Classical deity Silenus Marsyas, playing a double flute. Rare coins of Agathokles (*c*. 180 BC) from Ai Khanum follow the Classical tradition by depicting the Hindu deity Samkarshana in iconic form as a male figure in Oriental dress and winged headdress holding a plough, while his younger brother Vasudeva Krishna is similarly shown bearing the attributes of a conch shell (*saṅkha*) and wheel (*cakra*) (Kabul Mus.; see Allchin and Hammond, fig. 4.13). The enthroned and radiate Zeus on Indian tetradrachms of Hermaios (*c*. 90–70 BC) represents Zeus syncretized with Mithra, an Iranian pre-Zoroastrian solar deity (see 1992 exh. cat., p. 61, no. 24).

There were similar developments when the Kushanas extended their empire across Afghanistan in the 1st century AD. The first ruler, Kujula Kadphises, used Herakles, the Greek form of the Iranian war god and personification of victory, Verethragna. King Soter Megas used the rayed head of Mithra. All the gold and copper coins of his successor Vima Kadphises use the type of Shiva and his bull Nandi, showing the king's personal devotion to the war god, appropriate to his campaigns of conquest and to the support he required from his new Indian subjects. Kanishka was more eclectic, and his coins show a pantheon of primarily Iranian gods. Initially he used Greek legends, even to the extent of using the female name Selene for the male Iranian moon god. The Greek names were subsequently replaced by Bactrian ones, such as Mao (moon god), Mioro (sun god), Athsho (fire god) and Nana (water goddess, the Bactrian Anahita).

The Mauryan ruler Ashoka (*reg c*. 269–*c*. 232 BC) promoted Buddhism in Afghanistan as elsewhere, and inscriptions giving his edicts have been found in Laghman and at Kandahar; but it was only from the late 1st century BC onwards, under the Indo-Parthians and Kushanas, that Buddhism spread widely and numerous stupas were built in Afghanistan. During this period there were some remarkable developments in Buddhist iconography. Whereas previously the Buddha's presence had simply been indicated by symbols, such as a footprint or vacant throne, a new school of Buddhist thought stressing the miraculous life of the Buddha led to the representation of the Buddha in human form. A gold medallion from Tillya Tepe (see Sarianidi, pp. 188–9, no. 131), dated *c*. 50 BC–*c*. AD 50, has a reverse design of a lion and a *triratna* ('three jewels' symbol representing Buddha, the Law and the Buddhist community). The Kharoshthi inscription *siho vigatabhayo* ('the lion who chased away fear') refers to the Buddha, as does the obverse *dharmacakrapravatako* ('he who sets in motion the Wheel of the Law'; see Fussman, pp. 71–2), which is inscribed beside a bearded image of Herakles, complete with lion skin, pushing a wheel. The equation of a Classical deity with the Buddha suggests that the token was made in the aniconic period of Buddhist art, but within the Greco-Bactrian milieu, where religious images were traditionally represented in human form.

The gold reliquary from Bimaran Stupa 2 (*see* §II, 1(iv)(c) and fig. 14 below) also belongs to an early phase and has niches containing the standing images of the Buddha, Indra, Brahma and a fourth figure, variously thought to represent a *bodhisattva* or a donor. The billon coins found with the reliquary were issued posthumously in the name of Azes and date from the time of Kujula Kadphises (*c*. mid-1st century AD). Kanishka, who convened a Buddhist council in Kashmir to settle doctrinal disputes, issued coins in both gold and copper bearing an image of the Buddha. It was, however, a rare coinage, perhaps intended simply to commemorate the council. In spite of Kanishka's patronage of Buddhism, his dynastic shrine at SURKH KOTAL provides evidence of an indigenous religion associated with the cult of fire. His successor, Huvishka, shows the same eclectic approach in his coinage, but later Kushanas reverted to the more limited representation of the Hindu god Shiva with his mount Nandi and the enthroned Ardochsho, the Iranian goddess of good fortune, increasingly represented as her Hindu equivalent, Lakshmi. Kushana and Kushano-Sasanian kings are often depicted on coins with flames issuing from their shoulders, a divine symbol in Iranian terms of a universal ruler. A relief of the 3rd century AD from SHOTORAK similarly depicts the Dipankara Buddha (the first of 24 predecessors of the historical Buddha) as a substantially larger figure with flames rising from his shoulders (see Snellgrove, fig. 137; *see also* §II, 1(ii)(c) and fig. 6 below).

The two colossal images (h. 55 m and 38 m) in rock-cut niches at Bamiyan were clearly intended to inspire respect and show the Buddha as Lord of the world. Paintings in the niche containing the 38 m figure depict Sasanian donors and Buddhas, with a solar divinity in a quadriga above to indicate Buddha's solar character (see Tarzi, pls B8–27). The larger figure (see fig. 8 below) is set in a niche decorated with a pantheon of *bodhisattvas* encircling the cosmic Buddha (see Tarzi, pls B119–129). A late 7th-century AD Buddha statue from the monastery at FONDUKISTAN (see fig. 9 below) is depicted wearing heavy earrings and a jewelled chasuble over his monastic garment, i.e. the ascetic Buddha transformed into the glorified transcendent form also seen in India in the later iconography of Maitreya (the future Buddha; *see also* §II, 1(ii)(d) and (iii) below).

The ascendancy of Hinduism in the 7th–8th centuries AD, associated with the Hindu Shahi kings of Kabul, is represented by statues of the elephant god Ganesha from Koh Daman and Gardez; fragments of sculpture representing Shiva and his consort Durga killing the buffalo demon from Sa'robi; and two Surya images from Khair Khana near Kabul. Islam, brought by the advancing Muslim armies from the 8th century AD onwards, became the dominant religion of Afghanistan by the 10th century.

BIBLIOGRAPHY

B. Rowland: *The Evolution of the Buddha Image* (New York, 1963)
B. Y. Stavisky: *Kushanskaya Baktriya: Problemy istorii i kul'tury* (Moscow, 1977); Fr. trans. as *La Bactriane sous les Kushans: Problèmes d'histoire et de culture* (Paris, 1986)
Z. Tarzi: *L'Architecture et le décor rupestre des grottes de Bāmiyān*, 2 vols (Paris, 1977)
F. R. Allchin and N. Hammond, eds: *The Archaeology of Afghanistan: From Earliest Times to the Timurid Period* (London and New York, 1978)
D. L. Snellgrove, ed.: *The Image of the Buddha* (London, 1978)
V. Sarianidi: *The Golden Hoard of Bactria from the Tillya-tepe Excavations in Northern Afghanistan* (New York and Leningrad, 1985)
G. Fussman: 'Numismatic and Epigraphic Evidence for the Chronology of Early Gandharan Art', *Investigating Indian Art*, ed. M. Yaldiz (Berlin, 1987), pp. 67–88
The Crossroads of Asia: Transformation in Image and Symbol in the Art of Ancient Afghanistan and Pakistan (exh. cat., ed. E. Errington and J. Cribb; Cambridge, Fitzwilliam, 1992)
J. Harmatta: 'Religion in the Kushan Empire', *The Development of Sedentary and Nomadic Civilizations, 700 BC to AD 250*, ed. J. Harmatta, G. F. Etemadi and B. N. Puri (1993), ii of *UNESCO History of Civilizations of Central Asia* (Paris, 1992–)

D. W. MACDOWALL

II. Historical survey.

The study of art in Afghanistan can conveniently be divided into three broad periods. The rich and varied traditions of early historic Afghanistan gave way in the late 1st millennium AD to the influence of Islam, which dominated artistic output for 1000 years. Twentieth-century art has tended to imitate Western styles.

1. Before *c.* AD 900. 2. *c.* AD 900–*c.* 1900. 3. After *c.* 1900.

1. BEFORE *c.* AD 900.

(i) Architecture. (ii) Sculpture. (iii) Painting. (iv) Other arts.

(i) Architecture. At different periods in its history, Afghanistan has been subject to Harappan, Greek, Persian, Indian, Central Asian, Chinese, Islamic and Russian influences. The architecture of Afghanistan is the syncretic fusion of these divergent traditions, the origins of which can be traced in the prehistoric, Achaemenid and Hellenistic periods, culminating in the 1st millennium AD in the predominantly Buddhist architecture of GANDHARA (*see also* INDIAN SUBCONTINENT, §III, 3(ii)(a)).

2. Mundigak, 'Palace', north-west façade, *c.* 2500–*c.* 2000 BC

(a) Prehistoric. (b) *c.* 4th–*c.* 1st century BC. (c) *c.* 1st–*c.* 5th century AD. (d) *c.* 6th–*c.* 9th century AD.

(a) Prehistoric. Excavations at the Bronze and Iron Age town of Mundigak (founded *c.* 4000 BC) near Kandahar revealed a long history of simple mud and mud-brick domestic architecture. Monumental town walls were constructed in Period IV (later 3rd millennium BC), a date contemporary with the Urban Phase of the Harappan civilization at the great Indus Valley cities of MOHENJO-DARO and HARAPPA to the east. Two buildings, tentatively identified as a 'Palace' and a 'Temple', have massive exterior walls and buttresses built of fired brick with a surface coating of plaster. The 'Palace', located on the highest point of the site, has a façade on the north-west side, surviving some 35 m in length and nearly 3 m in height (see fig. 2). The line of semicircular buttresses or 'colonnade of pilasters' fronting this façade was capped by a frieze of stepped merlons. The interior plan, in contrast to the regularity and solidity of the exterior, appears haphazard and comprises small rooms of flimsy mud-brick construction around a central courtyard. Much, however, had been lost through erosion, particularly since the building was first excavated in the 1950s. The 'Temple' is more regular in plan, with a façade of decorative triangular buttresses traceable on three sides, although erosion had reduced the height of the building almost to foundation level.

When extant, these buttressed façades must have presented a very impressive aspect. This type of structure appears to have been a favourite form of architectural adornment, as even the ramparts are distinguished by more closely spaced, square buttresses than would be required for either structural or defensive reasons. The Late Bronze Age palace at Dashli 3 in Bactria (northern

Afghanistan) is similarly decorated with regular lines of square buttresses, on both the interior and exterior façades. The form recalls late 4th-millennium BC monumental architecture at Uruk (*see* MESOPOTAMIA, §II, 3), where semicircular, triangular and square buttressing were all used to decorate exterior façades. The semicircular buttresses of the 'Palace' at Mundigak seem to have a particularly close affinity with the 'Pillar Hall' at Uruk, while the merlons perhaps recall Mesopotamian prototypes.

The tradition of monumental building continued in the 1st millennium BC. Massive structures, usually on immense brick platforms, include Nad-i Ali in Sistan, south-west Afghanistan, the citadels at Maiwand and Kandahar in the south-east, and fortifications at Altin 1, Altin Dilyar Tepe, Kutlug Tepe, DILBERDJIN and Dashli in Bactria to the north (*see* CENTRAL ASIA, §I, 2(i)(a)). The same monumentality is also found in Iron Age and Achaemenid buildings of Pakistan (e.g. Bannu) and Iran (e.g. Tureng Tepe and the immense palace platform of PERSEPOLIS).

Altin 1 and Altin Dilyar Tepe in Bactria are both fortified towns with a high citadel surrounded by a town and massive outer defensive walls. This type of urban layout was to characterize Central Asian town planning for several millennia. The ramparts of Altin Dilyar are, furthermore, in the form of an immense circle, a feature of subsequent Parthian and Sasanian town planning that was still utilized in AD 762 at BAGHDAD. The Achaemenid citadel at Dilberdjin is also circular (though the surrounding town is largely later), as is a building at Kutlug Tepe, tentatively identified as a temple, that comprises three massive concentric mud walls pierced by embrasures.

Altin 1 was probably the administrative centre for a group of settlements. The most significant settlement was Altin 10, which contained two buildings, probably palaces, the one consisting of two porticoed courtyards with roofs supported by massive brick pillars, the other comprising a single courtyard dominated by a wide central entrance on one side. Both features subsequently evolved into two important architectural elements of the Middle East: the columned hall and the monumental portal.

The 1st millennium BC, therefore, was one in which the prototypes of certain basic architectural features were established: monumental buildings, the circular form, the columned hall and the monumental portal. That so many standard architectural elements of Afghanistan and neighbouring Iran were formulated in Afghanistan assumes significance in the light of the Central Asian origins of the Iranians themselves: when they arrived on the Iranian plateau, they already had a developed and vigorous architectural tradition.

(b) c. *4th*–c. *1st century* BC. New architectural traditions from the west arrived with the conquests of Alexander of Macedon and his Seleucid successors in the 4th–3rd century BC. The survival of the subsequent Greco-Bactrian and Indo-Greek kingdoms in the Central Asian and Indo-Iranian borderlands ensured the continuation and development of an independent Hellenistic artistic and architectural tradition that was open to more Oriental influences.

The only Greek city that has been excavated in Afghanistan is AI KHANUM (probably anc. Alexandria Oxiana). The city, founded at or soon after the time of Alexander's conquest (329–325 BC), occupies a naturally fortified position at the confluence of the Amu and Kokcha rivers. A low ridge on the third side is further reinforced by ramparts and, in places, a ditch. A north–south main thoroughfare divided the upper and lower town. The upper town has a necropolis and a citadel and is separated from the lower town by a main thoroughfare running from north to south. The lower town consists of three distinctive parts: an almost empty area to the north; a central administrative quarter and a palace; and living quarters to the south. The adjacent plain has an extensive irrigation system. The remains belong well within standard Hellenistic architectural traditions.

The earliest building is the temple dedicated to Kineas (*c.* 325–*c.* 300 BC), a leading citizen and probably one of the founders of the city. Other excavated buildings include a gymnasium, theatre, monumental mausoleum, propylaeum, monumental fountain, arsenal, several temples and some houses. The architectural decoration is typically Hellenistic, with stone columns bearing Corinthian, Ionic and Doric capitals throughout. A number of Oriental architectural features were nevertheless retained. Mudbrick was the primary building material, with stone used only for important structural purposes, such as columns. Even many of the Corinthian columns are Asiatic variations of the form, rather than true Greek. The great courtyard of the palace is dominated in the centre of one side by a monumental opening and reception hall supported by three rows of six columns each, in which it is easy to see the local elements of monumental portal and columned hall. While the mausoleum is a standard peripteral style temple, the Temple of Kineas and the temple 'à redans' or 'à niches indentées' are each situated in a large enclosure, or temenos. Such large temple enclosures are typical Asian features (*see also* CENTRAL ASIA, §I, 2(i)(a)). The layout of Ai Khanum conforms to standard Hellenistic town planning principles, with its grid system of streets and main north–south thoroughfare, though the division into citadel and lower town might be seen as a local influence. But elsewhere in Hellenistic Bactria, the Iranian circular plan remained popular: for example Jiga Tepe is a circular fortification, while Emshi Tepe is an entire circular city, like the earlier site of Altin Dilyar.

Evidence of major conflagrations at Ai Khanum in about 130 BC and again in 90 BC point to the final destruction of the city by invaders, possibly the Kushanas. But the unique blend of western and eastern elements found at the site continued to influence the subsequent cultures of Afghanistan for almost a millennium. Before the discovery and excavation of Ai Khanum in the 1960s, knowledge of this important formative period when the two cultures first became fused was almost non-existent.

(c) c. *1st*–c. *5th century* AD. The arrival of the originally nomadic KUSHANAS from Central Asia added a new element to the already eclectic nature of the architecture of Afghanistan. The establishment of the Kushana empire invigorated existing traditions and re-asserted international connections, particularly with the Indian subcontinent,

thereby encouraging the spread of Buddhism into Afghanistan. Under the Kushanas, the widely divergent traditions of architecture in Afghanistan became a cultural and political whole. The first Kushana political capital was at BEGRAM, north of Kabul. Subsequently the capital was moved to TAXILA in Pakistan and eventually to MATHURA in India. The site of KHALCHAYAN in Tajikistan has been identified by its excavators as an early Kushana dynastic shrine. The Kushanas established a similar dynastic cult centre at SURKH KOTAL, north of the Hindu Kush. The complex, dated *c.* 1st–*c.* 4th century AD, is reached by a monumental mud-brick and masonry staircase, flanked by four massive terraces cut from the hillside (see fig. 3). The main temple has a cella facing east, which is enclosed by a corridor on the three other sides and contains a square masonry platform with the remains of four Hellenistic column bases at each corner. The building was first thought to be a fire temple, but more recent research suggests that it may have had a more public ceremonial function. Abutting the south side of the temple is a later complex of two small fire temples linked by a courtyard. These each have a square central sanctuary enclosed by corridors. A Greek-letter inscription in the Bactrian language describes the construction of a well and the restoration of the complex by an official called Nokonzok in the year 31 of the Kanishka era (*c.* first half of the 2nd century).

The great staircase of Surkh Kotal is unique in the architecture of the region. The only contemporary parallel occurs at Wadi Hadhramaut in southern Arabia, where the monumental staircase approaches to a series of shrines bear many similarities to Surkh Kotal, although there is no apparent connection between the two sites. The associations with fire worship at Surkh Kotal have obvious Zoroastrian affinities, while the ambulatory in the form of corridors around the sanctuary is an essential feature of Buddhist architecture at sites such as ADZHINA TEPE. The syncretic fusion of different religious ideas and elements into a cult focused on the person of the emperor was apparently intended to symbolize the unity of different regions of the empire and the cultural tolerance of the Kushanas.

During the Kushana period Buddhism was the dominant religion in Afghanistan. The main architectural manifestation of Buddhism, the STUPA, is one of the most distinctive architectural features of eastern Afghanistan. In the long, complex evolution of the stupa form, Afghanistan played a major role, not least because contact with Hellenism gave rise to the distinctive art and architectural style of Gandhara. Many new forms of Buddhist architecture evolved, the Buddha image was given artistic and architectural expression, and numerous monastic complexes were built in the regions east of Kandahar in the south to Balkh in the north. Most importantly, it was during this formative period that Buddhism and its associated architecture spread from Afghanistan northwards into Central Asia and ultimately eastwards to China, Japan and South-east Asia, rather than directly from the Indian heartland.

The stupa, originally built to house relics associated with the Buddha, became both the centre for great monastic communities and the symbol of far-reaching philosophical ideas. In eastern Afghanistan the stupas number in hundreds, if not thousands. A well-preserved and architecturally outstanding example of the stupa form is found at GULDARA, south-east of Kabul (see fig. 4). The stupa consists of a dome and two drums positioned on a high, square platform and socle with a stairway on the south-west side. The core of the structure is faced with the distinctive 'diaper masonry' that is the hallmark of architecture of the Gandharan period throughout the region: large stones, dressed on one side with small, flat stones filling the interstices. The platform and both stupa drums are decorated with blind arcades of Indo-Corinthian pilasters (an Oriental variation of the Greek prototype). A

3. Surkh Kotal, fortified terraced enclosure and monumental stairs to the dynastic shrines on the acropolis, *c.* late 1st century AD to *c.* 4th

4. Guldara, main stupa, north-east façade, *c.* 2nd–*c.* 4th centuries AD

fortified monastery to the north comprises a central unexcavated courtyard, which possibly contained a central stupa and smaller votive stupas surrounded on four sides by an ambulatory and cells for monks. To the south of the principal stupa stands a second stupa of similar style also constructed of diaper masonry. The complex is dated on stylistic, epigraphic and numismatic grounds to the 2nd–4th century.

The Buddhist sites of HADDA, near Jalalabad in eastern Afghanistan, comprise numerous stupas, monasteries and artificial cave complexes extending over an area of approximately 39 sq. km. The major monastic complexes often have more than one large stupa and always have numerous votive stupas. The stupas, shrines and caves were decorated with a wealth of clay, stone and stucco sculptural decoration and wall paintings (*see* §§(ii)(c)–(d) and (iii)(b) below). The most spectacular sites were Tepe Kalan (three main stupas surrounded by dozens of decorated votive stupas) and Tepe Shotor (one main stupa with many votive stupas, richly decorated niches and shrines). All the excavated sites at Hadda have been destroyed, either soon after excavation in the 1920s or during fighting in the 1980s.

Although Afghanistan was incorporated into the SASANIAN empire in the 3rd century AD, under the Kushano-Sasanian rulers local cultural forms continued uninterrupted, albeit evincing increasing Sasanian influence. The Hephthalites who migrated southwards from Central Asia in the 5th century are often associated with great destruction, but in Afghanistan the Buddhist civilization not only continued but flourished following their invasion. Indeed, it is often difficult to distinguish any differences in the material culture of the Kushana, Sasanian and Hephthalite periods.

(d) c. *6th–*c. *9th century* AD. The numerous minor principalities that emerged in eastern Afghanistan during the 7th century AD were often little more than city states ruled by Hephthalite or Turkish lords who enjoyed considerable independence and frequently encouraged the religious arts. Although there was no great central unifying power, Buddhism imposed a cultural unity throughout, and some of the greatest Buddhist monuments were built during this period. At FONDUKISTAN, for example, the monastery contains a courtyard with niches that were elaborately decorated with painted clay sculptures and frescoes (*see* §§(ii)(d) and (iii)(c) below). Near Ghazna (probably the site of a minor principality), excavations also revealed a stupa and monastery complex at TEPE SARDAR that was almost Baroque in the richness of its sculptural decoration. The main stupa, the largest in Afghanistan, is surrounded by many votive stupas and chapels, richly decorated in clay reliefs. The remains in the sanctuary include clay fragments of several colossal Buddha statues. Most significantly, there is also a Brahmanical shrine in the Tepe Sardar complex, where a statue of Durga Mahishasuramardini was found. Following the establishment of the Hindu Shahis at Kabul in the 8th century AD, many significant Hindu works of art were created, but there are no great works of architecture belonging to this period, except perhaps the controversial Minar-i Chakri, a stone pillar on a mountain overlooking the Kabul valley.

By far the most spectacular Buddhist site in Afghanistan is BAMIYAN, in the central Hindu Kush. The cliffs on the north side of the valley are honeycombed for a length of about 1800 m by some 750 artificial caves, forming part of a Buddhist centre. Among the caves are two colossal, almost free-standing statues of the Buddha (55 m and 38 m high) and a smaller, seated Buddha, carved out of niches in the cliff face in high relief. Details of the robes are applied in stucco over a framework of ropes (representing the folds) attached to the bedrock with wooden pegs. The top halves of the faces have been destroyed by iconoclasts. In the niches surrounding the two standing Buddhas are the remains of frescoes. Frescoes and sculptures also decorate many of the caves, and plaster applied to the bedrock to represent architectural details often imitates wooden prototypes. Indeed, rock-cut architecture is characteristic of Bamiyan, in contrast with other eastern regions of Afghanistan, where architectural structures, particularly stupas, predominate. The only stupa discovered at Bamiyan was excavated to the east of the 38 m Buddha, though mounds of debris might indicate other examples.

In the architecture and art generally of Bamiyan there exists a surprising paradox. For Bamiyan was only a minor principality of the federation known as the Empire of the Western Turks, the capital of which was at Qunduz in north-eastern Afghanistan, where no monuments on such a scale exist. It has been suggested that Bamiyan may have been a dynastic centre for the Western Turks, in much the same way as Surkh Kotal functioned for the Kushanas. Whether or not this is true, Buddhist architecture reached a peak at Bamiyan. The caves cut out of the mountainside housed thousands of devotees; the colossal statues were the ultimate embodiment of the Buddha image, while the painting and sculpture combined Hellenistic, Iranian and Indian elements that influenced subsequent Chinese and Islamic art.

BIBLIOGRAPHY

J. Barthoux: *Les Fouilles de Hadda*, 2 vols, Mém.: Dél. Archéol. Fr. Afghanistan, iv–v (Paris and Brussels, 1930–33)

J. Hackin and J. Carl: *Recherches archéologiques au col de Khair Khaneh près de Kâbul*, Mém.: Dél. Archéol. Fr. Afghanistan, vii (Paris, 1936)

J. Meunié: *Shotorak*, Mém.: Dél. Archéol. Fr. Afghanistan, x (Paris, 1942)

J. Carl, J. Hackin and J. Meunié: *Diverses recherches archéologiques en Afghanistan, 1933–1940*, Mém.: Dél. Archéol. Fr. Afghanistan, viii (Paris, 1959)

J.-M. Casal: *Fouilles de Mundigak*, 2 vols, Mém.: Dél. Archéol. Fr. Afghanistan, xvii (Paris, 1961)

S. Mizuno, ed.: *Haibak and Kashmir-Smast: Buddhist Cave Temples in Afghanistan and Pakistan Surveyed in 1960* (Kyoto, 1962)

B. Dagens, M. Le Berre and D. Schlumberger: *Monuments préislamiques d'Afghanistan*, Mém.: Dél. Archéol. Fr. Afghanistan, xix (Paris, 1964)

S. Mizuno, ed.: *Durman Tepe and Lalma: Buddhist Sites in Afghanistan Surveyed in 1963–1965* (Kyoto, 1968)

——: *Chagalag Tepe: Fortified Village in North Afghanistan Excavated in 1964–1967* (Kyoto, 1970)

——: *Basawal and Jelalabad-Kabul: Buddhist Cave Temples and Topes in South-east Afghanistan Surveyed Mainly in 1965* (Kyoto, 1971)

P. Bernard and others: *Fouilles d'Aï Khanoum*, 9 vols, Mém.: Dél. Archéol. Fr. Afghanistan, xxi, xxvi–xxxi, xxxiii (Paris, 1973–92)

I. T. Kruglikova: *Dil'berdzhin (raskopki 1970–1972 gg.)* [Dilberdjin (excavations 1970–1972)], i (Moscow, 1974)

G. Fussman and M. Le Berre: *Monuments bouddhiques de la région de Caboul, I: Le Monastère de Gul Dara*, Mém.: Dél. Archéol. Fr. Afghanistan, xxii (Paris, 1976)

I. T. Kruglikova, ed.: *Drevnyaya Baktriya* [Ancient Bactria], 3 vols (Moscow, 1976–84)

Z. Tarzi: 'Hadda à la lumière des trois dernières campagnes de fouilles de Tapa-é-Shotor (1974–1976)', *Acad. Inscr. & B.-Lett.: C. R. Séances* (1976), pp. 381–410; Eng. trans. by A. A. Motamedi with C. Grissman as 'Hadda after the Three Last Seasons of Excavations at Tepe Shotor (1974–1976)', *Afghanistan Q.*, xxxii/2 (Sept 1979), pp. 60–89

I. T. Kruglikova and G. Pugachenkova: *Dil'berdzhin (raskopki 1970–1973 gg.)* [Dilberdjin (excavations 1970–1973)], ii (Moscow, 1977)

Z. Tarzi: *L'Architecture et le décor rupestre des grottes de Bāmiyān*, 2 vols (Paris, 1977)

F. R. Allchin and N. Hammond, eds: *The Archaeology of Afghanistan: From Earliest Times to the Timurid Period* (London and New York, 1978)

H. G. Franz: 'Das Chakri Minar als buddhistische Kultsäule', *Afghanistan J.*, v/3 (1978), pp. 96–101

M. Taddei and G. Verardi: 'Tapa Sardār: Second Preliminary Report', *E. & W.*, xxviii (1978), pp. 33–136

H.-P. Francfort: *Les Fortifications en Asie centrale de l'âge du bronze à l'époque kouchane* (Paris, 1979)

W. Ball: *Archaeological Gazetteer of Afghanistan/Catalogue de sites archéologiques d'Afghanistan*, 2 vols (Paris, 1982)

D. Schlumberger, M. Le Berre and G. Fussman: *Surkh Kotal en Bactriane, I: Les Temples, architecture, sculpture, inscriptions*, 2 vols, Mém.: Dél. Archéol. Fr. Afghanistan, xxv (Paris, 1983)

T. Higuchi, ed.: *Bamiyan: Art and Archaeological Researches on the Buddhist Cave Temples in Afghanistan, 1970–1978*, 4 vols (Kyoto, 1983–4)

S. Kuwayama: 'Tapa Shotor and Lalma: Aspects of Stupa Court at Hadda', *AION*, xlvii (1987), pp. 153–76

For further bibliography *see* §§(ii) and (iii) below.

W. BALL

(ii) Sculpture. The sculpture of Afghanistan reflects the diverse cultural traditions brought by trade and a series of foreign invaders to the region. Stylistic links with Iran and the Indian subcontinent are already evident in the prehistoric period. From the late 4th century BC onwards, the predominant Hellenistic and subsequent Buddhist influences formed the basis of Gandharan art (*c.* 1st–5th century AD); later sculptures provide increasing evidence of the resurgence of Hinduism. Apart from a few free-standing statues, the sculpture primarily comprises friezes and relief images that were designed to be placed against a wall. Stone, particularly schist and limestone, was used until *c.* 3rd century AD; stucco and particularly unbaked clay were also used extensively throughout all periods, later to the almost total exclusion of stone. A proportion of the finds from the French excavations at Bamiyan, Begram, Hadda, the Kapisa sites and Fondukistan are in Paris, Musée Guimet. Tepe Shotor, Hadda, was enclosed as a protected archaeological site, with the sculptures retained *in situ* (since destroyed). The Bamiyan rock-cut images and large items such as the columns and capitals at Ai Khanum were also left *in situ*, but the majority of sculptures were placed in the Kabul Museum (destroyed by bombing in 1993).

□

(a) Prehistoric. (b) *c.* 4th-*c.* 1st century BC. (c) *c.* 1st-*c.* 3rd century AD. (d) *c.* 4th-*c.* 9th century AD.

(a) Prehistoric. A carving of a human head (*c.* 635×381 mm) on a soft limestone pebble was found during the 1965–6 excavation of the cave Aq Kupruk II (Ghar-i Mar or 'Horse Cave') on the Balkh River, south of Mazar-e Sharif (see Dupree, 1968, 1972; Marshak, figs 138–40). Despite the crude carving, the eyes are clearly depicted and the curve of a distorted mouth can also be seen. This object is associated with an Upper Palaeolithic blade industry (Kuprukian A) and can tentatively be dated 20,000–15,000 BP. The site of Mundigak on the upper

reaches of the Helmand River near Kandahar became a major centre in Period IV (*c.* 2500–*c.* 2000 BC; *see* §(i)(a) above). Finds from this period include terracotta figurines, compartmented seals and copper or bronze tools (see Shaffer, figs 3.39–40). A male head of white limestone (h. 915 mm; see fig. 5), broken high at the neck and assigned to Period IV, 3, was found in a complex of rooms associated with a niched wall (see Casal, pp. 76–7, 255; pls XLIII–XLIV). It is a rather colourless representation of a beardless man with a full (now broken) nose. The chin has been defaced and only faint traces remain of a mouth. Ears are shown as simple 'C' shapes, much like those on Mohenjo-daro sculptures. The eyes are oval and rather large, could not have accommodated inlays and have prominent eyebrows above which a hairline is indicated. There is a slight indication that the hair may have been parted in the middle and worn wide and full at the shoulders. There is also a fillet around the forehead, extending down the back of the head in twin flat bands, just as with the 'Priest–King' (*see* INDIAN SUBCONTINENT, fig. 137). This piece of sculpture fits well within the corpus of Harappan material in terms of size, material and some stylistic features.

An Afghan tribal leader from Sistan owns a small stone head said to come from the environs of the village of Khwabgah (see Dales, p. 219). This is also broken at the neck and survives to a height of 94 mm. It is fashioned from a soft, creamy buff stone, with many pits and white veins. The beardless head has a small, tight mouth above a small chin and lacks vivacity. The nose comes from a steeply slanted forehead in a rather direct way and is slightly broken. Large, ovate eyes, capped by distinctive eyebrows, seem to have been without inlay. There is a prominent hairline, which could denote the original existence of a cap or some other headgear. A slight indentation towards the front of the top of the head may indicate a central parting. Details are lacking, but the hair seems to have been worn wide and full at the shoulders, as on the Mundigak head. A fillet goes around the forehead and extends down the back of the head in twin flat bands.

5. White limestone head, h. 915 mm, from Mundigak, *c.* 2500–*c.* 2000 BC (Kabul, Kabul Museum)

A team of Italian archaeologists exploring Iranian Sistan in 1977 found a small limestone head on the surface of the small site of Chah-i Torogh, *c.* 15 km south of SHAHR-I SOKHTA (see Jarrige and Tosi, pp. 131–3). Chah-i Torogh is a Shahr-i Sokhta IV site, dating to the earliest centuries of the 2nd millennium BC. The head, broken at the neck, survives to a height of 35 mm and is thus significantly smaller than the stone sculptures from the Indus sites or Mundigak. The expressionless countenance has a full but broken nose. The ears seem to be oval rather than 'C' shapes. The hair appears to have been parted in the middle and held in place with a fillet that hangs down the back in a pair of flat bands as in other examples.

BIBLIOGRAPHY

J.-M. Casal: *Fouilles de Mundigak*, 2 vols, Mém.: Dél. Archéol. Fr. Afghanistan, xvii (Paris, 1961)

L. Dupree: 'The Oldest Sculptured Head?', *Nat. Hist.*, lxxvii/5 (1968), pp. 26–7

——: 'Prehistoric Research in Afghanistan (1959–1966)', *Trans. Amer. Philos. Soc.*, lxii/4 (1972), pp. 3–84

A. Marshak: 'Aq Kupruk: Art and Symbols', in L. Dupree: 'Prehistoric Research in Afghanistan (1959–1966)', *Trans. Amer. Philos. Soc.*, lxii/4 (1972), pp. 66–72

P. Basaglia and others: *La città bruciata del deserto salato* (Venice, 1977)

J. G. Shaffer: 'The Later Prehistoric Periods', *The Archaeology of Afghanistan: From Earliest Times to the Timurid Period*, ed. F. R. Allchin and N. Hammond (London and New York, 1978), pp. 71–186

C. Jarrige and M. Tosi: 'The Natural Resources of Mundigak: Some Observations on the Location of the Site in Relation to its Economic Space', *South Asian Archaeology, 1979*, ed. H. Härtel (Berlin, 1981), pp. 115–42

V. M. Masson: *Altyn Depe* (Leningrad, 1981); Eng. trans. by H. N. Michael (Philadelphia, 1988)

G. F. Dales: 'Stone Sculpture from the Protohistoric Helmand Civilization, Afghanistan', *Orientalia Iosephi Tucci memoriae dicta*, ii (Rome, 1985), pp. 219–24

P. Amiet: *L'Age des échanges interiraniens, 3500–1700 avant J.-C.* (Paris, 1986)

GREGORY L. POSSEHL

(b) c. *4th–*c. *1st century* BC. The earliest historical sculptural production from the Afghanistan region is remarkably Hellenistic in both style and content. Until the 1960s Greco-Bractrian art was known only from large numbers of coins, as all attempts to locate the Greek cities of the region had been unsuccessful. The discovery of Ai Khanum (Alexandria Oxiana) at the confluence of the Kokcha and Amu (Oxus) rivers and subsequent excavations at the site by the Délégation Archéologique Française en Afghanistan (1965–78) dramatically increased knowledge of the period from 330 to *c.* 100 BC. Apart from a few metalwork pieces (*see* §(iv)(c) below), the most impressive sculptures from Ai Khanum are of limestone or marble.

A hermlike bust of a bearded man (*see* AI KHANUM, fig. 2) from the northern square of the gymnasium is dated archaeologically to Phase II (*c.* 150 BC), although the palaeographic characteristics of the dedicatory inscription point to an earlier date (see Veuve, pls 52–3). Though the bust resembles images of Herakles or the bearded Hermes, the strong individual characterization of the facial features suggests an actual portrait, perhaps of a gymnastic master, a typical Hellenic character.

The largest number of sculptures came from the temple 'à redans' (or 'à niches indentées') and its sanctuary. These sculptures included the colossal left foot of an acrolithic cult image; the unfinished statuette of a naked young athlete that is Lysippan in its posture and treatment of volumes (*see* LYSIPPOS); an unbaked clay female head and a stucco male head from statues that stood on either side of the cella entrance; an unbaked clay mould of a female bust (see Francfort, pl. XVII); and two ivory or bone figurines of an unknown naked goddess, one of which was perhaps a puppet, with movable jointed forearms (see Francfort, pl. V). The naked athlete and foot from the cult image (see Stavisky, pls VIIIb–IXa) are unmistakably Hellenistic in style and typology. The evidence provided by the athlete is particularly important, since the piece is unfinished and therefore certainly a local product. Even the two stucco and clay heads and the female bust are definitely in the Hellenistic tradition, though the treatment of their features, especially the rather heavy chins and eyelids, display local characteristics that survived until *c.* 5th century AD, at such sites as Tepe Sardar (Tapa Sardar) and Tepe Shotor, Hadda. The two ivory goddesses, although presumably derived from Mesopotamian prototypes, appear most closely comparable to Indian examples.

A lion-head gargoyle, perhaps from a fountain in the same sanctuary, is Greek in type but shows such pronounced 'provincial' features that it may be linked stylistically with Gandharan lion heads and protomes (see Francfort, p. 91, pl. XL). Other gargoyles from Ai Khanum are the comedy mask (see Stavisky, pl. IXb) and the dolphin and lion *protomai* that decorated a fountain on the bank of the Amu River (see Leriche and Thoraval, figs 19–21). Although the latter gargoyles more closely resemble Greek prototypes than the lion-head example from the sanctuary, they are certainly local products and not of such a high quality.

The use of ivory in the Greco-Bactrian period was probably much wider than the finds at Ai Khanum indicate. It has also been suggested that the famous rhyta from NISA in Turkmenistan were produced in Greek Bactria or in the Indo-Greek region. Afghanistan at the end of the 1st millennium BC was also greatly receptive to surrounding cultures, and it appears that Indian ivories in the BEGRAM treasure may have been imported into the region during the Greco-Bactrian or Indo-Greek period (*see also* §(c) below and CENTRAL ASIA, §I, 8(iv)).

(c) c. *1st–*c. *3rd century* AD. Only a few sites in Afghanistan are associated with the art production of the Kushana period, but the archaeological potential of the country is too little exploited for the apparent paucity of finds to be meaningful. The underlying culture is naturally Bactrian Greek, but the region certainly remained open to western influences even in the Kushana period, so that the presence of stylistic or iconographic elements of Hellenistic derivation cannot always be explained as Greco-Bactrian art. At the same time the region received ideas (and, in some instances, perhaps even artefacts) from the eastern Gandharan area, where some of the most vital centres of the 'Greco-Buddhist' art were situated: TAXILA, the monasteries of Peshawar, Mardan and Swat (e.g. SHAH-JI-KI-DHERI, SAHRI BAHLOL, BUTKARA). From India came not only new artistic stimuli but also luxury goods destined for customers of high rank. Symbolic of this receptiveness is the treasure from Begram (anc. Kāpishī), north of Kabul, which probably has a terminus date of the 3rd century AD. The hoard includes Indian ivories, Chinese lacquers, Hellenistic bronzes and plaster casts of metalware and Roman glass, which range in date between the 1st century BC and the beginning of the 3rd century AD. The princely owner of the collection seems to have had exquisite artistic interests, for some of the objects, especially the plaster casts (see Hackin and others, figs 274–320), would have had little intrinsic value or worth as status symbols, but great value as models for reproduction, or inspiration for locally manufactured pieces. The most ancient objects of the treasure are almost certainly those from India. It has been suggested that some of the ivories might be the produce of a local Indo-Parthian school. However, although an intermingling of Indian and, to a much lesser extent, Iranian motifs is certainly recognizable in the ivories, it is far more likely that they were all made in an Indian environment (see Hackin and others, figs 1–239). Perhaps the only object really posing a difficult problem of interpretation is the glazed *kinnarī*-shaped askos, the stylistic details of which are purely Indian (presumably of the first half of the 1st century BC), though the technique of glazing definitely refers to the Parthian world (see Hackin and others, figs 241–2).

In the Jalalabad region of eastern Afghanistan, Gandharan sculpture in stone, presumably attributable to the Kushana period, is indistinguishable from the more widely documented Gandharan output of the north-west Indian subcontinent (present-day north-west Pakistan). Dark grey schist reliefs were discovered at HADDA by the Délégation Archéologique Française en Afghanistan (1926–8), but the stratigraphic context and even the precise site provenance (either Tepe Kafariha or Bagh Gai) of the sculptures are unfortunately unknown (see Dagens, Le Berre and Schlumberger, pp. 11–34, pls I–XXI). Hadda is more famous for later stuccowork, but the discovery of this group of schist sculptures is important because it documents a substantial stylistic unity in the regions to the east and west of the Khyber Pass. However, the question of whether the schist sculptures at Hadda were produced locally or were imported from the Peshawar region, as certain circumstances suggest, is still open to debate. It should be noted that the so-called 'toilet trays' that abound in Pakistani sites of the 2nd century BC to at least the 1st century AD are almost completely missing from Afghanistan (*see* INDIAN SUBCONTINENT, §IV, 5(ii)).

It is certain, however, that the few limestone reliefs discovered at Hadda were locally produced, and they do not show any marked differences in style from the schist group. The formal elements taken from the late Hellenistic repertory can be clearly identified, while the architectural structures that frame the scenes are those of the mature phase of Gandharan sculpture. Nor are any stylistic links missing between the limestone reliefs and the stuccowork, even though the latter is mostly attributable to a later period (from the 4th century onwards).

Another more consistent group of schist sculptures was discovered during excavations at Paitava, SHOTORAK and Kham-e Zargar in Kapisa province, north of Kabul. The work from Kapishi is distinguished by a large number of images of the Buddha standing with flames on his shoulders and water flowing from his feet. The iconography has been related to the so-called Miracle of Shravasti (see fig. 6). It has also been suggested that the area was one of localized Iranian influence and was therefore strongly receptive to religious phenomena of a luminous nature. There is, however, no reason to consider a specifically Iranian origin for the iconography, since India provides an equally natural ideological context. Another characteristic element of these sculptures is the high occurrence of stiff, frontal compositions, with figures that stand out against the background of the relief, thus eschewing superimpositions and perspective effects, and suggesting a close link with works belonging to the so-called dynastic art of the Kushanas at SURKH KOTAL, near Pul-i Khumri, Baghlan province (see Schlumberger, Le Berre and Fussman, pls 58–64). This dynastic art is characterized by images of Kushana kings that are absolutely un-Indian from an iconographic point of view but are connected rather with the nomadic tradition of Central Asia whence the dynasty itself originally emerged. Such royal images (Kabul Mus., see Allchin and Hammond, fig. 5.37) have counterparts in the coinage, the Kushana images of MATHURA (Uttar Pradesh, India) and in a few other examples.

6. Schist relief of the Miracle of Shravasti, from Paitava, *c.* 2nd–*c.* 3rd centuries AD (Paris, Musée Guimet)

Stylistic affinities with this 'dynastic' production, confirmed by the frequent presence of figures in 'Kushana' dress, occur in another group of sculptures that are nevertheless wholly Gandharan in their choice of themes and composition. The sculptures comprise greyish limestone reliefs from the temple of Surkh Kotal (almost exclusively architectural elements, see Schlumberger, Le Berre and Fussman, pls 53–5, 66–8), Sham Qala near Baghlan, Chaqalaq Tepe near Kunduz and from other sites in the same region. The same stylistic characteristics and materials are shared by sculptures from beyond the Amu River in present-day Uzbekistan at such sites as AYRTAM, Kara Tepe and Fayaz Tepe (*see* TERMEZ, §2). The small sample of clay sculptures from Surkh Kotal seems to be contemporary with the limestone work, even if it is not really possible to date either category with any precision.

Widely diffused stucco and unbaked clay production, belonging at least in part to the Kushana period, is documented from numerous sites at Hadda (e.g. Tepe Kalan, Tepe Kafariha, Bagh Gai, Tepe Shotor), the site of Lalma, due south of Hadda, and Basawal on the Kabul River east of Jalalabad. At Tepe Sardar near Ghazna there is some stuccowork that perhaps dates to the 3rd century AD. Stucco from Afghanistan, particularly the eastern regions, exhibits the same iconographic and stylistic characteristics as work in the same medium from north-west Pakistan. The narrative scenes tend to disappear and isolated images of the Buddha and *bodhisattvas* predominate, repeated on the walls of the stupas to signify the multiplication of both historical and transcendental Buddhas, a visual expression of the divine experience as professed in the doctrine of Mahayana Buddhism.

Excavations from the 1960s onwards have revealed unbaked clay sculptures, especially at the Buddhist sites of Tepe Sardar, Tepe Maranjan near Kabul and Tepe Shotor II–IV at Hadda. Minor discoveries have also been made at Basawal, Guldara, Bamiyan and DILBERDJIN. Only a part of this production falls within the 2nd and 3rd centuries AD, but some of the early clay sculptures are real masterpieces. The same stylistic tendency already encountered in stucco is also visible in the clay images, but coupled with a genuine revival of the Hellenistic style. The immediate impression is that the Mediterranean 'sources' are more cultured and courtly than those that formed the earlier basis for so many Gandharan images in schist. The Vajrapani–Herakles (see fig. 7) and the Tyche of Niche V2 in the 'Great *Vihāra*' of Tepe Shotor (2nd–3rd century), for example, exhibit the reappearance after many centuries of iconographic types and stylistic forms that seem to have their roots in the Hellenism of the Greco-Bactrian and Indo-Greek kingdoms.

(d) c. *4th*–c. *9th century* AD. The quantity of Gandharan stuccowork, discovered particularly at Hadda in the 1920s,

7. Relief of Vajrapani–Herakles, unbaked clay, Niche V2, Tepe Shotor monastery, Hadda, *c.* 2nd–*c.* 3rd centuries AD

has been studied in detail, but no satisfactory chronological classification has yet been reached. It is, however, generally held that the majority of these stuccos must be later than the 3rd century AD. The fragments of stucco ornamentation, mainly from stupas, depict images of the Buddha, *bodhisattvas* and, more rarely, narrative scenes. The images were made by applying progressively refined layers of plaster to an inner core. Colour applied to surface details is still preserved on many examples.

The earliest phase of stucco production reworked images derived from Hellenistic stylistic prototypes, but there was a simultaneous development towards a greater idealization of the human figure. The Buddha image in particular lost many realistic traits in order to make room for an elegantly balanced play of simplified volumes, but certain subsidiary figures still retained the vivacity of Hellenistic naturalism. Clay images from the Buddhist sites follow the same stylistic trend, but display a greater preference for stylistic conventionalization and are often more 'Indianized'. Meaningful stylistic comparisons can be made with late examples from Taxila and the random collection of heads from Akhnur in Kashmir (see INDIAN SUBCONTINENT, §IV, 6(ii)). A relatively late date for the work is affirmed not only by the archaeological evidence but also by the appearance of many iconographic and stylistic elements reflecting the ideal of serenity that formed the basis of Indian art in the Gupta period: the facial features of the Buddha image, for example, show a strong reduction to geometric forms, in marked contrast to the fluent richness of the drapery.

Some sculptural groups at Tepe Shotor that also seem to belong to this period on the basis of their technical characteristics demonstrate a capacity for stylization of the human figure that anticipates the solutions of successive centuries. In particular, the 'aquatic niche' (?4th century AD), one of the greatest masterpieces of the region, shows a group of figures modelled in the round, including a Buddha (now missing) standing on a lotus flower, against a highly effective and dramatic background of fantastic fish and other aquatic animals amid the eddies of a pool. A date of the 4th–6th century has been suggested for Tepe Shotor V–VII, while the 6th–7th century has been proposed for the few sculptures from Tepe Maranjan. Excavations at SARDAR TEPE, however, tend to confirm that this production of unbaked clay work took place between the 4th and the 6th century.

The Tepe Sardar excavations are also important for showing conclusively that the so-called school of terracotta sculpture of the north-west Indian subcontinent and Afghanistan never existed. The sculptures were always, in origin, unbaked clay, any terracotta characteristics being merely the result of a later conflagration of the entire monument. The Tepe Shotor and Tepe Sardar excavations have also permitted a detailed analysis of the techniques employed in the manufacture of clay sculptures. In certain respects the process was similar to that used for stucco. The clay sculptures were often supported by a wooden framework, were also coloured and, occasionally, perhaps during the 5th and 6th centuries AD, gilded. Decorative details, such as jewellery, architectural motifs, curls of hair, and also the heads of small figures, were produced in moulds and then applied to the sculptures.

The period also marks the beginning of a trend towards gigantism in images of the Buddha. Tepe Sardar, in particular, provides eloquent examples; but the phenomenon was not exclusive to sites in Afghanistan, even if it was destined to become more important there (*see also* ADZHINA TEPE, TAKHT-I-BAHI). Representations of the Buddha increasingly appeared between two or more *bodhisattvas* of smaller size: an iconographic scheme that was perpetuated even in the most complex representations of the next period. Also perhaps assignable to the 4th–6th century AD is the small head of 'plâtre au grain grossier, de qualité médiocre' (i.e. ?stucco, see Hackin, in Carl, Hackin and Meunié, 1959, pp. 19–21, fig. 60) discovered in a monastery near Kunduz, a beautiful example of the working of Hellenistic motifs, which were subsequently destined to merge into more refined solutions such as those at the 7th-century site of Fondukistan. At Qul-i Nader, Kapisa province, some fragments show the use of yet another technique, also seen at Tepe Shotor, of raw earth covered with painted stucco. Fragments of stucco sculpture from Kama Dakka, between Jalalabad and the Pakistani border, perhaps dating from the 6th–7th century, provide possibly the latest evidence for this phase of artistic production in Afghanistan.

In the second half of the 6th century AD, political and military struggles, including the decline of the Hephthalites, undermined the north-west territories of the Indian subcontinent, formerly the heartland of Gandharan architectural and artistic production. Conversely, Kapisa and the Bamiyan region acquired greater importance, due to the opening of a new road, and thus assumed the function of artistic vanguard. The travel diary of the Buddhist Chinese pilgrim Xuanzang gives some idea of the importance of the kingdom of Bamiyan *c.* AD 632. The two colossal images of the Buddha (55 m and 38 m high), sculpted out of the rockface at BAMIYAN and finished in stucco, are without doubt the most famous works in Afghanistan. For a long time it was thought that the 55 m Buddha (considered the younger of the two; see fig. 8) was made between the 5th and 6th centuries, partly because paintings in the surrounding niche recalled subjects also present at Ajanta (*see* INDIAN SUBCONTINENT, §V, 3(i)(a)). The 38 m Buddha was variously thought to date from the 2nd–3rd century or the 4th. A more recent hypothesis suggests that the two Buddhas, whatever the time difference between them, should not be dated much before Xuanzang's visit, i.e. in the second half of the 6th century, for an undertaking of such importance and influence would only be justified after Bamiyan had emerged as a major centre on an important traffic route.

The 7th century was a turning-point in the artistic production of Afghanistan, both architecturally and in sculpture. Tepe Sardar is a typical example: following the destruction of the ancient sanctuary a partial reconstruction took place, using building techniques that are to a certain degree innovative and sculptural decoration that is also new in its conception. Stratigraphical evidence and stylistic comparisons with FONDUKISTAN place the beginning of these activities in the second half of the 7th century, presumably following one of the Arab raids that began shortly after the middle of the century. Both Fondukistan and Tepe Sardar have yielded a remarkable quantity of unbaked clay sculptures of very high quality and distinctive technique: a core of common clay, prepared round a wooden stick or pole, was covered with an outer layer of modelled red clay, on which colour and/or gilding were applied. The sculptures are innovative in both technique and style, though whether there was an actual gap between this phase of production and the sculptures of the earlier period is uncertain. The use of moulded details greatly increased, not only for parts of the jewellery and clothing but also, ever more prevalently, for curls, locks and tresses of hair and for architectural features such as small pilasters and scroll patterns. Moulds were also commonly used for architectural figural decoration, particularly the small atlantids and numerous small Buddha figures in various postures that decorated the unbaked clay stupas and row of 'thrones' along two sides of the main stupa. Stylistically, some patterns drawn from the late Gupta repertory became more flamboyant and the human figures more elongated, the Buddha image being practically the only one occasionally to show an archaizing trend. The sculptural compositions within the niches or chapels are generally more complicated: paradise scenes at Tepe Sardar, for example, comprise colossal images of the Buddha and *bodhisattvas* in the midst of myriad minor figures. Colour increasingly became an integral part of the sculpture. Although only a few fragments preserve their original polychromy (including gilding), both Fondukistan and Tepe Sardar have yielded enough specimens to provide some idea of the original overall effect, which was presumably closer to the strong contrasts of the earliest known works from the Himalayan regions than to the more elementary chromatism of Gandharan stucco and clay examples of the earlier periods.

8. Rock-cut image of the Buddha in a painted niche, h. 55 m, Bamiyan, *c.* 5th–*c.* 6th centuries AD

In the field of Buddhist iconography, besides the ever-increasing importance of representations that can be labelled 'paradise' scenes, there was a greater occurrence, both in sculpture and painting at Tepe Sardar, Fondukistan and Bamiyan, of image types unknown or at least unusual in the earlier period, such as the so-called 'Buddha paré' (bejewelled Buddha; see fig. 9), and the introduction into Buddhism of deities taken from the Hindu pantheon, such as Durga Mahishasuramardini at Tepe Sardar. Colossal images such as the *Parinirvāṇa* Buddha at Tepe Sardar (l. 16 m) were constructed by modelling unbaked clay around a brick core, a technique that continued from the preceding period. As the cores of votive stupas were also brick, it is apparent that the sculptures employed a masonry technique derived from architecture, while architectural structures (chiefly the stupas) were finished using typical modelling techniques. Since the discovery in 1934 of the Surya seated in a chariot from Khair Khana (Kabul Mus.), several marble sculptures have come to the light in Afghanistan, chiefly in the areas of Kabul, Tagao and Gardez, as well as in the North-west Frontier Province of Pakistan. The marble sculptures, while showing affinities with Buddhist clay images from Fondukistan and Tepe Sardar, also exhibit some idiosyncratic features, such as more rigidly conventionalized details of hair and clothing (usually Sasanian in origin), while the subjects represented

9. Painted clay image of the bejewelled Buddha, from Niche D, Fondukistan, late 7th century AD (Paris, Musée Guimet)

belong, almost without exception, to the Hindu and not the Buddhist repertory. Sculptures in this category include a standing Surya, also from Khair Khana, Kabul; the inscribed Umamaheshvara from Tepe Skandar, *c.* 30 km north of Kabul; two images of Durga Mahishasuramardini, one from Gardez (Kabul Mus.), the other known as the 'Scorretti marble' after its former owner (Rome, Pal. Brancaccio); the Ganesha image with an inscription referring to a *Khiṃgāla Uḍḍiyāna Śāhi* from Gardez in the Dargah Temple at Pir Rathan Nath, Kabul; another Ganesha, originally from Shakar Dara, in a Hindu temple in the Shur Bazaar, Kabul; and a third seated on a lion-*vāhana* (vehicle), allegedly from somewhere near Tagao, an area from which other cognate sculptures have also been found.

It has been convincingly suggested that this group of sculptures should be assigned to the period of the Turki Shahi dynasty (7th–8th century AD), while the closely linked marble sculptures primarily from the area of Hund, Pakistan, should be dated later (9th–10th century). It is interesting to observe that the Ghazna area appears to have remained outside the boundaries of this politico-cultural entity, for no Turki Shahi coins were found at Tepe Sardar, nor have any marble sculptures been reported from the region apart from the Brahma stele in the palace of the Ghaznavid ruler Mas'ud III (*reg* 1099–1115) and the Jaina stele (Kabul Mus.), presumably from the same site, which were taken as war booty from elsewhere. The production of these sculptures apparently came to an abrupt end during the 9th century, perhaps with the conquest of Ghazna by the Saffarid Ya'qub b. Layth in 869–70. As the heads from Akhnur were the eastern counterparts of the earlier clay sculptures from such sites as Tepe Sardar and Tepe Maranjan, so also do fragments from Ushkar, again in Kashmir, provide the closest comparisons for the later works from Afghanistan. The stylistic and iconographic elaborations that took place both in the 4th–5th and the 7th–8th centuries in Afghanistan were, moreover, of great importance for contemporary and later developments in Central Asia and China.

See also CENTRAL ASIA, §§I, 3(iii) and II, 3.

BIBLIOGRAPHY

GENERAL

D. Schlumberger: 'Les Descendants non-méditerranées de l'art grec', *Syria*, xxxvii (1960), pp. 131–66, 254–318
J. M. Rosenfield: *The Dynastic Arts of the Kushans* (Berkeley, 1967)
M. Hallade: *The Gandhara Style and the Evolution of Buddhist Art* (London, 1968)
D. Schlumberger: *L'Orient hellénisé* (Paris, 1970)
B. Rowland: *The Art of Central Asia* (New York, 1974)
S. Gaulier, R. Jera-Bezard and M. Maillard: *Buddhism in Afghanistan and Central Asia*, 2 vols, Iconography of Religions, xiii/14 (Leiden, 1976)
B. Y. Stavisky: *Kushanskaya Baktriya: Problemy istorii i kul'tury* (Moscow, 1977); Fr. trans. as *La Bactriane sous les Kushans: Problèmes d'histoire et de culture* (Paris, 1986)
G. A. Pugachenkova: *Iskusstvo Baktriy epokhi Kushan* [The art of Bactria in the Kushana period] (Moscow, 1979)
B. Stawiski: *Mittelasien: Kunst der Kuschan* (Leipzig, 1979)
S. L. Huntington and J. C. Huntington: *The Art of Ancient India: Buddhist, Hindu, Jain* (New York and Tokyo, 1985), pp. 125–62
L. Nehru: *Origins of the Gandhāran Style: A Study of Contributory Influences* (New Delhi, 1989)
S. Kuwayama: *Kāpishī–Gandāra shi kenkyū* [Studies in the history of Kāpishī–Gandhāra] (Kyoto, 1990)

ARCHAEOLOGICAL REPORTS

J. Barthoux: *Les Fouilles de Haḍḍa, III: Figures et figurines*, Mém.: Dél. Archéol. Fr. Afghanistan, vi (Paris and Brussels, 1930)
J. Hackin and others: *Nouvelles recherches archéologiques à Begram (ancienne Kâpicî), 1939–1940*, 2 vols, Mém.: Dél. Archéol. Fr. Afghanistan, xi (Paris, 1954)
J. Hackin, J. Carl and J. Meunié: *Diverses recherches archéologiques en Afghanistan, 1933–1940*, Mém.: Dél. Archéol. Fr. Afghanistan, xiii (Paris, 1959)
B. Dagens, M. Le Berre and D. Schlumberger: *Monuments préislamiques d'Afghanistan*, Mém.: Dél. Archéol. Fr. Afghanistan, xix (Paris, 1964)
S. Mustamandi and M. Mustamandi: 'The Excavation of the Afghan Archaeological Mission in Kapisa', *Afghanistan Q.*, xxi/4 (1968), pp. 67–79
P. Bernard: 'Quatrième campagne de fouilles à Aï Khanoum (Bactriane)', *Acad. Inscr. & B.-Lett.: C. R. Séances* (1969), pp. 313–55
M. Mustamandi and S. Mustamandi: 'Nouvelles fouilles à Haḍḍa (1966–1967) par l'Institut afghan d'archéologie', *A. Asiatiques*, xix (1969), pp. 15–36
P. Bernard: 'Fouilles de Aï Khanoum (Afghanistan): Campagnes de 1972 et 1973', *Acad. Inscr. & B.-Lett.: C. R. Séances* (1974), pp. 280–308
G. Fussman: 'Nouvelle découverte à Bamiyan', *Afghanistan Q.*, xxvii/2 (1974), pp. 57–78
P. Bernard: 'Campagne de fouilles 1975 à Aï Khanoum (Afghanistan)', *Acad. Inscr. & B.-Lett.: C. R. Séances* (1976), pp. 287–322
P. Leriche and J. Thoraval: 'La Fontaine du rempart de l'Oxus à Aï Khanoum', *Syria*, lvi (1979), pp. 170–205
V. M. Sokolovsky: 'Rekonstruktsiya dvukh skul'pturnykh izobrazheniy iz Dil'berdzhina (raskop X)' [A reconstruction of two sculptural images from Dilberdjin (excavation 10)], *Materialy sovetsko-afganskoy arkheologicheskoy ekspeditsii* [Findings of the Soviet-Afghan archaeological expedition], ii of *Drevnyaya Baktriya* [Ancient Bactria] (Moscow, 1979), pp. 113–19
D. Schlumberger, M. Le Berre and G. Fussman: *Surkh Kotal en Bactriane, I: Les Temples, architecture, sculpture, inscriptions*, 2 vols, Mém.: Dél. Archéol. Fr. Afghanistan, xxv (Paris, 1983)
H.-P. Francfort: *Le Sanctuaire du temple à niches indentées, II: Les Trouvailles*, Mém.: Dél. Archéol. Fr. Afghanistan, xxvii (1984), iii of *Fouilles d'Aï Khanum* (Paris, 1973–92)
M. Taddei and G. Verardi: 'Clay Stūpas and Thrones at Tapa Sardār, Ghazni', *Zinbun*, xx (1985), pp. 17–32

S. Veuve: *Le Gymnase: Architecture, céramique, sculpture*, Mém.: Dél. Archéol. Fr. Afghanistan, xxx (1987), vi of *Fouilles d'Aï Khanum* (Paris, 1973–92)

Z. Tarzi: 'Tapa-e-Top-e-Kalān (TTK) of Haḍḍa', *South Asian Archaeology, 1987*, ed. M. Taddei (Rome, 1990), pp. 707–26

——: *Haḍḍa à la lumière des fouilles afghanes de Tapa-é-Shotor et Tapa-é-Top-é-Kalan* (diss., U. Strasbourg II, 1991)

SPECIALIST STUDIES

J. Hackin: 'Sculptures gréco-bouddhiques du Kapiça', *Mnmts Piot*, xxviii (1925–6), pp. 35–44

A. C. Soper: 'Aspects of Light Symbolism in Gandharan Sculpture', *Artibus Asiae*, xii (1949), pp. 252–83, 314–30; xiii (1950), pp. 63–85

K. Fischer: 'Gandharan Sculptures from Qunduz and Environs', *Artibus Asiae*, xxi (1958), pp. 231–49

S. Kuwayama: 'The Turki Śāhis and Relevant Brahmanical Sculptures in Afghanistan', *E. & W.*, xxvi (1976), pp. 375–407

M. M. Rhie: 'Some Aspects of the Relation of 5th-century Chinese Buddha Images with Sculpture from N. India, Pakistan, Afghanistan and Central Asia', *E. & W.*, xxvi (1976), pp. 439–61

G. Verardi: 'Gaṇeśa Seated on Lion: A New Śāhi Marble', *E. & W.*, xxvii (1977), pp. 277–83

P. Bernard and F. Grenet: 'Découverte d'une statue du dieu solaire Surya dans la région de Caboul', *Stud. Iran.*, x (1981), pp. 128–46

M. Taddei and G. Verardi: 'Buddhist Sculptures from Tapa Sardâr, Ghazni', *Parola Passato*, cxcix (1981), pp. 251–66

G. Verardi: 'Osservazioni sulla coroplastica di epoca kuṣāṇa nel nord-ovest e in Afghanistan in relazione al materiale di Tapa Sardâr', *AION*, xliii (1983), pp. 479–504

——: 'The Kuṣāṇa Emperors as *Cakravartins*: Dynastic Art and Cults in India and Central Asia, History of a Theory, Clarifications and Refutations', *E. & W.*, xliii (1983), pp. 225–94

C. Mustamandy: 'Herakles, Ahnherr Alexanders, in einer Plastik aus Hadda', *Aus dem Osten des Alexanderreiches*, ed. J. Ozols and V. Thewalt (Cologne, 1984), pp. 176–80

M. Taddei: 'Neue Forschungsbelege zur Gandhāra-Ikonographie', *Aus dem Osten des Alexanderreiches*, ed. J. Ozols and V. Thewalt (Cologne, 1984), pp. 154–75

K. Tanabe: 'Iranian Origin of the Gandharan Buddha and Bodhisattva Images', *Bull. Anc. Orient Mus.*, vi (1984), pp. 1–27

G. Verardi: 'Gandharan Imagery at Tapa Sardâr', *South Asian Archaeology, 1981*, ed. B. Allchin (Cambridge, 1984), pp. 257–62

Z. Tarzi: 'La Technique du modelage en argile en Asie centrale et au nord-ouest de l'Inde sur les Kouchans: La Continuité malgré les ruptures', *Ktema*, xi (1986), pp. 57–93

S. Kuwayama: 'Literary Evidence for Dating the Colossi in Bāmiyān', *Orientalia Iosephi Tucci memoriae dicata*, ii, ed. G. Gnoli and L. Lanciotti (Rome, 1987), pp. 703–27

D. Klimburg-Salter: 'Bāmiyān: Recent Research', *E. & W.*, xxxviii (1988), pp. 305–12

M. M. Rhie: 'Interrelationships between the Buddhist Art of China and the Art of India and Central Asia from 618–755 AD', *AION*, suppl. no. liv (1988)

D. Klimburg-Salter: *The Kingdom of Bāmiyān: Buddhist Art and Culture of the Hindu Kush* (Naples, 1989)

S. Kuwayama: 'L'Inscription du Gaṇeśa de Gardez et la chronologie des Turki-Ṣāhīs', *J. Asiat.*, cclxxix (1991), pp. 267–87

M. Taddei: 'The Bejewelled Buddha and the Mahiṣāsuramardinī: Religion and Political Ideology in Pre-Muslim Afghanistan', *South Asian Archaeology, 1989*, ed. C. Jarrige (Madison, 1992), pp. 457–64

——: 'La plastica buddhistica in argilla in Afghanistan e nel nordovest del subcontinente indiano', *Oxus: Tesori dell'Asia Centrale* (exh. cat., Rome, Pal. Venezia, 1993–4), pp. 118–22

For further bibliography *see* §§(i) above and (iii) below.

(iii) Painting. Apart from a few remnants of the Greco-Bactrian period (*c.* 4th–*c.* 1st century BC), most of the evidence for painting in Afghanistan dates from the 3rd century AD onwards and comes from the sites of Hadda and Bamiyan. The medium used throughout is tempera. A large proportion of the paintings at Bamiyan was retained *in situ*; unless otherwise specified, the remaining finds were placed in the Kabul Museum. Following the bombing of the museum in 1993, their fate is uncertain.

(a) *c.* 4th–*c.* 1st century BC. (b) *c.* 1st–*c.* 5th century AD. (c) *c.* 6th–*c.* 9th century AD.

(a) c. 4th–c. 1st century BC. The excavations at Ai Khanum, so rich in architecture and sculpture, provide little direct evidence of figural painting. There is, however, clear evidence that the technique of painting was extensively used. Several architectural pieces, mostly from Rooms 6 and 9 of the Administrative Quarter's southern complex (mid-2nd century BC), still preserve traces of paint on their whitewashed stone surfaces. These traces show that heart-and-dart motifs were painted on mouldings and different artists' 'hands' are even recognizable (see e.g. Bernard and others, i, pl. 80). Another precious relic of painting, found in the sanctuary of the temple 'à niches indentées' (or 'temple à redans') at Ai Khanum, is attributed to the earliest phase of the city (4th century BC). The few fragments of painted canvas, pasted on a wooden frame (a typical Greek technique), depict a frieze of walking lions that presumably constituted the background scene for a cult image.

More substantial evidence of painting in Afghanistan only occurs at the end of the Greco-Bactrian period. Flanking either side of the entrance to the 'temple of the Dioscuri' at DILBERDJIN, north of the Hindu Kush, are the remains of a two-tiered wall painting defined at the bottom by a band of Greek fretwork. The scene depicts two naked young men, one on either side of the door and each accompanied by a horse. The painting, identified by its excavators as a representation of the Dioscuri, belongs to the first phase of the sanctuary (founded *c.* 150 BC), though it is not necessarily contemporary with the period of construction of the temple. The painting is in a very poor state of preservation; nevertheless it is apparent even from the published line drawings and watercolours that the painter's cultural background was intensely Greek. According to the excavation reports, the Dioscuri remained visible during the second phase of the sanctuary (dated to the period of Kujula Kadphises, 1st century AD) but were immured behind a new wall during the third phase (period of Kanishka, *c.* late 1st century to early 2nd). This important point suggests that the Greek religious tradition was not abandoned in this part of the Kushana empire until the time of Kanishka. There is no reason to think of a Vedic connection (the Ashvins) for the two young heroes. The painting technique consisted of the preparation of a loess surface, a sketch of the whole composition in diluted red colour, the use of a comparatively poor range of colours (no blue or green pigments) without chiaroscuro and finally the outlining of the faces and naked bodies in black or brown.

(b) c. 1st–c. 5th century AD. Afghanistan has yielded a fairly large number of wall paintings of the Kushana period. Close stylistic and technical comparisons are possible between these examples and other specimens found in Pakistan and north of the Amu River, for example at Kara Tepe. Although dating the various paintings is extremely difficult, all these remains bear witness to a highly sophisticated technique, and it is clear that the use of painting was far from exceptional in this period.

If the use of colour on stucco sculpture is not taken into consideration, painting of the Kushana period at

Buddhist sites is only known from very poorly preserved fragments at Hadda. Some examples in *Vihāra* B. 56 at Bagh Gai, Hadda, were ochre sketches that were never completed: the most impressive is a representation of the story of Angulimala, which follows the same iconographic models employed by Gandharan artists in stone reliefs. Another sketch in ochre of a moustached head was found on a stupa at Tepe Shotor, Hadda, in 1966–7. A niche from Tepe Kalan (TK.17; Paris, Mus. Guimet) is a good example of symbiosis of sculpture and painting: a modelled Buddha image is flanked by painted images of donors and surmounted by winged cupids who hold a wreath above his head. The typically Greco-Roman iconography, somewhat reminiscent of 3rd-century AD painting at Palmyra, underwent what might be called a Buddhist interpretation: a certain parallelism is noticeable in the paintings from MIRAN, Chinese Turkestan, which are also attributed to the 3rd century.

In the 'temple of the Dioscuri' at Dilberdjin a painting belonging to the fourth period of the sanctuary depicts a standing, high-ranking official beside a divine pair seated on a crouching bull. Since the male divine figure is ithyphallic, the pair can be identified as Shiva and his spouse Parvati. Though it is often doubtful whether this and other 'Hindu' images from Central Asia and Afghanistan (e.g. the Durga Mahishamardini figure at Tepe Sardar) should actually be interpreted as purely Hindu subjects, the derivation from an Indian iconographic model is clear and suggests a date for the painting not earlier than the 4th century AD, though the excavators attribute it to the time of Vasudeva I (3rd century). The painting technique differs from that of the Dioscuri, particularly since it includes the use of chiaroscuro in drapery and perhaps also in the naked parts of the human bodies.

The later north-east religious complex at Dilberdjin contained three rooms with important remains of wall paintings. The painting technique is closer to that of the wall paintings from Central Asia and of the contemporary sites in Afghanistan (e.g. Bamiyan, FONDUKISTAN, Tepe Sardar) insofar as the preparation of the mud-plaster coating and whitewash are concerned. The colour range includes lapis lazuli blue, which also occurs in the Shiva and Parvati painting in the 'temple of Dioscuri'.

The most problematic painting, in Room 12 of the complex, depicts a helmeted character between attendant figures (see fig. 10). It has been suggested that the main figure, seated front view with knees apart in a posture strongly reminiscent of the iconography of Sasanian kings, is a victorious 'hero' to whom homage is paid, but others have labelled this character a 'goddess'. Though the excavators suggest that Dilberdjin was abandoned immediately after the Hephthalite invasion in the 5th century AD, the helmeted figure may be attributed to the 6th–7th century or, if compared with the *bodhisattva* Maitreya in the soffit of Cave K3 at Bamiyan, late 7th century, or even, if compared with Maitreya in the soffit of Niche E at Bamiyan, dated to the 8th century.

(c) c. *6th–*c. *9th century* AD. A discovery in 1976 at Tepe Shotor, Hadda, provided the first impressive document of Buddhist painting south of the Hindu Kush: in a meditation cave at the site, ten disciples of the Buddha are shown seated cross-legged on either side of a skeleton (see fig. 11). The exact meaning of this representation is unclear, though the presence in the scroll frieze below the monks of what appear to be floral elements resembling phalli, seems to suggest a Tantric reading of the whole composition. The style can still be placed in the Greco-Buddhist tradition that gave rise to such compositions as the Buddha with monks and trees from Kara Tepe (Uzbekistan; *see* CENTRAL ASIA, fig. 28), attributed to the 2nd–3rd century. The scroll frieze is also very 'Hellenistic' in its free naturalism; nevertheless many details show signs of evolution: the heads are comparatively smaller, the drapery more elaborate, the faces less naturalistic and the shape of the eyes reminiscent of late works such as the manuscript covers from Gilgit (Pakistan). The archaeological evidence confirms a 6th-century date.

In the 6th century AD there was a westward shift of the main roads connecting India to Central Asia. The importance of the sites in Gandhara declined while those in the Hindu Kush flourished. The main archaeological centre in the Hindu Kush is Bamiyan, with four minor centres:

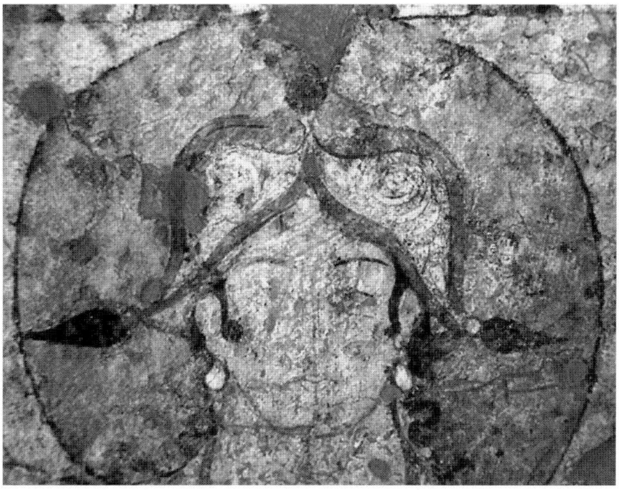

10. Wall painting (fragment) of a helmeted figure between attendants, from Room 12, Dilberdjin, *c.* 5th century AD or later (Kabul, Kabul Museum)

11. Wall painting of disciples of the Buddha flanking a skeleton, from meditation cave, Tepe Shotor, Hadda, *c.* 6th century AD

12. Wall painting (fragment) of seated Buddha images, from Cave K.10, Kakrak, *c.* late 7th century AD–*c.* early 8th (Paris, Musée Guimet)

Foladi and Kakrak, quite close to Bamiyan, Fondukistan, *c.* 130 km to the east, and Nigar (Dukhtar-i Nushirwan) to the north beyond the Kara Kotal Pass in the direction of Haibak (Samangan). Both Bamiyan and Fondukistan were investigated by the Délégation Archéologique Française en Afghanistan. In the 1960s and 1970s the wall paintings at Bamiyan were surveyed by scholars chiefly from Afghanistan and Japan and extensively restored by an Indian team.

The chronology of Bamiyan has often been the subject of controversy, also in connection with the formative process of various styles of painting, such as Gandharan, Syrian, Iranian (chiefly Sasanian) and Indian (Gupta). The early dating (Kushana period to the 4th–5th century AD) for the colossal Buddhas has now been abandoned, and most scholars are inclined to believe that neither image is earlier than the second half of the 6th century (*see* §(ii)(d) above). The paintings decorating their huge niches cannot therefore be any earlier in date. Research (see Klimburg-Salter, 1989) suggests the following working hypotheses: firstly, that the art of the Hindu Kush belongs to a single cultural period (7th–9th century); secondly, that it probably resulted from a consistent form of patronage; and thirdly, that the formal development indicates a possible movement towards a later Mahayana perspective.

The painting technique is common to Buddhist sites throughout Afghanistan and Central Asia. Like the wall paintings in India, those from Bamiyan and other sites in Afghanistan are not frescoes (as they are often unduly styled even in scientific literature), but rather tempera paintings. The wall surface first received a dressing of clay mixed with vegetable fibres (*kâhgel*), which functionally corresponds to the *arriccio* of the Italian medieval and later wall paintings. This dressing was coated with a thin white ground layer of burnt gypsum or plaster of Paris, on which the pigments were directly applied in a binding of animal glue. At other sites, such as Tepe Sardar, the ground layer was made of clay mixed with fibres obtained from the inflorescences of a kind of marsh reed (*simgel*); at DUNHUANG kaolin was employed for the same purpose.

A chronological classification of the wall paintings in the Hindu Kush has been attempted (see Klimburg-Salter, 1989) on the basis of style (morphology and representational conventions) and iconography. Phase Ia (mid- to second half of 7th century AD) is represented by paintings in the niche of the 38 m Buddha of Bamiyan; Phase Ib (*c.* second half of the 7th century) by the niche of the 55 m Buddha; Phase IIa–b (late 7th century–early 8th) by Bamiyan Cave K, Niches H and 'i', Fondukistan and Kakrak (see fig. 12); Phase IIc–d (8th century or later) by Bamiyan Niche E and Foladi.

Phase Ia appears to be linked to the 7th-century AD Sogdian paintings at PENDZHIKENT (*see also* CENTRAL ASIA, §I, 4(iv)(a)). Compositions are rather two-dimensional: there is no indication of shading and contours are obtained by using bands of colour separated by brown or black lines. Phase Ib, though essentially a linear style, is richer in shading and sometimes, at least in some subjects, even reflects conventions elaborated at Ajanta in India (*see* INDIAN SUBCONTINENT, §V, 3(i)(a)), though the most significant parallels are with the art of KIZIL and KHOTAN in Chinese Turkestan (*see also* CENTRAL ASIA, §II, 4(ii)(b)).

Phase II can be considered as the typical Bamiyan style, with such clear links with eastern Central Asia, especially Kizil and Kucha, as to suggest that after the Chinese invasion of Kucha *c.* AD 647, painters from there migrated to Bamiyan. The concurrent Chinese conquest of Kizil (647–8), the subsequent Tibetan conquest and Chinese reconquest perhaps also induced Kizil artists to flee their former large, cosmopolitan and free town. The tendency in Phase II is towards a high conventionalization of forms that abandons all interest in realism and develops into a somewhat linear elegance reminiscent of contemporary sculpture at Fondukistan. Characteristic features are thin double lines employed to define drapery, a swirl under the arms, and the use of contrasting black and white figures. At the end of the development, the human form is reduced to diagrammatic patterns.

Among the most interesting compositions at Bamiyan is one in the niche of the 38 m Buddha, which represents a *Pañcavārṣika* ceremony (as described by the Chinese Buddhist pilgrim Xuanzang in about AD 632), at precisely the point when the king presents the Buddha with all his worldly possessions. The ideological value of this ceremony is highly significant for understanding the role assumed by the kings of Bamiyan and the relationship between political and religious power. In the vault of the same niche a solar deity (possibly Surya) is also depicted.

The *Parinirvāṇa* in Cave K3, although poorly preserved, is one of the most impressive representations of this central scene of Buddhist devotion, with an abundance of detail that makes it and the companion painting in the soffit of Maitreya encircled by fifteen roundels, each containing six Buddhas, a rich source of information concerning jewellery, metalwork and (royal) garments (see Tarzi, figs 3–4, 6–12). Presumably the *Parinirvāṇa* was a 'reproduction' of the colossal reclining Buddha *c.* 300 m long that Xuanzang saw at Bamiyan (see Tarzi). The other *Parinirvāṇa* scenes at Bamiyan (Caves F, J and 222; see Miyaji, 1978) are not so rich or complicated and are rather reminiscent of traditional Gandharan representations of the same episode.

The remains of painting from more minor sites include the 'hunter king' in Sasanian style from Kakrak (Kabul Mus.) and the seated *bodhisattva* Maitreya from Niche E at Fondukistan. The Maitreya, together with a considerable number of modelled sculptures in unbaked clay in the same sanctuary, provide one of the most reliable links between sculpture and painting in the Hindu Kush region.

Various sites in other parts of Afghanistan preserve the remains of wall paintings. Those found by the Archaeological Mission of Kyoto University in Cave 130 at Basawal near Jalalabad depict a row of pairs of Buddhas facing each other. A similar setting is found in a painting excavated by the Italian Archaeological Mission in Room 52 at Tepe Sardar, Ghazna, where a row of alternating Buddhas and richly bejewelled *bodhisattvas* is perhaps intended to represent the revelation of Buddhas to *bodhisattvas*. Stylistically, these and other wall paintings from Tepe Sardar are close to those from Fondukistan, but comparisons are also possible with Khotan, Kizil and Pendzhikent. A dating in the 8th century AD seems quite reasonable.

The painting of pre-Muslim Afghanistan and Iran, even after the sanctuaries had been abandoned or (more rarely) destroyed, had a great impact on both art and literature of the subsequent period. At the end of the 10th century, the anonymous *Ḥudūd al-ʿālam* refers to the existence at Bamiyan of wall paintings 'in the Indian style' (see Melikian-Chirvani, p. 23). Even in the 13th century, Arab travellers still showed a lively interest in Bamiyan and its paintings: a description by Yaqut, of wall paintings depicting birds and other animals, is copied from an earlier account written by Samʿani in the mid-11th century (see Melikian-Chirvani, pp. 25–6).

BIBLIOGRAPHY

A. Godard, Y. Godard and J. Hackin: *Les Antiquités bouddhiques de Bāmiyān*, Mém.: Dél. Archéol. Fr. Afghanistan, ii (Paris, 1928)

J. Hackin and J. Carl: *Nouvelles recherches archéologiques à Bāmiyān*, Mém.: Dél. Archéol. Fr. Afghanistan, iii (Paris, 1933)

R. Gettens: 'Materials in the Wall Paintings of Bāmiyān, Afghanistan', *Tech. Stud.*, vi (Jan 1938), pp. 186–93

B. Rowland and A. Coomaraswamy: *The Wall Paintings of India, Central Asia and Ceylon* (Boston, 1938)

J. Hackin: 'Le Monastère bouddhique de Fondukistân: Fouilles de J. Carl, 1937', in J. Hackin, J. Carl and J. Meunié: *Diverses recherches archéologiques en Afghanistan, 1933–1940*, Mém.: Dél. Archéol. Fr. Afghanistan, xiii (Paris, 1959), pp. 49–58

U. Scerrato: 'A Short Note on Some Recently Discovered Buddhist Grottoes near Bāmiyān', *E. & W.*, xi (1960), pp. 94–120

K. Yamasaki: 'Saiiki hekiga no ganryo ni tsuite' [Pigments in the wall paintings of Central Asia], *Bijutsu Kenkyū*, 212 (1960), pp. 31–3

M. Bussagli: *Painting of Central Asia* (Geneva, 1963)

B. Dagens: 'Monastères rupestres de la vallée de Foladi', in B. Dagens, M. Le Berre and D. Schlumberger: *Monuments préislamiques d'Afghanistan*, Mém.: Dél. Archéol. Fr. Afghanistan, xix (1964), pp. 41–8

P. Bernard and others: *Fouilles d'Aï Khanoum, I: Campagnes 1965, 1966, 1967, 1968*, 2 vols, Mém.: Dél. Archéol. Fr. Afghanistan, xxi (Paris, 1973)

A. S. Melikian-Chirvani: 'L'Evocation littéraire du bouddhisme dans l'Iran musulman', *Monde Iran. & Islam*, ii (1974), pp. 1–72

V. P. Buryzh: 'Tekhnika zhivopisi' [Painting technique], *Materialy sovetsko–afganskoy ekspeditsiy, 1969–1973 gg.* [Findings of the Soviet–Afghan expedition], i of *Drevnyaya Baktriya* [Ancient Bactria] (Moscow, 1976), pp. 111–24

I. T. Kruglikova: 'Nastennye rospisi Dil'berdzhina' [The wall paintings of Dilberdjin], *Materialy sovetsko–afganskoy ekspeditsiy, 1969–1973 gg.* [Findings of the Soviet–Afghan expedition], i of *Drevnyaya Baktriya* [Ancient Bactria] (Moscow, 1976), pp. 87–110

A. Miyaji: 'Wall Paintings of Bāmiyān: A Stylistic Analysis', *Japan–Afghanistan Joint Archaeological Survey in 1974* (Kyoto, 1976), pp. 17–31

S. Sengupta: 'Preservation and Conservation of Bamiyan', *Bamiyan: Crossroads of Culture*, ed. A. Miyaji (Tokyo, 1976), pp. 9–15

A. Miyaji: 'The Parinirvāṇa Scenes of Bāmiyān: An Iconographical Analysis', *Japan–Afghanistan Joint Archaeological Survey in 1976* (Kyoto, 1978), pp. 13–22

P. Bernard and H.-P. Francfort: 'Nouvelles découvertes dans la Bactriane afghane', *AION*, xxxix (1979), pp. 119–48

V. P. Buryzh: 'Tekhnika rospisey pomeshcheniya 16' [The technique of the paintings of site 16], *Materialy sovetsko–afganskoy arkheologicheskoy ekspeditsiy* [Findings of the Soviet–Afghan archaeological expedition], ii of *Drevnyaya Baktriya* [Ancient Bactria] (Moscow, 1979), pp. 146–65

I. T. Kruglikova: 'Nastennye rospisi v pomeshcheniy 16 severo-vostochnogo kul'tovogo kompleksa Dil'berdzhina' [The wall paintings of site 16 at the north-eastern cultic complex of Dilberdjin], *Materialy sovetsko–afganskoy arkheologicheskoy ekspeditsiy* [Findings of the Soviet–Afghan archaeological expedition], ii of *Drevnyaya Baktriya* [Ancient Bactria] (Moscow, 1979), pp. 120–45

Z. M. Zhelninskaya and others: 'Analisy krasok nastennykh rospisey Dil'berdzhina' [An analysis of the colours of the wall paintings of Dilberdjin], *Materialy sovetsko–afganskoy arkheologicheskoy ekspeditsiy* [Findings of the Soviet–Afghan archaeological expedition], ii of *Drevnyaya Baktriya* [Ancient Bactria] (Moscow, 1979), pp. 166–72

A. Miyaji: 'The Wall Paintings of Bamiyan Caves (Continued): Stylistic Analysis', *Japan–Afghanistan Joint Archaeological Survey in 1978* (Kyoto, 1980), pp. 16–26

D. Klimburg-Salter: 'Ritual as Interaction at Bamiyan', *Systems of Communication and Interaction in South Asia*, ed. P. Gaeffke and S. Oleksiw (Philadelphia, 1981), pp. 65–9

C. Silvi Antonini and M. Taddei: 'Wall Paintings from Tapa Sardār, Ghaznī', *South Asian Archaeology, 1979*, ed. H. Härtel (Berlin, 1981), pp. 429–38

D. E. Klimburg-Salter, ed.: *The Silk Route and the Diamond Path: Esoteric Buddhist Art on the Trans-Himalayan Trade Routes* (Los Angeles, 1982)

Z. Tarzi: 'La Grotte K3 de Bâmiyân', *Arts Asiatiques*, xxxviii (1983), pp. 20–29

I. T. Kruglikova: *Dil'berdzhin: Khram Dioskurov* [Dilberdjin: the temple of the Dioscuri] (Moscow, 1986)

F. Grenet: 'L'Athéna de Dil'berdžin', *Cultes et monuments religieux dans l'Asie centrale préislamique*, ed. F. Grenet (Paris, 1987), pp. 41–5

D. Klimburg-Salter: 'Dukhtar-i Nushirwan: An Ideology of Kingship', *Kusumañjali: Sh. C. Sivaramamurti Commemoration Volume*, i, ed. N. Rao (New Delhi, 1987), pp. 62–76

——: *The Kingdom of Bāmiyān: Buddhist Art and Culture of the Hindu Kush* (Naples, 1989) [with app. on conservation by R. Sengupta]

M. Mode: 'The Great God of Dokhtar-e Noshirwān (Nigār)', *E. & W.*, xlii (1992), pp. 473–83

For further bibliography *see* §§(i) and (ii) above.

MAURIZIO TADDEI

(iv) Other arts.

(a) Coins. (b) Jewellery. (c) Metalwork. (d) Pottery.

(a) Coins. The official coinage of the Achaemenid (*see* ACHAEMENID, §2) period (550–331 BC) was the Persian gold Daric and silver siglos based on a gold:silver ratio of 13.3 to 1, but these coins are rarely found in Afghanistan (*see* ANCIENT NEAR EAST, §II, 8(i)). Normal currency during the 4th century BC consisted of worn Greek silver coins and their copies. The earliest of these coins had been exported from Athens and other cities of the Greek world as bullion. The hoard discovered in 1966 at Balkh comprised 170 old Greek silver coins of this category, 150 Athenian tetradrachms and coins from 13 other Greek states down to *c.* 380 BC. The group of Greek coins in the OXUS TREASURE had a similar composition. The 1933

13. Silver tetradrachm of Demetrios I of Bactria, obverse showing the king wearing an elephant headdress, diam. 33 mm, issued *c.* 200–*c.* 190 BC (London, British Museum); the reverse shows Herakles

hoard from Chaman-i-Hazuri, Kabul, dating from the mid-4th century BC, contained worn Greek silver with subsidiary denominations of bent bar silver coins weighing *c.* 11.7 gm and punch-marked silver (see Curiel and Schlumberger, pp. 31–45). Other hoards of similar bent bar silver coins with a wheel or sun symbol at each end of the bar have been found at Jalalabad and at Mir Zakah near Gardez (see Curiel and Schlumberger, pp. 65–91), as well as at sites in the Indus Valley such as TAXILA. Double the weight of a silver siglos and possibly derived from the bar coinage of Media, they appear to have constituted the silver coinage of the Achaemenid satrapies in north-west India before the invasion of Alexander the Great in 331 BC.

The fine coinage bearing the head of Herakles that Alexander issued was apparently based on a gold:silver ratio of 10 to 1. Another major change was the introduction of an Attic weight silver tetradrachm tariffed at 20 drachmae per gold stater that ensured the circulation of the new silver issues throughout the east as coins, not bullion. After Alexander's death in 323 BC, Bactria, as a Seleucid province, had a typically Hellenistic coinage with fine obverse portraits of the kings in gold and silver. The Greco-Bactrian kings who subsequently governed Bactria as an independent state after about 250 BC inherited this tradition. The tetradrachms of the first ruler Diodotos and his successor Eukhydemos are well engraved and show the king with a diadem. Demetrios, who invaded India in the early 2nd century BC, is shown with an elephant headdress (see fig. 13). Antimachos Theos is depicted with a Greek travelling cap (*petasos*) and Eucratides with a helmet. The reverse types of the coins show Greek divinities such as Zeus, Herakles, Artemis and the Dioscuri.

South-east Afghanistan was initially part of the Mauryan empire and used the Mauryan square silver punch-marked coinage and square copper coins. When the Greeks extended their rule to the south (*c.* 180 BC), they struck a distinctive coinage incorporating features from the existing Mauryan currency for their new Indian provinces. Pantaleon, Agathokles and their successors struck square copper coins with a reverse legend, initially in Brahmi and subsequently in Kharoshthi, which repeated the information given on the Greek obverse. Apollodotos I issued square silver drachms modelled on the Mauryan silver denomination, and all the Greek rulers of the regions south of the Hindu Kush struck a bilingual silver coinage on the reduced Indian weight standard. More than 80,000 coins collected in the 1830s by Charles Masson (*see* §III below) at BEGRAM, 60 km north of Kabul, and the hoard found in 1947 at Mir Zakah, 73 km north-east of Gardez, provide excellent evidence for the currency of this period in these regions. The Yueh-chih successors to the Greeks in Bactria from *c.* 130 BC onwards struck crude copies in base metal of the tetradrachms of Heliokles, the last Greco-Bactrian king, while the invaders of the Kabul Valley struck increasingly crude copies in copper of Hermaios, the last Indo-Greek king of the region. About AD 20 the Indo-Parthian king Gondophares established a powerful empire extending from Sistan across south Afghanistan to the Punjab. His coinage in Arachosia (Kandahar region) combined a striking portrait bust of the king with the Classical figure of Victory on the reverse. Successors to Gondophares in Arachosia and Sistan continued to strike copper tetradrachms until the Sasanian conquest by Ardashir and Shapur I (mid-3rd century AD).

The establishment of the Kushana empire in the 1st century AD led to the introduction of a standard coinage throughout Bactria and the Punjab. The nameless king Soter Megas struck a copper coinage with the radiate head of Mithra (*see* §I, 4 above) on the obverse and the mounted king on horseback on the reverse. His successor Vima Kadphises introduced the Kushana gold dinar and a large copper tetradrachm with the distinctive obverse motif of the king standing, sacrificing at a low fire altar. During the 2nd century Kanishka and Huvishka introduced a wide range of reverse types, such as Miiro (sun god), Mao (moon god), Oado (wind god) and Oesho (an Iranian wind god associated with the Hindu god Shiva). Under the later Kushanas the range of divinities was reduced to Shiva and Ardochsho, in an increasingly stylized form.

In the absence of an indigenous silver coinage, Sasanian silver drachms came to play an increasing role in the currency of Afghanistan during the 3rd century AD. The Sasanian coins have a portrait of the king on the obverse and a fire altar flanked by two attendants on the reverse, as do some associated Kushano-Sasanian gold and copper issues of Bactria and Gandhara. During the 4th century Hephthalite invaders of Bactria copied the types of the Sasanian king Shapur II (*reg* 309–79). Several Sasanian silver drachms from Afghanistan have Hephthalite countermarks and seem to have been coins paid in tribute in the time of Firuz (*reg* 457/9–84), which were countermarked to serve as Hephthalite currency. Rulers in the Turki Shahi period (early 7th century) followed the same tradition, as can be seen by the silver and copper drachms of Napki Malka and the coins of Vrahitigin. The silver currency of the Hindu Shahis of Kabul (750–1000) used a bull on the obverse and a horseman on the reverse. Most of the coins have an obverse legend in Sharada script, either *Sri Spalapati Deva* or *Sri Samanata Deva* (which are titles rather than personal names), and a letter or symbol in the field. The later debased coins of the currency, struck in billon, were extensively copied by the Islamic dynasties of Ghazna, Kanauj, Ajmer and Delhi (*see* INDIAN SUBCONTINENT, §VII, 6(ii)).

BIBLIOGRAPHY

H. H. Wilson: *Ariana Antiqua: A Descriptive List of the Antiquities and Coins of Afghanistan* (London, 1841/*R* Delhi, 1971)
R. Curiel and D. Schlumberger: *Trésors monétaires d'Afghanistan*, Mém.: Dél. Archéol. Fr. Afghanistan, xiv (Paris, 1953)
D. W. MacDowall and M. Taddei: 'The Early Historic Period: Achaemenids and Greeks'; 'The Pre-Muslim Period', *The Archaeology of Afghanistan: From Earliest Times to the Timurid Period*, ed. F. R. Allchin and N. Hammond (London and New York, 1978), pp. 201–14, 245–55
D. W. MacDowall: 'The Hazrajat Hoard of Indo-Greek Silver Drachms', *Pakistan Archaeol.*, xxvi/1 (1991), pp. 188–98
The Crossroads of Asia: Transformation in Image and Symbol in the Art of Ancient Afghanistan and Pakistan (exh. cat., ed. E. Errington and J. Cribb; Cambridge, Fitzwilliam, 1992)

D. W. MACDOWALL

(b) Jewellery. Northern Afghanistan has produced the richest finds of jewellery from the Achaemenid to the early Kushana period. The wealth of gold material suggests that during this time (*c*. 5th century BC–1st century AD) the region may have been a centre for goldwork of high artistic quality, but the lack of comprehensive excavation evidence makes the precise distinction between imported and indigenous wares unclear. Ornaments in the OXUS TREASURE, discovered near the Amu River, depict male figures, animals or mythical beasts. Prototypes for the stylized figures of fantastic animals occur in Achaemenid art, but the more vigorous appearance of the Oxus Treasure examples links them to the ANIMAL STYLE of the Central Asian steppes (*see* ANCIENT NEAR EAST, §II, 4(ii)(a)). Insets for stones on the haunches of the animals take the form of a dot between two curved triangles, a design that probably derives from the dot and comma motif on animal representations at Persepolis (*see* ACHAEMENID, §§2 and 4).

Six tombs of the 1st century BC–1st century AD at TILLYA TEPE yielded more than 20,000 gold objects, particularly buckles, clasps, collars, pendants and clothing plaques (*see also* §(c) below). The material shows that a local artistic tradition with roots in Achaemenid art continued until the beginning of the 1st century AD. The jewellery further reveals the co-existence of two other trends, the one influenced by the Animal style of the steppes, the other by Greek culture. Borrowed images are rather debased, as they usually lack the characteristic elegance and vitality of their sources of inspiration. A further distinct group shows a new stylistic development that combines Oriental, Greek and nomadic traditions. Elements borrowed from the decorative repertories of India and China appear on some items, while indigenous traditional motifs occur on others. Small drop-shaped insets of turquoise decorate the objects. Jewellery found in tombs on the opposite bank of the Amu River, in Uzbekistan, are, by contrast, all executed in a homogeneous style that follows well-defined local artistic traditions.

Jewellery of the 2nd–3rd century AD, recovered in excavations of the Kushana levels at Begram (see Ghirshman, pl. XVI.1–11), shows an increasing preference for polychromy and for ornaments encrusted with coloured, geometrically cut stones. Similar jewellery has also been found at Palmyra, Hatra and in south Russia (*see* ANCIENT NEAR EAST, §II, 4(ii)(b)). Although few extant examples have been found in Afghanistan, the wealth of ornaments depicted on the *bodhisattva* statues of Gandhara provide a comprehensive record of the jewellery of the Kushana period (*see* INDIAN SUBCONTINENT, §IV, 5(ii)(d)).

BIBLIOGRAPHY

O. M. Dalton: *The Treasure of the Oxus with Other Examples of Early Oriental Metalwork* (London, 1905, rev. 3/1964)
R. Ghirshman: *Bégram: Recherches archéologiques et historiques sur les kouchans*, Mém.: Dél. Archéol. Fr. Afghanistan, xii (Cairo, 1946), pp. 58–65
J. Hackin, J. Carl and J. Meunié: *Diverses recherches archéologiques en Afghanistan, 1933–40*, Mém.: Dél. Archéol. Fr. Afghanistan, viii (Paris, 1959), figs 228–55
A. M. Mandel'shtam: *Kochevniki ha puti v Indiya: Tradui tadzhikskoi arkheologicheskoi ekspeditsii* [The nomads on the Indian routes: results of the Tajik archaeological expedition] (Moscow, 1966)
——: 'Archäologische Bemerkungen zum Kuschana-Problem', *Beiträge zur alten Geschichte und deren Nachleben: Festschrift für Franz Altheim*, 2 vols, ed. R. Stiehl and H. E. Stier (Berlin, 1969–70), pp. 525–34
G. Pugachenkova: *Les Trésors de Dalverzine-tepe* (Leningrad, 1978), p. 47, pls 63–79
B. A. Litvinsky and I. R. Pichikyan: 'The Temple of the Oxus', *J. Royal Asiat. Soc. GB & Ireland* (1982), no. 2, p. 163
V. Sarianidi: *The Golden Hoard of Bactria from the Tillya-tepe Excavations in Northern Afghanistan* (New York and Leningrad, 1985)

C. FABRÈGUES

(c) Metalwork.

Prehistoric. In September 1966, a hoard of gold and silver vessels was uncovered near Sad Hazard village, between Kunduz and the lapis lazuli mines of Badakhshan, north-east Afghanistan. The hoard apparently came from an archaeological mound known as Fullol or Khosh Tapa ('happy mound'). The exact circumstances of discovery are not known; it is likely, however, that the hoard came to light while villagers were collecting earth from the site for their fields. Some of the vessels were cut up and sold to local goldsmiths and jewellers. Five gold and twelve silver vessels, almost all fragmentary and weighing *c*. 2 kg and 1 kg respectively, were placed in the Kabul Museum. Incised designs on the vessels include the stepped cross, so prevalent on Quetta ware and ceramics from Turkmenistan. Incised snakes recall examples from TEPE SIALK, Iran, and those on Anjira ware from Baluchistan. Two vessels have boars. Also present are the bearded bull, shown turned with a full face, as in finds from the Royal Cemetery of UR, and rows of romping bulls. One vessel has an eight-armed curl pattern and confronted bulls. None of the bovids depicted is of the humped Indian zebu type. The general conclusion of those who have handled the material is that the objects seem to come from diverse localities and different periods. Dupree, Gouin and Omer even entertain the possibility that the villagers assembled materials from several different find spots. Tosi and Wardak suggest that a local chieftain assembled the materials in antiquity. The bearded bulls suggest a date of

14. Reliquary decorated with repoussé images of the Buddha between Brahma and Indra, gold inset with garnets, h. 65 mm, from the relic deposit of Stupa 2 at Bimaran, 1st century AD (London, British Museum)

c. 2500 BC; other motifs place the date somewhat later, even extending into the early centuries of the 2nd millennium BC.

BIBLIOGRAPHY

L. Dupree, P. Gouin and N. Omer: 'The Kosh Tapa Hoard from North Afghanistan', *Afghanistan*, xxiv/1 (1971), pp. 44–54

M. Tosi and R. Wardak: 'The Fullol Hoard: A New Find from Bronze-Age Afghanistan', *E. & W.*, xxii/1 (1972), pp. 9–17

K. R. Maxwell-Hyslop: 'The Khosh Tapa–Fullol Hoard', *Afghan Stud.*, iii–iv (1982), pp. 25–37

GREGORY L. POSSEHL

Later periods. Excavated material from Greco-Bactrian and early Kushana sites (*c.* 3rd century BC–2nd century AD) provides most of the information on metalwork in the historical periods before *c.* AD 900, supplemented by a few stray finds from other periods. The material fits broadly into three categories: imported wares, local imitations (principally of contemporary Near Eastern and Iranian wares) and indigenous items.

The OXUS TREASURE, a hoard of primarily Achaemenid gold and silver objects, dated *c.* 550–*c.* 330 BC, was found in the banks of the Amu River, perhaps at Takht-i Kubad, in 1877. Achaemenid metal artefacts have also been excavated at TAKHT-I SANGIN, the fortress on the opposite bank of the river in Tajikistan. The earliest objects in the Oxus Treasure are in an assyrianizing style: a gold acinaces sheath decorated with hunting scenes and a gold phiale with addorsed lions. The hoard includes vessels (one in the form of a fish), a model of a chariot, human and animal figurines (deer, a goose, a silver handle in the form of an ibex), a silver disc with horsemen hunting reindeer, ibex and a hare depicted in ANIMAL STYLE, jewellery, coins and numerous votive plaques. The wide diversity of objects suggests the treasure may have been a temple hoard, but details concerning its precise context and original composition are lacking (*see also* §(b) above).

Excavated finds from the Greco-Bactrian city of AI KHANUM (*c.* 330–*c.* 100 BC) include a bronze cauldron handle with two female busts emerging from vine leaves and a copper crescent (probably a pectoral) with a female face (see Francfort, pp. 56–8, pl. XX.IV, nos 27–8). A bronze statuette of a thickset, wreathed Herakles is iconographically correct, but disproportionate, and was probably made locally (see Bernard, p. 302, fig. 13). A 3rd-century BC gilded silver medallion, thought to be imported from northern Syria, depicts Cybele and a winged Nike in a chariot pulled by two lions facing a figure on a stepped altar, with Helios, a crescent moon and star above (see Francfort, pp. 93–104, pl. XLI).

More than 20,000 metalwork objects, displaying a rich diversity of styles (e.g. Hellenistic, Greco-Bactrian, Animal style) and variously dated *c.* 1st century BC or early 1st century AD, were discovered in the royal burials at TILLYA TEPE. Most of these finds were pieces of gold jewellery (*see also* §I, 4 above), but also included were Chinese mirrors, a gold fluted phiale and a cylindrical container, both inscribed in Greek, several bowls and pots, some decorated with bands of Hellenistic vegetal motifs, a gold figure of a goat and, in the male grave, a gold handled dagger and two sheaths, inset with turquoise and decorated with animals, mythical winged beasts and dragons in Animal style.

At BEGRAM, bronze balsamaria or unguent vases in the form of busts of Athena, Hermes and Ares were probably imported from the west *c.* 1st century BC–*c.* 1st century AD, as were a bronze Harpokrates and an unusual syncretic image combining Serapis with Herakles. The bronze finds (Kabul Mus. and Paris, Mus. Guimet; see Ghirshman, pl. XII; Hackin and Hackin, figs 47–59; Hackin and others, figs 322–5) also include statuettes of a monk, a winged Eros and two horsemen, one Greek, the other of Scythian type, a cockerel with a human head, a mask of Silenus and a shield decorated with a gorgon head encircled by repoussé dolphins. Imported 1st–2nd century AD Alexandrian plaster mouldings of Hellenistic subjects are thought to have served as a source of reference for silversmiths at Begram. Several small bronze figurines of uncertain Afghan provenance (see 1992 exh. cat., nos 102–3, 105–6, 108, 110–12, 117) exhibit a similar range of Classical influences and subjects (e.g. a herm, Herakles, Demeter).

A quantity of metalwork was uncovered in the relic deposits of stupas near Kabul and Jalalabad in the 19th century (*see* §III below). Most famous is the Bimaran gold reliquary (see fig. 14), which is decorated with standing images of the Buddha, Indra, Brahma and perhaps a *bodhisattva* (London, BM; see 1992 exh. cat., pp. 186–92; *see also* §I, 4 above and INDIAN SUBCONTINENT, §IV, 5(ii)). These are the earliest datable Buddha images in Gandharan art, for which coins of *c.* mid-1st century AD included in the stupa deposit provide a *terminus ante quem.* Other reliquaries important for dating purposes are the gold amulet case from Ahinposh that contained Roman aurei of AD 100–136 and the inscribed bronze Wardak vase, which is dated year 51 of the Kushana king Kanishka and mentions his successor Huvishka (London, BM; see 1992 exh. cat., nos 170–71).

Two silver pateras, heirlooms of the Mirs of Badakshan, were acquired by a British officer, Dr P. Lord, in 1838. One is decorated with embossed and gilded sheet silver figures depicting the Triumph of Dionysos (London, BM; see Dalton, no. 196). Certain misunderstood details suggest a non-western, possibly local workshop of *c.* 1st century AD. The second patera, a Sasanian piece of *c.* mid-4th century, depicted a prince on horseback attacking a lion but was lost during the British retreat from Kabul in 1840 and is now known only from a drawing (see Harper, p. 134, pl. 11). A number of bronze Buddha and *bodhisattva* statues, purported to be principally from the eastern Afghanistan Hindu Kush region and variously dated *c.* 4th–*c.* 7th century (see von Schroeder, pl. V, figs 3a, 5a–b), are closely related to images from the Swat and Peshawar valleys, Pakistan. While Afghanistan is the most likely source of copper, tin and zinc for all these figures, preliminary technical analysis suggests there are identifiable regional variations in composition and manufacturing techniques (see 1992 exh. cat., pp. 241–56).

BIBLIOGRAPHY

O. M. Dalton: *The Treasure of the Oxus with Other Examples of Early Oriental Metalwork* (London, 1905, rev. 3/1964)
J. Hackin and J.-R. Hackin: *Recherches archéologiques à Begram*, 2 vols, Mém.: Dél. Archéol. Fr. Afghanistan, ix (Paris, 1939)
R. Ghirshman: *Bégram: Recherches archéologiques et historiques sur les kouchans*, Mém.: Dél. Archéol. Fr. Afghanistan, xii (Cairo, 1946)
J. Hackin and others: *Nouvelles recherches archéologiques à Begram, 1939–1940*, 2 vols, Mém.: Dél. Archéol. Fr. Afghanistan, xi (Paris, 1954)
P. Bernard: 'Fouilles de Aï Khanoum (Afghanistan): Campagnes de 1972 et 1973', *Acad. Inscr. & B.-Lett.: C. R. Séances* (1974), pp. 280–308
P. Harper: *Royal Imagery*, i of *Silver Vessels of the Sasanian Period* (New York, 1981)
U. von Schroeder: *Indo-Tibetan Bronzes* (Hong Kong, 1981)
H.-P. Francfort: *Le Sanctuaire du temple à niches indentées, II: Les Trouvailles*, Mém.: Dél. Archéol. Fr. Afghanistan, xxvii (1984), iii of *Fouilles d'Aï Khanoum* (Paris, 1973–92)
V. Sarianidi: *The Golden Hoard of Bactria from the Tillya-tepe Excavations in Northern Afghanistan* (New York and Leningrad, 1985)
G. Fussman: 'Numismatic and Epigraphic Evidence for the Chronology of Early Gandharan Art', *Investigating Indian Art*, ed. M. Yaldiz (Berlin, 1987), pp. 67–88
G. A. Pugachenkova and L. I. Rempel: 'Gold from Tillia-tepe', *Bull. Asia Inst.*, v (1991), pp. 11–25
The Crossroads of Asia: Transformation in Image and Symbol in the Art of Ancient Afghanistan and Pakistan (exh. cat., ed. E. Errington and J. Cribb; Cambridge, Fitzwilliam, 1992) [technical analysis app. by C. Reedy, pp. 241–63]

E. ERRINGTON

(d) Pottery. Prehistoric pottery (*c.* 4000–1000 BC) is characterized by painted decoration, which develops from simple curvilinear designs towards bolder and more complex geometric motifs and finally includes representations of stylized animals towards the end of the period. There are considerable stylistic links with southern Turkmenistan and Baluchistan throughout the prehistoric period. Burnishing, a distinctive new style of surface treatment, first appeared in the Achaemenid period (*c.* 530–330 BC) and soon became predominant. The initial simple wavy line or radial burnishes were superseded in the Hellenistic period (*c.* 3rd–1st century BC) by 'red spiral-burnished ware', that is spiral or horizontal line burnishing, usually on red/orange fabrics. Achaemenid and Hellenistic pottery shapes share some characteristics with Middle Eastern pottery of the same date, and Greek influence in the Hellenistic period can be seen with local imitations of Greek black-polished wares. Thereafter, foreign influences seem to recede, and the indigenous spiral-burnished wares predominate.

Red spiral-burnished ware was used almost exclusively in the Kushana period (*c.* 1st–3rd century AD). The ware occurs all over Afghanistan, much of Pakistan and in adjacent Parthian areas as far west as Khorasan in Iran. Although often considered a 'hallmark' for the Kushana period, it cannot be associated exclusively with the Kushanas, as was once thought, but is also found in the subsequent Sasanian, Hepthalite and Turki Shahi periods. Red spiral-burnished ware thus remained the most important pottery style, showing very little variation, throughout the 1st millennium AD until the beginning of the Islamic period (*c.* early 10th century).

BIBLIOGRAPHY

J.-C. Gardin: *Ceramiques de Bactres* (Paris, 1957)
L. Dupree: *Shamshir Ghar: Historic Cave Site in Kandahar Province, Afghanistan* (New York, 1958)
J.-M. Casal: *Fouilles de Mundigak*, 2 vols, Mém.: Dél. Archéol. Fr. Afghanistan, xvii (Paris, 1961)
A. W. McNicoll and W. Ball: *Excavations at Kandahar* (Oxford, 1995)

W. BALL

2. *c.* AD 900–*c.* 1900. Afghanistan was of particular importance for the arts of Islam between the 10th century and the 16th. Western Afghanistan was often included in the province of Khurasan (now limited to Iran). Although NISHAPUR was the provincial capital in early Islamic times, HERAT became increasingly important after the Mongol conquests in the 13th century and served as a capital of the TIMURID empire in the 15th. In the 11th–12th century, southern Afghanistan became important under the GHAZNAVID dynasty, which had capitals at GHAZNA and LASHKARI BAZAR. Eastern Afghanistan, with its centre at KABUL, flourished from the early 16th century under the patronage of the Mughal emperors of the Indian subcontinent. Northern Afghanistan, particularly the region of BALKH, became important from the 16th century under the SHAYBANID dynasty and their Uzbek successors.

The earliest Islamic buildings in Afghanistan date from the 9th century AD, when builders already employed materials, techniques and styles associated with the metropolitan centres of the Abbasid caliphate in Iraq. The nine-bay mosque at Balkh (9th century; *see* ISLAMIC ART, §II, 4(i)(c)), for example, was built of brick following a plan also found in North Africa and Spain and was decorated with carved stucco in the BEVELLED STYLE. Under the Ghaznavids and Ghurids (*reg c.* 1000–1215) there developed a progressive style of architecture distinguished by massive scale, occasional use of stone, distinctive arch profiles, new types of glazed tilework, terracotta decoration and inscriptions written in angular and cursive scripts (*see* ISLAMIC ART, §II, 5(i)(c)). Perhaps the most evocative example of this style is the towering late 12th-century minaret at Jam (*see* MINARET, fig. 3) in a remote valley in the centre of the country. Herat flourished under the Timurids, when the city and its environs were graced with splendid brick buildings enveloped in glittering webs of glazed tile (*see* ISLAMIC ART, §II, 6(i)(b)). Many of the most important monuments, however, were destroyed in the 19th century when the region was contested by the Russians and the British. The complex of Abu Nasr Parsa at Balkh exemplifies how shrines developed in the later period with the addition of madrasas and hospices around the grave of an earlier saint.

Many types of Islamic decorative art were produced in Afghanistan from early times. A group of hemispherical basins made of high-tin bronze is associated with the Ghaznavids because of the bifurcated hats worn by the courtiers depicted on them. Herat was a major centre of metalworking for centuries, to judge from the inlaid Bobrinski Bucket (*see* ISLAMIC ART, fig. 140) made in 1163, the huge cast bronze basin (dated 1374–5) in the congregational mosque, and the inlaid jugs made for the Timurid ruler Husayn Bayqara and other 15th-century patrons (*see* ISLAMIC ART, fig. 149). The arts of the book also flourished from an early date. Some idea of early manuscript illumination can be gained from a book (Leiden, Rijksuniv. Bib., MS. 437) formerly in the library of the Ghaznavid amir ʿAbd al-Rashid (*reg* 1049–51) and a copy of the Koran made at Bust in 1111–12 (Paris, Bib. N., MS. arab. 6041; *see* ISLAMIC ART, fig. 101). The apogee of the arts of the book in Afghanistan, and one of the great moments in all Islamic art, occurred in Herat under the patronage of the Timurid princes Baysunghur and Husayn Bayqara (*see* ISLAMIC ART, §III, 4(v)(d)). Splendid calligraphy by such masters as MIR ʿALI HUSAYNI HARAVI was embellished with beautiful illumination and paintings by such artists as BIHZAD and contained within sumptuous bindings (*see* ISLAMIC ART, fig. 138). After the collapse of Timurid power in the early 16th century, Herat ceased to be a major centre of patronage, but some painters worked in Kabul, temporary home of the Mughal court, in the middle of the century.

For bibliography see the individual articles cited in the text.

□

3. AFTER *c.* 1900. Creative expression in 20th-century Afghanistan resides in the artistry of diverse ethnic and tribal groups living mainly in rural villages and semi-nomadic camps. Western art styles, popularized during the early years of the 20th century by educated urban élites, tend to be imitative rather than innovative.

(i) Architecture. (ii) Painting and sculpture. (iii) Other arts.

(i) Architecture. The introduction of a more Western style of domestic architecture was accompanied by innovations in interior décor, furniture making, painting, landscape gardening and dress styles. When Amir Abdur Rahman (*reg* 1880–1901) acceded to the throne after living in exile in Central Asia for over a decade, he abandoned the traditional house plan with its interior courtyards and personally designed vaulted and domed palaces that faced outwards on to English gardens adorned with fountains.

The first 'European' home was built according to the same specifications as Dorchester House of Park Lane, London, in Kabul. This building heralded a period characterized by British Indian designs. These verandahed colonial styles fell out of fashion after the short 1919 war between Afghanistan and England, and King Amanullah (*reg* 1919–29) turned for inspiration to 18th-century European grand styles with their exuberant and eclectic mix of Neo-classical and pseudo-Rococo elements. By the mid-20th century this ebullience gave way to the utilitarian Soviet and Central European models that still dominate both domestic and public buildings.

Interior transformations mirrored changing lifestyles. In traditional homes each room served several purposes. White walls were decorated with floral ornamentation in pressed, moulded or carved stucco. Furnishings comprised richly coloured Afghan carpets and embroidered door hangings. There was no need for furniture, as mattresses and bolsters doubled for sitting and sleeping, fabric runners were spread on the floor for dining, and traditional clothing folded easily for storage in wall niches or decorated boxes.

Rooms in modern homes in Kabul, on the other hand, were set aside for specific purposes and filled accordingly with massive, ornately carved furniture, including commodious wardrobes to accommodate European clothes. While carpets were retained, stuccowork gave way to flocked and textured wallpaper, or stencilled approximations and daubed simulations of luxurious wood and marble wainscoting that provided a backdrop for a wealth of imported Victorian clutter.

(ii) Painting and sculpture. From the late 19th century onwards artists experimented with novel Western techniques, yet their landscapes and vivid abstract paintings incorporated no recognizable Afghan characteristics; even when the scenes were Afghan, the styles were clearly derivative. Sculpture, an innovation introduced many years later by students returning from Italy and the Soviet Union, was coolly received by this Muslim society. However, birds and animals carved from marble and lapis lazuli by artisans trained in Kabul by Chinese masters became popular with tourists.

Contemporary Afghan artists and sculptors have yet to enjoy either private patronage or public support despite official promotion by the government since the 1970s. In 1978 leftist urban leaders overthrew the élites who had set trends for almost 100 years. Their rise, closely followed by Soviet military intervention, ushered in a period dominated by socialist realism. Devastation caused by ground and air offensives forced more than a third of the Afghan population into exile in neighbouring Pakistan and Iran. Nevertheless, since 1989 an intrepid group of young artists has attracted growing numbers of students in their attempts to revive the Herati traditions of miniature painting and calligraphy renowned in Afghanistan during the 15th century.

Within the public domain, stylized floral mural painting (see fig. 15) enjoys a certain popularity in the decoration of mosques and teahouses. The most distinctive painting tradition in this genre, however, is displayed on truck bodies completely embellished with a wide range of themes including Swiss chalets, lovely ladies, trains, boats, telephones, animal combat scenes, birds and contemporary battle scenes.

(iii) Other arts. Of all Western innovations, dress probably had the most far-reaching, durable influence upon society. In the late 19th century hoops, bustles and wide-brimmed plumed and beribboned hats were introduced for the

ladies, along with splendid emblazoned uniforms, frock coats and tweeds fancied by the gentlemen at court. As fashions closely followed European changes, including mini-skirts and the ubiquitous T-shirt and jeans, Western dress became a measure of modernity throughout the educated urban populations and, for women, it symbolized emancipation.

More enduring indigenous examples of art and craftsmanship are found among the diverse creative traditions brought to Afghanistan over many centuries by artisans travelling to this pivotal Central Asian land from east, west, north and south along the routes of conquest and commerce. From 1978 onwards, however, the disruptions of war hastened the decline of crafts already affected by the introduction of modern materials, production methods, imports and commercialization. The art of ornamental stucco has all but disappeared; ikat weaving from an already limited number of northern workshops suffers equally; Nuristani wood-carving, Pushtun painted and lacquered wood decoration, tilemaking, copperwork and pottery and Herati glassblowing, silversmithing and silk weaving are all threatened. Nevertheless, since few items produced in Afghan villages and semi-nomadic camps are purely decorative and since most express personal and/or group identification and status, there is reason to hope for a craft revival once peace permits life to return to normal. The exquisite embroidery made by refugees for their personal use, in contrast to the lamentable pieces seen for sale, allows this note of optimism.

(a) Carpets and textiles. The richness of form and colour of the flat-woven, hand-knotted and felt carpets made by the Turkomen, Uzbek, Hazara, Aimaq, Kirghiz and Baluch place them among Afghanistan's most renowned artistic products. Ranking fifth among the country's exports before 1978, the carpet trade has continued on a reduced scale throughout the war, although the difficulties in obtaining quality raw materials coupled with local market demands on design and pricing have adversely affected the production of Afghan carpets by refugees in Pakistan and Iran. Carpet production contributes significantly to family income and is highly valued. Quality products are more particularly esteemed because they add to individual status. A bride gains heightened respect from her husband's family when her dowry includes fine examples of her own handiwork; a man's wealth and status is gauged by the quantity and quality of his household's production. Furthermore, since distinctive structures, designs, symbols and colours are proudly associated with specific groups, the excellence of the work of its individual producers enhances the reputation of the entire community.

While carpets represent a major portion of woven articles for sale, an inexhaustible variety of other items are made for both utilitarian and decorative use within the household. Long narrow woven bands both strengthen and decorate the wooden lattice framework of round felt-roofed yurts (*see* TENT, §II, 2(ii)). The Kirghiz, among others, entwine the reeds forming the skirting of yurts and interior partition screens with yarn in variegated designs. Almost all semi-nomadic groups use hand-knotted, often fringed, door hangings.

15. Floral mural painting

Furniture in most sedentary and semi-nomadic homes scarcely extends beyond an occasional wooden stool, one or two wooden chests and perhaps a cradle (*see* §(d) below). Possessions from clothing to food supplies are stored in flat-woven or knotted bags of various shapes and sizes. Uzbeks distinctively wrap bedding and clothing in flat-woven squares (2×2 m), which are stacked on top of chests. Finely embroidered V-shaped pieces and beaded tassels hung against these bundles provide the final adornment. Elsewhere, strings of pompoms and woollen tassels are used as cornices and wall hangings. By the mid-20th century, hand-woven textiles for clothing had largely given way to imported and locally manufactured materials. Exceptions are prized silk turbans, a speciality of the Herat area, and the popular striped cottons used for long-sleeved robes throughout the north.

Embroidery motifs and stitches serve to distinguish ethnic and regional goups. Embroidered items are made for family use and only rarely offered for sale. This handicraft is most importantly associated with marriage. Each male family member attending a wedding is presented with a finger-woven trouser drawstring with silk tassels and an intricately embroidered cummerbund. In addition to embroidered clothing, the bride's dowry typically includes up to 20 types of embroidered household items, from spoon bags, tray covers, sachets for money and make-up to dust covers for Korans and radios. Soft, knee-high leather boots embellished with fine embroidery by Turkic-speaking women of the north are especially prized. Every woman in the family takes part in spinning wool and silk, weaving, stitching and embroidering in order to amass this extensive collection. Kin-related girls often work together on the large embroidered and patchwork pieces. Mothers devise baby bonnets festooned with feathers, pompoms and protective charms. Intricately embroidered and beaded hats worn under men's turbans and women's headscarves are distinctive symbols of group identity. Ornaments, mirrorwork, gold braid, elaborate beading and fine embroidery decorate the high-waisted bodices, elbow-length cuffs and deep hems of women's dresses, the skirts of which may, among some groups, contain as much as 12 m of velvet or flowered cotton.

Among semi-nomadic groups, individual artistry is publicly displayed during their annual migrations in a variety of ornamental trappings for camels, donkeys and horses. In addition to saddle bags and blankets there are decorated leather harnesses, silver-studded saddles and neckpieces. A bridal camel, bedecked with a heavy, glass-beaded headdress and reins takes pride of place in any caravan. These sumptuous accoutrements proclaim wealth, status and power.

(b) Jewellery. Items for personal adornment have been zealously developed by all groups. Distinctive patterns distinguish each ethnic group, place of origin and, particularly among the Pushtun, tribe and sub-tribe. The most popular jewellery is made of silver, at times fire-gilded, a technique most employed by the Turkomen. Heavy, embossed torques of twisted silver are a speciality of Nuristan, but all bracelets, armlets, earrings, temple pendants and headdress ornaments tend to be massive and liberally hung with pendants. Insets of coloured glass or hardstones, including carnelian, turquoise and lapis lazuli, are frequently embued with symbolic meaning to avert sorrow, danger and disease or bring joy, serenity and marital bliss. Generous sprinklings of silver beads, discs, coins, medallions, dress fastenings, amulets and talismans are also sewn on to clothing in great profusion.

(c) Pottery. The shapes and designs of the primarily utilitarian pottery have survived unchanged for 5000 years. Glazes are rare, except for those found at Istalif, a hillside village just north of Kabul. The clear, bright blue pottery with black incised floral decorations and the bird and animal figurines from Istalif are unique. The Istalif double-headed horse must surely represent a tradition of considerable antiquity, although the potters themselves attribute their creations simply to 'custom'.

(d) Woodwork. Lacquered wooden boxes, stools, bed-legs and cradles are regional specialities, most notably in the east. Lacquerwork is normally restricted to colourful banding, but some artisans have developed a technique of applying several layers of different colours, which are then cut away to reveal intricate floral designs. The art of wood-carving in general is largely applied to such architectural elements as window-frames and panels, doorframes, lintels and pillars in homes and mosques. Much of this work exhibits affinities to Kashmiri floral, geometric and curvilinear traditions; unique motifs from Nuristan include animistic symbols that pre-date the conversion of this area to Islam in 1895. Distinctive snuff-boxes, made from small gourds, are traditionally shaped in wooden moulds as they ripen on the vine and are then highly polished, painted or adorned with silver stoppers and decorative collars.

BIBLIOGRAPHY

M. Kohzad: 'L'Inauguration du salon d'automne à Kaboul', *Afghanistan Q.*, i/4 (1946), pp. 30–34

B. Dupaigne: 'Aperçus sur quelques techniques afghans', *Obj. & Mondes*, viii (1968), pp. 41–84

A. Friedman: 'The Handicrafts of Afghanistan', *Afghanistan Q.*, xxv/2 (1972), pp. 11–12

N. Dupree: 'Archaeology and the Arts in the Creation of a National Consciousness', *Afghanistan in the 1970s*, ed. L. Dupree (New York, 1974), pp. 203–38

C. Naumann: 'Pamir und Wakhan', *Afghanistan J.*, i/4 (1974), pp. 91–104

G. O'Bannon: *The Turkoman Carpet* (London, 1974)

P. Centlivres: 'Les Uzbeks du Qattagnan', *Afghanistan J.*, ii/1 (1975), pp. 28–36

M. Centlivres-Demont: 'Les Peintures sur camions en Afghanistan', *Afghanistan J.*, ii/2 (1975), pp. 60–64

J.-C. Blanc: *Afghan Trucks* (London, 1976)

M. Centlivres-Demont: *Popular Art in Afghanistan: Paintings on Trucks, Mosques and Tea-houses* (Graz, 1976)

L. Dupree: *Afghan Women* (Hannover, 1976) [film; Afghanistan Ser., iv]

N. Dupree: 'Early Twentieth-century Afghan Adaptations of European Architecture', *A. & Archaeol. Res. Pap.*, xii (1977), pp. 15–21

R. Dor and C. Naumann: *Die Kirghisen des afghanischen Pamir* (Graz, 1978)

A. Janata: 'Ikat in Afghanistan', *Afghanistan J.*, v/4 (1978), pp. 130–39

A. Stucki: 'Horses and Women', *Afghanistan J.*, v/4 (1978), pp. 140–49

N. Dupree: 'A Building Boom in the Hindukush (Boom edilizio nell'Hindukush)', *Lotus Int.*, xxvi (1980), pp. 115–21

M. Klimburg: 'A Collection of Kafir Art from Nuristan', *Tribus*, xxx (1981), pp. 155–202

J. Kalter: 'Die Sammlungen des Linden-Museums aus Afghanistan und der Nachbargebieten', *Afghanistan J.*, ix/3 (1982), pp. 76–85

I. Rittmeyer: 'Die Sammlung Rittmeyer', *Afghanistan J.*, ix/4 (1982), pp. 112–14

R. Parsons: *The Carpets of Afghanistan* (Woodbridge, 1983)

N. Dupree: 'National Museum of Afghanistan', *Art Museums of the World*, i (Westport, 1987), pp. 26–30

——: 'Victoriana Comes to the Haremserai in Afghanistan (Viktorianischer Stil erobert den Haremserail)', *Bauen und Wohnen am Hindukush*, Stiftung Bibliotheca Afghanica, vii, ed. P. Bucherer-Dietschi (Liestal, 1988), pp. 111–49

The Decorative Arts of Central Asia (exh. cat., ed. J. Graham and H. Sandys; London, Zamara Gal., 1988)

J. Frembgen: *Naswar: Der Gebrauch von Mundtabak in Afghanistan und Pakistan*, Stiftung Bibliotheca Afghanica, viii (Liestal, 1989)

A. Szabo and T. Barfield: *Afghanistan: An Atlas of Indigenous Domestic Architecture* (Austin, 1991)

B. Dupaigne and R. Paiva: *Afghan Embroidery* (Lahore, 1993)

N. HATCH DUPREE

III. Historiography.

In the first centuries AD under KUSHANA rule, Afghanistan became established as a major centre of Buddhism, with many monasteries and stupas. Between the 5th and 8th centuries, a number of these Buddhist sites were visited and described by Chinese pilgrims such as Faxian (*c.* 400) and Xuanzang (*c.* 630).

Western interest in Afghanistan stems from the discovery in the 18th century by numismatists such as Theophilus Bayer, J. Pellerin and M. Mionnet that some fine portrait coins could be attributed to several Greek kings of Bactria (*see* BACTRIAN AND INDO-GREEK MONARCHIES) who were mentioned in Classical texts (see Wilson, pp. 3–4). At the beginning of the 19th century, the British in India became increasingly interested in Afghanistan, initially in order to forestall any potential designs of Napoleon I, and later for fear of Russian expansion in Central Asia. Various travellers who visited the country and recorded the monuments they saw were William Moorcroft and George Trebeck, on an ill-fated journey in 1825; Alexander Burnes and J. G. Gerard, who travelled to Bukhara in 1831; and

Martin Honigberger, a Transylvanian doctor, formerly in the service of the Sikh emperor Ranjit Singh, who explored several stupas in the neighbourhood of Kabul and Jalalabad in 1833. A major contributor was Charles Masson, a deserter from the East India Company army, who from 1826 onwards travelled extensively in the regions to the north of British India. He spent six years in Afghanistan (1832–8), during which time he surveyed and explored the archaeological remains near Kabul, Jalalabad and HADDA. The East India Company granted him a pardon in 1834 and funding to continue his investigations. He amassed a collection of more than 80,000 coins, primarily from BEGRAM, while his excavations of numerous stupas produced such remarkable objects as the Bimaran casket (see fig. 14 above; *see also* §IV below). His principal discoveries were published in *Ariana Antiqua* (see Wilson, pp. 55–118). He was also an early contributor to the journal (*J. Asiat. Soc. Bengal*) published from 1832 onwards by the Asiatic Society of Bengal (founded 1784), which under the editorship of JAMES PRINSEP became a principal source of information on the antiquities of India and neighbouring regions. Work on coins and their inscriptions, particularly by Prinsep and the German scholar Christian Lassen, resulted in the decipherment of the Kharoshthi script. But after the first Anglo-Afghan War (1839–42), little further fieldwork or research was undertaken, other than William Simpson's excavation of the Ahinposh Stupa near Jalalabad at the beginning of the second Anglo-Afghan War (1878–9) and incidental reports by members of the British border commissions in 1896–7 and 1903–5.

In the early 20th century the leading art historian in the field was undoubtedly ALFRED CHARLES AUGUSTE FOUCHER, who, fascinated by the extension of Hellenism in the east, contributed the monumental study, *L'Art gréco-bouddhique du Gandhâra*. The Franco-Afghan cultural convention of 1922 gave the French a virtual monopoly of archaeological research in Afghanistan for 30 years and a permanent institute in Kabul, with Foucher as first director. The Délégation Archéologique Française en Afghanistan has undertaken a major series of excavations and studies of the art and archaeology of Afghanistan. The results, published in more than 30 volumes (Mém.: Dél. Archéol. Fr. Afghanistan), include comprehensive excavation reports on Hadda, Begram, SURKH KOTAL and AI KHANUM. From the 1960s until 1978 Afghan archaeologists conducted extensive excavations at Tepe Shotor and Tepe Kalan, two important monastic complexes at Hadda. Since the 1960s other foreign missions have been allowed to work in Afghanistan: the Italian Istituto per il Medio ed Estremo Oriente at Ghazna (*see* SARDAR, TEPE), German and American teams in Sistan, a Japanese team from Kyoto University at Tepe Skandar, a Russian mission at TILLYA TEPE and the British Institute at Kandahar. This has led to much wider international interest in the art history of Afghanistan.

BIBLIOGRAPHY

A. Burnes: 'On the Colossal Idols of Bamian', *J. Asiat. Soc. Bengal*, ii (1833), pp. 561–4, pl. XIX

——: *Travels into Bokhara*, 3 vols (London, 1834/*R* Karachi, 1973)

J. G. Gerard: 'Memoir on the Topes and Antiquities of Afghanistan: From Jelalābād, 4th December 1833', *J. Asiat. Soc. Bengal*, iii (1834), pp. 321–9

E. Jacquet: 'Sur les découvertes archéologiques faites par M. Honigberger dans l'Afghanistan', *J. Asiat.*, n. s. 2, ii (1836), pp. 234–77; iv (1837), pp. 401–40; v (1838), pp. 163–97; vii (1839), pp. 385–404

W. Moorcroft and G. Trebeck: *Travels in the Himalayan Provinces of Hindustan and the Panjab from 1819 to 1825*, 2 vols, ed. H. H. Wilson (London, 1841); intro. G. J. Alder (*R* Karachi, 1979)

H. H. Wilson: *Ariana Antiqua: A Descriptive List of the Antiquities and Coins of Afghanistan* (London, 1841/*R* Delhi, 1971)

W. Simpson: 'Buddhist Architecture of the Jelalabad Valley', *Trans. RIBA* (1879–80), pp. 37–58

A. Foucher: *L'Art gréco-bouddhique du Gandhâra*, 2 vols (Paris, 1905–18)

M. Taddei and G. Verardi: 'The Italian Archaeological Mission in Afghanistan: Brief Account of Excavation and Study, 1976–1981', *Studi di storia dell'arte in memoria di Mario Rotili* (Naples, 1984), pp. 41–70

G. Whitteridge: *Charles Masson of Afghanistan* (Warmington, 1986)

For further bibliography *see* §II, 1(i), (ii) and (iii) above.

D. W. MacDOWALL

IV. Museums and collections.

The collections of material from Afghanistan are few in number but well published. The majority of pieces are located in the Kabul Museum and the Musée Guimet, Paris. The earliest collections date from the 19th century, when, notwithstanding political unrest and wars, a number of primarily British travellers and pioneers visited Afghanistan and sent a few stray finds, principally coins, to the British Museum, London. A major collection of coins and stupa relic deposits, made by Charles Masson in the 1830s (*see* §III above), was initially deposited in the East India Company Museum, London, then in 1880 divided between the British Museum and the Indian Museum, Calcutta.

After World War I cultural co-operation between the khan (later king) Aman-Allah (*reg* 1919–28) and France resulted in 1922 in the creation of the Délégation Archéologique Française en Afghanistan. The Délégation received exclusive rights to survey and excavate in Afghanistan for a period of 30 years. Following initial surveys by ALFRED CHARLES AUGUSTE FOUCHER at Balkh and Hadda (1922–3), finds from these investigations were shared between the Kabul Museum and the Musée Guimet, under the respective control of the king and the director of the Délégation. Even during World War II the scheme continued to benefit both countries. The majority of discoveries thus preserved were of outstanding importance, such as the well-known series of schist reliefs from Paitava (see fig. 6 above) and SHOTORAK, the stucco reliefs from HADDA, fragments of wall paintings, reliefs and clay statues from BAMIYAN, Kakrak and FONDUKISTAN (see figs 12 and 9 above), the famous hoard from BEGRAM and finds from the prehistoric city of Mundigak (see figs 2 and 5 above) and the large dynastic temple of SURKH KOTAL.

The French finally lost their exclusive rights to excavation in 1962, and from 1964 onwards no archaeological finds were legally allowed out of Afghanistan. Foreign teams worked under the control of the newly created Archaeological Survey of Afghanistan. The finds from British, American, German and Japanese excavations of prehistoric and historic sites, the French at AI KHANUM, the Italians at Ghazna (*see* SARDAR, TEPE) and Afghan and Soviet teams at Emshi Tepe and TILLYA TEPE were all placed in the Kabul Museum. In addition, site museums were created at Bamiyan, following restoration of the site

(1974–8), and at the Buddhist monastery of Tepe Shotor, Hadda (destroyed during bombing in 1979).

While Joseph Hackin was Director of the Musée Guimet in the 1930s, groups of 20 selected sculptures from the Hadda collection were distributed on permanent loan to various museums worldwide, in order that the material might become better known (Brussels, Musées Royaux A. & Hist.; Kansas City, MO, Nelson–Atkins Mus. A.; London, BM; Luxembourg, Mus. N. Hist. & A.; New Haven, CT, Yale U. A.G.; St Petersburg, Hermitage; Stockholm, Östasiat. Mus.; Tokyo, Ueno Royal Mus.; and a few others). In addition, about 12 ivory pieces from Begram were sent to India in 1960–63 as an exchange loan for some rare pieces of ancient Indian art. These ivories, the only examples outside Kabul or Paris, are in the National Museum, New Delhi. In the 1990s a programme was launched to expand the exhibit of Afghan material in the Musée Guimet beyond the original two galleries, in order to display additional, newly restored pieces from the reserve collection. Many other museums worldwide have Gandhara stucco pieces of uncertain provenance that are stylistically attributable to Afghanistan or Pakistan. It is to be hoped that the site origin of many of these pieces may be determined through the use of highly sophisticated methods of technical analysis that are increasingly available.

The Kabul Museum ranked among the most opulent depositories in the world, with a collection that recorded 50,000 years of the cultural history of Afghanistan. Although the artefacts were all boxed in 1991 for safekeeping during the civil war, the museum building was extensively damaged during bombing in 1993. Soon afterwards artefacts from the museum began to appear on the international art market and the ultimate fate of the collection is uncertain.

BIBLIOGRAPHY

O. Monod-Brühl: *Guide to the Musée Guimet* (Paris, 1966)
J. Auboyer: *L'Afghanistan et son art* (Prague, 1968)
N. Hatch Dupree and others: *The National Museum of Afghanistan: An Illustrated Guide* (Kabul, 1974)
F. R. Allchin and N. Hammond, eds: *The Archaeology of Afghanistan: From Earliest Times to the Timurid Period* (London and New York, 1978)
W. Ball and J. C. Gardin: *Archaeological Gazetteer of Afghanistan / Catalogue des sites archéologiques d'Afghanistan*, 2 vols (Paris, 1982)

F. TISSOT

Afinger, Bernhard (*b* Nuremberg, 6 May 1813; *d* Nuremberg, 25 Dec 1882). German sculptor. After an apprenticeship as a metal worker, having spent seven years as a journeyman in a silver-plating factory and having taught himself drawing and sculpting, he received a scholarship that allowed him to attend art school. In 1840 he met Christian Daniel Rauch who invited him to Berlin as his pupil, and there he was influenced by the prevalent Neo-classical style. However, his early works, such as the colossal figure of *Christ* that he carved in 1842 for the church in Dinkelsbühl, Mittelfranken, owe much to the tradition of the medieval sculptors of Nuremberg. In 1846 he founded his own workshop and in 1850 sculpted the much admired marble statuette of the actress *Elisa Rachel* (Berlin, Pfaueninsel). At the Great Exhibition in London in 1851 he won a commendation for his two medallions of the Prince and Princess of Prussia. During his long career Afinger produced 116 portraits in the form of medallions, busts and statuettes. He also carved a series of saints in sandstone for the castle church of Sagan. He received many public and private commissions for monuments of various kinds, such as the *Ernst Moritz Arndt* monument (1865) and the Christ Fountain (1878), both in Bonn. In 1873 he visited Italy, joined the Senat of the Königliche Akademie der Künste in Berlin in 1875 and in 1877 received a professorship there.

BIBLIOGRAPHY

Thieme–Becker
P. Bloch and W. Grzimek: *Das klassische Berlin: Die Berliner Bildhauerschule im neunzehnten Jahrhundert* (Berlin, Frankfurt am Main and Vienna, 1978), cols 149–50
Ethos und Pathos: Die Berliner Bildhauerschule, 1786–1914, 2 vols (exh. cat., ed. P. Bloch, S. Einholz and J. von Simson; Berlin, Staatl. Museen Preuss. Kultbes., 1990), esp. *Ausstellungskatalog*, pp. 11–12

HANNELORE HÄGELE

Aflalo, Roberto. *See under* CROCE, AFLALO AND GASPERINI.

Afonso, João (*fl* first half of the 15th century). Portuguese sculptor. He probably trained in the workshops of Batalha Abbey, where he absorbed the traditions of Coimbra, and he was the leading Portuguese sculptor of his time. In 1439–40 he worked on the tomb of *Fernão de Góis* in the church at Oliveira do Conde, where a Gothic inscription says that the work was carried out in 12 months by *João Afonso, mestre de Sinos*. The tomb is in the 14th-century tradition of MESTRE PÊRO and somewhat archaic in structure, comprising a chest borne by lions, with a recumbent figure on the cover and figures within aedicules at the sides. The treatment is more delicate than in most carving of the time; the arches and columns are slender and elegant, while the figures, with their animated poses and gracefully arranged drapery, are well modelled and show individual character. The same movement is found in the serene angels bearing the chalice in the *Corpus Domini* retable (1433; Coimbra), probably by the same hand. Many other works with similar characteristics are attributed to his workshop, albeit without documentary evidence. Numerous images of the Virgin and Child are considered to be by Afonso, including those at Tentúgal and Tábua (Dias); two figures of *St Michael* (Coimbra, Mus. N. Machado de Castro) and various figures in the Vilhena Collection (Lisbon, Mus. N. A. Ant.) have also been ascribed to him. If these attributions are correct, Afonso is the first Portuguese artist to have combined the sculptural tradition of Coimbra with that of Mestre Pêro's workshop and of the figure-carvers of Batalha Abbey; he in turn established a school that produced the fine sculptor Diogo Pires the elder.

BIBLIOGRAPHY

R. dos Santos: *A escultura em Portugal* (Lisbon, 1948), pp. 42–3, 46–7
V. Correia: *Obras*, iii (Coimbra, 1953), pp. 57–9
P. Dias: 'O gótico', *História da arte em Portugal*, iv (Lisbon, 1986), pp. 133–4
Sculpture et orfèvrerie: Aux confins du moyen âge (exh. cat. by L. Cardoso, Ghent, Sint-Pietersabdij, 1991), p. 91

MARIA ADELAIDE MIRANDA

Afonso, Jorge (*b* ?1470–75; *d* Lisbon, before 23 June 1540). Portuguese painter. He held a key position in

Portuguese art of the first half of the 16th century. He was the brother-in-law of Francisco Henriques, uncle of Cristóvão de Figueiredo and Garcia Fernandes, father-in-law of Gregório Lopes, and friend of the leading painter of Viseu, Vasco Fernandes. In his workshop, painters of the succeeding generation served their apprenticeships and completed their training, interpreting Afonso's Renaissance ideas in Mannerist style. By 1504 Afonso was living in Lisbon with a workshop close to the Monastery of S Domingos. In 1508 Manuel I appointed him *pintor régio* (court painter) and *examinador de todas as obras de pintura do reino* (examiner of all work in painting in the kingdom), appointments that were re-confirmed by John III in 1529. In this capacity he surveyed and evaluated work carried out at Tomar and various churches in Lisbon. Documents refer also to the execution of banners (1515) and to paintings (?1519–21; destr.) for the altarpiece of the church of the Conceição, Lisbon. In 1514 Afonso was ennobled and given the title of *araute Malaca* (Malacca Herald). In 1516 he received a substantial annuity from the Casa da Mina trading company for his services. The high valuation of his possessions and his will (1540) indicate the esteem in which his work was held.

All documented works by Afonso are untraced. Attributed to him is the group of paintings, formerly designated as by the Master of the Madre de Deus or the Master of 1515 (ii), from the polyptych executed for the Convent of Madre de Deus, Lisbon, and completed *c.* 1515, the date discovered during restoration of the panel of *Christ Appearing to the Virgin* (Lisbon, Mus. N. A. Ant.). The polyptych also included the *Annunciation* (Lisbon, Mus. N. A. Ant.), the *Adoration of the Shepherds*, the *Adoration of the Magi*, the *Ascension*, *Pentecost*, the *Assumption of the Virgin* and *St Francis Giving the Rules of the Order to St Clare* (all Lisbon, Convent of the Madre de Deus). This polyptych and the one painted for the Convent of Jesus, Setúbal, comprising fourteen panels (all Setúbal, Mus. Setúbal) divided in three series—the *Passion*, the *Childhood of Christ and Joys of the Virgin* and *Franciscan Saints*—were commissioned by Queen Eleanor, widow of John II, and probably executed (especially the second) with the assistance of artists in his workshop, Cristóvão de Figueiredo, Gregório Lopes and Garcia Fernandes, with whom he often worked. Both series of paintings show richer and more elaborate forms and pictorial clarification of the narrative, together with an adherence to the values of the northern Renaissance that is seen in the broad landscapes and use of aerial perspective. The iconography was often dependent on engravings and was influenced by texts that were close to the spirit of *devotio moderna.* An awareness of Italian art is seen in the monumental scale of the human figures, the knowledge of anatomy and the serene atmosphere of the settings. Afonso brought together these elements in a synthesis that is essentially Portuguese and that formed one of the strands in the development of early Portuguese painting.

BIBLIOGRAPHY

F. M. de Sousa Viterbo: *Noticia de alguns pintores portugueses e de outros que, sendo estrangeiros, exerceram a sua arte em Portugal*, 1 (Lisbon, 1903), pp. 8–25

A. de Gusmão: *O Mestre da Madre de Deus* (Lisbon, 1960)

L. R. Santos: *Jorge Afonso* (Lisbon, 1966)

D. Markl and F. A. Baptista Pereira: *O renascimento: História da arte em Portugal*, vi (Lisbon, 1986), pp. 123–38

F. A. BAPTISTA PEREIRA

Afonso V, King of Portugal. *See* AVIZ, (3).

Africa. Continent second only to Asia in size with a total area of 29,800,000 sq. km and a total population of 628 million (UN estimate, 1989). This survey focuses on the art traditions of Sub-Saharan Africa (i.e. south of the Sahara Desert), especially those of pre-colonial times as they continued into colonial and post-colonial times. It should be noted here that, while the major interest of scholars has been the study of unacculturated traditions, the fieldwork that makes such studies possible has been conducted many years, even centuries, after the time of first European contact. Furthermore, the notion of 'Sub-Saharan' Africa as a cultural entity, although still useful, is to some extent an arbitrary generalization: there has been both a high degree of internal diversity within the continent and much greater economic and political exchange between Africa and the outside world than was previously thought. Africa in the late 20th century comprises more than 50 independent nation states (see fig. 1); separate entries on most of these are found elsewhere in this dictionary. Other entries discuss specific civilizations, archaeological sites, cities and individual artists, as well as the art traditions of particular peoples.

For information on art produced in Africa *see also* EGYPT, ANCIENT, ISLAMIC ART and NUBIA.

BIBLIOGRAPHY

F. Willett: *African Art: An Introduction* (London, 1971, rev. 1993)

R. Brain: *Art and Society in Africa* (London, 1980)

Smithsonian Institution Libraries, National Museum of African Art Library, Library Acquisitions List (1981–)

W. Gillon: *A Short History of African Art* (London, 1984)

J. Vansina: *Art History in Africa: An Introduction to Method* (London and New York, 1984)

J. Kerchache, J.-L. Paudrat and L. Stéphan: *L'Art africain* (Paris, 1988; Eng. trans. by M. de Jager, New York, 1993)

□

I. Introduction. II. Art and aesthetics. III. Contexts of production and use. IV. Imagery and iconography. V. Materials, techniques and uses. VI. Art forms. VII. Regions. VIII. Diaspora. IX. Contemporary developments. X. Forgery. XI. Historiography. XII. Museums. XIII. Exhibitions. XIV. Collectors and dealers. XV. Art libraries and photographic collections.

DETAILED TABLE OF CONTENTS

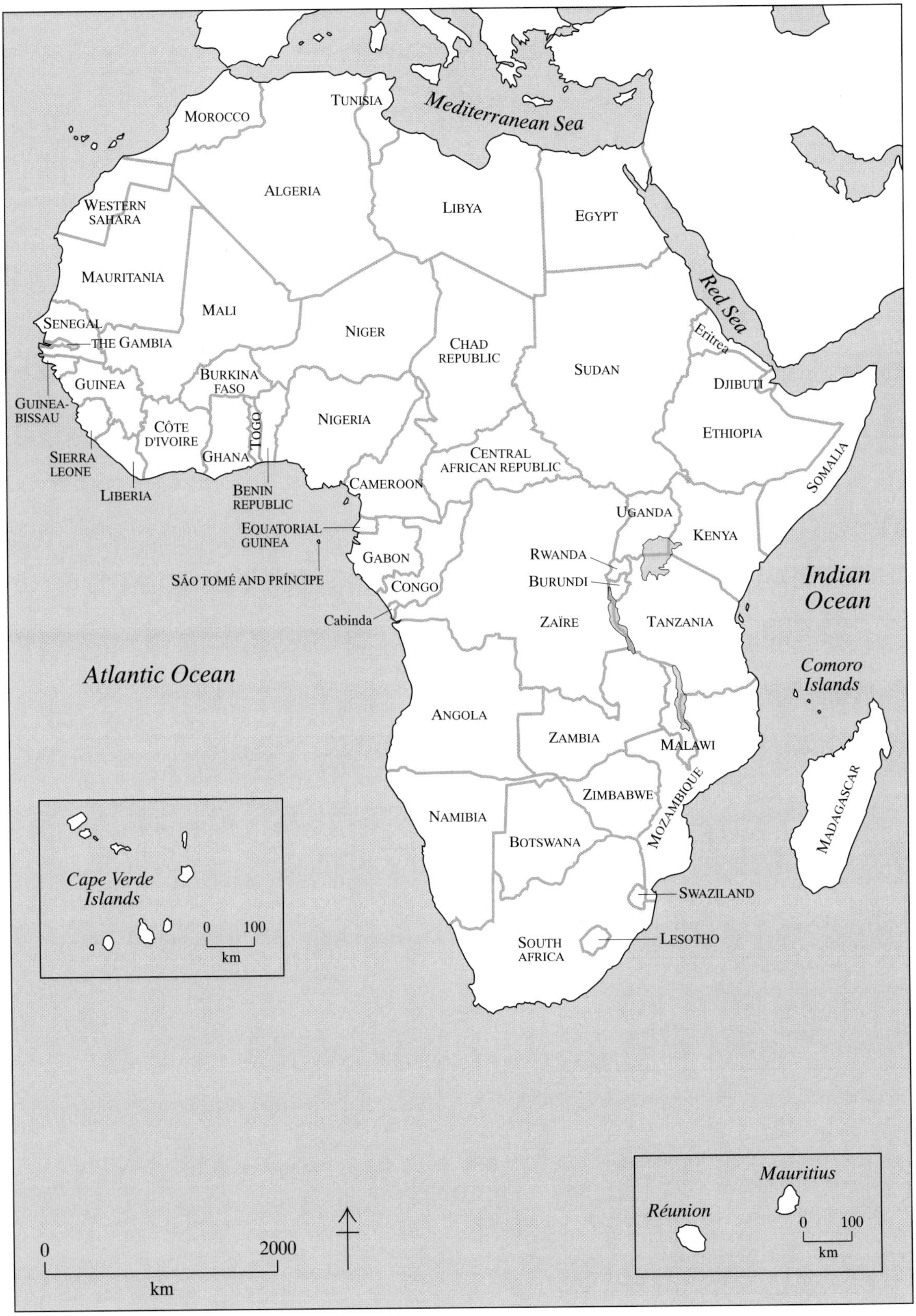

1. Map of Africa; those countries with separate entries in this dictionary are distinguished by CROSS-REFERENCE TYPE

I. Introduction.

1. Geography. 2. Ethnic and language groups. 3. History. 4. Religion.

1. Geography.

(i) Physical geography and climate. Much of Africa is plateau. The coastal plain is generally limited and backed by an escarpment where rivers break up into rapids and waterfalls, marking the limit for coastal shipping. Further upstream the great rivers are often navigable for long stretches by canoes and barges. Because the African coast is relatively lacking in estuaries or safe harbours, few African peoples developed ocean-going technologies or pursued overseas trade. Historically rivers were important for intra-continental contact, with the Nile being only one of several cases where major cultural and political developments took place around a riverine axis. A notable Sub-Saharan instance is the clustering of ancient bronze-casting technologies in the basin of the lower Niger. The interconnections between Nok, Nupe, Idah, Igbo-Ukwu, Ile-Ife and Benin are still obscure, but the proximity of all these places to the lower Niger and the intra-coastal network of creeks and lagoons linking the Niger Delta with Lagos to the west and Calabar to the east seems significant.

The interior plateau landscapes of Africa are diversified by bare-rock mountains (inselberge), upstanding tablelands and volcanic chains. In East Africa the landscape is diversified by a major sequence of intercontinental fault lines, responsible for the Rift Valley and its lakes. True mountain topographies are found in the Drakensberg of Natal, the Atlas Mountains in North Africa, the Ethiopian Highlands, parts of East Africa and the isolated massifs of the central Sahara. These areas are often characterized by considerable cultural and political distinctiveness—the result of specialized ecologies, isolation and freedom from invasion.

Seasonality in Africa is marked by a contrast between the rains and the dry season. At the northern and southern extremes of the continent a Mediterranean climatic regime (warm wet winters, hot dry summers) prevails. In the inter-tropical zone summer is the period of maximum rainfall, and here farming strategies are adapted to conditions of high humidity and extensive cloud cover in the growing season. Annual rainfall in the inter-tropical zones varies from over 3 m in the wettest districts to a few hundred mm on the edges of the Kalahari in the south and the Sahara in the north. Below 600 mm a settled agricultural way of life based on grain cultivation ceases to be viable, so drier districts have continued to be occupied by nomadic pastoralists. Except for a narrow band along the Equator, the contrast between wet and dry season is important throughout the greater part of the inter-tropical zone, even in high-rainfall districts. Parts of the upper Guinea coast in West Africa with over 3 m of rainfall still experience a severe dry season lasting from four to six months. In most cases rainfall follows a single maximum distribution, but in a band stretching from southern Ghana to Cameroon and in parts of East Africa there is a double maximum distribution pattern, in which the main rains and a second shorter period of rain are interrupted by a mid-season dry period. This rainfall pattern allows for double cropping of such short-duration grains as maize and is especially conducive to yam cultivation.

The importance of the dry and wet seasons is such that yearly variation in the start and end of the rains and the attendant uncertainty is socially and agriculturally disruptive. It is not surprising, therefore, that elaborate procedures for invoking or halting the rains are widespread, and in parts of Central Africa political authority is based on the perceived capacity to ensure the orderly progression of the seasons.

Seasonal rhythms affect pastoralists and settled cultivators differently. Pastoralists may follow the rains north and south, balancing the better grazing in wetter districts during the dry season against the reduced risks of disease for their animals in low-rainfall districts during the rainy season. For settled cultivators the rainy season is the time to stay at home and concentrate on agriculture, but during the dry season there may be scope to pursue a craft, join a hunting party, undertake a trading venture or take up seasonal work in towns. Festivals and major social occasions are concentrated in the dry season, when granaries

2. Hausa cushion-cover, leather, cotton and paint, 1.34×0.70 m, from Kano, Nigeria, *c.* 1920 (Edinburgh, Royal Museum of Scotland)

are full, people free of agricultural responsibilities and the paths and tracks more readily passable.

In addition to the normal irregularities connected with the passage of the seasons, account must also be taken of the phenomenon of long-term climatic change. There is much argument about whether the major droughts of the 1970s and 1980s represent a general trend. While available data are not yet adequate to settle the point, there is no disagreement that Africa entered a markedly drier phase *c.* 6000 years ago. This led to the dessication of the Sahara, which had been before then a favoured region for human habitation. The desertification of this area effectively separated the greater part of Africa from Europe. The cultural division this caused was offset to a limited degree by the expansion of cross-desert trade following the introduction of the camel *c.* AD 200.

(ii) Flora and fauna. The vegetation map of Africa is largely determined by rainfall, though in places topography also plays a part. North of the Sahara and at the Cape of Good Hope winter rainfall regimes are responsible for a Mediterranean-type vegetation (deciduous woodlands grading to scrub in low rainfall districts). On the Equator side of the Kalahari and Sahara deserts, savannah grassland gives way to savannah–woodland mosaic, semi-deciduous closed-canopy forest and full lowland humid rain-forest as rainfall totals increase towards the Equator.

About four-fifths of tropical Africa is savannah grassland that, left to itself, would mature into woodland. Where population pressure is high, however, the natural savannah vegetation has largely been replaced by farmland and grassy fallows. Wood is often very scarce, and remaining trees are largely such locally conserved economic species as the baobab, locust-bean and shea. Savannah is well suited to the production of cotton, which can only be grown with great difficulty in wetter districts, and to the raising of cattle, sheep and goats, especially where high population densities have eliminated the tsetse-fly. The relative scarcity of timber, combined with the ready availability of cotton yarn and animal hides, has influenced such arts and crafts of the savannah regions as the 'Morocco' leather and cotton cloth of the Hausa city states (see fig. 2).

The main belt of tropical rain-forest, much modified by cultivation and logging, centres around the Zaïre River basin and extends west towards southern Nigeria, with a western outlier running from Ghana to Sierra Leone. It is likely that the rain-forest presented an obstacle to initial settlement and that agricultural groups penetrated into the forest zone only at a relatively late date. Indeed, even in heavily farmed districts, islands of forest are carefully maintained for ritual activities.

The tropical rain-forest's species diversity makes it the richest and most complex of all ecosystems, and forest peoples have a vast store of knowledge concerning trees and plants, including how to obtain pigments and dyes for colouring the body, dyeing cloth and painting walls and carvings. Forest trees often have cultural as well as practical associations. In these respects, few African forest species surpass kola and the oil palm. Kola is an important stimulant, comparable to coffee or tea, and is an item of long-established commercial importance between the forest and the savannah. The oil palm provides oil for cooking and lighting and produces an important alcoholic beverage, palm wine. Both kola nuts and palm kernels are of importance in divination and ritual, and they often figure as decorative and symbolic motifs in the art of the forest zone.

The pastoral peoples of Africa are as interested in the aesthetics of living animals as in their artistic representation. Settled agriculturalists in drier savannah districts, where cattle are commonplace, think of domestic animals as sources of raw materials for artistic expression, but in the wetter savannahs and in the forest zone, where large domestic livestock are less common owing to disease, horses, cattle and sometimes even goats and sheep assume greater iconographic significance. In southern Nigeria, for example, rulers and title-holders kept horses and trypanosomiasis-resistant dwarf cattle more for prestige and sacrifice than for their economic utility, and these animals sometimes figure as motifs in the bronzework of the region.

The creatures that appear most often in African art are those that embody unusual mystical powers and confer the greatest prestige upon the hunter. Part of ivory's prestige derives from the difficulty and danger faced by the hunter of an elephant. Among other animals considered to possess particular mystical and symbolic force are antelopes, pythons, crocodiles, leopards and lions, which are frequently rendered in artistic terms (see fig. 3).

(iii) Minerals. Africa is a mineral-rich continent, with a long and widespread tradition of mineral-working. The African Iron Age may date back 2500 years, and until the colonial period iron was smelted from local deposits

3. Benin leopard figures, ivory, copper and mirrors, h. 815 mm, ?19th-century copies of earlier originals (London, British Museum)

throughout the continent and worked into agricultural implements, weapons and other items of domestic and ornamental hardware by a village blacksmith, who may also have served as gunsmith, goldsmith and jeweller. In some localities blacksmiths belonged to feared but socially inferior castes or clans. Although little ore has been smelted locally since the 1930s, the village blacksmith is as active as ever, using scrap metal as standard raw material.

Africa has long been famous for its gold. Until the opening up of New World sources in the 16th century, West Africa was the major supplier of gold to Europe and the Middle East. Gold from Central Africa was also important in the Indian Ocean trade and was a factor in the rise of Great Zimbabwe, while 20th-century output was dominated by mines in Southern Africa. Gold jewellery has long been appreciated in African societies, both for its aesthetic properties and as portable wealth. There are major deposits of copper in Central Africa, although these are not thought to have been the source of copper for the bronze of southern Nigeria. The exploitation of Africa's rich reserves of diamonds is a modern phenomenon, and diamonds have had little or no part to play in the story of African decorative arts.

Stone and brick have been used as building materials in North Africa since ancient times, for the monumental architecture of Egypt and of the Romans and Carthaginians. South of the Sahara, use of stone for building was uncommon in pre-colonial times (with such notable exceptions as Great Zimbabwe). Rapid chemical weathering in the tropical zone produces abundant supplies of lateritic mud, which provides a cheap, cool and flexible alternative to building in stone (*see also* §VI, 1 below).

BIBLIOGRAPHY

J. F. Griffiths: *Climates of Africa* (Amsterdam, 1972)
J. I. Clarke: *An Advanced Geography of Africa* (Amersham, 1975)
C. Buckle: *Landforms in Africa* (London, 1978)
P. Richards: *Indigenous Agricultural Revolution: Ecology and Food Production in West Africa* (London, 1985)

2. LANGUAGE AND ETHNIC GROUPS. By comparison with Europe or Asia, Africa is not a densely populated continent. The distribution, however, is very uneven. The major population concentrations are to be found in the Nile valley, Nigeria, the Kenyan and Ethiopian highlands, the Maghrib and in parts of South Africa. Nigeria alone accounts for perhaps one-fifth of the total population of the continent. Parts of the Sahel, east-central Africa and the Equatorial forest region are especially thinly peopled. Although there are few reliable population data before about 1950, it seems likely that this broad pattern of distribution is long established, since it correlates well with the general pattern of regional variation in soil fertility and rainfall reliability.

Africa is characterized by extraordinary linguistic diversity. Estimates vary, but it appears that the continent may have between 1000 and 1500 distinct languages. Of these perhaps 250 are spoken in just one country: Nigeria. Arabic is the main language of North Africa, and other important regional languages include Swahili in Central and East Africa and Hausa and Mandinka over much of the Sahel. Colonial languages (English, French and Portuguese) remain important for education and government

4. Rock painting of a pastoral scene, Tassili N'Ajjer, Algeria, ?*c.* 7000–*c.* 3000 BC

administration. Language classification is always a contentious issue and nowhere more so than in Africa. One widely accepted approach (see Greenberg) groups African languages into four major families (phyla): Niger-Kordofanian, Khoisan, Afro-Asiatic and Nilo-Saharan. (Malagasy, the language of Madagascar, belongs to Malayo-Polynesian, another language family altogether.)

Although it has long been conventional to identify pieces of African art by 'tribe', to produce a map of ethnic units is as contentious a task as producing a language map and will not be attempted here. It has been argued that ethnic consciousness was a phenomenon heightened or even created by the social and political conditions associated with colonialism. Furthermore, ethnic units are defined according to different criteria in different cases. In some parts of the continent ethnicity denotes membership of a linguistic community. Elsewhere it equates with class, occupational caste, regional origin, religious identity or even membership of a trading diaspora. Any generalization is likely to prove misleading, therefore, and the reader seeking further guidance must refer to specialist ethnographic publications, where such caveats are often dealt with in detail.

This complexity was made even greater in the 19th and 20th centuries through the immigration into Africa of Europeans (especially into Southern Africa), Asians (especially into East and Southern Africa) and freed black slaves and their descendants from the Americas.

BIBLIOGRAPHY

G. P. Murdock: *Africa: Its People and their Culture* (New York, 1959)
J. G. Greenberg: *The Languages of Africa* (The Hague, 1970)
J. Hiernaux: *The People of Africa* (London, 1974)
S. L. Kasfir: 'One Tribe, One Style? Paradigms in the Historiography of African Art', *Hist. Afr.*, xi (1984), pp. 163–93

PAUL RICHARDS

3. History.

(i) Before *c.* AD 600. (ii) *c.* AD 600–*c.* 1885. (iii) After *c.* 1885.

(i) Before c. AD *600.* The relatively late advent of indigenous literacy in many parts of Africa, especially south of the Sahara, means that there are very few documentary sources for African history and that archaeology is a prime source of knowledge about events, processes and developments in even the comparatively recent past. On the world stage, African archaeology is of major importance, not least because there is a strong probability that it was in Africa that humans first evolved. In addition the African experience provides an opportunity for interpreting major developments in human behaviour in the context of a landscape that has changed relatively little and is thus analogous to that exploited by past human populations.

Despite such potential, archaeological research in many parts of Africa remains in its infancy, being a low priority for the governments of recently independent nations. While intensive investigations have been undertaken in such areas as South Africa, Kenya and parts of the Nile Valley, huge regions remain almost completely unexplored.

(a) Human origins. Discoveries relating to the earliest periods of human activity have been made both in East Africa (from Ethopia southwards to Tanzania and inland as far as the western branch of the Rift Valley) and in Southern Africa, where conditions have favoured not only the preservation of the earliest hominids' bones and their stone tools but also their subsequent discovery by natural erosion or by quarrying. The concentrations of archaeological discoveries thus do not necessarily reflect the distribution of the earliest hominids. Precisely when modern man first appeared is not yet proven, but it may have been *c.* 200,000–100,000 BP. With the development of fully modern man, the African archaeological record indicates several features of particular relevance to the study of art. Formal disposal of the dead by burial is indicated, and graves and living sites provide evidence for personal adornment and clothing. Natural pigments, notably ochre, as well as bone and shell were frequently employed, probably with other more perishable substances. Particular interest attaches to the development of rock art, both painting and engraving (*see* §VI, 15 below), which was practised in Africa at least as long ago as in Europe (*see* PREHISTORIC EUROPE, §II, 2) and which, in its later phases in Southern Africa, may be closely linked with socio-religious practices of the SAN peoples.

(b) Development of agriculture. Between *c.* 10,000 and *c.* 6000 BC, in what is now the southern Sahara and in parts of East Africa, greatly increased rainfall resulted in the formation or enlargement of lakes and rivers in an area previously too arid to support human habitation. Beside these waters previously nomadic groups established semi-permanent habitations, identified by finds of pottery and barbed bone heads of harpoons. Between *c.* 5000 and *c.* 3000 BC the climate in the southern Sahara once again became more arid. It was at this time that people in this part of Africa began to control their plant and animal food supplies; this led ultimately to the development of farming.

The extent to which the domestication of animals and plants was an indigenous African development, rather than one caused by stimuli from outside that continent, has for long been a matter of controversy. Rock paintings in the Sahara, tentatively dated *c.* 7000–*c.* 3000 BC, provide numerous representations of domestic cattle indicating, among other features, the importance that was attached to body markings and the configuration of horns (see fig. 4). Later art in the Nile Valley and undated examples in the eastern Sahara show that attempts were made to tame such other species as giraffe and ostrich. Large numbers of heavily used grindstones on 4th-millennium BC sites in the Sudanese Nile Valley and parts of the Sahara probably indicate use of cereals, but the extent of their cultivation is still uncertain. By *c.* 1200 BC, if not before, bulrush millet was being intensively cultivated in the western Sahara of Mauritania.

5. Terracotta head, h. 155 mm, from Katsina Ala, Nok, Nigeria, *c.* 900 BC–*c.* AD 200 (Jos, National Museum)

The initial stages of African farming development almost certainly took place in the same general area as was occupied by the harpoon-fishers and at the time when established lifestyles were subject to stress from the lowering of water levels. It is easy to visualize how, in such circumstances, settled people might have controlled herds of formerly wild cattle and begun to protect and then to cultivate plant foods in order to maintain their supply in the face of reduced availability of fish.

It is reasonable to conclude, therefore, that during the last two millennia BC the peoples of the northern savannah belt between the southern fringes of the Sahara and the northern margin of the Equatorial forest turned increasingly to settled life and food production. To the south of the forest, however, the hunter-gatherer lifestyle of previous millennia continued.

(c) Discovery of metallurgy. During the 1st millennium BC, ironworking began in settlements south of the Sahara. The evidence for this comes primarily from the Jos Plateau of Nigeria, from sites that have also yielded the remarkable Nok terracottas (see fig. 5). Further evidence for ironworking rather more than 2000 years ago has been

6. Lydenburg head (no. 1), terracotta, h. 380 mm, from near Lydenburg, eastern Transvaal, South Africa, *c.* AD 500–700 (University of Cape Town, on loan to Cape Town, South African Museum); reconstruction

recovered around Lake Victoria, notably on its western shore in north-western Tanzania. In both areas the smelting technology used shows little sign of local antecedents, leading to suggestions that it was introduced from the north; however, no clear evidence for such long-distance connection has been cited. It is noteworthy that Sub-Saharan Africa generally lacked a distinct 'Bronze Age' when the softer metals were worked but techniques of ironworking had not yet been developed.

In the southern half of Africa the beginnings of farming and of metalworking seem to have been broadly concurrent. During the first few centuries AD, in territory previously inhabited by stone tool-using, mobile hunter–gatherer peoples, there were established villages of settled farmers, who worked metals and made pottery. Their pottery has a stylistic uniformity that, along with the apparent speed with which the lifestyle began over an enormous area and its marked contrast with what had gone before, led archaeologists to postulate rapid population migration, possibly of Bantu speakers.

By about the 3rd century AD farming peoples had begun to absorb and replace the hunter–gatherer populations of most of Southern Africa wherever environmental conditions were suitable for the cultivation of African cereal crops. Artefacts from this period other than pottery are scarce, but mention should be made of the remarkable series of seven life-size terracotta human heads of *c.* AD 500–700, reconstructed from fragments found at Lydenburg in the Transvaal (see fig. 6), which share many technological and stylistic features with the contemporary domestic pottery. In the south-westernmost regions pottery and domestic animals are attested by the 1st century AD, but metallurgy and crop cultivation remained unknown.

(d) Early settlements. During the 1st millennium AD peasant societies in several parts of Africa showed signs of increasing complexity and centralization. Indeed excavations at Jenne-Jeno, beside the inland Niger Delta in Mali, provide evidence for incipient urbanization 2000 years ago, probably supported by rice cultivation and by trade from an extensive hinterland. By the time that Arabic-speaking traders from North Africa crossed the Sahara in the 8th century AD, large centralized states had developed in the northern savannah. The most important of these was Ghana, centred on what is now southern Mauritania and south-western Mali. Although ancient Ghana and its successor, Mali, reached maximum prosperity through control of the gold production of the Bambuk area and by exploiting their intermediary position between the trans-Saharan Muslim traders and the rich savannah and forest lands of West Africa, their origin predates such long-distance links.

Within the forest itself states tended to be smaller because of restrictions on communication, but they included dense populations supported by yam cultivation. Information is largely derived from excavation at such sites as IFE and BENIN. The outstanding artistic works discovered here reveal the development of technological and artistic expertise together with a concentration of material resources. Although they reached a peak at these sites between the 13th and 18th centuries, at IGBO-UKWU in eastern Nigeria these developments may be traced back as far as the late 1st millennium AD. In East and Southern Africa broadly parallel developments occurred, again probably influenced by long-distance trade links, here involving the Indian Ocean coast, although its importance in African political centralization should not be exaggerated. Ivory, gum, spices, wood and slaves were exported together with, in later times, gold, in exchange for such luxury items as glass, beads, porcelain and textiles. Islam was introduced from a relatively early period. Despite the strong African roots of these maritime towns, it seems that their direct influence did not extend far inland. The interlacustrine kingdoms of East Africa, for example, seem to have arisen during the first half of the 2nd millennium AD, having virtually no contact with the Indian Ocean coast some 800–1200 km distant, but deriving their wealth primarily from large herds of cattle.

BIBLIOGRAPHY

C. Ehret and M. Posnansky: *The Archaeological and Linguistic Reconstruction of African History* (Berkeley, 1982)

T. H. Huffmann: 'Archaeology and Ethnohistory of the African Iron Age', *Annu. Rev. Anthropol.*, xi (1982), pp. 133–50
D. W. Phillipson: *African Archaeology*, Cambridge World Archaeology (Cambridge, 1985, rev. 1993)
——: 'An Archaeological Reconsideration of Bantu Expansion', *Muntu*, ii (1985), pp. 69–84
G. Connah: *African Civilizations* (Cambridge, 1987)
M. Hall: *The Changing Past: Farmers, Kings and Traders in Southern Africa* (Cape Town, 1987)
S. K. McIntosh and R. J. McIntosh: 'From Stone to Metal: New Perspectives on the Later Prehistory of West Africa', *J. World Prehist.*, ii (1988), pp. 89–133
J. Lewis-Williams and T. Dowson: *Images of Power* (Johannesburg, 1989)
T. Shaw, ed.: *The Archaeology of Africa: Food, Metals and Towns* (London, 1993)
D. E. Miller and N. J. van der Merwe: 'Early Metal Working in Sub-Saharan Africa: A Review of Recent Research', *J. Afr. Hist.*, xxxv (1994), pp. 1–36

DAVID W. PHILLIPSON

(ii) c. *AD 600–*c. *1885.* The diversity of societies, languages and cultures in the African continent is far too great to support generalizations about artistic and cultural trends. Some scholars have long recognized this and have attempted to group different cultural traditions by area. By 'culture' is understood not just the arts but whole distinctive ways of life, and by using the term 'tradition' the claim is made that cultures as they existed before the colonial period had been stable or even invariant for many generations. Classification by cultural area, however, has remained unsatisfactory, not only because it has proved impossible to apply the same set of criteria to different areas but also because this approach denies the existence of history, treating human cultures as if they were invariant geological strata or animal species. G. P. Murdock remedied this by focusing on the ways in which cultures had arisen, providing an early attempt at a genuine culture history of Africa. Since then, the main historical outlines of a cultural history have emerged.

The cultural map of Africa as it existed in the late 19th century took shape between *c.* AD 600 and 1100, and its traditions can be divided into four main cultural provinces: the *oikoumene*, the West African urban tradition and the western and eastern Bantu traditions. In addition there are other traditions of lesser geographic extent: several occur in the heart of the continent between the *oikoumene* and the cultures of the Bantu speakers, but they also include the Khoi-San traditions in south-western Africa and the Malagasy tradition.

(a) *Oikoumene.* (b) West African urban tradition. (c) Western Bantu tradition. (d) Eastern Bantu tradition. (e) Other traditions.

(a) Oikoumene.This term is derived from the Greek for 'inhabited world' and designates that part of Africa the cultures of which were polarized by the acceptance of Christianity or Islam and the peoples of which remained in continual contact with the old world. Encompassing almost half of the continent, the *oikoumene* includes all peoples north of a line linking the mouth of the Senegal River to the top of the Niger Bend to Lake Chad to the Nilotic Sudd, near Malakal, around the highlands of Ethiopia to the Somalia–Kenya border and then south to near the Indian Ocean following the shore inland to Mozambique. It also takes in the Comoro Islands and small parts of Madagascar.

The *oikoumene* grew out of many strands. First there was the civilization of ANCIENT EGYPT that developed in the Nile Valley, culminating in Pharaonic Egypt from *c.* 3200 BC onwards. Painting there shows influences from styles developed by the herders of the Sahara from *c.* 6000 BC, when Egypt was part of an intercommunicating zone that encompassed the Middle East. Its civilization did not spread widely to the west, although it interacted with older local traditions in the adjacent Nile Valley, perhaps as far south as present Khartoum. It was left to Phoenician (after *c.* 1000 BC) and Greek colonies (after *c.* 700 BC) to implant the cultures of the eastern Mediterranean on the northern shores of Africa. With the emergence of the Roman Empire, which incorporated Egypt in 30 BC, institutions of government, law and trade became more unified, although most aspects of indigenous culture remained relatively untouched. The Empire did not greatly influence Sudan, Ethiopia or even the peoples of the Sahara. More fundamental changes in culture and world view followed the spread of Christianity into Africa from the 1st century AD. In the next 500 years it unified all of North Africa as well as the Sudan south to the Sudd and highland Ethiopia. Christian artistic expression shows a striking uniformity over the whole area.

Islam was the core of the second *oikoumene.* By AD 640 Muslim armies had overrun Egypt before sweeping westwards, rapidly conquering the Maghrib. By *c.* 800 Muslim traders had reached the African shores of the Indian Ocean as well as towns south of the Sahara in West Africa. Islam did not, however, overrun Christian Sudan or Ethiopia, and the unification of the various branches of Islam took a long time, even in North Africa. By *c.* 1100 a single school of Muslim law dominated the Maghrib, while Sunni orthodoxy was regaining the heartland of Egypt. At this time the first West African rulers were beginning to convert, and Islam began to gain ground in the East African coastal towns. Between the 13th and 16th centuries northern Sudan also became Muslim, but highland Ethiopia remained Christian. After *c.* 1100 further Islamic advances were limited and slow. Inroads were made into West Africa, but the area retained its own character. In East Africa, Muslim traders made some converts as far south as Zimbabwe, but their advance had been lost by 1600.

Christianity and, later, Islam were extremely powerful forces, and persons from any part of the *oikoumene* shared, at least generally, the concerns, reasoning and customs of any other part. The practice of pilgrimage—to Mecca and Jerusalem—reinforced this unity. Nevertheless, within the Muslim tradition different cultural profiles developed. By 1100 this was evident in Egypt, Tunisia, Morocco, the Saharan desert cultures and the lowlands of the Horn of Africa. But, while Ethiopia redefined its cultural profile in reaction to Islam, and Sudan developed its own Muslim culture, such developments never threatened the fundamental unity of the culture of the *oikoumene.*

(b) West African urban tradition. Despite the vast linguistic and ethnic diversity of West Africa, there is an underlying unity based on an urban network linked by trade. The region also has a common tradition of state government and ideology that can be labelled sacred

kingship. This single ideology, once believed to have spread from one point to all the others, is not all-encompassing and probably evolved from a number of local village-based religions, becoming unified through centuries of mutual exchanges. The diversity of West African cultures stems from the strength of villages, which offered creative input into the urban cultures, taking only what was useful in return and resisting assimilation.

West Africa's cultural characteristics developed over a long period. Settlement in the savannah and on the desert fringe increased following the desertification of the Sahara from *c.* 2500 BC to *c.* AD 1. As population densities rose, trade based on the exchange of varying regional resources became important, and centres of trade developed. The first known city of the region, Djenné, illustrates this pattern of development. It was probably established *c.* 250 BC by peoples from the Sahara; by AD 400 its hinterland reached from the desert edge in Mauritania to the Atlantic Ocean to southern Mali. Some Hellenistic beads have even been found in Djenné. In this period other towns developed, so that by *c.* AD 700 a network of trade was taking shape in the western half of West Africa. Thus urbanization here should not be attributed to Muslim influences; indeed the first known large-scale states, with capitals located near the desert fringe, also pre-date Muslim trading contacts. One or two of them had begun to trade in gold with North Africa by the 7th century AD at the latest.

The trans-Saharan trade developed into a major trading network after the arrival of Islam in the Maghrib, spurring on the processes of urbanization and thus unifying West Africa. The earliest known trading centre in Nigeria, IGBO-UKWU, dates from *c.* 800, and the site shows evidence of intensive contact not only with North Africa but also with the ocean shore to the south. By *c.* 900 other cities were appearing, and by *c.* 1100 there was a town linked to the West African gold trade at Nyarko in southern Ghana. By this time the basic unity of West Africa was a reality: trading networks existed, and cities acted as crucibles of ideas, values and practices from afar that were then disseminated to the rural hinterlands.

An example of these processes is the history of terracotta art in West Africa. The earliest known centres of terracotta production were in northern Nigeria, where they had appeared by 900 BC. By AD 700 terracotta art was found all over the Sahel from Lake Chad to the Atlantic, with common stylistic features appearing from Nigeria to the Upper Niger and the coast. The tradition of building with sun-dried bricks also developed during the last centuries BC, so that by *c.* AD 1100 there were major monumental buildings in similar styles from Lake Chad to the Middle and Upper Niger. Finally, a common technique of metal-casting using the lost-wax process was established all over the West African savannah by *c.* 1000.

By *c.* 1100 a common cultural tradition linked all of West Africa (outside the forest areas between Sierra Leone and southern Ghana), and in the following centuries a gradual percolation of Islam and the expansion of specialized cattle herders, the Fulani, from Senegal to Sudan along the desert edge further strengthened common cultural features.

At the same time more localized cultural blocks were emerging in northern Nigeria, the area within the Niger Bend, the Upper Niger area, the area south of the River Senegal, southern Ghana and western Nigeria especially. These were urban, linked to the others and dominated by states but remaining culturally distinct.

(c) Western Bantu tradition. South of a line from the Atlantic Ocean near the border between Nigeria and Cameroon to the Indian Ocean in southern Somalia is an area occupied for the most part by Bantu-speaking peoples. These peoples migrated from their homelands in two directions. Western Bantu speakers settled most of Central Africa, while the eastern Bantu directly affected the cultural history of East and Southern Africa (*see* §(d) below).

The western Bantu speakers entered the rain-forests of Equatorial Africa *c.* 1800 BC, reached the savannah of Central Africa by 500 BC and arrived in southern Angola, the Middle Zambezi and eastern Zambia by *c.* the early 1st century AD. Their social organization was adapted to very low population densities. The basic units, 'houses', were led by 'big men'; several of them might group together for defensive purposes in ephemeral villages. The largest and most permanent social unit was the district, which consisted of a set of houses linked by alliance and marriage; this was the locus of ethnic identity. Ideologies of the big man and of kinship meshed well with religious beliefs and practices centring on the propitiation of spirits and the fear of witchcraft.

Cultural variation within the western Bantu tradition developed between the forest and the savannah peoples as a result not only of their physical separation and the difference of their physical environments but of varying degrees of interaction with autochthones and a later (*c.* AD 1–500) immigration of eastern Bantu speakers to the southern savannah. Despite the emergence of such localized cultural variants, a common core of beliefs and practices within the tradition remained. Evidence of early art in this area is sparse. Excavation of huge cemeteries found in the Upemba Depression of Zaïre and in the Shaba Province have revealed that wealth here was based on copper produced near by. Only a few objects in wood and pottery dating from before *c.* 1000 have survived in the savannah area, not enough as yet to speculate about common formal features for this early period. In south-eastern Zaïre (after *c.* 800) and in northern Angola (after *c.* 1500) enough works of art have survived to show a basic continuity.

(d) Eastern Bantu tradition. The earliest eastern Bantu speakers had moved from Cameroon to the Great Lakes by *c.* 1000 BC. There they met herders and farmers from the upper Nile and Ethiopia, and a stable, shared way of life developed, with world views and value systems that had become quite different from that of the western Bantu. By *c.* AD 400 the eastern Bantu had expanded both along the coast and inland from the Great Lakes as far south as Natal. The common culture that developed corresponds in part to that of the 'East African cattle area' designated by M. J. Herskovits; its best known works are terracotta masks from the Transvaal (see fig. 6 above).

Between *c.* 750 and *c.* 1000 a set of regional cultures, adapted to specific local conditions, grew out of the common tradition. In Southern Africa three main regional cultures can be discerned. Some farmer/herders moved back from Transvaal, first to the Limpopo River (*c.* 800) and then beyond to Zimbabwe (*c.* 900). These groups developed a centralized government based around hierarchical settlements, the largest of which were located on defensible hill-top positions, at which substantial herds of cattle were maintained. These sites, especially those in the Limpopo, show evidence of extensive ivory-working, apparently to produce items for export. Large quantities of glass beads were also produced and traded inland. From about the 11th century gold replaced ivory as the principal export, although it was also used locally, as is attested by élite graves at Mapungubwe, Transvaal. The layout of these central sites, the presence of dry-stone architecture and some aspects of the associated material culture are clearly ancestral to those of GREAT ZIMBABWE, which flourished during the 13th and 14th centuries and represents the culmination of this process of political centralization. At the same time the inhabitants of Botswana developed a different system based on more intensive herding and involving the creation of chiefdoms and structured interaction with the local hunter-gatherers, the San. In south-east Africa proper the Sotho–Nguni peoples retained more of the original culture, although their environments and autochthonic influences also helped to produce new cultural variants.

Beginning *c.* 750, four new major East African cultures emerged. Along the coast Swahili-speaking peoples adapted to the marine environment by founding fishing villages and becoming involved in overseas trade. Town sites on the coasts of Somalia, Kenya and Tanzania provide abundant evidence that by the 8th century maritime connections extended to at least as far south as Vilanculos Bay in Mozambique. In the Great Lakes new ceramics confirm immigration by non-Bantu-speakers from the north after *c.* 750. Well before *c.* 1400 this led to the creation of small states culminating in major kingdoms after *c.* 1500. In northern Tanzania and central Kenya a variety of foreign influences produced a highland variant of the original eastern Bantu culture, probably before 1000. A fourth variant of that heritage arose from *c.* 750 in south-eastern Zaïre, where eastern and western Bantu speakers had mixed. Chiefdoms and then states appeared in the area, and the culture expanded into all of Zambia and portions of Malawi after *c.* 1000.

(e) Other traditions. Several cultural traditions of lesser geographic extent must be mentioned. In south-western Africa the Khoi–San tradition derives from the cultures of the hunters and gatherers who have inhabited the area for thousands of years. As the Khoi expanded from their homeland in Botswana, cultural unification occurred as cattle were acquired and the new herders interacted with the hunters and gatherers.

During the early centuries AD, MADAGASCAR was settled by rice-growers from South-east Asia speaking Austronesian languages. Interaction with the eastern Bantu traditions followed, and a new cultural tradition arose. Later influences from all over the Indian Ocean contributed to Malagasy culture and arts without profoundly altering them. Unfortunately a lack of archaeological data means that a detailed chronology and cultural history for the island before *c.* 1500 have yet to be determined.

The cultural history of the peoples between the edge of the *oikoumene* and the Bantu traditions also remains obscure. The northern savannahs of Central Africa were settled by sedentary populations well before the 1st millennium BC. Where different cultural traditions confronted each other, as in the Ubangi–Uele basin, they fused, producing new variants. Further study is required to determine the age and stability of these traditions. Herders, farmers and hunter-gatherers from the southern Sudan, northern Uganda, Kenya and northern Tanzania have been better studied. Several traditions are involved, and their confrontations led to complex interactions and the creation of many local cultures. Many of the peoples concerned were highly mobile and left few archaeological traces. Several traditions (e.g. that of the Nilotic herders) can be traced, but, especially in Kenya and Tanzania, the dynamics of cultural interaction have been so intensive, complex and unstable for so long that the overall patterns remain unclear.

BIBLIOGRAPHY

J. Devisse: 'L'Apport de l'archéologie à l'histoire de l'Afrique occidentale entre le Vème et le XIIe siècle', *Acad. Inscr. & B.-Lett.: C. R. Séances* (1982), pp. 156–77

S. K. McIntosh and R. J. McIntosh: 'The Early City in West Africa: Towards an Understanding', *Afr. Archaeol. Rev.*, ii (1984), pp. 73–98

J. Vansina: 'Western Bantu Expansion', *J. Afr. Hist.*, xxv (1984), pp. 129–45

JAN VANSINA

(iii) After c. *1885.* From the end of the 19th century the colonial conquest and the intensive propagation of Christianity and Islam that attended it began to threaten Africa's cultural traditions and ways of life on a scale vastly exceeding the effects of the arrival of Europeans on the coasts after *c.* 1450 or the massive slave trade from *c.* 1660 to 1850. After 1885 five European powers (Belgium, Britain, France, Germany and Portugal) divided up the greater part of the continent between them. Colonial rule and expanded trade with Europe greatly increased the rate of urbanization and the power of the central institutions of the state. Although full colonial rule lasted for only 50 years (*c.* 1900–*c.* 1950), it was nevertheless largely through colonialism and the cultural and aesthetic climate of the colonial metropoles that the world developed its awareness of African art. From the African perspective, such metropolitan collections as the bronzes looted from Benin in the aftermath of the British military expedition of 1898 are particularly prone to stir up memories of injustices suffered under colonialism. It will be some time yet before the field of African art can be fully separated from the political geography of colonialism.

As far as post-colonial developments are concerned, the vigourous independence of rural African populations has kept alive many old art forms as well as adding new ones, often as elements in new religious cults. In addition, the growth of towns has led to the massive expansion of such popular arts as photography (see fig. 7), tourist art and 'bar art'. If measured by volume and brash, inventive vigour, then the surviving court arts of the old urban centres pale into insignificance beside these new forms of

7. Double portrait by an unknown photographer, 240×170 mm, Yamoussoukro, Côte d'Ivoire, 1970s (private collection)

artistic expression. As yet, however, the scholarly community has paid relatively little attention to popular arts in Africa's rapidly expanding urban centres.

BIBLIOGRAPHY

M. J. Herskovits: 'A Preliminary Consideration of the Culture Areas of Africa', *Amer. Anthropologist*, xxvi/1 (1924), pp. 50–64

L. Frobenius: *Kulturgeschichte Afrikas* (Zurich, 1934)

H. Baumann and D. Westermann: *Les Peuples et les civilisations de l'Afrique* (Paris, 1948)

G. P. Murdock: *Africa: Its Peoples and their Culture History* (New York, 1959)

J. Maquet: *Afrique: Les Civilisations noires* (Paris, 1962)

J. D. Fage and R. Oliver, eds: *The Cambridge History of Africa*, 8 vols (London, 1975–86)

J. Murray, ed.: *Cultural Atlas of Africa* (Oxford and New York, 1981)

UNESCO General History of Africa, 8 vols (Paris and London, 1981–)

C. Ehret and M. Posnansky: *The Archaeological and Linguistic Reconstruction of African History* (Berkeley, 1982)

D. Birmingham and P. Martin, eds: *History of Central Africa*, i (London, 1983)

W. Gillon: *A Short History of African Art* (London and New York, 1984)

J. Vansina: *Art History in Africa: An Introduction to Method* (London and New York, 1984)

Africa Explores: 20th Century African Art (exh. cat. by S. Vogel with I. Ebong, New York, Cent. Afr. A., 1991)

PAUL RICHARDS

4. RELIGION. By the late 20th century the religious map of Africa had become complex. In much of Sub-Saharan Africa 'traditional', often local, religions have continued to have many followers, especially in rural areas. In some areas, however, either Islam or Christianity has many adherents. Western Nigeria, for example, has a large Muslim population, while eastern Nigeria and such other areas as Uganda, Kenya and parts of Southern Africa have significant Christian populations. In addition, the East African coast and much of north-east Africa have been Islamic for centuries, although there is a long-established Christian Church in Ethiopia. Similarly, North Africa is predominantly Muslim, although a minority Coptic Christian Church exists in Egypt.

This section can provide only a brief introduction to religion in Africa. Further information on the many and complex links between religion and art in Africa will be found throughout the rest of this survey, in the entries on individual peoples and in the country entries.

BIBLIOGRAPHY

J. Relig. Africa (1967–)

Face of the Gods: Art and Altars of Africa and the African Americas (exh. cat. by R. F. Thompson, New York, Mus. Afr. A., 1993)

T. D. Blakely, W. E. A. van Beek and D. L. Thomson, eds: *Religion in Africa: Experience and Expression* (London and Portsmouth, NH, 1994)

(i) Indigenous religions. (ii) Christianity. (iii) Islam. (iv) Modern developments.

(i) Indigenous religions. Each 'traditional' or indigenous African religion is unique to a particular society. Each has its own 'high' God or Creator, often referred to as 'Divinity' in the anthropological literature. Each such Divinity is responsible for the creation of the world and for its protection. Divinity is all-powerful, while mankind is puny and helpless. In most indigenous African religions, people do not claim to know or understand Divinity or to know what Divinity looks like; Divinity is rarely if ever represented in art. Such qualities as compassion, anger, mercy and vengeance are, however, often attributed to Divinity. Much African myth is concerned with Divinity's creation of the world and with the activities of the first creatures, often half-human, half-divine, and with the actions of the first humans.

Divinity is typically remote and otiose. Once the world had been created, Divinity retired from any concern with everyday matters. Rather than being in any sort of contact with Divinity, therefore, the living communicate regularly with lesser forces. Generally these comprise ancestors, often referred to as ghosts, shades or ancestral spirits, and spirits, often referred to as deities or lesser divinities. These figures tend to be specific to individual societies, and they may be seen as symbolic representations of each society's experience of the world.

Ancestors are essentially the souls or spiritual essences of once-living people that have been transformed by the performance of mortuary rites into spiritual entities (*see* §III, 5(ii) below). They may be given shrines where they can be contacted by the living. Usually the ancestors are linked to lineages and kin-based groups and are concerned only with the affairs of their descendants. The senior members, those closest to the ancestors in life and who will join them soonest, are responsible for communication with them through prayer, sacrifice and ritual.

Spirits may be best understood as refractions of Divinity. They are aspects of Divinity as concerned with particular problems, such as illness, or with particular places. Generally spirits are not tied to lineages or other human groups but are free to wander where they will. The configuration of spirits with which any social group is concerned varies with their changing circumstances. People seek to control the power of spirits over them through sacrifice.

Communication with the ancestors and spirits is generally not sought haphazardly but rather undertaken in response to particular problems. The major forms of communication are prayer, sacrifice, possession, visions and dreams. Those mainly responsible for these forms of communication are often referred to as priests, prophets and diviners. Sacrifice to spirits tends to be more important in pastoralist societies, where the ancestors play a less significant role, while sacrifice to the ancestors is more important in agricultural societies. The great agricultural kingdoms place great emphasis on ritual for the royal ancestors.

Priests are generally regarded as possessing attributes of sacredness, often inherited, that enable them to make sacrifices and to act as repositories of divine truth and knowledge unknown to ordinary people. The elders of lineages and local groups share in these qualities of priests, at least in respect of the group's ancestors. Diviners are often held to be able to leave the immanent world and to enter that of the spirits and ancestors. They return from such trances with knowledge of the causes of misfortune or with knowledge of the future. Prophets bring messages from Divinity and often arise at times of disaster or of great stress (*see* §(iv) below).

In all traditional African societies a central problem is the occurrence of evil and misfortune, both to explain it and to cope with it. While the actions of Divinity, the spirits and the ancestors are one form of explanation, a belief in the human capacity to bring about misfortune through witchcraft and/or sorcery is widespread. Witchcraft involves an innate power to harm others merely by wishing to, while sorcery consists in the manipulation of substances. Beliefs in both witchcraft and sorcery are best understood as aspects of philosophies of misfortune. They are often part of sophisticated and complex belief systems that allow personal misfortune to be understood and dealt with. The term 'magic' has also been often used in accounts of African religion, especially by travellers and missionaries. Essentially it is an ethnocentric and derogatory term applied to the religious activities of indigenous practitioners. It has no defined meaning that can be usefully applied to the beliefs and practices of African religion and is best dispensed with.

BIBLIOGRAPHY

E. E. Evans-Pritchard: *Witchcraft, Oracles and Magic among the Azande* (Oxford, 1935; rev. and abridged 1979)
D. Forde, ed.: *African Worlds* (London, 1954)
M. Fortes: *Oedipus and Job in West African Religion* (Cambridge, 1959)
P. Tempels: *Bantu Philosophy* (Paris, 1959)
J. Middleton: *Lugbara Religion: Ritual and Authority among an East African People* (London, 1960)
R. G. Lienhardt: *Divinity and Experience: The Religion of the Dinka* (Oxford, 1961)
J. Middleton and E. Winter, eds: *Witchcraft and Sorcery in East Africa* (London, 1963)
M. Fortes and G. Dieterlen, eds: *African Systems of Thought* (London, 1965)
E. W. Smith: *African Ideas of God* (London, 1966)
J. Beattie and J. Middleton, eds: *Spirit Mediumship and Society in Africa* (London, 1969)
G. Parrinder: *Religion in Africa* (Harmondsworth, 1969)
J. Mbiti: *African Religions and Philosophy* (New York, 1970)
M. Douglas, ed.: *Witchcraft Confessions and Accusations* (London, 1971)
B. Ray: *African Religions: Symbol, Ritual and Community* (Englewood Cliffs, 1976)
J. W. Fernandez: *Bwiti: An Ethnography of the Religious Imagination in Africa* (Princeton, 1982)
T. Beidelman: *Moral Imagination in Kaguru Modes of Thought* (Bloomington, 1986)
J. Gray: *Àshe: Traditional Religion and Healing in Sub-Saharan Africa and the Diaspora—A Classified International Bibliography*, Bibliographies and Indexes in Afro-American and African Studies, 24 (Westport, CT, 1989)
R. Horton: *Patterns of Thought in Africa and the West* (Cambridge, 1993)

JOHN MIDDLETON

(ii) Christianity. By the late 20th century Christianity was probably the majority religion of Sub-Saharan Africa. This was especially so in such areas as eastern Nigeria, Uganda, Lesotho and parts of South Africa. In such areas, indeed, Christianity could be said to be the traditional religion, with some families having been Christian since the early 19th century. Like Islam (*see* §(iii) below), Christianity generally has more adherents in urban areas, while in rural areas it is more likely to exist side by side with other traditional beliefs. It is not uncommon for self-defining Christians to have recourse to pagan practices, and even Islamic ones, in response to particular problems or misfortunes.

Christianity in Africa is virtually as old as Christianity itself. In the very early Christian period, Egypt and North Africa were part of the Greco-Roman Mediterranean world and were thus visited by the early followers of the new religion. Churches were established in Egypt by the 2nd century AD, and Alexandria and Carthage became centres of Christian learning. Christianity was taken up the Nile, so that Christian churches flourished in Nubia into the 12th century. The Arab–Muslim advance into North Africa in the 7th century led eventually to the disappearance of Christianity from all the area, except for the Coptic Church in Egypt, which has continued to the present. Islam did not, however, affect the Christian Church in Ethiopia, which, with its links to the Christian Churches of Egypt and Syria, has maintained its rich and distinctive liturgical, architectural and painting traditions to the present day (*see* ETHIOPIA, §§I and II).

A second phase of the history of Christianity in Africa began with the European, especially Portuguese, contact with the West African coast from the late 15th century on. Missionary work began soon after and was spectacularly successful in the kingdom of the Kongo, where the king and many of his followers converted in 1491. Over the following centuries statues of saints with haloes were produced, as were crucifixes (see fig. 8) and other examples of Christian iconography. Given the almost archetypal status of the Kongo power figures (often erroneously referred to as 'nail fetishes') as primitive 'African' art, it is salutary to realize that there is a strong possibility that the very idea of driving nails into figures was derived by Kongo artists from Christian crucifixes and statues of martyrs (Jongmans; Thornton).

As trade with and, later, colonization of Africa increased, Christianity continued to make an impact in local areas.

8. Crucifix, copper alloy, h. 510 mm, from Kongo, Zaïre, ?17th century (Berlin, Museum für Völkerkunde, III C 44073)

Trading stations often had chaplains, and some local children received a partial Christian education. These developments had little effect on the interior until the late 18th century and the early 19th, when a new evangelism in Europe and America and the return of freed, and Christian, slaves to Africa combined to give Christianity in Africa a new impetus. With the partition of Africa by the colonial powers at the end of the 19th century and the development of road and rail transport, missionaries were able to establish themselves more securely, leading to the adoption of Christianity, in its myriad imported and local forms, as the major religion of Sub-Saharan Africa.

Christianity's effects on the visual arts in Sub-Saharan Africa have been mixed. They have often been negative, with members both preaching and practising the destruction of 'idols' and objects connected to traditional beliefs and practices. The cumulative effect of such attitudes and actions is difficult to judge, but thousands of objects must have been destroyed and whole art traditions, including those of body adornment and figure sculpture, wiped out. Presumably related knowledge and skills also disappeared. In discussing such questions, however, one must not forget that many of those who converted, as well as many of their descendants, probably came to share the worldview that encouraged the destruction of the 'pagan' traditions.

In many cases too, the abandonment, forcible or otherwise, of an art tradition presaged the adoption of new ones. Among the Baluyia of western Kenya, for example, the introduction of Christianity led to the abandonment of traditions of body painting but brought about the development of a vibrant tradition of mural painting in the later 20th century (Burt). Throughout the continent one of the most visible new art traditions is that of church and church-related architecture. By the late 20th century, however, the traditions (other than those of Ethiopia) had still not been widely studied, though the Angolan churches of the 16th, 17th and later centuries have received some attention (*see* ANGOLA, §2). Some works of the late 20th century, such as the basilica in Yamoussoukro, Côte d'Ivoire—a copy of St Peter's, Rome—have little architectural quality, being grandiose and uninspired monuments to political power rather than works of art.

In general by the late 20th century, however, the iconoclastic attitudes of earlier times had been replaced in many areas by new and more positive attitudes. A leading exemplar of these attitudes was the Roman Catholic priest Kevin Carroll (1920–93), who both studied and commissioned work by Yoruba artists, including sculptures and murals for churches and other buildings from the 1950s on. For example, he commissioned the Muslim Yoruba sculptor Lamidi Fakeye (*b c.* 1925) to carve panels with New Testament scenes for the doors of the Catholic church of the University of Ibadan in 1954 (Carroll, pls 85–6). (Examples of the work commissioned by Carroll and fellow priests are held by the African Art Museum at Tenafly, NJ.) By the early 1990s churches and other Christian buildings throughout the continent were decorated with African Christian art, and a related literature had begun to appear (e.g. Thiel and Helf; Harmsen).

BIBLIOGRAPHY

D. J. Fleming: *Heritage of Beauty: Pictorial Studies of Modern Christian Architecture in Asia and Africa Illustrating the Influence of Indigenous Cultures* (New York, 1937)

——: *Each with His Own Brush: Contemporary Christian Art in Asia and Africa* (New York, 1938)

D. G. Jongmans: 'Nail Fetish and Crucifix', *The Wonder of Man's Ingenuity*, Mededelingen van het Museum voor Volkenkunde, Leiden, xv (Leiden, 1962), pp. 50–62

A. Lehmann: *Afroasiatische christliche Kunst* (Berlin, 1966); Eng. trans. as *Christian Art in Africa and Asia* (St Louis, MO, and London, 1969)

K. Carroll: *Yoruba Religious Carving: Pagan and Christian Sculpture in Nigeria and Dahomey* (London, Dublin and Melbourne, 1967)

E. C. Burt: 'Mural Painting in Western Kenya', *Afr. A.*, xvi/3 (1983), pp. 60–63, 80

J. F. Thiel and H. Helf: *Christliche Kunst in Afrika* (1984)

Zimbabwe Christian Art: The First Collected Exhibition (exh. cat., Harare, Anglican Cathedral, 1986)

J. B. Waite: 'The African Art Museum of the S.M.A. Fathers', *Afr. A.*, xxi/1 (1987), pp. 64–7, 88

F. Harmsen: *The Way to Easter: Stations of the Cross in South Africa* (Pretoria, 1989)

J. Thornton: 'The Regalia of the Kingdom of Kongo, 1491–1895', *Kings of Africa: Art and Authority in Central Africa—Collection Museum für Völkerkunde Berlin* (exh. cat., ed. E. Beumers and H.-J. Koloss; Maastricht, Exh. & Congr. Cent., 1992), pp. 57–63 [see also figs 58–61 and captions]

JEREMY COOTE

(iii) Islam. As early as AD 640, followers of Islam had begun their conquest of Egypt. Further west and south,

Islam was probably first introduced into the western Sudan in the 8th and 9th centuries AD through the agency of Muslim merchants and scholars. The merchants exchanged goods from the Mediterranean lands and salt from the Sahara for gold, slaves, ivory and gum. Islam was introduced from North Africa along western routes, linking the Maghrib with the gold-trading centres of western Sudan, and along eastern routes that brought Tripoli, Tunis and Egypt into contact with such kingdoms of the central Sudan as Kanem, Bornu and the Hausa states. After Islam had been disseminated in the Sudan, partly by Berber armies, it was pushed further south by West African Muslim traders, who took it to the southern savannah and the Guinea Coast forest and to northern and central Nigeria. The growth of many towns was encouraged by the arrival of enterprising Muslim traders.

The Islamic colonization of the East African coast, meanwhile, began in the 8th century AD. Most of the early settlers were Arab or Persian merchants and clerics from southern Arabia and the Gulf. They intermarried with the indigenous populations and created numerous trading towns and city-states along the coastal strip. In these settlements Arab, Somali and, further south, SWAHILI cultures flourished, the latter being a synthesis of Bantu African and Islamic traits. Over the centuries these settlements maintained contacts with Arabia, the Gulf and western India.

The history of Islam in Sub-Saharan Africa has been one of interaction with the indigenous cultures it encountered. This interaction led to the development of a diversity of artistic traditions. In addition to the regions where the population converted to orthodox Islam, there were areas where pluralistic societies emerged or where Islamic beliefs and practices merged with the traditional culture in a syncretic pattern. In general, however, Islam became associated with processes of political centralization and urbanization. The construction of congregational mosques at fixed locations, for example, encouraged settlement. Notions of private property and private space were also encouraged and new working practices introduced. Skills and crafts that had traditionally been practised by women in nomadic societies often became the occupations of men as the societies became sedentary.

Many architectural and craft techniques were retained or reinvigorated. In this respect Islam had the ability to adapt itself region by region to the demands of the physical environment. In those regions where Islam was adopted, several new types of building were constructed, the most important being the congregational mosque. The arrival of Islam also led to the introduction of new building techniques. In the African savannah, for example, this is suggested by the continued use of indigenous terms for simple building techniques, while Arabic-derived terms are used for brick shapes.

The adoption of Islam also stimulated a number of other crafts. For example, Islamic prescriptions regarding body covering and the requirement for burial shrouds encouraged the textile crafts (see fig. 9). Islamic charms, talismans and similar items were also in great demand. Military exploits, meanwhile, stimulated a demand for the products of metalwork and leatherworking techniques.

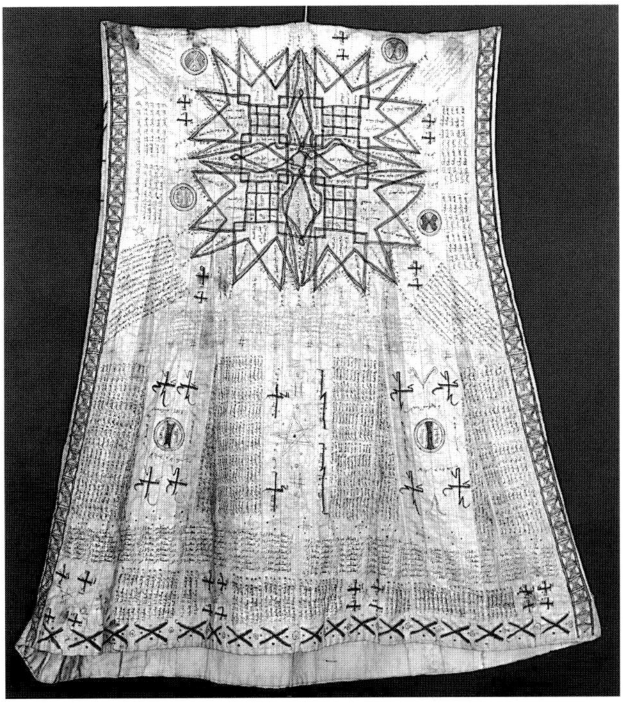

9. Cotton tunic, embroidered with patterns derived from the Koran, l. 890 mm, from northern Nigeria, before 1940 (London, British Museum)

Despite the common Islamic constraints on the representation of living beings, in many well-established Islamic communities in West Africa masking and figurative traditions were able to continue, either because they function at a level not treated by Islamic ritual or because they proved effective. As Islam recognized witchcraft and magic, the use of traditional methods of control when Muslim methods failed was not felt to be incompatible with the faith. The 14th-century Moroccan traveller Ibn Battuta, for example, recorded the use of masks and figurative art forms among the Muslim Mande élite of Mali. Such practices continued into the late 20th century. For example, of the various Bedu masks in use in the area of Bondoukou, Côte d'Ivoire, many were carved in the 1960s by the Muslim Hwela artist Sirikye (*b c.* 1925). Gbain masks have also been carved by Muslims, and evidence suggests that the Gbain cult, for protection against witchcraft, was originally a Muslim Mande tradition. Belief in the power of amulets is also very strong among Islamized Mande. The Do masking tradition, meanwhile, is exclusively Muslim. It follows Muslim procedures and is never used in a non-Muslim context, the ownership and custody of Do masks being invariably vested in the ulema. Masking traditions probably also exist in other Islamized regions of West Africa.

For an account of Islamic architecture in Sub-Saharan Africa, *see* §VI, 1(v) below.

BIBLIOGRAPHY

J. S. Trimingham: *Islam in West Africa* (London, 1959)
——: *A History of Islam in West Africa* (Oxford, 1962)
I. M. Lewis, ed.: *Islam in Tropical Africa* (London, 1966)
J. Kritzek and W. H. Lewis: *Islam in Africa* (New York, 1968)
J. S. Trimingham: *The Influence of Islam upon Africa* (New York, 1968)

R. A. Bravmann: *Islam and Tribal Art in West Africa*, African Studies Series (London and New York, 1974)
——: *African Islam* (Washington, DC, and London, 1983)
L. Prussin: *Hatumere: Islamic Design in West Africa* (Berkeley, 1986)
A. A. Mazrui: 'Islam and African Art: Stimulus or Stumbling Block', *Afr. A.*, xxvii/1 (1994), pp. 50–57

S. J. VERNOIT

(iv) Modern developments. The period of high European colonialism in the 19th and 20th centuries and the consequent opening up of the African interior to world trade and governmental systems encouraged Christian missionary endeavour throughout Africa. Moreover this has continued into post-colonial times. Islam also spread more widely in the same period and for similar reasons. In the late 20th century indigenous and 'intrusive' faiths exist side by side within the same society, within the same community, within the same family, and even within the same individual.

Virtually everywhere the spread of Christianity has been accompanied by the rise of prophets. These have tended to appear in opposition to the racially inegalitarian practices of most early mission churches. Some of these prophets have established their own breakaway or 'separatist' churches, free of European control, although many of these have been shortlived, rent by dissension and competition. Other churches have grown into large organizations in their own right. The Zaïrean Church of Jesus Christ on Earth through the Prophet Simon Kimbanqu is one example, as are the many churches of the Zambian Watch-Tower movement, which grew out of the Jehovah's Witnesses movement. In western Africa many churches with Christian antecedents have developed into faith-healing, often Pentecostalist-type churches with recreated 'traditional African' elements. The Aladura churches of Nigeria are an example. Other prophetic movements that began in opposition to mission churches have turned their backs on Western Christianity altogether and have adopted supposed original African symbols. They have also emphasized polygyny as an 'African' institution, descent from the Christian kings of Ethiopia, taboos on European-type foods, clothing and hairstyles and so on.

Modern reformist movements in Islamic societies in Africa have been similar, although they have not arisen in response to racial issues. The best known are the great Fulani *jihad* of the early 19th century, which was directed against what the Fulani leaders considered the lax practices of the more established Islam of the region, and the Mahdist movement in late 19th-century Sudan, which was directed against the presence of European and Egyptian power. The effects of such movements and developments on the visual art and architecture of Africa have yet to be fully explored.

BIBLIOGRAPHY

B. Sundkler: *Bantu Prophets in South Africa* (London, 1961)
F. Welbourn: *East African Rebels* (London, 1961)
J. D. Y. Peel: *Aladura: A Religious Movement among the Yoruba* (London, 1969)
W. MacGaffey: *Modern Kongo Prophets* (Bloomington, 1983)
——: *Religion and Society in Central Africa* (Chicago, 1986)
S. Barnes, ed.: *Africa's Ogun: Old World and New* (Bloomington, 1989)

JOHN MIDDLETON

II. Art and aesthetics.

The art-historical and aesthetic categories applied to African art are in a constant state of flux. The history of their usage has been dogged by misapprehensions and misrepresentations, although this is hardly surprising, given that they often represent the inappropriate application of Western intellectual and aesthetic concepts. This article provides an overview of the history of scholarly research into and discussion of African art and in particular figure sculpture (*see* §1 below), followed by an account of the vast increase in studies of indigenous systems of aesthetic evaluation since the 1960s (*see* §2 below).

1. Critical and scholarly approaches. 2. Aesthetic evaluation.

1. CRITICAL AND SCHOLARLY APPROACHES. The perception and identity of African art in universal art history are profoundly marked by two categories of art objects: wooden masks and figurative sculpture. In 1926 Paul Guillaume and Thomas Munro in *Primitive Negro Sculpture* went so far as to present a map of 'The Country of Negro Art' that drew a closed line around the regions of West and Central Africa and effectively limited African art to the mask and figurative art traditions that characterize these regions. Truly, however, the importance of figurative art to an understanding of African art history cannot be overestimated. Frank Willett (p. 27) stated that 'the greatest contribution Africa has made ... to the cultural heritage of mankind is its richly varied sculpture'. More recently, Susan Vogel (see 1986 exh. cat. *African Aesthetics*, p. xiv), in asserting the moral basis of much African art, in which 'beautiful' is intended and perceived also to be 'good', has argued that this conflation of beauty and goodness may explain why, in African art 'as in Greek art, the principal subject is the human figure—to the almost total exclusion of nature in the form of landscape, or plant motifs'. Consequently, while this discussion attempts a historical overview of scholarly understandings of African art as a whole, it is inevitably focused primarily on understandings of figure sculpture.

(i) Historical attitudes. (ii) Style and canon. (iii) Context and meaning. (iv) Appreciation of form.

(i) Historical attitudes. The predominance of figuration in African art traditions and in the history of Western collecting has left a legacy of countless thousands of African figures dispersed throughout the world in ethnographic and art museums as well as in private collections. These figures have been little understood in terms of the original intentionality and socio-historical context that brought them into being. The 'discovery' of primitive art, including African sculpture, in the early 20th century was a 'discovery' of its perceived formal qualities accompanied by an almost total, and indeed often wilful, ignorance of its cultural content. Figures acquired in Africa 'as curios rather than art, and as evidence of what [Europeans] considered to be the primitive barbarity of Africans' (see MacGaffey, p. 32) were taken back to Europe as 'found objects'; little or no documentation was acquired with them, and they survived as 'mute objects, themselves damaged in the processes of collection and storage' (MacGaffey, p. 33). The meanings subsequently attributed to these silent objects were invented ideas that reveal more about Western history than about African art history.

Looking back at common Western perceptions of African religion and art, Leon Siroto (p. 7) argued that one constant and fundamental assumption has been that 'representations of the human form fell into one or the other of two categories of iconographic identity. One kind of representation was thought to be positive: the ancestor figure. The other was thought to be negative: an impersonal image intended to hold combined substances capable of projecting magical force'. Each of these paired, common misperceptions of African figurative art is based on profoundly erroneous constructions of African thought and religion. The simplistic notion of 'magic', for example, has been based on a 'whole theory of African civilization, or the supposed lack of it, [that] has been developed under the term "fetishism"', according to which 'Africans were incapable of abstract and generalizing thought; instead their ideas and actions were governed by impulse' (see MacGaffey, p. 32). Likewise, the Western assumption that '"ancestor worship" was the prevailing religious and iconographic concern in traditional Africa' (Siroto, p. 7) has led to the idea that the highest form of artistic expression in Africa was the 'ancestor figure', interpreted as an 'imposing, finely worked depiction of the deceased parent', characterized by 'large size, dignified posture, a seemingly grave and aloof expression and the signs of social and political status, such as a beard, a prestigious stool, a headdress and one or more children' (Siroto).

Other historically determined notions that have continued to have a deleterious influence on Western understanding of African figurative traditions are the idea of the imagined 'expressiveness' of African sculpture and the related idea that African art results from cultural imperative rather than intellectual impulse. It is because 'much African art is extremely stylized compared to Western realism, [that] African art has been regarded as expressionistic and exaggerated' (see 1986 exh. cat. *African Aesthetics*, p. xvii). African figures have been perceived simultaneously as powerfully expressive works of creative invention and yet as almost accidental in their form, as though they were the result of some unleashed primal 'energy'. These seemingly opposed notions have in common a fundamental denial of any intentionality on the part of the artist. Close examination and appreciation of individual works, however, leads to the proper acknowledgement that 'African artists had complete mastery over their tools and materials', and thus 'we may assume that their work looks just as they intended, and that [any] irregularity and roughness were intentional' (see 1986 exh. cat. *African Aesthetics*, p. xii).

The notion that African art is simply a cultural product also denies the particular artistic intentionality of individual works of art and sees them as 'tribal' products, 'natural', or predictable outcomes of a certain world view or cultural system. The literature on African art commonly situates the production of art at the level of specific cultural systems (i.e. the 'tribe'), thus implicitly equating art with a collective activity. In this view, the production of art is almost always by 'artists', in the plural, and works are interpreted in generic cultural terms in which a gloss is given to entire genres of figurative art, for example 'the Baule other-world figure', 'the Dogon ancestor' or 'the Yoruba twin figure'. Such generic characterizations, however, have often been well-intentioned, constituting a necessary step in the understanding of art as a cultural product in their attempt to move beyond 'African' art as a totality to the art of particular cultural traditions. It is not surprising, therefore, that many studies of the cultural dimensions of specific African sculptural traditions were undertaken by anthropologists (e.g. Himmelheber, 1935; Olbrechts, 1946; Gerbrands, 1956; Horton, 1965; Ottenberg, 1975; Ben-Amos, 1980) and that, when art historians began to undertake field studies of African art, they borrowed the methodologies of anthropology (e.g. Sieber, 1961; Thompson, 1974; Vogel, 1977; Glaze, 1981; Cole, 1982; Ezra, 1986; McNaughton, 1988).

(ii) Style and canon. According to Leon Siroto (p. 7), 'the time-lag between academic and commercial interest in African art has led to a massive immigration of unidentified objects into the West', resulting in a plethora of objects whose place in the world had to be determined in some manner. In order to come to grips with, classify and posit cultural and geographical provenances to these otherwise anonymous objects, Western museum curators and scholars, as well as art dealers, have relied upon certain formal criteria of differentiation that collectively fall under the rubric of 'style'.

In African sculpture, it has been argued, style 'includes in essence: the total appearance of an object; the expressive effect of its subject matter; and the creative methods or techniques used to produce these effects' (Wingert, 'Style . . .', p. 38). 'Style' ultimately became a normative and essentialist framework in the categorization of African sculpture. It has been assumed that 'the essential properties involved in the characteristics of a style' could be readily identified (Wingert, 'Style...', p. 37). For example, in enunciating acquisition criteria for the collection of the National Museum of African Art, Washington, DC, Roy Sieber advanced the ideas that each object 'should be central to its style' and that it 'should be significant within that style', ideas that presuppose the possibility of establishing common denominators of style for each style and genre of traditional African art. The idea that style is culturally determined, however, potentially conflicts with the appreciation and acknowledgement of the creativity of individual artists as manifested in their work. The question of the relationship between 'cultural style' and 'individual creativity' has thus led African art scholars to investigate through field research 'the traditional artist in African societies' (the title of a compendium edited by Warren L. d'Azevedo and published in 1973). Within the culturally defined genre, what latitude does the artist have in expressing his own style? The push-and-pull contradictions of the paired opposites of cultural style and individual artistry are nicely captured in Vogel's commentary (see 1986 exh. cat. *African Aesthetics*, p. 129) on a Fang figure: 'some of its power comes from its size and bulk. Its formal complexity and ineffable expression place it at the summit of African artistic achievement. It both crystallizes and extends the canon of Fang art' (see fig. 10).

'Style' has been the critical framework for formal analysis of morphological form in African figurative art, even though, according to Paul Wingert ('Further Style Analysis...', p. 35), the term '"style" approaches the inexplicable, by virtue of its inclusion of practically every facet

10. Fang reliquary guardian figure, wood and metal, h. 700 mm (Paris, Musée Dapper)

of an art object'. The method of style analysis is based upon 'the separation of a design into its constituent parts so as to examine these elements and to determine their significance in the expressive and aesthetic character of the work as a whole' or in terms of common denominators within specific artistic traditions. In an attempt to systematize the study of style in Fang figurative sculpture, Louis Perrois examined a corpus of figures and measured proportions, such as the height of the head in relation to that of the torso, and described the positions of arms and legs, the style of coiffure and a number of specific details, such as the shape of eyes, nose, mouth, ears, navel and breasts. From his investigation he deduced that Fang style could be divided into the northern 'hyper- and longiform' styles and the southern 'equiform and breviform' styles. At one level Perrois' work can be seen as a somewhat obsessive attempt to codify the denominators of sub-styles, as if thereby to prove that artists necessarily work within culturally predetermined styles, albeit perhaps unconsciously.

Style analysis as objective description has resulted in the establishment of the canon of 'African art': the differentiation of styles in terms of their genres and their ethnic provenance. Some scholars, such as William Fagg, have made major contributions to the field of African art studies by advancing studies of 'tribal styles' (see Willett, p. 29). As Sidney Kasfir has argued, the approach has often been limited to an implicit 'one tribe, one style' paradigm, in which the framework of analysis is implicitly or explicitly the tribal unit with its attendant stylistic denominators. Tribal styles have also been seen, in turn, as building blocks to larger entities, the larger 'style regions' of African art (see 1968 exh. cat.; Roy), a version of which approach has been adopted in this survey (*see* §VII below). Jan Vansina has argued, however, that a distributional approach to African art is insufficient and that 'the historical evolvement of the [African] art forms, even the sculptural forms, has not been a subject of sustained research' (p. 1). He argues for a study of 'art in Africa and its history' rather than an 'art history of Africa', the latter not being possible owing to the lack of monographs as well as the fact that 'too many scholars in the field of "African art" have been allergic to historical pursuits'. It is unclear what place 'style regions' will occupy in the future development of an African art history. They have been a convenient way to explore and group larger stylistic tendencies of African sculpture, especially figurative, but as the study of African art develops to include the areas of Africa north of the Sahara and the relatively neglected art traditions of East and Southern Africa, the inadequacy and profound limitations of the 'style region' approach become more and more evident. The regional geographic paradigm allows for an examination of artistic traits and comparative cultural phenomena, but it has yielded little in terms of history, concentrating as it has on space rather than time.

(iii) Context and meaning. The classificatory approach to types of African figurative sculpture has resulted in incomplete understandings of questions of meaning in African sculpture as well as of the relationship between the form of an image and its original efficacy. Leon Siroto (p. 6) has argued that in field research 'the type-oriented question "What does this image (or object) represent?" can lead to crucial misunderstandings' and that 'equally crucial misunderstandings of imagery have resulted from failure to ask the person-oriented question "Whom does this image (or object) represent?"' (p. 7). A hypothetical exchange between an investigator and a field informant may be illustrative. In a Baule village in Côte d'Ivoire, a field

11. Baule figure sculpture of an 'other-world man' (*blolo bian*), wood and pigments, *c.* 1950s (Washington, DC, National Museum of African Art)

worker seeing a sculpted figure and asking, 'What is this?', may receive the reply, 'It is a wooden figure' (*waka sran*), or 'It is a figure of an "other-world man"' (*blolo bian*; see fig. 11). If, however, a further question were to be asked, 'Whom does this figure represent?', the answer would be the name of a specific individual, such as Gbaflin Kwami, 'Kwami the dandy'.

Approaches to African art that concentrate too much on the shared parameters and components of style in objects removed from their context have often overlooked the significance of the subtle differences in form that created the individuality and power of a specific work. Leon Siroto remarked (p. 7) that '[African] images often show great care in their sculptural rendering and seem individual enough to carry specific information about their personal identity'. He argued for a connection between a belief in animism—'belief in personalized, man-like supernaturals' (p. 8)—and the artistic interpretation of form, such that 'the carver's recognition of the spirit as a distinct individual compelled him to use its form as a way of differentiating it from all other spirits, and, in some cases, from humans as well' (p. 20). Wyatt MacGaffey argued convincingly for the 'personhood' of such ritual objects as Kongo power figures (*minkisi*; sing. *nkisi*; see fig. 12), claiming that they incarnate specific, named persons who are invoked, addressed and negotiated with in speech. Part of the identity of such figures is in their form and the accumulated materials or medicines added to it in use.

Arnold Rubin argued that 'the content of African sculpture has clearly not received the attention it deserves' (see 1974 exh. cat., *African Accumulative Sculpture*, p. 36).

12. Kongo figure sculpture, *nkisi nkondi*, mainly wood, glass and iron, h. 423 mm, from Congo or Zaïre (Washington, DC, National Museum of African Art)

In using the term 'content', Rubin described 'one dimension of the affective power and complex of multiple meanings embodied in a work of art'. In his consideration of the media of African sculpture, Rubin focused on 'accumulation'. The work of art is not just the original form fresh from the hands of the African artist; it also includes the embellishments or traces of use added to the work by its owner(s). He argued that, in visual terms, the substances and elements added to African works of art may provisionally be divided into two broad categories of 'power' and 'display'. According to Rubin:

> Display materials (beads, bells, fabrics, mirrors, etc) are primarily oriented toward enhancement of the splendor of the objects to which they are attached. They usually carry associations of prosperity and cosmopolitan association for the individual or group on whose behalf such sculpture is created . . . The second category of materials—horns, skulls, and sacrificial accumulations, for example—is connected with the organization and exploitation of power.

Although Rubin claimed to use the notions of power and display as a 'neutral frame of reference' to explore relationships between meaning and form in African art, these two notions are not in fact polar opposites, and much African sculpture combines attributes of both. All African figurative sculptures, for example, were created for specific uses, and their intended use necessarily had an effect on form, whether originally or as it changed through time. Sculpture used and displayed in public, for instance, is often larger than that intended for use in private shrines or in the context of a consultation between diviner and client. Within a specific cultural tradition there may well be stylistic relationships between different types of figures that differ in scale. Among the Senufo of Côte d'Ivoire and Mali, one genre of sculpture, known as 'the children of Poro' (see Glaze), is used in public displays by the men's or women's Poro society. These figures are large (h. 1 m or more), whereas the stylistically similar figures that represent the bush-spirits, sometimes equestrian, that empower diviners of the Sandogo society and are used in consultations are small (h. 150–350 mm; see fig. 44 below; *see also* SENUFO, §2).

(iv) Appreciation of form. Discussion of style in African art is based on formal qualities and relationships. For example, in 1926 Guillaume and Munro wrote (p. 35):

> Every part in a typical, fully-realized negro statue functions as an element in plastic design: an embodiment, a repetition in rhythmic, varied sequence, of some theme in mass, line, or surface . . . The figure must be dissociated into its parts, regarded as an aggregate of distinct units: the head, limbs, breasts, trunk, and so on, each by itself.

Such stylistic analysis, which represents subjective appreciation of individual works of art as aesthetic creations rather than as ethnographic documents, has a long history in African art studies. From Carl Einstein (1915) to Susan Vogel (1986) the fascination with the sculptural richness of African art has led to an often celebratory literature that asserts the universal value of African art. At times hostile to the contextualization of African sculpture (e.g. Einstein), at times sensitive to contextual information (e.g. Vogel), this literature is far more conclusive as art appreciation than art history. It fits into the larger historical context of the discovery of 'tribal art' or 'primitive art', the terms of convenience that have been used to link the arts of Africa, Oceania and the Americas. The 1984 exhibition *'Primitivism' in 20th Century Art: Affinity of the Tribal and the Modern* explored the crucial influence of 'tribal' art on modern painters and sculptors in the West. Kirk Varnedoe, co-director of the exhibition, stresses that 'modernist primitivism ultimately depends on the autonomous force of objects—and especially on the capacity of tribal art to transcend the intentions and conditions that first shaped it' (see 1984 exh. cat., p. x). It is these allied ideas of 'autonomy' and 'transcendence' that have made possible a history of stylistic appreciation of African art in which artistic meaning is posited by a direct reading of form. Such appreciation is also undertaken by Africanist art historians who seek to articulate the reasons for our response to particular works of art. Paul Wingert, for example, while arguing that 'sculpture from the Central Cameroon Grasslands area has one of the most distinctive styles in all of Black Africa' (see 'Further Style Analysis. . .', p. 35), analyses one particular figure as follows:

> It is apparent at first glance that the paramount importance in this carving is the expression of vigorous movement that is held in a state of momentary suspension. . . . all of the component parts of the figure have a strongly declared autonomy in space. . . . The figure has a compact organic unity of expression.

Such analyses are purely formal and take little, if any, note of the rich traditions of indigenous aesthetic evaluation that scholarship has begun to explore (*see* §2 below).

BIBLIOGRAPHY

C. Einstein: *Negerplastik* (Leipzig, 1915, rev. Berlin, 1992)

P. Guillaume and T. Munro: *Primitive Negro Sculpture* (London, 1926)

H. Himmelheber: *Negerkünstler* (Stuttgart, 1935)

F. M. Olbrechts: *Plastiek van Kongo* (Antwerp, 1946)

A. A. Gerbrands: *Kunst aus cultuur-element, in het bijzonder in Neger-Afrika* (Leiden, 1956); Eng. trans. by G. E. van Baaren-Pape, Mededelingen van het Rijksmuseum voor Volkenkunde, Leiden, 12 (Leiden, 1957)

The Sculpture of Northern Nigeria (exh. cat. by R. Sieber, New York, Mus. Primitive A., 1961)

R. Horton: *Kalabari Sculpture* (Lagos, 1965)

Sculpture of Black Africa (exh. cat. by R. Sieber and A. Rubin, Los Angeles, CA, Co. Mus. A., 1968)

F. Willett: *African Art: An Introduction*, World A. (London and New York, 1971/*R* 1993)

L. Perrois: *La Statuaire Fang* (Paris, 1972)

P. S. Wingert: 'Style Determinants in African Sculpture', *Afr. A.*, v/3 (1972), pp. 37–43

——: 'Further Style Analysis in African Sculpture', *Afr. A.*, vi/1 (1972), pp. 35–41

W. L. d'Azevedo, ed.: *The Traditional Artist in African Societies* (Bloomington and London, 1973/*R* 1992)

African Accumulative Sculpture: Power and Display (exh. cat. by A. Rubin, New York, Pace Gal., 1974)

African Art in Motion: Icon and Act (exh. cat. by R. F. Thompson; Washington, DC, N.G.A.; Los Angeles, UCLA, Wight A.G.; 1974)

S. Ottenberg: *The Masked Rituals of Afikpo: The Context of an African Art* (Seattle, 1975)

L. Siroto: *African Spirit Images and Identities* (New York, 1976)

S. M. Vogel: *Baule Art as the Expression of a Worldview* (diss., New York U., 1977; microfilm, Ann Arbor, 1977)

C. Roy: *African Sculpture: The Stanley Collection* (Iowa City, 1979)

P. Ben-Amos: *The Art of Benin*, Tribal A. (London, 1980)

A. J. Glaze: *Art and Death in a Senufo Village*, Trad. A. Africa (Bloomington, 1981)

H. M. Cole: *Mbari: Art and Life among the Owerri Igbo* (Bloomington, 1982)
S. L. Kasfir: 'One Tribe, One Style: Paradigms in the Historiography of African Art', *Hist. Afr.*, xi (1984), pp. 163–93
J. Vansina: *Art History in Africa: An Introduction to Method* (London and New York, 1984)
K. Varnedoe: 'Preface', *'Primitivism' in 20th Century Art: Affinity of the Tribal and the Modern*, 2 vols (exh. cat., ed. W. Rubin; New York, MOMA, 1984), p. x
African Aesthetics: The Carlo Monzino Collection (exh. cat. by S. Vogel, New York, Cent. Afr. A., 1986)
The Human Ideal in African Art: Bamana Figurative Sculpture (exh. cat. by K. Ezra, Washington, DC, N. Mus. Afr. A., 1986)
P. R. McNaughton: *The Mande Blacksmiths: Knowledge, Power, and Art in West Africa*, Trad. A. Africa (Bloomington, 1988)
W. MacGaffey: 'The Eyes of Understanding: Kongo Minkisi', *Astonishment and Power* (exh. cat., Washington, DC, N. Mus. Afr. A., 1993–4), pp. 21–103

PHILIP L. RAVENHILL

2. AESTHETIC EVALUATION. Aesthetics is here taken to be the valued formal qualities in things or experiences expressed as canons of taste or qualitative judgements. Broadly, visual aesthetics may be understood as a philosophy of form concerned both with objects and with activities and performances. These are evaluated by individuals whose judgements may be shared, to varying degrees, within and across cultures.

(i) Introduction. (ii) Cross-cultural criteria. (iii) Case-studies. (iv) Conclusion.

(i) Introduction. The presence of finely crafted images in ancient central Sahara, early Egypt and Nubia, as well as early works in other parts of the continent, suggests that aesthetic evaluation is ancient in Africa. We can, however, only conjecture about the criteria used. Western aesthetic evaluations of African cultural phenomena were first made at the end of the 19th century in the publications of the German scholar F. Ratzel and of E. Grosse. These authors focused on objects (primarily figure sculpture) that most closely resembled 'art' as then conventionally defined in the West. The interest in African art displayed a few years later by such artists as Vlaminck, Picasso, Derain, Matisse and Braque helped to validate its study (*see* PRIMITIVISM). At the same time, however, their personal, ethnocentric and formalist perspectives ignored consideration of indigenous African views and aesthetic judgements. Unfortunately, such an approach has continued to be adopted in some quarters.

Similar attitudes shaped the appreciation of African art in the USA. There, however, the emerging African consciousness among African Americans during the Black Renaissance of the 1920s led to the aesthetic value of African art receiving glowing praise from such writers as C. S. Johnson and, especially, Alain Locke. Locke urged African American artists to use African art as a source of inspiration, not simply because of its aesthetic qualities but also because its ancestral forms possessed both spiritual and cultural relevance for them.

It was only in the 1930s and 1940s, however, that African aesthetic evaluations began to be documented in detail. Moreover, the most sustained work has taken place since the 1970s. The limits of present knowledge and the vastness and cultural diversity of the continent make attempts to generalize about African aesthetics inevitable, although it is not always clear what they achieve. Pan-African and cross-cultural studies may be contrasted with cultural case-studies. While many are still based on the unverified observations and interpretations of a single authority, in some cases, for example that of the Akan- and Yoruba-speaking peoples of West Africa, there is an extensive literature by both African and non-African scholars. A 'critical mass' of scholarship has emerged that suggests the depth and richness of aesthetic thought in Africa.

BIBLIOGRAPHY

F. Ratzel: *Völkerkunde*, 3 vols (Leipzig, 1885–8; rev. as 2 vols, 1894–5); Eng. trans. of rev. by A. J. Butler as *The History of Mankind*, 3 vols (London, 1896–8)
E. Grosse: *The Beginnings of Art*, The Anthropological Series (New York, 1897)
C. S. Johnson: 'The Creative Art of the Negroes', *Opportunity*, i (1923), pp. 240–45
A. Locke: 'A Note on African Art', *Opportunity*, ii (1924), pp. 134–8
A. Locke, ed.: *The New Negro: An Interpretation* (New York, 1925)
A. Locke: *Negro Art: Past and Present*, Bronze Booklet, 3 (Washington, DC, 1936)
W. L. d'Azevedo: 'A Structural Approach to Esthetics: Toward a Definition of Art in Anthropology', *Amer. Anthropol.*, lx/4 (1958), pp. 702–14
J. Coote: 'The Anthropology of Aesthetics and the Dangers of "Maquetcentrism"', *J. Anthropol. Soc. Oxford*, xx/3 (1989), pp. 229–43

(ii) Cross-cultural criteria. Whether cross-cultural, pan-African or perhaps even universal criteria of aesthetic evaluation exist remains a largely unanswered question. For example, in specific comparisons between Baule and Yoruba aesthetic evaluations such criteria as resemblance, balance and youthfulness were shared, but there were also some significant divergences, such as in the evaluation of asymmetry (see Vogel). R. F. Thompson has suggested that there is a definable pan-African aesthetic, which he derived from widespread cultural ideas about composure and collectedness of mind and which he termed 'the cool'. In one case at least, however, among the Asante, it appears that, while works from a wide variety of African cultures are easily and willingly evaluated, this is done with Asante, not pan-African, criteria (see Silver).

The other elements of a supposed general African aesthetic that have been proposed include: the avoidance of straight lines and the use of exponential curves (see Fagg); a moral basis, such as among the Twi of Ghana where the word *fe* means both 'beautiful' and 'fitting' (see Appiah), which may explain why the human figure is so prevalent throughout African art; skill in the transformation of media, that is, technical excellence or workmanship; the attributes admired in sculpture being those admired in people; moderation; and innovation and invention within set cultural parameters (see 1986 exh. cat.). Perhaps another is the importance of the secular, artful and playful aspects of African arts (see Okpewho; Drewal).

As for the question of universal aesthetic criteria, through formal experiments some researchers have found substantial agreement among the responses to art between Africans and non-Africans. However, the reasons for the similar judgements (i.e. the evaluative criteria) differed significantly (see Child and Siroto; Child).

BIBLIOGRAPHY

W. B. Fagg: 'On the Nature of African Art', *Mem. & Proc. Manchester Lit. & Philos. Soc.*, xciv (1952–3), pp. 93–104
I. L. Child and L. Siroto: 'BaKwele and American Esthetic Evaluations Compared', *Ethnology*, iv/4 (1965), pp. 349–60; repr. in *Art and*

Aesthetics in Primitive Societies: A Critical Anthology, ed. C. F. Jopling (New York, 1971), pp. 271–89
I. L. Child: 'The Expert and the Bridge of Judgement that Crosses Every Cultural Gap', *Psychol. Today* (Dec 1968), pp. 24–9
R. F. Thompson: 'An Aesthetic of the Cool', *Afr. A.*, vii/1 (1973), pp. 40–43, 64–7, 89–91; also abridged in *Arts of Africa, Oceania, and the Americas: Selected Readings*, ed. J. C. Berlo and L. A. Wilson (Englewood Cliffs, 1993), pp. 22–35
African Art in Motion: Icon and Act (exh. cat. by R. F. Thompson; Washington, DC, N.G.A.; Los Angeles, UCLA, Wight A.G.; 1974)
I. Okpewho: 'Principles of Traditional African Art', *J. Aesth. & A. Crit.*, xxxv/3 (1977), pp. 301–13
S. M. Vogel: 'Baule and Yoruba Art Criticism: A Comparison', *The Visual Arts: Plastic and Graphic*, ed. J. M. Cordwell (The Hague, 1979), pp. 309–25
H. R. Silver: 'Foreign Art and Asante Aesthetics', *Afr. A.*, xvi/3 (1982), pp. 64–7, 79–80
A. Appiah: 'An Aesthetics for the Art of Adornment in Africa', *Beauty by Design: The Aesthetics of African Adornment* (exh. cat., ed. M.-T. Brincard; New York, Afr.-Amer. Inst., 1984), pp. 15–19
African Aesthetics: The Carlo Monzino Collection (exh. cat. by S. M. Vogel, New York, Cent. Afr. A., 1986)
M. T. Drewal: *Yoruba Ritual: Performers, Play, Agency*, African Systems of Thought (Bloomington, 1992)
K. Welsh-Asante: *The African Aesthetic: Keeper of the Traditions*, Contributions in Afro-American and African Studies, 153 (Westport, CT, 1993)

(iii) Case-studies.

(a) Survey. (b) Akan-speaking peoples. (c) Yoruba-speaking peoples.

(a) Survey. This survey is organized both geographically, to highlight possible cross-cultural interactions that may have helped shape aesthetic evaluations, and thematically.

The DAN and related peoples of Côte d'Ivoire value highly such features as finished and polished surfaces, colour, symmetry about the vertical axis, balance, rhythm and harmony among volumes, and carefully rendered linear patterns. For masks, there is also their suitability for seeing and breathing well. Such evaluations are often expressed by Dan artists not so much in words as in gestures, for example in the ways they handle works-in-progress, turning them upside-down, holding them at arm's length and so on (see Vandenhoute). For the Dan, form is meant to be evocative; specific emotions and reactions are for specific contexts and are evoked by a 'symbolism of forms' (see 1976 exh. cat., rev. 1984, p. 182). Thus, a mask that successfully conveys awe or terror (*gbuze*) is angular in form with a large mouth, tubular eyes, black feathers and red colouring. One expressive of grotesqueness or ugliness (*ya*) often has a low forehead, pendulous lips, a short flat nose and brown colouring. In contrast, a beautiful or fine (*se*) mask has a high forehead, slitted eyes, a narrow nose, full-lipped mouth and white paint about the eyes conveying gentleness. Other evaluative terms in the Dan vocabulary are *li* ('beautiful'), *yeiya* ('hateful'), *manyene* ('splendid') and *ga pe mu* ('something to look at'). Among the GURO, who are neighbours of the Dan to the north, the artists who make masks seem to take particular pleasure in smooth, subtle transitions from convex to concave shapes, and they also prize profile views. They have an extensive evaluative vocabulary based around such concepts as *ezima* ('beauty') and *nee* ('ugliness'; see 1986 exh. cat., p. 10).

Among the MENDE of Sierra Leone ideals of feminine beauty are guarded and passed on by the female elders (*sowei*) of the female initiation society, Sande; they are closely related to the attributes in terms of which sculptures and Sande headdresses (*sowo-wui*) depicting women are evaluated (see fig. 13). These attributes include three fundamental features and associated aesthetic ideas: a high, broad, smooth forehead, expressive of intelligence, good fortune and social responsibility; a full head of thick hair, neatly braided and decorated and expressive of energy, fertility and abundance; and 'rainbow' neck rings, expressive of high status, vitality, well-being, divine munificence and the beauty that benefits communities. Additional features include *ngakpango-jo*: completeness, correctness; *a gulo nya ma leke kinein*: comfortable to wear or danceable, suggesting useful, efficacious beauty; *gbong-bongo-bowobowo*: smoothness that epitomizes health; *mbema*: balance and symmetry connoting collectedness, composure; *ma ya-sahein*: clarity of form; *neku*: freshness, newness suggesting vitality; and *yengele*: delicacy, especially of the mouth, which is expressive of circumspection and good judgement. Sande headdresses thus embody a complex cluster of Mende social, aesthetic and spiritual aspirations (see Boone).

The Gola of Liberia, neighbours of the Mende, have an aesthetic preference for an air of nonchalance, for the ability 'to act as though one's mind were in another world ... to do difficult tasks with an air of ease and silent disdain'. Women are particularly admired for 'a detached expression, and somnambulistic movement and attitude during the dance or other performance'; this 'is considered very attractive' (see d'Azevedo, pp. 63–4).

The IDOMA of Nigeria focus on evaluations of the skill and technical proficiency demonstrated by artists (see Sieber). Among the Tiv of Nigeria people in general take an active role in aesthetic evaluation. Few art works are created by specialists, and thus most Tiv consider themselves both artists and critics. Expressing their appraisals both during and after the creation of a work, they explicitly judge its quality by such criteria as balance, symmetry and 'tasteful' asymmetry (see Bohannan). Among the Edo-speaking Okpella of Nigeria discussions revolve around the pleasing embellishments (*ene*) of form that make objects beautiful (*osomhotse*) as opposed to ugly (*oyemhosue*). The latter term is used for something that is broken, marred or flawed or that is frightful/grotesque (*ulishi*). The concept of beautiful overlaps with that of good (*ti*) but is not synonymous with it (see Borgatti, p. 19).

Among the KONGO peoples of central Africa the term *umbanqu* means the fusion of 'tradition and creation' and connotes 'creativity'. This suggests a preference for a dynamic, processual invention of tradition in aesthetic production (see Maesen). Knowing the reasons why persons may suspend aesthetic evaluations in certain circumstances can also reveal aesthetic preferences. Thus among the Lega (*see* LEGA AND RELATED PEOPLES) of Zaïre people refuse to comment on the objects of the Bwami society except to say that they are all 'good', which has been interpreted to mean that they fulfil their didactic and initiatory purposes (see Biebuyck, p. 17).

In several African cultures moral and aesthetic values intersect. Among the Chokwe of Angola and Zaïre (*see* CHOKWE AND RELATED PEOPLES), the concepts of 'good' and 'beautiful' (*chibema*) in relation to 'art' are shaped by such issues as colour preferences, age, craftsmanship,

13. Members of the Mende female initiation society, Sande, with Sowo mask, Sierra Leone; from a photograph by Rebecca Busselle

correctness, smoothness and precision of technique (see Crowley, 1966, 1973). Aesthetic comments by the Anang IBIBIO people of Nigeria identify an 'aesthetic feeling tone' (*mfon*) related to notions of beauty and moral goodness (see Messenger, p. 124). Among the FANG of Gabon aesthetic values also resonate with allusions to moral order. According to J. W. Fernandez (1966), important Fang aesthetic principles are the notions of vitality, the 'capacity to survive' (*enin*) and balance (*bibwe*), which together comprise 'a vitality of balanced opposites' that emerges in discussions of reliquary figures (*bieri*). Similar concepts are also seen in the spatial organization of villages whose survival depends on balancing the tensions between different sections of the community (see Fernandez, 1973).

Among nomadic or semi-nomadic pastoralists whose minimal material culture contains few objects that might be termed 'art', aesthetic evaluations focus on other things. For example, in Rwanda there is a concentration on performance arts (see Smith). Among some of the NUBA peoples of Sudan aesthetic evaluation centres around judgements of embellishment through cicatrization and painting of young, strong, healthy bodies. Evaluation concerns such visual attributes as symmetry, balance, colour, focus and the reinforcing impact of two-dimensional imagery on three-dimensional forms (see Faris).

According to H. K. Schneider, the Nilotic Pokot (Pakot) define 'art' from 'non-art', or rather aesthetic from non-aesthetic objects, on the basis of pleasing and non-utilitarian embellishment termed *pachigh*, 'beautiful, pleasant to look at'. A headrest that might be seen as a sculpture by Westerners is for the Pokot only art in its decorative aspects, the incised designs or smooth, shiny surfaces. Often the most highly prized, aesthetically valued embellished objects are the rare, novel or unusual ones. Among the Nuer, Dinka and other Nilotic-speaking cattle-keepers of southern Sudan aesthetic evaluations concentrate on their cattle, on the colour configurations, hide textures, horn shapes and the size and condition of the bovine body (see Coote). For example, cattle with variegated hides are highly valued and are set aside as display animals. The valued attribute of contrast in such cattle constitutes a maximizing of aesthetic satisfaction in an environment generally characterized by a colourless landscape and vast herds of off-white, greyish cattle (see fig. 14).

BIBLIOGRAPHY

P. J. L. Vandenhoute: *Classification stylistique du masque Dan et Guéré de la Côte d'Ivoire occidentale (A. O. F.)*, Mededelingen van het Rijksmuseum voor Volkenkunde, Leiden, 4 (Leiden, 1948)

H. K. Schneider: 'The Interpretation of Pakot Visual Art', *Man*, lvi (Aug 1956), pp. 103–6; repr. in *Art and Aesthetics in Primitive Societies: A Critical Anthology*, ed. C. F. Jopling (New York, 1971), pp. 55–63

R. Sieber: 'The Aesthetics of Traditional African Art', *Seven Metals of Africa* (exh. cat. by F. Rainey, Philadelphia, U. PA, Mus., 1959); repr. in *Art and Aesthetics in Primitive Societies: A Critical Anthology*, ed. C. F. Jopling (New York, 1971), pp. 127–31

A. Maesen: *Umbangu: Art du Congo au Musée Royale du Congo Belge* (Tervuren, 1960)

14. Dinka ox with bold black-and-white markings, near Pacong, southern Sudan; from a photograph by Jeremy Coote, 1991

P. Bohannan: 'Artist and Critic in an African Society', *The Artist in Tribal Society: Proceedings of a Symposium Held at the Royal Anthropological Institute*, ed. M. W. Smith, Royal Anthropological Institute Occasional Paper, 15 (London, 1961), pp. 85–94; repr. in *Anthropology and Art: Readings in Cross-cultural Aesthetics*, ed. C. M. Otten (New York, 1971/*R* Austin, TX, 1976), pp. 172–81
W. L. d'Azevedo: *The Artist Archetype in Gola Culture*, Desert Research Institute Preprint, 14 (Nevada, 1966, rev. 1970)
D. J. Crowley: 'An African Aesthetic', *J. Aesth. & A. Crit.*, xxiv/4 (1966), pp. 519–24; repr. in *Art and Aesthetics in Primitive Societies: A Critical Anthology*, ed. C. F. Jopling (New York, 1971), pp. 315–27
J. W. Fernandez: 'Principles of Opposition and Vitality in Fang Aesthetics', *J. Aesth. & A. Crit.*, xxv/1 (1966), pp. 53–64; repr. in *Art and Aesthetics in Primitive Societies: A Critical Anthology*, ed. C. F. Jopling (New York, 1971), pp. 356–73
D. Biebuyck: 'Introduction', *Tradition and Creativity in Tribal Art*, ed. D. Biebuyck (Berkeley, 1969/*R* 1973), pp. 1–23
J. C. Faris: *Nuba Personal Art*, A. & Soc. Ser. (London, 1972)
D. J. Crowley: 'Aesthetic Value and Professionalism in African Art: Three Cases from the Katanga Chokwe', *The Traditional Artist in African Societies*, ed. W. L. d'Azevedo (Bloomington, 1973), pp. 221–49
J. Fernandez: 'The Exposition and Imposition of Order: Artistic Expression in Fang Culture', *The Traditional Artist in African Societies*, ed. W. L. d'Azevedo (Bloomington, 1973), pp. 194–220
J. C. Messenger: 'The Carver in Anang Society', *The Traditional Artist in African Societies*, ed. W. L. d'Azevedo (Bloomington, 1973), pp. 101–27
Die Künste der Dan (exh. cat. by E. Fischer and H. Himmelheber, Zurich, Mus. Rietberg, 1976; Eng. trans. and rev., Zurich, 1984)
J. M. Borgatti: *From the Hands of Lawrence Ajanaku* (Los Angeles, 1979)
P. Smith: 'Aspects de l'esthétique au Rwanda', *L'Homme*, xxv/1 (1985), pp. 7–21
S. A. Boone: *Radiance from the Waters: Ideals of Feminine Beauty in Mende Art* (New Haven, 1986)
Masks in Guro Culture, Ivory Coast (exh. cat. by E. Fischer and L. Homberger, Zurich, Mus. Rietberg, 1986)
J. Coote: '"Marvels of Everyday Vision": The Anthropology of Aesthetics and the Cattle-keeping Nilotes', *Anthropology, Art, and Aesthetics*, ed. J. Coote and A. Shelton, Oxford Studies in the Anthropology of Cultural Forms (Oxford, 1992), pp. 245–73

(b) Akan-speaking peoples. The AKAN themselves have an elaborate taxonomy of art forms and an extensive aesthetic vocabulary. For example, they have categories of non-utilitarian forms termed *afefedee* or 'items of beauty' and of utilitarian forms, *adehunu* or 'things empty', many of which are regarded as *agyapadee*, treasured items or heirlooms. Among the Akan set of positive evaluative terms (given here without their prefixes) are *bere*: beautiful, delicate; *bereye*: fineness; *adwenemtew*: clearness of thought, intention; *fe/efe*: fine, pretty, beauty; *hare*: light, quick; and *ahoofe*: elegance. Among the set of negative terms are *kusuu*: unclear; *hima/kyea*: unbalanced, crooked; *kyim*: twisted; *omum*: ugliness; *tawee/bawee*: rough, shapeless, ugly; and *basa-basa*: unskilful (see Warren and Andrews, pp. 6, 33–8).

The BAULE comment critically on the morphology of their figural sculpture in evaluating such physical attributes of persons as the fullness and roundness of the head, arms and calves. Formal evaluations include such aspects as balance and appropriate asymmetry, segmentation and composition/placement (see Vogel). In the tourist arts of the Asante (*see* ASANTE AND RELATED PEOPLES) the distorted and grotesque works created for an external audience exaggeratedly violated indigenous aesthetic norms, thus serving to reinforce Asante aesthetic and cultural values (see Silver, 1979).

BIBLIOGRAPHY

D. Warren and J. K. Andrews: *An Ethnoscientific Approach to Akan Arts and Aesthetics*, Working Pap. Trad. A., 3 (Philadelphia, 1977)
H. R. Silver: 'Beauty and the "I" of the Beholder: Identity, Aesthetics, and Social Change among the Ashanti', *J. Anthropol. Res.*, xxxv/2 (1979), pp. 191–207
P. L. Ravenhill: *Baule Statuary Art: Meaning and Modernization*, Working Pap. Trad. A., 5 (Philadelphia, 1980) [pubd with S. M. Vogel, 1980, as special issue on Baule aesthetics]
S. M. Vogel: *Beauty in the Eyes of the Baule: Aesthetics and Cultural Values*, Working Pap. Trad. A., 6 (Philadelphia, 1980)

H. R. Silver: 'Calculating Risks: The Socioeconomic Foundations of Aesthetic Innovation in an Ashanti Carving Community', *Ethnology*, xx/2 (1981), pp. 101–14

(c) Yoruba-speaking peoples. YORUBA aesthetics are expressed in what is known as *oro ijinle* ('deep discourse'). This draws on such concepts as *jijora*: resemblance; *ifarahon*: visibility, clarity of line and form; *didon*: luminosity, shining smoothness of surface; *idogba*: balance; *gigun*: straightness; *odo*: ephebism, youthfulness; *itutu*: an expression of composure or 'cool'; *kekere*, *tinrin* and *we*: delicacy; *yo*: roundness/pleasing protrusions; *wiwu*: sinister swellings; and *sonso*: pleasing angularity (see Thompson, 1973). *Iwa l'ewa* ('essence/truth is beauty') refers to the criterion of capturing the essential character of a thing or person. This reflects an artist's *oju-inu*: inner-eye or insight; his *oju-ona*: design-consciousness, sensitivity to design and composition; his *yiye*: appropriateness (sense of propriety); his *imoju-mora*: appropriate innovation, inventiveness; his *ifarabale*: possession of a sense of disciplined authority; his *pipe*: correctness, which ensures that the work is *laaye*: alive; *tito*: enduring; and *dahun*: responding or evocative (see Abiodun; 1991 exh. cat.). These are some of the concepts and criteria that underlie the appreciation and evaluation both of sculpture and of masks and masquerade performances by their spectators (see fig. 15).

The carving process is divided into a number of stages: *ona lile*: blocking out the main volumes; *aletunle*: dividing the main volumes; *didon*, rounding and smoothing surfaces; and *fifin*, incising lines, linear details. These reveal some of the conceptual models of Yoruba art, such as a dynamic and ongoing view of creative activity, as well as the aesthetic preferences of Yoruba artists for such characteristics as completeness (see Carroll; 1980 exh. cat.). Close analysis of works by individual masters has shown how many of these aesthetic principles are manifested in their work (see Fagg; Thompson, 1969; Bascom; Abiodun, Drewal and Pemberton). A form of seriate or segmented composition, explained as *letoleto, l'ese ese* ('one by one, step by step'), is widespread in and fundamental to Yoruba sculpture, body arts and performance, as well as in Yoruba social organization. It seems to be linked with fundamental ontological concepts and a belief in *ase*: performative power or life-force (see M. T. Drewal and H. J. Drewal; H. J. Drewal; M. T. Drewal).

15. Yoruba Gelede masker surrounded by cheering spectators, Ilaro, Nigeria; from a photograph by Henry John Drewal, 1978

BIBLIOGRAPHY

W. B. Fagg: 'De l'art des Yoruba', *Présence Afr.*, x–xi (1951), pp. 103–35
K. Carroll: *Yoruba Religious Carving: Pagan and Christian Sculpture in Nigeria and Dahomey* (London, 1967)
R. Thompson: 'Abatan: A Master Potter of the Egbado Yoruba', *Tradition and Creativity in Tribal Art*, ed. D. Biebuyck (Berkeley, 1969/*R* 1973), pp. 120–82
W. Bascom: 'A Yoruba Master Carver: Duga of Meko', *The Traditional Artist in African Societies*, ed. W. L. d'Azevedo (Bloomington, 1973), pp. 62–78
R. F. Thompson: 'Yoruba Artistic Criticism', *The Traditional Artist in African Societies*, ed. W. L. d'Azevedo (Bloomington, 1973), pp. 19–61
African Artistry: Technique and Aesthetics in Yoruba Sculpture (exh. cat. by H. J. Drewal, Atlanta, GA, High Mus. A., 1980)
R. A. Abiodun: 'Identity and the Artistic Process in the Yoruba Aesthetic Concept of *Iwa*', *J. Cult. & Ideas*, i/1 (1983), pp. 13–30
M. T. Drewal and H. J. Drewal: 'Composing Time and Space in Yoruba Art', *Word & Image*, iii/3 (1987), pp. 225–51
H. J. Drewal: 'Beauty and Being: Aesthetics and Ontology in Yoruba Body Art', *Marks of Civilization: Artistic Transformations of the Human Body*, ed. A. Rubin (Los Angeles, 1988), pp. 83–96
Yoruba Art and Aesthetics (exh. cat. by R. Abiodun, H. J. Drewal and J. Pemberton III, Zurich, Mus. Rietberg, 1991)
M. T. Drewal: *Yoruba Ritual: Performers, Play, Agency*, African Systems of Thought (Bloomington, 1992)
R. A. Abiodun, H. J. Drewal and J. Pemberton, eds: *The Yoruba Artist: New Theoretical Perspectives in African Art Studies* (Washington, DC, 1994)

(iv) Conclusion. A few studies have attempted to document changes in aesthetic evaluation. A study of tourist art among the Edo people of southern Nigeria, that is, of the ebony sculptures made at Benin City, has revealed some of the factors shaping the changing dynamics of aesthetic judgements. Transformations in scale, motif and style show the ways in which artists have responded to new economic conditions and formulated new aesthetic preferences (see Ben-Amos, 1977). Other producers of African tourist arts have responded to the demand for instant recognition through the adoption of naturalistic styles and the manufacture of convenient portable objects (see Bascom). A study of economic factors in three African tourist art markets has illustrated other changes in aesthetic evaluations of skill, creativity and cultural expression (see Jules-Rosette).

In addition to further studies of aesthetic change it is hoped that future research will include fuller documentation of the commentaries and aesthetic terminologies of indigenous critics. Such studies would deepen and enrich an understanding of aesthetic evaluation in Africa. The development of video technology makes it possible for artists and performers to review and comment immediately on works they made or in which they participated. The interaction of members of a culture, the interplay of attitudes and opinions, seems to be at the very heart of the formulation of taste within cultures, and the study of it must therefore be essential to understanding aesthetic evaluation in Africa. Also, most scholarly discussions have concentrated on what object types are viewed as having aesthetic value rather than exploring why they have it, that is, they are concerned more with a category of object (art) than with a category of thought (aesthetics; see Coote, p. 250). Making such a distinction should help future understandings.

BIBLIOGRAPHY

W. Bascom: 'Changing African Art', *Ethnic and Tourist Arts: Cultural Expressions from the Fourth World*, ed. N. H. H. Graburn (Berkeley, 1976/*R* 1979), pp. 303–19

P. Ben-Amos: '"A la recherche du temps perdu": On Being an Ebony-carver in Benin', *Ethnic and Tourist Arts: Cultural Expressions from the Fourth World*, ed. N. H. H. Graburn (Berkeley, 1976/*R* 1979), pp. 320–33

——: 'Pidgin Languages and Tourist Arts', *Stud. Anthropol. Visual Communic.*, iv/2 (1977), pp. 128–39

B. Jules-Rosette: 'Aesthetics and Market Demand: The Structure of the Tourist Art Market in Three African Settings', *Afr. Stud. Rev.*, xxix/1 (1986), pp. 41–59

J. Coote: '"Marvels of Everyday Vision": The Anthropology of Aesthetics and the Cattle-keeping Nilotes', *Anthropology, Art, and Aesthetics*, ed. J. Coote and A. Shelton, Oxford Studies in the Anthropology of Cultural Forms (Oxford, 1992), pp. 245–73

HENRY JOHN DREWAL

III. Contexts of production and use.

1. Patronage. 2. Artists. 3. Trade. 4. Commercial production. 5. Ritual.

1. PATRONAGE. In Africa as elsewhere the patron is often the link by which the artist is made aware of society's demands and needs for art. This role has often been neglected in studies of artistic production in Africa. Although creative interpretation originates with the artist, it is the patron who sanctions such interpretation, thereby playing a critical role in supporting artistic production and championing artistic creativity. The final art object is the product of the patron–artist relationship and of the interacting factors of the artist's creativity, the patron's demands and the existing prototypes. The patron–artist relationship is often mediated by the role of the trader (*see* §3 below).

(i) General. (ii) Political. (iii) Religious.

(i) General. Within each act of patronage, the rules of interaction, the kinds of information exchanged and the form of the contract are affected by a number of factors. These include the type of art form, the socio-cultural context in which the art object functions, the patron's position in the local art world, the nature of the dominant social roles played by patron and artist during and after interaction and the degree of cultural understanding shared by patron and artist. Patrons commission, pay for and use art objects. As a consumer, the patron is the economic motivator who stimulates artistic production and thus not only influences stylistic continuity within a tradition but can also function as an agent of change. Of equal importance is the key role the patron plays in introducing the object into the social context where it may be evaluated by the wider community.

Patronage determines the range of art styles that develop and flourish in a society. For example, among the BAMANA of West Africa such men's socio-religious associations as N'tomo, Kore, Chi-wara and Komo commission stylistically distinct forms of wooden masks and headdresses. Moreover multiple art traditions, such as the production of wood and metal sculpture, architecture, textiles and ceramics, can co-exist in a single society if there is sufficient patronage to support them. Conversely, long-standing art traditions decline and disappear if patronage is withdrawn. The patron's impact is most clearly seen where patron and artist interact face-to-face. The patron's influence is most direct when the interaction takes place prior to production. During a pre-production transaction in the African context, artist and patron agree a verbal contract in which the patron's desires concerning materials, iconographic and decorative motifs and the time to be taken are articulated. Such specifications may be general, indicating only the type of object desired, or they may be precise, with detailed instructions given. In turn, the artist informs the patron about his requirements concerning materials, the rituals necessary for production and payment. The artist does not always wait for a patron but may build up a stock of objects ready for visits from patron-consumers. Non-ritual textiles, pottery, leatherwork and carved household utensils are often stockpiled in this way. In these cases the choices made from the artist's stock by patron-consumers have a delayed effect on subsequent production.

Most frequently patrons belong to the same ethnic group as the artists they support, and this may be labelled in-group patronage. Thus, patron and artist share a common artistic tradition and vocabulary as well as shared expectations about the degree of acceptable stylistic variation. For example, FULANI weavers in Mali must adhere to traditional patterns, colours and materials in their wool blankets, since their patrons demand conformity, choosing weavers on the basis of their ability to adhere to specific designs (Imperato, 1973). On the other hand, innovation in subject-matter at least is encouraged by the traditional patrons of brass-smiths among the ASANTE AND RELATED PEOPLES, who order distinctive forms of goldweights to display as prestige objects (McLeod, 1971).

An interesting form of in-group patronage is the phenomenon of self-patronage, when artist and patron are the same person. Among the Gurensi of northern Ghana, for example, women act as their own patrons when embellishing their house walls with painted designs (Smith, 1978). A senior woman of a compound organizes the necessary activities and solicits the help of other female relatives who together select the design motifs, divide the house wall into sections and paint them (see fig. 20 below). Similarly, young male initiates among the YAKA of Zaïre create highly original masks to be worn and judged by the community during their initiation ceremony (Adelman).

Where patron–artist interactions cross ethnic boundaries, in what may be labelled out-group patronage, a common cultural understanding may not exist. Prior to production, therefore, there may be a detailed exchange of information. Shared expectations are less important when the patron chooses from stockpiled goods. When out-group patronage becomes institutionalized, it can have long-term effects, even leading to the development of a distinctive new style. For example, an Afro-Portuguese ivory tradition emerged in the 16th century when Portuguese sailors commissioned Bulom (Sherbro) ivory-carvers from what is now Sierra Leone to produce intricate pedestal bowls with European motifs (*see* § 2(iii) below).

In general, it is the patron who takes the praise for the successful work of art or the blame for its failure. For this reason the creative process does not necessarily end when an artist finishes an object. Changes in its appearance may be demanded by the owner due to aesthetic preferences or for some other reason. Sometimes a ritual object's potency and efficacy need to be enhanced. For example, some KONGO figures (*nkisi*) are not considered complete until a ritual specialist acting on behalf of a patron has applied magical ingredients to them. Some are activated by having nails and blades driven into them; thus their appearance is continually transformed.

Some objects are subjected to a continual process of decorative embellishment by patrons or other artists. For example, among the YORUBA, patron-owners of Gelede masks repainted them before each public appearance (see fig. 16). Masks may also be enhanced with the application of cloth, beads, feathers and even attached carvings. Similarly, SENUFO patrons alter the appearance of their carved masks and figures by applying polychrome, decorative patterns to them (Glaze, 1981, p. 16).

The reactions to and evaluations of art objects by audiences and critics influence the future decisions of both artists and patrons. For example, the huge upstanding ears of Yoruba Egungun Erin masks were introduced when a patron demanded more imposing ears than usual. When the mask attracted favourable attention at a festival, other patrons asked for similar masks, and local carvers added the type to their repertories (Wolff, 1981).

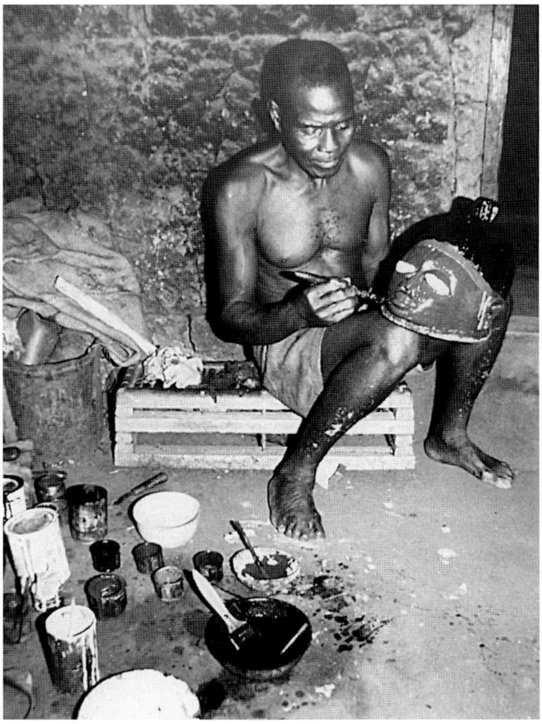

16. Yoruba patron–owner of a Gelede mask repainting it before a public performance, Ilaro, Nigeria; from a photograph by Henry John Drewal, 1978

Societies vary in the degree to which patron–artist interactions are formalized. In centralized societies with a high degree of social stratification and developed trade systems, for example among the Asante, NUPE, HAUSA and Kuba (*see* KUBA (iii)), the arts flourish. Here artists are needed to produce a wide range of products to meet the society's commercial, prestige and everyday needs, and patron–artist relations are direct, regular and tightly structured. Patrons are often traders, chiefs or leaders of some sort, and artists are often full-time specialists organized into structured workgroups. For example, in the 19th century the Nupe of central Nigeria were conquered by Muslim FULANI who imposed a guild system to ensure that artists would produce a wide range of trade and prestige objects. In this way the patronage of the Fulani ruling class, channelled through titled guild-heads, shaped the direction taken by Nupe crafts, bringing into existence, for example, a tradition of hammered brass vessels for Muslim ceremonies of protocol and gift exchange.

A less formal type of patronage, where contact between patron and artist is occasional and relatively unstructured, takes place in all societies but dominates where there is no centralized political system, for example among the DAN, SENUFO, FANG and IGBO. In such societies artists tend to be part-time, independent specialists, and it is the patron who takes the initiative by commissioning or purchasing objects. For instance, during the dry season in north-eastern Nigeria, Bata, Ungal and Fulani women decorate gourds that are used as gifts and dowry goods, but only on demand.

Patrons may operate both as individuals, motivated by their own needs, and as representatives of kinship, religious, leadership or age groups. Once displayed publicly art objects enhance the prestige and power of both the individual patron and the group. For example, the Yoruba mask Egungun Erin is known as 'the rich man's Egungun' because of its aesthetic quality and cost. To commission such a mask and costume often requires the resources of a whole kinship group, whose prestige is enhanced by its public appearances, as is that of the individual owner.

(ii) Political. Kings, emirs and chiefs of the centralized societies of West Africa (e.g. ASANTE AND RELATED PEOPLES, FON, YORUBA, NUPE, HAUSA), the Cameroon Grassfields (e.g. BAMUM) and the southern savannah of Central Africa (e.g. KONGO, KUBA, CHOKWE AND RELATED PEOPLES) are particularly important patrons in Sub-Saharan Africa. They exercise monopolies over scarce resources used in art production, have exclusive control of particular forms and motifs and control the labour and organization of craft workers. As patrons, such people largely control the production and distribution of highly valued prestige and leadership arts (Fraser and Cole). Prestige arts are those artistically embellished items of everyday life (household utensils, furniture, jewellery and clothing) that are used by persons of rank to display their wealth and special status. Leadership arts are more exclusive and include such items of regalia as dress and

17. Hausa emir in Sallah procession, dressed in ceremonial regalia and surrounded by retainers, Kano, Nigeria

accessories, sceptres, swords, thrones and ancestral sculptures. They function to stimulate loyalty to an office by instilling awe in beholders.

Items of regalia are commissioned by the emir and other Hausa nobility from local and regional craftsmen and figure prominently in public, ceremonial and political contexts where the very body of the leader becomes a focus of artistic elaboration. The appearance of the Hausa emir during the Sallah procession at the end of the Ramadan fast is such an event. Hand-embroidered gowns, layered one on top of the other, silver horse trappings, sceptres and a huge state umbrella draw attention to and magnify the importance of the emir (see fig. 17).

Such palace architecture as that of the Asante, the Yoruba and the Bamum also set rulers apart from the rest of the population. The massiveness and elaboration of the architecture express the special status of the leader (*see* §VI, 1(iii) below; *see also* PALACE, §VIII). Within the palace, art further enhances his special status. For example, the royal treasuries of the kings of the Cameroon Grassfields hold sculpture depicting royal ancestors, elaborately carved stools and thrones, drums, serving bowls, embroidered clothing, jewellery, tobacco pipes, drinking horns, fly-whisks, staffs and ceremonial swords. The leader is the guardian of such regalia and emblems of office and is responsible for the continuity of the various traditions, directly influencing the quality and quantity of objects produced. For example, after the emergence of the Asante kingdom in 18th-century Ghana, each king was required to commission two new, decorated swords, thereby assuring the continued vitality of the tradition (Ross, p. 25). Among the Kuba of Zaïre since the 17th century each king was required to commission a commemorative statue that functioned as his spiritual double.

To control production efficiently, leaders frequently have artists, whether freeborn or slave, who work in the vicinity of the palace, where they can be closely supervised. They may live in the palace complex itself, as in Bamum; in wards in the capital city, as in Benin and among the Nupe and Hausa; or in craft villages, as among the Asante, where shelter, board, financial support and regular employment are offered. The *Óbas* of BENIN, for example, established 40 to 50 guilds in wards near the palace. Members of these craft guilds were full-time specialists producing embroidered cloths, leather fans and sculpture in brass, ivory and wood for the *Óba* and for his chiefs and cult priests, if the *Óba* allowed. The kings (*fons*) of the larger kingdoms of the Cameroon Grassfields control wood-carving in a similar way, so that if a neighbouring ruler with no resident carvers wants a sculpture, he must commission and pay the local *fon*, not the artist (1984 exh. cat., pp. 61–2). Artists under royal patronage usually consider it a great honour to work for a leader and rarely request payment. Leaders, however, frequently reward artists with gifts.

The ability of leaders to recruit artists from a wide area, sometimes from different ethnic groups, is important in contributing to the mobility and spread of art styles. For instance, after the 19th-century Nupe conquest of northern Yoruba territories, the Fulani–Nupe emir settled Yoruba slaves, including weavers, in Bida, the capital city. Male Yoruba weavers introduced new cloth types and had a great impact on increasing textile production for the cloth trade, while female Yoruba weavers introduced weaving technology and new cloth types and designs to Nupe women (Perani, 1979). The patronage of leaders may encourage artists to be itinerant as, for example, in some 19th-century Liberian chiefdoms where weavers and wood-carvers attached themselves to households of wealthy chiefs in neighbouring or even distant chiefdoms, producing carvings and textiles in exchange for shelter and board.

The link between patron leaders and the origins of specific art forms is sometimes retained in a group's oral history. For example, Muhammadu Rumfa, a 15th-century Kano leader, is remembered for introducing red and green livery for retainers and leather sandals adorned with ostrich feathers as a royal prerogative. King Njoya of Bamum is credited with introducing weaving and tailoring to his court in the late 19th century and is said to have woven sample lengths so that his palace weavers could copy them (Geary, 1983). These attributions of royal artistic genius add legitimacy to the art traditions and, simultaneously, enhance the perceived qualities of the leader patrons.

(iii) Religious. Priests, diviners and members of religious associations and masquerade societies commission costumes, masks, shrine sculptures and prestige arts to honour and control supernatural beings and forces. The production of ritual art often involves calling upon supernatural forces to produce or activate masks or figures that then become receptacles for extraordinary powers. In this potentially dangerous activity the contract between patron and artist is both an economic agreement and a pledge of ritual cooperation. Patron–artist transactions regarding ritual carving are often highly structured. The interactions of male Gola artists and female Sande society officials in south-western Liberia offer an example. A transaction begins when the women commission a mask from a carver who thus becomes privy to the secret knowledge of Sande. While carving the mask the artist is supported by his Sande patrons who attempt to direct his work by insisting upon such details as specific coiffure designs and the form and

placement of neck rings. The patron–artist interaction is conceived here as a struggle: the carver may resist directives and, in extreme cases, destroy an unfinished work because of the continuous criticism of the patrons. Tension between the carver and the Sande officials may continue throughout the production period and sometimes, after the mask has been completed and performed, the artist may destroy it if he finds that it is treated with disrespect (d'Azevedo, 1973, pp. 145–7).

Occasionally whole communities may commission ritual objects from an artist. This is the case with the *ikoro* slit-drums of the IGBO of Nigeria. These huge signal drums, embellished with carved images of animals and humans, serve as symbols of village unity. Complex rituals are carried out before a giant tree is cut, and the lengthy carving process takes place in secret. Rituals of consecration have to be carried out at village expense to activate the drum before it can be used (see 1984 exh. cat., pp. 87–8).

In many cases of ritual patronage, the ultimate patron is a spirit with whom an individual makes a contract to act as mediator. The spirit often makes its demands known to an individual through a dream or vision or through a divination process. For example, among the DAN of Côte d'Ivoire masks are commissioned when a forest spirit appears in a person's dreams and requests the creation of a mask to allow that spirit to participate in the human world (Fischer, 1978). Similarly, BAULE nature spirits and spirit spouses, identified by a diviner as the source of an individual's misfortunes, may appear in dreams or trances to demand that figures be carved to portray them and act as a focus for offerings. The spirit then appears to the commissioning individual, diviner or carver to make its desires known, and a carving is prepared (Vogel, 1980). Illness and infertility are often taken to be signals that a spirit desires to be appeased with an act of art patronage. Among the CHOKWE AND RELATED PEOPLES of Zaïre, for example, if a man who has inherited a Pwo dance mask falls ill, a diviner may determine that the *pwo*, a female ancestor, is causing the sickness. The man must then reactivate the mask or have a new one carved (Bastin, p. 92).

BIBLIOGRAPHY

M. D. McLeod: 'Goldweights of Asante', *Afr. A.*, v/1 (1971), pp. 8–15
D. Fraser and H. Cole, eds: *African Art and Leadership* (Madison, 1972)
W. L. d'Azevedo: 'Sources of Gola Artistry', *The Traditional Artist in African Societies*, ed. W. L. d'Azevedo (Bloomington, 1973/*R* 1975), pp. 282–340
P. J. Imperato: 'Wool Blankets of the Peul of Mali', *Afr. A.*, vi/3 (1973), pp. 40–47, 84
K. L. Adelman: 'The Art of the Yaka', *Afr. A.*, ix/1 (1975), pp. 40–43
T. J. H. Chappel: *Decorated Gourds in North-eastern Nigeria* (Lagos, 1977)
D. Ross: 'The Iconography of Asante Sword Ornaments', *Afr. A.*, xi/1 (1977), pp. 16–25, 90–91
E. Fischer: 'Dan Forest Spirits: Masks in Dan Villages', *Afr. A.*, xi/2 (1978), pp. 16–23, 94
F. T. Smith: 'Gurensi Wall Painting', *Afr. A.*, xi/4 (1978), pp. 36–41, 96
P. R. McNaughton: *Secret Sculptures of Komo: Art and Power in Bamana (Bambara) Initiation Associations*, Working Pap. Trad. A., 4 (Philadelphia, 1979)
J. Perani: 'Nupe Costume Crafts', *Afr. A.*, xii/3 (1979), pp. 52–7, 96
P. Ben-Amos: *The Art of Benin*, Tribal A. (London, 1980)
——: 'Patron–artist Interactions in Africa', *Afr. A.*, xiii/3 (1980), pp. 56–7, 92
S. L. Kasfir: 'Patronage and Maconde Carvers', *Afr. A.*, xiii/3 (1980), pp. 67–70, 91–2
J. Perani: 'Patronage and Nupe Craft Industries', *Afr. A.*, xiii/3 (1980), pp. 71–5, 92
S. M. Vogel: *Beauty in the Eyes of the Baule: Aesthetics and Cultural Values*, Working Pap. Trad. A., 6 (Philadelphia, 1980)
A. J. Glaze: *Art and Death in a Senufo Village*, Trad. A. Africa (Bloomington, 1981)
N. H. Wolff: 'Headdress (Egungun Erin)', *For Spirits and Kings: African Art from the Tishman Collection* (exh. cat., ed. S. M. Vogel; New York, Met., 1981), pp. 110–12
——: 'Egungun Costuming in Abeokuta', *Afr. A.*, xv/3 (1982), pp. 66–70, 91
C. Geary: *Things of the Palace: A Catalogue of the Bamum Palace Museum in Foumban (Cameroon)*, Studien zur Kulturkunde, lx (Wiesbaden, 1983)
M.-L. Bastin: 'Ritual Masks of the Chokwe', *Afr. A.*, xvii/4 (1984), pp. 40–44, 92–3
J. Vansina: *Art History in Africa: An Introduction to Method* (London, 1984), esp. pp. 44–7
The Art of Cameroon (exh. cat. by T. Northern, Washington, DC, Smithsonian Inst. Traveling Exh. Serv., 1984)
Igbo Arts: Community and Cosmos (exh. cat. by H. M. Cole and C. C. Aniakor, Los Angeles, UCLA, Mus. Cult. Hist., 1984–6)

JUDITH PERANI, NORMA H. WOLFF

2. ARTISTS. The perceived role of artists in African society varies widely, depending on the nature and purpose of the work being produced and the traditions of a particular people or region. A major factor in the making of many types of art is that of gender (*see* §(ii) below). In general, the concept of an individual artist being associated with a personal style and oeuvre is a 20th-century development, following the introduction of Western views of art and teaching practices (*see* §IX below).

(i) Role and status. (ii) Gender.

(i) Role and status. In Africa the role of the artist ranges

18. *Mbari* master builder or 'man of skill' Akakporo, directing the construction of a *mbari* house at Umuedi Nworie, near Owerri, Igbo, Nigeria; from a photograph by Herbert M. Cole, 1967

from being the producer of ritual objects to the organizer of entertainments and rites of passage. He or she contributes to the establishment and maintenance of royal legitimacy as well as to new and emergent senses of identity. As for the artist's status, this ranges from being nobody of any importance to being of necessity a king, or, alternatively, a deviant. These variables are still insufficiently understood by scholars to enable the establishment of any precise correlation between role and status. For the moment, we have to be satisfied with the discussion of a few varied examples. This will give the reader an idea of the complexity of questions of artists' roles and statuses in 'traditional' African society. Some of the developments of colonial and post-colonial times are also addressed.

(a) Traditional examples. In the small-scale social groupings of traditional Africa it is not always obvious who the artist is. For example, for the building of a *mbari* house among the Owerri IGBO, a 'man of skill' is employed (see fig. 18). Such a man will already have a reputation for the successful direction of the construction of these buildings with their complex painting and sculpture. Similarly, in Afikpo Igbo communities, the 'play-leaders' who direct the performances of Okumkpa masked plays have established reputations for the successful direction of performances (see fig. 19). However, whereas the 'man of skill' is in essence affirming the authority of elders, whose responsibility it is to maintain appropriate relationships between people and deities, the subject-matter of Okumkpa plays is frequently derogatory of the elders who sanction the performances and are obliged to take the front-row seats. Perhaps not surprisingly, the status of 'play-leader' is adverse, and, for as long as one is directing plays that criticize and ridicule the elders, one is denied promotion within the local title system.

It is also useful to compare the Afikpo 'play-leader' with the 'preceptor', the senior man charged with the responsibility of organizing initiations into Bwami, the all-encompassing organization of the LEGA people of eastern Zaïre. Their roles are identical, yet in Afikpo the principle of the authority of the elders is confirmed by the criticism of those who are, in practice, in authority. In contrast, the successive phases of Bwami initiation entail a revelation of a philosophy. The Afikpo Igbo Okumkpa entails a revelation of practice, whereas Lega Bwami initiations entail a revelation of principle. If failure on the part of individual incumbents of senior office is enacted by Lega people, it is not within the context of Bwami. It is hardly surprising to learn that, in contrast to the Afikpo 'play-leader', the Lega 'preceptor' is a man of high regard.

This discussion suggests a perhaps obvious correlation between the purpose of the art work and the status of its producer, but other examples caution us against assuming such a necessary correlation. Thus, among the FANG people of Gabon, the carving of the figures that are placed with apotropaic intention upon boxes of ancestral bones

19. Afikpo Igbo 'play-leaders' directing the performance of an Okumkpa masked play, Amorie village, Afikpo, Nigeria; from a photograph by Simon Ottenberg, 1952

is, notwithstanding the ritual necessity of these figures, considered on a par with making fish-traps and is carried out in the public gaze of the men's club house. Here the role of producer attracts no particular esteem or status. Similarly, among the Tiv of Nigeria, sculptors attract no marked esteem, notwithstanding the social and ritual necessity of their work. In any case, for the Tiv, sculpture is something anyone can try, and, while some are better at it than others, no particular status attaches to this. The tradition of body-painting among some NUBA in Sudan might provide another example. A relevant factor is the extent to which, as determined within a received tradition of practice, an art form is considered to demand specialist knowledge. It is possible to suggest contrasts between contexts in which the practice of an art may broadly be categorized as commonplace (attracting no particular status), or specialist and clear-cut within an established order, or specialist but ambivalent, either because of the subject-matter of the art or because of the necessary circumstances of its making.

This is not a matter of the contrast between artists who support and those who subvert a political status quo; for the Afikpo 'play-leader' is not engaging in Okumkpa in an attempt to subvert chiefly authority but in its affirmation via the critique of the current incumbents of chiefly office. Among the Gola of Liberia, the wood-carver is perhaps an even more ambivalent character. While the status of a Gola chief is enhanced by the mere fact of having a famous sculptor within his retinue, success in sculpture is achieved through a relationship with a spirit mentor that encourages or entails behaviour that is locally regarded as deviant, to the extent that parents will take disciplinary action against a son whom they consider to be taking too much interest in the art. More to the point, the most significant artefact within a Gola sculptor's repertory is the mask worn by women of the Sande association in the relevant stage of the initiation of girls into adulthood (*see also* §VII, 4 below). The Sande association, however, is an institution the inner workings of which are secret and from which men are excluded except at the very highest levels of rank within Sande and the male equivalent association, Poro. The Gola carver thus is not a man of any particular authority, and yet in order to carve the mask the sculptor is the one man with access to the secret domain of women.

In contrast to the Gola carvers, and indeed those of the Tiv and Fang, the sculptors of Benin work within a hierarchical order of guilds, with the brass-casters at the top, followed by the ivory-carvers. Within each guild, there is a series of titled offices having responsibility for, among other things, negotiating the production of works of art. Moreover, guild titles are structured within an overall hierarchy of titled offices, and, while their status therein might be considered merely middle-ranking, the important point is that status is established and esteemed to the extent permitted within the title system. The role of the guilds is the production of artworks that participate in the enactment and definition of royal legitimacy, whether as ivory regalia worn by the king or brass regalia worn by titled men, or as ivory and brass furniture for altars within the royal palace (*see also* BENIN, §3). Even more marked is the contrast with the kingdoms of the Cameroon Grassfields, where sculptural expertise is an expected attribute of kings; even though much of the sculptural output is the work of palace servants, the king is nevertheless identified as its author (*see* BAMILEKE AND RELATED PEOPLES, BAMUM and BANGWA).

(b) Modern developments. By the early 1990s probably half the artists in any African country were working for an urban-based élite. Most of these were associated with an art gallery, having been trained in the fine art department of a university or college of higher education. While such institutions are colonial in origin, by the 1990s so many colonial elements had been either discarded or domesticated that they were thoroughly African. In particular, the subject-matter, the artists' intentions and the discourse of local historians and critics suggest that local cultural traditions and both local and national identities are dominant concerns.

In Nigeria, for example, some art movements have arisen out of pre-colonial decorative traditions. The Uli traditions of the Igbo were drawn on in the work of Uche Okeke and his followers, as they emerged from fine-art training at the time of Nigerian independence, determined to convey a sense of Nigerian identity by using forms associated with local traditions. Ibrahim El Salahi of Sudan drew upon both Islamic calligraphic and local craft patterns in his work. Moreover, in such countries as Kenya and Zaïre, such concerns have been manifested in work that can be seen as critical of the current state of political affairs. In South Africa, of course, artists took an often overt role in opposing apartheid. In the struggle for liberation from colonial rule in Mozambique, artists were prominent among the leaders of the Frelimo government in exile.

Thus, throughout Africa artists have taken up the role of mediator in a range of local and national concerns. The artist's status then depends upon his or her position *vis-à-vis* the élite and the position from which the status is being judged.

BIBLIOGRAPHY

P. Bohannan: 'Artist and Critic in an African Society', *The Artist in Tribal Society: Proceedings of a Symposium Held at the Royal Anthropological Institute*, ed. M. W. Smith, Royal Anthropological Institute Occasional Paper, xv (London, 1961), pp. 85–94; repr. in *Anthropology and Art: Readings in Cross-Cultural Aesthetics*, ed. C. M. Otten (New York, 1971/*R* Austin, TX, 1976), pp. 172–81

W. L. d'Azevedo: *The Artist Archetype in Gola Culture*, Desert Research Institute Preprint, xiv (Nevada, 1966, rev. 1970)

R. Brain and A. Pollock: *Bangwa Funerary Sculpture*, A. & Soc. Ser. (London, 1971)

D. Fraser and H. M. Cole, eds: *African Art and Leadership* (Madison, 1972)

W. L. d'Azevedo: 'Mask Makers and Myth in Western Liberia', *Primitive Art and Society*, ed. A. Forge (London, 1973), pp. 126–50

W. L. d'Azevedo, ed.: *The Traditional Artist in African Societies* (Bloomington and London, 1973/*R* 1993)

D. P. Biebuyck: *Lega Culture: Art, Initiation, and Moral Philosophy among a Central African People* (Berkeley, 1973)

P. J. C. Dark: *An Introduction to Benin Art and Technology* (Oxford, 1973)

S. Ottenberg: *Masked Rituals of Afikpo: The Context of an African Art* (Seattle, 1975)

R. Layton: *The Anthropology of Art* (Frogmore, 1981, rev. Cambridge, 1991)

H. M. Cole: *Mbari: Art and Life among the Owerri Igbo* (Bloomington, 1982)

Africa Explores: 20th Century African Art (exh. cat. by S. Vogel with I. Ebong, New York, Cent. Afr. A., 1991)

JOHN PICTON

(ii) Gender. Throughout Africa the division of labour by gender not only determines the everyday work of growing crops and trade but also strongly affects the production, use and imagery of visual art forms. This entry provides an overview of the role of women in the visual arts in Africa, both traditionally and in the modern situation.

(a) Traditional practices. In Africa generally men and women practise different arts, or at least different techniques. In many areas explicit rules restrict women from participation in wood-carving and metallurgy. Thus the wood sculptures and brass-castings for which Africa is most famous are the exclusive product of male artists. Beyond these two restricted pursuits, the division of artistic labour by gender varies from community to community. In North Africa, for example, women weave, while in the whole of Sub-Saharan Africa, apart from Nigeria and Madagascar, only men weave. Usually women are the potters, though there are a few communities, such as among the HAUSA of Niger, in which men are the potters. Although women modelled figures in clay or other soft materials among a number of peoples, for example the Dakakari and IGBO of Nigeria and the Kuba (*see* KUBA (iii)) of central Zaïre, it was more common that women's art comprised schematic forms or geometrical designs while the men produced the human and animal imagery.

Generally, where men and women engage in the same craft, whether for local use or for trade, there are clear distinctions between the equipment or materials they use or between the styles. In southern Nigeria, for example, where both men and women weave, men use a narrow, horizontal loom, while women weave on a broad, vertical loom. In the Fungom district of Cameroon, men produce tall, tapering baskets affixed to wooden slats with which to carry their burdens, while women plait a variety of bowl-shaped containers. In some instances the gender distinction lies in the type of imagery produced. For example, in mural painting in western Côte d'Ivoire and northern Ghana women paint schematic designs (see fig. 20), while men depict figurative scenes. Often efforts are complementary: men build house structures, and women shape the walls; men weave cloth, women decorate it by dyeing or embroidery. It was typical that both genders shared in the rewards of such complementary efforts, the initiating party retaining a claim on a share of the eventual profit.

Distinctions in production between the genders are reinforced in numerous ways, perhaps most obviously by social organization. For example, among the TUAREG, FULANI, BAMANA and Malinke in the populous Sahelian and light savannah region below the Sahara, where the social order prior to the rise of the modern state was explicitly hierarchical, with ranked status groups of nobles, freemen and servants, such artisans as smiths and leatherworkers belonged to named occupational groups ranked at the bottom of the status hierarchy. The wives of craftsmen often also pursued a craft. For example, smiths' wives among the HAUSA and Songhai of Niger usually engaged in tasks that, like smithing, were segregated from residential areas. Pottery, for example, was fired in open pits away from the town or village, and both tanning and indigo dyeing, with their offensive odours, also had their own areas. In the populous Yoruba cities of Nigeria, members of the women's weaving, dyeing and pottery guilds controlled their membership just as the male craftsmen did. Taboos or the possession of protective 'medicines' served to protect artists from encroachment in their field of expertise by members of the opposite gender. Sometimes also legends assigned the ownership of particular techniques to men or women within particular families; possession of the techniques by a particular gender could even be divinely authorized.

20. Kahnyno Thérèse of Medibli village painting a house, 1985; from a photograph by Monni Adams

Considerations of gender also entered into the actual production process. These are best known for male carvers and smelters/smiths, who must refrain from sexual activity prior to and during the work and whose workplace potentially fertile women must not approach. Taboos prevented men from entering the women's work area in a Kamba potting village in Kenya (see Gill). Also the work area was separated from the places where sexual relations took place, and the women potters had to refrain from sex for three days prior to their work. These Kamba potters produced cooking pots for the region and were held in high esteem for their skill. They were also feared, however, by other potters as well as by non-potters. These attitudes of fear and respect are similar to those towards male artisans in the West African Sahel. If reports on the social relations of women artisans were not so fragmentary, the basis for these ambivalent attitudes might be better understood.

In many parts of Africa rituals involving figures or featuring masked dancers were conducted solely by men, with women being prohibited from attending on pain of death or sterility. Where women were participants, they contributed in less spectacular fashion by lending costume elements, providing ceremonial containers, by repainting house walls or by singing and dancing to honour the spirits. In only one region of Africa, among the MENDE, Temne, Bullom and Gola of Sierra Leone and Liberia, did women organize public mask performances.

In spite of the general phenomenon of male leadership, in many contexts women did have formal public roles and responsibilities. Women were court officials, heads of urban markets and organizers of girls' initiation rites. Sometimes such women called attention to their achievements through art. Decorated pottery, painted houses, body and personal adornment and fashionable clothes silently convey success in a form that does not contradict the verbal leadership by which men demonstrate their superior authority.

(b) Modern developments. In spite of a tradition that only men work with metal, HAUSA Muslim women near Kano in Nigeria have been engraving designs on aluminium spoons used for daily and ceremonial use and for the tourist market. This relaxation of a rule was due to three factors: the lessening of sanctions surrounding metalwork; the relatively recent adoption of aluminium in the 1920s; and the spread of purdah in the area, which has prevented women from pursuing their former economic pursuits. Efforts to find a way to increase their earning power encouraged groups of women in Sierra Leone and Mali to learn weaving, a technique formerly reserved for men. To meet the expanded demands of the international tourist trade in Lusaka, Zambia, men took up the previously female activity of pottery-making, while women entered the formerly male activity of carving.

In the late 20th century some African women began to gain international recognition as contemporary artists. Perhaps because they were accustomed to producing surplus crafts in the market, in contrast to men producing only on commission, African women readily accepted the role of individual artists producing for sale. Among these were Kadiato Kamara (*b c.* 1933) of Sierra Leone who practised a traditional art of designing tie-dyed cloth; Nike Olaniyi Davis (*b* 1951) from northern Nigeria who used the imported technique of wax batik, which she learnt in a local art school, to express her own inspirations derived from dreams and books; and Ladi Kwali, a potter from Gwari, Nigeria, who learnt glazing at a pottery training centre. A number of women also trained as professional artists outside Africa. The Igbo potter Kate Ifejike-Obukwelu (*b* 1945) was educated in New York and produced both rounded pots of traditional shape and decorative ceramics, including paired male and female figures. Perhaps the outstanding example of an internationally trained, successful woman sculptor is the Kalabari Ijo artist Sokari Douglas Camp (*b* 1958), whose work includes large metal figures of women and children and male maskers (see fig. 21).

21. Sokari Douglas Camp: *Kalabari Masquerader with Boat Headdress*, steel and wood, mirror, bells and cloth, h. 2.18 m, 1987 (artist's collection)

BIBLIOGRAPHY

A. J. Glaze: 'Women, Power and Art in a Senufo Village', *Afr. A.*, viii/3 (1975), pp. 24–9, 64–8, 90–91

M. Etienne: 'Women and Men, Cloth and Colonization: The Transformation of Production–Distribution Relations among the Baule (Ivory Coast)', *Cah. Etud. Afr.*, xvii/1, no. 65 (1977), pp. 41–64

P. Ben-Amos: 'Owina n'Ido: Royal Weavers of Benin', *Afr. A.*, xi/4 (1978), pp. 48–53, 95–6

J. Teilhet: 'The Equivocal Role of Women Artists in Non-literate Cultures', *Heresies* (Winter 1978), pp. 96–102

M. Wahlman and E. Chuta: 'Sierra Leone Resist-dyed Textiles', *The Fabrics of Culture: The Anthropology of Clothing and Adornment*, ed. J. M. Cordwell and R. A. Schwarz, World Anthropology (The Hague, 1979), pp. 447–66

M. J. Adams: 'Afterword: Spheres of Men's and Women's Creativity', *Ethnol. Z. Zürich* (1980), no. 1, pp. 163–7

R. Richter: *Art, Economics and Change: The Kulebele of Northern Ivory Coast* (La Jolla, 1980)

M. Gill: *The Potter's Mark: Contemporary and Archaeological Pottery of the Kenyan Southeastern Highlands* (diss., Boston U., 1981)

L. Aronson: 'Popo Weaving: The Dynamics of Trade in Southeastern Nigeria', *Afr. A.*, xv/3 (1982), pp. 43–7, 90–91

S. Brett-Smith: 'Symbolic Blood: Cloths for Excised Women', *Res*, 5 (1982), pp. 15–51

22. Gourd stall at the daily market, Gombe, north-eastern Nigeria; from a photograph by Marla C. Berns, 1982

U. Wagner: *Catching the Tourists: Women Handicraft Traders in The Gambia* (Stockholm, 1982)
S. Ottenberg: 'Artistic and Sex Roles in a Limba Chiefdom', *Female and Male in West Africa*, ed. C. Oppong (London, 1983), pp. 76–90
L. Aronson: 'Women in the Arts', *African Women South of the Sahara*, ed. M. J. Hay and S. Stichter (London, 1984), pp. 119–38
B. Jules-Rosette: *The Messages of Tourist Art: An African Semiotic System in Comparative Perspective*, Topics in Contemporary Semiotics (New York, 1984)
R. Roberts: 'Women's Work and Women's Property: Household Social Relations in the Maraka Textile Industry of the Nineteenth Century', *Comp. Stud. Soc. & Hist.*, xxvi/2 (1984), pp. 229–50
M. Adams: 'Women and Masks among the Western Wè of Ivory Coast', *Afr. A.*, xix/2 (1986), pp. 46–55, 90
S. Afonja: 'Women, Power and Authority in Traditional Yoruba Society', *Visibility and Power: Essays on Women in Society and Development*, ed. L. Dube, E. Leacock and S. Ardener (Delhi, 1986/*R* 1989), pp. 136–57
P. Ben-Amos: 'Artistic Creativity in Benin Kingdom', *Afr. A.*, xix/3 (1986), pp. 60–63, 83–4
M. C. Daly, J. B. Eicher and T. V. Erekosima: 'Male and Female Artistry in Kalabari Dress', *Afr. A.*, xix/3 (1986), pp. 48–51, 83
W. J. Dewey: 'Shona Male and Female Artistry', *Afr. A.*, xix/3 (1986), pp. 64–7, 84
A. J. Glaze: 'Dialectics of Gender in Senufo Masquerades', *Afr. A.*, xix/3 (1986), pp. 30–39, 82
J. Perani: 'Hausa Calabash Decoration', *Afr. A.*, xix/3 (1986), pp. 45–7, 82–3
F. T. Smith: 'Compound Entryway Decoration: Male Space and Female Creativity', *Afr. A.*, xix/3 (1986), pp. 52–9, 83
——: 'Male and Female Artistry in Africa', *Afr. A.*, xix/3 (1986), pp. 28–9, 82
N. H. Wolff: 'A Hausa Aluminium Spoon Industry', *Afr. A.*, xix/3 (1986), pp. 40–44, 82
C. Geary: 'Basketry in the Aghem–Fungom Area of the Cameroon Grassfields', *Afr. A.*, xx/3 (1987), pp. 42–53, 89–90
B. Messick: 'Subordinate Discourse: Women, Weaving, and Gender Relations in North Africa', *Amer. Ethnol.*, xiv/2 (1987), pp. 210–25
B. La Duke: *Africa Through the Eyes of Women Artists* (Trenton, NJ, 1991)

MONNI ADAMS

3. TRADE. Scholarly knowledge is limited about the amount and extent of trade both within Africa and between Africa and the outside world. It is clear, however, that African societies have in general been far from isolated from one another or from the outside world. Trade has been an important factor in furthering and maintaining relations between local groups, between different geographical regions and between the continent and Europe, Asia and the Americas. Trade in both the raw materials out of which art is made and in finished art objects has played an important part in this. Moreover, trade has had important effects on art itself. The most obvious has been the introduction into communities of new objects to be adopted, adapted or copied. For example, North African goods and local imitations of them are found in Muslim areas of West Africa, Indian and Arab goods are found all over East Africa, and European goods are found throughout the continent. Often, though not always, these introductions have been at the expense of local production. This section can offer no more than a glimpse of the important relationship between art and trade in Africa.

(i) Local trade. (ii) Long-distance trade. (iii) External trade. (iv) Traders.

(i) Local trade. In many areas the village market is the place to which are brought not only foodstuffs but also such local craft products as iron hoes, wooden stools, baskets, mats, pots and gourds (see fig. 22). In larger markets some craftsmen may work in the market-place

itself, and in all but the smallest markets there are often non-local goods brought by enterprising local traders. In general, local exchanges provide markets for local craft production and encourage the emergence of specialist craft-workers. Tools made by one specialist, for example the smith, can be obtained by other specialists, for example the carvers, either for money or in exchange for their own product. Such craft products as cloth strips or hoes became forms of local currency, accepted even in the long-distance trade. Cloth strips were used over a wide area of the western and central savannahs of West Africa, and hoes were important on some East African trade routes.

(ii) Long-distance trade. In addition to providing wider markets for local crafts, long-distance trade brought in non-local raw materials. For example, the magenta-dyed silk favoured as an embellishment to Hausa gowns was waste silk from Mediterranean looms, dyed in North Africa and carried across the desert by camel. Historically, there were two major forms of long-distance trade in Africa: caravans, covering very long distances and stopping over at points on the route; and trade over shorter distances, from one major market to the next, never taking the merchants very far from their home base. In its most developed form the caravan trade followed circuits hundreds of miles long that took months or even years to complete, examples being some of the Saharan routes and the routes across East Africa. A well-documented West African caravan route led from the great Kola market in present-day Ghana to the Hausa cities of northern Nigeria (see Lovejoy). In west Central Africa, caravans travelled to Luanda in Angola from the Lake Mweru area of Zambia and Zaïre, an area that also traded with Mozambique. Traders from Omdurman in Sudan travelled to Hausaland in Nigeria along the ancient pilgrimage route from West Africa to Mecca; the same traders sought slaves and ivory as far away as the northern part of present-day Uganda. There was also a famous 'forty-day route' through the desert from the western part of present-day Sudan to Egypt.

In West Africa there were often traders' settlements along the trade routes, established by agreement with local chiefs who collected market tolls and 'gifts' from the merchants. Such towns became recognized stopping-places on the trade routes, with semi-permanent populations of resident traders from the same groups as the caravan traders. Such peoples as the Hausa and Dyula in West Africa and the Yao, Nyamwezi and coastal Swahili in East Africa established trading outposts far from their home areas. The markets of towns along the trade routes also attracted shorter-distance traders from nearby markets.

In addition to carrying raw materials, long-distance trade carried local crafts to markets far from their points of origin as well as providing markets en route that attracted local traders and craftsmen. The larger and more important markets themselves became significant centres of craft production, rivalled only by the courts of the major monarchs and the most important cult centres.

The trans-Saharan trade is the best-known long-distance caravan trade in Africa. The peculiar requirements of desert travel itself, for example for water storage, influenced the development of such crafts as leatherworking. In addition North African fashions, forms and motifs were introduced into northern West Africa where they were copied, often by different techniques. In Hausaland in northern Nigeria the North African burnous was adopted alongside shawls brought back from Mecca by pilgrims and garments made from local and imported cloth. Other developments that may be regarded as by-products of this trade include the way in which Hausa palaces and mosques imitate North African arch forms by an ingenious cantilever system in sun-dried mud reinforced with split palm trunk. Also, Hausa water-coolers can be seen as imitations of North African wheel-thrown pots. The export of West African cloth to the peoples of the desert was paid for from the proceeds of the desert trade. Much of the fine, indigo-dyed cloth produced in the area of Kano in northern Nigeria was made for export northwards (see fig. 23). A similar type of cloth was manufactured on the Senegal River, largely for sale to the Moors.

The Swahili trading empire stretched across East Africa to the Great Lakes and beyond. Some Swahili merchants even established political control over areas as far from their coastal base as present-day eastern Zaïre. Much of this trade was conducted by caravan, although some traders' towns were established, for example Tabora in present-day Tanzania. Until *c.* 1950 there was a Swahili village in the middle of Maasai country, a survival of one of the long-distance East African trade routes. Swahili villages also survived in Northern Rhodesia (now Zambia) into the 1950s. In addition to the Swahili, a number of other African peoples carried on long-distance trade in ivory and slaves across eastern Africa, the best known being the Yao. Earlier long-distance traders had carried ornaments made from conch shells; these have been found in excavations far inland.

(iii) External trade. The slave trade was probably the most significant external trade in African history. For centuries before Europeans reached Africa's Atlantic coasts slaves were exported by way of the Sahara and down the Nile to the Arab world. This trade continued in a small way into the 20th century. The Indian Ocean trade, though probably ancient, did not become large until the later 18th century and then only for *c.* 100 years. The Atlantic slave trade began when the Europeans reached the West African coast in the late 15th century, but it was not until the late 17th century, when the Dutch and the British became involved in sugar production in northern Brazil and the Caribbean, that there was large-scale export of slaves. This trade reached its peak in the late 18th century but did not finally end until towards the end of the 19th century. It has been estimated that *c.* 10 million or 11 million people were transported out of Africa, mainly between the 1660s and the 1860s. There has been much dispute as to the effects in Africa of the slave trade. It certainly caused great disruption in west Central Africa; but in West Africa the effects are much less certain. Many of the slaves came from areas already densely populated, and only in limited areas was there depopulation. Some small states disappeared in the course of attempting to obtain slaves for export, while other states became rich and powerful from

23. Indigo dyeing pits, Kano, Nigeria; from a photograph by H. Turner

the proceeds of the trade; along the coast, African merchants and merchant houses flourished.

The slave trade led to the introduction of many foreign goods into West Africa. The most important were textiles, for example cottons and silks from Asia and linens and woollens from Europe, and metals, including iron for tools and weapons, copper and brass largely for decoration and, in the form of bowls and basins, for domestic and ritual use of all kinds. A good part of these and other items were imported for direct consumption. There was, however, some recycling of raw materials: cloth was unwoven, brass melted down, and beads were ground up to form the raw materials for local industries. Only iron-smelting seems to have suffered seriously from competition with imports, although it survived in less accessible parts of West Africa until long after the end of the slave trade.

It is unlikely that many craftsmen were transported, since in many areas they belonged to a class that, while not wholly free, were not slaves and could not be sold. A craftsman could generally avoid being sold overseas, even if captured in war. Among the Asante, for example, he would be sent to one of the villages devoted to the making of ceremonial and domestic objects for the king's household. There was thus little transfer of African craft technology to the Americas. Weaving is a partial exception to this, since in some areas slaves were employed as weavers.

There appears to have been remarkably little transfer of technology into Africa either from Europe or from America in the slave-trade era. Claims have been made for the European origin of Benin and Ife brass-casting, but this can be discounted on chronological grounds (although it is just possible that certain refinements may have been contributed by European gunsmiths). It has been suggested that certain groupings found on Benin plaques may owe something to Christian iconography, but this seems very doubtful, although the art form of the plaque itself, so exceptional in African art, may possibly owe something to the influence of Portuguese traders. Even more improbable, on chronological and other grounds, is the suggestion that the West African loom owes anything to European technology. It is basically similar to the cotton looms of the eastern Sudan, the Yemen and India and was probably introduced originally by traders following the ancient trade route (marked by the use of cloth strips as currency) along what may be termed 'the cloth strip', where cotton and indigo can be grown, between the desert and the Middle Belt (see Johnson). There seems little or no indication of any transfer of technology from the Americas. It is just possible that the pedals and reed of the tripod loom of the Mende of Sierra Leone, described by one early traveller as 'worked entirely by hand', were inspired by the Portuguese.

In the 19th century trade patterns changed, with the export of slaves being increasingly replaced by trade in oil and oil-seeds, groundnuts from Senegambia and palm oil from Sierra Leone to the Niger Delta and thence overseas. By the later part of the century such areas as Gabon and the Congo were being opened up by traders in search of these and other goods; rubber became increasingly important. In East Africa ivory had long been one of the principal exports; it then went increasingly to Europe and America as well as to India. Ostrich feathers were for a time a major export across the Sahara and thence to Italy and France. Towards the end of the century, South Africa began exporting diamonds and then gold in addition to wool and ostrich feathers. Imports to Africa came increasingly from Europe and to a smaller extent from the USA. Indian hand-woven textiles, for example, were no longer competitive. Surprisingly, local weaving industries survived in West Africa, and efforts to persuade the people to export cotton and import cloth were still largely unsuccessful, though the simplest and poorest quality of local cloth was replaced by imported Lancashire cottons.

Generally, local crafts continued to be cheaper than their imported alternatives until the railways were built, and it was not until the coming of the motor lorry in the 1920s that European imports began to penetrate the remotest areas. By the 1930s Africans were again wearing Indian cottons, machine-made, often from cotton grown and exported from East Africa. Some local weaving industries survived, however, largely using imported machine-spun cotton yarn.

The world depression of the 1930s and import shortages during World War II led to revival of local industries in the villages. Generally, however, it is local industrialization and development in various forms that have caused the decline in local crafts rather than competition from imported goods. A craftsman can often earn more in shorter hours as a factory worker or a clerk than he can at his craft. It is thus mainly the most highly skilled craftsmen, producing prestige products for courts and wealthy commoners, who survive. These, however, are vulnerable to such trade crises as a decline in oil revenues or the failure of an export crop.

By the late 20th century it was generally impossible legally to export older works of art from Africa. No such prohibition existed in earlier times, and many pieces owe their preservation to the almost accidental trade that took thousands of objects, particularly figure sculptures and masks, to Europe (see Paudrat). During the 20th century the trade in African art became more organized and, in some contexts, commercialized.

MARION JOHNSON

(iv) Traders. The role of traders as both intermediaries between consumers and artists and as consumers and patrons in their own right is important in the African context.

(a) As intermediaries. In the complex network of supply and demand, traders communicate the needs and demands of art patrons and consumers to the artists. Traders in Africa tend to be conservative, but, as public tastes shift, they may take the lead in encouraging changes in art production. In the early 1970s, for example, urban market traders in Mali, in response to contemporary tastes, bought fewer traditional Bamana and Maninka cloths and encouraged local weavers to use modern dyes and new patterns (see Imperato). Similarly, in the 1960s Songye entrepreneurial traders in Zaïre encouraged changes in the forms and colours of raffia baskets to make them more appealing to European buyers (see Merriam).

Traders also act as agents of diffusion, carrying art objects over a broad geographical area and stimulating local demand for non-indigenous art forms. The traders' impact on the quantity, quality and distribution of goods produced is similar to that of leader-patrons (*see* §1 above). This can lead to a diaspora of artists, for example, as in the settlement of Hausa tailors, embroiderers, tanners, leatherworkers and other craftsmen throughout West and North Africa in the 19th and 20th centuries. Wood sculpture has become a 'market-driven' commodity only in the 20th century. Not only do trader-patrons encourage the fabrication of new forms to appeal to the tourist trade, they also promote the continuity of indigenous ritual carving styles that are redefined as commodities. For example, in the 1960s a flourishing Yoruba carving industry supported by trader-patrons emerged in Abeokuta, south-west Nigeria. Yoruba, Hausa and Ghanaian traders revived a lineage carving tradition that had largely disappeared for lack of ritual patronage. Stylistically, the carvings produced for trader-patrons adhered to the indigenous forms and aesthetics, but they were produced as commodities. As patrons, the traders encouraged a higher level of production than at any time in the past, and they spread the products across a wide geographical area. A similar industry occurred among the Senufo Kulebele of northern Côte d'Ivoire (Richter, 1980). Alternatively, traders may encourage local artists to copy foreign prototypes. This is particularly evident in the proliferation of such Western forms as salad bowls and servers, toothpicks and ashtrays offered by the purveyors of tourist arts (*see* §4 below). Hausa weavers and dyers of the Kano emirate produce a type of cloth known as *turkudi*, made up of narrow indigo-dyed strips, for leader-patrons and for the market-place. Although the cloth is used on ceremonial occasions by Hausa nobility, the most important consumers of it are the Tuareg. The production and distribution of *turkudi* for export involves a complex division of labour and a chain of economic interactions controlled by market agents. After buying cloth from the weavers, the agents commission cloth sewers to sew the bands together, dyers to dye the cloth a deep indigo colour and cloth beaters to pound it with powdered indigo to give it a glossy shine. The finished product is known as *yan kura* cloth and is sold to long-distance traders who carry it to Tuareg patrons in Niger and the Sahara.

JUDITH PERANI, NORMA H. WOLFF

(b) As consumers. Some African states grew rich from trade. Kings established elaborate courts and became patrons of all manner of court arts, for which they provided rich and exotic materials. However, not all the wealth passed into the hands of the kings and chiefs. There were wealthy merchants, too, and it was they who were largely responsible for the wealth and sophistication of the walled cities of Hausaland and the Swahili towns of the East African seaboard. Within established monarchies wealthy traders were not always able to display their wealth openly, although generally they did so when they could, often in the form of imported dress and other equipment. In the colonial period, many of the old sumptuary restraints were lifted, and there was an outburst of artistic elaboration in dress and, more recently, in such other consumer items as cars. Indeed, wealthy Swahili were once known as the Wana-Benzi, people of the Mercedes-Benz. Perhaps the most significant contribution of merchants to art patronage has been the development of the decorated houses of the Hausa cities in the colonial period.

MARION JOHNSON

BIBLIOGRAPHY

P. T. Bauer: *West African Trade: A Study of Competition, Oligopoly and Monopoly in a Changing Economy* (London, 1954/*R* 1965)

24. Kamba souvenir carvings, wood, female bust, h. 240 mm; warrior figure h. 250 mm; salad servers: l. 370 mm and 380 mm; mid-20th century (Berkeley, CA, University of California, Phoebe A. Hearst Museum of Anthropology)

K. O. Dike: *Trade and Politics in the Niger Delta, 1830–1885* (Oxford, 1956)
E. W. Bovill: *The Golden Trade of the Moors* (London, 1958, rev. 1970)
G. I. Jones: *The Trading States of the Oil Rivers* (London, 1963)
A. P. Merriam: 'Basongye Raffia Basketry', *Afr. A.*, ii/1 (1968), pp. 14–17, 73
The Development of Indigenous Trade and Markets in West Africa: Studies Presented and Discussed at the Tenth International African Seminar at Fourah Bay College: Freetown, December 1969
R. Gray and D. Birmingham, eds: *Pre-Colonial African Trade: Essays on Trade in Central and Eastern Africa before 1900* (London, 1970)
P. Martin: *The External Trade of the Loango Coast, 1576–1580: The Effects of Changing Commercial Relations on the Vili Kingdom of Loango* (Oxford, 1972)
P. J. Imperato: 'Bamana and Maninka Covers and Blankets', *Afr. A.*, vii/3 (1974), pp. 56–67, 91
E. J. Alpers: *Ivory and Slaves in East Central Africa: Changing Patterns of International Trade to the Later Nineteenth Century* (London, 1975)
P. Shea: *The Development of an Export Oriented Dyed Cloth Industry in Kano Emirate in the Nineteenth Century* (diss., U. WI, 1975)
M. Johnson: 'Cloth Strips and History', *W. Afr. J. Archaeol.*, vii (1977), pp. 169–78
D. Northrup: *Trade without Rulers: Pre-Colonial Development in South-Eastern Nigeria* (Oxford, 1978)
K. Arhin: *West African Traders in Ghana in the Nineteenth and Twentieth Centuries*, Legon History Series (London, 1979)
T. F. Garrard: *Akan Weights and the Gold Trade* (London, 1980)
B. W. Hodder: 'Indigenous Cloth Trade and Marketing in Africa', *Textile Hist.*, xi (1980), pp. 203–10
P. E. Lovejoy: *Caravans of Kola: The Hausa Kola Trade, 1700–1900* (Zaria, 1980)
D. Richter: *Art Economics and Change* (La Jolla, 1980)
R. W. Harms: *River of Wealth, River of Sorrow: The Central Zaire Basin in the Era of the Slave and Ivory Trade, 1500–1891* (New Haven, 1981)
J. E. Inikori: *Forced Migration: The Impact of the Export Slave Trade on African Societies* (London, 1981)
P. Shea: 'Approaching the Study of Production in Rural Kano', *Studies in the History of Kano*, ed. B. Barkindo (Ibadan, 1983), pp. 93–115
P. D. Curtin: *Cross-cultural Trade in World History* (Cambridge, 1984)
J.-L. Paudrat: 'From Africa', *'Primitivism' in 20th Century Art: Affinity of the Tribal and the Modern*, ed. W. Rubin (New York, 1984), pp. 125–75
J. Hogendorn and M. Johnson: *The Shell Money of the Slave Trade*, African Studies Series, 49 (Cambridge, 1986)
J. Perani: 'The Cloth Connection: Patrons and Producers of Hausa and Nupe Prestige Strip-Weave', *History, Design, and Craft in West African Strip-Woven Cloth* (Washington, DC, 1992), pp. 95–112
C. B. Steiner: *African Art in Transit* (Cambridge, 1993)

MARION JOHNSON, JUDITH PERANI, NORMA H. WOLFF

4. COMMERCIAL PRODUCTION. Much traditional African art has always been 'commercial production'. That is, it has been executed by master craftsmen in return for honours and/or bartered for livestock and farm produce. Traditionally, however, African artists do not commonly support themselves exclusively by their art. On the contrary, most make their living through subsistence agriculture, augmented by what they can obtain through the exercise of their art. This situation has altered with changing economic circumstances and particularly in response to the colonial presence, to tourism and to the arrival of the wage economy in many areas. These developments have led to an increase in commercial production, both of traditional and of non-traditional arts.

A major factor has been the artists' attempt to respond to Western tastes. Understanding has grown considerably more acute since the waning of colonialism and the arrival of political independence. The colonialists were replaced as potential consumers by tourists, who often have a positive attitude to Africa and a desire to take home art objects as evidence of their visit. The response has frequently been to produce what has been termed 'airport art', since so much of it has been made for sale in airport tourist shops. Understandably, such 'airport art' has usually been finest and most varied in those countries that attract the largest number of tourists, for example Kenya and Côte d'Ivoire. It has, however, also developed in virtually every other nation, even such less visited countries as Gabon and Rwanda.

(i) Chokwe. Since the late 19th century Chokwe people of north-eastern Angola have been immigrating into neighbouring Zaïre and Zambia. They went in search of economic opportunity and took with them their distinctive art style. Most Chokwe men practised a simple carving technique that they had learnt during their initiation. They used this to make small wooden amulets for their wives, and some also made small sculptures of humans and animals to be used in hunting magic. With the building of the Benguela Railway through their territory in the 1920s, however, Chokwe discovered an unexpected market for their arts. Portuguese and Belgian colonists and miners, as well as civil servants and their families, had time and money to spend in the various depots *en route* to and from their assignments. Chokwe artists began to produce baskets, wooden boxes, ashtrays and bowls with pyrographic decorations and, soon after, mask plaques, small wooden busts and figures in realistic European styles.

(ii) Kamba. Perhaps the most successful example of African 'airport art' is that produced by the Kamba people of Kenya, who like most East African peoples had no previous tradition of carving. Soon after World War II, Icelandic Lutheran missionaries encouraged some young Kamba male students to make carvings out of an attractive streaky tan-and-yellow local wood of such African animals as elephants and hippopotamuses, using European tools.

When these small carvings proved popular with tourists and expatriates on the streets of Nairobi, they broadened their subject-matter to include female busts, figures of warriors, letter openers and salad servers (see fig. 24) The latter had handles representing Maasai women, their long necks wrapped with imported steel wire to simulate the Maasai women's giant beaded necklaces. The carvings sold so well that local Kamba and East Indian entrepreneurs began exporting them. To cater to the growing market, factory-like 'production lines' were set up. Individual carvers were trained to specialize in a single operation, either adzing out the basic form, completing the figure, cutting in the details, sanding the surface or adding such extras as wire necklaces. But in spite of this process, usually so deadening to creativity, the Kamba have continued to change and modify their designs to assure their continued share of the market.

(iii) Makonde. Probably the second most successful 'airport art' also comes from East Africa, from Dar-es-Salaam, Tanzania. Here MAKONDE immigrant labourers from northern Mozambique, inspired in part by the Kamba example, began carving small human figures for the expatriate community and for the booming post-war tourist market. A more interesting genre featuring fantastic figures called *shetani* developed over time. *Shetani* had distorted bodies and weird, misshapen faces; sometimes several figures were entwined in one sculpture. Another development, also a uniquely Makonde expression, was the 'tree of life'. This comprised a number of small figures, not necessarily distorted or entwined, but clustered around a chunk or rough cylinder of hard wood. These complex sculptures are little understood but apparently represent mythological and lineage themes. Some seem to represent a family, with the founder of the lineage perhaps portrayed in the large head at the top (see fig. 25).

Later developments include the use of whole segments of a tree trunk, a metre or more high, and the exploitation of both the dark core of the wood and the softer yellow outer ring. Some such Makonde sculptures are spectacular, with small, finely carved and polished figures clambering over each other and seemingly struggling to emerge from the surface of the log. By the later 20th century such complex sculptures were no longer properly classifiable as 'airport art', although a few were still to be found in airport shops. More commonly, however, they were sold in elegant hotel shops and commercial art galleries, with prices often around US$1000. Heartening for the future of the arts in Africa, discriminating travellers have broadened their taste beyond wood sculpture to include African jewellery in brass, silver and gold; textiles such as batiks, 'mud-resist' *bokolonfini* and tie-dyes (using imported dyes), to say nothing of Manjaco and Asante narrow-strip weave cloths in non-traditional imported yarns or copied in print fabrics; furniture, hair combs, musical instruments, such long-overlooked crafts as baskets, carved gourds and even home-pictorial signboards.

25. Makonde *ujaama* ('tree of life') sculpture from Tanzania, wood, h. 305 mm, collected Cape Town, 1977 (USA, private collection)

BIBLIOGRAPHY

R. Dick-Read: *Sanamu: Adventures in Search of African Art* (London, 1964)

M. Shore-Bos: 'Modern Makonde: Discovery in East African Art', *Afr. A.*, iii/1 (1969), pp. 46–51, 80–81

D. J. Crowley: 'The Contemporary-Traditional Art Market in Africa', *Afr. A.*, iv/1 (1970), pp. 43–9, 80

——: 'The West African Art Market Revisited', *Afr. A.*, vii/4 (1974), pp. 54–9

J. A. Stout: 'The Eloquent Body...Sculptural Fantasy of Contemporary Makonde Tribesmen', *Cultural Resistance: Art from Guinea-Bissau, Mozambique and Angola* (exh. cat. by I. Hersey and others, New York, Afr.–Amer. Inst., 1975)

W. Bascom: 'Changing African Art', *Ethnic and Tourist Arts: Cultural Expressions from the Fourth World*, ed. N. H. H. Graburn (Berkeley, 1976), pp. 303–19

P. Ben-Amos: '"A la recherche du temps perdu": On Being an Ebony-Carver in Benin', *Ethnic and Tourist Arts: Cultural Expressions from the Fourth World*, ed. N. H. H. Graburn (Berkeley, 1976), pp. 320–33

B. H. Sandelowsky: 'Functional and Tourist Art along the Okavango River', *Ethnic and Tourist Arts: Cultural Expressions from the Fourth World*, ed. N. H. H. Graburn (Berkeley, 1976), pp. 350–65

U. Wagner: *Catching the Tourist: Women Handicraft Traders in The Gambia* (Stockholm, 1982)

B. Jules-Rosette: *The Messages of Tourist Art: An African Semiotic System in Comparative Perspective*, Topics in Contemporary Semiotics (New York, 1984)

J. Coote: 'Modern Makonde Carving: The Origins and Development of a New African Art Tradition', *Makonde: Wooden Sculpture from East Africa from the Malde Collection* (exh. cat.; Oxford, MOMA; Plymouth,

City Mus. & A.G.; Preston, Harris Mus.; and elsewhere; 1989–90), pp. 13–22
C. B. Steiner: *African Art in Transit* (Cambridge, 1994)

DANIEL J. CROWLEY

5. RITUAL. Art is an integral aspect of ritual throughout Africa. In puberty rituals in particular the arts of the body, adornment and dress are often highly elaborated and symbolically significant. In funerary rituals and others connected with death, body arts may also play a role, although sculpture is important. Masks and masquerades are common features of rituals throughout Africa, for it is frequently the masking societies that are responsible for organizing ritual ceremonies. A discussion of the ritual contexts of art illustrates the close relationship between art and life that is common in Africa.

This section can give only an indication of ritual as a context for art in Africa. Further discussion on art and ritual will be found throughout the rest of this survey and in the entries on the art traditions of individual peoples. □

(i) *Puberty.*

(a) Introduction. In most African societies individuals are required to undergo certain rites before they can participate fully in adult society. Although the form, scale and duration of the ceremonies vary considerably from one society to another, the arts customarily play a central role in even the most modest events. Because these rites are concerned with social as well as biological maturation, their timing often does not coincide with the onset of physiological puberty. Depending on the particular African society, youths may undergo 'puberty' rituals when as young as eight or as old as twenty or more.

With few exceptions, separate rituals are held for boys and for girls. In some areas the rites are performed for an individual, while in societies with institutionalized age-sets youth of the same sex and relatively the same age are initiated together as a group. In female rites much of the art and its related symbolism and instruction concentrate on domestic life, fertility, marriage and maternity. The emphasis in male rites tends to focus less on domestic life and more on men's roles in the more public spheres of politics, economics and ritual.

Most male rites and some female rites are organized into three phases of varying elaborateness. During the first phase, the novices are physically separated from their families and either taken to an initiation camp outside the village or sequestered inside it in specially designated areas. The second or transitional phase may last only a day or continue for many months. The ritual enactment of the death of the initiate as a child and his or her rebirth as an adult is a prominent symbolic theme in this transition. Often during this phase special rules and regulations apply to interactions between the initiates and other members of the community; the novices also receive instruction in practical and esoteric matters. In some societies the bodies of the initiates are subjected to permanent alteration through scarification or circumcision. The final phase of the ritual process almost always involves a public celebration at which the initiates' new status is acknowledged by the community at large.

(b) Body arts. Throughout Africa initiates decorate their bodies, don special costumes and ornaments or wear special hairstyles to proclaim their transformation into adults. Dress and adornment are simultaneously aesthetic statements and means of validating ethnic, age and gender identities. In a number of cultures, initiates begin the ritual process wearing children's costumes and emerge from their seclusion dressed in clothing and ornaments reserved for adults. Among the Herero of Southern Africa, for example, where the puberty ritual for a young girl is a small family affair, it is the girl's donning of a woman's headdress during the puberty ritual that symbolizes her transition to womanhood. Traditionally, a woman's headdress was a three-horned leather cap (*ekori*), often decorated with strands of metal beads, and her dress was a leather apron and cloak. In Christianized Herero households, the horned cap has been replaced by a cloth headtie (*ocikaeva*) and the leather apron and cloak by a long-sleeved, ankle-length cotton dress. Despite these substitutions, the ritual donning of the headdress remains one of the central symbolic acts of Herero puberty rituals.

Among the Ga'anda of north-eastern Nigeria, an elaborate programme of scarification, the *hleeta*, was the defining feature of girls' puberty rites until 1978. The full rites consisted of a series of six biennial ceremonies beginning when a girl was five or six years old and ending just before her marriage around the age of sixteen. Identical patterns were used throughout the dispersed Ga'anda communities, graphically proclaiming the ethnic identity of the initiates. The artful and intricate patterns made by specialists were closely placed cuts that scarred to form small, delicate dots slightly lighter than the surrounding skin (see fig. 26). The first patterns were cut on the stomach. Two years later the forehead was scarified. The third set was placed on the neck and forearm and the fourth set on the waist, buttocks and back of the neck. The fifth set filled in areas on the stomach and arms, and the sixth and final set decorated the thighs and filled in areas on the chest, back and abdomen. Ga'anda scarification constituted the permanent transformation through artistic means of a girl's body into that of a woman's. Traditionally, the various Ga'anda communities held an annual seven-day festival to honour all the young women who had completed the *hleeta* during the preceding year. The young women, their *hleeta* patterns enhanced by red camwood, danced with ornamental iron axes over their left shoulders and carried gourds decorated with incised patterns in their left hands to symbolize their new domestic and economic responsibilities as married women.

Elaborate coiffures and other forms of body adornment are part of everyday appearance among pastoralist groups in East Africa. Specific hairstyles, ornaments and modes of dress distinguish children from young adults and young adults from elders. The transition from boy to junior 'warrior' results in the most dramatic change in dress and ornament among young MAASAI, Samburu, Turkana and Pokot men. All these groups have highly articulated age-set systems through the different stages of which men pass in a gradual process of social maturation. The stages

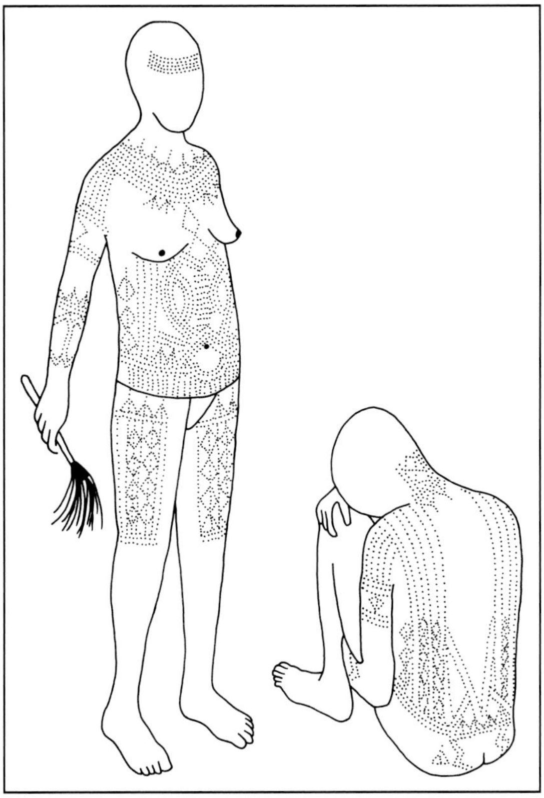

26. Ga'anda *hleeta* scarifications; after drawings by T. J. H. Chappel and Marla C. Berns

are marked by rituals. The first of these ceremonies transforms boys into young 'warriors' who thus acquire the right to wear certain coiffures and to use certain ornaments and colours. The young men invest great time and effort in the arts of personal adornment, and a man's dress is an emphatic statement of his personal aesthetic. The forms and types of ornamentation, however, also reflect and communicate ethnic affiliation and serve to manifest visually their bearer's position within the age-set system.

Many African puberty rites involve a series of elaborate and dramatic transformations in the form and style of costume and ornamentation as boys or girls move through the various ceremonies. Among the Okiek of Kenya, for example, girls are initiated as a group sometime between the ages of 13 and 17. Their puberty rites involve a series of ceremonies that last over a number of weeks. For the first ceremony, the girls appear wearing special dance costumes that consist of strands of beads wrapped around their wrists and forearms, bells on their calves, a beaded leather cloak on their shoulders, black-and-white colobus-monkey skins fitted on their arms and falling from their waists, and a decoratively painted headdress fitted over a tall mitre-like hat. The most elaborate of these headdresses are appliquéd with metal foil, and some even have battery-operated torch bulbs attached to them. The girls perform in full costume in the opening ceremonies of the ritual, after which they are taken to a house in the village where they are circumcised.

Following circumcision the girls are stripped of their elaborate costumes and jewellery and wrapped in blankets. They retire into the house for a period of healing, and during this phase their movements are greatly restricted. After they have healed sufficiently, their instruction in women's affairs and women's secret songs begins in earnest. The initiates are now dressed by their ritual leaders in calf-length skin skirts and skin cloaks. They wear a plain metal-band necklace and a chain with a round ring of yellow metal hanging from it. Each initiate also wears a beaded headband consisting of a single strand of dark blue beads, from the centre of which four pieces of chain hang down, reaching to the bridge of the nose. A bead of either red, white, yellow or black is fastened to the end of each chain. While in seclusion, the girls daily smear their arms, legs and faces with white clay and decorate each other's faces by drawing decorative lines in the clay. The girls may now venture out of the initiation house to visit female relatives living near by, to collect firewood and so on, but they are still expressly forbidden to have any contact with adult men.

On the morning of their coming-out ceremony, the initiates go to the river to bathe, their bodies are oiled, and they are dressed in a cloth sheet tied over one shoulder, a beaded leather skirt around the waist and a beaded leather cloak on the shoulders. Each young woman wears an elaborate array of beaded necklaces, bracelets and earrings. At the conclusion of the public festivity, the girl's beaded headband is removed and replaced by a beaded tiara that has two chain loops circling the eyes and a long beaded extension rising from the top of the head symbolizing the girl's transformation into a woman (see fig. 27). The young women return to their homes, put aside their ceremonial costumes and rejoin the daily life of their community. The next occasion when they will appear so elaborately dressed and adorned will be on their wedding day.

Among the BAMANA of the Baninko in southern Mali, boys' manhood rites take place once every seven years. The initiates into the men's Jo association range in age from 15 to 21. The various ceremonies take place over a period of eight or nine months. The novices are first taken to a bush camp, and, during the ritual called the Jo Faga (Jo killing), they enter the *sama so* (elephant house), a large mud plaster construction at whose summit is an enormous carved wooden horizontal mask representing an elephant. While they are in the belly of the beast the initiates are ritually killed as children and then reborn out of the beast as men. Following this ceremony, the novices spend a week in the bush in isolation, and they are stripped of all clothing and ornaments. (A mask symbolizing the principles of order and disorder protects the novices from harm. The masker is encased in a baglike form made from fibre or mud-dyed cloth that sports on its head a spread of porcupine quills.)

When the initiates emerge from the woods they cover themselves with unworked red fibres, which they gradually shed as they make their way to the outskirts of the village. There they each don a cache-sexe and bandoliers of red and white beans worn diagonally across their upper bodies; this comprises their daily dress for the period of their

27. Okiek woman wearing beaded tiara symbolizing her new status, Narok District, Kenya, 1983; from a photograph by Corinne A. Kratz

initiation. During the next few months the initiates wear more elaborate costumes and headdresses for a series of public ceremonies. Some groups of initiates may choose to devise their own distinctive costumes, but all are constructed from an array of bush materials in a variety of colours and textures, underscoring the initiates' association with the world of the bush. During their public performances the young men dance and sing special songs and often carry carved wooden statues of females that are decorated with strands of multicoloured beads. At a final ceremony of reincorporation, the young men discard the elaborate ritual costumes and put on plain country-cloth shirts, pants and caps made of handwoven unbleached cotton, the traditional everyday wear of adult men.

(c) Mask and masquerade. Puberty rituals are often the responsibility of mask-owning societies, and masks thus often feature in them. This is so, for example, in the male initiation complex known as Mukanda, which is found from south-western Zaïre into south-eastern Zambia among such peoples as the Ndembu, Suku, YAKA, KUBA (ii), PENDE and Chokwe (*see* CHOKWE AND RELATED PEOPLES). Most of these groups use a variety of fibre and wooden masks, both in the initiation camp and in the final coming-out ceremonies that take place in the village. Among the southern Kuba groups certain masks are created specifically for men's initiation and are intended to intensify the symbolic association between adult men, the forest and hunting. The masks are constructed from uncultivated forest palms, in contrast to the cultivated palm fibres used for weaving Kuba raffia textiles. Bird beaks, feathers and animal skins are often attached, and the masker carries bows and arrows and various hunting paraphernalia when performing in the forest camp. Among the Suku, the most important mask, the Kakunga, is worn by the ritual master. It is a large wooden mask with massive features including a bulbous forehead and cheeks. Kakunga appears on the day of the boys' circumcision to protect them, and in the final phase of the initiation cycle it leads the young men out of seclusion back to the village (*see also* YAKA, §1).

Masks appear in a large number of male initiation ceremonies throughout West and Central Africa. In West Africa they are central to BAGA, Diola, Bassari, BAMANA, Malinke, IGBO and IBIBIO rites, as well as appearing in the initiations of the Poro men's association among groups living in Liberia, Sierra Leone and Côte d'Ivoire. In Central Africa numerous peoples regularly use masks during male puberty rites. Besides those practising a form of Mukanda, the Lwalwa, Luluwa, Mbole and Bembe among others also use masks and figures in puberty rites.

Masks appear with less frequency during male initiations in East and Southern Africa, although the MAKONDE of Tanzania and Mozambique and the Chewa of Malawi are notable exceptions. During Chewa boys' initiation, a large fibre mask, Kisiyamaliro, is created. This representation of a mythical beast, resembling a bush cow or other large antelope, stands nearly 3 m high. It is constructed from dried maize leaves woven over a flexible wooden frame. The head of the beast has woven fibre horns and a large projecting snout. The boys are symbolically devoured by Kisiyamaliro and reborn out of it as men. In the final coming-out ceremony the mask leads the initiates back into the village and performs in a public ceremony. Following the initiation cycle, the mask is left to decay in the bush.

Masks and masquerades are less important in women's puberty rituals, although among the Ngbandi of Zaïre and the Makonde of Mozambique and Tanzania masks danced by males feature in both male and female puberty rites. Several Tanzanian Makonde masks collected in the early decades of the 20th century have fully carved, seated female figures attached to the crown of the mask. This motif seems to refer directly to the female puberty ritual itself, during which the initiates were carried on the backs of their adult sponsors.

One of the rare instances in Africa where masquerades are danced by women is during girls' initiation into the Sande association among the Vai, Gola, Temne and Mende of Liberia and Sierra Leone. The helmet mask, portraying a beautiful young woman with finely carved features, eyes modestly downcast, shining black skin and an elaborate coiffure, represents the Sande water spirit and symbolizes fertility and increase (*see* §II, 2(iii)(a) above; *see also* MENDE, §2).

(d) Other arts. Among the Bemba of Zambia, women's initiation traditionally involved a series of 18 different ceremonies and lasted for over a month. An initiation hut was built on the edge of the village, and its walls were

painted with a series of emblems. Some 40 or more clay images, painted white, black and red, were made by women potters for the initiation. These images represented a range of historical characters, common domestic objects, animals and birds as well as emblematic designs regularly found on pottery vessels. Each character or emblem had a name and was associated with a particular song.

During the various ceremonies, the girls were shown the figures, learnt their names and the songs and the multiple meanings associated with them. The pottery sculptures served as one of the primary means of instruction; through them the initiates learned the appropriate behaviour, values and beliefs associated with their future roles as Bemba wives and mothers. Among the Pedi, Tsonga and VENDA of Southern Africa free-standing carved wooden figures were once regularly used as didactic devices in boys', and occasionally girls', initiations. In south-central Zaïre, Kuba groups constructed an 'initiation' wall of raffia palm, to which they attached a variety of sculptures, masks and assorted objects in a graphic representation of men's secret lore and symbols.

BIBLIOGRAPHY

A. Van Gennep: *Les Rites de passage* (Paris, 1909; Eng. trans. by M. B. Vizedom and G. L. Caffee, London, 1960/*R* 1977)

J. Vansina: 'Initiation Rituals of the Bushong', *Africa*, xxv/2 (1955), pp. 138–53

A. I. Richards: *Chisungu: A Girls' Initiation Ceremony among the Bemba of Northern Rhodesia* (London, 1956); *R* as *Chisungu: A Girls' Initiation Ceremony among the Bemba of Zambia* (London, 1982)

G. D. Gibson: 'Herero Marriage', *Rhodes-Livingstone J.*, 24 (1959), pp. 1–37

J. Dias and M. Dias: *Os Macondes de Moçambique*, 3 vols (Lisbon, 1964–70)

P. Spencer: *The Samburu: A Study of Gerontocracy in a Nomadic Tribe* (London, 1965)

H. M. Cole: 'Vital Arts in Northern Kenya', *Afr. A.*, vii/2 (1974), pp. 12–23, 82

J. Buxton: 'Initiation and Bead-sets in Western Mandari', *Studies in Social Anthropology: Essays in Memory of E. E. Evans-Pritchard by his Former Oxford Colleagues*, ed. J. H. M. Beattie and R. G. Lienhardt (Oxford, 1975), pp. 310–27

H. M. Cole: 'Living Art among the Samburu', *The Fabrics of Culture: The Anthropology of Clothing and Adornment*, ed. J. M. Cordwell and R. A. Schwarz, World Anthropology (The Hague, 1979), pp. 87–102

M. Kecskesi: 'The Pickaback Motif in the Art and Initiation of the Rovuma Area', *Afr. A.*, xvi/1 (1982), pp. 52–5, 94–5

D. Biebuyck: *The Arts of Zaire*, 5 vols (Berkeley, 1985–)

J. S. La Fontaine: *Initiation: Ritual Drama and Secret Knowledge across the World* (Harmondsworth, 1985)

A Human Ideal in African Art: Bamana Figurative Sculpture (exh. cat. by K. Ezra, Washington, DC, N. Mus. Afr. A., 1986)

D. A. Binkley: *A View from the Forest: The Power of Southern Kuba Initiation Masks* (diss., Bloomington, IN U., 1987; microfilm, Ann Arbor, 1989)

M. C. Berns: 'Ga'anda Scarification: A Model for Art and Identity', *Marks of Civilization: Artistic Transformations of the Human Body*, ed. A. Rubin (Los Angeles, 1988), pp. 57–76

L. B. Faulkner: 'Basketry Masks of the Chewa', *Afr. A.*, xxi/3 (1988), pp. 28–31, 86

C. A. Kratz: 'Okiek Ornaments of Transition and Transformation', *Kenya Past & Present*, 20 (1988), pp. 21–6

A. Nettleton: 'History and the Myth of Zulu Sculpture', *Afr. A.*, xxi/3 (1988), pp. 48–51, 86–7

R. Sieber and R. A. Walker: *African Art in the Cycle of Life* (Washington, DC, 1988) [pubd in conjunction with exh., Washington, DC, N. Mus. Afr. A., 1987–8]

G. Meurillon: *Initiations septiennales et institutions du Jo bamanan du Baninko (Mali)* (Paris, 1992)

MARY JO ARNOLDI

(ii) Funerary.

(a) Introduction. (b) Sculpture. (c) Display.

(a) Introduction. In many African societies, burial and funerary celebration provide the stage for ritual action and the use and display of works of art that enact and reaffirm beliefs and societal values. Funerals conclude a person's passage through life, and death may be accompanied by elaborate ritual extending over many months or even years. The actual burial or interment of the remains is usually very brief and takes place immediately after the individual's demise, while subsequent commemorative funerary celebrations are carefully planned and prepared long in advance.

Although the content and form of funerary rites differ greatly from one African society to another, there are general principles underlying their structure. When death occurs, the community faces the upheaval of the biological and social order, for an important member has been lost. During the course of the funeral, this order needs to be re-established and asserted. Mortuary rituals also provide the setting for a symbolic discourse on life, death and the afterlife. In this context, works of art may be created to mediate between the living and the dead and to commemorate the deceased. Funerary rites facilitate the transition of the deceased into the afterlife, creating the conditions necessary for becoming an ancestral being. The living believe that the ancestors secure health and fecundity for those who attend to them, whether in the form of many offspring or in rich crop and animal yields. Dissatisfied and neglected ancestors may threaten their descendants for generations. They may bring misfortune, disease and death. Descendants therefore find it necessary to honour and propitiate the ancestors continuously.

Other concerns may be manifested during the public part of the mortuary ritual. Funerals sum up the social persona of the deceased, his or her conduct and achievements, and thus not all the deceased are accorded equal treatment. Age, sex and wealth determine the length and elaboration of the funerary process. Only important men and women who have lived a long life and gained respect and admiration in the community become ancestors.

(b) Sculpture. In West and Central Africa in particular, funerary celebrations and commemorations for important individuals are often accompanied by the commissioning and display of works of art. Among the better-known figurative funerary art forms are the terracottas of the AKAN of Ghana, which were first produced as early as the early 18th century. Made for display during formal funerary ceremonies, they represent deceased leaders and their retinues. Stylistically, the terracottas range from abstract forms, representing the head of the deceased only, to fully formed portrait heads and figures. In subsequent memorial ceremonies the terracottas were accorded the treatment befitting the deceased. Other forms of sculpture linked with mortuary ritual include the *nduen fobara* screens of the Kalabari Ijo (*see* IJO, §3). These complex constructions, made from wood and fabric and brightly painted, commemorated the leaders of big trading houses and became the surrogate residence for the spirit of the deceased. They

were kept in the group's meeting-houses and were propitiated when the living sought the protection of the powerful ancestral being.

Similar notions found expression in several of Nigeria's ancient traditions of funerary art. In and around NOK archaeologists have uncovered numerous terracotta sculptures dating back to *c.* 500 BC–AD 200. Terracotta heads with elaborate coiffures, headdresses and adornments, as well as other fragments, may have formed part of life-size sculptures used in a funerary context. Commemorative bronze and terracotta portraits of the rulers and other important male and female leaders in the ancient kingdom of IFE, which flourished from the 12th century AD to the 16th, are certainly conceptually, if not historically, linked to the Nok sculptures. In the Kingdom of Benin, whose dynasty can be traced back to the 14th century AD, the commissioning of brass heads portraying the kings and queen mothers was reminiscent of practices in both Nok and Ife (*see* BENIN). Upon succession, each new Benin king created an altar with numerous art works commemorating his predecessor, a place where the new king could communicate with the deceased.

Not all African funerary sculpture aspires to physical likeness or even takes representational form. The memorial effigies (*vigango*) of the Mijikenda of Kenya are distinguished by their minimalist elegance and clarity of design and only suggest the human form (see fig. 28). They were created and erected for important deceased members of the Chama ya Gohu, a men's secret society. Their particular characteristics, including the representation of such anatomical features on the planklike torso as the umbilicus, pectoral muscles or an indication of the waist, as well as the size of the head and their varying scale, indicate that they were 'personalized' sculptures and represented particular deceased individuals. The larger the effigy, the more important was the dead person's role in society.

28. Ritual installation of a Mijikenda memorial effigy (*vigango*), Kenya; from a photograph by Ernie Wolfe III

(c) Display. Funerary celebrations not only stimulate the creation of sculpture but also are often accompanied by spectacular displays of dances and masquerades. Different genres of performance may be enacted, among them dirges, laments and lyric songs, following a prescribed sequence. Their performance is a religious act as well as an aesthetic one, and they are often judged critically by the audience. Mortuary rites are both dramaturgical and aesthetic events. Such art forms as masquerade, dance, music and sculpture have a role to play in the discourse on life and the afterlife. The arts used in the mortuary rituals of many African societies express and enhance these societies' understanding of the person, the community and the cosmos. Besides mirroring these concepts, arts in the funerary context enact them and through repetitious enactment become instrumental in the constant process of constructing and consolidating the world of which death is very much a part.

Senufo. In her study on art and death in a SENUFO village in northern Côte d'Ivoire, A. J. Glaze discusses funerals as syntheses in which crucial components of social interaction manifest themselves. Most importantly, there is the interaction of man and spirit, then of male and female and lastly of the generations. Such art forms as figurative sculpture, masquerade, dance, music and song are vital parts of the funerals that the Senufo employ when dealing with the potential dangers of the spirits of the dead.

The death of an important elder sets into motion a prescribed chain of events. For a person who has lived a complete and full life, the burial and the funerary ceremony may take place on consecutive days. The corpse is wrapped in colourful and expensive funeral cloths, an expression of the riches he was able to accumulate through his hard work as a farmer. During his lifetime, he had purchased large quantities of finely woven cloth, which his kin now distribute as part of the inheritance. The mourners also contribute cloth to the funerary ceremony. The size and beauty of these cloths reflect upon the status of the dead member of the community and on the generosity of the givers. Social ties and obligations find their tangible and visible expression in this cloth-giving.

Among the main protagonists for the funeral ritual are the secret societies of which the deceased was a member. In the case of a man, the Pondo (Poro) society will be involved; in the case of a woman, the Sandogo (Sande) society will officiate. The maskers wear full raffia skirts and zoomorphic helmet masks with antelope horns, painted in bold black and white bands. The maskers execute their stunning dances in a prescribed sequence, and secret-society members carry out the ritual facilitating the transformation of the deceased into an ancestral being. The flow of events and the overall design of the funerary ritual has led Glaze to view the complete process as an orchestrated work of art.

Cameroon Grassfields. In the Grassfields of the Republic of Cameroon, burial and commemorative funerary ceremonies provide an ideal arena for the display of wealth. The Grassfields kingdoms and chiefdoms are hierarchically organized. Chiefs, office-holders and elders participate in a prestige economy in which each man strives to accumulate wealth in material goods and in people who follow and support him. The size of the funerals—participants may number thousands—and their duration visually express the deceased's importance. The grandeur not only serves to display the prestige and wealth acquired in this world but also ensures that the departed will secure a prominent position among the ancestors.

During his lifetime, a man also becomes a member of secret societies, warrior associations and dancing groups, which command high fees for admission. All these societies and associations have roles to perform at his funeral. In the north-western Cameroon Grassfields, the most important secret society for men is Kweifo, which wields political power. During burials and subsequent funerary celebrations for one of their own, Kweifo maskers give sinister and threatening performances. One mask, Nko, has a voluminous black raffia headdress with a stuffed monkey on its back. When Nko enters the funeral compound, all the women and the non-initiates flee in horror. Women who glance at Nko might bear deformed children. Nko destroys the dwelling of the deceased, throws stones, threatens the mourners and must be physically restrained and appeased by two attendants who 'cool' him down by sprinkling him with ritual substances prepared by an expert. Nko's appearance and actions mark the separation of the deceased from this world; his power lies in the visual expression of the anti-aesthetic, and he will ultimately carry the corpse to the grave and lay it to rest. The sombre messenger of dark, powerful forces disappears until he is called upon for the next funeral. Other masks and dance groups follow in the funerary process, providing entertainment.

Women who have led responsible lives, produced numerous offspring and grown food in abundance are accorded large funerals. While their funerals follow the general structure of the men's, the protagonists differ. Women of the female secret society Kefab, whose membership is open only to successful, wealthy women who have borne children, perform a solemn, slow dance at a woman's funeral, as will all the other associations of which the deceased was a member. Also, her husband may invite a single masker from a society to which he belongs to perform in the deceased's honour. After final farewells, she is laid to rest by the men of the compound.

The funerary rituals for a chief among the BANGWA of the southern Grassfields were observed (see Brain and Pollock). When a chief dies, men of the Night Society secretly perform the last rites before the death has even been announced to the public. The Night Society members, whose duties resemble those of the Kweifo, prepare the corpse for burial. The deceased's successor, a son who had been selected by the departed, anoints the body with medicines. It is then shrouded and buried. Until the day of the public funeral, the fiction is maintained that the chief is still alive. This lavish feast needs weeks, sometimes months, of preparation. Masks are cleaned and repainted, sometimes even newly carved, and costumes repaired. The royal sculptures, including carved wooden portraits of the former chiefs, musical instruments and elaborate objects of daily use, are publicly displayed in the dancing field, where the celebrations take place. The chief's palace is decorated with beautiful and rare cloths. Mourners in their finest attire assemble on the first day of the celebration. They present a stark contrast to the widows, who have smeared their naked bodies with mud. The women wail and lament the death of their husband, a reminder that this splendid celebration is one of death. Neighbouring chiefs bring the colourful masks of their chiefdoms to perform in honour of the deceased.

Bwende. The funerals of the chiefs of the Bwende and their neighbours on the Lower Congo River in the People's Republic of Congo and Zaïre have attracted much attention owing to their stunning visual aspects. In the past the Bwende used to honour departed chiefs with lavish sacrificial gifts of mats and cloths, out of which specialist artists created huge red anthropomorphic funerary bundles known as *niombo* (corpse) that enveloped the dried corpse (see fig. 29). The artist first built a frame for the torso, then constructed the limbs and added a head. The form of the *niombo* itself serves as a medium for communication with the people in the other world. Its open mouth alludes to this communication as does its colour, for red is the colour of mediation among the Bwende and their neighbours. On the day of burial, which followed days of dancing and celebration, the enormous figure was paraded to its grave. An orchestra of large figurated trumpets, slit-gongs and root trumpets accompanied the slow procession of hundreds of mourners. Women wailed and touched the figure one last time, while men carried it to its final resting-place. When the massive figure was lowered into the grave, the mourners leapt into the air simultaneously, thus marking the passage of one of their own. They resumed dancing and feasting and later returned to everyday life.

BIBLIOGRAPHY

A. Van Gennep: *Les Rites de passage* (Paris, 1909; Eng. trans. by M. B. Vizedom and G. L. Caffee, London, 1960/*R* 1977)

J. Goody: *Death, Property and the Ancestors: A Study of the Mortuary Customs of the LoDagaa of West Africa* (London, 1962)

R. Widman: *The Niombo Cult among the Babwende* (Stockholm, 1967)

V. W. Turner: *The Ritual Process: Structure and Anti-structure* (London, 1969/*R* 1974)

R. Brain and A. Pollock: *Bangwa Funerary Sculpture*, A. & Soc. Ser. (London, 1971)

R. Sieber: 'Kwahu Terracottas, Oral Tradition, and Ghanaian History', *African Art and Leadership*, ed. D. Fraser and H. M. Cole (Madison, 1972), pp. 173–83

The Arts of Ghana (exh. cat. by H. M. Cole and D. Ross, Los Angeles, UCLA, Mus. Cult. Hist., 1977–8)

R. Huntington and P. Metcalf: *Celebrations of Death: The Anthropology of Mortuary Ritual* (Cambridge, 1979)

Rites de la mort (exh. cat., Paris, Lab. Ethnol. Mus. Hist. Nat., 1979)

P. Ben-Amos: *The Art of Benin*, Tribal A. (London, 1980)

S. P. Blier: 'The Dance of Death: Notes on Architecture and Staging of Tamberma Funeral Performances', *Res*, 2 (1981), pp. 107–43

A. J. Glaze: *Art and Death in a Senufo Village*, Trad. A. Africa (Bloomington, 1981)

29. Bwende anthropomorphic funerary bundle (*niombo*), Kingoyi, with attendant orchestra, People's Republic of Congo; from a missionary's photograph, *c.* 1900

The Four Moments of the Sun: Kongo Art in Two Worlds (exh. cat. by R. F. Thompson and J. A. Cornet, Washington, DC, N.G.A., 1981–2)
M. Bloch and J. Parry, eds: *Death and the Regeneration of Life* (Cambridge, 1982)
L.-V. Thomas: *La Mort africaine: Idéologie funéraire en Afrique noire* (Paris, 1982)
Vigango: Commemorative Sculpture of the Mijikenda of Kenya (exh. cat., ed. E. Wolfe III; Williamstown, MA, Williams Coll. Mus. A., 1986)
Afr. A., xxi/1 (1987) [incl. 7 essays on 'Death, Ritual and Art in Africa']
N. Barley: *Foreheads of the Dead: An Anthropological View of Kalabari Ancestral Screens* (Washington, DC, 1988) [pubd in conjunction with exh., *Kalabari Ancestral Screens: Levels of Meaning*, Washington, DC, N. Mus. Afr. A., 1988–9]
R. Sieber and R. A. Walker: *African Art in the Cycle of Life* (Washington, DC, 1988) [pubd in conjunction with exh., Washington, DC, N. Mus. Afr. A., 1987–8]
C. M. Geary: 'Männerbünde in Kameruner Grasland', *Männerbande, Männerbünde: Zur Rolle des Mannes im Kulturvergleich*, 2 vols, ed. G. Völger and K. v. Welck; Ethnologica, n. s., 15 (Cologne, 1990), i, pp. 295–300
Likeness and Beyond: Portraits from Africa and the World (exh. cat., New York, Cent. Afr. A., 1990)
Niombo: Begräbnisrituale in Zentralafrika, Ethnologica, n. s., 16 (exh. cat. by A. Reikat, Cologne, Rautenstrauch-Joest-Mus.; Mannheim, Städt. Reiss-Mus.; 1990)

CHRISTRAUD M. GEARY

IV. Imagery and iconography.

1. Symbolism and ritual. 2. Gesture. 3. Portraiture. 4. Physical anomalies. 5. Mother-and-child imagery. 6. Animal imagery. 7. Equestrian imagery. 8. Tricksters.

1. SYMBOLISM AND RITUAL. The overall purpose of African ritual is to promote increase; that is, to stimulate (for example) the fecundity of mothers, the potency of fathers, the fertility of domesticated animals and of the land, spiritually guided sharpness of mind, physical dexterity in both earthly and spiritual contexts, social harmony in the community and good leadership. Symbols have an important role in ritual practices, and sexual symbolism in African art assumes an extremely wide range of expressive forms.

(i) Introduction. (ii) Human increase. (iii) Agricultural increase. (iv) Transition.

(i) Introduction. Africans frequently attribute the decline of particular communities to the neglect of ritual life and can hardly conceive of an existence without children; in addition to being a source of parental pride, children bring status to a family, they enlarge the labour force and the capacity for increase, and they serve after the death of the parent in paying ritual tribute to the deceased and, consequently, in ushering his or her spirit into a cycle of reincarnation and participation in the world of the living. There are overtly sexual sculptures and performances, as well as rituals that specifically address impotence and infertility (see Turner, 1967, pp. 12–14), but references to sexuality are more often embedded symbolically in ritual that appeals to a larger framework. This is because the universe functions as a body, and if one unit (e.g. man's realm) malfunctions, the whole must be treated. Ritual of increase generally functions by connecting the person and the community with fertile functions throughout the cosmos, in order to effect a holistic momentum that results in reproductivity in such specific areas as sexual performance.

The manmade environment often reflects this preoccupation with increase. The layout of villages of the DOGON of Mali symbolizes the human body, complete with male and female sexual organs in its centre. A pillar of earth serves as the male shrine, over which millet beer is poured during rituals. The female shrine consists of simple stones that are used to crush the *lannea acida* seed to produce oil (see Griaule, 1965, pp. 95–7). For the Batammaliba of Benin, the village plan represents the body of the goddess of the earth and underworld. At planting time, the villagers conduct a ritual procession around the village, tracing the outline of her body and identifying their reproductive capacities with hers (see Blier, pp. 90–96). The Batammaliba house, as the seat of reproduction, is a temple to the Creator, and its construction by men and women in concert is likened to the creation of a baby. Each part of the house is given an anatomical name (Blier, pp. 118–26, 199).

African ritual has a communal character. A male initiation, for example, functions not only to advance young men to an adult rank but serves to renew the society as a whole, promoting the entire participating community to a higher plane. Each initiation is, in turn, a re-creation of other markers of time such as original divine creation, birth and death and moments of cosmological significance. Through ritual, each member of the community internalizes cosmological forces to produce an atmosphere of fertilization; among the Temne of Sierra Leone, for example, women begin their initiation for girls by singing of a return to the mythical home of their ancestors (Futha), which is the place of primordial birth where the spiritual body politic meets.

It is often said that Africans think of time, at least symbolically, as cyclical (though some may pursue a linear path in mundane matters), and this is in itself a fertile view. Among the KONGO of Zaïre, the cycle is represented as a diamond or circle on which four cardinal points are indicated, symbolizing the four moments of the sun: rising, zenith, setting and nadir. This symbol relates to the life of man and is basic to motifs and gestures in sculpture, especially funerary sculpture (see 1981 exh. cat., p. 43). For the Temne, the four moments are related to four quadrants of space, indicated not only in the location of ritual sites and in dance movement but also in a small white quartered circle stamped all over the exterior walls of the sacred houses of the men's Pörö society (see fig. 30). As a central symbol of the men's initiation, its full meaning is known only to the elders. They will say only that it is the 'nucleus of the world', but it probably signifies, among other things, semen (see Lamp, in preparation). For the Malinke of Guinea, the fonio seed distributed in the pod of the okra—in cross-section a segmented circle—represents semen (see Dieterlen, p. 126). Among the Temne, okra is certainly a euphemism for semen.

(ii) Human increase. African art and ritual contain many explicit references to sexuality. The monolithic columns of the Nta Ejagham of Nigeria are clear phallic representations of the ancestral power to procreate (*see* EJAGHAM, fig. 2). These are generally *c.* 1.5 m high and are said to represent 30 or 40 generations of deceased chiefs and elders (see Allison, pp. 25–35). Masks used by boys in initiation among the YAKA of Zaïre are replete with images of the phallus, sexual intercourse and birth (see Bourgeois), intended to have an instructive effect on the initiates. Similarly, in the Chizungu initiation of girls among the Bemba of Zambia, the initiates are given clay figures; these often include pregnant or nursing females, nude males

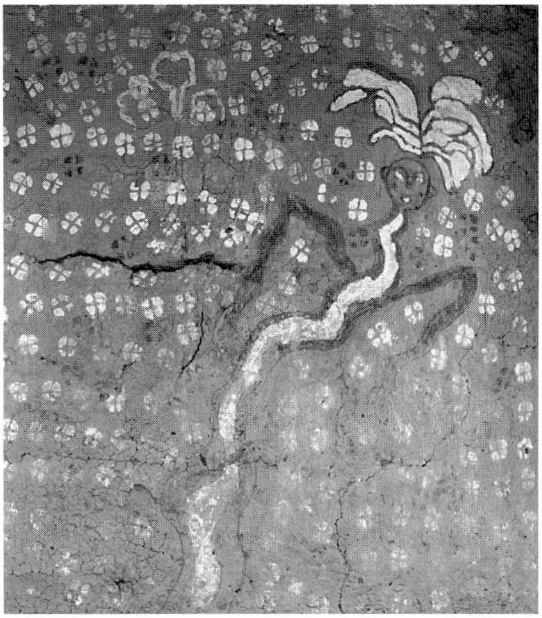

30. Wall painting on a house of the men's Pörö society among the Temne, Sierra Leone, h. *c.* 1 m, featuring serpent image and symbols of the 'nucleus'; from a photograph by Frederick Lamp, 1979

and phallic serpents (Richards, pp. 87, 209–11). Women of the Bamana of Mali maintain a nursing maternity figure called Daughter of the Gwan Society (Gwandusu). She is often surrounded by other figures, including one called 'the little pregnant one', and infertile women make sacrifices at the door of her shrine, promising to dedicate future children to her (see 1981 exh. cat., pp. 26–7). An object's function as a fertility figure, however, can only be ascertained when the ethnographic data confirm it. Geometric forms, especially vertical columns, are universal and clearly not always primarily phallic. Even explicit sexual images may have many subtle references peripheral to the goal of increase. For example, well-endowed male and female figures may simply be comic, or they may stress spiritual power, youthfulness or the importance of an ancestor. Public performances of sexually suggestive movement and form may express rebellion or chaos or a reversal of roles. Maternity images (*see* §5 below) have been shown to refer to the mother as progenitor, nurturer and punisher among the IGBO of Nigeria (see 1985 exh. cat., p. 9); as an instrument of divination among the Yombe of Zaïre (see 1978–9 exh. cat. fig. 21); and as the symbol of social prohibition, depicting a woman in sexual abstinence during the two years after a birth, among the YORUBA of Nigeria (see 1977 exh. cat., p. 5). Copulating images embellishing the chairs of Chokwe (*see* CHOKWE AND RELATED PEOPLES) and PENDE royalty in Zaïre are said to refer simply to the chief's dominion over even the most private aspects of community life (Vansina, p. 110).

In contrast, a sexual meaning is often conveyed by imagery that may seem non-sexual to the outside observer. Dogon women who wish to conceive keep a female figure in a shrine (see fig. 31), on which the only direct sexual gesture is the pointing of her hands to her abdomen.

31. Dogon female figure, wood, h. 730 mm, from Mali (New York, Paul and Ruth Tishman Collection)

G. Dieterlen has revealed deeper levels of meaning (see 1981 exh. cat.). The figure's long hair-braid represents the sheat-fish, which in turn symbolizes a foetus in uterine waters; a lip labret represents the fish's barbules. Four rows of beads around the head and four bracelets connect her with the female principle and indicate that she carries in her head the image of the child she wishes to conceive. Her pierced ear lobe suggests sexual penetration. The woman's ornaments denote original creation, the gift of speech. The weaving of words in turn indicates the symbolically rich act of weaving cloth with a shuttle, which has its own sexual connotations in the intersection of warp and weft (see Griaule, 1965, pp. 24–9, 69–74, 138–43). Another instance of such complexity of interpretation is to be found among both the BAGA of Guinea and the Yaka of Zaïre (Bourgeois, p. 48), for whom the house was an erotic image, often included on their masks and headdresses. For the young male still under sexual prohibition before initiation, the house evoked his future right to take a new bride, build his own home and engage there in previously unobtainable pleasures. The Asante of Ghana are well-known for a female figure called *akuaba* (*see* ASANTE AND RELATED PEOPLES, fig. 4), which is worn on a woman's back, tucked into her skirt, much as an infant would be carried. Although its purpose is to effect the birth of a beautiful child, and it is worn by both barren and expectant women (McLeod, pp. 162–6), its form is a simple disc or cylinder with only the slightest suggestion of sexual features or capacities.

Euphemism in sexual imagery relies on the power of the cosmological paradigm. Thus in the ritual of the girls' Chizungu initiation of the Bemba the penis is represented by the farmer's hoe, connecting the penetration of earth and women (see Richards, pp. 102–206). Proverbs of the Bondo (Bundu) association for Temne women refer to the opening and closing of a butterfly's fluttering wings as a symbol of a woman's legs, open in sexual receptivity (see Lamp, 1985, p. 33). A small head or a simple topknot carved on the top of the black helmet masks of the Bondo refers to conception, and the primordial child was said to have been born through a woman's head, both images suggesting that procreation begins in the mind (Lamp, 1985, p. 37). For the Temne, wearing a mask is a metaphor for bearing a child. Women say, 'I have carried the mask on my head' (Sayers, p. 111). Such containers as pots, spoons or gourds often symbolize the female as bearer of the seed or giver of sustenance (see Griaule, 1935; Turner, 1975, pp. 225–6). Among the Batammaliba, the word for gourd means 'multiplication', and when a woman marries she offers her gourd to her husband, who in turn presents it to the ancestors (Blier, pp. 39, 111, 186, 239).

Throughout Africa, the frog refers to birth and rebirth, as a creature of primordial water who emerges on land and heralds transitions in the daily and seasonal cycles (see Lamp, 1978; 1984 exh. cat., p. 50). The python is another powerful symbol of fertility and transition. Among the Baga it appeared to initiates in the form of a tall wooden headdress. As 'author of earthquakes, master of river sources', the python is the spirit of ends and beginnings, or the cycle of death and life (see Appia, p. 161). Among the Batammaliba also, it is a patron of male initiates, who trace its winding path through the village, enter its bedroom shrine and climb out one by one from a circular portal to be reborn (Blier, pp. 101–5).

Among the NDEBELE of South Africa, the progress and propriety of a family are celebrated and measured by the accumulation of elaborate beadwork worn on a woman's body (Schneider, pp. 62–4). She chronicles her own life and the life of the family by wearing, for example, a different type of beaded apron upon marriage or a long strand of beads from the head when her son goes into initiation. Her image, furthermore, becomes transfigured into the beaded doll in the form of a cylinder enveloped in heavy rings given to girls expressly to engender maternal instincts. Here the image of the woman bears a heavy load of generative import.

Royal display is frequently concerned with community increase. On state occasions the king of the Kuba of Zaïre (*see* KUBA (iii)) is surrounded by his scores of wives. This expresses the fecund nature of his own household and, by extension, the fertility of the Kuba community. In the Cameroon Grasslands, an annual ceremony is held to honour the ancestors in which the royal and noble families display their material wealth with maskers (see 1984 exh. cat.). Greater prestige is assumed by families with greater displays of masks. The display itself is a tribute to the achievement of the ancestors, but it could also be said that it perpetuates the well-being and productivity of the family.

(iii) Agricultural increase. The earth is considered to be female in much of African thought, and its working by man is often likened in ritual to coitus (see Blier, p. 39; 1981 exh. cat., p. 22). Dogon female images display on their abdomens a chequerboard pattern that symbolizes the ploughed field. In female initiation ceremonies among the Temne, the men sing of their betrothal: 'I've secured my own plot of ground; when I get there, I'll sow the seed' (see Lamp, 1988, 'Heavenly Bodies'). Champion cultivators among the SENUFO of the Côte d'Ivoire are given a trophy staff with a voluptuous female figure as its finial that had earlier been displayed in the field to encourage the young men. It promises the champion 'a beautiful fiancée, increase for the kinship unit, abundant harvests and many children' (see 1981 exh. cat., p. 48). For the Baga, the image of a beautiful mother with long pendant breasts, called D'mba or Nimba, was danced at both agricultural rituals and marriages. This honouring of the mother for her nurturing of many children served metaphorically to commemorate a bountiful harvest and celebrate the spirits that made it possible. Granary buildings in Africa are, by their very form, often clear symbols of female fecundity and nurturing (see Prussin, pp. 144–69), most notably among the Bororo of Niger. Among the Dogon, the thatched roof of the granary is tied with a cord spiralling down from the peak in reference to the descending acts of original creation, and its door locks are constructed of movable intersecting forms, suggesting sexual intercourse (see Griaule, 1965, pp. 30–34, 41–2, 71–2, 138–41; Laude, p. 60).

The Bamana celebrate agricultural success through the dance of the Chi Wara, whose headdress takes the form of a composite of the antelope, anteater and hornbill. The antelope, whose pawing movements are imitated in dance, suggests male prowess and potency. The anteater is celebrated as a burrowing animal that resembles the farmer tilling the soil and also the penis in penetration. The hornbill is frequently associated with fertility, combining a long, phallic beak with a pot-bellied body. Dancing the Chi Wara in male and female pairs, the male represents the sun and the female the earth. This confluence of the male and female principles links human sexual intercourse, the fertility of the earth, the movements of heavenly bodies and the activities of the natural world (see 1981 exh. cat., pp. 22, 25; Imperato, p. 72; Zahan).

(iv) Transition. Concern for the fate of the dead is based on more than nostalgia and a feeling of personal loss. They enter another world of former and future beings, a world in which the germination of new life takes place. From the Sapi culture of the 15th century in what is now Sierra Leone, small stone figures survive that were probably used in shrines dedicated to ancestors. Two sub-groups of their descendants, the Temne and KISSI, continue a version of the tradition (see Lamp, 1983; Paulme, pp. 141–9). Among the Temne, a stone is taken from the deceased's grave and placed in a shrine that contains many stones representing noble ancestors. To the west of the stones are anthills, representing the entry of the dead into the underworld. The anthills are 'hot' and the stones are 'cool', bathed in cool water during a ritual intended to reincarnate the dead, in concert with the birth of the sun in the cool eastern dawn. This 'House of Stones' is visited at every rite of passage in order to align all phenomena of birth and rebirth. The ancient stones of the Sapi, on the other hand, are revered today as representations of the primordial owners of the land by the immigrant MENDE, who now occupy most of the land where the stone figures are discovered in the fields. The Mende keep them in their fields to encourage the growth of crops, rewarding them for a bountiful harvest and punishing them with a flogging if the crop is poor.

Among the Kongo, death and the continuity of the lineage coincided in the placing of stone images on the graves of the noble dead. Although not actual portraits, they represented the deceased in his or her aspects of highest moral and physical authority. Numerous examples depict nursing mothers. On the chest of such female figures, three keloids are often indicated, representing the three stages of life (child, leader and elder) and by extension the qualities of vitality, leadership and wisdom.

Initiation into adulthood is the quintessential ritual devoted to increase, as children are considered asexual and initiation is thus crucial to their metamorphosis into sexual beings. Among the Loma and Gbande of Liberia, visitors (see Harley; Schwab and Harley) have described an institution called Bön or Pölö that is responsible for the transformation of young men into adults. Although procedure varies greatly from area to area, similar events characterize men's initiation throughout the region. Every four years, boys between the ages of about 8 and 20 are taken into the forest to be guided by their elders for a period ranging from a few days to a full four-year term. In an act symbolizing their death as boys and their rebirth as men, they were formerly thrown over a fence in the darkened forest, believing that they would be impaled on spears or disappear into the open jaws of the ancestral spirit, Landa or Dandai. Landa, the founder of Bön/Pölö, was said to ingest the boys of the village in his belly and, at the end of the initiation, to regurgitate them, fully metamorphosed into adult men, as if giving birth. He appeared in a mask resembling a crocodile head, and the scarification marks given to the boys during initiation were advertised as his tooth-marks.

For the Temne, the organization known as Bondo transforms girls into marriageable young women. Motifs found throughout the initiation are the butterfly and its chrysalis, the serpent that sheds its skin and devours whole living beings, the planted and germinating seed, and the moon that waxes and wanes, dies and is reborn. The final ceremonies of Bondo are a microcosm of fertile processes that turn the girls, through their ritual immersion in universal flow, into reproductive women. These 'graduation' ceremonies are probably scheduled to coincide with the girls' period of most likely fertilization, when they are released to their new husbands (see Lamp, 1988, 'An Opera...').

Their graduation (the 'pouring out' or 'birth-giving') involves four distinct acts. In the first (the 'transferring') the girls, still painted white (symbolizing spiritual invisibility) from their year in initiation, 'sweep the way' through the village in a probable reference to the cleansing action of menstruation. Nurturing and death are then contrasted in a dance involving a black cooking pot and a mysterious white bundle. A chaotic rampage follows, in which the villagers perform a symbolic 'uprooting' and 'transplanting'. Finally the villagers come together in a circle of cooperation to re-enact the cultivation of their fields and allude through song to the 'sowing of the seed', that is, the impregnation of the new brides. In the second act (the 'uprooting by the serpent') the ancestral serpent spirit returns in the night in the medium of a woman whining eerily through the village. Shut inside the initiation house, the initiates are said to have been devoured by the serpent. In the darkness of the early morning, the house is demolished as a metaphor for the opening of the serpent's belly, and the girls are rushed to the river to re-enact primordial birth, emerging through water.

The third act is the dance of the mask in the form of a butterfly chrysalis (Nöwo or Sowo). Beginning in the dimness of pre-dawn and ending at the rising of the sun, she symbolizes not only metamorphosis but also an enlightening of the mind that is essential to productivity. In the final act, all 'birth-givers' are saluted, a symbolic womb is created in the central village meeting-house, and the women 'descend' from the river through the village in a serpentine spiral to deposit the initiates, concealed under a canopy, in the meeting-house. Here they are described in song as 'germinating greens'. Thus, through the metaphorical association of the ritual acts of the girls and their community with productive forces throughout the cosmos, the increase of that community is ensured for another year.

BIBLIOGRAPHY

E. Sayers: 'A Few Temne Songs', *Sierra Leone Stud.*, x (1927), pp. 109–11
M. Griaule: 'Calebasses', *A. & Métiers Graph.*, 45 (1935), pp. 45–8
G. W. Harley: *Notes on the Poro in Liberia*, Pap. Peabody Mus. Archaeol. & Ethnol., xix/2 (Cambridge, MA, 1941)
B. Appia: 'Masques de Guinée française et de Casamance', *J. Africanistes*, xiii (1943), pp. 153–82
G. Schwab and G. Harley: *Tribes of the Liberian Hinterland*, Pap. Peabody Mus. Archaeol. & Ethnol., xxxi (Cambridge, MA, 1947)
M. Griaule: *Dieu d'eau: Entretiens avec Ogotemmêli* (Paris, 1948; Eng. trans. as *Conversations with Ogotemmêli: An Introduction to Dogon Religious Ideas*, London, 1965)
D. Paulme: *Les Gens du riz* (Paris, 1954)
A. I. Richards: *Chisungu: A Girls' Initiation Ceremony among the Bemba of Northern Rhodesia* (London, 1956/*R* as *Chisungu: A Girls' Initiation Ceremony among the Bemba of Zambia*, 1982)
G. Dieterlen: 'The Mande Creation Myth', *Africa*, xxvii/2 (1957), pp. 124–38
V. Turner: *The Forest of Symbols: Aspects of Ndembu Ritual* (Ithaca, NY, 1967/*R* 1970)
P. Allison: *African Stone Sculpture* (London, 1968)
P. J. Imperato: 'The Dance of the Tyi Wara', *Afr. A.*, iv/1 (1970), pp. 8–13
L. Prussin: 'West African Mud Granaries', *Paideuma*, xviii (1972), pp. 144–69
J. Laude: *African Art of the Dogon* (New York, 1973)
V. Turner: *Revelation and Divination in Ndembu Ritual*, Symbol, Myth and Ritual (Ithaca, NY, 1975)
Traditional Art of the Nigerian Peoples: The Milton D. Ratner Family Collection (exh. cat. by H. J. Drewal, Washington, DC, Mus. Afr. A., 1977)
F. Lamp: 'Frogs into Princes: The Temne Rabai Initiation', *Afr. A.*, xi/2 (1978), pp. 34–49, 94–5
A Survey of Zairian Art: The Bronson Collection (exh. cat. by J. Cornet; Raleigh, NC Mus. A.; Washington, DC, Mus. Afr. A.; Los Angeles, CA, Nat. Hist. Mus.; 1978–9)
D. Zahan: *Antilopes du soleil: Arts et rites agraires d'Afrique noire* (Vienna, 1980)
M. McLeod: *The Asante* (London, 1981)
For Spirits and Kings: African Art from the Paul and Ruth Tishman Collection (exh. cat., ed. S. M. Vogel; New York, Met., 1981)
The Four Moments of the Sun: Kongo Art in Two Worlds (exh. cat. by R. F. Thompson and J. A. Cornet, Washington, DC, N.G.A., 1981–2)
A. P. Bourgeois: 'Yaka Masks and Sexual Imagery', *Afr. A.*, xv/2 (1982), pp. 47–50, 87
F. Lamp: 'House of Stones: Memorial Art of Fifteenth-century Sierra Leone', *A. Bull.*, lxv/2 (1983), pp. 219–37
J. Vansina: *Art History in Africa: An Introduction to Method* (New York, 1984)
The Art of Cameroon (exh. cat. by T. Northern, Washington, DC, Smithsonian Inst. Traveling Exh. Serv., 1984)
F. Lamp: 'Cosmos, Cosmetics, and the Spirit of Bondo', *Afr. A.*, xviii/3 (1985), pp. 28–43, 98–9
E. A. Schneider: 'Ndebele Mural Art', *Afr. A.*, xviii/3 (1985), pp. 60–67
Mother and Child in African Sculpture (exh. cat. by H. Cole, Los Angeles, CA, Co. Mus. A., 1985)
S. P. Blier: *The Anatomy of Architecture: Ontology and Metaphor in Batammaliba Architectural Expression*, Res Monographs in Anthropology and Aesthetics (Cambridge, 1987)
F. Lamp: 'An Opera of the West African Bondo: The Act, Ideas and the Word', *Drama Rev.*, xxxii/2 (1988), pp. 83–101
——: 'Heavenly Bodies: Menses, Moon and Rituals of License among the Temne of Sierra Leone', *Blood Magic: The Anthropology of Menstruation*, ed. T. Buckley and A. Gottlieb (Berkeley, 1988), pp. 210–31
——: *The Art of Balancing Spatial and Temporal Valuation among the Temne* (in preparation)

FREDERICK LAMP

2. GESTURE. In African art, as in other contexts, gestures can both express an emotional condition or use established conventions to convey meaning (*see* GESTURE). In other words they define unspoken aspects of a work's meaning and significance. Some gestures have symbolic meanings; others provide visual cues expressive of emotions. Aesthetic concerns also influence gesture. Among the YORUBA of Nigeria, for whom the predominating aesthetic is one of symmetry, sculptures often emphasize the balanced placement of hands on parts of the body or on objects that are held (see fig. 32), while among the BAULE of Côte d'Ivoire, where asymmetry is a widespread feature, slight shifts from a strictly symmetrical portrayal are often introduced. Material and medium may affect the gestures portrayed in African art. DOGON works in iron (Mali) show a distinctive resistant bend in their gestures, a feature imparted by the material itself. The gestural expressions of LOBI wood sculptures in Burkina

32. Yoruba *edan* Ogboni staffs, brass, h. 195 mm (Amsterdam, private collection)

Faso and Côte d'Ivoire often intentionally draw on the natural curves, bends and texture of the wood (see fig. 38 below), with artists using the twisting form of a branch to reinforce the angling of an arm. Among the Batammaliba (Tamberma), the living branch is considered an essential component of the vitality of the sculpture. A group of artists, gazing up at the branches of a tree, will discuss the virtues of a particular section as they mentally superimpose a figure on it, noting the placement of the head, hands, torso and legs. After reaching a decision, one of them will climb up to cut the chosen branch for carving. Sometimes gestures are incorporated or omitted for functional reasons. The outstretched arms of Fanti and Asante *akuaba* figures, for example (*see* ASANTE AND RELATED PEOPLES, fig. 4), serve as a means of support when such figures are worn tucked into a woman's wrapper against her back. In FON, TEKE and some KONGO power figures the torso is sometimes bound, wrapped or otherwise covered, and one frequently finds a minimalization or outright elimination of gestures that would be hidden from view. Some of the most interesting figural representations in African art are those associated with body alterations and deformities, the one-legged, no-headed, no-armed images and similar forms that deviate from nature (*see* §4 below). For the Lobi, figures with more than two arms (see fig. 38 below) denote enhanced protective power.

(i) Religious themes. (ii) Social roles. (iii) Emotional expression.

(i) Religious themes. With no single gestural language employed throughout African art, gestures must be understood according to their cultural context. This is perhaps best illustrated by the examples of gestures for prayer. In Kongo art, prayer is defined by the gesture of palms drawn to the stomach. Among the Kaka, prayer to the deity Nwie, creator of earth and sky, is defined by the gesture of the right hand outstretched, palm up. In contrast, Mambila sculptures depict a person praying with arms held tightly to the chest. Among the Baule the right hand clasped in the palm of the left is identified with ceremonies to supplicate the earth, particularly after a crime against the earth has been committed. For the Dogon, raised arms are identified with prayers to the deity Amma.

Gestures in African art also convey other religious themes. In Yoruba sculptures, the diversity of such gestures is particularly striking and is used to identify affiliation to a religious association. Sculptures of the Ogboni society, dedicated to the deity of the earth, are recognized by the gesture of left hand fisted over right hand to hide an extended right thumb (see fig. 32). The sculptures of Ogun, god of iron and war, are characterized both by actions related to smithing and by the holding aloft of fanlike Ogun insignia. Sculptures dedicated to Eshu, the trickster–messenger deity (*see* §8 below), are often associated with thumb-sucking or whistle-blowing gestures. Shango, the god of lightning and thunder, is represented both by the action of balancing two celts on top of the head and by gestures in which Shango staffs and rattles are displayed. Memorial twin figures (*ibeji*) are recognized by their characteristic frontal pose, the hands held rigidly to the side.

(ii) Social roles. Gestures can be used to convey social roles and identities. This is particularly well defined in the Cameroon Grassfields, where gestures identify works as representing ruler, court servant, criminal or slave (*see* BAMILEKE AND RELATED PEOPLES; *see also* BAMUM). Kings are frequently seated, one hand supporting the chin, the other resting on the knee. This is a gesture assumed by judges when reflecting on legal matters, and it underscores the king's important subsidiary role as adjudicator. Royal retainers are most frequently identified by a gesture in which one hand is placed in front of the mouth, a pose traditionally assumed by servants when approaching the king. In other examples, servants are shown presenting objects of state (as would be done at prescribed times during ceremonies). Criminals and prisoners are often shown with anguished, angled and uncomfortable gestures and postures, in marked contrast to the more formally composed gestures of royalty.

Further examples of gestures being used to identify social position are found in Zaïre among the Chokwe, where powerful men and elders are frequently portrayed in the seated 'hocker' position, with elbows resting on upraised knees (*see* CHOKWE AND RELATED PEOPLES). Teke sculptures representing diviner-healers (*nganga*) are defined by a modified version of this same gesture. Baule elders, in contrast, are often identified by gestures in which the hand touches their carefully braided beards, and Lega sculptures of Zaïre representing elderly *bwami* initiates are recognized through gestural caricature, with rounded back and stooped body suggesting the weight of their years and responsibilities (*see* LEGA AND RELATED PEOPLES).

Gestural reference may be used to identify gender and social role. In Yoruba art, female sculptures with hands on the solar plexus are said to represent expectant women. Among the Dogon, pregnancy is suggested by the gesture of forearms resting against the abdomen (see fig. 31 above); sculptures with this gesture are found on altars dedicated to women who died while pregnant. In Kongo art the female gesture of palms against the stomach represents a woman communicating with the child she carries. Another important female gesture shows the placement of hands on the breast. For the Yoruba this gesture suggests the nursing mother and, by extension, the general idea of motherhood and generosity (see fig. 32). Among the Baule and Asante, hands supporting the breasts allude to the importance of maternal nurturing.

(iii) Emotional expression. Other gestures are used to convey emotion. For the Lobi the arms drawn behind the back imply anguish, while among the BANGWA and other Cameroon Grassfield groups the placement of the arms behind the head represents a brooding person or a child who is contemplating. Gestures used to portray sadness, sorrow, hardship and distress vary between peoples. The standard image of mourning and sorrow in such Zaïre cultures as the Kongo, Chokwe, LUBA and Ndembu is the hand drawn upwards to clasp or support the head, neck, cheek or chest while weeping or pondering in grief. Variations on this basic form include the Chokwe gesture of the hand on the mouth, which signifies someone with no chance in life. In Kongo sculptures sadness is conveyed in a number of ways. Both arms drawn upwards towards the mouth connote enormous grief; arms held aloft indicate crying or lamentation; touching the chin or cupping it with one's hand suggests the state of pondering and sadness; wrapping one arm about the body portrays loneliness and self-comfort; an outstretched arm indicates hunger; the arm crossed in front of the chest communicates coldness and silence; hands placed on the stomach or in an akimbo position express idleness; and a hand hanging loosely by the side suggests shame.

Gestures may be used in place of verbal messages, as an extension of speech. One of the most frequently seen has the hand being brought up towards the chin or mouth. This gesture is common in sculptures of the Bafo and Bakundu of southern Cameroon, where it suggests the action of swearing an oath. A single finger drawn up to the mouth represents the same idea among Kongo and Cameroon Grassfields groups. Pende sculptures that incorporate a hand gesturing towards the mouth define instead the moment of surprise when hearing some shocking news. Similarly, the hand-to-the-mouth gesture in Chokwe art is used to portray one who is startled on receiving secret information. Among the Luba, figures with this gesture are worn by women during childbirth, suggesting the newsworthiness and heightened excitement of the occasion.

Gesture may be used to elicit specific responses in the onlooker. Thus the Mambila gesture of arms outstretched to the side, frequently seen in sculptures of this society, is identified as a pose of protection or guardianship and may be intended to effect in the Mambila viewer a response of either security or fear depending on the person's role and relationship to the sculpture. The gestures of certain Lobi sculptures, believed to have a protective role in the house, can also be best understood in this way. Some figures turn their heads to the side as a signal of attentiveness; others raise one or both arms above the head defensively. Still others are depicted stretching out their arms horizontally to bar enemies from entering the house. Seeing such figures may invoke a response of restraint on the part of those intending harm to the house or its occupants. Gestural forms also play a significant part in helping to channel the viewer's emotional response to a work. A sculpture of an exuberant mother presenting her child in public invites an emotional response with the enthusiastic, forward-thrusting movement of her arms and the child she holds within them. A shrine figure may similarly draw an onlooker to the image through the gesture of outstretched hands, an action that for the IGBO of Nigeria conveys both the idea of a deity's request for recognition and devotion and the wish on the part of his or her faithful worshippers for generous aid.

As the eye will generally follow the dominant line of a work, attention may be directed by gesture to important details. A mother portrayed with hands reaching towards her child, for example, directs attention to the child's face, reinforcing the maternal theme. A hand raised to stroke a beard draws the eye to the beard, underscoring both the masculinity of the figure and his status as elder. In seated or kneeling figures, the depiction of hands resting on the knees reinforces the stability of persons portrayed in these works.

BIBLIOGRAPHY

R. Lecoq: *Les Bamileke* (Paris, 1953)
K. E. Laman: *The Kongo*, 3 vols, Studia Ethnographica Upsaliensia, iv, viii, xii (Uppsala, 1953–68)
L. de Sousberghe: *L'Art Pende* (Brussels, 1958)
P. Gebauer: *Spider Divination in the Cameroons*, Milwaukee, WI, Pub. Mus. Publications in Anthropology, x (Milwaukee, 1964)
W. Fagg: *Tribes and Forms in African Art* (New York, 1965)
M. Griaule and G. Dieterlen: *Le Renard pâle: Le Mythe cosmogonique*, Trav. & Mém. Inst. Ethnol., lxxii (Paris, 1965; Eng. trans., 1986)
K. Krieger: *Westafrikanische Plastik*, 3 vols, Veröff. Mus. Vlkerknd., Berlin, n. s. 7, Abt. Afrika, ii (Berlin, 1965–9) [col. cat.]
M.-L. Bastin: 'L'Art d'un peuple d'Angola, I: Chokwe'/'Arts of the Angolan Peoples, I: Chokwe', *Afr. A.*, ii/1 (1968), pp. 40–47, 60–64
W. Fagg: *African Tribal Images: The Katherine White Reswick Collection* (Cleveland, 1968)
R. Brain and A. Pollock: *Bangwa Funerary Sculpture*, A. & Soc. Ser. (London, 1971)
M. Lima: *Fonctions sociologiques des figurines de culte Hamba dans la société et dans la culture Tshokwe (Angola)* (Luanda, 1971)
C. Odugbesan: 'Femininity in Yoruba Religious Art', *Man in Africa*, ed. M. Douglas and P. M. Kaberry (London, 1971), pp. 199–211
R. F. Thompson: *Black Gods and Kings: Yoruba Art at UCLA* (Los Angeles, 1971/*R* Bloomington and London, 1976)
D. P. Biebuyck: 'The *Kindi* Aristocrats and their Art among the Lega', *African Art and Leadership*, ed. D. Fraser and H. M. Cole (Madison, 1972), pp. 7–20

N. B. Schwartz: *Mambila: Art and Material Culture*, Milwaukee, WI, Pub. Mus. Publications, iv (Milwaukee, 1972)
D. P. Biebuyck: *Lega Culture: Art, Initiation, and Moral Philosophy among a Central African People* (Berkeley, 1973)
R. Lehuard: *Statuaire du Stanley-Pool* (Villiers-le-Bel, 1974)
African Art in Motion: Icon and Act (exh. cat. by R. F. Thompson, Washington, DC, N.G.A.; Los Angeles, UCLA, Wight A.G.; 1974)
V. Guerry: *Life with the Baule* (New York, 1975)
The Arts of Ghana (exh. cat. by H. M. Cole and D. H. Ross, Los Angeles, UCLA, Wight A.G.; Minneapolis, MN, Walker A. Cent.; Dallas, TX, Mus. F.A.; 1977–8)
Traditional Art of the Nigerian Peoples: The Milton D. Ratner Family Collection (exh. cat. by H. J. Drewal, Washington, DC, Mus. Afr. A., 1977)
A. P. Bourgeois: 'Mbwoolo Sculpture of the Yaka', *Afr. A.*, xii/3 (1979), pp. 58–61
P. Gebauer: *Art of Cameroon* (Portland, OR, 1979)
P. Ben-Amos: *The Art of Benin*, Tribal A. (London, 1980)
P. L. Ravenhill: *Baule Statuary Art: Meaning and Modernization*, Working Pap. Trad. A., v (Philadelphia, 1980)
S. M. Vogel: *Beauty in the Eyes of the Baule: Aesthetics and Cultural Values*, Working Pap. Trad. A., vi (Philadelphia, 1980)
G. Dieterlen: 'Female Figure', *For Spirits and Kings: African Art from the Paul and Ruth Tishman Collection* (exh. cat., ed. S. M. Vogel; New York, Met., 1981), pp. 16–17
C. Geary: 'Bamum Thrones and Stools', *Afr. A.*, xiv/4 (1981), pp. 32–43
R. Kauenhoven-Janzen: 'Chokwe Thrones', *Afr. A.*, xiv/3 (1981), pp. 69–74
Kunst und Religion der Lobi (exh. cat. by P. Meyer, Zurich, Mus. Rietberg, 1981)
The Four Moments of the Sun: Kongo Art in Two Worlds (exh. cat. by R. F. Thompson and J. A. Cornet, Washington, DC, N.G.A., 1981–2)
Gestures in African Art (exh. cat. by S. P. Blier, New York, Kahan Gal. Afr. A., 1982)
Igbo Arts: Community and Cosmos (exh. cat. by H. M. Cole and C. C. Aniakor, Los Angeles, UCLA, Mus. Cult. Hist., 1984–6)

SUSAN PRESTON BLIER

3. PORTRAITURE. African portraits are simultaneously personal, because recognition of the subject's identity depends upon knowledge of the community and person portrayed, and impersonal, in that they stress social identity rather than individual likeness. Characteristically, name and context particularize the image, and representation of the subject is correct rather than idiosyncratic. Such is the economy of African sculpture that portraits embody individual and social identities simultaneously: the image of a king may represent a particular king and all kings; a woman's commemorative mask may stand for a particular woman and all similarly entitled women.

(i) Introduction. (ii) Anthropomorphic images. (iii) Representational and idealized images. (iv) Emblematic portraits.

(i) Introduction. African portraits identify important individuals within the often overlapping frameworks of ancestor cult, political organization and ritual activity. Most African portraits serve as memorials and so represent specific ancestors whose responsibility it is to aid the living by solving vital problems, by shielding them from harm and by contributing to their material success. Individuals who have demonstrated their capabilities during a lifetime of success are selected as most likely to be efficacious ancestral forces. Thus, African memorial portraits recognize, for example, heads of household, heads of state, women of strength and courage, priests and ritual actors, presenting them in terms of social identity rather than idiosyncratic personality and holding them up as embodying ideals of society and exemplifying correct behaviour. While portraiture is the successful person's privilege and honour, and remembrance his or her reward, a portrait's generalized nature shows that he or she is not differentiated for individual qualities but for being an admired example of the ideal. Nigerian Ijo funerary screens (*see* IJO, fig. 2) show the subject of the portrait as a member of a group but distinguish him by centrality and size rather than by physiognomic characteristics. The Oron of south-eastern Nigeria show their respect for successful individuals by the relative articulation of the memorial image: ordinary individuals are represented by uncarved sticks or staffs, leaders by stylized but highly differentiated and elaborately rendered figural sculpture (see Nicklin).

Any account of portraiture in African art is complicated by lack of recognition of images as portraits by cultural outsiders. Factors contributing to this failure include stylized ideals of comportment, an aesthetic of generalization and conventions of identification and record-keeping that differ from Western conventions. The specific identities of many African portrait subjects are unknown, because the works have been separated from their cultural context. Thus many images labelled by scholars 'ancestor figures' are actually unidentified portraits.

The general problem of recognition is demonstrated by FON commemorative tableaux (see 1985 exh. cat.; *see also* §(ii) below). In these tableaux the links between object and individual identity are extra-aesthetic and often ephemeral, dependent on cultural knowledge not readily accessible to an outsider. Tableau messages originate in discussions between donor and artist on the sentiments to be conveyed and on the selection of appropriate symbols. No-one is responsible for preserving a narrative explanation of the cryptic visual allusions and metaphoric references in the tableau; so, unless it contains a particularly striking or cleverly conceived message, the meaning will be lost with the passage of time.

The identity of African portraits is established or confirmed by association with the subject through siting, biographical references, use of actual clothing, relics or—most importantly—name rather than by literal physical description. Because name and context particularize the African image rather than physical likeness, dramatically disparate visual configurations work as portraits. The Kurumba of Burkina Faso, for example, represent high-ranking elders by masquerades depicting the protective antelope (*Hippotragus koba*), the totem of most Kurumba clans. Headdresses are carved at the death of an individual to enhance his prestige, and, when danced at funerals and public performances following the funeral, the masquerades serve as physical re-embodiments of the deceased and are addressed with his name (see Roy, pp. 198–202; *see also* §VI, 3 below). In Benin, Battamaliba families honour recently deceased elders by giving them the attribute of youth, portraying them in the form of houses wearing the garments of initiation (see Blier, 1987; *see also* §1(ii) above).

In contrast, the YORUBA of southern Nigeria use generalized human figures to commemorate deceased twins. These diminutive figures are linked to their subjects by being gender-specific and having appropriate lineage and scarification marks. The family addresses the image by name and makes gifts appropriate to the deceased child's place in the lineage (see Drewal). The DAN of Liberia and Côte d'Ivoire commission portraits of favourite wives from skilled carvers. These images, made after a meeting between artist and subject, are unusually specific, reflecting individual physiognomies, and, like most African portraits, they also bear the name of the subject (see 1976 exh. cat.).

Even the most representational African portrait, however, tends to be idealized, since the African aesthetic is a generalizing one. A realistic depiction of age or peculiarity implies a lack of respect for the subject (see Brain and Pollock; Ben-Amos, 1980). Completeness rather than verisimilitude may be the representational ideal, as it is for the exceptionally naturalistic commemorative portraits used by the Owo Yoruba (Abiodun, 1976).

An overview of African portrait images produces three broad and slightly overlapping categories. The largest category is that of generalized anthropomorphic images; the others are representational and idealized images and emblematic portraits.

(ii) Anthropomorphic images. Portraits taking this form are individuated by means of such specific references to the subject as naming. The Okpella of southern Nigeria recognize a woman's commemorative masquerade by personal and praise names. Although such a masquerade may dance in public during the lifetime of its subject, it assumes her name only after her death. It is not obviously distinguishable as a likeness, with its stylized features and elaborate coiffure. Instead, identity is established by its name and its location within the kin group that accompanies the masquerade when it appears in public during the annual ancestral festival (see fig. 33; Borgatti, 1979).

Images may be further identified through specific sculptural references to the subject's coiffure and personal decoration, a method used by AKAN artists to personalize commemorative terracotta portraits (see 1977–8 exh. cat.; Preston; Sieber; Soppelsa; Visona). Iconographic devices may also 'name' subjects: for example, portraits of Kuba kings (*see* KUBA (iii)) in Zaïre reflect ideals of body image and comportment, individuated only by an emblem shown at the base of the figure (see Vansina; Rosenwald). The 17th-century King Shyaam A-Mbul A-Ngoong is recognized by his game-board, while the 18th-century King Misha Mi-Shyaang A-Mbul (formerly Bom Bosh) is identified by a carved cup with its handle carved in the form of a human hand (see fig. 34).

The EDO of Benin depict kings in relief sculpture by associating a generalized figure with specific attributes or images linked to events occurring during his reign. The 16th-century Oba Ozolua, known as 'the conqueror', wears full battledress and carries a shield on his left arm; he brandishes a sword in his right hand and holds the severed head of an enemy in his left. His son, Esigie (1515–20), is portrayed wearing the red parrot-feather regalia of a senior priest of the Ovia cult, which he introduced to the palace during his rule (see Blackmun, 'Remembering . . .'). More complex biographical references are incorporated into the images of 17th- and 18th-century kings. The early 17th-century ruler Oba Ewuakpe's idiosyncratic headgear and staff and pair of emaciated attendants are explained by oral traditions of the period and the known problems he faced in acceding to the throne (see Ben-Amos, 1983).

33. Okpella memorial portrait mask of Olimi Elewo (made 1935) sitting with her mask herald and family members at the Olimi festival, New Iddo, Nigeria; from a photograph by Jean M. Borgatti

Fon memorial tableaux commemorate the honoured dead by depicting them in positions of authority through the idiom of royal dress, stance or regalia or by showing an individual at work. The subject of the sculpture holds a central position in the composition, with the donor's figure often occupying a more peripheral zone. Although the figures are generic in form, specific names may be directly represented in rebus form within the composition, as in an example where images of fish (*hue*) and a grinding stone (*li*) created the proper syllabic references to the subject's name (see 1985 exh. cat., p. 20). Alternatively, visual puns on the family or given name may establish identification, or the name may be spelt out in letters on a small metal plate.

The IBIBIO living in the area of Ikot Ekpene in Nigeria celebrate men of distinction with banners of cloth appliqué and patchwork. In the past, the banner-maker would be invited to stay at the compound of the deceased for several months in order to learn his life history, especially his acts of bravery, so that the shrine cloth would portray his achievements in full (see Salmons). A more recent practice is for the artist to absorb information about his subject during funeral ceremonies, where the exploits of the deceased are praised in song and mime.

34. Figure of the Kuba king Misha Mi-Shyaang A-Mbul, wood, h. 495 mm, from Zaïre, *c.* 1750 (New York, The Brooklyn Museum)

In southern MADAGASCAR, the Antanosy, Bara, Sihanaka, Antaimoro and Mahafaly remember individuals with sculptures that present them in the context of their actual possessions or in terms of their life history. One memorial sculpture by the Antanosy sculptor Fesira depicts the subject seated at the side of a large monument comprising two images that recall important aspects of his life: his service with the French authorities as a mounted policeman and his purchase of the first motor-car in the village (see Mack).

Such groups as the KONGO, BEMBE and Bwende of Zaïre identify a portrait by incorporating relics from the body of the deceased into the memorial figure. The Bwende artist Makoza of Kingoyi (*fl c.* 1900) also studied the face and body of the deceased whose mummy he was making in order accurately to represent such features as filed teeth and scarification (see 1981–2 exh. cat., pp. 60–61).

Contextual association of image and subject is stressed by the BAULE, whose portrait masks publicly express the admiration evoked by some exceptional quality associated with the subject (see Vogel). In such examples, identification is completed by the subject's partnering the portrait mask in performance. The masks also bear the names of their subjects and often wear clothing or accessories owned by them.

(iii) Representational and idealized images. Representational images are physiognomic likenesses, the subject (or an appropriate relative) having sat for the artist. Such portraits are found among the Bamileke (*see* BAMILEKE AND RELATED PEOPLES) and BANGWA of Cameroon (see Brain and Pollock; Lecoq; Rudy; Harter) and the Hemba of Zaïre (see Neyt and de Stryker). In other cases, the artist may simply familiarize himself with the individual, executing the work without further visual reference to the subject (see Himmelheber; 1981–2 exh. cat.).

Even the most representational African portraits idealize and generalize their subjects, demonstrating what Rowland Abiodun (1976) has called a 'controlled naturalism' in contrast to the idiosyncratic or literal naturalism of much Western portraiture. An Ijebu Yoruba artist's rendering of Queen Victoria based on her 1887 Jubilee portrait clearly illustrates this bias in African portraiture (see fig. 35). In keeping with Yoruba principles of representation, the artist has depicted the Queen as a respected and powerful member of society, treating her fan as the equivalent of the Yoruba royal fly-whisk and dramatizing her head and hand to signal their importance. (In Yoruba thought the head is the seat of an individual's luck, wisdom and destiny and consequently is emphasized, comprising up to a quarter of the total composition.) Additionally, the artist has honoured the Queen with youth, smoothing her wrinkles, firming up her chin and regularizing her features to reveal the strength and beauty within.

(iv) Emblematic portraits. Just as the most representational images may be seen to draw upon the generalizing aesthetic that informs all African portraits, the emblematic portrait takes the cultural and historic markers present in all the images and raises them to a further degree of abstraction. Emblematic portraits use symbolic devices to evoke an image of the subject in the mind's eye of the viewer. They are often non-anthropomorphic and may include an assemblage of goods or visual referents that recall the individual to the spectator. Generally, they may be said to represent an intellectualized vision of the subject and his personality or the spiritual side of the individual not normally visible. The imagery may be either personal and subtle, and therefore dependent upon the viewer's specialized knowledge, or public and dramatic, to impress more firmly on the audience the particular characteristics or achievements of the individual portrayed.

Many Nigerian groups remember male ancestors with non-anthropomorphic characterizations based on shrouds, a classic 'ghost form' (see fig. 36). The distribution of this commemorative masquerade follows the path of the Niger and the Benue rivers with a clustering in the

35. Ijebu Yoruba figure of Queen Victoria, wood, h. 622 mm, from Nigeria, after 1887 (Los Angeles, CA, University of California, Fowler Museum of Cultural History)

confluence area. Among the Edo-speaking Okpella, these Dead Fathers return for an annual celebration with their living kin during a festival of ancestors. The masquerade takes the form of a cloth sack constructed of expensive, handwoven cloth, some of it with ritual significance, held together at the top around a stick that may be used to extend its height. A Dead Father may be simultaneously general and specific: the commemorative masquerade with the greatest seniority represents simultaneously all deceased heads of household in the congregation as well as the specific individual whose name it bears. The masquerade's vigorous performance asserts masculinity in the dynamic expression of energy, and visual references to men's title status may be included to indicate a social ideal of achievement. Relics from the body of the deceased may be sewn into the costume to personalize the representation in an incontrovertible way. Attendants related to the deceased accompany the masquerade, thus placing the apparition in a lineage group, and members of the community salute it by name, using the greetings for welcoming someone who has come back from a long journey and thus offering further evidence of its identity. Comparable commemorative masks for men occur among the Yoruba, the IDOMA, the Igbira, the IGALU, the IGBO and other northern Edo groups besides the Okpella. The nuancing of the imagery varies from group to group.

The Fon of Benin (see Blier, 1990) make masterful emblematic portraits in both sculpture and cloth appliqué, relying for identification upon literary reference (proverbs

36. Okpella commemorative masks of the deceased chiefs Ikor and Sado, Afokpella, Imaiamune Quarter, Nigeria; from a photograph by Jean M. Borgatti, 1972

and history) and indirection (using images in a rebus fashion to spell the name of the subject). Fon royal portraits range from such large-scale wooden sculptures as the allegorical portrait of *King Glele* (Paris, Mus. Homme), depicting a man with the head of a lion, to such two-dimensional works as the wall hanging dedicated to him and featuring the lion image, used because his name-sentence states, 'I am the lion's whelp who sows terror as soon as his teeth have sprouted'. Glele's mission as king was to avenge his father's defeat at the hands of the neighbouring Yoruba at Abeokuta: the name he chose upon ascending the throne clearly states this goal.

BIBLIOGRAPHY

GENERAL

K. Nicklin: *Guide to the National Museum, Oron* (Lagos, n.d.)
R. Lecoq: *Les Bamileke* (Paris, 1953)
R. Horton: *Kalabari Sculpture* (Lagos, 1965)
R. Brain and A. Pollock: *Bangwa Funerary Sculpture*, A. & Soc. Ser. (London, 1971)
R. F. Thompson: *Black Gods and Kings: Yoruba Art at UCLA* (Los Angeles, 1971/*R* Bloomington and London, 1976)
G. Dieterlen, ed.: *La Nation de personne en Afrique Noire* (Paris, 1973)
R. Lehuard: *Statuaire du Stanley-Pool* (Villiers-le-Bel, 1974)
J. Rosenwald: 'Kuba King Figures', *Afr. A.*, vii/2 (1974), pp. 26–31, 92
F. Neyt and L. de Stryker: *Approche des arts Hemba*, Col. A. Afrique Noire, xi, suppl. (Villiers-le-Bel, 1975)
P. Ben-Amos: *The Art of Benin*, Tribal A. (London, 1980)
P. Harter: *Arts anciens du Cameroun* (Arnouville, 1986)
J. Mack: *Madagascar: Island of the Ancestors* (London, 1986)
C. Roy: *Art of the Upper Volta Rivers* (Meudon, 1987)
J. Borgatti and R. Brilliant: *Likeness and Beyond: Portraits from Africa and the World* (New York, 1990)

SPECIALIST STUDIES

B. Holas: 'Remarques sur la valeur sociologique du nom dans les sociétés traditionelles de l'ouest africain', *J. Soc. Africanistes*, xxiii/1–2 (1953), pp. 77–86
——: 'Nom, invocation, prière: Transposition du problème général sur le terrain des recherches negro africain', *Bull. Inst. Fr. Afrique Noire*, ser. B, xvii/1–2 (1956), pp. 109–28
H. Himmelheber and W. Tame-Tabmen: 'Wunkirle: Die gastichste Frau', *Festschrift Alfred Buhler*, ed. C. M. Schmitz (Basle, 1965), pp. 171–81
H. Himmelheber: 'Das Porträt in der Negerkunst', *Baessler-Archv*, xx (1972), pp. 261–311
S. Rudy: 'Royal Sculpture in the Cameroon Grasslands', *African Art and Leadership*, ed. D. Fraser and H. M. Cole (Madison, 1972), pp. 123–36
R. Sieber: 'Kwahu Terracottas, Oral Traditions, and Ghanaian History', *African Art and Leadership*, ed. D. Fraser and H. M. Cole (Madison, 1972), pp. 173–84
J. Vansina: 'Ndop: Royal Statues among the Kuba', *African Art and Leadership*, ed. D. Fraser and H. M. Cole (Madison, 1972), pp. 41–56
B. Söderberg: 'Les Figures d'ancêtres chez les Bambémbé', *A. Afrique Noire*, 13 (1975), pp. 21–33; 14 (1975), pp. 14–37
R. Abiodun: 'A Reconsideration of the Function of Ako, Second Burial Effigy in Owo', *Africa*, xlvi/1 (1976), pp. 4–20
S. M. Vogel: *Baule Art as the Expression of a World View* (diss., New York U., Inst. F.A., 1977)
J. M. Borgatti: 'Dead Mothers of Okpella', *Afr. A.*, xii/4 (1979), pp. 48–57
M. J. Adams: 'Fon Appliqued Cloths', *Afr. A.*, xiii/2 (1980), pp. 28–41, 87–8
J. R. Salmons: 'Funerary Shrine Cloths of the Annang-Ibibio, South East Nigeria', *Textiles of Africa*, ed. D. Idiens and K. Ponting (Bath, 1980), pp. 99–141
P. Ben-Amos: 'Who is the Man in the Bowler Hat? Emblems of Identity in Benin Royal Art', *Baessler-Archv*, n. s., xxxi (1983), pp. 161–83
B. W. Blackmun: 'Remembering the Warrior Kings', *The Art of Power, the Power of Art: Studies in Benin Iconography*, ed. P. Ben-Amos and A. Rubin, Museum of Cultural History Monograph, xix (Los Angeles, 1983), pp. 49–50
——: 'Reading a Royal Altar Tusk', *The Art of Power, the Power of Art: Studies in Benin Iconography*, ed. P. Ben-Amos and A. Rubin, Museum of Cultural History Monograph, xix (Los Angeles, 1983), pp. 59–70
H. J. Drewal: 'Art History and the Individual: A New Perspective for the Study of African Visual Traditions', *IA Stud. Afr. A.*, i (1984), pp. 87–114
E. Fischer: 'Self-portraits, and Copies among the Dan: The Creative Process of Traditional African Mask Carvers', *IA Stud. Afr. A.*, i (1984), pp. 5–28
S. P. Blier: *The Anatomy of Architecture: Ontology and Metaphor in Batammaliba Architectural Expression*, Res Monographs in Anthropology and Aesthetics (Cambridge, 1987)
R. Poynor: 'Ako Figures of Owo and Second Burials in Southern Nigeria', *Afr. A.*, xxi/1 (1987), pp. 62–4, 81–3, 86
N. Barley: *Foreheads of the Dead: An Anthropological View of Kalabari Ancestral Screens* (Washington, DC, 1988)
R. T. Soppelsa, J. Hellman and C. Keim: 'Western Art-historical Methodology and African Art: Panofsky's Paradigm and Ivorian Mma', *A. J.* [New York], xlvii/2 (1988), pp. 147–53
W. E. A. Van Beek: 'Functions of Sculpture in Dogon Religion', *Afr. A.*, xxi/4 (1988), pp. 58–65, 91
Afr. A., xxiii/3 (1990) and xxiii/4 (1990) [special issues on 'Portraiture in Africa']
S. P. Blier: 'King Glele of Danhome—Part One: Divination Portraits of Lion King and Man of Iron', *Afr. A.*, xxiii/4 (1990), pp. 42–53
G. N. Preston: 'People Making Portraits Making People: Living Icons of the Akan', *Afr. A.*, xxiii/3 (1990), pp. 70–76
R. T. Soppelsa: 'A Mna in the Metropolitan Museum of Art', *Afr. A.*, xxiii/3 (1990), pp. 77–8
M. B. Visona: 'Portraiture among the Lagoon Peoples of Côte d'Ivoire', *Afr. A.*, xxiii/4 (1990), pp. 54–61
S. P. Blier: 'King Glele of Danhome—Part Two: Dynasty and Destiny', *Afr. A.*, xxiv/1 (1991), pp. 44–55, 101–03

EXHIBITION CATALOGUES

Die Kunst der Dan (exh. cat. by E. Fischer and H. Himmelheber, Zurich, Mus. Rietberg, 1976; Eng. trans., rev., Zurich, 1984)
The Arts of Ghana (exh. cat. by H. M. Cole and D. H. Ross; Los Angeles, UCLA, Wight A.G.; Minneapolis, MN, Walker A. Cent.; Dallas, TX, Mus. F.A.; 1977–8)
The Four Moments of the Sun: Kongo Art in Two Worlds (exh. cat. by R. F. Thompson and J. A. Cornet, Washington, DC, N.G.A., 1981–2)
Asen: Iron Altars of the Fon People of Benin (exh. cat., ed. E. G. Bay; Atlanta, Emory U. Mus. A. & Archaeol., 1985)

JEAN M. BORGATTI

4. PHYSICAL ANOMALIES. Among the most visually powerful African works of art are those associated with physical anomalies. Although not every African society seeks to portray deformity in its arts, many do. The function of such works is quite varied, and artistic examples of physical anomaly, deformity and deficiency have important cultural associations. Some, including many of the two-faced figures that show a surfeit of bodily features, use their excess powers to convey greater than normal strength, force and status. Other works suggest, through the absence or distortion of body parts, ideas of stigmatized behaviour or social incompleteness. Spiritual and physiological sickness is suggested through body deformity as well. Still other sculptures through their inclusion of monstrous attributes are associated with antisocial qualities and those persons who depart from tradition and the interests of the group.

(i) Figures and dolls. Among the FON of Benin, certain genres of *bocio* power figures show body deformation in provocative ways. Known as *bocio-bigble* ('corrupted *bocio*'), such works display striking visual and emotional power (see Blier, 1995). While some such figures have missing legs or arms (see fig. 37), by far the most common forms incorporate two heads, faces or bodies. In these works faces may be carved on two sides of the head, or two or more heads set on a single pair of shoulders, or a single pair of legs and hips may support two torsos. Questions

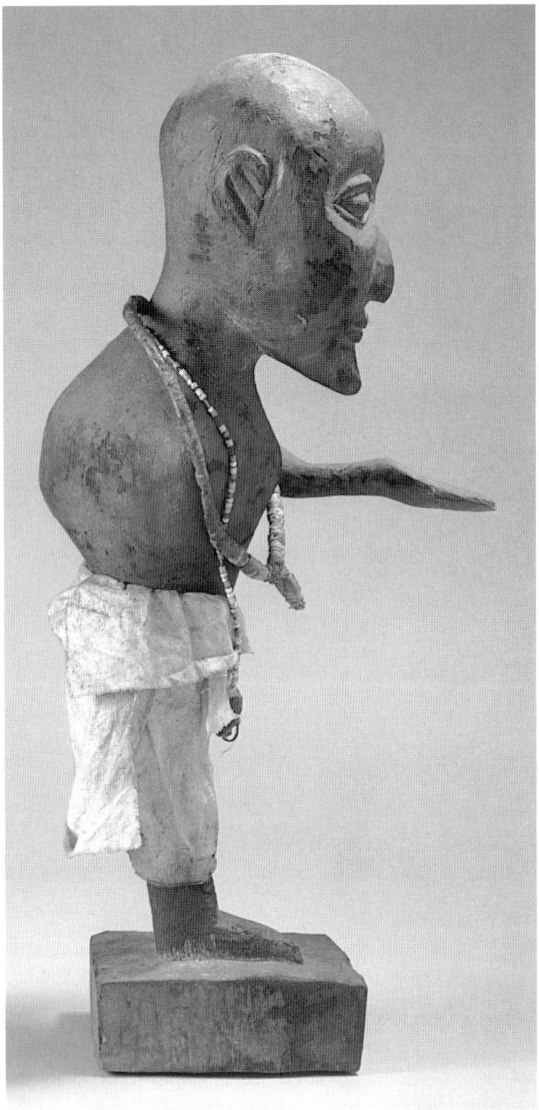

37. Fon deformed figure sculpture (*bocio-bigble*), wood, h. 584 mm, from Benin (Indianapolis, IN, Museum of Art)

of psychological power and social difference are often addressed in Fon *bocio* through aberrant visual imagery of this sort. These works are identified with individual danger, sorcery and empowerment. Accordingly they are often employed as guardian figures to protect the house, compound, temple or city. The perceived ability of multi-headed works to observe activity both inside and outside the compound is of considerable importance. Fon deformity imagery of this sort carries with it important associations not only with protection (and a wish to see in front and behind at the same time) but also with the desire to control one's personal and social landscape through the fragmentation and replication of key body parts. Such works also convey provocative ideas of gender conflation, with many incorporating the sexual attributes of both sexes. Most of these *bocio* draw their potency from tiny invisible *aziza* spirits who are believed to inhabit the forests. These spirits are generally described as having a single foot and arm. Also important to *bocio* figural empowerment are various *vodun* forces such as the *hoho* (twins) or Mawu (the solar god), both of whom are said to have clairvoyant, four-eyed vision. Sorcerers and kings are also believed to have this power. Fon deformity figures in this and other ways reinforce the vital interconnections between religion, power, psychology and art.

Deformity sculptures produced by LOBI artists in northern Ghana are also of interest. Lobi sculptures show a range of physical anomalies, including a head surmounting a single leg, a person missing an arm or leg, a figure with three or more arms, a person with two or more heads and a person with three or more legs supporting a single torso. These figures, which represent *ti bala* ('extraordinary persons'), are said to protect the house by frightening away all who would do it harm (see fig. 38). Because of their body incompleteness and/or deformities, they are viewed as especially dangerous (see 1981 exh. cat., p. 95).

Deformity figures that show missing or distorted body attributes suggest similarly important sociological concerns in other African cultures (see 1982 exh. cat.). Many are

38. Lobi deformity sculpture (*ti bala*), wood, h. 350 mm (Paris, private collection)

associated with antisocial attributes. Among the PENDE of Zaïre, sculptures with a single arm and leg are identified with loneliness, with persons who have neither close relatives nor friends (de Sousberghe, p. 109). It has been suggested that deformity figures of the Lega, another Zaïrean group (*see* LEGA AND RELATED PEOPLES), are identified with antisocial individuals as well (see Biebuyck, 1972, p. 17). Thus Lega figures displaying a single arm are described as representing an individual given to quarrelling, the deformity deriving from his aggressive character. A Lega work missing both arms is associated with adultery (see Biebuyck, 1973, pl. 69).

Physiological and mental illness is also suggested through features of physical anomaly. In the Cameroon Grasslands sufferers of disease, witchcraft ills and spiritual trauma are depicted in figural form through distortions of the abdomen (see Brain and Pollock). With the Nguu of Tanzania illness-causing sorcerers are shown turned on their heads (Cory, pp. 48–9). Illness-causing bush spirits among the SENUFO of the Côte d'Ivoire are represented in turn by figures with feet turned backwards or transformed into fins (Glaze, p. 65). A Rotse work with body attributes articulated on only half the figure represents a madness-causing, half-human creature called Mwenda-Njangula or Mwenda Lutaka (Reynolds, pp. 50, 65). Physiological or spiritual anomaly and figural distortion are in this way conjoined.

Carved doll forms that display deliberately underdeveloped limbs also are of interest in the context of physical anomaly. It has been suggested (see McLeod, p. 174) that Asante doll forms known as *akuaba* (*see* ASANTE AND RELATED PEOPLES, §4(i)) lack essential human attributes because of their identity as potential rather than fully realized beings. As McLeod explains, children cannot assume their own characters and roles until much later in life. Robert Farris Thompson notes similarly (see 1974 exh. cat., p. 53) that the lack of feet on many of these figures reinforces their association with social dependency. Doll-form figures that lack full body development or attributes are also employed by the MOSSI (Burkina Faso) and ZULU (South Africa) among other groups. These works too may suggest ideas of dependency, disempowerment and immaturity.

African sculptures that are characterized by a surfeit of features through their incorporation of multiple heads and/or members also form an important corpus of anomaly works. As with the Fon multi-headed figures discussed above, what unites this group is the increased power and presence that is identified with bodily surplus or abundance. Among the Bini of Nigeria, four-legged figures are identified with Ofoe, a death-associated deity who is said to be able to travel readily between the earth and sky (see Ben-Amos, p. 149). With the DOGON of Mali, figures with multiple arms or legs are said to be identified with the increased power of two sky *nommo* (see Griaule and Dieterlen, pl. 18). A seven-legged figure that is believed to be able to outrun thieves with ease is used by the Mburi of northern Cameroon to protect palm-wine stocks (Gebauer, p. 185). Added power is also attributed to two-faced sculptures because they have increased sensory properties. The TEKE of Zaïre employ such figures as a special prerogative of great chiefs (Lehuard, p. 37).

(ii) Masks and masquerades. Among the IGBO, IBIBIO and neighbouring Cross River peoples in Nigeria, masquerades displaying physical anomalies also have important power associations. With the EJAGHAM some such masks portray humans with distorted features including huge noses or off-centre mouths. These 'beast' personifiers often wear dirty or torn costumes and display aggressive dance steps and fierce actions (see Jones, 1945, pp. 194, 196). M. Ruel states that the Ejagham 'beast' masker Emanyankpe 'presents the more "fearsome" aspect of the association and when it appears non-members are expected to flee and hide' (p. 266).

Among the nearby Ibibio, Ekpo members wearing masks with various physical anomalies represent ancestors of bad character such as murderers, sorcerers, poisoners, paupers without kin and stealers of sacred objects. These ancestors are said to be responsible for the sickness and accidents of their descendants and townsmen (Messenger, pp. 120–21). Maskers of this sort, which are known as *idiok ekpo* ('evil Ekpo'), often have exaggerated features that jut out from the mask surface at irregular angles (see fig. 39). Many such works combine human and animalistic elements in terrifying compositions. Others portray horrible deforming diseases such as lupus, yaws (gangosa is an indicator of religious impurity), syphilis and leprosy (see Jones, 1984, p. 77; Messenger, p. 122). These diseases are represented in such features as sores, split tongues, twisted or eaten-away lips or noses, protruding teeth and tongues, mouths out of line and flapped eyes (symbolizing blindness). Skulls, snakes, lizards (witch familiars) and tortoises are often incorporated into these masks as well. Reinforcing the dangerous identity of these masks,

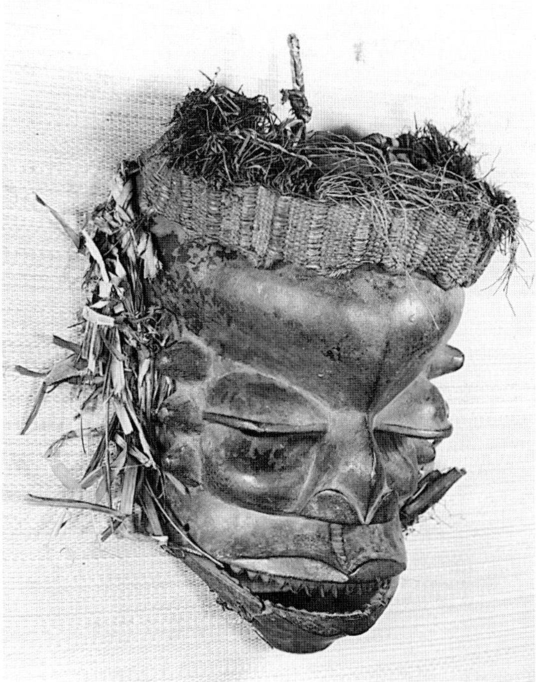

39. Ibibio *idiok ekpo* mask, wood, h. 355 mm (Stuttgart, Linden-Museum)

associated performers carry weapons such as machetes or bows and arrows. Their choreographed actions are frequently wayward and violent, with related maskers often shaking their bodies furiously, running through the village, climbing trees or houses, destroying property or harming people.

Okoroshi and Mwo 'beast' masquerades of the nearby Igbo also display various body anomalies. Southern Igbo Okoroshi masks often have ugly, diseased and animalistic features, which are either carved into the mask surface or glued on to it with a thick gum. These features include bloody fangs, thrust-forward mouths, furrowed foreheads and eyebrows, protruding, bent and tubular tongues, broken noses and twisted mouths (see Deji, p. 177; Cole, p. 38). Northern Igbo Mwo masks display complementary forms. Some of the latter masks are carved to represent terrifying animalistic monsters with a mixture of leonine, elephant and buffalo features. As with the Okoroshi 'beasts', the Mwo works draw analogies between human aggressiveness and the fierceness and violence of wild animals (Boston, p. 58).

BIBLIOGRAPHY

Deji: 'Okorosia', *Niger. Field*, iii/4 (1934), pp. 175–7
G. T. Basden: *Niger Ibos* (London and New York, 1938)
G. I. Jones: 'Masked Plays of South Eastern Nigeria', *Geog. Mag.*, xviii/5 (1945), pp. 190–200
H. Cory: *African Figurines: Their Ceremonial Use in Puberty Rites in Tanganyika* (London, 1956)
L. de Sousberghe: *L'Art Pende* (Brussels, 1959)
J. Boston: 'Some Northern Ibo Masquerades', *J. Royal Anthropol. Inst. GB & Ireland*, xc (1960), pp. 54–65
B. Reynolds: *Magic, Divination and Witchcraft among the Barotse of Northern Rhodesia* (Berkeley, 1963)
M. Griaule and G. Dieterlen: *Le Renard pâle: Le Mythe cosmogonique*, Trav. & Mém. Inst. Ethnol., lxxii (Paris, 1965; Eng. trans., 1986)
H. M. Cole: 'Art as a Verb in Iboland', *Afr. A.*, iii/1 (1969), pp. 34–41
M. Ruel: *Leopards and Leaders: Constitutional Politics among a Cross River People* (Cambridge and New York, 1969)
R. Brain and A. Pollock: *Bangwa Funerary Sculpture*, A. & Soc. Ser. (London, 1971)
D. P. Biebuyck: 'The *Kindi* Aristocrats and their Art among the Lega', *African Art and Leadership*, ed. D. Fraser and H. M. Cole (Madison, 1972), pp. 7–20
——: *Lega Culture: Art, Initiation and Moral Philosophy among a Central African People* (Berkeley, 1973)
J. C. Messenger: 'The Carver in Anang Society', *The Traditional Artist in African Societies*, ed. W. L. d'Azevedo (Bloomington and London, 1973), pp. 101–27
R. Lehuard: *Statuaire de Stanley-Pool* (Villiers-le-Bel, 1974)
African Art in Motion: Icon and Act (exh. cat. by R. F. Thompson; Washington, DC, N.G.A.; Los Angeles, UCLA, Wight A.G.; 1974)
S. P. Blier: *Masking Traditions of Southeastern Nigeria* (diss., New York, Columbia U., 1976)
A. J. Glaze: 'Senufu Ornament and Decorative Arts', *Afr. A.*, xii/1 (1978), pp. 63–71
P. Gebauer: *Art of Cameroon* (Portland, OR, and New York, 1979)
P. Ben-Amos: *The Art of Benin*, Tribal A. (London, 1980)
M. D. McLeod: *The Asante* (London, 1981)
Kunst und Religion der Lobi (exh. cat. by P. Meyer, Zurich, Mus. Rietberg, 1981)
Gestures in African Art (exh. cat. by S. P. Blier, New York, Kahan Gal. Afr. A., 1982)
G. I. Jones: *The Art of Eastern Nigeria* (Cambridge, 1984)
Igbo Arts: Community and Cosmos (exh. cat. by H. M. Cole and C. C. Aniakor, Los Angeles, UCLA, Mus. Cult. Hist., 1984)
S. P. Blier: *African Vodun: Art, Psychology and Power* (Chicago, 1995)

SUZANNE PRESTON BLIER

5. Mother-and-child imagery.

(i) Introduction. (ii) Formal interpretation. (iii) Religious context.

(i) Introduction. The mother-and-child group is for many the most affecting and compelling theme in African art. Partly owing to the biological model of a mother with her baby and partly to the Christian icon of the Virgin and Child, the subject is easily related to art elsewhere in the world, even if information is lacking on its values in specific cultures. The varied uses and meanings of African versions of this representation both illuminate the universal character of the icon and reveal aspects of the richness of African thought.

Renderings of the mother and child have a long history on the continent: paintings on the rock surfaces of Tassili and nearby sites in the Sahara date from *c.* 3000–2000 BC. The earliest known sculptural versions are pottery figures ascribed to the NOK cultures of northern Nigeria (*c.* 500 BC–AD 200). The most important prehistoric cluster of maternities is the corpus of pottery sculptures (*c.* AD 1000–1500) from the inland delta of the Niger River in Mali. Some of these are quite naturalistic renderings in lifelike poses, but others, showing a mother with one or two diminutive 'adult' children, are conventionalized and clearly symbolic, although their precise meanings are unknown. The majority of surviving examples of this form, however, come from the vast ethnographic corpus of 19th- and 20th-century artefacts, which, unlike many works from archaeological contexts, are informed by quantities of anthropological and art-historical data. While most maternities of this period are wood-carvings, fine pottery figures such as those of the AKAN peoples are also known, as are examples in sun-dried clay or mud, brass or bronze, and occasional examples in iron, stone, fibre and appliqué beadwork. Virtually all were made by well-trained professional artists, usually male, although there are pottery examples produced by Akan and IGBO female potters.

(ii) Form and interpretation. Most mother-and-child images are free-standing wood sculptures destined for shrines, but such representations, including birth scenes, may also be found on masks, chairs, stools, doors, house-posts, wooden gongs, combs, bowls and other utilitarian artefacts. In rare instances, too, the mother-and-child form may appear in wholly secular contexts, for example on Akan goldweights. Generally, however, the image has a spiritual connotation and use. The prevalence and recurrence of the maternity group attests to its importance in African life and thought (for discussion of the theme of 'increase' *see* §1 above), although its uneven distribution among various peoples is difficult to explain. The sculptors and patrons of the KONGO (e.g. Yombe, Vili) and YORUBA peoples, for example, are prolific in their use of the theme (see fig. 40), producing many variations in pose, size, shape, object type and even style. Neighbouring and other Central and West African cultures, for whom the biological imperative of motherhood is no less important, however, have exploited the theme far less fully, and occasionally not at all (e.g. Benin, Lega, Kalabari Ijo). There is no apparent correlation between matrilineal or patrilineal descent in a society and its preoccupation with the mother-and-child image, for the theme occurs unevenly in each. Pluralism in cultural preferences and local tradition seem to be better (although unsatisfying) explanations for distribution patterns. Clearly biological and demographic reality are not the same as artistic and spiritual reality, since

40. Mother and child, wood, glass beads, glass inlay and metal, h. 258 mm, from the Yombe group, Kongo people, Congo or Zaïre, collected before 1914 (Washington, DC, National Museum of African Art)

productive women are highly valued among all African peoples.

Basic to the elucidation of the theme are the identities of the mothers and children represented. It is easiest to say who they are not, since they are rarely portraits of real people. Even if ancestral images, they are usually not specifically named; rather, they are symbols of lineage or clan forebears, the generalized, idealized, 'incarnate dead'. In other cases the woman may be the primordial mother, the legendary founder of the people. Most DOGON maternities can probably be so identified, and it is certainly true of some large SENUFO examples, known as 'Ancient Mother'. Research indicates that the latter refer primarily to a complex of ideas about culture and social relationships rather than to the biological unit of a mother with her baby. Suckling here does refer to nurture, but the emphasis is not so much on a mother's nutritional provision for her infant as on the Ancient Mother's protection and guidance of all Senufo males during the 21-year cycle of initiation and education, which imparts the 'milk of knowledge' and results in the development of 'complete human beings' (see 1981 exh. cat., pp. 45–6). In the dualistic opposition between nature and culture so characteristic of African thought, the mother-and-child image refers more often to culture than to nature, while also acknowledging their interdependence.

A well-known 'maternity' among the Owerri Igbo of Nigeria is Ala, the earth goddess, who is portrayed larger than (presumed) life-size as the honoured recipient of elaborate temple-like structures (*mbari*), which are filled with dozens of human images in sun-dried clay. All of these, including the two who sit on her lap or beside her, are her 'children'. Ala also has the pendulous breasts and title regalia of an older woman. As a major tutelary deity, she presides over village morality and health, and, as the greatest of mothers, she yields or withholds children, crops and animals. She nurtures, but she also kills swiftly when offended. She incarnates cyclical regeneration, life, death and rebirth. She is revered and feared. All villagers and many deities are her children, and she demands their respect and honour.

It is notable that an intimate, emotional bond between the mother and her child is rarely expressed, even when the baby is suckling. Equally, the sculptor seldom gives the child any real personality. This can be partly accounted for by Africa's high rates of infant mortality. Moreover, children, however much desired by parents, were often regarded as useful property rather than as individual personalities, especially during infancy. Children were not always raised by their biological parents and might be pawned or sold into slavery. High infant mortality also accounts for the tradition of the changeling, the child who, it was believed, was born to die, often just as its parents began to cherish it. Believed to appear on earth several times, dying and being born again, a changeling plagued its parents with its mysterious actions and caused them not only anguish but also expense in the form of sacrifices to avert its death. In such circumstances, an emotional and psychological distance between mother and baby in a work of art and the child's lack of personality or character are understandable.

Mother-and-child sculptures are often called 'fertility figures'. Human productivity, of course, is crucial to the continuity of the race, and it is certainly true that many shrines and cults emphasize the fertility of women, their health during pregnancy and the infant's survival. Rather than being celebrated in and for itself, however, the biology of maternity serves the more important social states of motherhood and fatherhood, the creation of a family. An African female normally is not recognized as a real woman unless and until she is a mother, and her ideal status is as the mother of a large family. Children are social and economic assets, and they are also expected to honour parents and, at death, to organize a proper burial, which is often in fact a delayed funerary festival (*see* §III, 5(ii) above) that in turn ensures their beneficence as ancestors.

That there is ancestral intervention in daily life is widely believed, and this helps to maintain the institution of ancestor veneration. It is thought that dead parents, as ancestors, will stimulate and promote the fertility of their children and the productivity of farmlands. Ancestral cults are therefore difficult to separate from fertility cults, and the mother-and-child icon serves both (*see* §1 above).

Several such images from the Cameroon Grassland kingdoms (*see* e.g. BAMILEKE AND RELATED PEOPLES) commemorate royal ancestors, who may occasionally be named; they are placed in ensembles of statuary, housed in kings' treasuries (see fig. 41). Royal ancestors and retainer figures are not themselves the focus of the ancestral cult. They are, however, honoured and attended as memorials to the wealth and dignity of the court and the strength of the dynasty. In addition, they are occasionally brought out as display pieces and backdrops for kingship rituals. Female figures in this genre represent a chief's favourite wives or his queen mother (who is in fact his sister), and they celebrate womanhood, fertility and maternity. Most, though not all, of these sculptures of women are dressed with ivory bracelets and anklets, which are male attributes of royal status. They embody the frequent coalescing of socio-political and spiritual meanings.

(iii) Religious context. Elsewhere mother-and-child images were, and still are, housed in shrines of tutelary deities responsible for general protection and well-being. Statuary is more common in such contexts and in diviners' shrines than it is in ancestral cults. Tutelary deities (e.g. Ala) are accorded broad positive and negative powers. In return for blood sacrifices they offer guidance and succour and they regulate human behaviour. Their images are generic, and they may be named after the deity or considered to be his or her children, messengers, servants or worshippers. Placed beside other shrine images, they refer especially to the protection, nurture and productivity expected of wives and mothers while also representing the mysterious power of woman as child-bearer and the critical role of wife and mother. Ensembles of family members are common in shrines as projections of idealized domestic life, for the gods in their realm, it is believed, lead lives parallel to those of real people.

Specialist practitioners of the Yoruba, Baule, Igbo, Senufo, Kongo and other peoples interact with spirits, ascertaining their desires through divining practices (*see* §VI, 7 below) and passing them on to the clients who consult them. The greatest variety of mother-and-child images is found in the shrines and workplaces of Yoruba diviners and doctors, where they often embellish bowls, tappers and divining trays. The complexity and the value of such iconography on these implements has been noted by H. J. Drewal (see 1977 exh. cat., p. 5): 'Images of women in ritual contexts and mother and child figures represent much more than symbols of fertility. They communicate sexual abstinence [of a nursing mother], inner cleanliness [because her menses are suppressed, and therefore], ritual purity, female force, and spirituality'. Many Yoruba maternities show the woman kneeling in a position of respect, devotion and even submission to the gods: an appropriate posture when it is recalled that most women in Yoruba sculpture represent worshippers, not the gods themselves.

Sculptures of mother-and-child groups embellish various types of shrines, where they serve as display pieces, as evidence of the spiritual and material success of the ritualist and as an advertisement for his or her expertise. Accomplished, and therefore wealthy, diviners and cult priests are more likely to have statuary than mediocre ones, so such images can, to some extent, be considered an index of wealth and prosperity, although this also suggests that the presence of sculpture in a shrine may have an arbitrary element.

Mother-and-child imagery is metaphorical and value-laden far beyond its limited biological reference. To see such imagery merely as a collection of fertility figures or specific mothers with their babies is to undervalue the richness of African thought. This prevalent, recurrent icon is an archetype: Great Mother as earth and water, childbirth and initiation as repetitions of cosmogony, the mother as symbol of a compound or village, her children its inhabitants, the genetrix as the source of social institutions. African thought and symbolism accord with those of the rest of the world in creating from this icon a universe far greater than the sum of its parts. Dynamic and regenerative, the mother-and-child symbol reflects the verities and complexities of African spiritual thought and the continuity of culture.

BIBLIOGRAPHY

D. Zahan: *The Religion, Spirituality and Thought of Traditional Africa* (Chicago and London, 1970)

R. Brain and A. Pollock: *Bangwa Funerary Sculpture*, A. & Soc. Ser. (London, 1971)

Traditional Art of the Nigerian Peoples: The Milton D. Ratner Family Collection (exh. cat. by H. J. Drewal, Washington, DC, N. Mus. Afr. A., 1977)

The Arts of Ghana (exh. cat. by H. M. Cole and D. H. Ross; Los Angeles, UCLA, Mus. Cult. Hist.; Minneapolis, MN, Walker A. Cent.; Dallas, TX, Mus. F.A.; 1977–8)

A. J. Glaze: *Art and Death in a Senufo Village*, Trad. A. Africa (Bloomington, 1981)

For Spirits and Kings: African Art from the Paul and Ruth Tishman Collection (exh. cat., ed. S. M. Vogel; New York, Met., 1981)

Icons: Ideals and Power in the Art of Africa (exh. cat. by H. M. Cole, Washington, DC, N. Mus. Afr. A., 1989)

6. ANIMAL IMAGERY. Images of animals are found in Africa wherever the visual arts exist. Animals are depicted in such contexts as rock art, shrines, masquerades, regalia and jewellery, body decoration (tattoo and scarification) and household settings, forming a major subset within the larger corpus of arts.

(i) Introduction. (ii) Types. (iii) Perceived functions.

(i) Introduction. In most sub-Saharan cultures, even today, people contend with both wild and domestic animals. These are hunted and herded, chased from fields and sacrificed in rituals, while their spirit counterparts are consulted in divination and evoked in song, story and dance. Men are believed to transform themselves into animals, and animal spirits are called upon or avoided because of their mystical powers. Animals killed ritually are divided, each meaningful part being given to a certain person or group according to time-honoured rules.

Animal behaviour is closely observed and well understood, but it is also mythic and imagined. Hence animals

41. Queen Nana and child, wood with ochre pigment, h. 1.01 m, by Mbeudjang, Batufam Kingdom, Bamileke, Cameroon, *c.* 1912 (Toronto, Murray and Barbara Frum Collection)

figure in many creation myths and arts not as they exist in the forest or plain but as proto-humans, indeed meta-humans, furnished with such specifically human traits as language.

They also appear as legendary heroes in proverbs and folktales, as spirits, ancestors and oracles, often with extraordinary powers. Beliefs about animals are possibly more important to an understanding of this imagery than are empirical facts, since animal images are seldom merely decorative but usually also convey metaphorical and symbolic meanings, even if they are naturalistically rendered in their own environment, as in rock art (*see* §VI, 15 below). Animal representation is therefore selective and depends on the purpose served by the art object and/or its messages.

(ii) Types. Although some animal imagery is cross-cultural, the variety of forms employed and the diversity of local significances mean that much interpretation is culture-specific. For example, while leopards and elephants are everywhere associated with leadership and authority, unrelated qualities may be locally ascribed to their representations. Thus an AKAN proverb—'rain will not wash the spots off a leopard'—associates the animal not with chiefs or authority but with the idea that people's essential nature is not easily changed.

Animal imagery includes representations of most of the important classes of animals. They fall into two basic groups: the arthropods (crustacea, insects, arachnids) and the vertebrates (fish, amphibians, reptiles, birds and mammals). Over a hundred identifiable species are found in the corpus of cast-brass goldweights of Akan peoples in Ghana and Côte d'Ivoire (*see* ASANTE AND RELATED PEOPLES). These entirely secular counterbalances of known weight, used in commercial transactions from the 16th century to the late 19th, include miniatures of most animals found in West African forest and savannah zones, supplemented by fanciful creatures.

Many of these creatures, including those fashioned in such other media as ceramics, wood-carving and textiles, are associated with Akan proverbs, folktales and aphorisms. It is notable that the owl and the cat are never seen as goldweights, the former because it is a bird of ill omen, the latter because the word for cat, *okra*, is also the word for soul. In contrast, the rarity of goldweights fashioned into spiders, which are otherwise common in Akan arts and folklore, may be more practical, caused by the difficulty of casting such delicate creatures. Akan goldweights, gold-leaf linguist staffs and Asante cast-gold sword ornaments bear animal motifs the meanings of which are logical to us as well as to their makers and users (see fig. 42): the spider is seen as clever, the hen represents a mother or a chief, the porcupine is a warrior, the goat stupid, the chameleon changeable and the crocodile dangerous.

In addition to such universal symbols, a number of Akan objects bear single or multiple animal imagery with associations that are more arbitrary, involved and cryptic to outsiders. For example, if an object bore images of a monkey, an anthill and an antelope, a correct interpretation would depend upon knowledge of a proverb that refers to wishful thinking: when the monkey rubs an anthill, it does not become an antelope (see 1977–8 exh. cat., p. 152). Sword ornaments showing a viper catching a hornbill refer to patience, a meaning understood only in the light of a

42. Fante linguists with staffs surmounted by images of a leopard (right) and perhaps a porcupine (centre), Enyan Abassa, Ghana; from a photograph by Herbert M. Cole, 1975

folktale about a debt, a drought and the viper's long wait at the world's last waterhole, where the debtor hornbill had to come to drink (see 1977–8 exh. cat., p. 16).

Such examples are selected from thousands. It should be remembered that, within and across ethnic groups, variations of meaning arise out of local interpretations that are repeated and then harden into convention. In addition, of course, both the images used and their meanings are subject to temporal change. A further level of complication is introduced by the range of images produced, from highly schematic, compressed symbols to more elaborate representational images.

(iii) Perceived functions. Leaders throughout Africa have long used animal imagery to consolidate, symbolize and broadcast their powers. In the kingdom of Benin (*see* BENIN), for example, the divine king, court and chiefs have used brass, ivory and some wooden animal sculptures for about 500 years to express values, contrasts and hierarchies seen as parallel in human and natural realms. As P. Ben-Amos puts it (1976, p. 244): 'The ontological distinction between human and animal is expressed symbolically in art, myth, and ritual in the contrast between their respective spheres of activity—the home (the social world of the village) versus the bush (the wild forest areas)'. Within each sphere, relationships are hierarchical and orderly: the king dominates home and bush, day and night, as the leopard, elephant, crocodile and eagle dominate their species and habitats. The more accessible, docile or domestic animals—cow, mudfish, fowl, goat, ram—are associated with home and commoners and may be freely sacrificed, while only the king may sacrifice his mythological and metaphorical counterpart, the leopard, a frequent symbol of royal strength. Images of animals abound in Benin as free-standing brass shrine sculpture, on high-relief plaques used as architectural decoration and on such ritual implements as diviners' staffs. Depictions on the latter include animals considered dangerous and liminal—snakes, chameleon, frogs and the night heron—because they violate boundaries and order. Their magical powers come from the bush, and they, or their unseen spirits, are invoked firstly by leaders to help them govern, secondly by diviners to read omens, heal, and fight witches and thirdly by witches themselves to hurt or kill.

Leopard, buffalo, elephant and eagle sculptures are common in the kingdoms of West Africa (Akan, FON, Yoruba, Cameroon Grassfields) and in other less famous chiefdoms (see 1992 exh. cat.). Such emblems occur frequently in regalia and are supplemented by such tangible parts of the animals as skins, horns, tusks and feathers. Depictions of these animals and their parts relate to leadership in many cultures. Also, although less frequently, the lion, shark, python, crocodile, pangolin, scorpion and other creatures serve as leadership and power symbols. Given that leaders are overwhelmingly the major patrons of African artists, it is not surprising that much animal imagery, directly or indirectly, refers to leaders' putative qualities.

A general distinction can be made between the uses of animal symbols by paramount leaders in large, hierarchical polities and the animal imagery seen among more egalitarian societies. In the former, many of the animals are emblematic, conveying fairly simple political messages to the people. In smaller-scale cultures, on the other hand, animal imagery has stronger spiritual orientations and concerns itself with the complexities of social relationships in daily life, with fertility, the food supply and threats to the socio-spiritual order. Animal emblems in Fon or Akan kingdoms refer mostly to the varied powers of different kings, while for the BAMANA and SENUFO animal motifs are constellations of spirit forces, many from the bush (savannah or forest) rather than the village.

The physical, mystical and metaphorical powers of animals are especially evident in masquerades (*see* §VI, 3 below). In general, masquerades are more important in non-hierarchical societies than they are in large, centralized kingdoms, although there are exceptions to this tendency (e.g. the Yoruba and Cameroon kingdoms). Masks act as embodiments of unseen spiritual forces and are used to initiate, instruct, regulate and entertain. All masking cultures have animal masks that use dance and music, mime, free interpretation and even satire to amplify the character of the animal spirits: antelopes are majestically acrobatic, goats are lewd and stupid, buffaloes are marauding bullies. The danced character sometimes alludes only to the animal, but more often it also refers to human traits, for it is playing in an arena of belief and social force that it seeks to emulate, mock, idealize or otherwise influence.

Although masks may refer to single animals, artists often interpret these creatures freely, using a kind of structural shorthand. This stylized, symbolic nature is exemplified by the elephant masks danced by Bamileke (Cameroon) and Kuba peoples (Zaïre). Bamileke examples are made of beaded appliqué over cloth, the trunk is a long rectangular panel, and the ears are large circular discs (*see* fig. 43; *see also* BAMILEKE AND RELATED PEOPLES). These are worn with sumptuous royal cloths by noble, wealthy members of Elephant societies. They are deputized by kings, and in former times the maskers had powerful regulatory and executive roles. Mukyeem masks, used by leaders among Kuba-related peoples (*see* KUBA (iii)), are humanoid helmets made of such prestigious materials as leopard-skin, with a schematic bead and

43. Elephant masks worn by Kuosi society members, Bandjoun, Cameroon; from a photograph by Father Christol, 1930

cowrie-covered elephant trunk springing from the crown of the head. In both instances rich costume materials and abbreviated elephant references project the wealth, dignity, grandeur and authority of chiefs.

Composite animal masks are common in West Africa, if less prevalent than those referring to specific species. Several cultures (Baga, Toma, Senufo, Baule, Bamana, Bobo and others) have variations on horizontally or diagonally worn three-part (horns, head, snout) masks, which are often a metre or more in length. Because both the artistic structure and the symbolism of such masks are similar, they may all have developed from a single form. Various aspects of crocodile, antelope, buffalo and wart-hog are imaginatively combined in these composite masks, often with human eyes and noses and sometimes with added eagle feathers and porcupine quills. Most represent aggressive bush spirits, who operate as messengers and mediators in a zone between the gods and mankind, between wild nature and ordered civilization. These bristling, ferocious, magic-laden power-images, often considered ugly and dangerous, are invoked for social benefit by elders and others in authority and are danced in rituals to combat witchcraft, disease and other forms of evil and disorder.

Numerous animal images decorate the instruments used by diviners and other ritual specialists. Acting as mediators, oracles and doctors, they tap the esoteric, charged realms of nature and its sources of spiritual energy and arcane knowledge and bring their wisdom to the service of mankind. Pythons, turtles, chameleons and certain birds serve these specialists and figure in their shrines and equipment because their zone-crossing (i.e. land to water) qualities and their consequent intermediary existence suit the role of messenger between the spirit and human realms. Senufo diviners use images of pythons in mud reliefs, as portable props in shrines and in amuletic jewellery worn by ritual specialists and some of their clients. Small brass castings of simplified python, chameleon, tortoise, lizard, mudfish and other animal motifs are worn as protective and redemptive charms by Senufo, Lobi and other peoples. These symbols of zoomorphic spirits, often mentioned in creation myths, are accorded a variety of special traits. Common among them is their ability to transform themselves into human beings and to cause and cure physical and mental disorders. The mysteries and energies of the animal kingdom are repeatedly brought to bear in the uncertain realm of human affairs in man's ceaseless effort to rebalance the cosmos and maintain health in the specific human body and in the body politic.

BIBLIOGRAPHY

F. Willett: *Ife in the History of West African Sculpture* (London and New York, 1967)

D. P. Biebuyck: *Lega Culture: Art, Initiation, and Moral Philosophy among a Central African People* (Berkeley, 1973)

P. Ben-Amos: 'Men and Animals in Benin Art', *Man*, n. s., ii/2 (1976), pp. 243–52

D. H. Ross: 'The Iconography of Asante Sword Ornaments', *Afr. A.*, x/1 (1977), pp. 16–25, 90
The Arts of Ghana (exh. cat. by H. M. Cole and D. H. Ross, Los Angeles, CA, UCLA, Wight A.G.; Minneapolis, MN, Walker A. Cent.; Dallas, TX, Mus. F.A.; 1977–8)
P. Ben-Amos: *The Art of Benin*, Tribal A. (London, 1980)
B. de Grunne: *Terres cuites anciennes de l'ouest africain*, Pubns Hist. A. & Archéol. U. Cath. Louvain, xxii (Leuven, 1980)
A. J. Glaze: *Art and Death in a Senufo Village* (Bloomington, 1981)
J. Mack: 'Animal Representations in Kuba Art: An Anthropological Interpretation of Sculpture', *Oxford A.J.*, iv/2 (1981), pp. 5–56
Elephant: The Animal and its Ivory in African Culture (exh. cat., ed. D. H. Ross; Los Angeles, UCLA, Mus. Cult. Hist., 1992)

7. EQUESTRIAN IMAGERY. Ownership of a horse in tropical Africa indicates affluence. The wealth, elevation and speed represented by the rider and his mount derive not only from the power and swiftness of a warrior on horseback but also from the symbolic power of a leader or spirit personage. Riders are literally and figuratively superior beings, higher than their animal mounts and dominant over the common people. Such dominance is more important than mobility alone, and African equestrian sculpture thus expresses ideology and belief more than it depicts daily life. The identity of the rider depicted in sculptures varies. In many cases he may be a spirit, a deity or a legendary ancestor. Some are actual ancestors, while others are feared and respected alien leaders from the 'north', whence horses originally came. Rider sculptures may also commemorate élite hunters, warriors and chiefs. Equestrians appear on rulers' staffs and sceptres and on a number of YORUBA and SENUFO doors that were the property of kings and chiefs and symbolized their prestige, wealth and patronage. Most, however, were housed in shrines, where they reflected the powers and leadership traits attributed to spirits and deities, not to mention the authoritative positions of patron priests and priestesses. Sometimes shrine sculptures represented deities, but just as often they depicted worshippers.

The materials, styles and forms of these works vary considerably. The most common sculptural medium is wood, followed by bronze, then wrought iron, terracotta and unfired clay. In such exceptional cases as the large bronze castings from Benin (e.g. London, BM), both rider and beast are rendered in naturalistic detail. Simplification and generalization, however, are more usual, especially in the representation of the animal. Indeed these images were frequently conceived as metaphors; horses may thus look more like crocodiles or dogs or unidentifiable quadrupeds with tails and elongated heads. The fact that horse and rider symbolize spirits may help to account for their non-specific character. Other renderings often appear schematic and highly distorted anatomically. The rider is frequently rendered on a larger scale, overwhelming the animal and manifesting what may be called ideological scale, since the human is more significant than the beast.

Among the earliest equestrian sculptures are large ceramic images from Djenné and other sites in the inland delta of the Niger River, dating perhaps to AD 1000. Although these have little firm cultural data accompanying them, it is probable that their riders were prominent leaders. Such peoples of the Western Sudan as the BAMANA, DOGON and Senufo and the Yoruba of Nigeria were Africa's most prolific producers of equestrian statuary. In the areas occupied by these peoples horses were able to survive, whereas in most forested regions they fell prey to diseases borne by the tsetse fly. Despite the hostile environment, however, some leaders of forest peoples imported horses to ride in occasional ceremonies for heightened prestige, for example the Oba of Benin, divine king of the EDO people of southern Nigeria.

Mythology and the legendary ancestors that populate their creation stories 'explain' equestrian imagery among the Dogon, the Bamana and the nearby Senufo of Mali and Burkina Faso. Dogon equestrians in the form of small, cast-brass finger-rings, as well as larger wooden images of horsemen, probably depict the mythic, primordial *hogon*, called Lebe, whose priestly, human counterpart is a ritual and temporal leader of great importance. Probably employed as display pieces in shrines, these equestrian images have a wealth of associations set forth in myth, including fertility and the origin of death, as well as referring to wealth, chiefship and leadership in warfare. Bamana art from Mali includes numerous wrought-iron shrine sculptures of equestrians (e.g. New York, Met.; Paris, Mus. N.A. Afr. & Océan.), which were manufactured by the powerful blacksmith group who act as prominent priests, educators, diviners and doctors and thus hold critical leadership positions. Iron horsemen represent the smiths and their mythical forebears in their roles as ritual specialists responsible for harnessing and directing spiritual energy for the benefit of society.

In common with other African peoples, the Senufo associate horses with leadership, wealth, status, hunting and militarism. Riders sculpted by Senufo artists are often armed with spears or hold guns at the ready. They represent the multi-dimensional powers of forest or bush spirits (see fig. 44). In equestrian statuary a bush spirit is appropriately shown as a forceful, well-armed leader, since these spirits are capricious, fast-travelling, nocturnal, mysterious and aggressive. Senufo equestrian figures are executed in many sizes, using wood, brass and sometimes iron, and they appear on the clay façades of shrines and carved in relief on doors and locks. Such figures are optional display pieces in a diviner's or priest's shrine, where, like much display sculpture in African shrines, they connote luxury, good taste and prestige (see Glaze, p. 72). Although the equestrian theme is not found in all leadership contexts, wherever the rider occurs the power of leadership is being evoked.

Yoruba equestrians provide the most varied and numerous examples of the rider theme. The forms they take are diverse—small, schematic renderings, sculptures elaborated far beyond observable realities, monumental figures—and they appear as shrine statuary, mask superstructures, divination objects and house-posts and doors for palaces and shrines. Although meanings vary, the power of leaders, whether divine or temporal, is always implicit. Updated versions of the theme, for example cyclists, are also found, especially on doors. Equestrian figures are favoured subjects in the large Yoruba Epa and Elefon helmet masks that are danced in the Ekiti region. The rider here is often identified as the culture hero and warrior Jagunjagun and is depicted as a chief equipped for battle, sometimes with retainers at his side, ideologically scaled down. Ironically perhaps, these massive headdresses

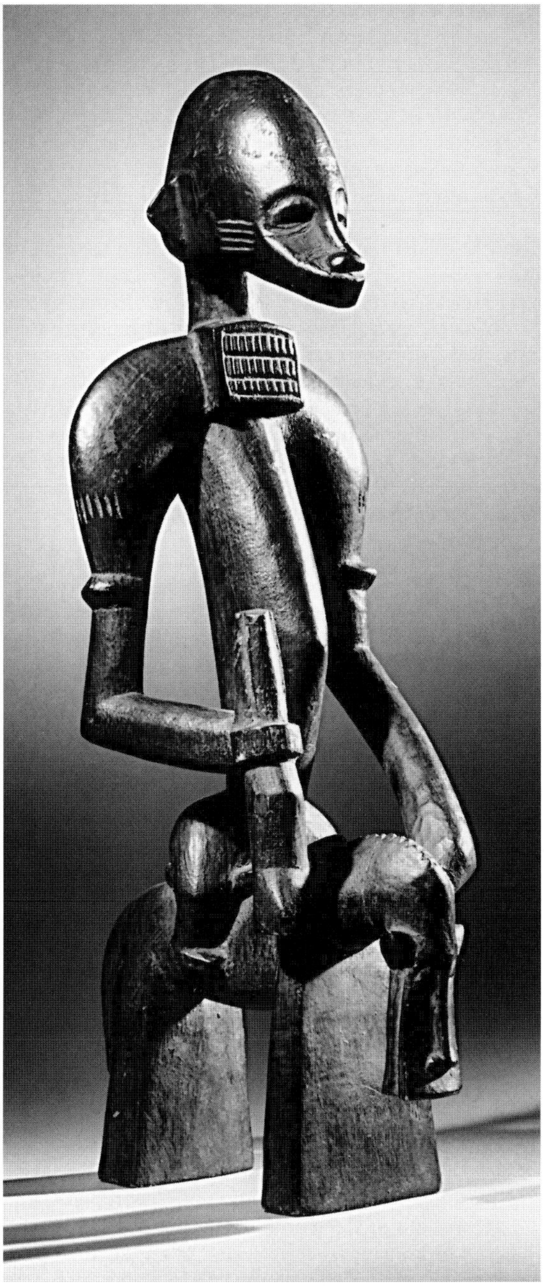

44. Senufo equestrian figure representing a bush spirit, wood, h. 320 mm, from Côte d'Ivoire or Mali, 19th–20th centuries (London, British Museum)

themselves 'ride' on the heads of agile young men as they dance a masquerade that, as one of its meanings, identifies them as bearers of their culture, extolling heroes and upholding, as it were, its ancient values. Equestrian figures also support Yoruba divination bowls, which themselves support and contain the sacred palm kernels used by diviners. Such diviners' bowls are understood to be temples of Orunmila (see Fagg and Pemberton, p. 64), and the equestrian theme implies the elevated status of this crucial god of divination, who imparts balance, control and order to a world beset by chaos and mystery. As the divination bowl supports the diviner's implements, so equestrian house-posts in the palaces of Yoruba kings support the edifice of kingship: ancestral heroes uphold the powers and privileges of divine rulers, who are thereby elevated and idealized in the eyes of their people.

Socio-spiritual aggrandizement and propaganda are no doubt factors among the Yoruba and others in the production of equestrian figures. Yet much more is involved, reaching deeply into the values and psychology of the people. The exercise of power by leaders and the response of those led are complex and critical factors in African life: equestrian statuary has had important, multi-dimensional roles in projecting and reinforcing these values.

BIBLIOGRAPHY

African Art in Motion: Icon and Act (exh. cat. by R. F. Thompson; Washington, DC, N.G.A.; Los Angeles, UCLA, Wight A.G.; 1974)

Iron Art of the Blacksmith in the Western Sudan (exh. cat., ed. P. R. McNaughton; West Lafayette, IN, Purdue U., 1975)

A. J. Glaze: *Art and Death in a Senufo Village*, Trad. A. Africa (Bloomington, 1981)

W. Fagg and J. Pemberton III: *Yoruba Sculpture of West Africa* (New York, 1982)

Icons, Ideals and Power in the Art of Africa (exh. cat. by H. M. Cole, Washington, DC, N. Mus. Afr. A., 1989)

HERBERT M. COLE

8. TRICKSTERS. In Africa tricksters figure prominently, not only in oral narrative and in such visual representations as those of the Yoruba deity Eshu/Elegba but also in philosophic and aesthetic concepts expressed through iconographic and morphological elements.

(i) Concepts. (ii) Eshu/Elegba complex.

(i) Concepts. A character in universal folklore, the trickster personifies apparent disorder. He is the enemy of fixed hierarchies and boundaries, ordered social and sexual roles and categorical separations. In psychological terms, he is the undifferentiated energy of the unconscious. In whatever form and medium he is made manifest, the trickster expands the terms of discourse by introducing what is selfishly desired within the fixed boundaries of what is socially permitted (see Kerenyi, p. 185). In African folklore and mythology, the trickster is realized diversely in trickster deities, in such characters as *enfants terribles* and, most elementally and pervasively, in tales about such morphologically ambiguous animals as Ananse the spider of the Akan, Hlakanyana the mongoose of the Southern Nguni, the mantis of the Khoisan, the hare of the Wolof and the Kagura or the tortoise of the Guinea Coast. The list could be extended to all African groups, since trickster tales are quantitatively the most numerous in African oral narrative traditions. Nevertheless, physical representations of these animal tricksters are surprisingly scarce: the Tiv of central Nigeria fabricate a copy of the hare trickster for their Kwagh Hir puppet tradition, the Nupe of the lower Niger valley of Nigeria create aluminium tortoises for the tourist markets, and wax printed cloths throughout West Africa are now adorned with images of the spider. Contemporary versions of the animal trickster are likely to be borrowed from universal mass-media imagery, which has spread depictions of Mickey Mouse and Donald Duck almost

45. Mende Gonde and Suwi masks, wood and raffia, 305×203 mm, from Sewa Mende area, Sierra Leone, before 1970 (New York, private collection)

everywhere, from the walls of ice-cream shops in Mogadishu, Somalia, to commemorative stamps in Sierra Leone.

Implicit in the dualistic concept of order and disorder that generates the trickster character is the 'principle of opposition', which operates at the core of many African cultures. The animal trickster is most representative of this principle in oral tradition, but African artists have also expressed the principle in diverse material forms. Thus in their construction of Eyima, the FANG of Gabon incorporate into wooden ancestral figures such infantile features as large head and torso, disproportionately small legs, a protruding stomach and a ruptured umbilicus. These contradictory qualities of infantile physical features in an ancestral figure give the Eyima a vitality it would not have if it were simply a figure of an aged person or an infant (see Fernandez, pp. 365–6). In African mythology, the same disproportion between the physical and the spiritual is realized in such diminutive or crippled heroes as Mwindo of the Nyanga of Zaïre and Sundiata of the Mande. Like the Eyima and all trickster figures, these epic heroes achieve power by disregarding the categorical separation between youthful energy and the cunning of age.

The TABWA of Zaïre and northern Zambia use a generic term (*mulalambo*) to express this principle of opposition, which they perceive in all phenomena, from the Milky Way's division of the sky to the fine line (*linea nigra*) that splits the human belly from navel to genitals. Tabwa artists give physical expression to this dualistic principle in the two-faced figures they carve on staffs, whisks, headrests and medicine containers (see Roberts, p. 31). Defying categorical separation by incorporating double-faced motifs, these diverse objects are used ritually to effect transitions from one state to another, and such expressions of transition as gates, doorways and the advent of a new year are the special province of the African trickster.

Since tricksters respect no boundaries or social conventions, their spirit is manifested in satiric and derisive images. The MENDE of Sierra Leone and Liberia mock the Suwi masker, their most sacred image of female beauty, by sometimes making her dance with Gonde, a grotesque parody often constructed from a discarded Suwi mask embellished with junk (Cosentino; see fig. 45). For similarly satirical reasons, the Egungun cult of ancestral power and entertainment among the YORUBA of south-western Nigeria brings out a mask called Big Nose. In sunlight its eyes become opaque, its mouth a lipless gash over stumps of teeth. All organic detail is obliterated down to the bone structure. Yoruba audiences laugh at this misshapen horror, and thus Big Nose satirizes the pompous and vain, mirroring their spiritual distortions with physical ones (see Thompson, 1971, p. 379). Both of these 'anti-masquerade' figures highlight the artificiality of categorical divisions, the trickster's special target.

(ii) Eshu/Elegba complex. Yoruba culture provides the most complete realization of the trickster in African art. In folktales, the Yoruba celebrate the misadventures of the tortoise Ijapa (or Obarun), whose motif analogues may be found throughout Congo–Kordofonian oral narrative traditions. But the Yoruba go on to attribute cosmic dimensions to the trickster. In a complex of myths, festival performance and ritual art, they celebrate the apotheosis of the trickster deity, who is known as either Eshu or Elegba, interchangeably. The trickster traits already described—animal cunning, the contrarieties of Gonde or Eyima, the perversity of Big Nose, the liminality of the Tabwa double-faced figure—all reach full development in Eshu/Elegba. His cult has spread from its Nigerian homeland westward to the Fon kingdom of Dahomey, to the Ewe of Togo and Ghana and across the Atlantic to the diaspora African American communities in Cuba, Brazil and Haiti (*see* §VIII below).

In Yorubaland, Eshu takes his place within a vast pantheon; many of these deities are grouped into a dozen or so cults for which the profusion of Yoruba ritual art has been created. Eshu's place within these cults varies. Worshippers of the hot/hard gods (Ogun of iron, Shango of lightning, Shapona of smallpox) say Eshu is their brother and is vain, handsome and sexually prolific. Icons of him, in mud or terracotta, are sometimes included in Shango's shrines. In Oshogbo, centre of the cult to Oshun, the cool mother of terrestrial waters, Oshun herself is held to be Eshu's wife and possessed of his cunning. For devotees of the Funfun cult, who worship the beneficent 'white gods', Eshu is totally evil and very ugly, with no wife and children, while to Muslims and Christians Eshu is simply Satan, the devil. The mythological Eshu is consistent with these contradictory interpretations: one myth tells of him wearing a two-sided hat so that farmers who were the best of friends would quarrel over his appearance and cause dissension in the world. Another myth tells how he enticed the sun and moon to change places, thereby reversing the primal order of things (see Wescott, p. 340). Despite their other cult affiliations, all Yoruba recognize Eshu and respect his control of the market-place and the crossroads. They also generally recognize him as an instigator who tricks men into offending each other and the gods (*orisha*). At the same time, however, Eshu is the mediating force who makes men turn to the gods in both expiation and propitiation and without whom they would starve for lack of sacrifice. His double role of instigator and mediator commands Eshu's presence wherever there is trouble or a state of transition.

Originally, Eshu may have been worshipped using 'stones of atonement', which commemorate a myth about the origin of his eyes (see Thompson, 1983, p. 21). However, more common Eshu representations are laterite pillars or mounds of mud called *yangi*. These are 0.3–1.2 m tall and are found at crossroads and in market-places and shrines. Daily offerings of palm oil are made on behalf of the town by cult officials. Smaller chunks of laterite (diam. 250–300 mm) protrude from the right side of passageways at the entrance of domestic compounds and serve as entrance shrines (see Pemberton, p. 20). According to myth, all *yangi* are part of Eshu's mystical body.

Eshu is also worshipped in household shrines. In some compounds a large chamber is reserved for him; this contains a raised altar, elaborately decorated with pieces of broken pottery inset in a blackened mud base. Other shrine rooms might contain sacred calabashes, painted with three black concentric circles (*igba eshu*), which are placed on large, open-mouthed terracotta pots (*ikoko*). These are framed by ritual cloth, wands and vestments, just as a dossal frames the cross on a Christian altar (Pemberton, p. 22).

The representations of Eshu most familiar to scholars are wood sculptures, although these are regarded by cult members as less ancient and less essential than the *yangi*. Such carvings may be divided into three categories: paired male and female supplicant figures united by cowrie strands; figural dance hooks that rest on the shoulders of ritual performers; and large votive images for decorating shrines and gates.

The sculptures are invariably painted black and are decorated with cowrie-shell dresses that may contain combs, pieces of calabash, spoons, knives and strings of coins. Some hold whistles, flutes, clubs, pipes or calabashes in their hands, while others suck their thumb. The most distinctive feature shared by these sculptures is a long, curved headdress, which may be overtly or suggestively phallic (see fig. 46). The priests of Eshu sometimes wear their hair in this manner, as do the possession priests of the lightning god, Shango. The figures are worn over the shoulder of a male worshipper, or a pair may be worn, one over each shoulder. When not in use, they are put back in the shrine. Female worshippers normally hang the images over their breasts or wear wrist sculptures of Eshu. The latter have a small head and limbless torso but retain the characteristic headdress and cowries; repeated arrowhead motifs may be used, possibly to represent stylized phalluses (see Wescott, p. 339). There are also more elaborate representations, some on horseback or wearing the two-coloured hat of dissension, which are used to decorate house and palace roof-posts and are also carved in low relief on doors.

46. Yoruba figure of Eshu/Elegba, wood with fluted coiffure and leather collar with cowrie shells, h. 395 mm, before 1960 (Los Angeles, CA, University of California, Fowler Museum of Cultural History)

Scholars concur on the symbolic significance of cowrie costumes that connect the Eshu of the market-place to this ancient form of currency (*see* §VI, 10 below). They also associate the knife and club with aggression, the comb and mirror with vanity, and the pipe and whistle with offensive, assertive behaviour or, like the thumb-sucking and the long-tailed phallic headdress, with libidinous behaviour. The precise nature of Eshu's sexuality, however, is debated. J. Wescott argues that the pubic apron Eshu usually wears indicates that his concern is with erotic energy, not procreation. J. Pemberton (p. 68) argues, from the iconography of a very old drum depicting Eshu with a snake above his head and juxtaposed (*inter alia*) with two couples copulating, that he gains vitality from sexual oppositions and from his mediating power, which overcomes such oppositions.

One of the oldest known pieces of Yoruba wood sculpture, the Ifa divination tray (Ulm, Ulm. Mus.), carved before 1659, includes images of Eshu with tailed headdress sucking his thumb and one of him smoking a pipe (see Thompson, 1983, p. 32). The association of Eshu with Ifa divination is of supreme philosophic importance to the Yoruba: the god Ifa is the master of the world's order, while Eshu is the personification of its chance. The Yoruba say, with profound simplicity, that Eshu and Ifa eat together. Eshu's bowl must be present at each divination, and a part of every sacrifice commanded by Ifa must be offered to Eshu, hence the spoon that adorns his statues. This is the greatest source of Eshu's power (*ashe*), for sacrifice is at the heart of Yoruba religious life and Eshu is at the heart of sacrifice.

The mythology of Eshu/Elegba was borrowed by the FON of Dahomey (now Benin Republic). They transformed him into their deity (*vodun*) Legba, maintaining his relationship with divination, while increasing his procreative sexuality and his intimacy with their highest god (Mawu) and reinventing his iconography. Travelling through Dahomey at the end of the 19th century, Sir Richard Burton observed (see Herskovits, p. 222):

> Legba himself is a horrid spectacle. A mass of red clay is roughly moulded by the clumsy, barbarous artist into an imitation man, who is evidently like Jupiter, 'a devil of a god for following the girls'. The figure is at squat, crouched, as it were, before its own attributes, with arms longer than a gorilla's, huge feet, and no legs to speak of. The head is of mud or wood, rising canonically to an almost pointed poll; a dab of clay represents the nose; the mouth is a gash from ear to ear, and the eyes and teeth are of cowries, or painted ghastly white.

These mud-sculpture representations of Legba spread further west to the Ewe, where they still decorate town gateways (see Gilbert), and also, via the forced migrations of the slave trade, to Cuba and Brazil, where local artists continue to create clay forms of the deity and to honour him in ritual services (see Thompson, 1983, pp. 18–33). In Haiti, Papa Legba is the first of the deities (*loa*) to be invoked at *vodun* services, at which his devotees remember his authority over crossroads by imploring him to 'open the barriers' for the other spirits from 'Guinee' (Africa).

Eshu/Elegba, Lord of Unpredictability, is the most manifold and generative personification of the trickster, conceived in a continent that has devoted much of its mythology, religion and art to the expression of this shadowy aspect of the human condition.

BIBLIOGRAPHY

L. Frobenius: *Und Afrika sprach* (Berlin, 1912; Eng. trans. in 2 vols, London and New York, 1913)
M. K. Herskovits: *Dahomey: An Ancient West African Kingdom*, ii (New York, 1938/*R* Evanston, IL, 1967)
J. Wescott: 'The Sculpture of Eshu-Elegba', *Africa*, xxxii/4 (1962), pp. 336–53
J. W. Fernandez: 'Principles of Opposition and Vitality in Fang Aesthetics', *J. Aesth. & A. Crit.*, xxv/1 (1966), pp. 53–64; repr. in *Art and Aesthetics in Primitive Societies: A Critical Anthology*, ed. C. F. Jopling (New York, 1971), pp. 356–73
R. F. Thompson: 'Aesthetics in Traditional Africa', *ARTnews*, lxvi/9 (1968), pp. 44–5, 63–6; repr. in *Art and Aesthetics in Primitive Societies: A Critical Anthology*, ed. C. F. Jopling (New York, 1971), pp. 374–81
K. Kerenyi: 'The Trickster in Relation to Greek Mythology', *The Trickster*, ed. P. Radin (New York, 1969), pp. 173–91
J. Pemberton III: 'Eshu-Elegba: The Yoruba Trickster God', *Afr. A.*, ix/1 (1975), pp. 20–27, 66–70, 90–92
R. D. Pelton: *The Trickster in West Africa* (Berkeley, 1980)
D. Cosentino: *Defiant Maids and Stubborn Farmers* (Cambridge, 1982)
M. V. Gilbert: 'Mystical Protection among the Anlo Ewe', *Afr. A.*, xv/4 (1982), pp. 60–66, 90
R. F. Thompson: *Flash of the Spirit: African and Afro-American Art and Philosophy* (New York, 1983)
A. F. Roberts: 'Duality in Tabwa Art', *Afr. A.*, xix/4 (1986), pp. 26–35, 86–7, 91–2

DONALD J. COSENTINO

V. Materials and techniques.

1. Earth. 2. Metal. 3. Paint. 4. Wood. 5. Stone. 6. Ivory. 7. Fibre. 8. Beads. 9. Leather. 10. Mixed media. 11. Gourds.

1. EARTH. In its raw state as soil, earth is the basic component of mud and ceramics, two of the commonest materials in African art and architecture, as well as being an ingredient in the manufacture of bricks and paints. Earth is both the simplest of materials and the most malleable. Its uses range from the simple smeared designs of some traditions of body decoration to complex sculptural and architectural forms.

(i) Mud. Depending on the amount of water present mud can be a liquid, paste or solid. Technically mud is a very wet soil or clay, forming a sub-aqueous sediment, with a particle size of not less than 0.004 mm. Any mineral substance can be made into mud with sufficient liquid, and the liquid is the medium by which the substance is applied. While the term 'mud' is used here, it should be noted that some scholars have preferred the term earth, since 'mud' is said to have pejorative connotations (e.g. see Cranstone). With clay and water mud can be fashioned into almost any shape or form. It can be used to make sculptures and items of personal adornment, to make dwellings or to decorate buildings.

There is no reliable method for dating works in mud. Some African buildings of mud and mud brick, however, notably the mud mosques of the Western Sudan, are possibly 1000 years old, and the technique of building with mud is probably much older. Sculpting in mud is also probably ancient in Africa; it is certainly widespread. Building in mud is practised over a more limited area, as it is impractical in areas of heavy rainfall.

Mud is an efficient insulator against the heat of the sun and can thus significantly reduce indoor temperatures during the summer months. This makes it a highly suitable building material for houses and compounds. Another advantage of using mud for dwellings is that it is not a permanent form, and buildings made out of it can be easily adapted to fit the changing requirements of the inhabitants (see Tobert, 1989). Mud buildings are also themselves used as a medium for art, the mud providing a kind of canvas. Painting of mud walls is done in many parts of Africa. Among the NDEBELE of Southern Africa women paint the exterior walls of their dwellings with bold, highly coloured designs. Ornate mud reliefs are also found, for example, on the royal palaces of Abomey and Benin and on the palaces and houses of the Hausa. Among the Gurens of north-eastern Ghana women use coloured mud to decorate the walls of their houses with figurative and geometrical designs, and some walls are so well burnished they shine. Mud walls of royal houses in Kano, Nigeria, are inset with small pieces of mica that glint in the light, while in southern Nigeria cowrie shells may be inset into the mud walls of Igbo houses.

While building in mud has received a lot of scholarly attention, its use within a dwelling has been sadly neglected. Mud can be used in many functional and yet artistic ways, for example to make a hearth, a pot stand or a granary. Among the Zaghawa of Northern Darfur, Sudan, mud has been used in the construction of beds and to construct modesty walls that protect the interior of a dwelling from view. Such walls, built for the houses of brides, are often decorated with raised and coloured patterns (see Tobert, 1989).

Mud has also been used as a paint and in body arts. Paintings in rock shelters in Southern Africa were produced using earth colours mixed to a paste and may have been applied with brushes made of animal hair attached to a stick (see Woodhouse). In some parts of Africa, mud is believed to have curative properties and may be applied to the body. In Zaïre, widows mourning the death of their husbands covered their bodies in a white clay (see Cannizzo). Among the Ndebele of Southern Africa young men paint their bodies with white clay during the three-month seclusion of their initiation rites. Among the Hamar of southern Ethiopia and other pastoral peoples of eastern Africa men construct elaborate coiffures out of clay smoothed over the head (see Ebin, pp. 74–9). Among the Bamana of Mali solutions of mud are applied with a bamboo stick to make designs on cotton textiles, known as *bogolanfini* or 'mud cloth' (see Imperato and Shamir; *see* MALI, fig. 1).

BIBLIOGRAPHY

H. C. Woodhouse: 'Rock Paintings of Southern Africa', *Afr. A.*, ii/3 (1969), pp. 44–9
P. J. Imperato and M. Shamir: 'Bokolanfini: Mud Cloth of the Bamana of Mali', *Afr. A.*, iii/4 (1970), pp. 32–41, 80
F. T. Smith: 'Gurensi Wall Painting', *Afr. A.*, xi/4 (1978), pp. 36–41
V. Ebin: *The Body Decorated*, Tribal A. (London, 1979)
N. Tobert: *The Ethnoarchaeology of the Zaghawa of Darfur (Sudan): Settlement and Transience*, Brit. Archaeol. Rep., 445/Cambridge Monographs in African Archaeology, 30 (Cambridge, 1988)
J. Cannizzo: *Into the Heart of Africa* (Toronto, 1989)
N. Tobert: 'Domestic Architecture and the Occupant's Life Cycle', *Traditional Dwellings & Settlements Rev.*, i/1 (1989), pp. 18–37
B. A. L. Cranstone: 'Earth as a Building Material', *J. Mus. Ethnog.*, 2 (1991), pp. 3–14

NATALIE TOBERT

(ii) Ceramics. Fired clay objects have been called variously, and with generally little scientific distinction, ceramics, pottery, earthenware and terracotta. 'Ceramics' is the umbrella term, with 'terracotta' frequently used to distinguish figurative ceramic sculpture from ceramic vessels and what is taken to be 'art' from 'craft'. Generally it is women who produce African ceramics, although it is often men who are responsible for figurative sculpture. Ceramics are among the earliest and most ubiquitous forms of art produced in Africa. Archaeological evidence indicates that Africans have been making pottery and sculptures of fired clay since Neolithic times. Although the evidence is fragmentary, it appears that domestic pottery was introduced into northern Africa shortly after its discovery in the Levant in the 6th millennium BC. Objects made of fired clay from sites in the Sahara Desert have been dated to the 8th millennium BC, a fact that might indicate independent invention of pottery in Africa. Pottery was produced in the area that is now Kenya as early as the Upper Paleolithic and was probably being produced throughout the continent by the 2nd millennium BC. Controlled excavations in Ghana and Mali have indicated dates in the 1st and 2nd millennia BC for terracotta sculptures, while radiocarbon dating of the Nok finds in northern Nigeria shows that the terracottas are from the early 1st millennium BC, and there is evidence that indicates a date of the mid-1st millennium AD for terracottas in Southern Africa. Despite the availability of mass-produced metal containers in Africa in the late 20th century, the production of ceramics has persisted, often quite vigorously.

(a) Manufacture. The clays used for making pottery in Africa vary from region to region but are generally coarse, and crushed potsherds are often mixed into the clay. The resulting material fires very rapidly and at low temperatures to a remarkably lightweight terracotta that is highly tolerant of thermal shock and functions well for both cooking pots and water vessels. Before the introduction of the potter's wheel from Europe all African pottery was hand-built, except in Egypt, where the potter's wheel was in use from at least the 2nd millennium BC. Even in the late 20th century almost all African pottery was still being built by hand, using one of several methods. The techniques vary from place to place and usually combine moulding, that is punching and pulling, and building with coils and slabs. Depending on the size of the desired pot, the potter either sits on the ground or on a low stool, turning the work between her legs, or moves around the pot as she works. Generally she begins either by coiling and modelling a long rope of clay on to itself using no support or, more frequently, by punching and pulling a mass of clay with her hands or a hammer over or within a mould, usually a fragment of an older pot, a gourd or a rounded stone. For spherical pots, top and bottom are built separately, left to stiffen until leather-like, then finally luted together.

The techniques for modelling and firing sculptures are similar to those used for pots, and the same clays and tools are used. Most small sculptures are solid, consisting of an interior of coarse clay, which establishes the basic shape of the object, and a surface of much finer clay, which is used for the detailing. Solid pieces up to 500 mm high are known; however, large pieces are more often hollow and sometimes very thin. Armatures of wood or palm fibre are sometimes used to support the clay during the modelling of larger objects.

Firing is done after the pots or sculptures have been preheated in one of two ways. They are either inverted over small fires or filled with grass that is burnt before the firing. This preheating dries out the clay so that only a brief firing at rather low temperatures is required. For the firing itself, which is most often done in the open, the preheated items are stacked in a pyramid that includes straw, wood and often dung. This is then covered with wood and potsherds. The whole is set afire and burns for an hour or two. The pots are removed from the stack immediately after firing and left to cool.

(b) Decoration. The greatest variation in African utilitarian ceramics lies in their decoration. Surfaces may be modified by burnishing, by applying slips before firing or pigments after firing (generally red, white and black), by blackening the entire vessel in a reduction atmosphere and by dipping or splashing the pots immediately after firing in a vegetal solution. Most distinctive to African pottery is

47. Ga'anda woman decorating a clay pot with a gourd chip, north-eastern Nigeria; from a photograph by Marla C. Berns, 1981

its range of impressed ornamentation (see fig. 47), done by means of rouletting, grooving, incising and comb stamping. Less typical is the application of clay pellets, spikes or bands.The amount and type of decoration is partly determined by function. Cooking pots have minimal ornamentation, for they are quickly blackened by the soot from open fires.

BIBLIOGRAPHY

D. Drost: *Topferei in Afrika: Ökonomie und Soziologie* (Berlin, 1968)

M. Cardew: *Pioneer Pottery* (London, 1969)

R. Thompson: 'Abatan: A Master Potter of the Egbado Yoruba', *Tradition and Creativity in Tribal Art*, ed. D. P. Biebuyck (Berkeley, 1969/*R* 1973), pp. 120–82

B. Fagg and J. Picton: *The Potter's Art in Africa* (London, 1970/*R* 1978)

R. Guardi: *African Crafts and Craftsmen* (New York, 1970)

S. Leith-Ross: *Nigerian Pottery* (Lagos, 1970)

C. Roy: *West African Pottery Forming and Firing Techniques* (diss., Bloomington, IN U., 1975)

J. Picton, ed.: *Earthenware in Asia and Africa* (London, 1984)

A. Stossel: *Afrikanische Keramik: Traditionelle Handwerkskunst südlich der Sahara* (Munich, 1984) [excellent plates and geographical coverage]

N. David, J. Sterner and K. Gavua: 'Why Pots are Decorated', *Current Anthropol.*, xxix/3 (1988), pp. 365–89

M. C. Berns: 'Ceramic Arts in Africa', *Afr. A.*, xxii/2 (1989), pp. 32–6, 101–02

N. Barley: *Smashing Pots: Feats of Clay from Africa* (London, 1994)

MARLA C. BERNS, ROBERT T. SOPPELSA

2. Metal. Historically, the main metals worked in Sub-Saharan Africa were iron, copper (including alloys) and gold. In addition, there was some localized use of lead, tin and, to a minor extent, silver. Africa is particularly well endowed with deposits of alluvial and reef gold and with iron ores, especially oxides in the form of haematite, magnetite and limonite, which are found in the laterite crust of the continent and in river sands. Copper is sparse in West Africa but plentiful in parts of Central and Southern Africa.

(i) Introduction. The earliest evidence for the smelting of metallic ores (as opposed to the working of native metals) comes from the southern Sahara, where copper was being worked by the early 1st millennium BC in the Aïr region of Niger and, shortly thereafter, to the west at Akjoujt in Mauritania. Even earlier dates for both copper and iron smelting have been claimed, but the evidence remains problematical. Although archaeological research is still too fragmentary to plot the course of diffusion, metal technology gradually spread through the subcontinent, albeit somewhat discontinuously, until by *c.* AD 1000 virtually all the peoples of the African mainland, with the exception of the Pygmy and Khoisan groups, used and probably also worked iron to some degree.

The ultimate source of this technology is uncertain. Some have contended that metalworking techniques were independently invented in Sub-Saharan Africa, but present evidence argues against this. It is now generally assumed that metalworking spread southward from North Africa and the Mediterranean, a view bolstered by the early dates of Saharan metallurgy. There seems to have been no chronological sequence from copper to copper alloys to iron, that is from simpler to more complex metallurgies, as happened in the ancient Near East and Europe. Rather, the introduction of iron and copper seems to have been roughly contemporaneous throughout the continent, except in the southern Sahara. There were few peoples of colonial Africa who did not themselves work metals, but some were far more skilled than others. In some cases metalworkers were itinerant craftsmen, for example the Awka of south-eastern Nigeria; in others they were hereditary occupational groups, sometimes referred to as 'castes', as among the Mande of Western Sudan; in still others they were people recognized as ethnically distinct, for example the smiths associated with the pastoral Tuareg and those associated with the Maasai.

In many areas the smith is socially marginalized and despised but also feared and respected, a set of attitudes reinforced by the smith's frequent role as circumciser, burier of the dead and maker of magical charms. In West Africa smiths are often also sculptors, creating works in both iron and wood, and their wives are potters. The separateness of smiths is commonly perpetuated by endogamy among metalworkers. In contrast, in Western Equatorial Africa and the interlacustrine region there is a strong association between the smith and the kingship and political authority. Here, oral traditions attribute the introduction of metalworking to culture heroes or even known kings. The smith's peculiar power, like that of the chief or the hunter, derives only in part from his technical skills; more especially it derives from his ability to invoke supernatural forces through his command of medicinal and ritual knowledge. His long apprenticeship teaches him not only to make the constant adjustments that variable ores, fuels and weather conditions demand but also to perform ritual sacrifices and offerings to the ancestors and other spirits without whom his work cannot prosper. He also learns how to protect the enterprise from malevolent forces or spiteful competitors through the use of medicines and prescribed behaviour. Indeed, medicines are often built into the structure of a smelting furnace or placed in its base to strengthen and protect it, or the furnace may be decorated with materials for the same purpose.

Metallurgy is often highly sexualized. It is very common for smelters to observe sexual abstinence during the construction of furnaces and during the smelting process and for menstruating women or women of childbearing age to be forbidden from going near the operation. Moreover, in regions as widely scattered as the Ader (Niger), Bassar (Togo), southern Tanzania, Zambia and Zimbabwe the furnace is said to be a woman gestating iron in a 'womb' and delivering a bloom as a mother delivers a child.

In areas where rich ores and sufficient fuels sustained intensive production, different villages specialized in smelting, refining, forging or charcoal-making. Such was the case among the Bassari of western Togo, where smelting dates back at least to the 12th century AD, reaching a quasi-industrial scale by the 19th. Similar levels of iron production were probably reached on the Ndop Plain of north-western Cameroon about the same time. By the late 20th century metal smelting had almost entirely died out in Africa owing to the availability of cheap imported scrap metal and the dwindling supplies of fuel. While smithing has continued to thrive, its practitioners are more often called on to repair objects than to create them.

(ii) Iron. African ironworking presents a bewildering variety of technological adaptations expressed in an almost infinite array of furnace types, bellows and tool kits. The primary distinctions relate to size and to the use or absence of bellows. Some furnaces are scarcely more than pits or shallow bowls, capable of smelting only small quantities of ore at a time; they are difficult to distinguish from forges in the archaeological record. The largest (3–4 m in height) tend to be those relying on a natural draught rather than forced air (see fig. 48). Some furnaces must be broken down after smelting to extract the bloom; others may be used repeatedly over many years. Wide variations in type are found even within a limited area, as they are adapted to local ores, fuels and other constraints.

The induced-draught furnace seems to have been an independent African innovation, since there is no record of it anywhere else except Burma. This type of furnace has a number of holes around the base that draw in air, which then rises as it heats, setting up a natural draught and achieving the desired temperatures without the need for bellows and someone to work them. Such furnaces have been documented in parts of West and Central Africa but have not been found south of the Zambezi River nor in the equatorial forest. While some scholars regard them as more sophisticated and therefore later than either the bowl furnace or the low shaft furnace, both of which rely on forced air, their introduction may be a response to social rather than technological factors. For example, in areas of heavy and sustained production, there may not have been adequate manpower to keep bellows operating for long periods.

An unusual feature of African ironworking was the ability, in some areas at least, to produce steel through the smelting process itself, rather than in subsequent forging. This carburization could be accomplished in the natural-draught furnace, if it was tall enough, or in an ordinary-sized furnace, if the twyers were inserted deep inside with the other end close to but not attached to the bellow's mouth, allowing more air to be drawn in. Cast iron, on the other hand, was rarely if ever produced by African smelters. In many cases the raw iron contained too many impurities

48. Iron-smelting furnace under construction, Banjeli, Togo; from a photograph by Carlyn Saltman, 1985

to be worked directly and needed to go through a refining process. This customarily involved breaking up the bloom and reheating it, sometimes in crucibles, in a small refining furnace or fire. It could then be forged by a smith through repeated heating and hammering.

The two main types of bellows used in Africa are bag and bowl, but the materials and forms vary almost as much as the furnaces and probably for the same reasons. Because bellows are more perishable than furnaces, the archaeological record is too incomplete to allow a reconstruction of their geographical diffusion. A cylindrical form, with pistons operated by sticks, is found only in Madagascar, bearing witness to the island's connections with Indonesian metalworking traditions. Bellows were always used in refining operations and in forging the metal.

While smiths produced a range of metal tools, weapons, jewellery and sculpture, they themselves often worked with stone anvils and hammers and with wooden tongs. Their dexterity was such that with unhafted stones they could pound red-hot metal into the various shapes required. Where iron anvils were used, they frequently took the form of large spikes or wedges, with the pointed end implanted in the ground.

(iii) Other metals. The main indigenous sources of copper in Sub-Saharan Africa are carbonates, such as malachite. Copper smelting requires lower temperatures than iron, and it was carried out in smaller-bellows furnaces. The copper was refined in crucibles and then worked or alloyed with other metals, principally lead. In the eastern Transvaal and possibly in the Aïr region and south-eastern Nigeria it was alloyed with local tins to produce bronze. Brass, the copper alloy found most commonly in Sub-Saharan Africa, was an imported metal, transported across the desert from the Muslim world or by sea from Europe.

Copper and its alloys were frequently worked by hammering and ornamented by heightening the colour of the metal or by the addition of chiselled, stippled or encrusted designs. A large number of West African peoples, from

Senegal to Lake Chad and south to the Cameroon Grassfields, perfected the art of lost-wax casting. The delicately detailed bronze corpus from Igbo-Ukwu in south-eastern Nigeria is dated to the late 1st millennium AD. It is very different in style and in metal content from the better-known, later works of Ife, which depict much larger human figures and life-size heads cast in either pure copper or brass. The enormous repertory of Benin castings, created over a period of perhaps 500 years, reveals the virtuosity of casters, who were able to produce complex free-standing figures, plaques in high relief and an array of ceremonial objects, using an elaborate system of armatures and runners in the casting process. Akan casters excelled in miniature work, producing thousands of brass goldweights, which illustrated with refined detail proverbs and activities of daily life. Akan casters used not only conventional wax models but also direct casting of such items as beetles, seeds and crustaceans.

While lost-wax casting was limited to West Africa, peoples in Equatorial and Central Africa used open-mould casting, especially in the production of massive collars and bracelets. In areas of Southern and Eastern Africa wire-drawing of both iron and copper was practised. Wiredrawing equipment dated to *c.* AD 1400 has been found in the archaeological site of Ingombe Ilede on the middle Zambezi River, and coils of wire are a common feature of graves in south-western Zaïre. While an abundance of coiled wire was found at Igbo-Ukwu, it seems to have been made by hammering rather than drawing.

Working gold is simpler than working either iron or copper, because it does not need to be smelted but can be simply separated from its rocky or alluvial matrix by crushing, washing and winnowing. The gold is then melted at low temperatures and cast into ingots in open moulds or into objects by means of the lost-wax method. Among the Asante of Ghana it was also pounded into leaf to cover items of regalia (*see* ASANTE AND RELATED PEOPLES, §3(i)). Goldsmiths in the Senegambian region produced gold jewellery, finely worked in spirals and filigree, that was undoubtedly influenced by North African conventions.

BIBLIOGRAPHY

W. B. Cline: *Mining and Metallurgy in Negro Africa* (Menasha, 1937)

M. Eliade: *Forgerons et alchimistes* (Paris, 1956); Eng. trans. by S. Corrin as *The Forge and the Crucible* (New York, 1972)

N. Echard: 'Notes sur les forgerons de l'Ader (Pays Hausa, République du Niger)', *J. Africanistes*, xxxv/2 (1965), pp. 353–72

G. Dieterlen: 'Contribution à l'étude des forgerons en Afrique occidentale', *Annu.: Ecole Pratique Hautes Etud.*, lxxiii (1965–6), pp. 5–28

J. A. R. Wembah-Rashid: *Iron Working in Ufipa* (Dar es Salaam, 1973)

P. McNaughton: *Iron Art of the Blacksmith in Western Sudan* (West Lafayette, IN, 1975)

G. Célis and E. Nzikobanyanka: *La Métallurgie traditionnelle au Burundi* (Tervuren, 1976)

N. Neaher: 'Awka Who Travel', *Africa*, xlix/4 (1979), pp. 352–66

J. P. Warnier and I. Fowler: 'A Nineteenth-century Rhur in Central Africa', *Africa*, xlix/4 (1979), pp. 329–51

P. de Maret: 'Ceux qui jouent avec le feu: La Place du forgeron en Afrique centrale', *Africa*, i/3 (1980), pp. 263–79

C. Goucher: '"Iron is Iron 'Til it is Rust": Trade and Ecology in the Decline of West African Iron Smelting', *J. Afr. Hist.*, xxii/3 (1981), pp. 179–89

B. Martinelli: *Métallurgistes bassari: Techniques et formation sociale* (Lome, 1982)

The Art of Metal in Africa (exh. cat. by M.-T. Brincard, New York, Afr.–Amer. Inst., 1982)

N. Echard, ed.: *Métallurgies africaines* (Paris, 1983)

F. J. Kense: *Traditional African Iron Working* (Calgary, 1983)

E. W. Herbert: *Red Gold of Africa: Copper in Precolonial History and Culture* (Madison, 1984)

R. Haaland and P. Shinnie, eds: *African Iron Working: Ancient and Traditional* (Oslo, 1985)

P. R. McNaughton: *The Mande Blacksmiths: Knowledge, Power, and Art in West Africa*, Trad. A. Africa (Bloomington, 1988)

T. Childs: 'Style, Technology, and Iron Smelting Furnaces in Bantu-speaking Africa', *J. Anthropol. Archeol.*, x (1991), pp. 332–59

E. W. Herbert: *Iron, Gender and Power: Rituals of Transformation in African Societies* (Bloomington, 1993) [extensive bibliog.]

Iron Master of Them All (exh. cat. by W. J. Dewey and A. F. Roberts, Iowa City, U. IA Mus. A., 1993)

FILM AND VIDEO RECORDINGS

N. Echard: *Noces de feu* (Paris, 1968) [film, 16 mm]

E. W. Herbert, C. Goucher and C. Saltman: *The Blooms of Banjeli: Technology and Gender in West African Ironmaking* (Bloomington, 1986) [videotape; study guide, 1987]

EUGENIA HERBERT

3. PAINT. By the late 20th century, African artists had access to the full range of local 'natural' and commercial 'manufactured' paints. Local pigments include those derived from natural earth or mineral elements, ground in a stone mortar and mixed with animal fat, tree sap or a similar substance to produce a type of oil paint. Such pigments were used in rock art, which has a long history in Africa (*see* §VI, 15 below). They were probably applied with the hand or an implement made from fibre, animal hair or bone. The use of ochres was especially widespread. This article provides an overview of the other uses to which paint has been put in African art.

(i) Body and shrine art. Throughout Africa people embellish their bodies with paint (*see also* §VI, 4(ii) below). This is an ancient practice. In the Sudan, for example, the use of ochre as a cosmetic dates back to at least 4000 BC. Among the Kuba and related groups in Zaïre, camwood mixed with palm oil is rubbed on the skin to increase its beauty; the mixture is also applied to a corpse before burial. Among the Nuba of the Sudan, men paint the body in order to enhance its form (see fig. 89 below). Among the Turkana of Kenya, men cake their hair with clay and red colour to celebrate a successful hunt or the end of planting (see fig. 141 below). Among the Igbo of Nigeria, women paint curvilinear designs, derived from plant and animal forms, on their faces and torsos (see fig. 49). The designs, called *uli*, demonstrate the wearer's status and beauty. The pigment used is a stain extracted from the fruit or pods of plants, for the application of which the body is prepared by covering the appropriate areas with a mixture of camwood and palm oil. The pigment is then applied with a quill feather or thin stick of palm frond.

The use of white clay or kaolin chalk is widespread in West Africa and is often used as a marker of spirituality. In Benin, kaolin is used for both body and shrine decoration and symbolizes the essence of ritual purity. Among the Asante and other Akan-speaking groups in Ghana and Côte d'Ivoire, white on the face, arms, shoulders and torso is the mark of a priest or priestess. Among the Fulani, or Peul, in Niger and Burkina Faso women paint white and black designs on their faces for protective purposes. During puberty ceremonies among the Dan of Côte d'Ivoire young women decorate themselves, especially their faces, with bold geometric patterns. Body painting is also practised during men's initiation among a number of

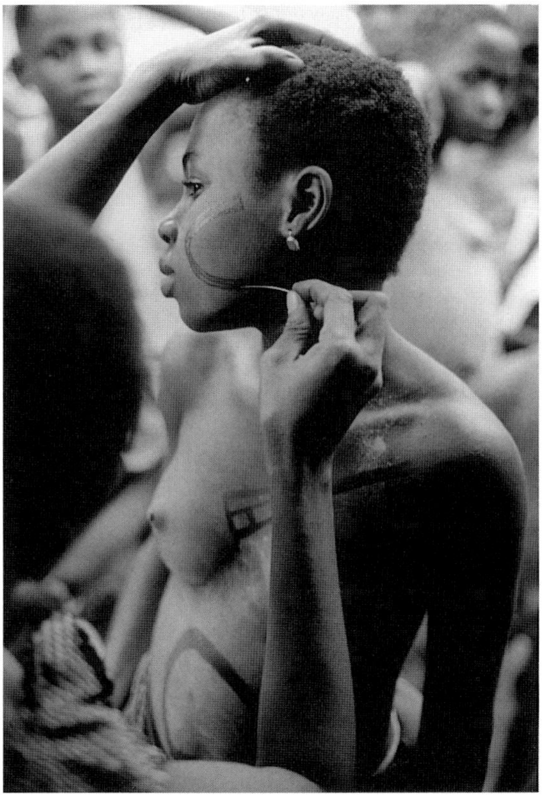

49. Igbo girl being painted with *uli* designs, Nigeria; from a photograph by H. M. Cole, 1983

groups in Liberia and Côte d'Ivoire. In the Tikar area of Cameroon, a red camwood paste is worn by women to mark the death of a chief or other important individual.

The appearance of shrines and religious structures is frequently enhanced by painting. This ranges from simple geometric decoration on ancestor shrines in northern Ghana and southern Burkina Faso, through the more elaborate shrines associated with various Yoruba and Benin deities in Nigeria, to the painted walls of women's initiation huts among the Bemba of Zambia. The *mbari* houses of the southern Igbo are particularly striking, as are the *asafo* shrines of the traditional warrior organizations of the Fante of Ghana (see fig. 79 below). The *mbari* house is a shrine, usually dedicated to Ala, the earth goddess, and has an exterior niche filled with figures representing a range of human and animal forms. These, as well as the walls themselves, are painted with complex representational and non-representational motifs that are both symbolic and decorative. The traditional pigments used provide white, red-brown, yellow, green and pink colours, while black is made from charcoal and red from camwood; blue is obtained from European washing blue. More recently, commercial paints have been used as well (*see also* IGBO, §3).

(ii) Decoration of domestic structures. In many parts of the continent, both the interior and exterior walls of domestic structures are painted. This is usually done by women (see fig. 50). Among the Frafra of northern Ghana, for example, wall decoration consists of a limited number of painted geometric motifs from which the artist chooses. Before a wall is painted, it is plastered with a mixture of cow-dung, clay and water. Compound walls usually need replastering every four or five years, but whether or not they are decorated, or redecorated, depends on the women's initiative. Three colours are used: red-brown, made from a clay of limited availability; black, from a soft, pulverized stone; and white, from a soft, chalklike stone. The wall is initially painted red-brown with a small wicker broom. Black is then applied with a feather or fibre brush. Usually black lines define the specific motifs. Next, the white is added, also with a fibre brush. After the wall has been painted and allowed to dry, it is burnished with a stone. Finally, it is sprayed with a varnish-like fixative made from the seed pods of the African locust-bean tree. The use of these three colours is characteristic of painting traditions from Mali to northern Ghana. Among the Frafra, walls are painted in order to embellish the compound and as a statement of female unity and support for the entire family.

The painted walls that traditionally frame the entrance of Igbo compounds are also executed by women and may be said to symbolize the status of the family head. The motifs used in Igbo wall painting have been strongly influenced by *uli* designs (*see* §(i) above). In fact, wall painting is called *uli aja* or 'wall *uli*' in Igbo. The walls are embellished with various plant and mineral pigments. In addition charcoal, soot, indigo and kaolin are used. In parts of Sudan, especially in the Nubian area near the Egyptian border, both men and women decorate compound walls. Many of the men are professional artists who use commercial paints bought in the market. Women, in contrast, use earth colours and lime from nearby hills. The women also sometimes use washing blue. Much of this art disappeared as a result of the construction of the Aswan dam.

Probably the most polychromic walls on the continent are those decorated by the southern NDEBELE and other peoples of Southern Africa. Here compound walls are decorated by women in a basically geometric style. Among regional variations are differences in colour, consequent upon the type of clay available in any particular area. Other Southern African groups, such as the Swazi and Pedi, are also noted for their painted compound walls. Throughout Africa, by the late 20th century commercial establishments (especially small businesses) advertised their products and services by having images or slogans painted on their walls. Various kinds of shop signs have also been popular; the barber's sign illustrating different hairstyles is probably the best-known type. These are done with commercial paints, usually by self-taught artists.

(iii) Decorations of vehicles, textiles, masks and other objects. Many types of secular objects are painted. Boats, donkey carts, vans and lorries are frequently decorated with proverbs, prayers, statements of status or affiliation, advertisements, and figurative and non-figurative motifs, often combined. Vans and lorries, for example, may carry such sayings as 'No condition is permanent' or 'God's word' along with a figure of a reclining lion or intertwined floral patterns. Most commonly, however, painted decoration is applied to pottery. The majority of painted pottery

50. Group of Gurensi women (co-wives) painting a hut wall, Zuarungu, Frafra region, northern Ghana; from a photograph by Fred T. Smith

designs are geometric, and with only a few exceptions they are executed by women, who are also the potters. The motifs may be symbolic for ritual vessels or purely aesthetic for utilitarian ware. Most unpainted African pottery is either red or black. Paint made from charcoal, earth pigments or white kaolin may be used for decoration.

Gourd bowls and spoons, drums, stools, staffs, shields and textiles may also be decorated with colour. Although pyro-engraving and carving are the most important techniques of gourd decoration, painting and dyeing also occur. Again, earth or vegetable pigments, charcoal, soot and chalk are commonly used, although imported enamel paints were in use throughout the continent by the late 20th century. In East Africa wooden and hide shields are painted with earth pigments and chalk. Among the Senufo of Côte d'Ivoire, black or dark brown human and animal forms are painted on a coarsely woven white cloth with a small brush or knife, the dye being made from a mud solution. In decorating Asante *adinkra* cloth, bamboo or wooden combs are used to outline square or rectangular areas in black. These areas are then filled in with a geometric stamped motif. A thick, black paint produced from tree bark and iron slag serves as the dye.

Masks and figures are also decorated with paint. Traditionally, various earth colours (especially ochres), charcoal, soot, indigo, ground eggshell, kaolin and chalk were employed, the pigments usually being mixed with water or egg white before application. By the late 20th century, the use of enamel paint was common in many areas. The Yoruba of Nigeria have decorated masks and some figures with enamel paint since the mid-19th century. Elaborate designs embellish the surfaces of masks and figures among the Dogon, Mossi, Bwa, Kuba, Teke, Pende and Yaka, among others. Among these groups, colour minimizes form while emphasizing the surface. Complex and elaborate decoration, especially the combination of triangles and parallel lines, is particularly characteristic of the aristocratic art of the Kuba. Moreover, paint is an important component of almost all masking styles. White-faced masks, for instance, usually with a heart-shaped face, are found over a wide area from eastern Nigeria to eastern Zaïre. Among some Igbo groups, white-faced masks are associated with beauty and harmony, while darker examples are associated with bravery and aggression. A similar dichotomy is also found among the Okpella, a northern Edo group. Among some peoples, for example the Yoruba of Nigeria, masks may be repainted if they begin to show signs of wear or if they are to appear at a particularly significant event (see fig. 16 above).

Increasingly throughout the 20th century, easel painting and other originally Western art forms have been taken up by African artists. For an overview of the use of paint by such artists *see* §IX below and entries on modern developments in individual countries; *see also* COLOUR, colour pl. I, fig. 2.

BIBLIOGRAPHY

H. Lhote: *The Search for the Tassili Frescoes* (London and New York, 1959)
D. Mazonowicz: 'Prehistoric Rock Painting at Tassili', *Afr. A.*, ii/1 (1968), pp. 24–5, 74–5

African Arts of Transformation (exh. cat. by H. M. Cole, Santa Barbara, U. CA, A. Gals, 1970)
F. Willett: *African Art: An Introduction*, World A. (London, 1971, rev. 1993)
M. Wenzel: *House Decoration in Nubia*, A. & Soc. Ser. (London, 1972)
African Textiles and Decorative Arts (exh. cat., ed. R. Sieber; New York, MOMA, 1972)
M. W. Mount: *African Art: The Years since 1920* (Bloomington, IN, and London, 1973, rev. New York, 1989)
The Arts of Ghana (exh. cat., ed. H. M. Cole and D. H. Ross; Los Angeles, UCLA, Wight A.G.; Minneapolis, MN, Walker A. Cent.; Dallas, TX, Mus. F.A.; 1977–8)
F. T. Smith: 'Gurensi Wall Painting', *Afr. A.*, xi/4 (1978), pp. 36–41
R. Brain: *Art and Society in Africa* (London, 1980)
R. Sieber: *African Furniture and Household Objects* (Bloomington, IN, 1980)
African Artistry: Technique and Aesthetics in Yoruba Sculpture (exh. cat. by H. J. Drewal, Atlanta, GA, High Mus. A., 1980)
H. M. Cole: *Mbari: Art and Life among the Owerri Igbo* (Bloomington, IN, 1982)
J. Vansina: *Art History in Africa: An Introduction to Method* (London and New York, 1984)
P. Ben-Amos: 'Artistic Creativity in Benin Kingdom', *Afr. A.*, xix/3 (1986), pp. 60–63
F. T. Smith: 'Compound Entryway Decoration: Male Space, Female Creativity', *Afr. A.*, xix/3 (1986), pp. 52–9

FRED T. SMITH

4. WOOD. The techniques and tools for carving wood are remarkably consistent throughout Sub-Saharan Africa. Almost invariably carved items are monoxylous or carved from one piece of wood. The few exceptions include such items as Chokwe and Akan chairs and Kalabari Ijo funerary screens. In these cases, however, the artists were influenced by European prototypes and/or European carpentry techniques. The type of wood used depends upon the object's intended use. Stools and doorposts are usually carved of heavy woods, while masks are carved of woods that are light but sturdy. There have been few studies of the species used in African wood-carving (but see Dechamps). Similarly, little work has been done to determine whether there are correlations between the symbolic attributes of species and the types of carvings for which they are used.

Traditionally the main tools used for carving were adzes and knives. Adzes are axelike tools with the blade set at a right angle to the handle. The most common type of adze in Africa has the narrow shaft of the metal blade set into or through a slot in the wooden handle. Another, rarer type has the rear section of the blade flattened and curved to form a socket into which the handle is inserted. Each carver uses a variety of sizes of adze. Often the blades can be removed from their handles to be employed as chisels. Knives are primarily used in the finishing stages for carving fine details, for incising surface decorations or for scraping down rough spots. Final smoothing was often done with a rough leaf or sand. Such tools as saws, files, drills and sandpaper had become quite common throughout Africa by the late 20th century, but adzes and knives were still the main tools used.

Usually the wood is carved while it is still moist. As it dries it is very carefully monitored, so that, if necessary, action can be taken to prevent cracking. The Mossi, for example, periodically bury carvings in moist earth during the carving process to slow down the drying. In the initial stages of carving the carver uses the adze blade almost perpendicularly and cuts deeply into the wood. The basic shapes are quickly roughed out. When more detailed work begins, smaller, sharper adzes are used, the angle at which the blade strikes the wood decreases and the shavings being cut away become progressively thinner (see fig. 51). An account of carving among the Jukun describes a process seen throughout Africa (see Rubin):

> The easy virtuosity of the carvers must be acknowledged. With the left hand, the work was braced on the ground against each adze stroke but kept almost constantly in motion. Whether the carver worked with or across the grain, whether he took off large chunks of wood in the early stages of the work or shavings as fine as any plane would make as the mask neared completion, adze strokes were unerringly accurate.

Distinct stages of the carving may be recognized explicitly. For example, the Yoruba distinguish blocking out, dividing up the masses, smoothing the forms and cutting the details (see Carroll). In a study in which a Yoruba carver was filmed at work it was found that, while the early stages were shorter than the later ones, and more

51. Large wooden spoon being carved with an adze by Si, a Dan sculptor, Nyor Diaple, north-east Liberia; from a photograph by Eberhard Fischer, 1960

wood was removed in them, a greater amount of time was spent in the early stages on 'thinking' (see Willett). Indeed, African sculptors frequently characterize the 'thinking' part of carving as the most difficult aspect of their work. As they do not use models or sketch out what they are going to carve beforehand, all the details must be conceived mentally. The early stages are, of course, the most important, and master carvers will often do these themselves, leaving the final stages to their apprentices. In many parts of Africa rituals must be carried out to ensure the success of the 'technical' processes. This is especially so for carvings that will have a ritual usage. Among the Mijikenda of Kenya, for example, elaborate rites are performed and offerings made before a tree can be cut down in order to be carved into a commemorative sculpture for a deceased elder. Often ritual prohibitions are placed on the behaviour of the carver throughout the carving process, and magical incantations are pronounced to ensure the efficacy of the mask or sculpture. Carvers frequently work in private, especially if the product of their work is to have a restricted audience.

Generally, wood-carvers are part-time specialists who are also subsistence farmers. They learn their skills growing up in a carving family or by undergoing a period of apprenticeship. In many cases all males are expected to be able to carve such simple utilitarian items as spoons and handles, while specialists are commissioned to carve more complex items. In most parts of Africa wood-carving is a male activity. Among the pastoral Turkana of Kenya, however, women carve elegantly shaped containers (see Donovan).

See also WOOD, colour pl. III, fig. 2.

BIBLIOGRAPHY

K. Carroll: *Yoruba Religious Carving: Pagan and Christian Sculpture in Nigeria and Dahomey* (London, 1967)
R. Dechamps: 'L'Identification anatomique des bois utilisés pour des sculptures en Afrique' [series of articles in *Africa-Tervuren*, beginning with xiv (1970)]
W. Bascom: 'A Yoruba Master Carver: Duga of Meko', *The Traditional Artist in African Societies*, ed. W. L. d'Azevedo (Bloomington, 1973), pp. 62–78
J. C. Messenger: 'The Role of the Carver in Anang Society', *The Traditional Artist in African Societies*, ed. W. L. d'Azevedo (Bloomington, 1973), pp. 101–27
F. Willett: 'An African Sculptor at Work', *Afr. A.*, xi/2 (1978), pp. 28–33, 96
C. Roy: 'Mossi Zazaido', *Afr. A.*, xiii/3 (1980), pp. 42–7, 92
A. Rubin: 'Akuma: Carving the Masks at Takum', *Afr. A.*, xviii/2 (1985), pp. 60–62, 103
D. Hersak: *Songye Masks and Figure Sculpture* (London, 1986), pp. 56–68
Vigango: Commemorative Sculpture of the Mijikenda of Kenya (exh. cat., ed. E. Wolfe, III; Williamstown, MA, Williams Coll. Mus. A., 1986)
A. Donovan: 'Turkana Functional Art', *Afr. A.*, xxi/3 (1988), pp. 44–7

5. STONE. Stone-carving traditions are comparatively rare in Sub-Saharan Africa. Moreover no traditional stone-carving practices have survived, so the techniques used can only be surmised from the extant carvings themselves. Soft-stone carvings are much more common than hard-stone ones and are mainly of steatites or talcs (commonly referred to as soapstone). The best-known examples are the bird pillars of Great Zimbabwe (for illustration *see* GREAT ZIMBABWE), the statues of Esie, memorial figures found among the Kissi and other peoples of Sierra Leone and Guinea, which are commonly known as *nomoli* or *pomdo*, and the funerary sculptures of the Kongo kingdom. From an unfinished stone in a quarry in the Kongo area, it has been deduced that the carvers of these figures made an initial blocking out before the stone was moved and so the method of stone-carvers is thought to be similar to that of wood-carvers. The carving tools used seem to have been essentially the same as those used by Kongo wood-carvers.

African hard-stone carvings are commonly of granite gneiss or basalt. The best-known examples include the *akwanshi* memorial carvings of the Cross River area of Nigeria, the archaic monoliths of Ife and the rock engravings of the San of Southern Africa. In both cases shallow surface decoration appears to have been scratched, pitted or ground away with stone tools.

BIBLIOGRAPHY

P. Allison: *African Stone Sculpture* (London, 1968)
P. Stevens: *The Stone Images of Esie, Nigeria* (Ibadan, 1978)
The Four Moments of the Sun: Kongo Art in Two Worlds (exh. cat. by R. F. Thompson and J. A. Cornet, Washington, DC, N.G.A., 1981–2)
F. Lamp: 'House of Stones: Memorial Art of Fifteenth-century Sierra Leone', *A. Bull.*, lxv/2 (1983), pp. 219–37
T. A. Dowson: *Rock Engravings of Southern Africa* (Johannesburg, 1992)

WILLIAM J. DEWEY

6. IVORY. Elephant tusks are the source of most African ivory, although hippopotamus and warthog teeth are also used. In general, the tools used to carve wood (i.e. adzes and knives) are also used in carving ivory, and ivoryworkers are usually also woodworkers. Ivory's hard, fine grain allows for very delicate, detailed carving as well as for undercutting and extensive openwork. The form of the tusk itself is often followed in the carving process, artists thus incorporating its natural curvature. This can be seen in such works as the divination tappers of the Yoruba (see fig. 98 below), the royal ancestral tusks of Benin, and across the continent in trumpets with side-blown embouchures used to announce the beginning of funerals, wars and initiations and the arrival of rulers. Cross-cut sections of tusk are frequently carved as bracelets or anklets. Some, such as those worn by titled Igbo women, are left unadorned, while in Benin, Owo and elsewhere specialist artists have created *tour de force* pieces, splitting one tusk section to form two interlocking, openwork cylinders. For example, a pair of interlocked armlets from Benin depict kings in their coral-bead regalia, carved in high relief, surrounded by royal emblems such as elephant and crocodile heads, leopards and mudfish (London, BM; see fig. 52).

The colour of African ivory objects is highly varied. In some areas the natural white of the ivory is associated with purity and so retained through bleaching with citrus juice or scrubbing with sand. In other areas the ivory is reddened or browned with palm oil or camwood and given a glossy surface.

In Africa elephant ivory has been a precious commodity since ancient times and generally signifies wealth. Throughout much of Africa the medium is associated with royalty. At Benin one tusk from each slain elephant belonged to the ruler, and he had the right to purchase the second. Such ivory objects of authority as sceptres, fly-whisks, staffs and snuff containers are features of Yoruba, Benin, Kongo, Mangbetu and other courts. In non-royal contexts,

52. Ivory armlet with bronze inlay, h. 150 mm, diam. 100 mm, from Benin City, 16th century (London, British Museum)

ivory is still usually associated with high status. Among the Igbo of Nigeria, titled men own tusks and on personal wooden shrines are often depicted holding them. Similarly, among the Lega of Zaïre only the highest-ranking members of the Bwami society are entitled to own ivory masks and objects.

The prestige of ivory is partially symbolic, for in Africa the power of a leader is often metaphorically likened to that of an elephant. Like antelope horns, porcupine quills, leopard's teeth and other media (*see* §10 below), tusks have both protective and aggressive functions, as do leaders who are empowered by the possession and/or representation of these material symbols. Indications of this empowerment can be seen in the ivory-hung costumes (*orufanran*) of Owo Yoruba chiefs and in the encircling of the body of the ruler of Benin with ivory bracelets and waist pendants.

While many African peoples carve ivory, a few areas stand out as important centres of ivory production. These include the peoples of Sierra Leone and Benin who produced the so-called Afro-Portuguese ivories (*see* §VI, 2(ii) below), the Yoruba and Benin kingdoms of Nigeria, and several regions of Zaïre (*see* LEGA AND RELATED PEOPLES, §2; KONGO, §4; PENDE, §3).

BIBLIOGRAPHY

African Textiles and Decorative Arts (exh. cat. by R. Sieber, New York, MOMA; Los Angeles, CA, Co. Mus. A.; San Francisco, CA, de Young Mem. Mus.; Cleveland, OH, Mus. A.; 1972–3)

R. Poynor: 'Edo Influence on the Art of Owo', *Afr. A.*, ix/4 (1976), pp. 40–45, 90

A Survey of Zaïrian Art: The Bronson Collection (exh. cat. by J. Cornet, Raleigh, NC Mus. A., 1978)

P. Gebauer: *Art of Cameroon with a Catalog of the Gebauer Collection of Cameroon Art at the Portland Art Museum and the Metropolitan Museum of Art* (Portland, 1979)

Treasures of Ancient Nigeria (exh. cat. by E. Eyo and F. Willett, Detroit, MI, Inst. A.; Oslo, N.G.; London, RA; and elsewhere; 1980–83)

J. Henggeler: 'Ivory Trumpets of the Mende', *Afr. A.*, xiv/2 (1981), pp. 59–63

F. Neyt: *Traditional Arts and History of Zaïre* (Brussels, 1981)

For Spirits and Kings: African Art from the Paul and Ruth Tishman Collection (exh. cat. by S. M. Vogel, New York, Met., 1981)

M.-L. Bastin: *La Sculpture Tshokwe* (Meudon, 1982)

African Ivories (exh. cat., ed. K. Ezra; New York, Met., 1984)

Igbo Arts: Community and Cosmos (exh. cat. by H. M. Cole and C. C. Aniakor, Los Angeles, UCLA, Mus. Cult. Hist., 1984–6)

African Masterpieces from Munich (exh. cat. by M. Kecskesi, New York, Cent. Afr. A., 1986)

N. Barley: 'Africa', *Ivory: An International History and Illustrated Survey* (London, 1987), pp. 170–87

Sounding Forms: African Musical Instruments (exh. cat., ed. M.-T. Brincard; Washington, DC, N. Mus. Afr. A.; Richmond, VA Mus. F.A.; Kansas City, MO, Nelson–Atkins Mus. A.; Paris, Mus. A. Afr. & Océan.; 1989)

Yoruba: Nine Centuries of African Art and Thought (exh. cat. by H. J. Drewal and J. Pemberton III, with R. Abiodun, New York, Cent. Afr. A., 1989)

H.-J. Koloss: *A Survey of Zaïrean Art* (New York, 1990)

African Reflections: Art from Northeastern Zaïre (exh. cat. by E. Echildkrout and C. A. Keim, New York, Amer. Mus. Nat. Hist., 1990)

Elephant: The Animal and its Ivory in African Culture (exh. cat., ed. D. Ross; Los Angeles, UCLA, Fowler Mus. Cult. Hist., 1992–3)

KATHY CURNOW

7. FIBRE.

(i) Weaving. (ii) Basketry.

(i) Weaving.

(a) Raw materials. In North Africa and in limited areas immediately south of the Sahara, sheep's wool is used in weaving, while goat's wool is most fully exploited in southern Madagascar. Silk, the other animal-derived fibre used traditionally in Africa, has a more restricted distribution. The main traditional production is in West Africa, especially in Nigeria, although waste silk from Europe was imported in the 19th century, and in Ghana European silk textiles were once unravelled and rewoven by local weavers. Silk is also produced in Madagascar.

Cotton, raffia and bark are the principal vegetable fibres used. Cotton is widely cultivated in West and North-East Africa and was exploited into the 20th century by weavers in the east and south of the continent. Raffia is woven in West Central Africa and Madagascar. Bark has been used mainly to produce a beaten and felted fabric rather than a woven textile. It can, however, be prepared for weaving and has been so used in parts of West Africa and Madagascar.

(b) Preparation. Wool, silk and cotton are all prepared for mounting on the loom by spinning. Each type of material is subjected to different procedures. Wool is soaked and then combed or carded (drawn across a series of spikes to yield a sheet of fibre); it may then be rolled and mounted on a distaff ready to be spun. Silk is prepared by boiling up the silk cocoons in an alkaline solution to release the fibres of which they are constructed. Cotton is

ginned to squeeze out its seeds and then bowed (fluffed out by flicking a bowstring against it). All three are spun in an essentially similar manner. A length of fibre is drawn from the distaff and twisted by hand. This is attached to the spindle, which is allowed to spin in mid-air, drawing out further lengths. These are wound on to the spindle giving a continuous yarn.

Raffia is the most easily prepared fibre. Derived from the upper epidermis of the cut leaves of the raffia palm, it is simply peeled off and then split lengthways. The bark of appropriate trees is retted to yield bast fibre. It is immersed in water, and the longitudinal fibres are separated out. As with raffia fibres, bark fibres may be tied together neatly or twisted to give longer lengths.

(c) Manufacture. While both men and women weave in Africa, in most areas the occupation is exclusive to one or the other gender. Thus in Berber North Africa and in Madagascar it is reserved to women, and in many parts of West Africa, Zaïre and East Africa it is a male activity. In Nigeria and Arab North Africa, however, both men and women weave, but they use different types of loom. Furthermore, while in some areas men weave professionally, for women weaving is generally a domestic activity.

African looms vary in the angle at which they are mounted, the means of creating tension in the warp system and how they are addressed in weaving. Perhaps the most basic distinction, however, is in the nature of the shedding device, the means of creating the shed and countershed whose alternation with each pick of the weft is the essential act performed by the loom. Two main possibilities are exploited in Africa. The loom may be furnished with a shed stick and a single heddle tied to one group of warp elements (see fig. 53). The shed stick creates the shed, and the weft may be passed through; pulling the heddle forward brings the warp elements from behind to the front and forms the countershed ready for the next pick of the weft. Varieties of this simple mechanism are widely distributed throughout the continent and are used by women in North Africa, Nigeria and Cameroon and in Madagascar; men weave on equivalent looms in West Central Africa and in the east and south of the continent. All such looms are fixed horizontal structures, with the exception of a foot-pedal loom in some isolated parts of Zaïre and a rare backstrap loom in Madagascar.

Alternatively, paired heddles are used, each attached to a group of warp elements. The heddles are connected by a cord that passes over a pulley and that is worked by pedals beneath. Pressing one pedal pulls one of the heddles down and simultaneously raises the other, enabling shed and countershed to be formed rapidly. This type of double-heddle loom is used exclusively by men in West and North-East Africa and by women in isolated parts of Madagascar. In Madagascar only one end of the warp is attached to the loom; the other is held either by a weight or tied to a pole. In West Africa the cloth woven on such looms is characteristically in the form of narrow strips that are sewn together selvage to selvage to give greater width.

(d) Decoration. The weaving process itself, dyeing, printing, appliqué and embroidery are the main techniques used in decorating African textiles. In weaving, variations of texture and colour are widely exploited as a means of introducing design, as are most of the structural possibilities familiar in other weaving traditions. Both warp- and weft-faced textiles (*see* TEXTILE, colour pl. VIII, fig. 1) are widely distributed, and the Asante of Ghana incorporate both in a single cloth. Tapestry weaves are characteristic of some Berber textiles. Perhaps the most common method of introducing pattern, however, is the use of float weaves. In an unusual subtractive technique the Kalabari Ijo of Nigeria cut and remove threads from manufactured cloth to create new patterns.

53. Raffia fibre being woven on an upright loom, Ndundu region, Zaïre

A wide variety of vegetable dyes is used. Indigo is the most common, yielding either a blue or a red colour. Ikat techniques, though rare in Africa, are found among the Baule of Côte d'Ivoire and were formerly used by the Sakalava in Madagascar. Resist-dyeing of woven cloth is widespread, and the techniques of tying, stitching and applying starch are used. The Bamana of Mali use a unique method of discharge-dyeing in the manufacture of their *bogolanfini* or 'mud cloth'.

The techniques of printing, drawing and stencilling cloth are all rare in Africa. In one of the few historic traditions, among the Asante of Ghana, a black dye produced from tree bark is applied with stamps cut from gourds. In many parts of the continent the technique of applying both cloth and other materials, including beads, shells, animal fur and medicine bundles, to a textile base is common. Prominent examples of applying cloth to other textiles are the banners and flags of the Sudanese Mahdists in the 19th century, those of the Akan peoples of Ghana and those of the Fon of the Republic of Benin. The Kuba of Zaïre make raffia appliquéd skirts. Embroidery techniques are applied in many parts of West and North-East Africa to gowns, trousers and cloaks. Those from West Africa are associated with Islamic fashions. The Kuba of Zaïre are noted for their production of pile cloth using techniques known in Europe as Richelieu embroidery.

BIBLIOGRAPHY

H. Loire: 'Le Tissage du raffia au Congo Belge', *An. Mus. Congo Belge, Anthropol. & Ethnog.*, iii/3 (1935) [whole issue]

R. Boser-Sarivaxevanis: *Textilhandwerk in Westafrika* (Basle, 1972)

K. P. Kent: 'West African Decorative Weaving', *Afr. A.*, vi/1 (1972), pp. 22–7, 67–70, 88

B. Menzel: *Textilien aus Westafrika*, 3 vols (Berlin, 1972)

R. Boser-Sarivaxevanis: *Recherche sur l'histoire des textiles traditionnels tissés et teints de l'Afrique occidentale* (Basle, 1975)

V. Lamb: *West African Weaving* (London, 1975)

J. Picton and J. Mack: *African Textiles* (London, 1979, rev. 1989)

D. Idiens and K. Ponting, eds: *Textiles in Africa* (Bath, 1980)

V. Lamb and J. Holmes: *Nigerian Weaving* (Lagos, 1980)

C. Polakoff: *Into Indigo: African Textiles and Dyeing Techniques* (Garden City, 1980)

Pelete Bite: Kalabari Cut-thread Cloth (exh. cat. by J. Eicher and T. Erekosima, Saint Paul, U. MN, Goldstein Gal., 1982)

JOHN MACK

(ii) Basketry.

(a) Raw materials. Nearly all the materials used in African basketry are vegetable. Stems such as grasses, reeds, sedges and creepers are used, as are the split leaves from various palm trees and irises. Wood is widely used in the form of withies, roots and timber in wattle-and-daub. Bark, both the outer bark of trees and the fibrous inner bast, is used as a twining material or for oversewing. Fibres are obtained from the scraped and soaked leaves of various sanseverias and from the leaves of the raffia palm. Animal materials such as rawhide, leather and sinew are also used in basketry. In the 20th century plastic fibres from grain sacks and telephone wire have been added to the range of African basketry materials.

(b) Preparation and manufacture. Preparation of these materials varies but often involves cutting and splitting or sometimes flattening with a mallet. Fibre cords are rolled on the leg and twisted and are often used two-ply. Basketry materials are commonly soaked in water to make them pliable.

The tools used are minimal. A small knife may be used for trimming off raw ends or for preparing the material for use. An awl, of iron, pointed wood or thorn, is used to pierce holes in coil-sewn baskets, to allow threading of the sewn element or the passage of a needle. An iron needle is used in mat-making, to join lengths of split cane and plaited strips or in making coiled baskets. By the late 20th century African basketry and its techniques had not yet been studied in depth, except for Southern Africa, where almost 300 different techniques have been identified (see Shaw). These vary according to the fabric, whether chequered, twilled, wrapped, twined, wickerwork, wattle-work or plaited, and according to form, whether sewn, flat, straight, circular or cylindrical. Other variations concern the starting foundations, shaping, edging and finishing off; the combinations of materials; and different weaves and stitches. Such functional additions as leather-reinforced rims and bases or carrying slings (which may also be decorative), basal feet and lids, with or without hinges, also require their own techniques.

(c) Decoration. A great variety of decorative interlacing techniques are used in African basketry. Some materials, such as split reeds, are used so that the glossy outside contrasts with the matt inner surface. Similarly, different materials may be used in the same piece of basketry to provide variety in texture and hue. The use of dyed elements, to contrast with the natural pale creamy yellow or pale brown of the undyed material, is widespread. Black is usually obtained from immersion in swamp mud; shades of red, yellow or brown are obtained from vegetable dyes; while red, green, violet and yellow synthetic dyes are also used. Further decoration is achieved through the addition of animal skin, leather, cowries, beads, brass buttons and animal fur. Bentwood rims may be ornamented with pyrogravure or stained black.

For royal use, ceremonial presentations and special occasions such as weddings, baskets with extra fine stitching (see fig. 54) are made; they may also be patterned and embellished with beads. In Ethiopia they take the form of hanging inverted cones covered in beadwork, in Kenya baskets with beads and metal dangles; women of the Ganda royal households in Uganda make minutely stitched baskets with conical lids, coloured in black and pale straw.

(d) Uses. Domestic containers are the most common form of basketry. A great variety of baskets for storing food, spoons and trinkets and for serving food are made almost everywhere in Africa. In some areas, for example among the Shilluk of Sudan and the Somali, baskets are so tightly sewn that they become waterproof as the fibres swell. In these areas, therefore, baskets can be used for storing milk, water and other liquids. Winnowing baskets are often made from square mats, their corners trimmed off before they are pressed and stitched into a circular hoop. Another specialist basket is bottle-shaped, for sifting cassava flour. In Southern Africa traditional beer-making involves the use of long strainer baskets and openwork basketry spoons. Around Lake Victoria basketry drinking straws with fine sieves at the ends are used. Some large gourds and earthenware pots are reinforced with a twined basketry casing; other vessels may be encased in a basketry sling; and some have a basketry rim added for strength and decoration. Pottery and gourd vessels often have a decorative basketry lid.

Basketry techniques are used in some traditional house-building where the roof framework is of wattles, trimmed branches or stems twined with bast ties and the walls are of wattle-and-daub. Basketry is also used in making various forms of granaries, pigeon houses and chicken coops. Some houses in the Zaïre basin area and around Lake Victoria may be walled with large, screenlike mats, often patterned in black. Elsewhere others are roofed with

54. Basket with lid, split palm-leaf, l. 760 mm, from Lower Zaïre or northern Angola, early 19th century (London, British Museum)

decoratively plaited mats. In many parts of Africa, house doors are made of reeds twined together. Basketry mats are used as tent roofs among nomadic peoples in Somalia. Almost everywhere in Africa mats are used for sleeping or sitting on. In north-eastern Zaïre, beds traditionally were made of mats tied on to a wooden frame. The headrests of the Turkana of Kenya have twined thongs between the legs to prevent splitting.

In some areas basketry is used to make conical fish traps, sometimes of great size; where fish poison is employed oval floating baskets are used to gather the catch. Finger-stall-shaped traps that contract and grip cane rats and other small animals have a wide distribution. In the Sahel, a special basket is used to harvest grain knocked off the plant. Large, open-mesh baskets of various forms are made for carrying tubers and other crops. Crudely made baskets are used for carrying chickens to market, while twined nets are used for stacks of pottery. Among the Lozi of Zambia and the Ndebele of Zimbabwe, basketry sleds made of wattlework on wooden runners are used for transporting bulk. In north-eastern Zaïre strong basketry shields made of split cane of palm leaf patterned in black on natural straw colour were used.

Basketry hats come in a great variety of forms, often embellished with fur, feathers, beads and tufts of raffia. In Zaïre basketry visors were used to protect the wearer's face from being cut by long, sharp grass. In Uganda basketry hoods protect a baby on its mother's back from the sun, and baby-carriers of wickerwork and wood were used in Liberia. Long ear-plugs covered with finely plaited, colourful grass were made in Uganda and Rwanda; in Mali fine straw is plaited in imitation of filigree gold; plaited bracelets of split palm leaves are made in Southern Africa. Basketry masks, though uncommon, do exist. The Chewa of Zambia make vast basketry masks, while in north-western Zambia and eastern Angola masks are made of painted barkcloth on a basketry frame.

By the late 20th century baskets were also being made for the export market. Bowl-shaped carrying bags made of twined sisal fibre have been exported in large numbers from Kenya, while coiled baskets from Nigeria and Botswana and shallow baskets of varicoloured telephone wire from South Africa have also been successful export items.

BIBLIOGRAPHY

M. Trowell and K. P. Wachsmann: *Tribal Crafts of Uganda* (London, 1953)

African Furniture and Household Objects (exh. cat., ed. R. Sieber; Indianapolis, IN, Mus. A., 1980)

R. Levinsohn: *Art and Craft of Southern Africa* (Craighall, 1984)

M. Shaw: 'The Basketwork of Southern Africa: Part I. Technology', *An. S. Afr. Mus.*, c/2 (1992), pp. 53–248

T. Katzenellenbogen: 'Imbenge', *J. Mus. Ethnog.*, 4 (1993), pp. 49–72

M. E. Terry and A. Cunningham: 'The Impact of Commercial Marketing on the Basketry of Southern Africa', *J. Mus. Ethnog.*, 4 (1993), pp. 25–48

N. Tobert: 'Rizekat Wedding Baskets', *J. Mus. Ethnog.*, 4 (1993), pp. 73–82

MARGRET CAREY

8. Beads. In Africa beads are fashioned from natural objects, such as seeds and seed pods, shells, nuts, teeth and bones, as well as from clay, stone, glass and metals, including gold, iron and copper alloys. Beads are worn as simple strings or attached to cloth, leather or other material. Beads are also fashioned into bead embroidery, while in some areas bead strings are wrapped around a central coil of cloth or fibre and the coils fashioned into necklaces, belts and other articles. Beads are found among African peoples inhabiting all geographic regions and ecological zones, among hunter-gatherers, herders and subsistence farmers as well as among peoples living in large, politically centralized chiefdoms and kingdoms. In centralized societies, beadwork is traditionally the domain of professional artisans, while elsewhere it is women who are generally responsible for making the beaded ornaments worn by themselves and members of their families.

(i) History. There is substantial evidence of early beaded ornamentation in archaeological remains. A Nok terracotta figurine (*c.* 500 BC–AD 200) shows a male wearing what appears to be a stone bead necklace. Cast-copper alloy figures and heads from Ife (*c.* 11th–15th centuries) portray kings wearing beaded necklaces, anklets, bracelets and crowns. Elaborate beaded ornamentation is also depicted on Benin art objects from the 14th century to the 19th. Life-size cast-copper alloy heads depict kings wearing high, beaded collars and crowns of coral or stone beads. Commemorative queen mother heads are similarly embellished with beaded collars and netlike hair coverings representing coral or stone beads.

There have been a number of bead-making centres in Africa. Stone beads were worked in Ilorin, Nigeria, while quantities of stone and coral beads were crafted in Benin. The manufacture of glass beads in Africa has never been widespread, although glass beads recovered from Mapungubwe in southern Africa are believed to have been locally crafted. The glass industry of Bida, Nigeria, has continued to flourish into the late 20th century. The Krobo of Ghana also have continued to produce powder-glass beads, made with scrap glass ground to a fine powder, then poured into moulds and fired in a furnace. Powder-glass beads are also produced in Kiffa and neighbouring centres in Mauritania.

Historically, however, most of the glass beads and stone beads found in Africa are either of Indian or European origin. From early times glass beads of Indian manufacture were brought by Arabs, Persians, Indians and Chinese traders through Egypt, Zanzibar and other Muslim trading centres along the East African coast. From there they were dispersed through much of East and Central Africa. The earliest European traders continued the trade in Indian beads, gradually introducing beads of European manufacture into eastern and southern Africa. In West Africa, Europeans imported enormous quantities of glass beads manufactured in such European beadmaking centres as Amsterdam, Venice, Idar-Oberstein, Bohemia and Moravia.

(ii) Uses. In subsistence-level economies, generally characterized by a dearth of material wealth, artistic expression frequently focuses on body ornamentation, and glass beads are among the materials used. In Kenya and the Sudan, among the Pokot, Turkana, Samburu, Maasai, Kikuyu, Dinka and other peoples, the colours of beads, as well as the specific types and quantity of ornaments worn, reflect different stages and statuses in life. The degree of elaboration increases with the age and status of the wearer. Children's ornamentation tends to be minimal, such as single or multiple bead strings worn round the waist or neck. Through adolescence and into adulthood, the amount of beaded ornamentation worn increases. Examples are the massive assemblages of beaded necklaces worn by adolescent girls and married women among the Samburu, the beaded corsets of young Dinka men and women and the richly beaded leather garments worn by Turkana married women (see fig. 55).

The San of Botswana and Namibia make beads from ostrich eggshells to fashion decorative ornaments and decorate leather garments. Elsewhere in southern Africa the Nguni-speaking peoples, for example the Zulu, Swazi,

55. Turkana woman's beaded skin apron, glass beads and iron beads, from Kenya (Cambridge University, Museum of Archaeology and Anthropology)

Ndebele, Xhosa and Thembu, use glass beads in elaborate beaded ornamentation. Following the emergence of the Zulu and Swazi kingdoms in the late 18th and early 19th centuries, kings strictly controlled the distribution and use of beads among their subjects. Ornaments fashioned from beads and such other prestige materials as brass, prized animal skins and feathers, were an important means of visually enhancing the power and prestige of the king and other high-ranking individuals. The smaller chiefdoms of the Xhosa, Thembu and others had similar restrictions on the use of beads. With the increased availability of beads in the second half of the 19th century, these restrictions became increasingly difficult to enforce, and the fabrication of beaded ornaments gradually proliferated among the general population. Specific styles of beaded ornaments and garments visually signify a girl's progression from childhood to womanhood, and on special occasions young men may also wear beadwork provided by their girlfriends and sisters. Nguni beadwork is often characterized by sharp contrasts of brightly coloured beads against a white background. This is especially evident among the Ndebele, where the designs in traditional beadwork can also be seen in the painted murals for which they have become particularly well known.

Beads are frequently used in the production of objects of prestige. Stone and glass beads are relatively durable and long-lasting in contrast to much traditional African material culture and may thus convey a sense of permanence and immortality. The relative scarcity of beads also serves to enhance their importance. When first introduced into Africa, imported beads were extremely rare, difficult to obtain and relatively costly. Only the wealthier members of society had the means to obtain them. In centralized chiefdoms and kingdoms the right to possess and display beads, as personal adornment or symbols of status, often continues to be restricted to higher-ranking members.

Among the Yoruba of Nigeria, the use of beads is reserved for those individuals who possess the power to communicate between the world of the living and the world of the gods. Thus beads are prominent in the regalia of kings and in the ceremonial or ritual objects used by priests and devotees of important sacred cults (*see* BEADWORK, colour pl. I, fig. 3). The most important element of the king's regalia is the veiled, beaded crown (see fig. 56). The veil conceals the wearer's identity, focusing the spectator's attention on the spiritual power of the king as the embodiment of the dynasty. Besides crowns, beaded regalia of the king include ceremonial staffs and sceptres, hats and other elements of clothing. Yoruba diviners are also permitted to use ceremonial or ritual objects featuring elaborate bead embroidery. Beaded sheaths 'clothe' or cover the metal staff of Oku, deity of the farm, when it is not in ritual use, and beautifully beaded dance panels are worn in pairs by devotees at the annual festivals for a number of Yoruba deities. Yoruba twin figures, *ibeji*, carved on the advice of a diviner as memorials to deceased twins, may also be clothed in elaborate, bead-embroidered garments.

Beads and beadwork are also important indicators of wealth and status in the stratified and hierarchically organized kingdoms of the Cameroon Grassfields. Formerly used as a medium of exchange, beads literally represent wealth and denote affluence and high status within the community. Beads and other prestige materials, including ivory and brass, embellish articles of personal adornment worn by high-ranking individuals on important occasions. The accoutrements range from beaded staffs and dance-whisks to necklaces, bracelets and earplugs, as well as beaded caps, loincloths, belts and bags. Thrones or stools, used by men of rank and carved in the form of human or animal caryatids, are sometimes lavishly decorated with beads and other valued materials; the degree of elaboration indicates the owner's status (*see* BAMUM, fig. 2). Ancestor figures may also be richly adorned with beaded ornamentation.

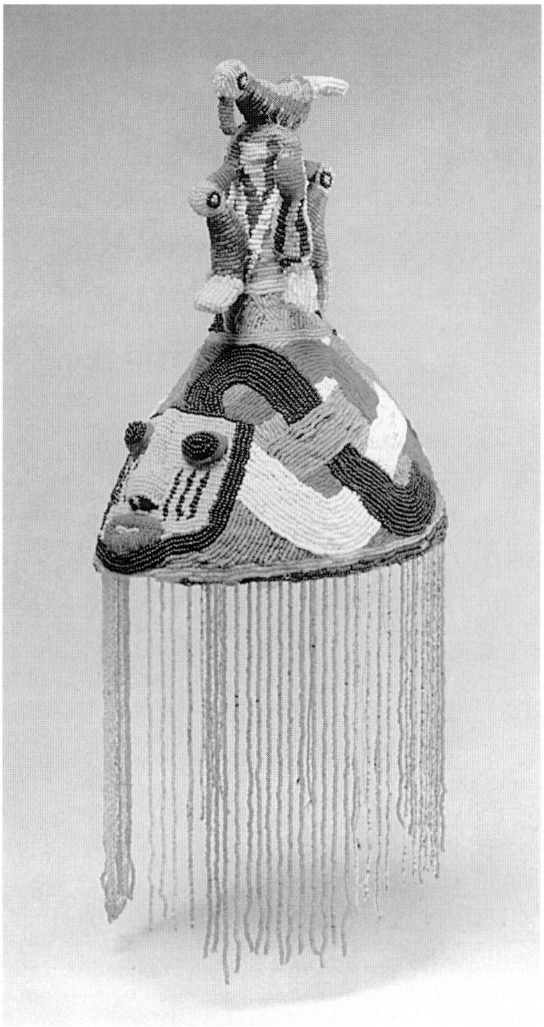

56. Yoruba beaded crown with veil, raffia, cloth and beads, h. without veil 254 mm (Los Angeles, CA, University of California, Fowler Museum of Cultural History)

Elephant masks, found throughout the Bamileke area of the Cameroon Grassfields, are among the most striking examples of bead-embellished art works (see fig. 43 above). Typically the mask consists of a tightly fitting cloth hood with long front and back panels representing the animal's trunk. The facial area and panels of the mask are elaborately decorated with beads, which when the mask dances become a whirling kaleidoscope of colour.

Beads, like cowrie shells, are important symbols of status among the Kuba of Zaïre. Wooden masks and masks of raffia fibre are richly decorated with glass beads, cowrie shells, fur, seeds and copper. The royal regalia of the Kuba king and his court likewise incorporate vast quantities of glass beads and cowrie shells, as well as raffia-embroidered cloth.

BIBLIOGRAPHY

R. F. Thompson: 'The Sign of the Divine King: An Essay on Yoruba

Bead-embroidered Crowns with Veil and Bird Decorations', *Afr. A.*, iii/3 (1970), pp. 8–17, 74–80
H. M. Cole: 'Artistic and Communicative Values of Beads in Kenya and Ghana', *Bead J.*, i/3 (1975), pp. 29–37
The Sign of the Leopard: Beaded Art of Cameroon (exh. cat. by T. Northern, Storrs, U. CT, Benton Mus. A., 1975)
S. Priebatsch and N. Knight: 'Traditional Ndebele Beadwork', *Afr. A.*, xi/2 (1978), pp. 24–7
W. Fagg: *Yoruba Beadwork* (New York, 1980)
U. Beier: *Yoruba Beaded Crowns: Sacred Regalia of the Olokuku* (London, 1982)
M. Carey: *Beads and Beadwork of East and South Africa*, Shire Ethnography, 3 (Princes Risborough, 1986)
L. S. Dubin: *The History of Beads from 30,000 BC to the Present* (New York, 1987)
M. Carey: *Beads and Beadwork of West and Central Africa*, Shire Ethnography (Princes Risborough, 1991)

CAROLEE G. KENNEDY

9. LEATHER. The ability to work animal hides and skins is known throughout Sub-Saharan Africa and has been employed since prehistoric times to serve a variety of utilitarian, social and aesthetic needs. With the introduction of the loom and cotton to Africa, textiles began to replace leather and skin products as the primary form of dress. The protective qualities of leather and hide and their durability and pliability, however, have continued to make them ideal for a wide variety of objects.

The best-known hide products of eastern and southern Africa are perhaps the elaborate rawhide shields of warriors and hunters, made from the thick skins of domestic cattle and buffalo. The skins are not dressed but are usually pegged a few inches from the ground, allowed to dry and cut to shape. Sometimes they are beaten with a stone to toughen and shape them. Among the Luo of Tanzania, the raw skins are stretched on to a basketry framework that gives shape and additional strength to the finished product. A variety of methods are used to decorate these shields. Most commonly the surfaces are rubbed or painted with red and yellow ochres or other natural pigments. Less commonly the short hairs left on the hide are shaved into a decorative pattern, or the hard surface is carved, and white kaolin is rubbed into the recessed areas to produce a stark design.

To produce the pliable leather required for items of dress, the peoples of eastern and southern Africa treat the skins of calves, goats and other small animals with fats and oils in a process that stabilizes the skin without actually tanning it. This process is generally a collaborative effort between men and women. The raw skins are moistened and either stretched on a frame or pegged on the ground. The flesh side is scraped to clean, compress and level the surface. If desired, the hairs are also scraped off; fresh dung is sometimes spread on the hairy side to facilitate this part of the process. The skins are then softened by rubbing with grease, fat or oils until they are quite supple. Among the Xhosa, women raise a rough nap on the surface with the thorny leaves of the aloe plant or a rough stone before working the fat into the skin. Aside from the surfaces being coloured with ochre or charcoal, these skins may be left undecorated or may serve as a backing for elaborate beadwork designs.

The Sudanic region of West Africa has long been known for its fine leatherwork. Among the Tuareg and Moor peoples in the north, women are the principal tanners and leatherworkers. Elsewhere, these crafts are a monopoly of men, although wives often assist their husbands. Cow hides, as well as those of other large animals such as giraffes and camels, are used untanned for shields and the soles of sandals and slippers. Although the skins of wild animals, including those of snakes, crocodiles and lizards, are sometimes tanned, goats and sheep are the primary source of skins in West Africa. The hair is usually removed prior to tanning by soaking in a caustic alkaline or lye solution and scraping the surface with a blunt knife or wooden implement. The skins are immersed and rubbed in a container of chicken manure and water and allowed to steep for several hours or overnight. The skins are then cleansed with a solution of fermented millet bran and water and scraped. These processes prepare the skin to accept and absorb the tannin. Throughout West Africa, acacia pods are the most common source of tannin. The skins are allowed to soak in a solution of macerated acacia pods and water of varying degrees of strength and frequently rubbed and kneaded. When the skins are sufficiently tanned, after between one and four days, they are washed and allowed to dry, then scraped, stretched and beaten to make them smooth and pliable.

Throughout West Africa, there are many ways by which leather is manipulated for decorative effect. The most widespread technique is perhaps that of dyeing or painting the surface of the leather. Although a variety of European chemical pigments and dyes have been available in the region since the beginning of the 20th century, leatherworkers tend to prefer the colours previously obtained exclusively with vegetable and mineral dyes. Traditionally, a deep maroon red was produced from the sheaths and kernels of specially cultivated millet or sorghum, while yellow was obtained from a variety of roots and leaves. Before the introduction of commercial pigments, green leather was highly prized and difficult to produce. Hausa and Tuareg leatherworkers had several ways of obtaining it, including a complex process using copper or brass filings and a mineral salt on untanned skin. Despite the availability of imported inks, leatherworkers have continued to mix their own black dye in the traditional manner using an acidic liquid such as lemon juice, iron residue and sugar or honey. Mande and Fula leatherworkers of the Western Sudan paint the surface of the leather with these same colours as part of the creation of the object. Geometric designs are the most common, either painted on in broad swathes or delicately applied with a reed pen or, more recently, with felt-tip and ball-point pens. Circular designs are sometimes made with the aid of a pair of compasses.

Appliqué is also quite widespread in West Africa, particularly in Northern Nigeria where the whole skins are dyed before being sold to leatherworkers. Shapes cut out of leather and cloth are secured to the surface with commercial or homemade paste and carefully stitched to the foundation piece with leather or cotton threads. Reverse appliqué, in which a pattern is cut into a piece of cloth or leather of one colour and layered over that of another colour, is especially common in Nigeria. Embroidery techniques are employed with a variety of materials, including leather, cotton, wool and occasionally silk or rayon. The technique of embroidery with palm fibres is

57. Leatherworker Sulemani Kouyaté incising patterns after embroidering a knife sheath; from a photograph by Barbara E. Frank, 1988

particularly characteristic of Mande leatherwork in the Western Sudan.

One technique takes particular advantage of the special properties of leather. In this, the smooth surface is incised with geometric patterns and selected portions are peeled off, revealing the soft suede underneath and providing a contrast in both texture and colour (see fig. 57). Designs impressed or stamped into a dampened surface become permanent when the leather dries. Leather may also be stretched and shaped around various objects, and craftsmen often build up the surface in patterns or ridges over which the leather is moulded.

Finally, one of the most visible features of leatherwork throughout much of West Africa is the fringe. Leather is cut into thin strips by hand to adorn objects to be suspended and, in the case of some trappings, to serve the useful purpose of keeping flies away. In addition, there are a variety of twisting and plaiting techniques used to create durable straps, cords, loops and ties.

For further illustration see fig. 142 below.

BIBLIOGRAPHY

J. M. Dalziel: 'African Leather Dyes', *Kew Bull.*, vi (1926), pp. 225–38

S. Ben Sai: 'Plantes à tannins, tannage et teinture indigène au Soudan', *Notes Afr.*, xxiii (1944), pp. 20–22

J. Gabus: *Arts et symboles* (1958), ii of *Au Sahara*, 3 vols (Neuchâtel, 1955–8)

J. Nicolaisen: *Ecology and Culture of the Pastoral Tuareg*, Nationalmuseets Skrifter, Ethonografisk Roekke, ix (Copenhagen, 1963)

M. Trowell: *African Design* (London, 1965)

V. Z. Gitywa: 'The Arts and Crafts of the Xhosa in the Ciskei: Past and Present', *Fort Hare Pap.*, v/2 (1971), pp. 111–16

D. Heathcote: 'A Leatherworker of Zaria City', *Niger. Field*, xxxix/1 (1974), pp. 12–26; xxxix/3 (1974), pp. 99–117

E. M. Shaw and N. J. Van Warmelo: 'The Material Culture of the Cape Nguni', *An. S. Afr. Mus.*, lviii/2 (1974), pp. 178–83

F. L. Lambrecht and D. J. Lambrecht: 'Leather and Beads in N'gamiland', *Afr. A.*, x/2 (1977), pp. 34–5

M. Lamb: 'The Hausa Tanners of Northern Nigeria (and the Production of Sokoto Tanned Goatskins)', *New Bkbinder*, i (1981), pp. 58–62

A. Hodge: *Nigeria's Traditional Crafts* (London, 1982)

P. J. Imperato: 'Luo Shields from Tanzania', *Afr. A.*, xvi/1 (1982), pp. 73–7, 96

I. Anagbogu: *The History of the Indigenous Leather Industry in Sokoto and Kano, Northern Nigeria, 1903–1960* (diss., U. Birmingham, 1986)

B. E. Frank: *Mande Leatherworking: A Study of Style, Technology and Identity* (diss., Bloomington, IN U., 1988)

L. Hooper, P. Davison and G. Klinghardt: 'Some Nguni Crafts Part 4: Skin-working Techniques', *An. S. Afr. Mus.*, lxx/4 (1989), pp. 313–404 [published as self-contained monography]

BARBARA E. FRANK

10. MIXED MEDIA. Virtually every traditional art form in Africa incorporates mixed media. An examination of any artistic endeavour, including those discussed below as well as, for example, the construction of shrines and performance arts, reveals a combination of materials embodying sophisticated aesthetic criteria and a rich and complex artistic symbolism. The range of materials and techniques used is vast. This entry can only hint at this range through a discussion of some of the main arenas for mixed-media arts in the traditional African context.

Much African sculpture may be characterized as mixed media or accumulative in nature, incorporating a variety of natural and manmade materials with the predominant sculptural medium of wood. The sculptural surface may be painted with natural and commercial pigments, embedded with seeds, shells, beads and metal, rubbed with vegetable oils or camwood, wrapped with cloth, skin or fibre, and encrusted with earth and the libations of millet beer, palm wine, water mixed with flour, and the blood of animal offerings. Both local and imported objects and materials may be attached to embellish sculptural forms. A partial inventory of such materials in African art would include: wooden and metal objects; locally made and imported cloth; natural fibres; animal skulls, horns, skins, claws, bones and teeth; bird beaks and feathers; beads and shells; and a variety of imported items such as mirrors, shotgun shells and European Christmas decorations.

In a discussion of the accumulative nature of African sculpture a distinction is made between display materials that 'are primarily oriented toward enhancement of the splendor of the objects to which they are attached' and materials 'connected with the organization and exploitation of power' (see Rubin, p. 8). These broad categories provide a useful approach to understanding the layers of meaning and intention in the variety of forms and materials of mixed-media African sculpture. Thus, Kalabari Ijo water-spirit masquerades include inventive combinations of local and imported materials, such as cloth, mirrors and Christmas ornaments, that heighten the visual splendour of the masquerade performances, provide information on the kinds of materials appropriate for the depiction of water spirits and point to the important position of the Kalabari Ijo in long-standing trade networks with their neighbours and with Europeans.

58. Mixed-media Kuba mask, Mwaash aMbooy, wood, fabric, feathers, cowries, beads and metal, h. 446 mm, from Zaïre (Washington, DC, National Museum of African Art)

In some African societies the capacities associated with the wilderness and nature are drawn on to imbue art objects with power. Thus, porcupine quills, leopard's teeth, tusks, horns, feathers, hides and other materials are used to suggest the powers of the wilderness and the abilities of certain individuals to manage that domain. The use of these materials refers both visually and symbolically to the distinctive capacities for survival that characterize animals of the wilderness and, by association, provides a commentary on the powerful capacities of those individuals and organizations that utilize such materials and motifs in their arts and regalia. Indeed, there are specific categories of African art that tend towards the use of mixed media derived from the wild. Many initiation, age grade and secret societies draw on powers associated with the wilderness in the construction of their masquerades and cult paraphernalia and in the spatial orientations of their rituals. Some of the masks made by the Bamana, Senufo, Igbo and Kuba, for example, are accumulative sculptures that embody both opposing and complementary categories of knowledge and experience and contrast concepts and powers of the wilderness with the civilized, orderly realm of village and community life.

Arts associated with hunters, healers and diviners often use materials derived from the wild. They emphasize the ritual specialists' mediating qualities and spiritual powers within their communities and validate their assertions to control, to some extent, aspects of nature and the wild. Medicines are used to imbue with power both individuals and the objects they use or make. Earth, bark, stones, leaves and other natural materials, as well as metals (themselves the product of a process of transformation), are used as medicines in many parts of Africa and are incorporated into sculptural forms to enhance their effectiveness. Although these medicines are often derived from the natural world, manmade objects are also used, including glass, mirrors and manufactured nails, as in the power figures of the Chokwe, Kongo, Yaka and Suku of Zaïre. The physical appearance of these sculptural forms changes over time as more and more materials are accumulated.

The arts associated with leadership often employ a variety of materials derived from both nature and culture, including animal skins and teeth, feathers and elaborate gold, ivory and beaded ornaments, that visually display royal wealth and prestige and state the king's capacity to control the disruptive, unpredictable and aggressive forces that threaten orderly domestic society. Masquerades associated with royalty embody many of these same characteristics. The full costumes of two Kuba royal masks,

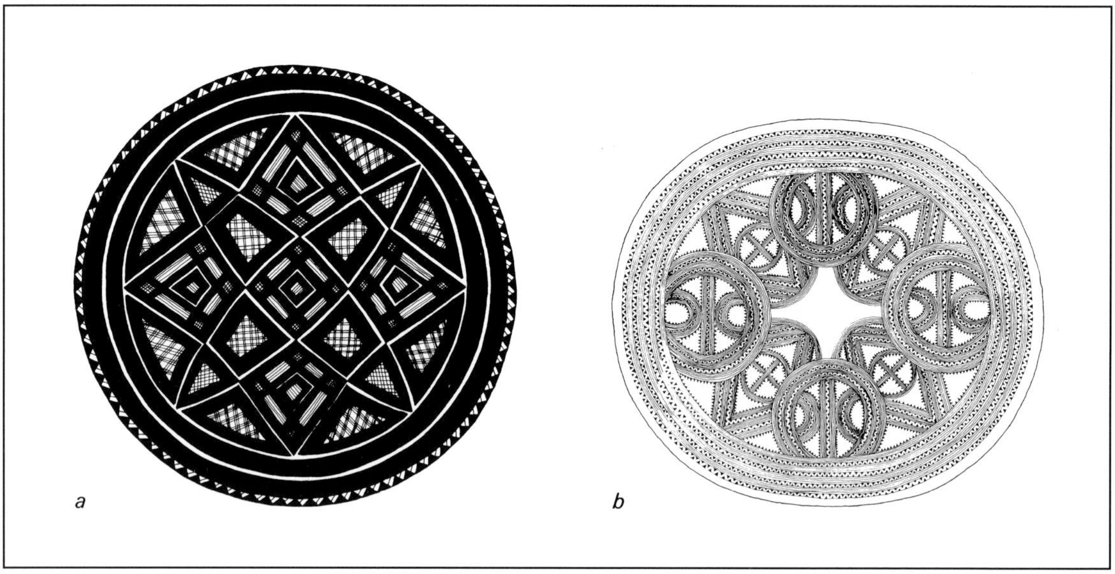

59. Gourd designs: (a) pyro-engraved gourd design, diam. 322 mm, settled Fulani, Song, Song District, Adamawa State, Nigeria, *c.* 1965; (b) pressure-engraved gourd design, diam. 305 mm, Yungur, Suktu, Yungur District, Adamawa State, Nigeria, *c.* 1959 (Lagos, National Museum)

Mwaash aMbooy, for example, include feather head-dresses, animal skins, leaves, textiles, cowries and beads; even the mask headpieces are mixed-media objects (see fig. 58).

BIBLIOGRAPHY

A. Rubin: *African Accumulative Sculpture: Power and Display* (New York, 1974)

Wild Spirits, Strong Medicine: African Art and the Wilderness (exh. cat., ed. M. G. Anderson and C. M. Kreamer; New York, Cent. Afr. A., 1989)

CHRISTINE MULLEN KREAMER

11. GOURDS. The decoration of these African hard-shelled fruit (*Lagenaria siceraria*) in some parts of Africa has been developed into an art form. The term 'calabash' is often used to refer to the African gourd, although strictly speaking it should be used only for the South American equivalent. The African gourd was one of the continent's earliest cultivated plants and remains a staple commodity, especially in rural areas. There are four main shapes—globular, flattened, bottle-shaped and tubular—rendering it suitable for numerous practical uses, whether preserved whole or cut into pieces. Its primary function, however, is as a domestic utensil, since the hollowed-out shell of the predominantly symmetrical gourd provides an inexpensive, durable, light and portable receptacle for transporting, storing and serving foodstuffs and liquids. In many parts of Africa a woman's collection of gourds, which enables her to fulfil her domestic and economic roles in the community, is reckoned among her most prized possessions. Its intimate association with female attributes and activities also ensures the gourd's wide association with femininity and motherhood, and in some areas it may even serve as a symbol of a bride's integration into her husband's family (*see* FULANI, §2).

Gourds are also used as protective bonnets for children, as fishing floats, seed-drills, henna baths, smoking pipes, drinking canteens, toys and small tools, and as personal containers for snuff, medicines and cosmetics. Gourds figure prominently in many social and ritual contexts, ranging from communal beer-drinking to agricultural and marriage ceremonies, burial rites and divination. They are also used in a wide range of musical contexts, both as percussive and wind instruments and as resonators on drums, harps and xylophones. Gourds used in ceremonial and ritual contexts often remain undecorated, a restriction that probably serves to emphasize the non-secular aspects of the occasion. Moreover, in such areas as north-eastern Nigeria, where gourd decoration is practised mainly by women (elsewhere this is a predominantly male art form), the use of undecorated gourds in ceremonial and ritual contexts probably reflects the exclusion of women from these areas of activity. Conversely, in many domestic and social contexts a decorated gourd is more highly valued than its undecorated counterpart, and not only for aesthetic reasons.

(i) Decorative techniques. The multiplicity of uses to which the African gourd is put is matched by the diverse methods employed, singly or in combination, in its decoration. Among the most common of these is pyro-engraving (see fig. 59a) or poker-work, including scorching, which involves the use of a heated metal engraving tool, usually consisting of a leaf-shaped blade with elongated shaft hafted into a circular wooden handle. Working with a succession of knives, carvers often facilitate the passage of the heated instrument across the work surface by simultaneously rotating the gourd with the non-carving hand (see fig. 60). Different colour and texture effects may be achieved by, for instance, a 'rocking' technique with a partially cooled blade, which produces a bronze or reddish-brown tone, or by scorching with the flat of the blade to produce a contrasting matt finish, as in the leaf pattern designs typical of south-eastern Nigeria.

The two other most common techniques are pressure-engraving (including scraping) and carving. In the former

60. Waja woman pyro-engraving a gourd bowl, Dela Waja, Nigeria; from a photograph by Marla C. Berns, 1982

a metal point is dragged, dagger-like, across the work surface towards the carver's body in a laborious and painstaking technique that in many areas pre-dates the introduction of pyro-engraving. First an outline of the design is made, and then, in the scraping or filling-in stage, the surface shell is wholly or partially removed, often between alternate pairs of engraved lines (as among some pastoral Fulani groups in West Africa), either by scraping or some form of hatching. The design is then reversed by filling in the engraved areas with a blackening agent. Among some groups, such as the Kamba of Kenya and a number of groups in north-eastern Nigeria, including the Longuda, the scraping stage is unnecessary, the whole design being composed of finely engraved lines that are then reversed (see fig. 59b). Carving is the reverse of pressure-engraving: after the design has been outlined with a sharp knife, the background is cut or scraped away, leaving the unmarked shell as a relief pattern (e.g. among the Hausa of northern Nigeria or the Bariba and Fon of Benin). To increase the contrast between white background and yellow relief, chalk or clay may be applied to the engraved areas and the shell stained or engraved with a texture pattern. Deep carving with an angled blade (e.g. among the Yoruba of south-western Nigeria) produces shadows that give an additional three-dimensional effect.

Less common techniques include painting, which only rarely serves as a group's primary technique (for example in the Potiskum area of north-eastern Nigeria). For practical reasons, such designs tend to be confined to the interior of the gourd, which is likely also to have an exterior decoration (e.g. among the settled Fulani of north-eastern Nigeria and Cameroon). Traditionally, locally produced pigments are used, often mixed with various oils in order to improve adhesion. Uniform interior coatings, polished to an enamel-like finish, help to make gourds watertight, to render them impervious to termite attacks and to improve their insulating properties. A recent innovation in north-eastern Nigeria, one of the richest areas of gourd decoration in Africa, is the use since *c.* 1960 of imported enamel paints and stamped designs. Among some peoples (such as the Ga'anda and settled Fulani of north-eastern Nigeria) gourds are dyed, although this is a subsidiary technique, invariably used as an adjunct to an engraved design. The favoured colour is red, produced from a mixture of guinea corn stalks and indigo leaves. A further refinement is the introduction of a resist-dye pattern through the application of an oily paste to those areas that are to remain undyed, producing an intricate polychrome effect (e.g. among the settled Fulani of north-eastern Nigeria and Cameroon). Gourds may also be decorated by adding extraneous materials, ranging from leather, basketry and elaborate coverings of patterned beadwork (as in the Cameroon Grassfields) to stitched 'embroidery' patterns using such prestigious materials as glass beads, cowrie shells and metal wire, including gold thread (as among the Asante of Ghana).

(ii) Designs. The designs used are partly determined by the gourd's curved surface and partly by the technique employed. For instance, in the case of the most commonly decorated receptacle, the hemispherical bowl, the whole surface is usually treated as a single compositional field, delimited by an outer rim band of decoration. The technique of pyro-engraving favours a broad, rapid treatment, in which the division and subdivision of the design field by a process of reduction tends to establish a rather formal, geometric framework, where the individual design units are filled in with incised lines and texture patterning (see fig. 59a). The relationship of figure to ground is sometimes ambiguous, but in most designs the engraved area serves as the background, while the untreated shell emerges as the relief pattern. Although pyro-engraving and especially pressure-engraving (which encourages the use of small design units) do not obviously favour free-flowing, curvilinear forms, these are nevertheless common among some groups, such as the Hausa, Tiv, Igbo and Ibibio of Nigeria and the Kiga of Uganda.

Design motifs tend to be non-figurative in most parts of Africa, even where there are no religious restrictions on figurative representations. Invariably, they have acquired conventional pattern names based on perceived associations either with objects in the environment or technical processes, but generally gourd designs seem to have no dominant subject-content, consisting instead of a composite arrangement of heterogeneous elements inspired largely by abstract aesthetic considerations. The Hausa, Kanuri and some pastoral Fulani groups (in northern Nigeria), the Kamba (in Kenya) and the Bariba and Fon (in Benin), among others, do, however, include representational imagery in their designs, and in the latter case these carved pictographs, alluding to well-known stories and proverbs, may be used to convey messages of love.

BIBLIOGRAPHY

G. Lindblom: *The Akamba in British East Africa: An Ethnological Monograph*, Archvs Etud. Orient., 17 (Uppsala, 1920)

M. Griaule and G. Dieterlen: 'Calebasses dahoméennes (Documents de la Mission Dakar-Djibouti)', *J. Africanistes*, v/2 (1935), pp. 203–46, pls xxvi–xxvii

M. J. Herskovits: *Dahomey: An Ancient West African Kingdom*, 2 vols (New York, 1938)

K. C. Murray: 'The Decoration of Calabashes by Tiv (Benue Province)', *Nigeria*, 36 (1951), pp. 469–74

C. Jest: 'Décoration des calebasses foulbées', *Notes Afr.*, 72 (1956), pp. 113–16

P. Malzy: 'Les Calebasses', *Notes Afr.*, 73 (1957), pp. 10–12

D. J. Stenning: *Savannah Nomads: A Study of the Wodaabe Pastoral Fulani of Western Bornu Province, Northern Region, Nigeria* (London, 1959)

M. Trowell: *African Design* (London, 1960, rev. 1965)

M. Dupire: *Peuls nomades: Etude descriptive des Wodaabe du Sahel Nigérien*, Trav. & Mém. Inst. Ethnol., lxiv (Paris, 1962)

B. Rubin: 'Calabash Decoration in North East State, Nigeria', *Afr. A.*, iv/1 (1970), pp. 20–25

L. E. Jefferson: *The Decorative Arts of Africa* (New York, 1973/*R* London, 1974)

T. J. H. Chappel: *Decorated Gourds in North-eastern Nigeria* (Lagos, 1977)

The Arts of the Hausa (exh. cat. by D. Heathcote, London, Commonwealth Inst., 1977)

S. Kay: 'Peter Nzuki: Calabash Carver of Kenya', *Afr. A.*, xii/1 (1978), pp. 40–41, 108

R. Sieber: *African Furniture and Household Objects* (Bloomington, 1980)

The Art of Cameroon (exh. cat. by T. Northern, Washington, DC, Smithsonian Inst. Traveling Exh. Serv., 1984)

J. Perani: 'Hausa Calabash Decoration', *Afr. A.*, xix/3 (1986), pp. 45–7, 82–3

The Essential Gourd: Art and History in Northeastern Nigeria (exh. cat. by M. C. Berns and B. R. Hudson, Los Angeles, UCLA, Wight A.G.; Honolulu, HI, Acad. A.; New York, Cent. Afr. A.; Washington, DC, N. Mus. Afr. A.; 1986–8)

T. J. H. CHAPPEL

VI. Art forms.

1. Architecture. 2. Sculpture. 3. Mask and masquerade. 4. Body arts. 5. Dress. 6. Regalia. 7. Divination instruments. 8. Musical instruments. 9. Arms and shields. 10. Currency, weights and measures. 11. Tools and implements. 12. Furniture. 13. Tobacco containers and pipes. 14. Household utensils. 15. Rock art.

1. Architecture.

(i) Introduction. (ii) Materials. (iii) Vernacular architecture. (iv) Christian architecture. (v) Islamic architecture. (vi) Western architecture. (vii) Further developments.

(i) Introduction. Discussion of African architecture is beset with problems of definition, scope, timespan and identity. North Africa may be seen as part of the Middle East, coastal East Africa as part of Arabian culture and South African cities as part of a Western cultural tradition. Much of the eastern and southern parts of the continent were only settled by Bantu-speaking peoples comparatively recently; Trans-Saharan trade, Islamic jihads and Fulani migrations in the western Sudan have all influenced architecture; while European colonization and subsequent national independence have also affected building types, methods of construction and settlement patterns.

This survey is concerned principally with the architecture of Sub-Saharan Africa, although reference is also made to northern, eastern and Saharan regions. Archaeological study of all but the largest sites in Africa is in its infancy, and information on the architecture of African cultures is often fragmented and unsystematic where it exists at all. Future studies may well change substantially the picture presented here.

Although by the late 20th century a third of Africans were living in cities, the majority were still rural, and their buildings may be loosely classified as 'vernacular architecture', i.e. indigenous buildings of community origin, not designed by specialist architects. Environmental factors influence the economies of different regions, which in turn affect population densities, settlement types and hence architecture. About 95% of the continental land mass has less than 80 people per sq. km, with densities conditioned by access to water. Such rivers as the Nile in Egypt and Sudan and the Niger in Mali have made a broad band of cultivation possible. In contrast, such desert regions as the Sahara in the northern half of the continent support fewer than eight persons to the sq. km. Here, water reserves are tapped through tunnelled water courses, cultivated depressions in the *erg* (sand desert) or by such oases as Touggourt and El Oued (both Algeria). Many desert inhabitants are camel- and goat-herding nomads, who live in tents or collapsible and transportable frame-and-mat structures. Other inhabitants of desert regions live in small concentrations in the mountains. The Matmata Berber, for example, excavate deep shafts off which are burrowed rooms, stables and an access ramp. At the bottom of the shaft a well, cistern and latrine may be sunk. This modifies the climate by means of the slow transmission of radiated heat through the rock, which warms interior spaces at night and, after re-radiation, keeps them cool during the day.

In the grassland steppes and savannah regions, permanent settlements are to be found, with dispersed farms worked by family units growing maize, sorghum and millet. Houses in these regions must afford protection from both solar radiation and seasonal rains. Those in open areas must also be able to resist high winds, while in areas of higher humidity, through-ventilation is important. In the tropical forests of West and Equatorial Africa, where farming of copra and plantains is year-round, protection from heavy rains is necessary. Permanent settlements are more clustered in these areas, and indigenous towns and cities are concentrated there. Trading complexes and market centres, sometimes with specialized functions, are widely distributed. Such centres have developed as cities and grew either indigenously or under colonial and post-colonial administrations.

(ii) Materials. The earliest forms of human shelter include cave dwellings. In Southern Africa artefacts and midden heaps provide evidence of continuous cave occupation over hundreds, even thousands, of years. In the Erongo Mountains, Namibia, rock shelters with collapsed screens still *in situ* have been uncovered. Caves were still in use in Nakapapula, northern Zambia, in the 1960s, and nomadic Hadza on the borders of Lake Eyasi, northern Tanzania, were using rock shelters into the 1990s. For peoples living in areas with no caves and for those requiring more adaptable shelters, however, vernacular architecture was dependent on available resources. Although such materials as mangrove poles from the swamps off the Kenyan coast were sent by dhow to the Gulf states, there is limited

evidence of any other extensive trading of building materials before the colonial period.

(a) Stone. (b) Soil. (c) Brick. (d) Wood and palm. (e) Grass. (f) Hair and hide.

(a) Stone. Historically, there were few tools appropriate for excavating, cutting and trimming stone. Where schists and other limestones cleaved naturally into suitable blocks, these were used. The best-known use of stone for indigenous building is in Zimbabwe, where, as well as GREAT ZIMBABWE, many other stone ruins survive, including Naletale, Dhlo Dhlo and the complex of walls and passages of the Khani Ruins. There are also numerous domestic rock sites, suggesting widespread knowledge of dry-stone building. Some of these sites are characterized by skilled and sophisticated use of decorative chevron patterning. In other parts of Southern Africa a number of corbelled, stone-domed dwellings have been found. In the 1990s stone was still being used by the Tigre and other Ethiopian peoples for domestic building, the rubble being bonded with mud. In West Africa stone plinths have been constructed to support earthen buildings, and some settled Tuareg build stone houses. Further west in Mauritania such ancient trading cities as Tegdaoust and Tichitt were constructed of coursed sandstone blocks. Stone is widely used in Morocco and Algeria, where it is often bonded with earth or used in association with sun-dried earth blocks. The settled Berber of northern Algeria employ stone for the construction of their one- and two-storey farm buildings. The techniques for building with stone may have spread to these areas with the advance of Islam, as was the case with the use of local coral ragstone in the building of the trading cities on the East African coast.

(b) Soil. The local soils are complex in the eastern and central parts of the continent and simpler in the northern and southern regions. Desert soils of broken rock, sand and pebbles are spread across the north, where pockets of calcareous crusts provide gypsum, used for making a building plaster. Gypsum-plastered barrel vaults and domes displaying a high level of craftsmanship are to be found in Tunisia and Algeria, in such towns as Takrouna and El Oued. South of the desert, in the semi-arid savannah steppe, a transcontinental band of brown soils gives way to ferralitic tropical red soils or laterites, which cover a third of Africa. Red in colour and friable in the well-drained and leached areas, the soils become black clays in poorly drained, humid areas. Low in fertility, the laterites make a good building material, being malleable, yet hardening to a stonelike surface. They are laid spirally in a technique (known as *banco*) closely related to that of coil pottery to form the cylindrical huts and linking-walls of compounds. These are often built by the compound head with his family participating in the preparation of the material. Women mould clay to make interior sleeping platforms, cooking areas and storage spaces for gourds and pottery vessels, all of which may be finished with ornamented edges.

In some parts of tropical West Africa the use of a wooden framework for building has been replaced by the use of mass walling of laterite mud. The earth is compressed in large balls, and the walls are laid in 'lifts', or layers, of *c.* 500 mm, each of which is allowed to dry before the next lift is raised. This technique, known as 'swish', was used in the historic city of Benin and has become widespread. Many savannah and Sahelian peoples build with excavated earth, mixed with water and straw and allowed to cure. The mixture is then formed into egg-shaped balls (*tabale*), which are laid in rows with the narrow ends uppermost and interlocking with the next row. Such peoples as the Sanga of Togo use pronounced, inclined lifts to produce a series of overhangs, off which the water runs in the seasonal rains. Erosion, however, remains a problem: the rapid passage of water over the walls causes considerable surface damage, while splash-back and run-off water deeply undercut the walls at ground-level. In addition, severe cracks may form as the walls dry out after the rains. Repairs are made to these cracks and may be painted over with a water-repelling preparation of locust-beans.

See also §2(iii) and (iv) below; §V, 1(i) above.

(c) Brick. In areas where there is considerable influence from the north, adobes or earth blocks have been used for building. Shaped by hand or cast in a wooden mould, the bricks are sun-dried before use. In the Nigerian centres of Katsina and Kanuri two- and three-storey houses have been built by this method. Their cubic forms, flat roofs and common walls all reduce the surface area on to which sunlight falls, helping to lower the level of solar radiation. Thick walls slow the transmission of heat from the outside to the inside of the building: by night, when the heat has passed through the walls, the rooms are warmed; during the day, rooms remain cool and comfortable.

Fired brick is not widely used in Sub-Saharan Africa, although evidence of early use has been found in Chad. In areas of European influence such bricks have been used for prestigious buildings. In Sudan the 'clamp' type of kiln is used, in which bricks are stacked so that the lower ones make a furnace and the flames pass around those above. The whole structure is covered with clay during the firing. There is, however, high consumption of palm for fuel and high wastage of bricks broken in the kiln. Although firing makes bricks more durable and less prone to erosion, their use is still limited. Successful experiments have been conducted in Sudan in producing bricks bonded with waste engine oil. These have proved to be considerably more durable than sun-dried bricks and less wasteful of resources.

See also BRICK, §V, 5.

(d) Wood and palm. More than a third of Africa has little or no vegetation suitable for building use, but the savannah and steppe regions produce baobab, dom palm and, in the more vegetated regions, acacia. Palm is not a structurally strong building material, but it is used for beams by the Hausa and Bornu and for the reinforcement of the parabolic arches by which the shallow domes of their houses are supported. Shorter lengths of palm are also employed, in a corbelling technique, to span the corners of a square room to produce a dome. Palm leaves are used extensively as a roof cover, either in layers alternating with brushwood and earth, as in the Sudan, or

61. Agar Dinka raising grass-thatched roof on to a house on wood posts, near Pacong, Agar Dinka, Southern Sudan; from a photograph by Jeremy Coote, 1981

as a thatching material. The splines are an effective tensile material for light spans, while the leaves may be woven to form mat walls. The gnarled lengths of acacia are not suitable for structural use. Slender poles from local trees are used by the Maasai and other East African peoples in the construction of huts, cattle kraals and so on. Young stands of pole wood are generally preferred to heavier timber. Here, as elsewhere in Africa, however, trees may be valued more for the shade they provide than as a source of building material.

Among nomadic peoples thin poles, often preformed into arcs to facilitate rapid erection, are used as armatures for their movable huts. These are usually domed structures with curved ridges. The north-east African Borana, Somali and Danakil, among others, use this form of structure, which may have been introduced southwards by the nomadic Beja. It is also used by southern Tuareg and by those other Tuareg who are becoming more settled. Here the roof frame may be supported on short poles to give more headroom. Some frame-and-mat structures, such as those used by the Baggara of Sudan, reach 10 m across. Covering mats may be of woven grass, palm leaves or similar material, which can be rolled up and packed on donkeys or camels as the group seeks new pasture.

Light wood and pole frames are also used by hunter-gatherer peoples in Africa's desert and scrub regions. In the Kalahari Desert the San built temporary camps of shelters erected from a few branches and a grass cover. When a longer stay was anticipated, these were more carefully made, with horizontal wands interwoven with the vertical members and covered with bunched grass, sometimes with its roots. In regions with plentiful wood such hunters as the Hadza of Tanzania used wands and branches to make thatched temporary shelters, while the Mbuti and other pygmy bands of the Ituri Forest in Zaïre constructed domical shelters of branches interwoven with lighter wands and covered with large leaves. Such light, temporary shelters may be built in a few hours and then used for two to three months, until the area's game has been hunted out and the group moves on.

In forested regions where timber is readily available, houses with a square or rectangular plan are commonly found. While these are often referred to as examples of 'carpentered' or trabeated architecture, most are not made of sawn and squared timber, even those built after European tools became generally available. African timber-framed buildings generally have no sill, the house-posts being driven directly into the ground. Many do not have roof trusses, but the ridges are supported by central poles and the wall plates by end- and side-poles. Such structures are often framed with a ring-beam of poles or intertwined, pliable branches, and further lateral poles or branches may be used to strengthen the side walls. The roof structure may have true purlins, but common rafters, with horizontal rafters laid to take thatching, are customary.

In such timber buildings most joints are secured by bark-strip lashing. Mortice-and-tenon, and even lap joints, were known but were often used only for doorways and door sills. Such skills in working timber with an adze, as are evident in sculpture throughout West and Central Africa, indicate that it was not for the lack of ability or tools that such methods were not employed. Although triangulation is sometimes employed to stabilize a structure, bracing tends to be horizontal unless considerable live loads from wind pressure are to be withstood. In very tall buildings, such as those of the Bafut of Cameroon, diagonal bracing is used both functionally and decoratively.

Although some peoples (e.g. the Kikuyu) use such termite-resistant woods as cedar, most timber buildings are constructed from soft woods that are subject to both termite infestation and wood rot. The damage these cause frequently necessitates rebuilding after a few years. In both forest and savannah woodland regions wood may be used in association with mud daub. A double layer of poles may be used, as among the Lamba of Zimbabwe, to produce a thicker wall section that may be strengthened both inside and out with horizontal woven branches and withies. Mud is used to pack the intervening space and for plastering the whole wall surface, both internally and externally. When smoothed and polished the building may appear to be constructed totally of earth.

(e) Grass. Bamboo is employed widely as a structural material. This is especially so in the lusher grassland areas, where it is most ambitiously used in the high structures of the Bamileke of the Cameroon Highlands. Here the main living space is constructed as a cube out of vertical bamboo poles with stout, timber corner posts. A platform of thin bamboos is raised on top of the dwelling space and the pyramidal roof erected above. A second stabilizing platform may be inserted in the roof structure, which frequently reaches 6 m in height. Roof structures are prefabricated from triangles of bamboo, lashed and braced, and the whole roof is thickly thatched by specialists.

Although a few nomadic groups (e.g. some pastoral Fulani) use unsupported grass as a temporary shelter, it is most often used for roof thatching or as a cladding material, for which purpose some South African peoples have developed intricate grass-weaving techniques. In some areas where grass is abundant it may be pulled in bunches with the roots still attached, these being used to secure the grass to the roof frame. Grass is usually layered from the eaves to the ridge, sometimes over a hipped roof among rain-forest peoples. Circular-plan houses have conical roofs that are thatched in layers from the eaves. Among the Dinka of Sudan the grass roof is made separately on the ground and then lifted onto the hut walls (see fig. 61). The peak of the roof is capped with a woven and bound grass finial or a pad of packed earth. Sometimes, for example among the Kipsigis of Kenya, the last bundles of grass are attached to a pole inserted at the crest, and an upturned broken pot is slid over the pole. In each case the purpose is to make the roof watertight at its weakest point. Where reeds or elephant grass are available these are used, tightly secured with bound straw. Forked sticks inserted through the wall structure at the eaves take the weight of the thatch.

(f) Hair and hide. Cattle nomads and camel nomads commonly use tents relating to the intercontinental tent culture. Bedouin and Berber tribes of the northern Sahara construct tents from strips of woven goat-hair, made on ground looms and sewn together to form a membrane. This membrane is held in tension by guy-ropes affixed with wooden stay fasteners. Strong, supporting webbing-bands take the lateral strains that would otherwise separate the strips. The centre of the tent is supported by a curved length of wood raised on two poles, its length varying from tribe to tribe, thus giving the tent a characteristic profile. The edge of the membrane is held up with poles. The Kababish of the Sudan often have boxlike tents, while among the Tuareg and the Fulani a Berber tent type is used, differing in that the membrane is made of goatskins sewn together (see fig. 62). Usually 40 such skins are used, but as many as 200 may be used in the membrane of a chief's tent. The trailing ends of the hides are cut and plaited by the women to provide internal decoration, and dyed patterns are also used. Among many tent cultures decorative hangings are used as side walls, to cover openings and to divide the internal spaces of the tent.

62. Fulani goatskin tent, Niger; from a photograph by Sarah Errington

(iii) Vernacular architecture.

(a) Building types. (b) Scale. (c) Spatial organization. (d) Symbolism. (e) Decoration.

(a) Building types. Most African buildings are domestic. Among these a distinction may be made between a 'hut', which is single-celled and conceived as one unit of space, and a 'house', which has not been divided but rather conceived and built as a number of separate units, or to accommodate a variety of discrete functions. Huts with a more temporary function are related to the dwelling and are often virtually identical in form. These include 'menstrual' huts, where pubertal girls may be confined prior to a celebration to mark their transition to womanhood, and circumcision huts, constructed for young boys awaiting initiation rites.

Movements of peoples and the persistence of building types in areas settled in modern times have meant that differing systems may be found in proximity to each other. Nevertheless, it is broadly possible to identify major areas where specific building forms occur. The cylindrical hut is the most widely dispersed, occurring in Southern and East Africa and through the savannah belts of West Africa. In Southern Africa it is commonly known as the rondavel.

In the tropical rain-forest and savannah woodlands rectangular- and square-plan buildings are common, while the so-called 'beehive' style of dome was built by many peoples.

Vernacular buildings that are similar in form may vary considerably in construction: a cylindrical, single-dwelling unit may be built wholly of mud, or it may be constructed of poles driven into the soil, bound with creepers or bark, mud daubed and mud plastered over; or it may be built of sun-dried blocks or bricks, which, when plastered, display similar formal characteristics. Rectangular-plan buildings, though constructed by different techniques, may also be rendered, and thus the structural differences between the building systems employed are obscured.

Basic forms. The dome is the simplest form, being an undifferentiated structure with no separation of roof from walls. Structural members are inserted in the ground and bent over to join at the apex to form a peaked, ribbed dome, held in tension. Such buildings are found as far west as among the Conagui of Guinea, as far east as among the Chencha of Ethiopia and as far south as among the Zulu of South Africa. Frequently the domes are thatched in layers of bundled grass. An alternative form of dome, developed by the Zulu and Nguni, consists of semicircular hoops, inserted into the ground concentrically to form a tight mesh, over which layers of grass thatch and woven grass mats are placed. Generally the grass dome receives a final thatch layer that is secured with a net of weighted grass ropes.

Though structurally more complex, the cylindrical hut with a differentiated, conical roof has a number of advantages, allowing not only additional headroom but also space for smoke from internal fires. In addition, the eaves can protect the exterior from both sun and rain. A low verandah with an outer ring of poles may take some of the roof's weight. Traditionally such houses were rarely subdivided, as the introduction of ceilings or walls reduces air circulation.

Centrally located on a line drawn from the Bight of Benin to the Horn of Africa, the territory of the Zande may be seen as a fulcrum of African shelter forms, a nodal region through which the main currents of influence appear to have passed. Zande house types include the *buguru* with mud walls and a timber door lintel for the senior wife; the *dondoma* with low eaves and no walls for other wives; and the *basura*, or temporary sleeping hut. They have also adopted such other forms as the *naderugi* hut, built on a platform of beaten clay; the *kata*, a type constructed of blocks of termite hill earth; the *basa*, formed in the shape of a tunnel; and a square hut, the *gbiliki*, influenced by European 'rest-houses'. Even 'traditional' Zande huts built at the end of the 20th century differ somewhat from 19th-century forms, which had high, pointed, conical roofs and verandahs offering protection from the rain. Although not all societies are as eclectic in their architectural tastes as the Zande, the diversity of forms adopted and built by them indicates the problem of ascribing a single type to any people or of assuming that types existing today are those of the past. In areas of West Africa with relatively low rainfall, cylindrical huts may have crossbeams supporting a flat roof and layers of brush and earth as well as, perhaps, a low parapet. Roofs of this type are used to dry and store grains and fruits and as outdoor sleeping areas that catch any available breeze. Flat-roofed cylindrical huts are not found in East Africa.

Houses with a square or rectangular plan occur most frequently in forested regions, where the availability of timber and bamboo permits a frame construction. Regular-square plans are comparatively unusual: most buildings with right-angled corners tend to be rectangular, with the entrance often on one of the shorter sides. As the ridge is usually supported by poles rather than by a roof truss, and the roofs take a burden of thatch, pitches of *c.* 45° are common. In some rain-forest regions there are thatched, hipped roofs. An extended eaves structure may permit a covered verandah, and, more rarely, thatched porches may be added. Wall openings other than doorways are rare, enhancing security but reducing light and cross-ventilation. Interiors can be subdivided relatively easily with a rectangular plan, and the simplest form of this—the erection of a cross-wall to create two rooms—is most common.

Stone, earth and mud-brick buildings of rectangular plan are also found throughout North Africa. Here more complex internal subdivision is common, both horizontally and vertically. Islamic requirements for the segregation of women also necessitated the further partitioning of rooms, which usually had small window openings.

Under Islamic influence, indigenous, circular forms south of the Sahara were replaced by houses of earth construction and rectangular plan, although both types existed in such areas as the northern Nigerian Hausa emirates. Flat roofs also superseded conical roofs, although arches and domes were used by the Hausa and Fulani to span larger spaces.

Palaces. Although the architecture of chiefs' compounds is closely based on that of ordinary dwellings, many African rulers expressed their power and influence architecturally. They did so by using the finest craftmen and by developing spatially elaborate complexes to accommodate not only themselves, their kinsmen, wives and children but also other retainers, courtiers, visitors and supplicants. At the time of early European contact, West African domestic architecture was in many ways comparable with that of Europe, with wattle-and-daub and timber-framed houses with thatched roofs. As a result, early Western observers were impressed not so much by essentially similar African building types and techniques as by the formal sophistication and decorative embellishment of the 'palaces'. As early as the 16th century, for example, accounts of the palace of the Oba of Benin reached Europe, with details of its sanctuaries, shrines and ceremonials (*see* BENIN).

Of all such palaces, the citadel of the Mambo Mutota (King Monomotapa) of Zimbabwe, with its impressive scale, skilful building in stone and evidence of a sophisticated culture has attracted most attention from archaeologists and historians (*see* GREAT ZIMBABWE). The lavish palace of the Shaykh of Mogadishu, further north, was described by the Moroccan traveller Ibn Battuta as early as 1332; all the east-coast shaykhdoms may have had similar palaces. Many Bantu chiefdoms and kingdoms had large compounds for their principal lineages, and these were also identified as 'palaces' by Europeans. King Mutesa of the Baganda built his capital, Kasubi Nabulagala, by covering a hillside with immense, domed houses, finely thatched in reed, laid out so that his regional chiefs lived in the part closest to their lands. The royal enclosure included a house for the keeper of the sacred fire, the house of the King's wives, the royal drum-room, the royal smithy, a waiting-room, court rooms and an Ivory Court, where the King discussed matters of state. Such neighbouring peoples as the Bunyoro and the Banyankole also had large palace complexes.

In the Bamenda highlands of Cameroon a number of Tikar tribes built notable palace compounds. That of the chief of Batoufam featured a cluster of tall, conically thatched buildings of bamboo construction of the traditional Bamileke form. Its arrangement was similar to the palace of the Fon of Bafut, which was approached through a courtyard flanked by enclosures for the older and the younger wives and their respective children. In the 1950s the Fon's enclosure included a reception hall, medicine huts, the storage and assembly halls of secret societies, dormitories and burial houses, but only two traditional buildings remained, the others having been replaced by earth-block houses with tiled roofs. The King of Bamum also had an impressive palace (*see* BAMUM).

Peoples inhabiting the rain-forests built large and complex palaces, although few survive. Such palaces include the *afins* of the Yoruba. These were the seats of the Obas of each city and comprised large complexes of courtyards surrounded by rectangular thatched buildings. Such palaces normally faced the city market, from which access was gained by a portico and gate to the main courtyard, overlooked by the Oba's verandah (*kobi*). The portico and arcade of the Oni at Ife was of immense dimensions with a frontage more than 100 m long.

See also PALACE, §VIII.

Shrines and other religious buildings. Palace complexes are often also spiritual centres, containing temples and shrines, a reflection of the concept of divine kingship that prevails in many African kingdoms. Among those peoples who build sanctuaries and cult houses are the Asante of Ghana. Their 'fetish-house' (*abosomfie*) is in the form of the customary dwelling, with four rectangular buildings around a court (*paito*). One open-fronted unit houses a drum orchestra: a shrine-room, the domain of the village priest, is opposite. The Yoruba of Nigeria, who follow a complex religion with many gods, build large temples, shrines and cult houses, among the most significant of which are a temple to Ogun Igbo at Isheda Benin, the cult houses to Sango the god of thunder and the river god Oshun at Oshogbo, and a number in various places to Omolu, the god of smallpox. Yoruba shrine-rooms have painted and sculptured pillars, and they and the cult objects they contain are guarded by a priest or priestess.

Among the peoples of eastern Nigeria members of Ekpe and other secret societies build houses for the performance of fertility rites. The Igbo construct open-fronted mud temples, from which are hung the skulls of

63. Dogon men's meeting-house (*togu na*), Ireli, Mali; from a photograph by Angela Fisher, 1981

sacrificial animals, fenced with a sacred shrub. The Ibibio build commemorative funerary shrines (*see* IBIBIO, §4). Often, however, a village priest works magic or invokes spirits in a sacred place that may be marked only by a ring of stones or protective charms. Ancestral hunters' shrines among the Ndembu of Zambia are encircled with animal horns, and each shrine contains a forked stick, a square of termite earth and a grass braid, all of which have symbolic connotations. Among many savannah peoples ancestral shrines may be built within the domestic hut or compound. They may take the form of cones or phallic columns and may sometimes contain the ancestor's remains.

Meeting-houses. In some societies, large communal meeting-houses served as council chambers. The most impressive include those of the MANGBETU of Zaïre, often being nearly 100 m long, 50 m wide and some 15 m high at the ridge. Rows of internal posts supported the interior roof framework, which was constructed of bamboo and palm fronds. Others, open at one end and of considerable size, were built by the Igbo of eastern Nigeria and used by masking societies. These and the meeting-houses of the Yakö (also of eastern Nigeria) were substantial constructions built of logs.

Special houses were often built for use by male clan members or by members of societies. These are often open-sided shelters with flat roofs supported on piers, on which may be stored reeds and firewood that act as insulation during the day. Such shelters are made by the Senufo and other peoples of Côte d'Ivoire and Mali, but the best-known type is the *togu na* of the Dogon, with its supporting forked pillars carved with female breasts and symbolically rich motifs (see fig. 63; *see also* DOGON).

Granaries and stores. The grain stores of the West African savannah generally take the form of large clay pots resting on short piers of rock or timber. Those of East and Southern Africa, in contrast, generally take the form of large baskets raised off the ground on stilts. Some attain great size; those of the Songhai of Mali, for example, being 3 or 4 m high. Among such savannah peoples as the Lobi of Burkina Faso and the Mofou of Cameroon, however, granaries are built inside an ordinary hut. Within, the grain stores may be built to roof-height and shaped like immense pottery vessels with internal subdivisions. Access to granaries is usually through the top of the container, which may have a removable lid or thatch roof (see fig. 64). When the level of the grain is low, a door in the side may be used. Such doors are hung on hinges, or on projections that turn in recesses, and have wooden locks. Other kinds of storage baskets and jars, often free-standing, at times rivalling in size associated sleeping huts, are found throughout Africa. They need to be constructed well to resist the thrusts of their loads and will often last without maintenance for long periods.

The stores of the Kiga of Uganda are as much as 3 m high and 1.5 m in diameter. Woven of pliable papyrus or bamboo lengths, they are highly resilient and fill out their shape as the container is filled. The *ngula* baskets of the Tonga of Zambia were built only after the size of the

64. Kirdi granary being filled, Mandara Mountains, Cameroon; from a photograph by Angela Fisher, 1980

65. Zulu settlement with central cattle *kraal*, South Africa

harvest had been ascertained. Many cylindrical grain stores are made of reeds or canes, the structure supported by strong poles, sometimes daubed with mud, and topped with a conical thatched roof. These are to be found in many eastern and southern regions, reflecting the southward movement of former migrant peoples. There is evidence that the basket-weave, cylindrical wattle or wattle-and-daub granary and the pottery grain store are all traceable historically to the inter-lacustrine region. Among some peoples, such as the Zulu, storage pits are also used for keeping root crops.

(b) Scale. In parts of Morocco and Algeria, fortified towns often had look-out towers and houses that were several storeys high. These were built around central shafts or light-giving wells and were accessed via stairways of timber and stone. In Sub-Saharan Africa the buildings of Islamicized societies are generally lower than those in the north, although two-storey houses are not uncommon, and some defensive towers are higher. Non-Islamic Sub-Saharan buildings are rarely more than one storey, although there are exceptions, including the two-storey, cylindrical houses of the rural Tigre in Ethiopia and the two- and sometimes three-storey dwellings of the Somolo of Burkina Faso and the Fante of Ghana. Platform dwellings on stilts are used by the Dinka of Sudan (see fig. 61 above) as well as by such riverain and lacustrine fishing peoples as the Nyasa of Tanzania and the Tofinou of Lake Nokwé, Togo.

The prevalence of single-storey, low-profile buildings may be accounted for by a variety of factors. There was no lack of space, they were considered relatively inconspicuous, and their low level was also seen as a defensive measure. Height is often associated with prestige, however, and many peoples, while still building single-storey dwellings, construct accentuated, high roofs. The narrow, pyramid-shaped huts of the Ngelima of Zaïre (more than 8 m high, though little more than 3 m sq. at the base) are examples.

(c) Spatial organization. It is in the disposition of structures and their lateral arrangement that African building is spatially most varied. Quadrangular-plan houses are often grouped around a courtyard either with individual units making contact only at the corners, as among the Asante, or with a continuous articulated roof, as in the traditional compound of the Yoruba or of the Fon of the Republic of Benin. Low dwellings arranged in lines facing each other or around a courtyard may be extended by adding further courts, some of which may function as impluvia, collecting rain-water from the roofs in large pottery vessels or a central circular tank. Another building arrangement based around a rectangular courtyard is the *tembe* of the Iraqw and Barangi of Tanzania. This is a continuous structure, which can be 100 m long, with a backward-sloping roof. The largest could provide refuge for, perhaps, a hundred people at times of attack. Some were made less conspicuous by being built in a deep trench or even totally below ground-level, with trench or tunnel access.

Kraal arrangements are common in Southern and East Africa and often take a circular or oblate form. Among, for example, the Ila Tonga, they may be of considerable size, as much as 0.5 km in diameter. Circular-plan huts may be unconnected but arranged in an approximate arc, circle or horseshoe-shape and surrounded by a defensive thicket or hedge of euphorbia (see fig. 65; *see also* MILITARY ARCHITECTURE AND FORTIFICATION, §IX). Among the Bahima of Uganda a number of clusters may be contained within one enclosure, while in Lesotho, where there is little danger from predators or from attack and population densities are low, dwellings may be widely dispersed and without any significant arrangement. Where there is considerable pressure on land, however, as among the Tswana and Ndebele of Botswana, fences may define family territory. Within the boundary a number of huts may be grouped around a cleared and carefully maintained area, often encircled by a low, sculptured wall. The area is used, in effect, as an outdoor room. Storehouses, latrines and screened washplaces may also be constructed within the larger area.

The greatest variety of settlement types occurs in the savannah regions of West Africa, in an arc from Sudan to Senegal. Among those peoples using circular dwelling units the customary settlement is the compound. For example, in the mountains of Southern Kordofan, Sudan,

Nuba often locate their houses on defensive positions on rocky edges overlooking their fields and cattle. Constructed as small cylinders, houses remain discrete units while being built close together, with narrow passages and gaps closed with stones and brush. A Nuba family compound comprises a hut for the wife, additional sleeping huts and granaries and an open communal space that is sometimes partially shaded. Among the Moro sub-group there are separate huts for the daughters, huts containing storage pots, a cooking space and an 'access' hut (*khodo*), divided by low walls and with sleeping ledges for the sons.

The dwellings of such craftsmen as smiths and metalworkers, who often belonged to a separate caste and were considered to be magically dangerous by virtue of the transformative nature of their work, were often set apart. This separation also had the advantage of keeping the forge and bellows ventilated and away from inflammable thatch. Other craft buildings such as workshops, dye-pits, potteries, tanneries, weaving sheds and furnaces (see fig. 48 above) were often located in specific areas within the community. In smaller settlements a local market may be held under a light, monopitch structure, under awnings or with little cover at all. In the towns, long rows of market stalls occupy designated spaces under monopitch or pitched roofs. Village shops, often comprising a single dwelling with an open side or room adapted for the sale of mixed commodities and imported goods, may be found in rain-forest areas. In the towns, of course, the mix of building types is correspondingly greater, including a variety of shops, schools and urban housing.

Although individual circular-plan huts are not easily extensible, the compound settlement form is extremely adaptable, and many examples of great beauty and complexity have been recorded in Burkina Faso, Togo, Mali, Guinea and elsewhere. Although in general such compounds are limited to the dwellings of extended families, each under a household head who may have more than one wife, in some areas several may be grouped together to form a village.

Throughout the Sahel, compounds have been adapted to meet cultural requirements for domestic privacy and the seclusion of women. In rural areas the curvilinear plans of traditional West African compounds persisted into the late 20th century, dwelling-units being usually circular with conical or flat roofs and linked by encircling and dividing walls. However, Mande influence has led in some areas to more regular, square-plan units sharing common side walls and clustered in rectilinear groupings. Many compounds have internal walls to distinguish the domain of the male household head from those of the women and children. Among the Hausa an entrance room (*zaure*) opens on to the head's area, which may include a stable and bachelor hut. The female section is situated beyond the vestibule (*sigife*). While seldom strict in their geometry, such compound plans are found in peri-urban areas of Mali, Burkina Faso and northern Côte d'Ivoire, but they are most characteristic of the towns. Even in the Hausa emirates of the western Sudan rural settlements may consist largely of circular-plan huts or a mixture of these with rectilinear forms; in the cities, however, round huts have become increasingly rare in the 20th century.

(d) Symbolism. Although some vernacular African architectural forms may have arisen out of functional considerations, it is rare for any to be without symbolic associations. The partly subterranean houses of the western Kassena of Burkina Faso, for example, display great formal originality in the use of sculpted platforms, tiers of steps, partitioning walls, dwelling spaces, tunnels and openings and in such functional structures as fish-drying kilns, hearths and storage shelves for gourds and pottery vessels. Similar moulded structures are also used by the Tallensi of Ghana and other peoples of the region. These forms have anthropomorphic associations, with parts identified with the mouth, the head or the 'face of the deceased'. The Dogon of Mali have a complex symbolic system that encompasses within it the settlement and compound architecture. Thus the smithy and the men's meeting-house (*togu na*; see fig. 63 above) were conceptualized as the head; individual families' houses as the chest; the women's house as the hands; the oil-crushing stones and village altar as the male and female genitalia; and other altars as the feet. In the individual dwelling, units are similarly conceptualized, and the whole compound is perceived as a man lying on his side in the act of procreation.

The architectural symbolism of the Fali of Cameroon is no less complex. They similarly associate parts of the village and the dwelling with human form and with procreation. The principal groups associate themselves with cardinal points within the settlement. Modelled and painted surfaces enrich Fali compounds, which are virtually autonomous, although communality is reinforced by the shared meeting-house. Fali cosmology is bipartite and related to a creation myth involving an ancestral toad and turtle. Each house represents this, with the cylindrical shape representing the female toad, in union with the conical roof-shell of the male turtle. There are, however, other layers of meaning: the settlement at the nodal centre is male, the encircling ring of cultivation is female, while the structure of the dwelling and the space it contains reflect the symbolic duality of earth and sky. The Batammaliba of northern Togo and the Republic of Benin regard their houses and settlements as icons of their cosmology. Concepts of the individual in society are expressed not only in the buildings' forms but also in the construction processes and in their subsequent use.

(e) Decoration. Much of the appeal of African architecture is due to its sculptural quality. Among many peoples the use of earths in pottery-related techniques has resulted in forms of great aesthetic beauty. Moreover, the use of curvilinear walls and details, door openings and mouldings in shell-like structures of considerable resilience gives a feeling of movement to the constructions.

Painted decoration is frequently executed by women, as among the Frafra of Ghana, using either their fingers or frayed sticks as brushes (see fig. 50 above). Traditionally, such earth colours as white, red and black were used, often with no fixing medium. Certain colours often have specific connotations: white is frequently linked with purity, power and health, red with blood and power and black with disease and death. (The traditional range of colours was extended in the second half of the 20th century with the

66. Ndebele decorated mud house inside enclosing wall, built and decorated by Christina Skosana and family, near Devon, Transvaal, South Africa; from a photograph by Elizabeth A. Schneider, 1980

adoption of washing 'blue' and commercial paints.) It should not be concluded, however, that the use of a colour always carried such connotations. Nor do all motifs convey meaning: the extensive use of triangles and simple geometric shapes on Shona houses may be purely decorative.

The townships in South Africa have been the location for the emergence of a 20th-century development in painted decoration. Highly abstract, simplified but forceful designs serve the dual purpose of visually increasing space and enriching the environment. Such decoration often comprises large shapes painted in bold colours, sometimes differentiated by textures in the plaster. Razor-blades and other objects have been the inspiration for some motifs.

Figurative wall painting, common in both ancient and modern Egyptian vernacular architecture, is not unknown in other African societies but normally appears only in such conventionalized and two-dimensional forms as the hunting scenes and totemic birds and animals painted in 'stick-figures' and silhouette on the external walls of some Lunda (Angola) and Ngere (Côte d'Ivoire) houses. With the growth in 'Chop Bars' and shops a lively and popular form of wall art has evolved featuring highly modelled figures, vignetted in decorative borders, often captioned with epigrams and representing images of affluence and sophistication.

Decorative wall painting may be used in conjunction with modelled decoration. Such Southern African peoples as the southern Sotho and Taung use finger-furrows on wall surfaces, with mosaics of pebbles and broken china to increase the textural contrast and curvilinear designs to define shapes. Among the Tswana the apron-court (*lolwapa*) is often decorated with a painted and sculpted defining wall. It is, however, among the Ndebele that the richest forms of wall painting are to be found (see fig. 66; *see also* NDEBELE). The walls of their cylindrical dwellings are decorated with strong abstract motifs, which became more geometric and rectilinear as rectangular plans were adopted. Exteriors of houses have continued to be lavishly painted with marked symmetry in patterning, the entrances to the compounds defined by high gateways or ziggurat-form gate-posts. Motifs were originally derived from blanket and beadwork patterns, but car number plates and the Victorian buildings of Pretoria later became design sources. The Ndebele also decorate the interiors of their homes: a painted sideboard of moulded clay, with clay fittings, is a typical feature.

Some West African peoples also use a combination of paint and high-relief modelling to decorate their dwellings. Asante houses were formerly decorated with abstract symbolic motifs painted in white and red, some of which were modelled as open-fret screens, with interlaced strapwork, spirals and volutes. These motifs had similar meanings to those of designs found on goldweights and *adinkra* cloth and may be Islamic in origin. After the sacking of Kumasi by the British in 1874, this art declined on houses, but it was retained for many years in shrines (*abosomfie*), where moulded walls, pillars, pilasters, plinths and openwork screen walls survived. Open screens, more heavily moulded and less formal, were also used elsewhere. Perhaps the most structurally daring are the arcades of the earth houses of the Fouta Djallon, Senegal, where abacus-like columns support massive loads and openings are pierced in a variety of audacious shapes, symmetrically disposed.

A combination of moulded and painted decoration also adorned the walls of the former palace of King Gozo of

Abomey in the Republic of Benin. Here deeply recessed, moulded panels once contrasted with the surface painting. Heavily weathered, many of these panels are now only distinguishable by their polychrome paintwork. Yoruba palaces in western Nigeria were often similarly decorated, and, by the 1990s, concrete was regularly used for the sculpting of three-dimensional figures and heraldic animals, notably lions, often derived from motifs imported from Brazil. Such heraldic animals are moulded on parapets and positions of prominence on the houses of the wealthy.

Other types of sculpted relief include carved doors, an important feature of many palace buildings, shrines and houses of important people (*see also* DOOR, §VII). Among the Dogon, granary doors had sculptured protective figures and elaborately carved locks. The Senufo and the Baule carve high-relief fertility devices, closely related in form to their buffalo and ram masks, on door panels. Under Baule influence the Senufo have developed door panels with spatially inventive arrangements of fish, bird and water motifs. Although some were polychromatically painted, Baule doors were often wholly in red and those of the Senufo in black. The palaces of the Yoruba also had elaborately carved doors, though their design was more constrained than that of the Senufo, being arranged in horizontal bands of figures with supporting panels of interlaced designs. Apart from the door, the entrance frame itself has sometimes been the focus of sculptural detail: Bamileke bamboo houses have heavy, wood surrounds carved with heads and figures symbolic of increase.

Three-dimensional architectural sculpture reached a high level in the *mbari* houses built by the Owerri Igbo to honour Ala, the earth goddess and guardian of morality. Square in plan and open-sided, they frequently have tiers or steps on which figures are moulded in mud. Other sculptures, often life-size, may include both traditional and modern totemic animals and ribald or witty representations of figures of authority (*see also* IGBO).

Larger, although perhaps not as inventive, are the so-called 'monuments' of the Asafo military companies of the Fante of Ghana. Each company has a polychrome, concrete command post (*posuban*), whose form is thought to derive ultimately from European trading forts (see fig. 79 below). Monumental in form, they may have verandahs, flights of stairs, arcades and life-size figures of men and lions and may terminate in a metal palm tree. They are used to store the company's drums and act as a focus for its ceremonial life.

(iv) Christian architecture. African architectural interpretation of Christian forms dates to at least the 4th century AD when Christianity was first established in Nubia. In Adulis and Aksum in Ethiopia, monasteries and churches existed in large numbers by the 6th century, although their numbers later declined as Islam was adopted in the region. The 13th-century Zagwe dynasty in the Lasta region of Ethiopia left 11 churches, carved from solid rock under

67. Christian church, Debre Libonos, Eritrea, probably before 1500; from a photograph by David Buxton, 1930s

the direction of King Lalibela (*see* ETHIOPIA, fig. 1). The church of St George was formed by digging a trench to create its cruciform plan. Aksumite influences include such exterior architectural features as simulated 'monkey-head' beam ends (see fig. 67). Links with more distant traditions are evident in the interior details of some of the churches. Although the churches of Lalibela are the most celebrated, many other churches, adapted from caves or carved into rock faces, have been documented in the Tigre region. These include the great churches at Cherkos, Wkro, Abreha Atsbehj and Medhane Alem, as well as the extraordinary plateau stronghold of Debra Damo with its almost inaccessible monastery.

Many of the churches and monasteries of the Ethiopian Christian enclave were destroyed by the non-Christian Galla in the 16th century. The establishment of the kingdom of Gondar under Fasiladas led to the building of a splendid palace–fortress, over 40 churches and the monastery of Kusquam with the now ruinous round church of Debra-Tsahay. It is possible that this circular church was based on wooden, thatched prototypes: a church of this form still stands at Manz and is locally attributed to Nagassi, a prince of Shoa at the time of Gondar's flourishing. Fasiladas was also responsible for rebuilding the cathedral at Aksum, the holiest place in Christian Africa, but Gondar was levelled by Theodore II in the mid-19th century. At the end of the 19th century Menelik II, the founder of Addis Ababa, built the three-tiered and domed octagonal church of Debra Raguel at his first capital of Entotto. With colonial partition of the continent a new ecclesiastical architecture appeared, but this had little effect on the development of indigenous forms.

See also COPTIC ART, §II, 3; ETHIOPIA, §I; NUBIA, §VI. For information on colonial and post-colonial Christian architecture in Africa see individual country entries.

(v) Islamic architecture. The impact of Islam on architecture in Africa has been profound. It has been felt through the influence of Islamic calligraphy, patterns and decorative forms, as well as through domestic house forms and the larger forms of religious architecture. Islam brought to Africa a taste for the monumental, with tombs, mosques and minarets introducing a vertical dimension that was new to African architecture south of the Sahara. Islam also brought with it some technological changes, including the occasional use of kiln-dried bricks. More importantly, it led to the concentration of dwellings in trading centres and entrepôts, where mosques, palaces, markets and people's homes were clustered together. Islam's impact has been felt throughout the continent, especially in urban areas, but has been at its strongest in the Muslim areas of the western Sudan, in the towns and cities of the East African coast and, of course, in North Africa and the Maghrib. Seen as the near and distant west by their Arab colonizers, North Africa and the Maghrib may be considered stylistically part of the Middle East.

(a) Building types. (b) Decoration.

(a) Building types.

Secular. From Cairo in Egypt to Salé in Morocco characteristically Islamic house and settlement forms are seen. There are medinas, souqs and kasbas; there are courtyard houses, linked by interconnecting lanes and passages, with their shared walls and flat roofs; and there is also the segregation of the women's quarters. At the coastal town of Sousse in Tunisia, an Islamic city was built next to the pre-existing medieval city, leaving the latter largely intact. In contrast, such towns as Ghadames, El Oued and those, such as Ghardaia, in the valleys of the Mzab, as well as Constantine, MARRAKESH and FEZ, developed environments that were responsive to the urban economies and social mores of Islam.

In such towns as Djenné in Mali a more syncretic response to Islam resulted in the development of regional styles. In the Dambougalsoria quarter, for example, there is a cluster of houses said to date from the Moroccan invasion of 1591. Their marked portals, known locally as *potigé*, flanking the entrances and the reception chamber above are topped with a row of pre-Islamic-style pinnacles. The Djenné masons, mostly of Songhay or Bamana origin, were renowned in the region into the late 20th century.

By the 10th century AD Muslims were established on the east coast of Africa. Indeed, the town of Manda may have been settled in the 9th century, while Mogadishu, Malindi, Zanzibar and other ports are of later date. Many of these Islamic towns were highly developed. Excavations at Gedi, a former sultan's palace on the Kenyan coast abandoned in the 14th century, revealed coral ragstone walls and portals, reception-rooms and audience courts, apartments, ablution chambers and lavatories. Extensive archaeological evidence of sophisticated spatial organization has been uncovered at the Husuni Kubwa palace, Kilwa, which, in the 13th century, was the largest building south of the Sahara.

Early in the 16th century many Swahili towns were sacked by the Portuguese. Lamu, an island town off the Kenyan coast, largely escaped destruction, and later a treaty of protection with Oman helped to preserve it. While none of its buildings dates from before the 18th century, their form may well reflect earlier domestic architecture. Two-storey merchants' houses made of stone have servants' quarters on the ground-floor and the main living spaces above. Flat roofs made of mangrove poles covered in lime span the walls. A succession of narrow, shallow rooms with plastered walls and rows of moulded display niches, though elegant, are climatically more appropriate to the Persian Gulf than to the Kenyan coast. While these town houses reveal a taste for sophisticated urban living, the central complex of stone houses was surrounded by smaller houses, with walls of wattle-and-daub and deep, open-gabled thatched roofs, which were more suitable climatically.

Palaces were built for the emirs of Muslim societies in West Africa as expressions of their religious authority and secular power and as the focus of the community. They include the elaborately decorated palaces of Zaria and KANO. Other Hausa palaces such as that of the Emir of Daura are less decorated, and the strength of the structural detail is clearer. The arches that provide structural support are typically made with stepped mud corbels, reinforced with lengths of termite-resistant *azara* wood from the dom palm and plastered with mud to produce a simulated continuous curved arch. Although the construction differs, the form may derive from the armatures of the frame-and-mat structures of the local nomads (*see* §(ii)(d) above). Arches may intersect at a central apex, often marked by an inset brass plate, or may form a grid of crossed parabolas. Although this technique can be seen in palaces and other important buildings, the normal method of spanning roofs in domestic houses is with lengths of *azara*. Spans are increased by crossing the corners and making a shallow, corbelled-roof platform, which may be further supported by piers or a central pillar to take the weight of the covering of sticks and earth.

Sacred. The earliest Sub-Saharan mosques to have been discovered are those at Koumbi Saleh, the capital of the former empire of Ghana. Trade links had been established with this area as early as the 9th century AD through the trans-Saharan camel caravans. The Koumbi Saleh mosque type comprised a court, a sanctuary and a square minaret. Elements of this mosque type were common in other parts of the Sudanic region and may be regarded as comprising a distinct Sudanic tradition, which nevertheless had many variants owing to the different currents of influence over many centuries. For example, although the square tower minaret of the Great Mosque at KAIROUAN in Tunisia may have been the source for the Sudanic square-based minaret-towers (*ṣawma'a*), such examples as the tower at Chinguetti, Mauritania, where the mosque may date from the 14th century, differ by having a tapering form, with reinforcements and projecting beams.

The rulers of the successive empires of Ghana, Songhai and Mali embraced a vast territory, which became progressively Islamicized. Cities on the trans-Saharan routes adopted elements of Berber culture, and, under Songhai influence, pyramidal minaret structures on three levels were built. The mosque–tomb of Askia-al-Hajj Muhammed at Gao (Mali) is characteristic, with its bristling, stepped tower that reaches only half the height it was in the mid-19th century. The Sankoré Mosque at TIMBUKTU, a seat of Islamic scholarship in the 15th century, had a buttressed, tapering minaret and arcaded sanctuary. Contacts with the Mzab are evident at Gao and even more marked at Agades in Niger where the pyramid tower of the great mosque is related stylistically to that at Ghardaia in Algeria.

As Islam penetrated further south, building styles were developed that incorporated traditional non-Islamic forms. The mosques built under the influence of Dyula mullah-traders, for instance those in Kong, a Dyula centre of learning and commerce in present-day Mali, though changing through time, were notable for such features reminiscent of traditional Dogon forms as slender, tapering pyramidal minarets and walls buttressed with tall pinnacles. Sculptural in form, these are reinforced by horizontal cross-poles between, or projecting from, the buttresses. The mosques of Bobo-Dioulasso in Burkina Faso, Kawara in Côte d'Ivoire and Banda Nkwanta in Ghana show a lively variety of forms that are, nonetheless, clearly related.

Such Hausa mosques as the Shehu Mosque at Sokoto and the Friday Mosque at Bauchi (both Nigeria) had different forms. Made of reinforced earth, they had pillared prayer-halls supporting flat roofs of palm and mud. Regarded as the finest of the Hausa type, the Friday Mosque at Zaria (also Nigeria) had an undulating roof of shallow domes supported by internal parabolic arches of mud, reinforced with palm and sculpted in high relief.

68. Djenné, Mali, Great Mosque, eastern façade and qibla wall, with the market-place in the foreground; from a photograph by Mick Csaky, *c.* 1980

This remarkable building was substantially altered during restoration in 1975. Other types of mosque also exist in Africa. In the Futa Jallon and Guinea highlands an indigenous savannah building type has accommodated the formal requirements of Islam without sacrificing regional identity: thatched mosques, including those at Manou Degala and Fougoumba, were built by Fulani in the form of vast, ribbed domes. Entirely covered with layered grass thatch, each has a large cap or crest to deflect the rains. Within, a cubic earth sanctuary surrounded by the posts of the supporting structure is oriented to Mecca. Other hybrids are to be found, as in Lagos, where slaves repatriated to Nigeria from Brazil built a number of mosques in a style that derived from the Latin American ecclesiastical Baroque, with classical pilasters and broken pediments, but that bore in their polychrome façades such Islamic motifs as the star and crescent.

An external influence with even greater impact was that of the French engineers who, in 1935, remodelled the great mosque at Mopti in Mali, giving it a greater symmetry and tall, tapering external pilasters. Similarly, although the original structure of the mosque at Djenné dated from the 14th century, it was largely demolished in the early 19th century and then reconstructed in similar form under French colonial direction in 1907 (see fig. 68). Although both are hybrids, their much-photographed images established a popularized form of Sahelian architecture that is evident, for example, in the substantial rebuilding and considerable enlargement of the Great Mosque of Niono, Mali, by the designer, contractor and mason Lassine Minta (*b c.* 1920). The original building was finished in 1948; Minta's rebuilding and extension of it was completed in 1973.

Elsewhere the reconstruction of mosques was less happily resolved. Earlier mud mosques were replaced by new ones, often in stone with conventional minarets and prayer-halls on the Egyptian pattern. Among these was the four-minaret Friday Mosque in Kano, Nigeria, and the somewhat heavily proportioned mosque at Bouake, Côte d'Ivoire, which, nevertheless, has finely cut screens and balustrades and ogee domes of almost Mughal character. Mosques built towards the end of the 20th century tended to be similar, if smaller, and generally undistinguished. The Niliem Mosque at Omdurman, Sudan, designed by Jamal Abdullah, is a radical departure from this, being in the form of a tetrahedral dome standing on tapering pillars over an open prayer-hall.

(b) Decoration. Islamic influence is clearly seen in the decorative details of much African architecture. These may be drawn from ideograms and calligraphy and from such geometric patterns as the subdivided rectangular magic squares known as *hatumere.* Other motifs have been derived from textile patterns, wood-carving and so on. Decorations found among the settled Kabyle Berber in Algeria include cursive patterns created in white plaster on internal, red earth walls, the rugged stone exteriors of such houses preventing external ornamentation. These patterns are used to frame windows and doorways and recall the decorated bed-frames of the nomadic Berber peoples. They are widespread, being found on the other side of the Sahara in Oualata, Mauritania. Strongly associated with the privacy of the women's domain, they were created by members of the lower castes (*harratin*) for wives of aristocrats as symbols of fertility and maternity. Other decorative elements include sculptures, water vessels and moulded sideboards.

Abstract forms are sculpted on the façades of the houses of important men in central Mali. More impressive are the age-set houses (*saho*) of the Sorko of the Niger River in Mali in such centres as Kolenze and Aore. These structures, built by youths in preparation for marriage, are deeply moulded with phallic motifs, verandahs and crenellated roof terraces. The use of clay bricks in this region also permits high-relief framing and structural expression, with geometric openings and recessed patterns achieved by omitting bricks from the outer wall layers. More dramatically moulded, houses in the Djenné style with tall, flanking *potigé* piers beside the entrances and phallic pinnacles are the apogee of Malian architectural decoration (see fig. 65 above).

The *zanen gida* decorations on the façades of the houses of Hausa merchants are notable for their complexity and richness. They are based on the surface enrichment of the walls, ceilings, arch ribs and coffers of Hausa palaces and mosques. Moulded over the mud-plastered surfaces of walls and coated with a locally made cement (*laso*), the motifs are in deep relief, emphasizing doorways or window openings and sometimes extending over the entire façade (see fig. 69). The endless knot (*dagi*) is a common motif, and others are rifles, bicycles, cars and even aeroplanes. The *zanen gida* technique is probably of 18th-century origin and may be derived from the tent hangings of the nomadic Fulani. It was popularized in the 20th century but was in decline by the 1990s.

In contrast to the internal relief plasterwork of Swahili houses (*see* §(a) above) external surfaces were simply treated, emphasis being mainly on the massive doors, with iron studs, spikes and bosses: a style as common in Bahrain as in Lamu, Kenya. Direct decorative influence from Arabia was evident in the now deserted coral stone city of Sawakin, Sudan, once an island trading port on the Red Sea coast and the focus for African pilgrims on their way to Mecca. It was built by Hijazis and had a number of Ottoman-style houses of a considerable size and three storeys in height. Richly decorated internally with banded walls infilled with geometric designs etched in plaster, these houses had doorways with carved stone hoods and cusped stone heads embellishing the wall niches. Windows were fitted with carved, boxed shade screens (*rowshan*s or *mashribiyya*s), some of which have ornately carved grilles and opening panels. After 1866 an Egyptian style emerged in Sawakin, sometimes including European details.

Indeed, Egyptian domestic architectural styles permeated northern Sudan during the 19th century, especially along the Nile. A further development in African Islamic decoration occurred in Nubia, where the internal walls of houses were painted and sometimes sculpted and external decorations painted or applied around the entrance. In Wadi Halfa an elaborate and prestigious style was developed by Ahmad Batoul, who began to make mud reliefs and incised patterns in the early 1930s. Craftsmen competed to invent new motifs, borrowing from contemporary Art Deco sources in Egypt and using saucers and ceramics

69. Hausa decorated house, Tudun Wada, Zaria, Nigeria; from a photograph of 1962

inset in the plaster. Local people also decorated their own houses, men favouring scenes of pilgrimages to Mecca and women painting banded abstract wall friezes. This style of Nubian wall paintings ended with the flooding of the valley by the Aswan Dam in 1970.

(vi) Western architecture. European architecture was first introduced to Africa through the building of trading posts and forts, the first probably being built by the Portuguese on Arguin Island, Cape Blanco, in 1445. Over the centuries others were built along the western seaboard, from Goree to the Kongo, with the greatest concentration on what were known as the Ivory, Slave and Gold coasts. The great Portuguese citadel of Fort Jesus was begun in 1593 at Mombasa. A number of forts were founded by one European power and taken over by another, with the Portuguese-built slave court and dungeons of Elmina in Ghana being taken over by the Dutch in 1637, while the British built a fort on Swedish foundations at Cape Coast. These forts, which often included barracks, chapels, slave quarters, stores and armouries, were frequently quadrangular in plan and had typically Renaissance defensive fortifications at the corners, designed to deflect missiles and to give good artillery command over the approaches. Traders' and merchants' houses were often built near by, either of stone, as at Dixcove, Ghana, or of timber with shaded balconies, as at Calabar, Nigeria (*see also* MILITARY ARCHITECTURE AND FORTIFICATION, §III, 2(v)).

(a) Colonial influences. Away from the coasts, mission churches, built in local materials with thatched roofs or with imported stone in neo-Gothic form, and the houses of the missionaries were among the few European buildings to be seen. The exception was the Cape Colony, settled in the mid-17th century by the Dutch. Their simple, linear farmhouses had stoeps along the front and evolved into both a T-plan, with the kitchen set back from the front, and a larger H-plan. These larger farmhouses were notable for their fine 17th–18th-century CAPE DUTCH STYLE and Cape Flemish gables, with double curved outlines and decoration. Such villages as Philippolis and Graaff-Reinet, the 'gem of the Karoo', retained their 19th-century charm and quality into the 1990s. Later settlements in Southern Africa included the fortified farmsteads of the eastern frontier and the homes of the first Voortreker settlers and were simple and sturdy, some being built of rammed earth or stone with thatched roofs.

Extensive European settlement did not occur until after the partition of Africa was completed at the turn of the 20th century, when small towns were established in the colonies. Although indigenous techniques were sometimes used by early settlers, stone structures were built where possible to replace the pole-and-daub. In addition, prefabricated houses were brought from England, and, from the mid-19th century, corrugated iron was imported in large quantities. The bungalow, originally developed in India, became the ubiquitous colonial house type. Raised on piers, these mostly one-storey buildings had verandahs, spacious interiors and high roofs that permitted air circulation. Their light, corrugated-iron roofs could make the interiors uncomfortably hot, but, despite this, bungalows fitted with mosquito screens were popular with settlers. With Europeanization the bungalow became a desirable urban house type among Africans, gradually replacing traditional compounds. Europeans in West Africa also favoured an alternative type of dwelling—the Basle Mission house. This was raised on piles to a high level and had a projecting upper storey fitted with louvred screens. Immigrant Malays may have had some effect on house types in Cape Town, while Indians influenced architecture in Kenya and Uganda, where Indian-styled rows of shop-houses developed between the World Wars, often with modest Art Deco details in the rendered façades.

In the mid-19th century, ex-slaves returning from the Americas introduced a number of architectural elements: those resettled in Liberia built wooden houses, entirely clad in shingles, applying a roofing technique developed in the USA. More significant and lasting was the *Pètési* (upstairs) house that was developed by repatriated slaves from Brazil, which appeared in Lagos, Abeokuta and, later, Ibadan (*see* NIGERIA, §IV). Such buildings had grand façades comprising elaborately detailed balconies, window mouldings, pillars and porticos. Each consisted of some three floors, perhaps eleven rooms and a rear courtyard. One family would occupy each room of such houses, which continued to be built until the mid-1950s.

(b) Modernism. Until World War II, many towns developed by Europeans were modest in scale, with low-rise architecture dominated only by government buildings of conventional European form. Such colonial cities as Dakar, Senegal, were well planned, its superb peninsula site having government buildings arranged about a star-plan crossing of main thoroughfares. Such others as JOHANNESBURG, DURBAN and Salisbury (now Harare, Zimbabwe) were laid out in a conventional grid plan, and their rigid formalism contrasted with the relaxed disposition of traditional African settlements.

Modernism was introduced with the direct involvement of such European architects as Ernst May, who worked in Kenya. In the early 1930s the Transvaal Group led by Rex Martienssen and including W. Gordon McIntosh and Norman Hanson enthusiastically followed the works of Le Corbusier and Walter Gropius. High-rise building with reinforced concrete or steel framing was not extensively developed until after the 1950s, when the growth of such towns as Lusaka, Zambia, and Blantyre, Malawi, was rapid. At this time the central business and administrative districts of cities throughout the continent assumed an increasingly uniform appearance. In Nigeria, annual concrete imports multiplied elevenfold in 20 years, branches of West African Portland Cement were opened, and the impact on the African urban environment was considerable.

Post-war modern architecture in Africa has been the work of both expatriates and African architects trained in European schools of architecture or at such African universities as Khartoum, Kumasi, Nairobi, Addis Ababa and the Witwatersrand, Johannesburg (*see also* SOUTH AFRICA, §III). University buildings in themselves presented challenging opportunities to architects: James Cubitt built a number at the Kumasi University of Science and Technology (1952–4) as well as the Teachers Training College (1951–4) at Sekondi, Ghana. Julian Elliott undertook the building of the University of Zambia, Lusaka, and Alan Vaughan-Richards designed houses at the University of Lagos, Nigeria. Cubitt's firm designed over 70 projects for African clients, many in Ghana and Nigeria, while Maxwell Fry and Jane Drew were responsible for more than 80, including the University College, Ibadan. Attempts were made to make these buildings suitable for the climate, with deep relief, cross-ventilation and *brises-soleil.* At the same time their strongly rectilinear forms, flat roofs and contrasting masses, designed to cast strong shadows, show their indebtedness to Le Corbusier. The influence of these Modernist forms was pervasive and had few challengers.

Among the most original architects working in Africa was AMANCIO GUEDES, whose sculptural houses, designed in Mozambique, combined spatial innovation and surrealist imagery. A more controlled but still eclectic approach to design is evident in the prolific output of the French-trained Moroccan architect Jean-François Zevaco. His fertile inventiveness is well illustrated by such works of the 1960s as the low-lined Groupe Scolaire in Agadir, the strong forms and contrasting textures of the Palace of Justice (1962–3) at Mohammedia, the exposed concrete of the Post Office (1966) at Agadir and the hopper-like Pavilion (1970) that he and E. J. Duhon created for the International Fair at Casablanca. His compatriot Elie Azagury designed many houses in the De Stijl idiom, of which the Civic Centre (1967), Rabat, is a dramatic example (*see* RABAT).

A new generation of African architects, mainly Nigerian, came to prominence in the 1960s. Of these the best known is OLUWOLE OLUMUYIWA, whose long, unobtrusive school buildings, housing for the United Africa Company, and other projects in Lagos are obviously Modernist but not ostentatious. Fellow Nigerian architects include ALEX EKWEME, architect of the hospital at Ebutametta for the Nigerian Railway Corporation, ISOLA KOLA-BANKOLE and DAVID MUTISO. Ekweme's laboratory building at St Gregory's College, Lagos, has an upper-storey *brise-soleil* and is essentially within a Corbusian idiom. Although admired for their clean lines and white, primary forms broken by projecting frames, such Modernist buildings have not always been responsive to the prevailing climate conditions. Many concrete structures are now green with algae and leak in heavy rains. Nor are they always fully appropriate to local environments. They may exploit the light and shade of tropical sunlight, but they seldom reflect local architectural genres.

(vii) Further developments. Traditional forms are occasionally re-interpreted, an example being the cone-and-cylinder concrete housing units built early in the 20th century for African railway workers in the Sudan. A lead in this field was given by the Egyptian architect HASSAN FATHY who used local methods of passive cooling and employed Sudanese Nubian masons to build barrel vaults by traditional techniques without formwork for his town of New Gourna near Luxor in 1946. Local forms, materials and cooling systems were also used by ANDRÉ RAVÉREAU and his partners in their designs for houses and the post office

in Ghardaia, in the Mzab, Algeria. The same architect's work with the Historical Monuments Service of Algeria led to his invitation to design the Medical Centre (completed 1976; see fig. 70) at Mopti, Mali. It was sited near the Friday Mosque and executed in reinforced soil–cement and Cinva–Ram adobes to harmonize with its context.

Although such experiments have seldom been wholly successful, culturally or environmentally, African forms have provided architectural inspiration in, for example, the design of tourist hotels. Typical is the El Kalas complex (1971) by Faraoui and de Mazieres, which derives its style from a Moroccan *ksar*. Simpler, low-rise hotel complexes such as Olivier-Clement Cacoub's Tourist Centre (1966) at Skanes, Tunisia, were also based on local vernacular architecture, but it is evident that this was more to satisfy European perceptions of Africa than to meet indigenous requirements. While the work of such architects as the Islamic-influenced André Ravéreau and the French-trained CHARLES BOCCARA responded to traditional building cultures and contributed towards the development of a modern indigenous architecture, Western influences more frequently had an impoverishing effect. The West African deep-pitch roof, which arose in response to the tropical rainfall of the area and was widespread in Nigeria, virtually disappeared under the influence of international styles, being replaced by the concrete deck and long-span, shallow-pitch aluminium roofs, often hidden behind a fascia, which give the impression of being flat.

In the 1970s wars and economic problems in many countries reduced the numbers of new buildings erected, permitting a pause in development. Subsequent attempts to solve housing needs were made, but J. C. Laederach's experimental house type in 1969 was one of the few to attempt to respond to local traditions.

Although prestigious, European-style parliamentary, commercial, transport and hotel buildings have been extensively developed throughout Africa, their social and environmental impact was probably less than that of such dam-building projects as the Volta Dam (1961–8) at Akosombo, Ghana, the Kariba Dam (begun 1959), the Aswan (High) Dam (begun 1969) and the Limpopo Valley Irrigation and Settlement Scheme. The successes and failures of resulting resettlement projects such as that of the Volta River Authority have been carefully monitored (see Chambers). In the 1980s a number of low-cost housing schemes tackled the problems of increasing African urbanization, and extensive self-help projects are being supported by non-governmental organizations in Kenya, Angola, Ghana, Malawi, Mozambique, Zimbabwe, Botswana and elsewhere, with innovations in, for example, servicing and soil–cement block manufacture. As confidence in the evolving technologies grows and develop-

70. Medical Centre, Mopti, Mali, by André Ravéreau, 1976; from a photograph by Emmanuelle Roche, 1979

ments in the design and building of dwellings become evident, new vernacular forms may emerge with values and meanings related to the changing nature of African societies of the future.

BIBLIOGRAPHY

GENERAL

P. Oliver, ed.: *Shelter and Society* (London, 1969/*R* 1978)
A. Rapoport: *House Form and Culture*, Foundations of Cultural Geography (Englewood Cliffs, 1969)
C. Duly: *The Houses of Mankind* (London, 1979)
E. Guidoni: *Primitive Architecture* (London, 1979)
P. Oliver: *Dwellings: The House across the World* (Oxford, 1987)

MATERIALS

C. G. Feilberg: *La Tente noire: Contribution ethnographique à l'histoire culturelle des nomades*, Nationalmuseets Skrifter, Ethnografisk Roekke, ii (Copenhagen, 1944)
J. Walton: *African Village* (Pretoria, 1956)
J. Nicolaisen: *Ecology and Culture of the Pastoral Tuareg with Particular Reference to the Tuareg of Ahaggar and Ayr*, Nationalmuseets Skrifter, Ethnografisk Roekke, xii (Copenhagen, 1963)
R. Gardi: *Indigenous African Architecture* (New York, 1974)
P. Oliver: *African Shelter* (London, 1975)

VERNACULAR ARCHITECTURE

J. Poujade: *Les Cases décorées d'un chef du Fouta-Djallon* (Paris, 1948)
J.-P. Béguin and others: *L'Habitat au Cameroun* (Paris, 1954)
J. F. Glück: 'Afrikanische Architektur', *Tribus*, n. s., vi (1956), pp. 65–82; Eng. trans. in *The Many Faces of Primitive Art: A Critical Anthology*, ed. D. Fraser (Englewood Cliffs, 1966), pp. 224–43
J.-P. Lebeuf: *L'Habitation des Fali: Montagnards du Cameroun septentrional—technologie, sociologie, mythologie, symbolisme* (Paris, 1961)
R. Ritzenthaler and P. Ritzenthaler: *Cameroons Village: An Ethnography of the Bafut* (Milwaukee, 1964)
G. J. A. Ojo: *Yoruba Palaces: A Study of Afins of Yorubaland* (London, 1966)
L. Prussin: *Architecture in Northern Ghana: A Study of Forms and Functions* (Berkeley, 1969)
M. Swithenbank: *Ashanti Fetish Houses* (Accra, 1969)
P. Oliver, ed.: *Shelter in Africa* (London, 1971)
W. E. Knuffel: *The Construction of the Bantu Grass Hut* (Graz, 1973)
A.-P. Lagopoulos: 'Semiological Urbanism: An Analysis of the Traditional Western Sudanese Settlement', *Shelter, Sign and Symbol*, ed. P. Oliver (London, 1975), pp. 206–18
G. N. Preston: 'Perseus and Medusa in Africa: Military Art in Fanteland, 1834–1972', *Afr. A.*, viii/3 (1975), pp. 36–41, 68–71
J. Walton: 'Art and Magic in the Southern Bantu Vernacular Architecture', *Shelter, Sign and Symbol*, ed. P. Oliver (London, 1975), pp. 117–34
R. W. Hill: *African Cities and Towns before the European Conquest* (New York, 1976)
K. B. Andersen: *African Traditional Architecture: A Study of the Housing and Settlement Patterns of Rural Kenya* (Nairobi, 1978)
S. Denyer: *African Traditional Architecture: An Historical and Geographical Perspective* (London, 1978)
J.-L. Bourgeois and C. Pelos: *Spectacular Vernacular: A New Appreciation of Traditional Desert Architecture* (Salt Lake City, 1983)
G. Philippart de Foy: *Les Pygmées d'Afrique centrale* (Marseille, 1984)
J.-P. Bourdier and T. H. Minn-ha: *African Spaces: Designs for Living in Upper Volta* (New York, 1985)
R. Plant: *Architecture of the Tigre* (Worcester, 1985)
S. P. Blier: *The Anatomy of Architecture: Ontology and Metaphor in Batammaliba Architectural Expression*, Res Monographs in Anthropology and Aesthetics (Cambridge, 1987)

ISLAMIC ARCHITECTURE

H. Labouret: 'Afrique occidentale et équatoriale', *L'Habitation indigène dans les possessions françaises*, ed. A. Bernard and others (Paris, 1931)
C. Monteil: *Une Cité soudanaise: Djenné—métropole du delta central du Niger* (Paris, 1932)
J. Kirkman: *Gedi: The Palace*, Studies in African History (The Hague, 1963)
M. Wenzel: *House Decoration in Nubia*, A. & Soc. Ser. (London, 1972)
N. Chittick: *Kilwa: An Islamic Trading City on the East African Coast*, 2 vols (Nairobi, 1974)
D. Dalby: 'The Concept of Settlement in the West African Savannah', *Shelter, Sign and Symbol*, ed. P. Oliver (London, 1975), pp. 197–205
J.-P. Greenlaw: *The Coral Buildings of Suakin* (Stocksfield, 1976)
F. Ago: *Moschee in adobe: Storia e tipologia nell'Africa occidentale* (Rome, 1982)
F. W. Schwerdtfeger: *Traditional Housing in African Cities: A Comparative Study of Houses in Zaria, Ibadan, and Marrakesh* (Chichester, 1982)
J. C. Moughtin: *Hausa Architecture* (London, 1985)
L. Prussin: *Hatumere: Islamic Design in West Africa* (Berkeley, 1986)

FURTHER DEVELOPMENTS

J. Walton: *Homesteads and Villages of South Africa* (Pretoria, 1952)
U. Kultermann: *New Architecture in Africa* (New York, 1963)
——: *New Directions in African Architecture*, New Directions in Architecture (London, 1969)
A. W. Lawrence: *Trade Castles and Forts of West Africa* (London, 1963); rev. as *Fortified Trade-posts: The English in West Africa, 1645–1822* (London, 1969)
R. Chambers, ed.: *The Volta Resettlement Experience* (London, 1970)
J. Beinart: 'Patterns of Change in an African Housing Environment', *Shelter, Sign and Symbol*, ed. P. Oliver (London, 1975), pp. 160–82
A. Ravéreau: *Le M'Zab: Une Leçon d'architecture*, preface by H. Fathy (Paris, 1981)
A. D. King: *The Bungalow: The Production of a Global Culture* (London, 1984)

PAUL OLIVER

2. SCULPTURE. Without doubt, figure sculpture (especially in wood) has received more attention than any other African art form. This applies not only to scholars but also to Western artists and the lay public. The only rival to figure sculpture's perceived position as the African art form *par excellence* is mask and masquerade, and many African masks could themselves be classified as figure sculptures. This article provides a general introduction to this huge subject; further information on materials, forms, production and use will be found in other entries on African art, and discussion of particular traditions will be found in the entries elsewhere in this dictionary on individual peoples.

(i) Wood. (ii) Ivory. (iii) Ceramic. (iv) Mud. (v) Cement.

(i) Wood.

(a) Introduction. (b) Formal analysis.

(a) Introduction. Wood is the most commonly used material for sculpture throughout Sub-Saharan Africa. No doubt there are good practical and environmental reasons for this, but another point has been emphasized (see Schmalenbach): wood, with its strength and its sap, must be seen as a fragment of nature that artistic intervention has not completely subdued and that, as such, counts for a great deal in the expressive capacity of African sculpture, whether this strength is seen as a natural or as a supernatural phenomenon. Thus wood is seen more as the 'substance' of the work than as a material pure and simple. Moreover, the choice of wood is important, as are the ritual ways in which the tree is felled. The shape of the statue often reveals traces of the original form of the trunk. Not all surfaces are treated with the same care, as if the raw material were part of the finished sculpture. African figure sculpture in wood favours the representation of human beings. Usually modest in size, African sculptures are portable, even if the way the forms are structured sometimes fulfils criteria of monumentality. Most figures are between 200 and 800 mm high, and only occasionally do they measure less or more. They are made to be handled rather than looked at. The techniques of carving reinforce this impression, as the sculptor, with his adze or knife, turns the piece or wood again and again to give it its shape (*see* §V, 3 above).

The male or female figure is either a representation of the ancestor, the father or mother of the line, with an individual identity (as among the Bamileke of the Cameroon Grassfields, where every district houses a series of royal ancestor figures), or seen as a generic and symbolic ancestor (as among the Fang of Western Equatorial Africa, where the figure watches over the precious relics). Usually nude, ancestral figures are strongly sexuate. Combined male and female figures are not necessarily man and wife but may be twins or representations of humanity's two components. Sculpted scenes are less common than single figures, but, in addition to the primordial couple, figures of a mother, or occasionally a father, and child, as well as equestrian figures (*see* §IV, 5 and 6 above) and even groups of warriors, servants, women and concubines are also known.

Figures are often represented standing tensed, with half-bent knees, or seated (most often on a circular stool), stiffly immobile but apparently serene. Few African sculptures show people in movement, while the depiction of asymmetrical gesture is limited to a few rare schools of sculpture usually linked to such powerful societies as Benin, Asante, Bamileke, Yoruba and Kuba (*see* §IV, 2 above). Animals are also represented, though much less frequently than in masquerade. Among the better-known examples are great Senufo birds, Kurumba antelopes, Baule monkeys, Kongo dogs, Baga snakes and Benin leopards (*see* §IV, 3(vi) above).

BIBLIOGRAPHY

M. Leiris and J. Delange: *Afrique noire: La Création plastique* (Paris, 1967); Eng. trans. as *African Art* (London, 1968)

W. Schmalenbach: 'Force et mesure', *A. Afrique Noire* (1988)

LOUIS PERROIS

(b) Formal analysis. African sculpture in wood is very plastic and is characterized by many unique formal inventions. The following discussion focuses on some of those that are most characteristically and distinctively African.

Volume. African artists frequently switch from a full round, three-dimensional treatment of some parts of a sculpture to a flat, relief carving in others without any transition. For example, a Dogon mother-and-child figure may be rendered in sculptural rods and knobs except for the hands and feet, which are simply deep grooves cut in the surface (see fig. 71). Similarly, among the Chokwe a neckrest may switch without warning from the bulky, rounded presentation of the body to a shallowly engraved face, while among the Mambila the airy, billowing forms of a figure may suddenly stop at the face, which has no volume at all. African sculptors also freely mix an organic treatment of the body with a completely geometric, inorganic one, again without transitions. In Fang reliquaries the full round, muscular arms and softly curving stomach flow directly into a metal-capped, cylindrical peg representing the navel. There are many other examples of a shockingly abrupt change in the sculptural language used by African artists.

71. Dogon figure sculpture of a mother and child, wood, metal and leather, h. 665 mm (USA, private collection)

African sculpture also shows an extraordinary sense of mass, of weight and density occupying space, one of its fundamental qualities. Much African sculpture suggests, not an inert shell, but an inner mass pressing towards the viewer. Swelling, bulging forms are the clearest manifestation of this, but there are subtler ones. To sense the density of African sculptures, they should be experienced as displacing air, containing volume; their surfaces should be felt not as enclosing a hollow core but as full, as the edge of thickness, in order to sense the active interior. The alternative conception of sculpture that sees it not as volume, but as flat or curved surfaces and lines, as for example in Cycladic or Cubist sculpture, is rare in African art, though some Kota figures are examples of this approach. This quality of dense mass in African art partly accounts for what is often experienced as an aggressiveness, described as a projection of energy. Though the outward projection of mass is probably the real source, energy may be perceived as coming from such non-formal attributes as posture and gesture or such features as horns, teeth or puffed cheeks—frequent concentrations where the inner volume thrusts towards the viewer. The same aggressive energy can be seen in body parts not normally thought of as aggressive, such as foreheads, breasts or buttocks, when they are rendered as masses pushing outward.

This active inner volume is so pervasive, it can be seen even in unaggressive, naturalistic sculptures, for example many Fang heads, where the domed forehead expresses the tense containment of volume, suggesting the power of intellect and numinous presence within (*see* FANG, fig. 3). More obvious thrusting forms are often found in Fang figures, in Luba figures (*see* LUBA, fig. 3) and in Bangwa masks. Even slender, linear sculptures have this same quality—an active interior. They may barely show outward volumes but suggest instead a wild current running through tubular limbs, as with the Bamana female figure whose dangerously pointed breasts and smoothly rounded posterior thrust against the skin of the surface, while the strong movement of the sculpture as a whole courses down the coiffure, down the widening torso and legs (see fig. 72). By contrast, the masses of the Senufo figures called rhythm pounders generally move upwards in a slower, more majestic pulse, rising from the ankles, swelling (throbbing) at the hips, then rising again to the beat of the shoulders and breasts, and finally rising once more in the slender neck (*see* SENUFO, §2(ii) and fig. 1).

Active voids ingeniously used are another fundamental quality of African sculpture. African works do not passively occupy space; they interact with and interpenetrate space, most obviously through the use of pierced forms and open compositions. The most extreme and evident pieces capture space, which becomes a positive element, not a negative zone against which the sculpted parts are read. Voids contained in a sculpture often repeat the shapes of the volumes and become part of the composition, not empty air. The triangular spaces under the arms of a Shankadi neckrest, which are the same size and shape as the flaring coiffure, become parts of the design. The space between the legs of a Southern African figure of a young girl duplicates exactly the shape of the torso, creating a negative echo of the positive form above. Even sculptures that seem densely compact engage the surrounding space. The air in front of a Zulu meat dish becomes the face and stomach of the figure, shaped by the artist into two visible voids, as surely as he shaped the wood.

The volumes of African sculpture are usually articulated as segments rather than continuous form. In fact, African artists rarely compose a fluidly unified whole (though this is less rare in sculptures from East and Southern Africa). They may isolate parts of a work with deep grooves or treat them as completely discrete units; thus an eye or

72. Bamana figure sculpture, wood, h. 595 mm, late 19th century to mid-20th (USA, Horstmann private collection)

knee may become a clean cylinder quite separate from the flat surface of the face. The arm and breast are often rendered as a single unified segment, sharply demarcated from the neck and torso, as in a Baule figure of a mother and child (see fig. 73). The segments are organized into patterns that transform the face and body into designs.

The organization of African sculptures, like that of all art works, proceeds from the repetition and variation of a limited number of elements. A common device is to render the different parts of the body with the same shape: for example the calves, thighs and buttocks of a figure may be rendered as similar swelling ovals, while the knees are completely suppressed in the interests of design. Designs can also be created out of similar positive and negative shapes, as seen in Bangwa night masks. More interesting (and sometimes disconcerting) are sculptures in which dissimilar features are given equivalent shapes. African sculptures are often so tightly organized that the works acquire a quality of inevitability. The rigorous construction sometimes means that no single part could be changed without altering everything else.

73. Baule figure sculpture of a mother and child, wood, h. 495 mm, late 19th century to mid-20th (USA, private collection)

Symmetry. It is often said that African sculpture is symmetrical. While its overall design is usually balanced and symmetrical compared to some sculptural traditions, it is almost never literally symmetrical. Overtly asymmetrical compositions, however, are rare. In fact, traditional African artists tend to create symmetrical designs but deliberately avoid symmetry in the execution; their works mock symmetry to create interest. A close look at an apparently regular figure such as a Fang reliquary guardian, for example, may reveal that the left arm is much fuller than the right, creating a small imbalance and different spaces under the arms. Like the living face and body, African sculptures are animated by subtle irregularities. In a Baule mask the coiffure may tilt faintly to the right, the left ear be lower than the right, the eyes slightly uneven and the nostrils not the same size. African artists set the viewer up to expect the paired sides of a composition to match, then leave him to enjoy the interplay between what is expected and what is seen. Moreover, variations may be played, not just on the horizontal axis but through space, forming a spiral movement. The body of a small Luba figure rotates so that the elbows are not aligned with the knees, creating a disjunction at waist level (see fig. 74). A spiral stance is central to the Bangwa conception of figure sculpture, so that in many figures, in relation to the head, the shoulders rotate to the left.

Continuous view. African figure sculpture often has no principal view; in fact it often does not seem to have any privileged vantage points. An African work may be best understood from the continuous view obtained by walking around it or by holding it in the hand and turning it. As the viewer circles the object, the sculptural shapes move in relation to each other; the viewer can gain a complete sense of its three-dimensionality and watch the order of the piece unfold. African works may be so complicated formally that without circling the piece it may be impossible to understand how the different masses interact in the parts of the sculpture that are momentarily out of sight. As part of their exceptional plasticity, African sculptures have what may be termed a continuous view. Many sculptures in other traditions have a principal view; they were designed to be seen from a particular angle (examples of this are the pedimental sculptures on ancient Greek temples). This is sometimes related to the artist's preliminary sketch on paper or on the uncarved block and is especially true of sculpture made to stand in a niche. A principal view is akin to a low relief in that it appears as an arrangement of masses in front of a picture plane. Sculptures conceived more fully in the round may never-

74. Luba figure sculpture (neckrest) by the Master of the Cascading Coiffure, wood and beads, h. 160 mm, late 19th century to mid-20th (USA, Horstmann private collection)

theless have numerous points of view. These, however, are only a succession of single views.

African artists often say they see the sculpture inside the raw wood and cut away material to free it. Its exceptional plasticity may come from that approach—from the fact that African art is unrelated to two-dimensional images. Non-African artists of all eras often began work by drawing the outline of the future sculpture on the front and sides of the block of wood or stone, or they might sketch studies of sculptures before executing them. African artists conceive their works directly as three-dimensional, envisioning them as they would exist in space, not on paper.

African sculpture is often mistakenly described as frontal, probably because its conventional pose—arms to the sides, eyes forward, weight on both feet equally—corresponds to frontal figures from other traditions (such as Egyptian statues). African sculpture, however, is not frontal in a purely sculptural sense, because it is developed fully in the round and can be viewed from all sides. Moreover, African sculpture is not conceived for a predetermined kind of display. Most will not stand on a flat surface. Many were meant to be carried, to lean against something or to be sunk partially into the ground; in any case they were not meant to stand in a particular way and be viewed from a single point. African artists did not usually create their works mainly to be displayed and were not primarily concerned with the reactions of a human viewer.

Conclusion. In the context of Western art history, a striking feature of African art in general, and wooden figure sculpture in particular, is that it is not normally narrative, does not depict movement or groups of figures interacting and is not pictorial; it does not seek to create any illusion of motion, perspective or verisimilitude. If an artist wants hair on his figure that exactly resembles hair, he will not hesitate to attach some of the real thing. If movement is wanted, the figure is worn or carried in dance.

Since African art is not an illusion of reality and does not depict the visible world, we must recognize that it creates a new kind of reality. In carving, African artists introduce new beings into the world. Field research confirms the independent reality created in sculptures. A new figure is almost always given a personal name like a new child; the sculpture of a nature spirit makes newly visible a being that was not accessible before the carving was made.

African sculptures are generally single figures unframed by any space boundary that would set them in their own small stage. They are unaccompanied by any reference for scale (such as a carved shrub or rock). Perspective, frontality and a principal view all imply a viewer positioned in a particular place. African sculpture has none of these qualities. African artists created movable objects that were not destined to be seen in a single setting; almost all might have different settings according to phases of their use (in a cluttered shrine, wrapped in cloth or carried in the sun in an annual procession, for example). Consequently, such objects inhabit human space; they are small or large in relation to the human body and not in relation to an architectural background or setting conceived for them. This quality is fundamental, for it means that African sculptures intrude upon inhabited space, not separate, artistically created space, and they interact directly with the viewer. Further, it implies their existence as independent entities, as newly created beings with an existence as palpable as our own.

BIBLIOGRAPHY

A. Maesen: *Umbangu: Art du Congo au Musée royal du Congo Belge* (Brussels, 1960)

J. Laude: *Art de l'Afrique noire* (Paris, 1968); Eng. trans. by J. Decock (Berkeley, 1971/*R* 1973)

African Aesthetics: The Carlo Monzino Collection (exh. cat. by S. Vogel, New York, Cent. Afr. A., 1986)

Perspectives: Angles on African Art (exh. cat. by J. Baldwin and others, New York, Cent. Afr. A., 1986)

J. Kerchache, J.-L. Paudrat and L. Stéphan: *L'Art africain* (Paris, 1988); Eng. trans. by M. de Jager (New York, 1993)

Art of Central Africa: Masterpieces from the Berlin Museum für Völkerkunde (exh. cat. by H.-J. Koloss, New York, Met., 1990)

Closeup: Lessons in the Art of Seeing African Sculpture (exh. cat. by J. L. Thompson and S. Vogel, New York, Cent. Afr. A., 1990)

SUSAN VOGEL

(ii) Ivory. Among the best-known African ivory sculptures are those produced in West Africa for export to Europe in the late 15th and 16th centuries. These ivories incorporate a number of European forms and motifs and have commonly been dubbed 'Afro-Portuguese'. Generally, however, even the most heavily influenced works strongly retain local style and iconography and might therefore be better called 'Luso-African', reflecting their production under African rather than European control. These ivory

sculptures have been studied in detail, and this entry focuses on them. It should be noted, however, that African sculpture in ivory is not limited to these objects. For information on other uses of ivory in African art, *see* §V, 5 above.

(a) Introduction. Nearly 200 of these early export ivories are extant, although contemporary customs records suggest that hundreds more were imported. Spoons seem to have been the most popular items; the fragility of their openwork stems probably resulted in frequent breakage and disposal. The Portuguese were the first Europeans to sail to Sub-Saharan Africa, and they brought back a number of art objects, as well as raw materials. For the most part, these early artworks had been made for local consumption and obtained at public markets or through gift exchanges. From the late 15th century to the mid-16th, however, ivory sculptures were also created specifically for the Portuguese.

The ivories were produced in only two areas, coastal Sierra Leone and Benin, both of which had established ivoryworking traditions. Although the Portuguese recognized the craftsmanship of the traditional sculptures, they did not appreciate the objects themselves. Their styles were very dissimilar to those of Europe, and the forms and motifs were associated, in Portuguese minds, with paganism. The Portuguese thus began to commission works directly from the artists themselves, to their own tastes and drawing from European iconography. The types of object commissioned were those valued by the European aristocracy, namely salt-cellars, pyxides, hunting horns and cutlery. Produced in the valuable medium of ivory, and with an exotic origin, the works had great prestige value in Europe. Although these works took European forms and used European motifs, aspects of local style and iconography were also maintained. The ivories are thus visual and conceptual hybrids.

(b) Sierra Leonean production. More than half the extant works are Sierra Leonean. When first contacted by the Portuguese in 1462, coastal Sierra Leone was occupied by the Temne and Bullom, or Sherbro, peoples; population shifts occurred later in the 16th century. Speaking distinct but related languages, these peoples were organized into village clusters, each with its own leader, while powerful men's and women's associations exerted substantial social and political influence. Ivoryworkers and other artists worked for these societies, as well as for other traditional patrons, before and during the time of Portuguese contact.

The ivories from Sierra Leone share some general characteristics. They frequently include spectacular openwork sections and display a contrast of smooth, unadorned surface sections with clusters of beaded or zigzagged banding. Many include human figures in high relief, usually representing Portuguese men and African women. Stylistically, these figures are very close to the region's soapstone heads and figures, which seem to be contemporary with the ivories (*see* KISSI and MENDE). In general, the heads are prognathous, with a strong horizontal thrust, and are often one-third to one-quarter of the figures' total height. Eyes dominate the face, noses are curved and prominent, and lips are often lifted slightly at the corners. Despite

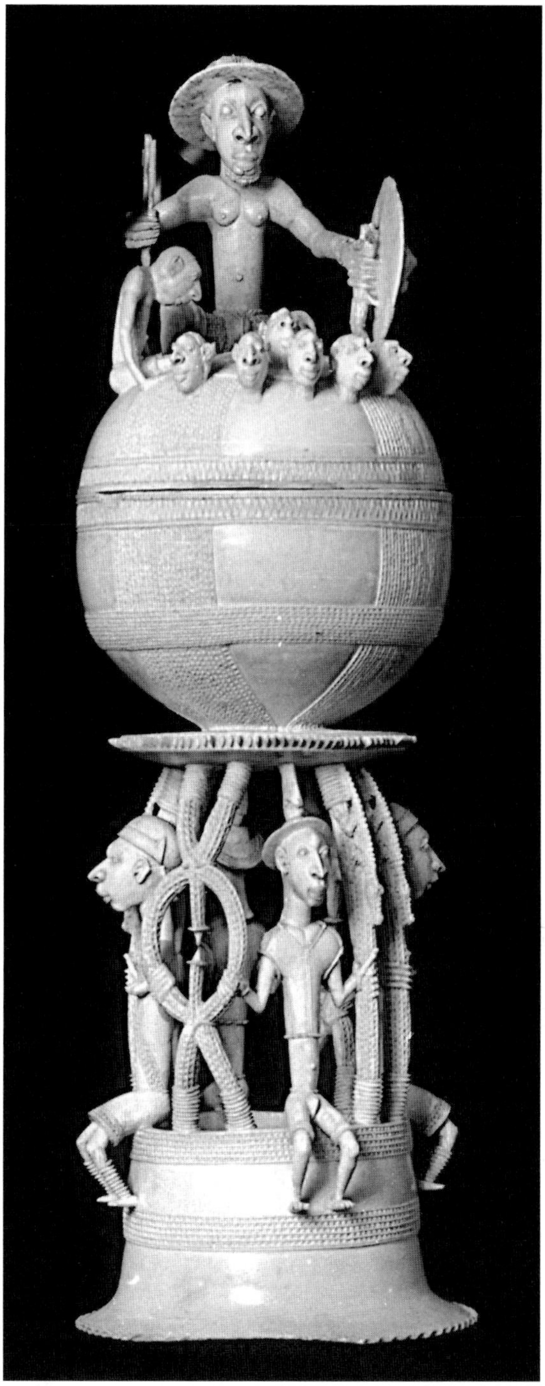

75. Ivory salt-cellar, h. 430 mm, from Sierra Leone, late 15th century to early 16th (Rome, Museo Nazionale Preistorico ed Etnografico Luigi Pigorini)

these general similarities, however, the works formally and iconographically fall into two distinct groups, apparently due to different geographic origins.

The first, and larger, set of Sierra Leonean ivories is the product of at least four workshops. It also shows the greatest evidence of European involvement. The decoration, for example, often includes the European surface treatment of spiralled gadrooning, producing undulations common on European metalwork of the period. In form, these objects also follow European patterns. Salt-cellars (average height 290 mm) have the sphere-on-cone structure of European covered metal cups. Circular pyxides are decorated with Christian scenes and derive from Portuguese metal models. Hunting horns are endblown in the European fashion, instead of employing the characteristic African side embouchure. Long-stemmed spoons (*c.* 230 mm long) are ribbed at the back in imitation of European metal prototypes. Their shallow, pointed bowls rise into virtuoso stems, often openworked in knotlike forms. Several two-tined forks are also known. These were not used in Africa and were still rare in 15th century Europe, so their occurrence confirms the patronage of upper-class Europeans.

The iconography of these works is a fascinating composite. Local motifs of pythons, crocodiles and parrots are frequently accompanied by images drawn from European heraldry and mythology, from Christian sources and from such aristocratic activities as stag hunting. The artists were supplied by their European patrons with drawings, printed materials, coins, textiles and religious articles as motif sources.

A second group of Sierra Leonean export ivories, fewer in number, includes salt-cellars, spoons and knife handles that show little evidence of direct contact with Portuguese patrons. Salt-cellars of this type have a sphere-on-cylinder structure, which is not European-derived. The imagery on these works is indigenous and includes anthropomorphized quadrupeds, double-faced heads and crocodiles. Only one extant example actually includes Western-derived motifs, although representations of long-haired Europeans accompanying Sierra Leonean women do occur on many pieces. Even these Portuguese are sometimes Africanized by their placement within local metaphors of leadership—astride an elephant or amidst captives. On the base of one example are figures of two seated Portuguese surrounded by African women and crocodiles, while the finial shows the figure of another Portuguese in a traditional Sierra Leonean leadership pose, surrounded by trophy heads (Rome, Mus. N. Preist. & Etnog.; see fig. 75). This non-European emphasis on form and symbolism suggests that these pieces had a non-coastal origin. They may have been carved upcountry along the Upper Scarcies River. This region, which an early account noted was a production centre of ivories for export, was the site of considerable trade between Cape Verdean smugglers and illegal Portuguese settlers. Living under African control, the settlers learnt the language, married local women and became initiates of the men's society; many of the Portuguese depicted on the 'upcountry' ivories bear initiation scarifications.

(c) Benin production. In contrast to the Sierra Leonean pieces, the export ivories from Benin are consistent in form and style. The Portuguese first reached the kingdom of Benin in the early 1470s, at which time it was a powerful centralized state. Its arts were centred on the royal court, with palace guilds producing elaborate brass, ivory and wooden objects for the ruler. Although Benin court ivories included ancestral tusks, jewellery and boxes, the objects made for export again followed foreign preferences. The salt-cellars (see fig. 76), hunting horns and spoons made at Benin, however, differ from Sierra Leonean examples in both form and decoration. The salt-cellars (h. *c.* 280 mm) are tripartite, as some contemporary Portuguese metal examples are, and have an unusual form, consisting of two globular, lidded compartments separated by a short stem. The exteriors are carved with high-relief figures of mounted or standing Portuguese dignitaries and

76. Ivory salt-cellar, from Benin, late 15th century to early 16th, (London, British Museum)

their attendants. The hunting horns are not endblown in the European style but sideblown, like traditional Benin court oliphants. Benin spoons (*c.* 250 mm long) have longer, deeper bowls than their Sierra Leonean counterparts, curving around at the front in a three-lobed 'duck-foot' formation, and have stems carved with animal figures.

The objects from Benin were created by at least eight artists within the royal carvers' guild. As in traditional Benin art, social hierarchy is stressed through detailed, rank-linked costumes and the use of hieratic scale. The figures of the most important people are static and frontal; figures shown in three-quarters view or with intimations of movement are of people of lower status, and, as in objects from Sierra Leone, are adaptations of European models. The figures conform to local style in proportion, the head being as much as one-quarter the length of the whole body. Surfaces are heavily decorated with crowded, small-scale designs from the Benin guild repertory, including guilloche, basketweave and scale patterns. Other than representations of Portuguese people, Portuguese motifs are minimal; although the horns contain a few European heraldic elements, the spoons are carved with animals of African, not European, origin, including crocodiles, snakes, snails and birds. They are often combined in relationships that suggest proverbial or metaphorical references of local significance, and some seem to share themes with art works of the neighbouring Yoruba peoples.

BIBLIOGRAPHY

F. Heger: 'Alte Elfenbeinarbeiten aus Afrika in den Wiener Sammlungen', *Mitt. Anthropol. Ges. Wien*, xxix (1899), pp. 101–09

C. H. Read and O. M. Dalton: *Antiquities from the City of Benin and from Other Parts of West Africa in the British Museum* (London, 1899)

W. Foy: 'Zur Frage der Herkunft einiger alter Jagdhörner: Portugal oder Benin?', *Abh. & Ber. Kön. Zool. & Anthropol.–Ethnog. Mus. Dresden*, ix (1900–01), pp. 20–22

R. Andrée: 'Alte westafrikanische Elfenbeinschnitzwerke im Herzoglichen Museum zu Braunschweig', *Globus*, lxxix (1901), pp. 156–9

R. Pettazoni: 'Avori scolpiti africani in collezioni italiane: Contributo allo studio dell'arte del "Benin"', *Boll. A.*, v (1911), pp. 388–98; vi (1912), pp. 56–74, 147–60; repr. as book (Rome, 1912)

R. Andrée: 'Seltene Ethnographica des Städtischen Gewerbe-Museums zu Ulm', *Baessler-Archv*, iv/1 (1913), pp. 29–38

J. Marquart: *Die Benin-Sammlung des Reichsmuseums für Völkerkunde im Leiden*, Veröffentlichungen des Reichsmuseums für Völkerkunde in Leiden, ser. 2, vii (Leiden, 1913)

F. von Luschan: *Die Altertümer von Benin*, 3 vols (Berlin, 1919)

K. Degen: 'Das Köllesche Elfenbeinhorn', *Heimatkundliche Bl. Kreis Tübingen* (1952), no. 4, pp. 14–15; (1953), no. 1, pp. 18–19

W. Fagg: *Afro-Portuguese Ivories* (London, 1959)

J. A. de Lasarte: 'La cope afro-portuguesa del Emperador', *Colóquio*, vii (1960), pp. 33–6

S. Wolf: 'Afrikanische Elfenbeinlöffel des 16. Jahrhunderts im Museum für Völkerkunde, Dresden', *Ethnologica*, n. s., ii (1960), pp. 410–25

C. Fyfe: *Sierra Leone Inheritance* (Oxford, 1964)

A. F. C. Ryder: 'A Note on the Afro-Portuguese Ivories', *J. Afr. Hist.*, v (1964), pp. 363–5

M. de Sampayo Ribeiro: 'O olifante de Drummond Castle', *Panorama*, ser. 4, ix (1964)

F. R. Cortez: 'O hostiário luso-africano de Museu de Grao Vasco', *Panorama*, ser. 4, xxi (1967), pp. 69–72

K. Dittmer: 'Bedeutung, Datierung und kulturhistorische Zusammenhänge der "prähistorischen" Steinfiguren aus Sierra Leone und Guinée', *Baessler-Archv*, n. s., xv (1967), pp. 183–238

P. Allison: *African Stone Sculpture* (London, 1968)

J. Atherton and M. Kalous: 'Nomoli', *J. Afr. Hist.*, xi/1 (1970), pp. 39–74

E. Bassani: 'Antichi avori africani nelle collezioni medicee', *Crit. A.*, cxliii (1975), pp. 69–80; cxliv (1975), pp. 8–23

V. L. Grottanelli: 'Discovery of a Masterpiece: A 16th Century Ivory Bowl from Sierra Leone', *Afr. A.*, viii/4 (1975), pp. 14–23

A. Teixeira da Mota: 'Gli avori africani nella documentazione portoghese dei secoli XV–XVII', *Africa* [Rome], iii (1975), pp. 580–89

P. Ben-Amos: *The Art of Benin*, Tribal A. (London, 1980)

G. Brooks: *Kola Trade and State-building: Upper Guinea Coast and Senegambia, 15th–17th Centuries*, Afr. Stud. Cent. Working Pap. (Boston, 1980)

E. Bassani: 'Trompes en ivoire du XVI siècle de la Sierra Leone', *Ethnographie*, lxxxv (1981–2), pp. 151–68

——: 'Antichi manufatti dell'Africa Nera nelle collezioni europee del rinascimento e dell'età barocca', *Quad. Poro*, iii (1982), pp. 9–34

K. Curnow: *The Afro-Portuguese Ivories: Classification and Stylistic Analysis of a Hybrid Art Form*, 2 vols (diss., Bloomington, IN U., 1983)

Africa and the Renaissance: Art in Ivory (exh. cat. by E. Bassani and W. Fagg, New York, Cent. Afr. A., 1988)

K. Curnow: 'Alien or Accepted: African Perspectives on the Western "Other" in 15th/16th Century Art', *Visual Anthropol. Rev.*, vi/1 (1990), pp. 38–44

——: 'Oberlin's Sierra Leonean Saltcellar: Documenting a Bicultural Dialogue', *Allen Mem. A. Mus. Bull.*, xliv (1991), pp. 12–23

W. A. Hart: 'A Rediscovered Afro-Portuguese Horn in the British Museum', *Afr. A.*, xxvi (1993), pp. 70–71

E. Bassani: 'Additional Notes on the Afro-Portuguese Ivories', *Afr. A.*, xxvii (1994), pp. 34–45

W. A. Hart: 'A Reconsideration of the Rediscovered "Afro-Portuguese" Horn', *Afr. A.*, xxvii (1994), pp. 92–3

A. Jones: 'A Collection of African Art in Seventeenth-century Germany: Christopher Weickmann's Kunst- und Naturkammer', *Afr. A.*, xxvii (1994), pp. 28–43

KATHY CURNOW

(iii) Ceramic. Fired clay is one of the earliest materials to be used for producing art objects in Africa (*see* §V, 1(ii) above). Ceramic sculpture is produced by either women or men depending on the practices maintained by particular African peoples. Examples of functional ceramic sculpture in Africa include finials used to secure the thatch of roofs and to prevent rain entering at the apex; these often designate the houses of important persons or structures serving as shrines. In the Mandara Mountains of the Nigeria–Cameroon border, finials made by women may be quite elaborate and may include clusters of human or animal figures. Throughout Africa functional vessels may be embellished with sculptural decoration.

Ceramic vessels modelled with a human head (sometimes referred to as cephalomorphic), which surmounts the neck, date mainly to the late 19th and 20th centuries, although some examples have been found in archaeological contexts. Cephalomorphic pots have been made by the Akye of southern Côte d'Ivoire; the Yoruba of south-western Nigeria; the Yungur, Jen, Tula, Longuda, Cham/Mwona, Bata and Mambila of north-eastern Nigeria; the Matakam, Koma and Mafa of northern Cameroon; the Mangbetu, Zande and related groups of the Uele region of north-eastern Zaïre; the Lunda, Lwena and Chokwe of the southern savannah of Zaïre, Angola and Zambia; and the Woyo of the Cabinda–Zaïre borderlands. Modelling of heads and bodies varies considerably from group to group. Some, such as those made by Lwena men, are very finely sculptured and have precisely incised linear decoration closely resembling the same group's style of wood-carving. Among the Yungur of north-eastern Nigeria, women produce animated and stylized images of deceased male leaders. Some of the best-known anthropomorphic pots from Africa are those made by men among the Mangbetu of Zaïre as prestige objects for local chiefs and for colonial officials and missionaries. The heads are idealized portraits of Mangbetu women, featuring elongated foreheads and elaborate fanlike coiffures (see fig. 77). Mangbetu ceramic sculpture flourished from the end of the 19th century to the early 1930s, after which production virtually ceased.

Detachable lids or stoppers for pots may also be conceived as heads. Among the Yoruba of south-western Nigeria, pots with figurative ceramic lids are made by women for cults honouring the river deity Erinle. One Egbado Yoruba woman, Abatan Odefunke Ayinke Ija (*b* ?1885), became well known in several Yoruba provinces for her lids, which are dominated by the half-figure of a woman (see Thompson). Voania Muba, an innovative male Woyo potter and chief (*d* ?1928), produced a unique group of pots with full-length figures and sometimes figurative groupings modelled on top of vessels with low, globular bases. His work was influenced by the Europeans who became his clientele, and each of Voania's pots bears his name in large capital letters.

It is common in West Africa to use figurative elements, in high or low relief, to adorn the walls of vessels generally used in ritual contexts. The best-known examples are from Nigeria and include bowls for worshipping the thunder god, Sango, among the Yoruba; pots used in shrines dedicated to the god of the seas and rivers, Olokun, in Benin; and vessels made for the cult of the yam spirit, Ifijioku, among the Igbo. The Fon and Gun peoples of the neighbouring Republic of Benin also make vessels with projecting human figures. Among other groups, decoration on ceramics includes a range of zoomorphic as well as anthropomorphic imagery. Several pots excavated from a disposal pit at Igbo-Ukwu, in south-eastern Nigeria, are remarkable for the combination of deep grooving, protruding bosses, multiple handles and relief images of coiled snakes, chameleons and rams' heads (*see* IGBO-UKWU). Dated to the 9th–10th centuries, these ceramics show the same elaborate surface decoration as Igbo-Ukwu artefacts cast in bronze. Although not as ornate, several pots unearthed at Ife, in south-western Nigeria, are modelled with arrangements of human figures and animals. Complex representational imagery is found on ritual vessels made by specialists among the Akan of Ghana and kept at grave sites and in shrine rooms. On these pots whole human figures or heads, snakes, lizards, frogs and crocodiles are worked in relief, often with reference to proverbs. Vessels made by the Bamana of Mali and by peoples of the Cameroon Grassfields have relief images of lizards, spiders, snakes, turtles and other animals.

Most early figurative ceramic sculpture is from West Africa, although a group of seven ceramic heads, dated to *c.* AD 500, have been found at Lydenburg in the Transvaal region of South Africa (now Cape Town, S. Afr. Cult. Hist. Mus.). The earliest known sculpture is associated with the Nok culture of northern Nigeria (500 BC–AD 200). These highly celebrated ceramic sculptures include nearly life-size hollow-built heads, which were probably once attached to full figures up to 1.2 m high, and small, solid figurines (h. 130 mm). Their function remains a mystery. NOK terracottas are remarkable for their technical sophistication and for their formal variation, despite such stylistic conventions as 'D'-shaped eyes and perforations in the pupils, nostrils, mouths and ears (features that aided their successful firing).

77. Ceramic double pot, h. 235 mm, from Mangbetu, Zaïre, collected 1913 (New York, American Museum of Natural History)

Also from Nigeria are the relatively naturalistic, though distinctively stylized, figurative ceramics associated with Ife, Benin and Owo royalty. The terracottas from Ife (12th–15th centuries) include free-standing heads, complete figures (and heads that have broken away from them) and such animals as rams and leopards (*see* IFE). The delicately modelled heads (h. 160–320 mm) often have faces bearing fine vertical lines and elaborately sculptured coiffures, crests or crowns. In Benin ceramic commemorative heads have continued to be associated with altars set up by members of bronze-casters' guilds. The ceramic heads and figures unearthed from sites in Owo have stylistic features typical of Ife and Benin, between which Owo lies. These ceramics date to the 15th century, and they are distinguished by the variety of subject-matter represented, including sacrificial offerings and severed heads.

Figurative ceramics associated with an ancient, and probably largely mythical, people called the Sao have been recovered from mound sites south of Lake Chad. Produced between the 11th and 13th centuries, the Sao corpus includes small, solid heads (h. 80–120 mm), human figurines (200–350 mm) and zoomorphic figurines (60–120 mm). Most have been described as grave goods, discovered in or near large, clay burial urns. The human figurines, most of which came from the site of Tago, have faces with thick, rather swollen features and bodies with such dress details as crossed baldrics and epaulets (see fig. 78).

Another major centre of sculptural ceramic production was the Middle Niger region of Mali. Hand-built figures (80–500 mm) have been recovered from a series of mound sites around the modern town of Jenne. Their complex postures and iconographical details have raised tantalizing questions about who produced them and how they were

78. Ceramic figure, h. 200 mm, Sao, Chad, 11th–13th centuries (Paris, Musée de l'Homme)

used (*see* MIDDLE NIGER CULTURES). Based on excavations made at Jenne-jenno, R. J. McIntosh and S. K. McIntosh have dated terracotta production in this area to AD 1000–1200, coinciding with the town's progressive urbanization.

In northern Ghana, Koma ceramics provide evidence of trade links with Jenne and other towns in the Middle Niger. Koma material in the form of animals and human heads and figures (70–300 mm) has been discovered, mostly in burial contexts. The treatment of the eye with its raised elliptical socket and bulging eyeball is distinctive of these rather schematically sculpted images. Koma involvement in the trans-Saharan trade network (*c.* 8th–16th centuries) is reflected in representations of riders on camels in the Koma corpus.

Also involved in this network were the Akan peoples of southern Ghana who, in addition to their ritual vessels discussed above, also produced commemorative ceramic heads used in post-burial funerary rites. They were mostly portraits of state chiefs, and they were displayed in groups on grave sites. Although there are certain stylistic consistencies in the sculpting of the faces, such as high, arching eyebrows and coffee-bean eyes and lips, it is in fact possible to identify from which specific Akan city-state each head comes. This funerary tradition dates to at least the 17th century, and among certain Akan groups women have continued to make portrait heads for funerary and shrine purposes.

Many African peoples have continued to use ceramic sculpture in ritual contexts into the late 20th century. For example, distinctive figurative shrine sculpture has continued to be made by Igbo women in Nigeria. Although it has generally been assumed that such ceramic archaeological treasures of Africa as those of Nok, Sao and the Middle Niger were made by men, the Igbo example, among others, raises the distinct possibility that some of them may have been made by women.

BIBLIOGRAPHY

R. Thompson: 'Abatan: A Master Potter of the Egbado Yoruba', *Tradition and Creativity in Tribal Art*, ed. D. Biebuyck (Berkeley, 1969/*R* 1973), pp. 120–82
B. Fagg and J. Picton: *The Potter's Art in Africa* (London, 1970/*R* 1978)
S. Leith-Ross: *Nigerian Pottery* (Lagos, 1970)
B. E. B. Fagg: *Nok Terracottas* (Lagos and London, 1977)
J.-P. Lebeuf and A. Lebeuf: *Les Arts des Sao* (Paris, 1977)
B. de Grunne: *Terres cuites anciennes de l'ouest africain/Ancient Terracottas from West Africa* (Louvain-la-Neuve, 1980) [bilingual text]
Treasures of Ancient Nigeria (exh. cat. by E. Eyo and F. Willett, Detroit, MI, Inst. A.; London, RA; 1980–82)
T. Maggs and P. Davidson: 'The Lydenburg Heads and the Earliest African Sculpture South of the Equator', *Afr. A.*, xiv/2 (1981), pp. 28–33, 88
J. Picton, ed.: *Earthenware in Asia and Africa* (London, 1984)
A. Stossel: *Afrikanische Keramik: Traditionelle Handwerkskunst südlich der Sahara* (Munich, 1984) [excellent pls and geog. coverage]
J. Anquandah and L. van Ham: *Discovering the Forgotten 'Civilization' of Komaland, Northern Ghana* (Rotterdam, 1985)
N. David, J. Sterner and K. Gavua: 'Why Pots Are Decorated', *Current Anthropol.*, xxix/3 (1988), pp. 365–89
M. C. Berns: 'Ceramic Arts in Africa', *Afr. A.*, xxii/2 (1989), pp. 32–6, 101–2
E. Schildkrout, J. Hellman and C. Keim: 'Mangbetu Pottery: Tradition and Innovation in Northeast Zaïre', *Afr. A.*, xxii/2 (1989), pp. 38–47
M. C. Berns: 'Pots as People: Yungur Ancestral Portraits', *Afr. A.*, xxiii/3 (1990), pp. 50–60, 102
——: 'Art, History and Gender: Women and Clay in West Africa', *Afr. Archaeol. Rev.*, xi (1993), pp. 129–48

MARLA C. BERNS

(iv) Mud. Sculpture in mud or non-baked clay is widespread in Africa, unsurprisingly, perhaps, given its easy availability and great malleability (*see* §V, 1(i) above). Most mud sculpture in Africa is associated with shrines and their related ritual activities. Indeed, shrine sculptures are most often made by priests rather than professional artists. In regions where there is heavy rainfall, mud sculptures have often been sheltered by fragile palm-thatch roofs; even when so protected, however, they have seldom lasted longer than a year. Given that mud sculptures anyway usually deteriorate and disappear after their ritual purpose has been fulfilled, the techniques used to produce them are difficult to document. Most African mud sculptures are massive with few or abbreviated details. In most cases their ritual efficacy is apparently more important than their aesthetic appearance or permanence. As a result, mud sculpture as an art form has been generally ignored by scholars, despite its wide distribution. In Benin, Nigeria, one of the most popular deities, Olukun, bringer of life-changes, wealth and children, is often represented by a mud figure. The material out of which these figures are made is brought from the river bank, a zone of transition

between land and water, and is itself considered a sacred substance that mediates between the world of the living and the world of the dead.

An exception to the general account given above, however, is provided by the *mbari* houses of the Igbo of Nigeria (*see also* IGBO). These often complex works are village projects, built by specialist sculptors with the help of the community at large, and are great sources of civic pride. Moreover, they have often been maintained long after their execution. In the later 20th century *mbari* made of mud and cement or just cement have become permanent (*see* §(v) below). The structure itself is built of heavily packed mud walls with painted, geometric designs on the surfaces. The *mbari* are alive with mud animals, people and 'monsters', all built on frameworks of bamboo. Some *mbari* have up to a hundred modelled images representing scenes from life; the iconography changes with the times and in the late 20th century commonly included radios, telephones and cars.

BIBLIOGRAPHY

U. Beier: *African Mud Sculpture* (Cambridge, 1963)

H. M. Cole: *Mbari: Art and Life among the Owerri Igbo* (Bloomington, 1982)

ROBERT T. SOPPELSA, NATALIE TOBERT

(v) Cement. This material first became available in Sub-Saharan Africa at the beginning of the 20th century, and by the 1980s it was the preferred material for monumental sculpture. More readily available than carvable stone and less expensive than bronze, cement is also easier to work and more durable than wood. Typically cement is modelled over iron rods or wire.

Generally it has replaced mud as a material in African art. The initial development of cement sculpture was concentrated within the coastal regions of what are now Nigeria and Ghana during the period just before World War I, although it quickly spread to neighbouring countries and probably developed independently in a number of areas at the same time. Its earliest manifestations followed European, and especially British colonial, practices of erecting cement headstones and crosses on the graves of their dead. In a merging of European and African belief systems, African funerary sculpture in cement developed first in those areas where there were similar but indigenous traditions of memorials to the dead.

The earliest documented cement sculptures are the grave markers in the Cross River area of south-east Nigeria (see Rosevear). Most are inscribed with dates in the 1920s, but one (in a graveyard at Okuni near Ikom) appears to be from 1911. Although several of these memorials are in the shape of an embellished Celtic cross, the predominant form is a schematic human figure with its right arm raised (*see also* EJAGHAM, §3).

One of the best-documented transitions from non-cement monuments to those made of cement is provided by the funerary memorials of the Ibibio peoples of south-east Nigeria. Traditionally, a bamboo and raffia-palm hut was constructed in the forest some years after the actual burial. Mud sculptures representing the deceased and selected relatives were often erected in front of the structure. The whole ensemble was subsequently allowed to deteriorate. During the 1920s, under the influence of Christianity and with a desire for more enduring forms, the Ibibio began to site memorials at the grave and began making the monuments in cement, eventually including angels and biblical figures, usually brightly painted, in the sculptural programme (*see also* IBIBIO, §4).

Among the Fante and neighbouring Akan-speaking peoples in southern Ghana a tradition of terracotta sculpture dates back at least 400 years. Images, occasionally life-size, were placed in groups near the burial ground; they represented the deceased and his family or, in the case of a chief, the court officials who served him. With the increased availability of cement in the 1920s, and again under the influence of British Christian practices, a tradition of polychrome-cement grave-site monuments was developed, with many of the same sculptural themes as found among the Ibibio.

Even outside the British sphere of influence, a similar pattern of development occurred in some places. Among the Kongo peoples of western Zaïre a rich and varied tradition of stone funerary sculpture was the foundation for a tradition of memorials in cement. On occasion, and perhaps initially, the stone figures were embedded in a concrete monument, but this gave way to figures fully realized in cement. One elaborate structure, dated 1926, features representations of cacti, lizards, spoked wheels, large bells and nesting hens (see 1981 exh. cat.). Another complex tomb, erected before 1949, includes two women with infants, an armed policeman, a blacksmith with bellows, a tailor with his sewing-machine and a man in Western dress with his right hand raised. By the 1970s some form of cement funerary monument had developed in most non-Muslim African countries, with elaborate examples proliferating in Kenya, Madagascar and Côte d'Ivoire, as well as in Nigeria, Ghana and Zaïre.

Cement has also been used to build shrines, with peoples in Ghana and Nigeria again leading the way. With the introduction of cement to the area in the 1920s, the shrines of the *asafo*, traditional warrior groups of the Fante, expanded, both in size and conceptually, into structures of up to three storeys, adorned by as many as twenty brightly painted, three-dimensional sculptures (see fig. 79). Images featured have included group leaders and respected elders, as well as motifs representing traditional proverbs, which incorporate lions, leopards, elephants and other animals. By 1981 there were at least 65 cement shrines in Fanteland.

From the early 1960s cement also became an increasingly common material in the construction of the *mbari* houses of the Owerri Igbo of south-east Nigeria, which typically displayed a complex array of mud sculptures of gods and village scenes. Originally designed as community-wide sacrifices to specific deities in the face of such problems as drought or disease, *mbari* were allowed to decay. As in other cases in Africa, the use of cement turned a deliberately ephemeral structure into a more permanent and, perhaps, more secular one, since religiously prescribed materials were ignored in favour of the modern.

The most famous and best-documented series of cement sculptures in Africa are those of the Yoruba shrines of Oshogbo in south-west Nigeria. Under the patronage and tutelage of the Austrian painter Susanne Wenger, a number of sculptors were employed during the 1960s to refurbish and embellish the town's shrines. The flowing

79. Cement shrine of a Fante *asafo* by Kwamina Amoaku, Gomoa Mankesim, Ghana, 1979; from a photograph by Doran H. Ross, 1980

forms of the shrine to Oshun (the riverain goddess of love and fertility) demonstrate a clear departure from the more rigidly posed and symmetrical tendency in traditional Yoruba art. The cement shrines of Oshogbo became a major tourist attraction, and the Sacred Grove of Oshun was designated a national monument.

Having become a substitute material for wood, stone, terracotta and mud in traditional religious sculpture, cement has also become the chosen material for secular sculpture bought by a growing population of middle- and upper-class African patrons to adorn homes and business premises. As early as the 1930s wealthy Yoruba were decorating the balustrades of their houses with cement lions and elephants. With the advent of national independence for most countries in Sub-Saharan Africa programmes of public sculpture were developed, honouring politicians, war heroes and other celebrated individuals, further increasing the number of commissions for cement sculptors. The technical and aesthetic aspects of cement sculpture became established components of the fine arts courses of many universities throughout Africa.

As the medium's popularity increased, individual artists achieved both national and, increasingly, international reputations. For example, the work of Koffi Mouroufié of Côte d'Ivoire was shown at the Centre Georges Pompidou, Paris, in 1977, while a number of life-size figures by the Ibibio artist Sunday Jack Akpan (*b c.* 1940) are owned by museums throughout the world (see fig. 80). Of the Oshogbo artists, Adebisi Akanji has received the most acclaim. The cement openwork screens he sculpted at the Esso petrol station opposite the Mbari Mbayo club, Oshogbo, comprise one of the most frequently published works of modern African art. The screens are composed of three tiers of stylized human and animal figures drawn from Yoruba myth and cosmology as well as from contemporary life (see, e.g., Kennedy, p. 62). Ovia Idah (1903–68) of Benin City, Nigeria, and Massinguitana (*b* 1926) of Mozambique have also gained international followings. (For further information on these cement artists see the works listed in the bibliography.)

80. Sunday Jack Akpan: *Portrait of a Man in Coat and Tie*, cement and acrylic paint, h. 1.92 m, 1989 (Lyon, Musée Saint Pierre Art Contemporain)

BIBLIOGRAPHY

U. Beier: 'Yoruba Cement Sculpture', *Nigeria Mag.*, 46 (1955), pp. 144–53

——: 'Ibibio Monuments', *Nigeria Mag.*, 51 (1956), pp. 318–36

——: 'Idah: An Original Bini Artist', *Nigeria Mag.*, 80 (1964), pp. 4–16

——: *Contemporary Art in Africa* (London, 1968)

——: *The Return of the Gods: The Sacred Art of Susanne Wenger* (Cambridge, 1975)

G. Preston: 'Perseus and Medusa in Africa: Military Art in Fanteland, 1834–1972', *Afr. A.*, viii/3 (1975), pp. 36–41, 68–71, 91–2

B. Schneider: 'Massinguitana of Mozambique', *Afr. A.*, x/1 (1976), pp. 24–9

K. Nicklin and J. Salmons: 'S. J. Akpan of Nigeria', *Afr. A.*, vii/1 (1977), pp. 30–34

Atelier aujourd'hui: Koffi Moroufié (exh. cat. by N. Beauthéac, Paris, Pompidou, 1977)

P. Breidenbach and D. Ross: 'The Holy Place: Twelve Apostles Healing Gardens', *Afr. A.*, xi/4 (1978), pp. 28–35

D. Ross: 'Cement Lions and Cloth Elephants: Popular Arts of the Fante Asafo', *Five Thousand Years of Popular Culture: Popular Culture before Printing*, ed. F. E. H. Schroeder (Bowling Green, 1980), pp. 287–317

The Four Moments of the Sun: Kongo Art in Two Worlds (exh. cat. by R. F. Thompson and J. A. Cornet, Washington, DC, N.G.A., 1981)

S. Domowitz and R. Mandirola: 'Grave Monuments in Ivory Coast', *Afr. A.*, xvii/4 (1984), pp. 46–52, 96

D. Rosevear: 'Cross River Tombstones', *Afr. A.*, xviii/1 (1984), pp. 44–7

Sculptures en ciment du Nigéria de S. J. Akpan and A. O. Akpan (exh. cat. by J. Soulillou, Calais, Mus. B.-A., 1985)

J. Kennedy: *New Currents, Ancient Rivers: Contemporary African Artists in a Generation of Change* (Washington and London, 1992) [discusses and illustrates the work of a number of Afr. cement artists]

DORAN H. ROSS

3. MASK AND MASQUERADE. The term 'mask' refers primarily to the object that is worn to hide the face of the masker. The term 'masquerade', however, refers to the multimedia activity of transforming a human being into a powerfully animated characterization. While much art-historical research has focused on the mask object itself, the African art form of masquerade comprises an entire ensemble of costume, dance, music and song. Indeed, masquerade is one of Africa's major contributions to world art; it is certainly the most spectacular. Further information on African mask and masquerade will be found in the entries on the arts of individual peoples, cross-references to several of which appear in the article below.

Mask forms have often been reproduced in other media. They have sometimes been adapted as architectural ornamentation or reproduced in miniature for personal adornment, as for example among the Pende of Zaïre (*see* PENDE, §2). There are several traditions of miniature masks, which are not worn over the face or head but simply displayed as symbols of status and achievement. Among the Lega of Zaïre, for example, small wooden and ivory masks are status objects that are displayed during the rituals of the multi-graded initiation societies (*see* LEGA AND RELATED PEOPLES, §2). Among the Dan and neighbouring peoples of Côte d'Ivoire and Liberia miniature masks are the personal property of young men and women whose families own full-size masks. The miniature masks represent the spiritual power embodied in the full-size mask and serve a variety of protective functions for their owners (*see* DAN, §2).

(i) Introduction. (ii) Forms and styles. (iii) Manufacture, preparation and performance. (iv) Contexts. (v) Women and masquerade. (vi) Boys' masquerades.

(i) Introduction. From a conventional Western perspective the aesthetic dynamism of an African mask emerges from analysis of the formal qualities of the static sculptural form, the wooden, facial portion of the mask, devoid of all costume and accompanying dance and music. Indeed, it was the startling sculptural inventiveness of African masks that first attracted the attention of European ethnographers, museum curators, painters and sculptors to African art in the early 20th century. In line with prevailing Western sensibilities and taste, the surfaces of masks in Western collections were cleaned and polished to accentuate their sculptural form; this practice further removed them from their original African context. The distortion of the true nature of African masks as elements of the performance of masked dancers in masquerade leaves the museum viewer devoid of the rich sights and sounds that are the essential aesthetic components of this art form.

Ethnographic reports on a variety of African cultures reveal dramatic differences in the elaboration of masking traditions. Some cultures have paid little attention to the creative potential of masking, while others have developed elaborate masquerades that appear throughout the year. The origins of masking on the African continent will probably never be known, for the perishable organic materials out of which masks are made (i.e. wood, fibre, cloth and so on) are highly susceptible to insect and environmental damage, and neither masks nor their accompanying costumes survive in the archaeological record. While it is thus impossible to trace the origins of mask-making in Africa, there is some evidence to suggest that it is very ancient. Rock paintings and engravings at the site at Tassili N' Ajjer and adjacent sites in southern Algeria have been interpreted as evidence that masquerade was already a fully established and vital form of artistic expression in the 5th and 4th millennia BC (see Cole, 1985, p. 15). In modern times the distribution of cultures that make and dance masks relates directly to the distribution of Bantu-speaking peoples throughout the area south of the Sahara Desert from the Atlantic to the Indian Ocean. It is within this vast area of West, Central and East Africa that the major masking traditions are found.

The origins of each mask are recorded in oral tradition for the peoples who make and perform them. Thus a mask may have come from the supreme god or from a tutelary deity, such as an ancestral or nature spirit. In a number of African cultures oral traditions state that women first made masks and that it was only later that mask-making was assumed by men. Masquerade continues to be predominantly a male activity. Throughout the continent, even in cultures where women may wear masks on occasion, only men ever carve masks. This is explained by men's exclusive role as wood-carvers and by the general dominance of men's secret societies, which ultimately control the manufacture and appearance of masks. Indeed, in many African cultures masquerade is a public assertion of male secular and spiritual dominance. Moreover, masking is often used to define gender and status differences in the community, separating men from women and the initiated from the uninitiated. Most African masking traditions are highly secret, and novices are taught the importance of retaining these powerful traditions within the male sphere. Women are nevertheless vital to the success of many masquerades, even if they appear to have only a passive role as observers (*see also* §(v) below).

In general, then, masked figures and the knowledge to make and dance them are associated with centres of political and/or spiritual authority in the community. These are often secret or semi-secret associations or societies whose members have passed through a period of initiation and instruction. In other cases masks 'belong' to the entire village, although they are often owned by aristocratic families, lineages or clans who control their appearance in the community and, when they are not in use, safeguard the masks and their costumes.

The disguise of the human face and body by the use of a mask creates powerful images. Masks suppress identity and transform the masked into powerful entities. In some African cultures the wearing of masks is likened to disappearance or even death. These are appropriate metaphors for masks that often appear at funerary rituals or during initiation rituals, when people 'die' from one status or identity to be 'reborn' in another.

In general masks represent two types of spirit forces: first, ancestral spirits who return to the land of the living in the form of masks to instruct, counsel, heal, aid and protect the living members of the secret cult or society; and, secondly, generalized nature spirits who, like ancestral spirits, demand respect through proper ritual observances but reward society members with good health, bountiful harvests and many children. The names given to masks suggest collective spirit forces rather than the names of actual people who once lived. Among the Mossi of Burkina Faso, masks are said to be the 'eyes' of clan ancestors (*see* MOSSI, §2), while among the Kuba of Zaïre masks are named *ngesh* or *mungici* after the names of nature spirits (see Binkley). Thus, when masks enter the community they do so as spirit forces. Masks are the visual embodiment of the power of the secret society that has brought them into being. Indeed, among the Yoruba there are some masks that still form part of the sacred paraphernalia placed on household shrines dedicated to tutelary deities even though they are damaged and no longer danced (see H. J. Drewal and M. T. Drewal, p. 250). Spirit forces in the form of masks provide the means by which the masking association or society conducts initiation rituals, buries its dead, promotes agricultural, animal and human fertility and passes judgement on those who have broken the society's rules.

During masquerade, other powers and values are expressed. These include the powers of elders over juniors and the power of men over women, as well as the power of the society's secret knowledge over the community's secular knowledge. Pride of membership in the secret society is also expressed, as is the self-respect and pride of the community as a whole in its masks and masquerades.

(ii) Forms and styles. African masks and mask costumes are stylistically varied. In general, masks can be grouped into three basic types. The first is the face mask, which is attached to or held in front of the face. The second is the helmet mask, which covers the entire head like a helmet or casque. The third and final category is the headdress or cap mask, which consists of a more or less elaborate superstructure worn on top of the head like a cap; in this case cloth or fibre attached to the base of the cap covers the face and sometimes the body of the performer, thus obscuring his identity. Within these three basic categories an immense variety of styles is found, ranging from a simple wooden or cloth face-covering to huge and complex sculptural forms that cover the entire body and may rise 5 m or more above the head of the masker. Such masks are immense mobile sculptures, especially when the masker wears stilts or incorporates other devices to increase overall height.

The form and style of African masks relate directly to the characters they embody in masquerade. These characters range from founders of the community, famous warriors and hunters to wild forest creatures. Even clowns, fools, drunkards and prostitutes may be subjects for characterization. The full style of a mask emerges during its performance. Masks may be male or female, young or old, wealthy or destitute. Masks may be benign and restrained or uncontrolled and dangerous. The characterization is completed by the adoption of appropriate gestures and sounds.

Often masks are made using the forms and materials symbolically associated with the realms of the hereafter and the wild: the savannah, forest, rivers and lakes. During masquerade these realms are contrasted with the civilized world of the community. These associations are reinforced by naming masks after ancestors and culture heroes and such, or after such forest creatures as birds, crocodiles and antelopes, or nature spirits. The forms and styles of masks visually evoke these other worlds and characters.

Physically, masks may represent everything from idealized beauty to grotesques or the results of disfiguring disease. In many African cultures, there is a direct link between outward physical beauty and inner moral and spiritual purity. Masks of good character and moral fortitude usually display marks of social status, wealth and achievement. For example, among the Mende of Sierra Leone and Liberia, a Sowei mask depicts a high-ranking member of the women's Sande society. The elaborate multi-crested hair arrangement, for instance, is carved in great detail. Carved scarification patterns on the face of this and other masks mark ethnic identity and social status but are also protective and decorative (*see* MENDE).

Other masks appear to glorify physical disease and deformity with an apparent disdain for aesthetic principles and artistic finesse. Often, these masks directly incorporate various natural materials, including dark, sticky resins and waxes, unworked raffia fibre and bark, as well as quills, bird beaks, animal horns and teeth (see fig. 81). Such masks represent unrestrained power and malevolent force and often serve as warnings to those in the community who are tempted to indulge in antisocial behaviour.

Colour plays an important role in the characterization of masks. While it is used to add decorative interest, it also often has important symbolic connotations. For example, black is generally associated with decay, death, ugliness and malevolent spirits, while white often symbolizes peace, purity, beauty and benevolent spirits. Red is more ambiguous: in some cultures it is associated with healing and well-being, while in others it is symbolic of blood, danger, power and death. In addition, the formal qualities of masks may convey quite specific meanings. Among the Igbo of

81. Mask representing Idu, a mythical bush monster, at the Otsa festival, Ekperi, Ugbekpe, northern Edo, southern Nigeria; from a photograph by Jean M. Borgatti, 1972

82. Mask representing Banda, Nalu, Guinea; from a photograph by Michael Huet, 1970s

Nigeria, for example, light-coloured masks with refined features often represent female characters, while dark-coloured masks with distorted features represent male characters from the forest or bush (*see* IGBO).

Many masks combine human and animal imagery, which may be enlarged, reduced or adjusted for both decorative and expressive purposes. Many mask-carvers use their understanding of human and animal facial anatomy and of the underlying skeletal structure to produce imaginative reinterpretations in a highly sophisticated abstract language while also taking into account the fact that the complete mask figure will be seen moving, rather than still, during masquerade. The deeply cut geometric planes and elaborate superstructure found on many masks are aesthetically powerful components.

Masks also frequently represent specific birds and animals. The heads may be realistic, or certain details may be exaggerated for added sculptural interest and visual impact. The jaws of forest animals are often enlarged in scale and carved open, with emphasis given to sharp teeth. Beaks, tusks and horns are often exaggerated in scale and multiplied in number for added dramatic impact. Masks may also represent such fantastic creatures as nature spirits or other potent forces, which have no single prototype in the visible world. Mask-makers thus often combine elements from a number of different animals to create powerful sculptural statements. For example, the Banda mask of the Nalu of Guinea does not represent just one animal but the collective danger, mystery and uncertainty of the forest world (see fig. 82).

Added visual and symbolic impact is obtained from using material directly appropriated from the bush and forest. Unworked raffia and other fibres, which often make up the voluminous costumes of masks, not only disguise the body of the dancer but also evoke the organic forms seen in the bush. Beaks, feathers, quills and animal skins are often integral parts of costumes. Masks may also carry paraphernalia associated with the forest, such as bows and arrows, spears, hunting nets and bells.

The costume accessories worn or carried by masks are often chosen for their symbolic power relating to an elevated station in life or supernatural power. The coiffure of the Sowei mask of the Mende, for example, is often carved with amulets and other protective charms. These power-related objects add to the efficacy, wealth and prestige of the mask. Among the Southern Kuba of Zaïre masks wear ornaments associated with wealth and high status, such as shell and beaded necklaces, bracelets and anklets (see fig. 83), and may also carry objects made of iron, copper or ivory. Among the Yoruba of Nigeria, Gelede and Egungun masks display expensive cloth. The display of such cloth and other objects of status on masks adds immeasurably to their aesthetic impact and also reflects favourably on the masking society that brought the mask into being and controls its appearance. Furthermore, the lavish display honours the spirit forces evoked by the masked performance.

Regardless of how dynamic the carving is, or how suggestive the various costume elements are, the mask is

83. Mask representing Inuba, an important titleholder, at a funerary masquerade, Northern Kete village, Southern Kuba area, Zaïre; from a photograph by David A. Binkley, 1981

still a static form that is only fully animated and defined by the movements and sounds of the masker. It is through such animation that the true nature of the forest and spirit world emerges. If the mask represents an animal or nature spirit its performance may be threatening or unpredictable. The mask may crawl on the ground, appear to fly in the air, breathe fire, run in all directions or be led into the village tethered on the end of a cord. Among the Mende of Sierra Leone and Liberia, the mask called Goboi is beaten by its attendants and then doused with cold water to 'cool' its rage. Among the Yoruba and other peoples, maskers representing females often wear false breasts and women's clothing and also dance and mime the behaviour traditionally associated with such women's roles as working in the fields, preparing food or nursing a child (see fig. 84). A female mask widely distributed among masking societies in Sierra Leone and Liberia even 'gives birth' to small costumed figures that have previously been hidden under its voluminous costume during the course of the performance. Unrefined and foolish masks may talk nonsensically and awkwardly meander through the village. In contrast, an important titleholder, such as the Kuba mask Inuba, struts its way through the village accompanied by an entourage of village titleholders, as is appropriate for a respected and influential visitor to the community (see fig. 83 above).

The voices of masks are as varied as their physical appearance. In some cultures maskers use voice disguisers to imitate swarming insects, screeching birds or the growl of a forest predator. A mask may also speak in a special language that has to be deciphered by an interpreter. Other sounds are also important components of masquerade. The sounds of gun shots, war trumpets and drums accompany the entrance into the village of certain Kuba masks in re-enactments of mythic battles in which the mask was originally captured. Among the northern Edo of Nigeria, complex instrumental and choral arrangements accompany masked performances, and music is considered essential to the success of a performance. Although musicians are not the centre of attention when masks perform, they may actually control the tempo and duration of the dances. Virtuosity and improvisation are essential ingredients of the ensemble presentation. The songs that are sung at masquerades often evoke the spirit under whose sanction the event is taking place. For example, for a funeral the qualities of the deceased and his family may be lauded. Songs also praise the power and authority of the masks and of the society under whose auspices the masquerade is being performed.

(iii) Manufacture, preparation and performance. Most masks, especially complex ones, are commissioned from a specialist in the particular type or style of mask required. Although mask-carvers are often specialists, they are not always full-time artists but often practise their skill as a part-time activity. The carving of a mask is by no means an everyday occurrence. The process of making a mask, whether carved from wood or made from some other materials, is often governed by strict rules of segregation and ritual observance. In many African cultures the artist is regarded as being in a state of ritual impurity during the carving process, and he will therefore segregate himself from the rest of the community. If a mask is to be carved from wood, the spiritual forces that inhabit the tree or surrounding forest may have to be contained or appeased before the tree is cut and the carving begun. Once the carving is completed, further sacrifices and prayers may be required to ensure that the spirit whom the mask represents will find favour with it and with the masquerade in which it will perform.

84. Mask of the Gelede society, representing a nursing mother, Yoruba, Benin; from a photograph by Michael Huet, 1970s

In addition to being carved from wood, masks may be made from a variety of other materials, including cloth, plaited fibre, leather, gourd, metal, hide and feathers. To prepare a single mask and its costume may require the skills of many individuals, including those of a woodcarver, a costume-maker, a blacksmith and a weaver. For example, if feathers, animal skins or other materials are required, these must be obtained from a hunter or trapper; if a sword, bow and arrows, iron gong, bells or mirrors are to be part of the mask's paraphernalia, then these must be made or purchased.

Mask-making may also be a part of the training novices undergo during initiation rituals (see fig. 85). While generally it is the elders who actually make the mask, by observation and participation the novices learn the techniques necessary both to make and to dance masks. This experience will be the novices' first sanctioned foray into the creative world of adult masquerade, although, in the spirit of imitation and play, they may have already made 'unofficial' examples of masks they have seen dance (*see* §(vi) below).

The presentation of the completed mask in performance requires the cooperation and skills of many individuals. Meetings are held to select the dancers and to plan the masquerade, which may consist of several distinct performances over a number of days. Since a mask rarely

85. Mask being made by initiation novices, Northern Kete village, Southern Kuba area, Zaïre; from a photograph by David A. Binkley, 1981

appears alone, other masks must be made or refurbished. In addition, musicians, singers and other specialists must be organized before the masquerade can take place. Generally each mask has one or more retainers who accompany it throughout its performance. One retainer may act as spokesman for the mask, interpreting its speech; others adjust its costume when necessary, clear the dance area and ensure that the performance is completed without incident.

Ritual precautions are also taken during the preparations for a masquerade performance. Among the Kuba of Zaïre, the Dan of Côte d'Ivoire and the Igbo of Nigeria, for example, maskers often believe themselves to be especially vulnerable during a performance. Through witchcraft, sorcery or the actions of a malevolent spirit they may injure themselves or find themselves weak and dance poorly. To ensure success, maskers may rub medicines on their joints and back or carry an efficacious charm in the mouth or hand during the performance. The behaviour of the community as a whole is also strictly regulated during the time of mask performances. Stealing, adultery, active disputes and other antisocial acts disruptive to community harmony are strictly forbidden during masquerade performances.

To keep the identity of the dancers secret from the uninitiated, maskers dress in a secluded location. The refurbishment of an older mask with a coat of paint may be augmented with additional sacrifices to the spirit forces, which 'call' it into being just before the performance begins. Through repeated sacrifice and application of pigment before each dance, a mask may be thought to gain in power. For example, among the Dan of Liberia and Côte d'Ivoire, masks that are first used purely for entertainment may become, after many years of dancing, powerful masks used as judges or hunters of witches and sorcerers. At the conclusion of the performance, before the mask is put away, it may be ritually 'cooled', thus dissipating the 'heat' generated in the performance.

Once the maskers are dressed, the masks enter the village as spirit forces, the maskers remaining 'in costume' throughout the performance, only returning to the forest or a designated enclosure at its conclusion. Often the audience and performers mingle and on occasion even change roles. For example, a musician may leave the dance area and be replaced by a member of the audience, or an elderly man, inspired by the performance, may walk to the centre of the dancing ground and imitate the dance of the mask. African masquerade is thus fluid and dynamic, following a loosely choreographed programme with its own rules of presentational style and decorum.

Some masks may only appear during the day, others only at night, or the masquerade cycle may last for several days including day and night performances. Generally masquerades take place in a prescribed area. This may be a central dancing area set aside for the purpose, although performances may also take place in specific locations, such as at the deceased's compound during a funeral. The masks may appear before the entire population of the village or only a select group of individuals, such as senior members of the masking society. Sometimes the masks may appear not in the village at all but deep in a forest enclosure.

Masks rarely perform alone. Although the appearance of dozens of masks on a single occasion has been documented, usually a much smaller number appear together. When several masks perform, they generally do so in the order of their relative importance. For example, among the Kuba of Zaïre, several lower-ranked masks perform on the day preceding the appearance of the senior mask. The hierarchy of masks corresponds to a similar hierarchy of membership in the masking society. Among the Senufo of Côte d'Ivoire, Mali and Burkina Faso, for example, lower-ranking masks are danced for entertainment by the junior members of the society, while the more powerful, senior masks appear under the aegis of the society's elders on more serious occasions. The senior masks, representing the highest political authority in the community, command great attention and respect (*see* SENUFO). The maskers, as well as the singers and musicians, are judged on their competence, aesthetic ability and, in the case of the maskers, athleticism. Competition between individual maskers, between masking societies and between families who own masks is a vital part of the dynamics of African masquerade.

(iv) Contexts. Masquerades are rarely held solely for entertainment. Masks most often appear during events

that mark periods of stress or transition in the life of the community. Such events include initiation and funeral rituals as well as such cyclical occasions as the onset of the planting season or harvest time. Masks also appear in response to such events as a long drought, a severe epidemic or a crop failure.

The most frequent occasions for masquerade in West and Central Africa are funerary rituals, especially those held for elders and other members of the masking society. Masks perform singly or in groups for several days at the funeral itself. Alternatively the masquerade may take place a year or more after the death; the masks then dance for all those who have died in the interim. Among the Dogon of Mali, for example, dozens of masks may appear at a second funeral to honour deceased members of the masking society (*see* DOGON). Among the Southern Kuba of Zaïre the powerful mask Inuba (see fig. 83 above) appears only at funerals of senior titleholders (see Binkley). During such funeral performances, masks are regarded as intermediaries between the living and the recently deceased. The masks dance to honour the latter and to dispel any ill feelings of the spirit of the deceased or members of his family because of his death. The memory of the deceased is honoured, and his spirit is conducted safely to the land of the dead.

Another frequent occasion for the appearance of masks is initiation rituals, in which young men (and sometimes young women) learn the secret knowledge that allows them to become full participating members of adult society. In many masking societies membership is mandatory for all who have reached the appropriate age. Masks play a major role throughout the initiation cycle, and they are often employed to 'steal' the uninitiated youths from the village and install them in a bush or forest camp. Among several groups in Liberia a large masked figure with exaggerated jaws and teeth stained red symbolically 'kills and eats' the novices at the onset of the rite before they are 'reborn' as adults through the initiation process. In the initiation enclosure, masks serve as guardians of the novices and, together with the elders, discipline and educate the novices. Masks also safeguard the novices' physical and spiritual well-being. In some cultures, masks are given the names of important deceased family members who are called upon to protect the novices from harm. This is especially important when circumcision is involved as the ancestral spirits, in the guise of masks, are thought to help the novices' wounds heal quickly. Masks also monitor the activities of the initiation camp and make certain that non-members keep their distance. Masks may also be used to obtain food and other materials for the camp. The making of masks is part of the secret knowledge imparted to the novices during initiation rituals. Indeed, masks are thought to be among the most secret of initiation-related lore; they are visible symbols of the secret nature of the institution. Depending on the stage of initiation, the masks dance for society members in the forest or enter the village to dance for the women and children. On these occasions masks express pride of membership in the society and the prestige of those who are undergoing the initiation rite.

In some societies masks form part of the regalia of aristocratic rulers and their families and appear at festivals and rituals, adding to the splendour of the royal court. For example, among the Kuba of Zaïre several masks are reported to form part of the ruler's patrimony. Maskers also appeared at the royal court of Bamum in the Cameroon Grassfields at festivals associated with the payment of tribute and at lavish feasts held to consolidate ties between the king and his subjects (see fig. 86; *see also* BAMUM).

Among the Dan, We and related groups in Côte d'Ivoire and Liberia masks play a multitude of roles. For example, some masks play a significant role in the judicial affairs of the community, while another is worn during competitive footraces, and another enters the village to control cooking

86. Mask representing a crocodile, at the Nja festival, Foumban, Bamum, Cameroon; from a photograph by Marie-Pauline Thorbecke, 1912

fires that, if left unattended, could burn the entire village. Historically, a very powerful Dan mask prepared and then led warriors into battle, while another was considered a judgement mask of great power and influence that sanctioned proceedings of various kinds, settled disputes and allocated fines (*see* DAN, §2).

The Bamana of southern Mali also have elaborate masking traditions. The Chi Wara society and its masks are primarily concerned with the fertility of the fields and proper farming practices. Members of the society dance in crest masks during agricultural rituals in honour of a mythic half-man/half-animal who was instrumental in bringing agriculture to the Bamana (*see* BAMANA, fig. 4). The powerful Komo society uses masks composed of an accumulation of symbolically charged material to identify and eliminate such destructive forces as thieves and sorcerers (*see* BAMANA, §3).

In parts of West Africa a number of elaborate regional initiation and masking societies developed. The masks of one of these, the Poro society, danced at the initiations and funerals of society members but also served important functions as agents of social control in protecting the community against antisocial behaviour. Some of these masks were sacred and had great power and authority. Acting in consort with a council of elders, the masks pronounced sentence on murderers, thieves and other deviants and then supervised the carrying out of the sentence.

Masks also appear in dramatic presentations of mythic or historical tales relating to village or clan histories. On these occasions masks represent important chiefs, warriors or culture heroes, while drunkards and fools may also appear. Masks also sometimes play important roles as social commentators. For example, masks may dance to comment on the antisocial behaviour of a specific community member, even if he or she is an elder. The mask may directly name the individual, or a skit may be enacted that graphically presents the immoral behaviour, such as drunkenness or adultery. In this role the mask stands in a privileged position as a third party protected by anonymity that can break the normal rules of decorum and comment on social behaviour without fear of reprisal.

In addition to all the above, masks in Africa are highly entertaining. Even on the most sombre of occasions a comical mask may appear to relieve the mood of seriousness or sadness. With increasing cultural influences from both the West and the Islamic world, however, many African masking traditions have lost or altered their ritual and ceremonial importance. By the late 20th century in some areas masks performed only for entertainment, often at such non-traditional occasions as Christmas or New Year festivals or in performances for tourists.

(v) Women and masquerade. Generally in Africa masquerade is regarded as a potentially dangerous occasion for people who are not members of the masking society, and this is especially the case for women. Masks are often regarded as dangerous to the health and fertility of women. If a woman touches a mask or even walks across the ground on which masks dance, infertility, still-births or illness may result. Precautions are taken, therefore, to ensure that women keep their distance and do not touch the masks during performance. These sanctions may also be explained by men's concern that the secrets possessed by their masking society are kept from the uninitiated. Thus, for the most part, women are excluded from direct participation in mask-making and dancing.

There are, however, several exceptions to this prohibition. Among the Mende and related peoples of Sierra Leone and Liberia, for example, women belong to a powerful initiation society called Sande. The society commissions the making of masks and organizes performances during initiation rites for society members (*see* MENDE; see also fig. 13 above). In some cultures the participation of elder women, usually those past the menopause, is crucial to the setting up of the men's initiation camp, and sometimes women are instrumental in the manufacture of some masks, even making a part of the costume worn by masked dancers. Among the southern Kuba of Zaïre, some masks cannot dance without a gift first being given to the women of the community, while among the Yoruba of Nigeria women actively participate in both Gelede and Egungun masquerades by contributing the expensive cloth for the mask costume. In a number of cultures women play the essential role of choral accompaniment at mask performances.

BIBLIOGRAPHY

The works listed below are only a very few of those devoted to mask and masquerade in Africa. For additional references see the bibliographies of the various entries on individual peoples, especially those cross-referred to above. Articles on African mask and masquerade appear regularly in such journals as *African Arts*.

G. Kubik: 'Masks of the Mbwela', *Geographica*, Revisita da Sociedade de Geografia de Lisboa, xx (1969)

S. Ottenberg: 'Humorous Masks and Serious Politics among Afikpo Ibo', *African Art and Leadership*, ed. D. Fraser and H. M. Cole (Madison, 1972), pp. 99–121

D. Biebuyck: *Lega Culture: Art, Initiation, and Moral Philosophy among a Central African People* (Berkeley, 1973)

S. Ottenberg: 'Afikpo Masquerades: Audience and Performers', *Afr. A.*, vi (1973), pp. 32–5, 94–5

R. A. Bravmann: *Islam and Tribal Art in West Africa* (Cambridge, 1974)

K. Nicklin: 'Nigeria Skin-covered Masks', *Afr. A.*, vii (1974), pp. 8–15, 67–8, 92

S. Ottenberg: *Masked Rituals of the Afikpo: The Context of an African Art* (Seattle, 1975)

A. Vrydagh: 'Makisi of Zambia', *Afr. A.*, x (1976), pp. 12–19, 88

H. J. Drewal: 'The Arts of Egungun among the Yoruba Peoples', *Afr. A.*, xi (1978), pp. 18–19, 97–8

B. DeMott: *Dogon Masks: A Structural Study of Form and Meaning*, Studies in the Fine Arts, 4 (Ann Arbor, 1979)

E. Tonkin: 'Masks and Power', *Man*, xiv (1979), pp. 237–48

From the Hands of Lawrence Ajanaku (exh. cat. by J. M. Borgatti, Los Angeles, UCLA, Mus. Cult. Hist., 1979)

Ethnol. Z. Zürich, i (1980) [special issue on masking and initiation societies in Sierra Leone, Liberia and Côte d'Ivoire]

A. J. Glaze: *Art and Death in a Senufo Village* (Bloomington, IN, 1981)

A. P. Bourgeois: 'Yaka Masks and Sexual Imagery', *Afr. A.*, xv (1982), pp. 47–50, 87

M. T. Drewal and H. J. Drewal: *Gelede: Art and Female Power among the Yoruba* (Bloomington, IN, 1983)

M.-L. Bastin: 'Ritual Masks of the Chokwe', *Afr. A.*, xvii (1984), pp. 40–45, 92–3, 95

A. P. Bourgeois: *Art of the Yaka and Suku* (Meudon, 1984)

E. Fischer and H. Himmelheber: *The Arts of the Dan in West Africa* (Zurich, 1984)

G. I. Jones: *The Art of Eastern Nigeria* (Cambridge, 1984)

The Art of Cameroon (exh. cat. by T. Northern, Washington, DC, Smithsonian Inst., 1984)

Igbo Arts: Community and Cosmos (exh. cat. by H. M. Cole and C. C. Aniakor, Los Angeles, UCLA, Mus. Cult. Hist., 1984–6)

H. M. Cole, ed.: *I Am Not myself: The Art of African Masquerade*, Los Angeles, Mus. Cult. Hist. UCLA, Monograph Ser., 26 (Los Angeles, 1985)
F. Lamp: 'Cosmos, Cosmetics and the Spirit of Bondo', *Afr. A.*, xviii (1985), pp. 28–43, 98–9
D. Biebuyck: *The Arts of Zaire*, 2 vols (Berkeley, 1985–6)
M. J. Arnoldi: 'Puppet Theatre: Form and Ideology in Bamana Performances', *Emp. Stud. A.*, iv (1986), pp. 131–50
D. Hersak: *Songye Masks and Figure Sculpture* (London, 1986)
D. A. Binkley: 'Avatar of Power: Southern Kuba Masquerade Figures in a Funerary Context', *Afr. A.*, lvii/1 (1987), pp. 75–97
J. W. Nunley: *Moving with the Face of the Devil: Art and Politics in Urban West Africa* (Urbana, 1987)
C. D. Roy: *Art of the Upper Volta Rivers* (Paris, 1987)
S. L. Kasfir, ed.: *West African Masks and Cultural Systems* (Tervuren, 1988)
D. A. Binkley: 'Masks, Space and Gender in Southern Kuba Initiation Ritual', *IA Stud. Afr. A.*, iii (1990), pp. 157–76
K. Yoshida: *Masks and Transformation among the Chewa of Eastern Zambia*, Osaka, N. Mus. Ethnol., Senri Ethnological Studies, xxxi (1992), pp. 203–73
Masks and the Art of Expression (exh. cat., ed. J. Mack; London, BM, 1994)

DAVID A. BINKLEY

(vi) Boys' masquerades. Children's masquerades are widespread in Africa, particularly in those areas where adult masking is found, that is, mainly in West and Central Africa. They are almost never performed by girls, however, even in Liberia and Sierra Leone where women's masquerades are as common as men's. A growing tendency to initiate boys into adult masquerade societies at a younger age means that boys have become less likely to have their own traditional masquerades. Even in the late 20th century, however, there was a great deal of boys' masquerading in Africa. Boys' masquerading can be usefully presented according to three categories: where its organization is linked to adult forms; where adult forms are emulated, but there is a great deal of autonomy; and where, if adult forms exist at all, they are not closely related. It should be noted that mask size alone is not a good criterion for identifying children's masks; adult forms are sometimes just as small, and boys' may be large.

Boys' masquerade among the Bamana of Mali can be taken to exemplify the first category (see Zahan). Each Bamana village has a number of masquerade associations based on residence, the boys' being the youngest association of six (*see also* BAMANA, §3). Each boys' group is highly organized, with established leadership positions, its own shrine and spirit and its characteristic wooden mask, which, though made by adult blacksmiths, is unique to boys. The mask has an elongated human face with a number of horns, the body being covered with a cloth shirt and long trousers. The masquerader is accompanied by other boys who drum and sing. He performs at festivals, receiving gifts from adults, and has important duties at the millet harvest, when the mask's spirit blesses the new crop of each farmer.

Among the Yoruba of Nigeria boys of all ages, though not yet really members, perform in the adult masquerades of Gelede, Egungun and other Orisa societies. They are individually integrated, joining the society of their father, unless advised by a diviner because of illness to join a different one. Boys as young as five years old often perform at the beginning of adult performances, guided by their fathers or other senior men. In Gelede the boys wear adult-style headpieces, usually representing human

87. Boy masqueraders prepared for Dodo, Bobo Dioulasso, Burkina Faso; from a photograph by René A. Bravmann, 1972

faces or animal forms, with cloth masks and body costumes. In Egungun they may wear a cloth hood and face piece and a variety of textile costumes. The close integration of uninitiated boys into adult masquerade societies also occurs among the Bobo of Burkina Faso (*see* BOBO, §2; see also Le Moal) and the Senufo of Côte d'Ivoire (*see* SENUFO).

Where boys' masking groups are separate from adult forms but emulate them, the religious aspect is less important. At Afikpo, among the Igbo of Nigeria, boys organize themselves into masking groups and perform masquerades in direct emulation of adult versions (see Ottenberg, 1975, 1982, 1989). Wood and gourd masks are reserved for adults, but masks of cloth, coconut or leaves are used with a raffia costume. During the festival season many boys perform together before an audience of children and some adults (*see* IGBO). Copying of adult forms also occurs in towns and cities, as has been described for Bo in Sierra Leone (see Cannizzo, 1978, 1979). Here, groups of boys perform as Alikali Devils in their local neighbourhoods and in the main streets, in imitation of the adult forms that derive from the capital, Freetown. Each boys' group performs a single masquerade with one of four different mask types, consisting of either a wood or cloth mask, various attachments and a variety of cloth body costumes. Despite their emulation of adult forms, these ethnically, religiously and socially mixed groups draw much of the imagery of their masquerades from popular Sierra Leone culture. Such emulating forms of boys' masquerades also exist among various other Igbo groups, among the Dogon of Mali, among the Gola of Liberia and among groups in Zaïre.

Boys' masquerades unrelated to prevalent adult forms are exemplified by the Dodo of Ouagadougou and other parts of Burkina Faso (see Hinckley, 1985, 1986). This secular form apparently originated among adults in northern Nigeria and was brought to Burkina Faso by Hausa traders in the 19th century, after which it became widespread in the country. By the late 20th century it had become a predominantly children's form. The outfit comprises a horned, white gourd mask with a costume of shorts, wristlets and anklets and sometimes body paint (see fig. 87). The boys' groups perform in their residential areas and in other parts of the town, and since the 1970s some of them have performed in a popular government-sponsored competition each year at Ramadan. The groups are often of mixed religious and ethnic background. One of their aims is to gain funds through performance, often the boys' major source of income. Other autonomous, non-emulating boys' masquerades are found in Ghana, where adult masking is uncommon (see Bravmann, 1979, 1983), and among the Igede in Nigeria. In various parts of Africa boys perform in a variety of costumes at Christmas, sometimes dressing as Father Christmas but also using traditional masks; some masquerading takes place during Ramadan.

Boys are only rarely directly taught the skills of masquerade by men, often learning from other boys of their own age or slightly older. Original praising, satiric and abusive songs are commonly composed by the boys, even when the mask and costume are conventional copies of adult types. Dance movements tend to be erratic, unlike in many adult masquerades, and the dress simpler, sometimes produced from odds and ends of materials. Receiving gifts for performances is generally very important. Musical instruments are often made out of tin cans, bits of metal and wood, although sometimes ordinary drums are used. The boys strive for autonomy and creativity, but parental encouragement, advice and assistance are common.

In the late 20th century changes in African life were leading to a decline in boys' masquerading in rural areas but to a growth in urban areas in forms that draw on the imagery of popular culture as seen in the media. These forms in turn were being adopted in rural areas.

BIBLIOGRAPHY

M. Griaule: *Jeux dogons*, Trav. & Mém. Inst. Ethnol., xxxii (Paris, 1938)
C. Béart: 'Jeux et jouets de l'ouest africain', *Mém. Inst. Fr. d'Afrique Noire: Mél. Ethnol.*, xlii (Dakar, 1955)
D. Zahan: *Sociétés d'initiation bambara: Le n'Domo, le kore, le monde d'outre-mer, passé et présent* (Paris, 1960)
U. Beier: 'The Agbegijo Masquerades', *Nigeria Mag.*, 82 (1964), pp. 189–99
H. Kreutzinger: *The Eri Devils in Freetown, Sierra Leone*, Ethnologische Gesellschaft Acta Ethnologica et Linguistica, ix (Vienna, 1966)
O. Balogun: 'Christmas at Aba in the Early 1950s', *Nigeria Mag.*, 101 (1969), pp. 436–41
E. Dahlschem: *Children in Zambia* (Ndola, 1972)
S. Ottenberg: *The Masked Rituals of Afikpo: The Context of an African Art* (Seattle, 1975)
M. Vander Heyden: 'The Epa Mask and Ceremony', *Afr. A.*, x/2 (1977), pp. 14–21, 91
C. Aniakor: 'Omabe Festival', *Nigeria Mag.*, 126–7 (1978), pp. 3–12
J. Cannizzo: *Alikali Devils: Children's Masquerading in a West African Town* (diss., Seattle, U. Washington, 1978)
R. Bravmann: 'Gur and Manding Masquerades in Ghana', *Afr. A.*, xii/4 (1979), pp. 44–51, 98–9
J. Cannizzo: 'The Alikali Devils of Sierra Leone', *Afr. A.*, xii/4 (1979), pp. 64–7, 90
M. Fellous: 'Socialisation de l'enfant bambara', *J. Africanistes*, v/1 (1981), pp. 201–15
G. Le Moal: 'Les Activités religieuses des jeunes enfants chez les Bobo', *J. Africanistes*, v/1–2 (1981), pp. 235–50
S. Ottenberg: 'Boys' Secret Societies at Afikpo', *African Religious Groups and Beliefs*, ed. S. Ottenberg (Meerut, 1982), pp. 170–84
R. Bravmann: *African Islam* (Washington, DC, 1983)
P. B. Hinckley: *'Let Them Dance before You': The Educative Role of Performance in a West African Children's Masquerade* (diss., U. Boston, MA, 1985)
——: 'The Dodo Masquerade of Burkina Faso', *Afr. A.*, xix/2 (1986), pp. 74–7, 91
S. Ottenberg: *Boyhood Rituals in an African Society: An Interpretation* (Seattle, 1989)

SIMON OTTENBERG

4. BODY ARTS. In Africa body arts, an integral part of dressing the body, are widely varied and include both permanent and temporary modifications of the body's contours and surface (*see also* §5 below). The head, neck, hair, teeth, nose, ears, lips, trunk and limbs may all be decorated or in some way altered for aesthetic or ritual purposes. Evidence of the antiquity of some of these body arts can be seen in Saharan rock art of *c.* 5000 BC, in Egyptian and Nubian mummies dating from *c.* 1800 BC, and in Nok terracotta sculpture (*c.* 500 BC–AD 200) and Igbo–Ukwu metalwork (*c.* AD 900) from Nigeria. The sculptural traditions of the more recent past often provide rich documentation of body arts practices. Although Euro-American practices and cosmetics are now employed in Africa, local customs of dressing the hair and painting, scenting, oiling, tattooing or cutting the skin continue to be performed in many areas and contexts.

The most extreme forms of body arts in Africa are those in which body shapes are transformed for aesthetic enhancement. Among the Ibibio and Ejagham of Nigeria and the Mende of Sierra Leone, girls are fattened before betrothal (*see* IBIBIO, §5; EJAGHAM, §6). In contrast, among the Kalabari Ijo of Nigeria, fattening occurs after childbirth. After being sequestered and pampered the new Kalabari mother displays her ample contours to the community in a series of outfits of cloth, cosmetics and jewellery. Alterations to the natural form of babies' heads are made by the Akan in Ghana and by the Mangbetu in north-eastern Zaïre. Among the Yoruba, mothers make two depressions with the thumb and a finger on the lower back of a newborn child to emphasize the separation of the back from the buttocks. Among such peoples as the Ovimbundu, Chokwe, Lwena and Songo in Angola, teeth are filed to a point, while among many peoples lips and ears are stretched and may be punctured to hold many types of ornament.

(i) Coiffure. (ii) Painting. (iii) Marking.

(i) Coiffure. Hairdressing is a widespread form of body art found in both rural and urban areas. Throughout the continent both men and women are expected to dress their hair, for being unkempt is considered a sign of mental

illness or grief. Though the wearing of veils, particularly in North Africa, often makes study of coiffure difficult, in Sub-Saharan Africa women are well known for fashioning a wide variety of intricate designs, both for themselves and for other women, and men also display and create elaborate coiffures, especially in East Africa. Hairdressing is often a domestic activity but may be a specialist occupation. The pliable nature of hair allows its transformation into an endless variety of sculptural designs through parting, packing, tying, weaving or plaiting (braiding and cornrowing) and coating with pomade, oils, mud or grease (see fig. 141 below). Early evidence of African hairdressing is found in rock paintings of Tassili N'Ajjer in southern Algeria. At Jabbaren a female figure is depicted with a hanging braid, and there are numerous figures with crested styles resembling those worn by Fulani women in Nigeria. Hair tied into buns is also found on Nok terracotta heads, as in an example from Rafin Kura (Lagos, N. Mus.).

Many techniques are used for shaping hair. Plaiting hair in many small braids, sometimes tied with decorative objects such as beads or shells, is common. Hair can be fluffed out by teasing and backcombing or clipped closely to the head. Shaved patterns on the scalp provide a contrast between textured hair and smooth scalp. Special thread, either glossy or dull, gives different textural effects when wound around bunches of hair separated to create a design on the scalp and a patterned effect for the hair. Adding pastes made from clay, ochre and various oils, for example, preserves the hair design and allows it to be moulded into a wide variety of sculptural forms. Such items as buttons, beads, pins and metal clippings are sometimes tied or woven into the hair to add colour and textural contrast. In order to increase the volume of their hair old Igbo women in Nigeria sometimes wear wigs made of fibres to imitate elaborate hair designs, while among the Mangbetu of Zaïre hair is interwoven with straw to create a halo-like form projecting from the crown of the head (see fig. 88). In contrast Maasai women shave their heads and smear them with red ochre and animal fat. Hair colour can be changed by bleaching or dyeing, for instance among the Mende, who admire deep black hair and enhance their hair colour with an indigo dye.

Some designs relate to a particular occupation. Fulani milk-hawkers, for example, wear elaborately worked sections of their coiffure on the sides of the head for greater comfort and visibility. Male priests of Sango, the Yoruba god of thunder, wear an elaborate hairstyle to show their devotion to the deity and to his authority. The attendants in Yoruba courts are distinguished by their partially shaved heads. Tonsure may be an indication of different phases of life or special status, or it may be a sign of mourning. The heads of Nuba women in the Sudan are shaved upon the consummation of marriage; this practice is abandoned during pregnancy and by those who are barren until the onset of the menopause. Among the pastoral Fulani, teenage boys grow long hair to display what is known as the 'courting style', but after undergoing their puberty ritual their heads must remain clean-shaven. In Kenya tonsure not only marks coming of age among many peoples but also indicates the esteemed status of an elder among the Mbeere. In contrast, young Afar males in Ethiopia have shaved heads, but upon reaching manhood

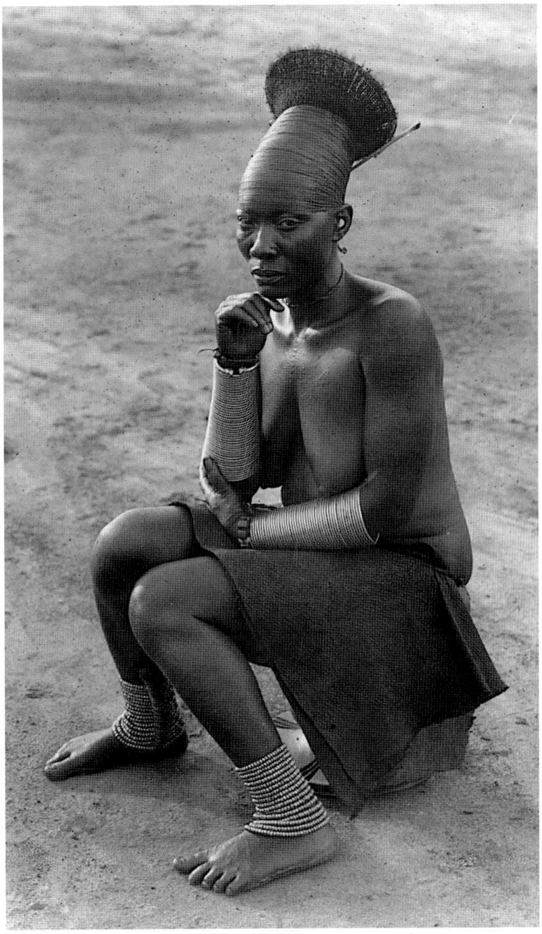

88. Mangbetu woman with artificially elongated head and coiffure, Okondo's village, north-eastern Zaïre; from a photograph by Herbert Lang, 1910

they grow their hair in a distinctive shape. Hair styles have even been given names relating to significant events, such as the Yoruba women's style called 'the war is over', which refers to the end of the Nigerian civil war in 1970. They may also be expressions of aesthetic preference and, as among the Mende of Sierra Leone, of ideals of female beauty, epitomized in the elaborate, plaited designs represented on Mende Sowei helmet-masks (*see* MENDE, fig. 1).

(ii) Painting. Temporary changes in status are frequently marked by temporary body modifications, especially of the skin. Skin colour and texture may be changed daily or occasionally with the application of cosmetics that wash or wear off. Camwood and henna are used for red hues, and white kaolin provides a stark contrast to dark skin. In many societies of North Africa, where skin colour is generally lighter, intricate henna designs are painted on the hands of brides. The colour of the design can range from red to a blue-black, depending on how long the henna is allowed to remain on the skin during the coloration process. Igbo women use the juice of a berry that temporarily stains the skin an indigo colour. Kalabari

Ijo women apply a similar dye to the legs, upper body, arms and face in patterns called *buruma.* To make the skin glisten and shine, the Baganda of Uganda apply an ointment, particularly to the face, producing a smooth, glossy, light-reflecting finish that is considered beautiful. Some Asante have been reported to grease the skin and sprinkle it with gold-dust twice daily. Kohl is used widely, especially by women, to darken the rims of the eyes. The lips and cheeks, however, are generally not stained or coloured.

The Baluyia of Kenya use body paint in funereal, martial and social contexts. Both men and women paint themselves in the first and last cases; in martial contexts men paint lines or dots in several colours across the forehead, cheeks and upper torso. Among the Maasai elaborate body painting is an important aspect of male initiation into warriorhood. Among the Nuba of Sudan men use red and yellow ochres, black ash, grey-white chalky limestone and even commercial blueing to produce a wide variety of representational and non-representational designs, many of which are zoomorphic (see fig. 89; *see also* NUBA, §1). These designs become progressively more elaborate and intense in colour as a man passes from one age-grade to another. The Baule have various uses for kaolin, using it to adorn and protect newborn babies and to paint the eyes and mouths of spirit mediums to aid in clairvoyance and ensure speaking and hearing the truth. Among the Dan in Liberia, the Mangbetu in Zaïre and the Mende in Sierra Leone body painting is also done for the initiation of girls. While the Dan do not keep to specific patterns, the Mangbetu produce an enormous variety of patterns, including stars, Maltese crosses, flowers, lines, zigzags, chequered patterns, ribbons, knots, bees, zebra stripes and leopard spots. Mende girls' bodies are smeared entirely with white clay for their initiation to show that they are under the control and protection of the Sande society. The Igbo, particularly women, decorate their bodies with continuous, asymmetrical and curvilinear motifs similar to those with which they decorate doors and walls. The patterns in Ibibio body painting are also curvilinear but are contained within small, independent units. Their body-painting designs are redolent of an ideographic writing system (*nsibidi*) that encoded messages of power and wisdom.

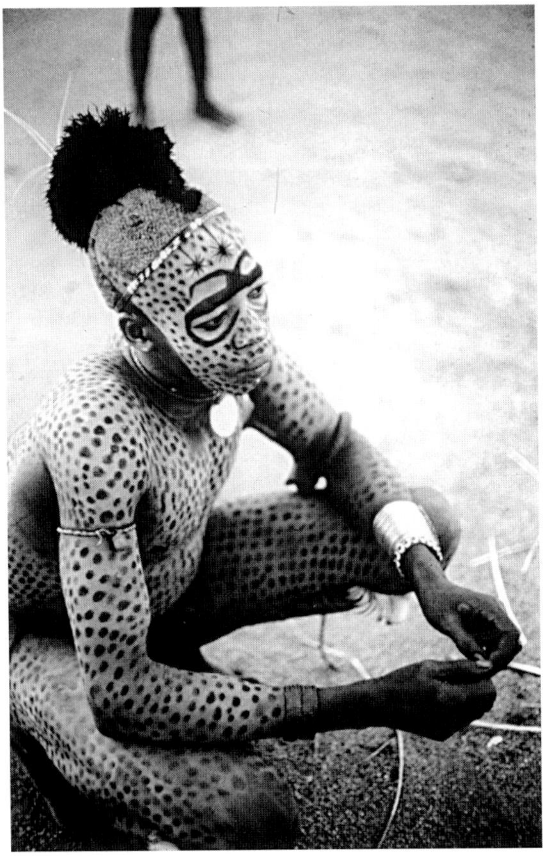

89. Nuba youth with body-paint design representing a species of leopard, south-east Nuba Mountains, Sudan; from a photograph by James C. Faris, 1969

(iii) Marking. Scarification, cicatrization and tattoo are three forms of permanent modification of the skin used in Africa. Markings made by simply cutting the skin are called scarification. Raised weals or keloids made by introducing foreign matter into the cuts are called cicatrizations. The term tattoo (from the Tahitian *tatau*), used incorrectly in the past to refer to all forms of body marking, is created by tapping and pricking the skin with colour. In Africa such designs are usually green and mostly figurative. Permanent body markings in Africa are generally combinations of bold or thin linear cuts variously arranged.

Although many African peoples, such as the Baule and the Tabwa, claim the permanent marking of the body to be a beautifying act that separates human beings from animals, reports have often related African body markings to the slave trade. Markings have been said to have been used as a device to identify and thus redeem members of one's group sold as slaves or as disfigurement to make the members of a group unattractive to slave-buyers. Both explanations are unsatisfactory, the former being based on the assumption that the captured member would be found, while there seems to be no factual evidence for the latter. Although records indicate that 19th-century slave-traders did not usually buy Igbo with *ichi*-type facial scarifications, this was not because the slave-buyers saw marking as disfigurement. Instead the marked Igbo were members of the Ozo title society and were respected by other Igbo, who usually followed their orders to mutiny or to commit suicide rather than submit to slavery. Indeed *ichi* markings have not been popularly adopted; they remain the exclusive preserve of Ozo title-holders and are seen mainly in northern Igboland.

Markings on some archaeological finds have designs that continue to be worn in the vicinity. A cylindrical Nok head from Katsina Ala (Jos, N. Mus.) displays bold lines from the corners of the mouth and diagonals by the side of the nose; such markings are still the characteristic facial scars worn by various peoples around the Niger–Benue confluence at the southern edge of the Nok area. The same components are also present among peoples on the same latitude west of the Niger–Benue confluence as far as the northern part of Côte d'Ivoire.

Items from Igbo Isaiah, such as a 9th–10th-century AD pendant with a human face (Lagos, N. Mus.; *see* IGBO-UKWU, fig. 1) and the male figure on an 'altar stand' (Lagos, N. Mus.), have their faces covered with raised, diagonal lines, which are probably an earlier version of present-day Igbo *ichi* scarifications. The female figure on the 'altar stand' has concentric, raised patterns on the forehead and a radiating sunflower pattern on the stomach that resembles the abdominal markings (*nbumbu* or *egbugbu*) displayed by Igbo women as a prerequisite for marriage and is also found among neighbouring peoples.

Facial scarifications are not found throughout Africa but were probably introduced in three independent regions (the Upper Nile Valley, West and Central Africa), gradually spreading and mixing with increased inter-cultural relations. Archaeological data from before the slave trade provide evidence for a long history of body marking, probably for decorative purposes. Patterns may derive from elements found in any of the three original areas or combinations of elements from any two. In northern Nigeria, for example, between the area of Kanuri influence near Lake Chad and the Niger–Benue confluence, face markings mainly comprise vertical elements, markings at the corner of the mouth or diagonals on the sides of the nose, typical of types in the Nuo–Chadean area and the Niger–Benue confluence. A mixture of simple scars (from the Niger–Benue confluence) and keloids (from south-east Nigeria) are also found among some peoples living south and east of the confluence. The face markings of south-west Nigeria and elsewhere in West Africa north of the Niger–Benue latitude are similar to those found in northern Nigeria outside the region of Kanuri influence.

(a) Scarification. Marking, particularly of the face, is sometimes associated with specific ethnic groups or with permanent and progressive status changes, especially among women (see fig. 90). Many such marks, however, are not made primarily for group identification but for aesthetic satisfaction, rituals, medicinal purposes or erotic sensation. Whatever the reason, the markings are usually made with aesthetic sensitivity and definite patterning. In most societies scarifications are executed by specialists: among the Oyo Yoruba, for example, these may be from particular lineages, while Hausa experts in scarification (*yan jarfa*) service various neighbouring ethnic groups.

According to the Yoruba, specific facial patterns, such as those called *keke* or *abaja*, are worn for beauty's sake. Their adoption as aspects of personal beauty is suggested in a traditional account of the origin of Yoruba scarification, which says that they are derived from the scars of bruises meted out to a slave for neglecting to carry out the orders of Sango, the first ruler of Oyo. The scars were found to be so attractive that they were adopted by members of the royal household. No single pattern is common to all sub-groups of the Yoruba. Even one of their most common patterns, *pele* (three thick, vertical lines on each cheek), is not seen among the Owo, Ondo, Ilaje and Ikale. Only the Oyo and related groups such as the Egba, Egbado, Ibolo and Igbomia have standard patterns, but these are reserved for lineages or extended families rather than being markings of ethnic identity. In many Yoruba areas in the late 20th century permanent

90. Adamawa woman with facial scarification, Benue-Gongola Valley, north-east Nigeria; from a photograph by Marla C. Berns, 1982

markings were frowned upon, leading to a decline in public or easily visible marking, but the practice of marking other parts of the body has continued, for example the incision on the stomachs of young children of their parents' (particularly their father's) names.

Some scarifications are employed as part of healing practices while still displaying a definite sense of composition. The Hausa create scarifications by using horns to draw 'impure' blood from ailing parts of the body. The practice of cupping mainly consists of making small, irregular cuts clustered around and over the ailing spots; after healing these are hardly noticeable. The same thing happens to *gbere*, the Yoruba method of inserting medicines under the skin. *Akara*, the marking used by the Igbo to ward off spirits believed to be causing frequent ailments in children, is made up of a distinctive pattern of parallel, vertical cuts (l. *c.* 10 mm) on both temples, close to the eyes. Between Igala country in the Niger–Benue confluence in Nigeria and the Dogoma area of northern Ghana, diagonal marks 20 mm long are made beside the nose to ensure that children believed to have been reborn after previous death in infancy live to adulthood. However, since half the Igala population has such markings it is likely that they were also popularly adopted. Participation in ritual may also involve scarification, particularly of the face. Among the Bamana of Mali men undergo scarification as part of agricultural rites, receiving two vertical marks at the base of the nose and three under each eye. This is in imitation of Chi Wara, the mythical being who taught them agriculture, and in the belief that through it Chi Wara will impart his agricultural zeal to the wearers: the more the marks are multiplied, the more plentiful the harvest will be.

(b) Cicatrization. Keloid marking is characteristic of body arts in the area from south-east Nigeria to Zaïre (see fig. 91). The common components are concentric shapes, dots and combinations of short, hatched lines. Raised weals are obtained through retarded healing. The Tabwa of Zaïre practised extensive cicatrization (*see* TABWA), sometimes covering their bodies with intricate, symmetrical designs that are said to signify the Tabwa world-view and its moral, social and cosmological order. Tabwa cicatrizations were executed by a skilled woman on young girls in preparation for marriage. Similarly, older women are responsible for the complex scarification programme (*hleeta*) that Ga'anda females of north-east Nigeria begin when aged five or six and that continues through six stages until the conclusion of the marriage contract. These markings are both a form of socialization and visible proof of positive spirit intervention (*see* §III, 5(i) above).

The Higis of Baza clan in Nigeria link the origin of their geometric keloid patterns to the scaly back of a crocodile. This association derives from the story of a man who had two wives, one of whom he confined to her room with a crocodile. The wife so admired the patterns on its back that the husband had these markings made on her body,

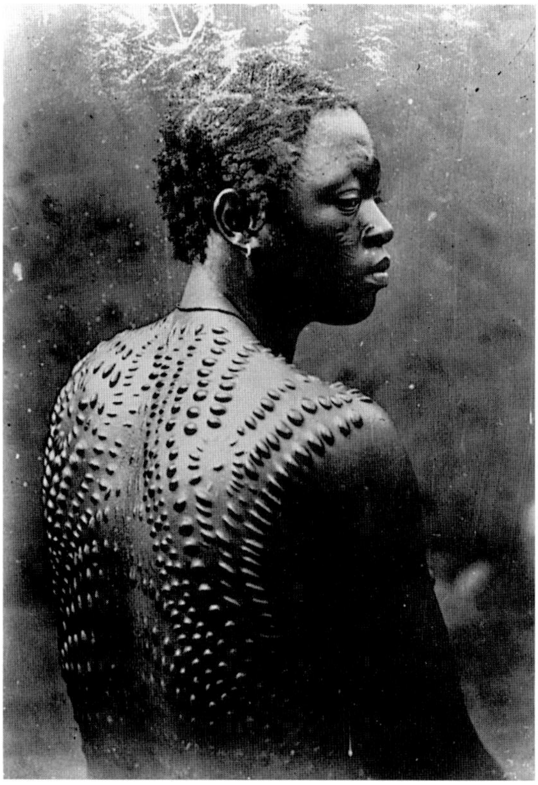

91. Tabwa woman with keloid markings, Kirungu, Zaïre; print by Allen F. Roberts, from a glassplate negative, early 1900s (Rome, Central Archives of the Missionaries of Our Lady of Africa)

and other women copied the patterns. Evidence of scarring females for erotic purposes has also been documented among groups including the Tiv of Nigeria and the Baluyia of Kenya. Among the Tabwa it is reported that the design and textural quality of scars on the stomach and buttocks make them intriguing for an intimate partner; moreover, the individual whose skin has been cut and scarred is said to be stimulated when touched.

(c) Tattoo. Generally in Africa tattoo is purely ornamental, and, despite its pictorial character and use of colour, it is more closely related to scarification than to body painting. African tattoos are made either by razor cuts or by tapping and pricking the skin with needles. Berber women in North Africa tattoo their chins, and in some parts of North Africa both men and women wear tattoos. In Sub-Saharan Africa razor designs are normally hatched, resembling some scarifications, and the same specialists are responsible for both. On the occasion of marking a baby, people sometimes request pictorial designs from the specialist markers. Among the Yoruba these are described as 'sympathy' marks, and they caution people on how to take care of the marked baby.

The art of tattoo was probably practised in Africa long before it was noticed on the coast by European travellers. The marks on a dessicated human skin from a Middle Nubian cemetery (*c.* 1800 BC), described as puncture tattoos, are actually scarified hatches like razor tattoos. The subsequent history of African tattoo is difficult to reconstruct owing to the scarcity of evidence. However, some early European travellers to the west coast of Africa mentioned pictorial decorations. Until the 18th century references were made to the practice of pictorial incisions or razor tattoos away from the coast. Needle tattoos, used alongside razor tattoos, are coastal phenomena. It would appear that the razor type was adopted first, followed by the needle type, which was perhaps introduced to coastal peoples by European sailors. Tattoos seem most prevalent in the area of Hausa influence across West Africa, and the practice may have been popularized by itinerant Hausa specialists. As the markings appear most clearly on light complexions, however, the presence of the light-skinned Fulani, who are very interested in tattoos, may also have contributed to its popularity.

The parts of the body covered with tattoos are usually the face, neck, chest, back, arms, legs and especially the calves. The thighs, although rarely exposed, may also be tattooed. Sometimes tattoo patterns are displayed alongside scarifications. The nature and quantity of the patterns generally reflect individual preferences and local fashions: in the area of Kontagora, Nigeria, for example, especially around Rijau and Zuru on the way to Sokoto, some people have their bodies almost entirely covered with tattoos. Both abstract and figural designs are employed. The former generally comprise individual or combined rectilinear shapes, such as squares, triangles, lozenges and simple straight lines. Sometimes these patterns are given names, often related to imagery suggested by the design; the Tiv, for example, describe two triangles set together at an angle as a sparrow, for each triangle suggests an outspread wing.

The graphic precision of tattooing and the pain involved in its execution demand that tattooers select motifs that can be easily recognized and executed without error. Such crawling animals as crocodiles, lizards, snakes, crabs and scorpions are invariably depicted as seen from above. Sometimes only the vital parts that enable identification are shown. Large animals or any creatures that walk rather than crawl are depicted in profile. In Nigeria those most commonly represented are elephants, cows, camels and such birds as the egret and duck. The chameleon, although a small creature, is also depicted in profile with its accentuated ridge back. Human figures are rarely represented. Plant motifs range from simple leaf shapes, attached on the sides to represent creepers or climbing plants, to big trees, especially distinctively shaped palms. Floral motifs were also noticed along the West African coast by early European travellers. In more recent times other commonly depicted objects with easily recognizable shapes include swords, daggers, umbrellas and aeroplanes. Graphic representations from printed sources and industrial goods are also sometimes adopted. In 1975 a design of two native hoes intersecting each other, derived from the symbol of a defunct Nigerian political party, was seen on a Hausa woman. Such insignia as the Nigerian coat of arms have also been recorded.

BIBLIOGRAPHY

J. Decorse: 'Le Tatouage: Les Mutilations ethniques et la parure chez les populations du Soudan', *L'Anthropologie*, xvi (1905), pp. 129–47
H. L. Roth: 'Tatu in Tunis', *Man*, v/72 (1905), pp. 129–31
P. Noel: 'Tatouages et leur technique au Cameroun Central', *Rev. Ethnog. & Trad. Pop.*, iii/11 (1922), pp. 241–4
C. H. Armitage: *The Tribal Markings and Marks of Adornment of the Natives of the Northern Territories of the Gold Coast Colony* (London, 1924)
W. D. Hambly: *The History of Tattooing and its Significance with Some Accounts of Other Forms of Corporal Marking* (London, 1925)
S. de Ganay: 'On a Form of Cicatrization among the Bambara', *Man*, xlix/5 (1949), pp. 53–5
M. D. W. Jeffreys: 'The Winged Solar Disk or Ibo Itzi Facial Scarifications', *Africa*, xxi/2 (1951), pp. 93–111
J. C. Froelich: 'Catalogues des scarifications en usage chez certaines populations du Dahomey et du Nord Togo', *Mém. Inst. Fr. Afrique Noire: Mél. Ethnol.*, xxiii (1953), pp. 253–64
R. Baker and M. Z. Yola: 'The Higis of Bazza Clan', *Nigeria*, 47 (1955), pp. 213–22
P. Bohannan: 'Beauty and Scarification amongst the Tiv', *Man*, 129 (1956), pp. 117–21
M. D. W. Jeffreys: 'Negro Abstract Art or Ibo Body Patterns', *S. Afr. Mus. Assoc. Bull.*, vi/9 (1957), pp. 218–29
E. de Negri: 'Hairstyling of Southern Nigeria', *Nigeria Mag.*, 65 (1960), pp. 191–8
M. Trowell: *African Design* (London, 1960, rev. 1965)
G. Neher: 'Chibuk Face Marks', *Niger. Field*, 29 (1963), pp. 16–27
B. de Rachewiltz: *Eros nero* (Milan, 1963); Eng. trans. by P. Whigham as *Black Eros: Sexual Customs of Africa from Prehistory to the Present Day* (London, 1964)
E. de Negri: 'Tribal Marks, Decorative and Painted Patterns', *Nigeria*, 81 (1964), pp. 106–16
J. B. Eicher: *African Dress: A Select and Annotated Bibliography of Subsaharan Countries* (East Lansing, 1969)
H. Cole: *African Arts of Transformation* (Santa Barbara, 1970)
J. C. Faris: *Nuba Personal Art* (London, 1972)
African Textiles and Decorative Arts (exh. cat. by R. Sieber, New York, MOMA; Los Angeles, CA, Co. Mus. A.; San Francisco, CA, de Young Mem. Mus.; Cleveland, OH, Mus. A.; 1972–3)
C. O. Adepegba: *A Survey of Nigerian Body Markings and their Relationship to other Nigerian Arts* (diss., Bloomington, IN U., 1976)
The Arts of Ghana (exh. cat. by H. M. Cole and D. H. Ross, Los Angeles, UCLA, Wight A.G.; Minneapolis, MN, Walker A. Cent.; Dallas, TX, Mus. F.A.; 1977–8)
C. O. Adepegba: 'Ife Art: An Enquiry into the Surface Patterns, and the Continuity of the Art Tradition among the Northern Yoruba', *W. Afr. J. Archaeol.*, xii (1982), pp. 95–109
E. C. Burt: 'Eroticism in Baluyia Body Arts', *Afr. A.*, xv/2 (1982), pp. 68–9, 88
E. Sagay: *African Hairstyles: Styles of Yesterday and Today* (London, 1983)
S. Searight: *The Use and Function of Tattooing on Moroccan Women*, 3 vols (New Haven, 1984)
Igbo Arts: Community and Cosmos (exh. cat. by H. M. Cole and C. C. Aniakor, Los Angeles, UCLA, Mus. Cult. Hist., 1984–6)
S. A. Boone: *Radiance from the Waters: Ideals of Feminine Beauty in Mende Art* (New Haven, 1986)
A. Rubin: *Marks of Civilization: Artistic Transformations of the Human Body* (Los Angeles, 1988), pp. 19–105

CORNELIUS ADEPEGBA, JOANNE BUBOLZ EICHER

5. DRESS. In the broadest sense the art of African dress involves totally or partially covering the body with garments, accessories, paint and jewellery and/or modifying the body itself (*see* §4 above). Both body modifications and body supplements involve manipulating colour, texture, shape, volume, scent and sound. For many Africans, to dress well involves proper decorum and elegant style. Display of appropriate apparel, cosmetics and coiffure is often accompanied by magnificent carriage, graceful movement, fastidious toilette and immaculate garments.

(i) Introduction. (ii) Dressing the torso. (iii) Headdress. (iv) Footwear. (v) Jewellery.

(i) Introduction. The understanding of African dress as an art form requires a consideration of both single items and total ensembles. Occasionally, only a single item is used to adorn the body of an individual, for example a string of beads around the waist. In such a case the texture, colour and shape of the beads, whether of seeds, pods, shells or glass, are judged in the context of the texture and colour of the skin and the body shape. African dress ensembles range from simple to complex. A simple ensemble may consist of a wrapper, body paint and uncomplicated hairdo; a complex one may combine several richly decorated garments, an intricate coiffure, opulent jewellery and other accessories. Both single items and total ensembles may have an additive, cumulative character; examples include clusters of beads, layers of cloth or layers of jewellery. Such clusters and layers are often necessary components, adding the sounds of rustling fabrics and jingling jewellery to the ensemble's visual impact. Layering of garments also provides the effect of bulk, as does the use of heavy fabric. The importance of an individual's social position may be visually reinforced by the size of his or her ensemble. The robes of a ruler are often massive, as is the wrapper set of a powerful and successful trader. Moreover, such accessories as canes, walking-sticks, horse-hair switches, umbrellas, fans, purses, handbags, handkerchiefs, linguist staffs and tusks are often needed to complete an ensemble.

In the late 20th century dress in Africa included items fashioned from local resources and tools (such as wrappers from Sierra Leone made of 'country cloth', handwoven from handspun cotton threads) and imported items made by complex machines and techniques (such as British top hats, French *haute couture* gowns, Italian shoes and handbags and Swiss laces). Purely indigenous ensembles were becoming increasingly rare. Borrowed items, however, are no less African for being borrowed when used creatively and juxtaposed with other items resulting in a readily identifiable ethnic style such as that of the dress of Kalabari Ijo men and women (see fig. 92). The term 'cultural

92. Characteristic dress of the Kalabari Ijo, Nigeria, *c.* 1980

authentication' may be used to designate adopted items that are selected, characterized by indigenous nomenclature, incorporated and transformed into a costume item or ensemble. The shape of the Nigerian Kalabari Ijo man's ceremonial hat, the *ajibulu*, for example, is adopted from the bicorne hat of military and naval officers of later 18th- and early 19th-century Europe. Decoration for the hat includes hair from the beard of a ram and such ornamentation as tiny mirrors, shiny balls, multicoloured feathers and hair ornaments. The total configuration is distinctively Kalabari. In contrast individuals of European and Asian descent ordinarily refrain from incorporating African items into their dress repertory and maintain forms of dress current in the lands from which their ancestors emigrated.

(ii) Dressing the torso. In general, dress may be classified as enclosing or attached. Enclosing dress may be further subdivided into categories of wrap-around, preshaped and suspended, all of which are found throughout Africa. Most attached and many suspended enclosing items of dress come into the category of jewellery, which is discussed separately (*see* §(v) below). To form a wrap-around garment, rectangular textile pieces are usually folded, crushed or twisted around the body. Throughout Africa variations of the wrapper (also called *lappa* or *pagne*) predominate for both men and women. The prevalent high temperatures (whether dry or humid), plus the availability of such materials as skins, bark (for barkcloth), or wool, cotton and raffia for handwoven cloth, make the loose fit of wrap-around apparel particularly appropriate. Preshaped garments in general, and trousered garments in particular for males, did not gain widespread use until contact with Europeans and Middle Eastern men and their clothing styles became frequent. Trousers or other bifurcated garments are not usually worn by Sub-Saharan African women.

The wrapper is ubiquitous in Sub-Saharan Africa. Women wear the cloth wrapped from the waist to the knees, calves or feet, with or without the upper body being covered, though sometimes wrapping the cloth under the armpits to cover the breasts. Men wrap a small length of cloth from their waist to their feet, with the chest bare or covered, or have a larger rectangle wrapped round their whole body with one shoulder covered, toga fashion. Wrap-around examples include the striped, handwoven silk *kente* of the Asante of Ghana; the handwoven shawls of sheer, white cotton of the Amharic women in Ethiopia; the hand-dyed indigo batik wrappers of Yoruba women in Nigeria; the raffia skirts of the Kuba in Zaïre; commercially woven blankets worn by Ndebele and Xhosa women in Southern Africa; the skin aprons of Zulu men; and the barkcloth garments worn by both sexes among the Baganda in Uganda.

With preshaped dress, lengths of cloth are cut and sewn before being worn. Examples include shirts, blouses, robes and trousers, or, for example, the *baba riga* (big gown) of the Hausa. Many preshaped garments show the influence of cross-cultural contacts. The long gown (*boubou*) of Wolof women in Senegal, for example, has a probable Muslim and Middle-Eastern origin. The gowns of Herero women in Namibia and of Efik women in Nigeria, and the 'granny' gown of women in Egypt, show 19th-century European influences. Trouser shapes vary from enormously large drawstring breeches worn by Hausa men in the north of Nigeria to some narrow ones worn by Yoruba men. With trousers or wrappers, men wear shirts and other preshaped, hip-length garments like tunics over the upper torso with a variety of details. Among the Fon of the Republic of Benin men wear an ensemble with a heavily embroidered, sleeveless tunic pleated at the neckline and flared at the hipline, embroidered trousers and embroidered cap. In Côte d'Ivoire and Ghana other male tunic-type garments include the war shirts and hunters' shirts of the Maninka and Akan. These are decorated with amulets comprising animal horns, claws, teeth or packets containing pieces of paper on which have been written magical words (see fig. 93). Yoruba men wear a three-piece outfit consisting of a robe (*agbada*) and shirt (*dansiki*), with either closely fitting or wide, loose trousers. The same style is regarded as less formal if tailored from a colourful, wax-printed cotton, and more formal if made from damask, lace, eyelet, brocade, or the handwoven textile of native silk known as *sanyan* or *alari*.

Suspended items of dress are generally of circular form with an opening to slip over a body part, for example necklaces and loose bangles. Two or more subtypes of enclosing garments may be used to produce a combination form, such as the royal cape worn by a Fulani emir in Nigeria that is preshaped and stitched but loose enough to be suspended from the shoulders.

The dress of different peoples is often distinguished by colour, texture and/or fabric motif. The textiles used in African dress range from handcrafted fabrics to commercially produced, both imported and domestic, textiles made of cotton, wool or synthetic fibres. Designs include prints of many kinds, plus woven patterns of plaids and checks (*see* DYE, colour pl. III, fig. 2, and TEXTILE, colour pl. IV, fig. 1). Fabric types range from plain broadcloth to laces,

93. Asante war shirt and shoulder-bag, cloth and leather, h. 1.09 m, before 1850 (Copenhagen, Nationalmuseum)

eyelets, damasks, brocades and velvets. Manufacturers in the UK, the Netherlands, Switzerland, India and Africa have been responsive to the specific textile motif and colour preferences of consumers in Africa. For example, printed cottons in brilliant pink and purple have been favoured in Zaïre; clear yellow, orange and green in eastern areas of Nigeria; burgundy and indigo in western Nigeria; and subdued purple, khaki and muted blue in Togo and the Republic of Benin. Sombre plaid designs are favoured by Ijo and Igbo groups in Nigeria. Some groups prefer monochrome textiles in soft pastels and dazzling white.

In parts of West Africa groups of people buy identical textiles to wear for special events. Frequently, the textile is commercially manufactured with a screenprinted portrait of a significant person (usually political) who is being honoured. This custom of wearing identical cloth is known as *aso ebi* (family dress) and *aso egbi* (association dress) among the Yoruba, where it began. It has also been adopted by some other groups, among the Igbo, for example, who call identical dress 'uniform'.

Decoration of garments includes the techniques of embroidery, beading (see fig. 142 below) and appliqué, the latter used particularly in ceremonial and masquerade gowns. Various male robes throughout West Africa are heavily embroidered, as among the Hausa (*see* HAUSA, fig. 1). Simpler embroidery is seen on some of the contemporary kaftans worn by women, especially those being made for the tourist market in the later 20th century. Beading is found on robes of some royalty; sequins and beads decorate women's blouses, for example among the Yoruba and Kalabari Ijo.

(iii) Headdress. Ensembles are often completed by modifications of the hair and face (*see* §4 above) and headdresses that reinforce information about gender, age, political position or community standing. Men's headwear includes caps, hats, veils and turbans and exhibits greater variety of type than the headties and veils of women. The wider range for men may be related to the wider range of statuses and political and religious positions, such as chieftaincy ranks and priesthood categories, available to them. The headties of women are often responsive to fashion change and are expressions of the fanciful imagination and flair of individuals.

Materials used for men's hats and caps include textiles, skins, feathers, straw, raffia and beads. Some hats, encrusted with precious metals or jewels or heavily embroidered with gold and silver threads, designate high (sometimes royal) status. Imported top hats, Derbys and fedoras are also worn by men in some areas as part of a dress ensemble, again indicating high status, if not that of chieftaincy, then achieved local honour or age grade. Veils and turbans may also be part of male dress. The wrapped veil of a Hausa male shows that he has been to Mecca. The shiny, deep indigo-dyed cotton veils of Tuareg males make them easily identifiable. Headties of cloth wrapped in numerous shapes and styles are most often worn by adult females, in particular by the Yoruba of Nigeria and the Ndebele of Southern Africa. In the 1800s Herero women of Southern Africa used skins. Some Muslim women wear a preshaped or suspended veil, revealing only the eyes.

(iv) Footwear. Much African footwear is preshaped and completes many ensembles, especially those of men and women of special ranks. Many types of sandal, boot and shoe are worn, made either by hand or commercially, locally or abroad. Decoration includes flamboyant and rare feathers, beads, precious metals or incised leather. The footwear of Hausa emirs, worn with ceremonial gowns and capes, has ostrich feathers over the insteps. Horsemen of the Hausa royal household wear leather boots. In his full ceremonial dress the Oba of Benin wears slippers covered with coral beads, whereas the Alake of Abeokuta, in his royal regalia, wears slippers covered with tiny imported glass beads.

BIBLIOGRAPHY

R. Murphy: 'Social Distance and the Veil', *Amer. Anthropologist*, lxvi/6 (1965), pp. 1257–74

J. B. Eicher: *African Dress: A Select and Annotated Bibliography of Subsaharan Countries* (East Lansing, 1969)

H. Cole: *African Arts of Transformation* (Santa Barbara, 1970)

A. A. Mazrui: 'The Robes of Rebellion: Sex, Dress, and Politics in Africa', *Encounter*, xxxiv/2 (1970), pp. 19–30

R. Boser-Sarivaxévanis: *Textilhandwerk in West-Afrika: Weberei und Farberei* (Basle, 1972; Eng. trans. as *West African Textiles and Garments from the Museum für Völkerkunde, Basel* (Minnesota, 1980))

J. B. Eicher: 'African Dress as an Art Form', *A Current Bibliography on African Affairs*, 5/5–6, n.s., ii (1972), pp. 516–20

African Textiles and Decorative Arts (exh. cat. by R. Sieber, New York, MOMA; Los Angeles, CA, Co. Mus. A.; San Francisco, CA, de Young Mem. Mus.; Cleveland, OH, Mus. A.; 1972–3)

A. Mertens and J. Broster: *African Elegance* (Cape Town, 1973/*R* London, 1974)

E. de Negri: *Nigerian Body Adornment* (Lagos, 1976)

The Arts of the Hausa (exh. cat. by D. Heathcote, London, Commonwealth Inst., 1977)
A. Elliott: *Sons of Zulu* (London, 1978)
J. M. Cordwell and R. A. Schwarz, eds: *The Fabrics of Culture* (New York, 1979), pp. 87–102, 103–17, 331–48, 349–97
Afr. A., xv/3 (1982) and xxv/3 (1992) [issues on Afr. dress and textiles]
J. M. Cordwell: 'The Art and Aesthetics of the Yoruba', *Afr. A.*, xvi/2 (1983), pp. 56–9, 93–4, 100
D. P. Biebuyck and N. Van den Abbeele: *The Power of Headdresses: A Cross-cultural Study of Forms and Functions* (Brussels, 1984)
A. Fisher: *Africa Adorned* (London, 1984/*R* 1989)
I. Pokornowski and others, eds: *African Dress II: A Select and Annotated Bibliography* (East Lansing, 1985)
M. C. Daly, J. B. Eicher and T. V. Erekosima: 'Male and Female Artistry in Kalabari Dress', *Afr. A.*, xix/3 (1986), pp. 48–51, 83
A. Rugh: *Reveal and Conceal: Dress in Contemporary Egypt* (New York, 1986)
O. C. Thieme and J. B. Eicher: 'African Dress: Form, Action, Meaning', *Afr. J.*, xiv/2–3 (1987), pp. 115–38
'History, Design and Crafts in West African Strip-woven Cloth', *Proceedings of the Symposium Organized by the National Museum of African Art, Smithsonian Institution, Feb 18–19, 1988* (Washington, DC, 1992), pp. 53–81, 95–112, 133–68
K. T. Hanson: 'Dealing with Used Clothing: Salaula and the Construction of Identity in Zambia's Third Republic', *Public Culture* (1994), pp. 503–22
J. Morris with E. Preston-Whyte: *Speaking with Beads* (New York, 1994)
Crowning Achievements: African Art of Dressing the Head (exh. cat. by M. J. Arnoldi and C. M. Kreamer, Los Angeles, UCLA, Fowler Mus. Cult. Hist., 1995)

JOANNE BUBOLZ EICHER

(v) Jewellery. The adornment of the body with jewellery is one of the most characteristic forms of African dress for both men and women, at least traditionally. The earliest evidence of African jewellery is in the form of the bead necklets, bracelets and anklets shown on the late 1st-millennium BC terracottas from Nok in Nigeria. Bronzes and terracottas of the 12th to 14th centuries AD from Ife, Nigeria, and terracottas of similar date from Jenne-Jeno in Mali add to this record. Much African jewellery was and has continued to be made of natural, often perishable materials, such as grasses, split palm leaves, wood, dried and scented clay, roots and furs. As a rule African jewellery uses no precious stones. Ivory arm-rings, usually left plain, are used as status symbols in many areas. Those of Benin City are finely carved and rate high in African art (see fig. 52 above). The pendants of elephant or hippopotamus ivory found among the Pende, Luba and Hungana of Zaïre are also of high quality. Amber, coral and low-grade silver are used where there has been Arab cultural influence, mainly in northern Africa, the Sahara and its southern fringe, the Horn of Africa and down the east coast. Coral, imported from the Mediterranean since the late 15th century, is essential to the regalia of the Oba of Benin City, Nigeria, and is highly valued by the Kalabari Ijo of southern Nigeria. Gold jewellery is virtually confined to Western Africa, where the Wolof of Senegambia make large earrings of beaten gold. Baule and Asante aristocrats of Côte d'Ivoire and Ghana have hollow gold pendants, rings and beads, cast by the lost-wax process. Bronze is widely used. The metal is either imported or derived from smelted ores and is worked by the lost-wax technique or by hammering and chasing. Copper, brass and iron wire are used in coiled neck, arm and leg ornaments. Thick wire may be drawn to make fine wire, which can be coiled around a fibre core to make flexible armlets; plaited vegetable fibre is used in a similar way. Stone beads, mostly

94. Samburu girl wearing characteristic beaded jewellery, Kenya; from a photograph by George Zaloumis

of cornelian and including those from Cambay (Khambhat), in western India, are made or traded over much of Sub-Saharan Africa. Stone bracelets are found in parts of the Sahel.

Beadwork is perhaps the best-known form of African jewellery; many beads are of African make, of brass, iron, wood, shell, stone or terracotta. Disc beads made of ostrich eggshell or snail shell are well known; by the late 20th century similar beads in red and black plastic had become popular. Glass beads have entered Africa since perhaps the early first millennium AD (*see* §V, 7(i) above). The most common bead is the small round 'seed' bead, used to make bead ornaments in great variety and number, especially among the Bantu peoples of Southern Africa. The larger and more elaborate beads were worn as status symbols or regalia by dignitaries or wealthy people in western and central Africa; they were usually worn singly or as a single string.

The types of jewellery found in Africa include necklaces and broad collars, armlets and anklets of different sorts, finger rings, earrings and earplugs, lip ornaments and head ornaments, as well as jewellery worn on the body. In general, women wear more jewellery than men.

African necklaces and neck ornaments range from heavy collars of cast or beaten brass, often with chased decoration, to single strings of beads or broad beadwork collars, sometimes strung on fine wire. The effect may be reinforced by wearing many strings of beads, as among the Samburu of Kenya, so that the breasts are partly covered (see fig. 94). The Ndebele women of Transvaal wear numerous massive ring collars of grass coils covered with beads and similar beaded rings on their arms, legs and body. Anklets similarly range from the heavy and unwieldy brass discs worn by Igbo women in Nigeria to numerous fine wire, beaded or plaited-fibre rings, sometimes covering the leg from knee to ankle. The heavy, iron-bead leg ornaments of the Herero of Namibia and Angola weigh up to 5 kg each. Several garters, usually beaded, form part of the festive dress of both sexes among the Bantu of Southern Africa.

Arm ornaments include ivory bracelets, some of which are very heavy. The royal burial at Igbo Richard (*c.* AD 850) in Nigeria contained cuff-shaped bead armlets; others occur among the Zulu of southern Africa. Among the Xhosa of South Africa, on special occasions women wear numerous bracelets covering the upper and lower arms. These may be bead strings, flexible rings wrapped with a bead string, plastic bangles or vegetable fibre rings, often finely plaited. Finger-rings are not much worn, apart from the elaborate gold rings cast by the lost-wax process among the Asante of Ghana. Silver rings are found in the areas of Arab culture contact.

Ear ornaments include earrings and earplugs. These range from the heavy gold earrings of the Wolof, through wooden discs to the cane cylinders used as snuff-boxes in eastern and southern Africa. Earplugs are often ornamented with pyrogravure, paint, beads or applied plastic. In Kenya and Tanzania, women wear a variety of beaded leather and wire ear pendants and earrings, sometimes combined with beaded headbands. Lip jewellery includes the large lip-discs formerly worn in both lips by women in Chad; smaller lip plugs, lip pegs and lip pendants were worn by both sexes among various peoples in eastern Africa, partly for adornment but also symbolically to protect the mouth.

African head jewellery includes headbands and types of headdresses. Detachable headdresses in a variety of styles and ornamented with beads were worn among the Fang of Gabon, the Ngbaka of Zaïre and the Lango of Sudan, among many others. In the late 20th century Zulu women wore headdresses ornamented with sundry beadwork ornaments. African body jewellery includes many sorts of waist- and hip-bands, pubic aprons, pendants, bandoliers and other ornaments found especially among the Bantu peoples of Southern Africa. The bead 'corsets' of the Dinka of Sudan, the ostrich eggshell 'corsets' of the Kwanyama of southern Angola, the bead 'waistcoats' of the Tembu and other Xhosa peoples of South Africa may also be better regarded as jewellery rather than clothing. The beaded waist-bands worn under their clothing by women in many parts of Africa constitute a private but important form of personal jewellery.

BIBLIOGRAPHY

A. Fisher: *Africa Adorned* (London, 1984/*R* 1989)
M. Carey: *Beads and Beadwork of East and South Africa*, Shire Ethnography, 3 (Princes Risborough, 1986)
J. Mack, ed.: *Ethnic Jewellery* (London, 1988)
T. F. Garrard: *Gold of Africa: Jewellery and Ornaments from Ghana, Côte d'Ivoire, Mali and Senegal in the Collection of the Barbier-Mueller Museum* (Munich, 1989)
M. Carey: *Beads and Beadwork from West and Central Africa*, Shire Ethnography, 21 (Princes Risborough, 1991)

MARGRET CAREY

6. REGALIA. In Africa regalia include the raiment that adorns a ruler, the insignia carried by a ruler and the emblematic devices that support or shelter the ruler as symbols of royal power. The interaction between ruler and emblems glorifies both the royal personage and the reign itself. Art objects commissioned by a king or queen, together with royal vestments, headgear, jewellery, thrones, stools, special weapons or other implements, constitute the regalia that embody the strength and spirit of each monarch's rule, and they are intimately involved in the exercise of leadership. The regalia of the Asante king, for example, are symbols of the kingly office, chronicles of royal history and evidence of traditional religion, cosmology and social organization (see Kyerematen, p. 1).

(i) Introduction. (ii) Elevation. (iii) Protection. (iv) Magnification.

(i) Introduction. In many African kingdoms a concept of divine right exists, wherein a ruler is chosen by virtue of his or her special relationship with the deities. There are, however, other modes of succession to office relating to the political position of a candidate, clan membership, consequences of gift exchange or victory in warfare. Whether considered divine or semi-divine, all rulers in Africa are perceived as larger than life and, as such, are vested at their coronations with material symbols expressing their rank and claim to power. Certain possessions are intended to reinforce this image both physically and metaphorically, thus legitimizing and validating the ruler's authority and right to rule.

There is often a degree of detachment and isolation inherent in the role of king or leader, and one of the functions of regalia is to distinguish the ruler from the ruled. Ownership of the regalia, a royal palace and special furnishings not only render the leader conspicuous but also emphasize his or her ability to control wealth and bestow privileges, often in the form of art objects or items of regalia that serve as documents of service or emblems of acquired rank. Regalia are not always conspicuously treated, however, but may be hidden from sight, creating an aura of secrecy. In addition to the regalia that cover or veil a ruler, there are those that are hidden by the ruler, as when a royal stool is occupied by an enrobed monarch sitting in state.

African rulers, whatever the size of their kingdoms or the extent of their power, tended to share certain common themes in the exercise of their rule. They claimed ownership of the land with rights to tribute, but at the same time they were responsible for the well-being of their people and carried out ceremonies on their subjects' behalf. The king, set apart from the people, lived in an elaborate establishment, attended by servants, wives and notables. These features, reflected in regalia, enhanced the ruler's image as an awe-inspiring figure. The degree of elaboration of the regalia was generally in direct proportion to the size, wealth, influence and political complexity of each kingdom.

The characteristic properties of African regalia include the use of rare or precious materials, usually durable and often lustrous or refractory, for example copper, bronze,

95. King Njoya of Bamum (*reg c.* 1887–1924) on his royal throne; from a photograph by Marie-Pauline Thorbecke, 1912

silver, gold, ivory, shells and beads. Cast-copper alloys, such as bronze and brass, were fashioned into royal jewellery, crowns, ceremonial weapons, implements, vessels and even stools and memorial royal portraits, especially among the ancient kingdoms of Ife and Benin in what is now Nigeria. In the Asante kingdom of Ghana a similar purpose has been served by worked gold, which was customarily reserved for the exclusive use of the ruling hierarchy. Cast or hammered, it was fabricated as embellishment for most items of regalia and sometimes for royal portrait masks. Ivory, a royal prerogative and favoured material in Benin, was fashioned into kingly portrait masks, worn at the hip by the monarch, or into royal zoomorphic aquamaniles, used for the ritual washing of the king's hands. In the Yoruba kingdoms of south-west Nigeria, elaborately carved ivory bracelets and ceremonial swords were signs of kingship. For centuries shells and beads have adorned the intricately worked and richly embellished state vestments and royal drums of the king of the Kuba peoples of Zaïre. Elaborate beaded decoration of royal garments, thrones and hand-held regalia is characteristic of other African kingdoms as well, especially those of the Cameroon Grassfields. Special textiles, animal skins or woven mats may also comprise part of a king's regalia. Several iconographic themes are prominently incorporated into African regalia design, particularly depictions of the elephant and leopard, whose formidable strength and courage make them suitable visual metaphors for the monarch. As such, they may be represented interchangeably with images of the king. In regalia their tusks, pelts, teeth, claws and other characteristic features are used to symbolize the king's power. Certain stylistic devices were commonly employed in the design of regalia to enhance the powerful image of the leader and were based on the principles of physical elevation, protection and extension.

The quantity, quality and elegance of all royal artistic expressions, used to glorify the ruler and sanction his reign, reflected the power of the king and the extent of his kingdom. African items of regalia function on several different levels. Aesthetically they are superbly crafted, dramatic and dazzling, but they can also be chronicles of historical events serving to recall and validate a king's right to rule. They may embody the meaning of religion, the history of statehood and the interpretation of cosmology and ethics. Items of regalia form part of a totality, and it is through the presentation of the panoply as a whole, in its intimate association with the person of the ruler, that its full impact can be perceived.

(ii) Elevation. The elevation of the ruler was intended to emphasize his or her exalted status and to proclaim his or

her royal power and grandeur. Thrones and stools dominate this category, but such other items of regalia as palanquins, cushions, sandals or even animal skins spread upon the ground also heighten and validate the ruler's position of leadership by separating him or her from the ground.

Among the most celebrated objects of regalia in Africa is the Golden Stool of the Asante (*see* ASANTE AND RELATED PEOPLES, fig. 1). A sacred symbol of kingship surrounded by myth and legend, it is considered to embody the soul of the Asante nation. The Golden Stool, with its elaborately curved seat and central supporting pedestal, is made of solid gold. Attached to the stool are other items of regalia, which include gold effigies of defeated enemies cast in the form of bells, along with two brass bells, a gold bell and precious beads. The stool rests on its own specially decorated throne, which in turn is placed on an elephant skin. On great public occasions the stool is carried in procession or is displayed resting on its side on its special chair under a splendid umbrella that shelters both the stool and the Asantehene as he sits in state beside it.

An elaborate type of beaded throne was the most significant item of regalia among the Bamum of the Cameroon Grassfields during the reign of King Njoya (*c.* 1887–1924). The complex anthropomorphic and zoomorphic iconography of the Bamum thrones expresses the essence of Bamum kingship, as they figuratively as well as literally elevate the monarch (see fig. 95). Two important beaded thrones from Njoya's reign survive today; one remains in the Bamum capital of Foumbam, the other is in the Museum für Völkerkunde, Berlin (*see* BAMUM, fig. 2). Their design, size, structure, materials and iconography are similar, although the former example is the older of the two, having been part of the regalia of Njoya's father and predecessor, King Nsangu. Both these large wooden thrones are intricately carved with multiple images and are covered by a solid overlay of beads arranged in complex polychrome designs. Their structure combines a cylindrical stool with carved base, two human figures that form the backrest, and a raised rectangular footrest surmounted by two figures with flintlock guns, one at each end. A dense mosaic of cowrie shells covers the tops of the stool and the footrest. Carved in openwork on the stool base are intertwined double-headed serpents, emblems of Bamum kingship reserved for the king's exclusive use. Carved in openwork on the footrest are five dancing figures. The male and female figures on the back and the warriors and dancers on the footrest represent the retainers and guardians of the king.

(iii) Protection. Items of regalia that enhance the image of a ruler and dazzle the populace may at the same time disguise, veil, shelter and protect the royal personage. These include garments that enshroud or envelop the wearer in massive folds or heavy and rigid materials, as well as veiled crowns, headdresses, umbrellas, canopies and even palace architecture. Beaded and veiled crowns, worn by all the Yoruba kings for example, exalt the ruler by their splendour while simultaneously shielding the king's face from public view (*see also* YORUBA). They serve as supreme royal attributes and are a symbol of the highest aspirations of Yoruba traditional civilization. Claiming

96. Ademuwagun Adesida II (*reg* 1957–76), Yoruba ruler of Akure, Nigeria, in his state robes and beaded crown; from a photograph by Eliot Elisofon, 1959

descent from Oduduwa, the mythic father of the Yoruba who initiated the wearing of the beaded crown, rulers of each of the Yoruba states have continued to wear them. The crowns are generally high and cone-shaped and are fully covered with beads of many colours in designs that represent a human face, birds, flowers, crosses and abstract interlace patterns (see fig. 96; see also fig. 55 above). The face on the front of the crown represents Oduduwa. Small representations of birds fashioned in the round and completely covered with beads are sewn on to the sides or sometimes attached to the crown's summit. For the Yoruba, bird imagery refers to the vital force held and controlled by women, living or dead, who are collectively known as 'our mothers'. The birds on the crown signify that the king rules only with the protection and cooperation of the mothers. From every crown falls a veil made of strands of beads that cover the face of the wearer rendering him more awesome because he is unseen. The only face visible to a viewer looking upon the crowned king is the face of Oduduwa that is depicted on the crown. By masking the face of the king, the veiled crown removes him from the world of mortals and places him in a sacred realm.

Beaded apparel also figures prominently as regalia in other African kingdoms. In Benin, for example, the ceremonial costume of coral beads is the emblem and the essence of the Oba's office. Only he can own the royal coral beads, and he alone can wear the full beaded regalia consisting of mantle, headgear and jewellery. Strands of the tubular beads, of a rich orange-red colour, are woven into a full gown of reticulated mesh that envelops the Oba's body; a fully beaded crown with winged projections covers his head; and masses of beaded necklaces, as well as baldrics, belt and pendants, create a virtual armour of coral. The royal beads are not merely ornamental but confer upon their possessor the power of *ase*, the ability to bring to pass proclamations or prophecies. Similarly, the full state costume of the king of the Kuba people of Zaïre provides both a physical and metaphorical shield of protection around him. The royal costume is so heavily embellished with beads, cowrie shells and other precious materials that it weighs 84 kg (see Cornet, p. 246).

Other regalia that shelter a ruler are exemplified by state umbrellas or canopies, which are used at important ceremonial events, for great processions or when the king sits in state. For example, the enormous fringed and decorated umbrellas of the Asante kingdom are made locally of richly woven and beautifully coloured textiles, including silk, brocade, damask and *kente*, elegantly patterned strip-woven cloth. Each umbrella may be surmounted by a gold- or silver-leafed symbol representing a person, an animal, an object or a scene, which usually refers to a proverb. The Asantehene owns at least 23 state umbrellas, each of which is used for a particular occasion as a symbol of his office. The use of canopies as sheltering devices was also a feature of royal protocol in the kingdom of Toro in Uganda. Ceremonies of royal burial and coronation were marked by the lavish use of regalia, which included drums, animal skins, bracelets, anklets and barkcloth. Worn at his coronation, the king's crown and royal shoes, his robes of barkcloth decorated with fringes of beads and elephant hair, the beads around his ankles and his necklace of lions' claws were all symbolic of wealth, power and courage. For the coronation ceremony, royal musicians played gourd trumpets, drums and flutes, and under a sheltering canopy of barkcloths the chiefs lined up on either side to signify their loyalty to the king.

(iv) Magnification. Regalia sometimes serve to extend or magnify a ruler's aura of authority, both literally and figuratively. The literal extension of the royal dimensions can be accomplished through the use of hand-held implements that physically enlarge the holder by extending his range. More abstractly, regalia that represent or allude to the ruler, such as royal portrait figures, serve also to magnify the royal personage.

Among the regalia that literally and metaphorically extend the ruler's reach are sceptres, swords, spears, axes, fly-whisks and knives. Though derived from purely utilitarian forms, their elaboration and iconography transform these otherwise functional tools and weapons into symbolic emblems of prestige. Of crucial importance to the kings of Benin were hand-held regalia, such as the ceremonial sword called *ada*. Fashioned with a long, curved and decorated iron blade with an elaborate hilt of bronze or brass, the *ada* symbolized the Oba's right to take human life. By presenting the sword to a subordinate chief, the Oba could thus delegate to the recipient his power of life and death over his subjects.

In the Asante kingdom of Ghana, swords were second only to stools as the most important items of ceremonial regalia (*see* ASANTE, §3(iii)). There are six different types of swords among the regalia of the Asantehene, each used for a different ceremonial purpose. The typical state sword consists of a wide curved blade of iron with a hilt of carved wood encased in gold leaf. The handle of the hilt is flanked by two globular spheres that strengthen the wielder's grip. A cast-gold ornament, usually depicting an animal and often representing a proverb, adorns the scabbard of the sword and symbolizes the power of the king. The importance of the sword is shown by the fact that at the coronation or enstoolment of the Asantehene it is held by the ruler-elect as he takes the oath of office. Swords are also used by subordinate chiefs to swear allegiance to the king, and they are carried by messengers of the king on official errands. Staffs and fly-whisks serve similar functions among the Asante. Cast or plated with gold, they convey messages through their rich decoration and iconography. Staffs are carried by royal messengers to identify themselves as spokesmen for the king, and fly-whisks, their handles carved with symbols alluding to proverbs, are carried by rulers as objects of prestige.

Staffs of office are among the most important items of regalia among many other hierarchical societies in Africa, for example among the Luba of south-eastern Zaïre. From about the 17th century and up to the 19th Luba rulers affirmed their positions of power through the use of regalia consisting of ceremonial stools, staffs, spears, bowstands, axes, bowls, cups and other items, of which staffs were among the most important. At his investiture the king, seated on a carved and decorated caryatid stool, held a staff in his right hand while taking the oath of office. Besides that of the ruler, passed down the royal line from king to successor, staffs could also be owned by chiefs, counsellors and noblemen, but the degree of the staff's sculptural elaboration depended on the rank, financial means or aesthetic taste of its owner.

The elegantly carved female figure that often surmounts Luba staffs refers to the founding female ancestor who represents the spirit of all Luba kings and the extent of their power (see fig. 97). Further down the staff, flaring oval or lozenge-shaped sections punctuate the lines of the slender shaft. These sections are engraved with geometric designs representing women's scarification patterns, which encrypt mythical and lineage information and map ancient centres of political organization. Oral history and tradition are thus recorded on these emblems, while affirming the owner's ties to the Luba dynasty.

In addition to the physical extension of the ruler, figurative extension can be achieved by portrait figures that replicate and thus magnify the ruler's person. The great commemorative royal heads of bronze commissioned by Benin rulers to grace their ancestral altars served to glorify the ruling dynasty. Among the Kuba peoples of

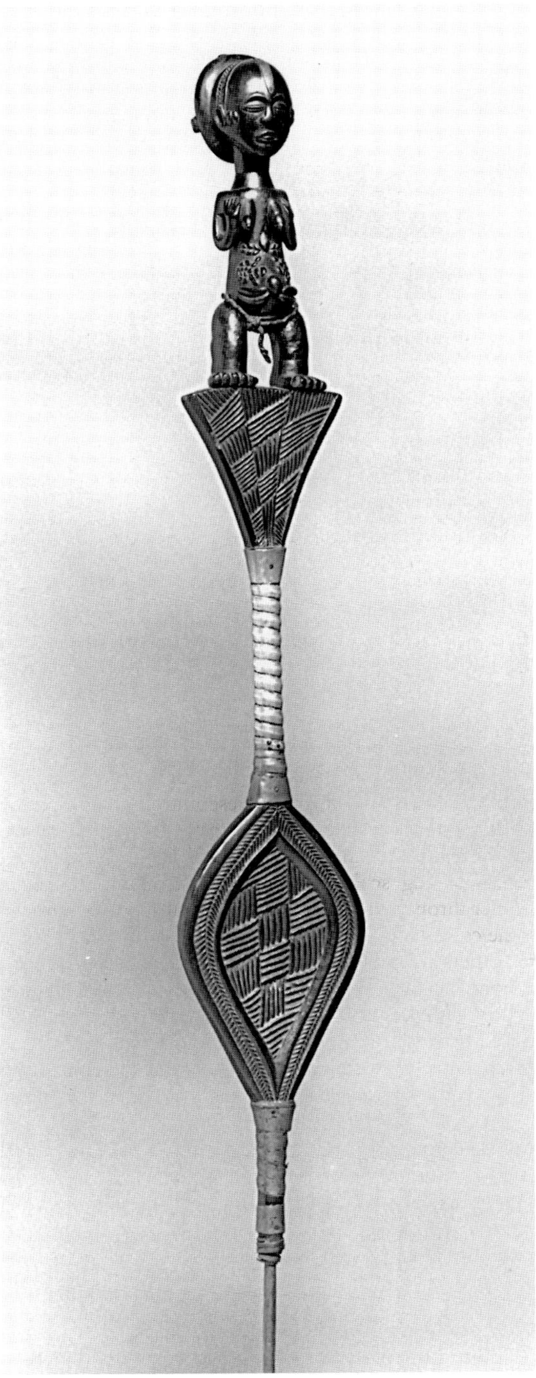

97. Luba staff of office, wood, metal, fibre and leather, h. 1.42 m (Toronto, private collection)

Zaïre the king maintained one of the most sumptuous of all African courts. Kuba regalia, consisting of portrait sculptures, drums, metalwork and textiles created by professional craftsmen, brilliantly expressed the wealth and power of the king and his court at Mushenge. Most important among the items of regalia were the *ndop* figures, or portrait statues of each reigning king, each carved with an identifying symbol associated with the ruler (*see also* KUBA (iii), §3). These figures functioned as effigies of past and existing rulers but also served as the vehicle for transferring the essence of kingship to the new king by means of a special ceremony of succession. Each king is portrayed seated cross-legged on a pedestal, resplendent in royal dress and regalia including bracelets, necklaces, belts and anklets, with a royal knife in his left hand. His form is symmetrical and contained, his expression calm and serene with an air of gravity. Before him is placed his personal emblem, or *ibol*, which distinguishes him from all others. Upon his enthronement, each king had a drum of office carved and elaborately decorated with copper, beads and cowrie shells. At the king's death, his drum and *ndop* figure were secreted in a storage room, to be brought out only for display on important occasions.

BIBLIOGRAPHY

A. Maesen: *Umbangu: Art du Congo au Musée royal du Congo belge* (Brussels, 1960)

A. A. Y. Kyerematen: *Panoply of Ghana* (London and Accra, 1964)

R. F. Thompson: 'The Sign of the Divine King: An Essay on Bead-embroidered Crowns with Veil and Bird Decorations', *Afr. A.*, iii/3 (1970), pp. 8–17, 74–80

D. Fraser and H. M. Cole, eds: *African Art and Leadership* (Madison, 1972)

Traditional Art of the Nigerian Peoples: The Milton D. Ratner Family Collection (exh. cat. by H. J. Drewal, Washington, DC, Mus. Afr. A., 1977)

The Arts of Ghana (exh. cat. by H. M. Cole and D. H. Ross, Los Angeles, UCLA, Wight A.G.; Minneapolis, MN, Walker A. Cent.; Dallas, TX, Mus. F.A.; 1977–8)

P. Ben-Amos: *The Art of Benin*, Tribal A. (London, 1980)

C. Geary: 'Bamum Thrones and Stools', *Afr. A.*, xiv/4 (1981), pp. 32–43

J. Cornet: *Art royal kuba* (Milan, 1982)

P. Ben-Amos and A. Rubin, eds: *The Art of Power, the Power of Art: Studies in Benin Iconography*, Mus. Cult. Hist. UCLA, Monograph Ser., xix (Los Angeles, 1983)

Princess Elizabeth of Toro: *African Princess: The Story of Princess Elizabeth of Toro* (London, 1983)

M. H. Nooter: *Luba Leadership Arts and the Politics of Prestige* (MA thesis, New York, Columbia U., 1984)

The Art of Cameroon (exh. cat. by T. Northern, Washington, DC, Smithsonian Inst. Traveling Exh. Serv., 1984)

T. F. Garrard: *Gold of Africa: Jewellery and Ornaments from Ghana, Côte d'Ivoire, Mali and Senegal in the Collection of the Barbier-Mueller Museum* (Munich, 1989)

M. H. Nooter: 'Secret Signs in Luba Sculptural Narrative: A Discourse on Power', *IA Stud. Afr. A.*, iii (1990), pp. 35–60

NANCY INGRAM NOOTER

7. DIVINATION INSTRUMENTS. The arts of divination are practised in a wide variety of African societies with a wide range of objects. An account of the divinatory process must be given before the objects themselves can be understood.

(i) Introduction. In most African societies where divination is practised it is a decision-making and problem-solving process rather than a fixed system of prediction. The future is not predetermined but can be influenced by human actions. Individuals or communities use divination to resolve problems ranging from the trivial to the cataclysmic: from finding a lost or stolen possession, deciding whom to marry, discovering how to cure an illness, to determining when and where to move a whole village during a drought. Moreover, in many African societies disease, otherwise unexplained deaths and other

98. Divination instruments of the Yoruba of south-west Nigeria, from left: Ifa tapper, ivory, h. 320 mm, 19th century (private collection); Ifa tray, wood, diam. 338 mm, *c.* 1920 (Los Angeles, University of California, Fowler Museum of Cultural History); Ifa bowl, wood, h. 273 mm, *c.* 1920 (private collection)

misfortunes are often attributed to neglected deities, offended ancestors or malevolent witches and sorcerers; a common goal of divination is therefore to identify the perpetrator and to divine a remedy. Solutions to the problem may range from a prescribed ritual sacrifice to execution of the identified guilty party.

The divination process is rarely straightforward and clearcut: interpretation by the diviner, or sometimes by his client, is generally required. Diviners typically undergo long periods of apprenticeship to religious specialists, since their role is to facilitate communication between the gods and the human world. Most African cultures practise some form of divination, and many practise several. Some diviners interpret the tracks of animals or the flights of birds, and others 'read' the entrails of animals. Poison oracles are employed by some societies to determine guilt, especially in instances of suspected murder: the suspect is administered the poison, and death or survival establishes the verdict. Spirit possession and dream analysis are also common means of gaining knowledge from the gods. In a few African cultures the divining process is embodied in a masquerade. Among the Bamana peoples of southern Mali, horizontal helmet masks of the Komo society feature an assemblage of such organic elements as antelope horns, porcupine quills and vulture feathers (*see* BAMANA, §2). These, along with an encrusted surface of sacrificial materials, bring power to the mask. Wearing a costume laden with amulets, and possessed by the powers of the mask, the dancer responds through song to questions posed prior to the performance. These songs are interpreted by the diviner.

Divination arts may be taken to include not only the manipulated objects discussed here but also the special ornaments and dress worn by the diviner, the containers for storing divining equipment and the charms and sculptures that are prescribed as remedies for various problems. Indeed, figurative sculpture representing ancestors, nature spirits and deities plays an important role in divination among many African peoples. These spirit forces and their corresponding sculptures are generally consulted by a diviner through possession trances or through dreams. In some cases only a limited range of problems is dealt with, but others are more far-ranging in their divinatory powers. Among the Yaka, Kongo and Songye of Zaïre, for example, figures with medicine bundles and charms are associated with divination. Among other objects that have been documented performing as oracles or otherwise involved in divination are Igbo terracottas, Ibibio shrine sculptures, Baga *elek* altars, Mende female figures, Kissi stone-carvings and Baule monkey and nature spirit images. The critical importance of divination is highlighted, however, by the large number of cultures that employ crafted instruments specifically for this purpose. These enhance the process aesthetically and bring prestige to the spirits and to the diviner.

(ii) Instruments. The best-studied and most artistically elaborate system of divination in Africa is that practised by the Yoruba of south-west Nigeria and known as Ifa. The focal object in the divination ensemble is a wooden tray with a smooth central surface framed by a band of relief carving (see fig. 98). The relief typically includes one or more faces of Eshu, the Yoruba trickster and messenger god (*see* §IV, 8 above). Other motifs depict a variety of sacrificial animals sacred to Ifa, equestrian figures, copulating couples and sometimes divination scenes. Simpler boards have geometric decoration, an interlace motif being common.

The Ifa divining process is begun by hitting the point of a wood, brass or ivory tapper against the tray to attract the attention of the gods. The tapper often features an image of a kneeling woman grasping her bare breasts in a gesture of supplication (see fig. 97 above). The tray is dusted with powdered wood and the diviner then repeatedly manipulates palm nuts to determine which one of sixteen set patterns to trace in the dust. Each pattern refers to a specific body of oral literature called *odu*. A repetition of this process determines another pattern that identifies one of sixteen sub-sections of the previously selected *odu*. These verses are then recited by the diviner. Usually the verses suggest rituals or sacrifices as solutions to the client's problem. The sacred palm nuts are stored in a cup with elaborately carved support figures such as female devotees, maternity figures, animals (especially roosters), and equestrian figures (see fig. 99). Larger containers and bowls, with many of the same motifs, may be used to store the entire assortment of divination instruments. Diviners also employ elaborately beaded bags displaying the face of Eshu to carry their equipment. All of these artefacts may be housed, possibly with additional sculpture, in an Ifa diviner's shrine.

A highly specific form of divination is found among the Guro, Yaure and Baule peoples of central Côte d'Ivoire. It employs field mice, whose proximity to the earth makes them ideal messengers of the ancestors and other spirits. A mouse is placed in the upper chamber of a two-tier wooden vessel (a hole connects the vessel's two chambers). This top chamber contains a small metal plate with ten thin, sticklike forms attached along one edge so they can pivot freely. The movements of the mouse in the chamber manipulate the sticks, and their resulting position is then interpreted by the diviner. The exterior surface of such vessels is sometimes embellished with representations of miniature masks or with figures carved in relief (*see* BAULE). These images are thought to be purely decorative, with no symbolic meaning.

Among the Kuba and related groups in central Zaïre friction oracles are commonly used to communicate with nature spirits; they are considered especially effective in identifying thieves, witches and adulterers. Generally the oracle is carved in the shape of a quadruped with a flat, polished area on its back. After dipping a wooden knob in oil, the diviner rubs it back and forth along the polished surface while reciting questions and possible answers. When the knob sticks firmly to the oracle, the correct answer has been reached. Warthogs and crocodiles are favoured decorative motifs, because they are closely associated with nature spirits and are respected for their ability to communicate with them. Dogs and elephants are also common and are thought to have special clairvoyant powers. Some friction oracles have a human head facing upwards on one or both ends, possibly referring to a revered ancestor or diviner.

Among the Luba, Hemba and Tabwa in south-eastern Zaïre carved figures attached to gourds were employed in divination. These figures were associated with the Buhabo secret society and were especially useful in determining cures for illness. The images are typically female, truncated at the waist and grasping their breasts. In some instances an ensemble of snail shells and animal skins, rather than a gourd, was tied to the base of the figures. In either case, a hole was drilled through the full length of the carving, which was either filled with medicines or left open so that small objects could be dropped through the head of the figure during the divination process. The Luba also use a rectangular block of wood with a hole in the centre and surmounted by a carving of a human head. Both the diviner and his client insert the first finger of their right hand into the hole and move the oracle back and forth on the ground or occasionally on a neckrest, which may also be carved with one or two caryatid figures. In order to identify an ancestor who has brought illness or misfortune to his client, the diviner interrogates the oracle, and when the pattern of movement changes abruptly the answer has been given.

The principal art form involved in divination among the Yaka of western Zaïre is a wooden slit-drum with a handle carved in the shape of a human head, sometimes two-faced. The drum serves multiple functions: it is used to announce the diviner's visits to other villages and as a stool; medicines prescribed by the divination process are prepared within it, and the client may subsequently drink from it. In some areas a male and female pair of slit-drums are played by the client and the diviner respectively as part of the consultation. Elaborately embellished slit-drums are also employed in divination by many neighbours of the Yaka, including the Suku, Mbala, Kongo, Holo and Pende. The Pende also use an unusual divination instrument called *galukoshi* (*see* PENDE, fig. 2).

Among the Chokwe peoples of northern Angola and adjacent parts of Zaïre, baskets containing an elaborate complex of up to 60 objects, including carved figures, are employed in divination. After shaking a pair of double rattles to remove evil forces, the diviner chants to enlist the participation of ancestral spirits. The basket is then shaken firmly, and the diviner interprets the specific meaning of each object in relation to its position in the basket. Carved images in such ensembles may include a headless figure representing a warrior killed in battle and a copulating couple. If the headless figure comes to rest on the edge of the basket, it indicates that the patient is troubled by the spirit of someone who has suffered a violent death. If the copulating-couple figure falls on the edge of the basket it could mean that the mother of one of the client's wives is causing trouble. Other small carvings, each with its own significance, include a woman carrying a load, a crying girl, a strong man, four people on a road, a gourd, a phallus, a neckrest and miniature masks. Elsewhere in Zaïre, the Songye and Holo have their own systems of divination involving various natural and carved objects that are tossed and read by the diviner.

The Senufo of northern Côte d'Ivoire and southern Mali also employ a combination of manmade and natural objects, which are thrown on the ground in front of the diviner and interpreted. The divination instruments include an assortment of human and animal images made of iron, brass and wood as well as non-figurative symbolic objects in various materials and such organic items as seeds, shells, and the teeth and horns of animals. Particularly important in Senufo divination are large forged iron and cast-brass bracelets in the form of a python, a primordial creature and principal messenger of the spirits.

Although these bracelets are particularly emblematic of the diviner's role, they are rarely worn but decorate the diviner's shrine or are kept beside him during consultations with clients. Also critical to the process is a pair of male and female figures representing bush spirits. These are placed facing the diviner, and an assortment of divining objects is tossed between them. The figures are thought to relate messages from the spirits to the diviner. These small carvings (h. 150–200 mm) include some of the most accomplished of all Senufo wood sculpture. Senufo divination sculpture also frequently includes a small equestrian figure that further evokes the power of the spirits and embellishes the visual display.

BIBLIOGRAPHY

L.Tucker: 'Divining Baskets of the Ovimbundu', *J. Royal Anthropol. Inst. GB & Ireland*, lxx (1940), pp. 171–201

T. Thomas: 'Les Itombwa: Objets divinatoires sculptés conservés au Musée royal du Congo belge', *Congo-Tervuren*, vi/3 (1960), pp. 78–83

G. Park: 'Divination and its Social Context', *J. Royal Anthropol. Inst. GB & Ireland*, xciii/2 (1963), pp. 195–209

W. Bascom: *Ifa Divination: Communication between Gods and Men in West Africa* (Bloomington, 1969)

R. F. Thompson: *Black Gods and Kings: Yoruba Art at UCLA* (Los Angeles, 1971/*R* Bloomington, 1976)

A. Hauenstein: 'L'Oracle à souris des Baoule de la Côte d'Ivoire', *Bull. Annu., Mus. Ethnog.* [Geneva], xv (1972), pp. 9–34

M. de Areia: 'Le Panier divinatoire de Tskokwe', *A. Afrique Noire*, xxvi (1978), pp. 30–44

P. McNaughton: *Secret Sculptures of Komo: Art and Power in Bamana (Bambara) Initiation Associations*, Working Pap. Trad. A., 4 (Philadelphia, 1979)

D. Biebuyck: '*Buhabo* Statues from the Benembaho (Bahoma)', *Africa-Tervuren*, xxvii/1 (1981), pp. 18–31

A. J. Glaze: *Art and Death in a Senufo Village*, Trad. A. Africa (Bloomington, 1981), pp. 54–72

J. Mack: 'Animal Representations in Kuba Art: An Anthropological Interpretation', *Oxford A. J.*, iv (1981), pp. 50–60

A. Bourgeois: 'Mukoku Ngoombu: Yaka Divination Paraphernalia', *Afr. A.*, xvi/3 (1983), pp. 56–9, 80

M. T. Drewal and H. J. Drewal: 'An Ifa Diviner's Shrine in Ijebuland', *Afr. A.*, xvi/2 (1983), pp. 60–67, 99–100

Igbo Arts: Community and Cosmos (exh. cat. by H. M. Cole and C. C. Aniakor, Los Angeles, UCLA, Mus. Cult. Hist., 1984–6), pp. 72–4

DORAN H. ROSS

8. Musical instruments.

(i) Introduction. (ii) Types.

(i) Introduction. Music forms an integral part of African life-cycle celebrations, festivals and rituals, as well as providing entertainment. Instruments are played solo, with vocal accompaniment or in ensembles. Four categories are represented: chordophones (instruments such as harps and zithers, in which a vibrating string produces the sound), membranophones (in which a vibrating membrane produces the sound, as with various kinds of drum), aerophones (in which the sound is produced by the passage of air, as with flutes, trumpets or reed instruments) and idiophones (a less precisely defined category that includes rattles, gongs, cymbals and *mbira*, a sub-category of instruments made of wooden or metal strips arranged flat on a soundboard and often mounted on a resonator). A variety of materials are used, including ivory and metal, but wooden instruments are by far the most numerous. Although both women and men may play, some instruments, such as the harp and the *mbira*, are the exclusive domain of men. While music has a central role in many African cultures, it is not only the sounds produced by the instrument that are important. A musician may be admired, for example, for the dexterity with which his fingers move on the keyboard of the *mbira*, creating a pattern that is itself perceived as a decorative motif. The aesthetic qualities of the instruments as objects are also important and are believed to reinforce the power of the player, both in enhancing his communication with the worlds of the spirits and of the ancestors and in signifying his status and prestige.

Instruments are commonly made by their players, who may also be responsible for their ornamentation, although if highly wrought decoration is required the player may enlist the help of a professional carver or blacksmith. The importance and extent of visual considerations in the design of instruments vary greatly; some are decorated with simple designs and abstract ornament, while others are elaborate sculptural objects in themselves. Generally, the immediately Sub-Saharan and Central African regions are particularly rich in such highly sculpted instruments, as are areas in Tanzania and Zambia, but examples of finely sculpted instruments may also be found in other areas, where two-dimensional abstract ornamentation is more usual. These sculptural objects are sometimes held in particularly high esteem for their value within a far-reaching system of symbolism, in which, for example, the instrument can also be designated as male or female (according to its pitch) or in which parts of the instrument may represent some aspect of social structure or illustrate some belief. Among the Dogon, according to one disputed interpretation (see Griaule and Dieterlen), for example, different parts of an instrument, such as the concave portion of a *gingiru*'s resonator, may symbolize the vault of the sky as opposed to the resonator itself, symbolizing the earth, and the inside of the trough, symbolizing the atmosphere. The four strings may refer to the four cardinal points. In the *ngombi* (harp) of the Bwiti (a religious cult found among the Fang of Gabon), the complementarity of male and female is translated into the parts of the harp: the resonator symbolizes the womb and the neck male virility, so that the junction of the two signifies sexual union. In this it repeats both the structure of a Bwiti chapel, which is divided into male and female halves, and the equal participation of men and women in the Bwiti cult (see 1989 exh. cat.). Furthermore, the harp can be seen to unite the microcosmic world of the living and the macrocosmic world of the gods and ancestors.

(ii) Types. Those instruments that can be claimed to be three-dimensional sculptural works fall readily into two principal categories—zoomorphic and anthropomorphic—with a third, minor category that comprises object-forms. The present discussion will limit itself to anthropomorphization only. The instruments that bear anthropomorphic representations show variations on the human theme ranging from the exquisite naturalism of a figure surmounting an instrument to the humanization of the instrument's abstract form (see figs 99 and 100). In some instances, the sculptor has sought with extravagant ingenuity to bend and subordinate (or integrate) the entire instrument to a recognizable human shape. The importance of this humanization probably derives from the symbolism these objects may bear: some Africans view

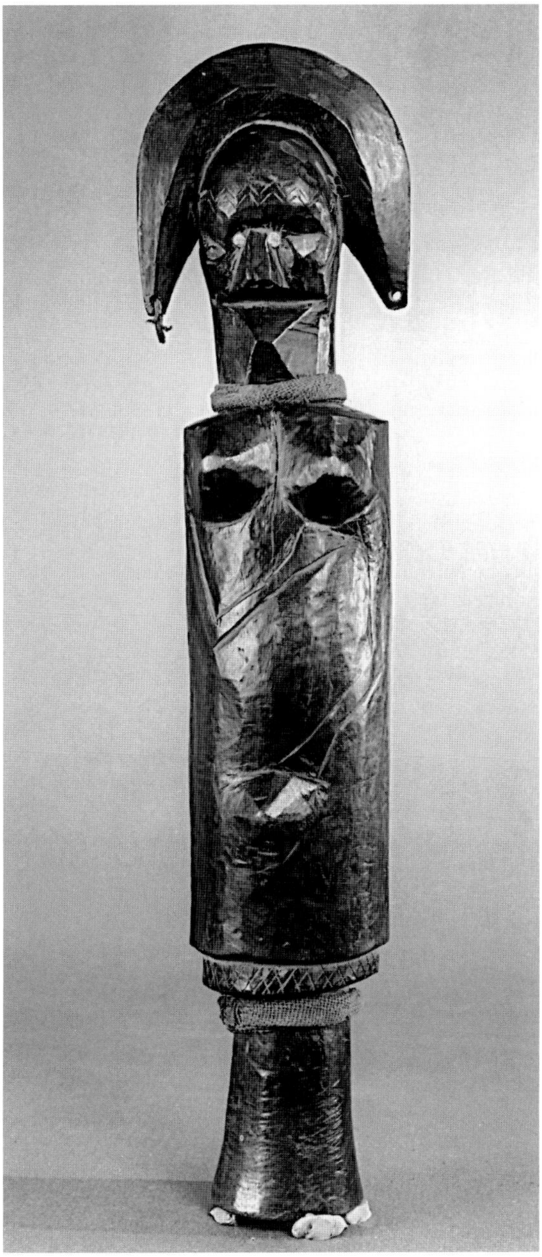

99. Kissi slit-gong, wood, h. 515 mm, from Guinea (Paris, Musée de l'Homme)

them as amplifications or extensions of the performer's soul and body and use terms of human anatomy to describe parts of the instruments; the sounds themselves are also characterized in terms of the human voice (see Laurenty).

(a) Chordophones. Examples of the total anthropomorphization of an instrument are remarkable but rare, even among peoples with strong traditions of figurative sculpture such as the Fang of Gabon and the Chokwe of Angola. There seems to be a concentration of fully anthropomorphized harps among the Mangbetu and the Nbaka in north-eastern Zaïre, an area also noted for incorporating the human figure in *mbira*, vessels and bark storage boxes for honey. In such harps, either the elongated neck of the harp ends in a finely carved head, with two flexed legs supporting the torso, which serves as the resonator, or the neck of the harp is carved as a complete human figure; one rare example (Zurich, Mus. Rietberg) presents a neck carved as a hermaphrodite figure with two

100. Zande *mbira*, wood and bamboo, h. 660 mm, from Uele region, Zaïre, collected 1908 (Tervuren, Koninklijk Museum voor Midden-Afrika)

finely modelled heads. Among the Nbaka three styles of harp stand out: the first is characterized by a prominent head, clearly defined facial features and flexed legs (see 1989 exh. cat., p. 86); the second is defined by a small head at the end of an elongated neck, and with straight legs (see 1989 exh. cat., p. 87); and the third style is characterized by a heart-shaped face on which the nose is only suggested by line, an enlarged rectangular cavity for the torso and short legs. The stylistic characteristics of this third group are shared by the Mongo, Ngombe and Ngbandi of Zaïre.

(b) Membranophones and aerophones. Examples of fully anthropomorphized membranophones include two monumental Luba-Kasai drums from Zaïre (Berlin, Mus. Vlkerknd.). Among the Bete of Côte d'Ivoire, some drums assume the form of a human torso. Stylistically, these are recognizable by linear bands around the waist, a prominent navel, scarification and stout legs, or by the navel only, with legs that have been reduced to an openwork support (see 1989 exh. cat., fig. 45).

Trumpets and horns are not commonly carved into a human figure, but such representations are found on megaphones or voice disguisers from Congo, Zaïre and Sudan. A few such examples have also been found in Sierra Leone, where such instruments belonged to the men's secret society known as Ghbandi. These instruments could not be seen by women or non-members and were only occasionally brought out for performance before members (see Hart, pp. 49–51). Some fully anthropomorphized examples of such instruments present the human figure in striking and significant poses. The hands, for example, may appear clasped against the back of the head, raised straight along the sides of the head, extended down along the sides of the torso or placed against the abdomen. Such positions recall for some Congolese peoples the classic poses of mourning, bewilderment or prayer (see 1981–2 exh. cat., pp. 74, 225). Among the Bembe of the Congo some of these instruments are carved in groups as a 'family' (father, mother, daughter and son), among the Dondo of Zaïre as female figures; among the Bongo of the Sudan at least one splendid human figure has been found with a face conveying an expression of awe (Rome, Mus. N. Preist. & Etnog., no. 29604). Whistles are particularly well suited to the human figure, many examples being found in Western Sudan and Central Africa, two regions particularly rich in sculpture where realism and abstraction are found side by side.

(c) Idiophones. Among idiophones, anthropomorphization of wooden slit-gongs (slit-drums) is prevalent among the Bamana of Mali, the Kissi of Guinea, the Dan of Côte d'Ivoire and the peoples of the Cameroon Grassfields. They range in size from small to monumental: the small slit-gongs are hand-held and serve as emblems for members of secret societies or associations, while the monumental slit-gongs often provide a focal point in community events. In style, the slit-gongs range from stylization of the human form to naturalistic representations. Indeed, in the case of one Dan instrument it has been argued that not merely naturalism but even portraiture is involved (see 1976 exh. cat., pp. 117, 120). Conversely, the slit-gongs of the Kissi are highly stylized: a long cylinder forming the bust terminates at the bottom in a cylindrical-conical base and is topped by a crescent coiffure. The figures, arms and hands are simply indicated by engraved lines (see fig. 99). In the Cameroon Grassfields, monumental slit-gongs carved with human-like figures at their top are kept in or near the palace. None of the older Bamum slit-gongs has survived, but smaller examples embodying the same theme are commonly found in the Grassfields region and span a broad spectrum of human forms, from the bold forms of the Mambila (e.g. Paris, Mus. Homme) to the stark, angular and expressive forms of the Bamileke (Berlin, Mus. Vlkerknd.). Monumental slit-gongs are found also among the Baule of Côte d'Ivoire and among the M'Bembe of Nigeria, who are noted for adorning either one or both ends of their slit-gongs with large figures called *idoro.* While only two such M'Bembe slit-gongs are known (Berlin, Mus. Vlkerknd.), several of the end-figurative sculptures survive (e.g. Paris, Mus. N.A. Afr. & Océan.). Both the fragments and the complete slit-gongs attest to a wide stylistic range, from naturalistic facial features, including scarification patterns, to abstraction and minimalization of features. Human figures can also be found adorning miniature slit-gongs among the Kongo groups (Vili, Yombe, Sundi). Not only do they have the fluid lines, attention to detail and fine execution of facial features characteristic of Kongo art but they also demonstrate unusual dynamism in the poses of the figures: kneeling with hands tied behind the back, standing in a group of four figures with knees bent and hand to abdomen, and seated with right knee raised and left leg stretched out (e.g. Rotterdam, Mus. Vlkenknd.).

Mbira and wooden bells from north-eastern Zaïre reflect the sculptural ideas familiar from the chordophones of the same region. In the case of examples of *mbira* of the Zande an entire woman's torso becomes the sounding chamber. A unique Zande bell is carved with swelling forms that might allude to a skirt, with semicircular handles as stylized arms and with two clappers suggesting the figure's legs (Antwerp, Etnog. Mus.). In the Lower Congo region there is an impressive diversity of very fine bells topped by figures in various positions: standing, kneeling, crouching and sitting. These are part of the paraphernalia of the *nganga* (healer).

Anthropomorphism may also be expressed in three other ways besides the above examples of full figurative representation. First, a full human figure may crown or support the instrument and may be depicted in high or low relief on its surface. As in African sculpture generally, these figures may assume a number of positions to which significance is often attached. Such sculptures are said 'to symbolize life and spirit in patterned sound' (see 1989 exh. cat., p. 39). Second, but less commonly, a pair of figures may appear facing each other on either side of the instrument. Finally, a single part of the human body, such as head, nose, mouth or phallus, may be incorporated into the instrument's design (this treatment tends to be restricted to drums, whistles and slit-gongs). The most frequently depicted feature is not surprisingly the head, the apparent seat of speech and sound. In some exceptional instances, such as bells from the Lower Niger and among the Kuba, as well as Senufo *mbira*, the instrument as a whole assumes the form of a human head.

BIBLIOGRAPHY

Grove Instr.
E. M. von Hornbostel and C. Sachs: 'Systematik der Musikinstrumente: Ein Versuch', *Z. Ethnol.* xlvi (1914), pp. 553–90
S. Chauvet: *Musique nègre* (Paris, 1929)
M. Griaule and G. Dieterlen: 'La Harpe-luth des Dogon', *J. Soc. Africanistes*, xx (1950), pp. 209–28
J. Laurenty: *Les Cordophones du Congo Belge et du Ruanda-Urundi*, 2 vols (Tervuren, 1960)
K. Krieger: *Westafrikanische Plastik*, 3 vols, Veröff. Mus. Vlkerknd., Berlin, n. s. 7, Abt. Afrika (Berlin, 1965–9) [col. cat.]
Sculptures africaines dans les collections publiques françaises (exh. cat., Paris, Mus. Orangerie, 1972)
H. Kamer: *Ancêtre Bembe* (Paris, 1974)
Die Kunst der Dan (exh. cat. by E. Fischer and H. Himmelheber, Zurich, Mus. Rietberg, 1976; Eng. trans. and rev., Zurich, 1984)
P. Berliner: *The Soul of Mbira* (Berkeley, 1978)
Oggetti e riti: Strumenti dell' Africa (exh. cat., Rome, Mus. N. Preist. & Etnog., 1980)
The Four Moments of the Sun: Kongo Art in Two Worlds (exh. cat. by R. F. Thompson and J. A. Cornet, Washington, DC, N.G.A., 1981–2)
Praise Poems: The Katherine White Collection (exh. cat., Seattle, WA, A. Mus., 1984)
W. A. Hart: 'Wood Carving of the Limba of Sierra Leone', *Afr. A.*, xxiii/1 (1989), pp. 44–53
Sounding Forms: African Musical Instruments (exh. cat., ed. M.-T. Brincard; New York, Amer. Fed. A., 1989)
African Reflections: Art from Northeastern Zaire (exh. cat. by E. Schildkrout and C. Keim, New York, Amer. Mus. Nat. Hist., 1990)
E. de Dampierre: *Harpes Zande*, Domaine Musicologique (Paris, 1991)

MARIE-THÉRÈSE BRINCARD

9. ARMS AND SHIELDS. African craftsmen have made many types of refined and elaborate weapons, including bows and arrows, knives, swords, spears, axes, clubs and firearms as well as a peculiarly African weapon, the throwing knife. Many of these are notable for their fine proportions, shapes and workmanship but still remain functional, while others may be elaborated or embellished to the extent that they can no longer serve the original purpose of their type, becoming instead identifying emblems and often serving as symbols of leadership and prestige. This is increasingly the case as weapons incorporating Western technology become more prevalent. Particularly in Central Africa, knives and other weapons were traded extensively, sometimes serving as forms of currency. This has made it difficult, if not impossible, in many instances to identify a specific form with a single ethnic group. One example is the throwing knife, designed to be thrown at human or animal targets and with an effective range of 20–30 m. This consists of a stem, which serves as the handle and is usually covered with fibre or skin, and two or more branching blades (see fig. 101). This multi-bladed design is unique and has allowed for an astonishing variety of shapes. Throwing knives are common over a wide area from Sudan to Gabon and the Zaïre River basin and are the African weapon most likely to be collected by Westerners.

Knife and sword blades are also found in a seemingly endless variety of shapes and sizes. Blades may be punctuated with openwork or, more commonly, incised, usually with linear and frequently asymmetric patterns. Among several Central African peoples, blades are divided into dark and light areas: the dark side is carbonized steel, a result of the forging process, while the light area is cleaned by abrasion after forging. In other cases, blades may be inlaid with, or may be made entirely from, precious metal such as copper. In some areas brass tacks, wire or thin

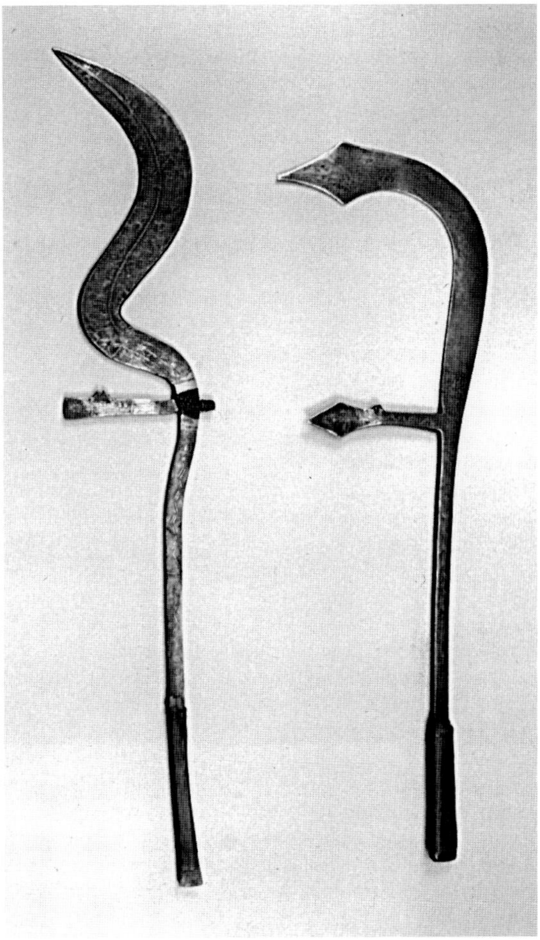

101. Ingessana throwing knives, metal, max. l. 830 mm, from Blue Nile Province, Sudan (London, British Museum)

strips of metal, gold ornaments, fur, reptile or animal skin often decorate wooden hilts, adding to a knife's prestige value. Handles may also be carved in figural forms or made from precious materials such as ivory or copper. In some areas knives and swords have assumed purely ceremonial functions. In the Nigerian kingdom of Benin, for example, a royal sword formerly used by the king's executioner is now carried in front of the king as a symbol of his right to take a human life, while in Ghana's Asante confederacy, swords, often with openwork patterns on the blades, were carried by envoys of the paramount chief as a symbol of their authority (*see* ASANTE AND RELATED PEOPLES, fig. 2). Among the Kuba of Zaïre, decorated wooden versions of the *ikula*, a knife with a leaf-shaped blade, serve as insignia of royalty or as indications of rank within the hierarchy of Kuba society. Axes too may serve several functions within a single culture. Among the Shona of Zimbabwe, for example, axes are not only weapons and tools but also part of the paraphernalia of spirit mediums and healers, as well as a symbol of resistance to colonial rule.

The shapes of blades vary with the area of origin: those from south-eastern Africa, for example, are shaped like half-moons with single tangs, while those of northern Nigeria are crescent-shaped with two places at which the blades fit into the shafts. Spears, either the light, throwing type or the heavier, longer, stabbing variety, are perhaps the most common traditional weapon in Africa. In some areas they are among the accoutrements of traditional dress for some social groups. When young Maasai men become warriors, for example, they are expected to carry their hunting spears at all times. Elsewhere spears may become exclusively display items through the intricate wrapping or decoration of the shaft, usually with metal strips or wire, or by elaboration of the spearhead. Among the Tutsi of Rwanda, for instance, such usually non-functional spears were carried as part of ordinary male attire. The spearheads of the Tutsi are known for their intricacy, often consisting of multiple points or multiple twists in the metal, a sign of skilled craftsmanship, adding to the spear's value.

Most bows and arrows, clubs and throwing sticks are in standard shapes and are undecorated. Exceptions include the arrows used by the Mangbetu in Zaïre, which have geometric relief patterns on the shafts; the fighting sticks made by the Turkana of Kenya, which are studded with nails or inlaid with wire; and Zulu clubs from South Africa, called knobkerries by Westerners, which are made from wood or rhinoceros horn and wrapped with elephant hair or wire in decorative patterns. Certain types of bracelets and rings with sharpened edges found among the pastoralist peoples of southern Sudan and northern Kenya and Uganda are also notable. These 'fighting' or 'razor' bracelets and rings are generally not meant for warfare but rather for spontaneous fights among men within the community. Although not indigenous to Africa, rifles and pistols are made by blacksmith specialists using both imported and locally made parts. Like simpler weapons, these too are sometimes embellished with such decorations as metal tacks or inlay.

Shields offer effective protection from all of these weapons except firearms and may be large enough to cover and protect the body or much smaller, affording greater visibility and mobility for the shield holder but necessitating quick reflexes and agility. A variety of shapes and materials can be found. The round hide shields of some peoples in Ethiopia, Somalia and Sudan have elaborate decoration, which includes not only patterns embossed into the hide but also additions of velvet and metal bosses and strips. Many of the latter are apparently made for display rather than serving as functional defensive weapons. Further south, the Maasai and the Zulu traditionally used colour and pattern both to decorate their elliptical hide shields and to identify the age grades or regiments of their owners, their ranks and their deeds of bravery. Maasai shields are painted in white, black and red, while those of the Zulu are fur-covered skins in particular colours and patterns. In the forest areas of Central Africa finely and tightly worked basketry shields, sometimes with painted decoration or coloured fibres, or wooden shields, sometimes covered with cane or other fibres, are more typical.

BIBLIOGRAPHY

P. R. McNaughton: 'The Throwing Knife in African History', *Afr. A.*, iii/2 (1970), pp. 54–60, 89

W. Fischer and M. A. Zirngibl: *African Weapons: Knives, Daggers, Swords, Axes, Throwing Knives* (Passau, 1978) [Ger. & Eng. text]

T. Northern: *The Ornate Implement* (Hanover, NH, 1981)

M. A. Zirngibl: *Seltene afrikanische Kurzwaffen/Rare African Short Weapons* (Grafenau, 1983)

P. Westerdijk: *African Metal Implements: Weapons, Tools and Regalia* (Greenvale, 1984)

——: *The African Throwing Knife: A Style Analysis* (Utrecht, 1988)

C. Spring: *African Arms and Armour* (London and Washington, DC, 1993)

DIANE M. PELRINE

10. CURRENCY, WEIGHTS AND MEASURES. There is considerable documentary information regarding the means of exchange used by traders in Africa. The caravans of the Egyptian Cosmas Indicopleustes, for example, trading in the early 6th century AD, bought gold on the Upper Nile with iron and salt, which were used in commercial transactions until the 20th century. Other commercial arrangements included *troc muet* (Fr.: 'silent barter'), in which the two parties did not meet, but each in turn left his merchandise in a prearranged spot, although no description of the rules governing such arrangements has survived.

Local currencies, including red cloth and pieces of iron, are mentioned in medieval documents (including Arabic, Jewish and Italian). These sources more usually refer, however, to their authors' own monetary systems, even where these had no validity in the place where the transaction occurred. The Arabs introduced not only the dinar but also the mitkal, which was the equivalent of the dinar in weight, and they must also have introduced the use of cowries, which came from the Maldives *c.* AD 1000. During the 14th century, shells were used as coins of small value in the area within the great curve of the River Niger.

During the 15th century, as they gradually advanced along the Atlantic coast, the Portuguese took up the trading customs of the Arab world, which were well known to the indigenous peoples they encountered. The Portuguese effectively devoted themselves to cabotage (coastal trade), ferrying local products from one region to another, but, after trying to introduce their own currency, they resorted to using cloth and metals (in the form of bars and bracelets) and often replaced local forms of currency with others that they controlled, such as glass beads or cheap trading goods. Metal rods, for example, were replaced by copper or iron bars (*barriferi*), and the squares of raffia used and made in the Congo had to compete first with others made in regions controlled by the Portuguese, then with pieces of cotton fabric introduced mainly by Portuguese soldiers, who received their pay in this form. In the late 18th century, thalers issued under the Austrian sovereign Maria-Theresa began to appear in Ethiopia. These silver coins came to be used across Northern Africa and even as far as Ubangi, Zaïre. During the 19th century, the coins were transported by caravan from Tripoli to the lands of the Hausa. One of the great Nigerian traders, Malan Yavoh, intercepted one such caravan at the end of the 19th century and, by virtue of the trading routes he controlled, introduced the coin into commercial circulation. As with the other silver pieces in use, the thaler was often considered as a piece of jewellery and was evaluated purely on the basis of the quality of the metal it contained.

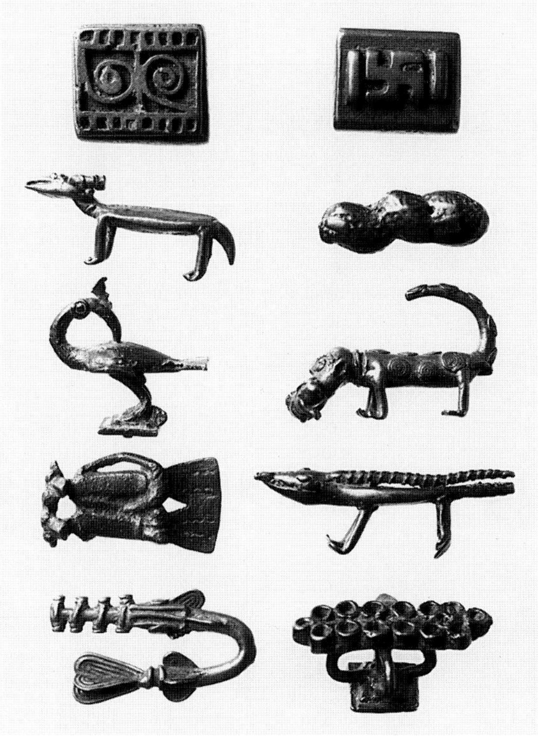

102. Brass weights for gold, Asante, Ghana, collected before 1930: (left, top to bottom) rectangular weight, 26×30 mm; antelope, l. 50 mm; Sankofa bird, l .35 mm; two men with heads placed side by side, l. 40 mm; sawfish, l .47 mm; (right, top to bottom) rectangular weight, 23×28 mm; peanut, l. 38 mm; leopard with porcupine in its jaws, l. 48 mm; crocodile swallowing mudfish, l. 75 mm; mancala game-board, l. 44 mm (Washington, DC, National Museum of Natural History)

Many other currencies have been used in Africa besides those adopted for trading purposes, but most of them have remained less well known. The oldest must have been the pierced shells of the Mauritania region, which may have been in use as early as the Neolithic age. Small copper crosses from *c.* 900 AD have been found in south-eastern Zaïre, and similar crosses of various sizes up to 250 mm in length continued to be used as currency from the Zambezi to the Kasai as late as the 20th century; trading caravans even disseminated them to the coast of Kenya to the east and that of Angola to the west. In this region, again *c.* 1000 BC, there were also strings of mollusc shell, which are still worked by older men among the Sakata. These currencies could include seeds, honey and drinks just as well as shells, stone or metal and were not constrained by any concern for durability, convenience or standardization: for example, although the strings of the Lega of Zaïre are all the same length, each varies slightly from every other. The same can be said of the metal rods used as currency, such as the *sompê* from central Côte d'Ivoire (which were very thin with flattened edges, varying from 180 mm to 250 mm in length), used by the Guro and the Malinke, and the *guinzé* of Guinea and Sierra Leone, with a twisted shaft, flattened edges and thickness varying from 250 mm to 800 mm, used by the Toma, the Kissi and the Mande.

Sometimes different currencies were used by a given people at the same time and for different types of payments. The function of these currencies was primarily ritual and social, with trading activities holding little importance for the societies concerned. Those using them often explained the value of such currencies in terms of their having been chosen by a founding ancestor, and indeed some of these coinages look similar to items of regalia, such as the *kul* of the Sara of Chad, which take the form of a miniature jet knife with two arms, 2 mm thick and 600 mm in length. In certain groups, the *kul* was the reference unit of value before the introduction of modern currency and was used alongside various iron ploughing tools (the crescent shaped *seme*), balls (*mbal*) or bars 200 mm to 500 mm in length and *c.* 2 mm in thickness. It was generally the village chief, the spokesperson for the founding ancestor, accompanied by the council of elders in whose keeping such items were stored, who took charge of the most important payments. These included marriage payments and the purchase of millet in case of food shortages. Payments were also made to the initiation priest or to the ancestors to help infertile women to conceive. This function of reinforcing social cohesion was also evident with the Kissi and the Toma: the *guinzé* were placed at the entrance to the village as a form of protection, or at the head of the tombs of heads of families; when one of their children left the village, they would take some *guinzé* with them and then replace them on their return.

There were fewer recognized currencies in the monarchies. Examples included the gold dust of the Asante kingdom, the *olivancillaria nana* or *n'zimbu* shells of the Kongo kingdom and the raffia squares and cowries of the Fon kingdom of Abomey. The entire range of a given kingdom's monetary usage is known only in a few cases, but the sovereigns exercised direct control over the production, entry into the kingdom and distribution of each currency. Each new dynasty may well have found the existing currency problematic, however, and for this reason it may have proved convenient to adopt means of exchange imported from abroad. A number of ancient currencies, impossible to dissociate from their ritual functions, can also be found decorating sculptures or masks in the form of jewellery, and all of these had a symbolic value. Imported products such as cowries or glass beads might be substituted for other, older local elements and could take on their names: thus cowries are still known as *n'zimbu* among the Kongo.

Weights and measures remained relative concepts in such societies. Some measures of length and volume served to evaluate certain types of currency, such as the cubit for valuing lengths of cotton, the string for beads or shellfish tests, the basket for *n'zimbu* and the gourd for grain. Weights appear to have been associated primarily with long-distance trade and could be made from stone, glass or seeds. They were used all along the trans-Saharan caravan routes and were all apparently calibrated in relation to the Arab unit of the mitkal. The other area to have produced a large number of weights, especially in brass, was the Akan in the forest regions of Ghana and Côte d'Ivoire. Here the weights were calibrated on the Arabic

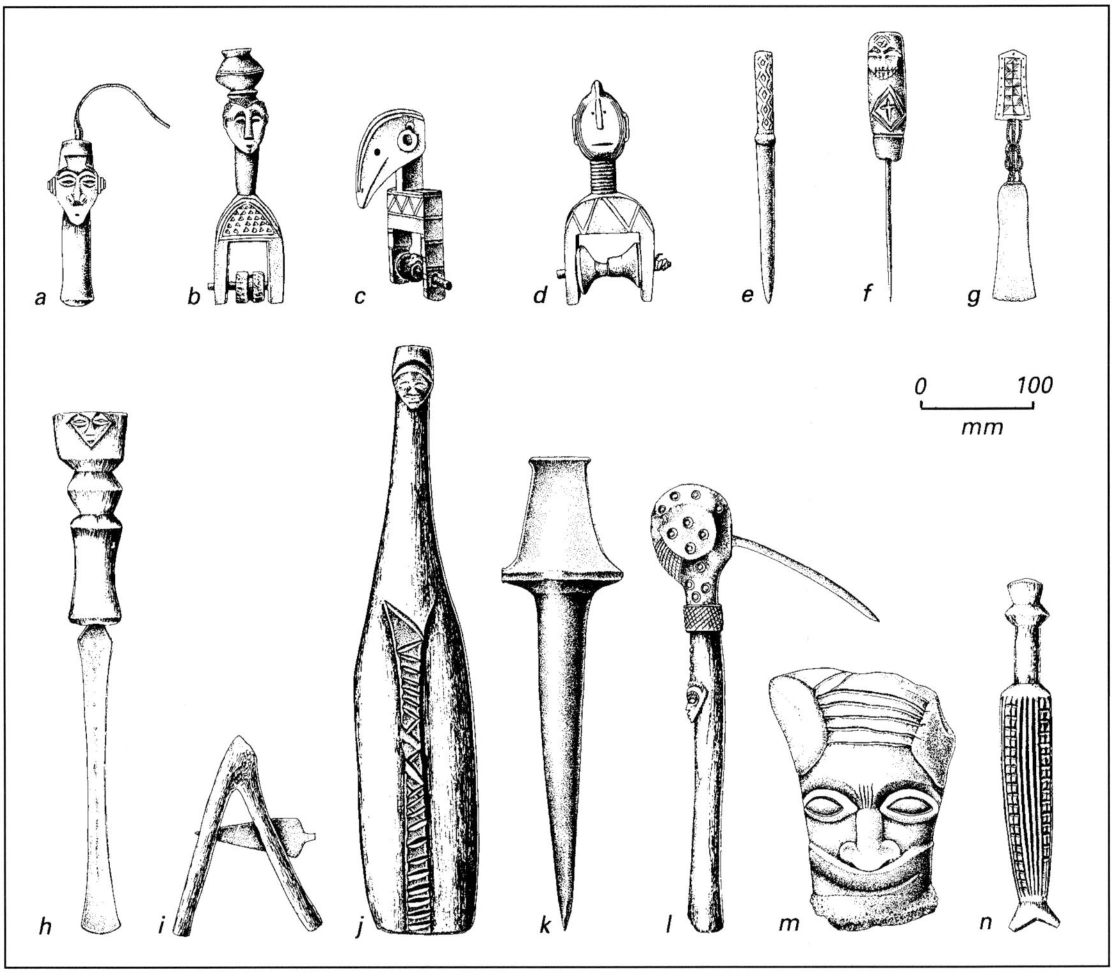

103. African tools and implements, 20th century unless otherwise stated: (a) Kuba bark scraper, wood and iron, h. 174 mm, from Zaïre; (b) Baule heddle pulley, wood, h. 210 mm, from Côte d'Ivoire; (c) Tura heddle pulley, wood, h. 155 mm, from Côte d'Ivoire; (d) Mossi heddle pulley, wood, h. 182 mm, from Burkina Faso; (e) Yombe weaving peg, wood, h. 201 mm, from Zaïre; (f) Kuba chasing chisel, wood and iron, h. 215 mm, from Zaïre; (g) Bushong (Kuba) razor, iron, h. 198 mm, from Zaïre; (h) Lulua chisel for palm-tree tapping, wood and iron, h. 414 mm, from Zaïre; (i) Lobo drawing knife, wood and iron, h. 163 mm, from Zaïre; (j) Gonge (Zande) clay paddle, wood, h. 470 mm, from Zaïre; (k) Mongo blacksmith's hammer, iron, h. 382 mm, from Zaïre; (l) Luba adze, wood and iron, h. 357 mm, from Zaïre; (m) Kissi twyer, soapstone, h. 210 mm, from Guinea, 19th century; (n) mallet, wood, h. 281 mm, from north-east Zaïre (Tervuren, Koninklijk Museum voor Midden-Afrika)

system in the northern regions and according to various European standards in the southern regions. They were closely linked with the trade in gold dust and played an important role in the families of the various kingdoms, where it appears that weight itself was of only relative importance. The decorations on these weights, using symbols associated with the different societies, were often considered to carry a coded message that guaranteed the value of the transaction (see fig. 102).

BIBLIOGRAPHY

M. M. Fischel: *Le Thaler de Marie-Thérèse: Etude de sociologie et d'histoire économique* (Paris, 1912)
P. Einzig: *Primitive Money in its Ethnological, Historical and Economic Aspects* (London, 1948)
E. Dartevelle: 'Les N'zimbu: Monnaie du royaume du Congo', *Bull. Soc. Royale Belge Anthropol. Préhist.*, n. s., 1, xliv (1953)
A. H. Quiggin: *A Survey of Primitive Money* (London, 1963)
M. Johnson: 'The Cowrie Currencies of West Africa', *J. Afr. Hist.*, xi/1 (1970), pp. 17–49; xi/2 (1970), pp. 331–53
A. Salifou: 'Malan Yavoh: Grand négociant du Soudan Central à la fin du XIXème siècle', *J. Soc. Africanistes*, xlii (1972), pp. 7–27
T. F. Garrard: *Akan Weights and the Gold Trade* (London, 1980)
R. Antoine: *L'Histoire curieuse des monnaies coloniales* (Nantes, 1986)
J. Cribb: *Money: From Cowrie Shells to Credit Cards* (London, 1986)
J. Hogendorn and M. Johnson: *The Shell Money of the Slave Trade*, Afr. Stud. Ser., xlix (Cambridge, 1986)
J. Rivallain: *Paléomonnaies africaines* (Paris, 1986)
F. A. Iroko: *Les Cauris en Afrique Occidentale du Xème au XXème siècle* (diss., U. Paris I, 1987)
M. Servet: 'La Monnaie contre l'Etat ou la fable du troc', *Droit et monnaie: Etats et espace monétaire transnational* (Lyon, 1988), pp. 49–62
J. Rivallain: *Poids akans à peser la poudre d'or: Collection Abel* (Paris, 1989)

JOSETTE RIVALLAIN

11. TOOLS AND IMPLEMENTS. The oldest known tools in the world are the African flaked cobbles and stone

flakes from *c.* 2.5 million years BC. From this time stone artefacts gradually became more elaborate. Acheulian tools, mainly hand axes, from *c.* 1.5 million years BC represent a remarkable intellectual achievement: the equilibrium of the shapes, the fine workmanship and the choice of the raw materials combine a functional approach with some concern for aesthetics. Later, polished tools, such as one made of haematite from Uele in Zaïre (see Van Noten), showed outstanding craftsmanship. Such materials as wood, vegetable and animal fibres, ivory, leaves, bones, horns, leather, eggshells, snail shells, seashells, gourds, clay and metal have also all been in use for millennia. In some places specific tools were developed to work these materials, which were used in turn to create numerous other implements, mainly for cultivating, hunting, fishing, animal husbandry, cooking and drinking. The number of tools owned by any given family, however, was quite small, with basic objects such as a knife, hoe or axe serving several purposes.

In African languages, usually one specific term is used to designate what in European languages is a rather vague category of objects. Often there is confusion, however, between the technical and symbolic use of an object, so that a ceremonial object may be in the same category as a simple knife; a very simple tool may have a more important symbolic role than highly decorated objects. This is the case with the hammer-anvil of the blacksmith (see fig. 103k), a sort of iron nail that is often used in enthronement rituals throughout Central Africa, where the king is often symbolically assimilated to the blacksmith. Like the blacksmith's other tools—pliers, wire drawing plate, cutter—it is not decorated unless it is used as regalia, as among the Kuba of Zaïre or in the interlacustrine zone. In some cases, as with the Kongo, the bellows can be carved, while the Kissi of Guinea carve cephalomorphic twyers in soapstone (103m).

As in other parts of the world, the simplest objects, those used for the most basic physical tasks, are rarely decorated, except with a few small designs as a sort of signature of the artisan or mark of the owner. The most widespread tool is the adze, which is highly versatile and can be used to carve with great precision (103l). Adzes and axes are usually associated with men's work, such as clearing the woods and war, and they are often decorated and used as objects of prestige. Knives and razors are usually not highly decorated but sometimes display remarkable craftsmanship; among the Kuba they are also used to cut velvet fabric (103g). Unusual and very characteristic drawing knives found in Central Africa and used to smooth wood of cylindrical objects, such as spear shafts or paddle handles, are composed of an arrowhead fixed across a forked branch (103i). The Kuba of Zaïre, well known for their careful decoration of many unusual objects, have chasing chisels (103f) and cephalomorphic bark scrapers (103a), used to collect the red powder used in many rituals.

Also relatively unusual are the large wooden paddles, sometimes decorated (103j), that are used to pack the clay floors and walls among the Zande of north-eastern Zaïre. Among fishermen, the very large paddles used in canoeing are often decorated with elaborate designs. Wooden or ivory mallets used to beat bark in order to make bark cloth are known in several parts of the forest area of West and Central Africa. Their grooving can be made in an elaborate and decorative pattern, as in some fine examples from north-east Zaïre (103n).

Weaving implements can also be decorated, the heddle pulleys in West Africa, for instance, being unusually beautifully carved (103b–d) in the shape of a man, an animal or even an inanimate object such as a headrest. In other areas, for weaving, wooden pegs (103e) are planted in the ground, and the warp is looped around them. Specialized tools are also employed in agriculture, the iron hoe being the most characteristic, often with the machete. Another tool characteristic of forest peoples is a big chisel used to cut the palm tree in order to collect the sap for palm wine (103h).

BIBLIOGRAPHY

F. Van Noten: *The Uelian* (Tervuren, 1968)

F. N'Diaye: 'Iconologie des poulies de métier à tisser Dogon', *Obj. & Mondes*, xi/4 (1971), pp. 355–70

African Furniture and Household Objects (exh. cat. by R. Sieber, New York, Amer. Fed. A., 1980–81)

'Les Instruments aratoires en Afrique tropicale', *Cah. ORSTOM Sci. Humaines*, xx/3–4 (1984)

R. Haaland and P. Shinnie, eds: *African Iron Working: Ancient and Traditional* (Oslo, 1985)

F. N'Diaye: *Poulies de métier à tisser: Masques et sculptures d'Afrique et d'Océanie* (Paris, 1986)

V. Bounoure: 'A propos des poulies de tisserance de la collection Liotard', *A. Afrique Noire*, 64 (1987), pp. 11–19

PIERRE DE MARET

12. FURNITURE. Some African peoples have rich traditions of furniture, almost all of which is made of wood and in the main out of single pieces. While no African household completely lacks furniture of some sort, large wooden objects are, for obvious reasons, scarce among nomadic peoples and in communities where villages are relocated at intervals.

In Africa the stool is the most basic item of furniture. A man's stool is extremely personal to him, as well as being a status symbol. There are some examples, for example from Liberia, of stools of composite construction made from palm-rib pieces. Generally, however, African stools are made from a section of tree trunk (see fig. 104). There is considerable stylistic variation in African stools, both between peoples and between those used by chiefs or elders and those used by commoners. That of an important person may be distinguished by the number of legs, by the elaboration of its carving or by its ornamentation with beadwork, metal plate or brass studs. For example, in northern Zambia, an ordinary man's stool has up to three legs, that of a headman five or more, while a chief's stool is also elaborately carved. Women, on the other hand, sit on a short piece of wood or a mat. In the Cameroon Grasslands the basic carved stool has a seat supported by a caryatid figure or by a hollow cylinder of openwork carving of such figures as stylized frogs and spiders. A chief's stool is larger and more elaborate, while a state stool is enhanced by an additional figure or figures carved to form a back- or armrest and beadwork covering. The Hemba of Zaïre also have caryatid stools (*see* HEMBA, fig. 2). Such stools are indeed not domestic furniture but form part of the regalia without which the chiefly succession is invalid. Footstools or footrests are also found in such contexts, since a chief, when sitting in state, may not

104. Tabwa high-backed stool with a human head, possibly of a tribal ancestor, wood, h. 858 mm, from south-eastern Zaïre (London, British Museum)

have his feet touching the ground. Some stools have backs formed from carved figures and are virtually chairs. In some cases, however, the seat is too shallow to sit on and the carved figure may then symbolize the presence of an ancestor (see fig. 104).

European chairs were brought as gifts for African kings and chiefs from at least the 16th century. In some areas European styles and forms were readily adopted. Among the Asante of Ghana there are two types of European-style chairs, both ornamented with brass studs. Among the Pende of Zaïre and the Chokwe of Angola, chiefs' chairs in European form occur, with the backs and cross-pieces carved with small figures in the local style, and are among the few pieces of African furniture carpentered from several pieces of wood. Another form of European seating is the small folding deckchair, with a skin or mat in place of canvas, used by village headmen in many areas. This form was copied from the travelling equipment of district commissioners.

Backrests are particularly common in Zaïre. They usually take a tripod form and are made from a tree trunk with its branches cut to shape. Those used by commoners may be quite basic, while those of Kuba chiefs, for example, are elaborately carved. Tip stools, found among the Bole of Zaïre, combine the functions of stool and backrest, having a central upright and a long surface to act as seat or backrest.

Headrests, which are almost always monoxylous, may be grouped with stools and backrests. The simplest headrests comprise a branch of which the surface has been smoothed, having perhaps three or four branchlet supports. Larger headrests double as stools. Among nomads headrests may be simple monopods or bipods with a neckpiece and carrying loop. Most African headrests are purely functional in form, although those of the Somali combine a graceful, basic shape with chip-carved decoration. Headrests with zoomorphic or other figural decoration are relatively uncommon and, when not carved for the Western market, may have been made for important people. The Zulu of Southern Africa have produced double headrests. The Bwaka of Zaïre make headrests comprising a lidded box, perhaps for holding trinkets.

Among such nomadic peoples as the San, beds are made on the ground, with a skin for both over- and underlay. Many traditional houses have an earth platform with sleeping-mats. Bedsteads, whether made by the local blacksmith-carpenter or constructed out of a framework of bamboo, palm ribs or long straight sticks with overlaid mats or mattress, have tended to replace the earth platform, since they give some protection against vermin and ants. Chiefs usually have more elaborate beds as befits their status; in the 1870s the king of the Mangbetu had a fine composite bed of bamboo and raffia matting. In the Cameroon Grasslands, a chief's bed was carved from one piece of wood, with supporting sides in the form of rows of carved figures.

Tables are hardly found outside Northern Africa and the Swahili coast, where Arab influence is strong. Swahili tables are small, like Western occasional tables, and often consist of a tray on a stand. In Ethiopia, food baskets were made with a circular tray top. Chests are only found where Arab influence is strong and are often ornamented with brass overlay. Wall niches, shelves and outdoor platform stands are otherwise common. Boxes made of wood or bark, lidded baskets and gourds, hanging nets and pots are also used for storage. Other belongings may be hung from a wooden hook in the wall or stuck into the thatch, which is a good place to keep small valuables safe or an axe or knife out of harm's way. Mats are an important item of African furnishing. Since many beds are 'built-in', mats serve as bedding. Where houses are built on a raised platform foundation, mats laid on the platform under the overhanging thatch provide sheltered built-in seating. Other pieces of African furniture are simple and multi-purpose, such as stout forked sticks that may serve as stands for waterpots.

See also BAMUM and SWAHILI, §3; for illustration *see* WOOD, colour pl. III, fig. 2.

BIBLIOGRAPHY

R. Sieber: *African Furniture and Household Objects* (Bloomington, 1980) [pubd in conjunction with an exh. organized by the Amer. Fed. A., New York, 1980–81]

C. Geary: 'Bamum Thrones and Stools', *Afr. A.*, xiv/4 (1981), pp. 32–43, 87–8

J. de V. Allen: 'The *kita cha enzi* and Other Swahili Chairs', *Afr. A.*, xxii/3 (1989), pp. 54–63, 88

The Art of the Personal Object (exh. cat. by P. Ravenhill, Washington, DC, N. Mus. Afr. A., 1991)

13. TOBACCO CONTAINERS AND PIPES. Tobacco was introduced into Africa from America by Europeans in the 15th century, while hemp, often called *dagga*, may have entered Africa from the east and north, via Arab contacts. In much of Sub-Saharan Africa, especially in the east and south, the preferred form of tobacco was snuff, made from dried, ground tobacco leaves, which in the late 20th century continued to be taken by both sexes. Snuff-boxes belonging to chiefs or important men might be distinguished by their size, superior workmanship or use of some exclusive material, such as elephant ivory. The great majority of snuff-boxes, however, are quite small and are portable as neck or waist pendants or, if they are made from a length of reed or wood, worn as an ear-plug. Small gourds are often used, either left plain or decorated in a variety of ways, such as pyrogravure, impressed beads or wire and beaded covers; and short lengths of cane or bamboo used to keep snuff may also be decorated by pyrogravure, shallow carving and beaded covers. In Malawi, for example, cane snuff-boxes have carved, wooden, mushroom-like stoppers. Among the Bantu of Southern Africa, ovoid snuff-boxes made from wood or ox-horn have a loop at the end for wearing as a pendant or are attached by a wooden link to the end of a headrest. A horn snuff-box of this shape might also be carved at the end of a long horn hairpin to wear in the hair, perhaps along with a carved bone snuff-spoon. Other horn snuff-boxes are carved as small conical flasks surmounted by the figure of an antelope or human head or torso. In Southern and South-eastern Africa, typically among the Shona, wooden chip-carved snuff-boxes are shaped like flasks or thistle-heads, with circular gourd stoppers. In Southern Africa containers in the shape of a flask or a miniature ox are made from a mixture of inner-skin scrapings and earth, shaped over a clay core. The surface is then lifted into numerous tiny spikes, and, after this has set, the clay core is removed through the neck of the flask or a hole cut in the ox's head. This method is known as 'blood and clay' (*tandu* in northern Nigeria).

Water-pipes occur in Central, South-eastern and Southern Africa but do not seem to exist in West Africa. They are the most common implement for smoking hemp (except in Northern Africa) and are also often used for smoking tobacco. The water container through which the smoke is inhaled and filtered is very often a gourd, but antelope horns, hollowed-out wood and bamboo stems also occur, again often decorated with pyrogravure, brass studs or twisted wire. The mouthpiece may be just a hole at one end of the water container, while the bowl for the tobacco or hemp is usually mounted on a short length of reed and can be made of stone (often soapstone), pottery or wood lined with sheet tin. The shapes vary but are basically like vases or funnels, often with a lug for securing to the water container and ornamented with grooved lines or chip-carving. In North-eastern Africa, notably the Nilotic Sudan, a small spherical gourd stuffed with bast is secured to the top of the long wooden stem by tight-fitting dried rawhide and acts as a filter.

Other forms of pipe include the earth pipes of Southern Africa, in which a short tube is connected to a small, hollow mound containing the hemp, and short pieces of stone or bone. Others again may be similar to European-style pipes but with the bowl carved to represent a human head, animal or other fancy shape. The bowls of these European-style pipes are made from such materials as metal, wood or clay, while the stems are made of reed, wood or a long gourd. In Northern Africa, for example,

105. Shilluk pipe, clay, bamboo, metal, beads and pigment, l. 740 mm, from Malakal area, Sudan (London, British Museum)

hemp is smoked from a straight reed stem attached to a small red clay bowl, decorated with incised Islamic ornamentation. Clay pipe-bowls are made, usually by men, using a technique somewhat akin to wood-carving. A rough clay form is made, with a smoke-hole pierced in it, and this is allowed to dry until 'leather-hard'. It is then carved to shape, and when the drying process is almost complete, the pipe-bowl is finished off with ornament in the local style and fired. Among the Asante of Ghana, pipe-bowls are made of red clay, with white kaolin in the grooves and in a variety of shapes, such as leopards, shells or human heads. In Uganda, traditional pipe-bowls were conical, burnished black, with fine red-and-white incised lines. The Tonga and Ila of southern Zambia make pipe-bowls of red or black clay carved with supports and representing antelope or buffalo forequarters. Pipe-bowls in the Nilotic Sudan are mostly vase-shaped, with a small foot, while among the Shilluk, ornamental pipe-bowls, representing a hyena's head, are carved from clay and burnished black, with white incised hatchings (see fig. 105). In the Cameroon Grasslands, while pipes for ordinary people or women are functional and plain, elaborate ceremonial pipes are owned by chiefs, with large bowls made of either carved clay or brass cast by the lost-wax process, perhaps in the shape of a mask or an elephant's head. These pipes have a long stem, often covered with beadwork in polychrome geometric patterns.

In Central Africa the favourite material is wood, with chiefs' pipes often being ornamented either with copper or brass wire strip wound around the stem or with brass domed nails, while the bowls are sometimes finely carved. Among the Bantu of Southern Africa, wooden pipes are usually carved from one piece of wood, with the bowl inlaid with zinc in a pattern or even carved with the bowl as a pot on a woman's head. The bowls are normally lined with sheet tin-plate; a separate short length of cane or wood is stuck in the end of the stem as a mouthpiece. Each smoker uses only his own mouthpiece, to prevent his spiritual essence falling into the hands of an enemy. Conversely, pipes with multiple wooden bowls are found among the Pondo of Southern Africa, and in Nigeria multiple vase-shaped pipe-bowls are made in carved clay.

BIBLIOGRAPHY

A. Dunhill: *The Pipe Book* (London, 1924)
M. Shaw: 'Some Native Snuff-boxes in the South African Museum', *An. S. Afr. Mus.*, xxiv/3 (1935), pp. 141–62
——: 'Native Pipes and Smoking in South Africa', *An. S. Afr. Mus.*, xxiv/5 (1938), pp. 277–302
——: 'South African Native Snuff-boxes', *An. S. Afr. Mus.*, xxiv/5 (1938), pp. 221–52

MARGRET CAREY

14. HOUSEHOLD UTENSILS. One of the most essential domestic items is the knife, which may be used for such diverse tasks as skinning animals, cutting meat or fish, peeling root vegetables, splitting reeds or cutting bark tie when making baskets, shaping wood, trimming fingernails or shaving the head. Generally, knives belong to the individual rather than the task. Forks feature little in African culture, other than as tourist commodities, but spoons are significant and are made in a wide range of forms and materials. The most important are those used for serving food, which have large bowls and are sometimes elaborate. The Dan people of Liberia, for example, have special rice spoons with a large bowl, sometimes decoratively carved at the back, and with the handle often carved in human or animal form (see fig.106 and fig. 51 above; *see also* DAN, fig. 4). Such spoons are used by women in lavish hospitality at times of festival and help celebrate women's social role. They are often the work of a master carver and are inherited. Many have decoratively carved handles or bowls, as they may be used for ritual feeding of respected elders, for making offerings to the

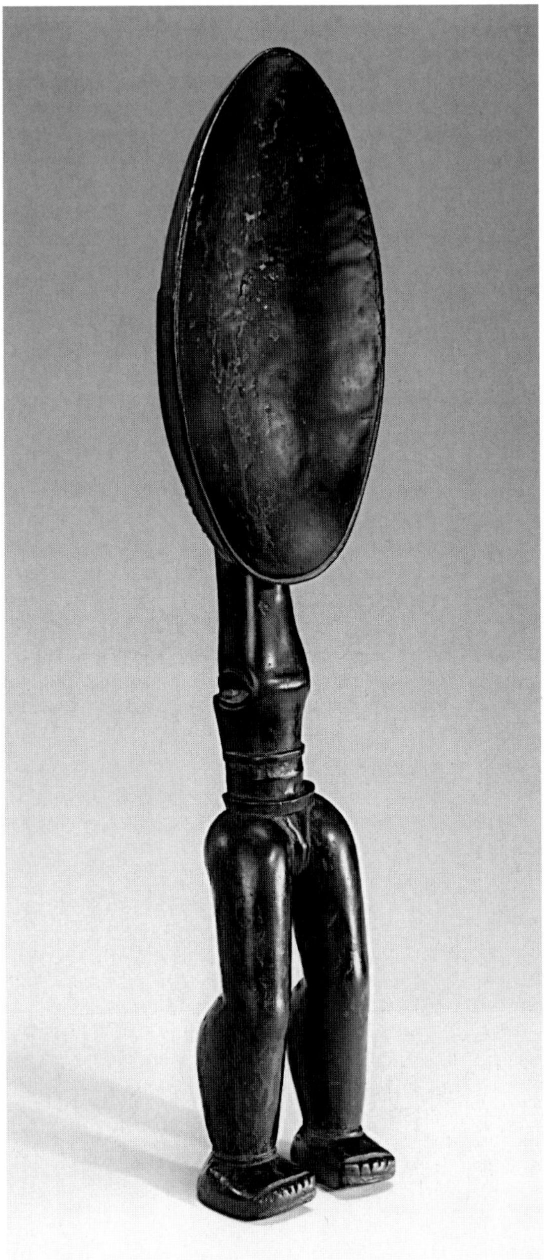

106. Dan spoon, wood, h. 465 mm, late 19th century–early 20th (Norwich, University of East Anglia, Sainsbury Centre for Visual Arts)

spirits or for serving food on special occasions. The Asante of Ghana have a unique form of spoon with a flat pestle-like end to the handle; this is used in levelling mashed yam (*fufu*). A paddle-shaped spoon is widely used to stir and serve the stiff porridge that provides the staple diet of much of Sub-Saharan Africa. In Northern and Eastern Africa, where the influence of Arabic culture is evident, spoons may be decorated with elaborate chip-carving (as among the Somali) or made of pearl-shell bowls mounted in a lacquered handle (as in Northern Africa).

Dippers, for ladling water out of a pot or for use as a drinking cup, are made from suitably shaped long-stemmed gourds or from coconut shells mounted on sticks, or carved from wood. Another special form is the strainer spoon, common among the Bantu-speaking peoples of Southern Africa, used to skim the floating mash from local beer. In general, spoons used for eating are rare but are made of wood, although brass alloys, iron and white metal are also used. In Central Africa the oval shell of the river-mussel is used as a spoon, while among the Zulu each person has his or her own spoon, often with an ornamented handle; these are kept in individual basketry wallets.

Water containers are often among the most highly decorated ceramic wares, and the variations in impressed decoration are striking. The water-carrying pots of the Makonde of Mozambique, for example, have all-over incised designs filled with kaolin, while the water-carrying jars of the Nupe of Nigeria have fine linear incisions and registers of rouletting (see fig. 107). The Nupe jars have elegantly clinched necks and hour-glass contours, reminiscent of the shape of some bottle gourds. In some cases (e.g. among the Bole of northern Nigeria and the Gbaya of the Central African Republic), highly ornamented pots are stacked around the interior of a woman's sleeping room and reflect her, or her household's, economic and social standing. Other ceramic vessels may be used for storing or transporting such items as beer, palm wine, grains, oils, butter, cosmetics, medicines, ink or dye solutions. Pots with perforations are used as sieves or as drying chambers for meat or fish; bowls with heavily incised interiors are used as grinders, and shallow dishes raised on stands can function as serving dishes or oil lamps. Pots for storing and cooling water are large, with little or no neck, for easy access and to allow the maximum surface area for evaporation. Vessels for transporting water, on the other hand, often have an elongated neck and sometimes a rim to minimize spillage. Other water containers can be made from gourds and, among nomadic peoples, of an entire animal skin, wood or closely sewn coiled basketry. The fibres of such baskets swell with the moisture to become virtually watertight, and the insides are coated with dried milk and are then smoked to increase impermeability. The San use ostrich eggshells as water containers. Such pots are not necessarily watertight, since seepage is a means of cooling the water inside. In Central Africa, especially large gourds or pots are also used in brewing beer, which is very important in social life.

107. Nupe water pot, ceramic and metal (?tin), h. 400 mm, from Bida, Nigeria (Washington, DC, National Museum of African Art)

Cooking vessels are usually either of earthenware or in the form of iron three-legged pots. The traditional earthenware pots are usually not elaborately decorated and generally have a round base, since they are designed to stand in a forked stick, on a ring-stand or on a traditional cooking hearth. Such hearths are made of a group of three stones, inverted pots (as among the Asante of Ghana), small shaped termitaries or moulded potter's clay, which hardens during use. Small charcoal stoves made from recycled oil drums have also become popular, especially in the less rural areas. The use of enamel basins as serving dishes has become common, although food is also served in bowls, dishes or trays made of earthenware, basketry, wood or gourd. For example, the Zulu have large, elaborately carved wooden meat dishes, while in eastern Africa a bride's trousseau may include decorated baskets and gourds made for serving her husband with his first meal in the new home and for subsequent special occasions.

Other culinary utensils include drinking straws covered with fine grass plaiting and ending in a fine bulbous strainer. These are used for drinking beer by the Interlacustrine peoples around Lake Victoria such as the Ganda. The pestle and mortar are almost ubiquitous, and sieves are used wherever yams or cassava are eaten, to sift the flour free of fibres; they are made of basketry with spaced elements or of perforated zinc or fine wire mesh on a wooden frame. Cleaning equipment generally comprises a hand broom, made of grass stems (with or without the feather heads), split palm leaves, a bunch of twigs or a bunch of stems with the leaves attached. Those made of grass or palm leaves are often carefully made and have a handle secured with ornamental plaiting. One unusual piece of cleaning equipment is the wash-table found among the Senufo of Côte d'Ivoire. It is shaped like an oblong-seated stool with four legs and made of hard, heavy wood so that it will not float in shallow water, and the women bang wet clothing on it.

BIBLIOGRAPHY

African Furniture and Household Objects (exh. cat. by R. Sieber, New York, Amer. Fed. A., 1980–81)

MARLA C. BERNS, MARGRET CAREY

15. Rock art.

(i) Introduction. (ii) Regional survey.

(i) Introduction. Rock art is widely distributed throughout the African continent in a number of independent traditions; some Southern African examples are among man's oldest artistic endeavour. Two principal techniques were employed: rock paintings, sometimes called pictographs, are almost exclusively found in shallow overhangs and rock shelters rather than in deep, underground caverns, as is Upper Palaeolithic art in Western Europe (*see* PREHISTORIC EUROPE, §II, 2); by contrast, rock engravings, or petroglyphs, made by incising and pecking, are found in open sites and in rock shelters. Incised engravings were cut through the patina, or outer skin, of rocks with a sharp stone implement. Pecked engravings were made by hammering the patina to remove it. Sometimes the engravers left part of the patina to represent features such as folds of skin or an eye and in some regions they polished the entire configuration.

African rock art research evinces two principal tendencies: interpretation of 'meaning', and formal chronological and geographical classification. At different times and for different regions of the continent one or other has predominated, although the desire to move beyond catalogues, counts and chronologies has seldom been fulfilled. Furthermore, since the 1980s there has been a shift away from various issues that were central to earlier rock art research. Formerly, much attention was accorded rock art as evidence for migrations, diffusions and cultural contacts. Often this evidence consisted merely of visual comparisons between arts from different cultures. Many students are now dubious about comparing superficial traits and prefer to seek the nature and social circumstances of any diffusions and contacts that may have taken place; the mere fact of contact tells us little. Another issue that has diminished in importance is that of artistic and cultural evolution. It was thought that art and society both evolved from simple, 'primitive' beginnings to more complex and sophisticated heights. Undoubtedly, art does change through time, but the technical simplicity of a work tells us little about the evolutionary status or the role of that work in its living social context. It follows from this that little can be gained from using Western notions and canons of art history to address prehistoric works.

(ii) Regional survey. Rock art regions are difficult to define, but the following are generally recognized (see fig. 108).

(a) North Africa. (b) Horn of Africa. (c) East Africa. (d) Southern Africa.

(a) North Africa. Most North African rock art is concentrated in the Saharan massifs of Adrar des Iforas, Tadrart Acacus, Tibesti, Ennedi, Hoggar and Tassili N' Ajjer. Further north, there is a considerable concentration in the Atlas Mountains. The proximity to the Iberian Peninsula of these northernmost depictions has raised questions of diffusion from Europe (*see* SPANISH LEVANTINE ROCK ART). Although there are some superficial points of similarity, most researchers now accept the African art as an independent tradition. Dating this tradition, or indeed any rock art, is notoriously difficult, however, and few reliable North African dates are available. Unlike organic archaeological finds, neither paintings nor engravings can be dated by radiometric methods. Most work is therefore based on the analysis of styles by superpositions. Despite these limitations and the debatable nature of some postulated stylistic sequences, four broad periods of Saharan rock art can be recognized: the *Bubalus antiquus* period; the 'Round Head' (or Bovidian) period; the Pastoral period; and the Post-Neolithic period.

Bubalus antiquus and Round Head periods. The earliest identified period of African rock art, termed *Bubalus antiquus*, comprises engravings of large game animals, including the eponymous extinct giant buffalo. These engravings are executed with remarkable élan. They are on rock walls outside shelters, where there is little hope of finding a connection between them and datable layers. However, F. Mori's work with an unusually indicative panel in the Acacus suggests that the engravings of this period belong to the Upper Pleistocene, more than 10,000 BP.

More is known about the Round Head period, a name bestowed by Abbé Breuil on account of the distinctive heads of many human figures. Rock art of this period mainly comprises paintings. Mori obtained a radiocarbon date of 8072±110 BP from samples of charcoal in a deposit that also contained fragments of a grindstone with traces of red and yellow pigment. Other excavations by B. Barich suggest an earlier date of 9080±70 BP (see Roset, 1984). It is, of course, difficult to link these dates to the paintings, but they do show the great length of occupation by hunter-gatherers. At this time the Sahara was experiencing a period of heavy rain; large lakes formed, and a Mediterranean type of vegetation prevailed.

The first human and animal depictions of this period are simple silhouettes, frequently with a darker outline. The later polychrome paintings are larger and have heavy, powerful shapes. Human figures often carry weapons such as spears, bows and other objects and have various body patterns (see fig. 109). They are usually drawn frontally, and their large heads merge with their bodies. The figures are frequently covered with networks of lines, chevrons, grids and rows of dots. Sometimes the heads are marked with semicircles and are crowned by lunate forms (see fig. 110). In the Tassili massif, one of the most remarkable of these is a painting of a striding woman in yellow ochre and white. The head has two large horns surrounded by dots. Beneath her is another, incomplete, female figure under a set of curving lines (see fig. 111). The animal depictions of this period, like those of the *Bubalus*, are of big game, sometimes very large and portrayed in awkward postures. Like the human figures, they are executed as outlined silhouettes. Among them are fantasy animals, bodiless hoofs and horns.

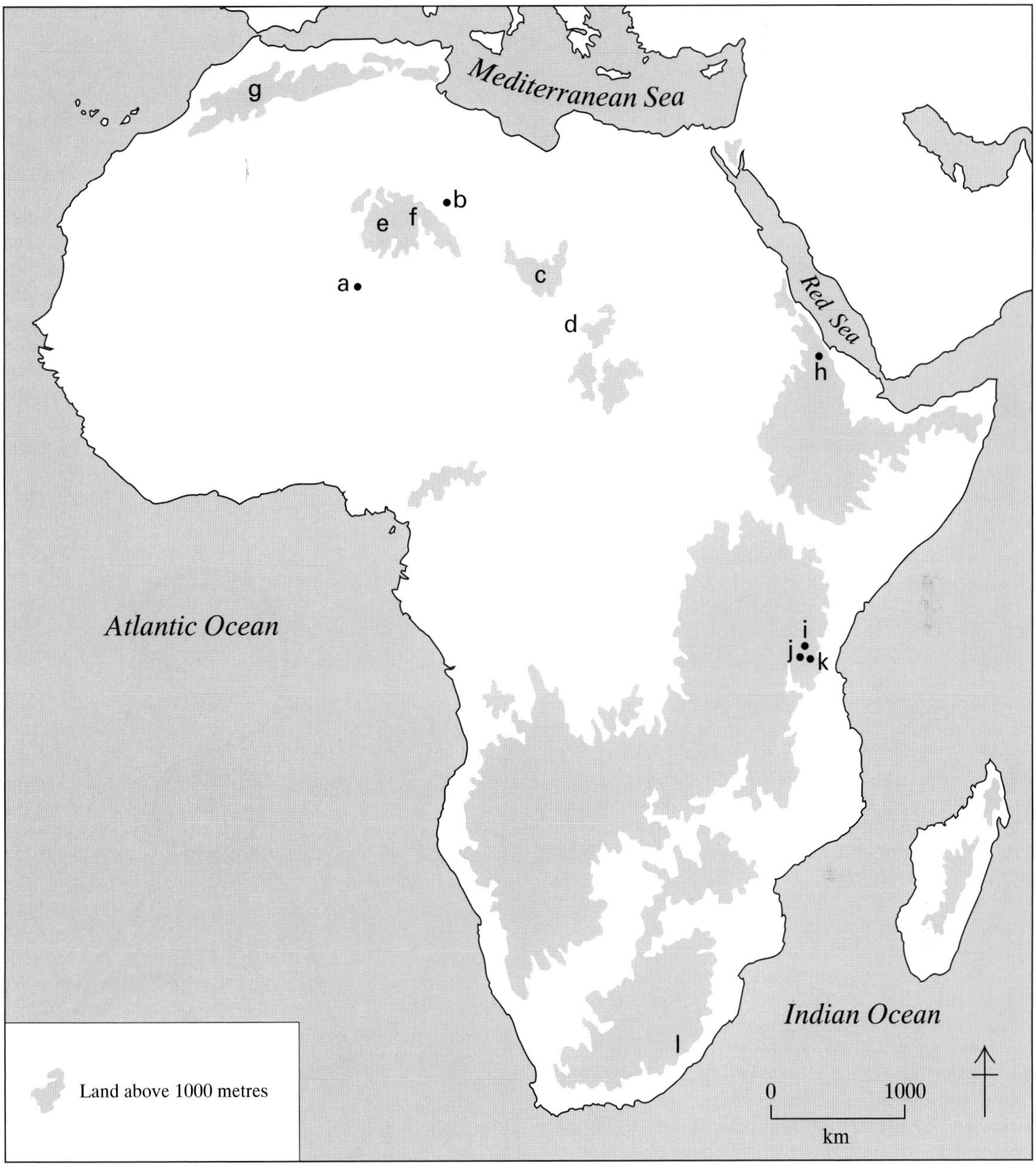

108. Map of Africa showing rock art sites: (a) Adrar des Iforas; (b) Tadrart Acacus; (c) Tibesti; (d) Ennedi; (e) Hoggar; (f) Tassili N' Ajjer; (g) Atlas Mountains; (h) Zeban Ona Libanos; (i) Kisese 2; (j) Fenga Hill; (k) Chungal 3; (l) Drakensberg

Because the paintings of both the *Bubalus* and the Round Head periods are ascribable to hunter-gatherers, and because the distinction between them is not clear, they may, for our purposes, be considered together. Recent research has developed a model of graphic depiction that appears to be applicable to both periods.

A widespread, perhaps universal, feature of hunter-gatherer religion is SHAMANISM: the exploitation of altered states of consciousness to gain access to the spirit world, to control animals and the weather and to cure the sick. Because the human nervous system is, of course, common to all people and has probably not changed much since the beginning of the Upper Palaeolithic, *c.* 30,000 BP, we can construct a generalized model of the experience of the altered state of consciousness known as trance. This model, derived from neuropsychological laboratory research, has been tested and found to fit known shamanistic arts. It can therefore be used to assess the content of arts not known *a priori* to be shamanistic.

Broadly speaking, the neuropsychological model identifies two stages through which people experience trance. In the first stage all people, irrespective of their cultural

109. North African rock painting of the Round Head period representing an archer, Sefar, Tassili N' Ajjer, Algeria

background, 'see' a range of luminous, geometric forms that pulsate, rotate, fragment and multiply in the visual field. These entoptic phenomena include grids, zigzags, sets of parallel lines, lunate forms and dots both in scintillating lines and in scatters. As the trance deepens, the culturally determined aspect increases. Entoptic phenomena persist but are now combined with true hallucinations, mainly of people, animals and emotionally charged objects. Accompanying these visual experiences are physical and aural hallucinations. People feel dissociated from their bodies; their bodies feel elongated and seem to have more digits and limbs than normal. They also hear sounds that they interpret as their culture directs them, for example rushing winds, waterfalls, crickets and bees.

If we apply this model to the art of the *Bubalus* and Round Head periods, we find not just one but a set of correspondences. Some of the body patterns may represent cicatrization, but others are more probably entoptic forms combined with human figures. Placed above the heads of some of these figures are lunate shapes and chevrons. Some are also surrounded by lines of dots, as are hallucinatory paintings in other cultures. These features lead us to believe that, like much hunter-gatherer rock art elsewhere, the art of these two periods contains a strong shamanistic element. However, the depictions were not necessarily executed by people actually in a trance. Rather, they were done subsequently upon recollection of such experiences. The rocks thus proclaim the reality of the other world and thereby underscore the status of the shamans, or medicine men, who were responsible for the well-being of the community and the renewal of nature.

Pastoral period. After the Round Head period there appears to have been a temporal hiatus during which new people settled in the Sahara. No transitional paintings have been found linking the Round Head period with the subsequent Pastoral period. The oldest date obtained by Mori for the Pastoral period is 7438±226 BP. A more recently obtained date for this period, 4730±310 BP, is particularly interesting because it was obtained from a hearth in a layer overlying a piece of fallen rock from the wall of the shelter; on it were painted two oxen (see Roset, 1984).

The pollen record suggests a comparatively humid climate at this time with conditions suitable for the keeping of large herds. This climatic condition and also, according to some writers, the Pastoral art, reached a turning point *c.* 6000 BP. Thereafter the climate became gradually drier and, although livestock keeping was still viable, xerophilous plants (i.e. plants adapted to extremely dry conditions) began to appear.

The herdsmen drawn into the Sahara during this climatically favourable period left behind them a wealth of striking art. Cattle are depicted singly and in large herds of up to a hundred. Mostly in profile and remarkably naturalistic, the creatures seem to move gracefully over the rock walls. There is also greater mastery of colour than in the Round Head period, the hide patterns of the cattle being faithfully reproduced. The presence of some fine

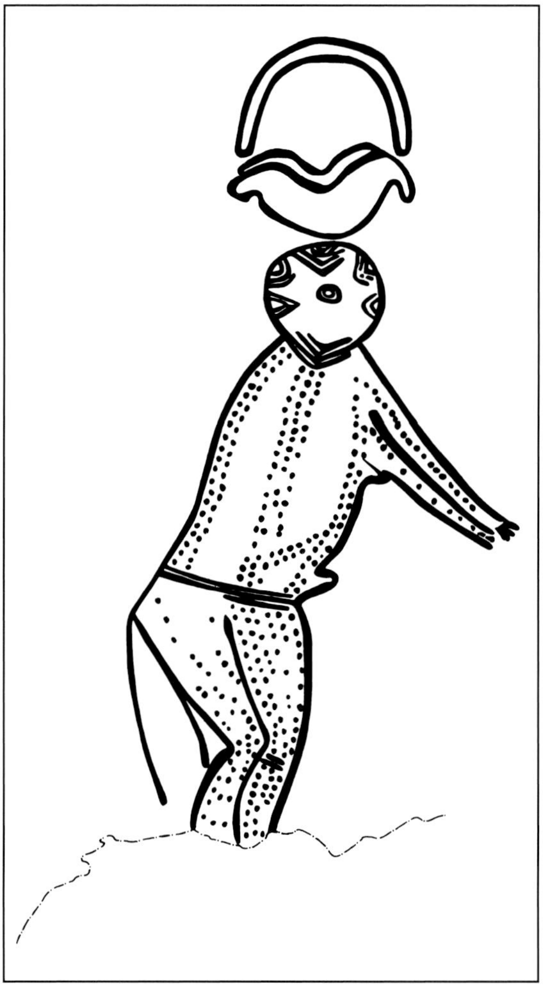

110. North African rock painting representing 'an ornate figure', Jabbanen, Tassili N' Ajjer, Algeria, Round Head period; redrawn from J. D. Lajoux, 1963, p. 57

111. North African rock painting representing 'a horned goddess', Aouanrhet, Tassili N' Ajjer, Algeria, Round Head period; redrawn from H. Lhote, 1959, fig. 35

engravings possibly indicates that the artists first scratched the outlines of the cattle before they coloured them.

Composed scenes also first appeared in the Pastoral period. What seem to be scenes of daily life abound. Figures are seated or recumbent, apparently dancing, hunting, herding cattle and fighting with bows and arrows. The basic shamanistic elements of Round Head-period rock art seem to be absent in the Pastoral phase, or at any rate far less prominent, but mundane interpretations cannot account for all images. For instance, the remarkable two-headed cows of Tassili would fit a hallucinatory context, as confirmed by both San and North American Shoshone shamanistic rock art. Similarly, some of the 'camp scenes' may depict rituals, as do many of the scenes in San rock art.

A ritual interpretation for the Pastoral period paintings has been strengthened by a Fulani man, Amadou Hampaté Ba, who interpreted copies of the paintings as pre-Islamic depictions of initiation rituals (see A. Hampaté Ba and Dieterlen). The Fulani have been thought to be the descendants of Saharan pastoralists who moved south as the desert dried out. Today they live nomadic lives in the basins of the Senegal and Niger rivers. One of the details on which Ba commented was the calf-rope that features so prominently in the art. He explained that this rope is used during the initiation of herdsmen and is considered sacred as it symbolizes the lifeline of the herd. Similarly, the herdsman's staff, also depicted in the art, is presented to initiates as part of the rituals and is used in oath swearing. A ceremony possibly associated with the paintings of two-headed animals is the ritual purification of cattle. Ba explained that on the rare occasion when a calf is born with two heads it is kept alive and then sacrificed during this ritual. If such an animal is not available, an effigy is made out of two cattle skins. Although there are, of course, objections to using modern informants to explain prehistoric art, Ba's interpretations suggest that we may at the very least be dealing with two similar, or cognate, belief systems.

Post-Neolithic period. The Pastoral period was followed by the Post-Neolithic period. Although there were moister times between 3500 and 3000 BP and again between 2500 and 2000 BP, the Sahara was becoming increasingly desiccated. In the Post-Neolithic period cattle are absent from the art, but there are depictions of camels, horses, chariots and shields as well as simple inscriptions. These paintings are generally less animated than those of the Pastoral period. Some depictions have been used in plotting migration and trail routes, but subsequent finds cast doubt on the conclusions.

The creators of this final phase of North African rock art have not been clearly identified. It is possible that the paintings were made not by the newcomers represented in the art but by small pastoral groups who remained in the Sahara. Certainly, the continued depiction of giraffe, elephant and lion (and the vegetation with which these species are associated) suggests that some pastoralism was still possible.

(b) Horn of Africa. Connections between the Saharan rock art and that found in the Horn of Africa (Somalia, Ethiopia and Eritrea) have been suggested (see Willcox, 1984), but the exact nature of these connections has not been established. In this area, it seems that pre-pastoral, hunter–gatherer art is absent for unknown reasons. The earliest art depicts cattle and people relatively naturalistically but to a much lesser degree than in the Saharan massifs. Clark (1954) tentatively dates the earliest art to *c.* 2000 BP; certainly, it must post-date the first appearance of cattle in the area during the preceding millennium. Like the Saharan cattle, those depicted in the Horn are long-horned and humpless, although the only cattle now in the area are humped zebu.

The Abbé Breuil attempted to define a series of eight successive styles, but subsequent writers have been unable to discern his groupings. Others have discovered what they believe to be affinities with San rock art. At Zeban Ona Libanos, for example, there are simplified human figures with spears and shields and a milking scene.

In addition to the paintings there are a number of petroglyph sites. The engravings depict human beings with shields and spears, cattle, camels and some geometric motifs. Many of these are thought to be no older than the 4th century AD.

The principal interest in the rock art of the Horn of Africa has been from a diffusionist perspective. Citing comparable stone industries from North Africa to the Cape and the fact that human figures tend to be less naturalistic than animals, some writers have postulated a diffusion route from Spain through the Sahara to the Cape with the Horn of Africa as an intermediate region. This view, however, has been seriously questioned by evidence considered below.

(c) East Africa. The rock art of Tanzania, Uganda, Kenya and Malawi, the next stage south on the supposed diffusion route, may be divided into two broad phases or groups: hunter–gatherer art and Iron Age art. As elsewhere, the dating of East African rock art is questionable and vague. At Kisese 2, in Tanzania, Inskeep (1962) uncovered 6 m of deposit. Red ochre, some pieces of which were faceted by wear, and 'palettes' on which ochre had been ground were found above the 29,000 BP level. In addition, rock spalls with paint were found in a layer said to be earlier than 8000 BP. A larger piece of rock with red and white paintings has been dated to *c.* 1500 BP. On the other hand, E. ten Raa shows that the Sandawe-speaking hunter-gatherers of this region were painting as late as the 20th century. The largely red hunter-gatherer paintings show closer affinities with San art to the south than with that of either the Sahara or the Horn of Africa. Mary Leakey, who remarks on this point, has recorded much Tanzanian rock art.

The neuropsychological model that suggested shamanistic elements in the Sahara can also be applied to the art of East Africa. In this area there are painted forms, some of which have been interpreted as traps, that conform to entoptic phenomena. These include dots, undulating lines, sets of short dashes and 'sun' images. The blending of entoptic shapes with human and animal forms, characteristic of a deep stage of trance, is also found (see fig. 112). Moreover, human and animal features are combined in therianthropic depictions, and there are distortions of the human form that can be explained as somatic hallucinations. These include elongations and 'hairiness'. Even more interesting are distortions of the human head that resemble the Round Head figures of the Sahara. (Persons in trance speak of the head appearing to swell and of marked tingling sensations in the scalp.)

The hallucinatory interpretation of these forms is greatly strengthened by other features. The art depicts dancers bending forward. San shamans speak of their stomach muscles contracting and so causing them to adopt this posture as their potency 'boils' in their stomachs. Tanzanian paintings also show short dashes falling from the noses of some figures (see fig. 113). For the rock art of Southern Africa this has been identified as the nasal haemorrhage experienced by San shamans as they enter trance. Some San shamans enter trance so violently that they execute a complete somersault. This probably accounts for the inverted figures in both San and Tanzanian rock art that appear to be cavorting around animals.

This shamanistic interpretation of East African hunter–gatherer art may well be correct, for there is evidence of an ecstatic 'spirit possession' cult among the Sandawe-speaking people that may have fulfilled a role comparable to the trance dance in San society.

Post-dating the hunter–gatherer art is a distinct series of thick white paintings that appear to have been done with a finger. They include zoomorphic figures, sometimes spreadeagled, birds and geometric forms such as dots, crosses and circles containing an inverted Y-shape. It is now known that many of these 'late whites', as they are often known, were connected with the Nyau societies. The Nyau are a society of male masked dancers who perform at funeral rites and female initiation ceremonies.

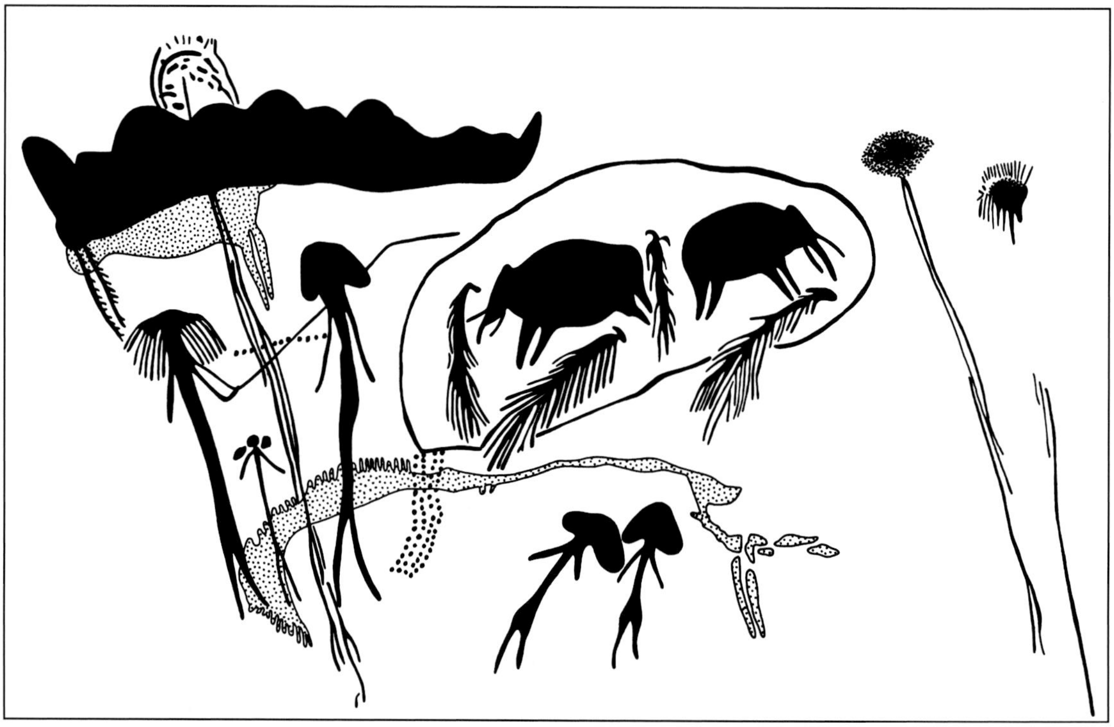

112. East African rock painting representing elephants, human figures and entoptic phenomena, Fenga Hill, Tanzania, hunter–gatherer phase; redrawn from H. A. Fosbrooke, 1950, pl. IIIB

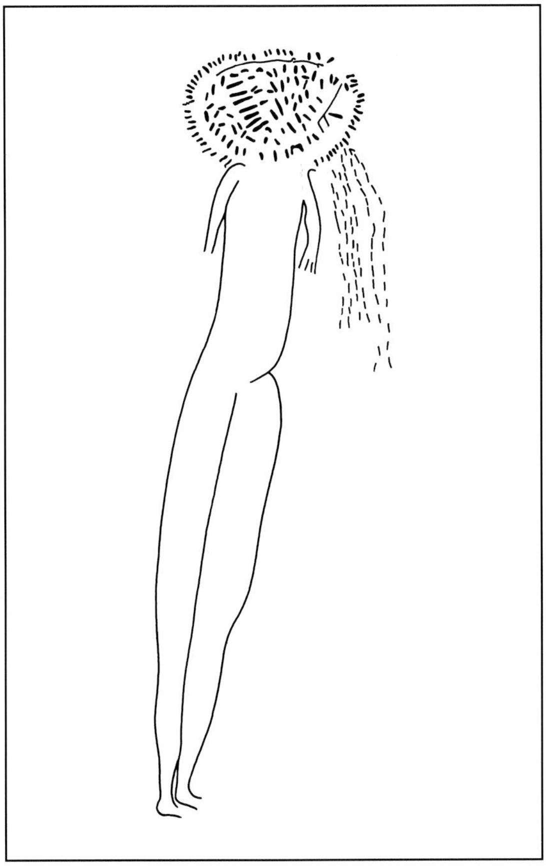

113. East African rock painting representing 'a shaman in trance bleeding from the nose', Chungal 3, Tanzania, hunter–gatherer phase; redrawn from M. Leakey, 1983, pl. 44

Some Nyau paintings mark the hiding places of masks and animal effigies used in the dance, and they also indicate meeting places for initiates. The paintings depict dancers and creatures associated with the ritual. The spreadeagled forms, for instance, probably depict crocodiles and mythical reptiles. Most Nyau paintings are associated with the Chewa and are found in Malawi. Similar paintings are known in Zambia. In Kenya, white geometric designs have been interpreted as depictions of cattle brands. These are associated with the Maasai warriors' practice of meat-feasting at sites distant from open-air settlements.

(d) Southern Africa. South of the Zambezi lies one of the richest areas of rock art in Africa, not only in the number of sites and depictions but also in the detail and elegance of the works. Although a fundamental distinction exists elsewhere in Africa between the art of hunter-gatherers and that of pastoralists or agriculturalists, in Southern Africa most depictions can be confidently ascribed to San hunter-gatherers. Some may have been made by the pastoral Khoi (Hottentots) and, in restricted areas, by mixed-farming Bantu-speaking groups.

SAN art is among the best understood hunter-gatherer rock art in the world because there is a considerable body of relevant ethnography—a vital component lacking for all the regions so far discussed. Some of the ethnography was collected in the 19th century and is thus contemporary with the last painters. The rest comes from the modern San of the Kalahari Desert. Striking correspondences between these two bodies of ethnography show that the San over a vast geographical area and probably for many millennia shared a fundamental cognitive system irrespective of local variations.

This system of belief derives from a shamanistic view of the world. The principal ritual, the trance or medicine dance, affords shamans access to the spirit world. Clapping, singing, hyperventilation and intense concentration induce trance. In this state the shamans cure the sick, drive off evil spirits and malign shamans in feline form, make rain and control antelope herds. San art depicts these activities as well as symbols of the supernatural potency harnessed by the shamans and the bizarre hallucinations they experience (*see* SAN, fig. 2). Trance imagery includes geometric entoptic forms, rain-animals, feline shamans and shamans blended with animal power in therianthropic figures. Apart from these 'non-realistic' elements, much San rock art is noteworthy for its remarkable portrayals of animals. In Zimbabwe graceful giraffes and kudu with finely drawn horns abound. Further south the eland predominates. This, the largest antelope, is, in the south-eastern mountains, depicted in the shaded polychrome technique many writers consider the apogee of all African rock art (*see* SAN, fig. 1). The red and white paint is delicately shaded to suggest the contours of the animal's body, and details, such as ears, mouth and cloven hoofs, are immaculately drawn. Some of the Saharan paintings show animals looking round; in the south, however, eland are drawn in every conceivable posture with an exceptional mastery of technique.

Also in the San area, there are complex scenes involving many individual depictions. They portray dances, fights, hunts (though much less frequently than often supposed) and rows of figures with their hunting equipment. The late 19th-century paintings sometimes show the conflict with the White colonists that effected the demise of the southern San. These apparently narrative scenes seem to argue for a literal component; however, on closer inspection, details can be found relating to religion and trance.

Unlike the Saharan and East African art, distinct periods are difficult to discern in any of the Southern African regions. None of the elaborate stylistic sequences that have been proposed stands up to scrutiny, although it appears that the shaded polychromes of the south-eastern mountains date from *c.* 1750.

BIBLIOGRAPHY

H. A. Winkler: *The Rock-drawings of Southern Upper Egypt* (London, 1938–9)

H. A. Fosbrooke: 'Tanganyika Rock Paintings', *Tanganyika Notes & Rec.*, xix (1950), pp. 1–61

J. D. Clark: *The Prehistoric Cultures of the Horn of Africa* (Cambridge, 1954)

H. Lhote: *The Search for the Tassili Frescoes* (London, 1959)

R. Summers, ed.: *Prehistoric Rock Art of the Federation of Rhodesia and Nyasaland* (Salisbury, 1959)

R. R. Inskego: 'The Age of the Kondoa Rock Paintings in the Light of Recent Excavations at Kiese II Rock Shelter', *Proceedings of the Fourth Panafrican Congress on Prehistory* (Tervuren, 1962), pp. 249–56

J. D. Lajoux: *The Rock Paintings of Tassili* (London, 1963)

F. Mori: *Tadrart Acacus* (Turin, 1965)

A. Hampaté Ba and G. Dieterlen: 'Les Fresques d'époque bovidienne du Tassili N'Ajjer et les traditions des Peul: Hypothèses d'interprétation', *J. Soc. Africanistes*, xxxci (1966), pp. 141–57
P. Hellstrom: *The Rock Drawings*, i of *Scandinavian Joint Expedition to Sudanese Nubia* (Odense, 1970)
H. Pager: *Ndedema* (Graz, 1971)
E. ten Raa: 'Dead Art and Living Society: A Study of Rock Paintings in a Social Context', *Mankind*, viii (1971), pp. 42–58
P. Cervicek: *Felsbilder des Nord-Etbai, Oberägyptens und Unternubiens* (Wiesbaden, 1974)
J. H. Chaplin: 'The Prehistoric Rock Art of the Lake Victoria Region', *Azania*, ix (1974), pp. 1–50
F. Mori: 'The Earliest Saharan Rock-engravings', *Antiquity*, xlviii (1974), pp. 87–92
R. M. Gramly: 'Meat-feasting Sites and Cattle Brands: Patterns of Rock-shelter Utilisation in East Africa', *Azania*, x (1975), pp. 107–21
H. Nowak, S. Ortner and D. Ortner: *Felsbilder der spanischen Sahara* (Graz, 1975)
D. W. Phillipson: *The Prehistory of Eastern Zambia* (Nairobi, 1976)
P. Vinnicombe: *People of the Eland* (Pietermaritzburg, 1976)
W. E. Wendt: ' "Art Mobilier" from Apollo 11 Cave, South West Africa: Africa's Oldest Dated Works of Art', *S. Afr. Archaeol. Bull.*, xxxi (1976), pp. 5–11
D. W. Phillipson: *The Later Prehistory of Eastern and Southern Africa* (London, 1977)
N. E. Lindgren and J. M. Schoffeleers: *Rock Art and Nyau Symbolism in Malawi* (Limbe, 1978)
J. D. Lewis-Williams: *Believing and Seeing: Symbolic Meanings in Southern San Rock Paintings* (London, 1981)
M. Leakey: *Africa's Vanishing Art: The Rock Paintings of Tanzania* (London, 1983)
W. Davis: 'Representation and Knowledge in the Prehistoric Rock Art of Africa', *Afr. Archaeol. Rev.*, ii (1984), pp. 7–35
J.-P. Roset: 'The Prehistoric Rock Paintings of the Sahara', *Endeavour*, viii (1984), pp. 75–84
A. R. Willcox: *The Rock Art of Africa* (Johannesburg, 1984)
P. Garlake: *The Painted Caves: An Introduction to the Prehistoric Art of Zimbabwe* (Harare, 1987)
J. D. Lewis-Williams: 'Beyond Style and Portrait: A Comparison of Tanzanian and Southern African Rock Art', *Contemp. Stud. Khoisan*, ii (1987), pp. 93–139
J. D. Lewis-Williams and T. A. Dowson: *Images of Power: Understanding Bushman Rock Art* (Johannesburg, 1989)
T. A. Dowson: *Rock Engravings of Southern Africa* (Johannesburg, 1992)

J. D. LEWIS-WILLIAMS

VII. Regions.

1. Northern Africa. 2. North-east Africa. 3. Western Sudan. 4. Guinea Coast. 5. Western Equatoria. 6. Central Africa. 7. East Africa. 8. Southern Africa.

1. NORTHERN AFRICA. Region to the north of the Sahara desert comprising the modern states of EGYPT, LIBYA, TUNISIA, ALGERIA, MOROCCO, WESTERN SAHARA and MAURITANIA (see fig. 114). Northern Africa shares the geography, climate, flora and fauna of the Mediterranean basin. Moreover, the sea was traditionally less of a barrier to the movement of men, materials and ideas than was the Sahara, although from early times important routes across the desert were established along the Nile Valley in the east and from Morocco to the Niger in the west. The southern border of the Mediterranean zone has been defined (see Braudel) as the limit of cultivation of wheat, grapes and olives; this line coincides with the northernmost limit of the compact palm grove. The close cultural ties between Northern Africa and southern Europe cannot be overemphasized: the straight-line distance between Tunis (anc. Carthage) and Rome, for example, is only 600 km.

(i) History. The history of Northern Africa over at least the last two millennia is known with remarkable precision, although most of the documents and all the histories were written by foreigners. The record of the arts in Northern Africa is equally rich and continuous, but it is normally studied in the discrete disciplines of prehistoric archaeology, ancient and Classical archaeology (*see* EGYPT, ANCIENT; GREECE, ANCIENT; and ROME, ANCIENT), EARLY CHRISTIAN AND BYZANTINE ART, ISLAMIC ART and archaeology and anthropology.

People later known as the Capsians or Proto-Mediterraneans appeared in the Maghrib (Maghreb, Magreb; a

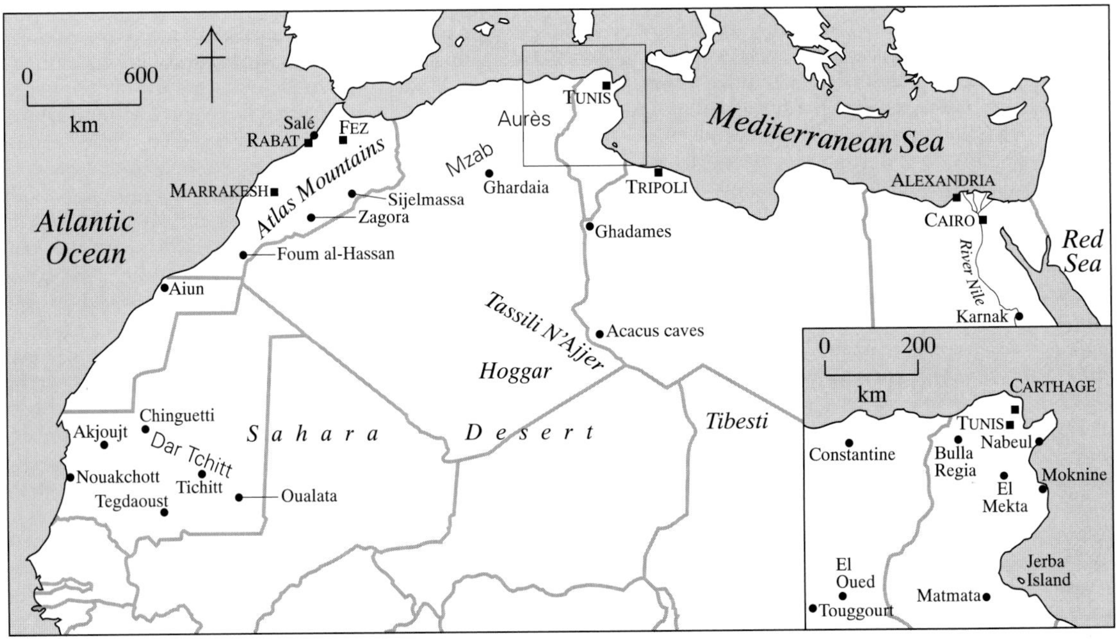

114. Map of Africa, northern regions; those sites with separate entries in this dictionary are distinguished by CROSS-REFERENCE TYPE

115. Mosaic pavement depicting *Ulysses and the Sirens*, 1.30×3.44 m, from Dougga, Tunisia, 3rd century AD (Tunis, Musée National du Bardo)

collective term often applied to Tunisia, Algeria and Morocco; from the Arabic word for 'west') in the 9th or 8th millennium BC. Rock engravings and sculptures with representations of elephants, rhinoceroses, giraffes and buffaloes have been found at sites such as El Mekta (near Gafsa, Tunisia); they date from the 7th millennium BC. The artefacts of settled agriculturalists and pastoralists (5th millennium BC) show evidence of stone-polishing, pottery-making and the use of grains. Megalithic cemeteries have been found with dolmens and sepulchral chambers carved into the rock. An inscription from Karnak, Egypt (*c.* 1220 BC), mentions the Libyans, one of the names for this indigenous population, later also known as Berber.

In the 9th century BC Phoenician traders from Tyre founded Carthage, which by the 6th century BC was the largest and richest city in the western Mediterranean, trading in tin from Cornwall, gold from West Africa, ivory from Central Africa and textiles (*see* PUNIC ART). In 146 BC the Romans invaded Northern Africa, destroyed Carthage, and made nearby Utica the capital of a new Roman province, which supplied Italy with wheat, wine and olive oil. The large estates of absentee landlords contrasted with the smaller holdings of settlers, who pressed further south and came increasingly in conflict with the semi-nomadic Berbers in their mountain retreats. In the 2nd and 3rd centuries AD Roman civilization spread from the cities, and great public monuments and baths were erected. In 439 AD, the Germanic Vandals seized Carthage and introduced Aryan Christianity. The first Muslim invasions took place in the 640s, and KAIROUAN, the first Muslim settlement west of the Nile, was established in the 670s. Carthage fell definitively in 698 (*see also* CARTHAGE, §§1, 2 and 3). After a century of direct control by caliphs, the region became increasingly self-governing from the late 8th century until about the mid-13th, when it again came under external rule. In the late 16th century Libya, Tunisia and much of Algeria became provinces of the Ottoman empire, while Morocco remained independent under the Sharifs. France, Germany, Italy and Spain gained colonies in the region and maintained them until independence was won in the 20th century.

(ii) Architecture, arts and crafts. Architecture has always been the most important art form in Northern Africa in the historical period. Public buildings were normally built of stone, which was easily quarried throughout the region, although unbaked and baked brick has also been used since Punic times (*c.* 3rd century BC) when stone was unavailable or impracticable. The building techniques and types generally belong to the Mediterranean traditions of trabeated stone construction roofed with wood, although vaulting was occasionally used, as in the early Islamic buildings from Sousse, Tunisia, or the more recent ones of the 10th century AD up to the 20th in the Mzab district of Algeria. The variety of religions followed in Northern Africa gave rise to a corresponding diversity of religious architecture, but congregational buildings, whether basilicas or mosques, were often hypostyle structures. Houses, as throughout the Mediterranean region, are single- or multi-storey, with rooms grouped around an open court. Variants include the houses of Bulla Regia, Tunisia (2nd–3rd centuries AD), with a subterranean level for relief from the summer heat; the troglodyte houses of Matmata, Tunisia, which have a circular pit serving as a court with chambers excavated in its walls; and the *ksour* of the north-western Sahara, which are Berber fortified farming villages with dwellings of rammed earth or unbaked brick.

Rock paintings at sites such as Tassili, Algeria (6th–2nd millennia BC), are the earliest examples of the visual arts in the region, while the most important and extensive are the thousands of mosaic pavements of Roman North Africa (*in situ* and in collections, e.g. Algiers, Mus. N. Ant.; Tunis, Mus. N. Bardo; see fig. 115). The earliest mosaic pavements at Carthage (?5th century BC) suggest that the mosaic technique may have been derived from *pavimenta punica*, in which mortar pavements were inlaid with bits of stone or glass. Black-and-white mosaics, based on Italian models, appeared in the 1st century AD, but the finest and most elaborate, which illustrate scenes of mythology and everyday life in many colours of marble, stone and glass tesserae, date from between the 3rd century and the 5th. The mosaic technique continued to be used under Christian patronage for tombs and church pavements but seems to have been abandoned soon after the coming of Islam.

Punic terracotta figurines (4th or 3rd century BC; Tunis, Bardo Mus.) show modes of representation based on the Greek or Egyptian models that had been imported into the region. Representational sculptures in terracotta, marble, limestone and other materials were produced throughout the Roman period; a few unusual figural sculptures were produced in Tunisia in the 10th and 11th centuries. These include a marble relief of a seated prince holding a cup (Tunis, Bardo Mus.). In the Islamic period tombstones and stucco revetments were decorated with geometric, plant and epigraphic sculptural designs. Some of the finest ceramics of antiquity, red wares with moulded decoration known as *terra sigillata*, were made over a long period in Tunisia and exported widely. Islam brought with it new ceramic techniques, including glazing and overglaze painting with metallic oxides to create a lustre effect. Lustre tiles were used in the mid-9th-century surround of the mihrab in the Great Mosque of Kairouan, but pavements and dados of glazed ceramic tile, one of the most characteristic features of western Islamic architecture, did not appear until the 11th century.

The Phoenicians may have introduced the eastern vertical loom to North Africa, and the Romans may also have introduced textile techniques, but the earliest fine weaving in the region is a textile inscribed with the name of the Umayyad caliph Marwan II (*reg* AD 744–50). Fine woollens were made from early Islamic times in many of the coastal cities (*see* ISLAMIC ART, §VI, 2(i)(c)), and, during the reign of al-Ma'mun (*reg* 813–33), 120 large carpets were sent from Tunisia to Baghdad in part-payment of taxes. North African woven and decorated textiles were eventually surpassed by those from Turkey and Iran, but the traditional textiles of Tunisia and Morocco, ranging from the exquisite silk embroideries of Fez to the sturdy carpets of Kairouan, have come to be highly appreciated. The traditional floor coverings in mosques are reed mats, and basketry is widely practised, particularly, for example, at Nabeul in Tunisia.

The arts of the book, including binding, calligraphy and illumination, became extraordinarily important in the Islamic period (*see* ISLAMIC ART, §III), as is clear from the exquisitely tooled leather bindings and fine parchment of a large collection of Koran manuscripts (*c.* 9th and 10th centuries; Kairouan, Great Mosque, Library). Glassmaking, probably also introduced by the Phoenicians, continued into the Islamic period, although Northern Africa was never a major centre of glass manufacture. Metals, including gold, copper alloys and lead, were used to make a wide range of tools, boxes, mirrors and jewellery and to mint coins from Punic times. Wood-carving and joinery, for which ample supplies of timber were to hand from the forests of North African mountains, were important throughout the Islamic period. The major congregational mosques have wooden minbars (pulpits) and *maqṣūra*s (enclosed area reserved for the sovereign, often marked by a screen). The earliest, among them that of Kairouan (mid-9th century), relied entirely on the effects of carving and turning, while later examples introduced colour effects through the use of marquetry in other woods and ivory.

The art of the region in colonial and post-colonial times is discussed in entries on individual countries.

BIBLIOGRAPHY

F. Braudel: *La Méditerranée et le monde méditerranéen à l'époque de Philippe II* (Paris, 1966); Eng. trans. by S. Reynolds as *The Mediterranean and the Mediterranean World in the Age of Philip II* (New York, 1972)
A. Laroui: *L'Histoire du Maghreb: Un Essai de synthèse* (Paris, 1970); Eng. trans. as *The History of the Maghrib: An Interpretive Essay* (Princeton, 1977)
D. Hill and L. Golvin: *Islamic Architecture in North Africa* (London, 1976)
From the Far West: Carpets and Textiles of Morocco (exh. cat. by P. L. Fiske, W. R. Pickering and R. S. Yohe, Washington, DC, Textile Mus., 1980)
De Carthage à Kairouan: 2000 ans d'art et d'histoire en Tunisie (exh. cat., Paris, Petit Pal., 1982–3)
I. Reswick: *Traditional Textiles of Tunisia and Related North African Weavings* (Los Angeles, 1985)
Carthage: A Mosaic of Ancient Tunisia (exh. cat., ed. A. B. A. Ben Khader and D. Soren; New York, Amer. Mus. Nat. Hist., 1987)
De l'empire romain aux villes impériales: 6000 ans d'art au Maroc (exh. cat., Paris, Petit Pal., 1990)

JONATHAN M. BLOOM

2. NORTH-EAST AFRICA. Region comprising the modern states of SUDAN, ETHIOPIA, Eritrea, DJIBUTI and SOMALIA (see fig. 116). Prehistoric art includes cave paintings depicting animals and figures (e.g. in Somalia), but the later dominant cultural and artistic traditions in the region are associated with two world religions: Islam in much of Sudan, in parts of Ethiopia and in Djibuti and Somalia; and Christianity in highland Ethiopia and, in vestigial forms, as late as the 15th century in NUBIA in the Sudan. In ancient times, Egyptian culture (*see* EGYPT, ANCIENT) impacted strongly on Nubia, as did the pre-Islamic civilization of South Arabia on Ethiopian or Aksumite culture (named after the city of AKSUM). Imported traditions were gradually assimilated to indigenous models, giving rise to quite independent and distinctive cultures. Sudan and Ethiopia, however, exhibit a wide degree of ethnic diversity, and some of their peoples, such as the NUBA in the Sudan and many of the Oromo in Ethiopia, have maintained their own artistic traditions.

Archaeology provides the sole evidence for the art of ancient Nubia and ancient Ethiopia. Monumental architecture and, to a lesser degree, pottery and metalwork have survived, but painting or sculpture in more perishable materials have not. The art and architecture of ancient Nubia or MEROË are clearly derived from those of ancient Egypt, but are sufficiently different to be considered as more than a mere provincial aberration. Distinctively Meroitic art dates from the 3rd century BC to around the beginning of the 4th century AD and is mostly known from monumental sculpture, both in the round and in relief, representing either royal persons and their activities or divine figures. In Ethiopia, too, the earliest examples of monumental architecture, such as the temple at Yeha, date from the last centuries BC and exhibit a South Arabian style, with a massive rectangular construction of fine ashlar masonry on a stepped plinth. The architecture of Aksum, dating from the first centuries AD, is somewhat different and probably represents an indigenous development from the older South Arabian tradition. Typical of Aksumite monuments are the famous obelisks or stelae, which faithfully copy in a single block of stone multi-storey

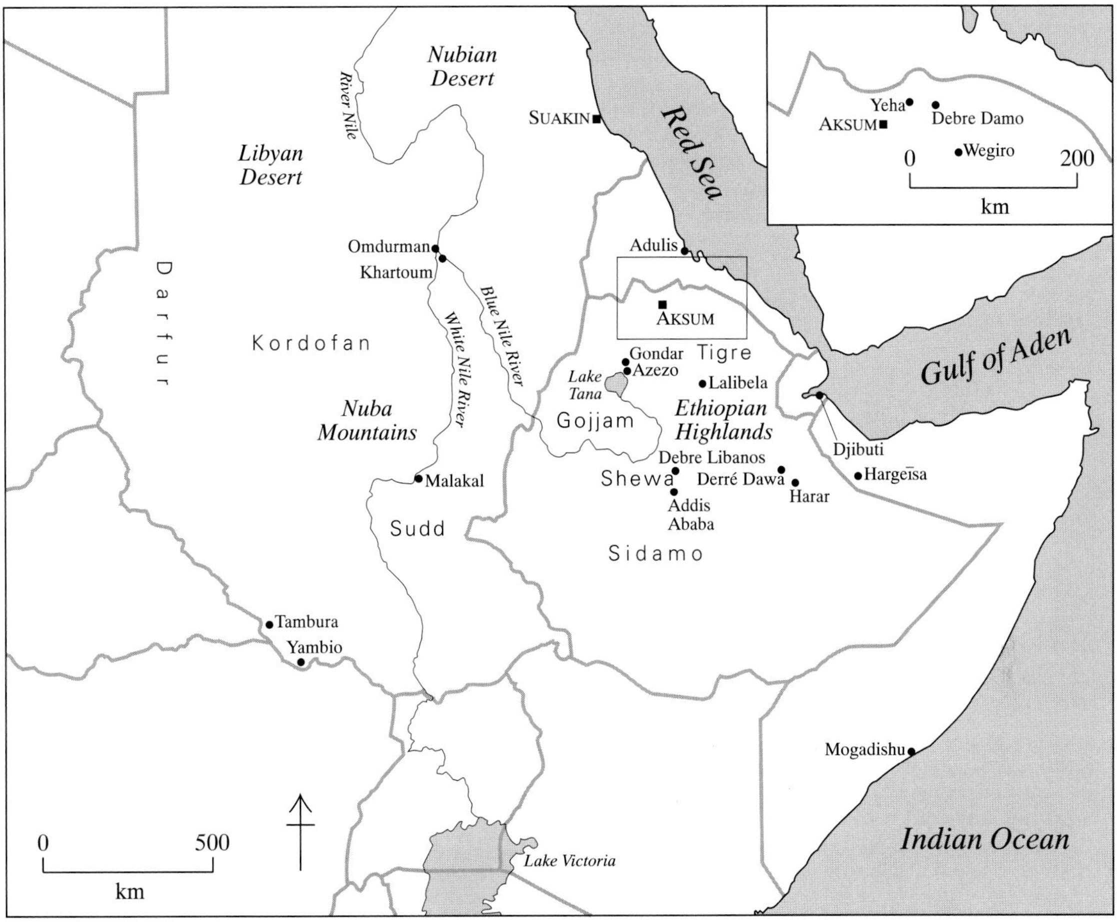

116. Map of North-east Africa; those sites with separate entries in this dictionary are distinguished by CROSS-REFERENCE TYPE

constructions with features such as door- and window-frames, protruding beams and corner joists (*see also* ETHIOPIA, §III). This architectural style was still in use in Ethiopia many centuries later, for example in the monastic church at Debre Damo (*c.* 11th century).

Christianity, adopted in both Ethiopia (mid-4th century) and Nubia, brought with it new artistic styles and genres. Paintings, on walls, on panels or as manuscript illuminations, were from then on all purely religious in content. Only wall paintings, such as those at the ruined cathedral at FARAS, survive from Christian Nubia (*see also* NUBIA, §VI). From Ethiopia, where Christianity still flourishes, examples of manuscript painting in illustrated Gospels and lives of saints, painted panels and murals are extant. The earliest Ethiopian Christian painting (13th and 14th centuries), though clearly derived from Syria and Armenia, as well as from Coptic Egypt, exhibits characteristics of its own, such as a marked tendency towards geometric design (for a 17th-century example see fig. 117). Like other Eastern Christian art, Ethiopian religious painting was highly conservative, developing markedly only in response to contacts with Western Europe, notably from the late 15th century to the early 17th, which gave rise to the Gondarene style, adopted in and around the old capital and cultural centre of GONDAR (*see also* ETHIOPIA, §II). In early Ethiopian church architecture (*see* ETHIOPIA, §I) a simplified basilican plan along the lines of Eastern Christian models became the standard form and persisted until the 19th century, when a circular plan became the norm in all but the north of the country. A remarkable development was the rock-cut church, the most famous examples being at Lalibela. Like the Aksumite obelisks, these faithfully imitate in stone constructions built of other materials. Also typical of Ethiopian Christian art is fine, pierced metalwork in the form of crosses, both hand-held and processional, and other church furniture and appurtenances such as thuribles and chalices.

In regions where Islam became the dominant religion different influences are detectable. For example, in the coastal towns of Somalia, such as Mogadishu, and in Harar, the centre of Ethiopian Islam, a tradition exists of complex and intricate geometrical carving in wood and stone belonging to the Azanian complex that extends down the East African coast as far as Mozambique. The Arab quarters of Mogadishu, which were once walled, contain mostly one- and two-storey stone houses. In north-western Somalia are the ruins of stone-built towns that flourished in the 15th and 16th centuries: porcelain,

117. Ethiopian illumination depicting *St Mark*, 268×249 mm, from a Gospel book, Lasta, 17th century (London, British Library, BM Or. 516, fol. 64*v*)

pottery, glass, metal and stone remains attest to their prosperity and to trading links with Egypt and western, Central and East Asia.

Much traditional or folk art in North-east Africa is concentrated in essentially portable personal and domestic objects, such as fabrics, weaving, bead- and needlework, leatherwork, basketwork, copper, silver and gold jewellery and metalwork, wood-carving and wood-engraving. Ivory-carving is widespread in Sudan. Dwellings among pastoral and agricultural communities may be made of clay, sun-dried mud, brick, branches, cow-dung plaster, mats and skins; conical thatched roofs are found among the sedentary agriculturalists of Somalia. Often, however, the artistic impulse, in settled as well as in semi-nomadic and pastoral societies, finds freer expression in language and oral literature than in visual art.

A notable form of artistic expression in North-east Africa is popular secular painting in Ethiopia, increasingly important since the beginning of the 20th century. These paintings, usually on canvas, often either illustrate events in recent history such as battles, splendid official ceremonies or scenes of everyday life or portray in strip-cartoon form the story of the Ethiopian national epic of King Solomon and the Queen of Sheba.

The art of the region in colonial and post-colonial times is discussed in entries on individual countries.

BIBLIOGRAPHY

P. L. Shinnie: *Meroe: A Civilization of the Sudan*, Ancient Peoples and Places (London, 1967)

G. Gerster: *Kirchen im Fels* (Stuttgart, 1968; Eng. trans., London, 1970; Ger. rev. Zurich and Freiburg im Breisgau, 1972)

D. Buxton: *The Abyssinians*, Ancient Peoples and Places (London, 1970)

S. Chojnacki: *Major Themes in Ethiopian Painting: Indigenous Developments, the Influence of Foreign Models and their Adaptation (from the 13th to the 19th Century)*, Äthiopische Forschungen (Stuttgart, 1983)

Somalia in Word and Image (exh. cat. by K. S. Loughran, J. L. Loughran, J. W. Johnson and S. S. Samatar, Washington, DC, Found. Cross Cult. Understanding, 1986)

Pittura etiopica tradizionale (exh. cat., Rome, Ist. It.–Afr., 1989)

DAVID APPLEYARD

3. Western Sudan.

Region between Lake Chad and the mouths of the Senegal and Gambia rivers, comprising NIGER, NIGERIA, MALI, BURKINA FASO, northern GHANA, SENEGAL and GAMBIA (see fig. 118). It is characterized by savannah grasslands, with patches of forest, and large river systems, including the Niger, Bani and Benue. The region has been subject to alternating wet and dry periods and consequently to tremendous changes in vegetation and desertification.

(i) Introduction. (ii) Regions.

(i) Introduction. In terms of cultural history, the Western Sudan includes, in the east, the NOK culture, which began in northern Nigeria in the latter half of the 1st millennium BC with the flourishing of complex societies based on metal technology and sophisticated ceramic sculpture, and, in the west, the early communities around a now extinct lake in the Dar Tchitt area of southern Mauritania, from which stemmed an era of great savannah state- and empire-building. Among these entities were the empires of Ghana, Mali and Songhai, the BAMANA states of Segou and Kaarta, the Fula state of Macina, the MOSSI states in southern Burkina Faso and the Kororofa and Hausa states in northern Nigeria. The northern Yoruba states such as Old Oyo may also have contributed to the character of Western Sudan.

In addition to sophisticated statecraft, the region has been typified by phenomenal commercial enterprise, dramatic religious developments and dynamic art traditions. Short- and long-distance trade have apparently long been a part of the area's economy, and many cultural groups have taken full advantage of ecological and technological developments to maximize the commercial potential in their human and natural environments. Western Sudan was one of the first African regions to be reached by Islam, which became both implanted and transformed as a powerful spiritual institution. Local religions, with their emphasis on special relations with ancestors and the earth, have also responded to new situations and changing conditions. Cult groups, which constitute a basic element of spiritual organization, are especially sensitive to their environments, moving in and out of regions and adjusting their tenets readily, thereby constantly reinvigorating the arts.

Although there is tremendous cultural variation across this area, as reflected in the proliferation of language and ethnic groups, artistic styles, while also encompassing great variety, nevertheless show a striking continuity. This is especially noteworthy in the 'Pole style' of maskmaking and figure sculpture, so called because of its abstract attenuation and elongation. Further characteristics are minimization of features and an orientation towards geometric interpretations of people and animals. This is obvious among the Voltaic peoples in Burkina Faso, whose masks are often decorated with basic geometric shapes in vivid colours, and in northern Nigeria, where many mask and figure types are reduced to geometric

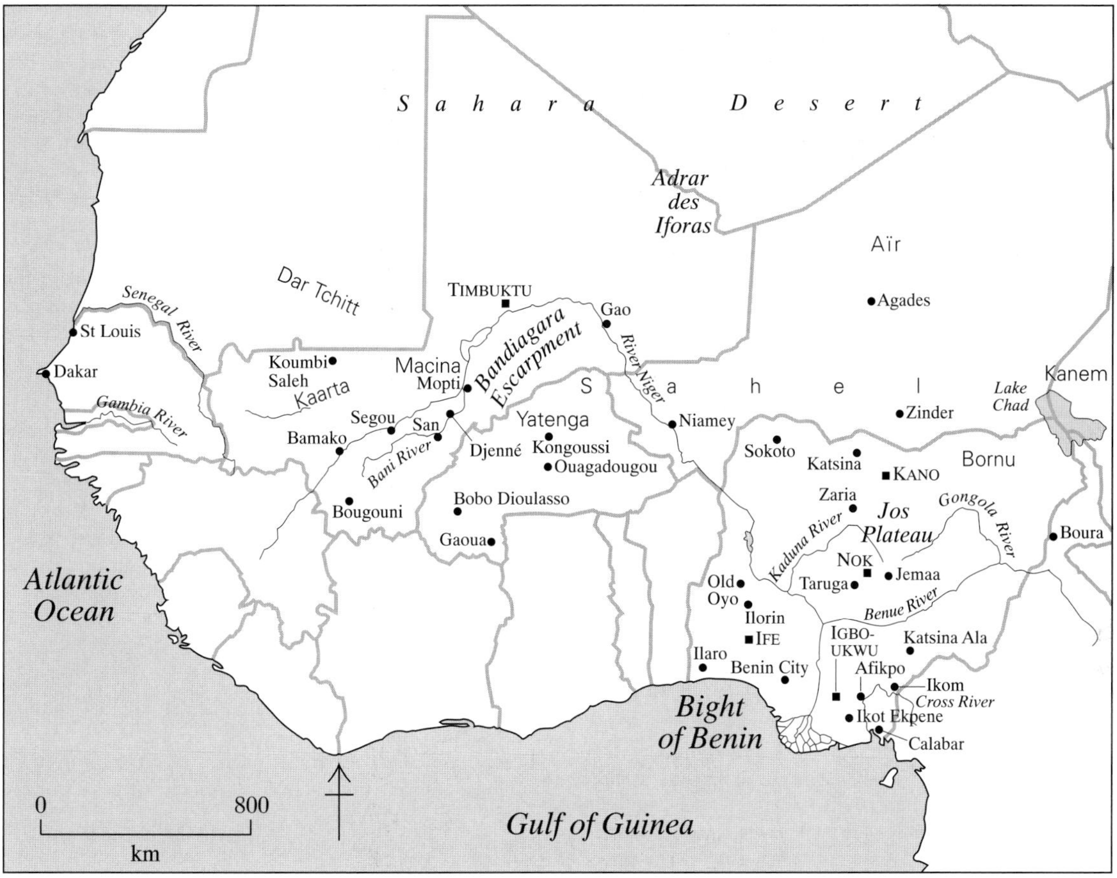

118. Map of Western Sudan; those sites with separate entries in this dictionary are distinguished by CROSS-REFERENCE TYPE

volumes, becoming almost the conceptual counterparts of 'primary form' sculptures of the West.

Knowledge of the history of Western Sudanic art is minimal. In the 1st millennium BC subtle ceramic sculpture was being manufactured extensively on and around the Jos Plateau in northern Nigeria; it portrayed humans, animals and, to a lesser extent, insects and vegetables. Many scholars associate this repertory with political and spiritual leadership complexes and the existence of an ancient and widespread social and economic unity. To the east, near Lake Chad, a slightly later ceramic sculpture tradition flourished. Later still, in the 1st millennium AD, clay sculpture was made to the west of the Niger–Benue confluence.

In the great bend of the River Niger another constellation existed of complex societies, active several centuries before and after the time of Christ and producing also terracotta sculpture, of which, unfortunately, very few pieces have been found in archaeological contexts, the rest having been illicitly removed to serve demand from Western collectors. Along the Bandiagara escarpment in Mali, art works of iron and wood have been found in burial caves. They date from the early 2nd millennium AD and are ascribed to people known to modern scholars as Tellem. Further west, in Senegal, large stone monuments have been found, built, apparently, over long periods during the 1st millennium AD.

Art, especially in the form of ornate precious-metal regalia, was associated with the courts of the Ghana and Mali empires. Arab sources indicate that Ghana's capital included a sacred forest housing secret sculpture. The Arab traveller Ibn Battuta (1304–68) observed carved wooden birds' heads worn with elaborate bird costumes by 'poets' who commented at court on the qualities of past and present leaders. Oral traditions suggest that sculpture associated with *komo* (initiation) may have existed early in the 2nd millennium AD. In the Mande expansion regions of the Gambia, occult iron staffs with figural tops may have been used as symbols of leadership by about the 15th century AD.

(ii) Regions.

(a) Eastern. (b) Central. (c) Western.

(a) Eastern. The eastern region is centred in northern Nigeria. In the Gongola River area clay and cultivated gourds are favoured media (see 1986–8 exh. cat.). Several ethnic groups, including the Bena, Cham, Ga'anda, Longuda, Tula and Yungur, create clay vessels of highly sacred character that can be found in shrines and are used in local medical practices and to honour ancestor and guardian

119. Kebere headdress, fibre and pigment, h. 1.13 m, Koro, Western Sudan (Bloomington, IN, Indiana University Art Museum)

spirits. They are elaborately embellished and, though anthropomorphic, often highly abstracted and stylized, sometimes to the extent that individual pots cannot be identified as portrayals without knowledge of important cultural practices such as scarification. Such is the importance of clay vessels that, for example, the culture hero among the Ga'anda is identified as a spirit pot.

In this area decorated gourds are a highly prized art form used by many ethnic groups, including the HAUSA and the Fulani (*see* FULANI, fig. 1). They often serve utilitarian purposes and include containers for storing and serving food and drink, head-balanced carriers, measuring devices, spoons and ladles, pipes and snuff bottles, and even sun bonnets for children. Others are used as musical instruments, such as drums, xylophones and horns, perhaps with sacred or occult associations. Gourds may constitute part of a bride's dowry or be given to her by husband or friends, and they are often central elements in carefully created displays indicating the married status of a woman. Gourds are often carried or worn at initiations, funerals and agricultural ceremonies. They may also symbolize membership of secret initiation associations, and several groups use them in soothsaying.

Like the ceramic pieces, gourds are embellished with carefully conceived and executed, sometimes three-dimensional, patterns that are extremely imaginative and greatly appreciated. Individual motifs have names and refer to the natural and social environments. The interpretations of both established and new designs respond to changing cultural situations, offering ways of contemplating and manipulating local experience.

To the west, in the Benue River area, among groups such as the Chamba (for illustration *see* CHAMBA (ii)), Jukun and MUMUYE, wooden masks and figures are the dominant art form. Great diversity in figure and especially mask forms have been recorded (especially by R. Sieber and A. Rubin; see 1961, 1974 and 1978 exh. cats, and Rubin, 1969), associated with a flexible approach to meaning and function. Among the mask and headdress types are some fantastic monumental raffia constructions (see fig. 119). The most widely known category of mask, which crosses at least ten ethnic boundaries, takes a variety of formal and conceptual configurations, emphasizing the horizontal plane. It apparently takes its inspiration from the awesome bush buffalo that formerly populated the entire savannah. Mama versions of the mask often display carved horns in the shape of an exaggerated crescent moon, attached to an abbreviated snout construction. The masks represent ancestor spirits and, providing access to occult power, are used in a cult called mangam which is involved in agricultural and funeral rites and the general well-being of the community.

Jukun versions are much more abstract, with a concave dish with cut-away designs serving as the horns, and other parts of the head attenuated in a creative fashion. Town chiefs claim that these masks, which also represent both bush cows and ancestors, are their own divine doubles, and wear them when performing at the funerals of leaders and other important persons. Goemai versions are similar formally, but, in addition to appearing at chiefs' funerals, are worn for dances at chiefs' installations and annual agricultural ceremonies. They are also employed in local medical practices. Chamba masks, worn at important funerals, embody the paramount female ancestors of the royal lineages. Mumuye versions are used in initiation rituals held every seven years. Each generation of neophytes commissions a new mask, which symbolizes that group at all subsequent performances.

Sculpted figures from this area are as reductionistically abstract as the masks. Jukun figures (for illustration *see* JUKUN) are used by chiefs to represent and communicate with ancestors; they are also used in a cult called Mam during propitiation ceremonies at planting and harvest seasons, and at times of duress. Mumuye figures are used in similar ways, bringing the spirits of ancestors into tangible focus, to be used by rainmakers greeting visitors, to help ascertain guilt at trials, to identify thieves by divination and as spiritual prophylactics to protect households. They are also linked to initiations, military activities and ironworking. Wurkun figures, used in male–female pairs, are believed to protect families as well as crops. Tiv figures, generally female, emerge from the tops of posts and are used in hunting, circumcision and prenuptial ceremonies. All these Benue figures, including those made by Chamba and other groups, have elongated torsos, arms, legs and necks and emphasize angularity and the lively, rhythmic interplay of shapes. Tiv figures are perhaps the least stylized. Brassworking in many areas of the Western Sudan was an important means of artistic expression, although it has gone undocumented (for illustration *see* BURKINA FASO). The Jukun are believed to have made brass pieces in various geometric configurations, such as cylinders and cones, with sonorific attachments, and openwork figures with fish-shaped legs, probably also as emblems of leadership.

Slightly to the west, in the Niger–Benue confluence area, the Idoma and the Igalu make art with strong stylistic affinities to Igbo groups to the south; indeed, the Igalu have imported mask types from their Igbo neighbours. These masks (for illustration *see* IDOMA and IGALU) are meant to call forth the spirits of ancestors of clan groups and thus help enhance the authority of community elders. Royal masquerades, also involving ancestors, reflect the ebb and flow of Igalu history. Idoma masks are associated not only with initiation into societies oriented towards military aggression but also with agricultural ceremonies and funerals. A formal eclecticism characterizes masks of both ethnic groups. Some take the helmet form, others are dance crests, and still others have horizontal configurations, some Idoma examples being of monumental size (l. *c.* 2 m). Both groups use figures in connection with health care, human fertility and general well-being and in particular with the protection of children.

The Igalu and the NUPE, the westernmost group in this region, used to carve doors for the entrances to family compounds. Elaborate collections of motifs asserted the wealth and prestige of the family heads who owned them. Made of several wood panels joined along vertical seams, Nupe doors (see fig. 120) were particularly large and were composed of many and elaborate motifs, from birds and Islamic writing-tablets to aeroplanes.

120. Nupe door, wood, from Western Sudan (Bloomington, IN, Indiana University Art Museum)

Several masquerades have been documented among the Nupe, who use cloth and cowrie compositions adapted from Yoruba Egungun masquerades (*see* YORUBA, §5 (i)) and, in an apotropaic practice called *ndako gboya*, tubes of cloth up to 3.5 m tall representing spirits and performing in twos or threes. A tradition of delicate face masks, surmounted by oval shapes and animals and figures aligned along a vertical shaft, is said to have reached the Nupe from sources to the south on the River Niger; these are brought into play in an entertainment masquerade performed on Muhammad's birthday.

The Hausa, commonly thought of primarily as craftsmen, in fact create arts that are sometimes subtle, sometimes flamboyant examples of rich expressive traditions. Their clay buildings and wall decoration (*see* HAUSA, fig. 2) constitute a vivid example, as seen in such structures as the 19th-century Friday Mosque in Zaria and the emir's palace in Kano (*see also* NIGERIA, §III). Exteriors are striking for their massive but elegant balustrades; interiors flow with arches and ribbing. Grand, geometric motifs, painted or in high relief, decorate the interiors and, since the 1930s, many exteriors too. Similar patterns are used in gourd decoration and in the embroidery that makes Hausa gowns (*see* HAUSA, fig. 1) among the most spectacular in West Africa. Modified, they are used also in leatherwork, such as sandals, cushion covers, bags, riding-boots and saddles. Hausa metalworking skill is evident in lovely jewellery and more practical items such as stirrups.

(b) Central. Dominant in this area are peoples who speak the Voltaic or Gur languages. Little scholarship has been devoted to their arts. Exceptions are Suzanne Blier's work on Tamberma iron jewellery, with its rich relationship to spirituality, myth and lore, and Fred Smith's studies on the sophisticated and aesthetically striking traditions of house-painting among certain groups in northern Ghana. Many of these groups also construct fantastic, two-storey, walled, clay family residences, using a coiling technique rather like that employed in making pottery; these buildings are sometimes referred to as castles.

Many Voltaic language-speaking ethnic groups, including the Mossi and LOBI, have become well known for their figure and, especially, their masking traditions, thanks largely to the work of Chris Roy (see 1979 exh. cat., and Roy). The Lobi make three-legged stools for men and four-legged stools for women; these artefacts are elegantly shaped, with highly imaginative leg shapes and angles, sweeping concave seats and often little sculpted human heads at the side. Lobi figures, which range in height from a few centimetres to *c.* 600–900 mm, frequently have minimally articulated torsos and limbs, the arms sometimes projecting in strange gestures, although the faces may be extremely sensitively carved. Research indicates (see 1981 exh. cat. by P. Meyer) that most are the embodiment of *thila* (spiritual beings), whom the creator god designed to assist and protect humankind. The Mossi produce chiefs' figures and dolls that are among the most refined, minimal abstractions created in Africa (*see* MOSSI, fig. 2). Figures made in this region are generally used in soothsaying

121. Bwa leaf mask for the cult of Do, worn at a funeral, Boni village, Western Sudan; from a photograph by Christopher D. Roy, 1985

and sorcery, both of which are practised in socially beneficial ways.

The masking traditions of these people are among the richest in Africa (see fig. 121). They are of major importance because they link individuals, clans and entire communities with the positive forces of the spirit world and serve in many capacities, including the regulation of commerce, the cleansing of communities, the practice of farming and the imparting of valuable cultural knowledge. Most groups have a mask society, admission to which may require extensive educational and socializing processes. The societies are linked, through the masks, to wilderness spirits, ancestor spirits or both, believed to be capable of bestowing blessings and benefits. The masks portray wild animals, such as antelopes (see fig. 122), buffalo, wild boar, hornbills, hyenas and snakes, as well as human characters, domestic animals, such as the cock, and unidentifiable, abstract conceptualizations. Even those that obviously depict animals are based on a central helmet form, with horns or other parts protruding up from it and snouts descending (*see*, for example, SENUFO, fig. 4). This format, though minimal, supports tremendous variation. Most masks are embellished with bold geometric patterns in black, white and red.

Masks appear, often in large groups, at funerals and burial ceremonies and agricultural cycle celebrations and in market-day entertainments, as well as in community problem-solving and initiation procedures. In the 20th century many young men have left Burkina Faso for employment and adventure elsewhere in West Africa, but they return for the farming season, a custom that is essential for the survival of their home communities. Mask performances are considered to have the power to draw the youth back home.

The DOGON are an intermediate group between the Voltaic language-speaking peoples of the central region

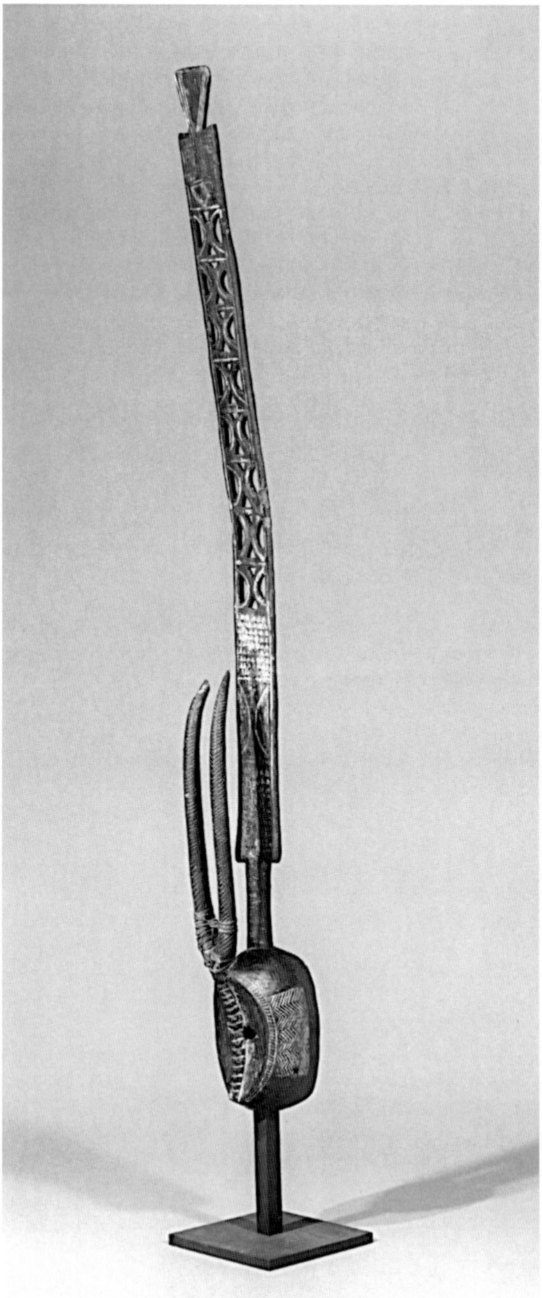

122. Mossi mask of Karanga type, wood, from Western Sudan (Bloomington, IN, Indiana University Art Museum)

and the Mande-speaking peoples of the western region. They speak a Voltaic language and, like many other Voltaic groups, have for many centuries interacted with the Mande, but with a greater intensity than most. Indeed, Mande oral traditions assert that the Dogon were of Mande origin, and the Dogon keep an earth shrine that allegedly contains soil brought during migrations from the Mande heartland in the mid-2nd millennium AD.

The Dogon are famous for their architecture, much of which graces the steep slopes of the Bandiagara escarpment. It features minimal, geometric house shapes, richly decorated shrines and spiritual residences, and elder men's public meeting-places (*togo na*) composed of massive, sculpted posts supporting thick straw roofs. Their figure sculpture is poorly documented, but in general it seems to serve as a means of warding off ill fortune and encouraging the intervention of benevolent spirits (*see* DOGON, fig. 1). Fine wrought-iron sculpture apparently functions as insignia for important priests (*hogan*): staffs are graced with extending arms that support small bells and are often topped with abstract, minimally articulated figures. In some examples iron strands on top are forged into cages that contain smooth stones.

Like other Voltaic peoples, the Dogon have a mask association. There are 78 recorded types of mask, which depict various characters, including humans and predators such as hyenas and crocodiles. The masks are often embellished with highly abstract, bold geometric patterns. Some extend a metre or more above the dancer's head. The masks are donned at funerals, at ceremonies to mark the end of formal periods of mourning and at *sigui*, dramatic ceremonies held every 60 years to mark the passing of the generations.

The SENUFO live to the south and the west of the Dogon, in southern Burkina Faso and Côte d'Ivoire. They too speak a Voltaic language, but their history includes a great deal of interaction with the Mande, and in many communities they live side by side with Mande Bamana. The Senufo make a vast array of sculpture, which exhibits many features of the savannah 'Pole style' but is sleeker and more curvilinear. Dramatic horizontal masks are used in their male initiation association (Poro) to help counteract negative spiritual forces. Almost antithetical are the face masks that depict great feminine beauty; these are used in initiation and funerary ceremonies by the Poro association and by the women's counterpart association (Sandogo). Tiny figures, along with miniature brass sculptures, are used in divination procedures by these women, while large, seated mother-and-child figures (*see* §IV, 5 above) represent a protective and nourishing female spirit force who plays a central role in Poro initiation. Large standing male and female figures also play important symbolic roles in Poro. Staffs topped by seated females or soaring birds with smaller birds balanced on their wings serve as prizes for young men who win annual cultivation contests (*see* SENUFO, figs 1–3).

(c) Western. The western region is dominated by Mande language-speaking groups such as the Bamana (Bambara), Maninka (Malinke) and Marka. Little art-historical research has been carried out on most Mande groups; the most dependable information relates to the Bamana, although the Maninka seem to have similar art forms.

The Bozo, who live in the western reaches of the Niger bend, share much with their Mande neighbours except language. They belong to a complex of peoples that includes the Bamana and the Marka, who are noted for marvellous and richly symbolic puppet performances staged by young people's volunteer work associations (*ton*). Boldly carved heads, masks and puppets, richly decorated with striking colours and perhaps dyed and woven cloth sewn into miniature clothing, are made to represent a cast of characters that includes not only people and animals but even objects such as jet aeroplanes. They are brought into play for skits and masquerades performed during the agricultural season.

The Bamana (*see* BAMANA, figs 3 and 4) also use masks in their secret initiation associations, which serve two principal types of function: soothsaying, healing and protection from evil; and education, individual contemplation and the opportunity for personal adjustment to the social and natural environment. The sculptures of one association, Chi Wara, which holds agricultural ceremonies and promotes good farming practice, take the form of an antelope headdress. Another society, N'tomo, which initiates young men into adulthood, has sculptures in the form of often delicate face masks presenting accepted ideas about intelligent, successful behaviour. Another association, Komo, stresses self-sufficiency, fulfilment and law and order: its major sculptures are dramatic, ambiguously carved horizontal masks, said to represent power and secrecy. Yet another association, Kore, reserved for mature male members of the community, also makes ambiguous masks, but these combine clearly recognizable human and animal features in highly imaginative compositions.

All these sculptures typify the geometric reductiveness that characterizes styles in the Western Sudan. One monumental form of Bamana sculpture is made for Gwan and Jo association activities and to celebrate the values of Mande society. These figures are much more curvilinear than the others and in many ways resemble the large Senufo sculptures mentioned above. Not surprisingly, these sculptures occur only in the southern portions of Bamana territory, where the Bamana live in close contact with the Senufo. Sadly, like other art objects in the Western Sudan, these figures have been subject to illicit collecting on a large scale.

Iron sculpture takes the form of lamps and figures on top of staffs and is often highly sophisticated, both aesthetically and technically. It too seems largely in decline. The staffs were used to grace the altars of the religious associations and of powerful individuals. In spite of the difficulties of working red-hot iron, the facial details often received delicate treatment. The staff portions were usually constructed of several pieces of metal, forge-welded together, with graceful hooks emerging from the joints to end in small conical knobs. The lamps consisted of a cup or cups of iron mounted on armatures attached to a central shaft. A lamp in the city of San is said to have had over 50 cups and was used to illuminate the popular night-time wrestling matches. Such iron lamps are still used in San for this purpose, although by and large iron lamps have been replaced by kerosene lanterns. Among the Mande small carved wooden figures are made, as playthings for children, as memorials in honour of the souls of deceased twins or for members of the male initiation association to enhance their public performances and emphasize their eligibility to young ladies.

See also articles on individual countries and §§II–VI above.

BIBLIOGRAPHY

Sculpture of Northern Nigeria (exh. cat. by R. Sieber, New York, Mus. Primitive A., 1961)

A. G. Rubin: *The Arts of the Jukun-speaking Peoples of Northern Nigeria* (diss., Bloomington, IN U., 1969)

R. A. Bravmann: *Islam and Tribal Art in West Africa*, African Studies Series (London and New York, 1974)

Interactions: The Art Styles of the Benue River Valley and East Nigeria (exh. cat., ed. R. Sieber and T. Vevers; West Lafayette, IN, Purdue U., 1974)

D. Heathcote: *The Arts of the Hausa: An Aspect of Islamic Culture in Northern Nigeria* (Chicago, 1977)

Bamana and Bozo Puppetry of the Segou Region Youth Societies (exh. cat. by M. J. Arnoldi, West Lafayette, IN, Purdue U., 1977)

Tellem: Een bijdrage tot de geschiedenis van de Republiek Mali (exh. cat. by R. M. A. Bedaux, Berg en Dal, Afrika Mus., 1977)

A. R[ubin]: '3: Masque-buffle/Buffalo Mask', *Vingt-cinq sculptures africaines/Twenty-five African Sculptures* (exh. cat., ed. J. Fry; Ottawa, N.G., 1978), pp. 54–7

T. Shaw: *Nigeria: Its Archaeology and Early History*, Ancient Peoples and Places, lxxxviii (London, 1978)

Three Rivers of Nigeria (exh. cat. by M. K. Wittmer and W. Arnett, Atlanta, GA, High Mus. A., 1978)

African Sculpture: The Stanley Collection (exh. cat. by C. D. Roy, Iowa City, U. IA Mus. A., 1979)

A. J. Glaze: *Art and Death in a Senufo Village*, Trad. A. Africa (Bloomington, 1981)

D. Idiens: *The Hausa of Northern Nigeria: A Catalogue of the R. E. Miller Collection and others in the Royal Scottish Museum*, Royal Scottish Museum Studies (Edinburgh, 1981)

F. T. Smith: 'Architectural Decoration of Northeastern Ghana', *Ba Shiru*, xi/1 (1981), pp. 24–32

For Spirits and Kings: African Art from the Paul and Ruth Tishman Collection (exh. cat. by S. M. Vogel, New York, Met., 1981)

Kunst und Religion der Lobi (exh. cat. by P. Meyer, Zurich, Mus. Rietberg, 1981)

T. Celenko: *A Treasury of African Art from the Harrison Eiteljorg Collection* (Bloomington, 1983)

S. P. Blier: 'Antelopes and Anvils: Tamberma Works of Iron', *Afr. A.*, xvii/3 (1984), pp. 58–63, 91

The Human Ideal in African Art: Bamana Figurative Sculpture (exh. cat. by K. Ezra, Washington, DC, N. Mus. Afr. A., 1986)

The Essential Gourd: Art and History in Northeastern Nigeria (exh. cat. by M. C. Berns and B. R. Hudson, Los Angeles, UCLA, Wight A.G.; Honolulu, HI, Acad. A.; New York, Cent. Afr. A.; Washington, DC, N. Mus. Afr. A.; 1986–8)

C. D. Roy: *Art of the Upper Volta Rivers* (Meudon, 1987)

S. K. McIntosh and R. J. McIntosh: 'From Stone to Metal: New Perspectives on the Later Prehistory of West Africa', *J. World Prehist.*, ii/1 (1988), pp. 89–133

P. R. McNaughton: *The Mande Blacksmiths: Knowledge, Power, and Art in West Africa*, Trad. A. Africa (Bloomington, 1988)

R. A. Sargent: 'Igala Masks: Dynastic History and the Face of the Nation', *West African Masks and Cultural Systems*, ed. S. L. Kasfir (Tervuren, 1988), pp. 17–44

African Art from the Rita and John Grunwald Collection (exh. cat. by D. M. Pelrine, Bloomington, IN U. A. Mus., 1988)

M. C. Berns: 'Ceramic Clues: Art History in the Gongola Valley', *Afr. A.*, xxii/2 (1989), pp. 48–59, 102–03

PATRICK R. McNAUGHTON

4. GUINEA COAST. Region of Africa comprising the countries of the Atlantic coast from GUINEA-BISSAU in the north-west to the BENIN REPUBLIC and including GUINEA, SIERRA LEONE, LIBERIA, the CÔTE D'IVOIRE, GHANA and TOGO (see fig. 123). Specifically, the region may be defined in cultural terms as the narrower strip of coast, generally 100–150 km wide, loosely delimited by the extent of tropical rain-forest and its adjoining areas of diffuse vegetation and high grassland. The topographical

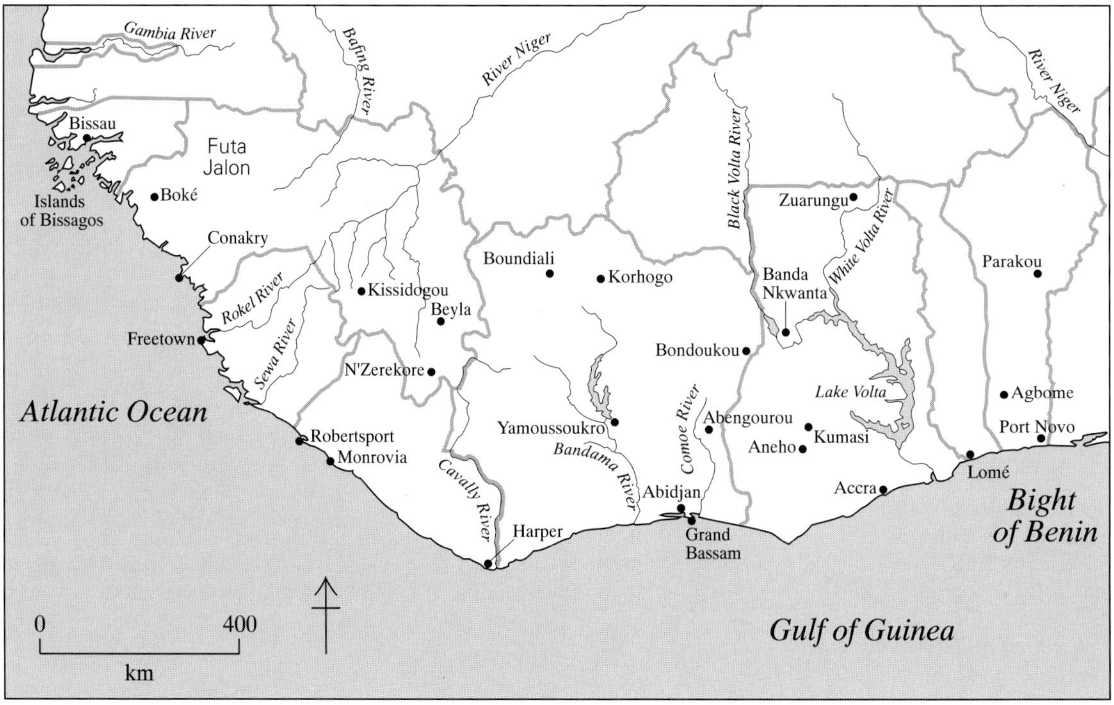

123. Map of the Guinea Coast

and climatic features of the land are factors in the formation of art styles. For example, the density of the forest in such places as Liberia and the Côte d'Ivoire has limited the mobility of peoples and thus insulated the indigenous groups from each other. Swampy, tidal lowlands along the coast, as in Guinea, often inaccessible for the annual six-month rainy season, compound this isolation. In most of the area, the rainy season extends fairly predictably from June to November and the dry from December to May.

(i) Historical introduction. (ii) Cultural traditions. (iii) Ritual organizations. (iv) Regional style clusters.

(i) Historical introduction. European contact with Africa has wrought a series of monumental transitions along this coast, where it penetrated early, from the 15th century, and has maintained a strong foothold. Before then, the coastal areas remained largely outside the reach of the centralized political movements of the Western Sudan and the trans-Saharan trade that so greatly affected the savannah. When commercial contact and, later, Christian missionary involvement began along the coast, West Africa turned its face towards the sea. This resulted in a scramble for the control of access, with an influx of northern immigrants, the creation of new lines of communication criss-crossing the forest zone, the realignment of power structures throughout the region and the creation of centralized kingdoms. The extant corpus of art derives from a period marked by fluidity in the movement of peoples and ideas and the consciousness of a cosmopolitan presence, resulting in immense cultural diversity. Urbanization has been a major factor throughout the 20th century, which has also been marked by familiarity with Western concepts and artistic forms and the introduction of many West African traditions.

During the period of the slave trade and the repatriation of slaves (*see* §VIII below), colonies of Afro-Americans were transplanted to the Guinea Coast; and in colonial times paid labourers migrated across international boundaries. In the two world wars, African subjects served their respective European colonial powers, which exposed them to each other's cultures and gave rise to new settlement patterns. By the end of the 19th century, Christian missionary activity involved cross-boundary exchanges, particularly between Nigeria and Sierra Leone. In the early 20th century coastal West African cities received an influx of immigrants from North Africa and the Middle East, attracted by the commercial possibilities. Further ethnic mixing, with the assignment of local administrators and the movement of labour forces, paved the road to political independence.

Cultural conventions continue to exhibit considerable dissemination. The power of the Yoruba (Nigerian) ancestral society for men continues to grow among the Temne in Sierra Leone. The cult of the water spirit, derived partly from the image of a female serpent-handler on Indian chromolithographs, has spread all along the coast. A Brazilian colonial style of architecture is often found in the Yoruba towns in Benin and Nigeria. Aeroplanes, motorcycles and European royal insignia have been used commonly in the 20th century on traditional forms of art. Ceremonial societies that were once unique have become unified and standardized, the most striking example being the Poro (more accurately Pörö) Society of Sierra Leone, Liberia, the Côte d'Ivoire and Guinea, reflecting political expediency in both its name and its international format. Trade in masks and linguist staffs exists between groups.

Nevertheless, in the rural areas of the interior and in many modern cities, the integrity of many ceremonial organizations and their artistic forms has remained relatively intact, as many examples attest. Masked ceremonies of the BAGA of Guinea survived until the 1950s much as described in the late 19th century. Both the Biri (Poro; men's society) and the Sande (women's society) of the Vai of Liberia were described by Olfert Dapper (?1635–89) in 1668 (Poro was mentioned as early as 1615 by Manuel Álvares (1573–?1617)) with many striking similarities to current conventions, and the present masks and costumes were illustrated as early as 1890 by J. Büttikofer. The description by de Faro (1664) of the shrines of the Temne of Sierra Leone, containing stones representing the ancestors, remained accurate in the 20th century. In Ghana, Krobo girls emerging from their period of initiation wear the same elaborate gold jewellery and long loincloths as they did in 1853, when described by Cruickshank (see 1977–8 exh. cat., p. 22).

(ii) Cultural traditions.

(a) Introduction. The length of the coast is dominated by six central language groups, divided into many subgroups and amalgamations. The largest is the Mande group, which is centred among the Malinke in the interior of Guinea but has spread with variants throughout the region. To a large extent, Mande has replaced Mel, which is now confined to small pockets along the littoral, in Guinea, Sierra Leone and Liberia. The Peul (or Fula, Fulani), speakers of the Pular languages, are believed to have subsumed and displaced Mande and Mel groups in parts of Guinea between the 14th and 18th centuries and are now prominent throughout coastal Guinea, Sierra Leone, Liberia and other parts of West Africa. A large area of southern Liberia and the Côte d'Ivoire is dominated by the Kru language group, also considered aboriginal. The Kwa group of languages includes Twi, which embraces nearly every ethnic group from the Côte d'Ivoire to Togo. Of these peoples, known as the AKAN, the best known are the Asante (*see* ASANTE AND RELATED PEOPLES). Ewe-related languages dominate in Togo and Benin.

Around the time of the first European contacts, several major kingdoms and larger alliances were developing, among them the Sapi of Sierra Leone and Guinea. Europeans described them as civil and prosperous, and they suffered invasions of Mande-speakers, who coveted their wealth. Before their conquest *c.* 1550 by the Mande groups known to Europeans as Mani, and perhaps from the 12th century onwards, the Sapi were known to carve miniature stone figures (*nomoli*; see fig. 124) and almost life-size stone heads now known as *mahen yafe* ('spirit of kings'). The figures probably represented royalty and nobility. For the European trade were also carved ivory trumpets and salt-cellars with intricate figural ornament.

By the mid-16th century, the interior of Sierra Leone was heavily infiltrated by Mande-speakers, who were

124. Sapi male figure sculpture, with two smaller figures and infant on back, steatite, h. 324 mm, 15th century (Oxford, Oxford University, Pitt Rivers Museum, 1934.24.2)

responsible for the formation of new kingdoms throughout the area and probably brought with them many continuing cultural conventions, including ironworking, strip-weaving, the ritual motif of the python and the bases of several ceremonial societies including the Poro.

(b) Kingdom of Asante. Further along the coast to the east, many smaller kingdoms rose and fell, but the most important political movement was the development of the great kingdom of the Asante on the Gold Coast (now Ghana). Having gained control of central Ghana in the 16th century, the Asante began a programme of expansion, beginning dramatically with the establishment of their capital at Kumasi under the leadership of the legendary Osei Tutu (*reg* 1697–1731). In the 17th century Tutu became the first Asantehene (king), when, it was said, the magnificent Golden Stool miraculously descended from heaven to rest on his knees (*see* ASANTE AND RELATED PEOPLES, fig. 1). The stool had long been an Akan symbol for the *sunsum* (spirit) of its owner, and the Golden Stool represented the divine right of the line of the Asantehene and the spirit of the whole nation, the prosperity of which depended on its ritual 'feeding' and care. It was exhibited at coronations, exclusive receptions and certain national festivals. Each Asantehene had his own personal, gold-plated stool, which occupied a chair at his side on state occasions. The queen mother and the chief also owned a gold- or silver-plated stool, and the more important officials had stools carved with supports in the form of a leopard or elephant, expressing the king's power, with abstract, openwork designs. When an important person died, his stool was blackened and placed in a shrine to be the focus of ancestral ritual.

The regalia of the Asante court, and, to a varying extent, the Akan court in general, included carved sceptres and sword hilts, plated in gold and carried by the royal staff on state occasions to indicate their official positions (see fig. 125). The most elaborate of the sceptres was held by the king's spokesman. The tradition may owe something to the silver- and gold-headed canes distributed by Europeans in the late 17th century and the 18th but is most likely to be a syncretization of foreign and indigenous sources. By the mid-20th century sceptres became elaborately ornamented with images of roosters and hens, elephants and leopards and with motifs derived from traditional Akan proverbs. Other important royal regalia included huge umbrellas topped with finials resembling the sceptres, caps with gold and silver ornament, intricately designed containers for gold dust and brilliantly coloured cloths made from strip-woven cotton and silk.

125. Asantehene Otumfuo Nana Opuko Ware II with sword-bearers and other attendants; from a photograph by Eliot Elisofon, 1971

The wealth of the Asante kingdom was based almost exclusively on gold and slaves, and its expansion was the result of an insatiable desire to control the markets of these commodities. The gold market existed before the coming of the Europeans, its trade directed northwards to the Western Sudan, but with the establishment of European trading forts along the Gold Coast, the Asante turned their attention to the elimination of the role of middleman occupied by surrounding states. By 1814 they controlled all access to the coast as well as most of modern Ghana and bordering areas. In 1874 the British sacked Kumasi, and in 1896 the Asantehene was exiled. On his return in 1924, however, the Asante confederacy was reconstituted, and in 1933 it was formally established, with Prempe II (*reg* 1892–1970) at its head, under British colonial rule. From this period date many of the most astounding forms of art.

(c) Kingdom of Dahomey. The coast of modern Togo and Benin, having no gold or safe harbours, experienced little early European contact. By the 19th century the powerful kingdom of Dahomey had emerged as a result of westward migrations of the Ewe and Aja peoples centuries earlier (*see* FON). The kingdom was famous principally for its role in the slave trade. While it never produced the volume of art of kingdoms to the east or west, its corpus includes some outstanding carved-wood memorials to the kings, monumental metal figure sculpture, decorative wooden figures and large, appliquéd textiles, originally made only for the king and his dignitaries and illustrating, in brilliant colours, the royal exploits. For the most part, the art of the kingdom of Dahomey served the royal court and was displayed in annual royal ceremonies. Its style reflects ethnic origins in, and continued connections with, the Yoruba kingdoms of Nigeria.

Much art production was instigated and inspired by King Glele of Dahomey. He came to the throne in 1858 and was the last great ruler of that kingdom, which fell only five years after his death. The son of a usurper, Glele was regarded by many of his subjects with ambivalence. During his reign he seems to have triumphed over many economic and military problems, but fires set by his antagonists destroyed the objects in the palace treasure houses, after which King Glele set about having new images produced that would reflect his reign and the reigns of his predecessors. His attributes and thus the predicted character of his rule were characterized by images derived from symbols in verse and narrative. An outstanding work from his reign, a lion-headed human figure in wood (Paris, Mus. Homme), refers symbolically to one of his titles, Lion of Lions. Huge figures in brass and iron refer to Gu, the god of iron and of war, decorative iron swords were used for display on state occasions, and iron and copper staffs with figurative scenes on a platform at the top refer to Glele's heritage, his right to rule and his numerous abilities. Common images were horses, dogs, umbrellas, pots and the right hand; the dog and the antelope symbolizing the spiritual sponsorship of the ancestors; a representation of a swirling storm symbolizing his immovability in the face of conflict; and the hornbill, with its heavy protrusion from the head symbolizing the bearer of burdens, much used in sculpture, architectural ornament and in appliqué textiles. Iron and brass memorial staffs (*asen*) continued to be used as ritual items in the 20th century, and the large, appliquéd cloths with symbols of royalty are still obtainable in markets.

The contribution to art made by the spirit-life of the region may be further exemplified in Vodun, the ritual employed to pay tribute to Dahomey spiritual beings, which has played an important part in African-American tradition in Haiti and later in the United States. The important trickster god, Legba, shown in wooden shrine figures in Dahomey, has a counterpart in both Cuba and Brazil in some physical representation and, more so, in ritual narrative and verse (*see* §VIII below). The diffusion of YORUBA imagery in the New World may be attributed to Dahomey's role in the traffic in slaves drawn during warfare largely from the neighbouring Yoruba groups to the east and especially from the sub-group Anago.

(iii) Ritual organizations. During the period of European contact, the western Guinea Coast has been noted not for its vast indigenous empires but for its powerful ritual organizations, which are mostly lacking in the eastern region. These organizations, usually restricted by gender, are spiritually and socially dominant throughout Guinea, Sierra Leone, Liberia and the Côte d'Ivoire. They usually serve as the major patrons of artistic activities that include the making of magnificent masks and figures, costumes and religious regalia and the performances at festivals that form the setting for much sculptural art. Their membership, often universal within any given ethnic group, is divided into distinct ranks, with separate initiation procedures and an elaborate structure of official titles and duties; the proceedings of ritual organizations are held in strict secrecy from outsiders. Such organizations often serve as a political counterbalance to the local, indigenous chiefs and their courts.

The most powerful and extensive ritual organization for men is the Poro, now generally thought to be a loose amalgamation of similar traditions generated from certain common origins but exhibiting some unique structures. Individual regional organizations of the Poro type go by different names but share a similar legend of origin and have many common titles, procedures and roles. Members of these organizations are responsible to a complex array of spiritual beings, and their rituals are designed to involve and channel some of the powers of the spirits into the world of mankind. Shrines, masks and figures are employed chiefly in the context of such ritual.

One important mask represents a founding spirit of Poro among peoples of the Sierra Leone–Guinea–Liberia border area. The monumental Landai (or Dandai) mask consists of a long, horizontal wooden head with open snout; a panache of plantain-eater feathers crowns its head, and black fur fringes its snout. The mask is worn with a costume of bleached raffia fibre. The masked dancer, who represents the founding spirit of the organization, appears during the boys' initiation, announcing their induction at the beginning, by figuratively devouring them, and their triumphal return to the village at the end, when he 'regurgitates' them (*see also* MENDE, fig. 2).

Among the Mende of Sierre Leone, dance costumes of cloth and yarn are worn over a substructure of rattan. The most important of the character costumes represent Gbini and Goboi, aspects of the great founding spirit of the Pö; they dance in sequence, with sudden occasional thrusts towards the audience. An essential feature of the dance is the frenetic movement of the masked dancer, which the guardians attempt to control. The dancers are magnificent in their colourful, pillbox-shaped headdresses, leopard-skin or antelope-skin capes and huge, billowing, bleached-raffia costumes.

The masks used among the ethnic groups of northern Liberia and adjacent areas of Guinea and Sierra Leone, such as the Dan, Kpalla, Mano and Loma (see fig. 126), are highly varied, not only in appearance but also in significance: in the north-western area they form part of the ritual regalia of the Poro organization, while in the south-east they do not. Sometimes identified in the literature as Poro masks, they are in fact an overlapping tradition. Although most studied by Western scholars among the DAN outside of the Poro area, the masks form the central core of Poro ritual among other groups. Among the Dan, 11 major mask types have been distinguished (see 1984 exh. cat., pp. 8–105; *see also* DAN, §2 and figs 1–3). Each mask incarnates a type of *du*, an ethereal force that makes itself known to a man and permits itself to be carved in wood. Its wearer speaks in unintelligible 'croaks, growls or twitters', which are interpreted by an accompanying savant. Masks are ascribed gender: the female masks are regarded as 'gentle', with smooth, oval faces; the male masks are angular, with a beard and tubular eyes, or in the form of an animal face or exceptionally large. Characters, given their own personal names as well as generic titles, include a female mask used in initiation, male or female 'miming' masks, a racing mask, a war-related mask with tubular eyes and ferocious mouth, and a mask with a bird's beak. A great variety of masking traditions exist throughout the Poro area that do not belong to the Dan complex. Some are local; others are distributed widely but differ greatly from each other in style of characterization and in role.

126. Loma female Nyangbai mask, wood, string and cowrie shells, h. 480 mm, early 20th century (Baltimore, MD, Baltimore Museum of Art)

In most of these societies membership is universal. Initiation into the organization is thought of as a metamorphosis of both body and spirit, without which a young man cannot marry, bear children or participate in the cultural life of the community. Procedures are quite similar from one area to the next, involving stages of initiation and an official hierarchy with a series of ritual roles.

The female counterpart to the Poro throughout most of the same area of Sierra Leone and Liberia is a group of related organizations best known by the names Sande or Bondo. In any area of Bondo/Sande, several types of spiritual beings, both masked and otherwise take part in the proceedings. The most powerful and feared are never revealed to outsiders and often take the form of a bundle carried on the head or an eerie voice heard in the night. The mask of one lesser spirit is well known, and examples exist in many collections: this is a helmet mask, painted or dyed black, consisting of a face, a heavily ringed neck, an elaborately carved coiffure and additional carved ornament (see Lamp, 1985). The masked dancer, called Nowo, Sowo or Zogba according to region, represents an idealized female type among all Sierra Leone groups but a male type among some Liberian groups. Best known among the former, she appears during initiation, in order to instruct the girls in moral comportment, and afterwards, when the female initiates return to the village. Her antithesis is Gonde, characterized by an anti-aesthetic, disorderly, dishevelled, masked dancer wearing a deteriorated or disfigured Nowo mask. The Bondo/Sande is a unique case in African art in that a wooden female mask is worn by women, although costuming and other forms of masking for women are common and distinctive in the upper Guinea Coast, from Guinea-Bissau to the border of Liberia and the Côte d'Ivoire.

(iv) Regional style clusters. Early studies of African art tended to group styles according to ethnic boundaries, assigning to each 'tribe' a definitive style, from which all departures were viewed as sub-styles. At the time, this was a valuable way of classifying objects in museums, but most modern scholars agree that such classification is somewhat misleading and that styles tend rather to develop around particular artists and their workshops, of whom some attract a large regional following, others not. Often this following adheres to ethnic boundaries, but in other cases it is cross-ethnic and not universal within any one ethnic

group. The style clusters described in this article are identified by their dominant ethnic designation, with the caveat mentioned.

(a) Bijogo. The northernmost cluster of importance is found off the shores of Guinea-Bissau, on the islands of Bissagos, inhabited by the BIJOGO. They are best known for their *iran*, highly schematized figures, often in the form of a head and torso, with reasonably naturalistic, concave face, and attached to a stool, on which the figure's legs may or may not be indicated. The figure often wears a flat hat with a narrow brim. Such figures were placed in community or personal shrines. Unlike most figural sculpture along the Guinea Coast, Bijogo sculpture is usually of unstained, natural, light wood. The Bijogo are also known for their varied masks and headdresses worn by neophytes and their masters in initiation proceedings. The best known is a bovine mask (Dugn'be) worn before initiation by a young boy, who crawls on the ground and imitates the movements of a village ox (see Galhano; Gallois Duquette).

(b) Nalu, Landuma, Baga and Mmani. From the southern border of Guinea-Bissau to the coastal border of Guinea and Sierra Leone, a number of different peoples carve monumental works in wood that are related in style and function. The peoples include the Nalu in the north, the Landuma somewhat inland, seven isolated groups calling themselves Baga (although all are not related linguistically) and the Mmani in the south. Common to all is a form of naturalistic figure sculpture characterized by large, bulging eyes and a long, aquiline nose, traits that recur in other of their art forms. Regional forms also exist. The Nalu and Baga are famous for an immense, horizontal mask (Banda) resembling a crocodile with long antelope horns and an anthropomorphic face (see fig. 127). The best-known Baga work is the huge wooden headdress commonly called Nimba (or D'mba; *see* BAGA, fig. 2), representing a female bust with an enormous nose, crested coiffure and long, pendant breasts. A tall, undulating wooden serpent carried on the head in ritual among the Nalu and the Baga is also an important work.

(c) Temne, Mende and Bullom of Sierra Leone. Many wooden female figures unconnected with the ritual organizations are used in private shrines dedicated to mental and physical health among the Temne, Mende and Bullom (Sherbro) of Sierra Leone. These are generally the property of women and are characterized by a naturalism that lacks, however, the consistent schema of the Bijogo or Baga. They have a blackened, highly polished surface, generally without a socle or base, with prominent buttocks and breasts and a ringed neck. Among these peoples many staffs of office are carved in similar manner, as well as many kinds of wooden and cloth masks used in ceremonial contexts both within Poro/Bondo/Sande and outside. A magnificently understated pattern of narrow-strip weaving is found especially among the Mende and their Mande neighbours.

(d) We, Kru, Grebo and Bete. Throughout the area of the We and also extending to the Kru and Grebo of south-eastern Liberia and the Bete in south-western Côte d'Ivoire, masks with horrific features occur, attached to elaborate costumes composed of frightful ensembles of objects. The Gela masks are best known. Female masks have a large, oval face studded with designs in carpet tacks, with bulging, oval eyes, a broad, flat nose and heavy,

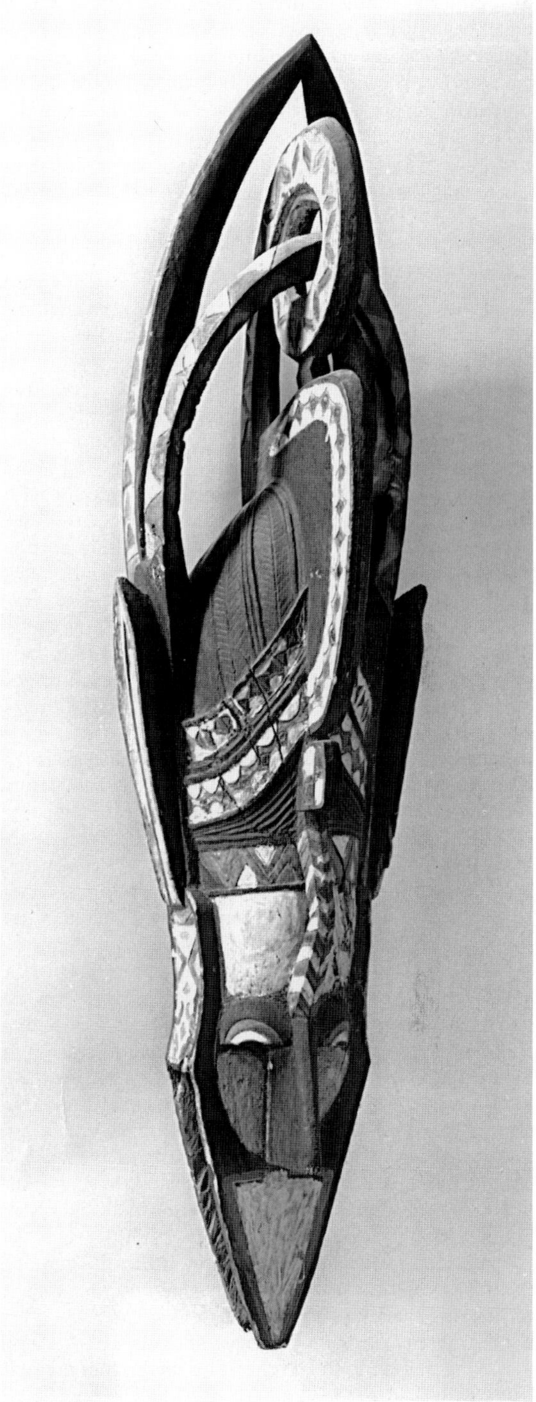

127. Nalu/Baga dance headdress (Banda), wood and paint, h. 1.42 m, early 20th century (Zurich, Museum Rietberg)

protruding lips. The entire mask is often fringed with metal bells. The male mask has tubular projections often described as warts, bulging bumps on the cheeks, an open jaw with teeth bared and wart-hog tusks carved on the forehead or cheeks. To the mask are attached wooden spikes, human and animal hair, shotgun cartridges, feathers and piles of overlapping fabric, producing an effect of chaos. The male masks appear to represent wild, uncontrollable forces of the forest. Like the Dan-complex masks, these are incarnations of the image of a spirit that has revealed itself to man (see Tiabas).

(e) Baule, Yaure and Guro. During the past few centuries the central Côte d'Ivoire has become a crossroads for the meeting of traditions and languages. The art style of the Baule, Yaure and Guro is characterized by a pleasing, serene refinement in figural sculpture and masking, and a schema that includes a concavity of the face sometimes recalling the sculpture of the Senufo to the north, gentle volumes resembling those of their neighbours to the west, the Dan, extensive carving of detailed body scarification patterns and a deep, dark, polished patina. Zoomorphic masks are in widespread use, their gentle, diminutive style contrasting sharply with the grotesque masks of their northern and western neighbours. The Baule bring an Akan influence from the east (whence they claim to have migrated in the early 18th century), while the Guro and Yaure derive from Mande origins (for illustration *see* BAULE, fig. 1, AKAN and GURO).

The best-known Baule objects are exquisite, small, human figures in wood, long prized by Western collectors. A standard aesthetic is followed in any one workshop, but the figures fall into two types serving different ritual functions. One type is the *blolo bla* ('other-world woman') or *blolo bian* ('other-world man'). These are commissioned by persons to whom it has been revealed that they are romantically involved with a being from a former spiritual existence. The figures are carved to represent the spiritual mate, kept in shrines and cared for lovingly, to appease the jealous intentions of the spiritual being. The figures are recognized by their highly polished patina. Masks of the other type represent *asie usu* ('nature spirits'), cantankerous beings who attempt to disrupt personal and community life. Though they are ugly, their representation is made pleasing in order to induce them to occupy the wooden body, so that they can be placated through ritual attention (see Vogel). These figures are usually encrusted on the surface from ritual applications.

Artists and craftsmen of the Baule–Guro area are among the most prolific in Africa, producing an enormous range of masks, including gentle, female face masks, often bearing petite, decorative images above the head, and masks incorporating certain characteristics of the antelope, leopard, buffalo and monkey (see 1985 exh. cat., pp. 108–20). Narrow-strip weaving has reached a peak of refinement in this area and is the context for small heddle pulleys carved with delicate figures, human and animal heads, and miniature representations of the masks. The Baule, especially, have retained the Akan fascination with gold, producing ornaments in intricate detail.

(f) Akan peoples. The Akan peoples have almost no masking tradition, but their other art forms are highly developed. Akan art is primarily court art, dedicated to the functions of prestige, the display of wealth and the veneration of nobility. This is an aspect of Baule art, found also among the Ebrie, Attie and Anyi in the Côte d'Ivoire, the Asante and Fanti in Ghana, and the Ewe on the coast of Togo and the Benin Republic.

Figural sculpture of the Akan is generally simpler and more direct than the polished work of the Baule and Guro, and in some cases highly abstract. The face tends to be round and flat, the neck bears the ringed creases that are found also in Sierra Leone figures, and limbs are often attenuated. Outside a royal context, the best-known figures of the Asante and Fanti are the schematized, wooden female figures known as *akua'ba* ('child of Akua'; *see* ASANTE AND RELATED PEOPLES, fig. 4). The form consists of a large, flat disc representing the head, a long, ringed neck, a simple cylinder representing the torso, brief indications of the breasts and two short, horizontal pegs for the arms. The *akua'ba*, symbolizing the epitome of female beauty, may be carried tucked into the back of a woman's wrapped skirt in the hope that it will help her conceive or that it will ensure a healthy pregnancy and the safe delivery of an attractive child. Once this is accomplished, the figure is returned to a private shrine, where it honours the woman's spiritual benefactors.

Gold weights are literally the trademark of the Asante, who use them as counterbalances in the weighing of golddust. Among other cast-brass items employed in this trade are containers, spoons, sieves and plates. Gold weights usually take the form of small, geometric abstractions, anthropomorphic and zoomorphic figures or miniaturizations of Asante material and agricultural elements. In addition to their function, they are designed as objects of delight, with proverbs and popular symbolic references (*see also* §VI, 10 above).

The Akan seem to have been less interested in the ethereal and more conscious of the real world including that of the departed ancestors. A group of important ceramics is found throughout the Akan area, especially among the Anyi, consisting of full or truncated figures or heads, which were used to commemorate the deaths of important elders in a period extending probably from 1875 to 1935. They were sculpted by women, like most clay artefacts throughout the Guinea Coast, and placed in a forest grove near the village but apart from the cemetery. The image was formed after the likeness of the deceased and served as the repository for his soul. The tradition of funerary sculpture continues in the Akan area in the form of monumental cement sculpture.

(g) Other styles. Throughout the Guinea Coast pockets of unique styles appear that do not conform to any of the above clusters: these include isolated ritual conventions and associated works of art, and examples of innovative brilliance by single artists and workshops, works that are highlighted rather than diminished by their exclusivity. The category includes the a-Rong-e-Thoma horned and snouted mask of the Temne, the flat Nyangbai mask of the Loma (see fig. 126 above), the disc-shaped Kplekple mask used by the Baule Goli association, the flat masks with tubular eyes used by the Grebo, and the fibre masks and costumes of the Djola and Tenda of Senegal, Guinea

and Guinea-Bissau. Certain peoples of the Guinea Coast, for example the Peul and Susu of Guinea, produce little in the way of plastic arts but are noted for their magnificent architecture, dance and music.

For further discussion of the art of the Guinea Coast region, *see* AKAN, AKYE, ASANTE AND RELATED PEOPLES, BAGA, BAULE, BIJOGO, DAN, FON, GURO, KISSI, MENDE and YORUBA. Art produced since colonial times is discussed in the relevant country entries.

BIBLIOGRAPHY

O. Dapper: *Nauwkeurige beschrijvinge der Africaensche gewesten* (Amsterdam, 1668; Eng. trans., London, 1670)
J. Büttikofer: *Reisebilder aus Liberia: Resultate geographischer, naturwissenschaftlicher und ethnographischer Untersuchungen, während der Jahre 1879–1882 und 1886–1887*, 2 vols (Leiden, 1890)
R. S. Rattray: *Religion and Art in Ashanti* (London, 1927/*R* 1954)
H. U. Hall: *Sherbro of Sierra Leone: A Preliminary Report on the Work of the University Museum's Expedition to West Africa* (Philadelphia, 1938)
G. W. Harley: *Notes on the Poro in Liberia*, Pap. Peabody Mus. Archaeol. & Ethnol., xix/2 (Cambridge, MA, 1941/*R* New York, 1968)
G. Schwab: *Tribes of the Liberian Hinterland*, Pap. Peabody Mus. Archaeol. & Ethnol., xxxii (Cambridge, MA, 1947)
G. W. Harley: *Masks as Agents of Social Control in Northeast Liberia*, Pap. Peabody Mus. Archaeol. & Ethnol., xxxii/2 (Cambridge, MA, 1950/*R* New York, 1975)
A. A. Y. Kyerematen: *Panoply of Ghana* (London and Accra, 1964)
F. Galhano: *Esculturas e objectos decorados da Guiné Portuguesa no Museo de Etnologia do Ultramar* (Lisbon, 1971)
D. Fraser and H. M. Cole, eds: *African Art and Leadership* (Madison, 1972)
R. Sieber: 'Art and History in Ghana', *Primitive Art and Society*, ed. A. Forge (London and New York, 1973), pp. 70–96
S. Vogel: 'People of Wood: Baule Figure Sculpture', *A.J.* [New York], xxiii/7 (1973), pp. 23–6
Die Kunst der Dan (exh. cat. by E. Fischer and H. Himmelheber, Zurich, Mus. Rietberg, 1976; Eng. trans., rev. Zurich, 1984)
M. Crowder: *West Africa: An Introduction to its History* (London, 1977)
The Arts of Ghana (exh. cat. by H. M. Cole and D. H. Ross, Los Angeles, UCLA, Wight A.G.; Minneapolis, MN, Walker A. Cent.; Dallas, TX, Mus. F.A.; 1977–8)
F. Lamp: 'Frogs into Princes: The Temne Rabai Initiation', *Afr. A.*, xi/2 (1978), pp. 34–49, 94
H. B. Tiabas: 'Masques en pays Guéré', *An. U. Abidjan*, ser. F, vii (1978), pp. 85–90
T. F. Garrard: 'Akan Metal Arts', *Afr. A.*, xiii/1 (1979), pp. 36–43
D. Gallois Duquette: 'Les Masques bovins des Iles Bissagos (Guinée-Bissau)', *Bull. Mus. Barbier-Müller*, xii (1981), pp. 3–4
M. V. Gilbert: 'Ewe Funerary Sculpture', *Afr. A.*, xiv/4 (1981), pp. 44–6
M. D. McLeod: *The Asante* (London, 1981)
For Spirits and Kings: African Art from the Paul and Ruth Tishman Collection (exh. cat. by S. M. Vogel, New York, Met., 1981)
D. H. Ross: 'The Verbal Art of Akan Linguist Staffs', *Afr. A.*, xvi/1 (1982), pp. 56–67
F. Lamp: 'House of Stones: Memorial Art of Fifteenth-century Sierra Leone', *A. Bull.*, lxv/2 (1983), pp. 219–37
B. Paxson: 'Mammy Water: New World Origins?', *Baessler-Archv*, n. s., xxxi (1983), pp. 407–46
S. F. Patton: 'The Asante Umbrella', *Afr. A.*, xvii/4 (1984), pp. 64–73
F. Lamp: 'Cosmos, Cosmetics, and the Spirit of Bondo', *Afr. A.*, xviii/3 (1985), pp. 28–43, 98–9
Die Kunst der Guro: Elfenbeinküste (exh. cat. by E. Fischer and L. Homberger, Zurich, Mus. Rietberg, 1985)
M. Adams: 'Women and Masks among the Western We of Ivory Coast', *Afr. A.*, xix/2 (1986), pp. 46–55
J. W. Nunley: *Moving with the Face of the Devil: Art and Politics in Urban West Africa* (Bloomington, 1987)
T. F. Garrard: *Gold of Africa: Jewellery and Ornaments from Ghana, Côte d'Ivoire, Mali and Senegal in the Collection of the Barbier-Mueller Museum* (Munich, 1989)
S. P. Blier: 'King Glele of Danhomé—Part One: Divination Portraits of a Lion King and a Man of Iron', *Afr. A.*, xxiii/4 (1990), pp. 42–53, 93–4
F. Lamp: 'Ancient Wood Figures from Sierra Leone: Implications for Historical Reconstruction', *Afr. A.*, xxiii/2 (1990), pp. 48–59, 103
S. P. Blier: 'King Glele of Danhomé—Part Two: Dynasty and Destiny', *Afr. A.*, xxiv/1 (1991), pp. 44–55, 101–3
——: *La Guinée et ses héritages culturels* (Conakry, 1992)

FREDERICK LAMP

5. WESTERN EQUATORIA. Region extending from the Central Cameroon Highlands in the north to the Ndogo Lagoon in the south, from Rio del Rey in the north-west to Bangui in the north-east, and from Setta Cama in the south-west to Kwamouth in the south-east. The west bank of the Zaïre River defines its eastern limit. It thus includes all or parts of the modern states of CAMEROON, CENTRAL AFRICAN REPUBLIC, CONGO, GABON and EQUATORIAL GUINEA (see fig. 128). For coverage of the colonial and post-colonial art and architecture of the region, refer to the entries on individual countries. *See also* BAMILEKE AND RELATED PEOPLES, BAMUM, BANGWA, FANG, KOTA and TEKE.

(i) Geography and cultural history. (ii) Contexts of production. (iii) Figure sculpture. (iv) Mask and masquerade. (v) Painting. (vi) Metalwork. (vii) Other arts.

(i) Geography and cultural history. Geographically the region varies greatly, from the forest–savannah mosaic pattern of the Cameroon Highlands to the central Sudanese parkland, with the equatorial rain-forest below this extending south until riven and then halted by the large forest–savannah mosaic west of the middle Zaïre River. With the exception of the central Cameroon Highlands and the north-eastern region, Western Equatorial Africa is peopled entirely by Bantu-speakers (including the bilingual pygmy groups associated with them). Bantu-speaking peoples form the core of the area. They have common origins and may generally be said to share a common culture. Over the last few centuries, however, previously related groups have become separated and their culture subject to fragmentation and recombination, leading to the development of different artistic styles.

To the north of this core area, in the central Cameroon Highlands, societies are characterized by strongly centralized and elaborated government, relatively stable settlements and extensively developed material cultures. Indeed, the distinctiveness of the area could justify its treatment as a separate region in its own right. There are only slight connections between its art forms and those of the core area; its art shows the influence of peoples to the north and west much more than of those to the south. To the south of the core area are the Kongo-speaking peoples, whose culture has affected that of the southernmost people of the region, the Shira-Punu, Nzabi and Teke-speakers. The southern Teke, moreover, share the pattern of divine kingship and centralized government long associated with the western Kongo states. Indeed, the intense development and sophisticated imagery of the arts of the Kongo kingdom seem to have been influential throughout a part of Western Equatorial Africa.

It is assumed that the Bantu-speaking cultivators, whose descendants now occupy the area, migrated from north to south. The earliest migrations seem to have bypassed the forest by following the large rivers and the Atlantic littoral. Later migrations, harder-pressed, also went southward, but in diverse directions. The oral histories of the region do not record the previous presence of any autochthonous

128. Map of the Western Equatorial region of Africa

(and conceivably non-Bantu-speaking) cultivators and hunters other than the pygmies who still live in the area. Either the pygmies were the only previous occupants of the core area or any non-pygmy autochthons were assimilated by the incoming Bantu-speakers. This latter possibility might be significant for the study of the distinctive features of the iconographies and rituals characteristic of the forest-dwelling peoples of the area.

The history of scattered and loosely cohesive groups of cultivators entering and adapting to the forest region with differing degrees of sophistication strongly affected the development of their arts. Each group that entered the forest had to follow a similar pioneering strategy involving the adoption of shifting residence, diffuse and ephemeral political authority, and competition for wealth and power based largely on trade for European goods. Moreover, the cultural and ideological climate created by the need to adapt to a dramatically new environment led to the development of religious beliefs based on enlisting supernatural aid through the interaction of familial spirits with autochthonous ones controlling fecundity, food, trade and power. These societies were essentially anarchic, lacking strong authority above the level of the minimal family lineage. This allowed for, if not encouraged, an extensive concern with competitive display, both in personal adornment and in the embellishment of religious objects. Similar principles sustained the development of art among societies outside the forest, but their longer intervals of fixed settlement and their elaboration of cults and chieftainship often led to the development of iconographic themes and contexts into more consistent, more widely observed and, generally, more secular institutions.

While these differences between forest pioneer and parkland sedentary societies, and the forms and contexts of their visual arts, may be partly due to ecological factors, any analysis must take into account both the particular historical circumstances of individual societies and the persistence of their pre-separation and pre-migration traditions. Unfortunately, there is little promise that archaeology might help in the reconstruction of the material culture of the core area before European contact, although the peripheral parklands may eventually yield more archaeological information. In the core area wood, other plant-derived materials and forged iron are for the most part quickly perishable. The advent of brass was relatively recent. It seems that most of the art traditions originated outside the region and that subsequent innovations from them did not precede the mid-18th century.

A firm chronology for the visual arts of the area has yet to be established. It seems, however, that such a chronology would rest upon five bases. The first and most substantial of these is provided by the records of Portuguese contact, from the late 15th century onwards, with the long-established kingdoms of the Kongo to the south of the region. This contact involved mainly Kongo-speakers along the Atlantic coast and along the Zaïre River from its mouth to the town of Matadi and the basin of the Lelunda River in northern Angola. The extensive presence of this group at the edge of the Western Equatorial region suggests that its southern part at least was well settled by Bantu-speakers when the Portuguese arrived. The second basis is provided by early 16th-century reports of settlements established on the coast from southern Cameroon to southern Gabon; the third by late 15th-century reports of the kingdom of the Tio in the south-east of the region; the fourth by early 19th-century accounts of peoples (presumably Bantu-speakers) in the forest country inland from the Atlantic coast; and the fifth by later 19th-century accounts of southward and westward population movements from northern parkland and forest margins into and through the forest. In addition, inferences from language distribution and shared elements of material culture support the idea of the established presence of Bantu-speaking groups along the Atlantic coast and quite possibly the middle bank of the Zaïre River. Moreover, a few of these material culture items indicate a persistence of sculptural style—stressing a distinctive mode of conventionalization—since at least the 17th century.

Early European accounts of the Kongo kingdoms record the existence of a plethora of images used for religious purposes. Few such figures have survived, making it difficult to substantiate these accounts, but the records of the Museo Nazionale Preistorico ed Etnografico Luigi Pigorini in Rome attest to the arrival in Italy in 1695 of two wooden female half-figures that had previously come to Portugal from West Africa. These seem to be in the same style and by the same hand, and authorities now attribute them to Kina, a district in the south-west of the Kongo kingdom, on the north bank of the Dande River and due south of the state of Bamba. Despite the obscurity of their origins, the existence of these two figures helps to make two points: first, that a conventionalizing tradition of sculpture probably flourished among the Kongo well before the great southward Bantu movements of the 19th century; and second, that the tradition relates significantly to much of the sculpture made in the 19th and early 20th centuries in Western Equatoria. Indeed, although the particular style of the Kina figures seems to be no longer extant, its elements are discernible in more recent styles, from central Angola to the western part of the Ogowe Basin.

(ii) Contexts of production. The contexts of art production in the region have developed out of religious beliefs and political institutions that are widespread in Sub-Saharan Africa. Most societies in the area attempted to deal with the supernatural world through men's cults. These associations were organized either on familial or local (i.e. supra-familial) principles, and their officiants were either individual family heads or important religious specialists. (The observance of individual or personal cults does not seem to have developed to the extent that it did in the societies of the Guinea Coast.) Village cults are concerned with autochthonous protective spirits, either directly or through the spirits of deceased cult members. In the latter case, the power of deceased men and women is thought to remain transitorily in such relics of their living form as bones, hair and nails. In the cults that depended on relics to influence the unseen world, apotropaic iconography was developed in which anthropomorphic images guarded and personified the power residing in the reliquaries. Many cults, whether or not they were based on a belief in the power of relics, personified their protective spirits in the form of statues and/or mask disguises worn by unidentified cult members. Again, these statues or masks symbolized either family groups or local groups made up of unrelated families. The institution of cult houses seems not to have been strongly developed through most of the area. Special buildings with large-scale architectural and liturgical elements representing mythic or supernatural figures are recorded only from central Gabon and the Lundu-Mbo complex near the northern Cameroon coast. Unfortunately, early European travellers recorded little about this practice.

The absence of stable political organization and centralized government over most of the area provided a context in which both individuals and families sought to emphasize their status through the enhancement of their appearance and that of the objects indicative of their position in society. Wealth and leadership often found expression in prestigious styles of personal attire and adornment and luxurious elaborations of such personal and professional effects as staffs, display weapons, musical instruments, bellows and eating-spoons. The representational imagery with which such objects were embellished may have been primarily secular, or it may invoke protective spirits. The ownership and performance of masks and masquerades were also matters of wealth and prestige, and their striking iconography may be seen as a product of this context of their production and use. The quest for prestige also extended to the decoration of house-doors and such parts of house interiors as room-screens, supporting pillars and beds.

The artistic skill required to produce these goods was generally diffused throughout society. In most of the region there were neither castelike groups nor family guilds of artisans. Otherwise family relationships or voluntary apprenticeships were the means by which individuals became practising artists. The status of the artist seems to have varied greatly over the region. Artists working in the kingdoms of Central Cameroon enjoyed the protection and support of rulers, but this relationship greatly limited their role in leadership and, in turn, their social prestige. Much less is known about the status of artists in the less fixed and centralized societies to the south and east, but the evidence suggests that outstanding carvers occupied an ambivalent position. While their work might gain them wealth, their status in the society as a whole depended, as it did for non-artists, on such other attributes as supernatural endowments and/or personality. While a connection between technical skill and supernatural power was recognized in most societies, that alone need not have led to wide renown. In the core area, the carver and the religious specialist who prescribed the carving could be the same man. Less frequently, that man could also be a political leader. The roles played by artist, religious specialist and political leader in the innovation of a form, the creation of a theme and the fixing of a tradition, whether formal or iconographic, remain unknown, although the ethnographic data strongly suggest that formal creativity and conformity did not always rest entirely with the artist. Such complex circumstances of production do not seem, however, to have especially complicated the meaning of the images themselves. Iconographic themes tend to be simple and religious imagery 'multivocal', although this quality has not been adequately investigated.

(iii) Figure sculpture. Most representational art of the region was carved in wood. The main tools were, in order of use, axe, occasionally a hewing knife, adze and fine knives, with finishing generally being done by smoothing with rough leaves and sometimes sealing and darkening with a glowing iron blade. A greater variety of materials and tools was used in the Central Cameroon area and in the areas immediately to the north and south of the region. Most figure sculptures take human form; representations of animals are less frequent. Male figures seem to predominate in the core area, while female figures prevail in the imagery of the south-western corner. Many of the numerous small magical figures made in the Lundo–Mbo area seem to be of inderterminate sex. Throughout most of the region, twins are credited with great supernatural power and held in great respect, so it is likely that some sculptures are surrogate figures representing dead twins.

So far, there is little evidence to suggest that statues in this region generally embodied deceased family members. In the core area, ancestors were represented more by relics than by images. Instead, statues served mainly to embody the protective spirits who watched over reliquaries, assemblages of magical materials, cult houses and homes. Some figures, kept carefully concealed, were made to be sent out at night by magicians in order to enthrall their rivals or punish their enemies. In the Central Cameroon area some groups used statues to commemorate deceased rulers and their first wives. Paired figures of men and women found standing in cult houses in the south of the region, for example among the Tsogho and probably other groups, are said to represent primal couples.

In the south-west corner of the region genre figures of women carrying bottles and gourds suggest the use of statuary to attain, and then flaunt, wealth and prosperity; the bottles probably symbolized European spirits and the gourds palm wine. Otherwise, such secular figures seem traditionally to have been more or less insignificant. There are no reports of carved figures being used primarily as dolls, and although statues seem to have been used in cult initiations there is little evidence of their having played primarily didactic roles. Compared with many other areas of west and central Africa, the formal themes of the statuary of the region tend to be simple and austere. Sculptural groups occur in the initiation tableaux of the northern Yaunde–Fang and the Sanaga regions, in the multiple figures of the Lundu–Mbo in the north-west corner and in the miniature figures of the Shira–Punu group. Otherwise, statues are usually single figures, representing people standing or crouching. Figures of women holding children are rare and of scattered distribution in the core area. Half-figures and heads on protracted necks are known. They are found mainly through a central belt. Integral compositions of a head or half-figure on a prestigious type of stool are quite distinctive of the core area but are also found in north-eastern Zaïre. In the west there are several traditions of openwork statuary in which the arms extend well away from the body, either holding an object (see fig. 129) or brought up to the chin or beard. In general, integral sculptural decoration, such as the representation in relief of elaborate scarification patterns (see fig. 130) and items of regalia, yields to incised surface effects, polychromy and metal appliqué.

Wooden statuary ranges in height from *c.* 150 to 900 mm. Early travellers noted life-size and even larger figures, apparently regarded as highly important, but their reports do not describe these figures. The importance of such images and the difficulty of transporting them probably precluded their coming into Western collections in any quantity. Such large figures came to the attention of Europeans mainly along the coast. They were later found to exist among relatively long-settled peoples in the south-western part of the Ogowe Basin, an occurrence that indicates a connection between a sedentary tradition

129. Ngumba-style figure sculpture, wood, mirror glass and brass, h. 566 mm, from Western Equatoria, before 1929 (Frankfurt am Main, Museum für Völkerkunde)

and an increase in the size of imagery. By the same token, the sculpture produced by nomadic societies tends to be of modest size. The colonial policy of fixing such groups in permanent villages may also have led, in certain instances, to an increase in the size of traditional statuary. The scale of representation in architectural sculpture, both structural and decorative, and in ritual tableaux exceeded the general limits observed in the production of free-standing figures. The lack of early accounts of the embellishment of traditional architecture with representational imagery between the western Cameroon Highlands and the Kongo states is striking. One would certainly have expected more from the south-western area, if only as a development out of a presumably long history of sculptural exuberance.

Traditions of miniaturism in three-dimensional representation are widely scattered. The finest miniature carving

130. Kuyu/Mboshi figure sculpture from Western Equatoria (Paris, Musée d'Art Moderne de la Ville de Paris)

131. Mbete reliquary figure, wood, pigment, cowrie shell and brass, h. 736 mm, from Congo, Western Equatoria, late 19th century–early 20th (San Francisco, CA, private collection)

seems to come from the south-western corner and probably reflects the influence of the north-western Kongo states.

It may be argued that, along with bold polychromy (*see* §(v) below), the distinctiveness of the art of this region, at least at its core, lies in its characteristically dramatic reduction of the human form (the northern and south-western areas encompass more naturalistic styles). Both the faces of masks and the composition of statues share an almost complete lack of naturalistic modelling of anatomical detail. This striking tendency to simplify expresses itself in highly contrasting modes. The intent to depart from nature is evident in all of them, but the nature of the stylization may vary greatly, ranging from a prevailing curvilinearity and roundness at one pole to a prevailing angularity and the use of flat, often steeply banked contours at the other (see fig. 131). Broadly speaking, the first type centres in the west and the second in the east. These contrasting stylistic canons frame a richly diversified continuum in which the distinctive features of both are combined in quite individual ethnic or local traditions. The intermingling of styles prevails to the extent that it is often impossible to infer the provenance of an image through the features generally thought to be the most salient and significant. In many cases insufficient background information prevents the assignment of an object to an ethnic style. Indeed, lack of secure evidence as to where objects were found might undermine many of the aesthetic conclusions on which current stylistic groupings are based.

For the moment, precision of attribution is at the level of geographical–cultural area rather than language family or ethnic group. The turbulent history of most of the area's peoples has encompassed migrations, dispersals, interactions, changes of group identity and, in some cases, extinction. In many, if not most cases, this precludes any assurance in the existence of precisely defined styles of sculpture.

(iv) Mask and masquerade. Masks of this region generally represent autochthonous spirits enlisted in the aid of a lineage group, village, religious specialist or dance association (see figs 132 and 133). There are reports that link masks with the shades of the dead, but these seem tenuous. Unlike other regions where masking is intensive, such genre themes as old dotards, easy women, village buffoons and overbearing warriors, brought forth to comment on antisocial behaviour, seem to be absent here. Instead, the didactic roles played by masks in this region tend to be direct rather than allegorical. References to masquerades involving different masks acting together or sequentially in a narrative performance are infrequent, and the extent of any such traditions is unknown. One early 20th-century report tells of Mboshi-speakers in the far east of the region acting out regional myths by means of disguised dancers (see Poupon). This might in fact be attributable to the western Mongo peoples on the other side of the Congo River. In some cases a cult owned a series of masks materializing different spirits, often in considerable numbers. In others, only one or two masks would embody paramount protective spirits. Although masks were employed mainly in religious contexts, a strong element of play can be identified in their forms and characteristic behaviour. Often masks appeared mainly as entertainers, although they doubtless always retained some supernatural

qualities. Except in the Cameroon Highlands, and perhaps in a few instances in central Gabon, masks do not seem to have participated significantly in funerary or 'second-burial' ceremonies. Their field of public, or quasi-public, activity was centred in rites of passage for the living and rites that dealt with general crises.

Some groups conceived of mask spirits as being predominantly animal in nature, while others visualize them in human form. These conceptions are not mutually exclusive but may be combined in many ways, especially in societies that use a variety of masks in their major cults, as in western Cameroon and central Gabon. The differences in conceptualization may nevertheless be important in tracing the cultural history of different groups. The question is, however, complicated by the tendency to give human faces to masks with salient animal attributes; and the reverse can also occur, especially in the case of monkey-associated spirits. Furthermore, some mask themes cross ethnic boundaries, while others do not.

The masks of the region represent a far wider sculptural range than that of its figure sculptures. This is especially so when the total configuration of form, colour and texture is taken into account; even just the part that covers the wearer's face or head is characterized by a wide range of forms. In the Cameroon Highlands, for example, the mask can sit atop or aslant the wearer's head, the wearer looking out through a cloth hood. To the south of the region an imposing and characteristic theme extends through the forest societies. Here, a large helmet- or bell-shaped wooden form covers the whole of the wearer's head. This disguise is usually embellished with great crests and/or multiple faces. The type coexists with a wide range of masks that are worn more or less over the face. These frontal masks are remarkably diverse in form, size and style. Their presence extends well beyond the central part of the region and reaches to the southern limit in the west. With a few exceptions, the main groups in the south-eastern area seem not to have had an important tradition of frontal masks. In southern Cameroon the Lundu–Mbo and Saa (Basa) peoples had distinctive dance-headdresses consisting of featureless helmets and caps surmounted by human figures.

133. Kwele mask, wood and pigments, h. 265 mm, from north-western People's Republic of the Congo, probably 1930s or 1940s (London, British Museum)

132. Shira–Punu mask, wood decorated with red and white paint, h. 280 mm, from Gabon, Western Equatoria, before 1904 (London, British Museum)

Many of the peoples who seem not to have employed such wooden masks devised other ways of representing fantasic personages. These included the use of more or less featureless garments and carapaces of plant bark, plant fibre and branchwork. Some Mboshi-speaking peoples invented a singular dance in which the performer, enveloped in a great cone of raffia cloth, held up a solid wooden head at arm's length as he whirled about.

(v) Painting. There is little evidence that two-dimensional graphic representation was important in this region, though this may be partly due to its generally ephemeral nature. The outer faces of the bark walls of traditional

houses were sometimes decorated with free-hand drawings, mainly of simplified human and animal figures, and silhouettes of weapons. These appear to have been done purely for diversion, and to have no symbolic, magical or even display purpose. On the other hand, colour was applied to many objects throughout the area, though again it was generally ephemeral. The range of pigments was generally limited to white, black, and shades of red and brown, which were applied to masks, statues, house-parts, drums and the bodies of those taking part in ritual events. Boldly contrasting and diversely shaped geometric fields were often further embellished by small motifs applied by improvised brushes and stamps. The intensive use of contrasting colours—most of them ephemeral—characterizes the use of paint on the sculpture of most of the area.

(vi) Metalwork. In Sub-Saharan Africa, techniques of applying copper alloy sheet and wire over shaped wooden forms probably reached their highpoint in this region. Iron was worked and brass cast with a high degree of skill and imagination. Bronze does not seem to occur. The secondary decorative treatment of metal forms, for example engraving, punchwork and repoussé, is also highly accomplished. Not all groups smelted iron, however, and some peoples enjoyed reputations as specialized ironworkers, supplying their neighbours with smelted metal, as well as implements and other objects. A few iron weapons have, or at least suggest, representational form, while many have quite distinctive abstract outlines. Many ironworkers embellished blades with graceful ridges and finely engraved geometric designs. For weapons, however, the main field of decoration was the wooden handle and the bark or hide scabbard, both of which were often covered with brass sheet or wire worked in various ways. The working of brass, mostly of European origin, is especially characteristic of the area. For example, massive, boldly contoured and often richly engraved penannuli were cast for personal adornment. The technique of brass-casting was limited to the use of moulds that were either open or partially closed. The lost-wax method appears to have been used only in the Central Cameroon area and possibly in the extreme south-west of the region.

(vii) Other arts. The other arts of the region included the making of the ivory side-blown horns and delicate hairpins used in some areas. Pipe bowls of soft stone are known from the south-west, otherwise stone was hardly used, except to a small extent in Central Cameroon. In most areas pottery was utilitarian and non-representational, though of some aesthetic quality. Surface decoration consists mainly of a few bands of incised or low-relief motifs. The ceramic art of the region reached its highest points in the furthest north and south. Some groups in the centre made earthen figures of men and animals, prone or supine, in varying degrees of relief. These ranged from life-size to immense and were limited to use by cults in their initiations and other ordeals. Textile techniques were more developed outside the core area. Traditionally, cotton cloth was woven in Central Cameroon, but its decorative effects are limited mainly to embroidery, which is likely to have been introduced from the north. Through much of the remaining area weaving is confined to raffia-strip cloth made on a vertical loom. Most of the material produced is monochrome and austere. Embroidery and resist-dyeing seem not to have been practised. In the core area ornamental mats were made with geometric patterns, both representational and 'abstract', produced through plaiting and twilling.

BIBLIOGRAPHY

EARLY TRAVEL WRITINGS

P. B. Du Chaillu: *Explorations and Adventures in Equatorial Africa* (London and New York, 1861)

——: *A Journey to Ashango-land* (London, 1867)

GENERAL WORKS

K. Krieger and G. Kutscher: *Westafrikanische Masken*, Veröff. Mus. Vlkerknd. Berlin, n. s. 1, Abt. Afrika, i (Berlin, 1960) [col. cat.]

A. R. Walker and R. Sillans: *Rites et croyances des peuples du Gabon* (Paris, 1962)

K. Krieger: *Westafrikanische Plastik*, 3 vols, Veröff. Mus. Vlkerknd. Berlin, n. s. 7, Abt. Afrika, ii; n. s. 17, Abt. Afrika, iv; n. s. 18, Abt. Afrika, v (Berlin, 1965–9) [col. cats]

I. Bolz: 'Zur Kunst in Gabon', *Ethnologica*, n. s., iii (1966), pp. 85–221, pls 38–62

L. Perrois: 'Gabon gestern und heute', *Z. Mus. Hildesheim*, n. s., xxiv (1973), pp. 1–72

M. Huet: *The Dance, Art and Ritual of Africa* (New York, 1978)

L. Perrois: *Arts du Gabon: Les Arts plastiques du Bassin de l'Ogooué* (Arnouville and Paris, 1979)

Masterpieces of the People's Republic of the Congo (exh. cat., New York, Afr.-Amer. Inst., 1980)

L. Perrois: *Ancestral Art of Gabon from the Collections of the Barbier-Mueller Museum* (Geneva, 1985)

SPECIALIST STUDIES

M. A. Poupon: 'Etude ethnographique de la tribu Kouyou', *L'Anthropologie*, xxix (1919), pp. 53–88, 297–335

G. Tessmann: *Die Bafia* (Stuttgart, 1934)

——: *Die Baja*, 2 vols (Stuttgart, 1934–7)

T. Thomas: 'Variation on a Theme: Analysis of Small Carved Figures from Bali, Cameroons, Africa', *Man*, xxxviii (1938), pp. 33–7, pl. C

M. Guthrie: *The Bantu Language of Western Equatorial Africa* (London, 1953)

J. Millot: 'De Pointe-noire au pays Tsogo', *Obj. & Mondes*, i/3–4 (1961), pp. 65–80

P. Harter: 'Les Courses de pirogues costumières chez les Doualas', *Bull. Assoc. Fr. Rech. & Etud.*, ii (1966), pp. 33–47

L. Perrois: *Gabon: Culture et technique, catalogue du Musée des Arts et Traditions de Libreville* (Paris, 1969)

L. Siroto: 'Gon: A Mask Used in Competition for Leadership among the BaKwele', *African Art and Leadership*, ed. D. Fraser and H. M. Cole (Madison, 1972), pp. 57–77

O. Gollnhofer, P. Sallée and R. Sillans: *Art et artisanat tsogho* (Paris, 1975)

L. Siroto: '*Njom*: The Magic Bridge of the Beti and Bulu of Southern Cameroon', *Afr. A.*, x/2 (1977), pp. 38–51, 90–91

E. Bassani: 'Les Sculptures Vallisnieri', *Africa-Tervuren*, xxiv/1 (1978), pp. 15–22

F. Bontinck: 'La Provenance des sculptures Vallisnieri', *Africa-Tervuren*, xxv/4 (1979), pp. 88–90

L. Siroto: 'Witchcraft Belief in the Explanation of Traditional African Iconography', *The Visual Arts: Plastic and Graphic*, ed. J. Cordwell, World. A. (The Hague, 1979), pp. 241–91

A. Fourquet: 'Chefs d'oeuvre de l'Afrique: Les Masques Pounou', *L'Oeil*, 321 (1982), pp. 52–7

T. Northern: *The Art of Cameroon* (Washington, DC, 1984)

A-M. Bénèzech: 'So-called Kuyu Carvings', *Afr. A.*, xxii (1988), pp. 52–9

LEON SIROTO

6. CENTRAL AFRICA. The area between the Atlantic coast and the Western Rift Valley, which corresponds to the modern nations of ZAÏRE, CONGO, Cabinda, ANGOLA and ZAMBIA (see fig. 134), is divided into several climatic zones, including high-altitude tropical forests, savannah-woodlands and semi-arid plains. The many rich and diverse categories of Central African art can be associated with three distinct spheres: politics, ritual and the home. Figure sculpture, masks, ceremonial stools, staffs (see fig. 135)

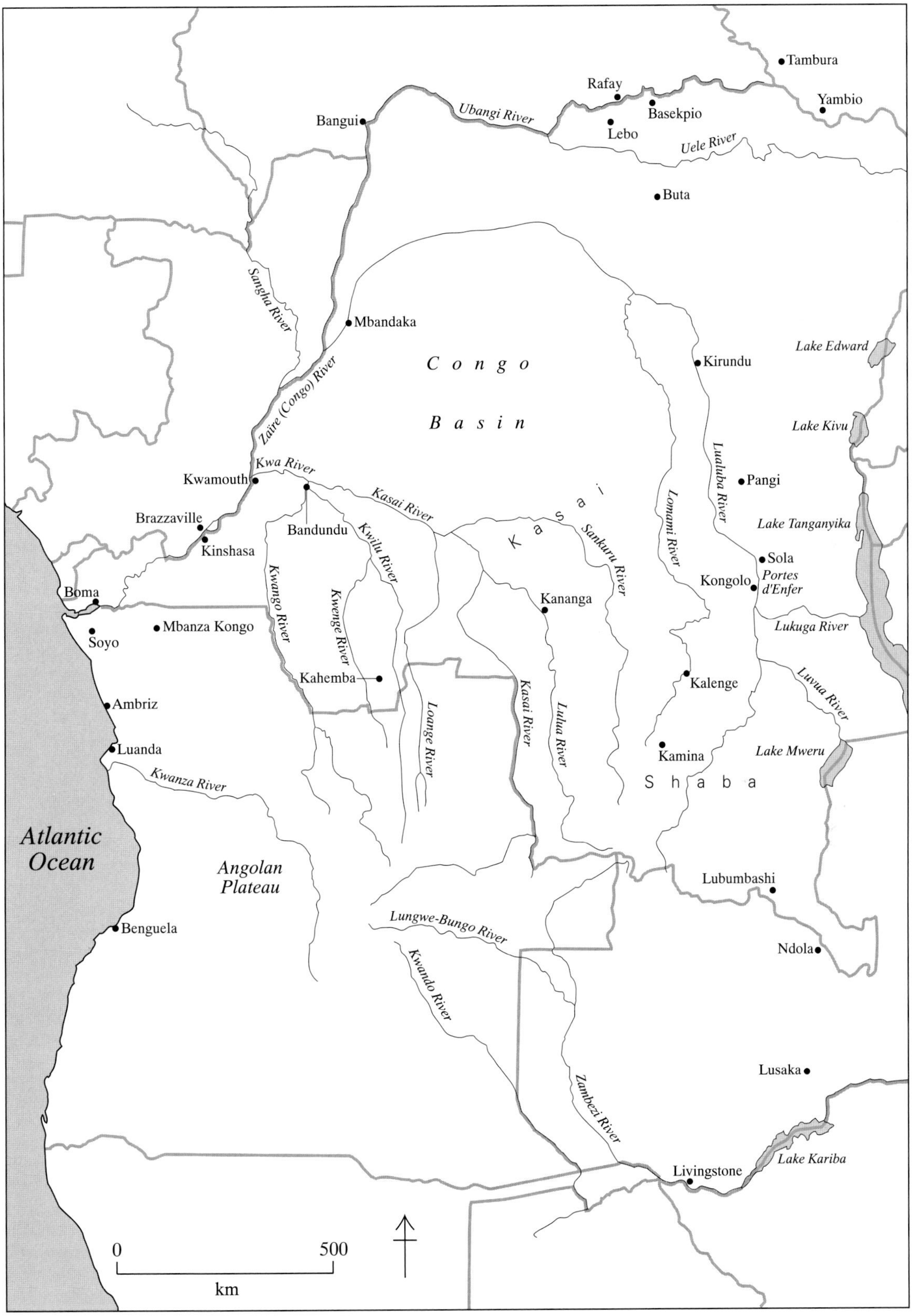

134. Map of Central Africa

135. Luba-Hemba (?or Eastern Luba) staff, wood, h. 250 mm (figures), 1.34 m (overall), from Zaïre (Prague, Náprstek Museum of Asian, African and American Culture)

and weapons symbolize political power and are used by ritual specialists, diviners and healers, while the domestic environment is the context for decorated utilitarian artefacts.

(i) Introduction. (ii) Sculpture. (iii) Masks. (iv) Textiles and ceramics. (v) Architecture. (vi) European influence.

(i) Introduction. The earliest human artefacts from Upper Acheulian and Post-Acheulian archaeological contexts are handaxes, cleavers, picks and leaf-shaped points made from polymorphic sandstones. Later artefacts—tanged arrowheads and polished axes—were made with greater care. Proto-Bushmen and early proto-Bantu-speaking peoples were probably the carriers of this Neolithic culture. Early Iron Age culture becomes apparent in the interlacustrian region by *c.* AD 200, and in the extreme south-east hemispherical pottery with the slight dimple base and rather short neck is commonly found in graves containing hoes, knives and iron spearheads. The oldest example of wood sculpture (Tervuren, Kon. Mus. Mid.-Afrika), attributed to the 8th century AD, was found in gravel banks along the Liavela River in Central Angola and represents an animal image. To the south-east around Lake Kisale, from the end of the 1st millennium AD, social stratification is evident with the presence of grave goods including ceremonial axes studded with nails, cylindrical iron anvils, copper bangles, anklets, belts, necklaces, bracelets, rings and copper cross-ingots.

Compared to other regions of Africa, rock art is poorly represented due to the limited number of exposed surfaces suitable for decoration. In the south-west, silhouettes of wild animals and a few human representations are found in rock painting regarded as the work of Final Neolithic hunter-gatherers, while schematic petroglyphs by Early Iron Age peoples consist of concentric and linked circles, chevrons, grids or ladder-like designs. In the lower Zaïre area, rock shelters present only zigzag engravings and black-and-ochre paintings thought to date from the 16th century. The general types of traditional ethnic art—so-called 'tribal' art—include both anthropomorphic and zoomorphic figures and masks, sculptured decoration of sceptres, staffs, ceremonial spears, adzes, knives, hairpins, pipes, cups, neckrests, ladles, caryatid stools, ritual implements, musical instruments and various items for building decoration. The principal medium is wood, although metal, stone and clay are occasionally used in three-dimensional work. Abstract designs are found in textiles, pottery and basketwork. Styles of art work are generally categorized by ethnic names, although recent field studies assert that a given style is not necessarily uniform within a given ethnic unit: borrowings of art objects between different groups appear, as well as unexpected forms of stylistic synthesis. Moreover, a style can be linked with ritual institutions that overlap ethnic groupings and thus are effectively 'trans-tribal'. Much of the literature on Central African art centres on broad regional and local stylistic classifications based upon the morphological study of carved statuettes. The classic work by Frans Olbrechts (1946) established the framework of classification for subsequent researchers. It recognizes five stylistic regions, each with several styles and substyles: the Lower Congo or South-west; Kuba or South Centre; Luba or South-east; the North-west; and the North-east.

(ii) Sculpture. The Lower Congo stylistic region, the western limit of which is the Atlantic Ocean, is subdivided into the

Coastal style area, the TEKE style to the north and the Kwango style to the east: the Coastal style includes sculptures of the Kongo (*see* KONGO, figs 1 and 3), Kakongo, Solongo, Yombe, Woyo, Sundi, Bwende and Vili peoples. Free-standing sculpture is noted for asymmetry and diversity in posture, with the head rendered in a naturalistic manner. Eyes are commonly picked out in kaolin or mirror fragments. Examples of the mother-and-child theme, together with the varied imagery of magical assemblages on the head or torso, are distinctive. Items attached to figures include metal rings and seed pods, inserted blades, nails and wrapped screws, tied packets, suspended containers and tufts of various materials, all of which offer sculptural qualities in an accumulative aesthetic mode. Research has identified independent style groups of the Bwende, BEMBE, Mboma and Sundi or simply designates given objects by the various Kongo ethnic components.

The Pool Malebo or Teke-style subdivision includes sculpture of the Lari, Mfinu and Wuum. Figures are shown in stiff standing postures, with striated faces, square beards, and on the head either a sagital crest or bunlike hairstyle. Back-to-back double statuettes among the Teke and Teke-related populations are known. Usually the magical load—diverse substances of metonymic and metaphorical reference—surrounds the torso enclosed in a resin adhesive, occasionally reinforced by cloth or skin. Thus arms are often omitted and sexual organs rarely shown. Related imagery appears among the Northern Mbala (see fig. 136), Yansi, Buma, Sakata and Npepe.

The Kwango-style subgroup includes sculpture of the YAKA, Mbala and PENDE, consisting of figures shown in a standing or squatting posture, with hands held up to chest or chin. Highly expressive eyes, noses, eyebrows, facial framing and elaboration of headgear are richly developed, with the spectrum of creativity ranging from simplified naturalism to grotesque caricature. The applied materials and textures that alter the sculptural form include antelope horns, packets, sticks, skins, bones, encrustations of camwood and other ingredients suspended, wrapped or otherwise attached to the statuettes. Further breakdown designates styles of the Suku, Nkanu, Hungaan, Holo, Southern Yaka, Tsotso, Kwese, Soonde, Lula, Dikidiki and Mbeko.

The South Centre or Kasai stylistic group centres on Bushoong court statues of the Kuba, in which sovereigns are depicted seated cross-legged with symbolic attributes carved on the plinth (*see* KUBA (ii), fig. 1). Rounded treatment of face and forehead, angled hairline and annulated neck are shared to varying degrees with the Ndengese, Biombo, Northern Kete, Mbagani and Salampasu, although figure sculpture may include a diversity of polychrome patterns painted on to the human face.

The South-east or LUBA stylistic cluster, stretching from Katanga to the Eastern Kasai, presents a smooth naturalism in human forms, with domed forehead, lowered eyes and pursed lips highlighted by an elaborate tiered hairdress that may cascade or end in a cross configuration. Hands and feet may be elongated and simplified, but more attention is given to body scarification. Characteristic are depictions of the young female with hands to breast or holding a bowl, or as a caryatid supporting a seat. Males

136. Northern Mbala headrest, wood, h. 175 mm (London, British Museum)

appear either holding regalia or standing with arms flanking a protruding stomach. Substyles of Luba Shankadi, Luba Upemba, Luba Kasai, Hemba, Eastern Luba, Zela, Kanyok, TABWA, Tumbwe, Holoholo, Bangubangu, Bemba, Sikasingo, Bembe and Boyo have been distinguished. The SONGYE substyle is differentiated by geometric treatment of the human face and body forms, which are segmented into distinct volumes. Apart from the figure-of-eight-shaped mouth, prominent chin and large flat hands and feet, there is the characteristic collage aspect, with attachments of copper sheeting, blades, tacks, feathers and cowrie shell together with the power packet enclosed in a protruding abdomen or inserted into a horn projecting vertically from the figure's head.

The Angolan Plateau stylistic group, formerly regarded as a Luba substyle tending to the baroque, centres on the Chokwe (*see* CHOKWE AND RELATED PEOPLES; see fig. 137). Distinct are the broad shoulders and slender torsos with arms thrown back in a dynamic stance. Attention is given to the flaring headgear and body detail down to fingernails and toes. Almond-shaped eyes can be recessed in deep sockets, and the beard projects laterally or is formed of fibre or human hair. Other attachments are usually limited to a proliferation of brass tacks. As with the Kuba and Luba, Chokwe styles overflow into many forms of minor arts with the decoration of pipes, combs, staffs, musical instruments and furniture. Mbunda, Lwena, Songo, Ovimbundu and Ngangela substyles present variations on scarification designs and headdresses but add new subjects, for example a figure mounted on an ox and both cruciform and framed figures of types shared on the Kwango River with the Holo.

In the North-eastern Equatorial stylistic region, various rudimentary human forms are produced in bone, ivory and wood. Diagnostic are the half figures, double-faced, double-headed or fully double figures with superimposed faces, heads or bodies placed in opposition or linked together, many without arms, with one arm or short stumps for arms. Relatively small, heart-shaped faces are distinctive, with arched eyebrows forming a single unit with a narrow ridge or flat triangular nose. Best-known is

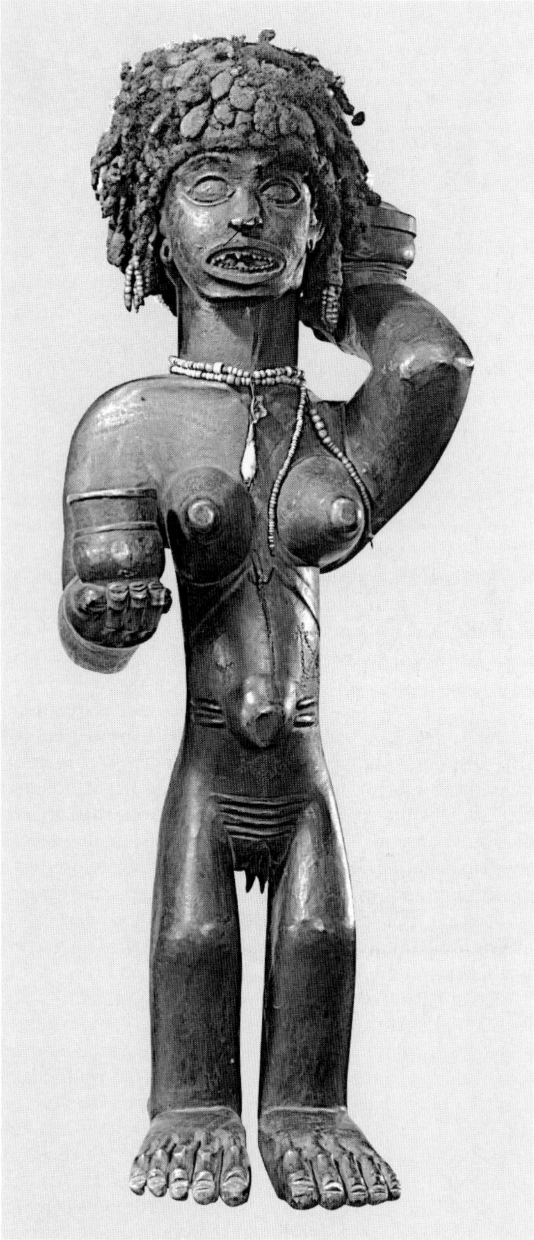

137. Chokwe figure sculpture, wood, human hair, glass beads, camwood powder, iron and traces of copper sheeting, h. 590 mm, collected 1883 (Berlin, Museum für Völkerkunde)

the imagery of the Lega (*see* LEGA AND RELATED PEOPLES), although similar anthropomorphic figurines are found among the Yela, Lengola, Mitoko, Bembe, Pere, Komo, Nyanga, Kwami, Nyindu, Songola and Zimba.

North-central and North-western stylistic groups are less uniform categories that include the MANGBETU (see fig. 138), ZANDE and Boa on the one hand and Ngbaka and Ngbandi further to the west. Figurative sculpture for the Mangbetu and Zande more commonly consisted of decoration on everyday objects rather than a prolific tradition in statuary. Delicate female figures decorate the bridges of harps covered with reptile skin. Their highly embellished realism shows distinct cranial deformation and expanding cylindrical headdresses. Zande styles of free-standing sculpture range from rounded forms to greatly abstracted figures with zigzag or stumplike legs

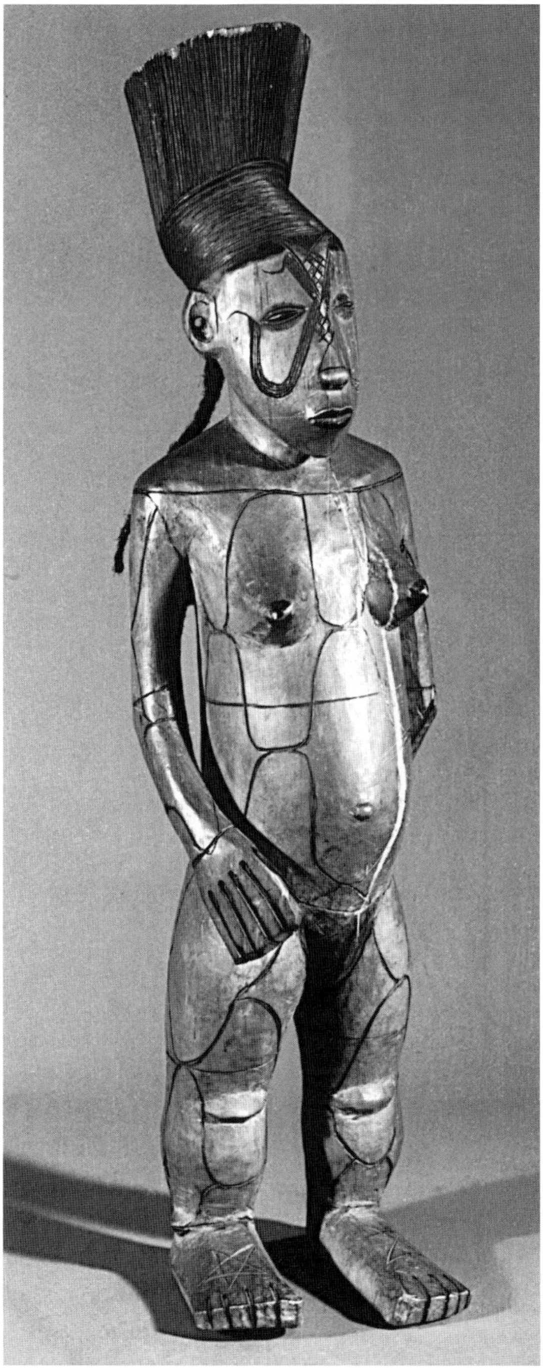

138. Mangbetu female figure sculpture, wood and hair, h. 485 mm, probably early 20th century, from Uele, Zaïre (Tervuren, Koninklijk Museum voor Midden-Afrika)

and underdeveloped arms, a characteristic shared with Ngbaka and Ngbande. Additives to such figures include multiple metal rings and strings of beads embedded in resin. Ngbandi and Ngbaka sculpture is equally rare; it is characterized by large spherical heads, often with heart-shaped faces and brows lined with ridges of scars that also bisect the forehead vertically. Flipper-like arms commonly hang freely at the side, and in highly abstract varieties human features are barely recognizable.

(iii) Masks. Central African masks range from miniatures to face coverings, from cap and helmet varieties that surround the wearer's head to massive creations that completely engulf the person beneath. Although the facial portion may be formed of woven materials, bark cloth or carefully carved and painted wood, masks are found decorated with strips of metal, tacks, shells, calabash segments, beads, feathers, fur, animal horns or constructed headgear and commonly include either a knitted hood or a free-flowing fibre fringe (see fig. 139). Representation includes humans, animals and composite creatures made up of elements of both. The system for classifying masks, like that of free-standing figures, is by ethnic unit or tribe, stressing the uniqueness of a chosen mask type. Resemblances in size or form are apparent both in contiguous ethnic groups and in isolated pockets within Central Africa. Miniature masks, small enough to be held in the palm of the hand, appear in the north-east among the Lega, Nyindu and Kwami, where they are carved of bone and ivory. In the south-west, amid the Pende, Southern Suku, Holo and Chokwe, such masks are made of wood, ivory, seed-pit, lead and other materials. In the south-west among the Songye, Luba-Hemba and northernmost Luba they appear in wood as miniature white-faced masks with striated markings.

Giant masks are defined as masks measuring 900 mm or more in any direction. They are reported across the southern savannah and the Angolan Plateau made of woven materials, bark cloth or carved from wood, often featuring a face with bloated cheeks or a horned animal. The massive fibre masks of the western or Kwilu Pende called *gikuku mingangi* are the largest recorded in Central Africa: during the dance five or six other masked personages emerge from the mask's flowing fringe skirt.

The white, heart-shaped face is characteristic of mask imagery across the equatorial forest region among Bantu-speaking peoples, including the Mbole, Komo, Tembo, Lega, Bembe, Jonga and Ngbaka, and into Gabon, where the form dominates. The heart-shaped face can also be found in isolated contexts on the southern savannah amid the Kwese and easternmost Kasai Pende, and indeed whiteness in faces and white areas around eyes of masks are prevalent throughout Central Africa. Contrasts between the schematization or abstract reductions in mask imagery of the equatorial forest and examples of naturalism among the Vili, Suku, Pende, Chokwe and Luba are readily apparent. Yet within the savannah belt alone fantastic exaggerations distantly removed from human facial physiognomy occur in masks of the Yaka, Pende, Kete, Luluwa, Lwalwa, Songye, Chokwe and HEMBA.

South of the Zaïre Basin two macrostyles encompass the diverse ethnic expressions in masking: an upper zone

139. Salampasu mask, fibres and feathers, h. 914 mm, from Zaïre (Los Angeles, CA, University of California, Fowler Museum of Cultural History)

of predominantly wooden helmet-shaped masks, found among populations living near the northern edge of the savannah and nearby forests (e.g. Suku, Kasai Pende, Kwese, Kete, Kuba, Binji, Kanyok and Luba), and a secondary tier of predominantly resin-and-fabric masks made by peoples across the savannah to the south (e.g. the Chokwe, Lwena, Lunda, Soonde, Yaka and Nkanu). Moreover, the towering projections, mitre-like elements, discs and painted decoration imply transtribal interaction of styles. The principal context for both resin-and-fabric masks and wooden helmet-shaped masks across southern Central Africa is that of *mukanda*, an institution involving collective circumcision and initiation to manhood with widespread similarities in terminology, sequence of events and use of masks at crucial moments of initiation and coming-out festivities. In north-eastern Zaïre, use of the white, heart-shaped face in masking of the Lega and their neighbours is associated with an age-graded association known variously as Bwami, Bukota, Lilwa and Nsubi.

Masks in these contexts serve as mnemonic devices that aid in learning an enormous number of proverbs and ritual actions, secrets reserved to members alone. Other trans-tribal examples in masking styles may be observed in the oblong or oval masks with patterns of incised facial striations among the Songye, Kalebwe and Luba-Hemba, which are associated with a secret organization known as Kifwebe. A still broader view might include diverse peoples using fibre masks and body coverings made of palm leaves and occasionally decorated with other materials. They generally signify bush monsters that terrorize the uninitiated; they are widespread and are the likely source from which more elaborate mask-making derives.

(iv) Textiles and ceramics. In the artistic production of textiles, Central African cut-pile embroidery, called 'Kasai velvets', has been admired by outsiders since first discovery. The oldest examples came to Europe between 1666 and 1674 from the mouth of the Zaïre River and Angola. Since the late 19th century production has been limited to Kuba-related peoples of the Kasai region, and it continues in the 20th century among the Shoowa and Ngombe of the Sankuru. The wide range of various rectilinear and abstract patterns are assigned individual names by their makers, although patterns bearing the same name are not necessarily identical. The classification of patterns is paralleled by distinctive social meanings of its use. Some were worn by women, others by men; some appeared on ceremonial occasions only, others were in everyday use and distinguished the social position of the wearer. Early accounts further describe a variety of uses: as blankets, in adornment of stools, as shrouds and as currency.

Pottery exists primarily as domestic ware. Forms range from jars with long, bottle-shaped necks made in the coastal region to the spherical forms made in the east, which bear short necks and a small mouth. Decoration of surfaces with bands of incised crosshatching and zigzag is common, as are impressions made with cords and other objects. Painting with mineral or vegetable pigments, as well as use of glazes, often enhances vessels. Noteworthy is the marbled or mottled effect achieved by splashing oil on the newly fired surface in Kongo and Teke wares. Although rare, figurative decoration on lids takes the form of birds, dogs or humans among the Kongo, while a few ceramic heads and busts used as containers appear among certain groups of the Kwango and Kasai rivers and the Mangbetu to the north. The influence of woven design is reflected in ceramic decoration, particularly in the Kasai region.

(v) Architecture. The most common traditional structure has a square or rectangular plan with walls of palm fronds and a hipped roof of thatch or palm leaf. Distinctive variations appear among Kuba-related peoples, who embellish this basic framework with interwoven materials and mats. The Mangbetu in the 19th century amplified it into a vast rectangular assembly hall some 15 m high. Roof structure and thatching could achieve a convex profile, found in structures from the Holo and Southern Suku to the Luba, or the pyramidal roof of leaves in the north among the Ngelima and Nalya. Granaries could be elevated versions of the pitched roof structure or miniature versions of cylindrical buildings with conical roofs, as found among the Chokwe and related peoples in Angola. Carved posts, panels or figures embellished the domestic dwellings of dignitaries, especially among the Kongo, Chokwe and Pende, while dressed wooden doorframes were made by the Southern Suku and Holo, and the Mangbetu elaborately painted pillars and walls.

(vi) European influence. Both stylistic diversity and traditional conservatism, apparent in the early 20th-century art of the region, were products of past isolation as well as of steady intergroup contacts, intermixing and political emulation or domination. Since then, the disruption of traditional structures of authority, religious proselytizing, the establishment of mission and government schools and rural projects and the external economic pressures of a cash economy have dramatically changed the traditional setting of art. In some areas a wholesale rejection of traditional ritual and accompanying paraphernalia has resulted. In others, masking in the context of initiations survived or has been revived, both in a quest for cultural authenticity and as a source of local revenue. Retention of the original significance or regulation of art works by traditional leadership is rare in the late 20th century.

The earliest influence of European imagery in Central Africa, however, dates from the beginning of the 16th century, following the arrival of Catholic missionaries. The Kongo king Alfonso I (*reg* 1509–41) gave the crucifix to clan chiefs and judges presiding over tribunals both in the Mbanza capital and outlying provinces. Later the crucifix became a standard item for the investiture of Kongo chiefs and was incorporated into a syncretic belief system. Cast by the lost-wax or open-mould methods, all brass *nkangi kiditu* ('attached Christ') are based on 14th–16th-century European examples, although African-like features illustrate indigenous adaptation. Wooden crucifixes and free-standing statuary of the Virgin and St Anthony were also produced. Within the south-western region, Christian religious influence into the 20th century is equally apparent in the *ntadi* stone funerary monuments of the Mboma, Holo framed figures and some Chokwe woodcarving.

For more information on continuing traditions, on colonial and post-colonial arts and on art patronage, museums and art education, *see* the individual country entries.

BIBLIOGRAPHY

F. M. Olbrechts: *Plastiek van Kongo* (Antwerp, 1946)
A. Maesen: 'Un Art traditionnel au Congo Belge: La Sculpture', *Les Arts au Congo Belge et au Ruanda-Urundi* (Brussels, 1950), pp. 9–33
L. de Sousberghe: *L'Art Pende* (Brussels, 1958)
J. Cornet: *Art d'Afrique noire au pays du fleuve Zaïre* (Brussels, 1971); Eng. trans. as *Art of Africa: Treasures from the Congo* (London, 1971)
D. Biebuyck: *The Arts of Zaire*, 5 vols (Berkeley, 1985–)
——: *The Arts of Central Africa: An Annotated Bibliography*, Ref. Pubns A. Hist. (Boston, MA, 1987)
M. L. Felix: *100 Peoples of Zaire and their Neighbors: The Handbook* (Brussels, 1987)
H.-J. Koloss: *Art of Central Africa: Masterpieces from the Berlin Museum für Völkerkunde* (New York, 1990)

A. P. BOURGEOIS

7. EAST AFRICA. For present purposes East Africa is taken to be the vast area occupied by the modern states of KENYA, UGANDA, RWANDA, BURUNDI, TANZANIA, ZAMBIA and MALAWI (see fig. 140). It thus includes what is often referred to as East Central Africa. Reference will

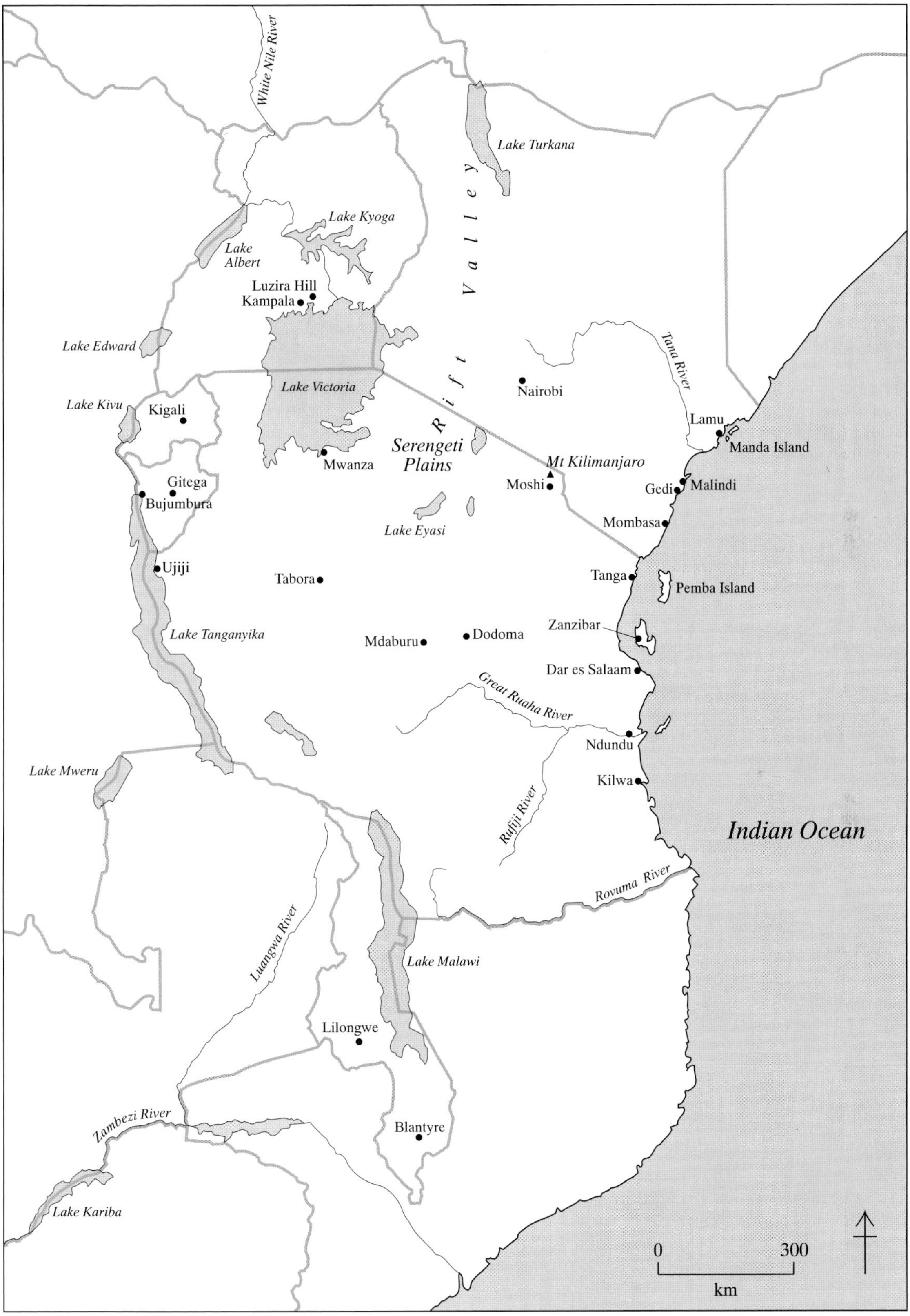

140. Map of East Africa

also be made to peoples living within the southern parts of Sudan whose cultural traditions link them with other East Africans rather than with the predominantly Islamic populations to their north, as well as to peoples living in adjacent areas of other neighbouring countries. The island of MADAGASCAR is often treated as part of East Africa, but it is dealt with separately in this dictionary.

(i) Introduction. (ii) Body arts. (iii) Mask and masquerade. (iv) Figure sculpture. (v) Architecture. (vi) Domestic and other arts.

(i) Introduction. The region whose art is discussed here straddles the Equator and lies well within the tropics, yet it does not experience a typical Equatorial climate, nor is it characterized by the dense lowland rain-forests found at similar latitudes on the west of the continent. The Ruwenzori Mountains, which constitute part of the western boundary of the area, are also the limit of the forests of the Zaïre River Basin. Generally, East Africa is high plateau country whose altitude ensures temperate conditions and a vegetation cover that, except in more mountainous parts, is typically that of dry woodland. In lower-lying areas, notably in the Rift Valley and the Serengeti Plains of northern Tanzania, there are vast areas of dry grassland. The north has the most arid climate, such that the area around Lake Turkana in northern Kenya includes large expanses of desert. The southern Sudan, through which flows the White Nile, includes both dry woodland and the vast swamps of the Sudd. With the Ethiopian Highlands this provides the northern limits of the region.

Most East and East Central Africans speak one of the innumerable Bantu languages and are descended from peoples who moved into the area from the west from *c.* AD 100. Today they live south of a line running through southern Uganda, including much of Tanzania and taking in eastern Kenya. The populations of Zambia and Malawi are almost entirely Bantu-speaking. Characteristically, such peoples practise mixed farming with an emphasis on cultivation, particularly in areas where cattle-keeping is made impossible by the presence of the tsetse fly.

Along the eastern coast and on such off-shore islands as Lamu, Pemba and Zanzibar, the SWAHILI established a series of Arab-style town states or sultanates. Their language, also Bantu though with many Arabic loan-words, and their political systems developed in parallel with their evolving cosmopolitan culture. Regular trading networks linked the East African coast to the Arabian Sea and beyond from the end of the 1st millennium AD, and Islam became the dominant faith of this maritime corridor. Swahili-speaking traders set up links with the interior, and forms of Swahili became the lingua franca throughout much of the region and into eastern Zaïre. Both Islam and the tradition of town states, however, have remained essentially coastal phenomena. Throughout the rest of the region, traditional political authority tends to be invested in local chiefs or village headmen. Only exceptionally did more elaborate kingdoms develop, for example those of the Ganda of Uganda, the Lozi or Rotse in Zambia, and among some of the peoples of Tanzania. None, however, attained the opulence that was achieved by some kingdoms in West and Central Africa.

In the north of the region the dominant languages are those of the Nilotic family, spoken by, for example, the Dinka in southern Sudan, the Karamojong in Uganda, the Turkana in Kenya and the Maasai in Kenya and Tanzania. Most of these peoples are noted for the attention they devote to their herds of cattle. These are of both economic and social importance and are sometimes in themselves vehicles for artistic expression and aesthetic contemplation, their hides being decorated and their horns twisted into pleasing shapes (see fig. 14 above; see also Coote). Pure pastoralism, however, is rare, and most East African cattle-keepers also grow crops. Among the peoples of the Kenya Highlands, known collectively as the Kalenjin, agricultural production is intensive and replaces cattle-keeping as the mainstay of the traditional economy. In general, political authority extending beyond the local level is rare among Nilotic peoples, although in Rwanda the Tutsi have established themselves as a local aristocracy. Despite being conquerors, however, they have adopted the language of the conquered and speak a Bantu dialect.

The Hadza of southern Tanzania are, along with Pygmy groups in Uganda, the last to maintain a hunter–gatherer economy in East Africa. Their material culture has been well documented (see Woodburn).

The region as a whole has often been described as being 'without art'. Such a statement, however, seriously misrepresents the situation. First, the assumption that art is limited to certain types of sculptural or graphic traditions can be challenged; and second, even on such a limited definition art is far from absent in the region. Since the 1950s more and more examples of East African sculptural traditions have come to light, both through the publication of previously unknown examples in museum collections and through fieldwork. Unfortunately, however, many pieces are only vaguely provenanced, and further information about context and use is often lacking. More importantly, until the early 1990s the art history of East Africa was still in its infancy. It is this fact and the restrictive definitions often applied, rather than any lack of materials, that has led to the perception of East Africa as being without art.

Indeed, there is evidence that artistic traditions are of considerable antiquity in the region. Among archaeological finds a striking head (and probably separate torso) found at Luzira Hill near Lake Victoria in Uganda remains undated and so far without parallel in the region (for illustration see *The Potter's Art in Africa* by W. Fagg and J. Pictor (London, 1970), p. 32). There are, however, paintings and petroglyphs on rock surfaces and in caves throughout most of the area, the largest concentrations being in central Tanzania (see figs 110 and 112 above). These works range from schematic designs to representations of both wild and domesticated animals, often in naturalistic styles, as well as human figures. Dating these works is difficult, and the overall timespan probably extensive. The depictions of wild animals are generally assumed to be among the oldest, though at Mt Elgon in Kenya depictions of long-horned cattle, which are not found anywhere in the area today, may date to the 1st millennium BC. To judge by its subject-matter, much of the rock art, except the very earliest, might most readily be associated with pastoralists. Certainly, pastoralists in the north have continued to make their own contributions to the rock art of the region late into the 20th century.

The principal and most visible subject of decoration among these peoples, however, is the human body.

(ii) Body arts. Among the Nilotic peoples of East Africa both men and women decorate their bodies using a wide variety of materials. For the Karamojong of Uganda and their Kenyan neighbours the Turkana and Pokot, mud is a major component in male decoration. This is applied particularly to the back of the head, where clay is pressed into the hair, building up successive layers. These dry to form a hard and smooth surface that can then be painted. Zips, pins and other small items may be incorporated, together with holders into which feathers are implanted (see fig. 141). Bead ornaments and other jewellery, often made of aluminium or brass from spent cartridge cases, are also worn. Again it is the head or parts of it that are emphasized. Ornaments may thus be attached to the ears, nose and lower lip, while beads and beaded discs are strung over the forehead. In addition, most of the men among these peoples carry with them a small headrest (*see* §(vi) below). This is used when lying down to prevent decorated areas from being crushed and destroyed.

Female decoration also frequently serves to focus attention on the head rather than the body. Here, however, it is not principally by altering or emphasizing the natural features of the head and face that the effect is achieved but by separating them visually from the rest of the body. Thus, typically, the neck is encircled by numerous strings of beads, often richly coloured and so massed as sometimes to give the illusion that the neck itself has been elongated (see figs 27 and 94 above; *see also* MAASAI). In the hot, dry regions clothing for both men and women is often minimal. Yet, where women clothe the body, it is normally in leather skins that are little embellished other than with small areas of beadwork usually applied to the back or skirts or small pubic aprons. Sometimes, however, as among the Turkana, the beadwork can be quite elaborate (see fig. 55 above). Otherwise, the most elaborate of such beaded skirts are those made not by Nilotic pastoralists but further south among the Cushitic-speaking Iraqw of Tanzania. Here red, blue, yellow and black beads may be applied in lazy stitch in bands and symbolic designs to a skirt consisting of three or four hides, thus producing a heavy and richly decorated garment (see fig. 142).

Understanding of these Nilotic styles of decoration would be advanced by greater knowledge of each people's conception of the body. For some of the Bantu peoples of the region there is more information. For them scarification is the most important form of body decoration, especially in western Tanzania and northern Zambia, where the elaborate traditions of cicatrization found in Zaïre also occur. Among Nilotic peoples, and most dramatically among the Dinka, Nuer and Shilluk of southern Sudan, such scarification is concentrated on the forehead. By contrast, the tendency among Bantu peoples around Lake Tanganyika is to embellish the natural symmetry of the body as a whole rather than to alter or emphasize specific parts of it. Thus, many systems of scarification are articulated around a central axis of the body running down the forehead to the tip of the nose and from the neck via the navel to the genitalia. The most

141. Turkana man with characteristically decorated head, northern Kenya; from a photograph by Fabby K. J. Nielsen

completely analysed case is that of the TABWA of Zaïre and adjacent parts of Zambia.

The patterns and designs thus created are also reproduced on figure sculpture in the area and are to be found in works associated with the Bemba and Bisa of Zambia as well as up the western coast of Lake Tanganyika to the cosmopolitan centre of Ujiji in Tanzania. The interpretation of such patterns is complex, but it is clear that particular motifs applied to particular parts of the body have specific significance. There are, however, a number of points where patterns of scarification concentrate or intersect. One is the navel, a reminder perhaps of birth and a place of transitions; another is the forehead, the seat of wisdom and the source of dreams and visions. In all such cases patterns of scarification are likely to take account of the symbolic topography of the body particular to different cultures. Our further understanding of such traditions of body arts thus depends on more studies of the symbolic systems of which they form a part.

Unsurprisingly, among the Muslim Swahili traditions of body art are very different from those discussed above. The focus here is on dress and elaborate jewellery (*see* SWAHILI, §4).

(iii) Mask and masquerade. Elaborate traditions of masking are found only among Bantu-speaking peoples of the region and then only in certain areas. Probably the best-known masking traditions are those of the two Makonde peoples of southern Tanzania and northern Mozambique. The wooden helmet masks of the Mozambican Makonde are often vividly realistic caricatures, though, with their characteristic scarification patterns applied with beeswax or carved into the wood, they are unmistakably Makonde (*see also* MAKONDE, §2). The best-studied masking tradition of the region, however, is probably that of the Chewa of adjacent parts of Zambia, Malawi and Mozambique (see Yoshida, 1992, 1993). Generally speaking, the Chewa

142. Iraqw hide skirt with beadwork decoration, l. 635 mm, from Tanzania (London, Commonwealth Institute)

tradition is similar to that of Central and West Africa (*see* §VI, 3 above). All the men are initiated into a secret masking association that performs at funerary rituals and other events including, at least in the later 20th century, some purely for entertainment. There are three types of mask among the Chewa. The first two, a feathered spirit mask and a wooden face mask, are used to represent spirits of the dead. The third, known collectively as *nyau yolemba*, are large zoomorphic basketwork structures, most of which represent wild animals, though cars, cattle, sorcerers and Europeans are also represented.

Masks, mostly in wood but also in hide and fibre, are known from a number of other East African peoples, especially in Tanzania. They are, however, mostly known from museum collections, and further details concerning their imagery and use are generally lacking (see Holy; Krieger).

(iv) Figure sculpture. In much of the region the dominant sculptural form is the pole, variously decorated and more or less anthropomorphized. Such pole sculptures have been recorded from the Bongo and Bari in the north of the region in the southern Sudan, from the Konso in southern Ethiopia and from numerous other peoples down to the Zaramo in Tanzania. Such sculptures are often associated with graves, or at least with the dead, or with entrances to villages. Among the best-known sculptures of this sort are the memorial posts (*vigango*, sing. *kigango*) of the Giriama and other Mijikenda-speaking peoples of Kenya. Among the Giriama the posts range in height from 1 to 3 m and are made of durable hardwoods. The dominant motif used in their decoration is the triangle—used to represent ribs, perhaps, or ropes or snakes entwined around the body or the snuff container and chain worn by elders around the neck. The carved triangles are painted in red, white and black, and this simple motif is combined and arranged in a vast variety of patterns (*see also* §III, 5(ii)(b) above). The top is either flat and disc-shaped or a three-dimensional head; some of the latter were given silver dollars for eyes.

Traditions of figure sculpture are known from many other areas of the region. The figures of the MAKONDE are well known, while many other traditions are represented in museum collections (see Holy; Krieger). Among the more spectacular examples are the zoomorphic iron figures of the Karagwe (e.g. Stuttgart, Linden-Mus.) and a particularly naturalistic male figure carved by a Nyamwezi artist among the Kerewe (Berlin, Mus. Vlkerknd.).

In the south of the region, in Tanzania and Zambia, there is a widespread tradition of using pottery figurines in initiation ceremonies and other rituals (see Cory, 1956; Corbeil).

(v) Architecture. East Africa's best-known architectural tradition is that of the Swahili towns of the coast and islands. The tradition can be traced from the ruins of Gedi and Kilwa to the bustling towns of Lamu and Zanzibar. The dominant features are the use of coral blocks and mangrove poles, decorative plasterwork and intricate wood-carving especially of doors and windows (*see* SWAHILI, §2).

In rural areas, traditional East African architecture is characterized by the use of wood, grass and mud. These deceptively simple materials have been combined in a vast variety of ways to produce a range of temporary and semi-permanent buildings for humans, animals and the storage of foodstuffs. The forms these structures take are often referred to as 'beehives' or 'cone-and-cylinder', but there are in fact a vast range of forms, architectural details, methods of construction and materials. The arrangement of buildings in compounds or villages also shows great variety. One of the most distinctive of such arrangements is that of the Maasai *manyatta*, constructed by women for their sons' circumcision and initiation ceremonies, in which 100 or more low, oblong cowdung-plastered huts are arranged in a circle with their doorways opening on to a large open area. Most grass, wood and mud buildings in East Africa are single-storey, but huts on stilts are found among some Dinka in southern Sudan (see fig. 61 above).

Many houses are decorated. Among the Kipsigis of Kenya houses may be topped with a carved finial, while generally throughout the area the arrangement of grass thatching on the roof and walls and the shapes and surfaces of mud walls and floors are the focus of much aesthetic attention. Both external and internal walls may be painted. Among the Hima of south-western Uganda the entrances and interior walls of houses are painted with bold geometric black-and-white designs. Among the Sukuma of Tanzania the interior walls of the lodges of the secret charmers' society are painted with images of humans, snakes and mythological figures.

(vi) Domestic and other arts. There are rich traditions of furniture, personal objects, weapons and other items throughout East Africa. Indeed, because of the perceived paucity of sculpture and masks, such objects have received proportionately greater attention from scholars and publishers anxious to fill the East African 'gap' in surveys of African art. For example, though not restricted to East Africa, the carved headrest has often served as the stereotypical example of East African art. The vast range of style and forms of this typically personal object makes it difficult to provide a generalized account. It is perhaps, however, useful to distinguish between headrests that are the product of opportunist carving, as among the Dinka, Nuer and their neighbours in Southern Sudan, and the more formal, geometric headrests produced by the Pokot and other peoples in Kenya. The simple forms produced by the Dinka and Nuer are often little more than the result of some judicious pruning of a found branch to produce a three- or four-legged stool-cum-headrest, a technique that also characterizes their production of poles and shrine posts (for illustration see Coote). Zoomorphic features, such as a tail, are sometimes 'brought out', or spots or stripes may be incised or scratched on the surface. The more formal carvings of the Pokot are sometimes elaborately decorated with the addition of metal, beads, hide and so on, though this could not be said to be typical (see fig. 143). The most elaborate type of East African furniture is probably the Indian-influenced chair produced by the Swahili, but high-backed chairs with sculptured figures are also produced by the Nyamwezi and neighbouring peoples in Tanzania (for illustrations see Krieger, pls 102–3). The range of other East African domestic arts includes pots, decorated gourds, snuff-containers, tobacco pipe-bowls, staffs, tools, implements and utensils.

Among the best-known of East African objects are the shields of the Maasai of Kenya and Tanzania. These are

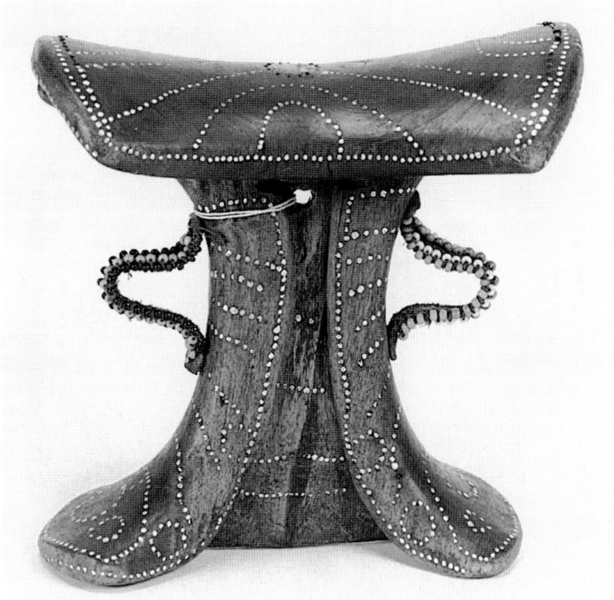

143. Tiati Pokot headrest (*ngachar*), wood, aluminium, copper, beads and hide, h. 170 mm, collected 1960s, from northern Kenya (Oxford, University of Oxford, Pitt Rivers Museum, 1978.20.35)

made of an oval of buffalo hide attached to a wooden 'backbone' and are painted with geometric designs whose complexity and significance have only rarely been appreciated (Winter). The 'shields' worn on the upper arm during initiation dances by young men among the Kikuyu of Kenya are also well known (see fig. 144). Carved from a single piece of wood (like the vast majority of East African carved objects), they are made by specialist craftsmen. The shield were painted with soot, a red paint and a white earth pigment. The shields were passed from older to younger brothers and the designs retained or scraped off and replaced with newly fashionable ones. As with most East African art forms, the art-historical study of Maasai shields and Kikuyu dance shields has hardly begun. The superficial simplicity of many of the forms has meant that they have only recently begun to receive the attention that they deserve from scholars.

For more information on continuing traditions, on colonial and post-colonial arts and on art patronage, museums and art education, *see* the individual country entries. *See also* MAASAI, MAKONDE, SWAHILI and TABWA.

BIBLIOGRAPHY

H. Cory: *Wall-painting by Snake Charmers in Tanganyika* (London, 1953)
M. Trowell and K. P. Wachsmann: *Arts and Crafts in Uganda* (London, 1953)
H. Cory: *African Figurines: Their Ceremonial Use in Puberty Rites in Tanganyika* (London, 1956)
C. M. Sekintu and K. P. Wachsmann: *Wall Patterns on Hima Huts*, Uganda Museum Occasional Papers (Kampala, 1956)
L. Holy: *The Arts of Africa: Masks and Figures from East and South Africa* (London, 1967)
G. W. Hartwig: 'East African Plastic Art Tradition: A Discussion of the Literature', *Genève Afrique*, vii/1 (1968), pp. 31–52
——: 'An Historical Perspective of Kerebe Sculpturing, Tanzania', *Tribus*, xviii (1969), pp. 85–102
——: 'The Role of Plastic Art Traditions in Tanzania: The Northeastern Region', *Baessler-Archv*, n.s., xvii (1969), pp. 25–31

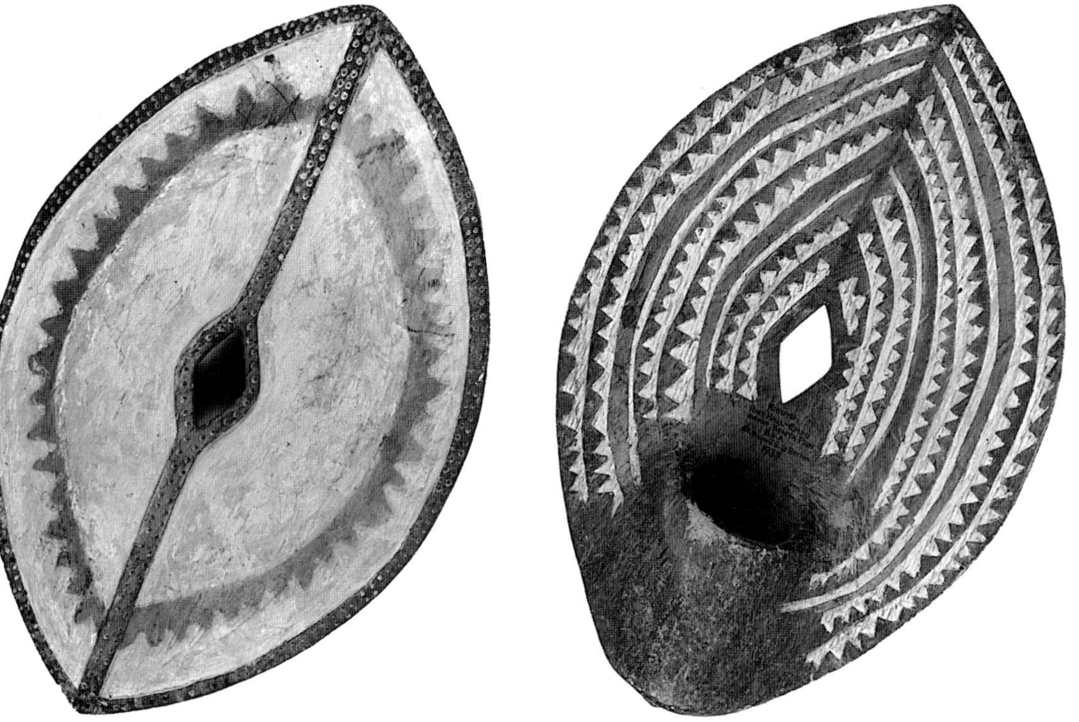

144. Kikuyu dance arm-shield (front and back views), wood, soot, paint and earth, l. 640 mm, from Embu, Kenya, *c.* 1930 (Oxford, University of Oxford, Pitt Rivers Museum, 1933.26.4)

A. M. Lugira: *Ganda Art* (Kampala, 1970); review by D. Banabakintu in *J. Afr. Relig. & Philos.*, i/2 (1990), pp. 137–40

J. M. Woodburn: *Hunters and Gatherers: The Material Culture of the Nomadic Hadza* (London, 1970)

H. M. Cole: 'Vital Arts in Northern Kenya', *Afr. A.*, vii/2 (1974), pp. 12–23, 82

J. A. R. Wembah-Rashid: *Introducing Tanzania through the National Museum* (Dar es Salaam, 1974)

D. W. Phillipson: *The Later Prehistory of Eastern and Southern Africa* (London, 1977)

J. C. Winter: 'Maasai Shield Patterns: A Documentary Source for Political History', *Zur Sprachgeschichte und Ethnohistorie in Afrika: Neue Beiträge afrikanistischer Forschungen*, ed. W. J. G. Möhlig, F. Rottland and B. Heine (Berlin, 1977), pp. 324–47

K. B. Andersen: *African Traditional Architecture: A Study of the Housing and Settlement Patterns of Rural Kenya* (Nairobi, Oxford and New York, 1978)

G. W. Hartwig: 'Sculptures in East Africa', *Afr. A.*, xi/4 (1978), pp. 62–5, 96

N. E. Lindgren and J. M. Schoffeleers: *Rock Art and Nyau Symbolism in Malawi* (Limbe, 1978)

H. M. Cole: 'Living Art among the Samburu', *The Fabrics of Culture: The Anthropology of Clothing and Adornment*, ed. J. M. Cordwell and R. A. Schwarz, World Anthropol. (The Hague, 1979), pp. 87–102

E. Burt: *An Annotated Bibliography of the Visual Arts of East Africa*, Trad. A. Africa (Bloomington, 1980); see also 'Bibliography of the Visual Arts in East Africa: Supplement', *Afr. J.*, xix/2–3 (1983), pp. 205–52

A. B. C. Ocholla-Ayayo: *The Luo Culture: A Reconstruction of the Material Culture Patterns of a Traditional African Society*, Stud. Kultknd., liv (Wiesbaden, 1980)

J. E. Arensen: *Sticks and Straw: Comparative House Forms in Southern Sudan and Northern Kenya*, International Museum of Cultures Publication, xiii (Dallas, 1982)

J. J. Corbeil: *Mbusa: Sacred Emblems of the Bemba* (Mbala, Zambia and London, 1982)

J. Mack: 'Material Culture and Ethnic Identity in Southeastern Sudan', *Culture History in the Southern Sudan: Archaeology, Linguistics and Ethnohistory*, ed. J. Mack and P. Robertshaw, British Institute in Eastern Africa Memoir, viii (Nairobi, 1982), pp. 111–30

M. Leakey: *Africa's Vanishing Past: The Rock Paintings of Tanzania* (London, 1983)

A. Fisher: *Africa Adorned* (London, 1984/*R* 1989) [excellent photographs of body adornment]

M. Carey: *Beads and Beadwork of East and South Africa*, Shire Ethnography, iii (Princes Risborough, 1986)

Vigango: The Commemorative Sculpture of the Mijikenda of Kenya (exh. cat., ed. E. Wolfe, III; Williamstown, MA, Williams Coll., Mus. A., 1986)

J. Barbour and S. Wadibba, eds: *Kenyan Pots and Potters* (Nairobi, 1989)

A Tanzanian Tradition: Doei, Iraku, Kerewe, Makonde, Nyamwezi, Pare, Zaramo, Zigua and Other Groups (exh. cat. by C. Bordogna and L. Kahan, Tenafly, NJ, Afr. A. Mus., 1989)

K. Krieger: *Ostafrikanische Plastik*, Veröff. Mus. Vlkerknd., Berlin, n.s. 50, Abt. Afrika, x (Berlin, 1990) [coll. cat.]

J. Coote: '"Marvels of Everyday Vision": The Anthropology of Aesthetics and the Cattle-keeping Nilotes', *Anthropology, Art, and Aesthetics*, ed. J. Coote and A. Shelton, Oxford Studies in the Anthropology of Cultural Forms (Oxford, 1992), pp. 245–73

K. Yoshida: 'Masks and Transformation among the Chewa of Eastern Zambia', *Africa 4*, ed. S. Wada and P. K. Eguchi, Senri Ethnological Studies, xxxi (Osaka, 1992), pp. 203–73

E. C. Burt, ed.: *Preliminary Study of the Distribution of Art and Material Culture in East Africa: Kenya, Tanzania, and Uganda* (Seattle, 1993)

W. J. Dewey: *Sleeping Beauties: The Jerome L. Joss Collection of African Headrests at UCLA* (Los Angeles, 1993)

S. Somjee: *Material Culture of Kenya* (Nairobi, 1993)

K. Yoshida: 'Masks and Secrecy among the Chewa', *Afr. A.*, xxvi/2 (1993), pp. 34–45, 92

C. A. Kratz: *Affecting Performance: Meaning, Movement, and Experience in Okiek Women's Initiation*, Smithsonian Series in Ethnographic Enquiry (Washington, DC, and London, 1994)

Tanzania: Meisterwerke afrikanischer Skulptur (exh. cat. by M. Felix and others; Berlin, Haus Kult. Welt; Munich, Lenbachhaus; 1994)

JEREMY COOTE, JOHN MACK

8. SOUTHERN AFRICA. Region comprising the area south of the Zambesi River Basin, the Okavango Delta and the Caprivi, including the modern states of ZIMBABWE, MOZAMBIQUE, NAMIBIA, BOTSWANA, SOUTH AFRICA, LESOTHO and SWAZILAND (see fig. 145). The people who inhabit this region speak different Bantu and Khoisan languages and display many different cultural traits. Among the larger language groups are the Ila-Tonga (Zambia–Zimbabwe), the SHONA (Zimbabwe; western Botswana), the NDEBELE (Zimbabwe), the Ovambo and Herero (Namibia), the Hambukushu (Botswana), the Tswana (Botswana; Northwest Province and western Transvaal, South Africa), the North-Sotho, VENDA and Ndebele (Northern Transvaal and Gauteng), the South Sotho (Lesotho; Orange Free State, South Africa), the Swazi (Swaziland), the ZULU (Kwazulu-Natal, South Africa), the Xhosa (eastern Cape, South Africa) and the Tsonga and Chopi of Mozambique. Many of these groups including the Shona, Tswana, North Sotho, Zulu, Xhosa and Tsonga can be subdivided further, both linguistically and culturally. The linguistic and cultural shifts reflect historical and political allegiances and splits among the peoples concerned. Khoisan peoples previously inhabited the whole region. Today they are largely confined to the Kalahari and Okavango areas of Namibia and Botswana.

(i) Introduction. (ii) Architecture. (iii) Wood-carving. (iv) Pottery. (v) Clay sculpture. (vi) Beadwork and costume.

(i) Introduction. Within the region as a whole, there are a number of shared and derived cultural and political institutions, such as initiations and forms of kingship, which cut across traditional linguistic and ethnic classifications. In some instances this is a direct result of impositions by expanding powers, as with the Zulu generals who carried Shaka-style military organizations and insignia to the far corners of the subcontinent. In other cases it reflects adoptions of institutions by neighbouring groups, as when the Lovedu, of Shona origins, adopted Pedi-style male initiations in two stages. Associated with these initiation institutions and following the same distribution in the Transvaal area are types of objects, such as carved figures or drums. However, there are also object-types with a wide distribution that are not linked directly to institutions; these include divining instruments and headrests. Where there is a wide distribution of the same object-type, similar stylistic and compositional features may obtain, but iconographic nuances may differ. There are some groups within the region whose cultural traits are closer to those of peoples in Central Africa (*see* §6 above). This is so in the case of the Ovambo, who are

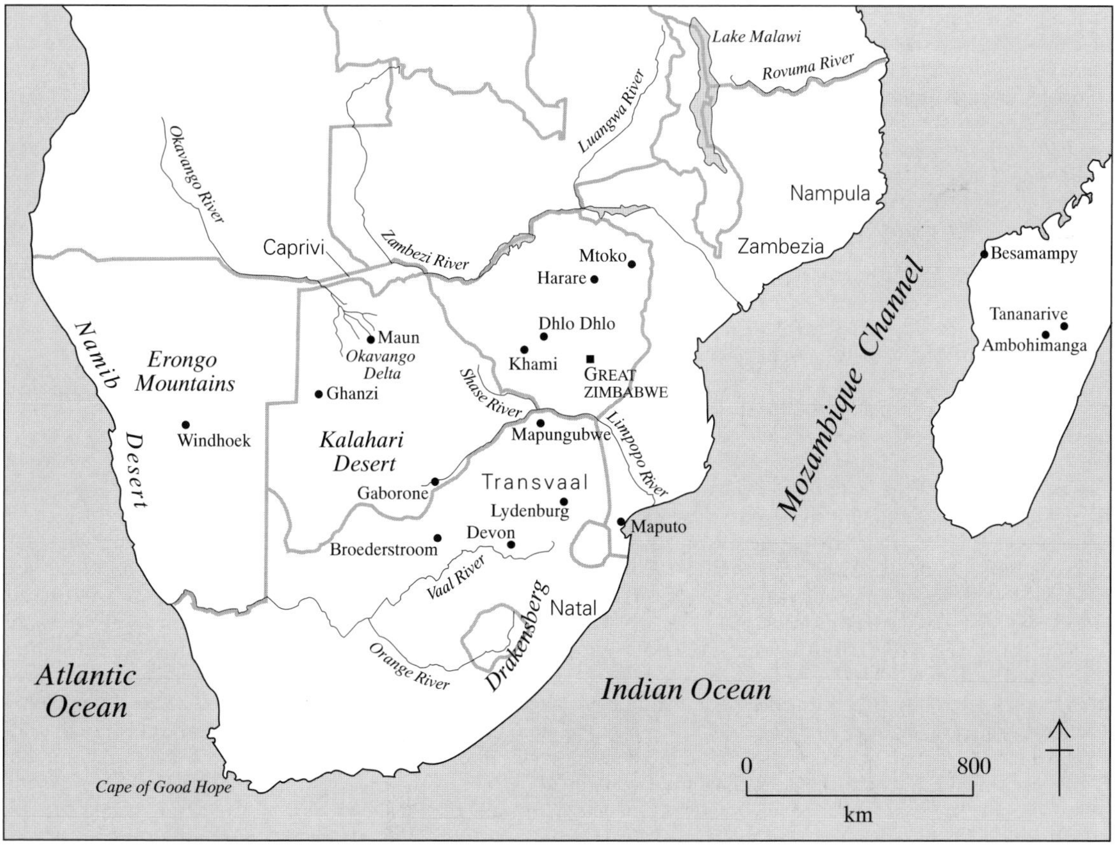

145. Map of Southern Africa; the site GREAT ZIMBABWE has a separate entry in this dictionary

clearly related to the Ovimbundu and Lunda-Chokwe of Angola.

Historically, a number of important states have risen and fallen within the region. The culture of Mapungubwe at the confluence of the Limpopo and Shase rivers flourished on trade in gold with the east coast as early as the 11th century. It was succeeded by the cultures of the Monomotapa empire at GREAT ZIMBABWE (*c.* 1250–*c.* 1450) and by that of Khami under the Changamire dynasty (*c.* 1450–*c.* 1640) in Zimbabwe itself. These cultures all shared the use of monumental stone architecture, clay figurines and, in Zimbabwe, soapstone sculptures (Masvingo, Great Zimbabwe N. Mnmt; Groote Schuur Zoo, Cape Town). In the Transvaal large empires were established by the Venda (*c.* 1700–1894), by the Pedi (*c.* 1750–1880) and the Ndebele (1820–92). The rise of the famous Zulu kingdom *c.* 1800 was thus part of a larger tendency to centralization in the region; it had many offshoots, such as the Swazi kingdom and the Zimbabwean Ndebele kingdom between 1820 and 1830. Other offshoots reached Mozambique (Matshangane) and Malawi (Ngoni). In all these states there was a tendency to produce prestige objects for a nobility who controlled trade and thus the sources of production. No large political conformations arose in the western part of the region, although in the areas of the northern Cape and Botswana there were some fairly centralized states before the invasions of the Ndebele under Mzilikaze (1820).

Trade links were established with the east coast as early as the 11th century and continued to the 19th century, first through the Arabs and later the Portuguese. White settlement in Southern Africa from the 17th century saw increasing encroachment on the lands of the indigenous populations and extensive culture contact. During the 19th century white rule expanded throughout the region, and acculturation among black peoples began. This brought with it the destruction and neglect of traditional institutions and many of the arts associated with them.

(ii) Architecture. Architectural structures and planning show great variation from one area to another but can be seen as falling into distinct settlement patterns. On the one hand are the highly concentrated settlements associated with the peoples of the plateau regions, from the Shona in the north to the Pedi and Ndebele and including the Tswana in the east. Stone-walled construction is a feature in many of the historical settlements of this type. The better known of these are those at Great Zimbabwe, Khami and Dhlo-Dhlo (Zimbabwe), but there are many others in the Transvaal and the northern Cape, including Mapungubwe, Dzata and Machemma's Kop. The Zimbabwean and northern Transvaal ruins all show the same architectural features, including decorative coursing in the walls of flat stones, whereas the Tswana and early Sotho stone constructions in the Magaliesberg area (e.g. Broederstroom, ?*c.* AD 600) used a much rougher stone construction. Stone walling was used only for the capitals of chiefs; it is still used by Venda chiefs. Within these walls homesteads of mud and thatch constructions were erected, often with mud or reed fences between the houses. The typical form of conical hut roofs on a circular base was found throughout the Zimbabwean, Botswanan and South African highveld area, with minor variations from one culture to the next.

Among some peoples in the western swamplands around the Okavango and in the Gwembe Valley, construction was predominantly wood or wattle-and-daub. Houses were built either on the ground or on stilts of wood, and little decoration occurs here on their walls. Wooden doors were used for ground-level houses. The Herero and Ovambo of Namibia use both mud construction and thatch, as well as some wooden construction. Little is known of traditional decoration in these areas.

In the coastal areas, particularly among the Nguni of Natal and the eastern Cape, beehive constructions of woven grass mats over wood and wicker framework were the norm in the past. Homesteads were widely spaced, lacking the degree of urban concentration more common in other regions. Perhaps as a result, boundary fences are less in evidence. Today most Zulu architecture follows the rondavel type and, as in most other areas, zinc sheeting is replacing the traditional thatch. In the construction of the homesteads and capitals men and women were responsible for different aspects of the labour. Men did all the work connected with the erection of stone walling, and all the wooden elements were prepared by them. In most cases men did the thatching, except among the Zulu, and men were responsible for the grass technology. Women were responsible for plastering the walls and the floors and for decorating the walls.

While finger-traced patterns on floor surfaces may be of some antiquity, the painting of walls with earth pigments or purchased paints developed much later. Walls in the ancient Zimbabwean cultures were decorated with patterns in the stone coursing. Wall decoration is found today throughout the Orange Free State, South Africa, in South Sotho homesteads, where designs of a predominantly organic nature are executed with textural elements, such as pebbles set into the plaster. In the Transvaal, Ndebele mural art with its predominantly geometric designs arose after 1945, and from this other forms have developed among the Pedi, Ntwane, Lobedu and Venda. While the patterns used in these later mural expressions are also mostly geometric, they are less flamboyant than Ndebele examples and show a tendency to divide walls into differing design fields rather than to treat a single wall as a compositional whole.

(iii) Wood-carving. Wood-carving was the sole province of men in this region. The traditional craftsman could produce many different kinds of items, and the degree of specialization varied from one group to another. In some areas, for example among the Venda and Tsonga, some carvers would specialize in carving figures and drums, while others would make bowls, mortars or milk-pails. In other instances, as among the Khakha (North Sotho), Zulu and Tonga, a carver might be called upon to carve the full range of items used within his society, from yokes and hoe handles to elaborately decorated headrests, stools and doors or free-standing figures. It was common, however, for only a few carvers to be involved in the manufacture of the more exclusive items such as figures, drums and doors, partly as a response to market forces and partly as a result of differing degrees of ability among

the carvers. Most carvers would have undergone some form of training, although formal apprenticeship outside of the patriline was uncommon. Styles thus tend to be identifiable in terms of areas and villages, i.e. in fairly localized distributions.

Evidence of the use of carved wooden prestige objects can be traced back to the use of wooden doors at Broederstroom (6th century AD) and the carved wooden rhinoceros figures from Mapungubwe that were plated with gold leaf (Pretoria, U. South Africa, Anthropol. Mus.). There is evidence of gold-plated headrests having been used at Khami (16th–17th centuries), and the carved soapstone birds, pillars and bowls from Great Zimbabwe are well known. There is no particular stylistic or cultural coherence among the objects from these successive cultures, but they bear witness to a long-standing artistic tradition within the area.

(a) Free-standing figures. (b) Decoration.

(a) Free-standing figures. Free-standing figurative carving was, in fact, produced only by a few groups within the region, the Venda, Tsonga-Shangane, Sotho and Tswana. It was made for use, generally in one of three contexts: as teaching aids in initiation lodges; for housing spiritual powers during healing or divination procedures; or as sentinels in homesteads or around fields.

Wooden sculpture was traditionally used in male initiation lodges by the Tswana, North Sotho, Tsonga-Shangane and Venda. It was only ever used in female initiation by the Venda and Valenge-Chopi. The main aim of the use of these figures was to instil in the initiates an understanding of and respect for sexual and social mores as well as some sense of group identity. Most of these initiations were held in two stages, at puberty and on a person's acceptance into full adult society. The sculptures of these different groups display some differences in style and iconography.

In the initiation lodges of Tswana and some North Sotho groups, wooden figures of animals representing group totems were used in various ways. Among the Gonanwa of the Blaauwberg, the initiates were required to eat their corn porridge from the hollowed underside of a large carved crocodile. Other groups required initiates to mime a killing of their own totem in order to reinforce the prohibitions. The style of the smaller animal figures used in this way is ubiquitous, as the figures were often produced by the fathers of initiates, not by specialist carvers. Some Tswana styles are identifiable, for example that of the Shatsi, but such particularity is not possible elsewhere in this region.

Other North Sotho groups, such as the Pedi and Khakha, made figures for teaching the initiates about sex and marriage. The fully rounded, naturalistic figures of the Pedi, with the head between one quarter and one third the size of the body in typical 'African proportion', are detailed in such a way that they clearly represent different ages and statuses—old man, young man, old woman and young woman. Other figures include representations of initiates and other functionaries. Among the Khakha, figures of humans and animals were carved by the initiates' fathers in a rather rough style and placed on the stockades erected around the initiation lodge. These figures were burnt with the rest of the lodge at the end of the initiation. Pedi figures, however, appear to have been kept from one initiation to another.

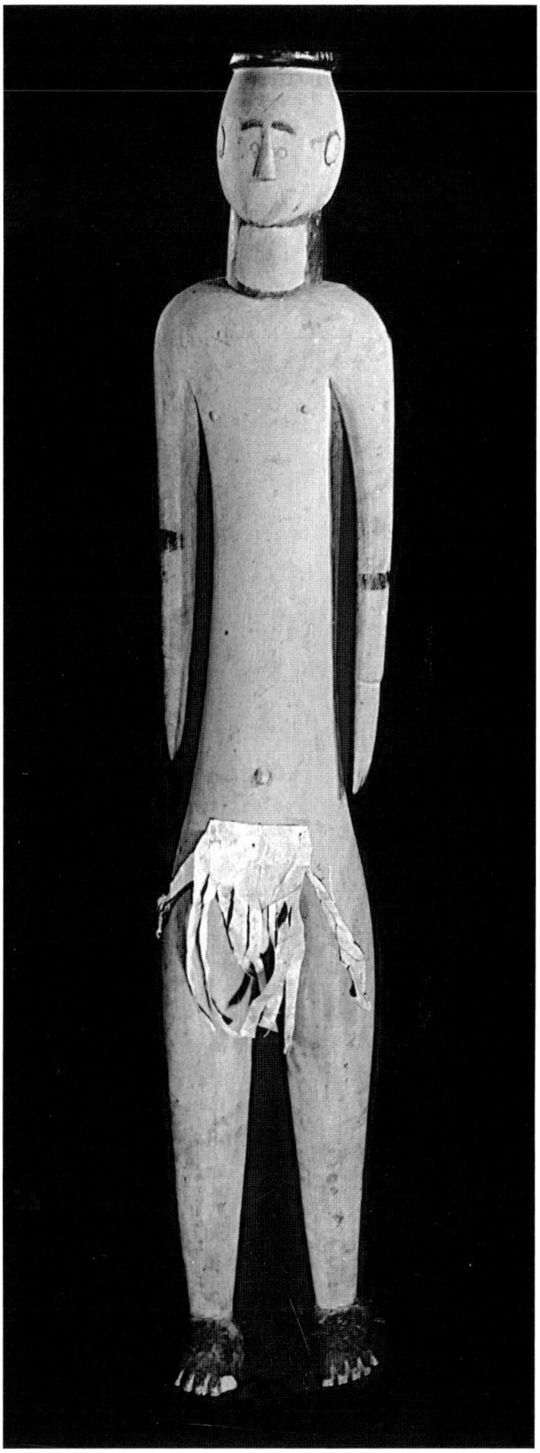

146. Tsonga figure sculpture, wood, h. 1.03 m, *c.* 1850–1900 (Tervuren, Koninklijk Museum voor Midden-Afrika)

147. Shona headrest, wood, h. 115 mm, 19th century (Johannesburg, University of the Witwatersrand, University Art Galleries)

Similar usages can be postulated for figures made both in the Transvaal and Mozambique by the Tsonga-Shangane, who were in contact with Sotho, whose initiation lodges the Tsonga often attended. Tsonga-Shangane figures are, however, distinctive in style and may have been used in other contexts as well.

Tsonga-Shangane figures tend to be much larger than those of the other groups in the area. They are elongated, with smallish heads, spatulate hands and domed feet. Most of them have clearly demarcated genitals and protruding buttocks, as well as clearly demarcated chests or breasts. In some the hair is rendered in Nguni fashion, a headring for the male (see fig. 146) and peaked hairstyles for the female: in others it is rendered as a raised chequered pattern. Details were often heightened by the burning and burnishing of the surface to render it black. In the past many of these figures were erroneously attributed to the Zulu. Figures of this type were used by the Tsonga-Shangane in initiations and as honorific markers outside the homes of important leaders or chiefs. The larger figures, some up to 1.75 m high, probably acted only in the capacity of markers. The figures with headrings may also have been displayed at the ceremonies where Tsonga-Shangane warriors were given their headrings. The figures always appear to have been used in pairs, one male and one female. The presence of the female figures at the headring ceremony may be explained by the fact that it was at this point that men were allowed to take wives.

The Venda also make and use wooden figure sculpture in their initiations, particularly in the Domba, the final stage of female initiation. These figures are executed in a style that combines some of the rounded naturalistic forms of Pedi sculpture and its small scale with the spatulate hands and domed feet of Tsonga sculpture. Venda carvers do not, however, appear to have used much burnt detail in their figures. Unlike the other groups the VENDA still make and use these figures. The Chopi also use a pair of wooden figures in their female initiation as didactic tools in explaining sexual matters. These figures are close in style to the Tsonga figures but are much smaller in scale and have rather stockier proportions, possibly as a result of the reduced scale. There are other figures that stylistically fall between the Chopi ones and the fully elongated Tsonga-Shangane type; these have been recorded as Nyai in origin but may be considered as part of the Tsonga complex.

Other forms of figure sculpture made by the peoples in the region include those used in divinatory or healing contexts. Among these are the articulated puppets used by many different groups, possibly originating in Mozambique among the Tsonga or Nyai. These puppets have been collected as far afield as Lesotho, Swaziland, Natal and the Transvaal as well as in Mozambique. They have a lesser degree of stylistic variation; although some idiosyncratic examples are known, they generally follow the same rather simplified forms. Their distribution may have followed the routes of famous itinerant Tsonga diviner-healers throughout the region. The Tsonga-Shangane healers also use other figures as containers for medicines: sometimes the whole figure may be carved of wood, or the head and shoulders may be carved, but the body formed by a calabash. There is evidence to suggest that in the past Shona diviners and spirit mediums used figures to represent their tutelary spirits. These figures are close in style to the Tsonga-Nyai style, although they are known only from photographs.

(b) Decoration. Objects carved for both daily and ceremonial use by most of the peoples in this region were decorated in some way. Often this took the form of sculptural embellishment with fully rounded figurative forms or relief designs. In this way useful objects were often given symbolic or figurative content. Thus the wooden doors carved by the Tonga, some Shona and the Venda were often decorated with compositions made up of chevrons and concentric circle motifs and were in some cases painted (Tonga). These designs may well have carried symbolic meaning. Stools and headrests made by the Tonga, Shona and Tsonga often had their caryatid sections carved as animal or human figures, but more often these sections were composed of geometric forms in apparently abstract conformations. Tonga stools had an open fretwork support composed of triangles and diamonds for the circular seat. Ovambo stools also used a fretwork support, in this case cylindrical, between the seat and base of the stool. Often a set of four mask forms typical of the Chokwe style were carved integrally with this support.

Headrests are ubiquitous throughout the Southern African region. They can be divided into two main groups: the Shona–Tsonga complex and the Zulu–Swazi complex. The headrest form of the Shona–Tonga complex is generally quite small and has a bilobed oval base with the thin horizontal and upward curving cross-piece supported by a caryatid of some decorative embellishment. In Northern and Central Shona headrests, the caryatid is composed of flat cut-out triangles with circles between them so that the whole has a form reminiscent of the female figure. The flat cut-out shapes are further embellished with relief patterns recalling the keloid scars used to decorate the human body, and on some headrests the circle elements bear three-dimensional 'breasts'. This type of Shona headrest is mostly stained black. In Tsonga and Southern and Eastern Shona headrests the supports vary more widely. Some use segmental arcs with cylindrical rods above them to support the cross-piece, while others have rectangular slabs in varying number and at varying angles between the base and the cross-piece. The slab-type caryatid is more common among the Tsonga and often has further relief embellishment. These latter headrest types have also spread far afield among Tswana and North Sotho groups such as the Ntwane. When animal figures are used by the Shona and Tsonga as caryatids (see fig. 147), the base may be dispensed with, but the cross-piece is always supported on rods or slabs above the back of the animal. These animals are most often horned and may represent cattle, goats or antelope, the last two being the most likely among the Tsonga.

The classic Zulu–Swazi headrest type rarely uses animal figures as caryatids. The classic form consists of two, three or four, but often more, generally square-shaped legs supporting a heavy rectangular cross-piece, which curves downwards towards the centre. At this point a cylindrical lug may be carved to project downwards, while at either end of the cross-piece other embellishments such as scrolls may indicate a 'head' or 'tail'. It is possible that in many of these headrests there is some reference to the bovine form, cattle being especially important in Zulu and Swazi society. On the legs themselves there is often geometric decoration in raised relief. There are many other variations on the basic form, but most follow the same scale and composition. Zulu headrests can be used as stools as well as pillows. Following a similar basic form, the headrests of some Pedi and Tau groups nevertheless show some differences. They are smaller in scale, the legs are generally cylindrical, and the cross-piece takes the form of an inverted triangle with its point replacing the lug of the Zulu type. The entire surface of the sides of these headrests is covered with engraved curvilinear, interlace patterns. A few headrests of similar type are known from Xhosa, Fingo and Bhaca sources, but there are not enough to outline any specific styles.

Among virtually all these groups, headrests could become associated with deceased members of a society and would then pass into use in ancestor veneration. Headrests were portable objects and were closely associated with their users. Among the Tsonga a man would make his first offering to his father as ancestor by rubbing tobacco on the cross-piece. Many of the headrests were further embellished with beads, and some had staffs or tobacco containers carved integrally with them.

Many other objects are embellished with carved decoration. These include snuff-containers, knives, milk-pails, mortars, drums, xylophones, plates, staffs and divining instruments. Among the Zulu, Swazi and Pedi four-legged plates are used to serve meat. The undersides of these plates are often given a composition of triangular designs or of interlace and may again recall animal forms, in that they are given handles at their 'heads' and 'tails'. Among the Shona, Swazi and Southern Sotho, knife-sheaths and

148. Zulu staffs, max. h. 675 mm, 19th century (Johannesburg, University of the Witwatersrand, University Art Galleries)

knife-handles were carved with abstract and figurative designs in both bone and wood, and among the Korana and the Tswana spoons were often elaborated with figures for handles and abstract designs under the bowl of the spoon. Venda and Tsonga carvers placed carved breasts as decoration on mortars, a motif also used on lintels over granary doors by the Tsonga. Many of these objects functioned as indices of status and prestige for their owners. Staffs probably also fall into this category. Staffs were used by both men and women among many groups. However, the longer and more elaborately carved (or beaded) examples were generally used by men or by women of extraordinary status, such as diviners or healers. The carving on such staffs varied from group to group. Shona staffs often used engraved designs along the entire stem of the staff; Zulu, Swazi and Tsonga staffs often had their tops carved with human heads or figures, animal figures or elaborate knobs (see fig. 148). They also, along with Southern Nguni and Zimbabwean Ndebele groups, produced staffs with snakes curling up around the stem. Among both Venda and Tonga a favourite staff motif was the hand-claw enclosing an egg. For the most part, these staffs were finely finished and given a shiny patina.

(iv) Pottery. Fired clay vessels were made by virtually every Southern African group. Some Khoi and Khoisan peoples, such as the San and the Hottentots, do not appear to have made any pottery, unless under direct external influence. Both fired and unfired pottery sculptures have a wide

distribution throughout the region. All pottery vessels were traditionally made by women using locally available clays. The pots were built up on a coiling method and fired in open fires. Pots were often burnished and decorated with graphite and incised designs. Patterns were generally engraved into the surface of the clay before firing and coloured after. Some women became specialists in the craft, selling their vessels to others within the group.

Fired pottery is one of the main tools used in dating the successive ancient cultures in the region. In many cases a stylistic range can be traced in historical depth for different Southern African Bantu-speaking cultures. Stylistic variation can also be traced synchronically across different cultures within the region. However, it is not always possible to do the same with clay sculpture (*see* §(v) below), as it does not always follow the same historical distribution as clay vessels. Both the shapes of the vessels and their decorations can be used as indices of stylistic affiliation. The decorative elements of style include the placing of the motifs on the vessel, the types of motifs and the technique of execution.

The pottery vessels made by the peoples of the Gwembe Valley, particularly the Tonga, are generally spherical with short necks that often flare towards the rim. The decoration is generally placed in two separate bands, one around the neck, the other around the shoulder of the pot. This decoration is composed largely of triangles or semicircles in a dark colour against the red of the pot. Shona domestic pots typically follow a similar form but do not have flaring necks. The decoration is largely engraved in a band around the shoulder of the pot, and the whole pot is burnished and blackened. Shona potters also make zoomorphic vessels for ceremonial use in ancestor veneration. These generally take the form of a headless 'zebra', the stripes being engraved into the surface of the pot and coloured red and black after firing.

North Sotho pottery, such as that made by the Pedi, Ntwane and Khakha, tends to follow a hemispherical shape with no neck on the vessel. The decoration is found in a wide band on the shoulder of the pot set away from the rim. The patterns are largely composed of arcs and triangles incised and coloured red or black. Venda pottery is similar today to Pedi pottery but in the past favoured the Shona style. Tsonga pottery is generally blackened and burnished with incised decoration around the shoulder of the pot, which has a slightly flattened profile. Here the designs are also geometric, using a combination of chevrons and triangles.

Zulu pots are also spherical in their basic shape, most pots traditionally having no necks. Their designs are placed largely lower down around the belly of the pot, rather than on the shoulder, and are rendered as raised geometric patterns and, often today, as engraved leaf- or shieldlike motifs. These pots are entirely blackened and do not use colour decoratively. Similar forms are found in some Southern Nguni groups, such as the Bhaca. There was generally a smaller range of types of vessels used among these peoples, as they used woven grass vessels rather than pots as containers for beer and milk.

(v) Clay sculpture. Clay sculpture is known throughout the Southern African region in two contexts. On the one hand there is the almost universal manufacture of generally unfired clay figurines for use as toys; usually given animal forms, most commonly cattle, these can be made by the women or by the children who play with them. On the other hand, fired clay figurines are known from archaeological sites dating back to the 6th century AD. Fired clay heads excavated in Lydenburg, Transvaal (Cape Town, S. Afr. Mus.), may well have been used in initiation contexts. They are made on the same coiling principle as the North Sotho pots in the area and bear similar decorative elements. Fired clay sculptures are also known from the Limpopo sites of Schroda (9th century AD; Pretoria, N. Cult. Hist. Mus.), Mapungubwe (11th–13th centuries; Pretoria, U. South Africa, Anthropol. Mus.), Great Zimbabwe (14th–16th centuries) and Dhlo-Dhlo (16th–17th centuries; Harare, Zimbabwe Mus. Human Sci.), all having similar stylistic characteristics. They have small heads, basically cylindrical bodies, often truncated limbs or no limbs, and emphasized genital areas. These figures were probably used in initiations, as are similar figures today among the Venda (Transvaal), the Bembe (Malawi) and the Nguu (Tanzania). Among the Tonga, fine pipe-bowls of zoomorphic form are made of a hard-fired clay. These pipe-bowls are modelled in the form of antelope cattle and occasionally bush-pigs.

(vi) Beadwork and costume. Throughout the Southern African region the making of beaded objects and fine costume is one of the major areas of artistic expression. The use of brightly coloured glass beads dates from the mid-19th century, and possibly the early 19th century in the south-east, with the expansion of European trade. Within the development of beadwork traditions, however, not only did different styles emerge but also different approaches to colour. The vast majority of early beaded items throughout the region was limited, by choice, to the use of white, red and blue or black; only occasionally were yellow and green used. Since the 1920s, however, the number of colours used has increased, particularly among the Ndebele, Xhosa, Tembu, Fingo, Zulu and Swazi. The beads were always strung by women.

In the past skin was the support on to which beaded finery was sewn. Generally cattle or goat skins were cured, decorated and sewn by men and then passed to women if they were to add any beaded motifs. Skins were decorated by patterns cut into the surface, by the retention of fur or hair in parts and by their shape. They could be used for short front aprons, long back aprons, capes and full skirts. Today beaded skin aprons, and occasionally some of the other forms, are still made, but are generally worn only on ceremonial occasions. In some areas, particularly on the south-east coast, decorated cloth with embroidered or appliquéd elements has largely replaced the older skin garments. In many areas even cloth was sewn by the men, but the effects of migrant labour have turned this into a female craft.

Possibly the best-known beadwork is that of the NDEBELE, but many other, as highly developed if not as flamboyant, traditions are known in the area. Among the Tonga, beaded front and back apron was worn by the women. The front aprons were short and completely beaded in patterns of triangles in red, white and black (see fig. 149). The back apron was long and had beaded triangular elements sewn on it in rows. Together with this, women wore fibre skirts, beaded headbands, necklaces and waist-bands as well as bands of beaded decoration around the upper arms. Beaded ropes were worn around the waist by women in many of the cultures in the region, including the Tswana, Venda, Shona, Pedi, Swazi, Zulu and Ndebele.

Beaded aprons vary in the amount of beaded elements used. Generally the short front aprons of women were more fully beaded than the back aprons. This is the pattern found among the Tswana, North Sotho, Venda, Tsonga-Shangane and Ndebele. Zulu and Swazi beaded aprons do not have leather backing. Longer skirts in use among some Nguni seem to have been preferred to short aprons.

The largest and most elaborate development of beaded costumes is found among the Nguni-speakers of the south-east coast, the Swazi, Zulu, Xhosa, Fingo, Bhaca, Tembu, Galeka, Pondo and Pondomise, and also the Southern Ndebele. In most of these groups, beaded items included headbands, neck-bands, necklaces, flaring collars, neck ropes, baldrics, waistbands, bracelets, armbands, anklets and today even sunglasses and handbags. Also beaded were staffs and clubs used in ceremonial dances; modern versions often feature cars or aeroplanes as finials. In many of the earlier examples the beadwork is predominantly white with coloured motifs woven in, but in the 20th century both colour and pattern have developed to a greater complexity. Generally patterns are geometric, based on triangles and chevrons. Stylistic differentiation between the groups concerned has not been definitely determined to date. In virtually all cases, however, one would find the most elaborate costumes reserved for certain occasions or for particular persons. Marriages were ceremonies where the bride and groom would be decked out with a great deal of finery not worn on other occasions. Diviners and healers engaged in any form of ceremony would also wear a great deal of very distinctive beadwork, this also being the case among non-coastal peoples.

In some areas the influence of missionary civilizing practices had led to the burgeoning of different dress arts. Among the Herero of Namibia, 19th-century Victorian dress is still worn today, and among the Pedi a similar kind of dress was adapted in cotton cloths and now forms an entirely distinctive style, with colourful patterns largely in the working of embroidery and appliqué.

Traditional Herero dress is reflected in the 'dolls' made by Herero women for their daughters or daughters-in-law. These 'dolls', made of stuffed cloth, have leather clothing of a short front apron and long back apron, a cloak and three-peaked cap with leather trains. Similarly, aspects of traditional dress are found in other dolls made within the region. Among the South Sotho and Southern Nguni, conical-shaped dolls were made, originally with clay or wicker cores, more recently with sand-filled bottles or stuffed cloth. These dolls were covered with cloth and some beaded elements and were carried by young wives who had difficulty conceiving or by those who had been given them by their husband's female relatives. Similar dolls were found among elements of the Zulu, among the Southern Ndebele and the North Sotho groups such as the Ntwane and the Pedi. The degree of beaded finery on these dolls varies, the Ndebele and Ntwane (see fig. 150) probably having most. Today these dolls are made for sale on the Western market, and many idiosyncratic elements have crept into their forms.

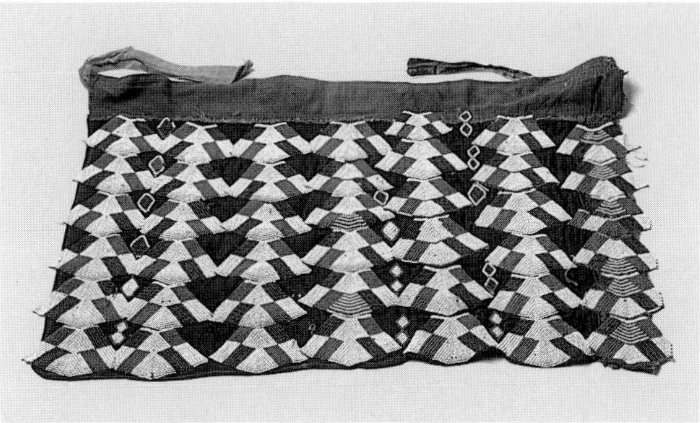

149. Tonga apron, beads and cloth, w. 600 mm, 20th century (Johannesburg, University of the Witwatersrand, University Art Galleries)

See also entries on individual countries.

BIBLIOGRAPHY

G. F. Angas: *The Kafirs Illustrated in a Series of Drawings Taken among the Amazulu, Amaponda and Amakosa Tribes etc.* (London, 1849)

J. T. Bent: *The Ruined Cities of Mashonaland* (London, 1893)

S. Schonland: 'Arts and Crafts of the Natives of South Africa', *Rep. Brit. Assoc. Adv. Sci., S. Africa*, iii/2 (1905), pp. 130–46

N. Roberts and C. A. T. Winter: 'The *Kgoma* or Initiation Rites of the Bupedi of Sekukuniland', *S. Afr. J. Sci.*, xii (1915), pp. 561–78

W. Blohm: 'Schöpferische Kräfte in der Gesellschaft der Xosa Gruppe', *Archv Anthropol.*, n. s., xiii (1916), pp. 159–95

R. McLaren: 'Arts and Crafts of the Xosas: A Study Based on Philology', *S. Afr. J. Sci.*, xv (1918), pp. 441–9

A. Muller: 'Zur materiellen Kultur der Kaffern', *Anthropos*, xxxi (1918), pp. 852–8

S. S. Dornan: 'Divination and Divining Bones', *S. Afr. J. Sci.*, xx (1923), pp. 504–611

E. A. T. Dutton: *The Basutos of Basutoland* (London, 1926)

P. Davidson and J. Hosford: 'Lobedu Pottery', *An. S. Afr. Mus.*, lxxv (1928), pp. 8–291

H. A. Junod: 'La Seconde Ecole de circoncision chez les Bakhakha du Nord Transvaal', *J. Royal Anthropol. Inst. GB & Ireland*, lix (1929), pp. 131–47

L. Fouché and G. A. Gardner: *Mapungupwe: Ancient African Civilization on the Limpopo*, 2 vols (Cambridge and Pretoria, 1937–63)

I. D. Krige and E. J. Krige: *The Realm of a Rain Queen* (London, 1943)

F. Goodall: 'Rhodesian Pots with Moulded Decorations', *Native Affairs Dept Annu.*, xxiii/1 (1946), pp. 36–49

J. Schofield: *Primitive Pottery* (Cape Town, 1948)

M. Shaw: 'Fertility Dolls in South Africa', *Native Affairs Dept Annu.*, xxv (1948), pp. 63–8

——: 'The Art of the Bantu', *The Studio*, cxxxvi/2 (1948), pp. 256–9

P. R. Kirby: *The Musical Instruments of the Native Races of South Africa* (Johannesburg, 1956)

R. Summers: 'Human Figures in Clay and Stone from Southern Rhodesia and Adjoining Territories', *Occas. Pap.: N. Mus. S. Rhodesia*, iii/21a (1957), pp. 61–75

K. R. Robinson: *Khami Ruins* (1959)

M. De Lange: 'Dolls for the Promotion of Fertility as Used by Some of the Nguni Tribes and Basotho', *An. Cape Prov. Mus.*, i (1961), pp. 86–101

L. Holy: *The Arts of Africa: Masks and Figures from East and South Africa* (London, 1967)

A. C. Lawton: 'Bantu Pottery of Southern Africa', *An. S. Afr. Mus.*, xlix (1967), pp. 1–440

P. Allison: *African Stone Sculpture* (London, 1968)

H. O. Mönnig: *The Pedi* (Pretoria, 1968)

B. Reynolds: *The Material Culture of the Peoples of the Gwembe Valley*, Kariba Studies, ii (1968)

150. Ntwane fertility 'doll', grass, beads, wool and plastics, h. 280 mm, 20th century (Johannesburg, University of the Witwatersrand, University Art Galleries)

J. Broster: *The Tembu: Their Beadwork, Songs and Dances* (Cape Town, 1976)
T. H. Matthews: 'Mural Painting in South Africa', *Afr. A.*, x/2 (1977), pp. 28–33
A. Kuper: 'Symbolic Dimensions of the Southern African Bantu Homestead', *Africa*, 1/1 (1980), pp. 7–23
A. Nettleton and W. D. Hammond-Tooke, eds: *African Art from Southern Africa: From Tradition to Township* (Johannesburg, 1989)
Art and Ambiguity: Perspectives on the Brenthurst Collection (exh. cat. by J. Lowen, Johannesburg A.G., 1992)
Ezakwantu: Beadwork from the Eastern Cape (exh. cat., ed. E. Bedford; Capetown, N.G., 1993)

ANITRA NETTLETON

VIII. Diaspora.

The African diaspora is principally a result of the slave trade, in the course of which millions of Africans were deported to the Americas and elsewhere. On a smaller scale, many other factors have contributed to the presence of active African cultural traditions outside Africa itself. This article discusses African art as retained, modified or blended with local traditions world-wide.

1. Historical introduction. Because African cultures have been misrepresented, many people, including many African Americans, believe that the slaves came from cultures so 'primitive' that they had nothing worth bringing to the New World and even welcomed Western technology as superior. Scholars have attempted to remedy this situation by showing the strength, beauty and complexity of African cultures so long denigrated in order to justify slavery. Anthropological and historical research has brought to light ample evidence of just how much of their intellectual and aesthetic traditions the enslaved Africans were able to preserve and transport intact and to re-establish in the New World. With little privacy and less power, the Africans managed to retain both those aspects of their cultures that their masters did not know or care about (i.e. religious beliefs, medical practices and folklore) and those which their masters needed or enjoyed (i.e. tool- and weapon-making, woodworking, weaving and other textile arts, narrative, music, dance and cuisine). Furthermore, it has become apparent that some of the slaves knew more about tropical agriculture than did their masters, while others possessed technical and artistic skills comparable to or surpassing those of their European counterparts.

This article is not primarily concerned with the myriad arts produced throughout the world by peoples of African descent but rather with African art itself as it developed and adapted in its many new milieux overseas. In evaluating the evidence, M. J. Herskovits (1941) suggested that the Africans were able to retain fully some African traits, while many other traits were reinterpreted or modified, and a few were blended or syncretized with local practices. All cultures, even the most conservative, are open to innovation, and the enslaved Africans, facing up to one of the cruellest displacements in human history, were certainly eager to grasp any appropriate practice, object or opportunity, from whatever source, that might alleviate their predicament. Thus while preserving the best, most beloved and most useful from Africa, they were far from conservative and adapted more or less willingly not only many Western culture traits, notably in language and religion, but also a considerable number from the Native Americans.

Sub-Saharan African slaves were known in ancient Egypt, Classical Greece (Aesop the fable-teller is thought to have been an African slave) and Rome. With the rise of Islam in the 8th century AD they spread across North Africa and the Near East and from there were taken with the Mughals into India, where some, such as the Siddis of Janjira and the Habshis of Gujarat, became mercenaries and established states (Harris, 1982). Domestic slavery through debt, crime or capture was widespread within African societies, and after the arrival of the Europeans in the mid-15th century Africans were again brought in significant numbers to Europe; this explains the presence of African faces in Spanish and other European paintings. The Atlantic slave trade began early in the 17th century, transporting Africans first to the Atlantic and Indian Ocean islands and then widely throughout the Americas until as late as 1888, when slavery was finally outlawed in Brazil.

The extensive documents of the slave trade analysed by P. D. Curtin demonstrate that virtually all Africans in the New World came either from West Africa (from Senegal to Nigeria) or from west Central Africa (present-day Congo, Zaïre and Angola), nearly always from within 300 km of the coast; only a few were brought from Southern or East Africa. For Europeans, slavery was a means of servicing a huge new market. The burgeoning plantations of the New World required cheap labour to produce sugar, cotton and other valuable crops. Although Europeans sometimes raided the coast for slaves themselves, it was easier and cheaper for them to encourage the local African states, some (such as Asante, Dahomey and Benin) built on slavery, to war among themselves in order to capture prisoners to be traded for guns, ammunition, liquor, cloth and other European trade goods. Thus most of the New World Africans came from those parts of Africa with the heaviest populations and the most developed technology. They can claim kinship with the Asante, Fanti, Baule and other Akan-speaking peoples, with the Ewe of Togo, the Fon, the Manding, Serer and Wolof of the western Sahel, the Kongo of Zaïre and especially the Yoruba and Igbo of Nigeria. An estimated one-quarter of the ancestors of African Americans were Igbo from south-eastern Nigeria, an independent-minded agricultural and trading people that resisted incorporation into a unified state, which might have been more effective in resisting enslavement than disunity proved to be. That is not to say, however, that the Igbos accepted slavery lightly: a warning proverb known throughout the plantation world was *Ibo pend li* ('the Igbos hang themselves').

By the time slavery ended in the New World in the late 19th century an estimated 12 million Africans had been transported (42% to the Caribbean, 38% to Brazil and a mere 6.8% to the USA), and they and their descendants, already much mixed with both European and Native American ancestry, could be found in every nation from Argentina to Canada. Today, by their own choice, Africans and their Caribbean cousins are again migrating, to the USA, Canada, Britain, France, Portugal, Scandinavia, even Australia, intermarrying everywhere.

Herskovits's system of retention, reinterpretation and syncretism works well for the arts, especially when they are combined with equally beloved religious and secular ritual. Indeed, the most African characteristic of the diasporic aesthetic is that all the arts combine in vibrant public displays, both religious and secular, which are quite different from the contemplative 'shrine' art central to much European and Asian religious artistic expression.

The widespread and increasingly popular New World religion that syncretizes Yoruba *orisa* and Fon *loa* (gods or spirits) with Catholic saints, termed Candomblé or Macumba in Brazil, Shango in Trinidad, Vodoun in Haiti and Santeria in Cuba and the USA (where it is spreading rapidly), is a leading vehicle bringing African arts to the New World. Sculptures, costumes, ritual objects (rarely masks) and finely embellished musical instruments, as well as songs, chants, prayers and incantations sometimes sung in the Yoruba language, are coming directly out of Africa. With the increasing ease in intercontinental travel, Yoruba priests can be found teaching their language and faith in Brazil, London and Miami, while prosperous West Indian faithful visit the shrines in Nigeria. There has been intermittent contact via Brazilian sailors between West Africa and Brazil for the past several centuries at least, and sizeable communities still exist in Cotonou, Accra and elsewhere that are descended from freed Brazilian slaves who returned to Africa, paralleling the Sierra Leone creoles from Britain and the Americo-Liberians from the USA.

2. ARCHITECTURE. As Stuckey and other revisionist historians have pointed out, some slaves arrived from Africa possessing advanced skills in such areas as tropical agriculture, metalwork and woodwork. In building construction they shared a knowledge of the two-room gabled house, thatching and wattle-and-daub. These skills were immediately employed in every kind of building, both Europeans and Africans needing to adapt the buildings they knew to the new climates, materials, techniques and requirements of the New World plantation societies.

While African artisans undoubtedly quickly learnt the architectural methods and styles of the transplanted Europeans, they also constructed truly African-inspired buildings, such as the circular house on the Keswick Plantation

151. 'Shotgun house', Port-au-Prince, Haiti; from a photograph by John Michael Vlach, 1973

in Virginia and the two-storey hip-roof structure at Natchitoches, Louisiana. On the Costa Chica on the Pacific coast of Mexico, circular houses with conical thatched roofs introduced by the Mande of Mali and Senegal were still being built in the 1990s. More important, the Africans discovered that their oblong 'shotgun house' (see fig. 151), which derived from the basic unit of the common traditional compound architecture, served well in both rural and urban settings. Unlike European-derived folk buildings, such as the classic American log cabin with its long side facing the street and gables at right angles to the street, the shotgun house has one gable-side facing the street, with the rooms of the house extending one behind the other and opening one into the next, so that a shotgun could be fired through the successive doorways without hitting anything. (The Yoruba word *to-gun*, 'place of assembly', is another possible derivation.) These houses, sometimes double or with a second floor at the back, can be found throughout the USA's southern states and the Caribbean, often with porches and/or Georgian or Victorian façades. The relatively small size of the rooms, rarely more than 4×4 m, and the widespread use of the front porch reflect African practice. CHARLESTON's I-shaped two-storey houses, with narrow façades and long side-porches, can be seen as adaptations of Caribbean–African origin to suit South Carolina's notoriously humid climate. The small, square, simple buildings of Africa became the models for the slave cabins 'behind the Big House', not only in the USA but throughout the plantation societies.

Porches, balconies, elegant wrought-iron fences, gates and window-grilles were all made by African ironworkers and their descendants, often working under European blacksmith-designers, throughout the southern USA. For instance a German artisan, Christopher Werner (*fl* 1828–70), employed five slave blacksmiths to produce much of the finest monumental ironwork in Charleston, and this tradition was continued and strengthened in the 20th century by the improvisational work of Philip Simmons, the son and grandson of slave-ironworkers.

African artisans and their descendants left their mark also on churches, theatres and public buildings throughout the New World. Perhaps the most famous of these was Antônio Francisco Lisboa (*see* LISBOA, (2)), a physically disabled mulatto freedman in late 18th-century Brazil, better known as Aleijadinho ('little cripple'). His spectacular Late Baroque churches and the monumental sculptures in wood and stone that surround them have made the old mining towns around Ouro Preto world-famous. His astonishing originality and unique ability to manipulate an otherwise drab and worked-out provincial style bear witness to his African roots.

3. SCULPTURE. In contrast to architectural ironwork, wood sculpture of African inspiration is richly preserved throughout the Americas, the most spectacular examples being the religious figures of Yoruba *orishas* (spirits or gods) found in north-eastern Brazil (see Verger). A sculpture of the popular goddess of the sea—Yemoja in Yoruba, Yemanja in Brazil—has been found in use in Afro-Brazilian Candomblé ceremonies in the old slaving port of Salvador da Bahia, so completely in Yoruba style that it is uncertain whether it was carved in Nigeria or in Brazil. Other sculptures of Candomblé divinities in wood, clay and wrought-iron with obvious African antecedents abound wherever the cult is found.

An example of secular sculpture from the USA is an early 19th-century near-life-size cigar-store Indian figure (Cooperstown, Mus. NY State Hist. Assoc.; see fig. 152), a common signpost type indicating a tobacco shop but in this case carved by an African named Job. The sculptor

152. Job: cigar-store Indian figure, painted wood, h. 1.5 m, early 19th century (Cooperstown, NY, Museum of New York State Historical Association)

recalls traditional African forms in the masklike head, which, however, is set atop a typical 19th-century American body made up of seven other pieces of wood. More common are finely carved canes decorated with human heads, snakes and reptiles, strikingly reminiscent in both subject and technique of the *bweji* canes produced by the Chokwe of Angola and Zaïre. In this west Central African area, such animals as lizards and frogs are associated with water and hence with divinity.

The African maroons who escaped from coastal plantations into the interior of Surinam (former Dutch Guiana) and French Guiana in northern South America from the late 16th century onwards set up what many consider to be the most 'African' societies in the Americas, having developed religious and political institutions. A complex pierced style of wood-carving, which may have carried arcane, multi-level, possibly erotic symbolism, was used to decorate superb combs (see fig. 153), stools, clothes-beaters, peanut-pounding boards, paddles and doorframes that suggest but do not duplicate the finest Asante and Fon sculpture. (*See* SURINAM, §III; FRENCH GUIANA, §III.)

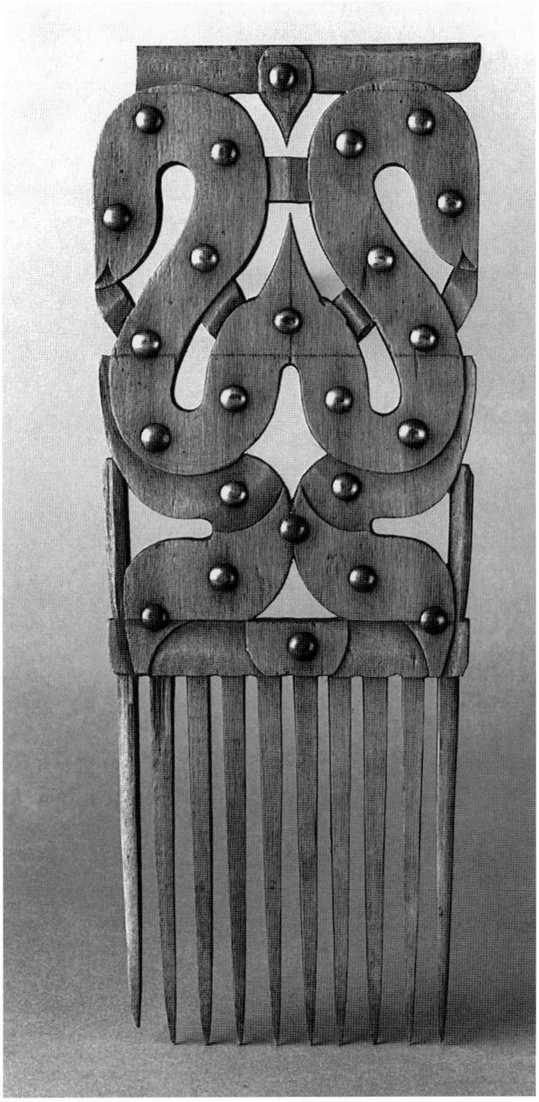

153. Comb, wood, h. 336 mm, from a village of the Djuka maroons on the Tapanahoni River, Surinam, collected late 1920s (New York, American Museum of Natural History)

4. MASK AND MASQUERADE. As the most popular sculptural expression in Africa, masks have managed to retain their central position in the secular carnival complex of theatrical arts throughout the New World, although they occur only rarely in religious art. Carnivals or carnival-like street parades exist widely, from cities in the USA such as New Orleans, Mobile and Philadelphia to virtually every Caribbean island and every Latin American city. They have recently spread, via Caribbean immigrants, to Miami, Brooklyn, Toronto and even London and Copenhagen.

In the mid-19th century, particularly in Brazil, Cuba and Trinidad, freed Africans recognized the possibilities of the European colonial carnival for their own individual and group self-expression and gradually took over the street parades previously dominated by the planter class (at which time they had been allowed to provide only music). With their brilliant masks and costumes, controversial and often witty themes, throbbing drum *baterías*, ecstatic dancing and huge, extravagant floats pulled by horses, humans and nowadays giant trucks, New World carnivals are quite distinct from their European antecedents. The choosing and development of an often historical or topical theme and the designing of the costumes and floats require the full- or part-time work of theme researchers, designers, sketch-artists, seamstresses, embroiderers, wire-workers, styrofoam-carvers, shoe- and bootmakers, tinsmiths (for armour and chain-mail), electricians and welders (for the immense floats and decorated double-decker trucks carrying maskers, musicians and literally earth-shaking sound equipment). Artistic innovation and creativity are expected and indeed required in all these crafts, some of them otherwise rarely considered as art forms.

Masks and masquerades are not associated, however, with secular ritual alone. A remarkable example of full retention of an African art form in the New World is in the cloth masks and richly embroidered costumes representing female ancestors of the Yoruba Egungun cult, still made near Salvador da Bahia in north-eastern Brazil. Their panels of cloth swinging around the dancing wearer and symbolic objects decorated with cowrie shells and glass beads are indistinguishable from their African antecedents. Some of the Candomblé divinities today wear nylon and spandex held on by velcro and carry chromium-plated staffs, while finely detailed oil paintings on canvas delineate the ritual details of their costumes.

5. TEXTILES. West African weavers long ago invented a distinctive horizontal loom, between 50 and 100 mm wide but with a warp that can extend many metres, producing with considerable speed and minimum effort a long, narrow strip of cloth, plain or intricately designed, which can be cut and stitched together to produce superbly complex textiles. Once slavery began, male and female

slave weavers were brought to the previously unpopulated Cape Verde Islands some 500 km off the coast of Senegal in West Africa and put to work producing the finest possible narrow-strip-weave textiles. Their products were then used to trade for more slaves with the African élites who gloried in the rich clothing made from these intricately designed textiles. Modern Caboverdianas and the Manjaco in nearby coastal GUINEA-BISSAU still make these superb weavings, among the finest in Africa, and some are displayed as part of the carnival costumes of the urban creoles in Guinea-Bissau. Somewhat similar *kente* cloth made by the Asante of Ghana, using imported Italian silk yarn, as well as cotton-print copies of it have become a popular symbol among African Americans to signify pride in their African heritage.

The maroons of Surinam and French Guiana have probably managed the cleverest variant on the African narrow-strip-weave aesthetic. More than a century ago, in their South American jungle homes, they cut European trade cloth of several contrasting designs into narrow strips and sewed them combined together in the African manner to make capes and covers of surprisingly traditional beauty and style (see fig. 154). Today similar print-cloth strip-design clothing can be found in West African markets.

Quilting is an ancient sewing technique known throughout Asia, Muslim Africa and Europe, where since the 14th century quilted bedcovers have been a powerful form of art expression for women. In the 19th century Polynesian, Native American and African American women also became adept, but whereas European American quiltmakers are famous for the precision and complexity of their designs and the fineness of their stitchery, African Americans have long defied the Western concept of symmetry with their wildly asymmetrical 'crazy quilts'. For example, on an otherwise neatly chequered quilt of alternating black and floral squares, the squares towards the right top corner are placed diagonally at uneven angles. In another quilt with three kinds of oblongs, most of the darker ones alternate with the paler oblongs, but the rest are grouped together along one edge. Although these quilts do indeed suggest lunacy to a 'straight' quilter, scholars of the African American tradition see in them the visual embodiment of 'offbeat' phrasing in music, as well as a form of magical protection, since 'the Devil can only go in straight lines'.

Closer and more specific parallels exist, however, between African and African American textile arts. Two appliqué 'Bible Quilts', made in the late 19th century by Harriet Powers (1837–1911) of Athens, Georgia, using brightly coloured trade cloth and associated with the Royal Court of Dahomey, so closely follow the style of Fon appliqué hangings that the similarity can hardly have been accidental, despite their Christian subject-matter (see fig. 155). Somehow, through at least a generation or two, the appliqué technique had been preserved and reinterpreted.

154. Shoulder-cape, cotton, l. 1 m, Saramaka maroons, Surinam, collected 1960s (Los Angeles, CA, University of California, Fowler Museum of Cultural History)

6. OTHER ARTS. Traditionally, African pottery is made by the built-up method of attaching one flattened piece of clay to another to form the desired shape rather than by coiling or by the potter's wheel. Women usually make pottery for their own use, but in areas where good clay produces superior pots, valuable for sale or barter, men are also potters. No built-up pottery has been found in the Americas, but, as in the other arts, African potters quickly adapted their traditional skills to the new methods, materials and forms needed in the plantation societies. Although African potters are known to have produced fine pottery in Brazil and the Caribbean, they are best known for elegantly turned bowls, urns and curiously animated 'face vessels' in the southern USA. With their inlaid eyes and teeth in contrasting colours, some of these face vessels, also known as devil jugs or monkey jugs, suggest African masks, particularly those of the Kongo peoples from the mouth of the great Congo (Zaïre) River. Some may have been made as grave ornaments in the manner of ceramic heads so used in coastal Ghana and Côte d'Ivoire.

Coiled grass baskets made in the creolized Gullah culture of the rice-growing Sea Islands off South Carolina are virtually interchangeable with baskets from Senegambia and Angola in technique, form and function (see fig. 156). Similar baskets are made, however, by Europeans and Native North Americans. As with other African arts, their New World exponents have felt free to modify and change their traditional ancestral designs to suit new uses and new markets, producing hats, table-mats and flower baskets with handles.

155. Harriet Powers: Bible Quilt, pieced and appliquéd cotton, embroidered with plain and metallic yarn, 1.75×2.67 m, *c.* 1895–8 (Boston, MA, Museum of Fine Arts)

The existence of other long-hidden or misunderstood African religious expression from the Mande, Fon, Yoruba, Ejagham and Kongo peoples, among others, has been revealed by the research of Robert Farris Thompson (1983) and his students. African form and colour symbols or cosmograms, somewhat modified or creolized, still exist throughout the New World, examples being the Haitian *vèvè* ground designs (*see* HAITI, fig. 3); protective charms made of cloth, leather and other materials; grave ornaments featuring shells, crosses and arrow-forms; and even one or more writing 'scripts', such as the *nsibidi* of the Ejagham (Ekoi) of south-central Nigeria (*see* EJAGHAM, §1). These different expressions suggest that many more persisting African beliefs and practices remain to be discovered in the New World.

Possibly the most 'African' people in the New World after the maroons, the Haitians have developed a strong painting tradition initiated in 1944 by an American teacher, De Witt Peters (1902–66), who exposed a number of young uneducated men to a wide range of foreign arts and then encouraged them to experiment, using their own local folklore and history as subject-matter. Besides the colourful street life, the rituals of Vodoun, the local religion syncretizing Catholicism with Fon cosmology, became the subject of many paintings and the source of national pride and much-needed income from avid tourist-collectors. Later, wood-carving and pierced sheet-iron panels (made from flattened steel oil drums) on the same subjects continued the tradition in sculpture as well. Although some painted wall decoration is known in Africa among the Mangbetu of Zaïre and the Ndebele of South Africa, Haitian mural and easel paintings on canvas or board using acrylic or oil paints have a Western form and a content paralleling that of other 'naive' (i.e. not academically trained) genre painters, including modern African sign-painters, whose work is now similarly appreciated abroad.

In virtually every other country of the New World, painters, sculptors and other artists of African or part-African ancestry, and with some knowledge and pride in their ancestral traditions, have made major contributions. They include WIFREDO LAM in Cuba, Agnaldo Manuel dos Santos and Rubem Valentim (*b* 1922) in Brazil, and in the USA Lois Mailou Jones (see fig. 157) and John Biggers (*b* 1925).

See also AFRICAN AMERICAN ART.

BIBLIOGRAPHY

M. J. Herskovits and F. S. Herskovits: *Rebel Destiny: Among the Bush Negroes of Dutch Guiana* (New York and London, 1934)

M. J. Herskovits: *The Myth of the Negro Past* (Boston, MA, 1941)

P. Dark: *Bush Negro Art: An African Art in the Americas* (London and New York, 1954)

P. Verger: *Dieux d'Afrique: Culte des Orishas et Vodouns à l'ancienne Côte des Esclaves en Afrique et à Bahia, la Baie de tous les Saints au Brésil* (Paris, 1954)

J. H. Rodrigues: *Brazil and Africa* (Berkeley, 1965)

P. D. Curtin: *The Atlantic Slave Trade: A Census* (Madison, 1969)

S. Lewis: *Art African American* (New York, 1969)

R. F. Thompson: *Black Gods and Kings: Yoruba Art at UCLA* (Los Angeles, 1971/*R* Bloomington and London, 1976)

156. Sewing basket, sweet grass, h. 380 mm, from Sea Islands, off South Carolina, 1975 (Washington, DC, National Museum of American History)

African Art in Motion: Icon and Act (exh. cat. by R. F. Thompson; Washington, DC, N.G.A.; Los Angeles, UCLA, Wight A.G.; 1974/*R* 1979)

J. Drachler: *Black Homeland, Black Diaspora: Cross-Currents in the African Relationship* (Port Washington, 1975)

G.-M. Fry: 'Harriet Powers: Portrait of a Black Quilter', *Missing Pieces: Georgia Folk Art* (Atlanta, 1976)

J. M. Vlach: 'The Shotgun House: An African Architectural Legacy', *Pioneer America*, viii (1976), pp. 47–80; also in *Afro-American Folk Art and Crafts*, ed. W. Ferris (Boston, MA, 1983) and *By the Work of their Hands: Studies in Afro-American Folklife*, by J. M. Vlach (Charlottesville and London, 1991), pp. 185–213

A. M. Pescatello: *Old Roots in New Lands: Historical and Anthropological Perspectives on Black Experiences in the Americas* (Westport, 1977)

S. Rodman: *Genius in the Backlands: Popular Artists of Brazil* (Old Greenwich, CT, 1977)

Haitian Art (exh. cat. by J. Stebich; New York, Brooklyn Mus.; Milwaukee, WI, A. Cent.; New Orleans, LA, Mus. A.; 1978–9)

The Afro-American Tradition in Decorative Arts (exh. cat. by J. M. Vlach; Cleveland, OH, Mus. A.; Milwaukee, WI, A. Cent.; Birmingham, AL, Mus. A.; and elsewhere; 1978–9)

Carybe: *Iconografia dos Deuses Africanos no Candomble da Bahia* (São Paulo, 1980)

Afro-American Arts in the Surinam Rain-Forest (exh. cat. by S. Price and R. Price; Los Angeles, UCLA, Wight A.G.; Dallas, TX, Mus. F.A.; Baltimore, MD, Walters A.G.; New York, Amer. Mus. Nat. Hist.; 1980–82)

The Four Moments of the Sun: Kongo Art in Two Worlds (exh. cat. by R. F. Thompson and J. A. Cornet, Washington, DC, N.G.A., 1981–2)

J. H. Harris: *Global Dimensions of the African Diaspora* (Washington, DC, 1982)

R. A. Perry: *What Is It? Black American Folk Art from the Collection of Regenia Perry* (Richmond, 1982)

W. Ferris, ed.: *Afro-American Folk Art and Crafts* (Boston, MA, 1983)

R. F. Thompson: *Flash of the Spirit: African and Afro-American Art and Philosophy* (New York, 1983)

D. J. Crowley: *African Myth and Black Reality in Bahian Carnival* (Los Angeles, 1984)

J. O. Horton: 'Double Consciousness: Afro-American Identity in the Nineteenth Century', *Sharing Traditions: Five Black Artists in Nineteenth Century America*, ed. L. R. Hartigan (Washington, DC, 1985)

D. E. Reno: *Collecting Black Americana* (New York, 1986)

S. Stuckey: *Slave Culture: Nationalist Theory and the Foundations of Black America* (New York, 1987)

Visionary Images from the South (exh. cat. by M. Wahlmann, Lafayette, U. SW LA, A. Mus., 1987–8)

J. Wilson: 'The Myth of the Black Aesthetic', *Next Generation: Southern Black Aesthetic* (Winston-Salem, 1990)

Free within Ourselves: African-American Artists in the Collection of the National Museum of American Art (exh. cat. by R. A. Perry; Hartford, CT, Wadsworth Atheneum; New York, IBM Gal. Sci. & A.; Sacramento, CA, Crocker A. Mus.; Memphis, TN, Brooks Mus. A.; Columbus, GA, Mus.; 1992–4)

R. F. Thompson: *Divine Inspiration from Benin to Bahia* (Albuquerque, 1993)

J. M. Vlach: *Back of the Big House: The Architecture of Plantation Slavery* (Chapel Hill, 1993)

——: *By the Work of their Hands: Studies in Afro-American Folklife* (Charlottesville and London, 1993)

Face of the Gods: Art and Altars of Africa and the African Americas (exh. cat. by R. F. Thompson, New York, Mus. Afr. A., 1993)

M. D. Harris: 'From Double Consciousness to Double Vision: The Africentric Artist', *Afr. A.*, xxvii (1994), pp. 44–53

DANIEL J. CROWLEY

IX. Contemporary developments.

Modern African art has largely developed since the mid-20th century. It is marked by the exploration of new media and engendered by aesthetic intentions very different from those that informed works from earlier times (*see* §II, 2 above). Any consideration of modernity in African art has

157. Lois Mailou Jones: *Les Fetiches*, oil on linen (Washington, DC, Museum of American Art)

to begin by examining its relationship to the ancient and continuing tradition. In each country, it is possible to determine whether a continuous development may be traced, within which the essential African culture is merely presented using different technical modes, or whether modern African art has to be considered a novel invention based upon foreign borrowings that, by their origins, distort the presentation of indigenous experience and reflect little of African antecedents.

1. Continuity and change. 2. Types of artist. 3. Art training and guidance.

1. CONTINUITY AND CHANGE. The power of art from Africa has been more appreciated since the earlier belief that it was pagan and primitive gave way in the 1930s to the respect of European artists such as Picasso, whose response moved beyond admiration into emulation. Their perception of the originality of the African aesthetic modified the formal qualities of Western art. It may be that in the 1990s the direction of influence was reversed, as African artists borrowed from those contemporary European styles that still showed residual evidence of prior influence from the African continent.

(i) Religious context. (ii) Adaptation to contemporary markets. (iii) Craft skills. (iv) New forms.

(i) Religious context. It has often been observed that traditional African art is closely linked to the religion it was designed to celebrate, although this thesis may have been over-emphasized by anthropologists, who tended to explain all cultural phenomena in terms of social function, and by missionaries who disapproved on theological grounds of representation of the animist beliefs they had arrived to supplant. The unwillingness to discriminate between form and purpose is based on the justification that sculpture is assessed by its efficacy rather than its appearance. In such a context beauty might have little relevance. However, experiment has shown that aesthetic evaluation can exist separately from any required function. Nevertheless, the concept of function remains predominant, and this assumption introduces a difficulty for the modern African artist. To a large extent he shares the secular principles of the West and therefore exists in a contextual framework that is no longer defined by the system of patronage, status and purpose established in the past. Recognition of this change requires deliberate artistic choices.

Many artists simply continue to carve in the traditional mode, for the demand and context for such work have not totally disappeared. African belief systems, though challenged by changing standards, have a remarkable resilience and adaptability. The Yoruba *ibeji* cult, for example, has survived generations of Christian conversion (*see* YORUBA, §4(i)). The production of personal twin figures requires artistic expression, and the designs have become increasingly transitional. Some are stylized as if to minimize their association with the orthodox forms. In other cases the wooden figures are replaced with manufactured dolls or photographs. Similarly, masking enactments remain popular, though the performances may be less closely connected to their religious origins. Even when such events lose some of their reverent intention and are subsumed into something approaching carnival, they still demand elaborate and familiar artefacts from established craftsmen.

(ii) Adaptation to contemporary markets. There are also established sculptors who continue to produce formally conventional figures but seek a market outside the local culture. Such works may be absorbed by the tourist trade. These carvers are not necessarily participants in the wholesale production of crude replicas, such as the *chiwawa* antelopes that line the pavements of Dakar, Senegal. The production of formal sculpture is a diversified wholesale industry ranging in quality from the excellent reproductions carved in the workshops of major museums, such as those in Abidjan or Bamako, to the crudest 'Senoufu' conveyor-belt factories. Experienced carvers may still exhibit great skill, regardless of the destination of their product and the intentions of its buyers. Strictly speaking, aesthetic excellence should be embodied in the work itself rather than dependent on the intention of either artist or patron, but that logic does not prevail in the assessment of collectable African art. Works are required to have been used in formal ritual. Fine carvings without that functional antecedent (or at least the intent of contextual use) have

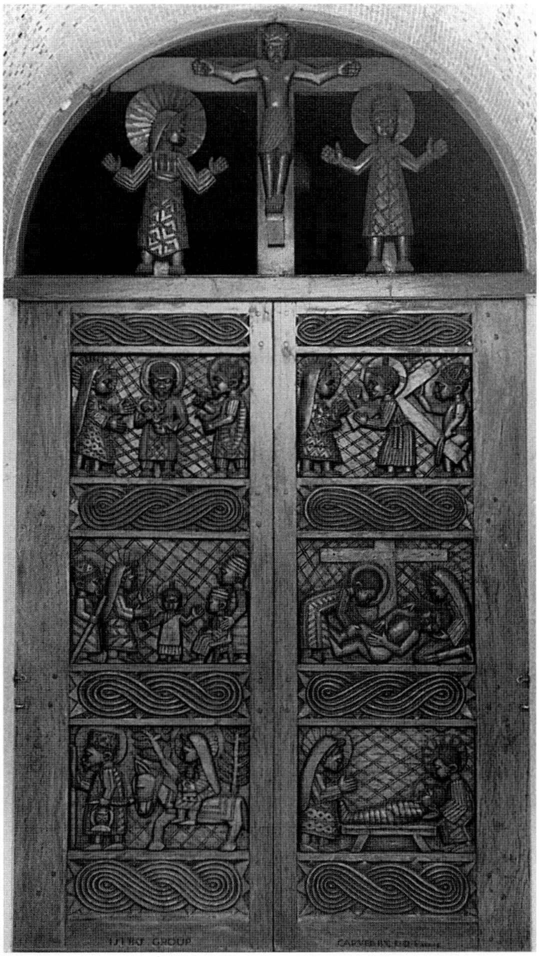

158. Lamidi Fakeye: church doors, wood, Oke-Padi, Nigeria, 1956–7

a limited market regardless of any abstract evaluation of their technical calibre. Inevitably, many modern sculptures, sometimes with visible demerits, are given false patina and deliberate termite damage to provide evidence of antiquity and usage, so allowing them to be more convincingly but fraudulently presented as 'genuine'. Their contrived appearance is sustained by spurious assurances that they have been actively 'danced' in the correct manner. This will enhance their collectability and value by means that have little connection with any purely aesthetic quality (*see* §X below).

A different kind of development allows modern carvers to incorporate tradition into an alternative product. This option, which sometimes offends purists, is exemplified by the Nigerian artist Lamidi Fakeye (see fig. 158), who was born into a family of Benin carvers. As well as absorbing traditional skills within this renowned artistic environment, he underwent an eclectic education, attending both Muslim and Catholic schools in his youth and the Paris Ecole des Beaux-Arts at maturity. He has achieved a considerable reputation for his ability to merge conventional styles with modern utility. For example, he works with the local adze to create the basic form but uses imported German chisels for the completion of fine detail. He adapts the characteristic design of Yoruba house-posts to local commercial architecture, and Yoruba figure-carving is the basis for his production of genre figures such as musicians in regional costume. His style has been widely copied by younger carvers. To meet demand he has established a workshop in which apprentices undertake the primary shaping. This arrangement, though common enough in the studios of European Renaissance painters, has been criticized as undermining individual authenticity. Most early carvers remain anonymous, but expectations have changed, and the name of the individual artist has become synonymous with value, as it is in Western galleries. (*See also* §III, 4 above.)

(iii) Craft skills. Traditional craft skills have continued into the later 20th century, although it must be recognized that the Western art–craft distinction is far less clear in Africa. The essential and active manufacture of pottery, vessels and textiles has had to be modified to cope with changing conditions and to maintain sales in the face of competition with manufactured goods. For common usage, cheap and sturdy imports have largely replaced many of the indigenous products: enamel bowls are preferred to breakable clay pots, while factory-made cloth is far cheaper and more uniform than the handwoven product, though sometimes these manufactured bales are printed to emulate the designs of the indigenous hand-dyed fabrics. Faced with the loss of trade the traditional craft-workers modify their products and survive by serving new ends, but some indigenous quality is lost. Etched gourds achieve a new market as bowls for cocktail peanuts; the skilful plaiting of raffia produces coasters and glass holders; the important Yoruba practice of indigo-dyeing is extended into the making of tablecloths, wall hangings and place-mats; clothing lengths are defined by shirt, not skirt, lengths. In these ways, traditional techniques survive, but at the expense of their original purpose.

The most intriguing examples of this adaptation are the familiar goldweights of Ghana. The early castings dating back into the 18th century were made specifically to measure gold dust but were superseded by more efficient measuring devices (*see also* §VI, 10 above). The residual pieces were very popular among visitors, who regarded them as unusual local novelties. Figurines and complex geometric shapes were so energetically exported that few genuine ones remained, yet demand remained unsatisfied, so the complex lost-wax technique was resumed for the new buyers. Some were merely replicas of original designs and thus could be described as fakes, but as market needs became more specific, Western-influenced designs such as cowboy figures were developed. Forming a substyle deemed to appeal to inhibited Europeans were the mildly pornographic figures called *bêtises* (Fr. 'naughty things'), which have no African antecedent at all. In this case it is arguable that the influence of tourism, generally condemned as meretricious, may be sustaining a traditional skill that would otherwise have died out.

(iv) New forms. In the examples of continuity and adaptation outlined above there is a direct if sometimes tenuous connection with the creative past. There is another kind of modern African art that develops where a similar form had once existed, but its association with the more recent expression is too remote to be demonstrable. The new variations are so different in style and purpose that it is hard to see them as other than a spontaneous creativity that occurred in a country where the indigenous inheritance has largely vanished. Modern art of the MAKONDE in Tanzania and the SHONA of Zimbabwe exemplify this renewed application of earlier techniques to modern demand. The Yoruba artists who work at Oshogbo certainly call upon a more resilient and continuing history, but their actual works indicate a similar gulf between production and tradition.

The Makonde people are divided by the Tanzania and Mozambique border. They have a well-known carving tradition, but this has little connection with the tourist phenomena of contemporary Makonde art. Its origin in the late 1950s has occasioned much controversy. Some have asserted that it was invented and commissioned by the Indian owner of a souvenir shop in Dar es Salaam; others look for some more mystic causation. Regardless of its precise beginnings, the idea took root, and Makonde carving has become an industry geared entirely to tourists. The works are a mix of unthinking repetition and real ingenuity, of sloppy chopping and polished refinement. Some types such as the tree of life—relief figures climbing around a heavy tree stump—are so recognizable that the design can be ordered by name (see fig. 25 above), while others are highly abstract. Pieces such as the *shetani* figures of bush spirits display a strikingly wild, surrealist imagination and, unusually for Africa, are sometimes grotesquely pornographic, a characteristic that confirms their export destination. Here one finds a vigorous community art style, for as yet only a few of the artists are identified by name, and whole families seem to be involved in the making and sale. It is hard to say whether this carving will develop into a more serious individualistic art or degenerate into the repeated production of cheap souvenirs.

The stone-carving of the Shona of Zimbabwe, although sustained by a more sophisticated critical acclaim, derives from a somewhat similar historical background (*see* ZIMBABWE, §3). There is an antecedent, most commonly observed in the carved birds that decorate the top of the walls of the Great Temple of Zimbabwe, yet no one has yet convincingly demonstrated a continuance of this medieval competence into modern times. There is little evidence of any interim production during the last 500 years. It took European intervention to reactivate the tradition. Frank McEwen, himself an artist, was appointed director of the Rhodesian National Art Museum in 1954. He urged his attendants to experiment with art. After some sporadic attempts at painting, they turned instinctively to the carving of the beautiful coloured stones found in the countryside. Their huge success, carefully nurtured by McEwen with exhibitions in Paris, engendered a recognizable regional style, and there are now many artists, some of whom have achieved acclaim for their individuality and have held one-man shows. The work of others is less distinctive, and generally there is a sense of a group functioning within a single medium. The artists often work in groups: Vukutu was founded as one such cooperative base, and a farmer, Tom Bloomfield of Tengenenge, also supported numerous carvers. All the sculptors choose to work in hard stone. The works are regularly explained as making reference to the old Shona creation myths, but their visual attraction derives rather from purely artistic elements, a sensitive exploitation of the colour and structure of the stone. Carefully introduced to the European market, these works have attracted critical respect and the highest prices, which have multiplied the number of producers. Demand, inspired by the better-known artists such as John Takawira and Bernard Takawira, has spawned a host of inferior imitators, though the difficulty of working in the hard material enforces some restriction on expansion. Each piece is individually worked, and there are as yet no production-line workshops equivalent to those of the Kamba people in Kenya.

Both these groups of artists reflect an external impetus that may have resuscitated a lost historical competence. McEwen has denied that he offered any training or guidance to his sculptors, but the presence of a sympathetic and responsible outsider who offers even general critical appreciation must have some effect on the direction of an artist's development. Since few work in isolation, emulation of the successful is an inevitable threat to personal style. The question of external influence takes on more complicated form in the venture established in the Nigerian town of Oshogbo, where a more complex involvement between tradition and foreign assistance became the basis of an important artistic enterprise established in IBADAN in 1961. This was a meeting-place and club that was known as Mbari, the Igbo word for a ritual building (*see* IGBO, §3). It was initially organized in Ibadan by Ulli Beier, a professor at the university. Subsequently other 'Mbaris' were set up to function as artists' cooperatives in Oshogbo (1962) and Enugu (1963). Later a similar venture was exported to Nairobi as Chemchemi, directed by the South African author Ezekial Mpahehlele.

In Nigeria, tradition is by no means as moribund as it seems to be in Zimbabwe. The extraordinary artistic imagination of the Yoruba people remains a virile and active presence after unbroken centuries of achievement. Nevertheless, Beier helped to focus this creativity into more modern modes of expression, with the international magazine *Black Orpheus* as its literary focus. He invited the attendance of young people who had artistic potential, requiring only that they had had no destructive formal art education. He did, however, arrange workshops to demonstrate techniques such as printmaking that would make efforts more profitable. Under Beier's encouragement the content remained identifiably Yoruba in both subject and design, but the materials were imported and the product contemporary. Oshogbo, which propelled several artists to considerable fame, must be considered one of the most imaginative programmes in Africa. An unemployed blacksmith named Ashiru was encouraged to experiment with repoussé designs that had something in common with the classical plaques from Benin but were beaten on to sheets of imported aluminium. Another artist, Fabunwe, stitched coloured thread pictures of Yoruba deities on black cloth using a Singer sewing-machine. Jimoh Buraimoh produced a new effect by gumming cheap imported beads on to hardboard to create designs that may make a passing satiric comment on the whole bead-trade culture in African history. All the artists take their subjects and patterns from their Yoruba inheritance. Because of their deliberate decision to use Western media, the manner in which they

159. Twins Seven Seven: *Baptist Church of Bush of Ghost*, etching, 375×305 mm, *c.* 1969 (Oxford, private collection)

160. Tshibumba Kanda-Matulu: *Colonie Belge 1885–1959*, paint on flour sack, 360×450 mm, 1970s (private collection)

explore these indigenous themes cannot be seen as a precise continuance.

One consistent feature of this work reveals the resilience of the tradition even in these circumstances. Perhaps because the local artistic antecedent is carving rather than painting, many artists seek to construct a three-dimensional effect by superimposing a raised level of material upon the flat surface characteristic of the usual pictorial format. One of the most famous Oshogbo artists is Twins Seven Seven (see fig. 159). His work embraces music and dance as well as design, demonstrating his attachment to Yoruba lore. His ink drawings are applied to cloth as well as paper, while his major paintings achieve the three-dimensional effect with fret-sawed plywood figures glued to the base. Other artists fix cut metal, cloth and strips of knitting wool to their surfaces to escape from the flat finish anticipated in much Western art. These efforts to maintain depth are philosophically more suggestive than collage, which might be considered the European equivalent. The formulation derives from an aesthetic conflict that arises whenever the African artist seeks to create a painted picture, which is primarily a Western form. There are many examples of depiction on wall surfaces, going back to the ancient Saharan petroglyphs (*see* §VI, 15 above), and textiles are displayed in a similar way. Nevertheless the concept of a separate illustration to be hung on a wall has little African antecedent except in Ethiopian ecclesiastical art (*see* ETHIOPIA, §II).

2. TYPES OF ARTIST. Within the field of contemporary art in Africa, there are two types of artists. Broadly, they can be described either as self-taught or as academic, depending on their educational background. The self-taught can in turn be subdivided according to their patron support as much as by style. Some predominantly cater to European buyers and are naive only in the technical sense. Others, local craftsmen, may be judged as more authentically connected to an African audience, because their efforts are available at a price that permits local purchase. They thus avoid the expectation of expatriate preference that sometimes compromises the integrity of artists when they become aware of another more lucrative, if foreign, market.

At the most functional level the craftsman artist creates murals on the walls of bars, perpetrates the elaborate decoration of mammy-wagon lorries and advertises hairstyles for barbers. There are also narrative shop-signs, showing a woman pounding *fou-fou* for a chop bar or humorously depicting the prosperous happiness of an owner who allows no credit and the misery of one so foolish as to do so. In this genre the artist has a clear function and fulfils a local service. Paintings at this level, constructed by using enamel house paint on sacking or denim, are touted in the streets, particularly in Zaïre. Their subjects are highly conventionalized. Forest fires and villages by the river are popular and repetitive themes—the 'canoe and palm tree' school. The ubiquitous water spirit Mamy Wata is sometimes drawn, by order, with a recognizable female face. The expectation is that Zaïrois may buy them to display on the walls of their urban quarters, even while multicoloured Indian chromo prints of Hindi mythology remain inexplicably popular. Curiosities that indicate the absorption of another dimension of neo-colonial influence are scenes using only black and white paint, which are claimed to reflect the images observed on local television screens.

A more political subject of paintings for this local audience in Zaïre is a sequence of popular history. The Belgian mismanagement of the Congo colony is illustrated by a judicially mandated public beating supervised by an arrogant colonial officer (see fig. 160). The series culminates with depictions of the battles fought during the period of UN intervention in the Congo after independence in 1960. Deposed premier Patrice Lumumba (1925–61) is invariably portrayed, in a version of his capture and murder entitled *La Calvaire*, as a cruelly treated martyr. The experiments of such artists when they become aware of alternative materials can produce fascinating works. An example of this process is to be seen in the work of Tito Zungu (*b* 1946), a South African Zulu who uses felt marking pens of various colours to depict such examples of modern progress as aeroplanes, trains and ocean liners (see fig. 161), with rigorous lines determined by the constant use of a ruler's edge. Originally these designs decorated envelopes for sale to goldminers for their letters home. Later his efforts, assisted by the Durban Art Institute, engendered a cult audience in South Africa and a nationally distributed calendar, which opened up another means by which patronage brings an unknown artist to prominence. Yet, like many African artists, Zungu has not subsequently chosen to explore any technique other than the one that brought him success. This adherence to a single idiosyncratic style may be explained by the need to maintain profitable commissions.

There is a considerable difference between such craftsmen artists, with their roots in the commerce of their community, and artists who though technically untaught are nonetheless patronized by predominantly non-African collectors. Two such painters who have achieved renown are Edward Saidi Tingatinga (1937–72) from Dar es Salaam (*see* TANZANIA, §3) and Jak Katarikawe of Kampala.

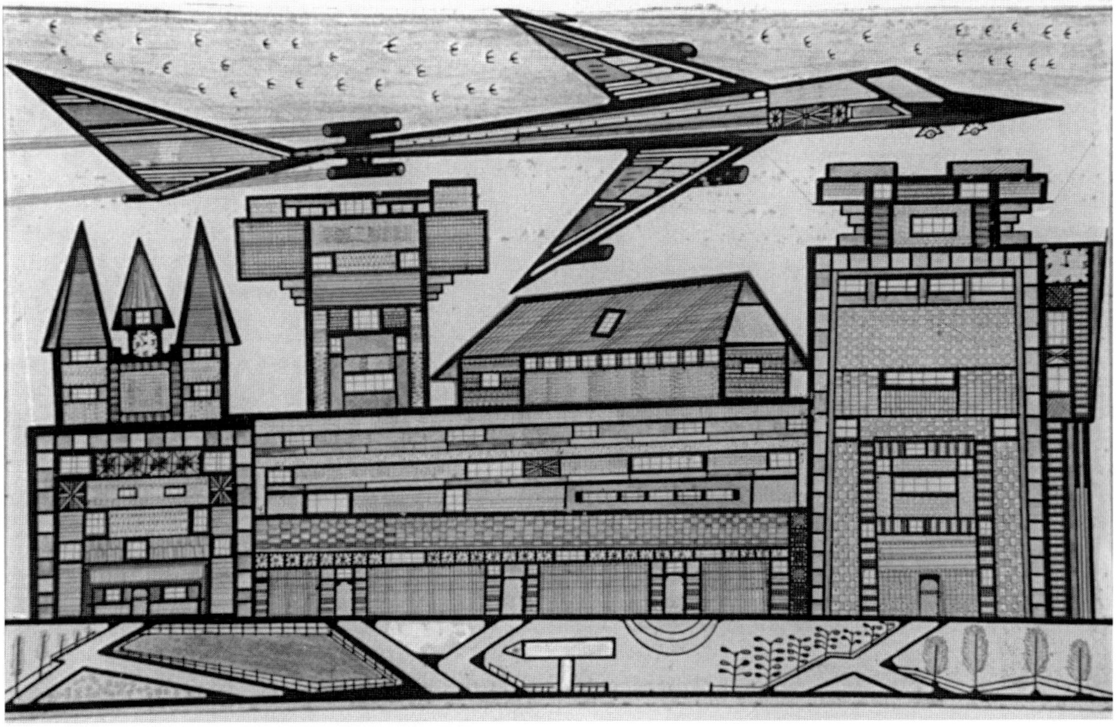

161. Tito Zungu: *Untitled*, ball-point pen ink on paper, 330×220 mm, *c.* 1972 (Durban, African Art Centre)

Tingatinga's works are highly distinctive. He depicts stylized animals in the boldest colours, controlled by cartoon-like black outlines. His pictures became so popular that at his death many borrowed his strikingly dramatic and sellable technique. Jak Katarikawe (see fig. 162) is naive in the conventional sense, as the word might be applied to Henri Rousseau. He uses both oil paints and crayon to present genre scenes of local myth, often enhanced by amusing anecdotal explanation. His style exhibits considerable wit and an extravagant design that has appealed to European collectors.

Much contemporary art derives from some measure of European intervention. Almost all of the more distinguished artists have had the opportunity of study and training abroad. An exception is Malangatana Valente Ngwenya (*b* 1936), detained in Mozambique during the period of political upheaval and an artist who has achieved international recognition without formal instruction (*see* MOZAMBIQUE, §3). It is clear that there must be some measure of alienation for an artist influenced by new techniques and exotic materials. Especially challenging to the modern African artist is the priority given in modern Western art to unfettered individuality and experiment, which contradicts his inherited expectation of modified replication of form. Despite assertions of aesthetic neutrality, European involvement cannot avoid becoming to some degree manipulative. Even teaching at the purely technical level imposes expectations in subsequent performance.

3. ART TRAINING AND GUIDANCE. The missionary schools sponsored several early schemes. Typical was the programme at the Cyrene Mission, Matopo Hills, near Bulawayo in Zimbabwe, which in 1939 was used as an educational centre offering little more than the teaching of manual skills to the handicapped. Under a period of direction by the Revd Edward Patterson up to 1953, a lively arts centre developed that, in spite of modest intentions, took on the Christian ambience around the resident artists. A similar influential programme was initiated in Nigeria by Father Kevin Carroll in 1947. He was commissioned by African Missions to set up a workshop in Oye-Ekiti to nurture local carving skills. With these ventures, there was a genuine desire to sustain local artists, but too often such projects encouraged the carving of wooden madonnas.

(i) Francophone Africa. In Francophone Africa the colonial artistic instruction was more deliberate and formal, so its consequences were more intrusive. One important institution was the Congolese Académie des Arts, which was established in Elisabethville in 1944 under the direction of a French artist from Brest, Pierre Romain-Defosse. Another, L'Académie des Beaux-Arts, was established somewhat later by Laurent Moonens (*see also* ZAÏRE). They were both organized on the same principles as similar art schools in Europe. The directors publicly announced that they would encourage indigenous expression and not suggest themes, propose models or impose styles and insisted that their students were free to explore their own inspiration, but in practice they failed to recognize how inevitably both overt and covert influences would affect any African attending an institution based on so European a pattern.

162. Jak Katarikawe: *Football Match*, oil on paper, 730×610 mm, *c.* 1986 (Frankfurt am Main, Museum für Völkerkunde)

Two artists of high reputation learnt their distinctive techniques from Romain-Defosse's academy: Pili-Pili Mulongoya, with his evocative pictures contrived out of spaced dots (see fig. 163), and Mwenze Kibwanga, who exploited short, separated brushstrokes. Both gained a profitable reputation among Belgian residents. How genuinely African their results are is debatable.

A similar art school, named after the Brazzaville suburb Poto-Poto, was founded under the direction of Pierre Lods in 1951 (*see also* CONGO). The enterprise inspired pottery, enamelling and weaving. The most familiar result appears to have been the origination of those now ubiquitous pictures of sticklike dancers drawn against a black background, which may have some antecedents in cave paintings. They are now touted throughout Africa. Lods moved on to Dakar, where the Académie Africaine des Arts Plastiques and, from 1961, the School of Arts and Letters were important centres of modern art, though the French influence remained paramount. Iba N'Diaye and Papa Ibra Tall were the most prominent artists; both were African but, after years of study and residence in Paris, steeped in French culture. Christian Lattier, from Côte d'Ivoire, chose to devise sculptural designs made of elaborately coiled ropes. Such are the complexities of transitional aesthetics, he announced that he had deliberately selected this unusual medium because it had no conceivable African antecedent that might impose upon him the expectation of some inherited style.

(ii) Nigeria. In Nigeria modern art teaching began in 1922 under the direction of Chief Aina Onabolu (1882–1963). In 1927 he arranged the appointment of Kenneth Murray, whose decades of work for Nigerian culture became legend. He taught Ben Enwonwu, who after achieving success as a sculptor became Federal Art Adviser. The best-known artists were trained in formal art departments attached to the major universities, first Zaria, then Ibadan and Lagos. As these were all staffed by expatriates, their curriculum did not vary greatly from the courses found in British art schools. Zaria was the most influential centre during the 1950s, producing an entire generation of modern Nigerian artists. Yusuf Grillo, Jimo Akolo, Uche Okeke and Bruce Onobrakpeya became the senior professionals; several in turn joined the faculty of other university art departments and thus passed on the principles they had learnt. Their work showed varied styles, but in each case a combination of international technique and African subject-matter was apparent, signalling the continuing dualism that remains so noticeable in modern African art. (*See also* NIGERIA, §VII.)

(iii) East Africa. In East Africa, formal art was substantially engendered by Margaret Trowell, who went to Kampala, Uganda, in 1929 and offered classes in her home. When Makerere became a college associated with London University, a School of Fine Art was founded under her direction and given her name after her retirement in 1958 (*see also* UGANDA). In 1964 Barbara Brown founded the prominent and influential Nommo Gallery, but it did not survive the Amin presidency (1971–9), and many artists, such as Eli Kyeyune, regrouped in Nairobi. This city offers a vigorous and sustaining market of residents and travellers; European cultural centres such as the German Goethe

163. Pili-Pili Mulongoya: *Termites and Birds*, acrylic on hardboard, 1970s (Bremen, Übersee-Museum)

Institute were generous with exhibitions, and white boutique entrepreneurs encouraged sales. Elimo Njau, a Makerere graduate, was a key figure in the fostering of new artists, at first through Paa-ya-paa Gallery, then from 1965 through an art colony that he set up with his author wife at Kibo across the border in Tanzania. Chemchemi also contributed support. Artists during the 1960s included a wide range, from university academics such as Francis Nnagenda to the brilliant untutored Herzbon Owiti. Foundation sponsorship released artists from total dependence on the tourist market, and the result was an exciting period of vigorous creativity. Work in Tanzania centred on the National Gallery. Another Makerere artist, Sam Ntiro (*b* 1923), combined support for art with important political appointments, while Francis Msangi (*b* 1937) achieved a reputation that led to teaching connections abroad. Generally economic conditions attracted Tanzanian artists to Nairobi rather than Dar es Salaam.

(iv) Other regions. There are comparable similarities in the growth of an African modern art in much of Africa. Three countries, because of their special histories, have acquired recognizably unique styles: Sudan, Ethiopia and South Africa. Art from the Sudan is primarily from the northern Muslim region and thus relates to the Middle East rather than Europe. Yet, unlike work from the Mediterranean coastal countries, it is usually considered African. Formal art training began in 1945 with the founding of the School of Design at the Gordon Memorial College in Khartoum by a young Englishman, Jean Greenlaw. He was succeeded in 1951 by J. Cottrell. After independence in 1956 Sudanese staff replaced the expatriates, and the name changed to the School of Fine Art. The school's most distinguished figure is IBRAHIM EL SALAHI, who employs characteristic Arabic calligraphic forms in his work. A major artist of the next generation is Mohamed Omer Bushara (*b* 1946), whose training in London did not seem to interfere with his highly idiosyncratic style and choice of media (inked cartoon-like outlines were drawn on a ground prepared with various pigments including coffee). Amir I. M. Nour (*b* 1936) moved to Chicago and experimented with sculpture. Many Sudanese artists seem inhibited from experimentation by the expectations of the formal teaching they receive and the Muslim environment the regime imposes. (*See also* SUDAN, §§4 and 5.)

The powerful Christian Orthodox Church has a profound influence in Ethiopia, where religious themes have dominated most art. In the late 20th century the senior artist was Afewerk Tekle, most renowned for his remarkable work in stained glass, a technique he studied in Paris in 1954. A major achievement is the window adorning the Organization of African Unity Hall in Addis Ababa. The black outlines of the patterning required by the medium recall the controlled boundaries of an icon and later became a personal characteristic when the style was transposed to his painting. The awareness of an extensive Church tradition may have originally been a stimulus to Ethiopian artists, but it also made for a confining obstacle to imaginative invention. Perhaps for this reason the two major young artists, Skunder Boghossian and Gebre Kristos Desta, chose to work abroad, the former training in Britain, the latter in Germany. Both have deliberately selected the technical freedom of non-representational forms. This is rare in Africa because, as is evident in traditional pieces, even the most extreme symbolic modification of naturalism does not totally divorce the residual design from the underlying realism of the object.

The peoples of South Africa, though they are supreme in the verbal art of poetry, have a more limited inheritance in the plastic arts compared with West Africans. Modern artists have less visual antecedent on which to draw. Even before the apartheid system was dismantled in the early 1990s, many worked quite closely with white artists and received both encouragement from galleries and a sympathetic, though perhaps too directive, audience for their work. The most important project was the Polly Street Art Centre established in 1952 and supervised by the renowned artist CECIL SKOTNES. This provided a place for work and an outlet for sales. An early associate was the sculptor SYDNEY KUMALO, who achieved the greatest reputation. But generally painting was the preferred medium. When Polly became the Jubilee Art Centre and moved to Soweto in 1960, there was a dramatic flowering of local art, presenting the black experience of life in Johannesburg. One characteristic style, rather casually called 'township art', portrayed urban existence in Soweto. Because of the anticipated audience the pictures tended to depict the cheerful vitality of the street scenes rather than signs of hardship and deprivation. As political antagonisms intensified, the emphasis changed and the art began to reflect the brutality of the system. A major figure who reacted with visceral anger was FENI DUMILE. His powerfully contorted lines were a direct challenge to the regime, and he was forced into exile in New York. In South Africa, however, his style continues to have a profound influence. His painting in Fort Hare, *African Guernica*, is a masterpiece linking the international theme with purely African imagery. Although Dumile himself now concentrates on clay sculpture, the characteristics of his early drawings have been repeatedly borrowed, as a shorthand expression of resistance. His preference for ink drawing, necessitated initially by limited equipment, prompted emulation from artists such as CYPRIAN SHILAKOE, who extended the technique to present poignant and ferocious displays of his environment.

One of the major preoccupations of South African artists during the apartheid years was to give artistic structure to the overwhelming oppression of their society, which tended to impose restrictions of content. In the search for a physical distancing, LOUIS KHELA MAQHUBELA, a Polly Centre artist, escaped to London, where he chose to experiment with brilliant, painterly colours and a semi-abstract style. Such modernist works would find few buyers in South Africa, where expectations of the familiar circumscribe style. (*See also* SOUTH AFRICA, §IV.)

(v) Economic context. In every African country the contemporary artist still finds it necessary to follow the dictates of the market. The problem is not only the too familiar international choice of teaching or starvation for all but a successful few. The additional dilemma derives from the predominantly non-African nationality of patrons and buyers, though exceptions are to be found. Educated Nigerians are beginning to acquire the work of local artists

for their homes, but the bulk of the art described has been bought by outsiders. Public galleries of modern art are few, and they are only just beginning to collect. Most nations have enough problems in financing the secure display of traditional works, which have achieved a higher degree of recognition and value, and governments are no more eager than many formal scholars to enter the uncharted sea of contemporary production. The exact effect of the primarily foreign source of available financial support by purchase is not easy to determine. Artists may resist direct pressures, but the nature of the audience must remain a factor. The development of modern African art often begins with a European impetus, initiated either by local programmes of assistance or by overseas scholarships. It regularly leads to European purchase. This may be judged as supportive or intrusive, and its power may be diminishing, but it nonetheless exists. Given this pattern, the variety and originality of so much of the work produced are remarkable and its authenticity convincing.

JOHN POVEY

BIBLIOGRAPHY

E. S. Brown: *Africa's Contemporary Art and Artists* (New York, 1966)

K. Carroll: *Yoruba Religious Carving: Pagan and Christian Sculpture in Nigeria and Dahomey* (London and New York, 1967)

U. Beier: *Contemporary Art in Africa* (London and New York, 1968)

R. B. Armstrong: *The Affecting Presence: An Essay in Humanistic Anthropology* (Urbana, IL, 1971)

J. DeJager: *Contemporary African Art in South Africa* (Cape Town, 1973)

M. W. Mount: *African Art: The Years Since 1920* (Bloomington and London, 1973, rev. New York, 1989)

M. Wahlman: *Contemporary African Arts* (Chicago, 1974)

Tradition and Change in Yoruba Art (exh. cat. by J. J. Arneson; Sacramento, CA, Crocker A. Mus., 1974)

J. von D. Miller: *Art in East Africa: A Guide to Contemporary Art* (London and Nairobi, 1975)

R. Jeffreys: *African Art Today* (New York, 1979)

K. Fosu: *20th Century Art of Africa* (Zaria, 1986)

G. Younge: *Art of the South African Townships* (London and New York, 1988)

H. M. Cole: 'Change and Continuity: The Icons in Twentieth-Century Art', *Icons: Ideals and Power in the Art of Africa* (exh. cat. by H. M. Cole, Washington, DC, N. Mus. Afr. A., 1989–90), pp. 160–74

J. Agthe: *Wegzeichen: Kunst aus Ostafrika, 1974–89/ Signs: Art from East Africa, 1974–89*, Frankfurt am Main, Mus. Vlkerknd. (Frankfurt am Main, 1990)

Art from the Frontline: Contemporary Art from Southern Africa (exh. cat.; Glasgow, A.G. & Mus.; Salford, Mus. & A.G.; Dublin, City Cent.; London, Commonwealth Inst.; 1990)

Africa Explores: 20th Century African Art (exh. cat. by S. Vogel, New York, Cent. Afr. A., 1991)

Africa Now (exh. cat.; Las Palmas de Gran Canaria, Cent. Atlantic. A. Mod.; Groningen, Groninger Mus.; Mexico City, Cent. Cult. A. Contemp.; 1991–2)

N. Guez: *L'Art africain contemporain/Contemporary African Art: Guide Edition 92–94* (Paris, 1992)

J. Kennedy: *New Currents, Ancient Rivers: Contemporary African Artists in a Generation of Change* (Washington, DC, and London, 1992)

C. B. Steiner: *African Art in Transit* (Cambridge, 1993)

For further bibliography *see* §III, 4 above. *See also* bibliographies for individual country entries and MAKONDE.

JEREMY COOTE

X. Forgery.

1. INTRODUCTION. In the traditional art of Sub-Saharan Africa, forgery almost always involves sculpture, primarily carvings of wood and ivory, and castings of cuprous alloys. The development of contemporary African art, such as printmaking, oil painting and other non-traditional work, is not considered in this article (*see* §§III, 4 and IX above). The market for this artwork is limited, and there is little reason for deception. Central to an understanding of forgery in African art is the issue of authenticity. In its purest sense, an authentic object is one of traditional form that was made by an African artist and used in a traditional context within the artist's own ethnic group. However, there are exceptions to this rule that make it difficult to establish a universally accepted definition for authenticity. For instance, a mask may be commissioned and carved for traditional use but, before it is worn, sold to a foreigner. This example should not be considered a forgery, unless it was misrepresented.

A forgery is a work intentionally made in the likeness of, or in imitation of, an original work of art; it is created to deceive and is always a fake. A fake, however, is not always a forgery. A fake is an inauthentic object that is presented as genuine. For example, in West Africa, tourist or airport carvings, mass-produced for sale to foreigners as well as to local élites, are frequently presented as old traditional artefacts by art dealers and other middlemen. They are only 'fakes' when presented in this way, and museum shops and other institutions sometimes sell them in a 'genuine' context at inexpensive prices. Three broad categories may thus be established: intentional forgeries, middlemen fakes and authentic objects.

Forgeries include newly created objects made to look old and presented as genuine. They may be copied from an original, constitute a pastiche or imitate a particular style and subject. They may be made by Africans or non-Africans. In some instances the same Africans who carve forgeries also carve objects for traditional use. A category of fraud that may be considered forgery of a special kind is misrepresented authentic objects that have been altered or falsified; for example an authentic figure with a newly made head, or a head from an authentic figure that is attached to another genuine figure that has lost its head.

Middlemen fakes are not necessarily made to deceive. Most are made by Africans in Africa. When attempting to present these artefacts as genuine traditional art works, traders, art dealers, collectors and other intermediaries use some of the same techniques as forgers in the falsification of surfaces and artificial ageing of objects by, for example, staining, scorching, burying and weathering. They also invent provenances and early dates of manufacture. Such fakes include handcarved but mass-produced contemporary tourist or airport pieces; early examples of tourist art, examples of which survive from as early as the 16th century; and copies made for visitors, researchers and museums.

Authentic objects are made by an African and used within his own ethnic group. However, there can be some flexibility to this definition (see above); for example, it may include an object made by a carver of one ethnic group but used by a neighbouring ethnic group, or an object of non-traditional form made by an African from imported material (e.g. plastic, aluminium) and used in a traditional context.

2. HISTORY. European interest in African objects as art was first shown during the first decade of the 20th century by such artists as Pablo Picasso and André Derain.

African sculptures could be viewed in ethnological museums and were accessible in curio shops. Despite this interest in African sculpture by some avant-garde artists of the day, the market demand was almost non-existent compared to that for European and Asian art. Indeed, before World War II the supply of African art was ample relative to the limited demand. Perhaps the best-known and earliest African fake is the 'Olokun' bronze head, collected by the German ethnologist Leo Frobenius in 1910 at the Yoruba town of Ife in south-western Nigeria. The following year British authorities forced Frobenius to return the head to its owners, and in 1934 it was placed in the Ife palace for safe-keeping. In the 1940s when the head was being cleaned at the British Museum, it was discovered to be a modern copy made by sand-casting rather than by the traditional lost-wax casting. Evidently, some time between 1910 and 1934 the original head, which probably dates to the 12th to 15th century, had been replaced with a forgery (see *Afr. A.*, 1976).

Since the 1950s and 1960s the demand for African art has grown steadily, as have prices; and only since this period has fraud become a serious matter. There are hundreds of collectors around the world, and many museums acquire African art. In a London auction at Christie's on 4 July 1989, a Benin bronze head (lot 86) realized more than £1 million; in a New York auction at Sotheby's on 21 April 1990, a Bangwa wooden figure (lot 127) was sold for over £3 million. There are reports of private sales with even higher prices. With escalating monetary values it is not surprising that fraud in African art has become a paramount concern to collectors, curators, dealers and appraisers. No one is exempt from making mistakes. For example, on 14 May 1981 Sotheby's, New York, had to withdraw an Ibibio-style wooden mask (lot 105), which was illustrated on the front cover of an auction catalogue, because it was discovered that the piece was a fake. Again, on 9 April 1984 Sotheby's, London, withdrew a metal-sheathed wooden reliquary figure in the Bwiti (Mahongwe) style and a Kwele-style wooden mask (lots 128, 133), apparently for the same reason.

Workshops both in and out of Africa have produced and still are producing forgeries. There is published documentation of forgers and forgery workshops in Africa (see Kamer; Cornet; Barbier), although their counterparts in Europe and America are not so well publicized. Particularly well documented are two groups of Asante woodcarvers in Kumasi, Ghana, who have been active since the 1970s (see Ross and Reichert). These carvers produce handsome sculptures of the highest quality with styles and iconographic elements drawn from authentic carvings as well as from their own imaginations. They then artificially age the surfaces. A number of their works have been published as authentic, and some can be found in museum and private collections.

3. Methods of detection. Despite the increasing number of scientific tools available, the most effective means for determining authenticity is a knowledgeable individual with an experienced eye who has seen and handled many objects. It is essential to have a full understanding of the use of objects in an African context. This understanding is critical when dealing with African and other 'ethnographic' art since, unlike much European art, which was intended to hang on a wall or sit on a table, authentic African sculptures were used during rituals, political ceremonies and other occasions.

In some instances, as with some types of Dogon or Bamana figures, wood-carvings are kept in shrines and, as part of rituals, are subjected to repeated applications of blood, beer or other substances. The surface of these objects can become heavily encrusted. In those instances where forgers have simulated an incrustation, this can usually be detected by the nature of the coating. A fraudulent incrustation is usually added in one application, whereas a traditional incrustation is applied in thin layers over a period of years. A microscopic or chemical analysis of the incrustation or pigmentation may also reveal forgery. Alernatively, some wooden figures, such as Yoruba twin figures, are not subject to ritual applications but rather are frequently handled, fondled and rubbed. This treatment results in a smooth surface associated with the traditional use of this type of object. Yet another class of African objects, such as some Ebrie cast goldwork, is simply displayed on rare occasions and stored away at other times. These castings have the traditional function of displaying an important man's wealth and may date from before the 20th century, but their physical condition may appear pristine. Thus every authentic object carries an expectation—based on traditional use patterns of a specific ethnic group and object type—of a particular patination and other physical features.

Among the most convenient, inexpensive and non-destructive tools available for determining authenticity is radiography (see Sieber and Celenko). Radiography can reveal a non-traditional means of manufacture, for example iron nails used to assemble a wooden figure that should be a monoxylous carving (i.e. from a single block). It can also expose hidden restoration that, if concealed, would increase the value of an object. Other visual analyses that do not require samples to be removed from objects include examination with high-powered microscopes and viewing under ultraviolet or 'black' light. Examination under infrared light is also useful but requires an expensive camera and monitor. These techniques can readily reveal repairs and restorations not seen by the unaided eye.

Some analyses are destructive to a minor extent, since they usually require a small sample from the object in question. Among these methods are pigment or accretion analysis by means of microchemical testing to determine non-traditional or inappropriate substances, microscopic wood cross-section analysis to determine tree species, and microscopic analysis and identification of plant fibre and animal hair to ascertain their nature and origin. X-ray fluorescence (no sample required), X-ray diffraction and atomic absorption spectrometry provide an elemental analysis of an object. With African art these techniques are especially useful when dealing with copper-alloy castings.

There are scientific dating methods that may be used to detect fakes. Thermoluminescence, which can determine the date when clay was last fired, has become an important technique in authenticating ceramic sculptures that may have been made centuries ago. The radiocarbon method can be applied to organic materials, either charcoal or other material from an archaeological context, or to actual art works of wood or other organic material. In some cases the size of the sample required precludes the use of this technique on small wooden and ivory objects. However, a recently developed radiocarbon procedure using an accelerator mass spectrometer requires a minimal sample.

A troublesome aspect of the radiocarbon method is that the technique dates only the wood of the object in question without necessarily giving a date of manufacture of the artwork. In other words, a fraudulent object could be carved from a much older piece of wood. This question most often arises with pieces from dry climates, where wood may survive for centuries, for example in Dogon country at the edge of the Sahara Desert. The base of a Dogon figure with a restored arm yielded a 16th- to 18th-century date. That the radiocarbon method provides an approximate date when the organic matter died, rather than when an artefact was created, demonstrates that a scientific test does not necessarily provide the definitive information sought.

BIBLIOGRAPHY

H. Kamer: 'De l'authenticité des sculptures africaines', *A. Afrique Noire*, 12 (1974), pp. 17–40

J. Cornet: 'African Art and Authenticity', *Afr. A.*, ix/1 (1975), pp. 52–5

Afr. A., x/3 (1976) [special issue on authenticity]

R. Sieber and T. Celenko: 'Rayons x et art africain: De l'utilisation des rayons x dans l'étude de l'art africain', *A. Afrique Noire*, 21 (1977), pp. 16–28

'This Matter of Fakes', *Primitive A. Newslett.*, i/4 (1978), pp. 1, 4–5

W. Gillon: *Collecting African Art* (London, 1979)

C. K. Provost: 'The Valuation of Traditional Art: Special Problems in Connoisseurship', *Valuation*, xxvi (1980), pp. 137–48

D. H. Ross and R. X. Reichert: 'Modern Antiquities: A Study of a Kumase Workshop', *Akan Transformations: Problems in Ghanaian Art History*, Museum of Cultural History, UCLA, Monographs Series, xxi (exh. cat., ed. D. H. Ross and T. F. Garrard; Los Angeles, UCLA, Mus. Cult. Hist., 1983), pp. 82–91

Is This for Real? Problems of Authenticity in Art (exh. cat., Bloomington, IN U.A. Mus., 1985)

E. M. Mauer: 'Art and Imitation: Original Works and Forgeries of Tribal Art', *Ant. & F.A.*, vii/1 (1989), pp. 45–52

W. M. Robbins: 'What African Art Is and What It Is Not', *African Art in American Collections: Survey 1989*, by W. M. Robbins and N. I. Nooter (Washington, DC, 1989), pp. 11–18

J. P. Barbier: 'Concluding Remarks', *Text*, i of *Art of Côte d'Ivoire: From the Collections of the Barbier-Mueller Museum*, 2 vols, ed. J. P. Barbier (Geneva, 1993), pp. 402–11

THEODORE CELENKO

XI. Historiography.

Despite the dramatic increase in the number of art historians specializing in Sub-Saharan Africa since 1960, the notion that African art has a history—and one that can be partially reconstructed—has yet to become firmly established (*see also* §II, 1 above). This is partly due to the nature of the source materials: the study of rock art is difficult, and only a fraction of the plastic art from Africa known today dates from before 1850. Moreover, early written sources are scarce, uneven in their coverage and mostly composed by outsiders.

A more fundamental reason is the preconceptions of scholars. African artefacts were collected by Europeans from *c.* 1500 onwards but were perceived as curiosities, fetishes or simply material culture. Only after relatively naturalistic works in bronze and ivory from Benin reached European collections in 1897 did scholars and artists begin to realize that Africa possessed something that could be called art. Since then writing on African art has been tied to aesthetics, including stylistic studies, and anthropology—at first evolutionist or diffusionist, then structural-functionalist, and today mainly fieldwork-orientated. Consequently, most art historians have implicitly adopted ahistorical models, such as the 'culture area' and 'one tribe, one style'.

Against this sombre background may be noted several efforts to place African art in a diachronic context. The key issues are spatial (provenance and distribution) and temporal (chronology). Where documentation is absent or unreliable, museum curators constantly face the question of provenance. Art historians, however, are frequently confronted by the wider problem of origin. Several 19th-century scholars speculated about the 'migration' of culture from North-east to West or Central Africa, and in the early 20th century European ethnologists pursued more sophisticated diffusionist approaches, trying to explain the present-day distribution of cultural traits—including art—in terms of historical movement. Although the early diffusionist hypotheses have been abandoned, the relationship between spatial distribution and time remains a historical issue.

Absolute chronology is often impossible, but relative chronology is essential if art is to have a historical meaning. F. M. Olbrechts demonstrated this weakness in African art studies and outlined some of the remedies, including the systematic documentation of objects, use of all printed and archival sources, and technical analysis of the materials used. In recent historical work the following four types of source have been used: an analysis of the art objects themselves; archaeological excavations; European writings and pictorial representations; and oral traditions.

A major impetus towards diachronic thinking came in the 1950s and 1960s from archaeologists working in southern Nigeria. The discovery of ceramic art from NOK, terracottas from Yelwa and metalwork from IGBO-UKWU, combined with more refined analysis of objects already known from the Kingdom of BENIN, IFE and elsewhere, prompted art historians to propose historical sequences linking various cultures. While the sequences remain controversial, they helped to stimulate historical thinking with reference to art. Subsequently attempts were made to refine the chronology with the help of oral tradition and written documents. Archaeological research in Mali and northern Ghana has transformed what is known about the art history of West Sudan, and progress has also been made with regard to other parts of Africa. Meanwhile, the study of changing art forms in the 20th century has gradually become accepted as a legitimate undertaking, thanks partly to the pioneering work of anthropologists. Most took as their starting-point the ahistorical notion of a 'traditional' tribal society. Nevertheless, important research has been conducted since 1960 on artistic change in the colonial and post-colonial periods, notably with reference to the effects of shifts in patronage. The journal *African Arts* has often provided a forum for such studies. For coastal regions with a long history of European contact it has been possible to document artistic change and continuity over a period of several centuries.

BIBLIOGRAPHY
F. M. Olbrechts: *Plastiek van Kongo* (Antwerp, 1946)
W. Gillon: *A Short History of African Art* (Harmondsworth, 1984)
S. L. Kasfir: 'One Tribe, One Style: Paradigms in the Historiography of African Art', *Hist. Afr.*, xi (1984), pp. 163–93
J. Vansina: *Art History in Africa: An Introduction to Method* (London and New York, 1984)

ADAM JONES

XII. Museums.

In the context of museum collections, Africa usually refers to Sub-Saharan Africa and excludes Ancient Egypt and the Islamic lands of North Africa. The way African material has been exhibited (*see also* §XIII below) indicates the evolution of Western attitudes to the continent. The first African artefacts to reach Europe in the early 16th century were treated as curiosities whose exact origins were often not acknowledged. A small group of West African pieces came to the museum at Ulm in the 17th century, and in the 18th century Sir Hans Sloane, whose collection became the nucleus of the British Museum collections, acquired several artefacts of African origin.

The colonial period saw the establishment of museums celebrating European empires in Africa, such as the Koninklijk Museum voor Midden-Afrika, Tervuren, which houses one of the most extensive collections of Central African art and material culture in the world. Increasing quantities of African material found their way into European collections as a by-product of missionary activity and trade, but the stimulus given to the study of ethnography by the imposition of colonial rule led to the establishment of ethnographic museums with strong colonial connections in the late 19th century, for example the Museum für Völkerkunde, Berlin, the British Museum, London, the Pitt Rivers Museum, Oxford, and the Musée des Arts Africains et Océaniens and the Musée de l'Homme, Paris. In the United States the colonial connection was absent, but the ethnological impulse was equally strong, as in the Peabody Museum of Archeology and Ethnology at the University of Harvard, Cambridge, MA, the American Museum of Natural History, New York, and the Field Museum of Natural History, Chicago. In the post-colonial period ethnography has made way for archaeology and anthropology. In 1970 the Ethnography Department of the British Museum was given an independent building in London as the Museum of Mankind. Other important anthropological collections are to be found at the Fowler Museum of Cultural History of the University of California in Los Angeles and the Barbier-Mueller Museum in Geneva. Apart from the Koninklijk Museum in Tervuren, the only other museum dedicated to Africa and maintained by public funds is the National Museum of African Art, opened in 1987 as part of the Smithsonian Institution, Washington, DC. The museums of the nation states of Africa, established either during or after the colonial period, are largely concerned with the exhibition of national material. The one exception is the National Museum of Accra, where an attempt has been made to situate Ghana in the Pan-African context. Art museums in the United States, notably the Metropolitan Museum, New York, and the Art Institute of Chicago, have led the way in collecting and exhibiting African art. Their only rival in Europe is the Rietberg Museum in Zurich. The Museum for African Art in New York, while hosting innovative exhibitions and maintaining an educational programme, does not yet have its own collection and depends entirely on grants and private donations; the same is true of the privately funded Fondation Olfert Dapper in Paris.

BIBLIOGRAPHY
H. J. Braunholtz: *Sir Hans Sloane and Ethnography*, ed. W. Fagg (London, 1970)
J.-L. Paudrat: 'From Africa', *'Primitivism' in 20th Century Art: Affinity of the Tribal and the Modern*, ed. W. Rubin, i (New York, 1984), pp. 125–75
Africa and the Renaissance: Art in Ivory (exh. cat. by E. Bassani and W. Fagg, New York, Cent. Afr. A., 1988)
E. Bassani and M. D. McLeod: *Jacob Epstein: Collector* (Milan, 1989)
S. Peters and others, eds: *Directory of Museums in Africa/Répertoire des musées en Afrique* (London and New York, 1990)
Africa Explores: 20th Century African Art (exh. cat. by S. Vogel, New York, Cent. Afr. A., 1991)
M. D. McLeod: 'Collecting for the British Museum', *Quad. Poro*, 8 (1993)

XIII. Exhibitions.

Long before the largely post-independence development of museums and galleries in the countries of Sub-Saharan Africa, the idea of display was an integral part of individual works of African art, many of which were intended to be seen in the performative context of the masquerade or royal procession. Works of art from Sub-Saharan Africa have been present in European collections since the 16th century. When these origins were acknowledged, the works themselves were accorded the status of curiosities. This changed with the arrival of works of art from the kingdom of BENIN (1897), and later the collection of works from colonized territories and the attention drawn to them by European artists (*see* §XIV below). The manner of display could be described as ethnographic, according to the perceptions of the time, with works of art placed on exhibition ordered according to tribal origins within a particular region, and with ritual artefacts representing particular communities and their ritual life. The notable exception was the Pitt Rivers Museum, Oxford, which displayed a typology of artefacts with the intention of illustrating a now untenable view of the temporally progressive development of human skill.

In more recent years in some museums, such as the Museum of Mankind, London, three modes of exhibition have emerged in contrast to ethnography or typology: concentrating on the work of art, the artefacts in context, and the 'cabinet of curiosities'. Each is problematic in its own way, and none is capable of resolving the problems contingent upon the circumstances in which the pieces were acquired or the previous mode of display. In the first mode, the artefact is carefully placed and lit, perhaps within a glass case. Although this enables the perception of form, it is also an appropriation to a 'fine art' conception that may have little to do with original context of the object. The second mode seeks to replicate the original context by recreating the environment with available materials. One of the finest of these exhibitions was the 'Yoruba Religious Cult' exhibition (London, Mus. Mankind, 1974). The problem here is not simply that of creating an ethnographic illusion but that the exhibition environment itself becomes the focus of the exhibition at the expense of the artefacts within it. The third mode (e.g.

'Lost Magic Kingdoms'; London, Mus. Mankind, 1985) is perhaps the most satisfactory because it makes apparent curatorial mediation without pretending to objectivity. In the late 1970s the Museum of Mankind had examples simultaneously of all three modes of exhibition.

Museums are now faced with the dilemma of how best to exhibit their African collections. The solution that is generally adopted (e.g. New York, Met.) is the tasteful display, in which objects are placed in uncluttered cases, suitably lit with brief descriptive labels, and ordered according to an ethnographic model. In the 1980s travelling or temporary exhibitions were used to explore inherent problems. Examples of problem-solving exhibitions are the 'Torday Exhibition' (London, Mus. Mankind), which placed an example of an early-20th-century collection in the context of anthropology and British Modernism; 'Art/Artefact' (1988), which considered different modes of display and representation; 'Africa and the Renaissance' (1988), which explored the ivory sculptures that reached European collections in the 16th century; 'Close-up' (1990), which focused on the artefact as form; 'Africa Explores' (1991), which concentrated on 20th century developments (all New York, Cent. Afr. A.); 'Echoes of the Kalabari' (1988–9), which featured the work of Kalabari sculptor Sokari Douglas-Camp; 'Astonishment and Power' (1993–4), which paired a deconstruction of Kongo sculpture with the work of African-American artist Renée Stout (both Washington, DC, N. Mus. Afr. A.); and 'Elephant' (Los Angeles, UCLA, Fowler Mus. Cult. Hist., 1992–3). European exhibitions, with the exception of those held at the Tropenmuseum, Amsterdam, tend to concentrate on the display of national masterpieces, adding little to the debate on how to display African material. The one other recent European exception was 'Lotte or the Transformation of the Object' (Graz, 1988), which explored the ethnographic mode of exhibition.

BIBLIOGRAPHY

C. H. Read and O. M. Dalton: *Antiquities of the City of Benin and from other Parts of West Africa in the British Museum* (London, 1899)

Lost Magic Kingdoms and Six Paper Moons from Nauhuatl: An Exhibition at the Museum of Mankind (exh. cat. by E. Paolozzi, London, Mus. Mankind, 1985)

N. Barley: *Foreheads of the Dead: An Anthropological View of Kalabari Ancestral Screens* (Washington, DC, 1988) [pubd on occasion of exh., Washington, DC, N. Mus. Afr. A., 1988–9]

Africa and the Renaissance: Art in Ivory (exh. cat. by E. Bassani and M. D. McLeod, New York, Cent. Afr. A., 1988)

Art/Artefact: African Art in Anthropology Collection (exh. cat. by A. Danto and others, New York, Cent. Afr. A., 1988)

Echoes of the Kalabari: Sculpture by Sokari Douglas Camp (exh. cat., Washington, DC, N. Mus. Afr. A., 1988–9)

Close-up: Lessons in the Art of Seeing African Sculpture (exh. cat. by J. L. Thompson and S. Vogel, New York, Cent. Afr. A., 1990)

J. Mack: *Emil Torday and the Art of the Congo* (London, 1991)

Africa Explores: 20th Century African Art (exh. cat. by S. Vogel, New York, Cent. Afr. A., 1991)

Elephant: The Animal and its Ivory in Africa Culture (exh. cat., ed. D. H. Ross; Los Angeles, UCLA, Fowler Mus. Cult. Hist., 1992–3)

Astonishment and Power (exh. cat., Washington, DC, N. Mus. Afr. A., 1993–4)

Africa: The Art of a Continent (exh. cat., London, RA, 1995–6)

JOHN PICTON

XIV. Collectors and dealers.

The earliest private collections of African art were those of European royalty and nobility, whose cabinets of curiosities preserved exotica brought back from overseas travels. The 19th century was marked by the acquisition of ethnographic objects either as scientific specimens, war trophies or curiosities, which found their way into museum collections. Early dealers in ethnographic objects and curios, such as W. D. Webster in Oxford or William O. Oldman in London, sold what would today be called art.

African art as a category of *objets d'art* has been defined largely by collectors, dealers, critics and artists, whose tastes and preferences restricted it almost exclusively to figural sculpture and masks. Modern collecting began in Paris in the early 20th century, with sculptures from the French colonies. Dan/Wobé masks, Baule and Fang figures, Mpongwe white-faced masks and Kota reliquaries began turning up in studios of artists and other Left Bank *cognoscenti* and in the few art galleries that catered for collectors. Negrophilism in Paris in the 1920s fuelled this passion for *art nègre.*

Among these early artist-collectors were Eduard von der Heydt (*b* 1882), Félix Fénéon, Tristan Tzara, Guillaume Apollinaire, Maurice de Vlaminck, Jacob Epstein, Modigliani, Matisse, Braque and Picasso, while some of the prominent dealers were PAUL GUILLAUME, Joseph and Ernest Brummer, Louis Carré, Charles Ratton (1895–1986) and ANDRÉ LEFÈVRE. The German Expressionists, too, developed a fascination with *art nègre.* Carl Kjersmeier (1889–1961), unique among these early collectors for his systematic approach to collecting and studying African art, travelled to West Africa in the 1930s to collect sculptures and subsequently published the landmark four-volume work, *Centres de style de l'art africain* (1935–9).

Although Parisian-based artists were the first serious collectors of African art, it was the American photographer and dealer ALFRED STIEGLITZ who mounted the first exhibition of African sculpture in the United States in 1914. The eccentric ALBERT C. BARNES acquired African sculptures in the 1920s, as did a few other Americans, including Frank Crowninshield (1872–1947), John Graham, John Quinn (1870–1924), Walter Arensberg (1878–1954) and Agnes Meyer (1887–1970). Authenticity was not an issue with these early collectors, who were attracted by the visual power of the works and were not concerned with origin, function and meaning. The influence of French ethnology in the 1930s and 1940s led dealers, such as PIERRE LOEB, systematically to mine new fields. Dogon, Senufo and Bamana works, for example, appeared in quantity for the first time in the 1950s and 1960s, and Africans themselves began dealing. The popularity of African art inspired the production of copies and forgeries (*see* §X above), and collectors and dealers were among the victims of fraud. Not surprisingly, authenticity became a major concern. But the motivations for collecting also became less pure, tainted by prestige, fashion and art as investment. The leading auction houses in Paris, London, Brussels and New York catered for the increasing demand for tribal art by private collectors, and the handful of commercial galleries devoted to African art gathered followers. Paris remains the centre of buying and selling, followed by Brussels, New York and London. The estimated number of serious collectors of African art worldwide in the period 1970–90 was around 500.

Decolonization, modern wars in Africa and archaeological discoveries since the 1960s have brought new objects to the art market. Prices have escalated as the supply of quality sculptures has diminished, due in part to the Unesco Treaty on Cultural Property (1970), which discouraged international trafficking in antiquities, and to increasing calls for the repatriation of art works. Some private collections have had high visibility, because they have been exhibited, published, donated to a museum or sold at auction. By the 1930s some of the first great early collections were going to auction, such as those of André Breton and Paul Eluard or Georges de Miré. These were followed by the sale of collections owned by Frank Crowninshield (1941), Jacob Epstein (1961), Helena Rubinstein (1966), James Hooper (1976) and Harry Franklin (1990). American private collections are often donated to museums. Nelson Rockefeller's collection led to the establishment of the Museum of Primitive Art and ultimately to the Rockefeller Wing of the Metropolitan Museum of Art (*see* ROCKEFELLER, (4)), and other donations include those of Clark Stillman (*b* 1907) to Dallas, Katherine White to Seattle, Max Stanley to the University of Iowa Museum of Art, and Lester Wunderman to the Metropolitan Museum of Art in New York. The visibility of African art in public art museums has in turn stimulated collectors' interest. Modern African art has yet to attract much critical attention and serious collectors. Ulli Beier's tireless devotion since the 1950s to African modern art and his collection (now at the University of Bayreuth, Iwalewa-Haus) are an exception.

BIBLIOGRAPHY

Arts primitifs dans les ateliers d'artistes (exh. cat., Paris, Mus. Homme, 1967)

W. Raymonde: 'Quelques Grands Amateurs et collectionneurs' and 'Les Grandes Ventes publiques', *Le Guidargus de l'art primitif: 1965–1985, 20 ans d'art primitif en ventes publiques* (Paris, 1985), pp. 19–21, 35–63

R. Lehuard: 'Charles Ratton et l'aventure de l'art nègre', *A. Afrique Noire*, lx (1986), pp. 11–33

P. Amrouche: 'Objets et collections d'art primitif: Réflexion sur les variations du goût de 1890 à nos jours', *Anthropologie de l'art: Formes et significations: Arts de l'Afrique, de l'Amérique et du Pacifique* (Paris, 1988), pp. 44–9

J. MacClancy: 'A Natural Curiosity: The British Market in Primitive Art', *Res*, 15 (Spring 1988), pp. 163–76

W. H. Robbins and N. Ingram Nooter: *African Art in American Collections: 1989 Survey* (Washington, DC, 1989)

L'Art d'Afrique noire dans les collections d'artistes (exh. cat. by F. N'Diaye, Arles, 1991)

XV. Art libraries and photographic collections.

The study of African art history has roots in the older field of cultural anthropology, which is primarily concerned with material culture rather than art. Most of the literature before 1960 falls into this category, and even today African art research still draws extensively on ethnography, history and archaeology (*see also* §§II, 1 and XI above). Serious study of the subject, therefore, remains dependent on libraries with strong collections in these fields.

Museums of ethnography, which were concerned with material culture and had colonial connections, sprang up in Europe during the late 19th century (*see* §XII above). They built library collections to support curatorial research and often also served as repositories for photographs, manuscripts and other official records. These institutions, such as the Museum für Völkerkunde, Berlin, the British Museum, London, the Pitt Rivers Museum, Oxford, the Koninklijk Museum voor Midden-Afrika, Tervuren, and the Musée de l'Homme, Paris, grew into significant research collections that remain only partially tapped. Although many are underfunded and their libraries are not being actively developed, their historical material makes them a critical group of repositories. In the United States libraries and photo-archives with extensive African material were developed by such institutions as the Peabody Museum of Archaeology and Ethnology at Harvard University, Cambridge, MA, the American Museum of Natural History, New York, and the Field Museum of Natural History, Chicago.

Colonial libraries with collections on African history, geography, law, economics, sociology and ethnology, with regional emphasis on colonial territories, are also essential sources. Although the development of the collections and financial support may have dwindled in the post-colonial era, these institutions, such as the libraries of the Royal Commonwealth Society and the Royal Geographical Society, both London, the Académie des Sciences d'Outre-Mer, Paris, and the Bibliothèque Africaine, Brussels, remain historically important. The Biblioteca Apostolica Vaticana in Rome holds even older material dating back to the earliest Catholic contacts with Africa. Missionary societies, such as the Baseler Mission, also retained photographs taken in the course of their work, although similarly they were not intended to document material culture. In addition, some of the European national and state libraries have surprisingly rich collections of African materials.

As the discipline of African art history emerged in universities, and African art was increasingly collected and exhibited (*see* §§XII and XIII above), libraries and photo-archives became more important. Important library collections of Africana were developed in the United States with the establishment of major graduate programmes from the 1960s at Indiana University, the University of California at Los Angeles, Yale University, the University of Iowa and Columbia University. Seminars in African art held at the Sorbonne, Paris, the School of Oriental and African Studies, London, and at many other universities, including Ghent, Brussels and Florence, created further demands for library collections. There were similar developments at contemporary German research centres, such as the Frobenius-Institut in Frankfurt am Main and Mainz University, although their emphasis is on ethnography and material culture rather than art history. The Frobenius-Institut is fortunate in having much early library and archival material while maintaining an active research programme that involves contemporary documentation.

Art museums in the United States (and to a lesser extent in Europe) have led the way in collecting and exhibiting African art, but their supporting libraries lack the earlier resources of their European ethnological counterparts. These newer centres, however, are developing true African art libraries with the acquisition of exhibition and auction catalogues, books, journals and dissertations documenting late 20th-century African art, including the work of contemporary artists who exhibit in galleries and museums. This shifting emphasis from ethnography to art history can be seen in Paris at the Musée National des Arts Africains et Océaniens and the Olfert Dapper Foundation; in Norwich, England, at the Sainsbury Centre for the Visual Arts, University of East Anglia; in New York at the Robert Goldwater Library of the Metropolitan Museum of Art and the Center of African Art; and at the Smithsonian Institution's National Museum of African Art, Washington, DC. The library at the last-named institution seeks to combine the historical and ethnographical with the artistic and art-historical streams of research materials within its collection policy. Although the newer repositories may lack the wealth of historical photographs found in those of the colonial era, their contemporary pictorial collections are focused directly on African art and contain many more studio photographs of individual objects and contextual field photographs taken by recent researchers.

Much older material has become available to newer collections through reprints and micro-publishing, and the increasing use of electronic technologies allows the sharing and transmission of images between institutions. The application of these technologies to the documentation and dissemination of African art has been pioneered by the Museum of Cultural History at the University of California in Los Angeles and by the University of Iowa.

Libraries and photo-archives in Africa remain sadly underdeveloped. The few isolated collections of note, such as those in Guinea-Bissau, Senegal and Nigeria, mostly date from the colonial period and are not being actively developed or preserved. The museums and archives in Zimbabwe and South Africa, however, have been more fortunate and are collecting printed and visual documentation on their material culture collections. They alone have been able to collect both historical and contemporary material at close range, but with an ethnographical rather than an art-historical emphasis.

BIBLIOGRAPHY

H. Hannam, ed.: *The SCOLMA Directory of Libraries and Special Collections on Africa in the United Kingdom and Western Europe* (Oxford, rev. 4/1983)

J. E. M. Gosebrink: *African Studies Information Resources Directory* (Oxford, 1986)

JANET L. STANLEY

African American [Afro-American; Black American] **art.** Term used to describe art made by Americans of African descent. While the crafts of African Americans in the 18th and 19th centuries continued largely to reflect African artistic traditions (*see* AFRICA, §VIII), the earliest fine art made by professional African American artists was in an academic western style.

1. Before *c.* 1920. 2. *c.* 1920–*c.* 1960. 3. *c.* 1960 and after.

1. BEFORE *c.* 1920. The first African American artist to be documented was JOSHUA JOHNSON, a portrait painter who practised in and around Baltimore, MD. Possibly a former slave in the West Indies, he executed plain, linear portraits for middle-class families (e.g. *Sarah Ogden Gustin*, *c.* 1798–1802; Washington, DC, N.G.A.). Only one of the *c.* 83 portraits attributed to Johnson is signed, and none is dated. There are only two African American sitters among Johnson's attributions. Among the second generation of prominent 19th-century African American artists were the portrait-painter William E. Simpson (1818–72) of Buffalo, NY, Robert Douglass jr (1809–87) and Douglass's cousin and pupil David Bowser (1820–1900) of Philadelphia. Douglass, none of whose works survives, started as a sign-painter and then painted portraits as a disciple of Thomas Sully. Engravings and lithographs were produced by Patrick Reason (*b* 1817) of New York, whose parents were from Haiti. His engravings included illustrations for publications supporting the abolition of slavery and also portraits (e.g. *Granville Sharp*, 1835; Washington, DC, Gal. A., Howard U.).

Julian Hudson (*fl c.* 1831–44) was the earliest documented African American painter in the South. Having studied in Paris, he returned to his home town, New Orleans, where he taught art and painted portraits. Although his quarter-length figures were rigidly conventional, Hudson was a skilful painter of faces. His *Self-portrait* (1839; New Orleans, LA State Mus.) is the earliest surviving self-portrait by an African American artist. Jules Lion (1810–66) also studied and practised in Paris prior to returning to New Orleans, where he produced paintings and lithographs. He was also credited with introducing the daguerreotype to the city, where he was one of the earliest professional photographers.

Throughout the 19th century African American artists in Louisiana apparently did not experience as much professional discrimination as their peers in other areas of the USA. However, even in Louisiana there are few examples of work commissioned by African Americans at this time. The Melrose Plantation House, built *c.* 1833 for the mulatto Metoyer family in Melrose, near Natchitoches, LA, is the only surviving plantation manor house built by an African American family in the southern states. It contained portraits of members of the family, probably executed by an unknown mulatto painter before 1830. The brick and timber African House, an out-house used in part as a prison for the control of slaves in the plantation at Melrose, was remarkable for the width and height of its roof: it was probably constructed during the early 19th century by African-born slaves owned by the Metoyer family.

Another artist from New Orleans, Eugene Warbourg (1826–59), was among the leading black sculptors of the 19th century. He worked in Rome, developing a Neo-classical style, as did Mary Edmonia Lewis, who trained in Boston before becoming the first professional African American sculptor, producing such works as *Hagar* (see fig. 1).

The most important African American landscape painters of the 19th century were ROBERT S. DUNCANSON, Edward Mitchell Bannister and Grafton Tyler Brown (1841–1918). Duncanson, who worked in Cincinnati and Detroit, was the earliest professional African American landscape painter. He studied in Glasgow and travelled extensively in Italy, France and England, as well as in Minnesota, Vermont and Canada. He was the first African American artist to receive international recognition. Although Duncanson painted portraits and still-lifes, he is best known as a Romantic realist landscape painter in the Hudson River school tradition. His largest commission came in 1848, when he painted eight large landscape panels and four over-door compositions in the main entrance hall of Nicholas Longworth's mansion 'Belmont' (now the Taft Museum) in Cincinnati.

1. Mary Edmonia Lewis: *Hagar*, marble, h. 1337mm, 1875 (Washington, DC, National Museum of American Art)

Bannister was the leading painter in Providence, RI, during the 1870s and 1880s. Born in Nova Scotia, he started by making solar prints and attended an evening drawing class in Boston. He is reported to have taken up painting in reaction to a newspaper statement in 1867 that blacks could appreciate art but not produce it. He was a moderately talented painter of poetic landscapes (e.g. *Landscape*, *c.* 1870–75; Providence, RI Sch. Des., Mus. A.), influenced by Alexander Helwig Wyant and the Hudson River school. He was the earliest African American artist to receive a national award when he received a gold medal for *Under the Oaks* (untraced) at the Philadelphia Centennial Exposition in 1876. He was also one of the seven founder-members in 1873 of the Providence Art Club, which became the nucleus of the Rhode Island School of Design. He was the only prominent African American artist of the 19th century not to travel or study in Europe.

Brown was the earliest documented professional African American artist in California. He was first employed in San Francisco as a draughtsman and lithographer, also printing street maps and stock certificates, before turning to landscape painting. His most productive years were during the 1880s, when he painted many Canadian landscapes and scenes of the American north-west. He also lived in Portland, OR, and Washington. After 1891 Brown apparently ceased painting and in 1892 moved to St Paul, MN, where he worked as a draughtsman.

The most distinguished African American artist who worked in the 19th century was HENRY OSSAWA TANNER. His early paintings of the 1890s included African American genre subjects and reflect the realist tradition of Thomas Eakins under whom Tanner studied at the Pennsylvania Academy of Fine Arts in Philadelphia. From 1903 he painted religious subjects, portraits and landscapes, primarily in subdued blues and greens. Like the majority of prominent 19th-century African American artists, Tanner went to Europe for further training and to escape racial and professional discrimination: he lived in Paris during most of his career and developed a painterly style influenced by Symbolism. He held his first one-man exhibition of religious paintings, however, at the American Art Galleries in New York in 1908, and in 1909 he became the first African American to be elected to the National Academy of Design.

In 1907 the Tercentennial Exposition in Jamestown, VA, included among the pavilions a 'Negro Building': its exhibits focused primarily on African American crafts, carpentry and inventions. Although there were 484 paintings and drawings, no works by prominent African American painters were included. The most important African American artist to be included in the Jamestown exhibition was the sculptor Meta Vaux Fuller, who had studied in Paris, where she had gained the approval of Rodin: she exhibited a series of dioramas depicting various aspects of black life in America. Other contemporary exhibitions, however, such as that of the Eight (*see* EIGHT, THE (ii)) in 1908 and the Armory Show in 1913, both held in New York, had little initial stylistic impact on African American art.

2. *c.* 1920–*c.* 1960. The most significant African American stylistic and aesthetic movement of the early 20th century was the Harlem Renaissance or 'New Negro' movement of the 1920s. The Harlem district of New York became, during the decade, the 'cultural capital of black America'. The ensuing Harlem Renaissance drew upon the community's African heritage and was the earliest race-conscious cultural movement by African Americans. Primarily political and literary, the spirit of the Harlem Renaissance was most eloquently expressed by Alain

Locke in his book *The New Negro* (New York, 1925). The earliest African American painter consciously to incorporate African imagery in his work was Aaron Douglas, a prominent figure in the Harlem Renaissance and later. Other significant artists who contributed to the movement included Meta Vaux Fuller, Palmer Hayden (1890–1964), who painted satirical images of life in Harlem, William E. Scott (1884–1964) and Malvin Gray Johnson (1896–1934). The most important African American photographer of that period was James Van Der Zee, who photographed people and scenes in Harlem for more than 50 years and also served as the official photographer for the Pan-Africanist Marcus Garvey during his frequent parades and rallies in Harlem.

The artists of the Harlem Renaissance received a great stimulus from the exhibitions of the Harmon Foundation. This was founded in New York in 1922 by William E. Harmon, a white Ohio-born philanthropist and real estate developer, and in 1926 it began promoting African American artistic talents and offering awards in the fine arts. The foundation's first *Exhibit of Fine Arts Productions of American Negro Artists* opened at International House in New York in January 1928. Following the success of the pilot exhibition, the foundation mounted additional shows at International House in 1929 and 1930. In 1931 it moved the location of its exhibitions to the galleries of the Art Center in E. 56th Street in New York. During the early years of the foundation's operation, annual travelling exhibitions were organized that introduced African American art to broad audiences for the first time. The exhibitions included artists working in traditional western, naive and modernist styles. Although some critics felt that the foundation's jurors were not critical enough in their selection procedures, the Harmon Foundation's awards, exhibitions and exhibition catalogues continued to promote African American art until 1966, when it closed. Its files, which formed the most comprehensive single body of materials relating specifically to African American art during the first half of the 20th century, were placed in the Library of Congress and the National Archives in Washington, DC. The large art collection that the foundation amassed was divided between the National Collection of Fine Arts (now the National Museum of American Art of the Smithsonian Institution) in Washington, DC, Fisk University in Nashville, TN, and the Hampton Institute (now Hampton University) in Hampton, VA.

The Stock Market crash of 1929 brought the golden era of the Harlem Renaissance to an end and plunged the USA into the Great Depression of the 1930s. The Depression paralysed the nation's economy, and President Franklin D. Roosevelt established the Federal Art Project (1935–43), a division of the Works Progress Administration (*see* UNITED STATES OF AMERICA, §VI), which provided employment for many African American artists. The early school of African American muralists reached its apogee during the 1930s, and numerous murals by African American artists were commissioned to decorate schools, hospitals, banks, post offices and other public buildings.

These murals ranged greatly in style: such artists as Charles White (1918–79) and Hale Woodruff executed historical murals that showed the influence of Mexican social realism, for example the *Amistad* murals (1939) by Woodruff in the Slavery Library in Tallageda College, Tallageda, AL, which depicted a slave mutiny in 1839. Other artists produced mural work in a primitivist style, for example Aaron Douglas, whose murals of African life included elongated, angular figures with stylized features, and Charles Alston (?1907–78), a painter and sculptor. Alston painted mural panels (1937) in the Harlem Hospital, New York, depicting tribal African and modern scientific medicine in a style also characterized by expressively distorted figures. Some murals had themes that were not specific to African Americans, for example the mural panel by Archibald J. Motley (1891–1980) entitled *United States Mail* (1936) in the post office in Wood River, IL. Motley also made easel paintings of scenes from African, American and even Parisian life, employing both a naive and a highly naturalistic style. Murals were also produced by such artists as the painter William E. Scott (1884–1964) and the sculptors Sargent Johnson (1887–1967) and Richmond Barthe (1901–89), who carved reliefs with highly formalized figures. Barthe was also an accomplished painter and figure-sculptor of black subjects (e.g. *Blackberry Woman*, 1932; New York, Whitney), as well as executing portraits of theatrical characters. The sculpture of Sargent Johnson was characterized by ingenuous figure studies in various materials such as porcelain, terracotta and lacquered wood (e.g. *Forever Free*, 1936; San Francisco, CA, MOMA).

The most important national commission received by an African American artist during the 1930s went to the sculptor Augusta Savage, who created a large sculpture, *The Harp* (later called *Lift Every Voice and Sing*, painted plaster, h. 4.87 m) for the Negro Pavilion of the New York World's Fair of 1939. It was intended to represent African American music and consisted of a receding line of singing figures arranged in the shape of a harp. The sculpture, cast in plaster and gilded to resemble bronze, never received permanent casting and was destroyed following the fair's closing (see Dover, pl. 72). Selma Burke was another important African American female sculptor whose career blossomed during the 1930s and 1940s. In 1935 she received a Roosevelt Foundation Fellowship, and in 1943 she participated in a competition sponsored by the Fine Arts Commission of the District of Columbia to depict a bust of President Roosevelt. The bust, which was completed and unveiled in 1945, was adapted in 1946 for use on the American dime coin.

During and immediately after World War II, there arose to prominence a new school of African American artists, many of whom were the so-called 'children of the Harlem Renaissance'. Such artists as Selma Burke, Charles White and William H. Johnson, who had attracted attention before the war, continued their achievements, for example in the social realism of the *Contribution of the Negro to American Democracy* (1953) in the Hampton Institute in Virginia. Johnson, who was influenced by Chaïm Soutine, worked in France, Denmark and Norway before returning to the USA in 1938. He painted Expressionist works and naive images of black life in the USA (e.g. *Going to Church*, *c.* 1940–44; see fig. 2). Over 1000 of his works were in the collection of the Harmon Foundation when it closed. The art of African Americans was encouraged by the exhibition of the *Art of the American Negro, 1851–1940*, assembled

2. William H. Johnson: *Going to Church*, oil on burlap, 968×1121 mm, *c.* 1940–44 (Washington, DC, National Museum of American Art)

by Alonso Aden with assistance from the Harmon Foundation and the Works Progress Administration, at the *American Negro Exposition* in Chicago in 1940. Among the artists exhibited was Jacob Lawrence (*b* 1917), who painted highly coloured naive images of black life and history, eschewing perspective (e.g. the 60 gouache panels of the *Migration of the Negro Northwards*, 1941; Washington, DC, Phillips Col. and New York, MOMA). Other prominent African American artists of this time were Elmer Simms Campbell, who contributed illustrations for such periodicals as *Esquire*, and the painters Romare Bearden (1912–88), Eldzier Cortor (*b* 1915), Frederick Flemister and Horace Pippin (1888–1947), whose paintings included depictions of figures from the history of black emancipation. Significant figure-sculpture was made by Elizabeth Catlett (*b* 1915) and William Artis (1914–77); the latter was a pupil of Augusta Savage and produced highly naturalistic portrait busts.

During the 1950s African American art was dominated by two stylistic trends: Abstract Expressionism and realism. Some artists developed an abstract style that was related to contemporary Abstract Expressionism but also was motivated by a belated interest in Cubism, most noticeable in the works of Charles Alston, Romare Bearden, Hale Woodruff and James Wells (*b* 1902). This contrasted with the realistic styles championed by Sargent Johnson and William Artis and heralded a new direction in African American art.

3. *c.* 1960 AND AFTER. In the 1960s and 1970s new classifications appeared in African American art based on continuing developments in abstract art and the rise of the figurative style known as Black Expressionism. A new generation of artists came to prominence, influenced by such developments as Abstract Expressionism, colour field painting and hard-edge painting. These artists produced large, colourful, non-representational art that was not racially identifiable: such work was more successful commercially and more likely to be included in museums, exhibitions and galleries than that of the Black Expressionists. The most prominent African American abstract painter was Sam Gilliam, based in Washington, DC, whose colour field painting employed folded, draped and hanging canvases as well as other forms of support (e.g. *Abstraction*, acrylic on aluminium-treated paper, 1969; Washington, DC, Evans-Tibbs Col., see 1989 exh. cat., p. 94).

3. Barbara Jones-Hogu: *Unite*, screenprint, 711×345 mm, 1969 (R. A. Perry private collection)

The leading African American abstract sculptor was Richard Hunt from Chicago: in his youth he worked under Julio González, after which he went on to produce elegant welded and cast metal sculpture that included figurative and organic elements. A variety of other abstract styles also appeared in the work of such sculptors as Barbara Chase-Riboud (*b* 1936), Martin Puryear (*b* 1941), Daniel Johnson (*b* 1938), Juan Logan (*b* 1946) and Fred Eversley (*b* 1941). Chase-Riboud produced expressive, distorted sculptures, using various media (e.g. *Monument III*, bronze and silk, 2134×914×152 mm, 1970; New York, Betty Parsons Gal.). Logan's sculpture, however, was concerned with the formal qualities of geometric shapes and the use of industrial materials (e.g. *Traditional Trap*, galvanized steel, 2.16×1.02×2.35 m, 1972; artist's col., see 1974 exh. cat., fig. 57), while Eversley's work aimed at producing complex optical effects (e.g. *Untitled*, polyester, 1970; New York, Whitney).

The 1960s and 1970s were also marked by fertile associations between the older and younger generations of abstract painters, such as the Spiral group, founded in New York in 1963 by Hale Woodruff, Romare Bearden and Norman Lewis (*b* 1909), which attracted such younger artists as Richard Mayhew (*b* 1934). Mayhew, who was also a jazz singer, expressed his love of music in lyrical, colourful abstractions (e.g. *Vibrato*, 1974; Washington, DC, Evans-Tibbs Col., see 1989 exh. cat., p. 86). Varying degrees of abstraction characterized the paintings of such artists as Norma Morgan (*b* 1928), Alvin Loving (*b* 1935), Bill Hutson (*b* 1936), William T. Williams (*b* 1942) and Robert Reid (*b* 1924). The development of innovative effects of colour and space also affected Robert Thompson (1937–66), who reinterpreted Renaissance themes with flat figures, colours influenced by Fauvism and rich impasto painting techniques (e.g. *Music Lesson*, 1962; Washington, DC, Evans-Tibbs Col., see 1989 exh. cat., p. 92).

Black Expressionism was a movement that grew out of the political unrest of the 1960s, in particular the struggle for civil rights. It also grew from the outrage of African American artists at the professional discrimination that they faced. As a result, many black artists began producing political art directed primarily towards black audiences. Black Expressionist art was always figurative and often employed bright colours, such as the black, red and green of the Black Nationalists' flag: the works frequently bore slogans and extolled the virtues of black Africa. The racial pride and political radicalism of this art led to regular depictions of such subjects as Angela Davis, the Black Panther Party (e.g. Eliot Knight's mural *Panther Tribute*, 10.97×7.32 m, early 1970s; Roxbury, MA, Warren Street, destr., see 1980 exh. cat., p. 10), Muhammad Ali and anti-Vietnam War slogans. The American flag was a constantly recurring motif and often appeared blood-spattered as a noose around the neck of a lynched black male or with yellow instead of white stripes to indicate the cowardice of the white American political structure.

Among the artists associated with Black Expressionism there was, however, a multiplicity of subjects, styles and techniques, ranging from the threatening images created by Dona Chandler (*b* 1941) even from such subjects as a domestic still-life, to the work of Faith Ringold (*b* 1934), who depicted ritualistic African subjects in so-called 'soft sculpture', while a preoccupation with unorthodox media is apparent in the collage paintings of Benny Andrews (*b* 1930), which contain real pieces of clothing. Other artists representative of the diversity of Black Expressionism included Charles Searles (*b* 1937), Murry DePillars (*b* 1939), David Hammonds (*b* 1943), Joe Overstreet (*b* 1934), Melvin Edwards (*b* 1939), John Riddle (*b* 1933), Malcolm Bailey (*b* 1947), Gary Rickson (*b* 1942), Phillip Mason (*b* 1942) and Vincent Smith (*b* 1929). Black Expressionism also influenced older artists such as Romare Bearden, Charles White, Elizabeth Catlett, Jacob Lawrence and John Biggers (*b* 1925).

One of the most important movements to develop out of Black Expressionism was the Black Neighborhood Mural Movement, which originated in Chicago during the early 1960s. Motivated partly by the fact that African Americans were not primarily museum-oriented and by the belief that American museums had few relevant programmes for African Americans, numerous artists transformed drab walls in run-down, predominantly black neighbourhoods with brilliant, glowing murals incorporating subject-matter with which almost every African American could identify. These served to instil black pride and a sense of heritage and racial identity. Chicago produced the largest number of murals, followed by Detroit; Boston; San Francisco; Washington, DC; Atlanta and New Orleans. The most famous were the *Wall of Respect and Community as One* in Chicago (1967; see 1989–91 exh. cat., p. 28) and the *Wall of Dignity* in Detroit, completed during the early 1960s: both were lost when the buildings on which they were painted were demolished.

The *Wall of Respect and Community as One*, which took as its general theme black heroes, was executed by the Visual Arts Workshop of the Organization of Black American Culture (OBAC). This included Barbara Jones-Hogu (*b* 1938) and Jeff Donaldson (*b* 1932). They were among a splinter group in Chicago which, after the mural was completed, formed the African Commune of Bad Relevant Artists (AfriCobra), 'bad' meaning 'good' in African American slang. AfriCobra artists employed fluorescent colours such as strawberry pink, 'hot' orange, lime green and grape purple in their highly rhythmic message-emblazoned art, which, they declared, was produced exclusively for African American audiences. They produced a series of high-quality screenprints that were originally sold very inexpensively to promote the doctrine of 'black art for every black home in America' (e.g. *Unite* by Barbara Jones-Hogu, 1969; see fig. 3).

Another important group that developed in the 1960s was Weusi Nyumba Ya Sanaa (Swahili: Black House of Art) in Harlem. Founded in 1965, it established an academy and a gallery (1967–78). The Weusi artists incorporated some aspects of African iconography in all of their art: many members abandoned their former 'slave' names, officially adopting African names and converting to African religions. Weusi's spokesman was Ademola Olugebefola (*b* 1941), who used traditional African materials such as cowrie shells to create ritualistic images.

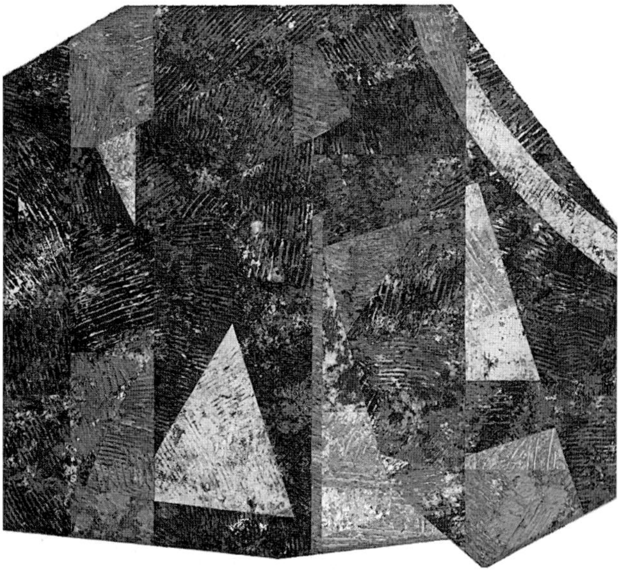

4. Sam Gilliam: *Bluesette*, acrylic on canvas, 2.03×2.29 m, 1980 (Washington, DC, Corcoran Gallery of Art); from the series *Chasers*

Following such reforms as the Public Accommodations Act of 1964, which made racial discrimination in public places illegal, and the Voting Rights Act of 1965, which enforced African Americans' right to vote, there was an increasingly heavy reliance on West African and sometimes Egyptian themes as the militancy of Black Expressionism gradually diminished. The Weusi and AfriCobra collaborations continued, however, to produce colourful, message-bearing art for African American audiences. In 1987 AfriCobra experienced its first cross-cultural exposure when it was invited to exhibit with Groupe Fromagé in Martinique at the 16th annual Sermac festival of the arts and culture. AfriCobra and Groupe Fromagé shared a similar philosophy and an aesthetic based on African, African American and Caribbean forms.

Such artists as Sam Gilliam and Richard Hunt continued meanwhile to explore abstract art, both completing a number of large-scale public commissions. Gilliam's paintings of the 1980s and early 1990s frequently employed metal, fabric and paint in dramatic impasto techniques, as well as using more conventional techniques such as acrylic (e.g. *Bluesette*, 1980; see fig. 4). Martin Puryear emerged during the 1980s as a leading African American abstract sculptor, working primarily in wood in a post-Minimalist style and frequently incorporating such materials as rope, leather and hide. During the late 1970s and early 1980s Puryear created a number of public projects and wall pieces that were ring-shaped or reflected biomorphic forms and organic materials.

In the 1980s African American art was the subject of a number of pioneering exhibitions. In particular, in 1982 the Corcoran Gallery of Art in Washington, DC, mounted the first major travelling exhibition of African American folk or self-taught artists. The artists, the majority of whom were born and still lived in the southern states of the USA, were frequently elderly when their careers began, following retirement or a work-related injury. Many were self-styled religious ministers, prophets and missionaries. As well as referring to childhood experiences they frequently used bird, animal and reptilian imagery: they also often represented figures associated with emancipation and civil rights, such as George Washington, Abraham Lincoln, John F. Kennedy and Martin Luther King. Such artists displayed an amazing ingenuity for converting *objets trouvés* and discarded materials, including costume jewellery, bones, bottle caps, chewing gum, foam packing, sawdust, mud, tree trunks, branches and Mardi Gras beads, into unique artefacts. The influence of traditional African culture on African American art was explored in an exhibition organized in 1989 by the Dallas Museum of Art. *Black Art—Ancestral Legacy: The African Impulse in African American Art* was the first major exhibition to bring together the works of African, Caribbean and African American academic and folk artists.

BIBLIOGRAPHY

J. A. Porter: *Modern Negro Art* (New York, 1943)
The Negro in American Art: One Hundred and Fifty Years of Afro-American Art (exh. cat. by J. A. Porter, Los Angeles, CA, Davis U. CA; San Diego, CA, State U., A. Gal.; Oakland, CA, Mus.; 1966–7)
The Evolution of Afro-American Artists, 1800–1950 (exh. cat., intro. C. Greene jr; New York, City Coll. City U., 1967)
M. J. Butcher: *The Negro in American Culture* (New York, 1969)
C. Dover: *American Negro Art* (London, 1969)
Harlem Artists 69 (exh. cat., intro. T. Gunn; New York, Stud. Mus. Harlem, 1969)
S. Lewis and R. Waddy, eds: *Black Artists on Art*, 2 vols (Los Angeles, 1969–71)
Afro-American Artists, 1800–1969 (exh. cat. by R. J. Craig, F. Bacon and B. Harmon, Philadelphia, PA, Mus. Civ. Cent., 1970)
Dimensions of Black (exh. cat., ed. J. Teihet; La Jolla, CA, A. Cent., 1970)
J. W. Chase: *Afro-American Art and Craft* (New York, 1971)
E. Fax: *Seventeen Black Artists* (New York, 1971)
Contemporary Black Artists in America (exh. cat. by R. Doty, New York, Whitney, 1971)
R. Bearden and H. Henderson: *Six Black Masters of American Art* (New York, 1972)
A New Vitality in Art: The Black Woman (exh. cat. by G. Garrison and P. Long, South Hadley, MA, Mount Holyoke Coll. A. Mus., 1972)
E. H. Fine: *The Afro-American Artist: A Search for Identity* (New York, 1973)
Blacks: USA: 1973 (exh. cat., intro. B. Andrews; New York, Cult. Cent., 1973)
Directions in Afro-American Art (exh. cat., intro. R. R. Jeffries; Ithaca, NY, Cornell U., Johnson Mus. A., 1974)
E. Fax: *Black Artists of the New Generation* (New York, 1977)
S. Lewis: *Art: African American* (New York, 1978)
Spirals: Afro-American Art of the '70s (exh. cat. by E. B. Gaither, Roxbury, MA, Mus. Afro-Amer. Hist., 1980)
L. M. Igoe: *Two Hundred and Fifty Years of Afro-American Art: An Annotated Bibliography* (New York, 1981)
J. Anderson: *This Was Harlem* (New York, 1982)
D. L. Lewis: *When Harlem Was in Vogue* (New York, 1982)
W. Ferris, ed.: *Afro-American Folk Arts and Crafts* (Jackson, MS, 1983)
R. F. Thompson: *Flash of the Spirit: African and Afro-American Art and Philosophy* (New York, 1984)
M. S. Campbell and others: *Harlem Renaissance: Art of Black America* (New York, 1987)
C. D. Wintz: *Black Culture and the Harlem Renaissance* (Houston, 1988)
African-American Artists, 1880–1987: Selections from the Evans-Tibbs Collection (exh. cat. by G. C. McElroy, R. J. Powell, S. F. Patton and D. C. Driskell, Washington, DC, Smithsonian Inst. Travelling Exh. Serv., 1989)
Black Art—Ancestral Legacy: The African Impulse in African–American Art (exh. cat., ed. R. V. Rozelle, A. J. Wardlaw and M. A. McKenna; Dallas, TX, Mus. A.; Atlanta, GA, High Mus. A.; Milwaukee, WI, A. Mus.; Richmond, VA Mus. F.A.; 1989–91)

REGENIA A. PERRY

Afro (Basaldella) (*b* Udine, 4 March 1912; *d* Zurich, 24 July 1976). Italian painter. He was the brother of MIRKO. He learnt to paint in the workshop belonging to his father and uncle, both of whom were painter–decorators. From 1926 to 1931 he studied at the Accademia di Belle Arti in Florence, with his brother Dino Basaldella (*b* 1909) and then in Venice. In 1932 he was in Milan, where he met Renato Birolli and Ennio Morlotti, and where an exhibition of his work was held the following year at the Galleria Il Milione. From 1933 he was in Rome working with such artists of the Scuola Romana as Corrado Cagli, whose influence is apparent in Afro's early figure-paintings and still-lifes, Fausto Pirandello, Giuseppe Capogrossi and Mirko. The artists were based in the Galleria della Cometa, where Afro exhibited in 1937. They opposed the classicism of Novecento Italiano, combining instead primitivism and metaphysical naturalism with expressionistic brushwork. During World War II Afro taught mosaic design at the Accademia di Belle Arti in Venice. After the war, between his participation in the Fronte Nuovo delle Arti (1946) and in the group of Otto Pittori Italiani (1952–4) his work was characterized by a tonal post-Cubist style. He held exhibitions in Rome at the Galleria Lo Zodiaco in 1946, at the Galleria dell'Obelisco in 1948 and at the Studio d'Arte Palma in 1951. Gradually he developed a style of lyrical abstraction that delicately balanced the expression of subconscious impulses with an objective vision, for example in *Still-life* (1948) and *Burnt Shadow* (1956; both Rome, G.N.A. Mod.). From 1949 he made numerous visits to the USA: he exhibited in New York and taught at Mills College in Oakland, CA. He also became acquainted with the Abstract Expressionism of Franz Kline, Willem de Kooning and especially Arshile Gorky, whose work he introduced in Rome in 1957 at the Galleria dell'Obelisco. He had one-man shows at the Venice Biennale in 1954, 1956 and 1960, and also participated in the *New Decade* exhibition (1955) at MOMA, New York, and the *Documenta* exhibition at Kassel. During the 1950s he received numerous public commissions for murals in Udine and, in 1958, in the UNESCO building in Paris (the *Garden of Hope*). During the 1960s his painting became more gestural and highly coloured, and he also employed collage. In the 1970s, however, he used crisper geometric forms.

BIBLIOGRAPHY

L. Venturi: *Afro*, Commentari (1954)
C. Brandi: *Afro* (Rome, 1977)
Afro (exh. cat., ed. B. Mantura; Rome, G.N.A. Mod., 1978)

ANTONELLO NEGRI

Afshar, Muhammad Hasan. *See* MUHAMMAD HASAN AFSHAR.

Afzal [Mir Afżal al-Ḥusaynī al-Tūnī] (*fl* Isfahan, 1640–51). Persian illustrator. Active during the reign of the

Safavid shah ʿAbbas II (*reg* 1642–66), Afzal produced manuscript illustrations and single pages for albums in different styles. Most of the 62 paintings he made for the voluminous copy (St Petersburg, Saltykov-Shchedrin Pub. Lib., Dorn 333) of Firdawi's *Shāhnāma* ('Book of kings') presented to the monarch by the head of the royal guard, Murtiza Quli Khan, are scenes of battles and combats in the metropolitan style that was transferred from Herat to Bukhara (*see* ISLAMIC ART, §III, 4(vi)(c)). Unlike the tinted drawings of his contemporaries, Afzal's single-page compositions use a rich, sombre palette highlighted with gold. Most depict the standard repertory of languid youths and lovers in the style of RIZA, but are more erotic. *Bishop with a Crosier* (Los Angeles, CA, Co. Mus. A., M.73.5.456) is the only known Persian portrait of an Armenian religious figure; it shows a broad-faced, sensitively modelled figure similar in style to those in the *Shāhnāma* illustrations.

BIBLIOGRAPHY

Enc. Iran.: 'Afżal al-Ḥosaynī'
M. M. Ashrafi: *Persian-Tajik Poetry in XIV–XVII Centuries Miniatures* (Dushanbe, 1974), no. 94
P. Pal, ed.: *Islamic Art: The Nasli M. Heeramaneck Collection* (Los Angeles, 1974), no. 248
M. Farhad: *Safavid Single Page Painting, 1628–1666* (diss., Cambridge, MA., Harvard U., 1987), pp. 85–101 and catalogue nos 1–11

□

Agabiti [Agapiti]**, Pietro Paolo** (*b* Sassoferrato, *c.* 1470; *d* Cupramontana, *c.* 1540). Italian painter and possible woodcutter. He spent his early years in Sassoferrato, where his family owned a ceramics workshop. Around 1497 he probably visited the Veneto region, since his *Virgin and Child with Saints* (Padua, Mus. Civ.) painted that year shows the strong influence of painters active there such as Cima da Conegliano. The painting also reflects the Bolognese style of Francesco Francia and that of the Romagnian Marco Palmezzano. In Venice, Agabiti may have made woodcuts after the illustrations for Francesco Colonna's *Hypnerotomachia Poliphili* (Venice, 1499). By 1502 he had returned to the Marches, where he executed a painting (untraced) for S Rocco, Jesi, the town where in 1507 he is documented as residing. After 1510 he was again in Sassoferrato, where in 1511 he signed and dated both the *Virgin and Child Enthroned with Saints* (Sassoferrato, Gal. A. Mod. & Contemp.) and the *Nativity* in S Maria del Piano. In 1518, for the same church, he signed and dated an altarpiece depicting the *Virgin and Child with SS Catherine and John the Baptist* (*in situ*). In S Fortunato, Sassoferrato, he executed the *Virgin and Child with Saints* (1521; *in situ*), in which the influence of Marco Palmezzano is even more evident.

Between 1522 and 1524, in collaboration with Andrea da Jesi the younger, Agabiti executed a series of frescoes in the Palazzo di Città, Jesi. In 1524, for Santa Croce, Sassoferrato, he painted a panel with *SS Benedict, Maurus and Placid* on the front and *SS Peter Damian and Scholastica* on the rear (Fonte Avellama, Abbazia; Urbino, Pal. Ducale). In 1528 he painted the *Virgin and Child Enthroned with SS John the Baptist and Anthony* (Jesi, Pin. Civ.). The lunette depicts *St Francis Receiving the Stigmata* and the predella shows the *Nativity*, the *Adoration of the Magi* and various *Saints*. Here the links with Cima da Conegliano and Marco Palmezzano are again in evidence, and there are also references to Carlo Crivelli's use of colour. In 1530 Agabiti painted the *Virgin and Child with Saints* for the Badia, San Lorenzo in Campo. The following year he retired to the Convento dell'Eremita, Cupramontana, where he remained until his death. Agabiti's work is retardataire; he did not adapt his style to suit 16th-century taste and remained instead nostalgically attached to the formal language of the 15th century.

BIBLIOGRAPHY

DBI; Thieme–Becker
R. Pallucchini: 'La pala dell'Agabiti per S Francesco di Corinaldo', *Festschrift Ulrich Middeldorf*, ed. O. Kosegarten and P. Tigler (Berlin, 1968), pp. 213–17
S. Salvadori: 'Pietro Paolo Agabiti', *Lorenzo Lotto nelle Marche* (exh. cat., ed. P. dal Poggetto and P. Zampetti; Ancona, Chiesa del Gesù, S Francesco alle Scale and Loggia Mercanti; 1981), pp. 132–4
A. Parronchi: 'Lo xilografo della *Hypnerotomachia Poliphili*: Pietro Paolo Agabiti', *Prospettiva*, 33–6 (1983–4), pp. 101–11 [Luigi Grassi *Festschrift*]

GENNARO TOSCANO

Agache, Donat-Alfred (*b* Tours, 1875; *d* 1934). French architect, urban planner and writer. He graduated in 1905 from the Ecole des Beaux-Arts, Paris, where he was a student in the atelier of Victor Laloux. In 1902 he came into contact with the Musée Social, a non-profit organization of bourgeois reformers, which sent him to visit the Louisiana Purchase International Exposition (1904) in St Louis, MO. Like a number of French architects of his generation such as Léon Jaussely and Marcel Auburtin (1872–1926), with whom he founded the Société Française des Architectes Urbanistes in 1913, he established a practice focused on urban design, achieving an international reputation in this field. Agache claimed to have coined the word 'urbanisme' and in 1914 he organized the first courses ever taught on the subject in France at the Collège Libre des Sciences Sociales et Economiques in Paris. His professional work included a prizewinning entry (1912; unexecuted) to the international competition for the design of Canberra, the new capital city of Australia, and master plans for Dunkerque (1912), Creil (1924) and Poitiers (1928). In 1927 he was invited to prepare a masterplan for Rio de Janeiro, then the capital city of Brazil. His proposals were based on traffic analysis; they stressed comprehensive zoning, with the establishment of a strong hierarchy between economic sectors and the creation of neighbourhood units separated by open space, as well as an architectural gradation from high-rise office buildings to small suburban houses. The plan was completed and published in 1930, but a change in government prevented its implementation. Agache produced several books on urban planning, including *La Remodélation d'une capitale* (1932), a comprehensive city planning manual based on his plan for Rio. His architectural work was limited but it is notable that in his Maison de Tous, a model communal house built in the precincts of the Village Français at the Exposition Internationale des Arts Décoratifs et Industriels Modernes (1925), Paris, this former advocate of a picturesque reconstruction of rural architecture was influenced by Tony Garnier's modernist architectural style.

WRITINGS

with J. M. Auburtin and E. Redont: *Comment reconstruire nos cités détruites* (Paris, 1915)
Nos Agglomérations rurales (Paris, 1918)

Où est l'urbanisme en France et à l'étranger? (Paris, 1923)
Cidade del Rio de Janeiro: Extensão, Remodelação, Embelezamento (Paris, 1930)
La Remodélation d'une capitale: Aménagement, extension, embellissement (Paris, 1932)

BIBLIOGRAPHY
J.-C. Tougeron: 'Donat-Alfred Agache: Un Architecte urbaniste', *Cah. Rech. Archit.*, 8 (1981), pp. 31–49

ISABELLE GOURNAY

Agalma. Term used for an ancient cult statue.

□

Agam, Yaacov (*b* Rishon-le-Zion, Palestine [now Israel], 11 May 1928). Israeli painter and sculptor. He studied at the Bezalel Academy in Jerusalem under Mordecai Ardon in 1946, and from 1951 in Paris at the Atelier d'Art Abstrait and at the Académie de la Grande Chaumière. The major influences on his early work were Kandinsky's *Über das Geistige in der Kunst* (1912), the Bauhaus ideas disseminated by Johannes Itten and Siegfried Giedion, with whom he came into contact in Zurich in 1949, and the work of Max Bill. Between 1951 and 1953 his work consisted of a series of *Contrapuntal* and *Transformable Pictures*, such as *Transformable Relief* (1953; Paris, R. N. Lebel priv. col., see Metken, p. 6). In 1953 he held his first one-man exhibition at the Galerie Craven in Paris. Although his claims that this was the first exhibition of kinetic art, and that he was the first optical-kinetic artist, have been disputed, he was certainly among the first artists to encourage spectator participation in such a direct way.

In the *Transformable Pictures* Agam allowed the spectator to arrange the elements either by plugging them into holes or by activating them manually or even by means of sound, as in *Sonore* (1961; Krefeld, Mus. Haus Lange), which he described as a tactile painting with acoustic effects; such works came to be called 'aleatoric' art. Agam's *Contrapuntal* and related later works, such as *Double Metamorphosis II* (oil on metal, 0.29×4.35 m, 1965; New York, MOMA), are as much optical as kinetic in their effects. They consist of a grid of painted strips that incorporate contrasting designs on opposite sides so that when viewed from the left or right a more or less distinct pattern takes form. These patterns merge, change and dissolve as the spectator passes from one side of the picture to another, conveying the impression of movement and changing colour. The transience of forms, and the power of light to dissolve them, could be said to have been Agam's real subject.

BIBLIOGRAPHY
J. Reichardt: *Yaacov Agam* (London, 1966)
Agam (exh. cat. by H. Gambu, New York, Marlborough-Gerson Gal., 1966)
Yaacov Agam: Pictures-sculptures (exh. cat. by H. Gambu, Tel Aviv, Tel Aviv Mus., 1973)
F. Popper: *Agam* (New York, 1976)
G. Metken: *Yaacov Agam* (London, 1977)

D. C. BARRETT

Agano. Japanese region in Buzen Province (now part of Fukuoka Prefect.), northern Kyushu, where stonewares were manufactured at various sites from *c.* 1600 (*see also* JAPAN, §VIII, 6(ii)).

The first potter to make Agano ware was the Korean master Chon'gye (Jap. Sonkai; 1576–1654). Deported to Kyushu during one of the Japanese invasions of Korea in 1592 and 1597, he entered the service of Hosokawa Tadaoki (1563–1645), the newly appointed governor of Buzen. On the completion of Tadaoki's fortress at Kokura (now Kitakyushu), Chon'gye built the Saienba kiln, probably within the castle precincts. A site thought to be Saienba was found beneath Myōkōji, the temple that replaced the castle in 1679, and excavations took place between 1979 and 1983. Sherds of both tea ceremony and everyday wares have been found there; they have transparent glazes made with a wood-ash flux, opaque glazes made with a straw-ash flux or brown-black glazes pigmented with iron oxide. Inscriptions on surviving pieces and entries in contemporary diaries indicate that these early products were also called Buzen or Kokura ware. After a few years the Saienba kiln closed, and Chon'gye, apparently still in Tadaoki's service, moved to the much larger Kamanokuchi kiln in the town of Akaike. Excavations there in 1955 uncovered thin-walled, finely finished wares mainly with transparent glazes; similar characteristics are found in early examples of Karatsu, Takatori and Hagi wares. Roughly coeval with the Kamanokuchi kiln was the Iwaya Kōrai kiln, a private enterprise that operated in nearby Hōjō. It made thick-walled vessels coated with an opaque glaze that is suggestive of north Korean origins. Both kilns produced wares for the tea ceremony and for utilitarian purposes.

A new phase began *c.* 1624, when the Saruyama Hongama kiln was opened, also in Akaike. It is believed to have been founded by Chon'gye and his assistants, who abandoned the Kamanokuchi kiln to a group of potters from the recently closed Takatori-ware kiln at Uchigaiso in the next valley. Initially the Saruyama Hongama kiln maintained the elegant standards of Kamanokuchi, but it ceased to make fine tea wares after 1632, when Hosokawa Tadaoki was made governor of the adjacent province of Higo (now part of Kumamoto Prefecture), and Chon'gye followed him there. Production of Agano wares continued for 250 years under the Ogasawara family, who succeeded the Hosokawa as lords of Buzen. In response to intense competition from the porcelain kilns at Arita, the Agano potters sought greater diversity and technical finesse. In the late 18th century Totoki Hoshō, a descendant of Chon'gye who worked at the Saruyama kiln, was sent to Kyoto and Edo to study the latest techniques, and the use of polychrome glazes and virtuoso textural effects dates from that time. Agano declined after the dissolution of the feudal domains in 1868, but production of wares in the Old Agano style was revived in the 20th century.

BIBLIOGRAPHY
G. Kōzuru: *Agano. Takatori* [Agano and Takatori] (1975), ii of *Nihon no yakimono* [Famous ceramics of Japan] (Tokyo, 1975–6, Eng. trans., 1981–4)
Nihon no tōji [Japanese ceramics] (exh. cat., ed. Y. Yoshiaki; Tokyo, N. Mus., 1985)

RICHARD L. WILSON

Agar, Eileen (*b* Buenos Aires, 1 Dec 1904; *d* London, 17 November 1991). English painter of Argentine birth. She arrived in England in 1906; in 1924 she studied with Leon Underwood (1890–1975), and she attended the Slade School of Fine Art, London, from 1925 to 1926; she also studied art in Paris from 1928 to 1930. She was a member of the LONDON GROUP from 1933, and her work was selected by Roland Penrose and Herbert Read for the International Surrealist Exhibition at the New Burlington Galleries, London, in 1936. Agar exhibited with the Surrealists both in England and abroad. From 1936 she experimented with automatic techniques and new materials, taking photographs and making collages and objects, for example *The Angel of Anarchy* (fabric over plaster and mixed media, 1936–40; London, Tate). By the 1960s she was producing Tachist paintings with Surrealist elements.

BIBLIOGRAPHY

Eileen Agar: Retrospective Exhibition (exh. cat., London, Commonwealth Inst., 1971)

W. Chadwick: *Women Artists and the Surrealist Movement* (London, 1985)

WHITNEY CHADWICK

Agar, Jacques d' (*b* Paris, 1640; *d* Copenhagen, 16 Nov 1715). French painter, also active in Denmark and England. He was probably a pupil of Jacob Ferdinand Voet (1639–?1700) and practised chiefly as a portrait painter. Having failed with his first submission to the Académie Royale in 1672, he was received (*reçu*) as a member in 1675 on submission of portraits of the sculptors *François Girardon* (untraced) and *Michel Anguier* (Versailles, Château). As a Protestant, he fled to London (where he became a denizen in October 1681) and as a result was expelled from the Académie Royale in 1682. He may also have travelled to the Netherlands but by 1685 had settled in Copenhagen, where he became chief court painter to Christian V (*reg* 1670–99) and then to Frederick IV (*reg* 1699–1730). Most of his portraits for the Danish court were destroyed in 1794, in the fire at Christianborg Castle. In 1699 he provided painted decorations for the funeral of Christian V, and between 1701 and 1706 he contributed several history paintings (destr.) to the decoration of Frederiksborg Castle. Among his authenticated surviving works are the portraits of *Jean-Baptiste Tavernier* (Copenhagen, Stat. Mus. Kst), *Christian V* (Copenhagen, Rosenborg Slot) and a *Self-portrait* (1693; Florence, Uffizi). His son Charles d'Agar (1669–1723) accompanied him to both London and Copenhagen; he settled in London in 1691, becoming a fashionable portrait painter. His few certain works, such as the full-length portrait of *Lord George Douglas as a Child* (1709; Duke of Buccleuch, priv. col.), are in the style of Michael Dahl. The works of father and son are often confused.

BIBLIOGRAPHY

Waterhouse: *16th & 17th C., 18th C.*

P. Lespinasse: 'Jacques d'Agar, portraitiste des rois de Danemark', *Gaz. B.-A.*, n. s. 5, xv (1927), pp. 241–9

D. BRÊME

Agar-Ellis, George James Welbore, 1st Baron Dover. *See* ELLIS, (2).

Agasse, Jacques-Laurent (*b* Geneva, 24 March 1767; *d* London, 27 Dec 1849). English painter of Swiss birth. Born into a wealthy and politically influential Huguenot family, Agasse spent his early childhood at the country estate of Crévin, where he may have developed the interest in animals and natural history that was to guide his later career as an artist in England. Agasse trained first at the Ecole du Colibri in Geneva and subsequently in Paris under Jacques-Louis David (beginning in 1787) and possibly under Horace Vernet. His early artistic output consisted chiefly of unpretentious silhouette 'cut-outs' in the style of Jean-Daniel Huber. At this time he also undertook a serious study of dissection and veterinary science.

Jacques-Laurent Agasse: *Nubian Giraffe*, oil on canvas, 1.27×1.01 m, *c.* 1827 (Windsor Castle, Berks, Royal Collection.)

Agasse first visited England in his early 20s, at the invitation of the Hon. George Pitt, 1st Baron Rivers (?1722–1803), whom he had met in either Geneva or Paris *c.* 1790. He stayed briefly at Rivers's home, Stratfield Saye, Hants, before returning to Europe for another decade, then emigrated permanently to England in 1800. He painted several animal and hunting scenes, for example *Lord Rivers's Stud-farm at Stratfield Saye* (1807; New Haven, CT, Yale Cent. Brit. A.), for Rivers and his sporting colleagues, who became his only steady source of patronage. A group of racing subjects was engraved from 1803 to 1807 by arrangement with Charles Turner, but Agasse's commercial contacts were generally few, and his business acumen was notably poor.

Despite exhibiting occasionally at the Royal Academy and British Institution, Agasse played little part in London's artistic society, preferring the company of, and sometimes collaborating with, fellow émigrés such as Adam-Wolfgang Töpffer. In his early years in London he stayed at the house of John James and Alfred Edward Chalon. Between 1810 and 1835 he was the permanent guest of George Booth, whose children modelled for some of his rural genre scenes. Although he produced several coaching, market and London street scenes (as well as a group of Thames views), and even designs for illuminations in Hyde Park, his strongest personal interest was in natural history. He frequented London's menageries, especially Polito's in the Strand, where he seems to have formed a tentative friendship with its owner, Edward Cross. In *Nubian Giraffe* (*c.* 1827; Brit. Royal Col.; see fig.), one of two pictures of exotic animals commissioned by George IV, Cross is thought to be portrayed in the group of figures standing prominently in the right foreground. Agasse's style, based on a detailed study of nature, bears some affinity to the work of George Stubbs. The combination of committed naturalism and an overall artificiality in the compositions of both artists received neither critical acclaim nor lucrative patronage.

A commission *c.* 1821 from the Royal College of Surgeons for a series of portrayals of wild animals suggests that there was some market for Agasse's art, but for these he was paid at the rate of little more than £10 per picture. Many of his studies of flowers, birds and animals were painted without particular buyers in mind, and they did not sell easily. His reputedly haughty demeanour and intransigent personality cannot have helped relations with patrons; he died poor and unrecognized. Most of his paintings can be closely dated from the record book that he maintained throughout his career in England.

UNPUBLISHED SOURCES

Geneva, Mus. A. & Hist. [*Le Livre de raison*; MS. record book]

BIBLIOGRAPHY

D. Baud-Bovy: *Peintres genevois du XVIII et du XIXe siècle* (Geneva, 1903–4)

C. Hardy: *La Vie et l'oeuvre de Jacques-Laurent Agasse* (Geneva, 1921)

Jacques-Laurent Agasse, 1767–1849, ou la séduction de l'Angleterre (exh. cat., Geneva, Mus. A. & Hist.; London, Tate; 1988–9)

STEPHEN DEUCHAR

Agatharchos (*fl* late 5th century BC). Greek painter. He was the son of Eudemos and came originally from Samos, but worked in Athens; none of his work survives. He was said to be self-taught. Vitruvius (*On Architecture* VII.praef.11) claimed that Agatharchos was the first artist to paint a stage set on wooden panels. This was for a tragedy by Aeschylus (525/4–456 BC), although it may have been a revival presented later in the 5th century BC. Vitruvius added that he wrote a commentary discussing the theoretical basis of his painted scenery and that the philosophers Demokritos (late 5th century BC) and Anaxagoras (*c.* 500–428 BC) followed him in exploring theories of perspective. It is unlikely that Agatharchos organized his compositions around a single vanishing point. More probably, individual objects and buildings or groups of buildings were depicted receding towards separate vanishing points. If Agatharchos' experiments in perspective were confined to stage scenery, they would have been limited to architectural backgrounds, before which the actor moved. Aristotle (384–322 BC), however, credited the tragedian Sophocles (*c.* 496–406 BC) with the introduction of painted scenery (*Poetics* 1449a.18–19), which creates some uncertainty about the accuracy of Vitruvius' account.

Two anecdotes about Agatharchos place him in the late 5th century BC. One, recounted by Plutarch (*Pericles* xiii.2), tells how Agatharchos boasted to his great contemporary Zeuxis of the speed and facility with which he painted, to which Zeuxis retorted that his own work both took, and lasted, a long time. Two versions exist of the other (Plutarch: *Alkibiades* xvi.4, and Pseudo-Andokides: *Against Alkibiades* xvii). Plutarch alleges that the brilliant and audacious Athenian Alkibiades (*c.* 450–404 BC) imprisoned Agatharchos in his house until he had decorated it with paintings. Alkibiades then dismissed the artist with a generous gift. Pseudo-Andokides writes that Agatharchos was confined despite his plea to finish other commissions. In the fourth month of his imprisonment, he fled. This story is the earliest extant evidence of wall paintings in private houses in Greece. The only contemporary wall paintings known to have been executed in a similar context were those by Zeuxis in the palace of Archelaos, King of Macedon (*c.* 413–399 BC), and the inference in the speech of Pseudo-Andokides was that Alkibiades had behaved in a manner more appropriate to a foreign monarch than to a citizen of democratic Athens. No ancient writer lists Agatharchos' works or describes his style.

BIBLIOGRAPHY

J. Overbeck: *Die antiken Schriftquellen zur Geschichte der bildenden Künste bei den Griechen* (Leipzig, 1868/*R* Hildesheim, 1959), nos 1118–25

C. HOBEY-HAMSHER

Ageladas [Hageladas] (*fl c.* 520–*c.* 450 BC). Greek sculptor. Said to be the teacher of Polykleitos, Myron and Pheidias, he was a bronze sculptor from Argos, active in the Late Archaic and Early Classical periods. His early works were statues at Olympia for victors of 520 BC, 516 BC and 507 BC. His monument at Delphi depicting captive Massapian women and horses may belong to the second quarter of the 5th century BC. The *Zeus Ithomatas* for the Messenians at Naupaktos was probably made in the 450s BC. Problematic is the date of his *Herakles Alexikakos* in Athens, said to be a dedication after the plague in the 420s BC. That has led to speculation on the existence of a second Ageladas. Unknown are the dates of his *Zeus Pais* and *Youthful Herakles* at Aigion. The statues for the Messenians and at Aigion seem to have been under life-size since they were easily transportable. A sense of their appearance is given by coins that show statues with stances like that of the *Zeus/Poseidon* from Cape Artemision (*see* GREECE, ANCIENT, fig. 43), which is sometimes connected with Ageladas. The Ludovisi *Herakles* herm has been proposed as a copy of the *Herakles Alexikakos*, but that is unlikely.

BIBLIOGRAPHY

Pauly–Wissowa: 'Hageladas'

A. Frickenhaus: 'Hageladas', *Jb. Dt. Archäol. Inst.*, xxvi (1911), pp. 24–34

C. A. Robinson jr: 'The Zeus Ithomatas of Ageladas', *Amer. J. Archaeol.*, xlix (1945), pp. 121–7

W. H. Gross: 'Kultbilder, Blitzschwinger und Hageladas', *Mitt. Dt. Archäol. Inst.: Röm. Abt.*, lxx (1963), pp. 13–19

H. von Heintze: 'Herakles Alexikakos', *Mitt. Dt. Archäol. Inst.: Röm. Abt.*, lxxii (1965), pp. 14–40

S. Woodford: 'Herakles Alexikakos Reviewed', *Amer. J. Archaeol.*, lxxx (1976), pp. 291–4

CHARLES M. EDWARDS

Agelii, John Gustaf. *See* AGUÉLI, IVAN.

Agha, Zubeida (*b* Faisalabad, 1922). Pakistani painter. She introduced non-traditional pictorial imagery in Pakistan and initiated a new era in painting. She completed a degree in political science at Kinnaird College, Lahore. Her introverted disposition and concentrated study of philosophy formed the background against which her abstract 'idea' paintings emerged. At the Lahore School of Fine Art (1945), Agha began a study of Western art. In addition to copying Old Masters, she came into contact with contemporary Indian painting and folk art.

Mario Perlinglieri, an Italian painter who had studied with Picasso, introduced Agha to abstraction in 1946. Unlike the majority of Pakistani artists in the 1950s and 1960s, who emulated Cubism (*see* CUBISM, §1), Agha evolved a personal style synthesizing East and West. Four years in London and Paris (1950–53) brought her face to face with modern European art. Agha's predilection for discordant shapes, tension, and mysterious and irrational juxtapositions link her art to that of Marc Chagall and Edvard Munch. Her work is in the collections of the Karachi Arts Council and the Pakistan National Council of Arts (both Islamabad), as well as in numerous private collections. An intensely private and cerebral individual, she was awarded the President's Medal for Pride of Performance in 1965.

See also PAKISTAN, §III.

BIBLIOGRAPHY

A. A. Hamid: 'Zubeida Agha', *Arts and the Islamic World*, ii/4 (Winter 1984–5), pp. 59–64
S. Hashmi: 'Beyond the Canvas', *The Star* (21 Feb 1985), p. iv
Paintings from Pakistan (Islamabad, 1988)
A. ul-Hasan: *Painting in Pakistan* (Lahore, 1991)
M. Nesom-Sirhandi: *Contemporary Painting in Pakistan* (Lahore, 1992)

MARCELLA NESOM-SIRHANDI

Aghlabid. Islamic dynasty that governed Tunisia, Algeria and Sicily from AD 800 to 909. The province of Ifriqiya, roughly corresponding to modern Tunisia, had been administered from KAIROUAN since the Islamic conquest in the 7th century by governors named by the Umayyad and Abbasid caliphs. The caliph authorized one of these governors, Ibrahim ibn al-Aghlab (*reg* 800–12), to appoint his own successor, thereby engendering a dynasty that maintained its position by paying the caliph an annual tribute. Ibrahim immediately built a satellite city, which he named al-ʿAbbasiyya, with a palace, known as the Qasr al-Abyad, and a congregational mosque. His sons ʿAbdallah I (*reg* 812–17) and Ziyadat Allah I (*reg* 817–38) continued to put down insurrections, and Tunis was temporarily outside the authority of the Aghlabid amir in Kairouan. The conquest of Sicily (827) was conducted like a holy war against the Byzantines, and the troops, encouraged by indoctrination in fortified convents (Arab. *ribāṭ*), were led by a wise man (*faqih*) of proverbial piety. The Great Mosque of Kairouan, founded *c.* 670 and rebuilt many times, was demolished in 836 and rebuilt in its present form (*see* ISLAMIC ART, §II, 4(iii)). The next rulers, Abu ʿIqal (*reg* 838–41) and Muhammad I (*reg* 841–56), had relatively peaceful reigns. The small mosque of Bu Fatata (838–41) was built at SOUSSE, and the congregational mosques of Sfax (*c.* 849) and Sousse (850–51) were erected.

The dynasty reached its apogee under Abu Ibrahim Ahmad (*reg* AD 856–63) when the Great Mosque of Kairouan was embellished: galleries were added around the court, the prayer-hall was given a splendid MINBAR of small carved panels of teak (*see* ISLAMIC ART, §VII, 1(iii)) and the mihrab received a magnificent covering of lustre-painted tiles imported from Iraq (*see* ISLAMIC ART, §V, 2(v)). Hydraulic improvements included an aqueduct feeding two enormous polygonal cisterns outside the walls of Kairouan. The Zaytuna Mosque in Tunis, a building that rivalled the Great Mosque of Kairouan, was restored in a campaign that was completed in 864–5. Kairouan became an important religious and cultural centre, attracting scholars and artisans who developed local variants of the ABBASID metropolitan styles. A group of manuscripts of the Koran found in the library of the Great Mosque of Kairouan, of which the earliest are traditionally attributed to the Aghlabid period, include some of the finest examples of early Islamic calligraphy and bookbinding (*see* ISLAMIC ART, §III, 7). Muhammad II (*reg* 863–75), known as Abu'l-Gharaniq, had a passion for hunting, pleasure and drink. Although Ibrahim II (*reg* 875–902) began his reign as an excellent prince, he soon slid into limitless absolutism, unleashing his bloodiest passions even on his own children. Nevertheless this strange ruler had the city of Raqqada built several kilometres from Kairouan, and Arab authors praised this splendid city for the beauty of its palaces, orchards and pools. Ibrahim's successors could not contain the growing strength of the FATIMID troops, and their taking of Kairouan in 909 put an end to the Aghlabid dynasty.

BIBLIOGRAPHY

Enc. Islam/2
K. A. C. Creswell: *Early Muslim Architecture*, 2 vols (Oxford, 1932–40; 2nd edn of vol. i in 2 parts, Oxford, 1969)
G. Marçais and L. Poinssot: *Objets kairouanais: IXe au XIIIe siècle: Relieures, verreries, cuivres et bronzes, bijoux*, 2 vols (Tunis, 1948–52)
M. Solignac: 'Recherches sur les installations hydrauliques de Kairouan et des steppes tunisiennes du VIIe au XIe siècle (J. C.)', *An. Inst. Etud. Orient. U. Alger*, x (1952), pp. 5–273 and xi (1953), pp. 60–170
G. Marçais: *L'Architecture musulmane d'occident* (Paris, 1954), pp. 1–54
A. Lézine: *Le Ribat de Sousse* (Tunis, 1956)
G. Marçais and L. Golvin: *La Grande Mosquée de Sfax* (Tunis, 1960)
A. Lézine: *Architecture de l'Ifriqiya: Recherches sur les monuments aghlabides* (Paris, 1966)
M. Talbi: *L'Emirat aghlabide, 184–296/800–909* (Paris, 1966)
L. Golvin: 'Le Mihrab de Kairouan', *Kst Orients*, v (1968), pp. 1–38
G. Kircher: 'Die Moschee des Muhammad b. Hairun ("Drei-Tore-Moschee") in Qairawân, Tunesien', *Mitt. Dt. Archäol. Inst.: Abt. Kairo*, xxvi (1970), pp. 141–68
L. Golvin: *Essai sur l'architecture religieuse musulmane*, iii (Paris, 1974), pp. 123–276
J. Bloom: *Minaret: Symbol of Islam* (Oxford, 1989), pp. 86–98

LUCIEN GOLVIN

Aght'amar. Island on Lake Van in south-eastern Turkey. It is the site of the church of the Holy Cross (Sourb Khatch), which was built in AD 915–21 as the palatine church of the Ardsruni king Gagik (*reg* 908–*c.* 943) of the Armenian kingdom of Vaspurakan. The church is of singular importance for the history of medieval art because of the form, content and iconography of its sculptural reliefs and wall paintings. It is the oldest surviving church almost entirely covered on the exterior with figural relief in stone (*see* ARMENIA, fig. 7).

According to information in a text of the late 18th century or early 19th and an inscription on the building's façade now hidden by a *gavit'* or assembly hall (1793; *see* ARMENIA, §II), the church was built by the King's

Armenian architect Manuel (Lalayan, 1910). An anonymous continuator of the 10th-century *History of the House of the Ardsrunik* described Gagik's other building activities on the island as including a harbour, citadel, towered walls, gardens and a palace (all destr.). He also reports that Manuel entrusted the sculptural programme to a monk.

In plan and construction, the church follows the classic 4th–7th-century Armenian tradition of building domed churches entirely in stone. Its plan (interior 14.8×11.5 m) is a variant of that of the Armenian churches of Avan (6th century) and of St Hrip'sime (618; *see* ĒDJMIADZIN), since it has four vaulted, axial niches and four smaller, diagonal niches and lacks only the four corner chambers of the earlier churches. The dome rests on a 16-sided drum and is covered by a conical roof (rest. 1292–6) that gives it the characteristic silhouette of Armenian churches; it rises 20.4 m above the ground. An unusual feature was the south façade's stone staircase (destr.), richly carved with figural reliefs, which once led to the royal gallery on the interior.

The encyclopedic sculptural programme includes themes and motifs drawn from the classic period of Armenian art and architectural sculpture as well as from Early Christian, Byzantine, Iranian, Sasanian and Islamic art. It consists essentially of four horizontal bands encircling the building at different levels. The three upper zones include an Evangelist carved under each gable, animals (real and mythical), hunting, harvesting and feasting scenes within a vine scroll, the bust of *Adam* and (on the east wall) a *Feasting Prince*. The main band includes Old Testament kings and prophets and *Adam and Eve*; deliverance scenes such as *David and Goliath* and *Jonah and the Whale* (south façade); *Daniel and the Three Hebrews* (north façade); *Christ*, the *Virgin and Child*, *St John the Baptist*, three cavalier saints and Armenian personages such as *St Grigor the Illuminator* (239–325/6), *King Gagik Presenting a Model of the Church to Christ* and two Ardsruni ancestors who were martyred in 786.

The church of the Holy Cross is also the oldest church in the Christian East (aside from 10th-century Cappadocian churches) in which the interior wall paintings have survived almost in their entirety. Its *Genesis* cycle, on the upper portion of the drum, is unique in a church of this period in either East or West, with certain features attributed by Mathews to Armenian traditions and nonscriptural sources. The lower walls have three horizontal zones of painting, with twenty-five scenes from the *Life of Christ* that incorporate modifications in accordance with Armenian church ritual; the eastern apse shows *Christ and the Apostles*.

BIBLIOGRAPHY

H. F. B. Lynch: *Armenia: Travels and Studies*, ii (London, 1901/*R* Beirut, 1967)

E. Lalayan: 'The Famous Monasteries of Vaspurakan: The Monastery of the Holy Cross at Aght'amar', *Azgagrakan Handes*, xii (1910), p. 208 [in Armen.]

J. Strzygowski: *Die Baukunst der Armenier und Europa*, i (Vienna, 1918)

A. Sakisian: 'Notes on the Sculpture of the Church of Akhthamar', *A. Bull.*, xv (1943), pp. 346–57

T'. T'ōramanyan: *Nyut er haykakan Tjartarapetut'yan patmut'yan* [Materials for the history of Armenian architecture], ii (Yerevan, 1948)

K. Otto-Dorn: 'Turkisch-Islamisches Bildgut in den Figurenreliefs von Achtamar', *Anatolia*, vi (1961), pp. 99–167

M. Ipsiroglu: *Die Kirche von Achtamar: Bauplastik im Leben des Lichtes* (Berlin, 1963)

S. Der Nersessian: *Aght'amar, Church of the Holy Cross* (Cambridge, 1965)

S. Der Nersessian and H. Vahramian: *Aght'amar* (Milan, 1974)

K. Maksoudian, ed.: *Armenian Architecture* (Zug, 1981–), i [in microfiche; incl. text by L. Der Manuelian and photographs of Aght'amar]

T. F. Mathews: 'The Genesis Frescoes of Alt'amar', *Rev. Etud. Armén.*, n. s., xvi (1982), pp. 245–57, 260–61

S. Mnac'akanyan: *Aght'amar Church of the Holy Cross, 915–921* (Finland, 1986)

C. L. Waltz: *Sources and Iconography of the Figural Sculpture of the Church of the Holy Cross at Aght'amar* (diss., Columbus, OH State U., 1986)

J.-M. Thierry and P. Donabedian: *Les Arts arméniens* (Paris, 1987; Eng. trans., New York, 1989)

P. Cuneo: *Architettura armena dal quarto al diciannovesimo secolo* (Rome, 1988)

LUCY DER MANUELIAN

Aghurmi. *See under* SIWA OASIS.

Agighiol. Iron Age burial mound in Dobrogea, Romania. It is important for a collection of figurally decorated, partly gilded silver objects that accompanied a Getic chieftain in death. The Getae had affinities to both Thracians and Scythians (*see* THRACIAN AND DACIAN ART and SCYTHIAN AND SARMATIAN ART). Imported Greek Red-figure pottery dates the burial to *c.* 350 BC, but the precious metalwork shows traces of wear and repair and was probably manufactured in the early 4th century BC.

The body armour recovered includes two sheet-silver greaves with knees in the form of human faces. Although their design is clearly adopted from Greek models with Medusa-head knees, the treatment is distinctively Thracian; one of the faces is covered with bands of gilding, probably representing the tattoos that both Thracians and Scythians are known to have had. One greave depicts a mounted huntsman holding aloft his bow and a seated huntsman drinking from a horn, with a hawk perched on his wrist, a motif clearly derived from representations of Zeus on Greek coinage. Hunting scenes also adorn the neck and cheek guards of an elaborate partly gilded silver helmet—one of only five known—which is remarkable for the dramatic representation of a pair of eyes, bordered by feathers, directly above the eyes of the wearer (*see* THRACIAN AND DACIAN ART, fig. 2). This device is based on apotropaic Greek models, in which the eyes served to avert evil or harm, especially in battle, but the local meaning also appears to relate to 'seeing twice' or having eyes like a hawk.

Two biconical silver drinking cups are decorated with animals of the chase, including wild goats, roe deer and a hawk-like bird grasping a fish in its beak and a hare in its talons; an image of a stag with eight legs is reminiscent of the confusion of paired horses' legs in Greek pottery painting and probably indicated extreme swiftness (*see* THRACIAN AND DACIAN ART, fig. 3).

BIBLIOGRAPHY

D. Berciu: *Arta traco-getica* (Bucharest, 1969)

——: 'Das thraco-getische Fürstengrab von Agighiol in Rumänien', *Ber. Röm.-Ger. Komm.*, l (1969), pp. 209–65

B. Goldman: 'Late Scythian Art in the West: The Detroit Helmet', *Jb. Prähist. Ethnog. Kst*, xxii (1969), pp. 67–75

TIMOTHY TAYLOR

Agitprop [Rus. *agitatsionnaya propaganda*: 'agitational propaganda']. Russian acronym in use shortly after the

Bolshevik Revolution of 1917 for art applied to political and agitational ends. The prefix *agit-* was also applied to objects decorated or designed for this purpose, hence *agitpoyezd* ('agit-train') and *agitparokhod* ('agit-boat'), decorated transport carrying propaganda to the war-front. Agitprop was not a stylistic term; it applied to various forms as many poets, painters and theatre designers became interested in agitational art. They derived new styles and techniques for it from Futurism, Suprematism and Constructivism.

The characteristics of the new art forms were defined as public, political and communal in purpose and execution. The poet Mayakovsky called for artists to abandon their studios and make the streets their brushes and the squares their palettes. Mass spectacular theatre provided vigorous examples of agitprop either by re-enacting recent events or by providing pageants of the progress of Communism. In 1920, for example, the theatre director Nikolay Yevreinov (1879–1953) re-enacted the *Storming of the Winter Palace* in Petrograd with a cast of 10,000 and an audience of 100,000. Concerts of factory sirens were performed in Petrograd (1918) and Moscow (1923). Trams were decorated with geometric designs, as were banners and posters, and, in response to Lenin's call in 1918 for monumental propaganda, temporary monuments to the Revolution and its heroes appeared in city streets. Tatlin's utopian design for his *Monument to the Third International* (1919–20; unexecuted) was a Constructivist response to this call. Printed works too played a role in agitprop, from the hand-stencilled posters of Mayakovsky's 'ROSTA-windows' (posters published by ROSTA, the Russian Telegraphy Agency, and displayed in shop windows; for illustration *see* MAYAKOVSKY, VLADIMIR) to Rodchenko's advertisements for state produce (*see* RODCHENKO, ALEKSANDR, fig. 2). Even sweet wrappers and tableware reflected the aims of agitprop. The state porcelain factory produced a dish elegantly bearing the word *Golod* ('Famine'), Sergey Chekhonin decorated a plate with the slogan *Kto ne s nami, tot protiv nas* ('Who is not with us is against us'), while another by Maria Lebedeva (1895–1942) declared *Kto ne rabotayet, tot ne yest* ('Who does not work does not eat'). Agitational vehicles included the trains *V. I. Lenin No. 1* (1918), *Oktyabr'skaya Revolyutsiya* ('October Revolution', 1919), *Krasnyy Vostok* ('Red East', 1920) and the boat *Krasnaya Zvezda* ('Red Star', 1920).

BIBLIOGRAPHY

I. I. Nikonova and K. G. Glont: *Agitatsionno-massovoye iskusstvo pervykh let Oktyabrya* [Agitational mass art of the first years of the October Revolution] (Moscow, 1971)

S. Bojko: *New Graphic Design in Revolutionary Russia*, trans. R. Strybel and L. Zembrzuski (New York, 1972)

The Avant-Garde in Russia, 1910–1930: New Perspectives (exh. cat., ed. S. Barron and M. Tuchman; Los Angeles, CA, Co. Mus. A., 1980)

JOHN MILNER

Ağlasun. *See* SAGALASSOS.

Aglio. *See* ALLIO.

Agneesens, Edouard(-Joseph-Alexandre) (*b* Brussels, 24 Aug 1842; *d* Uccle, Brabant, 20 Aug 1885). Belgian painter. He initially studied at the Académie Royale des Beaux-Arts in Brussels before entering Jean-François Portaels's studio in the same city, where he was one of Portaels's most important pupils. By the age of 18 he had already painted the mature work *Torso of an Adolescent* (1860; Brussels, Mus. A. Anc.). In 1863 he competed unsuccessfully in the Prix de Rome but he soon established himself with his exhibition of portraits at the Salon of 1866 in Brussels. In 1869 Agneesens went to St Petersburg, where he painted the portraits of various notable figures, including the actor *Vasily Vasil'evich Samoilov*. He returned to Brussels in 1870, where he settled.

In 1872 Agneesens exhibited his portrait of the sculptor *Gaston Marchant* (1868; Brussels, Mus. A. Anc.) in Vienna. The period between 1872 and 1875 was the most productive of his short life, during which time he painted such works as *Mother and Child* (1875; Brussels, Mus. A. Anc.). In 1875 he began to suffer from a nervous illness; during brief periods of lucidity he continued to paint, although there are no works dated after 1880. Most of his paintings consist of isolated figure and portrait works, such as the portrait of *Diane Vernon* (1876; Ghent, Mus. S. Kst.), executed in warm, harmonious colours. His painting marked an important step in the increasing freedom of Belgian art from traditional, academic styles.

BIBLIOGRAPHY

BNB [suppl. ii]

P. Colin: *La Peinture belge depuis 1830* (Brussels, 1930)

E. de Seyn: *Dictionnaire biographique des sciences, des lettres et des arts en Belgique* (Brussels, 1935)

□

Agnew, Tho(ma)s, & Sons, Ltd. English firm of art dealers and print publishers. Thomas Agnew (*b* Liverpool, 16 Dec 1794; *d* Fair Hope, Eccles, Greater Manchester, 24 March 1871) became a partner in the Manchester firm of Vittore Zanetti, framemaker, dealer in works of art and scientific instruments, and print publisher, in 1817. He took sole control of the business in 1835, opening a branch in London in 1860. His greatest achievement was to develop the market for contemporary English pictures among the newly wealthy class of northern businessman. He specialized in genre and modern-life subjects by such artists as William Mulready, William Collins, William Powell Frith, Edwin Landseer and John Phillip, which he sold for high prices. He was motivated by the utilitarian principles of Swedenborgianism, which encouraged him to help found the Salford Museum in 1850 and bequeath pictures to it. He retired in 1861 in favour of his sons, Sir William Agnew (*b* Salford, 20 Oct 1825; *d* London, 31 Oct 1910) and Thomas Agnew (1827–83). William was the most influential art dealer of the Victorian era, a figure of indefatigible energy and self-confidence. His deep purse and unrivalled eye for a profitable picture helped to keep the market for contemporary art buoyant. He paid William Holman Hunt £10,500 for the *Shadow of Death* (1873; Manchester, C.A.G.) and Edward Burne-Jones £15,000 for the *Briar Rose* cycle (1890; Buscot Park, Oxon, NT); these works were successfully exhibited and engraved by Agnew's. He did much to establish the career of Fred Walker.

The firm became a leading and highly successful print publisher, producing portrait mezzotints, commemorative engravings of such events as the Indian Mutiny, chromolithographs of John Leech's humorous sporting scenes, and reproductions of popular Royal Academy pictures;

the most lucrative was the photogravure issued in 1892 after Luke Fildes's *The Doctor* (exh. RA 1891; London, Tate). In a similar vein Agnew's commissioned Roger Fenton to photograph the Crimean War in 1855.

From the 1850s William Agnew was an increasingly dominant presence in the Christie's salerooms. He was one of the first to appreciate the change in fashion in the 1870s among rich collectors towards Old Masters and 18th-century English portraits, forming the collections of Sir Charles Tennant and E. C. Guinness along these lines. He also encouraged the growing internationalization of the art market in the late 19th century. He was a strong supporter of Gladstone and a Liberal MP from 1880 to 1886, and his political opinions were reflected in *Punch*, of which he was a director from 1872. He retired in 1895.

The London branch of the firm was taken over by William's son, Morland (1855–1931), and nephew, Lockett (1858–1918), who, in collaboration with Duveen and Knoedler's in New York, fostered the boom in the prices of Old Masters, particularly in America, which continued until 1931. The firm opened a branch in New York in 1925. Among their most important clients were J. Pierpont Morgan and George Salting. The economic slump of the 1930s almost destroyed the business and it did not regain relative prosperity until the Joseph Neeld sale in 1944. In the 1930s Agnew's began selling contemporary paintings by the London Group and the London Artists' Association, and it continued thereafter to show work by established living artists.

In the post-war years the business, primarily in top quality Old Master and 19th-century British paintings, grew with the revival of the international art market. Agnew's sold outstanding works to most of the major American museums, for example Murillo's *Return of the Prodigal Son* in 1948 to the National Gallery of Art, Washington, DC. The firm developed a particular expertise in Turner, an artist well represented in their watercolour exhibitions held annually since 1867. The firm handled many of Turner's greatest works, including *Dort or Dordrecht: The Dort Packet-boat from Rotterdam Becalmed* (New Haven, CT, Yale Cent. Brit. A.), sold to Paul Mellon in 1966. Evelyn Joll, who joined the firm in 1949, was the co-author of *The Paintings of J. M. W. Turner* (New Haven and London, 1977).

BIBLIOGRAPHY

DNB
A. J. [London], vii (1 Oct 1861), p. 319
G. Agnew: *Agnew's, 1817–1967* (London, 1967)
Great Victorian Pictures (exh. cat. by R. Treble, ACGB, 1978), p. 44
Presents from the Past: Gifts to Greater Manchester Galleries (exh. cat.; Bolton, Mus. & A.G.; Oldham, A.G.; Stockport, War Mem. Bldg A.G.; 1978), pp. 32–5
A Dealer's Record: Agnew's, 1967–81 (London, 1981)
E. Conran: 'Art Collections', *Art and Architecture in Victorian Manchester* (Manchester, 1985), pp. 71–2
Sir Geoffrey Agnew, 1908–1986: Dealer and Connoisseur (exh. cat., London, Thos Agnew & Sons, Ltd, 1988)

OLIVER GARNETT

Agniolo di Cosimo di Mariano Tori Bronzino. *See* BRONZINO, AGNOLO.

Agnolo, Andrea d'. *See* SARTO, ANDREA DEL.

Agnolo, Baccio d'. *See* BACCIO D'AGNOLO.

Agnolo del Moro. *See* ANGOLO DEL MORO, DELL'.

Agnolo di Polo (*b* Florence, 1470; *d* after 1498). Italian sculptor. He belonged to a family of well-known artisans; his grandfather Agnolo di Lippo di Polo had worked as an assistant on the stained glass for the cupola of Florence Cathedral and took the name de' Vetri, sometimes also used by his descendants. Agnolo's father, Polo di Agnolo, made masks and had his workshop on the Ponte Vecchio, Florence, and his brother Domenico engraved precious stones and medals. Vasari said that Agnolo was a pupil of Verrocchio, adding that 'he worked very well in clay and has filled the city with works from his hands'. Given the artist's birth date and that Verrocchio left Florence forever in 1483, Agnolo's apprenticeship would have been very brief; it is probable that he stayed on in the workshop when it was directed by Lorenzo di Credi.

Two of Agnolo's works are documented. On 16 August 1495 the Ufficiali della Sapienza commissioned a statue of *St Mary Magdalene* for the oratory of the Spedale della Morte at Pistoia, restored three years later by the artist himself because it was broken. This has been identified as the *Female Saint* (New York, Met.), which has many stylistic similarities with his only other known documented work, the terracotta bust of the *Redeemer* (Pistoia, Mus. Civ.), commissioned from him in 1498 by the same Ufficiali for their audience-chamber in Pistoia. Several versions of the bust of the *Redeemer* seem to derive either from the Pistoia bust or from a lost prototype by Verrocchio. Not all can be attributed to Agnolo, but a polychrome terracotta bust (Florence, Loggia del Bigallo) is of comparable size to another example (San Miniato, Mus. Dioc. A. Sacra) and perhaps even comes from the same mould; two other terracotta busts of the *Redeemer* (London, V&A; Florence, Mus. Horne) are very close. They are all derived ultimately from the head of Christ in the *Doubting Thomas* group (Florence, Orsanmichele).

Agnolo's documented works are stylistically very close to the work of Lorenzo di Credi, Pietro Torrigiani and of later members of the della Robbia family. He may have had contacts with the Dominicans of S Marco, Florence, where Savonarola was Prior. This might account for the profusion of small terracotta sculptures; the use of this malleable material enabled large numbers of comparatively inexpensive sacred images to be produced for private devotional use. The realistic representation of traditional subjects was designed to inspire intense spiritual fervour. Further works by Agnolo di Polo may yet be recognized among sculpture attributed to the della Robbia workshop.

BIBLIOGRAPHY

Thieme–Becker
G. Vasari: *Vite* (1550, rev. 2/1568); ed. G. Milanesi (1878–85), iii, pp. 371–2
P. Bacci: 'Agnolo di Polo, allievo del Verrocchio', *Riv. A.*, iii (1905), pp. 159–71
J. Mesnil: 'Polo del Maestro Agnolo dei Vetri', *Riv. A.*, iii (1905), pp. 256–8
J. Pope-Hennessy: *Catalogue of Italian Sculpture in the Victoria and Albert Museum*, i (London, 1964), p. 209
F. Rossi: *Il Museo Horne a Firenze* (Milan, 1967), p. 152
J. Goldsmith Phillips: 'A Sculpture by Agnolo di Polo', *Met. Mus. A. Bull.*, xxx/1 (1971), pp. 81–9
H. Kiel: *Il Museo del Bigallo a Firenze* (Milan, 1977), p. 127

La civiltà del cotto: Arte della terracotta nell'area fiorentina dal XV al XX secolo (exh. cat., Impruneta, Mus. Santuario, 1980), p. 102

FRANCESCA PETRUCCI

Agocchi, Giovanni Battista. *See* AGUCCHI, GIOVANNI BATTISTA.

Agocchiari, Barnaba. *See* BARNABA DA MODENA.

Agora. Place of public meeting or market place in an ancient Greek polis or city, the equivalent of a Roman forum (*see* GREECE, ANCIENT, §II, 1(i)(b))

□

Agorakritos (*b* Paros, *fl c.* 450–*c.* 420 BC). Greek sculptor. He was a prominent member of the group of artists led by Pheidias that executed the Periclean building programme on the Athenian Acropolis. Ancient literary sources provide little information on his career, and even this takes the form of later anecdotes, such as the story of his rivalry with Alkamenes in a competition to produce a statue of Aphrodite (Pliny: *Natural History*, XXXVI.iv.17), or has been distorted by the legends surrounding Pheidias, to whom two of his works were wrongly attributed: his statue of the *Enthroned Mother of the Gods* in the metroon in the Athenian Agora (Pausanias: *Guide to Greece*, I.iii.5) and his cult statue of *Nemesis* (*c.* 420 BC; Pausanias: I.xxxiii.3) for the temple at RHAMNOUS. The *Nemesis* was allegedly carved out of a colossal block of Parian marble brought to Marathon in 490 BC by the Persians, who intended to use it for a trophy after defeating the Athenians (Pausanias: I.xxxiii.2). Agorakritos was also credited with bronze statues of *Athena* and *Zeus-Hades* in the Boiotian Temple of Athena Itonia (Pausanias: IX.xxxiv.1).

A single fragment of the *Nemesis* head was discovered at Rhamnous in the late 18th century, and for a long time this formed the only basis for analysis of Agorakritos' style. However, Despinis's investigations in the storerooms of the Athens National Archaeological Museum have revealed a great number of other fragments from later excavations, which show that the statue of *Nemesis* was reproduced in several Roman copies (the best in Copenhagen, Ny Carlsberg Glyp.). Further investigation of the site by Petrakos has produced many fragments from the base of the statue, allowing its reliefs to be reconstructed (Athens, N. Archaeol. Mus.).

The identification of copies of the statue of *Nemesis* has also confirmed earlier theories that a Roman statue from Levadhia (Chaironeia, Archaeol. Mus.) reproduced Agorakritos' *Mother of the Gods*. However, attempts to identify copies of the cult statues in the Temple of Athena Itonia and to attribute to Agorakritos sculptures from the Parthenon have been less successful. Although some of the finest pedimental figures from the Parthenon, such as the group with the reclining *Aphrodite*, have been ascribed to Agorakritos, more research and perhaps other discoveries are needed to confirm this. Agorakritos' style is characterized by close adherence to the Classical ethos, structure and iconography. In his rendering of drapery, however, and his working of the marble he seems to look forward to the Rich Style of the last quarter of the century (*see* GREECE, ANCIENT, §IV, 2(iii)(b)).

BIBLIOGRAPHY

J. Overbeck: *Die antiken Schriftquellen zur Geschichte der bildenden Künste bei den Griechen* (Leipzig, 1868/*R* Hildesheim, 1959), nos 829–43

G. I. Despinis: *Symbole ste melete tou ergou tou Agorakritou* [Contribution to the study of the work of Agorakritos] (Athens, 1971)

V. Petrakos: 'Problemata tes bases tou agalmatos tes Nemeseos' [Problems of the base of the statue of Nemesis], *Archaische und klassische griechische Plastik: Akten des internationalen Kolloquiums: Athen, 1985*, pp. 89–107

A. DELIVORRIAS

Agostini, Angelo (*b* Vercelli, Italy, 1843; *d* Rio de Janeiro, 1910). Brazilian caricaturist and painter. He came to Brazil in 1859, having already acquired some knowledge of painting in Paris. He settled initially in São Paulo, where he at once started to publish caricatures attacking black slavery. There, in 1864, he was one of the founders of the comic newspaper *O Diabo Coxo*. His abolitionist spirit continued after he moved to Rio de Janeiro, through his frequent collaboration in periodicals such as *A Vida Fluminense*, *O Mosquito*, *Don Quixote* and *O Malho*. In the *Revista Ilustrada* he began to publish in 1884 the first long-running strip cartoon in Brazil, the adventures of Zé Caipora, a sertão (hinterland) character, depicting a lesser-known side of Brazil. As a painter he specialized in landscapes but also produced portraits with the same fervour that fired his enjoyable and impassioned satirical drawings, for example *Portrait of the Writer Joaquin Augusto Ribeiro de Sousa* (*c.* 1890; Rio de Janeiro, Mus. Hist. N.).

BIBLIOGRAPHY

L. Gonzaga Duque: *A arte brasileira* (Rio de Janeiro, 1888)

H. Lima: *História da caricatura no Brasil* (Rio de Janeiro, 1963)

Art of Latin America since Independence (exh. cat. by S. L. Catlin and T. Grieder, New Haven, CT, Yale U. A.G.; Austin, U. TX, A. Mus.; San Francisco, CA, Mus. A.; La Jolla, CA, A. Cent.; 1966)

J. L. Werneck da Silva: 'Angelo Agostini: 80 anos depois', *Cadernos Brasileiros*, 47 (1968)

ROBERTO PONTUAL

Agostino dei Musi. *See* MUSI, AGOSTINO DEI.

Agostino (di Antonio) di Duccio (*b* Florence, 1418; *d* ?Perugia, after 1481). Italian sculptor and architect. His father, Antonio di Duccio, a weaver, reported in his *catasto* (land registry declaration) of 1427 that Agostino was eight years old. On his father's death, the young Agostino enrolled in the company of the mercenary Giovanni da Tolentino, with whom he was serving in 1433. He may be the apprentice named Agostino who was working on the external pulpit for Prato Cathedral on 14 May 1437; this would suggest that he trained in the circle of Michelozzo and Donatello. What may be his earliest known work, datable *c.* 1440 (Rosenauer, 1977), is a marble statue of the *Virgin and Child* (Florence, S Maria del Carmine), influenced by Michelozzo.

Agostino's first certain work, commissioned by Ludovico Forni for Modena Cathedral, was an antependium that included four relief scenes from the *Life of St Geminian* (1442; dismembered, statue of *St Geminian* in Modena Cathedral sacristy, reliefs built into the cathedral's outer wall). The scenes are carved in high relief, the figures arranged in a stiff frieze formation. In 1446 he was in Venice, having apparently fled there after he and his brothers Costantino and Cosimo were accused in 1441 of stealing silver from the Compagnia dell'Osservanza in SS

Annunziata, Florence. Agostino may have worked in the Venice studio of Bartolomeo Bon (*d* 1529), whose influence is apparent in the statue attributed to him (Brunetti, 1950) of *St Louis of Toulouse* (Venice, S Alvise).

From 1449 to 1456 Agostino was in Rimini, employed by Sigismondo Pandolfo Malatesta on the decoration of the interior of the church of S Francesco (transformed and remodelled by Leon Battista Alberti and Matteo de' Pasti; *see* RIMINI, §1(ii)). There Agostino supervised a large group of sculptors working on the most richly sculptured Renaissance building in Italy. He was probably personally responsible for all the major figural carving in the six chapels that were built in the church (*see* RIMINI, fig. 4). In these he developed an individual, gothicizing linear style of great intensity, revealing a knowledge of Donatello's work and perhaps reflecting the use of line in paintings by Andrea del Castagno and Filippo Lippi. In 1454 Agostino also worked in Cesena, carving the elephant relief over the entrance to the Biblioteca Malatestiana, and at Forlì, making a tabernacle with a relief of the *Trinity* and a statue of the *Virgin and Child* on the façade for the sanctuary of the Madonna at Fornò. In 1456 his brother, Ottaviano di Antonio di Duccio (*b* 1422; *d* after 1478), a sculptor and goldsmith, joined him as an assistant at S Francesco, Rimini. (Ottaviano's only certain work is the tomb of *Antonio Malatesta* (1467) in Cesena Cathedral.)

Between 1457 and 1461 Agostino was working on the façade of the oratory of S Bernardino, Perugia. Although the architectural framework of the façade recalls Alberti's design for S Francesco, the sculpture, originally highly polychromed, is rich and intricate, emphasizing line and movement. Above a double door framed by reliefs of angels, a high tympanum contains a relief of *St Bernardino in Glory*. *God the Father* appears in the upper pediment, and four aedicules contain statues. Agostino also carved a large stone and terracotta dossal (dismantled and reconstituted in 1484) for the altar of S Lorenzo, in the church of S Domenico, Perugia, for the heirs of Lorenzo di Ser Giovanni. Between December 1462 and February 1463 Agostino was in Bologna, where he presented a wooden model (untraced) for the façade of S Petronio.

In 1463 Agostino returned to Florence and enrolled in the Arte dei Maestri di Pietra e Legname (the sculptors' guild). In 1463–4, for the Opere del Duomo, he made a colossal figure (untraced) to be placed in the cathedral tribune; they commissioned a second colossal statue from him in 1464, but this was abandoned, the marble block later being used by Michelangelo for his *David* (Florence, Accad.). For SS Annunziata he made a terracotta *Resurrection* (1470; untraced). Also belonging to this Florentine period are the marble relief of the *Virgin and Child with Angels* (Florence, Bargello), originally in the Carmine, Florence, and a tabernacle with *Two Angels Holding Back a Curtain* (Florence, Bargello) from the church of the Ognissanti, Florence; both works are carved in an intricate, linear style. The highly wrought marble relief of the *Virgin and Child*, known as the d'Aubervilliers *Madonna* (Paris, Louvre), and the terracotta statue of the *Angel of the Annunciation* (Budapest, Mus. F.A.) would seem to be of the same date.

In 1473 Agostino returned to Perugia as architect in charge of the design and execution of the Porta S Pietro, left unfinished at the time of his death. He also executed the altar of the *Pietà* (1473; destr. 1625; fragments Perugia, G. N. Umbria) for Perugia Cathedral, commissioned by the hospital of the Misericordia, and the marble low reliefs of *Christ Taking Leave of his Mother* (New York, Met.) and the *Virgin and Child* (*c.* 1473; Washington, DC, N.G.A.; see fig.). Among his other contemporary commissions, from small towns in Umbria and Lazio, are two *Archangels* for Acquapendente Cathedral (Viterbo) and two wall tombs, both originally in S Francesco, Amelia (Terni), those of *Giovanni Geraldini, Bishop of Catanzaro* (1476; Amelia Cathedral) and of *Matteo and Elisabetta Geraldini* (1477; *in situ*). Brunetti (1965) attributed the tomb slab of *Bishop Ruggero Mandosi* (Amelia Cathedral) to Agostino, which would imply that he was still alive in 1484, the year of the Bishop's death; however Agostino was last documented in 1481 working on the Porta S Pietro. He died before 1498, when his wife remarried.

BIBLIOGRAPHY

DBI; Thieme–Becker

A. Rossi: 'Prospetto cronologico della vita e delle opere di Agostino d'Antonio, scultore fiorentino, con la storia e documenti di quelle da lui fatte in Perugia', *G. Erud. A.*, iv (1875), pp. 3–25, 33–50, 76–83, 117–22, 141–52, 179–84, 202–11, 241–9, 263–75

A. Venturi: *Storia* (1901–40), vi, pp. 388–406, 1024

A. Pointner: *Agostino d'Antonio di Duccio* (Strasbourg, 1909)

A. Colasanti: 'La tomba di *Giovanni Geraldini*, opera di Agostino di Duccio', *Rass. A.*, iii (1916), pp. 38–42

C. Ricci: *Il tempio Malatestiano* (Milan, [1924]), pp. 103–37

C. L. Ragghianti: 'La mostra della scultura italiana antica a Detroit', *Crit. A.*, iii (1938), pp. 178–9

H. W. Janson: 'The Beginnings of Agostino di Duccio', *A. Bull.*, xxix (1942), pp. 330–34

Agostino di Duccio: *Virgin and Child*, marble relief, 720×573 mm, *c.* 1473 (Washington, DC, National Gallery of Art)